W9-AZA-995

social psychology

Elliot Aronson *University of California, Santa Cruz*

Timothy D. Wilson *University of Virginia*

Robin M. Akert *Wellesley College*

Beverley Fehr *University of Winnipeg*

SECOND CANADIAN EDITION

PEARSON

Prentice
Hall

Toronto

National Library of Canada Cataloguing in Publication

Social psychology / Elliot Aronson ... [et al.]. — 2nd Canadian ed.

Includes bibliographical references and index.
ISBN 0-13-120001-1

1. Social psychology. 1. Psychologie sociale. I. Aronson, Elliot

HM1033.S62 2004   302   C2003-901260-3

Copyright © 2004, 2001 Pearson Education Canada Inc., Toronto, Ontario.

Original edition published by Prentice-Hall, Inc., a division of Pearson Education, Upper Saddle River, NJ. Copyright © 2002 by Prentice-Hall, Inc. Earlier editions published by Addison Wesley Longman, Inc.

This edition is for sale in Canada only.

All rights reserved. This publication is protected by copyright and permission should be obtained from the publisher prior to any prohibited reproduction, storage in a retrieval system, or transmission in any form or by any means, electronic, mechanical, photocopying, recording, or likewise. For information regarding permission, write to the Permissions Department.

ISBN 0-13-120001-1

Vice President, Editorial Director: Michael J. Young
Executive Acquisitions Editor: Jessica Mosher
Senior Marketing Manager: Judith Allen
Senior Developmental Editor: Lise Dupont
Editorial Coordinator: Söğüt Y. Güleç
Copy Editor: Susan Broadhurst
Proofreader: Tara Tovell
Production Manager: Wendy Moran
Page Layout: Phyllis Seto
Permissions and Photo Research: Lisa Brant
Art Director: Mary Opper
Cover and Interior Design: Michelle Bellemare
Cover Image: Photonica

The credits appear on pages 681–684. They should be considered an extension of the copyright page.

Statistics Canada information is used with the permission of the Minister of Industry, as Minister responsible for Statistics Canada. Information on the availability of the wide range of data from Statistics Canada can be obtained from Statistics Canada's Regional Offices, its World Wide Web site at http://www.statcan.ca, and its toll-free access number 1-800-263-1136.

1 2 3 4 5   08 07 06 05 04

Printed and bound in the USA.

To my family, Vera, Hal, Neal, Julie,
  and Joshua Aronson

                                        —E.A.

To my family, Deirdre Smith, Christopher
  and Leigh Wilson

                                        —T.D.W.

To my mentor, colleague, and friend,
  Dane Archer

                                        —R.M.A.

To my family, Marvin, Genevieve,
  and Everett

                                        —B.F.

BRIEF CONTENTS

DETAILED CONTENTS

CHAPTER 10

Interpersonal Attraction
from first impressions to close relationships 344

CHAPTER 11

Prosocial Behaviour
why do people help? 387

CHAPTER 12

Aggression
why we hurt other people 423

CHAPTER 13

Prejudice
causes and cures 466

PREFACE

When we began writing this book, our overriding goal was to capture the excitement of social psychology. We have been pleased to hear, in many kind letters and e-mail messages from professors and students, that we succeeded. One of our favourites was from a student who said that the book was so interesting that she always saved it for last, to reward herself for finishing her other work. With this student—and, we hope, with others—we succeeded in making our book an enjoyable, fascinating story, not a dry report of facts and figures.

The excitement of social psychology is transmitted when students understand the whole context of the field: how theories inspire research, why research is performed as it is, how further research triggers yet new avenues of study. We have tried to convey our own fascination with the research process in a down-to-earth, meaningful way and have presented the results of the scientific process in terms of the everyday experience of the reader. However, we did not want to "water down" our presentation of the field. In a world where human behaviour can be endlessly surprising and where research results can be quite counterintuitive, it is important to prepare students by providing a firm foundation on which to build their understanding of this challenging discipline.

Our goal in *Social Psychology,* Second Canadian Edition, is to capture the excitement of social psychology for students in Canada by presenting the field in a Canadian context. In the novel *Tamarind Mem,* Indo-Canadian writer Anita Rau Badami (1996) tells the story of two young girls growing up in India whose parents sought to enhance their status by emulating British ways. To keep abreast of British fashion and hair styles, their mother faithfully subscribed to an expensive British magazine. One of the daughters, Kamini, recalls that the magazine also contained a children's story that usually focused on the sandwich and ginger beer picnics of two young British girls, Nora and Tilly. Kamini comments that, "I liked Nora and Tilly but wished that they had different names—Gauri and Geetha, perhaps, or Mini and Bani" (p. 24).

This quotation captures the sentiment of your Canadian author, Beverley Fehr, who taught social psychology for years using the American edition of this text. Although her students always enjoyed the book, she felt that they would have been happier if the news stories, historical examples, and statistics reflected their Canadian experience. In short, she was convinced that social psychology would come alive for students in Canada when they discovered the relevance of social psychological theories and concepts to the society in which they live.

A word on the organization of this text. We have seen a lot of syllabi from social psychology courses and spoken with many colleagues who teach the course, and have been impressed by the many different ways in which the course can be taught. To accommodate the diverse ways in which instructors may choose to present topics, we have tried to create a sensible, yet flexible, organization.

Each chapter of *Social Psychology,* Second Canadian Edition, is self-contained in terms of topics and concepts. Consequently, instructors can assign the chapters in any order they please; concepts are always explained in clear terms so that students won't need to have read earlier chapters in order to grasp the meanings of later ones. Further, the three Social Psychology in Action units at the end of the text may be integrated into the course at several points, or assigned at the end.

However you choose to arrange your course, we are confident that this text presents a rigorous, scientific approach to social psychology in a way that is sure to engage and fascinate students in Canada. Here's why:

A Storytelling Aproach

Social psychology is full of good stories, such as how the actions of Derek Kennedy—who risked his life to rescue drowning people in a Nova Scotia harbour—can be explained, how the Holocaust inspired investigations into obedience to authority, and how reactions to the marriage of the Crown Prince of Japan to Masako Owada, a career diplomat, illustrate cultural differences in the self-concept. By placing research in a real-world context, we make the material more familiar, understandable, and memorable.

OPENING VIGNETTES

Each chapter begins with a real-life vignette that epitomizes the concepts to come. We refer to this event at several points in the chapter to illustrate to students the relevance of the material they are learning. Examples of the opening vignettes include descriptions of a program sponsored by Pizza Hut Corp. called BOOKIT!, in which Canadian schoolchildren are rewarded with free pizzas for reading books (Chapter 5, Self-Knowledge); a television network called the Youth News Network that broadcasted news—and commercials—in some Canadian schools (Chapter 7, Attitudes and Attitude Change); the actions of John Rokosh, a young Winnipeg man, who stopped to help the front runner who had fallen during the snowshoe finals of the Canadian Special Olympics 2000 Winter Games, even though he could have won the gold medal by continuing (Chapter 11, Prosocial Behaviour); and the case of a Vancouver man, Thomas Sophonow, who was wrongfully convicted of murder based on faulty eyewitness testimony, and endured three trials and four years in prison as a result (Social Psychology in Action 3: Social Psychology and the Law). To illustrate more specifically the way in which the opening vignettes are tied to social psychological principles, here are a few examples in more detail:

- Chapter 6, Self-Justification and the Need to Maintain Self-Esteem, begins with the intriguing story of the Solar Temple Cult. The leader of the cult, Luc Jouret, believed that the world was about to be destroyed by fire and that the only salvation was to take a "death voyage" by ritualized suicide to the star Sirius, where they would be reborn. Jouret set up headquarters in villages in Quebec and Switzerland. The people in Quebec who joined the cult were mainly respected professionals including the mayor of Richelieu and his wife, people in upper management positions with Hydro Quebec, a civil servant, and a journalist. In 1994, 53 people, including the mayor of Richelieu and his wife, died in fires set in buildings owned by the cult. In all, 74 deaths linked to this cult have been documented.

    Why would respected, intelligent people willingly hand over their wealth and material possessions to a charismatic leader? How could they reach the point of handing over their very lives—and in some cases, even those of their children? Cognitive dissonance theory provides insight into what would otherwise seem as utterly incomprehensible human behaviour. By the end of this chapter, students will see that these behaviours are not unfathomable, but rather are an extreme manifestation of a basic human tendency—the need to justify our actions.

- In Chapter 10, Interpersonal Attraction: From First Impressions to Close Relationships, we draw students in by describing an incredible "love at first sight" experience in which a Winnipeg newspaper writer fell in love with a woman from Georgia (near Russia) on a bus to Istanbul, Turkey. Despite their difficulty communicating in English, within hours, they were intensely in love. They began to make plans for Nina to come to Canada. When Nina mentioned in a letter that he would need to travel to the Canadian Embassy in Turkey to plead her case, he dropped everything, including a teaching position that he had just secured, and booked a one-way ticket to Turkey and two tickets back to Canada. During this time, his attempts to reach Nina invariably failed. He finally managed to reach her sister who delivered the news that Nina had decided to return to her husband. Bradley Bird had never known there was a husband.

    Although one might have expected him to become extremely bitter, Bradley maintains that he will always be thankful to Nina for giving him the happiest hours of his adult life.

    This vignette serves to raise two key questions that are addressed in Chapter 10: What exactly is love? And why are people so motivated to seek it—so motivated that they might even rearrange their lives after a chance meeting with a stranger?

- Chapter 13, Prejudice: Causes and Cures, begins by introducing Mary Young, the Native Student Advisor at the University of Winnipeg. Mary was raised in Bloodvein First Nation, an Ojibway community in northern Manitoba. Growing up, she thought of herself as Anishinabe and was comfortable with that identity. It wasn't until she moved to Winnipeg, at the age of 14, with the dream of being the first person from her community to graduate from high school, that she discovered that she was perceived as Indian. Moreover, she quickly learned that being labelled as an Indian made her the target of racism and prejudice. Mary had never expected to feel embarrassed about her cultural heritage and identity. However, hearing comments such as "the only good Indian is a dead Indian" filled her with shame and resentment that she was Native. Mary's story serves to illustrate prejudice against groups such as Canada's Native people and provides a hearth-wrenching glimpse into the effects of prejudice and discrimination on their targets.

"MINI" STORIES IN EACH CHAPTER

Our storytelling approach is not limited to these opening vignettes. There are several "mini" stories woven into each chapter that illustrate specific concepts and make the material come alive. They each follow a similar format: First, we describe an example of a real-life phenomenon that is designed to pique students' interest. These stories are taken from current events (mainly Canadian), literature, and our own lives. Second, we describe an experiment that attempts to explain the phenomenon. This experiment is typically described in some detail, because we believe that students should learn not only the major theories in social psychology, but also understand and appreciate the methods used to test those theories. We often invite the students to pretend that they were participants in the experiment, to give them a better feel for what it was like and what was found. Here are a few examples of our "mini" stories (by thumbing through the book, you will come across many others):

- In Chapter 3, Social Cognition, we introduce the idea of schemas and discuss research showing that people will distort evidence to make it schema-consistent. We illustrate this point with a humorous anecdote from Pamela Wallin about an experience she had covering a G-7 summit hosted

by Canada. CTV had managed to secure interviews with the (then) British Prime Minister and the West German Chancellor. Ms. Wallin excitedly asked viewers to stay tuned for interviews with Margaret Thatcher and Helmut Shit. She was mortified at her mispronunciation of his name and left the studio, fully expecting that her broadcasting career was over. To her amazement, the people she ran into commented that they thought for a moment that she had mispronounced the Chancellor's name, but then realized that they hadn't had their coffee yet, or the vacuum cleaner was running, and so on. . . . In short, it was so inconsistent with Canadians' schemas that Pamela Wallin would make such a slip of the tongue on the air that they disbelieved their ears and concluded that she really had said "Schmidt."

- In Chapter 6, Self-Justification and the Need to Maintain Self-Esteem, we discuss that the need to justify our actions can become a self-perpetuating cycle in which we commit a questionable act, expend effort justifying it, and as a result, set the stage for further questionable actions. We illustrate this point by referring to the 1997 APEC summit in which the Prime Minister instructed the police to use pepper spray on protesters—mostly students—whose behaviour was well within their democratic rights. Rather than defuse the situation by apologizing, the Prime Minister continued to justify his actions by telling the protesters they should be thankful that the RCMP had used pepper spray instead of baseball bats. The need for justification didn't end there, as evidenced in his infamous "For me, pepper, I put it on my plate" quotation at the summit's closing conference.

- In Chapter 9, Group Processes, when introducing the concept of deindividuation, we offer the classic examples such as the My Lai incident in Vietnam and lynch mobs in the southern U.S. However, we also bring this concept closer to home by describing the recent, brutal attack on a Toronto teen, Matti Baranovski, who was approached in a park by a group of youths wearing balaclavas, bandannas, and ski goggles to conceal their identities. The injuries that resulted from this attack were so severe that Matti Baranovski later died in hospital.

Social Psychological Methods: Another Good Story

It might seem that a storytelling approach would obscure the scientific basis of social psychology. Quite to the contrary, we believe that part of what makes the story so interesting is explaining to students how to test hypotheses scientifically. In recent years, the trend has been for textbooks to include only short sections on research methodology and to provide only brief descriptions of the findings of individual studies. In this book, we integrate the science and methodology of the field into our story in a variety of ways.

SEPARATE CHAPTER ON METHODOLOGY

Unlike virtually all other texts, we devote an entire chapter to methodology (Chapter 2). "But wait," you might say, "How can you maintain students' interest and attention with an entire chapter on such dry material?" The answer is by integrating this material into our storytelling approach. Even the "dry" topic of methodology can come alive by telling it like a story. We set the stage by describing examples of pressing, real-world problems related to violence and aggression. For example, we open the chapter with the story of Virginie Larivière, a 13-year-old girl who was convinced that violent television programming was to blame for the brutal sexual assault and murder of her younger sister. The national publicity she garnered resulted in an investigation into the effects of violent television programming by the Standing Committee on Communications and Culture (1993). The committee interviewed people such as the chair of the CRTC and film and broadcasting executives. Their conclusion? There is little, if any, evidence that exposure to violent television programming produces violent behaviour. We contrast this report with one published by the Department of Canadian Heritage (1995) in which a social psychologist (Wendy Josephson) was commissioned to answer this question, based on an analysis of scientific studies. Her conclusion? Television violence does increase aggressive behaviour, particularly among children who are predisposed toward aggression. This example serves to illustrate the value of the scientific method in answering questions with important societal implications.

We then use actual research studies on this topic (as well as the related topic of why bystanders don't intervene to help victims of violence, as illustrated by the Kitty Genovese murder) to illustrate the three major scientific methods (observational research, correlational research, and experimental research). Rather than a dry recitation of methodological principles, the scientific method unfolds like a story with a "hook" (What are the causes of real-world aggression?) and a moral (such interesting, real-world questions can be addressed scientifically). We have been pleased by the reactions to this chapter in previous editions.

DETAILED DESCRIPTIONS OF INDIVIDUAL STUDIES

We describe prototypical studies in more detail than most texts. We discuss how a study was set up, what the research participants perceived and did, how the research design derives from theoretical issues, and how the findings offer support for the initial hypotheses. As we mentioned earlier, we often ask the reader to pretend that he or she was a participant, in order to understand the study from the participants' point of view. Whenever pertinent, we've also included anecdotal information about how a study was done or came to be; these brief stories allow the reader to see the hitherto hidden world of creating research. See, for example, the description of Aronson's jigsaw puzzle technique in Chapter 13 (pp. 513–516).

EMPHASIS ON CLASSIC, MODERN, AND CANADIAN RESEARCH

As you will see from flipping through the book, we include a large number of data figures detailing the results of individual experiments. The field of social psychology is expanding rapidly and exciting new work is being done in all sub-areas of the discipline. In this edition, the vast majority of the more than 150 new Canadian references were published in the 2000s. In addition to that, approximately 250 new references from the U.S. fourth edition, upon which this Second Canadian Edition is based, were incorporated. Thus, the book includes thorough coverage of up-to-date, cutting-edge research in Canada and in the field as a whole.

In emphasizing what is new, many texts have a tendency to ignore what is old. We have striven to strike a balance between current, up-to-date research findings and classic research in social psychology. Some older studies deserve their status as classics (e.g., early work in dissonance, conformity, and attribution) and are important cornerstones of the discipline. For example, unlike several current texts, we present detailed descriptions of the Festinger and Carlsmith (1959) dissonance study (Chapter 6), the LaPiere (1934) study on attitude–behaviour inconsistency (Chapter 7), and the Asch (1956) conformity studies (Chapter 8). To illustrate to students how research on the classics has been updated, we follow a discussion of the classics with modern approaches to these same topics, such as research conducted at the University of British Columbia on the process of dissonance reduction in different cultures (Heine & Lehman, 1997a, in Chapter 6). We also place the issue of attitude–behaviour inconsistency in a modern context by including a section on the implications of attitude–behaviour inconsistency for safe sex (Chapter 7). In this section, we describe studies conducted at the University of Waterloo (MacDonald, Zanna, & Fong, 1996) and at McGill University (Hynie & Lydon, 1996), among others, that provide insight into why people report positive attitudes toward condoms, yet fail to use them. In Chapter 8, we follow Asch's classic conformity studies with research conducted at the University of Waterloo (Buehler & Griffin, 1994; Griffin & Buehler, 1993) on the role of construal processes in conformity and dissent. This way, students see the continuity and depth of the field, rather than viewing it only as a mass of studies published in the past few years.

As these examples illustrate, the inclusion of Canadian research is not gratuitous. We highlight how current Canadian research builds on classic contributions to social psychology (Canadian and non-Canadian, alike) and showcase the role of Canadian research in moving the field forward. Perhaps most importantly, this coverage does not come at the expense of omitting other important classic and modern contributions made by non-Canadian researchers.

A Canadian Context

Canadian research and cultural examples are integrated throughout the text to provide a familiar context and comfortable learning environment for Canadian students. Here is just a partial listing of the rich Canadian content you will find woven into every chapter of *Social Psychology,* Second Canadian Edition:

Chapter 1, Introduction: Opening vignette contains stories taken from across the country that act as springboards for the social psychological investigation: Altruism is introduced with the story of Derek Kennedy, hero from Nova Scotia who rescued three people drowning in the North Sydney Harbour; Jean-François Caudron and his university hockey team's hazing rituals exemplify suffering and self-justification; and the tragic story of the Order of the Solar Temple cult points to a later discussion of our need to justify our actions. The example of the David Milgaard–Larry Fisher case illustrates what can go wrong in the legal process; Canada's decision to participate in NATO bombings in Kosovo illustrates basic, conflicting human motivations; the story of Dee Brasseur shows a woman forced to retire from the military because of continual sexual harassment, yet still defending the institution; studies by MacDonald, Zanna, and Fong (1996) and Maticka-Tyndale, Herold, and Mewhinney (1998) show that people reduce their fears about engaging in dangerous sexual behaviour by denying that the problem exists.

Chapter 2, Methodology: Opening vignette about Virginie Larivière, a 13-year-old Quebec girl who became an activist against violence on television after the murder of her younger sister, prompting a government committee to publish a report on the effects of TV violence, in contrast to another government report that reached the opposite conclusion; Canadian study out of the University of Western Ontario (Roese and Olson, 1996) on hindsight and predictability; Pepler and Craig (1995) study out of York University on methods of observing bullying in school playgrounds; studies conducted at the University of Manitoba (Morry & Staska, 2001) and at York University (Spizter, Henderson, & Zivian, 1999) on ideal male and female body images; study by Fletcher and Chalmers (1991) finding that Canadians who were asked their opinions on affirmative action provided very different answers depending upon how the questions were asked; the story of "Tillie the Rainmaker," showing the difference between correlation and causation; a classic reading added to If You Are Interested section: Adair, J.G. (1973), *The human subject: The social psychology of the psychological experiment.*

Chapter 3, Social Cognition: Opening vignette focuses on the story of Kevin Chappell, an Ottawa man who is unable to perceive objects due to a brain injury. This story is intended to illustrate the usefulness of schemas in navigating through the physical and social world and how difficult it would be to function without them. The chapter also contains studies by Roese and Olson (University of Western Ontario) and Mandel and Lehman, 1996, (University of British Columbia) and Kahneman, Slovic, and Tversky, 1982, (University of British Columbia) on counterfactual thinking; study by Sullivan, Rouse, Bishop, and Johnston (1997) out of Dalhousie University on the experience of pain; study by Mill, Gray, and Mandel (1994) of Concordia University suggesting that training in statistics and research methods does not necessarily guarantee the transfer of these concepts to everyday life.

Chapter 4, Social Perception: Studies by Russell and colleagues (Carroll & Russell, 1996; Russell & Fehr, 1987) at the University of British Columbia, demonstrating that context effects such as the presence of other facial expressions or the social situation in which an emotion is expressed can influence the perception of emotion; studies by Dion and Dion (1987) and Dion, Pak, and Dion (1990) of perceptions of attractive people, demonstrating implicit personality theories and cultural differences in those theories; the story of Nadia Hama, the B.C. woman who was suspected of dropping her baby off of the Capilano suspension bridge, to demonstrate attributions; studies by MacDonald and Ross (1999) and Murray and Holmes (1997) at the University of Waterloo on unrealistic optimism in romantic relationships; cross-cultural study of Canadian and Japanese students by Heine and Lehman (1995) showing that unrealistic optimism may not be a universal phenomenon; several studies on blaming the victim (Perrott, Miller, & Delaney, 1997; Perrott &

Webber, 1996, at Mount Saint Vincent University; Kristiansen & Giulietti, 1990, at Carleton University; Hafer, 2000a, b, 2002, at Brock University), including analyses of victim blaming in the Canadian legal system by the Honourable Madame Justice L'Heureux-Dubé (2001) and by Kwong-leung Tang (2000). The highly-acclaimed book, *The Justice Motive in Everyday Life*, edited by University of Waterloo's Michael Ross and by Dale T. Miller, was added to the recommended readings for this chapter.

Chapter 5, Self-Knowledge: Try It! box, "A Measure of Self-Concept Clarity," based on a scale developed by Campbell, Trapnell, Heine, Katz, Lavallee, and Lehman (1996) at the University of British Columbia; studies by Cathy McFarland and Roger Buehler (1997, 1998), at Simon Fraser University and at Wilfrid Laurier University on self-awareness and bad moods; studies by Vallerand and colleagues (Blais, Sabourin, Boucher, & Vallerand, 1990; Pelletier, Fortier, Vallerand, & Brière, 1996; Vallerand 1997) as well as Green-Demers, Pelletier, Stewart, and Gushue (1998), Losier and Koestner (1999), Koestner and Losier (2002) on intrinsic and extrinsic motivation in a variety of domains; studies by Baldwin and Holmes (1987) and Baldwin et al. (1990) at the University of Waterloo on how priming significant relationships affects one's momentary sense of self; studies by Lockwood and Kunda (1997, 1999, 2000; Lockwood, 2002) at the University of Toronto and the University of Waterloo looking at how we feel if we compare ourselves to someone who is better than we are. The chapter also includes studies by Wilson and Ross (2000, 2001, Ross & Wilson, 2002), Wilfrid Laurier University and the University of Waterloo, on people's appraisals of earlier and current selves. Finally, Céline Dion's make-overs are used to illustrate impression management in a Canadian context.

Chapter 6, Self-Justification: Studies by Heine and colleagues (Heine, 2001; Heine, Kityama, & Lehman, 2001; Heine, Takata, & Lehman, 2000) on self-enhancement in Canadian and Japanese students; new research by Ross, Xun, and Wilson (2002) on activation of bicultural selves among Chinese Canadian students; example of the Somalia scandal used to illustrate how people use dissonance to justify cruel actions toward others; example of the APEC pepper-spray incident used to illustrate self-justification; study by Shultz, Léveillé, and Lepper (1999) on dissonance reduction when choosing between unattractive alternatives; findings by Wright, Rule, Ferguson, McGuire, and Wells (1992) at the University of Alberta on dissonance reduction and the misattribution of arousal. New research on close relationships as a self-affirmational resource by Sandra Murray and colleagues (Murray, Bellavia, Feeney, Holmes, & Rose, 2001; Murray, Holmes, & Griffin, 2000).

Chapter 7, Attitudes: Numerous studies on attitudes by Haddock and Zanna at the University of Waterloo and Esses at the University of Western Ontario (Esses, Haddock, & Zanna, 1993; Haddock, Zanna, & Esses, 1993; Haddock & Zanna, 1994; Haddock & Zanna, 1998; Haddock, Zanna, & Esses, 1994); research by Bassili (1995, 1996) at the University of Toronto on attitude accessibility and strength; new research by Bell and Esses (2002) and Newby-Clark, McGregor, and Zanna (2002) on attitudinal ambivalence; research by Shestowsky, Wegener, and Fabrigar (1998) on low-need-for-cognition and high-need-for-cognition people and their ability to persuade or be persuaded; study by Hafer, Reynolds, and Obertynski (1996) on whether people are swayed by peripheral cues when issues are described using complicated, jargon-laden language. A section on attitude–behaviour inconsistency as applied to condom use (MacDonald, Fong, Zanna, & Martineau, 2000; MacDonald & Martineau, 2002; Maticka-Tyndale, Herold, & Mewhinney, 2001).

Chapter 8, Conformity: Opening vignette on the need to conform, featuring the story of the vicious beating and murder of B.C. teenager Reena Virk; study by Vorauer and Miller at the University of Manitoba on conformity by students exposed to other students' negative or positive self-evaluations; a figure and studies out of the University of Waterloo (Griffin & Buehler, 1993; Buehler & Griffin, 1994) on construal processes following the decision to conform or dissent; the case of a Canadian soldier who complained publicly about an out-of-date Anthrax vaccine he was given during the Gulf War, who was consequently silenced and assigned menial tasks as punishment for his nonconformity; study out of the University of British Columbia by Campbell and Fairey (1989) suggesting that the effects of group size depend on the kind of social influence that is operating. The chapter also includes Guimond's (1999) study of informational versus social influence among Canadian military college students and a new University of Western Ontario study on heightened conformity in response to ridicule (Janes & Olson, 2000). The conformity pressures experienced by bicultural minority students are explored in a study conducted by Tafarodi, Kang, and Milne (2002) at the University of Toronto.

Chapter 9, Group Processes: Opening vignette on faulty group decision making: the story of allegedly unsafe vaccines given to Canadian military personnel; study by Cooper, Gallupe, Pollard, and Cadsby (1998) at Queen's University on anonymity and idea generation; example of the murder of Toronto teen Matti Baranovski, in which some of his assailants wore disguises, illustrating deindividuation; study by James Cameron (1999) at Mount Allison University suggesting that the groups to which we belong play an important role in defining who we expect to be in the future; research on personality correlates of leadership by Suedfeld and colleagues at the University of British Columbia (Suedfeld, Conway, & Eichorn, 2001) and by Bradley, Nicol, Charbonneau, and Meyer (2002). The Meech Lake Accord failure is used as an example of groupthink. The chapter also includes research by Vorauer and Claude (1999) on negotiations, showing that the assumption that our goals are obvious to everyone is not necessarily warranted. Finally, a major review paper by Kenneth Dion at the University of Toronto on group cohesion is featured in the suggested readings section (Dion, 2000).

Chapter 10, Interpersonal Attraction: This chapter begins with a University of Calgary study on the risks associated with intimate relationships (Boon & Pasveer, 1999). Research conducted at various Canadian universities on how ordinary people define love is highlighted (Button & Collier, 1991; Fehr, 1988, 1994, 1993; Fehr & Russell, 1991). Another focus is research on the attachment theory perspective on close relationships, including studies on attachment and relationship satisfaction by Keelan, Dion, and Dion (1994) at the University of Toronto, coping strategies (Lussier, Sabourin, & Turgeon, 1997), interpersonal expectations (Baldwin, Fehr, Keedian, Siedel, & Thomson, 1993), and reactions to breakups (Sprecher, Felmlee, Metts, Fehr, & Vanni, 1998). In addition, the chapter addresses the conceptualization of avoidant attachment by Bartholomew (1990) and

Bartholomew and Horowitz (1991); research by Baldwin and Fehr and colleagues on the instability of attachment styles and a reconceptualization of attachment styles as schemas (Baldwin & Fehr, 1995; Baldwin, Fehr, Keedian, Siedel, & Thomson, 1993; Baldwin, Keedian, Fehr, 1996); as well as new research on general versus relationship-specific attachment (Pierce & Lydon, 2001; Ross & Spinner, 2001). The chapter also features research by Lydon and colleagues (Lydon, 1999, Lydon, Meana, Sepinwall, Richards, & Mayman, 1999, Lydon & Zanna, 1990) on the role of adversity in maintaining relationships; research by Murray and Holmes and colleagues at the University of Waterloo on the role of positive illusions in romantic relationships (Murray & Holmes, 1993, 1997, 1999, 2002; Murray, Holmes, & Griffin, 1996a, 1996b; Murray, Holmes, Dolderman, & Griffin, 2000).

Chapter 11, Prosocial Behaviour: Opening vignette on altruism featuring some of the winners of the "Year 2000 Canada Day People Who Make a Difference Awards"; Roberts and Strayer (1996) study conducted with children in British Columbia finding that empathy is related to helping even among children as young as five; Prancer and Pratt's (1999) research on volunteering among Canadian youth; cross-cultural research by Fu, Lee, Cameron, and Xu (2001), Lee, Cameron, Xu, Fu, and Board (1997), and McCrae, Yik, Trapnell, Bond, and Paulhus (1997) on altruism; study by James McDonald and Stuart McKelvie (1992) at Bishop's University on embarrassment and prosocial behaviour. Brown and Moore's (2000) evolutionary analysis of prosocial behaviour is also included.

Chapter 12, Aggression: A number of studies by Pihl and colleagues at McGill University on alcohol and aggression (Hoaken & Pihl, 2000; Pihl & Haoken, 2002; Pihl & Peterson, 1995; Pihl, Peterson, & Lau, 1993; Pihl, Young, Harden, Plotnick, Chamberlain, & Ervin, 1995). New research by Graham and colleagues on alcohol and aggression in various Ontario bars (Graham & Wells, 2001a, 2001b, Graham, West & Wells, 2000; Wells, Graham & West, 2000). The chapter also features a study by Wright et al. (1990) with students at McGill on relative deprivation; study by Van Oostrum and Horvath (1997) on aggression and the attribution of hostile intentions; research by Josephson (1987) finding that violent television programming increases aggression among those who are predis-

posed toward aggression; research by Neil Malamuth and James Check (1981) on the effects of watching sexual violence in movies on men's attitudes toward violence against women. Malamuth and Addison's (2001) evolutionary analysis of aggression is featured in the suggested readings.

Chapter 13, Prejudice: Try It! exercise titled "Multiculturalism: Is It Working?" examining Canada's multiculturalism policy in light of research by Osbeck, Moghaddam, and Perreault (1997); studies by Corenblum and colleagues, including Cornblum and Annis, (1993), in which Native children were more likely to want to play with a white child than a Native child. Corenblum, Annis, and Young (1996) on the effects of prejudice against Natives in Brandon, Manitoba, as well as more recent research examining Natives' attitudes toward white Canadians (Corenblum & Stephan, 2001). The chapter also includes research by Peter Grant (1992, 1993) finding that if a person's sense of social identity is threatened, that person might be especially likely to discriminate against an out-group; research by Sinclair and Kunda (2000) on the selective activation of social and gender stereotypes as a function of self-enhancement goals; a series of studies on meta-stereotypes conducted at the University of Manitoba by Vorauer and colleagues (Vorauer, in press; Vorauer & Kumhyr, 2001; Vorauer, Main, & O'Connell, 1998; Vorauer, Hunter, Main, & Roy, 2000) showing that our attitudes toward out-groups are determined, in part, by the stereotype we believe they hold of us; research by Esses at the University of Western Ontario and Zanna at the University of Waterloo and their colleagues on emotions, cognitions, and behaviour as predictors of prejudice toward various ethnic groups (Esses & Dovidio, 2002; Esses & Zanna, 1995; Esses, Haddock, & Zanna, 1993; Esses, Dovidio, Jackson, & Armstrong, 2001; Haddock, Zanna, & Esses, 1993, 1994); extensive research by Altemeyer at the University of Manitoba, (1981, 1988, 1996, 2001) on right-wing authoritarianism and prejudice; studies on self-blaming attributions for discrimination by Ruggiero and Taylor (1995, 1997), Dion (2001), Dion and Kawakami (1996), Taylor, Wright, Moghaddam, and Lalonde (1990), Foster and Matheson (1999), and Quinn, Roese, Pennington, and Olson (1999). The chapter also includes research conducted by Mark Schaller at the University of British Columbia on the origins of stereotype content (Schaller &

Conway, 1999, 2001; Schaller & O'Brien, 1992; Schaller, Conway, & Tanchuk, 2002). An award-winning address by Kenneth Dion, University of Toronto, on the social psychology of prejudice appears in the suggested readings (Dion, 2002).

Social Psychology in Action 1, Social Psychology and Health: Opening vignette on Manitoba senior Katy Simons, who received an award for her efforts in saving Jews during World War II; she fulfilled her dream of attending university—but not until after she retired; study on the benefits of perceived control and rape victims (Regehr, Cadell, & Jansen, 1999); new studies on coping with traumatic events such as the Holocaust (Sigal & Weinfeld, 2001) or the residential school experiences of First Nations people (Hanson, & Hampton, 2000); longitudinal research by the Canadian Aging Research Network on the benefits of perceived control and aging (Chipperfield, Perry, & Menec, 1999; Menec, Chipperfiled, & Perry, 1999; Menec & Chipperfield, 1997) as well as new research on perceived control and academic achievement (Perry, Hladkyj, Pekrun, & Pelletier, 2001); Allison, Dwyer, and Makin (1999) study of Toronto high-school students on exercise and self-efficacy; study by Walters, Lenton, French, Eyles, Mayr, and Newbold (1996) on the relationship between friendship and health problems; research by Allison, Adlaf, and Mates (1997) on gender differences in how high-school students handle stress. The chapter also includes new research on the effectiveness of social support in dealing with stress (Lefrançois, Leclerc, Hamel, & Gaulin, 2000; Stewart, Craig, MacPherson, & Alexander, 2001).

Social Psychology in Action 2, Social Psychology and the Environment: Study by Cramer, Nickels, and Gural (1997) at the University of Manitoba on loud noise and perceived helplessness; studies by Canadian biologists on deformities in fish and frogs caused by toxic substances in the Great Lakes and along the St. Lawrence River, which could indicate danger to humans; new research on the effects of toxic waste sites on well-being, including Nova Scotia's Tar Ponds (O'Leary & Covell, 2002) and landfill sites in Ontario (Wakefield & Elliott, 2000); studies on predictors of recycling in various Ontario communities (Pelletier, Dion, Tuson, & Green-Demers, 1999; Scott, 1999); McKenzie-Mohr, Nemiroff, Beers, and Desmarais (1995) study showing that B.C. residents' environmental

and cost-saving concerns predicted the use of energy-saving devices such as compact flourescent bulbs and programmable thermostats; studies on recycling in Edmonton (Wall, 1995), communities in the Greater Toronto area (Scott, 1999), and a 1991 Statistics Canada survey on the environment (Berger, 1997) demonstrating that if proenvironmental programs are made convenient enough, people will participate in them.

Social Psychology in Action 3, Social Psychology and the Law: Opening vignette on Thomas Sophonow's wrongful conviction for the murder of a Winnipeg teen forms a running thread through the entire chapter, illustrating the psychological concepts involved in wrongful conviction; studies by Yarmey et al. (1996) and Tollestrup et al. (1994), finding that the longer the time that elapses between seeing a suspect and being asked to identify the person from a lineup, the greater the likelihood of error; research conducted at York University (Schuller & Paglia, 1999) and at Simon Fraser University (Rose & Ogloff, 2001) on jurors' understanding of judges' instructions; studies by Haddock and Zanna (1998) and Vidmar (1974) suggesting that Canadians who favour capital punishment tend to believe that it has a deterrent effect. The chapter also presents various perspectives (judges', lawyers', and psychologists') on the debate over the value of expert testimony in the courtroom (Ogloff & Cronshaw, 2001; Peters, 2001; Saunders, 2001; Yarmey, 2001a). Schuller and Ogloff's (2001) new book on Canadian perspectives on psychology and the law is featured in the suggested readings.

Integrated Coverage of Culture and Gender

To understand behaviour in a social context, we must consider such influences as culture and gender. Rather than adding a chapter on these important topics, we discuss them in every chapter, as they apply to the topic at hand. In many places, we discuss the wonderful diversity of humankind, by presenting research on the differences between people of different cultures, races, or genders. We also discuss the commonalities people share, by illustrating the applicability of many phenomena across cultures, races, and genders. Here are examples:

- Chapter 1, Introduction: The issue of universality versus the cultural relativity of social psychological principles is introduced.
- Chapter 2, Methodology: The issue of how to generalize the results of studies across different types of people is discussed in the section on external validity. In addition, we discuss issues involved in conducting cross-cultural research.
- Chapter 3, Social Cognition: The chapter touches on the issue of gender differences and achievement (e.g., girls' math performance), raising the question of whether these differences are due to the expectations about gender held by teachers and parents. There is also a section on the cultural determinants of schemas that discusses classic work by Bartlett.
- Chapter 4, Social Perception: This chapter includes a good deal of material on culture and gender, including a discussion of controversy over the universality of facial expressions of emotion; cultural differences in other channels of nonverbal communication, such as eye contact, gaze, and personal space; cultural variation in implicit personality theories; and cultural differences in attribution processes. The chapter also describes how the gender of the victim influences victim-blaming attributions.
- Chapter 5, Self-Knowledge: A major focus of this chapter is cultural differences in the definition of self, featuring research by Heine, Lehman, Markus, Kitayama, and others. There also is a section on gender differences in the definition of the self. These lines of inquiry are integrated in research by Adair, Watkins, and colleagues that examines gender differences in the definition of the self in different cultures. We also discuss cultural differences in impression management.
- Chapter 6, Self-Justification: This chapter includes a section on cultural differences in dissonance and dissonance reduction. We also have included two new sections, "Self-Discrepancies and Culture" and "Self-Affirmation and Culture," which focus on striking differences between Canadians' and Asians' self-esteem maintenance processes.

- Chapter 7, Attitudes: This chapter includes a section on culture and the basis of attitudes. We also present research on effectiveness of different kinds of advertisements (e.g., in Korea and the United States in Han & Shavitt, 1994). In the context of a discussion of the effects of advertising, we consider ways in which the media can transmit cultural stereotypes about race and gender.
- Chapter 8, Conformity: This chapter includes a discussion of the role of normative social influence in creating and maintaining cultural standards of beauty. We also discuss gender and cultural differences in conformity and a meta analysis by Bond and Smith (1996) comparing conformity on the Asch line task in 17 countries.
- Chapter 9, Group Processes: We discuss research on gender and culture at several points in this chapter, including gender and cultural differences in social loafing, gender and cultural differences in leadership styles. In addition, we discuss social roles and gender and include a student exercise in which students are asked to deliberately violate a gender role and keep a journal of people's responses to them.
- Chapter 10, Interpersonal Attraction: The role of culture comes up at several points in this chapter, including sections on cultural standards of beauty, comparisons between Canada, the United States, and Korea in the "what is beautiful is good" stereotype (Wheeler & Kim, 1997). We also discuss cultural and gender differences in the effects of physical attractiveness on liking, conceptions of love, and reactions to the dissolution of relationships.
- Chapter 11, Prosocial Behaviour: In this chapter we include a section on gender differences in prosocial behaviour and a section on cultural differences in prosocial behaviour (e.g., comparisons between Canada and Asian countries; McCrae et al., 1998; Lee et al., 1997).
- Chapter 12, Aggression: There is a major section in this chapter on cultural differences in aggression, including a discussion of differences in

homicide rates in different countries. We also discuss research on gender differences in aggression and the effects of violent pornography on violence against women. A new Try It! student exercise focuses on gender differences in spousal violence.

- Chapter 13, Prejudice: Issues about in-groups and out-groups and ways of reducing prejudice are central to this chapter. For example, we present research on stereotype threat, including American and Canadian studies on achievement in minority groups and men versus women. We also discuss recent research by Sinclair and Kunda (1999, 2000) on motivational factors underlying the activation of racial and gender stereotypes. In addition, a new Try It! exercise prompts students to evaluate Canada's multiculturalism policy in light of social psychological findings.

- Social Psychology in Action units on Health, Environment, and Law: These chapters include numerous discussions relevant to culture and gender. For example, in the Health unit, we discuss research on cultural differences in the Type A personality as well as gender and cultural differences in social support. In the Environment unit, we discuss cultural differences in how density and crowding are perceived. In the Law unit, we compare crime rates in countries (and states) that use capital punishment with crime rates in regions that do not invoke the death penalty.

- Chapter 1, Introduction to Social Psychology: We introduce the evolutionary perspective in this chapter. We also recommend Crawford and Kreb's (1998) *Handbook of Evolutionary Psychology* in the reading list as a resource for students who wish to learn more about this theory.

- Chapter 4, Social Perception: We discuss the controversy over whether some facial expressions are universal, including Darwin's view that they are.

- Chapter 9, Group Processes: We discuss whether we have inherited the need to belong from our evolutionary past.

- Chapter 10, Interpersonal Attraction: We present the evolutionary perspective on gender differences in romantic attraction and on why people fall in love. We also include Buckle et al.'s (1996) evolution theory analysis of marriage and divorce patterns in Canada.

- Chapter 11, Prosocial Behaviour: Evolutionary psychology is presented as one of the major theories of why humans engage in prosocial behaviour. We present evidence for and against this perspective and contrast it to other approaches, such as social exchange theory.

- Chapter 12, Aggression: We include a section on whether aggression is inborn or learned, including a discussion of an evolutionary explanation of aggressive behaviour.

- Chapter 13, Prejudice: We touch on the issue of whether there might be an evolutionary basis for prejudice.

The Evolutionary Approach

In recent years, social psychologists have become increasingly interested in an evolutionary perspective on many aspects of social behaviour. Once again, our approach is to integrate this perspective into those parts of chapters where it is relevant, rather than devote a separate chapter to this topic. We present what we believe is a balanced approach, discussing evolutionary psychology as well as alternatives to it. Here are examples of places in which we discuss the evolutionary approach:

Social Psychology: The Applied Side

One of the best ways to capture students' interest is to point out the real-world significance of the material they are studying. From the vignette that opens each chapter and runs throughout it to the discussions of historical events, current affairs, and our own lives that are embedded in the story line, the narrative is highlighted by real, familiar examples. Applications are an integral part of social psychology, however, and deserve their own treatment. In addition to an integrated coverage of applied topics in the body of the text, we include additional coverage in two ways.

TRY IT! STUDENT EXERCISES

In each chapter, we feature a series of Try It! exercises, in which students are invited to apply the concepts they are learning to their everyday life. These exercises include detailed instructions about how to attempt to replicate actual social psychological experiments, such as Milgram's (1963) lost letter technique in Chapter 11, and Reno and colleagues' (1993) study on norms and littering in the Social Psychology in Action 3 unit. Other Try It! exercises reproduce self-report scales and invite the students to fill them out to see where they stand on these measures. Examples include Campbell and colleagues' (1996) measure of self-concept clarity in Chapter 5, and the Passionate Love Scale in Chapter 10. Still others are quizzes that illustrate social psychological concepts, such as a Reasoning Quiz in Chapter 3 that illustrates judgmental heuristics, or demonstrations that explain how to use a particular concept in a student's everyday life, such as an exercise in Chapter 9 that instructs students to violate a sex role norm and observe the consequences. The format of, and the time frame required for, each of these exercises varies. You might want to flip through the book to look at other examples in more detail.

Try It! exercises are not only in the text itself, but built into the website as well. Students will find a new Try It! exercise for each chapter on the *Companion Website*. You can use Try It! exercises as class activities or as homework.

We believe that the Try It! exercises will generate a lot of interest in learning social psychological concepts by making them more memorable and engaging.

SOCIAL PSYCHOLOGY IN ACTION UNITS

You will note from the Detailed Contents that there are three chapters devoted to applied topics in social psychology: one on health, one on environment, and one on law. Each has the subtitle of Social Psychology in Action. You might wonder why these chapters have a different name and numbering system than the other chapters. The reason is that they are designed to be free-floating units that

can be assigned at virtually any point in the text. Although we do occasionally refer to earlier chapters in these units, they are designed to be independent units that could fit into many different points of a course in social psychology.

In talking with many professors who teach social psychology, we have been struck by how differently they present applied material. Some prefer to assign these chapters at the end of the course, after they have covered the major concepts, theories, and research findings. Others prefer to integrate the applied chapters with the more theoretical material when relevant. Our applied units are designed to be used in either way.

Supplements to the Text

A really good textbook should become part of the classroom experience, supporting and augmenting the professor's vision for his or her class. *Social Psychology,* Second Canadian Edition, offers a number of supplements that will enrich both the professor's presentation of social psychology and the student's understanding of it.

INSTRUCTOR'S SUPPLEMENTS

- **Pearson Education Canada/CBC Video Library.** (ISBN 0-13-122467-0) Few will dispute that video is one of the most dynamic supplements you can use to enhance a class. The authors and editors of Pearson Education Canada have carefully selected videos on topics that complement *Social Psychology,* Second Canadian Edition, from popular CBC series such as *The National, The Health Show*, and *Undercurrents*. An excellent video guide will help you integrate the videos into your lecture. The guide has a synopsis of each video, a list of the psychological principles it reinforces with respect to the text chapter, advance preparation, discussion questions, and in-class activities to help students focus on how concepts and theories apply to real-life situations.

- **PowerPoint Presentations.** Contain figures and tables from the text. Available through the *Companion Website* by chapter.

- **Instructor's Manual and Resource Kit.** (ISBN 0-13-121776-3) Includes lecture ideas, teaching tips, suggested readings, chapter outlines, student projects and research assignments, Try It! exercises, critical thinking topics and discussion questions, and a media resource guide.

- **Test Item File.** (ISBN 0-13-121775-5) Each question in this 2000-question test bank is referenced to parent text page number, topic, and skill level.

- **Pearson TestGen.** The *Pearson TestGen* is a special computerized version of the *Test Item File* that enables instructors to view and edit the existing questions, add questions, generate tests, and print the tests in a variety of formats. Powerful search and sort functions make it easy to locate questions and arrange them in any order desired. TestGen also enables instructors to administer tests on a local area network, have the tests graded electronically, and have the results prepared in electronic or printed reports. Issued on a CD-ROM, the *Pearson TestGen* is compatible with IBM or Macintosh systems.

- **Instructor's Resource CD-ROM.** (ISBN 0-13-121771-2) This CD-ROM features the textbook graphics, the *Instructor's Manual*, the *Pearson TestGen*, and the *PowerPoint Presentations*, along with the appropriate viewers to read and use these materials.

STUDENT SUPPLEMENTS

- **Student Study Guide.** (ISBN 0-13-121772-0) Contains chapter overviews, learning objectives and outlines, study questions, key terms, and practice tests.

- **Companion Website (www.pearsoned.ca/aronson)** Includes additional Try It! exercises, two Practice Tests with instant self-scoring and coaching for each chapter, Critical Thinking and Writing activities, links to other sites, and a key terms glossary. The Instructor's Resource area of the site features

the *Instructor's Manual* and the *PowerPoint Presentations*.

Acknowledgments

Elliot Aronson is delighted to acknowledge the general contributions of his best friend (who also happens to be his wife), Vera Aronson. Vera, as usual, provided a great deal of inspiration for his ideas and acted as the sounding board for and supportive critic of many of his semiformed notions, helping to mold them into more sensible analyses. He would also like to thank his son, Joshua Aronson, a brilliant young social psychologist in his own right, for the many stimulating conversations that contributed mightily to the final version of this book. For the U.S. fourth edition, Linda Tropp provided valuable specific research assistance.

Tim Wilson would like to thank his graduate mentor, Richard E. Nisbett, who nurtured his interest in the field and showed him the continuity between social psychological research and everyday life. He thanks his graduate students, Sara Algoe, David Centerbar, Elizabeth Dunn, Debby Kermer, Jaime Kurtz, Jay Meyers, and Thalia Wheatley, who helped keep him a well-balanced professor—a researcher as well as a teacher and author. He thanks his parents, Elizabeth and Geoffrey Wilson, for their overall support. Most of all, he thanks his wife, Deirdre Smith, and his children, Christopher and Leigh, for their love, patience, and understanding, even when the hour was late and the computer was still on.

Robin Akert would like to thank her students and colleagues at Wellesley College for their support and encouragement. In particular, she is beholden to Patricia Berman, Jonathan Cheek, Regan Bernhard, and Alison Bibbins. Their advice, feedback, and senses of humour were vastly appreciated. She is deeply grateful to her family, Michaela and Wayne Akert, and Linda and Jerry Wuichet; their inexhaustible enthusiasm and boundless support have sustained her on this project as on all the ones before it. Once again she thanks C. Issak for authorial inspiration. Finally, no words can express her gratitude and indebtedness to Dane Archer, mentor, colleague, and friend, who opened the world of social psychology to her and who has been her guide ever since.

Beverley Fehr would like to thank her colleagues at the University of Winnipeg and her social psychology colleagues at the University of Manitoba for their enthusiasm and support throughout this project. She is indebted to Lisa Sinclair, Wendy Josephson, and Marian Morry for their emotional and practical support, which included offering incisive feedback on individual chapters. Beverley would also like to express gratitude to her capable, highly skilled research assistants, Cheryl Harasymchuk and Joanne Wong. On a more personal note, Beverley's dear friends Lydia Friesen Rempel and Lorrie Brubacher provided the unfailing emotional support and good cheer that have sustained her through many a project over the years. Beverley is also grateful to her husband, Marvin Giesbrecht, for his generosity and kindness in doing "more than his share" of domestic chores and the more mundane aspects of childcare so that she could focus on writing this book. Even though Beverley's children, Genevieve and Everett, are probably too young to realize it, their smiles and antics were an invaluable source of joy and energy. Finally, Beverley would like to thank the staff at Bread and Circuses Café, where much of her writing was done, for their warmth, friendliness, and the countless refills of coffee.

No book can be written and published without the help of a great many people working with the authors behind the scenes, and this book is no exception. Beverley would like to thank the people at Pearson Education Canada who worked with her on this text. She would like to express appreciation to Lise Dupont, Senior Developmental Editor, for her competence, good judgment, and unfailing cheerfulness. Beverley would also like to thank Executive Acquisitions Editor Jessica Mosher for her encouragement and willingness to lend a listening ear no matter how busy she was; Editorial Coordinator Söğüt Y. Güleç, and Copy Editor Susan Broadhurst for their competence, conscientiousness, and good-natured patience in dealing with an author who constantly wanted to make "just one more little change."

Finally, we would like to thank the many colleagues who read one or more chapters of previous editions of the book.

REVIEWERS OF THE SECOND CANADIAN EDITION

James Cameron, St. Mary's University
Jennifer D. Campbell, University of British Columbia
Steve Charlton, Kwantlen University College
Andrew J. Howell, Grant MacEwan College
Patrice Karn, University of Ottawa
Barry N. Kelly, University of Winnipeg
David Mandel, University of Victoria
Donald Sharpe, University of Regina
Warren Thorngate, Carleton University

REVIEWERS OF THE U.S. FOURTH EDITION

John Bargh, New York University
Ellen S. Berscheid, University of Minnesota
Jeff Bryson, San Diego State University
Brad Bushman, Iowa State University
Russell Geen, University of Missouri
Elaine Hatfield, University of Hawaii, Manoa
Alan Lambert, Washington University, St. Louis
Allen R. McConnell, Michigan State University
Lee D. Ross, Stanford University
Alex Rothman, University of Minnesota
Delia Saenz, Arizona State University
Brad Sagarin, Northern Illinois University
Norbert Schwartz, University of Michigan
Jonell Strough, West Virginia University
Scott Tindale, Loyola University of Chicago
Paul Windschitl, University of Iowa
Gwen Wittenbaum, Michigan State University

Thank you for inviting us into your classroom. We welcome your suggestions, and we would be delighted to hear your comments about this book.

Elliot Aronson
elliot@cats.ucsc.edu

Tim Wilson
tdw@virginia.edu

Robin Akert
rakert@wellesley.edu

Beverley Fehr
bfehr@uwinnipeg.ca

A Great Way to Learn and Instruct Online

The Pearson Education Canada Companion Website is easy to navigate and is organized to correspond to the chapters in this textbook. Whether you are a student in the classroom or a distance learner you will discover helpful resources for in-depth study and research that empower you in your quest for greater knowledge and maximize your potential for success in the course.

Companion
Website

[www.pearsoned.ca/aronson]

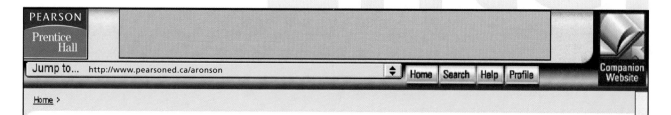

PEARSON
Prentice
Hall

Jump to...   http://www.pearsoned.ca/aronson   ⬍   Home | Search | Help | Profile

Companion
Website

Home >

PH Companion Website

Social Psychology, Second Canadian Edition, by Aronson, Wilson, Akert, and Fehr

Student Resources

The modules in this section provide students with tools for learning course material. These modules include:

- Chapter Objectives
- Additional Try It! exercises
- Practice Tests
- Links
- Net Search
- Glossary

In the quiz modules students can send answers to the grader and receive instant feedback on their progress through the Results Reporter. Coaching comments and references to the textbook may be available to ensure that students take advantage of all available resources to enhance their learning experience.

Instructor Resources

This module links directly to additional teaching tools. Downloadable Powerpoint Presentations, Electronic Transparencies, and an Instructor's Manual are just some of the materials that may be available in this section.

ABOUT THE AUTHORS

ELLIOT ARONSON

When I was a kid, we were the only Jewish family in a virulently anti-Semitic neighbourhood. I had to go to Hebrew school every day, late in the afternoon. Being the only youngster in my neighbourhood going to Hebrew school made me an easy target for some of the older neighbourhood toughs. On my way home from Hebrew school, after dark, I was frequently waylaid and roughed up by roving gangs shouting anti-Semitic epithets.

I have a vivid memory of sitting on a curb after one of these beatings, nursing a bloody nose or a split lip, feeling very sorry for myself and wondering how these kids could hate me so much when they didn't even know me. I thought about whether those kids were taught to hate Jews or whether, somehow, they were born that way. I wondered if their hatred could be changed—if they got to know me better, would they hate me less? I speculated about my own character. What would I have done if the shoe were on the other foot—that is, if I were bigger and stronger than they, would I be capable of beating them up for no good reason?

I didn't realize it at the time, of course, but eventually I discovered that these were profound questions. And some thirty years later, as an experimental social psychologist, I had the great good fortune to be in a position to answer some of those questions and to invent techniques to reduce the kind of prejudice that had claimed me as a victim.

Elliot Aronson graduated from Brandeis University (where he worked with Abraham Maslow) and received his Ph.D. from Stanford University, working under the guidance of Leon Festinger. He has done pioneering research in the areas of social influence, persuasion, prejudice reduction, and AIDS prevention. Aronson has written or edited 18 books, including The Social Animal, The Handbook of Social Psychology, Age of Propaganda, The Jigsaw Classroom, Methods of Research in Social Psychology, *and* Nobody Left to Hate. *He is among the world's most distinguished social psychologists. He is the only person in the 107-year history of the American Psychological Association to have earned all three of its major academic awards: for Distinguished Teaching, for Distinguished Research, and for Distinguished Writing. He has served as president of the Society of Personality and Social Psychology and president of the Western Psychological Association. In 1992, he was elected a Fellow of the American Academy of Arts and Sciences. He is currently professor emeritus at the University of California at Santa Cruz and a visiting professor at Stanford University.*

TIM WILSON

One day, when I was 8, a couple of older kids rode up on their bikes to share some big news: They had discovered an abandoned house down a country road. "It's really neat," they said. "We broke a window and nobody cared!" My friend and I

hopped onto our bikes to investigate. We had no trouble finding the house—there it was, sitting off by itself, with a big, jagged hole in a first-floor window. We got off of our bikes and looked around. My friend found a baseball-sized rock lying on the ground and threw a perfect strike through another first-floor window. There was something exhilarating about the smash-and-tingle of shattering glass, especially when we knew there was nothing wrong with what we were doing. After all, the house was abandoned, wasn't it? We broke nearly every window in the house and then climbed through one of the first-floor windows to look around.

It was then that we realized something was terribly wrong. The house certainly did not look abandoned. There were pictures on the wall, nice furniture, books in shelves. We went home feeling frightened and confused.

We soon learned that the house was not abandoned: It was the residence of an elderly couple who were away on vacation. Eventually my parents discovered what we had done and paid a substantial sum to repair the windows.

For years, I pondered this incident: Why did I do such a terrible thing? Was I a bad kid? I didn't think so, and neither did my parents. How, then, could a good kid do such a bad thing? Even though the neighbourhood kids said the house was abandoned, why couldn't my friend and I see the clear signs that someone lived there? How crucial was it that my friend was there and threw the first rock? Though I didn't know it at the time, these reflections touched on several classic social psychological issues, such as whether only bad people do bad things, whether the social situation can be powerful enough to make good people do bad things, and the way in which our expectations about an event can make it difficult to see it as it really is. Fortunately, my career as a vandal ended with this one incident. It did, however, mark the beginning of my fascination with basic questions about how people understand themselves and the social world—questions I continue to investigate to this day.

Tim Wilson did his undergraduate work at Williams College and Hampshire College and received his Ph.D. from the University of Michigan. Currently a professor of psychology at the University of Virginia, he has published numerous articles in the areas of introspection, attitude change, self-knowledge, and affective forecasting. His research has received the support of the National Science Foundation and the National Institute for Mental Health. He has been associate editor of the Journal of Personality and Social Psychology *and a member of the Social and Groups Processes Review Committee at the National Institute of Mental Health. He has been elected twice to the Executive Board of the Society for Experimental Social Psychology and is a Fellow in the American Psychological Society. Wilson has taught the Introduction to Social Psychology course at the University of Virginia for more than twenty years. He was recently awarded an All University Outstanding Teaching Award.*

ROBIN AKERT

One fall day, when I was about 16, I was walking with a friend along the shore of the San Francisco Bay. Deep in conversation, I glanced over my shoulder and saw a sailboat capsize. I pointed it out to my friend, who took only a perfunctory interest and went on talking. However, I kept watching as we walked, and I realized that the two sailors were in the water, clinging to the capsized boat.  Again I said something to my friend, who replied, "Oh, they'll get it upright, don't worry."

But I was worried. Was this an emergency? My friend didn't think so. And I was no sailor; I knew nothing about boats. But I kept thinking, "That water is really cold. They can't stay in that water too long." I remember feeling very confused and unsure. What should I do? Should I do anything? Did they really need help?

We were near a restaurant with a big window overlooking the bay, and I decided to go in and see if anyone had done anything about the boat. Lots of people were watching but not doing anything. This confused me, too. Very meekly, I asked the bartender to call for some kind of help. He just shrugged. I went back to the window and watched the two small figures in the water. Why was everyone so unconcerned? Was I crazy?

Years later, I reflected on how hard it was for me to do what I did next: I demanded that the bartender let me use his phone. In those days before "911," it was lucky that I knew there was a Coast Guard station on the bay, and I asked the operator for the number. I was relieved to hear the guardsman take my message very seriously.

It had been an emergency. I watched as the Coast Guard cutter sped across the bay and pulled the two sailors out of the water. Maybe I saved their lives that day. What really stuck with me over the years was how other people behaved and how it made me feel. The other bystanders seemed unconcerned and did nothing to help. Their reactions made me doubt myself and made it harder for me to decide to take action. When I later studied social psychology in college, I realized that on the shore of the San Francisco Bay that day, I had experienced the "bystander effect" fully: The presence of other, apparently unconcerned bystanders had made it difficult for me to decide if the situation was an emergency and whether it was my responsibility to help.

Robin Akert graduated summa cum laude from the University of California at Santa Cruz, where she majored in psychology and sociology. She received her Ph.D. in experimental social psychology from Princeton University. She is currently a professor of psychology at Wellesley College, where she was awarded the Pinanski Prize for Excellence in Teaching. She publishes primarily in the area of nonverbal communication and is the co-author of Interpretation and Awareness: Verbal and Nonverbal Factors in Person Perception.

BEVERLEY FEHR

I suspect that many social psychologists, like me, didn't start out with the intention of becoming social psychologists. I was attending university as a music major, taking psychology courses for interest. I enjoyed them, but kept experiencing a vague sense of disappointment—each course wasn't quite what I had thought psychology would be about. When I enrolled in a social psychology course that was offered one summer, I was delighted to have finally found a course that captured what I had been

looking for. One day, as part of a class exercise, our professor handed out copies of Rubin's (1970) love and liking scale for us to complete with reference to a romantic partner and a friend. (This scale is still widely used in close relationships research today.) I was dating someone at the time about whom I cared deeply, although I had a feeling that he was not a particularly good choice as a long-term partner. I was astonished, when we scored the scale, that the love score for this person was extremely high, but the liking score was distressingly low! Quite aside from the personal implications of this result, I was utterly fascinated that social psychologists could use the scientific method to gain insight into issues that are highly relevant to people's everyday lives. This, and other experiences in that class, prompted me to reconsider my career choice and I ended up changing my major to psychology. I suspect that this experience also may have played a role in my eventual decision to become a social psychologist who studies close relationships.

Beverley Fehr graduated with a B.A. (Hons.) from the University of Winnipeg where she was awarded the Gold Medal for the highest standing in psychology. She received her M.A. (under the guidance of Jim Russell) and her Ph.D. (under the guidance of Dan Perlman) from the University of British Columbia. Her doctoral thesis on lay people's conceptions of love and commitment won the Iowa/International Network for the Study of Personal Relationships Dissertation Prize. She has published numerous articles and book chapters on the topics of emotion and close relationships. Her book Friendship Processes *(1996) was awarded the 1997 Outstanding Academic Book Award by Choice: Current Reviews for Academic Libraries. Beverley's research is supported by grants from the Social Sciences and Humanities Research Council of Canada and the Fetzer Institute.*

Introduction to Social Psychology

▼ Derek Kennedy was awarded a medal of bravery by the Governor General in December 1999, for rescuing three drowning people in North Sydney Harbour, Nova Scotia.

THE TASK OF THE PSYCHOLOGIST IS TO TRY TO UNDERSTAND AND predict human behaviour. Different kinds of psychologists go about this in different ways, and in this book we will attempt to show you how social psychologists do it. Let's begin with a few examples of human behaviour. Some of these might seem important; others might seem trivial; one or two might seem frightening. To a social psychologist, all of them are interesting. Our hope is that by the time you finish reading this book, you will find all of these examples as fascinating as we do. As you read, try to think about how you would explain why each event unfolded as it did.

1. Derek Kennedy was watching the boats in North Sydney Harbour in Nova Scotia on August 6, 1998, when a pleasure boat exploded and five adults and two children were forced into the water. Kennedy immediately dove into the water and swam the 20 metres to rescue the children, who were clinging to a struggling woman. When Kennedy got to them, the panicking woman repeatedly pulled him under the water. Kennedy managed to get away from her, then helped her swim to shore while he brought the children in safely. Once they were ashore, he went back into the water to help another woman who was refusing to let go of a dinghy. Eventually, with the help of other witnesses, all the other boaters got safely to shore. Kennedy was awarded a medal of bravery by the Governor General in December 1999 (The Governor General of Canada, 1999).

What makes a person risk his life to save another? What made Kennedy go back into the water a second time, when he had already nearly been drowned by a panicking adult? Would you or anyone you know have done what Kennedy did?

2. Sally was watching TV with a few friends. On the tube, Premier Ralph Klein was making an important policy speech. This was the first time Sally had listened really carefully to one of Klein's substantive speeches. She was favourably impressed by his homey, down-to-earth quality; she felt he was smart, honest, sincere, and compassionate. As soon as the speech was over, her friend Melinda said, "Boy, what a phony—I wouldn't trust that guy with my dirty laundry—I can't believe he's running our province. No wonder our health care has gone down the tubes!" The others quickly chimed in, voicing their agreement. Sally felt uncomfortable, and was frankly puzzled. Finally, she mumbled, "Yeah, I guess he did come off as a bit insincere."

What do you suppose was going on in Sally's mind? Did she actually come to see Premier Klein in a new light, or was she simply trying to "go along" in order to get along?

3. On the cover of the March 6, 2000, issue of *Maclean's* magazine, a headline reads, "A barbaric rite of passage: Hazing in university athletes." The article begins with the story of Jean-François Caudron from St-Hubert, Quebec, the recipient of a hockey scholarship from the University of Vermont. As a rookie, he would be subjected to a hazing that involved shaving his pubic hair, painting his toenails, and drinking warm beer until he vomited. Based on his experiences on Canadian hockey teams, Jean-François knew there was no

escaping rookie night: "You knew about this night and you were nervous. You feel pressure that you have to do it." One might expect that Jean-François would have nothing but bad memories about his hazing experiences. However, he describes it this way, "[O]nce it was over, I was so happy. I really felt part of the team" (O'Hara, 2000).

Why would Jean-François feel so happy to be part of a team that inflicted pain, embarrassment, and humiliation?

> 4. In the mid-1980s, Quebecers were introduced to the Order of the Solar Temple—a cult founded by Luc Jouret and his partner Joseph Di Mambro. Prominent citizens, including the highly respected mayor of Richelieu and his wife, joined the cult. They were taught that the only redemption from their sins was to experience death by fire, which would transport them to the star Sirius, where they would be reborn. Suicides were to take place during the spring or autumn equinox. The cult attracted worldwide attention in October 1994, when 53 cult members, including the mayor of Richelieu and his wife, died in a combined mass murder–suicide. An elaborate system of explosives set fire to the buildings they inhabited in Quebec and Switzerland. Nearly a year later, another 16 cult members, including several children, died in a remote village in France. So far, at least 74 members of this cult have died.

How can people agree to kill themselves and their own children? Were they crazy? Were they under some kind of hypnotic spell? How would you explain it? We now have several questions about human social behaviour—questions we find fascinating. Why did Derek Kennedy put his life at serious risk to save the victims of the boating accident? Why did Sally change her opinion about the sincerity of Premier Klein and bring it in line with her friends' opinion? Why did Jean-François Caudron like being part of hockey teams that forced him to endure barbaric hazing rituals? And how could large numbers of people be induced to kill their own children and themselves in Quebec, Switzerland, and France? In this chapter, we will consider what these examples have in common and why they are of interest to us. We will also put forth some reasonable explanations based upon social psychological research.

What Is Social Psychology?

At the heart of social psychology is the phenomenon of social influence: We are all influenced by other people. When we think of social influence, the kinds of examples that readily come to mind are direct attempts at persuasion, whereby one person deliberately tries to change another person's behaviour. This is what happens in an advertising campaign when creative individuals employ sophisticated techniques to persuade us to buy a particular brand of toothpaste, or during an election campaign when similar techniques are used to get us to vote for a particular political candidate. Direct attempts at persuasion also occur when our friends try to get us to do something we don't really want to do ("Come on, have another beer—everyone is doing it") or when the schoolyard bully uses force or threats to get smaller kids to part with their lunch money or completed homework.

These direct social influence attempts form a major part of social psychology, and will be discussed in our chapters on conformity, attitudes, and group processes. To the social psychologist, however, social influence is broader than attempts by one person to change another person's behaviour. For one thing, social influence extends beyond behaviour—it includes our thoughts and feelings, as well as our overt acts. In addition, social influence takes on many forms other than deliberate attempts at persuasion. We are often influenced merely by the presence of other people. Moreover, even when we are not in the physical presence of other people, we are still influenced by them. Thus, in a sense we carry our mothers, fathers, friends, and teachers around with us, as we attempt to make decisions that would make them proud of us.

On a more subtle level, each of us is immersed in a social and cultural context. Social psychologists are interested in studying how and why our thoughts, feelings, and behaviours are shaped by the entire social environment. Taking all these factors into account, we can define **social psychology** as the scientific study of the way in which people's thoughts, feelings, and behaviours are influenced by the real or imagined presence of other people (Allport, 1985). Of particular interest to social psychologists is what happens in the mind of an individual when various influences come into conflict with one another, as is frequently the case when young people go off to university or college and find themselves torn between the beliefs and values they learned at home and the beliefs and values their professors or peers are expressing.

Other disciplines, such as anthropology and sociology, are also interested in how people are influenced by their social environment. Social psychology is distinct, however, primarily because it is concerned not so much with social situations in any objective sense, but rather with how people are influenced by their interpretation, or **construal**, of their social environment. To understand how people are influenced by their social world, social psychologists believe, it is more important to understand how they perceive, comprehend, and interpret the social world than it is to understand the objective properties of the social world itself (Lewin, 1943).

In a murder trial, for example, the prosecution may present evidence such as DNA tests that it believes will have a decisive impact on the verdict. But no matter how powerful the evidence might be, the final verdict will always hinge on precisely how each member of the jury construes that evidence—and these construals may rest on a variety of events and perceptions that may or may not bear objective relevance to the matter. Such construal processes can produce very different outcomes. In the O.J. Simpson trial in the United States, even though objective evidence concerning DNA and hair and fibre samples was presented, the jury decided that Simpson was not guilty of murdering his ex-wife and her friend. In contrast, in the case of Larry Fisher—who was tried for the murder of Gail Miller after David Milgaard was finally exonerated—the same kind of objective evidence (results of DNA tests) led to a first-degree murder conviction, even though the defence tried to persuade the jury that the DNA evidence proved only that he had raped Gail Miller, not that he was her killer.

Another distinctive feature of social psychology is that it is an experimentally based science that tests its assumptions, guesses, and ideas about human social behaviour empirically and systematically, rather than relying on folk wisdom, common sense, the opinions and insights of philosophers, novelists, political pundits, grandmothers, and others wise in

Social psychology

the scientific study of the way in which people's thoughts, feelings, and behaviours are influenced by the real or imagined presence of other people

Construal

the way in which people perceive, comprehend, and interpret the social world

the ways of human beings. As you will see, doing systematic experiments in social psychology presents a great many challenges, primarily because we are attempting to predict the behaviour of highly sophisticated organisms in a variety of complex situations. As scientists, our goal is to find objective answers to a wide array of important questions: What are the factors that cause aggression? How might we reduce prejudice? What variables cause two people to like or love each other? Why do certain kinds of political advertisements work better than others? The specific ways in which experimental social psychologists meet these challenges will be illustrated throughout this book and discussed in detail in Chapter 2.

We will spend most of this introductory chapter expanding on the issues raised in the section above: what social psychology is and how it is distinct from other, related disciplines. A good place to begin is with what social psychology is *not*.

SOME ALTERNATIVE WAYS OF UNDERSTANDING SOCIAL INFLUENCE

Let's take another look at the examples at the beginning of this chapter. Why did people behave the way they did? One way to answer this question might simply be to ask them. For example, we could ask Derek Kennedy why he was willing to risk his life—twice— to save the drowning women and children; we could ask Sally why she changed her opinion of Premier Ralph Klein. The problem with this approach is that people are not always aware of the origins of their own responses (Nisbett & Wilson, 1977a). It is unlikely that Derek Kennedy knows why he went back into the water, or that Sally knows why she changed her mind about the premier of her province.

Folk Wisdom   Journalists, social critics, and novelists have many interesting things to say about these situations. Such commentary is generally referred to as *folk wisdom* or *common sense*. A great deal can be learned about social behaviour from journalists, social critics, and novelists—and in this book we quote from all of these. There is, however, at least one problem with full reliance on such sources: More often than not, they disagree with one another, and there is no easy way of determining which of them is correct. Consider what folk wisdom has to say about the factors that influence how much we like other people. On the one hand, we know that "birds of a feather flock together," and, with a little effort, each of us could come up with many examples in which we liked and hung around with people who shared our backgrounds and interests. But on the other hand, folk wisdom *also* tells us that "opposites attract," and, if we tried, we could come up with examples in which people with backgrounds and interests different from our own did attract us. Which is correct?

Similarly, are we to believe that "out of sight is out of mind" or that "absence makes the heart grow fonder"; that "haste makes waste" or that "he who hesitates is lost"?

There is no shortage of folk theories for events such as the Solar Temple tragedy. When cult members kill themselves and their children at the request of their leader, explanations range from the view that the leader must have employed hypnotism and drugs to weaken the resistance of his followers, to suspicion that the people who were attracted to his cult must have been disturbed, self-destructive individuals in the first

▲ Although attorneys do their best to convince a jury, in the end the verdict will depend on how the individual jurors construe the evidence. In the case of Larry Fisher, pictured here, the jury was shown DNA evidence proving that Fisher raped Gail Miller, and decided he must have murdered her as well.

place. Such speculations, because they underestimate the power of the situation, are almost certainly incorrect—or at the very least oversimplified. Indeed, what is most striking about members of the Solar Temple cult is that they tended to be highly respected, well-functioning members of society—including a mayor, a journalist, a civil servant, and a sales manager.

Unfortunately, because so-called common sense frequently turns out to be wrong or oversimplified, we tend not to learn from previous incidents. The Solar Temple was probably the first mass suicide involving Canadians, but certainly not the first or the last event of this kind. In 1978, nearly 800 members of a California-based religious cult died when they drank a deadly mixture of Kool-Aid and cyanide in response to a command from their leader, the Reverend Jim Jones. A few years ago in Waco, Texas, the followers of cult leader David Koresh barricaded themselves into a fortress-like compound, and, when surrounded, apparently set fire to their own buildings; this resulted in the deaths of 86 people, including several children. Still more recently, doomsday cults capitalized on fears that the millennium would bring about the end of the world, and managed to persuade their followers to take their lives and those of their children. A particularly chilling example of such a doomsday cult is a Uganda cult known as the Movement for the Restoration of the Ten Commandments of God. One of the cult's beliefs is that childhood is sinful. The leaders managed to persuade parents that handing over their children to die was the only way to prevent them from falling into the hands of Satan. On March 17, 2000, hundreds of people, many of whom were children, were led into a sealed chapel that was set on fire (Associated Press, 2000). Hundreds of other cult members and their children died in other ways. Although it is difficult to determine the exact number of casualties, most

▶ Why would reasonable persons blindly agree to hand themselves and their children over to a painful death? Though it may be easy to dismiss the followers of the Ugandan cult as foolish, such oversimplifications and denial of the power of social influence can lead us to blame the victims. Shown here are the primary leaders of Uganda's Movement for the Restoration of the Ten Commandments of God: (left to right) Ursala Kamuhangi, Cledonia Mwerinde, Joseph Kibweteere, and Dominic Kataribabo.

reports suggest that between 800 and 1000 people perished, placing this cult on the same horrific scale as the California-based Jonestown cult (Wasswa, 2002).

It is difficult for most people to grasp just how powerful a cult can be in affecting the hearts and minds of relatively normal people. Accordingly, the general population is eager to find someone to blame. Often people blame the victims themselves, accusing them of stupidity or of suffering from mental illness. Fixing blame may make us feel better by resolving our confusion, but it is no substitute for understanding the complexities of the situations that produced those events.

Philosophy Throughout the history of humankind, philosophy has been, and continues to be, a major source of insight about human nature. Indeed, the creativity and analytical thinking of philosophers are a major part of the foundation of contemporary psychology. This has more than mere historical significance. During this decade alone, psychologists have used current philosophical thinking in an attempt to gain greater understanding of such important issues as the nature of consciousness (e.g., Dennett, 1991) and how people form beliefs about the social world (e.g., Gilbert, 1991). Sometimes, however, even great thinkers find themselves in disagreement; when this occurs, how is one to know who is right? Are there some situations in which philosopher A might be right and other conditions in which philosopher B might be right? How would you determine this?

We social psychologists address many of the same questions that philosophers address, but we attempt to look at these questions scientifically. Just as a physicist performs experiments to test hypotheses about the nature of the physical world, the social psychologist performs experiments to test hypotheses about the nature of the social world. The major reason we have conflicting philosophical positions (just as we have conflicting folk aphorisms) is that the world is a complicated place. Small differences in the situation might not be easily discernible; yet these small differences might produce very different effects. For example, in 1663, the great Dutch philosopher Benedict Spinoza came out with a highly original insight about love. He wrote that if we love someone whom we formerly hated, that love will be greater than if hatred had not preceded it. Spinoza's proposition is beautifully worked out. His logic is impeccable. But how can we be sure that it holds up? Does it always hold? What are the conditions under which it does or does not hold? These are empirical questions for the social psychologist.

To elaborate on this point, let us return for a moment to our earlier discussion about the kinds of people we like, and the relationship between absence and liking. Almost certainly, there are some conditions under which birds of a feather do flock together and other conditions under which opposites do attract; similarly, there are some conditions under which absence does make the heart grow fonder and others under which out of sight does mean out of mind. Each of these can be true. If you really want to understand human behaviour, however, knowing that both can be true is not sufficient. One of the tasks of the social psychologist is to design experiments sophisticated enough to demonstrate the specific situations under which one or the other applies. This enriches our understanding of human nature and allows us to make accurate predictions once we know the key aspects of the prevailing situation. In Chapter 2, we will discuss in more detail the scientific methods social psychologists use.

SOCIAL PSYCHOLOGY COMPARED TO SOCIOLOGY

Social psychology's focus on social behaviour is shared by several other disciplines in the social sciences, most notably sociology. Both disciplines are concerned with the influence of social and societal factors on human behaviour. There are important differences, however. One such difference is the level of analysis. Social psychology is a branch of psychology, and as such is rooted in an interest in individual human beings, with an emphasis on the psychological processes going on in our hearts and minds. For the social psychologist, the level of analysis is the individual in the context of a social situation. For example, to understand why people intentionally hurt one another, the social psychologist focuses on the specific psychological processes that trigger aggression in specific situations. To what extent is aggression preceded by a state of frustration? Is frustration necessary? If people are feeling frustrated, under what conditions will they vent their frustration with an overt, aggressive act? What factors might preclude an aggressive response by a frustrated individual? Aside from frustration, what other factors might cause aggression? We will address these questions in Chapter 12.

Sociology is more concerned with broad societal factors that influence events in a given society. Thus, the focus is on topics such as social class, social structure, and social institutions. It goes without saying that because society is made up of collections of people, some overlap is bound to exist between the domains of sociology and social psychology. The major difference is this: Sociology, rather than focusing on the psychology of the individual, tends toward a more macro focus—that of society at large. Although sociologists, like social psychologists, are interested in aggressive behaviour, for example, sociologists are more likely to be concerned with why a particular society produces different levels and types of aggression in its members. Why, for example, is the murder rate in the United States so much higher than in Canada? Within Canada, why is the murder rate higher in some social classes than in others? How do changes in society relate to changes in aggressive behaviour?

The difference between social psychology and sociology in level of analysis reflects another difference between the disciplines—namely, what they are trying to explain. The goal of social psychology is to identify universal properties of human nature that make everyone—regardless of social class or culture—susceptible to social influence. The laws governing the relationship between frustration and aggression, for example, are hypothesized to be true of most people in most places—not just members of one social class, age group, or race. Social psychology is a young science that, until recently, had developed mostly in North America; thus, many of its findings have not yet been tested in other cultures to see if they are indeed universal. However, cross-cultural research is increasing, and as it continues to grow, we are learning more about the extent to which these laws are universal. This type of cultural expansion is extremely valuable because it sharpens theories, either by demonstrating their universality or by leading us to discover additional variables, the incorporation of which will ultimately help us make more accurate predictions of human social behaviour. We will encounter several examples of such cross-cultural research in subsequent chapters.

SOCIAL PSYCHOLOGY COMPARED TO PERSONALITY PSYCHOLOGY

Like social psychology, some other areas of psychology focus on studying individuals and the reasons they do what they do. Paramount among these is personality psychology. Let's discuss how social psychology and personality psychology differ in their approach and concerns.

If you are like most people, when you read the examples presented at the beginning of this chapter and began to think about how those events might have come about, your first thoughts were about the strengths, weaknesses, flaws, and quirks of the personalities of the individuals involved. When people behave in interesting or unusual ways, it is natural to try to pinpoint what aspects of their personalities led them to respond as they did. Most of us explain these kinds of behaviours in terms of the personalities of the people involved.

What might these be? Some people are leaders and others are followers; some people are bold and others are timid; some people are public-spirited and others are selfish.

When trying to find explanations of social behaviour, personality psychologists generally focus their attention on **individual differences**—the aspects of an individual's personality that make him or her different from other individuals. For example, to explain why the people in the Solar Temple cult ended their own lives and those of their children, it seems natural to point to their personalities. Perhaps they were all "conformist types" or weak-willed; maybe they were even psychotic. An understanding of personality psychology increases our understanding of human behaviour, but social psychologists are convinced that explaining behaviour primarily in terms of personality factors can be superficial because it leads to a serious underestimation of the role played by a powerful source of human behaviour: social influence. Remember that it was not just a handful of people who died in a ski resort in Quebec and in two villages in Switzerland—53 people died in October 1994, and almost a year later, another *16* cult members died in a village in France. It is thought that, in all, 74 people lost their lives. In the U.S., the Jonestown tragedy claimed 800 lives, and in Uganda, at least that many, and perhaps up to 1000 people, many of whom were children, perished. While it is conceivable that all of these people were psychotic, that explanation is highly improbable. If we want a deeper, richer, more thorough explanation of these tragic events, we need to understand what kind of power and influence the charismatic leaders of these cults possess, the nature of the impact of living in a closed society cut off from other points of view, and myriad other factors that might have contributed to the deaths.

Individual differences
the aspects of people's personalities that make them different from other people

These two different approaches can be illustrated with an everyday example. Suppose you stop at a roadside restaurant for a cup of coffee and a piece of pie. The waitress comes over to take your order, but you are having a hard time deciding which kind of pie to order. While you are hesitating, the waitress impatiently taps her pen against her order book, rolls her eyes toward the ceiling, scowls at you, and finally snaps, "Hey, I haven't got all day, you know!"

What do you conclude about this event? When faced with such a situation, most people would conclude that the waitress is a nasty or unpleasant person; consequently, they would be reluctant to enter that particular restaurant again—especially when that nasty person was on duty. That would certainly be understandable.

However, suppose we were to tell you that (a) the waitress is a single parent and was kept awake all night by the moaning of her youngest child, who has a painful terminal illness; (b) her car broke down on her way to work, and she has no idea where she will find the money to have it repaired; (c) when she finally arrived at the restaurant, she learned that her co-worker was too drunk to work, requiring her to cover twice the usual number of tables; and (d) the short-order cook keeps screaming at her because she is not picking up the orders fast enough to please him. Given all this information, you might revise your judgment and conclude that she is not necessarily a nasty person—just an ordinary person under enormous stress.

The important fact remains that in the absence of obvious situational information, when trying to account for a person's behaviour in a complex situation, the overwhelming majority of people will jump to the conclusion that the behaviour was caused by the personality of the individual involved. And this fact—that we often fail to take the situation into account—is important to a social psychologist, for it has a profound impact on how human beings relate to one another.

In sum, social psychology is located somewhere between its closest intellectual cousins, sociology and personality psychology (see Table 1.1). Social psychology shares with sociology an interest in situational and societal influences on behaviour, but focuses more on the psychological makeup of individuals that renders them susceptible to social influence. Social psychology shares with personality psychology an emphasis on the psychology of the individual, but rather than focusing on what makes people different from one another, it emphasizes the psychological processes shared by most people that make them susceptible to social influence.

The Power of Social Influence

When trying to convince people that their behaviour is greatly influenced by the social environment, the social psychologist is up against a formidable barrier: the inclination we all have for explaining people's behaviour in terms of their personalities (e.g., the case of the waitress discussed above). This barrier is known as the **fundamental attribution error**—the tendency to explain our own and other people's behaviour in terms of personality traits, thereby underestimating the power of social influence. While reading this book, try to suspend judgment for a short time and consider the possibility that to under-

Fundamental attribution error

the tendency to overestimate the extent to which people's behaviour is due to internal, dispositional factors and to underestimate the role of situational factors

TABLE 1.1		
Social psychology compared to related disciplines		
Sociology	**Social Psychology**	**Personality Psychology**
Provides general laws and theories about societies, not individuals.	Studies the psychological processes people have in common with one another that make them susceptible to social influence.	Studies the characteristics that make individuals unique and different from one another

 **Social Situations and Behaviour**

1. Think about one of your friends or acquaintances whom you regard as a shy person. For a moment, try not to think about that person as "shy," but rather as someone who has difficulty relating to people in some situations but not in others.

2. Make a list of the social situations that you think are most likely to bring out your friend's "shy" behaviour.

3. Make a list of the social situations that might bring forth more outgoing behaviour on his or her part. (For example, if someone showed a real interest in one of your friend's favourite hobbies or topics of conversation, it might bring out behaviour that could be classified as charming or vivacious.)

4. Try to create a social environment in which this would be accomplished. Pay close attention to the effect it has on your friend's behaviour.

stand why people do what they do, it is important to look closely at the nature of the social situation. Try It!, above, may help you do just that.

UNDERESTIMATING THE POWER OF SOCIAL INFLUENCE

When we underestimate the power of social influence, we experience a feeling of false security. For example, when trying to explain why people do repugnant or bizarre things—such as the members of the Solar Temple cult taking their own lives or killing their own children—it is tempting, and in a strange way comforting, to write off the victims as flawed human beings. Doing so helps the rest of us believe that it could never happen to us. Ironically, this in turn increases our personal vulnerability to possibly destructive social influence, because we lower our guard. Moreover, by failing to appreciate fully the power of the situation, we tend to oversimplify complex situations; oversimplification decreases our understanding of the causes of a great deal of human behaviour. Among other things, this oversimplification can lead us to blame the victim in situations where the individual was overpowered by social forces too difficult for most of us to resist—as in the Solar Temple tragedy.

Here is an example of the kind of oversimplification we are talking about: Imagine a situation in which people are playing a two-person game wherein each player must choose one of two strategies: They can play competitively, where they try to win as much money as possible and ensure that their partner loses as much as possible, or they can play cooperatively, where they try to ensure that both they and their partner win some money. We will discuss the details of this game in Chapter 9. For now, it is important to note that there are only two basic strategies people can use when playing the game—competitive or cooperative. Now think about some of your friends. How do you think they would play this game?

Few people find this question hard to answer; we all have a sense of the relative competitiveness of our friends. "Well," you might say, "I am certain that my friend Sam, who

▶ Suppose these students were asked to play a game for money. Would they play cooperatively or competitively? Do you think their characters or the situation will be most likely to influence them?

is a cutthroat business major, would play this game more competitively than my friend Anna, who is a really caring, loving person." That is, we think of our friends' personalities and answer accordingly. We usually do not think much about the nature of the social situation when making our predictions.

But how accurate are such predictions? Should we think about the social situation? To find out, Lee Ross and Steven Samuels (1993) conducted the following experiment. First, they chose a group of students at Stanford University who were considered by the resident assistants in their dorm to be either especially cooperative or especially competitive. The researchers did this by describing the game to the resident assistants and asking them to think of students in their dormitories who would be most likely to adopt the competitive or cooperative strategy. As expected, the resident assistants had no trouble thinking of students who fit each category.

Next, Ross and Samuels invited these students to play the game in a psychology experiment. There was one added twist: The researchers varied a seemingly minor aspect of the social situation—namely, what the game was called. They told half the participants that it was the Wall Street Game and half that it was the Community Game. Everything else about the game was identical. Thus, because people who were judged as either competitive or cooperative played the game under one of two names, the experiment resulted in four conditions.

Again, most of us go through life assuming that what really counts is an individual's personality—not something as trivial as what a game is called. Some people seem competitive by nature and would thus relish the opportunity to go head to head with a fellow student. Others seem much more cooperative and would thus achieve the most satisfaction by ensuring that no one lost too much money and no one's feelings were hurt. Right? Not so fast! As seen in Figure 1.1, even as trivial an aspect of the situation as the name of the game made a tremendous difference in how people behaved. When it was called the

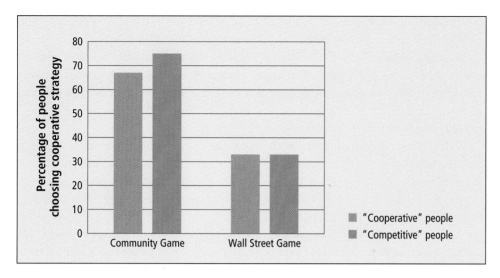

◀ Figure 1.1

WHAT INFLUENCES HOW
COOPERATIVE PEOPLE WILL
BE—THEIR PERSONALITIES
OR THE NATURE OF THE
SOCIAL SITUATION?

Ross and Samuels (1993) found
that university students'
personalities, as rated by the
resident assistants in their
dormitories, did not determine
how cooperative or competitive
they were in a laboratory game.
The name of the game—whether
it was called the Wall Street
Game or the Community Game—
did, however, make a tremendous
difference. Such seemingly minor
aspects of the social situation
can have powerful effects on
people's behaviour, overwhelming
the differences in their
personalities.

(Adapted from Ross & Samuels,
1993)

Wall Street Game, approximately two-thirds of the people responded competitively, whereas when it was called the Community Game, only a third of the people responded competitively. The name of the game conveyed strong social norms about what kind of behaviour was appropriate in this situation, and, as we will see in Chapter 8, social norms can shape people's behaviour in powerful ways.

In this situation, a student's personality made no measurable difference in how he or she behaved. The students labelled "competitive" were no more likely to adopt the competitive strategy than those who were labelled "cooperative." This pattern of results is one we will encounter frequently in this book: Seemingly minor aspects of the social situation can have powerful effects, overwhelming the differences in people's personalities (Ross & Ward, 1996). This is not to say that personality differences do not exist or are unimportant. They do exist and frequently are of great importance. But we have learned that social and environmental situations are so powerful that they have dramatic effects on almost everyone. This is the domain of the social psychologist.

THE SUBJECTIVITY OF THE SOCIAL SITUATION

We have argued that the social situation often has profound effects on human behaviour. But what exactly do we mean by the social situation? One strategy for defining it would be to specify the objective properties of the situation, such as how rewarding it is to people, and then to document the behaviours that follow from these objective properties.

This was the approach taken by **behaviourism**, a school of psychology maintaining that to understand human behaviour, one need only consider the reinforcing properties of the environment—that is, how positive and negative events in the environment are associated with specific behaviours. For example, dogs come when they are called because they have learned that compliance is followed by positive reinforcement (e.g., food or fondling); children memorize their multiplication tables more quickly if you praise them, smile at them, and give them a gold star following correct answers. Psychologists in this tradition, such as John Watson (1924) and B. F. Skinner (1938), suggested that all behaviour could be

Behaviourism
a school of psychology
maintaining that to
understand human behaviour,
one need only consider the
reinforcing properties of the
environment—that is, how
positive and negative events
in the environment are
associated with specific
behaviours

understood by examining the rewards and punishments in the organism's environment, and that there was no need to study such subjective states as thinking and feeling. Thus, to understand why Derek Kennedy risked his life to rescue victims of a boating mishap, a behaviourist would analyze the situation to see what specific, objective factors were promoting helpful actions. What were the objective rewards and punishments implicit in taking a specific course of action? What were the rewards and punishments implicit in doing nothing?

Behaviourists chose not to deal with issues such as cognition, thinking, and feeling, because they considered these concepts too vague and mentalistic, and not sufficiently anchored to observable behaviour. Elegant in its simplicity, the behaviourist approach can account for a great deal of behaviour. But because behaviourism does not deal with cognition, thinking, and feeling—phenomena vital to the human social experience—this approach has proven inadequate for a complete understanding of the social world. We have learned that social behaviour cannot be fully understood by confining our observations to the physical properties of a situation. Instead, it is important to look at the situation from the viewpoint of the people in it, to see how they construe the world around them (Griffin & Ross, 1991; Ross & Nisbett, 1991). For example, if a person approaches us, slaps us on the back, and asks us how we are feeling, is that rewarding or not? On the surface, it might seem like a reward, but it is, in actuality, a complex situation that depends on our thoughts and feelings. We might construe the meaning differently, depending on whether the question is asked by a close friend of ours who is deeply concerned that we might be working too hard, a casual acquaintance simply passing the time of day, or an automobile salesperson intending to sell us a used car—even if the questions are worded the same and asked in the same tone of voice. In responding to the salesperson's question, it is unlikely that we will begin a detailed description of the pains we've been having in our kidney.

This emphasis on construal has its roots in an approach called Gestalt psychology. Initially proposed as a theory of how people perceive the physical word, **Gestalt psychology** holds that we should study the subjective way in which an object appears in people's minds (the gestalt, or whole), rather than the way in which the objective, physical attributes of the object combine. For example, one way to try to understand how people perceive a painting would be to break it down into its individual elements—such as the exact amounts of primary colours applied to the different parts of the canvas, the types of brushstrokes used to apply the colours, and the different geometric shapes they form—and to attempt to determine how these elements are combined by the perceiver to form an overall image of the painting. According to Gestalt psychologists, however, it is impossible to understand the way in which an object is perceived simply by studying these building blocks of perception. The whole is different from the sum of its parts. One must focus on the phenomenology of the perceiver—that is, on how an object appears to people—instead of on the individual elements of the objective stimulus.

The Gestalt approach was formulated in Germany in the first part of this century by Kurt Koffka, Wolfgang Kohler, Max Wertheimer, and their students and colleagues. Among these was Kurt Lewin, generally considered to be the founding father of modern experimental social psychology. As a young German-Jewish professor, Lewin directly experienced the intolerance for cultural diversity rampant in that country in the 1930s.

Gestalt psychology

a school of psychology stressing the importance of studying the subjective way in which an object appears in people's minds, rather than the objective, physical attributes of the object

This experience had a major impact on his thinking. After he moved to the United States, he helped shape social psychology and directed it toward a deep and abiding interest in the exploration of causes and cures of prejudice and ethnic stereotyping.

As a theorist, Lewin took the bold step of applying Gestalt principles beyond the perception of objects to social perception—how people perceive other people and their motives, intentions, and behaviours. Lewin was the first scientist to fully realize the importance of taking the perspective of the people in any social situation to see how they construe (e.g., perceive, interpret, distort) this social environment. Social psychologists soon began to focus on the importance of considering subjective situations (how they are construed by people). These early social psychologists and their key statements are presented on the next page.

Such construals can be rather simple, as in the example of the question "How are you feeling?" discussed earlier. Other construals might appear simple but are, in reality, remarkably complex. For example, suppose Maria gives Shawn a kiss on the cheek at the end of their first date. How will Shawn respond to the kiss? We would say that it depends on how he construes the situation: Does he interpret it as a first step—a sign of awakening romantic interest on Maria's part? Or does he see it as an aloof, sisterly expression—a signal that Maria wants to be friends but nothing more? Or does he see it as a sign that Maria is interested in him but wants things to go slow in their developing relationship?

Were Shawn to misconstrue the situation, he might commit a serious blunder; he might turn his back on what could have been the love of his life—or he might express passion inappropriately. In either case, we believe that the best strategy for understanding Shawn's reaction would be to find a way to determine Shawn's construal of Maria's behaviour, rather than to dissect the objective nature of the kiss itself (its length, degree of pressure, etc.). But how are these construals formed?

Where Construals Come from: Basic Human Motives

How will Shawn determine why Maria kissed him? If it is true that subjective and not objective situations influence people, then we need to understand how people arrive at their subjective impressions of the world. What are people trying to accomplish when they interpret the social world? Again, we could address this question from the perspective of people's personalities. What is it about Shawn, including his upbringing, family background, and unique experiences, that makes him view the world the way he does? As we have seen, such a focus on individual differences in people's personalities, while valuable, misses what is usually of far greater importance: the effects of the social situation on people. To understand these effects, we need to understand the fundamental laws of human nature, common to all, that explain why we construe the social world the way we do.

We human beings are complex organisms; at a given moment, myriad intersecting motives underlie our thoughts and behaviours. Over the years, social psychologists have found that two of these motives are of primary importance: the need to be as accurate as possible and the need to feel good about ourselves.

As we go through life, there are times when each of these motives pulls us in the same direction. Often, however, we find ourselves in situations where these two motives tug us in opposite directions—where to perceive the world accurately requires us to face up to the fact that we have behaved foolishly or immorally.

Leon Festinger, one of social psychology's most innovative theorists, was quick to realize that it is precisely when these two motives tug an individual in opposite directions that we can gain our most valuable insights into the workings of the human heart and mind. An example will clarify. Imagine you are Jean Chrétien, prime minister of Canada, and NATO is putting pressure on your country to assist in attacking Serbia with the intent of stopping genocide in Kosovo and forcing the Serbians to retreat. Serbian leader Slobodan Milosevic is portrayed as inflicting a reign of terror. His goal is to exterminate the Kosovar Albanians, or at least drive them from their homeland. Moreover, he is presented as making a laughingstock of the world—arrogantly operating as though no one could stop him. NATO calls on you to help stop the genocide, promising that only air power will be used and that this approach will be effective in a few days. As prime minister of Canada, you want to help stop the slaughter of innocent people and the abuses of human rights.

There is, however, another side to this issue that causes you to wake up in the middle of the night bathed in a cold sweat. The United Nations opposes the invasion of a

Fritz Heider—"Generally, a person reacts to what he thinks the other person is perceiving, feeling, and thinking, in addition to what the other person may be doing" (1958).

Leon Festinger—"The way I have always thought about it is that if the empirical world looks complicated, if people seem to react in bewilderingly different ways to similar forces, and if I cannot see the operation of universal underlying dynamics, then that is my fault. I have asked the wrong questions; I have, at a theoretical level, sliced up the world incorrectly. The underlying dynamics are there, and I have to find the theoretical apparatus that will enable me to reveal these uniformities."

Kurt Lewin—"If an individual sits in a room trusting that the ceiling will not come down, should only his 'subjective probability' be taken into account for predicting behavior or should we also consider the 'objective probability' of the ceiling's coming down as determined by engineers? To my mind, only the first has to be taken into account" (1943).

◀ Social psychology focuses on how even intelligent and powerful individuals can make a grievous error when faced with conflicting advice on a monumental decision. Here Prime Minister Chrétien addresses the House of Commons regarding the decision to participate in the NATO bombing of Kosovo—a decision that many Canadians viewed as a tragic mistake.

sovereign country, and Canada has traditionally only taken on peacekeeping roles sanctioned by the UN. Should Canada ignore the UN and its policies (and tarnish its image as an international peacekeeper)? And what if the war in Kosovo does not succeed? How will Canada look then?

In speeches made to the House of Commons, the prime minister made it clear that this was an agonizing decision for him. There were strong, vocal supporters on each side of the issue. In the end, he decided to follow the advice of those who supported the NATO position, and in March 1999, Canada joined NATO in launching air attacks on Serbia. The operation took much longer than expected, and the loss of life was horrific: 5000 people died as a result of the bombings, and most were civilians.

And how did the prime minister construe the situation? He maintained that Canada's only option was to take military action—or do nothing. And while many people regarded this as a war that Canada lost, Jean Chrétien interpreted the situation quite differently. In his words, "The fact that we and our NATO allies carried the day gives us hope. Hope that the world has truly learned . . . about the importance of resisting aggression."

Sometimes the need for self-justification can fly in the face of the need to be accurate. This is how many Canadians would construe Canada's involvement in Kosovo.

THE SELF-ESTEEM APPROACH: THE DESIRE TO FEEL GOOD ABOUT OURSELVES

Most people have a strong need to maintain reasonably high **self-esteem**—that is, to see themselves as good, competent, and decent (Aronson, 1992; Aronson, 1998; Baumeister, 1993; Harter, 1993; Kunda, 1990; Tice, 1993). The reason people view the world the way they do can often be traced to this underlying need to maintain a favourable image

Self-esteem

people's evaluations of their own self-worth—that is, the extent to which they view themselves as good, competent, and decent

of themselves. Given the choice between distorting the world in order to feel good about themselves and representing the world accurately, people often take the first option.

Justifying Past Behaviour   Suppose a couple gets divorced after 10 years of a marriage made difficult by the husband's irrational jealousy. Suppose the husband blames the breakup of his marriage on the fact that his ex-wife was not sufficiently responsive or attentive to his needs, rather than admitting the truth: that his jealousy and overpossessiveness drove her away. His interpretation serves some purpose, in that it makes him feel better about himself—it is very difficult to own up to major deficiencies in ourselves, even when the cost is seeing the world inaccurately. The consequence of this distortion, of course, is that it decreases the probability that the individual will learn from experience; that is, in his next relationship the husband is likely to run into the same problems.

We do not mean to imply that people totally distort reality, denying the existence of all information that reflects badly on them; such extreme behaviour is rare outside of mental institutions. Yet it is often possible for normal people like you and us to put a slightly different spin on the existing facts, one that shows us in the best possible light. Consider Roger—everybody knows someone like Roger. He's the guy whose shoes are almost always untied and who frequently has coffee stains on the front of his shirt or mustard stains around his lips. Most observers might consider Roger to be a slob, but Roger might see himself as casual and non-compulsive. Or consider Heather—if Heather is playing basketball and has missed six or seven easy layups in succession, her teammates might consider her to be untalented and begin to think twice about passing the ball to her; on the other hand, Heather might simply feel that she hasn't yet gotten into her rhythm.

The fact that people distort their interpretation of reality so that they feel better about themselves is not surprising, even to the most casual observer of human behaviour. The ways in which this motive operates, however, are often startling—and shed a great deal of light on behaviour that would otherwise be mystifying.

Suffering and Self-Justification   Let's go back to one of our early scenarios: the case of Jean-François Caudron. Why did Jean-François feel happy to be a part of hockey teams that made him endure rookie-night hazings? Perhaps his teammates were usually such a great bunch of guys that he was able to overlook their behaviour on rookie night. That is quite possible. But a far more compelling possibility involves the hazing itself. Specifically, we would contend, a major factor that increased Jean-François's liking for his teammates was, in fact, the unpleasant hazing ritual he experienced. That sounds a little strange. Why would something so unpleasant cause Jean-François to like his team? Didn't behaviourist psychology teach us that rewards, not punishments, make us like things associated with them? Quite so. But as we indicated earlier, in recent years social psychologists have discovered that this formulation is far too simple to account for human thinking and motivation. Unlike rats and pigeons, human beings have a need to justify their past behaviour, and this need leads them to thoughts, feelings, and behaviours that don't always fit into the neat categories of the behaviourist.

Here's how it works. If Jean-François goes through a hazing in order to be accepted by a team of mean-spirited players who do nasty things to one another, he will feel like a fool: "Why did I go through all that pain and embarrassment in order to be accepted by a bunch of jerks? Only a moron would do a thing like that." To avoid feeling like a fool, he will try to justify his decision to undergo the hazing by seeing his team in the best possible light.

But what about situations in which people experience severe hazings—more severe than having their toenails painted and being forced to drink warm beer until they vomit? Surely, under these conditions people wouldn't decide that they really want to belong to the group, would they? As it turns out, they often do. Consider the case of Dee Brasseur, one of Canada's first female military pilots. Her applications to fly with the elite all-male Snowbirds jet team were repeatedly turned down because of her gender. She also endured harassment, assault, and even rape during her 21-year career in the military. "Battle fatigue" caused by years of gender discrimination eventually forced her to retire. How does Dee Brasseur sum up her feelings toward the military? "I still love it . . . I would recommend it to anybody, despite what occurred" (Branswell, 1998).

Though an unmotivated observer might consider these costs of belonging to a group to be high, people such as Jean-François Caudron and Dee Brasseur who have experienced them are motivated to see the experiences differently. Jean-François Caudron, like many athletes, considers hazing a small price to pay for the sense of team solidarity that it creates. And Dee Brasseur remains fiercely loyal to the military.

Does this sound unbelievable? Are people actually more attracted to groups that subject them to pain and abuse? As far-fetched as it may sound, a series of well-controlled laboratory experiments conducted in the 1950s and 1960s demonstrated conclusively that the more unpleasant the procedure the participants underwent to get into a group, the more they liked the group (Aronson & Mills, 1959; Gerard & Mathewson, 1966). This phenomenon will be discussed more thoroughly in Chapter 6. The important points to remember here are that (a) human beings are motivated to maintain a positive picture of themselves, in part by justifying their past behaviour; and (b) under certain specific conditions, this leads them to do things that at first glance might seem surprising or paradoxical—for example, to prefer people and things for whom they have suffered to people and things they associate with easiness and pleasure.

Again, we want to emphasize that the results of this research tradition should not be taken to mean that behaviourist theories are dead wrong; those theories explain some behaviour very well (e.g., see our discussion in Chapter 10 of the research on social exchange theory). In our view, however, behaviourist approaches are inadequate to account for a huge subset of important attitudes and behaviours. This will become much clearer as you read on; in future chapters, we will try to specify the precise conditions under which one or the other set of principles is more likely to apply.

▲ Our desire to maintain self-esteem can have surprising consequences. Social psychological research demonstrates that when people submit to a painful or embarrassing initiation in order to join a group, they need to justify the experience to avoid feeling foolish. One way they do that is to decide that the initiation was worth it because the group is so wonderful. Jean-François Caudron, pictured here, was subjected to severe initiations as a rookie, but remembers his teammates with fondness.

THE SOCIAL COGNITION APPROACH: THE NEED TO BE ACCURATE

As mentioned earlier, even when people are bending the facts to cast themselves in as favourable a light as they can, they do not completely distort reality. It would not be very adaptive to live in a fantasy world, believing, for example, that the car speeding toward us as we step off the curb is really a mirage, or that our future spouse will be Denzel

Washington or Kim Basinger. In fact, human beings are quite skilled at thinking, contemplating, and deducing. One of the hallmarks of being human is the ability to reason. As a species, we have developed truly amazing logical and computational abilities. In our lifetimes, we have witnessed such extraordinary cognitive achievements as the invention and development of computers, the exploration of outer space, and the conquering of many human diseases.

Moreover, on a more common (but perhaps more important) level, it is impossible to observe the cognitive development of a child without being awestruck. Just think of the vast gains in knowledge and reasoning that occur in the first few years of life. In a relatively short time, we see our child transform from a squirming, helpless newborn, who seems to do little but eat, cry, and sleep, into a sophisticated, garrulous four-year-old, who can utter complex sentences, hatch diabolic plots to frustrate a younger sibling, and evoke consternation (and pride) in parents.

Social Cognition   Given the amazing cognitive abilities of our species, it makes sense that social psychologists, when formulating theories of social behaviour, would take into consideration the way in which human beings think about the world. We call this the cognitive approach to social psychology, or **social cognition** (Fiske & Taylor, 1991; Kunda, 1999; Nisbett & Ross, 1980). Researchers who attempt to understand social behaviour from the perspective of social cognition begin with the assumption that all people try to view the world as accurately as possible. Accordingly, human beings are viewed by researchers as amateur sleuths who are doing their best to understand and predict their social world.

But this is by no means as easy or as straightforward as it may seem. We human beings frequently run into problems because we almost never know all the facts we need to in order to make the most accurate judgment of a given situation. Whether it is a relatively simple decision, such as which breakfast cereal is the best combination of nutrition and tastiness, or a slightly more complex decision, such as our desire to buy the best car we can for under $1800, or a much more complex decision, such as choosing a marriage partner who will make us deliriously happy for the rest of our lives, it is almost never easy to gather all the relevant facts in advance. Moreover, we make countless decisions every day; even if there were a way to gather all the facts for each decision, we simply lack the time and the stamina to do so.

Does this sound a bit overblown? Aren't most decisions fairly easy? Let's take a closer look. We will begin by asking you a simple question: Which breakfast cereal is better for you, Lucky Charms or 100% Natural from Quaker? If you are like most of our students, you answered, "100% Natural from Quaker." After all, Lucky Charms is a kid's cereal, full of sugar and cute little marshmallows. There is even a picture of a leprechaun on the box, for goodness' sake. And 100% Natural has a picture of raw wheat on the box, the box is the colour of natural wheat (light tan)—and doesn't *natural* mean "good for you"? If that is the way you reasoned, you have, understandably, fallen into a common cognitive trap—you have generalized from the cover to the product. A careful reading of the ingredients (in small print on the package) will inform you that although Lucky Charms has a bit more sugar in it than 100% Natural, the latter contains far more fat—so much so that the respected journal *Consumer Reports* has judged it to be less healthful

---

Social cognition

how people think about themselves and the social world; more specifically, how people select, interpret, remember, and use social information

◀ Which of these cereals is better for you? The answer may surprise you (see the discussion in the text). Even when we are trying to make accurate judgments about the social world, we often make mistakes.

than Lucky Charms. Things are not always as they appear; thus, coming up with an accurate picture of the social world is not always easy.

Expectations about the Social World   To add to the difficulty, sometimes our expectations about the social world get in the way of our perceiving it accurately. Our expectations can even change the nature of the social world. Imagine, for example, that you are an elementary school teacher dedicated to improving the lives of your students as best you can. You are aware at the beginning of the academic year of how each student performed on standardized intelligence tests. Early in your career, you were pretty sure, but not *entirely* sure, that these tests could gauge each child's true potential. But after several years of teaching, you have gradually become certain that these tests are accurate. Why the change? Almost without fail, you have come to see that the kids who got high scores on these tests are the ones who did the best in your classroom, and the kids who got low scores performed poorly in class.

This scenario doesn't sound all that surprising, except for one key fact: You might be wrong about the validity of the intelligence tests. It might be that the tests weren't very accurate but that you unintentionally treated the kids with high scores and the kids with low scores differently, making it look as if the tests were accurate. This is exactly what Robert Rosenthal and Lenore Jacobson (1968) found in their investigation of a phenomenon called the *self-fulfilling prophecy*. They first entered elementary school classrooms and administered a test. They then informed each teacher that, according to the test, a few specific students were bloomers—that is, they were about to take off and perform extremely well. In actuality, the test showed no such thing; the children labelled as bloomers were chosen by drawing names out of a hat and thus were no different, on average, from any of the other kids. Lo and behold, on returning to the classroom at the end of the school year, Rosenthal and Jacobson found that the bloomers were performing extremely well. The mere fact that the teachers were led to expect these students to do well caused a reliable improvement in their performance. This striking phenomenon is no fluke; it has been replicated a number of times in a wide variety of schools (Rosenthal, 1995).

How did it come about? Though this outcome seems almost magical, it is imbedded in an important aspect of human nature. If you were one of those teachers and were led to expect two or three specific students to perform well, you would be more likely to treat those students in special ways—such as paying more attention to them, listening to them with more respect, calling on them more frequently, encouraging them, and trying to teach them more difficult material. This in turn would almost certainly make these students feel happier, more respected, more motivated, and smarter, and voila—a self-fulfilling prophecy. Thus, even when we are trying to perceive the social world as accurately as we can, there are many ways in which we can go wrong, ending up with the wrong impressions. We will see why—and the conditions under which social perception is accurate—in chapters 3 and 4.

OTHER MOTIVES: ENSURING OUR SURVIVAL

We want to reiterate what we stated earlier: The two major sources of construals we have emphasized here—the need to maintain a positive view of ourselves (the self-esteem approach) and the need to view the world accurately (the social cognition approach)—are the most important of our social motives, but they are certainly not the only motives influencing people's thoughts and behaviours. As noted earlier, we human beings are complex organisms, and under various conditions a variety of motives influence what we think, feel, and do. Biological drives such as hunger and thirst, of course, can be powerful motivators, especially under circumstances of extreme deprivation. At a more psychological level, we can be motivated by fear or by the promise of love, favours, and other rewards involving social exchange. These motives will be discussed at length in chapters 10 and 11.

Our genes also play a role in determining what we think, feel, and do. For example, in Chapter 7 we shall see that our attitudes may be at least partly determined by our genes.

Finally, at a fundamental level, human behaviour is motivated by the need to survive. This is a central tenet of evolutionary psychology, a theory that is receiving increasing prominence in social psychology. **Evolutionary psychology** is a theoretical branch of psychology that attempts to explain social behaviour in terms of genetic factors that evolved over time according to the principles of natural selection (Buss, 1994, 1996; Buss & Kenrick, 1998; Simpson & Kenrick, 1997; Wright, 1994). The theory of evolution was originally articulated by Charles Darwin, and the key idea underlying it is natural selection, the assumption that characteristics that help an organism survive will be passed on to its offspring. The application of this idea to human behaviour has generated considerable controversy. The theory has often been interpreted to mean that human behaviour is driven by biology alone and therefore that the environment has little or no effect. However, current evolutionary theorists take the perspective that biological influences on human behaviour are, in fact, responsive to the environment (Buss & Kenrick, 1998; Crawford & Krebs, 1998). As we will see, evolutionary explanations have been offered for a variety of human social behaviours, including situations under which help will be

Evolutionary psychology
the attempt to explain social behaviour in terms of genetic factors that evolved over time according to the principles of natural selection

offered to others (Chapter 11), our choice of dating and mating partners, and how we go about trying to attract them (Chapter 10).

Social Psychology and Social Problems

To recapitulate, social psychology can be defined as the scientific study of social influence. Social influence can best be understood by examining the basic human motives that produce the subjective views people form about their environment. It might have occurred to you to ask why we want to understand social influence in the first place. Who cares? And what difference does it make whether a behaviour has its roots in the desire to be accurate or in the desire to bolster our self-esteem or in the desire to pass on our genes?

There are several answers. The most basic is simple: We are curious. Social psychologists are fascinated by human social behaviour and want to understand it on the deepest possible level. In a sense, all of us are social psychologists. We all live in a social environment, and we all are more than mildly curious about such issues as how we become influenced, how we influence others, and why we fall in love with some people, dislike others, and are indifferent to still others.

▼ Among the many kinds of relevant issues social psychologists investigate are the following: (a) Does watching violence on TV produce violent behaviour in children? (b) Does cooperation reduce prejudice? (c) Does fear motivate people to change dangerous sexual practices?

Many social psychologists have another reason for studying the causes of social behaviour—namely, to contribute to the solution of social problems. From the beginnings of our young science, social psychologists have been keenly interested in such social problems as the reduction of hostility and prejudice, and the increase of altruism and generosity. Contemporary social psychologists have continued this tradition and have broadened the issues of concern to include such endeavours as inducing people to conserve natural resources such as water and energy (Dickerson et al., 1992), educating people to practise safer sex in order to reduce the spread of AIDS (Aronson, 1997a, 1998; Stone et al., 1994), understanding the relationship between viewing violence on television and the violent behaviour of television-watchers (Eron et al., 1996; Josephson, 1987), developing effective negotiation strategies for the reduction of international conflict (Kelman, 1997), finding ways to reduce racial prejudice (Aronson & Patnoe, 1997), and helping people adjust to life changes such as the entry to college or the death of a loved one (Harris, 1986).

The ability to understand and explain complex and dysfunctional social behaviour brings with it the challenge to change it. For example, given the health risks associated with smoking, there has been increased pressure on governments to persuade people to stop smoking.

As of June 2000, Canadian cigarette packages displayed the largest, most graphic warning images and messages anywhere in the world. The federal government's intent was to frighten people into stopping (or not starting) smoking. The images include pictures of a cancerous mouth, pictures of premature infants with warnings to pregnant women not to smoke (because of the link between smoking and sudden infant death syndrome), and pictures of brain fragments with a warning that smoking leads to increased risk of strokes. This seems consistent with common sense: If you want people to do something they aren't inclined to do, why not scare the daylights out of them?

This is certainly not a stupid idea. As we shall see in subsequent chapters, there are many dysfunctional acts (e.g., cigarette smoking, drunk driving) for which the induction of fear can and does motivate people to take rational, appropriate action to preserve their health (Petty, 1995). However, based on years of systematic research on persuasion, social psychologists have realized that this approach is not effective in all situations. For example, the fear-inducing approach has been applied in the case of AIDS, where it does not produce the desired effect of persuading people to practise safer sex. Rather, the research evidence suggests that most people do not want to be thinking about dying or contracting a painful illness while they are getting ready to have sex. Such thoughts can interfere, to say the least, with the romance of the occasion. Moreover, most people do not enjoy using condoms because they feel that interrupting the sexual act destroys the mood. As demonstrated in a study with French-Canadian university students, people who feel that condoms are inconvenient are less likely to use them (Hébert et al., 1989). Given these considerations, when people have been exposed to frightening messages, instead of engaging in rational problem-solving behaviour, most tend to reduce that fear by engaging in denial. For example, in research conducted at various universities in Ontario (MacDonald, Zanna, & Fong, 1996; Maticka-Tyndale, Herold, & Mewhinney, 1998), students expressed beliefs such as, "It can't happen to me," "Surely none of my friends have

AIDS," "This person I've just met doesn't seem like the type who would sleep around," and so on.

The astute reader will see that the process of denial stems not from the desire to be accurate but from the desire to maintain one's self-esteem. That is, if people can succeed in convincing themselves that their sexual partners do not have AIDS, then they can continue to engage in unprotected sex while maintaining a reasonably positive picture of themselves as rational individuals. By understanding the conditions under which self-esteem maintenance prevails, social psychologists have been able to contribute important insights to AIDS education and prevention, as we shall see (Aronson, 1997a; Aronson, Fried, & Stone, 1991; Stone et al., 1994).

Throughout this book, we will examine many similar examples of the applications of social psychology. Likewise, throughout this book we will discuss some of the underlying human motives and characteristics of the social situation that produce significant social behaviours, with the assumption that if we are interested in changing our own or other people's behaviour, we must first know something about these fundamental causes. Although most of the studies discussed are concerned with such fundamental causes, in the process they also address critical social problems, including the effects of mass media on attitudes and behaviour (Chapter 7), violence and aggression (Chapter 12), and prejudice (Chapter 13). For the benefit of the interested reader, we have also included three separate "modules" that apply social psychology to contemporary issues involving health, the environment, and law. These are briefer and less detailed than regular chapters; the instructor may assign them at any time during the semester.

SUMMARY

People are constantly being influenced by others. **Social psychology** is defined as the scientific study of the way in which people's thoughts, feelings, and behaviours are influenced by the real or imagined presence of other people. Social influence is often powerful, usually outweighing and frequently overwhelming **individual differences** in people's personalities as determinants of behaviour. As a result, we must try to avoid making the **fundamental attribution error**—the tendency to explain our own and others' behaviour entirely in terms of personality traits, thus underestimating the power of social influence.

To appreciate the power of social influence, we must understand how people form **construals** of their social environment. We are not computer-like organisms who respond directly and mechanically to environmental stimuli; rather, we are complex human beings who perceive, think about, and sometimes distort information from our environment. By emphasizing the way in which people construe the social world, social psychology has more roots in the tradition of **Gestalt psychology** than in that of **behaviourism**.

Although human behaviour is complex and non-mechanical, it is not unfathomable. A person's construals of the world derive primarily from two fundamental motives: the desire to maintain **self-esteem** and the desire to form an accurate picture of oneself and the social world (the **social cognition** approach). Accordingly, to understand how we are influenced by our social environments we must understand the processes by which we do the perceiving, thinking, and distorting.

Human behaviour also is motivated by a very basic need: the need for survival—of oneself and one's offspring. This **evolutionary** perspective has recently been used to explain various social psychological phenomena, including prosocial behaviour (helping) and human mate selection.

We also discussed another important point about social psychology: It is an empirical science. Social psychologists attempt to find answers to key questions about social influence by designing and conducting research, rather than by relying on common sense or the wisdom of the ages. In Chapter 2, we will discuss the scientific methods social psychologists use when conducting such research.

IF YOU ARE INTERESTED

Aron, A., & Aron, E. (1992). *The heart of social psychology.* Lexington, MA: Lexington Books. A highly readable look behind the scenes at how eminent social psychologists view their discipline.

Crawford, C., & Krebs, D. L. (Eds.). (1998). *Handbook of evolutionary psychology*. Mahwah, NJ: Lawrence Erlbaum. This volume, edited by two Simon Fraser University psychologists, is a comprehensive, up-to-date assessment of evolutionary theory and its application to the study of human behaviour. Topics covered include evolutionary analyses of mate selection, sexual aggression, prosocial behaviour, sex differences, and so on.

Dion, K. L. (2000). Canada. In A. E. Kazdin (Ed.), *Encyclopedia of psychology* (Vol. 2, pp. 5–12). Washington, D.C.: American Psychological Association & New York: Oxford University Press. In this brief article, University of Toronto social psychologist Kenneth Dion traces the history of psychology in Canada, covering such events as the birth of the Canadian Psychological Association, the establishment of research granting agencies, prominent research centres, and so on. In addition to providing an overview of the field, the author provides a trenchant analysis of the state of the field today. Issues such as the relation between researchers and practitioners are discussed.

Festinger, L. (Ed.). (1980). *Retrospections on social psychology.* New York: Oxford University Press. A collection of articles by many of the most eminent scientists in the field of social psychology. Even though this book is almost two decades old, it remains an excellent source of articles about the origins of the field and its current research trends.

Jones, E. (1998). Major developments in social psychology during the past six decades. In D. Gilbert, S. Fiske, & G. Lindzey (Eds.), *The handbook of social psychology.* (4th ed., Vol. 1). New York: McGraw-Hill. A thorough treatment of the history of social psychology from a leading researcher in the field. This chapter discusses the roots of the field, plots the changes in its emphases and trends, and details its intellectual history.

Moghaddam, F. M., Taylor, D. M., & Wright, S. (1993). *Social psychology in cross-cultural perspective.* New York: W. H. Freeman. This book, written at McGill University, provides a fascinating look at the role of cultural factors in social psychology. The authors demonstrate that various phenomena that have been taken for granted in social psychology (e.g., cognitive dissonance, social influence) take a rather different form when examined outside the North American context.

Ross, L., & Nisbett, R. E. (1991). *The person and the situation: Perspectives of social psychology.* New York: McGraw-Hill. An entertaining, insightful look at many of the ideas presented in this chapter, including the importance of considering people's construals of social situations and the ways in which those construals are often more powerful determinants of people's behaviour than are their personalities.

Taylor, S. (1998). Conceptualizations of the social being. In D. Gilbert, S. Fiske, & G. Lindzey (Eds.), *The handbook of social psychology* (4th ed., Vol. 1). New York: McGraw-Hill. A scholarly analysis of the different theoretical approaches to understanding human social behaviour.

WEBLINKS

www.cpa.ca

Canadian Psychological Association

The Canadian Psychological Association represents the interests of all aspects of psychology in Canada, and includes a section devoted to social psychology.

www.apa.org

American Psychological Association

www.apa.org/journals/psp.html

Journal of Personality and Social Psychology

This is the flagship journal for the field of social psychology. At this APA site, you can read the contents and abstracts of current issues of the journal.

www.spssi.org

The Society for the Psychological Study of Social Issues

This is the Web site for the Society for the Psychological Study of Social Issues (SPSSI). Traditionally, members of this society have been primarily social psychologists.

www.uiowa.edu/~grpproc/crisp/crisp.html

Current Research in Social Psychology

This site hosts a peer reviewed, electronic journal covering all aspects of social psychology.

www.socialpsychology.org

Social Psychology Network

Arguably the best online resource for social psychology, this page provides several links to topics related to social psychology, links to the home pages of social psychologists, and a search engine specifically for the information contained at the site.

CHAPTER 2

Methodology
how social psychologists do research

In 1993, THE STANDING COMMITTEE ON COMMUNICATIONS AND Culture published a report on the effects of television violence titled "Television Violence: Fraying Our Social Fabric." This report was triggered, at least in part, by a petition initiated by 13-year-old Virginie Larivière, whose 11-year-old sister had been robbed, sexually assaulted, and murdered. Virginie Larivière was convinced that television violence was responsible for her sister's death. She and her family gathered more than 1.3 million signatures from Canadians across the country. The petition called for a boycott of violent television programming and for federal government legislation to reduce the violent content of television programming. The 11 members of Parliament who served on the Standing Committee on Communications and Culture interviewed the chair of the CRTC, professors, executives from the Canadian Association of Broadcasters, and the president of the Canadian Film and Television Production Association, among others. Based on these interviews and various reports, the committee decided there is not enough evidence to support the conclusion that violence on television contributes to violent behaviour. In their words, "many factors contribute to violence in society and the part played by television violence can only be estimated and amounts to an unknown fraction" (p. 17). As a result, they recommended against legislating a reduction in violent content in television programming, preferring industry self-regulation and public education instead.

The question of whether television violence produces violent behaviour is an extremely important one, particularly in light of allegations, such as those made by Virginie Larivière, that violence on television plays a role in brutal, deadly assaults on innocent people. However, as the Standing Committee on Communications and Culture discovered, different experts have different opinions, making it difficult to draw firm conclusions. How can we decide who is right? Is this a case where majority opinion rules, or is there a more scientific way to determine the answers?

Consider, now, a 1995 report commissioned by the Department of Canadian Heritage to address the same question. This report, titled "Television Violence: A Review of the Effects on Children of Different Ages," was prepared by social psychologist Wendy Josephson, who analyzed the results of hundreds of scientific studies. Her conclusion was that television violence does increase aggressive behaviour—at least among children predisposed toward aggression to begin with. She pointed out that "although the group especially at risk might be a minority of viewers, they are likely to be the majority of aggressors." Thus, Josephson's conclusion, based on a careful analysis of scientific evidence, was quite different from the conclusion reached by the Standing Committee on Communications and Culture, which relied on reports and interviews with individuals—many of whom were from the television industry. In this chapter, we will examine the kinds of research methods that allow us to scientifically answer important questions about the causes of violence.

As social psychologists, we also are interested in finding ways of stopping violence when it occurs. If you happen to witness someone being attacked by another person you might not intervene directly, out of fear for your own safety. Most of us assume that we would help in some way, though, such as by calling the police. This very assumption was the reason people were so shocked by an incident that occurred in the early 1960s, in the

Kitty Genovese was attacked in this area in full view of her neighbours. Why didn't anyone call the police?

Queens section of New York City. A woman named Kitty Genovese was attacked while walking to her car and brutally murdered in the alley of an apartment complex. The attack lasted 45 minutes. No fewer than 38 of the apartment residents admitted later that they had rushed to their windows after hearing Genovese's screams for help. However, not one of the bystanders attempted in any way to help her—none of them even telephoned the police.

As you might imagine, the Kitty Genovese murder received a great deal of publicity. Reporters, commentators, and pundits of all kinds came forward with their personal theories about why the bystanders had done nothing. The most popular explanation was that there is something dehumanizing about living in a metropolis that inevitably leads to apathy, indifference to human suffering, and lack of caring. The blame was laid on New York and New Yorkers; the general belief was that this kind of thing would not have happened in a small town, where people care about each other (Rosenthal, 1964). Was big-city life the cause of the bystanders' behaviour? Or was there some other explanation? Again, how can we find out?

Social Psychology: An Empirical Science

A fundamental principle of social psychology is that many social problems, such as the causes of and reactions to violence, can be studied empirically (Aronson, Wilson, & Brewer, 1998; Judd & McClelland, 1998; Kenny, Kashy, & Bolger, 1998). As mentioned in Chapter 1, it is insufficient to rely on personal beliefs, folk wisdom, hope, or magazine polls when answering questions about human behaviour. Many personal observations are astute and accurate reflections of social reality, whereas others are far off the mark. To tell the difference, our observations must be translated into hypotheses that can be tested scientifically. In the case of violent television programming, as we have seen, respected experts disagree as to its effects; scientific investigations are the true arbiters of such disputes.

Because we will describe the results of many empirical studies in this book, it is important to discuss how social psychological research is done. We begin with a warning: The results of some of the experiments you encounter will seem obvious, because the topic of social psychology is something with which we are all intimately familiar—social behaviour and social influence. Note that this fact separates social psychology from other sciences. When you read about an experiment in particle physics, it is unlikely that the results will connect with your personal experiences and have a ring of familiarity. We don't know about you, but we have never thought, "Wow! That experiment on quarks was just like what happened to me while I was waiting for the bus yesterday," or "My grandmother always told me to watch out for quarks, positrons, and antimatter." When reading about the results of a study on helping behaviour or aggression, however, it is quite common to think, "Aw, come on, I could have predicted that. That's the same thing that happened to me last Friday."

The thing to remember is that such findings appear obvious because most examples of human behaviour seem to make sense and to have been easily predictable—once we know the outcome (Fischhoff, 1975; Hertwig, Gigerenzer, & Hoffrage, 1997; Nario & Branscombe, 1995). Hindsight is 20/20, as the saying goes. This phenomenon was illustrated in a study by Roese and Olson (1996). They asked students at the University of Western Ontario to read a story, based on First World War events, about a young British soldier who devised a plan to save a small village that was about to be invaded. In one condition, participants were told that the soldier managed to convince others in the military to accept his plan and the village was saved. When asked how predictable this outcome was, they felt it was obvious all along that the village would be saved. In another condition, participants were told that the soldier's plan was rejected and the village was destroyed. When asked how predictable this outcome was, these participants thought it was obvious that the village would be destroyed! As this study shows, the opposite finding of an experiment might seem just as obvious as the results that actually were obtained. The trick is to predict what will happen in an experiment *before* you know how it turned out. To illustrate what we mean when we say that not all obvious findings are easy to predict in advance, take the Try It! quiz on page 32. Each answer is based on well-established social psychological research. In our experience as teachers, we have found that few of our students get all the answers correct. Findings that seem obvious in retrospect may not be easy to predict in advance.

Social psychology is an empirical science, with a well-developed set of methods to answer questions about social behaviour, such as the ones about violence with which we began this chapter. These methods are of three types: the observational method, the correlational method, and the experimental method. Any of these methods could be used to explore a specific research question; each is a powerful tool in some ways and a weak tool in others. Part of the creativity in conducting social psychological research involves choosing the right method, maximizing its strengths, and minimizing its weaknesses.

In this chapter, we will discuss these methods in detail. We, the authors of this book, are not primarily textbook writers—we are social scientists who have done a great deal of experimental research in social psychology. As such, we will try to provide you with an understanding of both the joy and the difficulty of doing research. The joy comes in

Social Psychology Quiz

Take a moment to answer the questions below, each of which is based on social psychological research. Though the correct answers may seem obvious in retrospect, many are hard to guess in advance.

1. Suppose an authority figure asks university students to administer near-lethal electric shocks to another student who has not harmed them in any way. What percentage of these students will agree to do it?

2. If you give children a reward for doing something they already enjoy doing, they will subsequently like that activity (a) more, (b) the same, or (c) less.

3. Who do you think would be happiest with their choice of a consumer product, such as an art poster? (a) people who spend several minutes thinking about why they like or dislike each poster; (b) people who choose a poster without analyzing the reasons for their feelings.

4. Repeated exposure to a stimulus, such as a person, a song, or a painting, will make you like it (a) more, (b) the same, or (c) less.

5. You ask an acquaintance to do you a favour—for example, to lend you $10—and he or she agrees. As a result of doing you this favour, the person will probably like you (a) more, (b) the same, or (c) less.

6. True or false: It is most adaptive and beneficial to people's mental health to have a realistic view of the future, an accurate appraisal of their own abilities and traits, and an accurate view of how much control they have over their lives.

7. In Canada and the United States, female university students tend not to do as well as male students on math tests. Under which of the following circumstances will women do as well as men? (a) When they are told that there are no gender differences on a test, (b) when they are told that women tend to do better on a difficult math test, because under these circumstances, they rise to the challenge, or (c) when they are told that men outperform women under almost all circumstances.

8. Which kind of advertising is most effective? (a) subliminal messages implanted in advertisements, or (b) normal, everyday advertising, such as TV ads for painkillers or laundry detergents.

unravelling the clues about the causes of interesting and important social behaviours, just as a sleuth gradually unmasks the culprit in a murder mystery. Each of us finds it exhilarating that we have the tools to provide definitive answers to questions that philosophers have debated for centuries. At the same time, as seasoned researchers we have learned to temper this exhilaration with a heavy dose of humility, for the practical and ethical constraints involved in creating and conducting social psychological research are formidable.

Formulating Hypotheses and Theories

There is a lore in science that brilliant insights come all of a sudden, as when Archimedes shouted, "Eureka! I have found it!" when the solution to a problem flashed into his mind. Though such insights do sometimes occur suddenly, science is a cumulative process, and people often generate hypotheses from previous theories and research. We define a **theory** as an organized set of principles that can be used to explain observed phenomena.

Theory

an organized set of principles that can be used to explain observed phenomena

9. In public settings, (a) women touch men more, (b) men touch women more, or (c) there is no difference—men and women touch each other equally.

10. Which things in their past do people regret the most? (a) actions they performed that they wish they had not, (b) actions they did not perform that they wish they had, or (c) it depends on how long ago the events occurred.

ANSWERS

1. In studies conducted by Stanley Milgram (1974), up to 65 percent of participants administered what they thought were near-lethal shocks to another subject. (In fact, no real shocks were administered.)

2. (c) Rewarding people for doing something they enjoy will typically make them like that activity less in the future (e.g., Lepper, Greene, & Nisbett, 1973; Lepper, 1995, 1996).

3. (b) Wilson et al. (1993) found that people who did not analyze their feelings were the most satisfied with their choice of posters when contacted a few weeks later.

4. (a) Under most circumstances, repeated exposure increases liking for a stimulus (Zajonc, 1968).

5. (a) More (Jecker & Landy, 1969).

6. False (Taylor & Brown, 1988, 1994).

7. (a) Research in Canada (Walsh, Hickey, & Duffy, 1999) and in the United States (Spencer, Steele, & Quinn, 1997; Steele, 1997) has found that when women think there are sex differences on a test, they do worse because of stereotype threat—the fear that they might confirm a negative stereotype about their gender. When women are told that there were no gender differences in performance on the test, they do as well as men.

8. (b) There is no evidence that subliminal messages in advertising have any effect, whereas there is substantial evidence that normal, everyday advertising is quite effective (Chaiken, Wood, & Eagly, 1996; Merikle, 1988; Weir, 1984; Wilson, Houston, & Meyers, 1998).

9. (b) Men touch women more than vice versa (Henley, 1977).

10. (c) Gilovich and Medvec have found that in the short run, people regret acts of commission (things they did that they wish they hadn't) more than acts of omission (things they didn't do that they wish they had). In the long run, however, people come to regret acts of omission more than acts of commission (Gilovich & Medvec, 1995; Gilovich, Medvec, & Chen, 1995).

Many studies stem from a researcher's dissatisfaction with existing theories and explanations. After reading other people's work, a researcher might believe that he or she has a better way of explaining people's behaviour (e.g., why they fail to help in an emergency). In the 1950s, for example, Leon Festinger was dissatisfied with the ability of a major theory of the day, behaviourism, to explain attitude change. He formulated a new approach—dissonance theory—that made specific predictions about when and how people would change their attitudes. Social psychologists, like scientists in other disciplines, engage in a continual process of theory refinement: They develop a theory, test specific hypotheses derived from that theory, and, based on the results, revise the theory and formulate new hypotheses.

Theory is not the only way to derive a new hypothesis in social psychology. Researchers often observe a phenomenon in everyday life that they find curious and interesting. They then construct a theory about why this phenomenon occurred, and design a study to see if they are right.

Consider the murder of Kitty Genovese discussed earlier. As we saw, most people blamed her neighbours' failure to intervene on the apathy, indifference, and callousness that big-city life breeds. Two social psychologists who taught at universities in New York, however, had a different idea. Bibb Latané and John Darley got to talking one day about the Genovese murder. Here is how Latané describes it: "One evening after [a] downtown cocktail party, John Darley . . . came back with me to my 12th Street apartment for a drink. Our common complaint was the distressing tendency of acquaintances, on finding that we called ourselves social psychologists, to ask why New Yorkers were so apathetic" (Latané, 1987, p. 78). Instead of focusing on "what was wrong with New Yorkers," Latané and Darley thought it would be more interesting and more important to examine the social situation in which Genovese's neighbours found themselves: "We came up with the insight that perhaps what made the Genovese case so fascinating was itself what made it happen—namely, that not just one or two, but 38 people had watched and done nothing" (Latané, 1987, p. 78).

The researchers had the hunch that, paradoxically, the more people who witness an emergency, the less likely it is that any given individual will intervene. Genovese's neighbours might have assumed that someone else had called the police, a phenomenon Latané and Darley (1968) referred to as the *diffusion of responsibility*. Perhaps the bystanders would have been more likely to help had each thought he or she alone was witnessing the murder.

Once a researcher has a hypothesis, whether it comes from a theory, previous research, or an observation of everyday life, how can he or she tell if it is true? How could Latané and Darley tell whether the number of eyewitnesses in fact affects people's likelihood of helping a victim? In science, idle speculation will not do; the researcher must collect data to test his or her hypothesis. Let's look at how the observational method, the correlational method, and the experimental method are used to explore research hypotheses such as Latané and Darley's. These methods are summarized in Table 2.1.

Descriptive Methods: Describing Social Behaviour

One goal of the social psychologist is to systematically describe human social behaviour. There are a number of tools, or methods, that are at the social psychologist's disposal in this enterprise. We will focus on three such methods: the observational method, archival analysis, and the correlational method.

TABLE 2.1	
A summary of research methods	
Method	**Questions Answered**
1. Observational/Archival	Description: What is the nature of the phenomenon?
2. Correlational	Description: What is the relation between variable X and variable Y?
3. Experimental	Causality: Is variable X a cause of variable Y?

THE OBSERVATIONAL METHOD

As its name implies, the **observational method** is the technique whereby a researcher observes people and systematically records measurements of their behaviour. This method varies according to the degree to which the observer actively participates in the scene. At one extreme, the observer neither participates nor intervenes in any way; instead, the observer is unobtrusive and tries to blend in with the scenery as much as possible. For example, Debra Pepler at York University and Wendy Craig at Queen's University have developed a particularly unobtrusive method for observing bullying behaviour in school settings (Craig & Pepler, 1997; Pepler & Craig, 1995; Atlas & Pepler, 1998). The children wear waist pouches containing small microphones, while a hidden video camera films their interactions. Thus, children can freely roam over relatively large areas (e.g., school playgrounds) while having their behaviour recorded. This combination of audio and visual technology allows the researchers to observe overt physical acts of aggression, as well as more subtle forms of bullying, such as indirect aggression, and verbal threats or insults. (Subtle forms of bullying are especially difficult to detect when researchers rely on more traditional methods, such as standing outside a playground fence and making check marks whenever they notice particular behaviours.)

The waist-pouch microphone technology also addresses an age-old problem in observational research, namely that people change their behaviour when they are being observed. Bullies, for example, tend not to engage in bullying when adults are around (Craig & Pepler, 1997). Thus, an advantage of using unobtrusive measures, such as Pepler and Craig's, is that researchers can observe spontaneous, naturally occurring behaviour.

In all observational research—regardless of whether observers are on the spot or later analyze video- or audiotapes—it is important for the researchers to clearly define the

Observational method
the technique whereby a researcher observes people and systematically records measurements of their behaviour

© 1985 FarWorks Inc./Distributed by Universal Press Syndicate. All rights reserved.

◀ The hazards of the observational method.

"For crying out loud, gentlemen! That's us! Someone's installed the one-way mirror in backward!"

behaviours of interest. For example, in Pepler and Craig's research an episode is classified as bullying only if there is a power imbalance between the individuals involved, if there is intent to harm on the part of the person doing the bullying, and if the victim shows distress (Atlas & Pepler, 1998; Craig & Pepler, 1997).

Note that the importance of clearly defining the behaviours of interest applies to all psychological research, not just to observational studies. The term **operational definition** refers to the precise specification of how variables are measured or manipulated. Recall, for example, that a power imbalance is one of the criteria that Pepler and colleagues use to define bullying. Are you able to come up with an operational definition of this variable that would be useful in the context of observing playground interactions? Pepler and Craig operationally defined a power imbalance as a discrepancy, between the children involved, in terms of height and weight. In other words, in situations involving aggression on the playground, the researchers assumed that a bigger child was likely to be in a position of power relative to a smaller child.

If, on the other hand, the researchers were interested in observing bullying in a corporate boardroom, they presumably would specify a different operational definition of power imbalance—perhaps the discrepancy between the individuals' status in the corporation (e.g., manager versus secretary).

Some situations, by their nature, require **participant observation**. Participant observation is a form of the observational method whereby the observer interacts with the people being observed, but tries not to alter the situation in any way. For example, in the 1950s, a group of people in the U.S. Midwest predicted that the world would come to an end in a violent cataclysm on a specific date. They also announced that they would be rescued in time by a spaceship that would land in their leader's backyard. Assuming that the end of the world was not imminent, Leon Festinger and his colleagues thought it would be interesting to observe this group closely and chronicle how they reacted when their beliefs and prophecy were disconfirmed (Festinger, Riecken, & Schachter, 1956). However, unlike the case of observing children at play, the researchers couldn't stand on the other side of the fence and unobtrusively observe the subtleties of the group members' behaviour. (Even if Pepler and colleagues' technology had been available, it is doubtful that cult members would have agreed to be video- and audiotaped.) To monitor the hour-to-hour conversations of this group, the social psychologists found it necessary to join the group and pretend that they too believed the world was about to end. More recently, Raphael Ezekiel (1995) was interested in the nature and workings of extreme political cults. To find out more about them, he attended meetings of neo-Nazi groups and the Ku Klux Klan. While he did not join these groups, he did interact with and interview many group members.

We should point out that the observational method has some significant drawbacks. First, certain kinds of behaviour are difficult to observe because they occur only rarely or only in private. To return to our earlier example, had Latané and Darley chosen the observational method to study the effects of the number of bystanders on people's willingness to help a victim, we might still be waiting for an answer. To determine how witnesses react to a violent crime, the researchers would have had to linger on street corners throughout a city, wait patiently for assaults to occur, and then keep careful track of the responses of any and all bystanders. Obviously, they would have had to wait a long time

---

Operational definition
the precise specification of how variables are measured or manipulated

Participant observation
a form of the observational method whereby the observer interacts with the people being observed, but tries not to alter the situation in any way

before an assault happened in their presence, and they would have found it difficult to gather data while a real-life emergency occurred before their eyes.

Finally, there is another issue that arises when we use the observational method: How can we be sure that the observers are presenting an accurate portrayal of social behaviour? In such studies, it is important to establish **interjudge reliability**, which is the level of agreement between two or more people who independently observe and code a set of data. By showing that two or more judges independently come up with the same observations, researchers ensure that the observations are not the subjective, distorted impressions of one individual. For example, the analysis of bullying should not reflect the opinion of one individual, but should be an objective, scientific rating of what behaviours are actually taking place on the playground.

ARCHIVAL ANALYSIS

Another form of the observational method is **archival analysis**, whereby the researcher examines the accumulated documents, or archives, of a culture (Simonton, 1999). For example, diaries, novels, suicide notes, popular music lyrics, television shows, movies, magazine and newspaper articles, and advertising all tell us a great deal about how a society views itself. Much like our earlier example, specific, well-defined categories are created and then applied to the archival source.

Archival analysis is a powerful form of observational research because it allows a unique look at the values and interests of a culture. (If you want to try your hand at archival analysis, see Try It! on page 38.) For example, researchers at York University used archival analysis to examine the relation between body ideals (as portrayed in magazines such as *Playboy* and *Playgirl*) and the body sizes of average young women and men (Spizter, Henderson, & Zivian, 1999). To assess the image of the *ideal* male and female body, Spitzer and colleagues calculated the body mass index (an indicator of body fat obtained by dividing weight by height squared) of *Playboy* and *Playgirl* centrefolds and Miss America Pageant winners from the 1950s to the 1990s. They found that the body sizes of *Playboy* models and beauty pageant winners have decreased over time to the point where, currently, nearly 100 percent of these women are underweight according to Health and Welfare Canada's guidelines. Moreover, approximately one-third of the *Playboy* models and 17 percent of pageant winners meet the World Health Organization criteria for anorexia nervosa. The researchers comment that "clearly the North American ideal for female beauty as portrayed in the media is at a weight deemed to be dangerous by Canadian and World Health officials" (p. 559).

And what about the bodies of average young women? To answer this question, Spitzer and colleagues calculated the body mass index of young adults in Canada and the U.S. based on health and weight information as recorded in national health surveys conducted in each country. They found that the body mass index of North American women actually has increased in the past four decades (somewhat more so for American than Canadian women). Thus, the average woman's body is now further from the cultural ideal than it was 40 years ago. As for men's bodies, Spitzer and colleagues found that the body sizes of *Playgirl* centrefolds and average young men have both increased over time. However, as a look around your classroom probably will verify, the average guy doesn't look like a *Playgirl* centrefold. The reason is that the bodies of *Playgirl* centrefolds have

Interjudge reliability
the level of agreement between two or more people who independently observe and code a set of data; by showing that two or more judges independently come up with the same observations, researchers ensure that the observations are not the subjective impressions of one individual

Archival analysis
a form of the observational method, whereby the researcher examines the accumulated documents, or archives, of a culture (e.g., diaries, novels, magazines, and newspapers)

Archival Analysis: Body Image and the Media

▲ Today's media are replete with images of physiques, like this one, that are nearly impossible to achieve without steroids.

Try doing your own archival analysis to see how the ideal body types for women and men are portrayed in the media. Choose three or four magazines that differ in their topic and audience; for example, a "women's" beauty magazine such as *Glamour,* a "men's" magazine such as *GQ,* and a fitness magazine such as *Shape* or *Muscle and Fitness.* For each magazine, open the pages randomly until you find a photograph of a woman's or a man's body. Repeat this so you look at two or three such photographs in each magazine.

What is the ideal body type for *women* portrayed in these magazines? What is the ideal body type for *men* portrayed in these magazines? In answering these questions, note the following:

(a) the ideal weight portrayed

(b) the ideal muscle versus fat ratio

(c) other characteristics (e.g., width of shoulders relative to waist, size of bust/chest).

Does the ideal body type portrayed in the magazines seem attainable for each gender? Are the ideals that are portrayed healthy?

According to a recent study conducted by researchers at the University of Manitoba and the University of Winnipeg (Morry & Staska, 2001), internalizing the body ideals portrayed in the media can be harmful to your health. The researchers found that women who frequently read beauty magazines were more likely to accept the societal ideal of thinness for females. Internalization of this ideal was associated with greater body dissatisfaction and with higher incidence of eating disorders. And what about men? Men who frequently read fitness magazines were more likely to internalize the muscular ideal, which in turn was associated with body dissatisfaction, disordered eating behaviours, and steroid use. The bottom line, regardless of your gender, is to beware of too readily accepting the ideals portrayed in the media—it could be dangerous to your physical and emotional health.

increased dramatically in muscle, not fat, whereas for average men, increases have tended to occur in the other direction.

Results such as these lead us inexorably to some disturbing questions: Does the ideal of thinness for women contribute to body dissatisfaction, low self-esteem, and destructive behaviours such as bulimia or excessive exercise? Does the muscular ideal for men contribute to dangerous behaviours such as anabolic steroid use? To answer such questions, researchers must use research methods such as the correlational method and the experimental method. These methods will be discussed next.

Like the observational method described earlier, archival analysis has some drawbacks. Returning to our earlier example of bystander intervention, Latané and Darley could have used archival analysis to investigate this issue. For example, they could have examined newspaper accounts of violent crimes and noted the number of bystanders and how many offered assistance to the victim. Yet here, too, they would have quickly run into problems: Did each journalist mention how many bystanders were present? Was the number accurate? Were all forms of assistance noted in the newspaper article? Clearly, these are messy data. As is always the case with archival analysis, the researcher is at the mercy of the original compiler of the material; the journalists had different aims when they wrote their articles and may not have included all the information researchers would later need.

THE CORRELATIONAL METHOD

Often social scientists want to do more than document social behaviour—they want to understand relations between variables. For example, is there a relation between the amount of violence children see on television and their aggressiveness? To answer such questions, researchers frequently use a different approach: the correlational method.

The **correlational method** is the technique whereby two variables are systematically measured and the relation between them—how much you can predict one from the other—is assessed. For example, using the correlational method, researchers might be interested in testing the relation between children's aggressive behaviour and how much violent television they watch. They also might observe children on the playground, but here the goal is to assess the relation, or correlation, between the children's aggressiveness and other factors, such as TV viewing habits, that the researchers also measure.

Often researchers want to judge the relation between variables that are difficult to observe. In these situations, they rely on questionnaires or surveys, in which people are asked about their beliefs, attitudes, and behaviours. For example, Herold and Mewhinney (1993) wanted to know whether people who had positive attitudes toward the use of condoms would be more likely to engage in safer sex. To answer this question, they asked women and men in various singles bars in southern Ontario to complete a survey that assessed their agreement with attitude statements such as, "If I were to have sex with someone I just met, I would be uncomfortable suggesting to my partner that we use a condom." Respondents also were asked about the frequency with which they actually used condoms.

Researchers look at such relations by calculating the **correlation coefficient**, which is a statistic that assesses how well you can predict one variable based on another; for example, how well you can predict people's weight from their height. A positive correlation means that increases in the value of one variable are associated with increases in the value of the other variable. Height and weight are positively correlated; the taller people are, the more they tend to weigh. A negative correlation means that increases in the value of one variable are associated with decreases in the value of the other. If height and weight were negatively correlated in human beings, we would look very peculiar—short people, such as children, would look like penguins, whereas tall people, like NBA basketball players, would be all skin and bones! It is also possible, of course, for two variables to be completely uncorrelated, so that a researcher cannot predict one variable from the other.

Correlation coefficients are expressed as numbers that can range from –1.00 to +1.00. A correlation of 1.00 means that two variables are perfectly correlated in a positive direc-

▼ Many people believe that pornography is a cause of sexual violence against women. How could this hypothesis be tested scientifically? Which research method would you use?

Correlational method
the technique whereby researchers systematically measure two or more variables, and assess the relation between them (i.e., how much one can be predicted from the other)

Correlation coefficient
a statistical technique that assesses how well you can predict one variable based on another; for example, how well you can predict people's weight from their height

tion; thus, by knowing people's standing on one variable, the researcher can predict exactly where they stand on the other variable. In everyday life, of course, perfect correlations are rare. For example, one study found that the correlation between height and weight was .47, in a sample of men ages 18 to 24 (Freedman et al., 1991). This means that, on average, the taller people were heavier than the shorter people, but there were exceptions. A correlation of –1.00 means that two variables are perfectly correlated in a negative direction, whereas a correlation of zero means that two variables are not correlated. And what is the correlation between having positive attitudes toward condoms and actually using them? Most studies find that this correlation is disturbingly low—as low as .23 (Hébert et al., 1989). Recall that a correlation of zero means that two variables are not associated at all. Thus, if you know that someone has positive attitudes toward using condoms, this information will not allow you to make an accurate prediction about whether the person actually will use one the next time he or she has sex.

Surveys

research in which a representative sample of people are asked questions about their attitudes or behaviour

Surveys   The correlational method is often used in **surveys**, research in which a representative sample of people are asked (often anonymously) questions about their attitudes or behaviour. Surveys are a convenient way to measure people's attitudes; for example, people can be telephoned and asked which candidate they will support in an upcoming election or how they feel about a variety of social issues. Researchers often apply the correlational method to survey results, to predict how people's responses to one question predict their other responses. Political scientists, for example, might be interested in whether people's attitudes toward a specific issue, such as gun control, predict how they will vote. Psychologists often use surveys to help understand social behaviour and attitudes—for example, by seeing whether the amount of pornography people say they read is correlated with their attitudes toward women.

Surveys have a number of advantages, one of which is that they allow researchers to judge the relationship between variables that are often difficult to observe, such as how often people engage in safer sex. The researcher looks at the relationship between the questions asked on the survey, such as whether people who know a lot about how AIDS is transmitted are more likely than other people to engage in safer sex.

Another advantage of surveys is the ability to sample representative segments of the population. Answers to a survey are useful only if they reflect the responses of people in general—not just the sample of people actually tested. Survey researchers go to great lengths to ensure that the people they sample are typical. They select samples that are representative of the population on a number of characteristics important to a given research question (e.g., age, educational background, religion, gender, income level). They also make sure to use a **random selection** of people from the population at large, which is a way of ensuring that a sample of people is representative. As long as the sample is selected randomly, we can assume that the responses are a reasonable match to those of the population as a whole. (Random selection also is important when researchers conduct experiments—which we discuss later.)

Random selection

a way of ensuring that a sample of people is representative of a population, by giving everyone in the population an equal chance of being selected for the sample

There are some famous cases whereby people tried to generalize from samples that were not randomly selected—to their peril. In the fall of 1936, a weekly magazine called *The Literary Digest* conducted a large survey asking Americans whom they planned to vote for in the upcoming presidential election. The magazine obtained the names and addresses of its sample from U.S. telephone directories and automobile registration lists. The results of its survey of 2 million people indicated that the Republican candidate, Alf Landon, would win by a landslide. There never was a President Landon; instead, Franklin Delano Roosevelt won every state but two. What went wrong with *The Literary Digest*'s poll? In the depths of the Great Depression, many people could not afford telephones or cars. Those who could afford these items were, by definition, doing well financially, were frequently Republican, and overwhelmingly favoured Alf Landon. However, the majority of the voters were poor—and overwhelmingly supported the Democratic candidate, Roosevelt. By using a list of names that excluded the less affluent members of the population, *The Literary Digest* created a nonrepresentative sample. (*The Literary Digest* never recovered from this methodological disaster and went out of business shortly after publishing its poll.)

Another potential problem with survey data is the accuracy of the responses. Straightforward questions—regarding what people think about an issue or what they typically do—are relatively easy to answer. For example, in a recent plebiscite, residents of Brandon, Manitoba, were asked two questions about a hotly contested issue: "Do you favour the establishment of a casino in the city of Brandon?" and "Do you support having a casino built on an urban reserve in the city of Brandon?" This kind of straightforward questioning tends to produce straightforward answers. More than half of voters (56 percent) responded "no" to the first question, and 64 percent responded "no" to the second question. As a result, the mayor announced that no casino would be built (Nickel, 2002).

◀ The importance of random selection in surveys. In 1936, an American magazine, *The Literary Digest,* conducted one of the first political polls. It randomly selected names from telephone directories and automobile registration lists and asked people for whom they planned to vote in the presidential election: Alf Landon or Franklin Roosevelt. As seen here, the poll indicated that Landon would win by a landslide. He didn't; Roosevelt carried virtually every state in the union. What went wrong with this poll?

However, asking respondents to predict how they might behave in some hypothetical situation or to explain why they behaved as they did in the past is an invitation to inaccuracy (Schuman & Kalton, 1985; Schwarz, Groves, & Schuman, 1998). Often people simply don't know the answer—but they think they do. Richard Nisbett and Tim Wilson (1977a) demonstrated this "telling more than you can know" phenomenon in a number of studies in which people often made inaccurate reports about why they responded the way they did. For example, if there was a distracting noise while they were watching a film, they indicated that the noise reduced their enjoyment of the film—even though it actually hadn't. (Participants who viewed the film under noisy conditions rated the film just as favourably as did participants who viewed it without background noise.) We discuss these studies at greater length in Chapter 5.

Finally, survey researchers have to be careful that they do not influence people's responses by the way they phrase questions (Hippler, Schwarz, & Sudman, 1987). For example, in a survey of attitudes toward affirmative action, Fletcher and Chalmers (1991) found that if Canadians were asked, "How important is it to guarantee equality between women and men in all aspects of life?" nearly everyone agreed that it was "most important" or "very important." There was, however, considerably less agreement when people were asked, "Do you think the government in Ottawa should make sure that a certain proportion of top jobs in government go to women?" Thus, depending on which question was asked, quite different conclusions would be drawn about the extent to which Canadians are in favour of affirmative action.

Limits of the Correlational Method: Correlation Does Not Equal Causation

The major shortcoming of the correlational method is that it tells us only that two variables are related, whereas the goal of the social psychologist is to identify the causes of social behaviour. We want to be able to say that A causes B, not just that A is related to, or correlated with, B.

If a researcher finds that there is a correlation between two variables, it means that there are three possible causal relations between these variables. For example, researchers have found a correlation between the amount of violent television children watch and how aggressive they are (Eron, 1982). One explanation of this correlation is that watching TV violence causes kids to become more violent. It is equally probable, however, that the reverse is true: that kids who are violent to begin with are more likely to watch violent TV. Or there might be no causal relation between these two variables; instead, both TV watching and violent behaviour could be caused by a third variable, such as having neglectful parents who do not pay much attention to their kids. (In Chapter 12, we will present experimental evidence that supports the first causal relation.) When we use the correlational method, it is wrong to jump to the conclusion that one variable is causing the other to occur. Correlation does not prove causation.

Unfortunately, one of the most common methodological errors in the social sciences is for a researcher to forget this adage. Drawing causal conclusions from correlational data also frequently occurs in everyday life. Consider, for example, a recent column in the *Winnipeg Free Press* featuring Tillie the Rainmaker. It all began in 1986 when Tillie took a trip to Sacramento, California. As soon as she stepped off the plane, the skies poured with rain, ending a six-week drought. Until then, Tillie had seen herself as an average

◀ Tillie Goren believes that she has the ability to end droughts because on several occasions when she has visited a drought-stricken area, it has started to rain. Is this a case of correlation or causation?

Jewish grandmother. But at that moment, she realized that she had special powers. Tillie claims to have ended many droughts and extinguished major forest fires since then. Winnipeg rabbi Alan Green is a strong supporter of Tillie and her work. "I can't prove scientifically that there is cause-and-effect," says Green. But he does believe that such things are possible. Besides, "It's a freely offered gift . . . There can be no harm." (Reynolds, 2000).

In a letter to the editor the next week, a psychology professor suggested that a more likely explanation for Tillie's special powers is that she and her rabbi inferred causality from correlational events ("Double deception," 2000). In some cases, this might be quite harmless, as Rabbi Green points out. However, it is not sound scientific practice, and the consequences can be quite serious, as demonstrated by a study of birth control methods and sexually transmitted diseases (STDs) in women (Rosenberg et al., 1992). These researchers examined the records of women who had visited a clinic for STDs, noting which method of birth control they used and whether they had STDs. Surprisingly, the researchers found that women who relied on condoms had significantly more STDs than women who used diaphragms or contraceptive sponges. This result was widely reported in the popular press, along with the conclusion that the use of diaphragms and sponges caused a lower incidence of disease. Some reporters urged women whose partners used condoms to switch to other methods.

Can you see the problem with this conclusion? The fact that the incidence of disease was correlated with the type of contraception women used is open to a number of causal interpretations. Perhaps the women who used sponges and diaphragms had sex with fewer partners. (In fact, condom users were more likely to have had sex with multiple partners in the previous month.) Perhaps the partners of women who relied on condoms were more likely to have STDs than the partners of women who used sponges and diaphragms. There is simply no way of knowing. Thus, the conclusion that any of the three types of birth control offered protection against STDs cannot be drawn from this correlational study.

Latané and Darley also might have used the correlational method to determine whether the number of bystanders is related to helping behaviour. They might have surveyed victims and bystanders of crimes and then correlated the total number of bystanders at each crime scene with the number of bystanders who helped or tried to help the victims. Let's say that a negative correlation was found in these data: The greater the number of bystanders, the less likely it was that any one of them intervened. Would this be evidence that the number of bystanders caused helping behaviour to occur or not? Unfortunately, no. Any number of unknown third variables could be causing both the number of bystanders and the rate of helping to occur. For example, the seriousness of the emergency could be such a third variable, in that serious, frightening emergencies, as compared to minor mishaps, tend to draw a large number of bystanders and make people less likely to intervene. Other examples of the difficulty of inferring causality from correlational studies are shown in Try It! on page 45.

The Experimental Method: Answering Causal Questions

Experimental method
the method in which the researcher randomly assigns participants to different conditions and ensures that these conditions are identical except for the independent variable (the one thought to have a causal effect on people's responses)

The only way to determine causal relations is with the **experimental method**, whereby the researcher systematically orchestrates the event so that people experience it in one way (e.g., they witness an emergency along with other bystanders) or another way (e.g., they witness the same emergency but are the sole bystander). The experimental method is the method of choice in most social psychological research, because it allows the experimenter to make causal inferences. The observational method is extremely useful in helping us describe social behaviour; the correlational method is extremely useful in helping us understand what aspects of social behaviour are related. However, only a properly executed experiment allows us to make cause-and-effect statements. For this reason, the experimental method is the crown jewel of social psychological research design.

The experimental method always involves direct intervention on the part of the researcher. By carefully changing only one aspect of the situation (e.g., group size), the researcher can see whether this aspect is the cause of the behaviour in question (e.g., whether people help in an emergency). Sound simple? Actually, it isn't. Stop and think for a moment how you might stage such an experiment to test Latané and Darley's hypothesis about the effects of group size. A moment's reflection will reveal that some rather severe practical and ethical difficulties are involved. What kind of emergency should be used? Ideally (from a scientific perspective), it should be as true to the Genovese case as possible. Accordingly, you would want to stage a murder that passersby could witness. In one condition, you could stage the murder so that only a few onlookers were present; in another condition, you could stage it so that a great many onlookers were present.

Clearly, there are some glaring ethical problems with this scenario. No scientist in his or her right mind would stage a murder for unsuspecting bystanders. But how can we arrange a realistic situation that is upsetting enough to be similar to the Genovese case without it being too upsetting? In addition, how can we ensure that each bystander

Correlation Does Not Equal Causation

It can be difficult to remember that correlation does not allow us to make causal inferences, especially when a correlation suggests a particularly compelling cause. It is easy to forget that there are alternative explanations for the obtained correlation; for example, other variables could be causing both of the observed variables to occur. For each of the following examples, think about why the correlation was found. Even if it seems obvious which variable was causing the other, are there alternative explanations?

Correlation Does Not Equal Causation Quiz

1. Recently, a politician extolled the virtues of the Boy and Girl Scouts organizations. In his salute to the Scouts, the politician mentioned that few teenagers convicted of street crimes had been members of the Scouts. In other words, he was positing a negative correlation between activity in Scouting and frequency of criminal behaviour. Why might this be?

2. A research study found that having a pet in childhood is correlated with a reduced likelihood of one becoming a juvenile delinquent in adolescence. Why is this?

3. A recent study of soldiers stationed on army bases found that the number of tattoos a soldier had is correlated positively with his becoming involved in a motorcycle accident. Why?

4. Recently, it was reported that a correlation exists between people's tendency to eat breakfast in the morning and how long they live, such that people who skip breakfast die younger. Does eating Cheerios lead to a long life?

5. A few years ago, newspaper headlines announced, "Coffee suspected as a cause of heart attacks." Medical studies had found a correlation between the amount of coffee people drank and their likelihood of having a heart attack. Are there any alternative explanations?

6. A positive correlation exists between the viscosity of asphalt in city playgrounds and the crime rate. How can this be? When asphalt becomes viscous (softer), is some chemical released that drives potential criminals wild? When the crime rate goes up, do people flock to the playgrounds, such that the pounding of feet increases the viscosity of the asphalt? What explains this correlation?

7. A news magazine recently reported that the more time fathers spend with their children, the less likely they are to sexually abuse them. Why might this be?

ANSWERS

1. The politician ignored possible third variables that could cause both Scouts membership and crime, such as socioeconomic class. Traditionally, Scouting has been most popular in small towns and suburbs among middle-class youngsters; it has never been very attractive or even available to youths growing up in densely populated, urban, high-crime areas.

2. Families who can afford or are willing to have a pet might differ in any number of ways from families who neither can afford nor are willing to have one.

3. Did tattoos cause motorcycle accidents? Or, for that matter, did motorcycle accidents cause tattoos? The researchers suggested that a third (unmeasured) variable was in fact the cause of both: a tendency to take risks and to be involved in flamboyant personal displays led to tattooing one's body and to driving a motorcycle recklessly.

4. Not necessarily. People who do not eat breakfast might differ from people who do in any number of ways that influence longevity—for example, in how obese they are, in how hard-driving and high-strung they are, or even in how late they sleep in the morning.

5. Coffee drinkers may be more likely to engage in other behaviours that put them at risk, such as smoking cigarettes or not exercising regularly.

6. Both the viscosity of asphalt and the crime rate go up when the temperature is high—for example, on a hot summer day or night.

7. The news magazine concluded that spending time with one's child reduces the urge to engage in sexual abuse (Adler, 1997). But perhaps child abuse leads to less time with children, due to feelings of guilt or fear of being caught. Or perhaps there is a third variable, such as an antisocial personality, that contributes to parents abusing and spending less time with their child.

experiences the same emergency except for the variable whose effect we want to test—in this case, the number of bystanders?

Let's see how Latané and Darley (1968) dealt with these problems. Imagine you were a participant in their experiment. You arrive at the scheduled time and find yourself in a long corridor with doors to several small cubicles. An experimenter greets you and takes you into one of the cubicles, mentioning that five other students, seated in the other cubicles, will be participating with you. The experimenter leaves after giving you a pair of headphones with an attached microphone. You put on the headphones, and soon you hear the experimenter explaining to everyone that he is interested in learning about the kinds of personal problems college students experience. To ensure that people will discuss their problems openly, he explains, each participant will remain anonymous; each will stay in his or her separate room and communicate with the others only via the intercom system. Further, the experimenter says, he will not be listening to the discussion, so that people will feel freer to be open and honest. Finally, the experimenter asks that participants take turns presenting their problems, each speaking for two minutes, after which each person will comment on what the others said. To make sure this procedure is followed, he says, only one person's microphone will be turned on at a time.

The group discussion then begins. You listen as the first participant admits that he has found it difficult to adjust to college. With some embarrassment, he mentions that he sometimes has seizures, especially when under stress. When his two minutes are up, you hear the other four participants discuss their problems, after which it is your turn. When you have finished, it is the first person's turn to speak again. To your astonishment, after he makes a few further comments, he seems to begin to experience a seizure:

> I—er—um—I think I—I need—er—if—if could—er—er—somebody er—er—er—er—er—er—er—give me a little—er—give me a little help here because—er—I—er—I'm—er—er—h—h—having a—a—a real problem—er—right now and I—er—if somebody could help me out it would—it would—er—er s—s—sure be—sure be good . . . because—er—there—er—er—a cause I—er—I—uh—I've got a—a one of the—er—sei—er—er—things coming on and—and—and I could really—er—use some help so if somebody would—er—give me a little h—help—uh—er—er—er—er—c—could somebody—er—er—help—er—uh—uh—uh (choking sounds) . . . I'm gonna die—er—er—I'm . . . gonna die—er—help—er—er—seizure—er (chokes, then quiet) (Darley & Latané, 1968, p. 379).

Stop and think for a moment: What would you have done in this situation? If you are like most of the participants in the actual study, you would have remained in your cubicle, listening to your fellow student having a seizure, and done nothing about it. Does this surprise you? Latané and Darley kept track of the number of people who left their cubicle to find the victim or the experimenter before the end of the victim's seizure. Only 31 percent of the participants sought help in this way. Fully 69 percent of the students remained in their cubicles and did nothing—just as Kitty Genovese's neighbours failed to offer her assistance in any way.

Does this finding prove that the failure to help was due to the number of people who witnessed the seizure? How do we know that it wasn't due to some other factor? Here is the major advantage of the experimental method. We know because Latané and Darley included two other conditions in their experiment. In these conditions, the procedure was identical to that described above, with one crucial difference: the size of the discussion group was smaller, meaning that fewer people were witnesses to the seizure. In one condition, the participants were told that there were three other people in the discussion group aside from themselves (the victim plus two others). In another condition, participants were told that there was only one other person in their discussion group (namely, the victim). In this latter condition, each participant believed that he or she was the only one who could hear the seizure. Did the size of the discussion group make a difference? As you'll see in a moment, it did.

INDEPENDENT AND DEPENDENT VARIABLES

The number of people witnessing the emergency was the **independent variable** in the Latané and Darley study, which is the variable a researcher changes or varies to see if it has an effect on some other variable. The **dependent variable** is the variable a researcher measures to see if it is influenced by the independent variable; the researcher hypothesizes that the dependent variable will be influenced by the level of the independent variable. That is, the dependent variable is hypothesized to depend on the independent variable (see Figure 2.1). Latané and Darley found that their independent variable—the number of bystanders—did have an effect on the dependent variable—whether they tried to help. When the participants believed that four other people were witnesses to the seizure, only 31 percent offered assistance. When the participants believed that only two other people were aware of the seizure, the amount of helping behaviour increased to 62 percent of the participants. When the participants believed that they were the only person listening to the seizure, nearly everyone helped (85 percent of the participants).

Independent variable

the variable a researcher changes or varies to see if it has an effect on some other variable

Dependent variable

the variable a researcher measures to see if it is influenced by the independent variable; the researcher hypothesizes that the dependent variable will depend on the level of the independent variable

Independent Variable	Dependent Variable
The variable that is hypothesized to influence the dependent variable. Participants are treated identically except for this variable.	The response that is hypothesized to depend on the independent variable. All participants are measured on this variable.

Example: Darley and Latané (1968)	
The number of bystanders	**How many subjects helped?**
Participant + Victim	85%
Participant + Victim + Two others	62%
Participant + Victim + Four others	31%

◀ **Figure 2.1**

INDEPENDENT AND DEPENDENT VARIABLES IN EXPERIMENTAL RESEARCH.

These results indicate that the number of bystanders strongly influences the rate of helping, but it does not mean that the size of the group is the only cause of people's decision to help. After all, when there were four bystanders, a third of the participants still helped; conversely, when participants thought they were the only witness, some of them failed to help. Obviously, other factors influence helping behaviour—such as the bystanders' personalities and their prior experience with emergencies. Nonetheless, Latané and Darley succeeded in identifying one important determinant of whether people help: the number of bystanders present.

INTERNAL VALIDITY IN EXPERIMENTS

How can we be sure that the differences in help across conditions in the Latané and Darley (1968) seizure study were due to the different numbers of bystanders who witnessed the emergency? Could this effect have been caused by some other aspect of the situation? Again, this is the beauty of the experimental method. We can be sure of the causal connection between the number of bystanders and helping because Latané and Darley made sure that everything about the situation was the same in the different conditions *except* the independent variable: the number of bystanders. Keeping everything the same but the independent variable is referred to as *internal validity* in an experiment (we'll provide a more formal definition of this term shortly). Latané and Darley were careful to maintain high internal validity by ensuring that everyone witnessed the same emergency. They pre-recorded the supposed other participants and the victim, and played their voices over the intercom system.

The astute reader will have noticed, however, that there was a key difference between the conditions of the Latané and Darley experiment other than the number of bystanders: different people participated in the different conditions. Maybe the observed differences in helping were due to characteristics of the participants instead of the independent variable. The people in the sole witness condition might have differed in any number of ways from their counterparts in the other conditions, making them more likely to help. Maybe they were more likely to have had loving parents, to know something about epilepsy, or to have experience helping in emergencies. Were any of these possibilities true, it would be difficult to conclude that it was the number of bystanders, rather than something about the participants' backgrounds, that led to differences in helping.

Fortunately, there is a technique that allows experimenters to minimize differences among participants as the cause of the results: **random assignment to condition**. This is the process whereby all participants have an equal chance of taking part in any condition of an experiment; through random assignment, researchers can be relatively certain that differences in the participants' personalities or backgrounds are distributed evenly across conditions. Because Latané and Darley's participants were randomly assigned to the conditions of their experiment, it is very unlikely that the ones who knew the most about epilepsy all ended up in one condition. Knowledge about epilepsy should be randomly (i.e., roughly evenly) dispersed across the three experimental conditions. This powerful technique is the most important part of the experimental method.

However, even with random assignment there is always the (very small) possibility that different characteristics of people did not distribute themselves evenly across conditions. For example, if we randomly divide a group of 40 people into two groups, it is possible that more of those who know the most about epilepsy will by chance end up in one group than in the other—just as it is possible to get more heads than tails when you flip a coin 40 times. This is a possibility we take seriously in experimental science. The analyses of our data come with a **probability level (*p*-value),** which is a number, calculated with statistical techniques, that tells researchers how likely it is that the results of their experiment occurred by chance and not because of the independent variable. The convention in science, including social psychology, is to consider results significant if the probability level is less than 5 in 100 that the results might be due to chance factors, and not the independent variables studied. For example, if we flipped a coin 40 times and got 40 heads, we

Random assignment to condition

the process whereby all participants have an equal chance of taking part in any condition of an experiment; through random assignment, researchers can be relatively certain that differences in the participants' personalities or backgrounds are distributed evenly across conditions

Probability level (*p*-value)

a number, calculated with statistical techniques, that tells researchers how likely it is that the results of their experiment occurred by chance and not because of the independent variable(s); the convention in science, including social psychology, is to consider results significant if the probability level is less than 5 in 100 that the results might be due to chance factors and not the independent variables studied would probably assume that this was very unlikely to have occurred by chance and that there was something wrong with the coin. (We might check the other side to ensure that it wasn't one of those trick coins with heads on both sides!) Similarly, if the results in two conditions of an experiment differ significantly from what we would expect by chance, we assume that the difference was caused by the independent variable (e.g., the number of bystanders present during the emergency). The p-value tells us how confident we can be that the difference was due to chance rather than to the independent variable.

To summarize, the key to a good experiment is to maintain high **internal validity**, which we can now define as making sure that the independent variable, and only the independent variable, influences the dependent variable. This is accomplished by controlling all extraneous variables (other variables that could conceivably affect the independent variable) and by randomly assigning people to different experimental conditions (Campbell & Stanley, 1967). When internal validity is high, the experimenter is in a position to judge whether the independent variable causes the dependent variable. This is the hallmark of the experimental method that sets it apart from the observational and correlational methods: Only the experimental method can answer causal questions.

EXTERNAL VALIDITY IN EXPERIMENTS

For all of the advantages of the experimental method, there are some drawbacks. By virtue of gaining enough control over the situation so as to randomly assign people to conditions and rule out the effects of extraneous variables, the situation can become somewhat artificial and distant from real life. For example, one could argue that Latané and Darley strayed far from the original inspiration for their study, the Kitty Genovese murder. What does witnessing a seizure while participating in a laboratory experiment in a college building have to do with a brutal murder in New York? How often in everyday life do we have discussions with other people through an intercom system? Did the fact that the participants knew they were in a psychology experiment influence their behaviour?

These are important questions that concern **external validity**, which is the extent to which the results of a study can be generalized to other situations and other people. Note that two kinds of generalizability are at issue: (a) the extent to which we can generalize from the situation constructed by an experimenter to real-life situations (generalizability across *situations*), and (b) the extent to which we can generalize from the people who participated in the experiment to people in general (generalizability across *people*).

Generalizability across Situations A possible criticism of research in social psychology is that it is often conducted in artificial situations that cannot be generalized to real life. To address this problem, social psychologists attempt to increase the generalizability of their results by making their studies as realistic as possible. However, it is important to note that there are different ways in which an experiment can be realistic. By one definition—the similarity of an experimental situation to events that occur frequently in everyday life—it is clear that many experiments are decidedly unreal. In many experiments, people are placed in situations they would rarely, if ever, encounter in everyday life, such as occurred in Latané and Darley's group discussion of personal problems over an intercom system. We can refer to the extent to which an experiment is similar to real-life situations as the experiment's **mundane realism** (Aronson & Carlsmith, 1968).

Internal validity
ensuring that nothing other than the independent variable can affect the dependent variable; this is accomplished by controlling all extraneous variables and by randomly assigning people to different experimental conditions

External validity
the extent to which the results of a study can be generalized to other situations and to other people

Mundane realism
the extent to which an experiment is similar to real-life situations

Psychological realism

the extent to which the psychological processes triggered in an experiment are similar to psychological processes that occur in everyday life; psychological realism can be high in an experiment, even if mundane realism is low

It is more important to ensure that a study is high in **psychological realism**, which is the extent to which the psychological processes triggered in an experiment are similar to psychological processes that occur in everyday life (Aronson, Wilson, & Brewer, 1998). Even though Latané and Darley staged an emergency that in significant ways was unlike ones encountered in everyday life, was it psychologically similar to real-life emergencies? Were the same psychological processes triggered? Did the participants have the same types of perceptions and thoughts, make the same types of decisions, and choose the same types of behaviours that they would have in a real-life situation? If so, then the study is high in psychological realism and the results are generalizable to everyday life.

Psychological realism is heightened if people find themselves engrossed in a real event. To accomplish this, it is often necessary to tell the participants a **cover story**—a false description of the study's purpose. You might have wondered why Latané and Darley told people that the purpose of the experiment was to study the personal problems of college students. It certainly would have been simpler to tell participants, "Look, we are interested in how people react to emergencies, so at some point during the study we are going to stage an accident, and then we'll see how you respond." We think you will agree, however, that such a procedure would be very low in psychological realism. In everyday life, we do not know when emergencies are going to occur and we do not have time to plan our responses to them. Thus, the kinds of psychological processes triggered would differ widely from those of a real emergency, reducing the psychological realism of the study.

Cover story

a description of the purpose of a study, given to participants, that is different from its true purpose; cover stories are used to maintain psychological realism

Further, as discussed earlier, people don't always know why they do what they do, or even what they will do until it happens. Thus, describing an experimental situation to participants and then asking them to respond normally will produce responses that are, at best, suspect. For example, after describing the Latané and Darley seizure experiment to our students, we often ask them to predict how they would respond, just as we asked you earlier. Invariably, most of our students think they would have helped the victim, even when they know that in the condition where the group size was six, most people did not help. Unfortunately, we cannot depend on people's predictions about what they would do in a hypothetical situation; we can only find out what people will really do when we construct a situation that triggers the same psychological processes as occur in the real world.

Generalizability across People One question we can ask about experiments such as Latané and Darley's is whether their findings are limited to university students, or whether we have learned something about human behaviour in general. As we mentioned earlier in our discussion of survey research, we can be more confident that findings from experiments apply to people in general when research participants are randomly selected from the population at large. Unfortunately, it is impractical and expensive to select random samples for social psychology experiments. It is difficult enough to convince a random sample of people to agree to answer a few questions over the telephone as part of a political poll, and such polls can cost thousands of dollars to conduct. Imagine the difficulty Latané and Darley would have had convincing a random sample of Americans to board a plane to New York to take part in their study, not to mention the cost of such an endeavour.

Of course, concerns about practicality and expense are not good excuses for poor science. More importantly, given the goal of social psychology, it is unnecessary to select random samples for every experiment performed. As noted in Chapter 1, social psychologists attempt to identify basic psychological processes that make people susceptible to social influence. If we accept the premise that there are fundamental psychological processes shared by all people in all places, and that it is these processes that are being studied in social psychology experiments, then it becomes relatively unimportant to select participants from every corner of the earth. Many social psychologists assume that the processes they study—such as the diffusion of responsibility caused by the presence of others in an emergency—are basic components of human nature, common to New Yorkers, Nova Scotians, and Japanese alike.

Replications Suppose a researcher claims that her study is high in psychological realism, that it has thus captured psychological functioning as it occurs in everyday life, and that it doesn't matter that only Introductory Psychology students at one university participated because these psychological processes are universal. Should we take her word for it?

Not necessarily. The ultimate test of an experiment's external validity is **replication**—conducting the study over again, often with different subject populations or in different settings. Do we think that Latané and Darley found the results they did only because their participants knew they were in a psychology experiment? If so, we should try to replicate their study in an experiment conducted outside the laboratory. Do we think that their results are limited to only certain kinds of emergencies? Then we should try to replicate the results with a different emergency. Do we think that only New Yorkers would be so unhelpful? Then we should try to replicate the study with participants from different parts of the United States and in different countries. Only with such replications can we be certain about how generalizable the results are.

Often, when many studies of one problem are conducted, the results are somewhat variable. Several studies might find an effect of the number of bystanders on helping behaviour, for example, whereas a few do not. How can we make sense out of this? Does the number of bystanders make a difference or not? Fortunately, there is a statistical technique called **meta analysis** that averages the results of two or more studies to see if the effect of an independent variable is reliable. Earlier we discussed p-levels, which tell us the probability that the findings of one study are due to chance or to the independent variable. A meta analysis essentially does the same thing, except that it averages across the results of many different studies. If, say, an independent variable is found to have an effect in only one of 20 studies, the meta analysis will tell us that that one study was probably an exception and that, on average, the independent variable is not influencing the dependent variable. If an independent variable is having an effect in most of the studies, the meta analysis is likely to tell us that, on average, it does influence the dependent variable. For example, Wendy Wood and her colleagues (Wood, Wong, & Chachere, 1991) conducted a meta analysis of 28 experiments examining the effects of television violence on aggression during social interactions. Although there was variability in the findings from one study to the next, when the findings of all these studies were aggregated, there was evidence that exposure to violent television does, in fact, produce aggressive behaviour.

Virtually all findings we will discuss in this book have been replicated in a number of different settings, with different populations, thus demonstrating that they are reliable phenomena that are not limited to the laboratory or to Introductory Psychology students.

▼ Some psychological processes are common to all people, whereas some differ across age, gender, and culture. To see if the results of an experiment are generalized to other groups of people, the study must be replicated with diverse populations.

Replication

repeating a study, often with different subject populations or in different settings

Meta analysis

a statistical technique that averages the results of two or more studies to see if the effect of an independent variable is reliable

For example, Latané and Darley's original findings have been replicated numerous times. Increasing the number of bystanders has been found to inhibit helping behaviour with many kinds of people, including children, university students, and future ministers (Darley & Batson, 1973; Latané & Nida, 1981); in Israel (Schwartz & Gottlieb, 1976); in small towns and large cities in the U.S. (Latané & Dabbs, 1975); in a variety of settings, such as psychology laboratories, city streets, and subway trains (Harrison & Wells, 1991; Latané & Darley, 1970; Piliavin et al., 1981; Piliavin & Piliavin, 1972); and with a variety of types of emergencies, such as seizures, potential fires, fights, and accidents (Latané & Darley, 1968; Shotland & Straw, 1976; Staub, 1974), as well as with less serious events, such as having a flat tire (Hurley & Allen, 1974). In addition, many of these replications have been conducted in real-life settings (e.g., on a subway train) where people could not possibly have known that an experiment was being conducted. We will frequently point out similar replications of the major findings we discuss in this book.

Generalizability across Cultures More and more social psychological experiments are being performed in other cultures, and this activity will enrich our understanding of the external validity of many findings. Cross-cultural research has two main goals. The first is to try to demonstrate that a particular psychological process or law is universal, in that it operates the same way in all human beings. This type of research emphasizes what we as human beings have in common, regardless of our backgrounds and culture. For example, Charles Darwin (1872) argued that there is a basic set of human emotions (e.g., anger, happiness) that are expressed and understood throughout the world. As we will see in Chapter 4, a lively controversy has arisen as to whether Darwin was right (Russell, 1994; Russell & Fehr, 1987). However, it is generally accepted that there are some similarities in the facial expression of emotions across cultures, even in remote cultures (Ekman, 1994; Izard, 1994; Ekman & Friesen, 1971).

Clearly, however, the diversity of our backgrounds shapes our lives in interesting ways. The second goal of cross-cultural research is to explore the differences among us, by examining how culture influences basic social psychological processes (Fiske et al., 1998; Moghaddam, Taylor, & Wright, 1993). Some findings in social psychology are culture-dependent, as we will see at many points throughout this book. In Chapter 5, for example, we will see that there are cultural differences in the very way people define themselves. Many Western cultures tend to emphasize individualism and independence, whereas many Asian cultures emphasize collectivism and interdependence (Heine et al., 1999; Markus & Kitayama, 1991; Triandis, 1989).

We do not have the space to discuss how to conduct cross-cultural research and the many nuances involved (see van de Vijver & Leung, 1997). Suffice it to say that it is not a simple matter of travelling to another culture, translating materials into the local language, and replicating a study there. Researchers have to be careful that they are not imposing their viewpoints and definitions, learned from their own culture, onto another unfamiliar culture. They also have to be sure that their independent and dependent variables are understood in the same way in different cultures (Bond, 1988; Lonner & Berry, 1986). Most cross-cultural researchers are sensitive to these issues, and as more and more cross-cultural research is conducted carefully, we will be able to determine which social psychological processes are universal and which are culture-bound.

Doonesbury

BY GARRY TRUDEAU

Universal Press Syndicate © G. B. Trudeau

◀ As researchers conduct more and more social psychological studies in diverse cultures, they document interesting cultural differences.

THE BASIC DILEMMA OF THE SOCIAL PSYCHOLOGIST

One of the best ways to increase external validity is by conducting **field experiments**. In a field experiment, people's behaviour is studied outside the laboratory, in its natural setting. A field experiment is identical in design to a laboratory experiment (e.g., the researcher controls the occurrence of an independent variable to see what effect it has on the dependent variable), except that it is conducted in a real-life setting. The participants in a field experiment are unaware that the events they experience are in fact an experiment. The external validity of such an experiment is high, since, after all, it is taking place in the real world, with real people who are more diverse than a typical university student sample.

Many such field studies have been conducted in social psychology. For example, Latané and Darley (1970) tested their hypothesis about group size and bystander intervention in a convenience store outside New York City. Two "robbers"—with full knowledge and permission of the cashier and manager of the store—waited until there were either one or two other customers at the checkout counter. Then they asked the cashier to name the most expensive beer the store carried. The cashier answered the question and then said he would have to check in the back to see how much of that brand was in stock. While the cashier was gone, the robbers picked up a case of beer in the front of the store, declared that "They'll never miss this," put the beer in their car, and drove off.

Given that the robbers were rather burly fellows, no one attempted to intervene directly to stop the theft. When the cashier returned, how many people would help by telling him that a theft had just occurred? The number of bystanders had the same inhibiting effect on helping behaviour as in the laboratory seizure study: Significantly fewer people reported the theft when there was another witness/customer in the store than when they were alone.

When we conduct experiments in psychology, there is almost always a trade-off between internal and external validity—that is, between (a) having enough control over the situation to ensure that no extraneous variables are influencing the results and to randomly assign people to conditions, and (b) ensuring that the results can be generalized to everyday life. Control is best exerted in a laboratory setting, but the laboratory may be unlike real life. Real life can best be captured by doing a field experiment, but it is difficult to control all extraneous variables in such studies. For example, the astute reader will have noticed that Latané and Darley's (1970) beer theft study was unlike laboratory

Field experiments

experiments conducted in natural settings, rather than in the laboratory

experiments in an important respect: People could not be randomly assigned to the alone or in-pairs conditions. If this were the only study Latané and Darley had performed, we could not be certain whether the kinds of people who prefer to shop alone, as compared to the kinds of people who prefer to shop with a friend, differ in ways that might influence helping behaviour. By randomly assigning people to conditions in their laboratory studies, Latané and Darley were able to rule out such alternative explanations.

The trade-off between internal and external validity has been referred to as the basic dilemma of the experimental psychologist (Aronson & Carlsmith, 1968). The challenge is to devise a study that maximizes both. Wendy Josephson's (1987) study on the relation between television violence and aggressive behaviour is an example of one that rose to this challenge and elegantly captured both internal validity and external validity. In this study, boys in grades 2 and 3 from 13 schools in Winnipeg watched either a violent or a nonviolent television show. Internal validity was achieved by controlling the television show the participants watched. For example, Josephson ensured that the violent and nonviolent shows were equivalent in terms of excitement, liking, and physiological arousal. This level of control ensured that any differences in subsequent behaviour between the two groups were due to differences in violent content, rather than to other variables that might be associated with violent programming, such as excitement. Internal validity was further enhanced by random assignment of participants to either the violent or the nonviolent condition. External validity was maximized by having the participants play floor hockey in their school gymnasium (an activity typical for boys this age) after they had finished viewing the television segment. (As you will see in Chapter 12, in social psychological research, aggression is often assessed in terms of the severity of electric shocks administered to another research participant—a procedure that may be high in internal validity, but that certainly lacks external validity.) Observers who were unaware of whether the boys had seen the violent or nonviolent segment (a procedure known as keeping observers "blind" to the experiment's hypothesis) recorded instances of aggression. To make the observation as natural as possible, participants were told that the observers would be doing "play by plays" just the way they do in "real" hockey games. The observers spoke into microphones, noted the number on a child's jersey, and recorded the kind of aggression that occurred. (One of the observers was Wendy Josephson's mother, who apparently had to swallow hard before recounting some of the instances of verbal aggression!) The results of this study indicated that exposure to violent programming did, in fact, increase aggression, but only among boys who were predisposed toward aggression.

Generally, both internal and external validity are not captured in a single experiment. Most social psychologists opt first for internal validity, conducting laboratory experiments in which people are randomly assigned to different conditions and all extraneous variables are controlled; here, there is little ambiguity about which variable is causing which result. Other social psychologists prefer external validity to control, conducting most of their research in field studies. And many social psychologists do both. Taken together, both types of studies meet the requirements of our perfect experiment. Through replication, researchers can study a given research question with maximal internal and external validity. This approach has worked well in many areas of inquiry, in which laboratory and field studies have been conducted on the same problem and have yielded similar findings (Anderson, Lindsay, & Bushman, 1999).

Ethical Issues in Social Psychology

Now that we have discussed the three major research methodologies in social psychology (observational, correlational, experimental), there are two remaining issues about research that we need to address. First, it is important to discuss ethical issues that arise in research in social psychology. Earlier, we mentioned that in order to maintain high psychological realism in experiments, researchers sometimes construct cover stories that mislead people about the true purpose of the study. Also, as we saw with the Latané and Darley study, people are sometimes put in situations that are upsetting. This study illustrates that in their quest to create realistic, engaging situations, social psychologists frequently face an ethical dilemma. On the one hand, for obvious scientific reasons, we want our experiments to resemble the real world as much as possible and to be as sound and well controlled as we can make them. On the other hand, we want to avoid causing our participants undue and unnecessary stress, discomfort, or unpleasantness. These two goals often conflict as the researcher goes about his business of creating and conducting experiments.

Researchers are concerned about the health and welfare of the individuals participating in their experiments. Researchers are also in the process of discovering important information about human social behaviour—such as bystander intervention, prejudice, conformity, aggression, and obedience to authority. Many of these discoveries are bound to be of benefit to society. Indeed, given the fact that social psychologists have developed powerful tools to investigate such issues scientifically, many scholars feel it would be immoral *not* to conduct these experiments. However, in order to gain insight into such critical issues, researchers must create vivid events that are involving for the participants. Some of these events, by their nature, are likely to produce a degree of discomfort for the participants. Thus, what is required for good science and what is required for ethical science can be contradictory. The dilemma cannot be resolved by making pious claims that no participant ever experiences any kind of discomfort in an experiment, or by insisting that all is fair in science and forging blindly ahead. Clearly, the problem calls for a middle ground.

The dilemma would be less problematic if researchers could obtain informed consent from their participants prior to participation. **Informed consent** is the procedure whereby the researcher explains the nature of the experiment to participants before it begins and asks for their consent to participate. If the experimenter fully describes to participants the kinds of experiences they are about to undergo and asks them if they are willing to participate, then the ethical dilemma is resolved. In many social psychology experiments, this sort of description is feasible—and where it is feasible, it is done. In other kinds of experiments, however, it is impossible. Suppose Latané and Darley had told their participants that a seizure was about to be staged, that it wouldn't be a real emergency, and that the hypothesis stated they should offer help. As we saw earlier, such a procedure would be bad science. In this kind of experiment, it's essential that the participant experience contrived events as if they were real; this is called a deception experiment. **Deception** in social psychological research involves misleading participants about the true purpose of a study or the events that transpire. (It is important to note that not all research in social psychology involves deception.)

Informed consent

the procedure whereby researchers explain the nature of the experiment to participants before it begins, and obtain their consent to participate

Deception

the procedure whereby participants are misled about the true purpose of a study or the events that will actually transpire

▶ It is unlikely that an ethics committee would have approved this study.

THE FAR SIDE By GARY LARSON

© 1993 FarWorks Inc./Distributed by Universal Press Syndicate. All rights reserved.

Over the years, a number of guidelines have been developed to deal with these dilemmas about the ethics of experiments and to ensure that the dignity and safety of research participants are protected. For example, the Canadian Psychological Association has published a set of ethical principles that apply to psychology research and clinical practice; these guidelines are summarized in Figure 2.2. In addition, there is a set of ethics guidelines, the Tri-Council Policy Statement, that governs research conducted at universities. All psychology research is reviewed by a Research Ethics Board to ensure that the strict guidelines of the Tri-Council Policy are met. Any aspect of the experimental procedure that this committee judges to be stressful or upsetting must be changed or deleted before the study can be conducted.

In all research studies, participants must be told that they can withdraw at any time, for any reason, without fear of consequences for doing so. They also are assured of the anonymity and confidentiality of their responses.

Debriefing

the process of explaining to the participants, at the end of the experiment, the purpose of the study and exactly what transpired

When deception is used, the post-experimental interview, called the debriefing session, is crucial and must occur. **Debriefing** is the process of explaining to the participants, at the end of the experiment, the purpose of the study and exactly what transpired. If any participants experienced discomfort, the researchers attempt to undo and alleviate it. Finally, the debriefing session provides an opportunity to inform the participants about the goals and purpose of the research, thereby serving an important educational function. The best researchers question their participants carefully and listen to what they say, regardless of whether deception was used in the experiment. (For a detailed description of how debriefing interviews should be conducted, see Aronson, Ellsworth, Carlsmith, & Gonzales, 1990.)

Ethical Principles of Psychologists in the Conduct of Research

1. **Respect for dignity of persons.** The central ethical principle underlying psychological research is respect for human dignity. This principle forms the foundation for the other principles that follow.

2. **Informed consent.** As much as possible, the researcher should describe the procedures to participants before they take part in a study, and document their agreement to take part in the study as it was described to them.

3. **Minimizing harm.** Psychologists must take steps to avoid harming their research participants.

4. **Freedom to withdraw.** Participants must be informed that they are free to withdraw from a study at any point, and that there will be no negative consequences for doing so.

5. **Privacy and confidentiality.** All information obtained from individual participants must be held in strict confidence.

6. **Use of deception.** Deception may be used only if there are no other viable means of testing a hypothesis, and only if a Research Ethics Board rules that it does not put participants at undue risk. After the study, participants must be provided with a full description and explanation of all procedures, in a post-experimental interview called the debriefing.

▲ **Figure 2.2**

PROCEDURES FOR THE PROTECTION OF PARTICIPANTS IN PSYCHOLOGICAL RESEARCH.

Source: Adapted from *Canadian code of ethics for psychologists*, Canadian Psychological Association, 1991, and *Ethical principles of psychologists in the conduct of research*, American Psychological Association, 1992.

In our experience, virtually all participants understand and appreciate the need for deception, as long as the time is taken in the post-experimental debriefing session to go over the purpose of the research and to explain why alternative procedures could not be used. Studies that have investigated the impact of participating in deception studies have consistently found that people do not object to the kinds of mild discomfort and deceptions typically used in social psychological research (e.g., Christensen, 1988; Finney, 1987; Gerdes, 1979). This was also the case in a study at the University of Manitoba where attitudes toward deception research were assessed in 1970 and again, 20 years later, in 1990 (Sharpe, Adair, & Roese, 1992). At each time period, there was no evidence that students who had participated in deception studies felt negatively about their experience. In fact, participants who had been deceived were more likely to agree with arguments in favour of deception research than were those who had not experienced deception. And, importantly, those who had experienced deception did not show greater distrust of psychologists. Some studies have even found that people who participated in deception experiments said they had learned more and enjoyed the experiments more than did those who participated in nondeception experiments (Smith & Richardson, 1983). For example, Latané and Darley (1970) reported that during their debriefing, the participants said that the deception was necessary and that they were willing to participate in similar studies in the future—even though they had experienced some stress and conflict during the study.

We do not mean to imply that all deception is beneficial. Nonetheless, if mild deception is used and time is spent after the study discussing the deception with participants and explaining why it was necessary, the evidence shows that people will not be adversely affected.

Basic versus Applied Research

You might have wondered how people decide which specific topic to study. Why would a social psychologist decide to study helping behaviour, bullying, or the effects of violent television on aggression? Is he or she simply curious? Or does the social psychologist have a specific purpose in mind, such as trying to reduce violence?

In general, we can distinguish between two types of research, each having a different purpose. The goal in **basic research** is to find the best answer as to why people behave the way they do, purely for reasons of intellectual curiosity. No direct attempt is made to solve a specific social or psychological problem. In contrast, the goal in **applied research** is to solve a particular social problem; building a theory of behaviour is usually secondary to solving the specific problem, such as alleviating racism, reducing violence, or stemming the spread of AIDS.

The difference between basic and applied research is easily illustrated by examples from other sciences. Some biology researchers, for example, are concerned primarily with fundamental theoretical issues—such as the role DNA plays in the transmission of genetic information—without an immediate concern as to how these issues can be applied to everyday problems. Other biology researchers are concerned primarily with applied issues—such as how to develop a strain of rice that has more protein and is more resistant to disease—to help solve problems of world hunger.

In most sciences, however, the distinction between basic and applied research is fuzzy. Even though many researchers label themselves as either basic or applied scientists, it is clear that the endeavours of one group are not independent of those of the other group. There are countless examples of advances in basic science that at the time had no known applied value but later proved to be the key to solving a significant applied problem. Basic research on DNA and genetics has led to a technology that enables researchers to create new strains of bacteria, with several important real-world applications in medicine and environmental control. For example, genetically engineered bacteria are now used in oil spills to help break up and disperse the oil. The same is true in social psychology. As we will see later in this book, for instance, basic research with dogs, rats, and fish on the effects of feeling in control of one's environment has led to the development of techniques to improve the health of elderly nursing home residents (Langer & Rodin, 1976; Schulz, 1976; Seligman, 1975). Similarly, observational research on bullying led to the development of an anti-bullying intervention program that has been used in Toronto schools (Pepler et al., 1994).

Most social psychologists would agree that in order to solve a specific social problem, it is vital to have a good understanding of the psychological processes responsible for it. Kurt Lewin (1951), one of the founders of social psychology, coined a phrase that has become a motto for the field: "There is nothing so practical as a good theory." He meant that to solve such difficult social problems as violence or racial prejudice, one must first understand the underlying psychological dynamics of human nature and social interaction. In the early years of social psychology as a discipline, differences emerged in the extent to which researchers focused directly on solving a social problem versus studying basic aspects of human nature. Lewin's own research group fell into these two camps. This dichotomy is still present in the field today, with some social psychologists doing basic research primarily in laboratory settings and others doing applied research primarily in field settings.

This book reflects the first school of social psychologists, those concerned mainly with basic theoretical issues. The subject matter of social psychology, however, is such that even

Basic research

studies that are designed to find the best answer as to why people behave the way they do and that are conducted purely for reasons of intellectual curiosity

Applied research

studies designed specifically to solve a particular social problem; building a theory of behaviour is usually secondary to solving the specific problem

when the goal is to discover the psychological processes underlying social behaviour, the findings often have clear applied implications. Thus, throughout this book we will see many examples of research that have direct applications. We also include at the end of the book three Social Psychology in Action units that discuss how social psychology has been applied to important social problems.

SUMMARY

The goal of social psychology is to answer questions about social behaviour scientifically. The principal research designs used are descriptive methods (observational, archival, and correlational) and experimental methods. Each has its strengths and weaknesses and is appropriate for certain research questions. Each method causes the researcher to make a different type of statement about his or her findings.

Descriptive methods allow a researcher to observe and describe a social phenomenon. **Observational methods** vary in terms of how visible the researcher is. In some cases, the researcher is unobtrusive; in other cases, the researcher interacts with the people being observed (this is known as **participant observation**). In **archival analysis**, the researcher examines the accumulated documents or archives of a culture. The **correlational method** allows the researcher to determine if two or more variables are related—that is, whether one can be predicted from the other. **Survey** research is one kind of correlational research. The **correlation coefficient** is a statistical technique that reveals the extent to which one variable can be predicted from another. Correlations are often calculated from survey data, in which there is **random selection** of a sample from a larger population. This ensures that the responses of the sample are representative of those of the population. The major drawback of the correlational method is that it cannot determine causality. It is not possible to determine from a correlation whether A causes B, B causes A, or some other variable causes both A and B.

For this reason, the **experimental method** is the preferred design in social psychology; it alone allows the researcher to infer the presence of causality. Experiments can be conducted in the laboratory or in the field; **field experiments** are those conducted in natural settings. In experiments, researchers vary the level of an **independent variable**, which is the one hypothesized to have a causal effect on behaviour. The **dependent variable** is the measured variable hypothesized to be caused or influenced by the independent variable. The researcher ensures that participants are treated identically except for the independent variable, and randomly assigns people to the experimental conditions. **Random assignment to condition**, the hallmark of true experimental design, minimizes the possibility that different types of people are unevenly distributed across conditions. A **probability level (p-value)** is calculated, telling the researcher how likely it is that the results are due to chance versus due to the independent variable.

Experiments are designed to be as high as possible in **internal validity** (ensuring that nothing other than the independent variable is influencing the results) and in **external validity** (ensuring that the results can be generalized across people and situations). **Mundane realism** reflects the extent to which the experimental setting is similar to real-life settings. **Psychological realism** reflects the extent to which the experiment involves psychological responses like those occurring in real life. The best test of external validity is **replication**—repeating the experiment in different settings with different people, to see if the results are the same. A statistical technique called **meta analysis** allows researchers to see how reliable the effects of an independent variable are over many replications.

Researchers engage in both **basic research** and **applied research**. While the line between these is often blurred, basic research aims to gain understanding of human social behaviour, without trying specifically to solve a particular problem, whereas applied research aims to solve a specific problem, often one with social policy implications. Finally, a major concern in social psychological research is the ethical treatment of participants. Canadian researchers carefully follow the Canadian Psychological Association's guidelines, which specify procedures such as obtaining **informed consent**, the participant's right to leave the study at any time, ensured anonymity and confidentiality, and **debriefing** following

an experiment, particularly if **deception** (involving a **cover story** about the supposed purpose of the study or the independent or dependent variables) has been used.

IF YOU ARE INTERESTED

Adair, J. G. (1973). *The human subject: The social psychology of the psychological experiment.* Boston: Little, Brown, and Company. This timeless treasure, written by a University of Manitoba social psychologist, covers all of the important methodological issues in conducting social psychological research. Topics include experimenter–participant interactions, participants' interpretation of experiments, the use of deception in research, and debriefing.

Aron, A., & Aron, E. N. (1990). *The heart of social psychology* (2nd ed.). Lexington, MA: Heath. A behind-the-scenes look at how social psychologists conduct research, based on interviews with leading researchers.

Aronson, E., Ellsworth, P., Carlsmith, J. M., & Gonzales, M. (1990). *Methods of research in social psychology* (2nd ed.). New York: Random House. An entertaining, thorough treatment of how to conduct social psychological research.

Aronson, E., Wilson, T. D., & Brewer, M. (1998). Experimental methods. In D. Gilbert, S. Fiske, & G. Lindzey (Eds.), *The handbook of social psychology* (4th ed., Vol. 1, pp. 99–142). New York: McGraw-Hill. An expanded discussion of many of the issues discussed in this chapter, for those considering social psychology as a profession.

Reitman, Ivan (Director). (1984). *Ghostbusters* [Film]. At the beginning of this movie there is a scene in which Bill Murray, playing a psychologist, conducts an experiment on ESP. It is an amusing illustration of how not to do experimental research.

Rosenthal, R., & Rosnow, R. L. (1991). *Essentials of behavioral research: Methods and data analysis* (2nd ed.). New York: McGraw-Hill. A detailed guide to methodology and statistical analyses, for professionals and the advanced student.

WEBLINKS

www.nova.edu/ssss/QR/web.html

Qualitative Research Web Sites

This is a good starting point to find out more about qualitative research methodology.

www.uwinnipeg.ca/~clark/research/cpaethics.html

Canadian Code of Ethics for Psychologists

This site contains the full text of the Canadian Psychological Association's code of ethics for psychologists.

http://psych.hanover.edu/research/exponnet.html

Psychological Research on the Net

This site includes some ongoing social psychological studies being conducted via the Internet.

http://trochim.human.cornell.edu/kb/index.htm

Research Methods Knowledge Base

This interesting online textbook is devoted to the topic of methods with a unique approach.

CHAPTER 3

Social Cognition
how we think about the social world

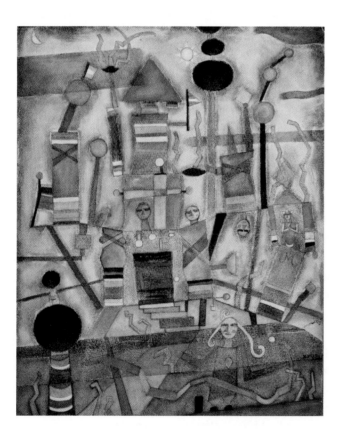

▼ Because of a brain injury, Kevin Chappell, shown here standing between his two sons, lives in a world of unidentifiable objects.

KEVIN CHAPPELL WAS ON HIS WAY TO THE TOP. It was 1988 and the 29-year-old man with an IQ of 147 had just been accepted to medical school, had graduated at the top of his class from Trent University, and was working on a master's degree. He was also an avid soccer player and had played lead guitar in a rock and roll band. On January 30, 1988, he decided to go for a run after a hard day of studying. It was a dark, rainy evening and, as he crossed a street, he was hit by a car. From that moment, Chappell's life was changed immeasurably. He sustained severe brain damage, leaving him unable to recognize things. He could see objects, but didn't know what they were—a condition known as visual agnosia. There are very few people in the world with visual agnosia—perhaps only two or three—so, not surprisingly, Chappell's condition attracted the attention of neuropsychologists.

Psychologist Gordon Winocur, a specialist in memory at Trent University, met Chappell just after he had been diagnosed with visual agnosia. Chappell didn't touch the cup of coffee that Dr. Winocur had served him, which wasn't unusual for someone with this diagnosis. How can you drink a cup of coffee if you don't recognize what it is? However, one day Chappell happened to run into Winocur and greeted him by name. Dr. Winocur was stunned. How could someone who didn't recognize objects know who he was?

It became apparent that Chappell does recognize one thing—faces. He doesn't recognize arms, legs, or feet. He doesn't recognize faces that are upside down or sideways, but he does recognize faces that are upright (Scott, 2002). This ability probably makes him unique in the world. Dr. Winocur teamed up with two neuropsychologists, Morris Moscovitch from the University of Toronto and Marlene Behrman from Carnegie Mellon University in Pittsburgh, to formally study Kevin Chappell. Their findings were published in the highly prestigious science journal *Nature* in 1992 (Behrman, Winocur, & Moscovitch, 1992). Chappell's case is teaching scientists that the brain may use different systems for recognizing faces, for recognizing objects, and for forming a mental image of things. In order to recognize an object, we have to be able to perceive its parts, synthesize them, and match them to the representation of that object stored in our brains. According to Dr. Moscovitch, "Kevin seems to be fine at identifying the bits and pieces . . . . It's his ability to integrate the information rapidly and then match it to the internal representation that seems to be impaired" (Scott, 2002).

A writer, interviewing Chappell, now age 44, shows him a pair of sunglasses. "It's brown with bits of silver and two horns," Chappell says. But what is it? Chappell has no idea. "I don't know what I see," he replies, "I have to guess" (Scott, 2002). It is hard to imagine what Kevin Chappell's world must be like. When we enter a classroom, for example, we do not see a bunch of objects that have platforms parallel to the floor connected to four legs with another flat surface at a right angle, that we then mentally assemble to figure out what they are. Instead of having to pause and think, "Let's see. Oh, yes, those are chairs," we quickly, unconsciously, and effortlessly categorize the objects as chairs. The fact that we do this automatically allows us to use our conscious minds for other, more important purposes ("What's going to be on the quiz today?" or "Should I strike up a conversation with that cute guy in the third row?"). Similarly, when we encounter people we know, the process of recognizing them requires little effort on our part, thereby allowing us to focus on our interaction with them.

In this chapter we will explore **social cognition**, which is the way people think about themselves and the social world—how they select, interpret, remember, and use social information to make judgments and decisions. Not only are we able to recognize chairs and other physical objects without any apparent effort, but we are also able to make complex judgments about people at lightning speed. Of course, we also occasionally make mistakes, and sometimes these mistakes are costly. In this chapter we will see how sophisticated we are as social thinkers, as well as the kinds of mistakes we are prone to make.

To understand how people think about the social world, we will first consider the procedures, rules, and strategies they use. It is often impossible to consider the overwhelming amount of information we have about the people around us. Consequently, individuals rely on a variety of mental shortcuts that serve them well. As we will see, people are quite practical, adopting different procedures and rules according to their goals and needs in that situation. Even so, human reasoning is not perfect, and in the last section we will consider methods of improving the way that people think.

Social cognition

how people think about themselves and the social world; more specifically, how people select, interpret, remember, and use social information to make judgments and decisions

People as Everyday Theorists: Schemas and Their Influence

We have knowledge about many things—objects, such as chairs and sunglasses; other people; ourselves; social roles (e.g., what a librarian or an engineer is like); and specific events (e.g., what usually happens when people eat a meal in a restaurant). **Schemas** are mental structures people use to organize their knowledge around themes or topics (Bartlett, 1932; Kunda, 1999; Markus, 1977; Taylor & Crocker, 1981). There are a number of different kinds of schemas. As already discussed, we have schemas of objects, such as chairs. However, social psychologists have tended to focus more on schemas pertaining to the social world. For example, our schema about car salespeople might be that they're smooth talkers, insincere, male, and knowledgeable about cars. As this example illustrates, our stereotypes of different groups can be thought of as a kind of schema (we will discuss stereotypes further in Chapter 13). Another important kind of schema is a self-schema—our knowledge of ourselves—what we are like as a person, our likes, our dislikes, and so on. (Self-schemas are the focus of Chapter 5.) We also have schemas about typical patterns of relating with other people. Such schemas are known as relational schemas (Baldwin, 1992). Schemas profoundly affect what information we notice, think about, and later remember (Kerr & Stanfel, 1993; Trafimow & Schneider, 1994; Trafimow & Wyer, 1993; von Hippel et al., 1993). If you see a car salesperson who is sincere and honest, this information will be inconsistent with your schema, and under most circumstances you will forget it, ignore it, or fail to even notice it. Thus, schemas act as filters, straining out information that is contradictory to or inconsistent with the prevailing theme (Fiske, 1993; Higgins & Bargh, 1987; Olson, Roese, & Zanna, 1996; Stangor & McMillan, 1992).

Sometimes, of course, a fact can be so inconsistent with a schema that we cannot ignore or forget it. If we encounter a car salesperson who fumbles for words, is honest, and is female, this person is such a glaring exception to our schema that she will stick in our minds—particularly if we spend time pondering how she could ever have ended up

Schemas

mental structures people use to organize their knowledge about the social world around themes or subjects; schemas affect what information we notice, think about, and remember

in car sales (Burgoon, 1993; Hastie, 1980; Stangor & McMillan, 1992). In most cases, however, we are likely to notice and interpret the behaviour of other people in ways that fit our preconceptions about them.

One of your authors, Beverley Fehr, recently heard a rather humorous story that illustrates this phenomenon at a fundraising breakfast for a counselling centre. Guest speaker Pamela Wallin described an early incident that nearly cost her her broadcasting career—or so she thought. The setting was the G-7 economic summit in Quebec, and CTV had managed to arrange interviews with the British prime minister and the chancellor of West Germany. Wallin excitedly announced to viewers that they should stay tuned, because after the commercial break they would be interviewing Margaret Thatcher and Helmut Shit. Convinced that she had just committed career suicide, Wallin left the studio. The first few people she ran into commented that for a moment they had thought she had mispronounced Chancellor Schmidt's name, but then realized that the vacuum cleaner had been on, or that they hadn't had their morning coffee yet, or . . . In short, the fact that Pamela Wallin said "shit" on television was so inconsistent with people's schema of her that they convinced themselves they must have heard wrong—that she really must have said "Schmidt."

The power of schemas has been demonstrated in numerous laboratory studies. For example, participants in a study by Linda Carli (1999) read a story about a woman named Barbara and her relationship with a man named Jack. After dating for a while, Barbara and Jack went to a ski lodge for a weekend getaway. In one condition, the story ended with Jack proposing to Barbara; in the other condition, the story ended with Jack raping Barbara. Two weeks later, participants took a memory test in which they read several facts about Jack and Barbara and judged whether these facts had appeared in the story. In the marriage-proposal condition, people were likely to misremember details that were consistent with a proposal schema, such as "Jack wanted Barbara to meet his parents" and "Jack gave Barbara a dozen roses." Neither of these details had been in the story, but people in the proposal condition tended to think they were (see Figure 3.1). Similarly,

Figure 3.1

MISREMEMBERING DETAILS ABOUT A STORY.

People's schemas about a story, based on its outcome, led them to misremember details that were consistent with this schema.

(Adapted from Carli, 1999)

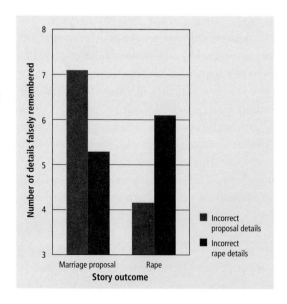

people in the rape condition were likely to misremember details that were consistent with a rape schema, such as "Jack liked to drink" and "Jack was unpopular with women."

As this study demonstrates, people don't remember exactly what occurred in a given setting as if their minds were a film camera recording precise images and sounds. Instead, they remember some information that was there (particularly information our schemas leads us to notice and pay attention to) and other information that was never there but that they have unknowingly added later (Darley & Akert, 1993; Markus & Zajonc, 1985). For example, if you ask people what is the most famous line of dialogue in the classic Humphrey Bogart and Ingrid Bergman movie *Casablanca,* they will probably say, "Play it again, Sam." Similarly, if you ask them what is one of the most famous lines from the original (1966–69) *Star Trek* television series, they will probably say, "Beam me up, Scotty."

Here is a piece of trivia that might surprise you: Both of these lines of dialogue are reconstructions—the characters in the movie and the television series never said them.

THE FUNCTION OF SCHEMAS: WHY DO WE HAVE THEM?

If schemas can sometimes make us misperceive the world, why do we have them? Think back, for a moment, to our opening story about Kevin Chappell, a man who lives in a world of unidentifiable objects. What would it be like to have no schemas about the social world? What if everything you encountered was inexplicable, confusing, and unlike anything else you'd ever known? Tragically, this is what happens to people who suffer from a neurological disorder called Korsakov's Syndrome. Similar to Kevin Chappell's visual agnosia, people who suffer from Korsakov's Syndrome also have difficulty forming schemas. This can be so unsettling—even terrifying—that some people with Korsakov's Syndrome go to great lengths to try to impose meaning on their experiences. The neurologist Oliver Sacks gives the following description of a Korsakov patient named Mr. Thompson:

◀ "Beam me up, Scotty." Did the characters in the original *Star Trek* television series ever speak this line?

He remembered nothing for more than a few seconds. He was continually disoriented. Abysses of amnesia continually opened beneath him, but he would bridge them, nimbly, by fluent confabulations and fictions of all kinds. For him they were not fictions, but how he suddenly saw, or interpreted, the world. Its radical flux and incoherence could not be tolerated, acknowledged, for an instant—there was, instead, this strange, delirious, quasi-coherence, as Mr. Thompson, with his ceaseless, unconscious, quick-fire inventions, continually improvised a world around him . . . *for such a patient must literally make himself (and his world) up every moment* (Sacks, 1987; emphasis in original).

In short, it is so important to us to have continuity, to relate new experiences to our past schemas, that people who lose this ability invent schemas where none exist.

As already mentioned, schemas also reduce the amount of information we have to process. As the writer of an article on Kevin Chappell notes, "For most people, recognizing things is a no-brainer. You see a chair; you know what it is" (Scott, 2002). If we don't have to go through the painstaking process of trying to figure out what this object with a seat, four legs, and a back is, we are able to concentrate on those aspects of our social world that require our full attention.

Schemas also are important when we encounter information that can be interpreted in a number of ways, because they provide us with a way of reducing ambiguity. Consider a classic study by Harold Kelley (1950), in which students in different sections of an economics class were told that a guest lecturer would be filling in that day. In order to create a schema about what the guest lecturer would be like, Kelley told the students that the economics department was interested in how different classes reacted to different instructors and that the students would thus receive a brief biographical note about the instructor before he arrived. The note contained information about the instructor's age, background, and teaching experience. It also gave one of two descriptions of his personality. One version said, "People who know him consider him to be a rather cold person, industrious, critical, practical, and determined." The other version was identical, except

▲ People who know him consider him to be a very warm person, industrious, critical, practical, and determined.

▲ People who know him consider him to be a rather cold person, industrious, critical, practical, and determined.

that the phrase "a rather cold person" was replaced with "a very warm person." The students were randomly given one of these personality descriptions.

The guest lecturer then conducted a class discussion for 20 minutes, after which the students rated their impressions of him: How humorous was he? How sociable? How considerate? Given that there was some ambiguity in this situation—after all, the students had seen the instructor for only a brief time—Kelley hypothesized that they would use the schema provided by the biographical note to fill in the blanks. This hypothesis was confirmed: The students who expected the instructor to be warm gave him significantly higher ratings than did the students who expected him to be cold, even though all of the students had observed the same teacher behaving in the same way. Students who expected the instructor to be warm were also more likely to ask him questions and to participate in the class discussion.

It is important to note that there is nothing wrong with what Kelley's students did. As long as people have reason to believe their schemas are accurate, it is perfectly reasonable to use them to resolve ambiguity. If a suspicious-looking character approaches you in a dark alley and says, "Take out your wallet," your schema about such encounters tells you the person wants to steal your money, not admire pictures of your family. This schema helps you avert a serious, and perhaps deadly, misunderstanding. If you bring to mind the wrong schema, you can get yourself into hot water—not many muggers want to *ooh* and *ah* over your pictures of Uncle Jake and Aunt Lisa.

WHICH SCHEMAS ARE APPLIED? ACCESSIBILITY AND PRIMING

The social world is full of ambiguous information that is open to interpretation. Imagine, for example, that you are riding on a city bus and a man gets on and sits beside you. You can't help but notice that he's acting a little strangely. He mutters incoherently to himself, stares at everyone on the bus, and repeatedly rubs his face with one hand. How would you make sense of his behaviour? You have several schemas you could use. What dictates your choice?

Your impression of the man on the bus can be affected by **accessibility**, defined as the extent to which schemas and concepts are at the forefront of our minds and therefore are likely to be used when we are making judgments about the social world (Higgins, 1996; Wyer & Srull, 1989). There are two kinds of accessibility. First, some schemas can be chronically accessible due to past experience (Chen & Andersen, 1999; Dijksterhuis & van Knippengerg, 1996; Higgins & Brendl, 1995; Rudman & Borgida, 1995). For example, if there is a history of alcoholism in your family, traits describing an alcoholic are likely to be very accessible to you, increasing the likelihood that this schema will come to mind when you are thinking about the behaviour of the man on the bus. If someone you know suffers from mental illness, however, then thoughts about how the mentally ill behave are more likely to be accessible than are thoughts about alcoholics, leading you to interpret the man's behaviour very differently.

Second, traits can also become temporarily accessible for more arbitrary reasons (Bargh, 1990, 1996; Higgins & Bargh, 1987). Whatever we happen to have been thinking or doing prior to encountering an event can prime a schema, making it more accessible and thus more likely to be used to interpret that event. Suppose, for example, that right before the man on the bus sat down, you were reading Ken Kesey's *One Flew over the*

Accessibility

the extent to which schemas and concepts are at the forefront of people's minds and are therefore likely to be used when making judgments about the social world

Cuckoo's Nest, a novel about patients in a mental hospital. Given that thoughts about mental patients are accessible in your mind, you would probably assume that the man's strange behaviour was due to mental illness. If, on the other hand, thoughts about alcoholism were fresh in your mind—for example, you had just looked out the window and seen an alcoholic leaning against a building drinking a bottle of wine—you would probably assume that the man on the bus had had a few too many drinks (see Figure 3.2). These are examples of **priming**, whereby a recent experience, such as reading Kesey's novel, increases the accessibility of certain traits, such as those describing the mentally ill, making it more likely that you will use these traits to interpret a new event—such as the behaviour of the man on the bus—even though this new event is completely unrelated to the one that originally primed the traits.

Tory Higgins, Stephen Rholes, and Carl Jones (1977) illustrated this priming effect in the following experiment. Research participants were told they would take part in two unrelated studies. The first was a perception study, in which they would be asked to identify different colours while at the same time memorizing a list of words. The second was

Priming

the process by which recent experiences increase a schema's or trait's accessibility

▶ **Figure 3.2**

HOW WE INTERPRET AN AMBIGUOUS SITUATION: THE ROLE OF ACCESSIBILITY AND PRIMING.

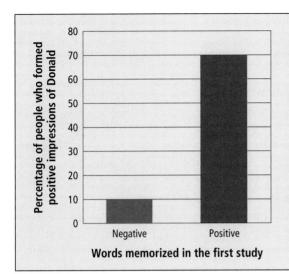

Description of Donald
Donald spent a great deal of time in his search for what he liked to call excitement. He had already climbed Mt. McKinley, shot the Colorado rapids in a kayak, driven in a demolition derby, and piloted a jet-powered boat—without knowing very much about boats. He had risked injury, and even death, a number of times. Now he was in search of new excitement. He was thinking, perhaps, he would do some skydiving or maybe cross the Atlantic in a sailboat. By the way he acted, Donald seemed well aware of his ability to do many things well. Other than business engagements, Donald's contacts with people were rather limited. He felt he didn't really need to rely on anyone. Once Donald made up his mind to do something it was as good as done no matter how long it might take or how difficult the going might be. Only rarely did he change his mind even when it might well have been better if he had.

▲ Figure 3.3

PRIMING AND ACCESSIBILITY.

People read the paragraph about Donald and formed an impression of him. In a prior study, some people had memorized words that could be used to interpret Donald in a negative way (e.g., reckless, conceited), while others had memorized words that could be used to interpret Donald in a positive way (e.g., adventurous, self-confident). As seen in the graph, those who had memorized the negative words formed a much more negative impression of Donald than did those who had memorized the positive words.

(Adapted from Higgins, Rholes, & Jones, 1977)

a reading comprehension study, in which they would be asked to read a paragraph about someone named Donald and then give their impressions of him. This paragraph is shown in Figure 3.3. Take a moment to read it. What do you think of Donald?

You might have noticed that many of Donald's actions are ambiguous, interpretable in either a positive or a negative manner. Take the fact that he piloted a boat without knowing much about it and wants to sail across the Atlantic Ocean. It is possible to put a positive spin on these acts, and decide that Donald has an admirable sense of adventure. It's just as easy, however, to put a negative spin on these acts, and assume that Donald is a rather reckless and foolhardy individual.

How did the participants interpret Donald's behaviour? Higgins and his colleagues (1977) found, as expected, that it depended on whether positive or negative traits were primed and accessible. In the first study, the researchers divided people into two groups and gave them different words to memorize. People who had first memorized the words *adventurous, self-confident, independent,* and *persistent* later formed positive impressions of Donald, viewing him as a likeable man who enjoyed new challenges. People who had first memorized *reckless, conceited, aloof,* and *stubborn* later formed negative impressions of Donald, viewing him as a stuck-up person who took needlessly dangerous chances.

We should note that it was not memorizing just any positive or negative words that influenced people's impressions of Donald. In other conditions, research participants memorized words that were also positive or negative, such as *neat* or *disrespectful*. However, these traits did not influence their impressions of Donald because the words did not apply to Donald's actions. Thus, thoughts have to be applicable before they will act as primes, exerting an influence on our impressions of the social world.

SCHEMAS CAN PERSIST EVEN AFTER THEY ARE DISCREDITED

There is another way in which schemas can take on a life of their own: They persist even after the evidence for them has been completely debunked. Sometimes we hear something about an issue or another person that later turns out not to be true. For example, a jury might hear something in the courtroom about a defendant that is untrue or labelled as inadmissible evidence, and be told by the judge to disregard that information. The problem is that due to the way schemas operate, our beliefs can persist even after the evidence for them proves to be false.

To illustrate this point, imagine you were a participant in a study by Lee Ross, Mark Lepper, and Michael Hubbard (1975). You are given a stack of cards containing both real and fictitious suicide notes. Your job is to guess which ones are real, supposedly to study the effects of physiological processes during decision making. After each guess, the experimenter tells you whether you are right or wrong. As the experiment progresses, you find out that you are pretty good at this task. In fact, you guess right on 24 of the 25 cards, which is much better than the average performance of 16 correct.

At this point, the experimenter tells you that the study is over and explains that it was actually concerned with the effects of success and failure on physiological responses. You learn that the feedback you received was bogus; that is, you had been randomly assigned to a condition in which the experimenter said you were correct on 24 of the cards, regardless of how well you actually did. The experimenter then gives you a final questionnaire, which asks you how many answers you think you really got correct and how many times you think you would guess correctly on a second, equally difficult test with new cards. What would you say? Now pretend you were in the other condition of the study. Here everything is identical, except you are told that you got only 10 of the 25 answers correct, which is much worse than average. How would you respond to the questionnaire after you found out the feedback was bogus?

Depending on which condition you were in, you would have formed a schema that you were either very good or very poor at the task. What happens when the evidence for this schema is discredited? Ross and colleagues (1975) went to some pains to ensure that the participants realized the feedback had been randomly determined and had nothing to do with their actual performance. Even though the participants believed this, those who had received the "success" feedback still thought they had gotten more of the items correct and would do better on a second test than did people who had received the "failure" feedback. In addition, when asked how they would do on a new test, success participants said they would do better than failure participants did (see Figure 3.4).

▶ **Figure 3.4**

THE PERSEVERANCE EFFECT.

People were told they had done very well (success feedback) or very poorly (failure feedback) on a test of their social sensitivity. They were then told that the feedback was bogus and had nothing to do with their actual performance. People's impressions that they were good or bad at the task persevered, even after learning that the feedback was bogus.

(Adapted from Ross, Lepper, & Hubbard, 1975)

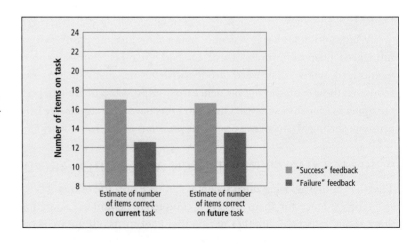

This result is called the **perseverance effect** because people's beliefs persisted even after the original evidence was discredited. When people received the feedback, they explained to themselves why they were doing so well or so poorly, bringing to mind evidence from their past that was consistent with their performance (e.g., "I am really very perceptive. After all, last week I was the only one who realized that Jennifer was depressed" or "Well, I'm not so good at this stuff; my friends always say I'm the last to know"). Even after learning that the feedback was false, these thoughts were still fresh in people's minds, making them think they were particularly good or bad at the task (Anderson, 1995; Anderson & Lindsay, 1998; Davies, 1997).

Perseverance effect
the finding that people's beliefs about themselves and the social world persist even after the evidence supporting these beliefs is discredited

MAKING OUR SCHEMAS COME TRUE: THE SELF-FULFILLING PROPHECY

We have seen that when people encounter new evidence or have old evidence discredited, they tend not to revise their schemas as much as we might expect. People are not always passive recipients of information, however—they often act on their schemas, and in doing so can change the extent to which these schemas are supported or contradicted. In fact, people can inadvertently make their schemas come true by the way they treat others. This is called a **self-fulfilling prophecy**, and it occurs when people have an expectation about what another person is like that influences how they act toward that person, which in turn causes that person to behave consistently with people's original expectations—making the expectations come true. Figure 3.5 illustrates this self-perpetuating cycle.

Self-fulfilling prophecy
the case whereby people (a) have an expectation about what another person is like, which (b) influences how they act toward that person, which (c) causes that person to behave consistently with people's original expectations

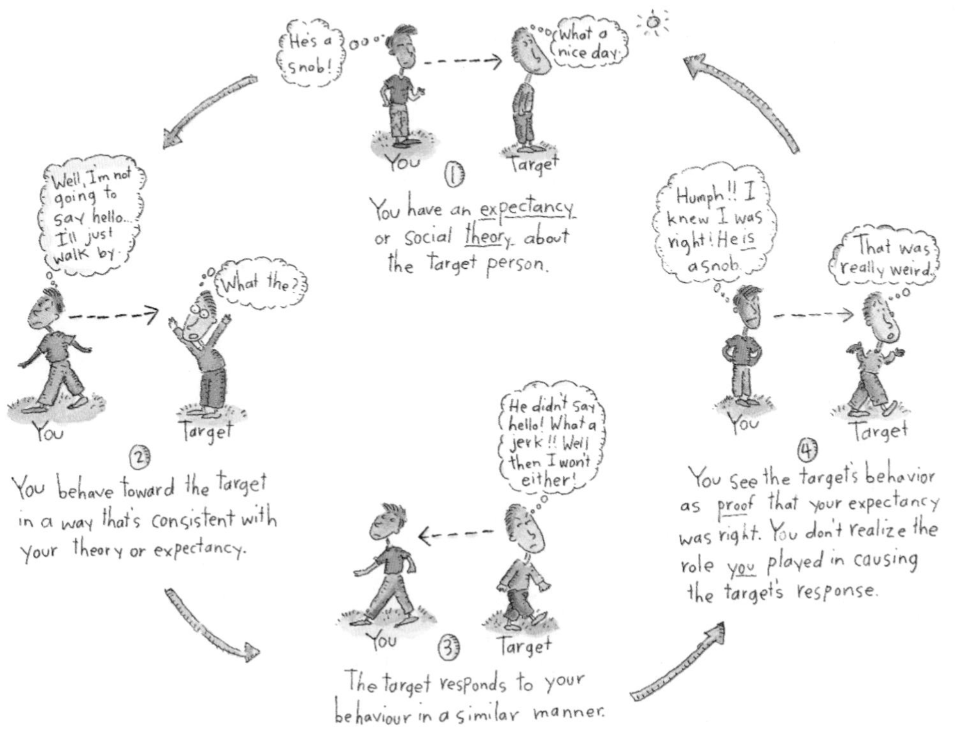

◀ **Figure 3.5**

THE SELF-FULFILLING PROPHECY: A SAD CYCLE IN FOUR ACTS

In what has become one of the most famous studies in social psychology, Robert Rosenthal and Lenore Jacobson (1968) examined whether teachers' expectations for students can have self-fulfilling effects. They administered an IQ test to all students in an elementary school and told the teachers that some of the students had scored so well that they were sure to "bloom" academically in the upcoming year. In fact, this was not necessarily true: The students identified as "bloomers" were chosen randomly by the researchers. As we discussed in Chapter 2, the use of random assignment means that on average the students designated as bloomers were no smarter or more likely to bloom than any of the other kids. The only way in which these students differed from their peers was in the minds of the teachers (neither the students nor their parents were told anything about the results of the test).

After creating the expectations in the teachers that some of the kids would do especially well, Rosenthal and Jacobson waited to see what would happen. They observed the classroom dynamics periodically over the school year, and at the end of the year they tested all of the children again with an actual IQ test. Did the prophecy come true? Indeed it did: The students in each class who had been labelled as bloomers showed significantly higher gains in their IQ scores than did the other students (see Figure 3.6). The teachers' expectations had become reality. Rosenthal and Jacobson's findings have since been replicated in a number of both experimental and correlational studies (Babad, 1993; Blank, 1993; Brattesani, Weinstein, & Marshall, 1984; Jussim, 1989, 1991; Madon, Jussim, & Eccles, 1997; Smith, Jussim, & Eccles, 1999).

Note that teachers do not callously decide to direct their limited time and resources to a few privileged students. Most teachers are incredibly dedicated and try not to treat some students in a more advantageous manner than others. Interestingly, the teachers in the Rosenthal and Jacobson (1968) study reported that they spent slightly *less* time with the students who were labelled as bloomers. In subsequent studies, however, teachers

▶ **Figure 3.6**

THE SELF-FULFILLING PROPHECY: PERCENTAGE OF FIRST- AND SECOND-GRADERS WHO IMPROVED ON AN IQ TEST OVER THE COURSE OF THE SCHOOL YEAR.

Those whom the teachers expected to do well actually improved more than did the other students.

(Adapted from Rosenthal & Jacobson, 1968)

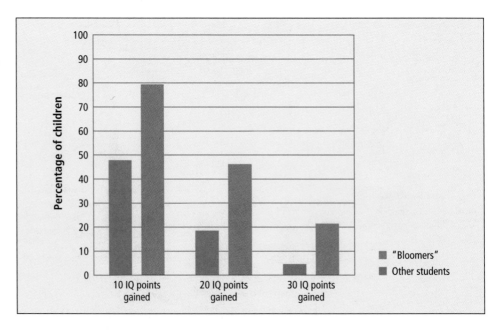

have been found to treat bloomers (the students they expect to do better) differently in four general ways: (a) They create a warmer emotional climate for bloomers, giving them more personal attention, encouragement, and support; (b) they give bloomers more material to learn and material that is more difficult; (c) they give bloomers more and better feedback on their work; and (d) they give bloomers more opportunities to respond in class and give them longer to respond (Brophy, 1983; Jussim, 1986; Rosenthal, 1994; Snyder, 1984).

Self-fulfilling prophecies are not limited to the way teachers treat students. Each of us has all sorts of schemas about what other people are like, and whenever we act on these schemas in a way that makes the schema come true, a self-fulfilling prophecy results (Darley & Fazio, 1980). Self-fulfilling prophecies have been found among diverse populations, with diverse expectations, including university students' schemas about what a potential dating partner is like, mothers' schemas about what premature babies are like, supervisors' expectations about the performance of assembly-line workers, judges' expectations about the guilt of a defendant, and physicians' expectations about their patients' health (Blank, 1993; Eden & Zuk, 1995; Friedman, 1993; King, 1971; McNatt, 2000; Snyder & Swann, 1978; Stern & Hildebrandt, 1986). In Chapter 10, we will discuss some of the ways self-fulfilling prophecies operate in intimate relationships.

A distressing implication of research on the self-fulfilling prophecy is that our schemas may be resistant to change because we see a good deal of false evidence that confirms them. Suppose a teacher has the schema that boys possess innate ability that makes them superior in math to girls. "But Mr. Jones," we might say, "how can you hold such a belief? There are plenty of girls who do very well in math." Mr. Jones would probably be unconvinced because he would have data to support his schema. "In my classes over the years," he might reply, "nearly three times as many boys as girls have excelled at math." His error lies not in his characterization of the evidence but in his failure to realize his role in producing it. Robert Merton (1948) referred to this process as a "reign of error," whereby people can "cite the actual course of events as proof that [they were] right from the very beginning." See Try It!, on page 74, for a way to overcome your own self-fulfilling prophecies.

To summarize, we have seen that the amount of information with which we are faced every day is so vast that we have to reduce it to a manageable size. In addition, much of this information is ambiguous or difficult to decipher. One way we deal with these problems is by relying on schemas, which help us reduce the amount of information we need to take in and help us interpret ambiguous information.

CULTURAL DETERMINANTS OF SCHEMAS

It may have occurred to you to wonder where schemas come from. One determinant is the culture in which people live; people learn all sorts of schemas from their culture. Have you ever met someone from another culture and been amazed at what he or she noticed and remembered about your country? A few years ago, a niece of one of the authors (Beverley Fehr), named Sheri, attended a youth conference in Saskatchewan. Students from several countries participated, including a young woman from Africa who was visiting Canada for the first time. She seemed quite intrigued by Sheri's braces, and eventually worked up the nerve to ask how much they cost. She expressed shock that Sheri's parents had spent a few thousand dollars on them. "They're really nice," she said, "but

Avoiding Self-fulfilling Prophecies

Examine some of your own schemas and expectations about social groups, especially groups you don't particularly like. These might be members of a particular race or ethnic group, of a rival university, of a political party, or people with a particular sexual orientation. Why don't you like members of this group? "Well," you might think, "one reason is that whenever I interact with francophones [substitute anglophones, Americans, Jews, gays, Canadian Alliance Party members, or members of any other social group], they seem cold and unfriendly." And you might be right. Perhaps they do respond to you in a cold and unfriendly fashion. Not, however, because they are this way by nature but because they are responding to the way you have treated them.

Try this exercise to counteract the self-fulfilling prophecy: Find someone who is a member of a group you dislike and strike up a conversation. For example, sit next to this person in one of your classes or approach him or her at a party. Try to imagine that this individual is the friendliest, kindest, sweetest person you have ever met. Be as warm and charming as you can be. Don't go overboard—if, after never having spoken to this person before, you suddenly act like Mr. or Ms. Congeniality, you might arouse suspicion. The trick is to act as if you expect him or her to be extremely pleasant and friendly.

Observe this person's reactions. Are you surprised by how pleasantly he or she responded to you? People you thought were inherently cold and unfriendly will probably behave in a warm and friendly manner themselves, in response to the way you have treated them. If this doesn't work on your first encounter with the person, try it again on one or two occasions. In all likelihood, you will find that friendliness really does breed friendliness.

---

that's just too much money." It was then that Sheri realized this young woman thought her braces were an item of jewellery—jewellery for her teeth!

Clearly, an important source of our schemas is the culture in which we grow up. In fact, schemas are a very important way in which cultures exert their influence—namely, by instilling mental structures that influence the very way we understand and interpret the world. In Chapter 5, we will see that across cultures there are fundamental differences in people's schemas about themselves and the social world, with some interesting consequences. For now, we point out that the schemas our culture teaches us have a large influence on what we notice and remember about the world. Frederic Bartlett (1932), for example, noted that different cultures have schemas about different things, depending on what is important to that culture. These schemas influence what people in different cultures are likely to remember.

To illustrate the relationship among culture, schemas, and memory, Bartlett interviewed a Scottish settler and a local Bantu herdsman in Swaziland, a small country in southeast Africa. Both men had been present at a complicated cattle transaction that had transpired a year earlier. The Scottish man had little memory about the details of the transaction; he had to consult his records to remember how many cattle were bought and sold and for how much. The Bantu man, when asked, promptly recited from memory every detail of the transaction, including from whom each ox and cow had been bought, the colour of each ox and cow, and the price of each transaction. The Bantu people's

◀ The Bantu have an excellent memory for their cattle, possibly because they have much better schemas for cattle than people in other cultures do.

memory for cattle is so good that they do not bother to brand them; if a cow happens to wander away and get mixed up with a neighbour's herd, the owner simply goes over and takes it back—having no trouble distinguishing his cow from the dozens of others.

Perhaps the Bantu simply have better memories overall. Bartlett (1932) argues convincingly, however, that their memories are no better than the memories of people in other cultures. Each of us has a superb memory, he suggests, in the areas that are important to us, areas for which we thus have well-developed schemas. Cattle are a central part of the Bantu economy and culture, and thus the Bantu have well-developed schemas about cattle. To a person who grew up in a different culture, one cow might look like any other. This person undoubtedly has well-developed schemas about, and an excellent memory for, things that are quite foreign to the Bantu, such as transactions on the Toronto Stock Exchange, foreign movies, or, for that matter, the reasons why people wear braces on their teeth.

To summarize, we have seen that the amount of information we face every day is so vast that we have to reduce it to a manageable size. In addition, much of this information is ambiguous or difficult to decipher. One way we deal with this "blooming, buzzing, confusion," in William James' words, is to rely on schemas, which help us reduce the amount of information we need to take in and help us interpret ambiguous information. We turn now to other, more specific mental shortcuts that people use.

Mental Strategies and Shortcuts: Heuristics

How did you decide which university to apply to? One strategy would be to investigate thoroughly each of the more than 70 universities in Canada (as well as all of the community colleges). You could read every catalogue from cover to cover, visit every campus, and interview as many faculty members, deans, and students as you could find. Getting tired yet? Such a strategy would, of course, be prohibitively time-consuming and costly. Instead of considering every university and college, most high-school students narrow down their choice to a small number of options and find out what they can about these schools.

This example is like many decisions and judgments we make in everyday life. When deciding which job to accept, what car to purchase, or whom to marry, we usually do not conduct a thorough search of every option ("Okay, it's time for me to get married; I think I'll consult the Census lists of unmarried adults in my city and begin my interviews tomorrow"). Instead, we use mental strategies and shortcuts that make the decision easier, allowing us to get on with our lives without turning every decision into a major research project.

What kinds of shortcuts do people use? One, as we have already seen, is to use schemas to understand new situations. Rather than starting from scratch when examining our options, we often apply previous knowledge and schemas. We have many such schemas, about everything from colleges and universities (e.g., what community colleges are like versus what universities are like) to other people. When making specific kinds of judgments and decisions, however, we do not always have a ready-made schema to apply. At other times, there are too many schemas that could apply, and it is not clear which one to use. What do we do?

Judgmental heuristics

mental shortcuts people use to make judgments quickly and efficiently

At times like these, people often use mental shortcuts called **judgmental heuristics**. The word *heuristic* comes from the Greek word meaning "to discover"; in the field of social cognition, heuristics refers to the mental shortcuts people use to make judgments quickly and efficiently. Before discussing these heuristics, we should note that they do not guarantee people will make accurate inferences about the world. In fact, we will document many mental errors in this chapter. Reliance on heuristics also does not always lead to the best decision. For example, had you exhaustively studied every university and college in Canada, you may have found one you liked better than the one you are at now. However, the bottom line is that mental shortcuts are efficient, and usually lead to good decisions in a reasonable amount of time (Gigerenzer & Goldstein, 1996; Griffin, Gonzalez, & Varey, 2002; Nisbett & Ross, 1980).

HOW EASILY DOES IT COME TO MIND? THE AVAILABILITY HEURISTIC

Suppose you are sitting in a restaurant with several friends one night, when it becomes clear that the waiter made a mistake with one of the orders. Your friend Michael ordered the veggie burger with onion rings but instead got the veggie burger with fries. "Oh, well," he says, "I'll just eat the fries." This starts a discussion of whether he should have sent back his order, and some of your friends accuse Michael of being unassertive. He turns to you and asks, "Do you think I'm an unassertive person?" How would you answer this question?

One way, as we have seen, would be to call on a ready-made schema that provides the answer. If you know Michael well and have already formed a picture of how assertive he is, you can recite your answer easily and quickly: "Don't worry, Michael, if I had to deal with a used-car salesman, you'd be the first person I'd call." Suppose, though, that you've never really thought about how assertive Michael is and have to think about your answer. In these situations, we often rely on how easily different examples come to mind. If it is easy to think of times Michael acted assertively (e.g., "that time he stopped someone from butting in line in front of him at the movies"), you will conclude that Michael is a pretty assertive guy. If it is easier to think of times Michael acted unassertively (e.g., "that time he let a phone solicitor talk him into buying a Veg-O-Matic for $29.99"), you will conclude that he is pretty unassertive.

This mental rule of thumb is called the **availability heuristic**, which is basing a judgment on the ease with which you can bring something to mind (Dougherty, Gettys, & Ogden, 1999; Manis et al., 1993; Rothman & Hardin, 1997; Schwarz, 1998; Wänke, Schwarz, & Bless, 1995). Note, that **availability** is not the same as *accessibility* (which we discussed earlier). Accessibility is defined as the extent to which schemas and concepts are at the forefront of people's minds—in other words, accessibility refers to the information that is on your mind at any given moment. Availability, on the other hand, refers to how easy or difficult it is for you to bring a schema or concept to mind. And when we speak of the availability heuristic, we are referring to a mental rule of thumb whereby people base a judgment on the ease with which they can bring something to mind. The first studies demonstrating the availability heuristic were conducted by Tversky and Kahneman (1973). In one of their studies, participants were presented with the names of famous and non-famous people. When asked to recall the names, participants were more likely to remember the famous ones, even though there were fewer famous than non-famous names on the list. Presumably, the famous names were more available in memory. When other participants were asked to estimate the number of male and female names, they gave higher estimates for the gender that was famous. For example, if a list contained the names of 19 famous women and 20 non-famous men, participants believed there had been a greater number of women's names than men's on the list. Similar findings were obtained when this study was replicated with Canadian participants (McKelvie, 1995, 1997).

There are many situations in which the availability heuristic is a good strategy. If you can easily bring to mind several times when Michael stood up for his rights, he probably is an assertive person; if you can easily bring to mind several times when he was timid or meek, he probably is not an assertive person. The trouble with the availability heuristic is that sometimes what is easiest to bring to mind is not typical of the overall picture, leading to faulty conclusions.

One example is medical diagnosis. It might seem as if it is a relatively straightforward matter for a doctor to observe your symptoms and figure out what disease, if any, you have. Sometimes, though, medical symptoms are quite ambiguous and might be a sign of several different disorders. Do doctors use the availability heuristic, whereby they are more likely to consider diagnoses that come to mind easily? Several studies of medical diagnoses suggest that the answer is yes (Eraker & Politser, 1988; Fox, 1980; Travis, Phillippi, & Tonn, 1989; Weber et al., 1993).

Consider Dr. Robert Marion's diagnosis of Nicole, a bright, sweet, nine-year-old patient. Nicole was normal in every way, except that once or twice a year she had strange, neurological attacks, characterized by disorientation, insomnia, slurred words, and strange mewing sounds. Nicole had been hospitalized three times, had seen more than a dozen specialists, and had undergone many diagnostic tests, including CT scans, brain-wave tests, and virtually every blood test there is. The doctors were stumped; they could

Availability heuristic
a mental rule of thumb whereby people base a judgment on the ease with which they can bring something to mind

Availability
how easy or difficult it is for someone to bring a schema or concept to mind

▶ Physicians have been found to use the availability heuristic when making diagnoses. Their diagnoses are influenced by how easily they can bring to mind different diseases.

not figure out what was wrong with her. Within minutes of seeing her, however, Dr. Marion correctly diagnosed her problem as a rare, inherited blood disorder called acute intermittent porphyria (AIP). The blood chemistry of people with this disorder often gets out of sync, causing a variety of neurological symptoms. It can be controlled with a careful diet and by avoiding certain medications.

How did Dr. Marion diagnose Nicole's disorder so quickly, when so many other doctors failed to do so? Dr. Marion had just finished writing a book on the genetic diseases of historical figures, including a chapter on King George III of England, who—you guessed it—suffered from AIP. "I didn't make the diagnosis because I'm a brilliant diagnostician or because I'm a sensitive listener," reports Dr. Marion. "I succeeded where others failed because [Nicole] and I happened to run into each other in exactly the right place, at exactly the right time" (Marion, 1995).

In other words, Dr. Marion used the availability heuristic. AIP happened to be available in his memory, making the diagnosis easy. Though this was a happy outcome of the use of the availability heuristic, it is easy to see how it can go wrong. As Dr. Marion says, "Doctors are just like everyone else. We go to the movies, watch TV, read newspapers and novels. If we happen to see a patient who has symptoms of a rare disease that was featured on the previous night's 'Movie of the Week,' we're more likely to consider that condition when making a diagnosis" (Marion, 1995). That's all well and good if your disease happens to be the topic of last night's movie. It's not so good if your disease doesn't happen to be available in your doctor's memory, as was the case with the 12 doctors Nicole had seen previously.

Do people use the availability heuristic to make judgments about themselves? It might seem that we have well-developed ideas about our own personalities, such as how assertive we are. Often, however, people do not have firm schemas about their own traits

(Markus, 1977; Kunda et al., 1993) and thus might make judgments about themselves based on how easily they can bring to mind examples of their own behaviour. To see if this is the case, Norbert Schwarz and his colleagues (1991) performed a clever experiment in which they altered how easy it was for people to bring to mind examples of their own past behaviours. In one condition, they asked people to think of six times they had acted assertively. Most people found this to be pretty easy; examples came to mind quickly. In another condition, the researchers asked people to think of 12 times they had acted assertively. This was much more difficult; people had to try hard to think of this many examples. All participants were then asked to rate how assertive they thought they really were.

The question was, did people use the availability heuristic (the ease with which they could bring examples to mind) to infer how assertive they were? As seen on the left-hand side of Figure 3.7, they did. People asked to think of six examples rated themselves as relatively assertive, because it was easy to think of six examples ("Hey, this is easy—I guess I'm a pretty assertive person"). It might surprise you to learn that people asked to think of 12 examples rated themselves as relatively unassertive, because it was difficult to think of 12 examples ("Hmm, this is hard—I must not be a very assertive person"). Other people were asked to think of either 6 or 12 times they had acted *un*assertively, and similar results were found—those asked to think of 6 examples rated themselves as more unassertive than those who were asked to think of 12 examples (see the right-hand side of Figure 3.7). In short, people use the availability heuristic—the ease with which they can bring examples to mind—when making judgments about themselves and other people.

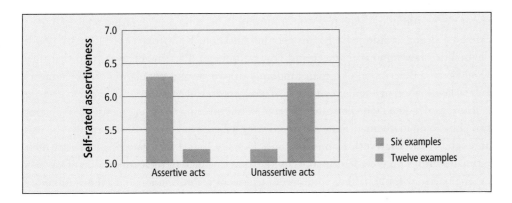

▲ Figure 3.7

AVAILABILITY AND HOW ASSERTIVE WE THINK WE ARE.

People asked to think of six times they behaved assertively found it easy to do so and thus concluded that they were pretty assertive people. People asked to think of 12 times they behaved assertively found it difficult to think of so many examples and thus concluded that they were not very assertive people (see the left-hand side of the graph). Similar results were found among people asked to think of either 6 or 12 times they behaved unassertively (see the right-hand side of the graph). These results show that people often base their judgments on availability, or how easily they can bring information to mind.

(Adapted from Schwarz et al., 1991)

HOW SIMILAR IS A TO B? THE REPRESENTATIVENESS HEURISTIC

People use another mental shortcut when trying to categorize something: They judge how similar it is to their idea of the typical case. Suppose, for example, that you attend a university in Alberta. One day you meet a student named Lyne in a lineup for one of the food outlets on campus. Lyne is fashionably dressed, orders a café au lait and a croissant, and from the way she pronounces "croissant," it's apparent she speaks French. Which province do you think Lyne is from? Because Lyne seems similar to many people's stereotype of a Quebecer, you might guess Quebec, or at least seriously entertain this possibility. If so, you would be using the **representativeness heuristic**, which is a mental shortcut whereby people classify something according to how similar it is to a typical case—such as how similar Lyne is to your conception of Quebecers (Dawes, 1998; Garb, 1996; Kahneman & Tversky, 1973; Lupfer & Layman, 1996; Thomsen & Borgida, 1996; Tversky & Kahneman, 1974).

Categorizing things according to representativeness is often a perfectly reasonable thing to do. If we did not use the representativeness heuristic, how else would we decide where Lyne comes from? Should we just randomly choose a province? Actually, there is another source of information we might use. If we knew nothing about Lyne, it would be wise to guess that she was from Alberta, because at Albertan universities there are more in-province than out-of-province students. If we guessed Alberta, we would be using what is called **base rate information**, or information about the relative frequency of members of different categories in the population (e.g., the percentage of students at Albertan universities who are from Alberta).

What do people do when they have both base rate information (e.g., knowing that there are more Albertans than Quebecers at a university) and contradictory information about the person in question (e.g., encountering Lyne, who dresses fashionably and likes café au lait and croissants)? To answer this question, Kahneman and Tversky (1973) devised the now-famous engineer-and-lawyer problem. Participants were told that they would read a description of a man randomly drawn from a population of 70 engineers and 30 lawyers (or, in another condition, 70 lawyers and 30 engineers). They then received a description of Jack, who possessed stereotypic engineering traits (e.g., conservative, careful, likes doing mathematical puzzles) and were asked what the chances were that he was an engineer (or a lawyer). Kahneman and Tversky found that participants based their estimates simply on whether the traits used to describe Jack fit their conception of lawyers or engineers, without taking into account base rate information (i.e., the number of lawyers or engineers in the population). Thus, participants were just as likely to assume Jack was an engineer when there were 30 engineers in the population as when there were 70, because in making their judgments they only focused on individuating information (i.e., Jack's qualities). This study was recently replicated by Griffin and Buehler (1999) with students in Canada and Britain. They added some changes designed to increase the salience of base rate information. For example, they showed participants a clear bowl containing 70 white and 30 green balls as a vivid reminder of the number of engineers and lawyers in the population. However, even under these conditions, participants still failed to take base rates into account, and instead based their answers to questions about Jack's profession on information about Jack's traits.

Representativeness heuristic

a mental shortcut whereby people classify something according to how similar it is to a typical case

Base rate information

information about the frequency of members of different categories in the population

Before leaving this topic, we should note that although this is not a bad strategy if the information about the person is reliable, it can get us into trouble when the information is flimsy. Returning to our example of Lyne, given that the base rate of Quebecers attending universities in Alberta is low, you would need to have very good evidence that Lyne was a Quebecer before ignoring the base rate and guessing that she is one of the few exceptions. And given that it is not unusual to find people from Alberta who dress well, speak French, and enjoy café au lait and croissants, you would, in this instance, be wise not to ignore the base rate.

TAKING THINGS AT FACE VALUE: THE ANCHORING AND ADJUSTMENT HEURISTIC

Suppose you are trying to quit smoking and are sitting around with a group of friends who also smoke. "How likely am I to get cancer anyway?" you say, reaching for a cigarette. "I bet that not all that many people end up with lung cancer. In fact, of all the students at our university, I wonder how many will get cancer in their lifetimes?" One of your friends throws out a number: "I don't know," he says, "I'd guess maybe 2500." Would your friend's response influence your answer to the question? It would if you use the **anchoring and adjustment heuristic** (Tversky & Kahneman, 1974), a mental shortcut whereby people use a number or value as a starting point and then adjust their answer away from this anchor. You might begin by saying, "Hmm, 2500—that sounds high. I'd say it's a little lower than that."

Like all of the other mental shortcuts we have considered, the anchoring and adjustment heuristic is a good strategy under many circumstances. If you have no idea what the answer is, but your friend is a medical resident specializing in oncology, it is wise to stick pretty close to his answer. However, like the other heuristics, this one can get us into trouble. The problem with anchoring and adjustment is that people sometimes use completely arbitrary values as starting points and then stick too close to these values. For example, Tim Wilson and colleagues (1996) asked university students to copy several words or numbers, supposedly as part of a study of handwriting analysis. In one condition, people copied several pages of numbers, all of which happened to be around 4500. In the other condition, people copied down words, such as *sofa*. Then, as part of what was supposedly an unrelated study, everyone was asked how many students at his or her university would get cancer in the next 40 years. Those who copied down numbers gave much higher estimates (average answer = 3145) than did those who copied down words (average answer = 1645). Similar anchoring effects have been found in many other studies (e.g., Allison & Beggan, 1994; Cadinu & Rothbart, 1996; Chapman & Bornstein, 1996; Czaczkes & Ganzach, 1996; Jacowitz & Kahneman, 1995; Slovic & Lichtenstein, 1971; Strack & Mussweiler, 1997).

The examples of anchoring and adjustment we have seen so far have concerned numerical judgments. This process, however, also occurs with many other kinds of judgments. When we form judgments about the world, we often allow our personal experiences and observations to anchor our impressions, even when we know our experiences are unusual (Gilovich, Medvec, & Savitsky, 2000). Suppose, for example, that you go to a popular restaurant that all your friends rave about. As luck would have it, the waiter is rude and your entrée is burned. You know your experience is atypical; after all, your

Anchoring and adjustment heuristic

a mental shortcut that involves using a number or value as a starting point, and then adjusting one's answer away from this anchor; people often do not adjust their answer sufficiently

friends have had great meals at this restaurant. Nonetheless, your experiences are likely to anchor your impression of the restaurant, making you reluctant to return. When generalizing from a sample of information we know to be biased (e.g., one meal in a restaurant) to the population of information (e.g., all meals in that restaurant), we are engaging in a process called **biased sampling**: making generalizations from samples of information that we know are biased.

Even when we know that a piece of information is biased or atypical, it can be hard to ignore it completely. We all know that reporters, television producers, and authors seldom present information that is typical; their job is to present what is unusual, interesting, and attention grabbing, not what is average. (Imagine that a reporter said, "Leading the news tonight: Barbara Kowalski did not have a car accident on her way to the office, and Jerome Smith had an average day driving his city bus up and down Main Street.") Nonetheless, we seem to find it hard to avoid making generalizations from what we see.

For example, Ruth Hamill, Tim Wilson, and Richard Nisbett (1980) asked people to read a story about a welfare mother whose life was irresponsible and bleak. They told some participants that this woman was typical of people on welfare, and others that she was very atypical of people on welfare. Not surprisingly, the participants who thought she was typical became more negative in their attitudes toward all welfare recipients (see Figure 3.8). More surprisingly, people who thought she was atypical also became more negative toward all welfare recipients. This is another example of the anchoring and adjustment heuristic. People have a starting point, or an anchor ("This welfare recipient is irresponsible and undeserving"), from which they should adjust their judgment ("But she is not at all typical, thus I shouldn't generalize from her to welfare recipients in general"). As with many other kinds of anchoring effects, however, people do not adjust sufficiently and are influenced too much by their initial judgment.

To summarize, we have discussed two general types of strategies used by the social thinker: schemas and judgmental heuristics. Schemas are organized bits of knowledge about people and situations that have a powerful effect on what information we notice,

Biased sampling

making generalizations from samples of information that are known to be biased

▼ Biased sampling: How would you feel about a region if you visited only one of these places? People have been found to generalize from small samples of information, even when they know that these samples are biased, not typical.

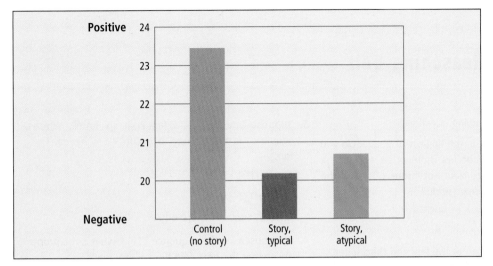

◀ Figure 3.8

ATTITUDES TOWARD WELFARE RECIPIENTS.

People who read a story about one unlikeable welfare recipient had more negative attitudes toward welfare recipients in general, regardless of whether they believed she was typical or atypical.

(Adapted from Hamill, Wilson, & Nisbett, 1980)

think about, and remember. When we make judgments about the social world, however, we do not always have a ready-made schema or we may not know which schema is most appropriate to use. In such cases, we rely instead on judgmental heuristics. The availability heuristic refers to judgments based on the ease with which something can be brought to mind. The representativeness heuristic helps us decide how similar one thing is to another; we use it to classify people or situations on the basis of their similarity to a typical case. When using this heuristic, we have a tendency to ignore base rate information—the probability that someone or something belongs in that classification. People also rely on the anchoring and adjustment heuristic, wherein an initial piece of information acts as an anchor, or a starting point, for subsequent judgments. Now that you have learned about some of the ways in which people reason, take the Try It! reasoning quiz on page 84.

One final comment before leaving this topic: We have been focusing on research that demonstrates errors or biases in people's thinking. However, some researchers have argued that what is biased is not so much people's thinking, but rather the methods that psychologists have used to study how they think. Remember the research showing that people tend to ignore base rate information, relying instead on individuating information? Krosnick, Li, and Lehman (1990) offer a different perspective on this research. They maintain that participants in such studies are making the reasonable assumption that the researchers are adhering to normal rules of conversation. One such rule is that speakers don't convey information unless it is informative and relevant. Thus, when researchers provide information about Jack's personality, for example, it may be absurd to expect participants to disregard it and focus only on the number of engineers in the population. Another rule of conversation is that if two conflicting pieces of information are presented, the speaker generally intends the last piece of information to be the most important. Krosnick and colleagues note that in studies on the use of base rates, base rate information is typically presented first (e.g., there are 70 lawyers and 30 engineers in a population), followed by individuating information (e.g., a description of Jack). This may be another reason that people tend to rely on individuating information, rather than base rates, when making judgments. In a series of studies with Canadian and American students, these

Reasoning Quiz

Answer each of the following questions:

1. Consider the letter *R* in the English language. Do you think that this letter occurs more often as the first letter of words (e.g., *rope*) or more often as the third letter of words (e.g., *park*)?

   A. the first letter

   B. the third letter

   C. about equally often as the first and third letter

2. Which of these do you think causes more fatalities in Canada?

   A. accidental death

   B. death from strokes

   C. each causes about the same number of deaths

3. Suppose you flipped a fair coin six times. Which sequence is more likely to occur? (H = heads, T = tails)

   A. HTTHTH

   B. HHHTTT

   C. both sequences are equally likely

4. After observing the sequence TTTTT, what is the probability that the next coin flip will be heads?

   A. less than 0.5

   B. 0.5

   C. greater than 0.5

ANSWERS

1. The correct answer is (b), the third letter. Tversky and Kahneman (1974) found that most people thought that the answer was (a), the first letter. Why do people make this mistake? Because, say Tversky and Kahneman, they find it easier to think of examples of words that begin with *R*. By using the availability heuristic, they assumed that the ease with which they could bring examples to mind meant that such words were more common.

2. The correct answer is (b). According to 1997 Statistics Canada information (Statistics Canada, 1997), deaths due to cerebrovascular disease (stroke is a major component) are nearly twice as likely as accidental deaths (16 051 cases versus 8626 cases). Fischhoff and Lichtenstein (1976) found that most people think that (a) is correct (accidental deaths). Why did people make this error? Again, it's the availability heuristic: Accidental deaths are more likely to be reported by the media, thus people find it easier to bring to mind such deaths than they do deaths from strokes.

3. The correct answer is (c). Both outcomes are equally likely, given that the outcomes of coin flips are random events. Tversky and Kahneman (1974) argue that due to the rep-
resentativeness heuristic, people expect a sequence of random events to "look" random. That is, they expect events to be representative of their conception of randomness. Thus, many people choose HTTHTH, because this sequence is more representative of people's idea of randomness than HHHTTT. In fact, the chance that either sequence will occur is 1 out of 26 times, or 1/64. As another illustration of this point, if you were to buy a lottery ticket with four numbers, would you rather have the number 6957 or 1111? Many people prefer the former number, because it seems more "random" and thus more likely to be picked. In fact, both numbers have a 1/1000 chance of being picked.

4. The correct answer is (b). Many people choose (c), because they think that after five tails in a row, heads is more likely "to even things out." This is called the gambler's fallacy, which is the belief that prior random events (e.g., five tails in a row) have an influence on subsequent random events. Assuming that the coin is fair, prior tosses have no influence on future ones. Tversky and Kahneman (1974) suggest that the gambler's fallacy is due in part to the representativeness heuristic: Five tails and one head seems more representative of a chance outcome than does six tails in a row.

---

researchers found that when they presented base rate information first (i.e., the number of lawyers and engineers in the population), followed by individuating information (i.e., the description of Jack), participants showed the classic tendency to rely on the latter.

However, when individuating information was presented first, followed by base rate information, questions about Jack's profession were now more likely to be answered in terms of base rates.

Research along the same lines conducted at Mount Allison University in New Brunswick suggests that several other cognitive "biases" can be attributed to the participants' reasonable, but incorrect, assumption that researchers are following normal conversational conventions (Slugoski & Wilson, 1998). In fact, Slugoski and Wilson found that the participants with the best conversational skills were most likely to show cognitive "biases," such as the underuse of base rate information.

Automatic versus Controlled Thinking

Think back to what it was like to learn a new skill, such as riding a bicycle or using in-line skates. The first time you rode a two-wheeler, you probably felt awkward and ungainly as you wobbled across the pavement, and you may have paid for your inexperience with a skinned elbow or knee. You were probably concentrating on what you were doing with your feet, knees, and hands, and it seemed as if you would never figure it out. Once you became an experienced rider, however, your actions became automatic, in the sense that you no longer had to think about what you were doing.

Just as our actions can become automatic, so too can the way we think (Bargh, 1994, 1996; Wegner & Bargh, 1998). The more practice we have in thinking in a certain way, the more automatic that kind of thinking becomes, to the point where we can do it unconsciously, with no effort. **Automatic processing** can be defined as thinking that is nonconscious, unintentional, involuntary, and effortless.

As with all of the strategies and properties of social cognition we have considered, however, efficiency comes with a cost. If we automatically categorize a thing or person incorrectly, we can get into trouble. For example, when Wendy Josephson was hired at the University of Winnipeg about 20 years ago, it was still relatively rare to find young women among the professoriate. (Most young women employed by the university were secretaries.) One day, as Wendy was waiting in the dean's office for a secretary to return, a senior male professor marched up to her and handed her some sheets of paper. He failed to notice her expression of puzzlement, and matter-of-factly asked her to please have them typed by Monday. He was extremely embarrassed when she pointed out that she was a professor, not a secretary. As this example suggests, we pigeonhole people quickly, such that our schemas based on race, gender, age, or physical attractiveness are invoked automatically (Devine, 1989a, 1989b; Fiske, 1989a). This is one reason stereotypes are so difficult to overcome—they often operate without our knowing it.

Clearly, not all thinking is automatic; like Rodin's statue of the thinker, sometimes we pause and think deeply about ourselves and the social world. This kind of thinking is called **controlled processing**, defined as thinking that is conscious, intentional, voluntary, and effortful. An example of controlled processing is the kind of conscious musing people often engage in: "I wonder what's for lunch today?" or "When will the authors get on with it and finish this chapter?" You can "turn on" or "turn off" this type of thinking at will, and you are fully aware of what you are thinking.

Automatic processing
thinking that is non-conscious, unintentional, involuntary, and effortless

Controlled processing
thinking that is conscious, intentional, voluntary, and effortful

One purpose of controlled thinking is to provide checks and balances for automatic processing. Just as an airline captain can turn off the automatic pilot and take control of the plane when trouble occurs, our controlled thinking takes over when unusual events occur. Unlike automatic processing, however, controlled thinking requires motivation and effort. We have to want to do it, and we have to have the time and energy to devote to it. Thus, when the stakes are low and we do not particularly care about the accuracy of a decision or judgment, we often let our automatic thinking do the job, without bothering to check or correct it.

According to Daniel Gilbert (1991, 1993, 1998), people are programmed to automatically believe everything they hear and see. This automatic "seeing is believing" process is built into human beings, he suggests, because pretty much everything we hear and see is true. If we had to stop and deliberate about the truthfulness of everything we encountered, life would be difficult indeed ("Let's see, it looks like a car careening toward me down the street, but maybe it's really an illusion" . . . *CRASH!*). Occasionally, however, what we see or hear is not true; thus, we need a checks-and-balances system to be able to "unaccept" what we have initially believed. When we hear a political candidate say, "If elected, I will lower your taxes, balance the budget, reduce crime, and wash your car every Sunday afternoon," we initially believe what we hear, argues Gilbert (1991), but the "unacceptance" part of the process quickly kicks in, making us doubt the truth of what we've just heard ("Now wait just a minute . . ."). This process is depicted in Figure 3.9.

The interesting thing about this process is that the initial acceptance part occurs automatically, which, as we have seen, means that it occurs non-consciously and without effort or intention. The assessment and unacceptance part of the process is the product of controlled processing, however, which means that people have to have the energy and motivation to do it. If people are preoccupied, tired, or unmotivated, the acceptance part of the process will operate unchecked, and this can lead to the acceptance of falsehoods. If we mindlessly watch television and do not think carefully about what is said, for example, we might mindlessly accept the outlandish claims being made in commercials (see Chapter 7).

When people care enough to analyze a problem thoughtfully, though, they can sometimes avoid the kinds of biases that result from automatic thinking. In some of the studies we reviewed earlier, the tasks were not all that important to the participants. There is, however, considerable evidence that when more consequential tasks are used, people do make more complex and accurate inferences (Chaiken, Liberman, & Eagly, 1989; Hilton

▶ Figure 3.9

GILBERT'S THEORY OF AUTOMATIC BELIEVING.

According to Gilbert (1991), people initially believe everything they hear and see. They then assess whether what they heard or saw is really true and "unaccept" it if necessary. The second and third parts of the process, in which people assess and unaccept information, take time and effort. If people are tired or preoccupied, these parts of the process are difficult to execute, increasing the likelihood that they will believe false information.

(Adapted from Gilbert, 1991)

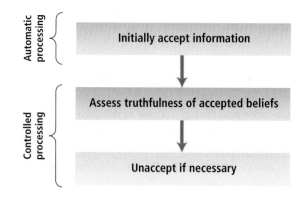

& Darley, 1991; Fiske, 1993; Kruglanski & Webster, 1996; Martin, Seta, & Crelia, 1990; Strack & Hannover, 1996). For example, Allan Harkness, Kenneth DeBono, and Eugene Borgida (1985) gave female participants information about a person named Tom Ferguson, whom they had never met. The participants learned how interested Tom was in dating each of several women. They also were given some information about the characteristics of the women, such as how good a sense of humour each had. Finally, participants judged the relationship between the qualities of the women (e.g., their sense of humour) and Tom's willingness to date them.

As with many other studies that have examined people's ability to judge such relationships, Harkness and colleagues (1985) found that the participants used simple strategies that, while not totally wrong, were not particularly accurate. Unless, that is, the participants were highly motivated to make careful judgments. Some of the participants thought they were taking part in a dating study and that they themselves would be dating Tom for several weeks. Now that the women cared more about what Tom liked and disliked in a dating partner, they used more complex mental strategies and made judgments that were more accurate.

In general, when the stakes are high, people use more sophisticated strategies than when the stakes are low, make more accurate judgments, and are more likely to notice facts that conflict with their prior schemas (Darke, Chaiken, Bohner, Einwiller, Erb, & Hazelwood, 1998; Dunn & Wilson, 1990; Fiske, 1993; Kruglanski, 1989; Neuberg, 1994; Petty & Cacioppo, 1986; Tetlock, 1992).

We do not mean to imply that with a little motivation, people become perfect reasoners. We will see several examples in later chapters in which people make erroneous judgments about the social world, in spite of their best efforts and intentions. Nevertheless, it is often true that the more motivated people are to form unbiased judgments, the greater the likelihood that they will do so.

THOUGHT SUPPRESSION

There is another interesting consequence of being preoccupied and unable to engage in much controlled processing: It reduces our ability to engage in **thought suppression**—the attempt to avoid thinking about something we would just as soon forget, such as a lost love, an unpleasant encounter with one's boss, or a delectable piece of cheesecake in the refrigerator. According to Daniel Wegner (1992, 1994), successful thought suppression depends on the interaction of two processes, one relatively automatic and the other relatively controlled. The first, automatic part of the system, called the *monitoring process,* searches for evidence that the unwanted thought is about to intrude upon consciousness. Once the unwanted thought is detected, the second, more controlled part of the system, called the *operating process,* comes into play. This is the effortful, conscious attempt to distract oneself by finding something else to think about.

In a recent study, Smart and Wegner (1999) suggested that people with nonobvious stigmas might be especially likely to experience the cycle of thought intrusions and subsequent attempts to suppress them. To test this idea, they asked a group of women with eating disorders to pretend that they did not have an eating disorder while having a conversation with another woman. (This condition was designed to approximate the real-life experience of people with nonobvious stigmas.) In another condition, women with eating

Thought suppression
the attempt to avoid thinking about something we would just as soon forget

◀ Sometimes we try our best not to think about something, such as fattening foods when we are on a diet. According to research by Daniel Wegner (1994), trying not to think about something can backfire. Particularly when we are under cognitive load, trying to suppress a thought can make that thought come to mind all the more.

disorders were told to come across as a person who had an eating disorder. Thus, these women were not required to keep their stigma a secret. The researchers found that the women who were trying to conceal their disorder experienced the most thought intrusions about eating habits and body image, and were most likely to engage in thought suppression.

What happens, though, when the controlled, operating process is unable to do its job because the person is tired or preoccupied? The monitoring process continues to find instances of the unwanted thought, which then intrude upon consciousness unchecked by the conscious, controlled system. Consequently, a state of hyperaccessibility exists, whereby the unwanted thought occurs with high frequency.

To illustrate this process, Wegner, Erber, and Bowman (1995) asked people to try not to make sexist responses when completing sentences during a laboratory task. If people had a lot of time to respond, they were able to suppress sexist responses, because their monitoring and operating processes worked together: One process looked for sexist answers and the other process suppressed these answers. Another group, however, was instructed not to be sexist and was asked to respond immediately. Under these conditions, the operating process did not have time to suppress. The automatic monitoring process that searched for sexist thoughts found many examples, and people reported them at a high rate, unchecked by the operating process. Consequently, people in this condition gave the highest number of sexist responses of all. The irony is that when it is most important to people not to express prejudiced thoughts (e.g., you are on guard not to make any jokes about short people because your four-foot-eight boss is standing next to you), if you are tired or preoccupied—that is, under cognitive load—these thoughts are especially likely to spill out unchecked.

Attempts at thought suppression can have other unfortunate effects, as demonstrated by Sullivan, Rouse, Bishop, and Johnston (1997). Students at Dalhousie University who had agreed to participate in an experiment on the experience of pain were shown a cooler with ice water, and were given a detailed description of how their arms would be immersed in it. Prior to this experience, some participants were instructed not to think about the ice-water immersion for the next nine minutes. Other participants were simply asked to record their thoughts. Those who were instructed not to think about the procedure experienced more thought intrusions (e.g., "The water looks really cold"; "I wonder if it will hurt?") than those who had not received this instruction. Importantly, they also rated the ice-water immersion as more painful. The authors suggest that the effort required to suppress their thoughts may have prevented these participants from engaging in active coping strategies. The Try It! exercise below shows what happens when you are trying your hardest not to do something.

 **The Amazing Pendulum**

Make a pendulum by tying a small weight to the end of a 0.5-metre piece of string or fishing line (a large nut or bolt works well). Then, draw a large plus sign on a piece of paper. Each of the two lines should be about 10 centimetres long. The point of this exercise is to hold the pendulum over the middle of the plus sign, keeping it as steady as possible.

Specifically, hold the string in your dominant hand, about 30 centimetres up from the weight. Wrap the rest of the string around your index finger. Then hold the weight about 2.5 centimetres over the paper as steady as you can. Make absolutely sure that the weight does not move from side to side. That is, make sure it does not move parallel to the horizontal line on the page. Do this for 30 seconds, and have a friend keep track of how many times the pendulum moved side to side and how many times it moved up and down. How did you do?

Now try it again, with one additional instruction: While you are holding the pendulum and trying to make sure that it does not move sideways, count backwards from 1000 by threes in your head. Again, have a friend count the number of times the pendulum moved sideways and how many times it moved up and down. How did you do this time?

This is a version of an experiment by Daniel Wegner, Matthew Ansfield, and Daniel Pilloff (1998) on the mental control of action. Just as it can be difficult to suppress a thought, it can be difficult to suppress movements. The same processes are involved: a monitoring process that looks for examples of what is being suppressed (e.g., sideways movements of the pendulum) and an operating process that attempts to avoid the undesired state (e.g., by making sure that the pendulum doesn't move sideways). The operating process requires more mental effort, so if people are distracted, it does not work very well. The consequence? The monitoring process operates unchecked, creating the very state the person is trying to avoid.

You can probably figure out the prediction for the pendulum test. It should be especially hard to keep the pendulum from moving side to side when you are counting backwards by threes, because here the operating process is unable to correct for sideways movements that the monitoring process detects. In the Wegner and colleagues study (1998), participants moved the pendulum sideways an average of 3.1 times when they had to count backwards by threes, whereas they moved it sideways an average of only 2.2 times when they did not have to count backwards by threes.

THINKING ABOUT WHAT MIGHT HAVE BEEN: COUNTERFACTUAL REASONING

There is one final condition under which people are likely to go off automatic pilot and think about things more slowly and consciously: when they experience a negative event that was a "close call," such a failing a test by just a point or two. Under these conditions, people engage in **counterfactual thinking**: mentally changing some aspect of the past as a way of imagining what might have been (Kahneman & Miller, 1986; Markman et al., 1995; Kahneman & Tversky, 1982; Roese, 1997; Roese & Olson, 1997). "If only I hadn't fallen asleep while studying the night before the test," you might think, "I would have gotten a better grade," or "If only I had worked up the courage to ask out Michelle, she might be going out with me instead of my best friend."

And what if you had mustered up the courage to ask out Michelle and the two of you were now head over heels in love? Chances are you probably wouldn't be spending much time agonizing over how the outcome could have been different. We are most likely to engage in "if only" thinking when negative events occur, especially if those events are unusual. Consider, for example, the following incident:

> Mr. Caution never picks up hitchhikers. Yesterday, however, he broke his rule and gave a stranger a lift. The stranger repaid his kindness by robbing him.

Now consider the following:

> Mr. Risk frequently picks up hitchhikers. Yesterday, he gave yet another stranger a ride. The stranger repaid his kindness by robbing him.

Who do you suppose will engage in more "if only" thinking? If you answered "Mr. Caution," your thinking is very much like that of students at the University of British Columbia who were asked this question (Kahenman & Tversky, 1982; Kahneman & Miller, 1986). Mr. Caution is more likely to be thinking, "If only I had followed my rule of never picking up hitchhikers . . ." Who do you suppose will experience greater regret? If you replied, "Mr. Caution again," you are right. Why does counterfactual thinking lead us to conclude that Mr. Caution will experience more regret? Because it is easier to imagine alternative outcomes to unusual behaviour—in this case, picking up hitchhikers—than it is to imagine alternative outcomes for behaviours that are usual or normal. Based on this reasoning, one might expect that people would feel more sympathy for those who experience negative outcomes following unusual, rather than usual, events. In fact, according to research conducted at Simon Fraser University, this is precisely what occurs. Miller and McFarland (1986) constructed a scenario about a man who was injured during a store robbery. Participants who were told that this was a store he rarely visited awarded him greater compensation than did those who were told that this was his regular store.

We also are more likely to engage in counterfactual thinking when we were nearly able to avoid a negative event. For example, missing a plane by five minutes causes more counterfactual thinking ("If only I had driven a little faster"; "If only I hadn't stopped to pick up a coffee") and more regret than missing a plane by half an hour (Kahneman & Miller, 1986; Miller, Turnbull, & McFarland, 1990). Similarly, if you sold a winning lottery ticket to your sister one hour before the draw, you would experience more regret than

Counterfactual thinking

mentally changing some aspect of the past as a way of imagining what might have been

if you had sold the ticket two weeks before the draw (Miller & Taylor, 2002). As you might expect, people also feel greater sympathy for others in near-miss situations. To demonstrate this, Miller and McFarland (1986) had students at Simon Fraser University read a scenario in which a man attempted to walk to safety after his plane crashed in an isolated northern area. Those who were told that the man perished 0.4 kilometres from the nearest town awarded greater compensation to his family than did those who were told that he died 120 kilometres from the nearest town.

The use of hypothetical scenarios such as these is common in counterfactual research. For example, students at the University of British Columbia have been asked to imagine a man taking an unusual route home and having an accident (Kahneman & Tversky, 1982; Mandel & Lehman, 1996), and students at the University of Western Ontario have been asked to imagine a man catching or missing a flight out of Pearson Airport in Toronto (Roese & Olson, 1996), getting a good or poor grade on a project with a classmate (Roese & Olson, 1993), or going on a blind date that ends in disaster (Roese & Olson, 1995). The effects we have been discussing, however, are not limited to people's reactions to hypothetical scenarios (Branscombe et al., 1996; Davis & Lehman, 1995). Indeed, as Davis, Lehman, Wortman, Silver, and Thompson (1995) have demonstrated, counterfactual thoughts have a great impact on people's emotional reactions to actual events. These researchers interviewed people who had experienced the trauma of losing a spouse or child in a car accident or the death of an infant due to Sudden Infant Death Syndrome. They discovered that thoughts such as "If only I had done something differently, my spouse [child] would still be alive" were common. In fact, for half of their participants, these kinds of thoughts persisted four to seven years later. Sadly, the more people engaged in such counterfactual thinking, the greater their distress. Similar findings were obtained when Davis and colleagues interviewed spinal cord injury victims (Davis et al., 1996). As expected, the more people imagined ways in which the tragedy could have been averted, by mentally "undoing" the circumstances preceding it, the more distress they reported.

Counterfactual reasoning can also lead to some paradoxical effects on our emotions. For example, who do you think would be happiest: an Olympic athlete who won a silver medal (came in second) or an Olympic athlete who won a bronze medal (came in third)? Though it might seem like the athlete who performed better (the silver medal winner) would be happier, that is not what Victoria Medvec, Scott Madey, and Tom Gilovich (1995) predicted. They reasoned that the silver medal winner should feel worse, because he or she could more easily imagine having won the event and would thus engage in more counterfactual reasoning. To see if they were right, they analyzed videotapes of the 1992 Olympics. Both immediately after their event and while athletes received their medals, silver medal winners appeared less happy than bronze medal winners. And during interviews with reporters, silver medal winners engaged in more counterfactual reasoning, saying things such as "I almost pulled it off; it's too bad . . . ." In subsequent research, Medvec and colleagues (2002) targeted an athletic competition at which they could interview the athletes immediately after their events, namely New York's Empire State Games. Consistent with their previous findings, the thoughts of silver medallists were focused on "I almost won . . ." whereas bronze medallists focused on "At least I did this well . . . ."

▶ Who do you think would be happier: the silver or bronze medallist in an Olympic event? Research by Medvec, Madey, and Gilovich (1995) suggests that bronze medallists are happier because it is harder for them to engage in counterfactual reasoning— imagining ways in which they could have won the event. This certainly seems to have been true for Canada's Beckie Scott, shown here after finishing in third place in the 2002 Winter Olympics. Headlines described Scott as "jumping for joy." By contrast, Kevin Martin, whose curling team won the silver medal, hangs his head after watching a gold medal slip through his fingers.

Finally, we should note that our discussion so far has centred on a particular kind of counterfactual thinking—namely, imagining outcomes that are better than reality (e.g., imagining winning a gold medal instead of the silver that was actually won). Roese and Olson (1997) refer to imagined outcomes that are better than reality as *upward counterfactuals*. These researchers point out that sometimes we imagine outcomes that are worse than reality (e.g., "Even though it's no fun being on crutches, I'm lucky to have survived the accident . . . ."). Roese and Olson refer to imagined outcomes that are worse than reality as *downward counterfactuals*.

According to Roese (1997), each kind of counterfactual serves a particular purpose. Downward counterfactuals help us feel better. By imagining that things could have turned out much worse than they actually did, we experience relief. In contrast, upward counterfactuals make us feel prepared for the future—if we are able to figure out how an unpleasant event could have been avoided, it feels less likely that we will find ourselves in the same situation again. Roese (1994) tested this reasoning by asking students at the University of Western Ontario to think of an exam they had written in the past year "that went especially poorly, and that you were especially disappointed with." Some participants were asked to generate upward counterfactuals for this event. They were asked to "list some specific actions that, in retrospect, could have been taken to have improved your exam score." Other participants were asked to generate downward counterfactuals— actions that could have made the situation even worse. As expected, students who generated downward counterfactuals felt better (experienced more relief) than did those who generated upward counterfactuals. Those who generated upward counterfactuals expressed greater intentions to perform success-enhancing behaviours in the future (e.g., studying). In a follow-up study, students who generated upward counterfactuals actually worked harder to improve their performance than did students who generated downward counterfactuals (Roese, 1994). These findings are consistent with research conducted at the University of British Columbia (Mandel & Lehman, 1996) showing that counterfactual thinking involves thinking not only about why an event occurred, but also about how various outcomes could have been avoided. Thus, counterfactual thinking can be useful when it motivates us to take steps to prevent similar outcomes from occurring in the future (Nasco & Marsh, 1999; Roese & Olson, 1997). This kind of thinking can be problematic, however, when people are trapped in their thoughts about an unpleasant event and are unable to think about anything else.

A Portrayal of Social Thinking

By now we have seen two rather different modes of social cognition, one that is effortless, involuntary, unintentional, and unconscious (automatic thinking) and another that is more effortful, voluntary, intentional and conscious (controlled thinking). We have also seen some ways in which these two kinds of thinking interact. Controlled thinking, for example, can provide checks and balances for automatic thinking by "unaccepting" false assumptions that people make more quickly.

Which kind of thinking—automatic or controlled—is more important in human functioning? There is a lively debate among social psychologists over the answer to this question. It is fair to say that there has been an increasing appreciation of the role of automatic thinking in human thought; more and more research has shown that people operate on automatic pilot when thinking about the social world. Some researchers have gone so far as to argue that the role of conscious, controlled thinking may be quite limited in human functioning (Bargh, 1999; Bargh & Chartrand, 1999; Wegner, in press; Wegner & Wheatley, 1999). Others have argued that although it can be difficult, it is possible to gain conscious control over unwanted automatic responses, such as prejudiced ones (Devine, 1989b; Devine & Monteith, 1999; Fiske, 1989a). Debate over these fundamental issues, such as the role of consciousness in human functioning, is likely to generate a good deal of research in the next several years.

What is clear is that both kinds of thinking are extremely useful. It would be difficult to live without the ability to process information about the social world automatically and make quick assumptions about our environment; we would be like a primitive, extremely slow computer, chugging away constantly as we tried to understand what was happening around us. And it is clearly to our advantage to be able to switch to controlled mode, where we can think about ourselves and our social world more slowly and carefully.

We have also seen, however, that both kinds of thinking can lead to consequential errors. So, what are we to conclude? How good a thinker is the typical human being anyway? Despite a number of thorny issues involved in trying to answer this very basic and important question (for an in-depth discussion, see Gigerenzer, 1993; Gigerenzer & Goldstein, 1996; Gilovich, 1991; Kahneman & Tversky, 1983; Nisbett & Ross, 1980), the following portrait of the social thinker has emerged: First, when people are motivated to make careful inferences and have the time and capacity to think, they often think in quite sophisticated ways. No one has yet been able to construct a computer that comes close to matching the power of the human brain. However, there is plenty of room for improvement in human thought. The shortcomings of social thinking we have documented can be quite consequential (Gilovich, 1991; Nisbett & Ross, 1980; Quattrone, 1982; Slusher & Anderson, 1989). For example, in Chapter 13 we will see that racial prejudice can, in part, be traced back to faulty reasoning processes. Tim Wilson and colleagues have gone so far as to use the term *mental contamination* to describe the kinds of biases in our thinking that are pervasive in everyday life (Wilson & Brekke, 1994; Wilson, Centerbar, & Brekkle, 2001). Perhaps the best metaphor of human thinking is that people are "flawed scientists"—brilliant thinkers who are attempting to discover the nature of the social world in a logical manner. This metaphor also captures the idea that people are not perfect scientists. We are often blind to truths that don't fit our schemas and sometimes treat others in ways that make our schemas come true—something that good scientists would never do.

IMPROVING HUMAN THINKING

Given that human reasoning is sometimes flawed and can have unpleasant and even tragic consequences, it is important to consider how these mistakes can be corrected. Is it possible to teach people to make better inferences, thereby avoiding some of the mistakes we have discussed in this chapter? If so, what is the best way to do it? Educators, philosophers, and psychologists have debated this question for decades, and recently some fascinating experiments have provided encouraging answers.

One approach is to make people a little more humble about their reasoning abilities. Often we have greater confidence in our judgments than we should (Lichtenstein, Fischhoff, & Phillips, 1982; Vallone et al., 1990; Griffin & Tversky, 1992). For example, research conducted in Canada and Great Britain shows that if people are able to answer a few difficult questions correctly, they tend to overestimate just how much general knowledge they have (Griffin & Buehler, 1999). Anyone trying to improve human inference is thus up against an **overconfidence barrier** (Metcalfe, 1998). Many people seem to think that their reasoning processes are just fine the way they are, and hence that there is no need for remedial action. One approach, then, might be to address this overconfidence directly, getting people to consider the possibility that they might be wrong. This tack was taken by Lord, Lepper, and Preston (1984), who found that when they asked people to consider the opposite point of view to their own, people realized there were other ways to construe the world and were less likely to make errors in their judgments (see also Anderson, Lepper, & Ross, 1980; Hirt & Markman, 1995; Mussweiler, Strack, & Pfeiffer, in press; Plous, 1995).

Another approach is to teach people directly some basic statistical and methodological principles about how to reason correctly, with the hope that they will apply these principles in their everyday lives. Many of these principles are already taught in courses in statistics and research design, such as the idea that if you want to generalize from a sample of information (e.g., a group of welfare mothers) to a population (e.g., all welfare mothers), you must have a large, unbiased sample. Do people who take such courses apply these principles in their everyday lives? Are they less likely to make the kinds of mistakes we have discussed in this chapter? A number of recent studies have provided encouraging answers to these questions, showing that people's reasoning processes can be improved by university statistics courses, graduate training in research design, and even brief, one-time lessons (Fong, Krantz, & Nisbett, 1986; Nisbett et al., 1987; Nisbett et al., 1983;

Overconfidence barrier
the barrier that results when people have too much confidence in the accuracy of their judgments; people's judgments are usually not as correct as they think they are

Schaller, Asp, Rosell, & Heim, 1996). Thus, there is reason to be cautiously optimistic—cautiously because a study conducted at Concordia University found that training in statistics and research methods does not guarantee the transfer of these concepts to everyday life. Specifically, Mill, Gray, and Mandel (1994) found that it in order to improve reasoning abilities, it was necessary to introduce tutorial sessions that focused explicitly on the application of course material to reasoning in everyday contexts (e.g., evaluating claims made by politicians, choosing between competing products).

In summary, there is reason to be hopeful about people's ability to overcome the kinds of mistakes we have documented in this chapter. And you don't have to go to graduate school to do it. Sometimes it helps simply to consider the opposite, as participants in the Lord and colleagues (1984) study did. Beyond this, formal training in statistics helps, at both the graduate and undergraduate levels—especially if your instructor illustrates how these principles apply in real-life situations. So, if you were dreading taking a university statistics course, take heart: It might not only satisfy a requirement for your major but improve your reasoning as well!

SUMMARY

Social cognition is the study of how people select, interpret, and use information to make judgments and decisions. People have developed several strategies and rules to help them understand the social world. **Schemas** are cognitive structures that organize information around themes or subjects. Schemas have a powerful effect on what information we notice, think about, and remember. One determinant of the schema that people apply in a given situation is **accessibility**, the extent to which a schema is at the forefront of one's mind and therefore are likely to be used when we are making judgments about the social world. Schemas can become accessible through **priming**, the process by which recent experiences increase the likelihood that a particular schema, trait, or concept will be brought to mind. Relying on schemas is adaptive and functional up to a point, but people can be overzealous. At times, we distort information so that it fits our schemas. We also have a tendency to persevere in our beliefs even when they're disproved, as shown in research on the **perseverance effect**. Finally, schemas also affect our behaviour—we act on the basis of our schemas. The most fascinating example of this is the **self-fulfilling prophecy**, wherein our schemas come true when we unconsciously treat others in such a way that they begin to act consistently with our schemas.

In addition to schemas, we use **judgmental heuristics** to help us deal with the large amount of social information with which we are faced. Heuristics are rules of thumb people follow to make judgments quickly and efficiently. The **availability heuristic**, the ease with which we can think of something, has a strong effect on how we view the world. The **representativeness heuristic** helps us decide how similar one thing is to another; we use it to classify people or situations on the basis of their similarity to a typical case. We also have a tendency to ignore **base rate information**—the prior probability that something or someone belongs in that classification. People also rely on the **anchoring and adjustment heuristic**, wherein an initial piece of information acts as an anchor, or starting point, for subsequent thoughts on the topic. One example of anchoring and adjustment is **biased sampling**, whereby people make generalizations from samples of information they know are biased or atypical. Whereas all three heuristics are useful, they can also lead to incorrect conclusions.

Finally, an important kind of social thinking is **automatic processing**—thinking that is non-conscious, unintentional, involuntary, and effortless. Engaging in automatic processing is very efficient, freeing up cognitive resources for other purposes. However, this kind of thinking can lead to errors such as making faulty, snap judgments about others. Another kind of social thinking is **controlled processing**—thinking that is conscious, intentional, voluntary, and effortful—to counteract the negative effects of automatic processing. When people are unmotivated or preoccupied, however, controlled processing is difficult. In such cases, people are more likely to accept false information and to have difficulty engaging in **thought suppression**: the attempt to avoid thinking about something they are trying to forget. Another example of controlled thinking is **counterfactual thinking**—thinking about what might have been. This kind of thinking can influence people's emotional reactions to events and can serve a preparative function for the future.

The issue of whether people are good thinkers has been the subject of considerable debate. Perhaps the best metaphor of the social thinker is that people are like flawed scientists—brilliant thinkers who often blind themselves to truths that don't fit their theories and who sometimes treat others in ways that make those theories come true. Though people often use strategies effectively, there is room for improvement in social thinking. For one thing, people are up against an **overconfidence barrier**, whereby they are too confident in the accuracy of their judgments. Fortunately, recent research has indicated that some of the shortcomings of human reasoning can be improved, particularly by training in statistics.

IF YOU ARE INTERESTED

Dostoevsky, Fyodor. (1945). *Notes from underground.* A classic discourse on the role of consciousness in human thinking and feeling.

Fiske, S. T., & Taylor, S. E. (1991). *Social cognition* (2nd ed.). New York: McGraw-Hill. An encyclopedic review of the literature on social cognition by two experts in the field.

Gilovich, T. (1991). *How we know what isn't so: The fallibility of human reason in everyday life.* New York: Free Press. An entertaining overview of the many ways in which mental shortcuts can get us into trouble.

Gilovich, T., Griffin, D. W., & Kahneman, D. (Eds.). (2001). *The psychology of judgment: Heuristics and biases.* New York: Cambridge University Press. A state-of-the-art compilation of research on people's use of heuristics and other mental shortcuts assembled by a stellar cast of editors. Dale Griffin is now at the University of British Columbia. Daniel Kahneman, formerly at the University of British Columbia, received the Nobel Prize for Economic Science in October 2002 for his research on judgment and uncertainty.

Kahneman, D., Slovic, P., & Tversky, A. (1982). *Judgment under uncertainty: Heuristics and biases.* New York: Cambridge University Press. A classic collection of chapters by researchers in the area of human inference.

Kunda, Z. (1999). *Social cognition.* Cambridge, MA: MIT Press. A comprehensive, up-to-date summary and analysis of social cognitive theory and research written by a prominent expert in the field from the University of Waterloo. This book was written with an undergraduate audience in mind. It is clear, readable, and infused with everyday examples to illustrate social cognitive concepts.

Menendez, Ramon (Director). (1988). *Stand and deliver* [Film]. A tough math teacher in an inner-city school challenges his students to do well in calculus. Based on a true story, the teacher expects the students to do well—and they do. An interesting portrayal of the power of social expectations.

Nisbett, R. E., & Ross, L. (1980). *Human inference: Strategies and shortcomings of human judgment.* Englewood Cliffs, NJ: Prentice Hall. A lively, poignant review of mental shortcuts and biases in human reasoning by the people who discovered many of them.

Plous, S. (1993). *The psychology of judgment and decision making.* New York: McGraw-Hill. An interesting review of how people form judgments and make decisions, one that expands upon many of the strategies and heuristics we have discussed.

Pollack, Sydney (Director). (1982). *Tootsie* [Film]. An unemployed, male, New York actor finally lands a role on a popular soap opera—as a woman. An amusing, poignant look at the expectations we have about each other based on gender.

WEBLINKS

www.psych.purdue.edu/~esmith/scarch.html

Social Cognition Paper Archive and Information Center

A recommended set of papers on social cognition research. This site provides the abstracts of many social cognition papers as well as several links to topics related to social cognition.

www.sfu.ca/counterfactual

Conterfactual Research News

Get the latest information on counterfactual research. References, background information, and cartoons are provided.

www.mentalhelp.net/poc/view_doc.php?type=doc&&id=289&&cn=0&&clnt%3Dclnt00001&&

Being Human and the Illusory Correlation

From baseball announcers to stereotyping, this article discusses human inference and the illusory correlation.

CHAPTER 4

Social Perception
how we come to understand other people

Chapter Outline

AS YOU HAVE NO DOUBT NOTICED, OTHER PEOPLE ARE NOT EASY TO figure out. Why are they the way they are? Why do they do what they do? The frequency and urgency with which we pose these questions are demonstrated in this touching story, sent in by a reader to the *New York Times*:

> After ending an office romance, a female friend of mine threw a bag full of her former paramour's love letters, cards, and poems into an outside Dumpster. The following day he called and wanted to know why she would throw out his letters. She was stunned. He explained that a homeless person going through the garbage read the correspondence and called the number found on a piece of stationery. The homeless man was curious as to why two people who seemed so in love could now be apart. "I would have called you sooner," he told the former boyfriend, "but this was the first quarter I was given today" (DeMarco, 1994).

The homeless man was down on his luck—no home, no money, reduced to rifling through garbage cans—and yet that endless fascination with the human condition still asserted itself. He needed to know why the couple broke up. He even spent his only quarter to find out.

We all have a fundamental fascination with explaining other people's behaviour. But the reasons for why others behave as they do are usually hidden from us. All we have to go on is observable behaviour: what people do, what they say, their facial expressions, gestures, and tone of voice. Unfortunately, we don't have the ability to read other people's minds—we can't know, truly and completely, who they are and what they mean. Instead, we rely on our impressions and theories, putting them together as well as we can, hoping they will lead to reasonably accurate and useful conclusions.

Our desire to understand people is so fundamental that it carries over into our hobbies and recreational lives. We go to movies, read novels, watch soap operas, and "people-watch" at airports because thinking about the behaviour of even strangers and fictional characters fascinates us. This basic aspect of human cognition has been exploited brilliantly by "reality TV" programmers, who have recently begun to cast television shows with real people instead of actors, and to place them in unusual or difficult situations. One such show was *Survivor*, which marooned 16 men and women for 39 days on the remote and uninhabited island of Pulau Tiga, off the coast of Borneo in the South China Sea. Every few days, the contestants had to vote one person off the island. The final "survivor" won US$1 million.

Almost immediately, the contestants began scheming, lying, and forming secret alliances as one by one they voted their fellow contestants off the island. One correspondent summed up the show's action like this: "The contestants ate grilled rat while competing to see who was the biggest rat" (Dowd, 2000). A typical segment of the show featured one contestant confiding to another her plans and strategy for remaining on the island, then presenting a totally different story to another contestant, and finally, speaking directly into the camera to us, the TV audience, telling yet a third version that contradicted the other two. What was the truth? What would she really do?

▶ *Left*: *Survivor* contestants eat a typical meal of rice while being filmed by the ever-present crew. *Right*: Richard, the confident and scheming contestant on *Survivor* who eventually beat 15 others to win US$1 million. Richard said, "I feel good about who I am. I was never mean or nasty. I played a game. I wasn't there to make friends."

Survivor was a huge ratings hit for CBS from start to finish. Why was it such a hit? Because it posed fascinating questions about what people are going to do next, what motivates them to do what they do, and what they're really like. Viewers were caught up in answering these questions for themselves, while at the same time watching the contestants (filmed 24 hours a day) trying to answer these same questions about one another.

Why do we expend so much time and energy trying to explain the behaviour of others? Because doing so helps us understand and predict our social world (Heider, 1958; Kelley, 1967). In this chapter, we will discuss **social perception**—the study of how we form impressions of other people and how we make inferences about them. One important source of information that we use is people's nonverbal behaviour, such as their facial expressions, body movements, and tone of voice.

Social perception

the study of how we form impressions of and make inferences about other people

Nonverbal Behaviour

What do we know about people when we first meet them? We know what we can see and hear, and even though we know we should not judge a book by its cover, this kind of easily observable information is critical to our first impressions. Physical characteristics such as people's attractiveness and facial configuration (e.g., a "baby face") influence others' judgments of them (Berry & McArthur, 1986; Hatfield & Sprecher, 1986a; McArthur, 1990; Zebrowitz, 1997; Zebrowitz & Montepare, 1992). We also pay a great deal of attention to what people say. After all, our most noteworthy accomplishment as a species is the development of verbal language.

But people's words are not the full story. There is a rich source of information about people other than their words—the ways they communicate nonverbally (Ambady & Rosenthal, 1992, 1993; DePaulo & Friedman, 1998; Gifford, 1991, 1994). **Nonverbal communication** refers to a large body of research on how people communicate, intentionally or unintentionally, without words. Facial expressions, tones of voice, gestures, body positions and movement, the use of touch, and eye gaze are the most frequently used diagnostic channels of nonverbal communication (Henley, 1977; Knapp & Hall, 1997).

Nonverbal communication

the way in which people communicate, intentionally or unintentionally, without words; nonverbal cues include facial expressions, tones of voice, gestures, body position and movement, the use of touch, and eye gaze

How does nonverbal communication work? Nonverbal cues serve many functions in communication. The primary uses of nonverbal behaviour are (a) *expressing emotion* (your eyes narrow, your eyebrows lower, you stare intently, your mouth is set in a thin, straight line—you're angry), (b) *conveying attitudes* (e.g., "I like you"—smiles, extended eye contact—or "I don't like you"—eyes averted, flat tone of voice, body turned away), (c) *communicating one's personality traits* ("I'm outgoing"—broad gestures, changes in inflection when speaking, an energetic tone of voice), and (d) *facilitating verbal communication* (you lower your voice and look away as you finish your sentence so that your conversational partner knows you are done and it is his or her turn to speak) (Argyle, 1975).

In addition, some nonverbal cues repeat or complement the spoken message, as when you smile while saying, "I'm so happy for you!" Others actually contradict the spoken words. Communicating sarcasm is the classic example of verbal–nonverbal contradiction. Think about how you'd say, "I'm so happy for you" sarcastically. (You could use your tone of voice, stressing the word *so* with an ironic twist, or you could roll your eyes as you speak, a sign of sarcasm in our culture.)

Nonverbal cues can also substitute for the verbal message. Hand gestures such as flashing the "okay" sign—in which one forms a circle with the thumb and forefinger and the rest of the fingers curve above the circle—or drawing a finger across your throat, convey clear messages without any words at all (Ekman, 1965).

Nonverbal forms of communication have typically been studied individually, in their separate "channels" (e.g., eye gaze or gestures), even though in everyday life nonverbal cues of many kinds occur all at the same time in a quite dazzling orchestration of information (Archer & Akert, 1980, 1984, 1998). Let's focus on a few of these channels.

FACIAL EXPRESSIONS OF EMOTION

Without doubt, the crown jewel of nonverbal communication is the facial expressions channel. This aspect of communication has the longest history of research, beginning with Charles Darwin's (1872) book *The Expression of the Emotions in Man and Animals*; its primacy is due to the exquisite communicativeness of the human face (Kappas, 1997; McHugo & Smith, 1996; Wehrle et al., 2000). Look at the photographs on the next page; you can probably figure out the meaning of these expressions with very little effort.

Darwin's research on facial expressions has had a major impact on the field in many areas; we will focus on his belief that the primary emotions conveyed by the face are universal—all human beings everywhere **encode** or express these emotions in the same way, and all human beings can **decode** or interpret them with equal accuracy. Darwin's (1872) interest in evolution led him to believe that nonverbal forms of communication were "species-specific" and not "culture-specific." He stated that facial expressions were vestiges of once-useful physiological reactions—for example, if early hominids ate something that tasted terrible, they would have wrinkled their noses in displeasure (from the bad smell) and expelled the food from their mouths. Note that the photograph on the next page showing the disgusted expression demonstrates this sort of reaction. Darwin (1872) states that such facial expressions then acquired evolutionary significance; being able to communicate such emotional states (e.g., the feeling of disgust, not for food but for another person or a situation) had survival value for the developing species (Hansen & Hansen, 1988; Izard, 1994; McArthur & Baron, 1983). Was Darwin right? Are facial expressions of emotion universal?

Encode

to express or emit nonverbal behaviour, such as smiling or patting someone on the back

Decode

to interpret the meaning of the nonverbal behaviour other people express, such as deciding that a pat on the back was an expression of condescension and not kindness

According to Paul Ekman and Walter Friesen, the answer is yes, at least for six major emotions: anger, happiness, surprise, fear, disgust, and sadness (Ekman and Friesen, 1986). (Subsequently these researchers added "contempt" to this list.) To demonstrate that the facial expression of these emotions is universal, Ekman and Friesen (1971) travelled to New Guinea, where they studied the decoding ability of the South Fore, a preliterate tribe that had had little contact with Western civilization. They told the Fore people brief stories with emotional content and then showed them photographs of American men and women expressing the six emotions; the Fore participants' job was to match the facial expressions of emotion to the stories. The researchers concluded that the Fore people were almost as accurate as Western subjects had been. They then asked the Fore people to demonstrate, while being photographed, facial expressions that would match the stories they were told. When these photographs were shown to American research participants, they were also decoded quite accurately. Based on these and other data, it is generally accepted that the ability to interpret these six emotions is universal—part of being human, and not a product of people's cultural experience (Biehl et al., 1997; Buck, 1984; Ekman, 1993, 1994; Ekman, Friesen, & Ellsworth, 1982a, 1982b; Ekman et al., 1987; Haidt & Keltner, 1999; Izard, 1969, 1994).

Are There Six (and Only Six) Universal Facial Expressions of Emotion?

Not all emotion theorists have agreed with Ekman's conclusion that there are six (or seven, if one includes contempt) universal facial expressions. As we will see, there are

▶ These photographs depict facial expressions of the six major emotions. Can you guess the emotion expressed on each face? (Adapted from Ekman & Friesen, 1975)

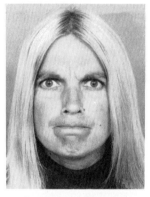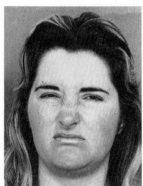
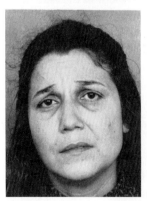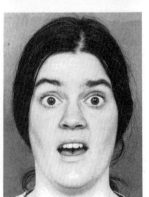

ANSWERS: (clockwise, beginning with upper-left photo): Anger, fear, disgust, surprise, happiness, and sadness.

some thorny issues involved in drawing conclusions about universality. One issue concerns the level of accuracy that participants must demonstrate in order to conclude that a given facial expression is being perceived in the same way across cultures. For example, when Ekman and Friesen (1975) showed photographs of their six basic emotions to participants in the U.S., Brazil, Chile, Argentina, Japan, and New Guinea, at least 82 percent of participants in each culture labelled their happiness facial expression as such. However, these percentages were substantially lower for some of the other emotions. For example, the fear expression was identified by only 54 percent of participants in both Argentina and New Guinea, and less than half (44 percent) of the New Guineans recognized the disgust expression.

According to Russell, Suzuki, and Ishida (1993), there is even less agreement when participants are asked to name the emotion shown in a face, rather than to select emotion terms from a list in which the number of emotion terms matches the number of faces (a common procedure in Ekman and Friesen's studies). Russell and colleagues approached adults in various public places in Canada, Greece, and Japan, and showed them Ekman's photographs of the six basic (plus "contempt") facial expressions of emotions. Once again, the facial expression of happiness was identified by the majority of respondents in each country, whereas recognition rates for the other emotions were much lower. For example, only 14 percent of Japanese participants generated fear-related words for the fear expression. The contempt photograph was not labelled as such by participants in any of the cultures. Similar findings have been obtained in studies involving Canadian, Chinese, and Japanese respondents (Yik, Meng, & Russell, 1998; Yik & Russell, 1999). Other research involving students from the University of Quebec at Montreal and the University of Belgium confirms that it is generally more difficult to "read" facial expressions of negative emotions, such as anger, than facial expressions of positive emotions, such as happiness (Hess, Philippot, & Blairy, 1998). If the perception of certain basic emotions is universal, people in all cultures should be able to identify these emotions with relative ease—even the negative ones. In fact, this does not appear to be the case. The Try It! box on page 104 encourages you to come up with your own answer to the question of how many basic facial expressions of emotion exist.

The claim of universality also suggests that basic facial expressions of emotion should be easily identified regardless of the context in which they are perceived. This also does not appear to be the case. In a series of studies conducted at the University of British Columbia, James Russell and Beverley Fehr (1987) found that the judgment of a given facial expression depended on what other faces were presented. If, for example, participants were exposed to a happy face and then a neutral face, the neutral face was perceived as sad. If a sad face was encountered first, the neutral face appeared happy. Most important, these effects were not limited to neutral faces. An angry face was perceived as sad, for example, when participants were first exposed to an expression such as disgust.

Finally, the situation a person is in also can influence the emotion read from a face. Imagine the following scenario:

> A man wanted to treat his brother to the most expensive, exclusive restaurant in their city. Months ahead, he made a reservation. When he and his brother arrived, they were told by the maitre d' that their table would be ready in 45 minutes. Still, an hour passed, and no table. Other groups arrived and were

How Many Universal Facial Expressions of Emotion Exist?

How many universal facial expressions of emotion are there? Come up with your own answer the next time you are with a group of friends. You can take turns posing facial expressions of emotion while the others in the group try to guess the emotion that is being conveyed. Here are some emotions you may wish to focus on:

1. Happiness, Sadness, Anger, Fear, Disgust, Surprise

These are the six facial expressions originally identified by Paul Ekman as universal. If these are basic, universal facial expressions, it should be relatively easy for the people doing the posing to show those emotions on their faces. It should also be easy for the rest of the group to identify the emotion being displayed.

2. Contempt

This is an emotion that Paul Ekman has more recently added to his list of universal facial expressions. Is contempt easily conveyed via facial expression? Was it easily recognized?

3. Embarrassment

Research by Dacher Keltner (1995; Keltner & Buswell, 1996) suggests that embarrassment has a distinctive facial expression—the person turns his or her head away, looks down and to the side, and smiles with pressed lips. Is this how embarrassment looked when it was posed in your group? Should it be considered a universal facial expression?

4. Heroism, Humour/Amusement, Love, Peace, Wonder

Are these emotions easily conveyed via facial expression? According to an analysis of ancient Hindu writings, these emotions, along with anger, disgust, fear, sadness, and shame/embarrassment, may be universal (Hejmadi, Davidson, & Rozin, 2000). When participants in India and the United States were presented with videotaped expressions of these emotions (conveyed via facial expression and body movement), they were quite accurate at identifying them.

So, exactly how many universal facial expressions of emotion are there? Which emotions should be included in that set? If you and your friends disagree, take heart. Emotion researchers aren't quite sure, either.

seated after a short wait. The man went to the maitre d' and reminded him of his reservation. The maitre d' said that he'd do his best. Ten minutes later, a local celebrity and his date arrived and were immediately shown to a table. The man went to the maitre d', who said that the tables were now all full and that it might be another hour before anything was available.

Now, imagine that the person you have been reading about is the man shown in the top row of facial expressions featured on page 102. What emotion is he experiencing? If you are like the University of British Columbia students who read the story (Carroll & Russell, 1996), you would probably say "anger." However, if you had not read this story, chances are you would have identified this facial expression as "fear" (see Answers section on page 102). The emotion of anger as depicted in the story "wins out" over the emotion of fear depicted on the face. Thus, context effects, such as the presence of other facial expressions or the social situation in which an emotion is expressed, can have powerful influences on the perception of emotion. Such findings challenge the idea of universality of facial expressions of emotion and have generated lively debate among researchers (e.g., Ekman & O'Sullivan, 1988; Russell & Fehr, 1988; Russell, 1994).

Factors That Decrease the Accuracy with Which Facial Expressions Are Decoded

Emotion theorists do agree, however, on some other factors that limit the accuracy with which facial expressions are decoded. First, people frequently display **affect blends** (Ekman & Friesen, 1975), wherein one part of their face is registering one emotion and another part is registering a different emotion. Take a look at the photographs on this page and see if you can tell which two emotions are being expressed in each face. In the photograph on the left, we see a blend of anger (the eye and eyebrow region) and disgust (the nose and mouth region). (It may help to cover half the photograph with your hand to see each emotional expression clearly.) This is the sort of expression you might display if a person told you something that was both horrible and inappropriate—you'd be disgusted with the content and angry that the person had told you.

Second, decoding facial expressions accurately can be difficult because culture plays a role as to when and how people display emotions on their faces. According to Ekman and his colleagues (Ekman & Friesen, 1969; Ekman & Davidson, 1994), **display rules** are particular to each culture and dictate what kind of emotional expression people are supposed to show. For example, North American cultural norms discourage emotional displays in men, such as grief or crying, but allow the facial display of such emotions in women. Thus, when Canadian novelist Robertson Davies portrays a funeral scene in *Murther and Walking Spirits* (1991) with the phrase "they sat in rows of weeping men and grim-faced women," he is fully aware that this description runs contrary to cultural norms, and adds an explanation: "For in our day there has been a reversal which makes it perfectly all right for a man to give way to feeling, whereas women must show no such weakness." So far, the reversal about which the author speaks appears to exist only in fiction. Women are still much more likely than men to express emotion by crying (Fehr & Baldwin, 1996).

Affect blend

a facial expression in which one part of the face is registering one emotion and another part of the face is registering a different emotion

Display rules

culturally determined rules about which nonverbal behaviours are appropriate to display

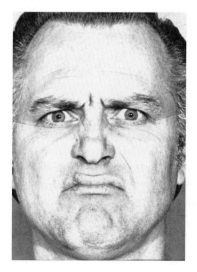

◀ Often people express more than one emotion at the same time. Can you tell which emotions these people are expressing? The answers are printed below. (Adapted from Ekman & Friesen, 1975)

ANSWERS: The man is expressing a blend of anger and disgust. The woman is expressing a blend of surprise and happiness.

In Japan, traditional cultural rules dictate that women should not exhibit a wide, uninhibited smile (Ramsey, 1981). Japanese women will often hide their wide smiles behind their hands, while Western women are allowed—indeed, encouraged—to smile broadly and often (Henley, 1977; La France & Hecht, 1999). In fact, the cultural display rules that govern Japanese nonverbal expression are surprisingly different from Western ones. Japanese norms lead people to cover up negative facial expressions with smiles and laughter and to display fewer facial expressions in general than is the case in the West (Aune & Aune, 1996; Friesen, 1972; Gudykunst, Ting-Toomey, & Nishida, 1996; Leathers, 1997). This is undoubtedly what lies behind the Western stereotype that Asians are "inscrutable" and "hard to read."

To give an example from another culture, Mandal, Bryden, and Bulman-Fleming (1996) showed Ekman's (American) photographs of the basic six facial expressions, as well as photographs of Indian faces portraying the same emotions, to students at the University of Waterloo and Banaras Hindu University in India. Canadians were able to recognize happiness, sadness, and disgust expressions on Indian faces, and vice versa. However, there were difficulties in identifying the other emotions, particularly anger and fear. These expressions were perceived as being less distinct on Indian faces by participants from both countries. Moreover, Indians judged fear and anger as more unpleasant than did Canadians. The authors suggest that in India, as in other collectivist cultures, the expression of strong negative emotions is discouraged because to do so can disrupt group harmony. As a result, Indians would have less experience in displaying such emotions on their faces and perceive them as more unpleasant when expressed.

Before leaving this topic, we should note that recent technological developments by a team of researchers in Quebec and Belgium (Blairy, Herrera, & Hess, 1999; Hess, Philippot, & Blairy, 1998) may allow us to pinpoint with precision the factors that determine the expression of emotion on a face on a moment-to-moment basis. In these studies, facial electrodes are attached to participants' faces to record movements of specific muscles involved in producing certain facial expressions. For example, in one study (Hess, Banse, & Kappas, 1995), facial activity was assessed while students at the University of Quebec at Montreal watched humorous films. The researchers found that the intensity of emotion shown on the face was determined by the emotion experienced (i.e., highly amusing films created more happiness/amusement than did moderately funny films), the sociality of the situation (i.e., whether participants viewed the films alone or with another person), and the nature of the relationship between the person expressing the emotion and the perceiver (e.g., friend versus stranger). Thus, a number of complex factors determine the emotion that is expressed and perceived on the face.

OTHER CHANNELS OF NONVERBAL COMMUNICATION

There are, of course, other channels of nonverbal communication. Eye contact and eye gaze are particularly powerful nonverbal cues. In North America, we become suspicious when a person doesn't "look us in the eye" while speaking, and we find talking to someone who is wearing dark sunglasses quite disconcerting. However, in other parts of the world, direct eye gaze is considered invasive or disrespectful. For example, in Nigeria, Puerto Rico, and Thailand, children are taught not to make direct eye contact with adults. Japanese also use far less direct eye contact than do North Americans.

◀ Cambodians in downtown Phnom Penh watch a television broadcast of the trial of Pol Pot, the leader of the Khmer Rouge, a Cambodian revolutionary group that was responsible for the murder of more than 1 million civilians during the country's civil war in the mid-1970s. The Cambodians' facial expressions show emotions such as anger and surprise (the two children in the foreground) as well as affect blends of surprise with fear or anger (the adults around them).

Another form of nonverbal communication is the way people use personal space. Imagine you are talking to a person who stands too close to you (or too far away); these deviations from "normal" spacing will affect your impressions of him or her. Cultures vary greatly in what is considered normative use of personal space (Hall, 1969). For example, in countries such as Canada and the U.S., most people like to have a bubble of open space, at least 0.5 metres in radius, surrounding them; in comparison, in some other cultures, strangers will think nothing of standing right next to each other, to the point of touching. Differences in personal space can lead to misunderstandings when people of different cultures interact. For example, when Neil Malamuth was at the University of Manitoba, he helped organize a student exchange program in which North American students travelled to Israel. On one occasion, he organized a dance so the students from the two countries could get to know one another. Due to cultural differences in personal space, there were some unintended consequences:

> The scripted behaviour for an Israeli female in slow dances is generally not to have direct bodily contact with her dancing partner unless she is intimately involved with him. North American scripts, as you know, frequently prescribe body contact in such dances even when no intimacy is involved or desired. The consequence of the different cultural scripts was that the Israeli males thought that the North American women with whom they danced desired immediate sexual intimacy. The North American males dancing with Israeli partners, on the other hand, seemed very uncomfortable in being kept at a physical distance and later reported that they had been thinking that the Israelis must have found something about them highly offensive (Malamuth, 1983).

Gestures of the hands and arms are also a fascinating means of communication. We are adept at understanding certain gestures, such as the "okay" sign, in which one forms a circle with the thumb and forefinger and the rest of the fingers curve above the circle, and "giving someone the finger" (also known as the "up yours" gesture; Wolfgang & Wolofsky, 1991), in which one bends all the fingers down at the first knuckle except the longest, middle finger. Gestures such as these, for which there are clear, well-understood definitions, are called **emblems** (Ekman & Friesen, 1975; Archer, 1997b).

Emblems

nonverbal gestures that have well-understood definitions within a given culture; they usually have direct verbal translations, such as the "okay" sign

The important point about emblems is that they are not universal; each culture has devised its own emblems, and these need not be understandable to people from other cultures. For example, Wolfgang and Wolofsky (1991) photographed actors displaying 23 different Canadian emblems. They asked Canadians and English as a second language students from Asian, Latin, and Mediterranean countries to identify them. Overall, identification rates were high because even the participants from the other countries already had some exposure to Canada. However, Canadians showed the highest rate of correct identification (97 percent). Thus, when the late Prime Minister Trudeau gave protesters "the finger," it was a clear, communicative sign that the protesters (and the media) had no difficulty interpreting. However, in some parts of Europe, one would have to make a quick gesture with a cupped hand under one's chin to convey the same message.

To summarize, we can learn quite a lot about people from their facial expressions and nonverbal behaviour. Specifically, we can use this information to infer what they are feeling or thinking. However, usually we are not content just to know what someone is feeling or thinking; we also want to know what this person is really like, and perhaps even more importantly, *why* they are feeling or thinking that way. In the next sections, we turn to the cognitive processes that people rely on to answer these questions.

Implicit Personality Theories: Filling in the Blanks

Implicit personality theory

a type of schema people use to group various kinds of personality traits together; for example, many people believe that if someone is kind, he or she is generous as well

As we saw in Chapter 3, when people are unsure about the nature of the social world, they use their schemas to fill in the gaps. An excellent example of this use of schemas is the way in which we form impressions of other people. If we know that someone is kind, we use an important type of schema called an **implicit personality theory** to determine what other qualities the person has. These theories consist of our ideas about what kinds of personality traits go together (Anderson & Sedikides, 1990; Sedikides & Anderson, 1994; Sherman & Klein, 1994; Schneider, 1973). For example, research on implicit personality theories of North Americans indicates that if people are perceived to be "helpful," they are also believed to be "sincere"; if they are thought to be "practical," they are also believed to be "cautious" (Rosenberg, Nelson, & Vivekananthan, 1968).

These implicit theories about personality serve the same function as does any schema: We can extrapolate from a small to a much larger amount of information (Fiske & Taylor, 1991; Markus & Zajonc, 1985). In this case, we can use just a few observations of a person as a starting point, and then, using our schema, create a much fuller understanding of what that person is like (Kim & Rosenberg, 1980). This way, we can form impressions quickly, without having to spend weeks with people to figure out what they are like.

However, this efficiency can come at some cost, and in some cases could even be fatal. How could our implicit personality theories cost us our lives? A team of researchers in the United States and Canada found that university students relied on implicit personality theories to determine whether they should use condoms (Williams et al., 1992). If they knew their partner and liked their partner, participants assumed that he or she couldn't possibly be HIV positive. If participants didn't know their partner, they relied on superficial characteristics, such as the person's age, the way he or she dressed, or even whether the person was from a large city versus a small town. Thus, if a potential sexual partner didn't dress provocatively or wasn't from a large city, participants assumed that a condom wasn't necessary. The researchers concluded that young people are placing themselves at considerable risk by relying on such implicit personality theories, because these variables are not accurate indicators of whether a sexual partner actually has HIV or AIDS.

Another strong implicit personality theory in our culture involves physical attractiveness. We presume that "what is beautiful is good"—that people with physical beauty will also have a whole host of other wonderful qualities (Dion, Berscheid, & Walster, 1972; Eagly et al., 1991; Jackson, Hunter, & Hodge, 1995). For example, when Dion and Dion (1987) showed visitors to the Ontario Science Centre photographs of attractive and unattractive individuals, more positive qualities (e.g., kind, considerate, sincere) were attributed to the attractive individuals. Participants also predicted that attractive individuals would experience more successes in life.

Dion, Pak, and Dion (1990) wondered whether physical attractiveness stereotyping might be less likely to occur in collectivist cultures (e.g., China) where social judgments are more likely to be based on group-related attributes (e.g., family, position in a social group) than on characteristics of the individual. Dion and colleagues tested this prediction in a sample of University of Toronto students of Chinese ethnicity. Indeed, students with a collectivist orientation (defined in this study as being highly involved in Toronto's Chinese community) were less likely to assume that an attractive person possessed desirable personality traits than were students who did not have a strong collectivist orientation (i.e., were less involved in the Chinese community).

Cultural variation in implicit personality theories also was demonstrated in an intriguing study by Hoffman, Lau, and Johnson (1986). They noted that different cultures have different ideas about personality types—that is, the kinds of people for whom there are simple, agreed-on verbal labels. For example, in Western cultures we agree that there is a kind of person who has an artistic personality: a person who is creative, intense, and

◀ Implicit personality theories differ from culture to culture. Westerners assume that there is an artistic type of person: someone who is creative, intense, temperamental, and unconventional—for example, poet–songwriter Leonard Cohen, pictured at left. The Chinese have no such implicit personality theory. The Chinese have a category of *shi gú* person—someone who is worldly, devoted to family, socially skillful, and somewhat reserved. Westerners do not have this implicit personality theory.

temperamental, and who has an unconventional lifestyle. The Chinese, however, do not have a schema or implicit personality theory for an artistic type. Conversely, in China there are categories of personality that do not exist in Western cultures. For example, a *shi gú* person is someone who is worldly, devoted to family, socially skillful, and somewhat reserved.

Hoffman and colleagues (1986) hypothesized that these culturally implicit personality theories influence the way people form impressions of others. To test this hypothesis, they wrote stories that described a person behaving like an artistic type of person or a *shi gú* type of person, without using those labels to describe the person. These stories were written in both English and Chinese. The English versions were given to a group of unilingual English speakers and to a group of Chinese–English bilinguals. Another group of Chinese–English bilinguals received the versions written in Chinese. Participants were asked to write down their impressions of the characters in the stories. The researchers then examined whether the participants listed traits that were not used in the stories but did fit the artistic or *shi gú* personality type. For example, "unreliable" was not mentioned in the "artistic personality type" story but is consistent with that implicit personality theory.

As seen in Figure 4.1, when the unilingual English speakers read about the characters, they formed an impression that was more consistent with the artistic type than with the *shi gú* type. This was also the case for the Chinese–English bilinguals who read the descriptions in English. However, Chinese–English bilinguals who read the descriptions in Chinese showed the opposite pattern of results. Their impression of the character was more consistent with the *shi gú* type than with the artistic type because the Chinese language provides a convenient label or implicit personality theory for this kind of person. These results are consistent with a well-known argument by Whorf (1956) that the language people speak influences the way they think about the world. Characters described identically were perceived differently by the bilingual research participants, depending on the language (and therefore the implicit personality theory) used. Thus, one's culture and

▶ **Figure 4.1**

IMPLICIT PERSONALITY THEORIES: HOW OUR CULTURE AND LANGUAGE SHAPE OUR IMPRESSIONS OF OTHER PEOPLE.

People formed an impression of other people that was consistent with the implicit personality theory contained in their language. For example, when Chinese-English bilinguals read stories about people in English, they were likely to form impressions consistent with a Western implicit theory, the artistic personality. When Chinese-English bilinguals read the same stories in Chinese, they were likely to form impressions consistent with a Chinese implicit theory, the *shi gú* personality.

(Adapted from Hoffman, Lau, & Johnson, 1986)

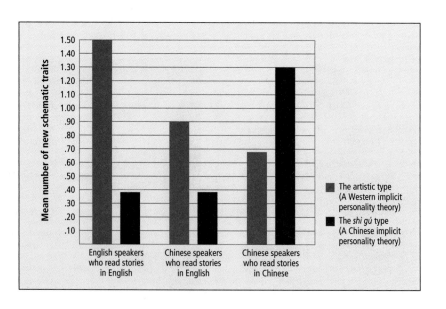

one's language produce widely shared implicit personality theories, and these theories can influence the kinds of impressions people form of each other.

Causal Attribution: Answering the "Why" Question

We have seen that when we observe other people, we make guesses about their personalities, such as how friendly or outgoing they are. And once we get this far, we use our implicit personality theories to fill in the blanks: If a person is friendly, she must be sincere as well. Or more disturbingly, if a person is likeable, he must not have AIDS. In addition to trying to figure out what people are like, it is human nature also to want to know *why* they behave as they do. How people go about answering this question is the focus of **attribution theory**, the study of how we infer the causes of other people's behaviour.

THE NATURE OF THE ATTRIBUTIONAL PROCESS

Fritz Heider (1958) is frequently referred to as the father of attribution theory. His influential book defined the field of social perception, and his legacy is still very much evident in current research (Gilbert, 1998a; Ross, 1998). Heider (1958) discussed what he called "naive" or "common sense" psychology. In his view, people were like amateur scientists, trying to understand other people's behaviour by piecing together information until they arrived at a reasonable explanation or cause.

One of Heider's (1958) most valuable contributions is a simple dichotomy: We can make an **internal attribution**, deciding that the cause of the person's behaviour was something about her—her disposition, personality, attitudes, or character—an explanation that assigns the causality of her behaviour internally. Conversely, we can make an **external attribution**, deciding that the cause of a person's behaviour was something about the situation (see Try It! on page 112). This dichotomy was vividly illustrated in an incident that occurred in North Vancouver, British Columbia, on September 22, 1999. Nadia Hama made newspaper headlines when her 18-month-old daughter Kaya fell 47 metres from the Capilano Suspension Bridge. People in the media and on the street were quick to blame Hama. They accused her of intentionally throwing Kaya off the bridge. These accusations mounted as it came to light that her daughter had Down's syndrome and that Hama had looked into placing her daughter for adoption. In short, Hama was portrayed as a bad mother who intentionally tried to kill her child.

Others agreed that Nadia Hama may have tried to kill her child, but made external attributions for her behaviour. They pointed to extremely high levels of stress in her life—the stress of raising a handicapped child, the stress of being embroiled in an ugly divorce, the stress of not receiving child-care payments from her estranged husband, and so on. Not surprisingly, Hama herself explained the situation in terms of external factors—stating that baby Kaya's fall was accidental.

Whether we make internal or external attributions for someone's behaviour can have serious consequences. In Hama's case, those who made internal attributions concluded that she was a cold-hearted murderer. In contrast, those who made external attributions felt compassion, sympathy, and pity. Quite a difference! Perhaps even more important, the fate of Nadia Hama rested on the attributions made for baby Kaya's fall. In this case,

Attribution theory

a description of the way in which people explain the causes of their own and other people's behaviour

Internal attribution

the inference that a person is behaving in a certain way because of something about him or her, such as his or her attitude, character, or personality

External attribution

the inference that a person is behaving a certain way because of something about the situation he or she is in; the assumption is that most people would respond the same way in that situation

try it !   Listen as People Make Attributions

Forming attributions is a major part of daily life—note the Rhona Raskin column on page 121! You can watch the attribution process in action, too. All it takes is a group of friends and an interesting topic to discuss. Perhaps one of your friends is telling you about something that happened to her that day, or perhaps your group is discussing another person whom everybody knows. As they talk, pay very close attention to what they say. They will be trying to figure out why the person being discussed did what she did or said what he said. In other words, they will be making attributions. Your job is to try to keep track of their comments and label the attributional strategies they are using.

In particular, do they make internal attributions, about a person's character or personality, or do they make situational attributions, about all of the other events and variables that make up a person's life? Do your friends seem to prefer one type of attribution over the other? If their interpretation is dispositional (internal), what happens when you suggest another possible interpretation, one that is situational? Do they agree or disagree with you? What kinds of information do they offer as "proof" that their attribution is right?

Observing people when they are making attributions in real conversations will show you just how common and powerful this type of thinking is when people are trying to understand each other.

police and Crown prosecutors did not find sufficient evidence to charge Hama with either attempted murder or criminal negligence causing bodily harm (D'Angelo, 2000).

Thus, attributions can play a pivotal role in determining whether someone is charged with a crime. As demonstrated in a study by Linda Coates (1997), attributions also play a role in the severity of sentencing when people are convicted of committing crimes. She recorded the kinds of attributions made by judges in transcripts of 70 cases of convicted

▶ According to Fritz Heider, we tend to see the causes of a person's behaviour as internal. So when a person asks us for money, we will most likely at first assume that he is at fault for being poor—perhaps lazy or drug-addicted. If you knew the person's situation—that perhaps he has lost his job due to a plant closing or has a spouse whose medical bills have bankrupted them—you might come up with a different, external attribution.

sexual assaults in British Columbia. The kind of attributions made had important implications for sentencing—if the assault was seen as the result of a decision to be violent or due to the offender's violent nature, the sentence was harsher than if situational or external attributions were made (e.g., the assault was attributed to stress or negative mood).

Another of Heider's (1958) important contributions was his observation that people generally prefer internal attributions over external ones. While either type of attribution is always possible, Heider (1958) noted that we tend to see the causes of a person's behaviour as residing in that person. We are perceptually focused on *people*—they are who we notice—while the *situation*, which is often hard to see and hard to describe, can be overlooked (Bargh, 1994; Carlston & Skowronski, 1994; Gilbert, 1998b; Newman & Uleman, 1993; Pittman & D'Agostino, 1985; Uleman & Moskowitz, 1994).

THE COVARIATION MODEL: INTERNAL VERSUS EXTERNAL ATTRIBUTIONS

Harold Kelley (1967, 1973) developed a theory of attribution that focused on the first step in the process of social perception, namely how people decide whether to make an internal or an external attribution. Kelley's major contribution to attribution theory was the idea that we notice and think about more than one piece of information when we form an impression of another person. For example, let's say that you ask your friend to lend you her car, and she says no. Naturally, you wonder why. In formulating an answer, Kelley's theory, called the **covariation model**, states that you will examine multiple instances of behaviour, occurring at different times and in different situations. Has your friend refused to lend you her car in the past? Does she lend it to other people? Does she normally lend you other possessions of hers?

Kelley (like Heider before him) assumes that when we are in the process of forming an attribution, we gather information, or data, that will help us reach a judgment. The data we use, according to Kelley, are how a person's behaviour covaries across time, place, different actors, and different targets of the behaviour. By discovering covariation in people's behaviour (e.g., your friend refuses to lend you his car; he agrees to lend it to others), you are able to reach a judgment about what caused their behaviour.

When we are forming an attribution, what kinds of information do we examine for covariation? Kelley (1967, 1973) states that there are three important types of information: *consensus*, *distinctiveness*, and *consistency*. Let's describe these three types of information through an example: You are working at your part-time job in a clothing store and you observe your boss yelling at another employee, Hannah, telling her in no uncertain terms that she's an idiot. Without any conscious effort on your part, you pose the attributional question: "Why is the boss yelling at Hannah and being so critical—is it something about the boss, or is it something about the situation that surrounds and affects him?"

Now let's look at how Kelley's model of covariation assessment answers this question. **Consensus information** refers to how other people behave toward the same stimulus—in this case, Hannah. Do other people at work also yell at Hannah and criticize her? **Distinctiveness information** refers to how the actor (the person whose behaviour we are trying to explain) responds to other stimuli. Does the boss yell at and demean other employees in the store? **Consistency information** refers to the frequency with which the

Covariation model
a theory stating that in order to form an attribution about what caused a person's behaviour, we systematically note the pattern between the presence (or absence) of possible causal factors and whether or not the behaviour occurs

Consensus information
information about the extent to which other people behave the same way as the actor does toward the same stimulus

Distinctiveness information
information about the extent to which one particular actor behaves in the same way to different stimuli

Consistency information
information about the extent to which the behaviour between one actor and one stimulus is the same across time and circumstances

observed behaviour between the same actor and the same stimulus occurs across time and circumstances. Does the boss yell at and criticize Hannah regularly and frequently, whether the store is busy with customers or empty?

According to Kelley's theory, when these three sources of information combine into one of two distinct patterns, a clear attribution can be made. People are most likely to make an *internal attribution* (deciding the behaviour was due to something about the boss) when the consensus and distinctiveness of the act are low but its consistency is high (see Figure 4.2). We would be pretty confident that the boss yelled at Hannah because he is a mean and vindictive person if we knew that no one else yells at Hannah, that the boss yells at other employees, and that the boss yells at Hannah every chance he gets. People are likely to make an *external attribution* (in this case, about Hannah) if consensus, distinctiveness, and consistency are all high. Finally, when consistency is low we cannot make a clear internal or external attribution, and so resort to a special kind of external or *situational attribution,* one that assumes something unusual or peculiar is going on in these circumstances—for example, the boss just received very upsetting news and lost his temper with the first person he saw.

The covariation model assumes that people make causal attributions in a rational, logical fashion. People observe the clues, such as the distinctiveness of the act, and then draw a logical inference about why the person did what he or she did. Several studies have confirmed that people often do make attributions the way that Kelley's (1967) model says they should (Gilbert, 1998; Hazelwood & Olson, 1986; Hewstone & Jaspars, 1987; Major,

▶ **Figure 4.2**

THE COVARIATION MODEL.

Why did the boss yell at his employee Hannah? To decide whether a behaviour was caused by internal (or dispositional) factors, or external (or situational) factors, people use consensus, distinctiveness, and consistency information.

Why Did the Boss Yell at His Employee, Hannah?			
People are likely to make an **internal attribution**—it was something about the Boss—if they see this behaviour as	**low** in consensus: the Boss is the only person working in the store who yells at Hannah	**low** in distinctiveness: the Boss yells at all the employees	**high** in consistency: the Boss yells at Hannah almost every time he sees her
People are likely to make an **external attribution**—it was something about Hannah—if they see this behaviour as	**high** in consensus: all the employees yell at Hannah too	**high** in distinctiveness: the Boss doesn't yell at any of the other employees	**high** in consistency: the Boss yells at Hannah almost every time he sees her
People are likely to think it was something peculiar about the particular circumstances in which the Boss yelled at Hannah if they see this behaviour as	**low** or **high** in consensus	**low** or **high** in distinctiveness	**low** in consistency: this is the first time the Boss has yelled at Hannah

1980; Ruble & Feldman, 1976)—with two exceptions. First, studies have shown that people don't use consensus information as much as Kelley's theory predicted; they rely more on consistency and distinctiveness information when forming attributions (McArthur, 1972; Wright, Luus, & Christie, 1990). Second, people don't always have the relevant information they need on all three of Kelley's dimensions. For example, you may not have consistency information because this is the first time you have ever asked your friend to borrow her car. In these situations, research has shown that people proceed with the attribution process using the information they do have, and, if necessary, making inferences about the "missing data" (Fiedler, Walther, & Nickel, 1999; Kelley, 1973).

To summarize, the covariation model portrays people as master detectives, deducing the causes of behaviour as systematically and logically as Sherlock Holmes would. However, as is evident in chapters 3 and 6, people sometimes aren't that accurate or rational when forming judgments about others. Sometimes they distort information to satisfy their need for high self-esteem (see Chapter 6). Other motivational factors can influence attributions as well. For example, Kafer, Hodkin, Furrow, and Landry (1993) examined attributions for the Montreal Massacre made by students at three Halifax universities. (As you will recall, on December 6, 1989, 14 women in Montreal, among them engineering students, were gunned down by Marc Lepine.) Men were more likely to explain the murders as the random act of a madman, whereas women were more likely to attribute the murders to societal sexism and violence toward women. The researchers suggest that men may have wanted to distance themselves from guilt by implication, whereas women's attributions reflected a tendency to identify with the victims.

Attributions also can be biased or distorted when people use mental shortcuts (see Chapter 3). In the next section, we will discuss some specific errors or biases that plague the attribution process. One shortcut is very common, at least in Western cultures: assuming that people do what they do because of the kind of people they are, not because of the situation they are in. This has been termed the fundamental attribution error.

THE FUNDAMENTAL ATTRIBUTION ERROR: PEOPLE AS PERSONALITY PSYCHOLOGISTS

In the early morning of August 31, 1997, Diana, Princess of Wales, died in a car accident in Paris. The worldwide reaction was immediate—disbelief, horror, and unmitigated sorrow. Nowhere was the public response stronger than in her own country, Great Britain. Bouquets of flowers were left in memorial at Buckingham Palace and at her home, Kensington Palace—so many flowers that they covered acres of ground. People waited in line for more than 12 hours just so they could pay their respects and share their feelings of loss in special remembrance books. However, most striking was the way in which the British people and the media turned against the royal family. During that week, the royal family had remained in seclusion in Scotland at Balmoral Castle. The British people and the media accused Queen Elizabeth and Prince Charles of being aloof and uncaring about Diana's death, in marked contrast to their own reaction of deep and very public grieving. The major newspapers openly criticized the Queen (an unheard-of event in Britain), running headlines such as, "Where is our Queen?" "Your people are suffering, speak to us, Ma'am" and "Show us you care" (Hoge, 1997).

The British public had made a strong and negative dispositional attribution about the Queen's absence and silence during that week: She was a cold, uncaring woman who had never liked Diana and wasn't as upset by her death as they were. Stung by this criticism and antagonism on the part of the people, the Queen released a statement via her press secretary, saying, "The Royal family have been hurt by suggestions that they are indifferent to the country's sorrow at the tragic death of the Princess of Wales" (Hoge, 1997). Queen Elizabeth then conducted her first-ever, unscheduled television statement to the British people, assuring them that she was grieving too. Why had she remained behind closed doors in Scotland? The Palace offered a situational explanation: "Prince William and Prince Henry [Diana's sons] themselves want to be with their father and grandparents at this time in the quiet haven of Balmoral. As their grandmother, the Queen is helping the Princes to come to terms with their loss" (Hoge, 1997). Thus, the Queen had been absent from London not because she is a remote, aloof individual who didn't care about Diana's death (a dispositional attribution), but because her grieving grandsons needed her and needed to be in a secluded setting, where the media could not intrude (a situational attribution) (Hoge, 1997; Lyall, 1997).

The pervasive, fundamental theory or schema most of us have about human behaviour is that people do what they do because of the kind of people they are, not because of the situation they are in. When thinking this way, we are more like personality psychologists, who see behaviour as stemming from internal dispositions and traits, than social psychologists, who focus on the impact of social situations on behaviour. This bias toward being personality psychologists is so pervasive that social psychologist Lee Ross (1977) termed it the **fundamental attribution error** (Heider, 1958; Jones, 1990; Ross & Nisbett, 1991).

Fundamental attribution error

the tendency to overestimate the extent to which people's behaviour is due to internal, dispositional factors, and to underestimate the role of situational factors

There have been many empirical demonstrations of the tendency to see people's behaviour as a reflection of their dispositions and beliefs, rather than as influenced by the situation (Allison et al., 1993; Miller, Ashton, & Mishal, 1990). In a classic demonstration of this effect, Edward Jones and Victor Harris (1967) asked university students to read a fellow student's essay that either supported or opposed Fidel Castro's rule in Cuba, and then to guess how the author of the essay really felt about Castro (see Figure 4.3). In one condition, the researchers told the students that the author freely chose which position to take in the essay, thereby making it easy to guess how he or she really felt. If the author chose to write in favour of Castro, then clearly he or she must indeed be sympathetic to Castro. In another condition, however, the students learned that the author did not have any choice about which position to take—he or she had been assigned the position as a participant in a debate. Logically, if we know someone could not choose the topic, we should not assume the writer believes what he or she wrote. Yet the participants in this study, and in the dozens of others like it, assumed that the author really believed what he or she wrote, even when they knew he or she could not choose which position to take. As seen in Figure 4.3, people moderated their guesses a little bit—there was not as much difference in people's estimates of the author's attitude in the pro-Castro and anti-Castro conditions—but they still assumed that the content of the essay reflected the author's true feelings.

Why is the tendency to explain behaviour in terms of people's dispositions called the fundamental attribution error? It is not always wrong to make an internal attribution;

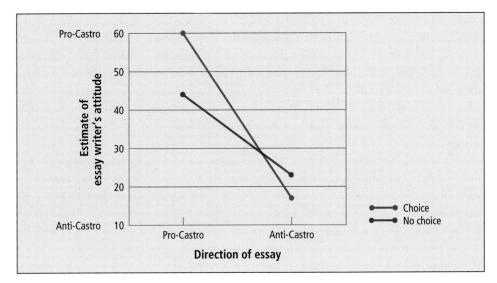

◀ Figure 4.3

THE FUNDAMENTAL
ATTRIBUTION ERROR.

Even when people knew that the
author's choice of an essay topic
was externally caused (i.e., in the
no-choice condition), they
assumed that what he or she
wrote reflected how he or she
really felt about Castro. That is,
they made an internal attribution
for the author's behaviour.

(Adapted from Jones & Harris,
1967)

clearly, people often do what they do because of the kind of people they are. However, there is ample evidence that social situations can have a strong impact on behaviour; indeed, the major lesson of social psychology is that these influences can be extremely powerful. The point of the fundamental attribution error is that people tend to underestimate these influences when explaining other people's behaviour. Even when a situational constraint on behaviour is obvious, as in the Jones and Harris (1967) experiment, people persist in making internal attributions (Lord et al., 1997; Newman, 1996; Ross, 1977; Ross, Amabile, & Steinmetz, 1977; Ross & Nisbett, 1991).

The Role of Perceptual Salience in the Fundamental Attribution Error

Why do people commit the fundamental attribution error? One reason is that when we try to explain someone's behaviour, our focus of attention is usually on the person, not on the surrounding situation (Heider, 1958; Jones & Nisbett, 1972). In fact, as Daniel Gilbert and Patrick Malone (1995) have pointed out, the situational causes of another person's behaviour are practically invisible to us. If we don't know what happened to a person earlier in the day (e.g., she received an *F* on her midterm), we can't use that situational information to help us understand her current behaviour. Even when we know "her situation," we still don't know how she interprets it—for example, the *F* may not have upset her because she's planning to drop the course anyway. If we don't know the meaning of the situation for her, we can't accurately judge its effects on her behaviour. Thus, information about the situational causes of behaviour is frequently unavailable to us or difficult to interpret accurately (Gilbert, 1998b; Gilbert & Malone, 1995).

What information does that leave us? Though the situation may be close to invisible, the individual is extremely perceptually prominent—*people* are what our eyes and ears notice. And as Heider (1958) pointed out, what we notice seems to be the reasonable and logical cause of the observed behaviour.

Several studies have confirmed the importance of perceptual salience—in particular, an elegant one by Shelley Taylor and Susan Fiske (1975). In this study, two male students engaged in a "get acquainted" conversation. (They were actually both accomplices of the experimenters and were following a specific script during their conversation.) At each session, six actual research participants also took part. They sat in assigned seats, surrounding the two conversationalists (see Figure 4.4). Two of them sat on each side of the actors; they had a clear, profile view of both individuals. Two observers sat behind each actor; they could see the back of one actor's head but the face of the other. Thus, who was visually salient—that is, who the participants could see the best—was cleverly manipulated in this study.

After the conversation, the research participants were asked questions about the two men—for example, who had taken the lead in the conversation, and who had chosen the topics to be discussed. As you can see in Figure 4.5, the person whom they could see the best was the person they thought had the most impact on the conversation. Even though all the observers heard the same conversation, those who were facing student *A* thought *he* had taken the lead and chosen the topics, whereas those who were facing student *B* thought *he* had taken the lead and chosen the topics. In comparison, those who could see both students equally well thought both were equally influential. **Perceptual salience**, or our visual point of view, helps explain why the fundamental attribution error is so widespread. We focus our attention more on people than on the surrounding situation because the situation is so hard to see or know; we underestimate (or even forget about) the influence of the situation when we are explaining human behaviour. But this is only part of the story. Why should the simple fact that we are focused on a person make us exaggerate the extent to which that person is the cause of her actions?

The culprit is one of the mental shortcuts we discussed in Chapter 3: *the anchoring and adjustment heuristic.* We saw several examples in which people began with a reference point when making a judgment and then did not adjust sufficiently away from this point. The fundamental attribution error is another byproduct of this shortcut. When making attributions, people use the focus of their attention as a starting point. For example, when we hear someone argue strongly in favour of Castro's regime in Cuba, our first

Perceptual salience

information that is the focus of people's attention; people tend to overestimate the causal role of perceptually salient information

▶ **Figure 4.4**

MANIPULATING PERCEPTUAL SALIENCE.

This is the seating arrangement for two actors and the six research participants in the Taylor and Fiske study. Participants rated each actor's impact on the conversation. Researchers found that people rated the actor they could see most clearly as having the largest role in the conversation.

(Adapted from Taylor and Fiske, 1975)

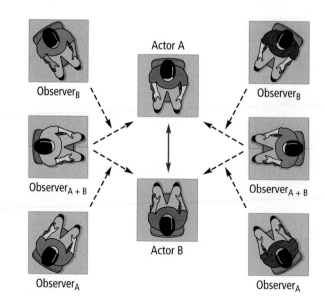

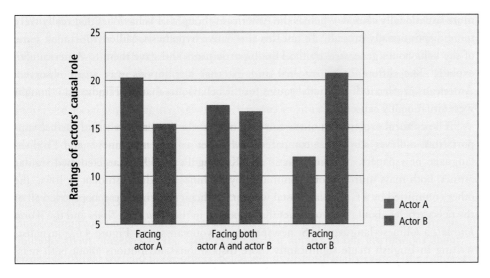

◀ **Figure 4.5**

THE EFFECTS OF PERCEPTUAL
SALIENCE.

These are the ratings of each
actor's causal role in the
conversation. People thought that
the actor they could see the best
had the most impact on the
conversation.

(Adapted from Taylor and Fiske,
1975)

inclination is to explain this in dispositional terms: "This person must hold radical political views." We realize this explanation might not be the whole story, however. We might
think, "On the other hand, I know he was assigned this position as part of a debate," and
adjust our attributions more toward a situational explanation. However, the problem is
that people often don't adjust their judgments enough. In the Jones and Harris (1967)
experiment, participants who knew that the essay writer did not have a choice of topics
nevertheless thought he believed what he had written, at least to some extent. They
adjusted insufficiently from their anchor, the position advocated in the essay.

The Role of Culture in the Fundamental Attribution Error Recent research has
suggested a second reason as to why the fundamental attribution error occurs: Western
culture, which emphasizes individual freedom and autonomy, socializes us to prefer dispositional attributions over situational ones (Dix, 1993; Rholes, Newman, & Ruble, 1990).
In comparison, collectivist (often Eastern) cultures emphasize group membership, interdependence, and conformity to group norms (Fletcher & Ward, 1988; Markus &
Kitayama, 1991; Newman, 1991; Triandis, 1990; Zebrowitz-McArthur, 1988). These cultural values suggest that people would be socialized to prefer situational attributions over
dispositional ones. As a result of this very different socialization, do people in collectivist
cultures make fewer fundamental attribution errors than Westerners do?

To find out, Joan Miller (1984) asked people of two cultures—Hindus living in India
and Americans living in the United States—to think of various examples of behaviours
performed by their friends, and to explain why those behaviours occurred. Consistent
with what we've said so far, the American participants preferred dispositional explanations for the behaviours. They were more likely to say that the causes of their friends'
behaviours were the kinds of people they are, rather than the situation or context in which
the behaviours occurred. In contrast, Hindu participants preferred situational explanations for their friends' behaviours (Miller, 1984).

"But," you might be thinking, "perhaps the Americans and Hindus generated different kinds of examples. Perhaps the Hindus thought of behaviours that really were

▲ People in collectivist
cultures such as China are
more likely to form
situational attributions than
are people in individualistic
cultures such as Canada or
the United States, who are
more likely to form
dispositional attributions.

have none of it. She responds with a strong, internal attribution—the woman herself, not her situation, is the cause of her problems. As you might guess, the actor/observer difference can lead to some striking disagreements between people. Why, at times, do the attributions made by actors and observers diverge so sharply?

Perceptual Salience Revisited One reason for such divergence is our old friend perceptual salience (Jones & Nisbett, 1972). As we said earlier, just as we notice other people's behaviour more than their situation, so too do we notice our own situation more than our own behaviour. None of us is so egotistical or self-centred that we walk through life constantly holding up a full-length mirror in order to observe ourselves. We are looking outward; what is perceptually salient to us is other people, objects, and the events that unfold. We don't (and can't) pay as much attention to ourselves. Thus, when the actor and the observer think about what caused a given behaviour, they are swayed by the information that is most salient and noticeable to them: the actor for the observer, and the situation for the actor (Malle & Knobe, 1997; Nisbett & Ross, 1980; Ross & Nisbett, 1991).

Michael Storms (1973) conducted a fascinating experiment that demonstrates the role of perceptual salience in both the fundamental attribution error and the actor/observer difference. In a design reminiscent of the Taylor and Fiske (1975) study presented earlier, Storms (1973) seated groups of four research participants in a special way (see Figure 4.7). Two of them were going to chat with each other (actor A and actor B), and two of them would observe this conversation, focusing on one of the conversationalists (observer of A and observer of B). In addition, two video cameras were present; one filmed actor A's face, and the other filmed actor B's face.

Following the conversation, the four participants were asked to make attributions about themselves (for actors) or about the actor they were watching (for observers). For example, they were asked to what extent the actor's behaviour was due to personal characteristics or to characteristics of the situation (the topic of conversation, the behaviour of the conversational partner, etc.). Storms (1973) found that the observers attributed more dispositional characteristics to the actor they were watching (demonstrating the

▶ **Figure 4.7**

SEATING ARRANGEMENTS IN THE STORMS STUDY.

People's behaviour was videotaped, so that some of them could view it later from a different perspective.

(Adapted from Storms, 1973)

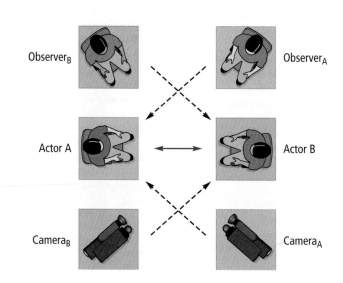

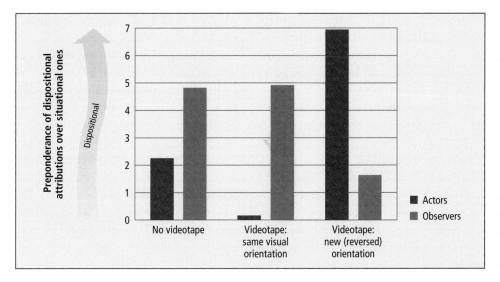

◀ Figure 4.8

EFFECTS OF PERCEPTUAL
SALIENCE (VISUAL ORIENTA-
TION) ON ACTORS' AND
OBSERVERS' ATTRIBUTIONS.

When people got to see their
own or another person's
behaviour from a new orientation
(see right-hand side of figure),
they made attributions very
different from those of people
who did not see the behaviour
from a new orientation (see
middle and left-hand side of
figure).

(Adapted from Storms, 1973)

fundamental attribution error, as in the Taylor & Fiske [1975] study), whereas the actors made more situational attributions about the same behaviour—their own (see the left-hand side of Figure 4.8).

In a creative addition to the study's design, Storms (1973) showed the videotapes to some of the participants before they made their ratings. Some of them saw on tape what they had experienced live—actor A saw a tape of actor B's face, and actor B saw the videotape of actor A's face; observer A saw a tape of actor A, and observer B saw a tape of actor B. When asked to make causal attributions, these participants showed the same actor/observer difference as before, although the actors made even stronger situational attributions about themselves when they had the chance to sit back and observe their situation again (see middle of Figure 4.8).

Another group of participants was placed in the most interesting position of all. After the conversation, they saw a videotape that had the opposite visual orientation to the one they had experienced in real life. Actor A and actor B each saw their own face; observer A saw the videotape of actor B, and observer B saw the tape of actor A. Now the object of perceptual salience was completely reversed. How did these participants assign causality? As can be seen on the right-hand side of Figure 4.8, this change in perceptual salience erased the typical actor/observer difference. After looking at themselves, actors made more dispositional attributions. After looking at their actor's (the conversational partner's) situation, observers made more situational attributions about their actor.

The Role of Information Availability in the Actor/Observer Difference The actor/observer difference occurs for another reason as well. Actors have more information about themselves than observers do (Greenwald & Banaji, 1989; Jones & Nisbett, 1972; Krueger, Ham, & Linford, 1996; Malle & Knobe, 1997). Actors know how they've behaved over the years; they know what happened to them that morning. They are far more aware than observers are of both the similarities and the differences in their behaviour across time and across situations. In Kelley's (1967) terms, actors have far more consistency and distinctiveness information about themselves than observers do. For example, if you are behaving in a quiet, shy fashion at a party, an observer is likely to make a dispositional attribution about you—"Gee, that person is quite an introvert." In fact, you may know that this is not your typical way of responding to a party setting. Perhaps you are shy only at parties where you don't know anyone, or you might be tired, or depressed by some recent bad news. Thus, it is not surprising that actors' self-attributions often reflect situational factors, because they know more about how their behaviour varies from one situation to the next than do most observers, who see them in limited contexts.

The Role of Culture in the Actor/Observer Difference

Is the actor/observer difference affected by culture? The results indicate that this attributional bias bears the imprint of cultural values, just as the fundamental attribution error does.

For example, Incheol Choi and Richard Nisbett (1998) examined the actor/observer difference among American and Korean research participants. These groups did not differ in the attributions they made to themselves—the "actors." They both made situational attributions for their behaviour. They differed only in the attributions they formed about another person, and in a familiar way. Americans were more likely to think that the other person's behaviour was due to his or her disposition (the fundamental attribution error), whereas Koreans were more likely to think that the other person's behaviour was due to the situation.

So far, our discussion of the mental shortcuts people use when making attributions has covered the role of perceptual salience, information availability, and culture. But what about a person's needs, desires, hopes, and fears—do these more emotional factors also create biases in our attributions? Are you motivated to see the world in certain ways because these views make you feel better, about both yourself and life in general? The answer is yes. The shortcuts we will discuss below have a *motivational basis*; they are attributions that protect our self-esteem and our belief that the world is a safe and just place.

SELF-SERVING ATTRIBUTIONS

Imagine that Alison goes to her chemistry class one day with some apprehension because she will find out how she did on the midterm. The professor gives her her exam. Alison turns it over. She sees that she has received an A. What will Alison think is the reason for her great grade? It probably will come as no surprise that people tend to take personal credit for their successes but explain away their failures as due to external events that were beyond their control. Therefore, Alison is likely to think that her success was due to her— she's good at chemistry and just plain smart.

Self-serving attributions
explanations for one's successes that credit internal, dispositional factors and explanations for one's failures that blame external, situational factors

How can we explain this departure from the typical actor/observer pattern? The answer is that when people's self-esteem is threatened, they often make **self-serving attributions**. Simply put, these attributions refer to our tendency to take credit for our successes (by making internal attributions) but to blame others (or the situation) for our failures (Miller & Ross, 1975). Many studies have shown that people make internal attributions when they do well on a task but make external attributions when they do poorly (Davis & Stephan, 1980; Elig & Frieze, 1979; McAllister, 1996; Sedikides et al., 1998; Whitley & Frieze, 1985).

A particularly interesting arena for studying self-serving attributions is professional sports. Consider, for example, a headline that appeared in the Sports section of the July 3,

An interesting area for studying self-serving attributions is sports. We can conjecture about what kinds of attributions were made by the Canadian men's volleyball team after its nine-game losing streak in early 2000. The team is shown here in a match against Mexico.

2000, *Winnipeg Free Press:* "Injured Canadians tagged with ninth straight loss." The article describes yet another loss by Canada's men's volleyball team—this time in Argentina. How did the team explain this loss? One of the players, Jules Martens, offered this comment: "We get here and our major offensive players are injured; it's a different lineup again; it's a patch-work job. . . ." The coach added that "People back at home don't understand the extreme conditions, that you rarely get a call (in a close situation), and in a rally point, that can swing a match." (The coach was referring to a call made by one of the officials that went against Canada.) Thus, both the players and the coach made self-serving attributions—blaming their loss on external factors, rather than on themselves.

Consider now another story in the same Sports section. In the U.S. Senior Open golf tournament, Hale Irwin defeated Bruce Fleisher, who led after the first three rounds. How did Irwin account for his victory? "I did what I wanted to do early on. . . . I let Bruce know I'm there, and put pressure on him."

These examples are consistent with the findings of social psychological research on the attributions made by professional athletes and coaches for why their team won or lost a game. For example, Richard Lau and Dan Russell (1980) found that when explaining their victories, the athletes and coaches overwhelmingly pointed to aspects of their own teams or players; in fact, 80 percent of the attributions for wins were to such internal factors. Losses were more likely to be attributed to things external to one's own team.

Scott Roesch and James Amirkham (1997) wondered if a player's skill, experience, and type of sport (team sports versus solo sports such as tennis) affected the type of attribution he or she made about a sports outcome. The researchers found that less experienced athletes were more likely to make self-serving attributions than were experienced ones. Experienced athletes realize that losses sometimes are their fault and that wins are not always due to them. For example, after losing the 2002 CFL Western final against the Edmonton Eskimos, the Winnipeg Blue Bombers' middle linebacker, Ryland Wickman, said, "I put the blame on my shoulders" (Tait, 2002). The Bombers' all-star defensive tackle, Doug Brown, said, "I was embarrassed with my own performance. . . . It was a horrid performance, individually . . . that was probably the worst game I've ever played" (Tait, 2002). Roesch ad Amirkhan (1997) also found that highly skilled athletes made more self-serving attributions than did those with lower ability. The highly talented athlete believes that success is due to her prowess, while failure, an unusual (and upsetting) outcome, is due to teammates or other circumstances of the game. Finally, athletes in solo sports made more self-serving attributions than did those in team sports. Solo athletes know that winning or losing rests on their shoulders.

As suggested in the Try It! box, it is interesting to examine Sports pages for evidence that teams or players tend to take credit for their successes but blame external factors (e.g., injuries, poor officiating) for their losses.

The self-serving bias has a number of important implications that extend well beyond the world of sports. For example, it leads people to believe that their actions are rational and defensible, but that the actions of others are unreasonable and unjustified. This phenomenon was demonstrated by Sande, Goethals, Ferrari, and Worth (1989), who found that American students attributed positive motives to the U.S. for both positive actions (e.g., saving whales trapped in ice) and negative actions (e.g., building more nuclear-powered submarines). However, these same actions were attributed to negative,

Self-serving Attributions in the Sports Pages

Do athletes and coaches tend to take credit for their wins but make excuses for their losses? Find out for yourself the next time you read the Sports section of the newspaper or watch television interviews after a game. Analyze the sports figures' comments to see what kinds of attributions they make about the cause of their performance. Is the pattern a self-serving one?

For example, after a win, does the athlete make internal attributions, such as, "We won because of excellent teamwork; our defensive line really held today," or "My serve was totally on"? After a loss, does the athlete make external attributions, such as, "All the injuries we've had this season have really hurt us," or "That line judge made every call against me"? According to the research, these self-serving attributions should occur more often than the opposite pattern—for example, where a winner says, "We won because the other team played so badly it was like they were dead" (external), or where a loser says, "I played terribly today. I stank" (internal).

Finally, think about why people make self-serving attributions. For example, if a famous athlete such as Donovan Bailey attributes his team's loss to factors outside himself, do you think he is protecting his self-esteem, trying to look good in front of others, or making the most logical attribution he can given his experience (i.e., he's so talented, most team losses really aren't his fault!)?

self-serving motives if participants were told they had been performed by the former Soviet Union. Apparently one participant remarked that the only reason Soviets would save trapped whales was to slaughter and eat them later; another participant assumed that the whales must have been blocking Soviet shipping lanes! In contrast, Canadian students tended to attribute similar motives to American and Soviet actions.

Self-serving biases also tend to creep in whenever we work on tasks with others (Shestowsky, Wegener, & Fabrigar, 1998; Zanna & Sande, 1987; Sande, Ellard, & Ross, 1986). For example, in a classic study conducted at the University of Waterloo, Ross and Sicoly (1979) found that students working on a group project had very good memories when asked to recall their contributions to the project. However, their memories were considerably poorer when asked to recall the contributions of the other group members. Ross and Sicoly found that this tendency extends even to our closest relationships. In another study, they asked married couples living in student housing at the University of Waterloo to indicate the extent to which each spouse assumed responsibility for 20 different activities (e.g., cooking, deciding how money should be spent, resolving conflicts). Each person tended to overestimate his or her contribution, such that when the husband's and wife's estimates of responsibility were added, the total was greater than 100 percent!

Culture and the Self-serving Bias
Recent research suggests that like the other attributional biases we have discussed, the self-serving bias has a strong cultural component. For example, traditional Chinese culture values modesty and harmony with others. Thus, Chinese students are expected to attribute their successes to other people (such as their parents or teachers) or to other aspects of the situation (such as the quality of their school), rather than to themselves (Bond, 1996; Leung, 1996). Indeed, in several experiments, researchers have found that Chinese participants take less credit for their successes than do American participants (Anderson, 1999; Lee & Seligman, 1997). In Chapter 6, we will discuss related research showing that Asian students tend not to believe success feedback, but readily accept failure feedback, whereas Canadian students show just the opposite tendency.

Defensive Attributions
People also alter their attributions to deal with other kinds of threats to their self-esteem. One of the hardest things to understand in life is the occurrence of tragic events, such as rapes, terminal diseases, and fatal accidents. Even when they happen to strangers we have never met, they can be upsetting. They remind us that if such tragedies can happen to someone else, they can happen to us. Of all the kinds of self-knowledge that we have, the knowledge that we are mortal and that bad things can happen to us is perhaps the hardest to accept (Greenberg, Pyszczynski, & Solomon, 1986; Greening & Chandler, 1997). We thus take steps to deny this fact. One way we do so is by making **defensive attributions**, which are explanations for behaviour that defend us from feelings of vulnerability and mortality.

One form of defensive attribution is **unrealistic optimism**, wherein people believe that good things are *more* likely to happen to them than to others, and bad things are *less* likely to happen to them than to others (Harris, 1996; Heine & Lehman, 1995; Klein, 1996; Regan, Snyder, & Kassin, 1995; Weinstein & Klein, 1996). Suppose we asked you to estimate how likely it is that each of the following will happen to you, compared to how likely it is that they will happen to other students at your college or university—owning your own home, liking your postgraduate job, living past age 80, having a drinking problem, getting

Defensive attributions
explanations for behaviour that avoid feelings of vulnerability and mortality

Unrealistic optimism
a form of defensive attribution wherein people think that good things are more likely to happen to them than to their peers and that bad things are less likely to happen to them than to their peers

divorced, and being unable to have children. When Neil Weinstein (1980) asked students these and similar questions, he found that people were too optimistic. Virtually everyone thought that the good things were more likely to happen to them than to their peers and that the bad things were less likely to happen to them than to their peers.

According to research conducted at the University of Waterloo, unrealistic optimism abounds when it comes to people's romantic relationships. For example, Murray and Holmes (1997) found that both dating and married couples claimed that they were unlikely to encounter the kinds of difficulties and conflicts that affect most relationships. They also believed that should problems arise, they were better equipped to deal with them than the average couple. When forecasting the fate of their relationship, these couples believed that their relationship had a brighter future than most.

MacDonald and Ross (1999) similarly found that University of Waterloo students who were in dating relationships expected that their relationship would last longer than that of the typical first-year student. In an interesting twist, they also asked each participant's parents and dormitory roommates how long they thought the participant's relationship would last. These "outsiders" were less optimistic about the longevity of these relationships than were the students. Who was right? To answer this question, MacDonald and Ross contacted the students again six months later and one year later to see whether their relationships were still intact. It turned out that the participants' parents and roommates were better at predicting how long these relationships would last than the participants were themselves. Why were the forecasts of "outsiders" more accurate than those of the people who were actually involved in these relationships? Apparently, when judging the likelihood of their relationship surviving, the participants tended to focus only on its positive aspects, whereas parents and roommates were more likely to take negative information into account. This more "balanced" approach resulted in more accurate predictions. Thus, if you are in a dating relationship and are wondering whether it will last, your best bet is to ask your friend or your mother!

Recent research conducted at McGill University shows that we are most likely to show this kind of unrealistic optimism when we have decided that we want a relationship to continue and are focusing on achieving that goal (Gagné & Lydon, 2001). In contrast, if we are in the process of assessing the pros and cons of staying in a relationship, we tend to be in a more realistic frame of mind. And this greater realism enables us to make more accurate forecasts about the chances of the relationship surviving.

On a much sadder note, battered women have also been found to be unrealistically optimistic about the personal risks they run when they return to live with their abusive partners. They estimate that their own risk is significantly lower than the risk of most battered women—even when the facts of their situation would suggest otherwise (Martin et al., 2000). Thus, although unrealistic optimism may help us feel better in the short term, in the long term it can be a potentially fatal attribution error.

Unrealistic optimism pervades all aspects of people's lives—not just their romantic involvements. Indeed, recent research has indicated that unrealistic optimism is evident in women's attitudes about getting breast cancer (Clarke et al., 2000), heroin users' attitudes about the risk of overdosing (McGregor et al., 1998), gamblers' attitudes about winning the lottery (Rogers, 1998), and motorcyclists' attitudes about having a serious accident (Rutter, Quine, & Albery, 1998). To give a final example, unrealistic optimism undoubtedly explains what lies behind the popularity of "extreme sports"—athletic activities that take place under very dangerous conditions in which the chance of death is definitely present. How can these athletes take such risks? Wendy Middleton and her colleagues (1996) interviewed British bungee jumpers immediately before they jumped. (To bungee, a person ties a high-strength cord around one ankle, leaps off a very high tower or bridge, free falling, and then bounces at the end of the tether.) The researchers found strong support for unrealistic optimism among the jumpers: Each jumper perceived his or her own risk of injury to be less than that of the typical jumper.

It is important to point out that risk-takers are not impulsive, reckless fools with no regard for danger. In a recent study on risk-taking conducted in Kingston, Ontario, Trimpop, Kerr, and Kirkcaldy (1999) found that among the young men interviewed, at least some planned ahead and carefully prepared for high-risk activities. Ironically, it may be just these "precautions" that fuel unrealistic optimism. As you probably recall, on November 13, 1998, Michel Trudeau was tragically killed by an avalanche while back-country skiing in British Columbia with friends. Reporters later asked his mother and brother whether Michel was a risk-taker. According to one reporter, "They laughed when at the same time Margaret denied Michel was a risk-taker and Justin wholeheartedly agreed that his brother was" (Moore, 2000). The Trudeaus have established a foundation to educate skiers and snowboarders about the dangers of avalanches. They acknowledge, however, that the foundation's message might not have saved Michel's life because he was experienced and was taking precautions the day he was killed.

Culture and Unrealistic Optimism   Recent research suggests that unrealistic optimism may be a Western phenomenon. In a study by Heine and Lehman (1995), students at the University of British Columbia showed classic unrealistic optimism: They assumed that negative events (e.g., contracting AIDS, becoming an alcoholic) were less likely to happen to them than the "average UBC student," and that positive events were more likely to happen to them. However, when students at Nagasaki University in Japan were asked to make the same judgments, the opposite was true: Japanese students believed that bad things were more likely to happen to them, and good things were less likely to happen to them, than to the average student at their university.

Given that Canadians have an independent view of self and Japanese have an interdependent view, Heine and Lehman wondered whether Japanese participants might show unrealistic optimism if they were asked questions that would be more relevant to their self-concept. Thus, the researchers repeated their earlier study, this time adding questions pertaining to interdependence (e.g., "How likely is it that you will do something that will make your family ashamed of you?"). However, once again, Canadian students showed unrealistic optimism and Japanese students showed unrealistic pessimism. In fact, Japanese showed even stronger unrealistic pessimism for interdependent events than for independent events.

BLAMING THE VICTIM: AN UNFORTUNATE BY-PRODUCT OF ATTRIBUTIONAL PROCESSES

Earlier, we discussed people's tendency to make dispositional attributions for the behaviour of other people, even when those behaviours are due to situational factors. This is known as the fundamental attribution error. Sadly, this error can lead to some tragic consequences, including a tendency to blame those who are victimized or stigmatized for their plight. Even if people are made aware of the situational factors responsible for the plight of disadvantaged members of our society (e.g., inadequate nutrition, disrupted family life), they may still see these individuals as responsible for their misfortune.

This tendency was demonstrated in a study by Guimond and Dubé (1989). They found that anglophone students viewed francophones themselves, rather than situational factors, as responsible for their lower economic status in Quebec. Perhaps even more unsettling, these kinds of attributions are prevalent in cases of rape and domestic violence. For example, suppose a female student on your campus was the victim of a date rape by a male fellow student. How do you think you and your friends would react? Would you wonder if she'd done something to trigger the rape? Was she acting suggestively earlier in the evening? Had she invited the man into her room?

Research by Elaine Walster (1966) and others has focused on such attributions (e.g., Burger, 1981; Lerner & Miller, 1978; Stormo, Lang, & Stritzke, 1997). In several experiments, they have found that the victims of crimes or accidents are often seen as causing their fate. For example, people tend to believe that rape victims are to blame for the rape (Bell, Kuriloff, & Lottes, 1994; Burt, 1980; Lambert & Raichle, 2000). A recent study conducted by researchers at the University of Manitoba found that those who believe in rape myths (e.g., "Women falsely report rape to get attention") are especially likely to engage in victim blaming (Morry & Winkler, 2001). This was true for both women and men.

Sadly, such myths can make their way into the courtroom. Consider, for example, the 1998 case of *R. v. Ewanchuk*. The complainant in this case was a 17-year-old woman who was sexually assaulted by a man while he was interviewing her for a job. The man was 45-year-old Steve Ewanchuk, a contractor with a history of convictions for rape and sexual assault. At the time of this incident, he had been court-ordered not to hire any females under the age of 18 to work for him. The young woman testified in the Alberta Court of Queen's Bench that she did not consent to Ewanchuk's advances and, in fact, felt very afraid during the incident. The trial judge, however, held her responsible for not having communicated her fear and ruled that consent had been implied. As a result, Ewanchuk was acquitted. The case then went to the Alberta Court of Appeal. One of the appeal judges commented that Ewanchuk's actions were "far less criminal than hormonal" and suggested that the 17-year-old should have taken actions to stop him by using "a well-chosen expletive, a slap in the face, or, if necessary, a well-directed knee" *(R. v. Ewanchuk,* 1998). Once again, Ewanchuk was acquitted. This decision was finally overturned by the Supreme Court of Canada in 1999, which ruled that there is no such thing as implied consent. One of the Supreme Court judges, Justice L'Heureux-Dubé, wrote, "This case is not about consent, since none was given. It is about myths and stereotyping." These myths include the belief that a woman could resist the attack of a rapist if she really wanted to, that women deserve to be raped because of the way they dress, and so on. Despite the Supreme Court's ruling, concerns remain that women who are the victims of sexual assault will be further victimized by rape myths and victim blaming when they appear in the courtroom (L'Heureux-Dubé, 2001; Tang, 2000).

Similarly, battered wives are often seen as responsible for their abusive husbands' behaviour (Summers & Feldman, 1984). One way in which people justify blaming victims of violence is to assume that the victims must have done something to provoke the attack. Researchers at Carleton University (Kristiansen & Giulietti, 1990) and at Mount Saint Vincent University (Perrott, Miller, & Delaney, 1997) have found that women are especially likely to be blamed for domestic assaults if they are seen as having done something to provoke their partner. For example, Kristiansen and Giulietti (1990) asked participants to read the following scenario:

> Mrs. X explained that, as she was late coming home from work, she was preparing leftovers. Upon hearing this, Mr. X became upset and angry. He argued that, as she has a family to attend to, Mrs. X should ensure that she get home on time.

Some participants received the provocation version of this scenario. For these participants, the scenario went on to read:

> Mrs. X then became upset. She began to yell at Mr. X and as her anger heightened, she began to shout various obscenities at him, calling him a "nagging bastard."

All participants then read the same ending:

> Mrs. X then went into the kitchen to prepare dinner. Mr. X. followed her . . . He grabbed her by the arm and slapped her, knocking her to the floor, and kicked her several times. He subsequently left the house.

In this study, participants who received the provocation excerpt blamed Mrs. X more than did those who did not receive this information.

The research we have been discussing so far has focused on situations in which women have been the victims of violence. Are male victims of violence also blamed? To find out, Perrott and Webber (1996) presented students at Mount Saint Vincent University with scenarios in which a man or a woman was attacked. In some of the scenarios, the victim knew the attacker; in other scenarios he or she did not. The researchers found that there was greater blaming of female victims than of male victims. Moreover, different attributions were made for the assault, depending on the victim's gender. Female victims were blamed for being "too trusting" and for not having anticipated the assault. Male victims, on the other hand, were blamed for not having been able to fight off the attackers. Perrott and Webber found the extent of victim blaming quite disturbing, given that most of their participants were female students attending a university that has a strong women's issues focus.

Finally, another way in which fundamental attribution leads to victim blaming is when we decide that victims could have exercised control over the situation but didn't. In a study conducted at the University of Manitoba, Menec and Perry (1998) constructed descriptions of people with stigmas (e.g., heart disease, AIDS) that varied in degree of controllability. For example, heart disease was attributed to the person's heredity (an uncontrollable factor) in one scenario and to excessive smoking and a high cholesterol diet (controllable factors) in another scenario. When a stigma was seen as uncontrollable, participants felt pity for the person and expressed a willingness to help. However, when a stigma was seen as controllable, participants responded with anger. In a study along the same lines, Rotenberg (1998) found that students at Lakehead University were less accepting of a lonely student if they attributed his or her loneliness to controllable factors. And finally, recent research shows that prejudice against overweight people is greatest in cultures where people are seen as personally responsible for being fat (Crandall et al., 2001). It will come as no surprise that the countries in which this is most likely to happen are ones high in individualism.

Thus, when we combine our tendency to explain other people's behaviour in dispositional terms (i.e., the fundamental attribution error) with our need to see the world as a safe, orderly place, the sad result is that we blame victims for their misfortunes.

Why are we so motivated to explain other people's misfortunes in dispositional terms, rather than to consider the situational factors that could have produced these negative outcomes? According to research on defensive attributions, one way we deal with these unsettling reminders that bad things happen is by explaining them, to make it seem as if they could never happen to us. We do so by believing that bad things happen only to bad people. Melvin Lerner (1980) at the University of Waterloo has called this **belief in a just world**—the assumption that people get what they deserve and deserve what they get. By using this attributional bias, the perceiver does not have to acknowledge that there is a certain randomness in life, that an accident or a criminal or unemployment may be waiting just around the corner for an innocent person. Indeed, in an ingenious set of experiments, Carolyn Hafer (2000a) at Brock University demonstrated that the greater people's belief in a just world was threatened by hearing about an attack on an innocent person, the more likely they were to derogate the victim's character and to distance themselves from the victim. Presumably, by doing so they were able to convince themselves that bad things happen to bad people—and since they themselves are good, surely no misfortune will befall them. More recently, Hafer (2000b, 2002) has identified another reason why we subscribe to just-world beliefs, namely that such beliefs motivate us to invest in our future. We will not be very motivated to plan ahead and make long-term investments if we believe that the world is an unfair, unjust place. For example, in one study (Hafer, 2000b), Brock University students were asked to write an essay about their plans after graduation; other students were asked to write about their current university courses and activities. Later, all students saw a video of a young woman, named Sarah, who was seeing a counsellor because she had recently contracted a sexually transmitted disease. In the "innocent victim" version of the videotape, Sarah said that she and her partner had used a condom, but it had broken during sex. In the non-innocent version, Sarah admitted that no condom had been used. Who was most likely to blame Sarah for contracting the disease, even when she was portrayed as an innocent victim? You guessed it—the students who earlier had been asked to focus on their long-term goals and plans. Presumably, these participants most needed to be reassured that their long-term investments would be rewarded according to principles of fairness and justice. By blaming Sarah for her fate, they were able to maintain this belief.

On a more positive note, you may be less vulnerable to making these kinds of attributions simply because you are taking this course! Guimond and Palmer (1996) studied the attributions of social science and commerce students at an Ontario university over a three-year period. The two groups of students made similar attributions for poverty and

Belief in a just world
a form of defensive attribution wherein people assume that bad things happen to bad people and that good things happen to good people

unemployment in their first year of university. However, by their third year, commerce students were more likely to make dispositional attributions—blaming the poor for their poverty and the unemployed for their unemployment, whereas social science students were more likely to make situational attributions. Similar results were obtained in a subsequent study comparing the attributions of social science and engineering students in a Canadian Armed Forces college (Guimond, 1999).

How Accurate Are Our Attributions and Impressions?

When we make attributions, our goal is to be able to understand other people and predict what they will do. It is obviously to our advantage to make attributions that are as accurate as possible. But how accurate are we? The answer, in a nutshell, is that under many circumstances we are not very accurate, especially compared to how accurate we *think* we are. For example, research has found that first impressions—the quick, attributional snapshots we form when we first meet someone—are not very accurate (DePaulo et al., 1987; Funder & Colvin, 1988). However, our impressions of others do become more accurate the more we get to know them (Wegener & Petty, 1995). For example, at the University of British Columbia, Delroy Paulhus and his colleagues (Paulhus & Bruce, 1992; Paulhus & Reynolds, 1995) had students complete a variety of standard personality questionnaires. They then interacted in groups on a weekly basis for a seven-week period. (Each group consisted of between five and seven students who did not previously know one another.) After weeks 1, 4, and 7, the group members rated one another's personalities. As shown in Figure 4.9, the correlation between students' self-ratings and the group members' ratings of them increased over time, suggesting that people's perceptions of one another were becoming more accurate.

Note that the accuracy of the group members' perceptions was far from perfect (you'll recall from Chapter 2 that a perfect correlation is 1.00), but did increase

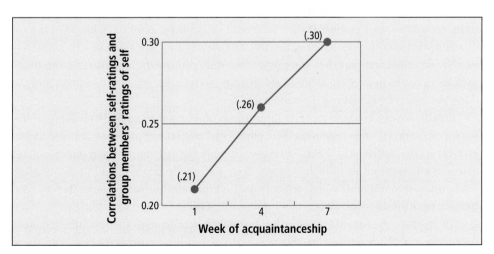

◀ Figure 4.9

ACCURACY OF IMPRESSIONS OF OTHER PEOPLE.

As we get to know people, our impressions of them correspond more closely to how they view themselves. In a study by Paulhus & Bruce (1992), students' impressions of one another became more accurate over time.

significantly with increased acquaintance. The researchers suggest that higher rates of accuracy might be found if comparisons were made between self-ratings and the ratings of close friends or family members. However, subsequent research conducted by Funder and Colvin (1988) found that this was not the case. They obtained a correlation of only .27 between students' ratings of their own personalities and their close friends' impressions of them.

Thus, the evidence suggests that our impressions of others do become more accurate as we get to know them. However, it is also apparent that there is plenty of room for improvement. Sometimes our impressions of other people—even those we know well—are just plain wrong. Why might that be?

The first culprit is our familiar friend, the fundamental attribution error. People are too ready to attribute others' actions to their personalities rather than to the situation. For example, suppose you meet Andrea at a party and she is acting in an outgoing, sociable manner. If you are like most people, you will conclude that Andrea is outgoing and sociable, rather than taking into consideration that you are meeting her in a situation where most people act sociably—a fun party.

We don't mean to imply that people are always wrong when making dispositional attributions, but when they overlook situational causes of another person's behaviour they are likely to end up with faulty impressions.

Another reason our impressions can be wrong concerns our use of schemas. As we have seen, people use implicit personality theories to fill in the gaps in their knowledge about other people and use schemas or theories to decide why other people do what they do. Thus, our impressions are only as accurate as our theories. While many of our theories are likely to be correct, there are some dramatic illustrations of how they can lead us astray.

For example, consider what happened to David Rosenhan (1973). He and several other researchers went to the admissions departments of local mental hospitals and pretended they had been hearing voices. All were admitted to the hospitals, most with the diagnosis of schizophrenia. Despite the fact that from then on they all behaved in a perfectly normal manner, the psychiatric staff continued to treat them as if they were mentally ill. Not one of the researchers was identified as a fake by the staff, and all were kept in the hospitals for several days. (One person had to spend more than seven weeks in the hospital before being released.) Interestingly, the staff interpreted behaviour that was perfectly normal as confirmation of their schema. For example, all of the fake patients kept diaries during their hospitalization, and the staff viewed this "engaging in writing behaviour" as an indication that they were psychologically disturbed. (Interestingly, the "real" patients in the hospital were more likely than the staff to discern that Rosenhan and the other researchers were faking their mental illness.)

Finally, we can create inaccurate impressions of others through self-fulfilling prophecies. For example, suppose you run into your social psychology professor at the mall and give her a curt, unfriendly "hello," because, after all, she is a stern person who wouldn't give you an extension on your last paper. Your unfriendly greeting will probably cause your professor to respond in a less friendly manner than she normally would, thereby confirming your (in this case, inaccurate) impression of her.

To improve the accuracy of your impressions, remember that the fundamental attribution error, implicit personality theories, and self-fulfilling prophecies exist, and try to counteract these biases. Before deciding that another person is shy, for example, ask your-self whether the situation that he or she is in might account for the seeming shyness. Even if a person actually is shy, try to resist the tendency to draw inferences about the other per-son's qualities based on your implicit personality theories. For example, University of British Columbia researchers Paulhus and Morgan (1997) found that if someone was shy, people also tended to assume that the person was unintelligent—an assumption that sim-ply was not true.

Let's cut to the chase. Yes, we are quite accurate perceivers of other people. We do very well most of the time. We are adept at reading and interpreting nonverbal forms of communication; in fact, most of us are actually better at this than we realize. We become more accurate at perceiving others as we get to know them better, and since most of our truly important social interactions involve people we know well, this is good news. In short, we are capable of making both blindingly accurate assessments of people and hor-rific attributional mistakes—it's up to you to determine the difference in your life.

SUMMARY

Social perception is the study of how people form impres-sions and make inferences about other people. People constantly form such impressions because doing so helps them understand and predict their social worlds.

One source of information people use is the nonver-bal behaviour of others. **Nonverbal communication** is used to **encode** or express emotion, convey attitudes, com-municate personality traits, and facilitate and regulate verbal speech. Many studies show that people can accu-rately decode subtle nonverbal cues, although there is debate surrounding the claim that six basic facial expres-sions of emotion are perceived accurately around the world. One reason that perception of emotion can be inac-curate is that the context in which a face is perceived can influence the emotion attributed to it. Also, sometimes facial expressions are **affect blends**, in which one part of the face registers one emotion and another part of the face registers another. In addition, facial expressions vary according to culturally determined **display rules**. These rules dictate which expressions are appropriate to display. **Emblems**—nonverbal gestures that have specific mean-ings—are also culturally determined.

Often it is difficult to tell how someone feels, or what kind of person he or she is, solely from his or her nonver-bal behaviour. As a result, we go beyond the information given in people's behaviour, making inferences about their feelings, traits, and motives. One way we do this is

to rely on an **implicit personality theory** to fill in the blanks. Such a theory is composed of our general notions about which personality traits go together in one person. Although the use of implicit personality theories allows us to form impressions of others efficiently, there can be some serious consequences when, for example, people decide that because a potential sexual partner is likeable, he or she must not have AIDS.

According to **attribution theory**, we try to determine why people do what they do, in order to uncover the feel-ings and traits that are behind their actions. The **covaria-tion model**, a theory of attribution, focuses on observations of behaviour across time, place, different actors, and dif-ferent targets of the behaviour, and examines how the per-ceiver chooses either an **internal** or an **external attribution**. We make such choices by using **consensus, distinctiveness**, and **consistency** information.

People also use various mental shortcuts when mak-ing attributions, including schemas and theories. One common shortcut is the **fundamental attribution error**, which is the tendency to overestimate the extent to which people do what they do because of internal, dispositional factors. A reason for this error is that a person's behaviour often has greater **perceptual salience** than the surround-ing situation. The initial, automatic attribution about another person's behaviour tends to be dispositional, but it can be corrected at the second step with conscious and effortful thinking, bringing to mind possible situational explanations. Culture also plays a role: People from Western cultures are more likely to engage in the fundamental attribution error than are people from Eastern cultures. The **actor/observer difference** is a qualification of the fundamental attribution error: We are more likely to commit this error when explaining other people's behaviour than when explaining our own behaviour. The actor/observer effect occurs because perceptual saliency and information availability differ for the actor and the observer.

People's attributions are also influenced by their personal needs. **Self-serving attributions** occur when people make internal attributions for their successes and external attributions for their failures. **Defensive attributions** help people avoid feelings of mortality. One type of defensive attribution is **unrealistic optimism** about the future,

whereby we think that good things are more likely to happen to us than to other people, and that bad things are less likely to happen to us than to others. Another type of defensive attribution is the **belief in a just world**, whereby we believe that bad things happen to bad people and good things happen to good people. The combination of the fundamental attribution error and defensive attributions can result in tragic consequences, such as blaming victims for their victimization and denying them the help they need.

Not surprisingly, the more we get to know someone, the more accurate we are. Even when judging people we know well, however, the shortcuts we use sometimes lead to mistaken impressions. In addition, the way we treat people can cause them to behave the way in which we expect them to (the self-fulfilling prophecy).

IF YOU ARE INTERESTED

Dorris, Michael. *A yellow raft in blue water.* New York: Warner Books, 1988. Three generations of women—a daughter, a mother, and a grandmother—tell the stories of their lives on a Native American reservation, and in the telling, indicate how they have both understood and misunderstood each other.

Fiske, S. T., & Taylor, S. E. (1991). *Social cognition* (2nd ed.). New York: McGraw-Hill. An encyclopedic review of the literature on social perception by two experts in the field.

Guterson, D. (1995). *Snow falling on cedars.* Both accurate and inaccurate attributions abound in this murder mystery and courtroom drama set in a small community haunted by the exile of its Japanese-American residents in internment camps during the Second World War. It is also a major motion picture.

Jones, E. E. (1990). *Interpersonal perception.* New York: Freeman. A review of social perception (with an emphasis on attribution theory) by one of the pioneers in the field.

Kunda, Z. (1999). *Social cognition.* Cambridge, MA: MIT Press. A comprehensive, up-to-date summary and analysis of social cognitive theory and research written by a prominent expert in the field from the University of Waterloo. This book was written with an undergraduate audience in mind. It is clear, readable, and infused with everyday examples to illustrate social cognitive concepts.

Kurosawa, Akira (Director). (1951). *Rashomon* [Film]. A classic film set in medieval Japan, and winner of the Academy Award for Best Foreign Film. A violent murder and rape occurs. In an exploration of truth, lies, and attributions, four people tell their own, very different versions of what happened.

McArthur, L. Z. (1990). *Social perception.* Pacific Grove, CA: Brooks/Cole. A general review of social perception and impression formation.

Ross, L., & Nisbett, R. E. (1991). *The person and the situation: Perspectives of social psychology.* New York: McGraw-Hill. A lively, in-depth discussion of many of the aspects of social perception we have discussed, such as the fundamental attribution error.

Ross, M., & Miller, D. T. (Eds). (2002) *The justice motive in everyday life.* Cambridge, UK: Cambridge University Press. This collection of works on justice motive is dedicated to the founder of the study of just-world beliefs, Melvin Lerner, Professor Emeritus, University of Waterloo. In addition to a chapter by Lerner, this volume contains contributions from an international cast of prominent scholars, including several Canadian social psychologists. The editors, Michael Ross of the University of Waterloo and Dale Miller of Princeton University, provide an instructive overview in their introductory chapter.

Topics covered include theoretical perspectives on the justice motive, victim derogation and the belief in a just world, and the justice motive and prosocial behaviour, to name a few. This state-of-the-art collection is a must-read for anyone interested in the justice motive.

WEBLINKS

www.as.wvu.edu/~sbb/comm221/chapters/attrib.htm

Attribution Theory

Attribution theory is thoroughly reviewed and discussed in the chapter provided at this site.

www3.usal.es/~nonverbal/introduction.htm

Nonverbal Behavior and Nonverbal Communications Links

Another site for nonverbal research. In addition to several links, pictures of current and past nonverbal researchers are provided.

CHAPTER 5

Self-Knowledge
how we come to understand ourselves

There is one thing, and only one in the whole universe which we know more about than we could learn from external observation. That one thing is [ourselves]. We have, so to speak, inside information; we are in the know.

—C. S. Lewis, 1960

We are unknown, we knowers, ourselves to ourselves; this has its own good reason. We have never searched for ourselves—how should it then come to pass, that we should ever find ourselves?

—Friedrich Nietzsche, 1918

STOP FOR A MOMENT AND THINK ABOUT HOW YOU FEEL RIGHT NOW. Are you happy or sad? Tired or energetic? Calm or irritated? Questions like these are usually pretty easy to answer; as C. S. Lewis says, we are "in the know" about ourselves. Few of us, however, would claim to know ourselves perfectly. Sometimes our thoughts and feelings are a confused jumble of contradictory reactions. And even if we know how we feel, it is not always clear why we feel that way. A lot about ourselves is inscrutable and difficult to determine, as Nietzsche implies.

How do we gain self-knowledge? According to social psychologists, it is not a simple matter of looking inward. Because it is often difficult to know exactly how we feel or why we are doing what we are doing, we look outward to the social environment for clues. This is why self-knowledge is a key social psychological topic: Our views of ourselves are shaped by the world around us. We learn a great deal by observing how people treat us and how we treat others.

Let's turn this question around for a moment. Not only do other people influence our self-views; *we* influence *their* self-views. The way in which we do so can have important consequences. Suppose, for example, that you are an elementary school teacher and want your students to develop a love of reading. In this case, you are deliberately trying to influence how your students view themselves—you want them to look in the mirror and see someone who loves books. How might you go about accomplishing this? If you are like many teachers and educators, you might arrive at the following solution: reward the kids for reading. Maybe that will get them to love books.

Teachers have always rewarded kids with a smile or a pat on the head, of course, but recently they have used more powerful incentives. In Canada, Pizza Hut Corp. has developed a five-month program called BOOK IT! which offers children a certificate for a free pizza when they meet their monthly reading goals. Teachers are instructed to "Present the certificate to the student as soon as he or she meets the reading goal. *This immediate reinforcement benefits the child.*" And that's not all. Each time children redeem a pizza certificate, they are showered with even more rewards—the restaurant manager and staff promise to lavish praise on them and present them with BOOK IT! buttons and stickers. There are even more incentives to encourage reading. Teachers are provided with Honour Roll Diplomas to be awarded to children who meet their reading goals each month. And, as if that's not enough, Pizza Hut will throw a party for classes in which 100 percent of the students meet their reading goals in at least four of the five months of the BOOK IT! program.

BOOK IT! is one of many programs that try to get children to read more by rewarding them. Do such rewards influence a child's self-concept? Do they increase or decrease a child's love of reading?

▶ Many programs try to get children to read more by rewarding them. Do such rewards influence a child's self-concept? Do they increase or decrease a child's love of reading?

Supporters of programs such as these argue that kids are better off reading than watching television or playing video games, and that whatever it takes to get them to read is well worth it. There is no doubt that rewards are powerful motivators and that pizzas and stickers will get kids to read more. One of the oldest and most fundamental psychological principles is that behaviour followed by rewards will increase in frequency. Whether it be a rat pressing a bar to obtain a food pellet or a child reading to get a free pizza, rewards can change behaviour.

But people are not rats, and we have to consider the effects of rewards on what's inside—people's thoughts about themselves, their self-concepts, their motivation to read in the future. The danger of reward programs such as BOOK IT! is that the kids will begin to think they are reading to earn the rewards, not because they find reading to be an enjoyable activity in its own right. Well-intentioned efforts to reward children might actually reduce their enjoyment of the activity by encouraging them to think they are doing it for the pizzas. When the reward program ends and the pizzas, praise, buttons, and stickers are no longer forthcoming, children may actually read less than they did before. In this chapter on the self and self-knowledge, we will see why.

The Nature of the Self

Who are you? How did you come to be this person you call "myself"? One of the founders of psychology, William James (1842–1910), described the basic duality of our perception of self. First, the self is composed of our thoughts and beliefs about ourselves, or what James (1890) called the "known," or, more simply, the "me." Second, the self is also the active processor of information, the "knower," or the "I." In modern terms, we refer to the known aspect of the self as the **self-concept**, which is the contents of the self (our

Self-concept

the contents of the self; that is, our knowledge about who we are knowledge about who we are) and to the knower aspect as **self-awareness**, which is the act of thinking about ourselves. These two aspects of the self combine to create a coherent sense of identity. Your self is both a book (full of fascinating contents collected over time) and the reader of that book (who at any moment can access a specific chapter or add a new one). In this chapter we will focus on these aspects of the self—the nature of the self-concept and how we come to know ourselves through self-awareness. In the next chapter, we will focus on self-esteem—whether we evaluate our self positively or negatively.

A good place to begin is with the question of whether we are the only species with a sense of self. Some fascinating studies by Gordon Gallup (1977, 1993, 1994; Gallup & Suarez, 1986) suggest that we are not alone in this regard. Gallup placed a mirror in an animal's cage until the animal became familiar with it. The animal was then briefly anesthetized and an odourless red dye was painted on its brow or ear (the "rouge test"). What happens when the animal wakes up and looks in the mirror? Chimpanzees and orangutans immediately touch the area of their heads that contains the red spot. Gorillas and many species of monkeys, on the other hand, do not seem to recognize that the image in the mirror is them. They rarely touch the red spot and, unlike chimps and orangutans, are no more likely to touch it when the mirror is present than when the mirror is absent. These studies indicate that chimps and orangutans have a rudimentary self-concept. They realize that the image in the mirror is them and not another ape, and recognize that they look different from the way they looked before (Gallup, 1997; Povinelli, 1993, 1994; Sedikides & Skowronski, 1997).

What about humans? When we are toddlers we seem to have a similar, rudimentary self-concept. Researchers have used a variation of the rouge test with humans and found that self-recognition develops at around two years of age (Povinelli, Landau, & Perilloux, 1996). Lewis and Brooks (1978), for example, found that 75 percent of 21- to 25-month-old infants touched their rouged noses, while only 25 percent of the 9- to 12-month-old infants did so.

As we grow older, this self-concept, of course, becomes more complex. Psychologists have studied how people's self-concept changes from childhood to adulthood, by asking people of different ages to answer the simple question "Who am I?" Typically, a child's self-concept is concrete, with references to clear-cut, easily observable characteristics such as age, sex, neighbourhood, and hobbies. In a study by Montemayor and Eisen (1977), for example, a nine-year-old answered the "Who am I?" question this way: "I have brown eyes. I have brown hair. I have brown eyebrows. . . . I'm a boy. I have an uncle that is almost seven feet tall." As we mature, we place less emphasis on physical characteristics and more emphasis on our psychological states (e.g., our thoughts and feelings), our traits or characteristics, and considerations of how other people judge us (Hart & Damon, 1986; Montemayor & Eisen, 1977; Sande, Goethals, & Radloff, 1988). Thus, we might define ourselves as an extrovert, a cautious person, a spiritual person, an only child, a worrier, someone who is not very interested in politics, and so on.

Research conducted by Jennifer Campbell at the University of British Columbia suggests that some of us may have a clearer sense of self than others. Self-concept clarity is defined as the extent to which knowledge about the self is clearly or consistently defined (Campbell, 1990). Campbell and her colleagues have found that the extent to which one's knowledge of one's self is stable, and clearly and consistently defined, has important

Self-awareness
the act of thinking about ourselves

▼ Research by Gordon Gallup (1977) has found that some apes (chimpanzees and orangutans) have a sense of self, whereas other mammals do not.

cognitive and emotional implications (Campbell & Fehr, 1990; Campbell, Assanand, & Di Paula, 2000).

For example, Campbell and colleagues (1996) found that people who were low in self-concept clarity were more likely to be neurotic and have low self-esteem, and were less likely to be aware of their internal states. They also tended to engage in chronic self-analysis and rumination—an involuntary, negative form of self-focus associated with threat or uncertainty (e.g., "Sometimes it's hard for me to shut off thoughts about myself"). People low in self-concept clarity also were less likely to engage in positive forms of self-focus such as reflection (e.g., "I love exploring my 'inner self'"). (We will discuss rumination and reflection in greater detail later in this chapter.) Thus, not having a clear, confident sense of who you are can have negative effects on your thoughts and emotions. To find out where you stand in terms of self-concept clarity, see the Try It! box on page 143.

THE FUNCTION OF THE SELF

Why do human adults have a multifaceted, complex definition of self? Researchers have pointed to three important functions served by the self (Baumeister, 1998; Cross & Madson, 1997; Higgins, 1996; Mischel, Cantor, & Feldman, 1996; Sedikides & Skowronski, 1997). First, the self has an *organizational function*, acting as an extremely important schema that helps us interpret and recall information about ourselves and the social world (Dunning & Hayes, 1996; Kihlstrom & Klein, 1994; Markus, 1977; Markus, Smith, & Moreland, 1985; Symons & Johnson, 1997). As discussed in Chapter 3, a schema is a mental structure people use to organize their knowledge about the social world around themes or subjects. As we will discuss later in this chapter, one of our most important schemas is the self-concept; the information we notice, think about, and remember is organized around our view of ourselves.

Second, the self has an *emotional function*, helping to determine our emotional responses (Higgins, 1987; Markus & Nurius, 1986; Pelham, 1991). For example, as we have already seen, people with self-concept clarity are less likely to experience negative emotions (Campbell, 1990; Campbell et al., 1996; Campbell, Assanand, & DiPaula, 2000). In addition, as will be seen later, we experience emotions such as anxiety or depression when we compare our sense of self with the self we want to be (our ideal self) or the self we feel we should be (our ought self; Higgins, 1987).

Third, the self serves an *executive function* that regulates our behaviour, makes choices, and plans for the future, much like the chief executive officer of a corporation. We appear to be the only species that can imagine events that have not yet occurred and engage in long-term planning, and it is the self that does this planning and exerts control over our actions. Regulating our behaviour and choices in optimal ways, of course, can be easier said than done, as anyone who has been on a diet or tried to quit smoking knows. Fascinating new research conducted by Roy Baumeister, Mark Muraven, and Dianne Tice suggests that the self is like a muscle, and success at self-control depends on how tired that muscle is or how much it has been strengthened through exercise (Baumeister, Muraven, & Tice, 2000; Muraven & Baumeister, 2000; Muraven, Tice, & Baumeister, 1998). The idea is that the self has a limited amount of energy to spend on self-control and that spending it on one task limits the amount that can be spent on another task, just as going for a 10-kilometre run makes it difficult to play tennis.

A Measure of Self-Concept Clarity

		strongly disagree				strongly agree
1. My beliefs about myself often conflict with one another.*		1	2	3	4	5
2. One day I might have one opinion of myself and on another day I might have a different opinion.*		1	2	3	4	5
3. I spend a lot of time wondering about what kind of person I really am.*		1	2	3	4	5
4. Sometimes I feel that I am not really the person that I appear to be.*		1	2	3	4	5
5. When I think about the kind of person I have been in the past, I'm not sure what I was really like.*		1	2	3	4	5
6. I seldom experience conflict between the different aspects of my personality.		1	2	3	4	5
7. Sometimes I think I know other people better than I know myself.*		1	2	3	4	5
8. My beliefs about myself seem to change very frequently.*		1	2	3	4	5
9. If I were asked to describe my personality, my description might end up being different from one day to another day.*		1	2	3	4	5
10. Even if I wanted to, I don't think I could tell someone what I'm really like.*		1	2	3	4	5
11. In general, I have a clear sense of who I am and what I am.		1	2	3	4	5
12. It is often hard for me to make up my mind about things because I don't really know what I want.*		1	2	3	4	5

Note: This is the Self-Concept Clarity Scale developed by Campbell, Trapnell, Heine, Katz, Lavallee, & Lehman (1996) to measure the extent to which people have a stable, clear, and consistently defined sense of self. The items with asterisks (*) are reverse-scored. Thus, to find out how you score on this scale, first reverse your answers to the items with asterisks. If you answered "5," change it to a "1"; if you answered "4," change it to a "2," and so on. Then add your ratings on all 12 questions. The higher your score, the more clearly defined your sense of self is. Among Canadian students, average scores on this scale range from 38 to 43. In a study comparing UBC students with students from Japan (where it was expected that self-concepts would be less clearly defined), the average was 40 for UBC students and 35 for Japanese students.

Source: Adapted from Campbell, J. D., Trapnell, P. D., Heine, S. J., Katz, I. M., Lavallee, L. F., & Lehman, D. R. (1996). Self-concept clarity: Measurement, personality correlates, and cultural boundaries. *Journal of Personality and Social Psychology*, 70, 141–156. Copyright 1996 by the American Psychological Association. Reprinted with permission.

Baumeister and colleagues have demonstrated this point in a number of studies in which people are asked to exert self-control on one task to see if this reduces their ability to exert self-control on a subsequent, completely unrelated, task. For example, they have asked participants to try not to show emotions while watching a sad movie or to resist delicious cookies while hungry. These participants show less self-control on a subsequent task (e.g., trying not to laugh during a comedy) compared to those who have not already performed a self-control task. These findings explain why people often fail at attempts at self-control when they are under stress; for example, former smokers are more likely to take up smoking again when they are under stress. Dealing with stress depletes the "self resource," such that there is less to spend in other areas. Similarly, efforts at self-control are more likely to fail at night when our self-resources have been depleted by a day of making choices and resisting temptations; dieters are more likely to break their diets at night, and bulimics are more likely to engage in binge eating at night (Baumeister, Muraven, & Tice, 2000). People are best at self-control when they are well rested and under minimal stress.

The good news is that self-control, just like our muscles, can be strengthened through exercise. The idea is that in the short run, depleting the self resource makes it more difficult to engage in self-control, just as going for a long run tires the muscles and makes it more difficult to do other physical activities. Long-term exercise, however, strengthens the muscles, increasing endurance on physical tasks. And the same seems to be true for self-control. For example, alcoholics who succeed at stopping drinking are better than average at quitting smoking. And Muraven, Baumeister, and Tice (1999) found that students who were instructed to improve their posture for two weeks subsequently showed greater stamina on an unrelated task (squeezing a handgrip), compared to those who did not "exercise" their self-control.

Thus, the self serves a number of basic adaptive functions (organizational, emotional, executive). This does not mean, however, that people define themselves in exactly the same way. As we will now see, the way in which people define themselves can vary a lot, even though these different self-concepts serve the same functions.

CULTURAL DIFFERENCES IN THE DEFINITION OF SELF

In June 1993, Masako Owada, a 29-year-old Japanese woman, married Crown Prince Naruhito of Japan. Masako was a very bright career diplomat in the foreign ministry, educated at Harvard and Oxford. She spoke five languages and was on the fast track to a prestigious diplomatic career. Her decision to marry the prince surprised some observers, because it meant she would have to give up her career. Indeed, she gave up any semblance of an independent life, becoming subservient to the prince and the rest of the royal family and spending much of her time participating in rigid royal ceremonies. Her primary role was to produce a male heir to the royal throne.

Independent view of the self

defining oneself in terms of one's own internal thoughts, feelings, and actions, and not in terms of the thoughts, feelings, and actions of other people

How do you feel about Masako's decision to marry the prince? Your answer may say something about the nature of your self-concept and the culture in which you grew up. As mentioned in Chapter 4, in many Western cultures, people have an **independent view of the self**, which is a way of defining oneself in terms of one's own internal thoughts, feelings, and actions, and not in terms of the thoughts, feelings, and actions of others (Cross, 1995; Heine et al., 1999; Kitayama & Markus, 1994; Markus & Kitayama, 1991; Markus, Kitayama, & Heiman, 1996; Tafarodi & Swann, 1996; Triandis, 1989, 1995). Westerners learn to define themselves as quite separate from other people and to value independence and uniqueness. Consequently, many Western observers were mystified by Masako's decision to marry the crown prince. They assumed she was coerced into the marriage by a backwards, sexist society that did not properly value her worth as an individual with an independent life of her own.

Interdependent view of the self

defining oneself in terms of one's relationships to other people; recognizing that one's behaviour is often determined by the thoughts, feelings, and actions of others

In contrast, many Asian and other non-Western cultures have an **interdependent view of the self**, which is a way of defining oneself in terms of one's relationships to other people and recognizing that one's behaviour is often determined by the thoughts, feelings, and actions of others. Connectedness and interdependence between people is valued, whereas independence and uniqueness are frowned upon. For example, when asked to complete sentences beginning with "I am . . . ," people from Asian cultures are more likely to refer to social groups, such as one's family or religious group, than are people from Western cultures (Bochner, 1994; Triandis, 1989). To many Japanese and other Asians, Masako's decision to give up her career was not at all surprising, and was a positive, natural consequence of her view of herself as connected and obligated to others, such as her family and the royal family. What is viewed as positive and normal behaviour by one culture might be viewed very differently by another.

We do not mean to imply that every member of a Western culture has an independent view of the self and that every member of an Asian culture has an interdependent view of the self. Within cultures there are differences in the self-concept, and these differences are likely to increase as contact between cultures increases. It is interesting to note, for example, that Masako's decision to marry the prince was unpopular among at least some young Japanese women, who felt that her choice was not a positive sign of interdependence but a betrayal to the feminist cause in Japan (Sanger, 1993). Nonetheless, the differences between the Western and Eastern sense of self is real and has interesting consequences for communication between the cultures. Indeed, the differences in the sense of self are so fundamental that it is difficult for people with independent selves to appreciate what it is like to have an interdependent self, and vice versa. Western readers might find it difficult to appreciate the Asian sense of interdependence; similarly, many Japanese find it difficult to comprehend that North Americans could possibly know who they are, separate from the social groups to which they belong.

Consider again Jennifer Campbell's notion of self-concept clarity. It might already have occurred to you that self-concept clarity is probably a Western phenomenon, given that it is based on a premise that the self is a stable configuration of internal traits that govern behaviour across situations. One might expect, therefore, that the sense of self would be less clear in cultures in which the self is perceived as interdependent. To see whether this is the case, Campbell and her colleagues (1996) administered the Self-Concept Clarity Scale to Canadian and Japanese students. Japanese participants did, in fact, have lower self-concept clarity than Canadians. Moreover, self-concept clarity was not as strongly linked to self-esteem for the Japanese as it was for the Canadians (Campbell et al., 1996).

GENDER DIFFERENCES IN THE DEFINITION OF SELF

There is a stereotype that when women get together, they talk about interpersonal problems and relationships, whereas men talk about sports or politics—anything but their feelings. Research suggests that there is some truth to the stereotype (Fehr, 1996) and that it reflects a difference in women's and men's self-concept (Baumeister & Sommer, 1997; Cross, Bacon, & Morris, 2000; Cross & Madson, 1997; Gabriel & Gardner, 1999). Susan Cross and Laura Madson (1997) point out that starting in early childhood, girls are more likely to develop intimate friendships, cooperate with others, and focus their attention on social relationships. Boys are more likely to engage in competitive activities and focus on dominance over others (Maccoby, 1990). These differences persist into adulthood, such that men in North America are more likely to have an independent view of self, whereas women define themselves more in relation to other people. In other words, women have more *relational* interdependence (Brewer & Gardner, 1996). To see how much your

▲ People had very different reactions to Masako Owada's decision to give up her promising career to marry Crown Prince Naruhito of Japan, due in part to cultural differences in the importance of independence versus interdependence.

self-concept is based on a sense of relational interdependence, answer the questions in the Try It! exercise, below.

Research on the self conducted by a team consisting of David Watkins (University of Hong Kong), John Adair (University of Manitoba), and researchers from many other countries confirms this gender difference—at least in individualist cultures (Watkins, Adair, et al., 1998; Watkins, Akande, et al., 1998). These researchers have examined differences in self-concept by administering the sentence completion test ("I am . . .") to thousands of participants in as many as 15 different cultures. In these studies, gender differences in self-concepts typically are found only among individualist cultures (e.g., Canada, white South Africa, New Zealand). Specifically, the self-concepts of men are more likely to be independent (e.g., "I am honest"; "I am intelligent"), whereas the self-concepts of women are more likely to be relational/collectivist (e.g., "I am a mother";

A Measure of Relational Interdependence

Instructions: Indicate the extent to which you agree or disagree with each of these statements.

		strongly disagree						strongly agree
1.	My close relationships are an important reflection of who I am.	1	2	3	4	5	6	7
2.	When I feel close to someone, it often feels to me like that person is an important part of who I am.	1	2	3	4	5	6	7
3.	I usually feel a strong sense of pride when someone close to me has an important accomplishment.	1	2	3	4	5	6	7
4.	I think one of the most important parts of who I am can be captured by looking at my close friends and understanding who they are.	1	2	3	4	5	6	7
5.	When I think of myself, I often think of my close friends or family also.	1	2	3	4	5	6	7
6.	If a person hurts someone close to me, I feel personally hurt as well.	1	2	3	4	5	6	7
7.	In general, my close relationships are an important part of my self-image.	1	2	3	4	5	6	7
8.	Overall, my close relationships have very little to do with how I feel about myself.	1	2	3	4	5	6	7
9.	My close relationships are unimportant to my sense of what kind of person I am.	1	2	3	4	5	6	7
10.	My sense of pride comes from knowing who I have as close friends.	1	2	3	4	5	6	7
11.	When I establish a close friendship with someone, I usually develop a strong sense of identification with that person.	1	2	3	4	5	6	7

Note: To compute your score, first reverse the rating you gave to questions 8 and 9. That is, if you circled a 1, change it to a 7; if you circled a 2, change it to a 6; if you circled a 7, change it to a 1; and so on. Then total your answers to the 11 questions. High scores reflect more of a tendency to define yourself in terms of relational interdependence. Cross, Bacon, and Morris (2000) found that women tend to score higher than men; in eight samples of university students, women averaged 57.2 and men averaged 53.4.

Source: Adapted from Cross, Bacon, & Morris (2000).

"I am a sociable person"). In contrast, in collectivist cultures that emphasize interdependence (e.g., China, Ethiopia, black South Africa), women and men are equally likely to hold a relational/collectivist view of the self.

This is not to say that men in individualist cultures are completely lacking in interdependence. Quite the contrary. According to recent research by Cross and Madson, interdependence is part of men's conception of self, but it is not the kind of relational interdependence shown by women. Rather, men tend to define themselves in terms of social groups, such as the sports teams to which they belong (Cross, Bacon, & Morris, 2000; Cross & Madson, 1997). This is known as *collective* interdependence (Gabriel & Gardner, 1999). Shira Gabriel and Wendi Gardner (1999), for example, asked women and men to describe either a positive or a negative emotional event in their lives. Women tended to mention personal relationships, such as becoming engaged or the death of a family member. Men talked about events involving larger groups, such as the time they joined a fraternity or the time their sports team lost an important game (see Figure 5.1).

Research on gender differences is controversial, and we should be clear about what researchers are saying here. First, Cross and Madson (1997) are not arguing that women in North America have the exact same sense of self as women and men in collectivist countries. Second, they acknowledge that men desire intimate relationships as much as women do. Nonetheless there are differences in the kinds of relationships each sex desires and the way in which they manage these relationships. Women focus more on intimacy and cooperation with a small number of close others, whereas men focus more on power and status with a larger number of others (Baumeister & Sommer, 1997; Fehr, 1996; Gabriel & Gardner, 1999). Indeed, more than 20 years of research in personality psychology conducted at the University of British Columbia shows that men tend to define themselves in terms of high-dominance/low-nurturance traits (e.g., assured–dominant),

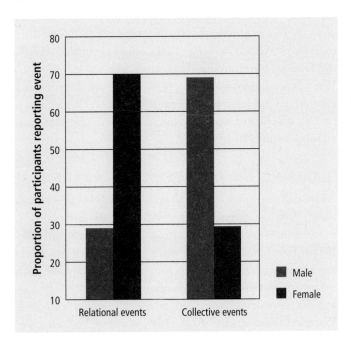

◀ Figure 5.1

GENDER DIFFERENCES IN TYPES OF INTERDEPENDENCE.

Male and female university students were asked to describe an important emotional event in their lives. Women reported more relational events, ones that had to do with close personal relationships. Men reported more collective events, ones that had to do with their membership in larger groups.

(From Gabriel & Gardner, 1999)

whereas women define themselves in terms of low-dominance/high-nurturance traits (e.g., warm–agreeable) (Paulhus, 1987; Wiggins & Holzmuller, 1981; Wiggins, 1979, 1993). This pattern was recently confirmed in a series of studies conducted at the University of Winnipeg (Fehr & Broughton, 2001). Importantly, Fehr and Broughton found that even though men defined themselves in terms of dominance-related traits and women defined themselves in terms of nurturance-related traits, both genders valued intimate relationships characterized by trust, intimacy, respect, and honesty.

The bottom line is that it is important not to overemphasize sex differences. As Kay Deaux and Marianne LaFrance (1998) point out, doing so stresses opposites rather than the vast overlap in the psychological makeup of women and men. Moreover, as recent research is suggesting, even though there may be differences in how men and women in our culture define themselves, both sexes desire and value close, intimate relationships.

To summarize, the self-concept serves basic adaptive functions common to all cultures (e.g., the executive function). There are also interesting differences across cultures and between women and men in how people define themselves. But how do people learn who they are in the first place? How did you discover those things that make you uniquely *you*? For the remainder of this chapter we will discuss how people gain self-knowledge.

Knowing Ourselves through Introspection

Introspection

the process whereby people look inward and examine their own thoughts, feelings, and motives

When we told you we were going to describe the sources of information you use to construct a self-concept, you may have thought, "Good grief! I don't need a social psychology textbook to tell me that! It's not exactly a surprise; I just think about myself. No big deal." In other words, you rely on **introspection**: You look inward and examine the "inside information" that you, and you alone, have about your thoughts, feelings, and motives. And indeed, you do find some answers when you introspect. But there are two interesting things about introspection: First, people do not rely on this source of information as often as you might think—surprisingly, people spend very little time thinking about themselves. According to one study, only 8 percent of thoughts are about the self; most of the time we are thinking about work, chores, and time (Csikszentmihalyi & Figurski, 1982). Second, even when people do introspect, the reasons for their feelings and behaviour can be hidden from conscious awareness (Wilson, in press). In short, self-scrutiny isn't all it's cracked up to be, and if this were our only source of knowledge about ourselves, we would be in trouble.

FOCUSING ON THE SELF: SELF-AWARENESS THEORY

As we just saw, we do not focus on ourselves very often. However, when we are thinking about ourselves, what happens? What are the consequences of turning the spotlight of consciousness on ourselves, instead of focusing our attention on the world around us? Recent research suggests that when we are feeling self-aware (because people are watching us, we are seeing ourselves on videotape, or we are staring at ourselves in a mirror), we tend to assume that we also are more transparent to others—not just to ourselves. In a series of studies conducted at the University of Manitoba and the University of Waterloo, Vorauer and Ross (1999; see also Vorauer, 2001) demonstrated that when people were made to feel self-aware, they tended to assume that another person also would have this heightened access to their traits. This assumption was incorrect, however. Outside observers did not discern the traits of self-aware participants any more accurately than the traits of participants who had not been made self-aware.

In subsequent research, Vorauer and Cameron (in press) predicted that this tendency to assume that others are aware of our inner states should be especially pronounced among people who are high in collectivism. The reason is that collectivists emphasize interdependence and perspective taking, and, importantly, perceive their self as merged with the self of in-group members. And, indeed, these researchers found that participants who were high, rather than low, in collectivism were especially likely to assume that others had access to their inner thoughts and feelings. (Interestingly, participants who were high in collectivism also were more confident that they could judge an in-group member's inner state. In reality, they were no more accurate than those who were low in collectivism.) Thus, when we are focused on our self, we have a tendency to erroneously assume that others also share this awareness—particularly if we are high in collectivism. Nevertheless, as we shall see next, the mere fact that we have focused on our self has some interesting and important effects.

According to **self-awareness theory**, when we focus our attention on ourselves, we evaluate and compare our current behaviour against our internal standards and values (Carver & Scheier, 1981; Duval & Wicklund, 1972; Wicklund, 1975; Wicklund & Frey, 1980). In short, we become self-conscious, in the sense that we become objective, judgmental observers of ourselves. Let's say that you believe it is important for you to be honest with your friends. One day, while conversing with a friend, you lie to him. In the midst of this conversation, you catch sight of yourself in a large mirror. How do you think you will feel?

According to Shelley Duval and Robert Wicklund (1972), seeing yourself will make you aware of the disparity between your behaviour and your moral standards. If you can change your behaviour to match your internal guidelines (e.g., say something particularly nice to your friend or admit that you lied and ask for forgiveness), you will do so. If you feel you can't change your behaviour, then being in a state of self-awareness will be very uncomfortable, for you will be confronted with disagreeable feedback about yourself. In this situation, you will stop being self-aware as quickly as possible (e.g., by turning so that your back is to the mirror or by saying goodbye to your friend and leaving the room). Figure 5.2 illustrates this process—how self-awareness makes us conscious of our internal standards and directs our subsequent behaviour.

This dissatisfaction with ourselves can be painful. Jane Bybee and her colleagues, for example, found that the more people thought about their ideal selves—the kind of person they most wanted to be—the more anxious and angry they felt (Bybee et al., 1997; Higgins, 1987). Sophia Moskalenko and Steven Heine (in press) took this research one step further and showed that if people are able to avoid self-awareness by engaging in a distracting activity such as watching television, they perceive less of a gap between their actual self and their ideal self.

This latter finding suggests that people might intentionally try to distract themselves to alleviate the pain of unpleasant realizations about the self. To see whether that is the case, Moskalenko and Heine (in press) conducted additional research in which some participants were told that they had done very poorly on a task that reflected their level of intelligence. Others were told that they had done well on the task (a control group did not receive any

Self-awareness theory

the idea that when people focus their attention on themselves, they evaluate and compare their behaviour to their internal standards and values

▶ Figure 5.2

SELF-AWARENESS THEORY:
THE CONSEQUENCES OF
SELF-FOCUSED ATTENTION.

When people focus on
themselves, they compare their
behaviour to their internal
standards.

(Adapted from Carver and
Scheier, 1981)

① You come across a self-focusing cue in the environment (eg, a mirror, camera or an audience).

② This cue creates a state of self-awareness... You become aware of and think about yourself...

③ You compare your current thoughts or behaviour to your internal standards or expectations for yourself. Do they match?

4a If NO—uh-oh! What to do? (either)

5a Change your behaviour so it matches your standard for yourself. Feel great!

5b If you can't or won't change your behaviour... Feel terrible! Flee from a state of self-awareness as quickly as possible!

4b If YES... everything's fine!

feedback). The authors reasoned that the participants who were given the failure feedback would be highly motivated to escape self-awareness, and therefore, would be most likely to pay attention to a video that was on in the room. And that is exactly what happened.

Sometimes people go even further in their attempt to escape the self. Roy Baumeister (1991) has pointed out that such diverse activities as alcohol abuse, binge eating, sexual masochism, and suicide have one thing in common: All are effective ways of turning the internal spotlight away from oneself. Getting drunk, for example, is one way of avoiding negative thoughts about oneself (at least temporarily). Suicide, of course, is the ultimate way of ending self-scrutiny. The fact that people regularly engage in such behaviours, despite the risks, is an indication of how aversive self-focus can be (Hull, 1981; Hull & Young, 1983; Hull, Young, & Jouriles, 1986).

We hasten to add that self-awareness does not inevitably have negative effects. Self-focus can also be a way of keeping you out of trouble, by reminding you of your sense of right and wrong. For example, several studies have found that when people are self-aware (e.g., in front of a mirror), they are more likely to follow their moral standards, such as avoiding the temptation to cheat on a test (Beaman et al., 1979; Diener & Wallbom, 1976; Gibbons, 1978). And Baumeister (1991) points out that people also escape self-awareness through more positive means such as religious expression and spirituality.

Whether self-awareness has positive or negative effects also depends on the kind of self-awareness we are experiencing. University of British Columbia researchers Paul

Trapnell and Jennifer Campbell (1999) have differentiated between two kinds of self-awareness: rumination and reflection. Rumination is an involuntary, neurotic form of self-focus associated with threat or uncertainty. Reflection, on the other hand, is an emotionally positive form of self-focus that involves an openness to self-exploration and an intellectual curiosity about the self. To find out whether you are more likely to engage in rumination or reflection, see Try It!, below.

It turns out that whether we engage in reflection versus rumination has important implications for how we deal with negative life events (Wood & Dodgson, 1996; McFarland & Buehler, 1997). For example, Cathy McFarland and Roger Buehler (1998)

 **The Rumination–Reflection Scale**

Reflection

1. I love exploring my "inner self."	1	2	3	4	5
2. I often love to look at my life in philosophical ways.	1	2	3	4	5
3. I love to meditate on the nature and meaning of things.	1	2	3	4	5
4. I don't really care for introspective or self-reflective thinking. (–)	1	2	3	4	5
5. My attitudes and feelings about things fascinate me.	1	2	3	4	5
6. I love analyzing why I do things.	1	2	3	4	5

Rumination

1. I tend to "ruminate" or dwell over things that happen to me for a really long time afterwards.	1	2	3	4	5
2. Often I'm playing back over in my mind how I acted in a past situation.	1	2	3	4	5
3. I always seem to be rehashing in my mind recent things I've said or done.	1	2	3	4	5
4. Long after an argument or disagreement is over with, my thoughts keep going back to what happened.	1	2	3	4	5
5. I don't waste time rethinking things that are over and done with. (–)	1	2	3	4	5
6. I spend a great deal of time thinking back over my embarrassing or disappointing moments.	1	2	3	4	5

The questions are taken from the Reflection–Rumination Questionnaire developed by Trapnell and Campbell (1999). The actual scale has 12 items to measure reflection and 12 items to measure rumination. The reflection scale assesses a positive form of self-focus associated with curiosity about the self and openness to exploring the self. The rumination scale assesses a negative form of self-focus associated with anxiety and obsessive thoughts. Campbell and colleagues (1996) found that people with low self-concept clarity (see Try It! exercise on page 143) are more likely to engage in rumination and less likely to engage in reflection than those with high self-concept clarity.

Source: Adapted from Trapnell, P. D., & Campbell, J. D. (1999). Private self-consciousness and the five-factor model of personality: Distinguishing rumination from reflection. *Journal of Personality and Social Psychology, 76,* 284–304. Copyright 1999 by the American Psychological Association. Reprinted with permission.

put students at Simon Fraser University and at Wilfrid Laurier University in a bad mood by telling them they had performed poorly on a test of social perceptiveness. The researchers predicted that when self-awareness takes the form of reflection, people will be open to exploring their negative feelings and will come up with strategies for alleviating these feelings. Indeed, participants in a reflective state cheered themselves up by remembering positive events in their lives—happy high school memories, recent academic successes, fun times with friends and family, and so on. In contrast, participants who engaged in rumination were not able to cheer themselves up. Instead, they dredged up memories that matched their bad mood—unhappy times in high school, academic failures, and unpleasant interactions with family and friends.

Thus, self-awareness can have negative or positive effects. It depends on the kind of self-awareness we are experiencing (i.e., rumination versus reflection). And in those cases where self-awareness feels aversive, we can alleviate those bad feelings in either a constructive or a destructive manner.

JUDGING WHY WE FEEL THE WAY WE DO: TELLING MORE THAN WE CAN KNOW

Another kind of self-knowledge is more difficult to obtain, even when we are self-aware and introspect to our heart's content: knowing why we feel the way we do. This can be difficult to understand because many of our basic mental processes occur outside of awareness (Kihlstrom, 1987; Mandler, 1975; Neisser, 1976). This is not to say that we are thinkers without a clue—we are aware of the final result of our thought processes (e.g., that we are in love or not in love); however, we are often unaware of the cognitive processing that led to the result. It's as if the magician pulled a rabbit out of a hat: You see the rabbit, but you don't know how it got there. How do we deal with this rabbit problem?

▶ The people on the couch look awfully smug; they must like what they see when they are self-aware.

"Steer clear of that group. They're all terribly self-aware."

Frascino © 1977 The New Yorker Collection. All rights reserved.

Whereas we often don't know why we feel a certain way, it seems we are always able to come up with an explanation. Richard Nisbett and Tim Wilson referred to this phenomenon as "telling more than we know" (Nisbett & Ross, 1980; Nisbett & Wilson, 1977b; Wilson, 1985, 1994, in press; Wilson & Stone, 1985). For example, Wilson, Laser, and Stone (1982) asked university students to keep journals of their daily moods every day for five weeks. The students also kept track of things that might affect their daily moods, such as the weather and how much they had slept the night before. At the end of the five weeks, the students estimated how much their mood was related to these other variables, such as their sleep habits. Wilson and colleagues found that in many cases, people were wrong about what predicted their mood. For example, most people believed that the amount of sleep they got predicted how good a mood they were in the next day, when in fact this wasn't true. Amount of sleep was unrelated to people's moods.

In a conceptually similar study, McFarlane, Martin, and Williams (1988) had students at the University of British Columbia keep track of their moods every day for a 70-day period. Later, students were asked to recall what their moods had been. These researchers found that participants "remembered" more positive moods on weekends and "bluer Mondays" than they actually experienced. Interestingly, women also reported having been in worse moods during their premenstrual and menstrual phases than was the case. In fact, during the menstrual phase of their cycle, female participants actually reported being in an especially pleasant mood!

What participants in studies such as these rely on, at least in part, are their **causal theories**. People have many theories about what influences their feelings and behaviour, and often use these theories to help them explain why they feel the way they do (e.g., "I am in a bad mood—I bet it's because I got only six hours of sleep last night, or because it's Monday, or because it's that 'time of the month'"). We learn many of these theories from the culture in which we grow up, such as the idea that people are in bad moods on Mondays, or good moods on weekends, or that women are miserable during their premenstrual and menstrual phases. The only problem, as discussed in Chapter 3, is that our schemas and theories are not always correct and thus can lead to incorrect judgments about the causes of our actions.

Consider this example of causal theories in action, from the researchers who have studied them. One night, Nisbett and Wilson were meeting in an office at the University of Michigan. They were trying to think of ways to test the hypothesis that we rely on causal theories when trying to uncover the reasons for our feelings, judgments, and actions. Brilliant insights were not forthcoming, and the researchers were frustrated by their lack of progress. Then they realized that a source of their frustration (or so they thought) was the annoying whine of a vacuum cleaner that a custodial worker was operating right outside their office. This realization led them to wonder whether distracting background noises are more bothersome than people think. Maybe this was an example of the very kind of stimulus they were looking for—one that would influence people's judgments but would be overlooked when people explained their behaviour.

Nisbett and Wilson (1977b), after shutting the door, designed a study to test this possibility. The researchers asked people to rate how interesting they found a documentary film. In one condition, a "construction worker" (actually, Dick Nisbett) ran a power saw right outside the door to the room in which the film was shown. The irritating burst of

Causal theories

theories about the causes of one's own feelings and behaviours; often we learn such theories from our culture (e.g., "absence makes the heart grow fonder")

noise began about a minute into the film. It continued intermittently until Tim Wilson, the experimenter, went to the door and shouted to the worker to please stop sawing until the film was over. The participants rated how much they enjoyed the film, and then the experimenter asked them to indicate whether the noise had influenced their evaluations. To see if the noise really did have an effect, Nisbett and Wilson included a control condition in which other participants viewed the film without any distracting noise. The hypothesis was that the noise would lower people's evaluation of the film but that people would not realize the noise was responsible for the negative evaluation.

As it happened, this hypothesis was completely wrong. The participants who watched the film with the annoying background noise did not like it any less than did those who saw the film without the distracting noise (in fact, they liked the film slightly *more*). When the participants were asked how much the noise had influenced their ratings, however, their hypothesis agreed with Nisbett and Wilson's. Even though the noise had no detectable effect on people's ratings, most people reported that it *had* lowered their ratings of the film.

In a further study, Nisbett and Wilson (1977b) asked people in a shopping mall to evaluate the quality of items of clothing, such as pantyhose. Much to the surprise of the researchers, the position of the items on the display table had a large effect on people's preferences. The more to the right an item was, the more people liked it. The researchers knew that it was the position that was influencing people's judgments because in fact all four pairs of pantyhose were identical. However, the participants were completely in the dark about this effect of position on their judgments. Instead, they generated other causal theories for their choices.

We do not mean to imply that people rely solely on their causal theories when introspecting about the reasons for their feelings and behaviours. In addition to culturally learned causal theories, we have a great deal of information about ourselves, such as how we have responded in the past and what we happen to have been thinking about before making a choice (Gavanski & Hoffman, 1987; Wilson & Stone, 1985; Wilson, in press). For example, Roger Buehler at Wilfrid Laurier University and Catherine McFarland at Simon Fraser University recently demonstrated that if we are asked to predict our emotional reactions to future positive and negative events, we tend to anticipate more extreme emotional reactions than we actually end up experiencing (Buehler & McFarland, 2001). If, however, we are instructed to focus on similar experiences we've had in the past, we become more accurate in our forecasts of future emotional reactions. The fact remains, however, that introspecting about our past actions and current thoughts does not always yield the right answer about why we feel the way we do.

Knowing Ourselves through Observations of Our Own Behaviour

As we have seen, it is often difficult to know exactly why we feel the way we do. If introspection has its limits, how else might we find out what sort of person we are and what our attitudes are? We turn now to another source of self-knowledge: observations of our own behaviour.

▲ People are not always correct about the causes of their feelings and judgments. People in a study by Nisbett and Wilson (1977b) reported that a distracting noise lowered their enjoyment of a film, when in fact the noise had no detectable effect on their enjoyment.

INFERRING WHO WE ARE FROM HOW WE BEHAVE: SELF-PERCEPTION THEORY

If you aren't sure how you feel about something, there is another way you can find out: observe your own behaviour. If you want to know whether you like country music, for example, you might think, "Well, I always listen to the country music station on my car radio," concluding that you like country tunes. It might seem a little strange to say that you find out how you feel by observing what you do, but according to Daryl Bem (1972), such observations are an important source of self-knowledge.

Bem's (1972) **self-perception theory** argues that when our attitudes and feelings are uncertain or ambiguous, we infer these states by observing our behaviour and the situation in which it occurs. Let's consider each part of this theory. First, we infer our inner feelings from our behaviour only when we are not sure how we feel. If you've always known that you are a country music lover, then you do not need to observe your behaviour to figure this out (Andersen, 1984; Andersen & Ross, 1984). However, if you aren't sure how much you like country music, you are especially likely to use your behaviour as a guide to how you feel. This effect was demonstrated by Chaiken and Baldwin (1981) with University of Toronto students. First, the researchers assessed whether the participants had well-defined attitudes or poorly defined attitudes toward being an environmentalist. Then they asked participants to check off which of a list of various pro-ecology or anti-ecology actions they had performed (e.g., "I frequently leave on lights in rooms I'm not using") as a way of reminding them of their past behaviour. The researchers expected that being reminded of their past behaviour would influence only the attitudes of those participants whose attitudes were poorly defined. Indeed, participants with poorly defined environmental attitudes were strongly affected by these behavioural cues; those who were reminded of their pro-ecology behaviour subsequently reported that they held pro-environmental attitudes, whereas those who were reminded of their anti-ecology behaviour later reported more negative environmental attitudes. In contrast, being reminded of their past behaviour had little effect on the participants who already had clear (well-defined) attitudes on this issue.

Second, people judge whether their behaviour really reflects how they feel or whether it was the situation that made them act that way. If you freely choose to listen to the country radio station—no one makes you do it—you are especially likely to conclude that you listen to that station because you love country music. If it is your roommate and not you who always tunes in to the country station, you are unlikely to conclude that you listen to country music in your car because you love it.

INTRINSIC MOTIVATION VERSUS EXTRINSIC MOTIVATION

Let's say you love to play the piano. You spend many hours happily practising, simply enjoying the act of making music and the feeling that you are getting better. We would say that your interest in playing the piano stems from **intrinsic motivation**, which is the desire to engage in an activity because you enjoy it or find it interesting, not because of **extrinsic motivation**—external rewards or pressures (Cordova & Lepper, 1996; Deci & Flaste, 1995; Deci & Ryan, 1985, 2002; Harackiewicz & Elliot, 1993, 1998; Sansone & Harackiewicz, 1996). Whether our behaviour is motivated by intrinsic, versus extrinsic, factors has a number of far-reaching effects. These effects have been explored by Robert

---

Self-perception theory
the theory that when our attitudes and feelings are uncertain or ambiguous, we infer these states by observing our behaviour and the situation in which it occurs

Intrinsic motivation
the desire to engage in an activity because we enjoy it or find it interesting, not because of external rewards or pressures

Extrinsic motivation
the desire to engage in an activity because of external rewards or pressures, not because we enjoy the task or find it interesting

Vallerand and his colleagues (Vallerand, 1997; Vallerand & Ratelle, 2002). For example, they have found that intrinsic motivation is positively correlated with persistence (over a two-year period) among competitive swimmers (Pelletier et al., 1996), and with maintaining interest in repetitive figure skating tasks, as demonstrated with competitive figure skaters from clubs in the Ottawa-Carleton area (Green-Demers et al., 1998). In the domain of academics, intrinsic motivation is associated with positive language learning outcomes (e.g., feeling competent speaking French in a sample of French immersion students; Noels, Clément, & Pelletier, 1999), and with remaining in school rather than dropping out (as shown in several studies with French-Canadian high-school students; Koestner & Losier, 2002; Vallerand, Fortier, & Guay, 1997). Intrinsic motivation is also correlated with actively seeking information from government and other groups about environmental issues (e.g., nuclear waste, pesticides in food) and engaging in pro-environmental behaviours (e.g., recycling, purchasing environmentally friendly products) as evidenced in several studies of Ontario residents (Pelletier, 2002; Séguin, Pelletier, & Hunsley, 1999).

The effects of intrinsic motivation have also been examined in the political arena (Losier & Koestner, 1999; see Koestner & Losier [2002] for a review). These researchers contacted students at the University of Moncton one week before the 1995 New Brunswick provincial election, and McGill University students one week before the 1995 Quebec referendum. They found that students who were high in intrinsic motivation were more likely to actively seek out information about the campaigns (e.g., reading newspaper articles or watching television coverage) than those who were low in intrinsic motivation, although they were not necessarily more likely to have made the effort to vote.

Finally, research conducted by Blais, Sabourin, Boucher, and Vallerand (1990) with French-Canadian couples suggests that intrinsic motivation is important even in our closest relationships. Couples who reported that they were in the relationship for reasons such as "the numerous crazy and amusing moments I have with my partner" (i.e., they were high in intrinsic motivation) were more likely to be happy and to have developed constructive problem-solving strategies than couples who were in the relationship because it would disappoint others if they broke up (i.e., they were high in extrinsic motivation). Thus, when we are intrinsically motivated to do something—be it sports, academics, interest in politics, or even remaining in a relationship—we are more likely to enjoy the activity (or the relationship) and are more likely to persist with it (or him or her).

The Overjustification Effect Return, for a moment, to our earlier example of the joy you experienced while playing the piano. Now let's say your parents get the brilliant idea of rewarding you with money for playing the piano. They figure that this will make you practise even harder. After all, rewards work, don't they? However, your parents have now added an extrinsic reason for you to play the piano. Unfortunately, extrinsic rewards can undermine intrinsic motivation. Whereas before you played the piano because you loved it, now you're playing it so you'll get the reward. What was once play is now work. The sad outcome is that replacing intrinsic motivation with extrinsic motivation makes people lose interest in the activity they initially enjoyed. This result is called the **overjustification effect**, whereby people view their behaviour as caused by compelling extrin-

Overjustification effect
the case whereby people view their behaviour as caused by compelling extrinsic reasons, making them underestimate the extent to which their behaviour was caused by intrinsic reasons

Making children read for external reasons can lead to an overjustification effect, whereby they infer that they have no intrinsic interest in reading.

sic reasons (e.g., a reward), making them underestimate the extent to which their behaviour was caused by intrinsic reasons (e.g., Deci, Koestner, & Ryan, 1999a, 1999b; Deci & Ryan, 1985; Harackiewicz, 1979; Kohn, 1993; Lepper, 1995; Lepper, Keavney, & Drake, 1996; Ryan & Deci, 1996; Tang & Hall, 1995).

Sound familiar? The danger of programs such as BOOK IT!, described at the beginning of this chapter, now becomes clear. Giving children pizzas to read books may backfire by lowering their intrinsic interest in reading. During the programs, children might well read more, in order to get the rewards. No one doubts that rewards are powerful motivators and can change what people do. It's the changes that occur inside people's heads that are often overlooked. Once the programs end, children might actually be less likely to read than they were before the programs began. Why? They might think, "I was reading to get pizza, stickers, and buttons. Now that there is nothing in it for me, why should I read? I think I'll play a video game."

The overjustification effect has been found in dozens of laboratory and field experiments, with several kinds of rewards, activities, and age groups (Deci, Koestner, & Ryan, 1999a). For example, in one study, teachers introduced four new math games to grade four and five students. During a 13-day baseline period they simply noted how long each child played with each game (Greene, Sternberg, & Lepper, 1976). As seen in the first panel of Figure 5.3, the children had some intrinsic interest in the math games initially, in that they played with them for several minutes during this baseline period. For the next several days, a reward program was introduced, whereby the children could earn credits toward certificates and trophies by playing with the math games. The more time they spent playing with the games, the more credits they could earn. As seen in the middle panel of Figure 5.3, this program was effective in increasing the amount of time the kids spent on the math games, showing that the rewards were an effective motivator.

The key question, however, is what happened after the program was terminated and the kids could no longer earn rewards for playing with the games? According to the overjustification hypothesis, the children would conclude that they were playing with the math games only to earn prizes; as a result, when the rewards were taken away, the children would spend significantly less time with the games than they had during the baseline period (e.g., "I can't earn prizes playing with these games any more—why play with them at all?"). This is exactly what happened (see right-hand panel of Figure 5.3.) (The researchers determined, by comparing these results to those of a control condition, that it was the rewards that made people like the games less, and not the fact that everyone became bored with the games as time went by.) In short, the rewards destroyed the

▶ Figure 5.3

THE OVERJUSTIFICATION
EFFECT.

During the initial baseline
phase, researchers measured
how much time elementary
school children played with
math games. During the reward
program, they rewarded the
children with prizes for playing
the games. When the rewards
were taken away (during the
follow-up), the children played
with the games even less than
they had during the baseline
phase, indicating that the
rewards had lowered their
intrinsic interest in the games.

(Adapted from Greene,
Sternberg, & Lepper, 1976)

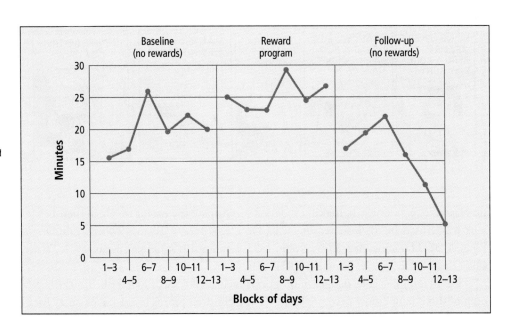

▼ "I remember that the
game lost some of its
magical qualities for me
once I thought seriously
about playing for a living."
—Basketball great Bill
Russell

children's intrinsic interest in the games, such that by the end of the study they were hardly playing with the games at all.

The results of overjustification studies are distressing, given the wide use of rewards and incentives by parents, educators, and employers. In the workplace, for example, people sometimes find themselves doing things they used to do for the pure joy of it but for which they are now getting paid. Consider basketball great Bill Russell's description of how becoming a professional affected his love of the game:

> I remember that the game lost some of its magical qualities for me once I thought seriously about playing for a living. This first happened in 1955, in my junior year, after USF [University of San Francisco] won the NCAA national championship. As a result, all through my senior year at USF I played with the idea of turning professional, and things began to change. Whenever I walked on the court I began to calculate how this particular game might affect my future. Thoughts of money and prestige crept into my head. Over the years the professional game would turn more and more into a business (Russell & Branch, 1979).

What can we do to protect intrinsic motivation from the slings and arrows of our society's reward system? Fortunately, there is room for some optimism, as recent research has identified conditions under which overjustification effects can be avoided. First, rewards will undermine interest only if interest was high initially (Calder & Staw, 1975; Tang & Hall, 1995). If you think a task is excruciatingly boring, rewards obviously can't reduce your interest any further. Similarly, if a child has no interest whatsoever in reading, then getting her to read by offering free pizzas is not a bad idea, because there is no initial interest to undermine. The danger arises when a child already likes to read, because then offering free pizzas is likely to convince the child that she is reading to earn pizzas, not because reading is interesting in its own right.

Second, the type of reward makes a difference. So far, we have discussed **task-contingent rewards**, meaning that people get them only for doing a task, regardless of how well they do it. Sometimes **performance-contingent rewards** are used, whereby the reward depends on how well people perform the task. For example, grades are performance-contingent because you get a high reward (an *A*) only if you do well in the class. This type of reward is less likely to decrease interest in a task—and may even increase interest—because it conveys the message that you are good at the task (Deci & Ryan, 1985; Sansone & Harackiewicz, 1997; Tang & Hall, 1995). Thus, rather than giving kids a reward for playing with math games regardless of how well they do (task-contingent), it is better to reward them for doing well at math.

Finally, another hopeful sign is that children can be taught to avoid the damaging effects of rewards. Because rewards can never be eliminated from our society, Beth Hennessey and her colleagues focused on ways of helping children to maintain intrinsic motivation even with rewards dangled all around them (Hennessey, Amabile, & Martinage, 1989; Hennessey & Zbikowski, 1993). They showed children a videotape in which a boy and girl noted that getting rewards was nice but that the real reason they did things, such as their schoolwork, was how much they enjoyed these activities. Did this video "immunize" the kids against the negative effects of rewards? To find out, the children came back the next day and took part in what they thought was another study. The researchers asked the kids to make up stories to accompany a series of pictures, and half of them were offered a reward for doing so.

The kids who did not see the videotape showed the usual overjustification effect—they lost interest and produced stories that were less creative than those produced by the nonrewarded children (see the left-hand side of Figure 5.4). What about the kids who had watched the videotape? As seen in the right-hand side of Figure 5.4, the reward had little effect on the creativity of their stories (in fact, the kids who were rewarded made up stories that were slightly more creative than the kids who were not rewarded). The

Task-contingent rewards
rewards that are given for performing a task, regardless of how well we do that task

Performance-contingent rewards
rewards that are based on how well we perform a task

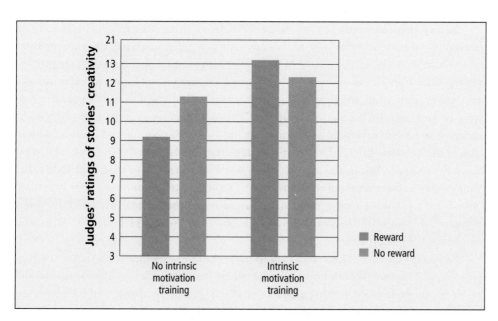

◀ **Figure 5.4**

AVOIDING THE OVERJUSTIFICATION EFFECT.

As seen on the left-hand side of the graph, children who were rewarded told stories that were less creative, demonstrating the standard overjustification effect. As seen on the right-hand side of the graph, children who were immunized—by watching a videotape that stressed the importance of intrinsic motivation—did not demonstrate the overjustification effect. That is, when they received a reward, they still wrote creative stories.

(Adapted from Hennessey & Zbikowski, 1993)

information they learned in the video seems to have kept them focused on their intrinsic interest in the task, thereby "short-circuiting" the negative effects of rewards. This research suggests an encouraging solution to the dilemma posed by our society's use of rewards. Your intrinsic interest in an activity can be maintained in the face of rewards if you try to ignore the reward and remind yourself of how much you enjoy doing the task for its own sake.

UNDERSTANDING OUR EMOTIONS: THE TWO-FACTOR THEORY OF EMOTION

We have just seen that people often use observations of their behaviour to determine what they think and what kind of person they are. You may have wondered whether the same is true of other kinds of views of yourself. For example, what about your emotions, such as how happy, angry, or afraid you feel at any given time—how do you know which emotion you are experiencing?

Though it may seem as if we just know how we feel, the experience of emotion is not as simple as it appears. Stanley Schachter (1964) proposed a theory of emotion that says we infer what our emotions are by observing how physiologically aroused we feel and then trying to figure out what is causing this arousal. For example, let's say your heart is pounding and your body feels tense. Is it because you just saw your professor—the one from whom you got a paper extension because supposedly you had to go to your grandmother's funeral that day? Or is it because you just saw the person standing next to the professor—the one on whom you have the most amazing crush in the universe? Are you feeling stomach-churning fear or stomach-churning love?

Schachter's theory is called the **two-factor theory of emotion**, because understanding our emotional states requires two steps. First, we must experience physiological arousal, and, second, we must seek an appropriate explanation or label for it. Because our physical states are difficult to label, we use information in the situation to help us make an attribution about why we feel aroused. Figure 5.5 illustrates the two-factor theory of emotion.

Stanley Schachter and Jerome Singer (1962) conducted an experiment to test this provocative theory. Imagine you are a participant. When you arrive, the experimenter tells you he is studying the effects of a vitamin compound called Suproxin on people's vision. After a physician injects you with a small amount of Suproxin, the experimenter asks you to wait while the drug takes effect. He introduces you to another participant, who, he says, has also been given Suproxin. The experimenter gives each of you a questionnaire to fill out, saying he will return in a little while to give you the vision tests. You look at the questionnaire and notice it contains some highly personal and insulting questions. For example, one question asks, "With how many men (other than your father) has your mother had extramarital relationships?" The other participant reacts angrily to these offensive questions, becoming more and more furious, until he finally tears up his questionnaire, throws it on the floor, and stomps out of the room. How do you think you would feel? Would you feel angry as well?

As you have no doubt gathered, the real purpose of this experiment was not to test people's vision. The researchers set up a situation where the two crucial variables—arousal and an emotional explanation for that arousal—would be present or absent, and then observed which, if any, emotions people experienced. The participants did not really receive an

Two-factor theory of emotion

the idea that emotional experience is the result of a two-step self-perception process in which people first experience physiological arousal and then seek an appropriate explanation for it

◀ **Figure 5.5**

THE TWO-FACTOR THEORY OF
EMOTION: PEOPLE FIRST
EXPERIENCE PHYSIOLOGICAL
AROUSAL AND THEN ATTACH
AN EXPLANATION TO IT.

injection of a vitamin compound. Instead, the arousal variable was manipulated in the following way: Half of the participants received epinephrine, a drug that causes arousal (body temperature and heart and breathing rates increase), and the other half received a placebo that had no physiological effects at all.

Imagine how you would feel had you received the epinephrine. As you read the insulting questionnaire, you begin to feel aroused. (Remember, the experimenter didn't tell you the drug was epinephrine, so you don't realize that it's the drug that's making you aroused.) The other participant—who was actually an accomplice of the experimenter—reacts with rage. You are likely to infer that you are feeling flushed and aroused because you too are angry. You have met the conditions that Schachter (1964) argues are necessary to experience an emotion—you are aroused, and you have sought out and found a reasonable explanation for your arousal in the situation that surrounds you. Thus, you become furious. This is indeed what happened—participants who had been given epinephrine reacted much more angrily than did participants who had been given the placebo.

A fascinating implication of Schachter's theory is that people's emotions are somewhat arbitrary, depending on what the most plausible explanation for their arousal happens to be. Schachter and Singer (1962) demonstrated this idea in two ways. First, they showed that they could prevent people from becoming angry by providing a nonemotional explanation for why they felt aroused. They did this by informing some of the people who received epinephrine that the drug would increase their heart rate, make their face feel warm and flushed, and cause their hands to shake slightly. When people actually began to feel this way, they inferred that it was not because they were angry but because the drug was taking effect. As a result, these participants did not react angrily to the questionnaire.

Even more impressively, Schachter and Singer showed that they could make participants experience a very different emotion by changing the most plausible explanation for their arousal. In other conditions, participants did not receive the insulting questionnaire and the accomplice did not respond angrily. Instead, the accomplice acted in a euphoric, devil-may-care fashion, playing basketball with rolled-up pieces of paper, making paper airplanes, and playing with a Hula-Hoop he found in the corner. How did the real participants respond? If they had received epinephrine but had not been told of its effects, they inferred that they must be feeling happy and euphoric, and often joined the accomplice's impromptu games.

The Schachter and Singer (1962) experiment has become one of the most famous studies in social psychology, because it shows that emotions can be the result of a self-perception process whereby people look for the most plausible explanation for their arousal. Sometimes the most plausible explanation is not the right explanation, and so people end up experiencing a mistaken emotion. The people who became angry or euphoric in the Schachter and Singer (1962) study did so because they felt aroused and thought this arousal was due to the obnoxious questionnaire or to the infectious, happy-go-lucky behaviour of the accomplice. The real cause of their arousal, the epinephrine, was hidden from them; all they had to go on were situational cues to explain their behaviour.

FINDING THE WRONG CAUSE: MISATTRIBUTION OF AROUSAL

To what extent do the results found by Schachter and Singer (1962) generalize to everyday life? Imagine that you go to see a scary movie with an extremely attractive date. As you are sitting there, you notice that your heart is thumping and you are a little short of breath. Is this because you are wildly attracted to your date, or because the movie is terrifying you? It is unlikely that you could say, "Fifty-seven percent of my arousal is due to the fact that my date is gorgeous, 32 percent is due to the scary movie, and 11 percent is due to indigestion from all the popcorn I ate." Because of this difficulty in pinpointing the precise causes of our arousal, we sometimes form mistaken emotions. You might think that most of your arousal is a sign of attraction to your date, when in fact a lot of it is due to the movie (or maybe even indigestion).

Misattribution of arousal

the process whereby people make mistaken inferences about what is causing them to feel the way they do

In recent years, many studies have demonstrated the occurrence of such **misattribution of arousal**, whereby people make mistaken inferences about what is causing them to feel the way they do (Ross & Olson, 1981; Savitsky et al., 1998; Schachter, 1977; Storms & Nisbett, 1970; Valins, 1966; Zillmann, 1978). Consider, for example, an intriguing field experiment by Donald Dutton and Arthur Aron (1974). Imagine you were one of the participants (all of whom were men). You are one of many people visiting the Capilano Canyon in scenic North Vancouver. Spanning the canyon is a narrow, 137-metre suspension bridge made of wooden planks attached to wire cables. You decide to walk across it. When you get a little way across, the bridge starts to sway from side to side. You feel as though you are about to tumble over the edge, and reach for the handrails. But they are so low that it feels even more likely that you will topple over. Then you make the mistake of looking down. You see nothing but a sheer 70-metre drop to rocks and rapids below. You become more than a little aroused—your heart is thumping, you breathe rapidly, and you begin to perspire. At this point, an attractive young woman approaches you and asks if you could fill out a questionnaire for her, as part of a psychology project on the effects of scenic attractions on people's creativity. You decide to help her out. After you complete the questionnaire, the woman thanks you and says she would be happy to explain her study in more detail. She tears off a corner of the questionnaire, writes down her name and phone number. How attracted do you think you would be to this woman? Would you phone her and ask her out?

Think about this for a moment, and now imagine that the same woman approaches you under different circumstances. You decide to take a leisurely stroll farther up the Capilano River. You notice a wide, sturdy bridge made of heavy cedar planks. The bridge has high handrails, even though it is situated only 3 metres above a shallow rivulet that runs into the main river. You are peaceably admiring the scenery when the woman asks you to fill out her questionnaire. How attracted do you feel toward her now? The prediction from Schachter's two-factor theory is clear: If you are on the high, scary bridge, you will be considerably aroused and will mistakenly think some of this arousal is the result of attraction to the beautiful woman. This is exactly what happened in the actual experiment. Half of the men (50 percent) who were approached on the high suspension bridge telephoned the woman later, whereas relatively few of the men (12.5 percent) who were approached on the low, sturdy bridge called her. (As you probably have guessed, the woman was a confederate—someone hired by the researchers—and she approached only men who were not accompanied by a woman.)

After one of your authors (Beverley Fehr) discussed this study in a class, one student had a new perspective on a recent experience in which she had found herself attracted to the person who was giving her a tattoo. The student had been feeling quite nervous about the procedure, but now realized that she might have misinterpreted her anxiety as attraction to the tattoo artist! The tattoo artist, who presumably was not experiencing the same level of arousal, apparently did not interpret whatever feelings he had as attraction. Alas, he turned her down when she asked him out. The moral is this: If you encounter an attractive man or woman and your heart is going *thump-thump,* think carefully about why you are aroused—you might fall in love for the wrong reasons!

▲ When people are aroused, in this case due to crossing a scary bridge, they often misattribute this arousal to the wrong source—such as attraction to the person they are with.

Knowing Ourselves through Self-Schemas

As we have seen, we can learn about ourselves in a variety of ways. What do we do with all of this information once we have it? Not surprisingly, we organize our self-knowledge in much the same way that we organize our knowledge about the external world—into schemas.

In Chapter 3, we noted that people use schemas—knowledge structures about a person, topic, or object—to understand the social world. It should come as no surprise that we form **self-schemas** as well, the organized knowledge structures about ourselves, based on our past experiences, that help us understand, explain, and predict our own behaviour (Andersen & Cyranowski, 1994; Cantor & Kihlstrom, 1987; Deaux, 1993; Markus, 1977;

Self-schemas

organized knowledge structures about ourselves, based on our past experiences, that help us understand, explain, and predict our own behaviour

Markus & Nurius, 1986; Malle & Horowitz, 1995). Schemas also influence how we interpret new things that happen to us. Suppose, for example, that you lose a close tennis match to your best friend. How will you react? In part, the answer depends on the nature of your self-schemas. If you define yourself as competitive and athletic, you are likely to feel bad and want a rematch as soon as possible, whereas if you define yourself as cooperative and nurturing, losing the match won't be such a big deal.

AUTOBIOGRAPHICAL MEMORY

Autobiographical memories

memories about one's own past thoughts, feelings, and behaviours

Self-schemas also help us organize our pasts by influencing our **autobiographical memories**, which are memories about our own past thoughts, feelings, and behaviours. If being independent is part of your self-schema but being competitive is not, you will probably remember more times when you acted independently than competitively (Akert, 1993; Bahrick, Hall, & Berger, 1996; Markus, 1977; Thompson et al., 1996).

Recent research by Ziva Kunda and her colleagues suggests that motivational factors such as the desire to see ourselves in a positive light influence which of our past actions we are most likely to bring to mind. For example, in one study (Sanitioso, Kunda, & Fong, 1990), participants were told that research shows that the trait of introversion is associated with professional success; others were told that extroversion is associated with success. All participants were then asked to list behaviours they had performed that were relevant to the dimension of introversion–extroversion. Those who were led to believe that introversion was associated with success were more likely to remember introverted, rather than extroverted, behaviours they had performed. The opposite was true for those who were led to believe that extroversion was associated with success. According to the researchers, when people are motivated to see themselves as possessing a desired quality or trait, they conduct a selective memory search for examples of past behaviours consistent with that trait. This body of evidence then allows them to draw the "rational" conclusion that they possess the desirable trait.

Even the way in which we are asked questions about ourselves can influence which memories we access, and, as a result, our current self-conception. This effect was demonstrated by Kunda, Fong, Sanitioso, and Reber (1993). In their first study, students at the University of Waterloo were asked one of two questions: "Are you happy with your social life?" or "Are you unhappy with your social life?" Next, they were instructed to list examples of past behaviours, thoughts, and feelings relevant to the question. Participants who were asked the "happy" question tended to list more happy thoughts and feelings, and subsequently rated their social life as happier, than did those who were asked the "unhappy" question. Thus, simply asking participants if they were happy with their social life had an effect on their self-conceptions in that they came to view themselves as happier than those who were asked if they were unhappy with their social lives. Thus, our schemas can determine which autobiographical memories we access, and those memories, in turn, can affect our sense of self at any given moment.

Before leaving this topic, we should note that our schemas or theories about how stable our feelings and attitudes are also colour the ways in which we remember our past. We tend to expect that some feelings, such as our moods or how happy we are in a new romantic relationship, will fluctuate over time. In contrast, we expect that other feelings, such as our attitudes about social issues (e.g., the death penalty), will be relatively stable—

we assume that the way we feel now is how we have always felt. At the University of Waterloo, Michael Ross and his colleagues have found that these theories are not always correct, leading to distortions in memory (Conway & Ross, 1984; Ross, 1989; Ross & McFarland, 1988). For example, attitudes toward social issues sometimes do change, but because people's theories are that these attitudes remain stable, they underestimate the amount of change that occurs. "I've always been against the death penalty," we might think, underestimating the extent to which our attitude has evolved over the years. Thus, not only do our memories define us, but also we define our memories.

Knowing Ourselves through Social Interaction

So far, we have seen that people learn about themselves through introspection and observations of their own behaviour, and that they organize this information into self-schemas. As important as these sources of self-knowledge are, there is still something missing. We are not solitary seekers of self-knowledge but social beings who often see ourselves through the eyes of other people. James (1890) stressed the importance of social relationships in our definition of self, noting that we can have different "selves" that develop in response to different social situations. For example, when one of your authors (Robin Akert) is at the stable, training her horse and chatting with other riders and stable hands, she presents a different aspect of herself than she does when she is at a psychology conference with her colleagues. Her "barn self" is more colloquial, less intellectual; she alters her vocabulary and topics of conversation. Not only is it true that we present ourselves differently to different people, but also we shape our self-definition according to how they view us. It's as if other people reflect their image of you back for you to see.

THE LOOKING-GLASS SELF

The idea that we see ourselves through the eyes of other people—either present or imagined—and incorporate their views into our self-concept is called the **looking-glass self** (Cooley, 1902; Mead, 1934). Mark Baldwin and his colleagues have explored this idea in an ingenious set of experiments (Baldwin, 1992; Baldwin & Meunier, 1999; Baldwin & Sinclair, 1996). Imagine you were a participant in one of their studies. Think of an older member of your family. Try to form a vivid picture of this person in your mind. Imagine that this person is sitting beside you. Focus on the colour of the person's eyes or hair, and then focus on the sound of the person's voice. Imagine talking to this person.

Now imagine reading a story about a woman who engages in sexually permissive behaviour. How much do you think you would enjoy the story? This is the situation in which female students at the University of Waterloo found themselves (Baldwin & Holmes, 1987). Half of the participants were asked to visualize older family members as a way of priming a conservative internal audience. In other words, participants were induced to see themselves through the eyes of significant people in their lives—in this case, older members of their family. The other participants were asked to visualize friends from campus as a way of priming a permissive internal audience. They were then asked to participate in a supposedly unrelated study in which they would evaluate pieces of fiction. One of the stories, taken from *Cosmopolitan* magazine, described a woman's sexually permissive behaviour. The researchers found that women who had previously

Looking-glass self
the idea that we see ourselves through the eyes of other people and incorporate their views into our self-concept

imagined older family members rated the story as less enjoyable than women who had imagined their university friends. Thus, participants responded in ways that they felt would be acceptable to whatever internal audience had been primed.

There was one additional finding of note. Recall that earlier in this chapter we discussed research showing that when people are self-aware, they are more attuned to their beliefs and moral standards. Baldwin and Holmes also added a condition in which some participants were made to feel self-aware (by the presence of a mirror) while they were rating the passages. Their findings were even more pronounced among self-aware participants; thus, if you were imagining your grandmother or great-uncle Ted, and then saw yourself in a mirror while reading a sexual passage, you were even less likely to enjoy it!

The effects of an internal audience on our sense of self has been demonstrated in other domains as well. For example, in another study (Baldwin, Carrell, & Lopez, 1990), graduate students at the University of Michigan were asked to evaluate their recent research ideas. For some of the students, an evaluative authority figure was primed by subliminal exposure (flashing a slide so quickly that the participants weren't consciously aware of what had been shown) to the scowling face of their program director. Other students were exposed to an approving figure—the warm, friendly face of John Ellard, a postdoctoral student (now a social psychology professor at the University of Calgary). Students who were exposed to the face of their program director subsequently evaluated their research ideas more negatively than did those exposed to the face of John Ellard.

In a second study, Baldwin and colleagues (1990) primed a sense of self as a Catholic among Catholic women at the University of Waterloo through subliminal exposure to a picture of Pope John Paul II looking disapproving. Other participants (also Catholics) were exposed to the scowling face of a man who was unfamiliar to them (and therefore should not have had implications for their sense of self). All participants then read a sexually permissive passage. As expected, women exposed to the disapproving countenance of the Pope rated themselves more negatively than did women exposed to the disapproving face of an unfamiliar man. However, this effect was obtained only for women who defined themselves as practising Catholics. Presumably for these women, the Pope was an especially relevant internal audience.

Thus, who we are is determined, at least in part, by the internal audience we have in mind. If we are reminded of a significant person in our lives who seems critical or disapproving, we will tend to see ourselves as possessing negative traits (e.g., immoral or incompetent). On the other hand, if we happen to have a supportive, approving internal audience in mind, we are more likely to view ourselves as having positive characteristics.

SOCIAL COMPARISON THEORY

We also come to know ourselves by comparison with other people (Brown, 1990; Collins, 1996; Kruglanski & Mayseless, 1990; McFarland & Miller, 1994; Niedenthal & Beike, 1997; Suls, Martin, & Wheeler, 2000; Wheeler, Martin, & Suls, 1997; Wood, 1989, 1996). Suppose, for example, we gave you a test that measured your social sensitivity, or how aware you are of other people's problems. The test involves reading excerpts from autobiographies and guessing the nature of the authors' personal problems, if any. After you've taken the test, we tell you that you achieved a score of 35. What have you learned about yourself? Not much, because you don't know what a score of 35 means. Is it a good

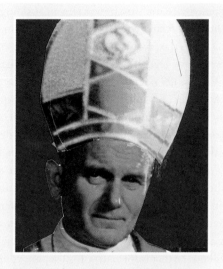

▲ The looking-glass self: In one study (Baldwin, Carrell, & Lopez, 1990), students were subliminally exposed either to a photo of the chair of their department, scowling, or to a photo of a postdoctoral student, smiling. Those exposed to their scowling chair subsequently rated their own research more negatively than did those exposed to the friendly postdoctoral student.

In a second study (Baldwin et al., 1990), participants were subliminally exposed either to a picture of a scowling man unknown to them, or to a picture of the Pope, altered to look particularly disapproving. Practising Catholic women rated themselves more negatively after reading a sexually permissive passage when they had been exposed to the picture of the Pope. Thus, how we see ourselves is determined at least in part by how we believe significant people in our lives see us.

score or a bad score? Suppose we told you that the test is scored on a scale from 0 to 50. Now what have you learned? A little more than you knew before, perhaps, but this is still pretty uninformative if you don't know how other people did on the test. If we told you that everyone else in your class scored between 0 and 20, you would probably say, "Wow—I really am an extremely sensitive person!" On the other hand, you might feel differently if we told you that everyone else scored between 45 and 50.

This example illustrates Leon Festinger's (1954) **social comparison theory**, which holds that people learn about their own abilities and attitudes by comparing themselves to other people. The theory revolves around two important questions: (1) When do you engage in social comparison, and (2) With whom do you choose to compare yourself? The answer to the first question is that you socially compare when there is no objective standard for you to measure yourself against and when you experience some uncertainty about yourself in a particular area (Suls & Fletcher, 1983; Suls & Miller, 1977). That is,

Social comparison theory the idea that we learn about our own abilities and attitudes by comparing ourselves to other people

when you're not sure how well you're doing or what exactly you're feeling, you'll observe other people and compare yourself to them.

As to the second question—With whom do you choose to compare yourself?—recent research by Daniel Gilbert and his colleagues reveals a surprising answer (Gilbert, Giesler, & Morris, 1995). Our initial impulse, they argue, is to compare ourselves with anyone who is around. This initial comparison occurs quickly and automatically (see Chapter 3, for a discussion of automatic judgment). After a quick assessment of how our performance compares to others', however, we then decide how appropriate that comparison is—realizing that not all comparisons are equally informative.

Not surprisingly, people find it most informative to compare themselves to others who are similar to them on important attributes or dimensions (Goethals & Darley, 1977; Miller, 1982; Wheeler, Koestner, & Driver, 1982; Zanna, Goethals, & Hill, 1975). For example, if you are wondering about your artistic ability, it will not be very informative to compare yourself to Picasso—one of the great artists of the twentieth century. It also will not be that informative to compare your artistic endeavours to the fingerpainting and scribbles of your four-year-old sister. It is better to compare yourself to the other people in your drawing class, if your goal is to assess your own abilities.

Using Social Comparison as a Self-Enhancement Strategy Constructing an accurate image of ourselves is only one reason that we engage in social comparison. We also use social comparison to boost our egos. Is it important to you to believe that you are a fabulous artist-in-the-making? Then compare yourself to your little sister—you have her beat! This use of **downward social comparison**—comparing yourself to people who are worse than you on a particular trait or ability—is a self-protective, self-enhancing strategy (Aspinwall & Taylor, 1993; Davison, Pennebaker, & Dickerson, 2000; Pyszczynski, Greenberg, & LaPrelle, 1985; Reis, Gerrard, & Gibbons, 1993; Wheeler & Kunitate, 1992; Wood & VanderZee, 1997). This research shows that if you compare yourself to people who are less smart, less talented, or sicker than you are, you'll feel very good about yourself. For example, Joanne Wood, Shelley Taylor, and Rosemary Lichtman (1985) found evidence of downward comparison in interviews with cancer patients. The vast majority of patients spontaneously compared themselves to other cancer patients who were more ill than they were, presumably as a way of making themselves feel more optimistic about the course of their own condition. More recently, Wood and her colleagues examined spontaneous social comparisons in everyday life by having students at the University of Waterloo keep track of times when they compared themselves to another person over a three-week period (Wood, Michela, & Giordano, 2000). An analysis of these diaries confirmed that people were most likely to spontaneously engage in downward social comparisons when they wanted to feel better about themselves.

In an interesting "twist" on this issue, Anne Wilson at Wilfrid Laurier University and Michael Ross at the University of Waterloo have suggested that we can even get a self-esteem boost by comparing our current performance with our own past performance (Wilson & Ross, 2000, 2001; Ross & Wilson, 2002). We are still using downward social comparison, but in this case the target of comparison is a "past self" instead of another person. For example, in one of their studies, a participant mentioned that her "university student self" was more outgoing and sociable than her shy, reserved "high-school student

Downward social comparison

the process whereby we compare ourselves to people who are worse than we are on a particular trait or ability

self." Thus, another route to self-enhancement is to focus on the ways in which we are better now than we were in the past. In related research, Cameron, Ross and Holmes (2002) showed that if we are forced to think about a time when we behaved badly in a relationship, we will "bend over backwards" to show how much we and our relationships have improved since then. In other words, when we are reminded of a negative past self, we restore our self-esteem by focusing on how much better our current self is.

Importantly, recent research conducted by Penelope Lockwood (2002) reveals that downward comparison does not inevitably result in self-enhancement. Specifically, Lockwood argues that comparing ourselves to worse-off others will make us feel good only if we don't feel vulnerable to the other person's negative outcomes. For example, in one of her studies, first-year students at the University of Toronto who were doing well academically read about the experiences of another first-year student who was struggling. In this situation, students showed the usual self-enhancement effect of downward social comparison. They could feel good about the fact that they, themselves, were not experiencing academic difficulties. Quite the opposite occurred, however, when participants were presented with a situation that could, in fact, happen to them. More specifically, this time first-year students read about a recent graduate who did well in university at the outset, but then declined in academic performance over his four years at the University of Toronto. Now that he had graduated, he could only find work in fast food restaurants. In this case, downward social comparison had a negative effect. First-year students who were asked to imagine experiencing a similar fate felt worse about themselves than students who did not engage in downward comparison. (These latter students had been asked, instead, to write about a typical day in their lives). Thus, comparing ourselves to someone who is worse off can make us feel better about ourselves—but only if we are confident that the other person's fate cannot befall us.

How do we feel if we instead compare ourselves to someone who is better than we are—thus engaging in **upward social comparison**? According to Lockwood and Kunda (1997, 1999, 2000), the answer is, it depends. You might feel better or worse, depending on the sense of self that is activated (brought to mind) at the time. Imagine you were a participant in one of their studies. Think of a peak academic experience that made you especially proud. If you are like the math, biology, and computer science students at the University of Waterloo who participated in this study, you would have no trouble coming up with an answer (Lockwood & Kunda, 1999). Now imagine reading an article in your campus newspaper that describes a student, the same gender as you, who has had a stellar academic career. This person has won all kinds of awards, and university officials are raving about how truly outstanding this student is. How do you feel now? If you suddenly don't feel so good, you are not alone. Lockwood and Kunda found that when participants' "best self" had been activated, it was depressing for them to be exposed to a superstar. They tended not to feel very good about themselves, and their motivation to study hard took a dive.

What if, instead of describing your "best" self, you focused on your "usual" self? Other participants in this study did just that—they were simply asked to describe what they had done the day before. For these participants, reading about the superstar student was inspiring. They imagined that they, too, could achieve greatness, and as a result they felt very good about themselves—even better than participants who focused on their usual self but did not read about the superstar. (These results are shown in Figure 5.6.)

Upward social comparison the process whereby we compare ourselves to people who are better than we are on a particular trait or ability

▶ This man has engaged in too much upward social comparison.

"Of course you're going to be depressed if you keep comparing yourself with successful people."

Hamilton © from the New Yorker Collection. All rights reserved.

The researchers conclude that when we focus on our actual or usual self, exposure to outstanding others inspires us to generate higher hopes and aspirations for ourselves than we would have if we hadn't been exposed to the superstar. However, if we happen to be focusing on our best or ideal self, it can be depressing to realize that someone else has already surpassed our highest hopes and dreams.

In sum, to whom we compare ourselves depends on the nature of our goals. When we want an accurate assessment of our abilities and opinions, we compare ourselves to people who are similar to us. When we want information about what we can strive

▶ **Figure 5.6**

EFFECTS OF UPWARD SOCIAL COMPARISON ON SELF-ENHANCEMENT.

People who focused on their usual self evaluated themselves more positively following exposure to a superstar than did people who were not exposed to a superstar. However, people who focused on their "best" self evaluated themselves more negatively following exposure to a superstar than did those who were not exposed to a superstar.

(Lockwood & Kunda, 1999)

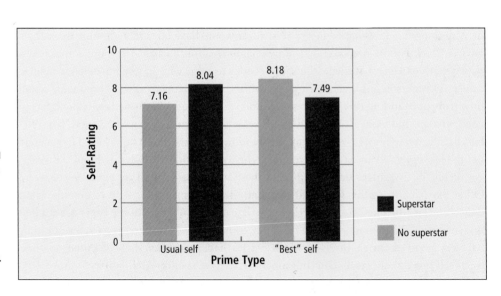

toward, we engage in upward social comparison. We also can feel good by engaging in upward social comparison, but only if we are focusing on our usual, ordinary self. Another route to feeling good is to engage in downward comparison and compare ourselves to our past selves or to those who are less fortunate. Doing so will make us look better by comparison—as long as we're convinced that we are not vulnerable to the same misfortunes.

Impression Management: All the World's a Stage

Now that you've come to know yourself, what do you do with all that knowledge? Being a member of a highly social species, you present yourself to others. You have many aspects to your self-concept; you can be many selves. Thus, a basic aspect of your social existence is **self-presentation**, whereby you present who you are (or who you want people to believe you are) through your words, nonverbal behaviour, and actions (Goffman, 1959; Leary, 1995; Martin & Leary, 1999; Schlenker, 1980; Schlenker, Britt, & Pennington, 1996; Tedeschi, 1981). However, self-presentation is not always a simple, straightforward process; there are times when you want people to form a particular impression of you. At these times, you engage in **impression management**, consciously or unconsciously orchestrating a carefully designed presentation of self that will create a certain impression, one that fits your goals or needs in a social interaction (Goffman, 1959; Schlenker, 1980; Schlenker & Britt, 1999; see Schlenker & Pontari, 2000 for a review).

The concepts of self-presentation and impression management were eloquently discussed by Erving Goffman (1955, 1959, 1967, 1971). His theory of social interaction was based on a dramaturgical model, which uses the theatre as a metaphor for social life. On the stage, the actors present certain aspects of self (or their roles) to each other; Goffman says that in everyday life, we do the same thing in our social interactions. Further, just as in the theatre, real life is made up of backstage and frontstage areas. Frontstage is when you're "on," when you are actively presenting a particular self to others so as to create or maintain a certain impression in their eyes. Thoroughly cleaning your room, apartment, or house before company arrives (and saying, "Oh, it's nothing," when they compliment you on how lovely it looks) is preparing for and being on frontstage. In contrast, backstage is when you are not actively managing or creating a particular impression. We become uncomfortable when people invade our backstage areas, for we are, by definition, unprepared. Witness how annoying and embarrassing it is when people you'd like to impress drop by to visit you unannounced and your place is a slovenly pigsty and you are looking your grungiest!

Some people have an easier time than others "pulling off" the impressions they want to create. Shy people, for example, have difficulties with impression management. According to a study conducted at the University of Windsor, people who are shy believe that they are not very competent in interpersonal interactions, and they expect others to reject them (Jackson, Towson, & Narduzzi, 1997). With these expectations in mind, it is perhaps not surprising that shy people end up not making a very good impression on others. Paulhus and Morgan (1997) studied these effects by having University of British Columbia students participate in seven weekly discussion groups. They found that

Self-presentation

the attempt to present who we are, or who we want people to believe we are, through our words, nonverbal behaviour, and actions

Impression management

our conscious or unconscious orchestration of a carefully designed presentation of self so as to create a certain impression that fits our goals or needs in a social interaction

people who were shy did not speak up in these meetings—with the result that they were perceived as less intelligent than the non-shy group members. As the researchers put it, group members assumed that "saying nothing means nothing to say." (Sadly, the students who were shy also thought of themselves as less intelligent—even though the researchers found no relationship between shyness and IQ.) The good news is that as the shy students became more comfortable with the group, they began to contribute more, such that by the end of the seven weeks they were no longer perceived as less intelligent than their non-shy peers.

It is undoubtedly true that people in all cultures are concerned with impression management. The form, however, differs considerably from culture to culture. Earlier, we mentioned that people in Asian cultures tend to have a more interdependent view of themselves than do people in Western cultures. One consequence of this identity is that "saving face," or avoiding public embarrassment, is extremely important in Asian cultures. In Japan, for example, it is very important that people have the "right" guests at their weddings and enough mourners at the funerals of their loved ones—so important, in fact, that if guests or mourners are unavailable, you can go to a local "convenience agency" and rent some. These agencies (or *benriya*) keep a staff of employees on hand to pretend they are your closest friends. A woman named Hiroko, for example, was concerned that not enough guests would attend her second wedding. No problem—she simply hired some. She rented six guests, including a man to pose as her boss, at a cost of US$1500. Her "boss" even delivered a flattering speech about her at the wedding (Jordan & Sullivan, 1995).

People from Western cultures are likely to chuckle at what to them seems like impression management taken to absurd lengths. However, Westerners also go to great lengths to influence what others think of them. Consider, for example, the impression management efforts of Céline Dion. It was the opinion of her manager (now husband), René, that Céline was going to have to transform her look in order to "make it big." Accordingly, her image received a substantial overhaul before she began recording in English. Dion mentions in her autobiography that René had big projects for her: "fix teeth, change hair and look" (Dion, 2000). According to other writers, the measures that Dion took to transform her look into that of a sexy superstar were even more drastic. Some biographers claim that she underwent extensive orthodontic work and even oral plastic surgery to give her a sexier look (Grills, 1997; Halperin, 1997). It is also claimed that she enrolled in intensive English classes, was taught to adopt a sophisticated British accent, and was put through a vigorous—if not gruelling—exercise regimen to develop a sexier body (Halperin, 1997). In addition, she spent months mastering dance moves that would enhance her onstage presence (Grills, 1997; Halperin, 1997). Apparently, one and a half years were devoted to perfecting her look, and when the overhaul was finished, the 18-year-old Dion had been transformed from a child star who spoke mostly French into a sexy, English-speaking pop diva (Halperin, 1997).

Clearly, concern with impression management is alive and well in our country, too! Most of us, of course, do not go to quite these lengths to manage the impressions we convey. All of us, however, attempt to manage our impressions to some extent.

◀ Impression management in action: Céline Dion before and after her image change.

SUMMARY

In this chapter, we have explored the nature of the self, the function of the self, and how people come to know themselves. The **self-concept** is the contents of the self—namely our perception of our own thoughts, beliefs, and personality traits. People differ in the extent to which their sense of self is clearly defined. Those who are high in self-concept clarity are more likely to have high self-esteem. The self-concept serves three important functions: organizational (acting as a schema that influences what we notice, think, and remember), emotional (determining how we feel about ourselves), and executive (regulating our actions and planning for the future). These functions of the self may well serve a survival function and are probably basic to all humans.

There are, however, interesting cross-cultural and gender differences in the self-concept. In many Western cultures, people have an **independent view of the self**, whereby they define themselves mainly in terms of their own thoughts, feelings, and actions. In many Asian cultures, people have an **interdependent view of the self**, whereby they define themselves primarily in terms of their relationships with other people. In North America,

women define themselves more in relation to other people and close intimate relationships than do men. This kind of interdependence is known as *relational* interdependence. Men are more likely to have an independent view of self. Men also show interdependence, but it takes a different form than in women. Specifically, men tend to focus on the groups to which they belong—a kind of interdependence known as *collective* interdependence.

There are four basic ways in which we come to know ourselves: through (1) **introspection**, (2) observations of our own behaviour, (3) self-schemas, and (4) social interaction. **Self-awareness** refers to the act of thinking about ourselves. Self-awareness can take two forms—either reflection (a positive form of self-focus) or rumination (a negative form of self-focus). Research on **self-awareness theory** has found that introspecting about ourselves can be unpleasant, because it focuses our attention on how we fall short of our internal standards. As a result, we may distract ourselves from these unpleasant feelings (e.g., by watching television). A benefit of self-focus is that it can make us more aware of our own feelings and traits. Thinking about why we feel the way we do, however, is more difficult. Many studies show that people's judgments about the reasons for their feelings and actions are often incorrect, in part because people rely on **causal theories** when explaining their behaviour.

Self-perception theory holds that we come to know ourselves through observations of our own behaviour, just as an outsider would. This occurs in particular when our internal states are unclear and there appears to be no external reason for our behaviour. One interesting application of self-perception theory is the **overjustification effect**, which is the discounting of our **intrinsic motivation** for a task, as a result of inferring that we are engaging in the task because of **extrinsic motivation**. That is, rewards and other kinds of external influences can undermine our intrinsic interest; an activity we once liked seems like work instead of play. The overjustification effect is especially likely to occur when **task-contingent rewards** are used. These rewards are given for completing a task, regardless of people's level of performance. **Performance-contingent rewards** are based on how well people perform a task; these rewards are less likely to decrease interest in a task and may even increase interest if they convey the message that people are competent without making them feel nervous and apprehensive about being evaluated. Another example of self-perception is the **two-factor theory of emotion**, whereby we determine our emotions by observing how aroused we are and making inferences about the causes of that arousal. **Misattribution of arousal** can occur, whereby people attribute their arousal to the wrong source.

People also organize information about themselves into **self-schemas**, which are knowledge structures about the self that help people understand, explain, and predict their own behaviour. Self-schemas also help us organize our pasts, by influencing what we remember about ourselves, or our **autobiographical memories**. There is evidence that our memories can be reconstructive: We view the past not as it really was but in ways consistent with our current theories and schemas.

Another way we come to know ourselves is through social interaction. According to the **looking-glass self**, our sense of who we are is based on others' perceptions of us. These perceptions become internalized and can influence our sense of self at any given time. We also know ourselves through comparison with others. **Social comparison theory** states that we will compare ourselves to others when we are unsure of our standing on some attribute and there is no objective criterion we can use. Typically, we choose to compare ourselves to similar others, for this is most diagnostic. **Downward social comparison**, comparing ourselves to our past selves or to those who are inferior on the relevant attribute, can make us feel better about ourselves—as long as we are confident that we are not vulnerable to their plight. **Upward social comparison**, comparing ourselves to those who are superior on the relevant attribute, can make us feel better about ourselves if we are focusing on our actual (usual) self, but it can make us feel worse about ourselves if we are focusing on our best or ideal self.

Once we know ourselves, we often attempt to manage the self we present to others through the processes of **self-presentation** and **impression management**. Social life is much like the theatre, where we present selves (or roles) to others. Shy people find it particularly difficult to make a positive impression on others. Impression management exists in both Western and Eastern cultures, although it may take different forms.

IF YOU ARE INTERESTED

Baumeister, R. F. (1991). *Escaping the self: Alcoholism, spirituality, masochism, and other flights from the burden of selfhood.* New York: Basic Books. An intriguing look at the many different ways in which people try to escape too much self-focus.

Deci, E. L., & Ryan, R. M. (Eds.) (2002). *Handbook of self-determination research.* Rochester, NY: University of Rochester Press. A state-of-the-art presentation and analysis of theorizing and research on intrinsic and extrinsic motivation (and related concepts). Several chapters were written by leading Canadian researchers, including Richard Koestner (McGill University) and Gaëtan Losier (Université de Moncton), Luc Pelletier (University of Ottawa), Robert Vallerand and Catherine Ratelle (Université du Québec à Montréal), as well as T. Cameron Wild and Michael Enzle (University of Alberta).

Fiske, S. T., & Taylor, S. E. (1991). *Social cognition* (2nd ed.). New York: McGraw-Hill. An encyclopedic review of the literature on social cognition by two experts in the field. Includes a chapter on social cognition and the self that covers in greater detail some of the same material we discussed in this chapter.

Gilovich, T. (1991). *How we know what isn't so: The fallibility of human reason in everyday life.* New York: Free Press. This book, written in an engaging, readable style, examines the cognitive, motivational, and social determinants of what the author refers to as "questionable beliefs," such as beliefs in ESP and in suspect "alternative" health practices (e.g., bogus cancer cures). This book is a must-read for anyone seeking an incisive analysis of why people cling to beliefs that fail to withstand the test of scientific scrutiny.

James, Steve (Director). (1994). *Hoop dreams* [Film]. A documentary about two high-school basketball stars from Chicago. In terms of research on the self and overjustification effects, it is fascinating to see what happens to these two players' love for the game as they are rewarded more and more for playing basketball.

Kitayama, S., & Markus, H. R. (Eds.). (1994). *Emotion and culture: Empirical investigations of mutual influence.* Washington, D.C.: American Psychological Association Press. A collection of chapters on culture and emotion by top researchers in the area. The topics include how emotions are experienced within a cultural context, the role of language in culture and emotion, and the relation between culture, emotion, and morality.

Kunda, Z. (1999). *Social cognition.* Cambridge, MA: MIT Press. A comprehensive, up-to-date summary and analysis of social cognitive theory and research written by a prominent expert in the field from the University of Waterloo. This book was written with an undergraduate audience in mind. It is clear, readable, and infused with everyday examples to illustrate social cognitive concepts.

Mann, Thomas (1932). *The magic mountain.* This novel was reportedly the inspiration for Stanley Schachter's two-factor theory of emotion. While Hans Castorp is at a tuberculosis sanatorium high in the Swiss Alps, he experiences feelings of arousal and shortness of breath due to the thin air. He interprets these feelings as signs of love for Clauvida Chauchat.

Proust, Marcel (1934). *Remembrance of things past.* This classic novel is full of insights about how people gain self-knowledge.

Schlenker, B. R., & Pontari, B. A. (2000). The strategic control of information: Impression management and self-presentation in daily life. In A. Tesser, R. B. Fleson, & J. M. Suls (Eds). *Psychological perspectives on self and identity* (pp. 199–232). Washington, D.C.: American Psychological Association. A conceptually rich, up-to-date review and analysis of the literature on impression management and self-presentation.

Tan, Amy (1989). *The joy luck club.* A poignant novel, also made into a feature film, about identity and growth within conflicting cultural contexts.

Vigne, Daniel (Director). (1982). *The return of Martin Guerre* [Film]. A film about a young husband who disappears and then returns to his wife years later. But is it the same man or an imposter? The film raises interesting questions about the continuity of one's identity and how that identity is perceived by others. A 1993 remake of the film, starring Jodie Foster and Richard Gere, was called *Sommersby*.

WEBLINKS

www.spsp.org

Society for Personality and Social Psychology

This is the division of APA that pertains to social psychology and personality.

www.personalityresearch.org

Great Ideas in Personality

This site contains original contributions by many authors on personality research programs ranging from psychoanalysis to behaviourism to sociobiology, as well as pages on psychology journals, psychologist home pages, and personality courses.

CHAPTER 6

Self-Justification and the Need to Maintain Self-Esteem

Chapter Outline

MARCH, 1997. QUEBEC POLICE WERE STUNNED WHEN THEY LEARNED that five people had committed suicide in St. Casimir, a village west of Quebec City. The people who died were members of the Solar Temple cult, discussed briefly in Chapter 1. The cult was lead by Luc Jouret and his right-hand man, Joseph Di Mambro. Those who joined the Solar Temple cult were mainly wealthy professionals, including the mayor of Richelieu, Quebec, and his wife, people in upper management positions at Hydro-Québec, a journalist, and a civil servant. Jouret was a charismatic spiritual leader with formidable powers of persuasion. A woman interviewed by *Maclean's* reported, "He asked all of us to empty our bank accounts" (Laver, 1994). She and her husband sold their property in Switzerland and handed over the proceeds—$300 000—to Jouret. Others followed suit. Most disturbing of all, Jouret convinced cult members that the world was about to be destroyed by fire, and that the only salvation was to take a "death voyage" by ritualized suicide to the star Sirius, where they would be reborn.

▲ Luc Jouret, leader of the Order of the Solar Temple cult, died in the 1994 mass murder–suicide along with 52 other members.

The cult attracted worldwide attention in October 1994, when buildings used by Jouret and his followers in a small village in Switzerland, and a chalet owned by Di Mambro in Morin Heights, Quebec, erupted in flames. Swiss firefighters discovered a chapel in which 22 cult members, cloaked in ceremonial robes, lay in a circle, with their faces looking up at a Christ-like figure resembling Jouret. In Morin Heights, police found the bodies of cult members clad in ceremonial robes and wearing red and gold medallions inscribed with the initials T. S. (*Temple Solaire*). At the end of the day, the death toll was 53 people, including several children. It is believed that both Jouret and Di Mambro died in the Swiss fires. So did the mayor of Richelieu, Quebec, and his wife (Laver, 1994).

Sadly, the 1994 deaths did not put an end to the cult. Some of the remaining followers continued to take death voyages. However, by 1997, Quebec police believed that the Solar Temple had finally run its course. Apparently that was not the case. The five suicides in St. Casimir, Quebec, brought the total to 74 deaths in Canada and Europe over a five-year period.

By what process do intelligent, sane people succumb to such fantastic thinking and self-destructive behaviour? For now, we will simply state that their behaviour is not unfathomable. Rather, it is simply an extreme example of a normal human tendency—our tendency to justify our actions. We will explore this process in greater detail in the latter half of this chapter.

The need to justify our actions is only one aspect of self-evaluation. As we will see, we also have a need to feel good about ourselves, and as a result we engage in all kinds of repair strategies when our self-esteem is threatened. We also have a need for accurate information about ourselves—even if that information is not necessarily flattering. These basic human needs are the focus of this chapter.

The Need to Feel Good about Ourselves

During the past half-century, social psychologists have discovered that one of the most powerful determinants of human behaviour stems from our need to preserve a stable, positive self-concept; that is, to maintain a relatively favourable view of ourselves, particularly when we encounter evidence that contradicts our typically rosy self-image (Aronson, 1969, 1992, 1998; Baumeister, 1993; Cooper, 1998; Devine, 1998; Harmon-Jones, 1998; Leippe & Eisenstadt, 1998; Wicklund & Brehm, 1998). In recent years, social psychologists have explored this basic premise—that people have a fundamental need to maintain a stable, positive sense of self—in greater depth and in new contexts.

SELF-DISCREPANCY THEORY

The work of E. Tory Higgins and his colleagues (Higgins, 1987, 1989, 1996, 1999; Higgins, Klein, & Strauman, 1987) is concerned with understanding how violations of personal standards influence people's emotional and motivational states. In particular, these researchers have taken a close look at the nature of the emotional distress that occurs when we perceive ourselves as not measuring up to our ideals and standards. **Self-discrepancy theory** posits that we become distressed when our sense of who we truly are—our actual self—is discrepant from our personal standards or desired self-conceptions. For Higgins and his colleagues, these standards are reflected most clearly in the various beliefs we hold about the type of person we aspire to be—our ideal self—and the type of person we believe we should be—our "ought" self. Comparing our actual self with our ideal and ought selves provides us with an important means of self-evaluation.

What happens when we become aware that we have failed to measure up to our own standards? Consider the predicament of Sarah, a first-year university student who has always had very high academic standards. In terms of self-discrepancy theory, academic competence is a central component of her ideal self. Moreover, she's become accustomed to living up to these high standards over the years. With only a modest level of effort in high school, she earned *A*s in most subjects and *B*s in the others. In her first semester at a competitive, prestigious university, however, Sarah has discovered that those *A*s are much harder to come by. As a matter of fact, in her introductory chemistry course—a prerequisite for her major—she barely managed to earn a *C*. Given this scenario, how is Sarah likely to experience this discrepancy between her ideal and actual selves?

To begin with, we might imagine that the threat to her self-concept as a high achiever would almost certainly generate fairly strong levels of emotional discomfort—for example, disappointment in herself and perhaps an unaccustomed sense of uncertainty regarding her abilities. Self-discrepancy research supports this view. In a series of studies, Higgins and his colleagues (Higgins, 1989; Higgins et al., 1986) have found that when people are made mindful of a discrepancy between their actual and ideal selves, they tend to experience a pattern of feelings involving dejection, sadness, dissatisfaction, and other depression-related emotions.

On the other hand, what if Sarah had encountered a self-discrepancy involving her ought self—that is, not the ideal self she aspired to but the "should" self she felt obligated to uphold? Imagine that being a top-notch student was not enormously significant to Sarah. Instead, suppose that her parents had always held this standard as highly important, and that Sarah, out of respect for them, tried to achieve academic excellence. How, then, would Sarah experience this discrepancy between her actual and ought selves, in the face of a mediocre performance in her first semester at university? Research by Higgins and his colleagues indicates that in this case, Sarah would be likely to experience fear, worry, tension, and other anxiety-related emotions.

Self-discrepancy theory
the theory that we become distressed when our sense of who we truly are—our actual self—is discrepant from our personal standards or desired self-conceptions

How might Sarah attempt to cope with the negative feelings generated by either of these two forms of self-discrepancy? According to the theory, self-discrepancies not only produce emotional discomfort but also provoke strivings to minimize the gap between the actual and the ideal, or ought, selves. Thus, Sarah might convince herself that the grading was unfair, that her chemistry instructor was totally inept, or in some other way interpret her mediocre performance in the most positive light possible. Of course, justifying her actions in order to maintain self-esteem—while a self-protective strategy in the short run—might not be the most adaptive approach Sarah could adopt. Rather, she would undoubtedly benefit far more from reassessing her situation—concluding, perhaps, that maintaining her high academic standards might require greater effort than she had been accustomed to exerting in the past when her courses were less challenging.

Self-Discrepancies and Culture In cultures that emphasize interdependence, self-criticism is valued because group members are expected to continually strive to improve themselves in order to function harmoniously with others (Heine et al., 1999). Heine and Lehman (1999) reasoned that this emphasis on self-criticism might lead people in Asian cultures to experience larger discrepancies between their ideal and actual self than people in Western cultures. Indeed, when the researchers compared students at the University of British Columbia with students at Ritsumeikan University in Kyoto, Japan, they found that Japanese students viewed their actual self as falling short of their ideal self (particularly on traits they regarded as important) to a greater extent than did the Canadian students. However, interestingly, for Japanese students, discrepancies between their actual and ideal self were not as depressing as they were for Canadian students. Heine and Lehman suggest that the Japanese participants may have been accustomed to thinking of their inadequacies as areas for improvement and therefore found it less upsetting that they weren't measuring up to their ideals.

SELF-COMPLETION THEORY

Robert Wicklund and Peter Gollwitzer have investigated how the need for self-maintenance plays itself out in the realm of social relationships (Brunstein & Gollwitzer, 1996; Gollwitzer & Wicklund, 1985; Wicklund & Gollwitzer, 1982). Specifically, their work on **self-completion theory** indicates that when people experience a threat to a valued aspect of their self-concept, or identity, they become highly motivated to seek some sort of social recognition of that identity. Once achieved, this acknowledgment allows people to restore their valued self-conceptions.

Imagine, for example, that you are an aspiring poet. You think your work has a good deal of promise, and one of your poems has already been published in a small, regional poetry journal. Bolstered by this success, you have recently sent out a new batch of poems to a more prestigious journal with a larger circulation. You are also committed to developing your talents further, so you sign up for a writing course offered by an up-and-coming poet whose work you greatly admire. As you're leaving the house on your way to the first class, you stop at your mailbox to pick up the mail. You discover a letter from the poetry journal to which you've submitted your work. With great excitement, you rip open the letter. To your dismay, however, you find an impersonal form letter from the journal's editor, informing you that your poems have been deemed unacceptable for publication.

▲ Self-discrepancy theory posits that we are distressed when our sense of who we truly are does not match our desired self-conception. For this high-achieving student, finding out she's done poorly on a test would generate strong levels of emotional discomfort.

Self-completion theory
the theory that when people experience a threat to a valued aspect of their self-concept, or identity, they become highly motivated to seek social recognition of that identity

Disappointed and annoyed, you tear up the letter, get into your car, and proceed to your writing class. When you arrive, the instructor announces that most of the class time will be spent listening to student poetry, but that given the unexpectedly large size of the group, only a few students will have the opportunity to read samples of their work. She then asks for volunteers.

Given the recent blow to your cherished identity as a poet, how do you think you would react to the instructor's request? Would you shrink back into your chair and let the others grab for the spotlight? Probably not. Rather, research on self-completion theory strongly suggests that even before the instructor had finished her sentence, your hand would have shot up into the air, as you vigorously vie for an opportunity to have your poems heard by the rest of the class. Why would this be the case? According to Wicklund and Gollwitzer (1982), when we experience a threat to an identity to which we are committed, we become highly motivated to restore that aspect of our self-concept through social recognition. We tend to look for ways to signal to others that we do in fact have a credible, legitimate claim to a particular identity that has been challenged. Through such self-symbolizing activities—in this case, reading poems to a group of strangers—we are able to restore our valued notions of self.

In an experiment very similar to this hypothetical scenario, participants who were committed to their identities as promising dancers wrote essays about their training in dance (Gollwitzer, 1986). Half the participants were asked to describe the worst dance instructor they had ever trained with; the other half wrote essays about their most gifted instructor. In the former condition, then, participants were made uncomfortably aware of an aspect of their training that undermined their identities as dancers (having a poor instructor), whereas in the latter condition subjects were asked to recall an aspect of their background that supported their identities as dancers (having a great instructor). Later, in an entirely different setting, all the participants were invited to participate in a dance concert and were given an opportunity to select a date for their performance. As self-completion theory predicts, dancers whose identities had been threatened—those who had recently been asked to recall an inadequate aspect of their training—expressed the desire to perform in public nearly two weeks earlier than those whose self-concepts as dancers had not been challenged. Similar results have been found in research involving medical students whose identities as aspiring physicians were threatened (Gollwitzer, 1986), as well as individuals who were made to feel inadequate about their identities as athletes (Gollwitzer & Wicklund, 1985).

SELF-EVALUATION MAINTENANCE THEORY

So far we have been focusing on situations in which our self-image is threatened by our own behaviour, such as failing to live up to our ideals. Abraham Tesser and his colleagues have explored how other people's behaviour can threaten our self-concept (Tesser, 1988; Tesser, Martin, & Mendolia, 1995; Beach et al., 1996).

Suppose you consider yourself to be a good cook—in fact, the best cook among all your friends and acquaintances. You love nothing better than playing with a recipe, adding your own creative touches, until, voilà—you have a delectable new creation. Then you move to another town, make new friends, and, alas, your favourite new friend turns out to be a superb cook, far better than you. How does that make you feel? We suspect you will agree that you might feel more than a little uneasy about the fact that your friend outdoes you in your area of expertise.

Now consider a slightly different scenario. Suppose your new best friend is not a superb cook, but a very talented artist. Are you likely to experience any discomfort in this situation? Undoubtedly not; in fact, you are likely to bask in the reflected glory of your friend's success. "Guess what?" you will probably tell everyone. "My new friend has sold some of her paintings in the most exclusive art galleries."

The difference between these two cases is that in the first one, your friend is superior on an attribute that is important to you and may even be a central part of how you define yourself. We all have abilities and traits that we treasure—we are especially proud of being good cooks, talented artists, gifted musicians, or inventive scientists. Whatever our most treasured ability, if we encounter someone who is better at it than we are, there is likely to be trouble—trouble of the self-esteem variety. It is difficult to be proud of your ability to cook if your closest friend is a far better chef than you are.

This is the premise of Tesser's (1988) **self-evaluation maintenance theory**. One's self-concept can be threatened by another individual's behaviour; the level of the threat is determined by both the closeness of the other individual and the personal relevance of the behaviour. As seen in Figure 6.1, there is no problem if a close friend outperforms us on a task that is not relevant to us. In fact, we feel even better about ourselves. However, we feel bad when a close friend outperforms us on a task that is relevant to our self-definition. For example, Campbell, Fairey, and Fehr (1986) had students at the University of British Columbia participate in an experiment in which they performed two tests—one that supposedly assessed their social sensitivity, and another that supposedly assessed their esthetic judgment. Some students participated in the experiment with a friend; others participated with a stranger. Later, the participants were given feedback indicating that they had done poorly on one of the tests—both they and their partner in the experiment got only 6 of the 12 questions right. On the other test, their performance was better—they got 8 of the 12 questions right and their partner got 11 right. Which situation did participants prefer? Campbell and colleagues found that when the partner was close to them (i.e., their friend), participants preferred the test on which they and their friend received the same score—even though their performance was worse on that test (6 versus 8 questions correct). On the other hand, when their partner was a stranger, participants preferred the test on which they received a higher score—despite the fact that their partner outperformed them. This study illustrated that it is less threatening to our self-esteem to have performed poorly than to have a close friend trump our good performance.

This conclusion is reinforced by a recent study of more than 1000 French-Canadian schoolchildren (Guay, Boivin, & Hodges, 1999). The children's self-esteem in the area of academics (an area that was relevant to their self-definition) increased when they compared themselves with low-performing close friends and decreased when they compared themselves with high-performing friends. Consistent with self-evaluation maintenance theory, comparisons with friends who were not close had no effect on the children's self-evaluation.

An astute reader may have noticed that there appears to be a contradiction between the finding that we feel bad when a friend outperforms us and the findings of research by Lockwood and Kunda (1997, 1999) presented in Chapter 5. Specifically, they found that

▲ Self-evaluation maintenance theory predicts that we will only feel threatened if a close friend outperforms us on a task that is important to our self-definition. If your friend earns his or her black belt, this success will threaten your self-esteem if you see yourself as good in martial arts.

Self-evaluation maintenance theory

the theory that one's self-concept can be threatened by another individual's behaviour and that the level of threat is determined by both the closeness of the other individual and the personal relevance of the behaviour

▶ **Figure 6.1**

SELF-EVALUATION
MAINTENANCE THEORY.

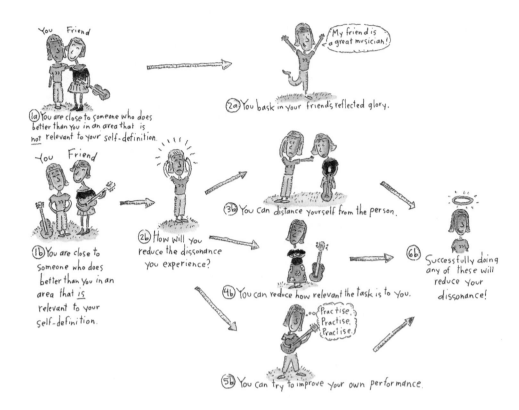

under some conditions, the outstanding behaviour of another person in a domain that is important to us can inspire us and make us feel good about ourselves. Can we resolve the issue of whether a friend's outstanding performance makes us feel good or bad? Lockwood and Kunda suggest that both can be true—the critical factor is whether we believe that our friend's success is attainable. If we think that we too can achieve such greatness, our friend's performance can be inspiring. However, if our friend's performance seems way out of our league, the effects on our self-evaluation will be negative—just as self-evaluation theory would predict.

Restoring Our Self-Esteem If we are vastly outperformed by a friend in an area that matters to us, how do we go about dealing with this threat to our self-esteem? According to self-evaluation maintenance theory, we have three options. First, we can distance ourselves from the person who outperforms us, deciding that he is not such a close friend after all. Pleban and Tesser (1981) tested this possibility by having university students compete against another student, who was actually an accomplice of the experimenter, on general knowledge questions. They rigged it so that in some conditions the questions were on topics that were highly relevant to people's self-definitions and the accomplice got many more of the questions correct. Just as predicted, this was the condition in which people distanced themselves the most from the accomplice, saying they would not want to work with him again.

Sadly, these effects are not limited to the laboratory. As Tesser (1980) found, they occur even in our closest relationships. He examined biographies of male scientists, noting how close these scientists were to their fathers. As the theory predicts, when the scientists' fields of expertise were the same as their fathers', they had a more distant and strained relationship with their fathers. Similarly, the greatest amount of friction between siblings was found to occur when the siblings were close in age and one sibling was significantly better on key dimensions, such as popularity or intelligence. Thus, when performance and relevance are high, it can be difficult to avoid conflicts with family members. Consider how the novelist Norman Maclean (1983) describes his relationship with his brother in *A River Runs Through It*: "One of the earliest things brothers try to find out is how they differ from each other. . . . Undoubtedly, our differences would not have seemed so great if we had not been such a close family."

A second way to reduce such threats to our self-esteem is to change how relevant the task is to our self-definition. If our new friend is a far better cook than we are, we might lose interest in cooking, deciding that auto mechanics is really our thing. To test this prediction, Tesser and Paulhus (1983) gave people feedback about how well they and another student had done on a test of a newly discovered ability: cognitive-perceptual integration. When people learned that the other student was similar to them (high closeness) and had done better on the test, they were especially likely to say that this ability was not very important to them—just as the theory predicts.

Finally, people can deal with self-esteem threats by changing the third component in the equation—their performance relative to the other person's. If our new best friend is a superb cook, we can try to make ourselves an even better cook. This won't work, however, if we are already performing to the best of our ability. If so, we can take a more diabolic route, wherein we try to undermine our friend's performance so that it is not as good as ours. If our friend asks for a recipe, we might leave out a critical ingredient so that her salmon *en brioche* will be certain to flop.

Are people really so mean-spirited that they try to sabotage their friends' performances? Certainly there are many times when we are extremely generous and helpful toward our friends. If our self-esteem is on the line, however, there is evidence that we are not as helpful as we would like to think. Tesser and Smith (1980) asked students to play a game of Password®—wherein one person gave clues to another to guess a word—with both a friend and a stranger. The students could choose to give clues that were helpful, making it easy for the other player to guess the word, or obscure, making it hard for the other player to guess the word. The researchers set it up so that people first performed rather poorly themselves and then had the opportunity to help the other players by giving them easy or difficult clues. The question was, who would they help more—the strangers or their friends?

By now, you can probably see what self-evaluation maintenance theory predicts. If the task is not self-relevant to people, they should want their friends to do especially well, so that they can bask in the reflected glory. If the task is self-relevant, however, it would be threatening to people's self-esteem to have their friends outperform them. So they might make it difficult for their friends, by giving them especially hard clues. This is exactly what Tesser and Smith found. They made the task self-relevant for some participants by telling them that performance on the game was highly correlated with intelligence and leadership skills. Under these conditions, people gave more difficult clues to their friends than to the strangers, because they did not want their friends to shine on a

▶ Figure 6.2

PEOPLE ARE MORE
INCLINED TO BE HELPFUL
TO A FRIEND IF THE
FRIEND'S SUCCESS DOES
NOT POSE A THREAT TO
THEIR OWN SELF-ESTEEM.

(Adapted from Tesser & Smith,
1980)

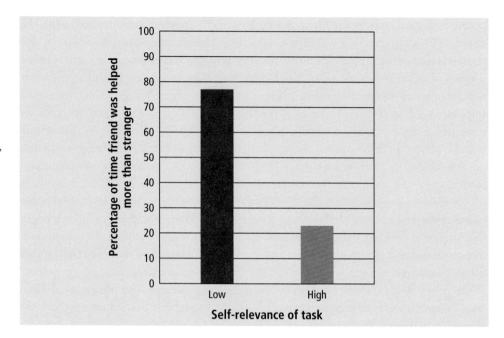

task that was highly important to them. When the task was not self-relevant, people gave more difficult clues to the strangers than to their friends (see Figure 6.2).

In sum, research on self-evaluation maintenance theory has shown that threats to our self-concept have fascinating implications for our interpersonal relationships. When we are feeling threatened, we are highly motivated to restore our self-esteem, even if that means distancing ourselves from someone who is close to us—or, if we are feeling really desperate for a self-esteem boost, even sabotaging their performance.

SELF-AFFIRMATION THEORY

Another kind of threat to our self-esteem occurs when we behave in ways that are contrary to our attitudes. For example, if we smoke cigarettes, we will experience *cognitive dissonance*—a feeling of discomfort created when our attitudes are inconsistent with our behaviour. (We will discuss cognitive dissonance theory more fully in the latter part of this chapter.) We know that smoking is bad for us, and yet here we are doing it. In this situation, people are motivated to alleviate the discomfort, a process known as *dissonance reduction*. Thus, we might try to quit smoking or we might convince ourselves that smoking is not really bad for our health.

Sometimes, however, threats to our self-concept can be so strong and difficult to avoid that the normal means of reducing dissonance do not work. It can be difficult to stop smoking, as millions of people have discovered. It is also difficult to ignore all of the evidence indicating that smoking is bad for us and might even kill us. So what can we do? **Self-affirmation theory** suggests that people will reduce the impact of a dissonance-arousing threat to their self-concept by focusing on and affirming their competence on some dimension unrelated to the threat.

Research by Claude Steele and his colleagues (Aronson, Cohen, & Nail, 1998; Steele, 1988) shows how self-affirmation comes about. "Yes, it's true that I smoke," you might

Self-affirmation theory

a theory suggesting that people will reduce the impact of a dissonance-arousing threat to their self-concept by focusing on and affirming their competence on some dimension unrelated to the threat

say, "but I am a great cook" (or a terrific poet, or a wonderful friend, or a promising scientist). Self-affirmation occurs when our self-esteem is threatened; if possible, we will attempt to restore our self-esteem by reminding ourselves of some irrelevant aspect of our self-concept that we cherish, as a way of feeling good about ourselves in spite of our stupid or immoral behaviour.

In a series of clever experiments, Steele and his colleagues demonstrated that if, prior to the onset of dissonance, you provide people with an opportunity for self-affirmation, they will often grab it (Steele, 1988; Steele & Liu, 1981). For example, Steele, Hoppe, and Gonzales (1986) conducted a classic dissonance reduction experiment. They asked students to rank-order 10 record albums, ostensibly as part of a marketing survey. As a reward, the students were then told that they could keep either their fifth- or sixth-ranked album. Ten minutes after making their choice, they were asked to rate the albums again. Participants spread apart their ratings of the record albums, rating the one they had chosen much higher than the one they had rejected. In this manner, they convinced themselves that they had made a smart decision.

However, Steele and his colleagues built an additional set of conditions into their experiment. Half the students were science majors, and half were business majors. Half the science majors and half the business majors were asked to put on a white lab coat while participating in the experiment. Why the lab coat? As you know, a lab coat is associated with the idea of science. Steele and his colleagues suspected that the lab coat would serve a "self-affirmation function" for the science majors but not for the business majors. The results supported their predictions. Whether or not they were wearing a lab coat, business majors showed standard dissonance reduction. After their choice, they increased their evaluation of the chosen album and decreased their evaluation of the one they had rejected. Similarly, in the absence of a lab coat, science majors reduced their dissonance in the same way. However, science majors who were wearing the lab coat resisted the temptation to distort their perceptions; the lab coat reminded these students that they were promising scientists and thereby short-circuited the need to reduce dissonance by changing their attitudes toward the albums. In effect, they said, "I might have made a dumb choice in record albums, but I can live with that because I have other things going for me; at least I'm a promising scientist!" A simplified version of these findings is presented in Figure 6.3.

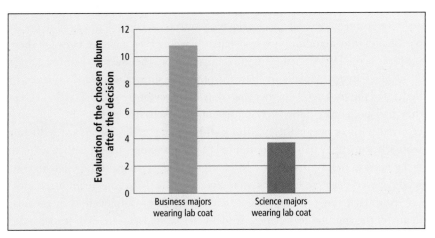

◀ Figure 6.3

DISSONANCE AND SELF-AFFIRMATION.

People who were allowed the opportunity to affirm their values (science majors wearing lab coats) were able to avoid the pressures to reduce dissonance by increasing the attractiveness of the chosen album.

(Adapted from Steele, Hoppe, & Gonzales, 1986)

We have seen that people can deal with threats to their self-esteem by reminding themselves of the areas in which they are competent and performing well. Recent research by Sandra Murray, John Holmes, and their colleagues (Murray et al, 2001; Murray et al., 1998) suggests that people also use their close relationships as a self-affirmational resource. These researchers conducted a series of studies with students at the University of Waterloo and at the State University of New York, Buffalo who were in dating relationships. In this research, some of the participants experienced a threat to their self-concept. This was done, for example, by giving them false feedback indicating that they were not very intelligent. How did these participants restore their self-esteem? By exaggerating how much their partners appreciated and accepted them. In effect, these participants were saying, "I may not be that smart, but I have a wonderful partner who thinks I'm great!" Interestingly, people with high self-esteem were most likely to engage in this self-affirmational strategy.

Self-Affirmation and Culture

According to Heine and Lehman (1997a), the experience of dissonance may be unique to cultures in which the self is defined as independent. If the focus in a culture is on the individual, it becomes important for the individual to behave in ways that are consistent with his or her attitudes, because the person's behaviour is seen as diagnostic of what he or she is really like. On the other hand, if the self is defined in relation to others, as is the case in Asian cultures, behaviour is more likely to be tailored to the demands of the group. If an individual behaves in an attitude-inconsistent way, others are likely to invoke situational explanations. (You may recall from our discussion of the fundamental attribution error in Chapter 4 that people in Asian cultures do, in fact, make more situational attributions for others' behaviour than those in Western cultures.) Based on this reasoning, Heine and Lehman hypothesized that people in Asian cultures should experience little dissonance when their attitudes and behaviours are inconsistent.

To test this idea, the researchers conducted a study similar to the one by Steele, Hoppe, and Gonzales (1986) we just described. Students at the University of British Columbia and Japanese students visiting Vancouver signed up for a marketing research study. First, the researchers administered a bogus personality test. Then participants were asked to rate the desirability of 10 CDs. In the meantime, their personality tests supposedly had been scored. Some participants received positive personality feedback and others received negative feedback. (Participants in a control group did not receive any personality information.) Next, participants were given a choice between their fifth- and sixth-ranked CDs. After they made their selection, they were asked to again rate all 10.

Canadian participants in the control group showed classic dissonance reduction—they rated the chosen CD higher than they had previously and the rejected CD lower than they had previously. However, consistent with self-affirmation theory, Canadians who received positive personality feedback did not engage in dissonance reduction. In other words, because they had been reminded of what wonderful people they were, they did not feel a need to reduce dissonance by changing their ratings of the CDs. In contrast, those who received negative feedback were especially likely to engage in dissonance reduction.

And what about the Japanese participants? They did not show dissonance reduction in any of the conditions. Japanese students felt as bad as Canadian students did about the negative personality feedback and were more likely than Canadians to believe that it was accurate. However, they did not reduce dissonance by changing their ratings of the CDs, even under these circumstances.

Self-Evaluation: Biased or Accurate?

So far we have been operating on the assumption that people (at least in Western cultures) have a need to feel good about themselves. One way of feeling good about ourselves is to distort or exaggerate our positive qualities. We could even convince ourselves that we are better than most other people. Such positive illusions could certainly bolster our self-esteem. On the other hand, probably most of us don't want to live in a fantasy world in which we are fooling ourselves about the kind of person we are. In fact, we might even want other people to "tell it like it is" so that we develop an accurate picture of who we are. Thus, it seems we are caught between wanting to view ourselves in the most positive possible light, and wanting an accurate assessment of what we are really like. Given these conflicting motives, do our self-evaluations tend to show a positivity bias, or do they tend to be accurate? Let's examine the evidence for each side of this issue.

SELF-ENHANCEMENT: WANTING TO FEEL GOOD ABOUT OURSELVES, REGARDLESS OF THE FACTS

Take a moment to answer the following questions: How attractive are you compared to the average student (of your gender) at your university? How adaptive are you compared to the average student? How well are you able to get along with others compared to the average student? Chances are, you see yourself as better than the average student with regard to at least some of these qualities, or perhaps even all of them. One way of boosting our self-esteem is to hold unrealistically positive views of ourselves, a tendency known as **self-enhancement**. "Well," you might be thinking, "in my case, it really isn't unrealistic to have a positive view of myself—I really am a great person." We don't doubt that you are a great person. The problem, however, is that most people have a tendency to think this way, and it really isn't possible for everyone to be better than most people, is it? This is why self-enhancement is defined as an unrealistically positive view of the self.

Self-enhancement
a tendency to hold unrealistically positive views about ourselves

Research confirms that we really do tend to paint quite a flattering picture of ourselves. For example, when Heine and Lehman (1999) asked students at the University of British Columbia the kinds of questions with which we began this section, they found that participants tended to view themselves as better than the average student. In research along the same lines, Jennifer Campbell (1986) found that students at the University of British Columbia showed a false uniqueness effect—they believed that many other students shared their weaknesses, but believed that they were unique in their strengths. Finally, researchers at Simon Fraser University found that people tend to rate themselves as happier, more intelligent, more ethical, and even as having stronger emotional reactions than those around them (McFarland & Miller, 1990; Miller & McFarland, 1987).

Does engaging in this kind of unrealistic thinking actually make us feel better about ourselves? Apparently so. Research conducted at the University of British Columbia by Del Paulhus and colleagues has found that the more we distort reality to paint a flattering picture of ourselves, the higher our self-esteem is (Paulhus, 1998; Yik, Bind, & Paulhus, 1998).

Self-Enhancement and Culture

As we have already discussed, self-enhancement appears to be largely a Western phenomenon. Unrealistically positive self views are not common in Eastern cultures. In fact, as mentioned earlier, in Asian cultures the tendency is to hold a negative view of oneself—a phenomenon known as self-effacement (Heine et al., 1999; Heine, 2001, under review). Yik, Bond, and Paulhus (1998) found evidence of this cultural difference in a study in which they asked students at the University of British Columbia who were working on a group project to rate one another's personality traits. Canadian students showed classic self-enhancement—they rated themselves more positively than the other group members rated them. However, when students at the Chinese University of Hong Kong made similar ratings, the findings were opposite—Chinese students rated themselves more negatively than their peers rated them. More recently, Heine and Renshaw (2002) examined how students in Japan and the United States rated themselves on various traits compared to how their university friends rated them. Americans perceived themselves more positively than their friends perceived them; Japanese perceived themselves more negatively than their friends perceived them. Similarly, Heine and his colleagues have found that Canadian students view themselves as superior to their peers, whereas Japanese students see themselves as worse than their peers. This tendency is particularly pronounced among Japanese students after they are given failure feedback. In contrast, failure feedback does nothing to tarnish the positive self-view of Canadians (Heine, Kitayama, & Lehman, 2001; see Endo, Heine, & Lehman, 2000 for related findings). Given findings such as these, you probably will not find it surprising that Asian university students score lower on measures of self-esteem than Canadian students do (Campbell et al., 1996; Endo, Heine, & Lehman, 2000; Heine & Lehman, 1997b; Sato & Cameron, 1999).

It appears that these tendencies are established at an early age. For example, Kwok (1995) found that grade-four students in Hong Kong rated themselves lower in scholastic competence, athletic competence, physical appearance, and overall self-worth than did grade-four students in Canada. Interestingly, this was the case even though the Chinese students performed better than the Canadian children on standardized math tests.

Heine, Takata, and Lehman (2000) wondered whether people in Asian countries might, in fact, secretly engage in self-enhancement but not feel comfortable openly bragging about themselves on questionnaires. To examine this possibility, they designed a study in which they measured self-enhancement in a subtle way—namely, by examining whether students believed or accepted certain kinds of feedback. In this study, students at the University of British Columbia and at Nara University in Japan took a computerized mathematical judgment test. Later, participants were asked who had performed better on the test—them or the average student at their university. In order to answer this question, they were given (false) information on how they had performed on each trial and how the average student had performed. Participants were told that they could keep viewing trials until they had enough information to answer the question. In the success condition, the participant had higher scores than the average student on most trials, whereas in the failure condition, the average student's scores generally were higher. The critical question was how many of these trials participants would want to view before making a decision about whether they had performed better than the average student. As shown on the left side of Figure 6.4, in Canada participants in the failure condition tended to view more trials than participants in the success condition. In other words, Canadians found it hard to believe that they had done worse than the average student, and therefore needed ample "proof" that they had done so. However, if the feedback indicated that they had outperformed the average student, they did not need to see many trials to be convinced of this. In other words, Canadians showed self-enhancing tendencies (see Figure 6.4).

In Japan, participants showed exactly the opposite pattern. They did not have to see many trials in which they had been outperformed before concluding that the average student had performed better than they had (see right side of Figure 6.4). However, when it came to concluding that they had performed better than the average student, they needed plenty of proof—Japanese participants in the success condition viewed the greatest number of trials. As the researchers note, these results are consistent with self-effacement.

Recall that Heine and colleagues conducted this study to see whether Japanese people's failure to show self-enhancement effects might be due to a reluctance to boast about their positive qualities on questionnaires. This study gave participants (in the success condition) an opportunity to self-enhance without being obvious about it. However, even under these conditions Japanese participants did not capitalize on the chance to feel good about themselves, whereas Canadians were eager to seize the opportunity.

In another study, Heine and Lehman (1997b) explored a different possibility—namely, that self-enhancement may simply take a different form in Asian cultures. Specifically, they proposed that in cultures that value interdependence, people might hold unrealistically positive views about the groups to which they belong, rather than about themselves as individuals. To test this possibility, they asked students in Canada and Japan to rate their own and their rival university. For example, students at the University of British Columbia and at

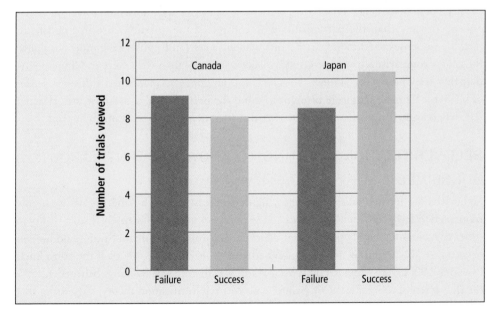

◀ **Figure 6.4**

CULTURAL DIFFERENCES IN SELF-ENHANCEMENT.

When Canadian participants received feedback that they had performed worse than the average student, they needed greater "proof" that this had been the case than when they received feedback that they had performed better than the average student. Japanese students found it easy to believe that they had performed poorly, but hard to believe that they had performed well.

(Based on Heine, Takata, & Lehman, 2000)

Simon Fraser University were asked how much they agreed with statements such as "I think that most UBC students are glad they went to UBC instead of SFU." They also rated themselves and students at each university in terms of independent (e.g., confident, intelligent) and interdependent (e.g., cooperative, loyal) traits. Students at rival universities in Japan (Ritsumeikan and Doshisha) completed the same measures.

By now it will not surprise you to learn that in Canada, students rated themselves and the students at their university more positively than they rated the students at their rival university. And what about the Japanese students? Did they show group-enhancement? Not at all—in fact, Japanese students rated their own university more negatively than the rival university.

These researchers obtained similar findings when they asked students in Canada and Japan to estimate the extent to which a close family member was better than the average family member of the same age and gender: Canadians thought their family members were better than average; Japanese participants thought their family members were worse than average. Thus, the hypothesis that people from Asian cultures might show group-enhancement rather than self-enhancement was not supported. Instead, Heine and Lehman found that Canadians engaged in both kinds of enhancement. The researchers suggest that in Western cultures, group-enhancement may simply be another route to self-enhancement. And as for self-enhancement among Easterners, Heine and Lehman have reached the conclusion that they simply don't do it! A recent meta analysis of 70 studies examining self-enhancement among North Americans and East Asians supports this conclusion (Heine, under review).

Before we leave this topic, we would like to consider a fascinating question posed by Ross, Xun, and Wilson (2002), namely whether people evaluate themselves differently, depending on the cultural identity that is activated. To find out, Ross and colleagues asked Chinese-born students (who had lived in Canada for an average of seven years) to complete a questionnaire on various aspects of the self. The questionnaire was written in either Chinese or English. Interestingly, participants who answered in Chinese described themselves in more collectivist terms, were more self-effacing, and scored lower on a self-esteem measure than the participants who completed the questionnaire in English. In fact, the responses of Chinese participants who answered in English were more similar to those of a comparison group of Canadian-born students than they were to Chinese participants responding in Chinese. In short, the language used primed different senses of self—the Chinese language brought to mind the participants' collectivist, self-effacing self, whereas the English language activated their independent, self-enhancing self.

SELF-VERIFICATION: WANTING TO KNOW THE TRUTH ABOUT OURSELVES

Self-verification theory

a theory suggesting that people have a need to seek confirmation of their self-concept, whether the self-concept is positive or negative; in some circumstances, this tendency can conflict with the desire to uphold a favourable view of oneself

So far we have focused on research showing that, at least in North America, we are highly motivated to feel good about ourselves, to the point where we will happily distort reality in order to maintain a highly positive self-concept. According to William Swann and his colleagues, we also are motivated to know the truth about ourselves—even if the truth hurts (Swann, 1990, 1996; Swann & Hill, 1982; Swann & Pelham, 1988; Swann & Schroeder, 1995; Giesler, Josephs, & Swann, 1996). Swann calls this **self-verification theory**, suggesting that people have a need to seek confirmation of their self-concept whether the self-concept is positive or negative. In some circumstances, this tendency can conflict with the desire to uphold a favourable view of oneself.

For example, consider Patrick, who has always thought of himself as a lousy writer with poor verbal skills. One day he is working on a term paper with a friend, who remarks that she thinks his paper is skilfully crafted, beautifully written, and superbly articulate. How will Patrick feel? He should feel pleased and gratified, we might predict, because the friend's praise gives Patrick's self-esteem a boost. On the other hand, Patrick's friend has given him feedback that challenges his long-standing view of himself as a poor writer, and he might be motivated to maintain this negative view. Why? For two reasons. First, according to self-verification theory, it is unsettling and confusing to have our views of ourselves disconfirmed; if we changed our self-concept every time we encountered someone with a different opinion of us, it would be impossible to maintain a coherent, consistent self-concept. Second, self-verification theory holds that it can be uncomfortable to interact with people who view us differently from the way we view ourselves. People who don't know us might have unrealistic expectations, and it would be embarrassing to have them discover that we are not as smart or as artistic or as creative as they think we are. Better to let them know our faults at the outset.

In short, when people with negative self-views receive positive feedback, opposing needs go head to head—the desire to feel good about themselves by believing the positive feedback (self-enhancement needs) versus the desire to maintain a consistent, coherent picture of themselves and avoid the embarrassment of being found out (self-verification needs). Which needs win out?

Several studies suggest that when the two motives are in conflict, our need to maintain a stable self-concept under certain conditions overpowers our compelling desire to view ourselves in a positive light (Aronson & Carlsmith, 1962; Brock et al., 1965; Marecek & Mettee, 1972; Swann, 1990). For example, Swann and his colleagues have found that people prefer to remain in close relationships with friends, roommates, and romantic partners whose evaluations of their abilities are consistent with their own (sometimes negative) self-evaluations (Swann, Hixon, & De La Ronde, 1992; Swann & Pelham, 1988). In other words, people prefer to be close to someone whose evaluations of them are not more positive than their self-concept. In a close relationship, most people find it better to be known than to be overrated.

We should point out, however, that, recently, Swann and colleagues (2002) have qualified this conclusion. Specifically, they suggest that whether we want to have accurate, rather than positive, feedback depends on two things—the dimension on which we are being evaluated and the nature of the relationship we have with the person doing the evaluating. For example, they found that when it comes to a quality such as physical attractiveness, we want dating partners to give us high marks—regardless of the facts. However, we want the truth when it comes to our other qualities. And if the person assessing our looks is a friend or a roommate, rather than a dating partner, it's honesty that counts. Similarly, if our artistic ability is being evaluated by our art instructor, or our athletic ability is being evaluated by our teammates, we prefer positivity over accuracy. However, if these people are evaluating our other qualities, the self-verification motive wins out.

Before leaving this topic, we should note that there are other limits to the need to self-verify. First, people generally strive to uphold their negative self-beliefs only when they are highly certain of those beliefs (Maracek & Mettee, 1972; Swann & Ely, 1984; Swann & Pelham, 1988). Thus, if Patrick had been less thoroughly convinced of his poor talents as a writer, he almost certainly would have been more receptive to his friend's praise. Second, if the consequences of being improperly evaluated are not too great—for example, if our contact with these individuals is rare so that it is unlikely they will discover we are not who we appear to be—then even people with negative views prefer positive feedback (Aronson, 1992). Finally, if people feel there is nothing they can do to improve their abilities, they generally prefer positive feedback to accurate feedback. Why remind ourselves that we are terrible if there is nothing we can do about it? If, however, people feel that a negative self-attribute can be changed with a little work, they prefer accurate feedback, because this information can help them figure out what they need to do to get better (Steele, Spencer, & Josephs, 1992).

The Need to Justify Our Actions

Another way in which we maintain a positive self-evaluation is to believe that we are reasonable, decent folks who make wise decisions, do not behave immorally, and have integrity. In short, we want to believe that we do not do stupid, cruel, or absurd things. But as we go through life, we encounter a great many challenges to this belief. The rest of this chapter will deal with how human beings handle those challenges.

THE THEORY OF COGNITIVE DISSONANCE

Cognitive dissonance

a feeling of discomfort caused by the realization that one's behaviour is inconsistent with one's attitudes or that one holds two conflicting attitudes

Earlier, in our discussion of self-affirmation theory, we introduced the idea of **cognitive dissonance**—the uncomfortable feeling we experience when our behaviour is at odds with our attitudes or when we hold attitudes that conflict with one another. Leon Festinger was the first to investigate the precise workings of this powerful phenomenon, and elaborated his findings into what is arguably social psychology's most important and most provocative theory—the theory of cognitive dissonance (Festinger, 1957). Cognitive dissonance most often occurs whenever we do something that makes us feel stupid or immoral (Aronson, 1968, 1969, 1992, 1998; Aronson et al., 1974; Thibodeau & Aronson, 1992; Harmon-Jones & Mills, 1998). Dissonance always produces discomfort and therefore motivates a person to try to reduce the discomfort, in much the same way that hunger and thirst produce discomfort that motivates a person to eat or drink. However, unlike satisfying hunger or thirst by eating or drinking, the ways of reducing dissonance are not simple; rather, they often lead to fascinating changes in the way we think about the world and the way we behave.

How can an individual reduce dissonance? There are three basic ways:
- By changing our behaviour to bring it in line with the dissonant cognition
- By attempting to justify our behaviour through changing one of the dissonant cognitions
- By attempting to justify our behaviour by adding new cognitions (see Figure 6.5)

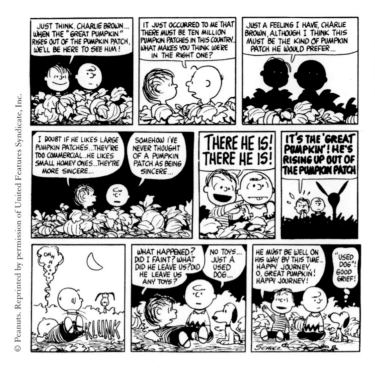

◀ Once we have committed a lot of time or energy to a cause, it is nearly impossible to convince us that the cause is unworthy.

To illustrate, let's look at an absurd example of behaviour that millions of people engage in several times a day—smoking cigarettes. Suppose you are a smoker. As we mentioned earlier in this chapter, you are likely to experience dissonance because it is absurd to engage in behaviour that stands a good chance of producing a painful, early death. How can you reduce this dissonance? The most direct way is to change your

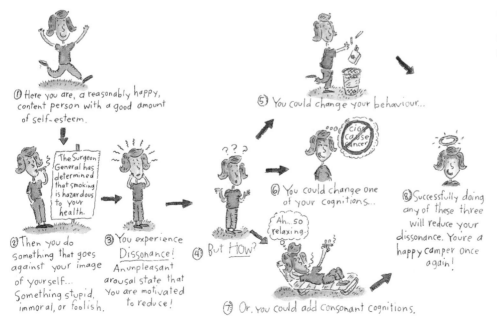

◀ **Figure 6.5**

HOW WE REDUCE COGNITIVE DISSONANCE.

▲ Like smokers, people who are overweight know that there are health risks involved, but have developed ways of rationalizing their decision to keep eating unhealthy, high-fat foods, deciding that our culture places too much emphasis on looks, or that they deserve a treat because the day was difficult. They may even feel that they are not that overweight. They will have to do something to ease the dissonance they are likely to feel when confronted with their weight and the health risks associated with it.

behaviour—to give up smoking. Your behaviour would then be consistent with your knowledge of the link between smoking and cancer. While many people have succeeded in doing just that, it's not easy—many have tried to quit and failed. What do these people do? It would be erroneous to assume that they simply swallow hard and prepare to die. They don't. Instead, they try to reduce their dissonance in a different way—namely, by convincing themselves that smoking isn't as bad as they thought. Rick Gibbons and his colleagues (1997) found that heavy smokers who attended a smoking cessation clinic, quit smoking for a while, and then relapsed into heavy smoking again, actually lowered their perception of the dangers of smoking.

Smokers can come up with pretty creative ways to justify their smoking; for example, some might try to convince themselves that the data linking cigarette smoking to cancer are inconclusive. Others will try to add new cognitions—for example, the erroneous belief that filters trap most of the harmful chemicals and thus reduce the threat of cancer. Some will add a cognition that allows them to focus on the vivid exception: "Look at old Sam Carouthers—he's 97 years old and he's been smoking a pack a day since he was 12. That proves it's not always bad for you." Still others will add the cognition that smoking is an extremely enjoyable activity, one for which it is worth risking cancer. Others may even succeed in convincing themselves that, all things considered, smoking is worthwhile because it relaxes them, reduces nervous tension, and so on.

These justifications may sound silly to the nonsmoker. That is precisely our point. People experiencing dissonance will often go to extreme lengths to reduce it. We did not make up the examples of denial, distortion, and justification listed above; they are based on actual examples generated by people who have tried and failed to quit smoking. Similar justifications have been generated by people who try and fail to lose weight, who refuse to practise safer sex, or who receive unwelcome information about their health (Aronson, 1997b; Croyle & Jemmott, 1990; Goleman, 1982; Kassarjian & Cohen, 1965; Leishman, 1988). To escape from dissonance, people will engage in quite extraordinary rationalizing.

To demonstrate the irrationality of dissonance-reducing behaviour, Edward E. Jones and Rika Kohler (1959) performed a simple experiment in a southern U.S. town in the late 1950s, before desegregation was widely accepted. First, they selected individuals who were deeply committed to a position on the issue of racial segregation—some of the participants were in favour of segregation, others were opposed to it. Next, the researchers presented these individuals with a series of arguments on both sides of the issue. Some of the arguments, on each side, were plausible, and others, on each side, were rather silly. The question was, which of the arguments would people remember best? As you might have guessed, they tended to remember the plausible arguments agreeing with their own position and the implausible arguments agreeing with the opposing position.

Subsequent research has yielded similar results on a wide variety of issues, from whether or not the death penalty deters people from committing murder, to the risks of contracting AIDS through heterosexual contact (e.g., Biek, Wood, & Chaiken, 1996; Edwards & Smith, 1996; Lord, Ross, & Lepper, 1979; Vallone, Ross, & Lepper, 1985). All of this research indicates that we human beings do not process information in an unbiased manner. Rather, we distort it in a way that fits our preconceived notions.

DECISIONS, DECISIONS, DECISIONS

Every time we make a decision—whether it is between two cars, two universities, or two potential lovers—we experience dissonance. Why? Because the chosen alternative is seldom entirely positive, and the rejected alternative is seldom entirely negative. Let's pretend that you are trying to decide which of two attractive people to date: Chris, who is funny and playful, but a bit irresponsible; or Pat, who is interesting and smart, but not very spontaneous. You agonize over the decision but eventually decide to pursue a relationship with Pat. After you've made the decision, you will experience dissonance because despite Pat's good qualities, you did end up choosing to be with someone who is not very spontaneous. Dissonance also is created because you ended up turning down someone who is playful and fun. We call this **postdecision dissonance**.

Cognitive dissonance theory predicts that in order to feel better about the decision, you will do some mental work to try to reduce the dissonance. What kind of work? You would convince yourself that Pat really was the right person for you and that Chris actually would have been a lousy choice. An early experiment by Jack Brehm (1956) illustrates this phenomenon. Brehm posed as a representative of a consumer testing service and asked women to rate the attractiveness and desirability of several kinds of appliances, such as toasters and electric coffee makers. Each woman was told that as a reward for having participated in the survey, she could have one of the appliances as a gift. She was given a choice between two of the products she had rated as being equally attractive. After she made her decision, her appliance was wrapped up and given to her. Twenty minutes later, each woman was asked to re-rate all of the products. Brehm found that after receiving the appliance of their choice, the women rated its attractiveness somewhat higher than they had done the first time. Not only that, but they drastically lowered their rating of the appliance they might have chosen but had decided to reject. In other words, following a decision, to reduce dissonance, we change the way we feel about the chosen and unchosen alternatives—cognitively spreading them apart in our own minds to make ourselves feel better about the choice we made.

Much of the research conducted since Brehm's classic study has adopted this kind of methodology. Participants first evaluate a set of items; they then are given a choice between two items they found attractive; once they have made their choice, they again rate the items to see if their evaluations have changed. For example, earlier (see the section on self-affirmation theory) we described studies in which participants were given a choice between two record albums that they had rated favourably (Steele, Hoppe, & Gonzales, 1986) or between two CDs that they liked (Heine & Lehman, 1997a).

In studies such as these, participants are required to choose between two attractive options. Shultz, Léveillé, and Lepper (1999) describe this situation as one of "choosing between two highly tempting desserts." In an interesting new twist, these researchers examined dissonance reduction in situations where one is forced to choose between two unattractive alternatives—having to decide between "two overcooked and unattractive green vegetables." For example, in one study, Shultz and colleagues asked 13-year-olds attending a day camp in Montreal to rate the attractiveness of various posters. Some children were allowed to choose between two posters they had rated highly. Consistent with classic cognitive dissonance research, these children rated the poster they rejected more negatively than they had previously. Other children had to choose between two posters

Postdecision dissonance
dissonance that is inevitably aroused after a person makes a decision; such dissonance is typically reduced by enhancing the attractiveness of the chosen alternative and devaluing the rejected alternatives

Justifying Decisions

Talk to one or two friends or family members who are trying to decide between two alternatives—between two vehicles, two jobs, two items of clothing in a store, or even two relationship partners. Take note of the pluses and minuses that are mentioned for each alternative. Then, wait until the person has made his or her decision. Take note of the pluses and minuses mentioned for the option chosen and for the one rejected. Is the person even more positive later about the chosen alternative than he or she was before making the choice? Is the person also more negative about the rejected alternative than he or she was before making the choice? Cognitive dissonance theory predicts that the answer to each of these questions would be yes.

that they didn't particularly like. These children also reduced dissonance—in this case, by increasing their liking for the poster they chose. The most striking finding was that dissonance reduction was greater when choosing between unattractive alternatives than when choosing between attractive alternatives. Thus, according to this research, if you are at a buffet dinner, trying to decide between the delectable strawberry shortcake and the scrumptious chocolate hazelnut torte, and you choose the torte, you will end up deciding that the strawberry shortcake didn't look so great after all. However, your thumbs-down rating of the strawberry shortcake will not be as emphatic as your thumbs-up rating on the limp, tasteless green beans if you chose them instead of the soggy, overcooked broccoli. To experience cognitive dissonance in action, see Try It!, above.

The Permanence of the Decision Decisions vary in terms of how permanent they are—that is, how difficult they are to revoke. For example, it is usually a lot easier to go back to a car dealership and trade in your new car for another one than to extricate yourself from an unhappy marriage. The more permanent and less revocable the decision, the greater the need to reduce dissonance.

An excellent place to investigate the significance of irrevocability is the racetrack. Experienced bettors typically spend a great deal of time poring over the "dope sheets," trying to decide which horse to put their money on. When they make a decision, they head for the betting windows. While they are standing in line, they have already made their decision, but, we would hypothesize, because it is still revocable they have no urge to reduce dissonance. However, once they get to the window and place their bet—even if it's for only $2—there is no turning back. Thirty seconds later, one cannot go back and tell the nice person behind the window that one has changed one's mind. If irrevocability is an important factor, one would expect greater dissonance reduction among bettors a few minutes after placing the bet than a few minutes before placing the bet.

In a simple but clever experiment, Knox and Inkster (1968) intercepted people at the Exhibition Park Race Track in Vancouver who were on their way to place $2 bets and asked them how certain they were their horses would win. The investigators also intercepted other bettors just as they were leaving the $2 window, after having placed their

◀ Once an individual makes a final and irrevocable decision, he or she has a greater need to reduce dissonance. For example, at the racetrack, once we've placed our bet, our certainty is greater than it is immediately *before* we've placed our bet.

bets, and asked them the same question. Almost invariably, people who had already placed their bets gave their horses a much better chance of winning than did those who had yet to place their bets. Since only a few minutes separated one group from another, nothing real had occurred to increase the probability of winning; the only thing that had changed was the finality of the decision—and thus the dissonance it produced.

The Decision to Behave Immorally Needless to say, life is made up of more than just decisions about cars, CDs, appliances, and racehorses. Often our decisions involve moral and ethical issues. When is it permissible to lie to a friend, and when is it not? When is an act stealing, and when is it borrowing? The area of resolving moral dilemmas is a particularly interesting one in which to study dissonance, because of the powerful implications for one's self-esteem. Even more interesting is the fact that dissonance reduction following a difficult moral decision can cause people to behave either more or less ethically in the future—it can actually change their system of values.

Take the issue of cheating on an exam. Suppose you are a third-year university student taking the final exam in a chemistry course. You have always wanted to be a surgeon and you know that your admission to medical school depends heavily on how well you do in this course. As you write the exam, you experience acute anxiety and draw a blank. You simply cannot come up with the answer to the most crucial question. You happen to be sitting behind the smartest person in the class and notice that she has just written down her answer to this question. You could easily read it if you chose to. What do you do? Your conscience tells you it's wrong to cheat—and yet if you don't cheat, you are certain to get a poor grade. And if you get a poor grade, there goes medical school.

Regardless of whether you decide to cheat, you are doomed to experience dissonance. If you cheat, your cognition "I am a decent, moral person" is dissonant with your cognition "I have just committed an immoral act." If you decide to resist temptation, your cognition "I want to become a surgeon" is dissonant with your cognition "I could have acted in a way that would have ensured a good grade and admission to medical school, but I chose not to. Wow, was that stupid!"

In this situation, some students decide to cheat; others decide not to cheat. What happens to the students' attitudes about cheating after their decision? For students who decide to cheat, an efficient path of dissonance reduction would be to adopt a more lenient attitude toward cheating, convincing themselves that it is a victimless crime that doesn't hurt anybody, that everybody does it and so it's not really that bad.

Students who manage to resist the temptation to cheat also could reduce dissonance by changing their attitude about the morality of the act—but this time in the opposite direction. That is, in order to justify giving up a good grade, they would have to convince themselves that it is very dishonest and immoral to cheat and that only despicable people would do such a thing.

How Dissonance Affects Personal Values The dissonance reduction that occurs for these students—regardless of whether they cheated or not—is not merely a rationalization of their behaviour but an actual change in their system of values; individuals faced with this kind of choice will undergo either a softening or a hardening of their attitudes toward cheating on exams, depending on whether they decided to cheat. The interesting and important thing to remember is that two people acting in the two different ways described above could have started out with almost identical attitudes toward cheating. Their decisions might have been a hairbreadth apart—one came close to cheating but decided to resist, while the other came close to resisting but decided to cheat. Once they made their decisions, however, their attitudes toward cheating diverged sharply as a consequence of their actions.

These speculations were put to the test by Judson Mills (1958) in an experiment he performed at an elementary school. Mills first measured the attitudes of sixth graders toward cheating. He then had them participate in a competitive exam, offering prizes to the winners. The situation was arranged so it was almost impossible to win without cheating. Moreover, Mills made it easy for the children to cheat on the exam, and created the illusion that they could not be detected. Under these conditions, as one might expect, some of the students cheated and others did not. The next day, the sixth graders were again asked to indicate how they felt about cheating. Children who had cheated became more lenient toward cheating, and those who had resisted the temptation to cheat adopted a harsher attitude toward cheating.

THE JUSTIFICATION OF EFFORT

Suppose you expend a great deal of effort to get into a particular club, and it turns out to be a totally worthless organization, consisting of boring, pompous people engaged in trivial activities. You would feel pretty foolish, wouldn't you? Such a circumstance would produce a fair amount of dissonance; your cognition that you are a sensible, adept human being is dissonant with your cognition that you worked hard to get into a worthless club. How would you reduce this dissonance? How would you justify your behaviour? You might start by finding a way to convince yourself that the club and the people in it are

◀ Going through a lot of effort to become a soldier will increase the recruit's feelings of cohesiveness and pride in the corps.

nicer, more interesting, and more worthwhile than they appeared to be at first glance. How can one turn boring people into interesting people and a trivial club into a worthwhile one? Easy. Even the most boring people and trivial clubs have some redeeming qualities. Activities and behaviours are open to a variety of interpretations; if we are motivated to see the best in people and things, we will tend to interpret these ambiguities in a positive manner. We call this the **justification of effort**—the tendency for individuals to increase their liking for something they have worked hard to attain.

In a now classic experiment, Elliot Aronson and Judson Mills (1959) explored the link between effort and dissonance reduction. In their experiment, university students volunteered to join a group that would be meeting regularly to discuss various aspects of the psychology of sex. In order to be admitted to the group, they volunteered to go through a screening procedure. For one-third of the participants, the procedure was an extremely effortful and unpleasant one; for one-third it was only very mildly unpleasant; and the final one-third were admitted to the group without undergoing any screening procedure.

Each participant was then allowed to listen in on a discussion being conducted by the members of the group they would be joining. Although they were led to believe that the discussion was a live, ongoing one, what they actually heard was a prerecorded tape. The taped discussion was arranged so it was as dull and bombastic as possible. After the discussion was over, each participant was asked to rate it in terms of how much they liked it, how interesting it was, how intelligent the participants were, and so forth. The major findings are shown in Figure 6.6.

The results supported the predictions. Participants who underwent little or no effort to get into the group did not enjoy the discussion very much. They were able to see it for what it was—a dull and boring waste of time. They regretted that they had agreed to participate. Participants who went through a severe initiation, however, succeeded in

Justification of effort

the tendency for individuals to increase their liking for something they have worked hard to attain

▶ Figure 6.6

THE TOUGHER THE
INITIATION, THE MORE WE
LIKE THE GROUP.

The more effort we put into
gaining group membership, the
more we like the group we have
just joined.

(Adapted from Aronson &
Mills, 1959)

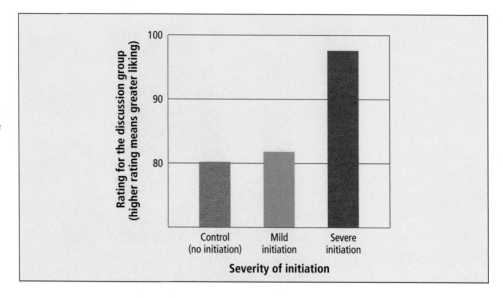

convincing themselves that the same discussion, while not as scintillating as they had hoped, was dotted with interesting and provocative tidbits, and therefore, in the main, was a worthwhile experience. In short, they justified their effortful initiation process by interpreting all the ambiguous aspects of the group discussion in the most positive manner possible.

It should be clear that we are not suggesting that most people enjoy effortful, unpleasant experiences—they do not. What we are asserting is that if a person agrees to go through a difficult or an unpleasant experience to attain some goal or object, that goal or object becomes more attractive (see Try It!, below). As we mentioned in Chapter 1, it is not unusual for people in the military or on sports teams to be subjected to barbaric, cruel hazing rituals. On the face of it, one might expect that the victims of hazings would

Justifying Actions

Think about something that you have tackled in the past that necessitated your going to a lot of trouble or effort. Perhaps you waited for several hours in a long line to get tickets to a concert; perhaps you knowingly sat in your car through an incredible traffic jam because it was the only way you could visit a close friend.

1. Specifically, list the things you had to go through in order to attain your goal.

2. Do you think you might have tried to justify all that effort? Did you find yourself exaggerating the good things about the goal and minimizing any negative aspects of the goal? List some of the ways you might have exaggerated the value of the goal.

3. The next time you find yourself in that kind of situation, you might want to monitor your actions and cognitions carefully to see if there is any self-justification involved.

despise those who made them suffer. However, by now you are probably in a better position to understand the reactions of people such as Dave Tremblay.

When Dave Tremblay, a former Quebec Nordiques prospect, joined the Pickering Panthers of the Ontario Hockey Association, he was blindfolded, shaved, and forced to sit in a hot liniment that badly burned his genitals. A few years later, he was hazed again when he received a hockey scholarship from an American university. That time, he was sick for days, suffering from alcohol poisoning. How does he remember the teammates who inflicted this cruelty on him? Remarkably, with fondness . . . "They came by and checked on us when it was over . . . They didn't just beat the crap out of us and leave us" (O'Hara, 2000). If it weren't for cognitive dissonance theory, such a reaction would be difficult to understand!

THE PSYCHOLOGY OF INSUFFICIENT JUSTIFICATION

When we were little, we were taught never to tell a lie. We also were taught to be kind to one another. Alas, the world is a complicated place—occasionally, in order to be kind to someone, we find it necessary to tell a lie. Your best friend invites you to the first performance of a band that he has proudly put together. The vocalist is awful, the bass player shows little talent, and, as it turns out, your friend should have kept up with his saxophone lessons. Afterwards, your friend excitedly asks you how you enjoyed the band. How do you respond? You hesitate. Chances are you go through something like the following thought process: "Jeremy seems so happy and excited. Why should I hurt his feelings and possibly ruin our friendship?" So you tell Jeremy that the band was great. Do you experience much dissonance? We doubt it. There are a great many thoughts that are consonant with having told this lie, as outlined in your reasoning. In effect, your cognition that it is important not to cause pain to people you like provides ample **external justification** for having told a harmless lie.

Counter-attitudinal Advocacy What happens, on the other hand, if you say something you don't really believe and there is no ample external justification for doing so? That is, what if Jeremy sincerely needed to know your opinion of the band because he was thinking of quitting school to devote his life to music? If you still tell him the band was great, you will experience dissonance. When you can't find external justification for your behaviour, you will attempt to find **internal justification**—you will try to reduce dissonance by changing something about your attitudes or behaviour. How can you do this? You might begin looking for positive aspects of the band—some evidence of creativity or potential that might be realized with a little more practice or a few new talented band members. If you look hard enough, you will probably find something. Within a short time, your attitude toward the band will have moved in the direction of the statement you made—and that is how saying becomes believing. This phenomenon is generally referred to as **counter-attitudinal advocacy**, a process that occurs when a person states an opinion or attitude that runs counter to his private belief or attitude. When this is accomplished with a minimum of external justification, it results in a change in the individual's private attitude in the direction of the public statement.

This proposition was first tested in a groundbreaking experiment by Leon Festinger and J. Merrill Carlsmith (1959). In this experiment, university students were induced to

▲ "How do I look?" your friend asks. Do you tell him or her the truth? Chances are you don't. Your concern about his or her feelings provides enough external justification for telling a white lie, so you experience little dissonance.

External justification
a person's reason or explanation for dissonant behaviour that resides outside the individual (e.g., in order to receive a large reward or avoid a severe punishment)

Internal justification
the reduction of dissonance by changing something about oneself (e.g., one's attitude or behaviour)

Counter-attitudinal advocacy
the process that occurs when a person states an opinion or attitude that runs counter to his or her private belief or attitude

spend an hour performing a series of excruciatingly boring and repetitive tasks. The experimenter then told them that the purpose of the study was to determine whether people would perform better if they had been informed in advance that the tasks were interesting. They were each informed that they had been randomly assigned to the control condition—that is, they had not been told anything in advance. However, he explained, the next participant, a young woman who was just arriving in the anteroom, was going to be in the experimental condition. The researcher said that he needed to convince her that the task was going to be interesting and enjoyable. Since it was much more convincing if a fellow student rather than the experimenter delivered this message, would the participant do so? Thus, with this request the experimenter induced the participants to lie about the task to another student.

Half of the students were offered $20 for telling the lie (a large external justification), while the others were offered only $1 for telling the lie (a very small external justification). After the experiment was over, an interviewer asked the lie-tellers how much they had enjoyed the tasks they had performed earlier in the experiment. The results validated the hypothesis. Students who had been paid $20 for lying—that is, for saying that the tasks had been enjoyable—rated the activities as the dull and boring experiences they were. But those who were paid only $1 for saying that the task was enjoyable rated the task as significantly more enjoyable. In other words, people who had received an abundance of external justification for lying told the lie but didn't believe it, whereas those who told the lie without a great deal of external justification succeeded in convincing themselves that what they said was closer to the truth.

Finally, in an important set of experiments, Mike Leippe and Donna Eisenstadt (1994, 1998) demonstrated that laboratory experiments on counter-attitudinal advocacy could be applied directly to important societal problems—in this case, race relations and racial prejudice. They induced white students at an American university to write a counter-attitudinal essay publicly endorsing a controversial proposal at their university—to double the funds available for academic scholarships for African-American students. Because the total funds were limited, this meant cutting by half the scholarship funds available to white students. As you might imagine, this was a highly dissonant situation. How might they reduce dissonance? The best way would be to convince themselves that they really believed deeply in that policy. Moreover, dissonance theory would predict that their general attitude toward African Americans would become more favourable and much more supportive. And that is exactly what Leippe and Eisenstadt found.

Hypocrisy and AIDS Prevention In the past decade, dissonance theory has also been applied to another important societal issue: the prevention of the spread of AIDS. As you know, since it first made its presence known in the early 1980s, AIDS has become an epidemic of epic proportions. Hundreds of millions of dollars have been spent on AIDS information and prevention campaigns in the mass media. While these campaigns have been somewhat effective in conveying information, they have not been nearly as successful in preventing people from engaging in risky sexual behaviour. For example, although university students are aware of AIDS as a serious problem, as we will see in the next chapter, a surprisingly small percentage use condoms every time they have sex. The reason seems to be that condoms are inconvenient, unromantic, and remind people of disease—the last thing they want to be thinking about when getting ready to make love. Rather, as researchers have consistently discovered, people have a strong tendency to experience denial where sexual behaviour is involved; in this case, they believe that while AIDS is a problem for most people, they themselves are not at risk.

If the media have been ineffective, is there anything else that can be done? In the past several years, Elliot Aronson and colleagues (Aronson, Fried, & Stone, 1991; Stone et al., 1994) have had considerable success at convincing people to use condoms by employing a variation of the counter-attitudinal advocacy paradigm. They asked university students to compose a speech describing the dangers of AIDS and advocating the use of condoms every single time a person has sex. In one condition, the students merely composed the arguments. In another condition, the students composed the arguments and then recited them in front of a video camera, after being informed that the videotape would be played to an audience of high-school students. In addition, half of the students in each condition were made mindful of their own failure to use condoms by having them make a list of the circumstances in which they had found it particularly difficult, awkward, or impossible to use them.

Essentially, then, the participants in one condition—those who made a video for high-school students after having been made mindful of their own failure to use condoms—were in a state of high dissonance. This was caused by their being made aware of their own hypocrisy; they were fully aware of the fact that they were preaching behaviour to high-school students that they themselves were not practising. In order to remove the hypocrisy and maintain their self-esteem, they would need to start practising what they were preaching. And that is exactly what Aronson and his colleagues found. Later, when the students were given the opportunity to purchase condoms very cheaply, those in the hypocrisy condition were the most likely to buy them. Figure 6.7 illustrates these findings. A follow-up telephone interview several months after the experiment demonstrated that

▼ Figure 6.7

PEOPLE WHO ARE MADE MINDFUL OF THEIR HYPOCRISY BEGIN TO PRACTISE WHAT THEY PREACH.

(Adapted from Stone et al., 1994)

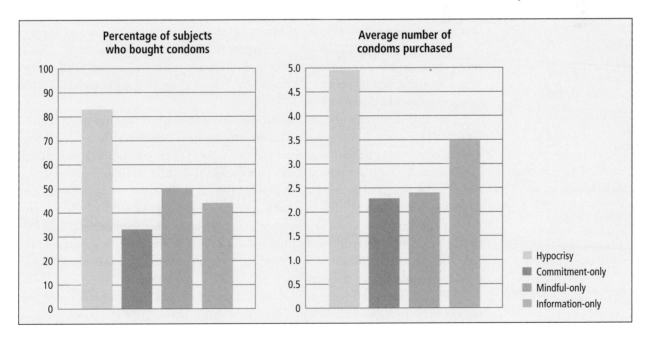

the effects were long lasting. People in the hypocrisy condition reported far greater use of condoms than did those in the control conditions.

Insufficient Punishment
Another form of insufficient justification is insufficient punishment. Complex societies run, in part, on punishment or the threat of punishment. For example, while cruising down the highway at 130 kilometres per hour, we know that if we get caught we will end up paying a substantial fine. If it happens often, we will lose our licence. So we learn to obey the speed limit when police cars are in the vicinity. By the same token, bullies know that if they get caught, they could be punished, so they learn not to bully while adults are around, but happily engage in bullying at other times (Atlas & Pepler, 1998; Craig & Pepler, 1997). It is extremely difficult to persuade children that it's not right or enjoyable to beat up smaller children. But theoretically, it is conceivable that under certain conditions they will persuade themselves that such behaviour is unenjoyable.

Imagine that you are the parent of a six-year-old boy who often beats up his four-year-old brother. You've tried to reason with him, but to no avail. Thus, in order to make him a nicer person (and in order to preserve the health and welfare of his little brother), you begin to punish him for his aggressiveness. As a parent, you have at your disposal a number of possible punishments, ranging from the extremely mild (a stern look) to the extremely severe (a hard spanking, forcing the child to stand in the corner for two hours, and depriving him of TV privileges for a month). The more severe the threat, the greater the likelihood the youngster will cease and desist—while you are watching him. But he may very well hit his brother again as soon as you are out of sight. In short, just as most drivers learn to be on the lookout for radar traps while speeding, your six-year-old has not lost his enjoyment of bullying his little brother; he has merely learned not to do it while you are around to punish him.

Suppose, now, that you threaten your six-year-old with a mild punishment. In either case—under threat of severe punishment or of mild punishment—the child experiences dissonance. He is aware that he is not beating up his little brother, and he is also aware that he would like to beat him up. When he has the urge to hit his brother and doesn't, he implicitly asks himself, "How come I'm not beating up my little brother?" Under severe threat, he has a convincing answer in the form of a sufficient external justification: "I'm not beating him up because if I do, my parents are going to really punish me." This serves to reduce the dissonance.

The child in the mild threat situation experiences dissonance too. But when he asks himself, "How come I'm not beating up my little brother?" he doesn't have a very convincing answer, because the threat is so mild that it does not provide a superabundance of justification. In short, this is **insufficient punishment**. The child is refraining from doing something he wants to do and lacks complete justification for doing so. In this situation, he continues to experience dissonance. How can this dissonance be reduced? By his convincing himself that he doesn't really want to beat up his brother. In time, he can go farther in his quest for internal justification and decide that beating up little kids is not fun. Allowing children the leeway to construct their own internal justification enables them to develop a permanent set of values.

Thus far, this has all been speculative. Will threats of mild punishment for performing any behaviour diminish the attractiveness of that behaviour to a greater extent than

Insufficient punishment
the dissonance aroused when individuals lack sufficient external justification for having resisted a desired activity or object, usually resulting in individuals devaluing the forbidden activity or object

severe threats? This proposition was first investigated by Elliot Aronson and J. Merrill Carlsmith (1963) in an experiment with preschoolers. In this study, the experimenter first asked each child to rate the attractiveness of several toys. He then pointed to a toy that the child considered to be among the most attractive, and told the child that he or she was not allowed to play with it. Half of the children were threatened with mild punishment (the experimenter said he would be annoyed) if they disobeyed; the other half were threatened with severe punishment (the experimenter said he would be very angry, would take his toys away, and would never come back again). The experimenter then left the room for several minutes to provide the children with the time and opportunity to play with the other toys and to resist the temptation of playing with the forbidden toy. None of the children played with the forbidden toy.

The experimenter then returned to the room and asked each child to rate how much he or she liked each of the toys. Initially, all the children had wanted to play with the forbidden toy. During the temptation period, all of them had refrained from playing with it. Clearly, this disparity means that dissonance was aroused in the children. How did they respond? The children who had received a severe threat had ample justification for their restraint. They knew why they hadn't played with the attractive toy, and they thus had no reason to change their attitude about the toy. These children continued to rate the forbidden toy as highly desirable; indeed, some even found it more desirable than they had before the threat.

But what about the others? Lacking an abundance of external justification for refraining from playing with the toy, the children in the mild threat condition needed an internal justification to reduce their dissonance. They succeeded in convincing themselves that the reason they hadn't played with the toy was that they didn't really like it. They rated the forbidden toy as less attractive than they had at the beginning of the experiment. What we have here is a clear example of **self-justification** leading to self-persuasion in the behaviour of very young children. The implications for child rearing are fascinating.

The Permanence of Self-Persuasion Importantly, attitudes generated by self-persuasion and self-justification can have long-lasting effects. To take one dramatic example, Jonathan Freedman (1965) performed a replication ·of Aronson and Carlsmith's (1963) forbidden toy experiment. In Freedman's version of the experiment, the forbidden toy was an attractive battery-powered robot; all of the children in the experiment were eager to play with it. However, Freedman forbade them from doing so, indicating that they could play with the other toys—which paled by comparison—if they wanted to. Just as in the original experiment, Freedman issued either a mild threat or a severe threat for breaking the rule. Just as in the original experiment, all of the children obeyed the rule.

Several weeks later, a young woman came to the school, supposedly to conduct an unrelated study. She administered her tests in the same room Freedman had used for his experiment—the room where the same toys were casually scattered about. Afterwards, she asked the children to wait for her while she went to the next room to score the tests. She casually suggested that the scoring might take a while and that—how lucky!—someone had left some toys around and the children could play with any of them.

As shown in Figure 6.8, the results were striking. The overwhelming majority of the children whom Freedman had mildly threatened several weeks earlier decided, on their

▲ How can we induce this child to give up playing with an attractive toy?

Self-justification

the tendency to justify one's actions in order to maintain one's self-esteem

▶ **Figure 6.8**

Several weeks afterwards, children who had received a threat of mild punishment were far less likely to play with the forbidden toy than children who had received a threat of severe punishment. Those given a mild threat had to provide their own justification by devaluing the attractiveness of the toy.

(Adapted from Freedman, 1965)

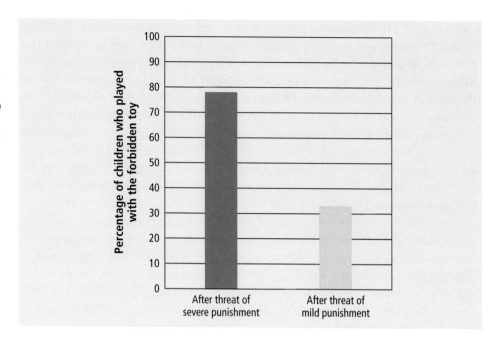

own, not to play with the robot; they played with the uninteresting toys instead. By contrast, the great majority of the children who had been severely threatened did, in fact, play with the forbidden toy. Thus, a single mild threat was still very effective several weeks later, while a severe threat was not.

Again, the power of this phenomenon rests on the fact that the reason the children didn't play with the toy was not that some adult told them the toy was undesirable; such admonitions would not have persisted very long after the admonishing adult had left the premises. The reason the mild threat persisted for at least several weeks was that the children were motivated to convince themselves that the toy was undesirable.

THE EVIDENCE FOR MOTIVATIONAL AROUSAL

The theory of cognitive dissonance is largely a motivational theory; in other words, the theorists maintain that discomfort and arousal are what drive the engine, what motivate the individual to change his or her attitude or behaviour. How do we know this is the case? Is there any independent evidence indicating that people who experience cognitive dissonance are in a state of discomfort or arousal? Before answering this question, take a moment to place yourself in the following situation.

If you are like most university students, the idea of taking a class at 6:30 a.m. isn't particularly inviting. Imagine, however, that you are asked to write an essay in favour of 6:30 a.m. classes and that your arguments might affect whether your university actually adopts such a policy. As you start writing, you begin to experience that uneasy feeling that you recognize as cognitive dissonance. You really do not want your classes to begin at 6:30 a.m., and yet here you are, formulating compelling arguments for why such a policy should be implemented. This is just the situation in which some students at the University of Alberta found themselves, and most of them showed classic dissonance reduction—

they changed their attitudes to become consistent with the position they were endorsing (Wright et al., 1992). In other words, they decided that the idea of 6:30 a.m. classes wasn't so bad after all. That's not the whole story, however. Before writing the essay, some participants were given a drug—supposedly to improve memory—and were told either that the drug would have no side effects or that the drug would make them tense. If you recall the research on misattribution of arousal discussed in Chapter 5, you can probably anticipate the researchers' hypothesis. They expected that participants who were told the drug would make them tense would not experience dissonance because they would attribute their uneasy feelings to the drug ("Oh, right—I took a pill that's supposed to make me feel tense; that's why I'm feeling this way"). And if they weren't experiencing dissonance, there would be no need to change their attitudes, would there? Indeed, participants in this condition were most likely to retain their negative views toward 6:30 a.m. classes, despite writing an essay promoting such a policy.

This study is similar to a classic study conducted by Zanna and Cooper (1974). In their experiment, some participants were told that the pill they had been given would arouse them and make them feel tense. Others were told that the pill would make them feel calm and relaxed. Participants in the control condition were told that the pill would not affect them in any way. After ingesting the pill, each person voluntarily wrote a counter-attitudinal essay, thus creating dissonance. Participants in the control condition underwent considerable attitude change, as would be expected in a typical dissonance experiment. Participants in the aroused condition, however, did not change their attitudes—they attributed their discomfort to the pill, not their counter-attitudinal essay. And what about participants in the relaxed condition? They changed their attitudes even more than did the control participants. Why might that be? These participants inferred that writing the counter-attitudinal essay had made them tense, since they were feeling aroused despite a relaxing drug ("Oh, no—I took a pill that's supposed to make me feel relaxed and I feel tense"). Thus, they concluded that their behaviour was very inconsistent with their perception of themselves as decent and reasonable people, and they changed their attitude to bring it in line with their essay contents. These data are illustrated in Figure 6.9.

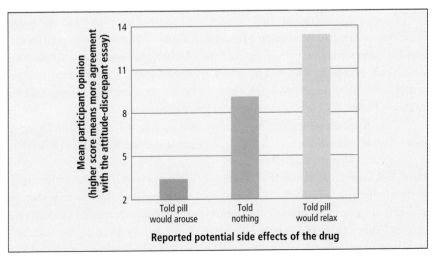

◀ Figure 6.9

IF PEOPLE CAN MISATTRIBUTE THE AROUSAL ASSOCIATED WITH THE DISSONANCE, THEY DO NOT SHOW THE TYPICAL ATTITUDE CHANGE FOLLOWING A COUNTER-ATTITUDINAL ESSAY.

This is strong support for the notion that dissonance causes physiological arousal.

(Adapted from Zanna & Cooper, 1974)

Before leaving this topic, let's return to the study at the University of Alberta (Wright et al., 1992). There was an additional condition in this study that we haven't described yet. Imagine that you were one of the participants who had been told that the pill would make you feel tense. As you write out the arguments in favour of 6:30 a.m. classes, you experience some tension that you attribute to the effects of the pill. However, the experimenter then enters the room and apologizes, saying there has been a mix-up and that you were accidentally given the wrong pill. The pill you received actually has no side effects. The researchers found that in this condition, participants decided that the unpleasant feelings they had experienced must have been due to dissonance after all, and therefore engaged in dissonance reduction. Thus, these participants ended up deciding that 6:30 a.m. classes would be just fine!

THE AFTERMATH OF GOOD AND BAD DEEDS

It is obvious that when we like people, we tend to treat them well, speak kindly to them, do them favours, and smile at them with warmth and joy. If we don't like them, we treat them less kindly, avoid them, say bad things about them, and perhaps even go out of our way to snub them. But what happens when we do a person a favour? In particular, what happens when we are subtly induced to do a favour for a person we do not like—will we like them more? Or less? Dissonance theory would predict that we will like the person more.

To see whether that's actually what happens, Jon Jecker and David Landy (1969) set up an intellectual contest in which students were able to win a substantial sum of money. After the experiment was over, one-third of the participants were approached by the experimenter, who explained that he was using his own funds for the experiment and was running short, which meant he might be forced to close down the experiment prematurely. He asked, "As a special favour to me, would you mind returning the money you won?" The same request was made to a different group of participants—except that this time the request was made not by the experimenter but by the departmental secretary, who asked them if they would return the money as a special favour to the (impersonal) psychology department's research fund, which was running low. The remaining participants were not asked to return their winnings. Finally, all of the participants were asked to fill out a questionnaire that included an opportunity to rate the experimenter. Participants who had been cajoled into doing a special favour for the experimenter found him the most attractive; after they did him a favour, they convinced themselves he was a wonderful, deserving fellow. The others thought he was a pretty nice guy, too, but not nearly as wonderful as he was thought to be by the people who had been asked to do him a favour. Figure 6.10 shows the results of this experiment.

Thus, if we do something nice for another person, we will end up liking the person more than if we had not done a favour for him or her (see Try It! on page 209).

How We Come to Hate Our Victims What happens in the opposite situation, if we harm another person? Sadly, it appears that we come to dislike or hate that person as a way of justifying our cruelty. This phenomenon was demonstrated in an early experiment performed by Keith Davis and Edward E. Jones (1960). Participants watched a young man being interviewed, and then, on the basis of this observation, provided him with an

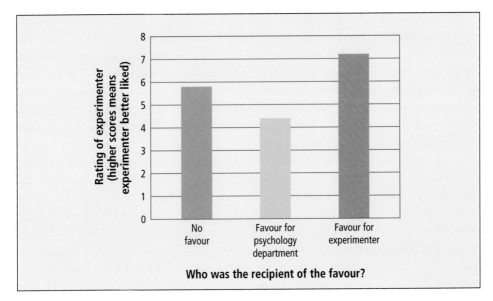

◀ Figure 6.10

IF WE HAVE DONE SOMEONE
A FAVOUR, WE ARE MORE
LIKELY TO FEEL POSITIVELY
TOWARD THAT PERSON.

(Adapted from Jecker & Landy,
1969)

analysis of his shortcomings as a human being. Specifically, the participants were told to tell the young man (a confederate) that they believed him to be a shallow, untrustworthy, boring person. The participants succeeded in convincing themselves that they didn't like the victim of their cruelty—after the fact. In short, after saying things they knew were certain to hurt him, they convinced themselves that he deserved it. They found him less attractive than they had prior to saying the hurtful things to him.

According to research conducted at the University of Western Ontario (Hobden & Olson, 1994; Maio, Olson, & Bush, 1997) such effects can operate on quite a subtle level, as when we tell disparaging jokes about a particular group. Even though it may seem like harmless fun, we end up evaluating the group more negatively as a means of justifying our put-downs. For example, in one study, University of Western Ontario students who were asked to recite disparaging jokes about Newfoundlanders later reported more negative stereotypes of this group than those who recited nondisparaging jokes.

Good Deeds

When you walk down a city street and view people sitting on the sidewalk, panhandling, or pushing their possessions around in a shopping cart, how do you feel about them? Think about it for a few moments and write down a list of your feelings. If you are like most university students, your list will reflect some mixed feelings. That is, most students feel some compassion mixed with the feeling that such people are a nuisance—that, if they really tried, they could get their lives together. Consider doing volunteer work at a shelter for the homeless—serving food, for example. After a few sessions, pay close attention to your feelings. Do you notice any changes?

Do people in real-world situations also use dissonance to justify cruel actions toward another human being? Sadly, the answer appears to be yes. In March 1993, Canadian soldiers from the elite Canadian Airborne Regiment on a peacekeeping mission in Somalia captured 16-year-old Shidane Arone trying to sneak into their compound. He was tied up, savagely beaten, and tortured to death. A court martial later learned that one of the soldiers beat Shidane Arone with a wooden riot baton, a metal pipe, and his feet and fists. Others soldiers joined in. According to newspaper reports, the young Somali boy's cries of "Canada, Canada, Canada" as he drifted in and out of consciousness could be heard across the compound. Canadians were shocked and deeply disturbed by this incident. Perhaps most shocking was that the soldiers posed for "trophy" photographs—in one photograph, soldiers posed beside the unconscious Somali boy; in another photograph a soldier held the boy's head up by jamming a wooden baton into his bloody mouth; still others showed a soldier holding a gun to Shidane Arone's head. What was so chilling about these photographs was the broad smiles on the soldiers' faces. As James Travers, the editor of the *Ottawa Citizen* (one of the newspapers that published these photographs), commented, "They not only tortured, beat and killed him, but were obviously playing when they did this" (Boadle, 1994). How could anyone gleefully torture and murder a 16-year-old boy? By deciding that he deserved it. It may seem absurd to suggest that Canadian peacekeepers could convince themselves that an unarmed, civilian boy deserved to be beaten to death for trying to enter their compound. However, as various inquiries into this tragedy revealed, some of the higher-ranking officers had issued orders to "abuse" any Somali intruders. Although the soldiers who committed these atrocities were aware that it was illegal to torture or kill anyone they captured, the fact that some of their superiors advocated punishing intruders appears to have been all the justification they needed. In short, the soldiers may have convinced themselves that Shidane Arone deserved what he got.

Another way in which people reduce dissonance for having committed cruel acts is to derogate or dehumanize their victims. During the Vietnam War, it was common for American soldiers to derogate Vietnamese people by referring to them as "gooks." Dehumanization was evident during the trial of William Calley, an American lieutenant who was court-martialled for his role in the slaughter of innocent civilians at My Lai in Vietnam. In a long and detailed testimony, Lieutenant Calley's psychiatrist made it clear that the lieutenant had come to regard the Vietnamese people as less than human. In the Somalia affair, the soldiers who killed Shidane Arone dehumanized him by blindfolding him. And there was evidence that the Somali people were derogated by Canadian peacekeepers. According to the Report of the Somalia Commission of Inquiry, the Canadian soldiers referred to the Somali people as "gimmes," "smufties," and "nignogs."

Presumably, the American soldiers in Vietnam and the soldiers in the Canadian Airborne Regiment would have experienced less dissonance if they had killed fully armed soldiers in a combat situation. However, hurting or killing an unarmed civilian—especially a child, and especially while on a peace mission—is likely to create massive dissonance. Sometimes, the dissonance created by the realization that one has engaged in cruel, reprehensible behaviour may be too great to bear. This may have been the case for Master Corporal Clayton Matchee, the alleged instigator of the Shidane Arone beating. He tried to hang himself two days later. Although he didn't die, his suicide attempt left

▲ When defenseless civilians such as the elderly, women, and children are targets of military violence, the soldiers committing the violence will be inclined to derogate or dehumanize their victims to reduce their own dissonance. Here, Master Corporal Clayton Matchee of the Canadian Airborne Regiment smiles and points at Somali teenager Shidane Arone, whom members of the regiment tortured and beat to death in 1993. This photo, taken by one of the soldiers, shows the dehumanization of the Somalians in the eyes of the soldiers.

◀ During wartime, especially when defenseless civilians such as old people, women, and children are targets of military violence, the soldiers committing such acts of violence will become inclined to derogate or dehumanize their victims, after the fact, in order to reduce their own dissonance.

him too brain-damaged to stand trial. He currently lives in a psychiatric hospital in Saskatchewan. Such a reaction is relatively rare. More often, people who inflict harm on those who cannot retaliate reduce dissonance by derogating their victims and deciding that the victims deserved their cruel treatment.

Ironically, success at dehumanizing the victim virtually guarantees a continuation or even an escalation of the cruelty. It becomes easier to hurt and kill "subhumans" than to hurt and kill fellow human beings. Thus, reducing dissonance in this way has sobering future consequences: it increases the likelihood that the atrocities people are willing to commit will become greater and greater through an endless chain of violence followed by self-justification (in the form of dehumanizing the victim), followed by greater violence and still more intense dehumanization. In this manner, unbelievable acts of human cruelty—such as the Nazi Final Solution that led to the murder of 6 million European Jews—can occur. Unfortunately, atrocities are not a thing of the past but are as recent as today's newspaper.

AVOIDING THE RATIONALIZATION TRAP

Dissonance-reducing behaviour is ego-defensive behaviour. It can be useful because it keeps our egos from being continually battered; it provides us with a feeling of stability and high self-esteem. But as we have seen, dissonance-reducing behaviour can be dangerous as well. The tendency to justify our past behaviour can lead us into an escalation of rationalizations that can be disastrous. We call this the **rationalization trap**: the potential is for dissonance reduction to produce a succession of self-justifications that ultimately results in a chain of stupid or irrational actions. The irony, of course, is that to avoid thinking of ourselves as stupid or immoral, we set the stage to increase our acts of stupidity or immorality.

LEARNING FROM OUR MISTAKES

As we have seen throughout this chapter, the process of dissonance reduction perpetuates error and can lead to tragedy. For example, people who hurt others can derogate their

Rationalization trap

the potential for dissonance reduction to produce a succession of self-justifications that ultimately result in a chain of stupid or immoral actions

victims to the point that their actions not only seem just, but might even become heroic in their own eyes (we will elaborate on this phenomenon in chapters 12 and 13, on aggression and prejudice). Similarly, we have seen how people who say something they don't really believe will come to believe the statement—and some of those beliefs might be tragically erroneous.

The press conferences and parliamentary speeches of politicians are full of the kind of self-serving, self-justifying statements that can best be summarized as "If I had it all to do over again, I would not change anything important." Consider, for example, the controversy surrounding the Asia Pacific Economic Co-operation (APEC) summit that was held in Vancouver in 1997. It was known that protesters would be on the scene to protest violations of human rights in countries such as Indonesia. Prime Minister Jean Chrétien wanted to spare the leaders of these countries embarrassment and apparently instructed the RCMP that protesters were to be dispersed. Ironically, as the protesters (mostly students) stood holding signs advocating human rights and freedom of speech, they were doused with pepper spray. Some were strip-searched and roughed up. Chrétien subsequently faced serious accusations of violating the constitutional and human rights of the protesters. Moreover, some constitutional experts argued that by directing the police to break up the protest, the prime minister had breached the barrier between legislators and the police force, thereby setting the stage for a constitutional crisis. There also were reports that Chrétien pressured the CBC into removing the reporter who publicized his involvement in the actions taken against the protesters. Amid calls for Chrétien's resignation, the beleaguered APEC inquiry was launched to investigate his actions. And how did Prime Minister Chrétien react to all of this? Did he apologize to the protesters and express regret that he had been more concerned with protecting other leaders from

▶ When RCMP officers were told to pepper-spray protestors at the APEC summit in Vancouver in 1997, it soon became a political disaster for Prime Minister Chrétien. The scandal was made worse by the rationalization to which the government resorted: Instead of apologizing, Chrétien justified his actions and actually joked that the protestors were lucky it was only pepper spray and not baseball bats—thereby fuelling public anger.

embarrassment than with the rights of protesters in his own country? Not at all. His response was that protesters should be glad that the RCMP had opted for a "civilized" method such as pepper spray, rather than using baseball bats. At the summit's closing press conference, he quipped, "For me, pepper, I put it on my plate."

Is there a way that people can be persuaded not to rationalize their behaviour when they make mistakes? It might be helpful to learn to tolerate dissonance long enough to examine the situation critically and dispassionately. We then stand a chance of breaking out of the cycle of action, followed by self-justification, followed by more intense action. For example, suppose Mary has acted unkindly toward a fellow student. In order to learn from that experience, she must be able to resist the need to derogate her victim. Ideally, it would be effective if she were able to stay with the dissonance long enough to say, "Okay, I blew it; I did a cruel thing. But that doesn't necessarily make me a cruel person. Let me think about why I did it."

We are well aware that this is easier said than done. However, a clue as to how such behaviour might come about is contained in some of the research on self-affirmation discussed previously (Steele, 1988). Suppose that immediately after Mary acted cruelly, but before she had an opportunity to derogate her victim, she was reminded of the fact that she had recently donated several units of blood to the Red Cross to be used by September 11, 2001, victims, or that she had recently gotten a high score on her physics exam. This self-affirmation would likely provide her with the ability to resist engaging in typical dissonance-reducing behaviour. In effect, Mary might be able to say, "It's true—I just did a cruel thing. But I am also capable of some really fine, intelligent, and generous behaviour."

Indeed, self-affirmation can serve as a cognitive buffer, protecting a person from caving in to temptation and committing a cruel or immoral act. This was demonstrated in an early experiment on cheating (Aronson & Mettee, 1968). In this experiment, university students were first given a personality test, and then given false feedback that was either positive (aimed at temporarily raising self-esteem) or negative (aimed at temporarily lowering self-esteem), or they received no information at all. Immediately afterwards, they played a game of cards in which, to win a large pot, they could easily cheat without getting caught. The results were striking. Students in the high self-esteem condition were able to resist the temptation to cheat to a far greater extent than were the students in the other conditions. In short, a temporary boost in self-esteem served to inoculate these students against cheating, because the anticipation of doing something immoral was more dissonant than it would otherwise have been. Thus, when they were put in a tempting situation, they were able to say to themselves, "Terrific people like me don't cheat." And they didn't (see also Spencer, Josephs, & Steele, 1993; Steele, Spencer, & Lynch, 1993). We find these results encouraging. They suggest a viable way of reversing the rationalization trap.

To summarize, throughout this chapter we've indicated that human beings generally have a need to see themselves as intelligent, sensible, and decent folks who behave with integrity. Indeed, what triggers the attitude change and distortion that can take place in the process of dissonance reduction is precisely the need people have to maintain this picture of themselves. At first glance, much of the behaviour described in this chapter may seem startling: people coming to dislike others more after doing them harm; people liking others more after doing them a favour; people believing a lie they've told only if there is little or no reward for telling it. These behaviours would be difficult for us to understand if it weren't for the insights provided by the theory of cognitive dissonance.

The Solar Temple Revisited

At the beginning of this chapter, we raised a vital question regarding the followers of Luc Jouret and Joseph Di Mambro of the Solar Temple. Similar questions were raised in Chapter 1 about the followers of other cult leaders in the U.S. and Uganda. How could intelligent people allow themselves to be led into what, to the overwhelming majority of us, is obviously senseless and tragic behaviour—resulting in mass suicide–murders? Needless to say, the situation is a complex one; there were many factors operating, including the charismatic, persuasive power of each of these leaders, the existence of a great deal of social support for the views of the group (from other members of the group), and the relative isolation of each group from dissenting views, producing a closed system—a little like living in a roomful of mirrors.

In addition to these factors, we are convinced that one of the single most powerful forces common to all of these groups was the existence of a great deal of cognitive dissonance within the mind of each participant. You know from reading this chapter that when individuals make an important decision and invest heavily in that decision (in terms of time, effort, sacrifice, and commitment), the result is a strong need to justify those actions and that investment. The more they give up and the harder they work, the greater the need to convince themselves that their views are correct; indeed, they may even begin to feel sorry for those who do not share their beliefs. The members of the Solar Temple cult sacrificed a great deal for their beliefs: They abandoned their friends and families, relinquished their money and possessions, and, if they were female, subjected themselves to sexual exploitation. All of these sacrifices served to increase their commitment to the cult. Those of us who have studied the theory of cognitive dissonance were not surprised to learn that intelligent, respected, professional people could be persuaded that through death by fire they could escape the imminent apocalypse on earth and be reborn on the star Sirius. To begin to question these beliefs would have produced too much dissonance to bear. Although tragic and bizarre, the death voyages of the Solar Temple members are not unfathomable. They are simply an extreme manifestation of a process—cognitive dissonance—that we have seen in operation over and over again.

SUMMARY

People are highly motivated to maintain their self-esteem. Social psychologists have proposed several fascinating theories as to how we go about maintaining a positive self-evaluation. According to **self-discrepancy theory**, we will feel bad about ourselves when our actual self falls short of the self we feel we should be (our "ought" self) or the self we would like to be (our "ideal" self). Discrepancies between our actual and ideal selves produce feelings of dejection and depression, whereas discrepancies between our actual self and our ought self produce feelings of anxiety. According to **self-completion theory**, when we experience a threat to an important aspect of our identity, we will try to restore our self-esteem by seeking social recognition for that aspect of our self-concept. **Self-evaluation maintenance theory** argues that we maintain our self-esteem by basking in the glory of a close other's accomplishments—as long as those accomplishments don't take place in a domain relevant to our self-definition. We feel threatened if a close other outperforms us in a relevant domain, and we seek to restore our self-esteem by distancing ourselves from the person, improving our performance, lowering the other person's performance, or reducing the relevance of the task. **Self-affirmation theory** argues that people deal with threats to their self-esteem by affirming themselves in some other area.

Research on **self-enhancement** suggests that the need to feel good about ourselves is so strong we tend to hold unrealistically positive views of ourselves. In contrast, **self-verification theory** holds that we want accurate information about what we are like—even if it is not flattering. Generally, people opt for self-enhancement rather than self-verification. Finally, it is important to realize that self-enhancement is limited to individualistic (Western) cultures. In Asian countries, people are more likely to be self-critical, a phenomenon known as self-effacement.

In the latter half of the chapter we focused on another powerful motivator of human behaviour: the need to justify our actions. According to **cognitive dissonance theory**, people experience discomfort (dissonance) whenever they behave in ways inconsistent with their attitudes or hold two conflicting attitudes. Consistent with the idea that dissonance is an uncomfortable state that people are motivated to reduce, there is evidence that dissonance is accompanied by physiological arousal. People reduce dissonance by either changing their behaviour or justifying their past behaviour. The resulting change in attitude stems from a process of self-persuasion.

Dissonance inevitably occurs after important decisions (**postdecision dissonance**), because the thought that "I chose alternative X" is inconsistent with the thought that "I might have been a lot better off with alternative Y." People reduce this dissonance by increasing their liking for the chosen alternative and decreasing their liking for the negative alternative. Dissonance also occurs after people choose to exert a lot of effort to attain something boring or onerous. A **justification of effort** occurs, whereby people increase their liking for what they attained.

Another source of dissonance occurs when people commit foolish, immoral, or absurd acts for **insufficient punishment**. For example, when people say something against their attitudes (**counter-attitudinal advocacy**) for low **external justification**, they find an **internal justification** for their behaviour, coming to believe what they said. Similarly, if people avoid doing something desirable for insufficient punishment, they will come to believe that the activity wasn't really all that desirable. And if people find themselves doing someone a favour for insufficient justification, they assume that they did so because the person is likeable. The flip side of this kind of dissonance reduction has sinister effects: If people find themselves acting cruelly toward someone for insufficient justification, they will derogate the victim, assuming he or she must have deserved it.

The problem with reducing dissonance in ways that make us feel better about ourselves (**self-justification**) is that it can result in a **rationalization trap**, whereby we set the stage for acts of increasing stupidity or immorality. As suggested by **self-affirmation theory**, we can avoid this trap by reminding ourselves that we are good and decent people, so we do not have to justify and rationalize every stupid or immoral act we perform.

IF YOU ARE INTERESTED

Aronson, E. (1992). The return of the repressed: Dissonance theory makes a comeback. *Psychological Inquiry, 3,* 303–311. A brief but penetrating discussion of the conceptual linkage between the theory of cognitive dissonance and recent developments in cognitive psychology.

Aronson, E. (1997). The theory of cognitive dissonance: The evolution and vicissitudes of an idea. In C. McGarty & S. A. Haslam (Eds.), *The message of social psychology: Perspectives on mind in society.* Oxford, England: Blackwell Publishers, Inc. A readable account, tracing the development and evolution of the theory in the context of general social psychology.

Aronson, E. (1998). Dissonance, hypocrisy, and the self-concept. In E. Harmon Jones & J. S. Mills (Eds.), *Cognitive dissonance theory: Revival with revisions and controversies.* Washington, DC: American Psychological Association Press. Bringing Festinger's original theory up to date—with special reference to the role of self-esteem and the self-concept.

Festinger, L. (1957). *A theory of cognitive dissonance.* Evanston, IL: Row, Peterson. The original presentation of dissonance theory. A classic in social psychology—clear, concise, and engagingly written.

Harmon-Jones, E., & Mills, J. S. (Eds.). (1998). *Cognitive dissonance theory: Revival with revisions and controversies.* Washington, D.C.: American Psychological Association Press.

Heine, S. J. (under review). In search of East Asian self-enhancement. In this paper, University of British Columbia social psychologist Steven Heine, a leading researcher on culture and the self, describes the controversy over whether self-enhancement doesn't occur in Asian cultures or whether it simply takes a different form. The author addresses this issue by conducting a meta-analysis of 70 studies in which the self-concepts of Asians and North Americans have been compared. He concludes that self-enhancement is alive and well in North America, but is largely absent in East Asian countries.

Ivory, James (Director). (1993). *Remains of the Day* [Film]. There are a great many films (available on video) that illustrate the workings of dissonance. Among the best is *Remains of the Day,* adapted from Ishiguru's classic novel. This stunning 1993 film explores self-justification from the perspective of a proper British butler, played by Sir Anthony Hopkins. Shying away from friendship and romance, the butler rationalizes his lonely lifestyle by reasserting his belief that such intimacy is improper for a man in his position, and is worth it because of the worthiness of his employer.

Tesser, A., & Cornell, D. P. (1991). On the confluence of self process. *Journal of Experimental Social Psychology, 27,* 501–526. The researchers conduct an ingenious set of experiments that integrate the self-affirmation, cognitive dissonance, and self-evaluation maintenance models. Their bottom line is that the basic motive underlying all of these models is a need to maintain, rather than maximize, self-evaluation.

Wicklund, R., & Brehm, J. (1976). *Perspectives on cognitive dissonance.* Hillsdale, NJ: Earlbaum. A scholarly, readable presentation of dissonance theory some two decades after its inception. Contains a description of much of the early research as well as some of the more important conceptual modifications of the theory.

WEBLINKS

www.usnews.com/usnews/issue/980518/18john.htm
The Media's Perception of Self-esteem Research
This is an article from *U.S. News and World Report* about recent findings that self-esteem is not as related to academic performance as much as was previously believed.

www.colorado.edu/communication/meta-discourses/Theory/festinger.htm
Cognitive Dissonance Theory
This site provides several links related to cognitive dissonance theory.

CHAPTER 7

Attitudes and Attitude Change
influencing thoughts and feelings

HOW MANY TIMES, IN A GIVEN DAY, DOES SOMEONE ATTEMPT TO change your attitudes? Be sure to count every advertisement you see or hear, because advertising is nothing less than an attempt to change your attitude toward a consumer product, be it a brand of laundry detergent, a type of automobile, or a political candidate. Don't forget to include ads you get in the mail, calls from telemarketers, and signs you see on the side of buses, as well as those ever-present television commercials. How many did you come up with? You might be surprised at the answer. According to some estimates, we encounter 300 to 400 advertisements per day (Asker & Myers, 1987; Pratkanis & Aronson, 1991).

As if this were not enough, advertisers are ever on the lookout for new ways of reaching consumers. Entire cable television channels are now devoted to pitching products, either through "home shopping networks" or "infomercials" designed to look like regular television programs. The World Wide Web has opened a new frontier for advertisers that did not exist until a few years ago. Even in our most private moments, we are not immune from advertisements, as witnessed by the proliferation of advertisements placed in public washrooms—above the hand dryers and even on the inside doors of washroom stalls. Yet advertisers are still not satisfied. We can only imagine the conversation that must have occurred between marketers trying to find new inroads for advertising to teenagers. Maybe it went something like this:

> Marketer 1: You know, one of our best audiences is teenagers. They see an awful lot of ads on television.
>
> Marketer 2: Yeah, but doggone it, kids are out of reach for several hours a day—when they're in school. That's so unfair; if only we could figure out a way to reach them during school hours.
>
> Marketer 1: Wait a minute—maybe you're on to something. Why don't we show kids advertisements in their classrooms?
>
> Marketer 2: Are you crazy? How are we going to show them ads during their English or math class? Teachers and principals would never stand for it.
>
> Marketer 1: I think I've got a way . . .

Sound far-fetched? In the summer of 1999, Athena Educational Partners of Montreal offered Canadian schools a "deal." They would broadcast 12 minutes of Youth News Network newscasts in classrooms every day so students would be abreast of current events. The catch was that students also would be exposed to two minutes of commercials. In exchange, schools would receive televisions, VCRs, computers, and even satellite dishes. This proposal created a storm of controversy. Some schools eagerly signed up, while others refused. Principals, teachers, students, and parents were divided on the issue.

In Manitoba, some schools had already agreed to Athena's proposal, when the New Democrat Party came into power. The NDP was opposed to using classroom time in this way, and in the fall of 1999 announced that schools would not be allowed to sign contracts with Athena. However, in Ontario Athena forged ahead, and in January 2000 initiated a pilot project at the Meadowvale Secondary School in Mississauga. The pilot project ended in May 2000. According to an evaluation report published by the Peel District School Board the following month, the reaction of students, teachers, and parents has been mixed. One concern that had been raised before the school implemented the project was that the ads would influence students. However, only 5 percent of the students reported that they felt like buying the products that were advertised. Nevertheless, it is quite possible that the 95 percent of students who claimed not to be persuaded by the ads, were, in fact, influenced by them. (As we shall see later in this chapter, people are not necessarily aware that they have been influenced by persuasive messages.) At this point, it is not known whether the ads have generated the expected revenue. However, a similar program launched in the United States in 1990 by Whittle Communications has been phenomenally successful. Many companies jumped at the chance to pitch their products to captive audiences of teenagers, and by 1992 Whittle Communications was earning $100 million a year in advertising income.

This might sound pretty harmless. After all, schools get much-needed equipment, and kids see only a couple of advertisements a day. As some of the Mississauga students and their parents pointed out, ads are a "fact of life." What are two more, on top of the hundreds that people see already? One troubling finding, however, is that advertisements shown in schools are especially powerful because students believe that the schools endorse the advertised products (Toch, 1992). And as you will see later in this chapter, there is evidence that advertising in general can be quite effective at shaping and changing people's attitudes.

How do advertisements try to change people's attitudes? Some go straight for the gut with the intent of manipulating your emotions, not your thoughts or beliefs. Many advertisements

◀ Advertisements shown in schools are especially powerful because students believe that the schools endorse the advertised products.

for perfume, soft drinks, and jeans, for example, tell you absolutely nothing about the product, but try to associate it with good feelings—often sexual feelings. (Interestingly, a recent study found that people actually have poorer memories for advertisements that are embedded in sexual or violent programs, as opposed to programs that are more neutral in content [Bushman & Bonacci, 2002]. Although this research examined the content of the programs in which ads were embedded, rather than the content of the ads themselves, the findings do raise the question of whether sex really does sell.) Other kinds of ads, such as those for mutual funds, CD players, or coffee makers, downplay emotions and instead throw lots of facts and figures at you. Often the same product can be advertised in either way. Consider a recent ad for the Dodge Caravan. The ad was packed with facts and figures about cupholders, cubbyholes, and cargo room. At least for us, it evoked little emotion (although one of your authors, Beverley Fehr, experienced the emotion of astonishment when she learned, while recently shopping for a vehicle, that one model of the 7-passenger Chevrolet Ventura van boasts 17 cupholders!). Compare an ad such as this to other car ads you've seen that try hard to elicit feelings of freedom, autonomy, and sexual prowess. Meanwhile, they tell you very little about the car.

Which type of ad works better? Obviously, advertisers are convinced that sex (and other emotions) sells. But surely facts and figures can be persuasive as well. More than likely, people's attitudes can be influenced in either way. Under some conditions, people are swayed by a logical consideration of the facts; under other conditions, people are swayed by appeals to their fears, hopes, and desires. What are these conditions? Exactly what is an attitude, and how is it changed? These questions, which are some of the oldest in social psychology, are the subject of this chapter.

The Nature and Origin of Attitudes

Attitude

an evaluation of a person, object, or idea

Most social psychologists define an **attitude** as an evaluation of a person, object, or idea (Eagly & Chaiken, 1993, 1998; Olson & Zanna, 1993). Attitudes are evaluative in that they consist of a positive or negative reaction to something. People are not neutral observers of the world but constant evaluators of what they see. It would be very odd to hear someone say, "My feelings toward anchovies, snakes, chocolate cake, and my roommate are completely neutral." We can elaborate further on our definition of an attitude by stating more precisely what we mean by an "evaluation." Attitudes are made up of different components, or parts. Specifically, attitudes are made up of an affective component, consisting of your emotional reactions toward the attitude object (e.g., another person or a social issue); a cognitive component, consisting of your thoughts and beliefs about the attitude object; and a behavioural component, consisting of your actions or observable behaviour toward the attitude object.

For example, consider your attitude toward a particular model of car. First, there is your affective reaction, or the emotions and feelings the car triggers. These feelings might be a sense of excitement and esthetic pleasure when you see the car, or feelings of anger and resentment (e.g., if you are a Canadian autoworker examining a new foreign-made model). Second, there is your cognitive reaction, or the beliefs you hold about the car's attributes. These might include your thoughts about the car's gas mileage, safety, steering and handling, and roominess. Third, there is your behavioural reaction, or how you act in regard to this type of car. For example, going to the dealership to test-drive the car and actually purchasing it are behaviours related to your attitude.

WHERE DO ATTITUDES COME FROM?

Social psychologists have focused primarily on the way that attitudes are created by people's cognitive, affective, and behavioural experiences. One important finding is that not all attitudes are created equally. Whereas attitudes have affective, cognitive, and behavioural components, any given attitude can be based more on one type of experience than another (Zanna & Rempel, 1988).

Cognitively Based Attitudes Sometimes our attitudes are based primarily on a perusal of the relevant facts, such as the objective merits of an automobile. How many kilometres per litre of gas does it get? Does it have air conditioning? To the extent that a person's evaluation is based primarily on beliefs about the properties of an attitude object, we say it is a **cognitively based attitude**. The function of such an attitude is "object appraisal," meaning that we classify objects according to the rewards and punishments they can provide (Katz, 1960; Smith, Bruner, & White, 1956; Murray, Haddock, & Zanna, 1996). In other words, the purpose of this kind of attitude is to classify the pluses and minuses of an object so we can quickly tell whether it is worth our while to have anything to do with it. Consider your attitude toward a utilitarian object such as a vacuum cleaner. Your attitude is likely to be based on your beliefs about the objective merits of particular brands, such as how well they vacuum up dirt and how much they cost—not on how sexy they make you feel!

Cognitively based attitude
an attitude based primarily on a person's beliefs about the properties of an attitude object

Affectively Based Attitudes An attitude based more on emotions and feelings than on an objective appraisal of pluses and minuses is called an **affectively based attitude** (Breckler & Wiggins, 1989; Zanna & Rempel, 1988). Sometimes we simply like a certain brand of car, regardless of whether it gets good gas mileage or whether it has 17 cupholders. Occasionally we even feel very positively about something—such as another person—in spite of having negative beliefs.

Affectively based attitude
an attitude based primarily on people's feelings and values pertaining to the attitude object

As a guide to which attitudes are likely to be affectively based, consider the topics that etiquette manuals suggest should not be discussed at a dinner party: politics, sex, and religion. People seem to vote more with their hearts than their minds, for example, basing their decision to vote for a political candidate on how they feel about the person, rather than on a well-reasoned evaluation of the policies (Abelson et al., 1982; Granberg & Brown, 1989).

Where do affectively based attitudes come from? They have a variety of sources. First, they can stem from people's values, such as their basic religious and moral beliefs. Attitudes about such issues as abortion, the death penalty, and premarital sex often express and validate one's basic value system (Murray, Holmes, & Griffin, 1996; Schwartz, 1992; Smith, Bruner, & White, 1956). For example, in a study conducted at the University of Western Ontario, Maio and Olson (1995) varied the message on posters soliciting donations for cancer research so that the messages either did or did not emphasize the values of helpfulness and altruism. In the value-expressive condition, the poster read, "Save people's lives, help researchers find a cure for cancer *and help others live,*" whereas in the

▶ Attitudes toward abortion, the death penalty, and premarital sex are examples of affectively based attitudes that are likely to be derived from people's value systems.

non-value condition, the message ended with *"and protect your future."* For participants in the value-expressive condition ("help others live"), there was a positive relation between altruistic values and having favourable attitudes toward donating to cancer research. In contrast, in the non-values condition ("protect your future"), there was no relation between altruistic values and attitudes toward donating money.

Other affectively based attitudes can be the result of a sensory reaction, such as liking the taste of chocolate (despite how many calories it has!), or an esthetic reaction, such as admiring a painting or the lines and colour of a car. Still others can be the result of conditioning. **Classical conditioning** is the case in which a stimulus that elicits an emotional response is repeatedly experienced along with a neutral stimulus, until the neutral stimulus takes on the emotional properties of the first stimulus. For example, suppose that when you were a child you experienced feelings of warmth and love when you visited your grandmother. Suppose also that there was always a faint smell of mothballs in the air at your grandmother's house. Eventually, the smell of mothballs itself will trigger the emotions you experienced during your visits, through the process of classical conditioning (Baldwin & Meunier, 1999; Baldwin & Main, 2001; Cacioppo et al., 1992; Groenland & Schoormans, 1994).

In **operant conditioning**, behaviours that we freely choose to perform increase or decrease in frequency, depending on whether they are followed by positive reinforcement or punishment. How does this apply to attitudes? Imagine that a four-year-old white girl goes to the playground with her father and chooses to play with an East Indian girl. Her father expresses strong disapproval, telling her, "We don't play with that kind of child." It won't take long for the child to associate interacting with minorities with punishment, thereby adopting her father's racist attitudes. Attitudes can take on positive or negative

Classical conditioning

the case whereby a stimulus that elicits an emotional response is repeatedly experienced along with a neutral stimulus that does not, until the neutral stimulus takes on the emotional properties of the first stimulus

Operant conditioning

the case whereby behaviours that people freely choose to perform increase or decrease in frequency, depending on whether they are followed by positive reinforcement or punishment

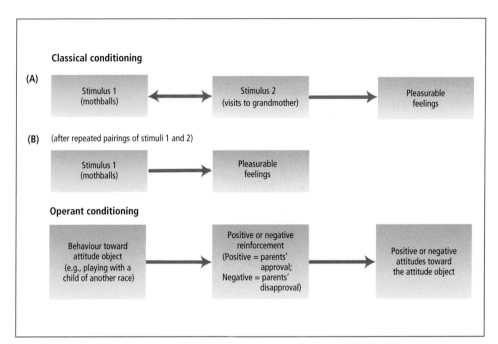

◀ **Figure 7.1**

CLASSICAL AND OPERANT
CONDITIONING OF ATTITUDES.

Affectively based attitudes can
result from either classical or
instrumental conditioning.

affect through either classical or operant conditioning, as shown in Figure 7.1 (Cacioppo et al., 1992; Kuykendall & Keating, 1990).

Although affectively based attitudes can have varied sources, we can group them into one family because they have certain key features in common: (a) they do not result from a rational examination of the issues; (b) they are not governed by logic (e.g., persuasive arguments about the issues seldom change an affectively based attitude); and (c) they are often linked to people's values, so that trying to change them challenges those values (Katz, 1960; Smith, Bruner & White, 1956). How can we tell if an attitude is more affectively or cognitively based? See Try It! on page 224 for one way of measuring the bases of people's attitudes.

Behaviourally Based Attitudes Just as an attitude can be based primarily on cognition or affect, so too can it be based primarily on behaviour. A **behaviourally based attitude** is one based on observations of how you behave toward an attitude object. This may seem a little odd—how do we know how to behave if we don't already know how we feel? According to Daryl Bem's (1972) *self-perception theory*, under certain circumstances people don't know how they feel until they see how they behave. For example, suppose you asked a friend how much she enjoys exercising. If she replies, "Well, I guess I like it, because I always seem to be going for a run or heading over to the gym to work out," we would say she has a behaviourally based attitude. Her attitude is based more on an observation of her own behaviour than on her cognitions or affect.

As noted in Chapter 5, people infer their attitudes from their behaviour only under certain conditions. First, their initial attitude has to be weak or ambiguous. If your friend already has a strong attitude toward exercising, she does not have to observe her behaviour to infer how she feels about it. Second, people infer their attitudes from their

Behaviourally based attitude

an attitude based primarily on observations of how one behaves toward an attitude object

Affective and Cognitive Bases of Attitudes

Fill out this questionnaire to see how psychologists measure the affective and cognitive components of attitudes.

1. Circle the number on each scale that best describes your feelings toward snakes:

hateful	−3	−2	−1	0	1	2	3	loving
sad	−3	−2	−1	0	1	2	3	delighted
annoyed	−3	−2	−1	0	1	2	3	happy
tense	−3	−2	−1	0	1	2	3	calm
bored	−3	−2	−1	0	1	2	3	excited
angry	−3	−2	−1	0	1	2	3	relaxed
disgusted	−3	−2	−1	0	1	2	3	accepting
sorrowful	−3	−2	−1	0	1	2	3	joyful

2. Circle the number on each scale that best describes the traits or characteristics of snakes:

useless	−3	−2	−1	0	1	2	3	useful
foolish	−3	−2	−1	0	1	2	3	wise
unsafe	−3	−2	−1	0	1	2	3	safe
harmful	−3	−2	−1	0	1	2	3	beneficial
worthless	−3	−2	−1	0	1	2	3	valuable
imperfect	−3	−2	−1	0	1	2	3	perfect
unhealthy	−3	−2	−1	0	1	2	3	wholesome

Instructions: Answer each of the above questions. Then, sum each of your responses to Question 1 and each of your responses to Question 2.

These scales were developed by Crites, Fabrigar, and Petty (1994) to measure the affective and cognitive components of attitudes. Question 1 measures the affective component of your attitude toward snakes; you were asked to rate your feelings on such scales as "hateful/loving." Question 2 measures the cognitive component of attitudes; you were asked to rate your beliefs about the characteristics of snakes on such scales as "worthless/valuable." Most people's attitudes toward snakes are more affectively than cognitively based. If this was true of you, your total score for Question 1 should depart more from zero (in a negative direction, for most people) than your total score for Question 2.

Now go back and fill out the scales again, but substitute "vacuum cleaners" for "snakes." Most people's attitudes toward a utilitarian object such as a vacuum cleaner are more cognitively than affectively based. If this was true of you, your total score for Question 2 should depart more from zero than your total score for Question 1.

behaviour only when there are no other plausible explanations for their behaviour. If your friend believes she exercises to lose weight or because her doctor has ordered her to, she is unlikely to assume that she runs and works out because she enjoys it.

Comparing Affective, Cognitive, and Behavioural Bases of Attitudes As we have been discussing, not all attitudes are created equally. They can be based on affect, cognition, or behaviour. Recently, Geoffrey Haddock, Mark Zanna, and Victoria Esses have conducted a series of studies to determine which attitudes are most likely to be based on affect, on cognition, or on behaviour (Esses, Haddock & Zanna, 1993; Haddock & Zanna, 1994, 1998; Haddock, Zanna, & Esses, 1993, 1994). In one of their studies, the researchers focused on attitudes toward homosexuals held by students at the University of Waterloo (Haddock, Zanna, & Esses, 1993). Affect was assessed by having participants describe the feelings they experienced when thinking about homosexuals. Two kinds of cognition were measured: the participants' stereotypes of homosexuals (the characteristics they believe homosexuals possess) and symbolic beliefs about homosexuals (the values they believed were promoted or hindered by homosexuals). Behaviour was assessed by asking participants to describe how frequently they interacted with homosexuals and whether their most recent experiences with homosexuals had been positive or negative.

Haddock and colleagues found that people's attitudes toward homosexuals were based on all three sources. However, the strongest effects were for symbolic beliefs (a cognitive component). In other words, if you wanted to know someone's attitude toward homosexuals and could ask only one question, you should ask, "Do homosexuals threaten your value system"? This would be a better question than asking, "How do you feel about homosexuals?" or "What is your stereotype of homosexuals?" or " Have your most recent interactions with homosexuals been pleasant?" The researchers obtained the same pattern of findings when they assessed attitudes toward Pakistanis.

Esses, Haddock, and Zanna (1993) note that in their research, attitudes toward homosexuals and Pakistanis are generally negative, and it is for these groups that attitudes tend to be based on symbolic beliefs. Attitudes toward other social groups that they have studied (English Canadians, French Canadians, and Native Indians) are more positive, and these attitudes are more likely to be based on affect (Haddock, Zanna, & Esses, 1993).

These researchers also have examined the basis of attitudes toward various social issues. For example, Haddock and Zanna (1998) assessed whether University of Waterloo students' attitudes toward capital punishment were based more strongly on affect (feelings about capital punishment) or on cognition (stereotypic beliefs and symbolic beliefs). The researchers found that on this issue, attitudes were more likely to be based on affect.

Thus, different attitudes have different bases. When it comes to our attitudes concerning different social groups, it appears that if we dislike the group, our attitudes are likely to have a cognitive basis—specifically, the belief that the group threatens our value system. Attitudes toward groups whom we like are more likely to be based on our feelings toward that group (i.e., affect). Attitudes toward issues such as capital punishment also are more likely to be based on how we feel about the issue, rather than on what we think about it.

DETERMINANTS OF ATTITUDE STRENGTH

Attitudes differ not only in their affective, cognitive, or behavioural origins, but also in their strength (Fazio, 1995; Petty & Krosnick, 1995; Pomerantz, Chaiken, & Tordesillas, 1995). This probably does not come as a surprise; for most of us, our attitude toward the current price of rutabagas is weaker, and held with less conviction, than our religious views or our feelings toward a loved one. As you might expect, attitudes that are strong are more resistant to change. What determines whether an attitude is strong or weak? There are a number of answers (Bassili, 1996). We will focus on four major determinants of attitude strength that have been identified in the research literature: ambivalence, accessibility, subjective experiences, and autobiographical recall.

Ambivalence   So far we have been discussing attitudes in an either–or fashion—as though they are either uniformly positive or negative. However, sometimes we experience ambivalence, or "mixed feelings," toward someone or something. For example, some University of Waterloo students have ambivalent attitudes toward feminists—they see feminists in both positive and negative terms (MacDonald & Zanna, 1998)—and toward issues such as capital punishment and abortion (Newby-Clark, McGregor, & Zanna, 2002). To give another example, some University of Western Ontario students have ambivalent attitudes toward Canada's Native peoples (Bell & Esses, 1997). Recent research by Newby-Clark and colleagues (2002) shows that not only do positive and negative aspects of an attitude come to mind equally quickly for those who are ambivalent, but such people actually experience feeling conflicted about the attitude in question.

As you might expect, ambivalent attitudes tend to be weaker, and therefore are more easily changed, than attitudes that are clearly positive or clearly negative. For example, Maio, Bell, and Esses (1996) assessed ambivalence toward Asian people among students at the University of Western Ontario. Participants then read an editorial (constructed by the researchers) that contained either strong or weak arguments in favour of immigration from Hong Kong to Canada. Those with ambivalent attitudes were more likely to be persuaded by the editorial, particularly when it contained strong arguments. On the other hand, those who held either positive or negative attitudes (i.e., were not ambivalent) did not change their attitudes after reading the editorial, regardless of the arguments presented. These researchers obtained similar findings in a recent study of attitudes toward Native people (Bell & Esses, 2002). Participants read an article that presented arguments either supporting or opposing Native land claims. Those who were ambivalent became more positive in their attitudes toward Native people after exposure to arguments in favour of land claims than those who read the negative article. Consistent with their earlier findings, participants who held nonambivalent attitudes failed to show attitude change—regardless of whether they were exposed to positive or negative arguments.

Accessibility   Another determinant of attitude strength is accessibility (Bassili, 1996; Roese & Olson, 1994). Consider this example: In a moment, we are going to give you the name of an object. When we do, simply think about that object for a few seconds. Ready? Here is the object: *a mountain bike.* Did positive or negative feelings come to mind immediately, or did you think about a mountain bike without much feeling? These questions concern **attitude accessibility**, which Russ Fazio (1989, 1990, 2000; Fazio, Ledbetter, & Towles-Schwen, 2000) defines as the strength of the association between an object and an evaluation of it. If an attitude is highly accessible, your attitude comes to mind whenever you encounter the object. For example, if your attitude toward mountain bikes is highly accessible, as soon as you read the words, feelings of liking or disliking are triggered. If an attitude is relatively inaccessible, feelings of liking or disliking come to mind more slowly.

Attitude accessibility
the strength of the association between an object and a person's evaluation of that object; accessibility is measured by the speed with which people can report how they feel about an issue or object

Simply expressing an attitude can increase its accessibility. In fact, even expressing the *opposite* of an attitude can increase its accessibility. Why? Because doing so reminds us of our true attitude. To demonstrate this effect, Maio and Olson (1998) asked some students at the University of Western Ontario about their attitude toward Albert Einstein (they were quite positive); others were asked to express the opposite of their true attitude. (Participants in the control group were not asked about their attitude toward Einstein.) Later, all participants read an article, supposedly written by Einstein, opposing the development of a particular technology. Participants who had expressed their attitudes earlier—either true or false—were more likely to agree that the technology should not be developed than were participants in the no-attitude control group.

The more accessible an attitude is, the stronger it is, and consequently the harder it is to change (Bassili, 1995, 1996; Houston & Fazio, 1989). For example, in one study (Bassili, 1996), University of Toronto students were telephoned and asked about their views on issues such as employment quotas for women, pornography laws, and hateful expression laws. The accessibility of the respondents' attitudes was assessed by recording how long it took them to answer the questions. The interviewers then presented counterarguments (arguments opposite to the respondent's position) on some of the issues. Participants whose attitudes were highly accessible (i.e., who responded quickly to the attitude questions) were less likely to change their attitudes in light of the counterarguments than were participants whose attitudes were less accessible.

Subjective Experience Another determinant of attitude strength is subjective experience, or the ease with which you are able to generate arguments for (or against) your attitudes. In Chapter 3, we described a study by Schwarz and colleagues (1991) in which people were asked to describe either 6 or 12 examples of assertive behaviour. As you may recall, ironically, participants who listed 6 instances of assertive behaviour rated themselves as more assertive than did participants who listed 12 instances. The reason? It was relatively easy to generate six examples, leading participants to conclude that they, in fact, must be quite assertive. In contrast, it was so difficult to come up with 12 examples that participants concluded they must not be very assertive after all.

Haddock, Rothman, and Schwarz (1996) suggested that a similar process might determine attitude strength. They asked participants to generate either three or seven arguments in favour of (or against) doctor-assisted suicide. The researchers reasoned that if attitude strength is based on the ease with which people can generate arguments, then attitude strength should be greater after generating three arguments ("I must hold strong attitudes toward this issue because it's easy for me to come up with reasons why doctor-assisted suicide is a good/bad idea") than after seven arguments ("I must not have very strong views on this issue because I'm having a hard time coming up with arguments"). And that is exactly what they found.

Autobiographical Recall Finally, research conducted at the University of Waterloo suggests that our attitudes are stronger if we recall personal behaviours relevant to that attitude (Ross et al., 1983; Lydon, Zanna, & Ross, 1988). For example, in one study (Ross et al., 1983), participants were exposed to arguments that brushing your teeth is actually a harmful practice and that people should floss instead. Participants in the relevant

▲ When you looked at this picture, how quickly did your attitude toward mountain bikes come to mind? The faster your attitude came to mind, the more accessible and resistant to change it is.

condition were asked how often they brushed their teeth, whereas those in the irrelevant condition reported on the frequency with which they used seat belts. Later, all participants were exposed to an attack on the anti-toothbrushing message they had heard earlier. Who was most likely to stick with their new anti-toothbrushing attitudes? As you might have guessed, it was the participants who had been asked to recall behaviours relevant to the message (i.e., how often they brushed their teeth). Participants who had recalled irrelevant behaviours (i.e., seat belt use) were more likely to be swayed by the counterarguments that were presented.

In summary, we have seen that attitude strength is determined by a variety of factors, including ambivalence, accessibility, subjective experiences, and autobiographical recall. Regardless of the path to attitude strength, once an attitude is strongly entrenched it will show greater resistance to change than will a weakly held attitude.

When Will Attitudes Predict Behaviour?

Advertisers assume that changing people's attitudes toward products will result in increased sales, and politicians assume that positive feelings toward a candidate will result in a vote for that candidate on election day. Sounds pretty straightforward, right?

Actually, the relationship between attitudes and behaviour is not so straightforward, as indicated by a classic study by Richard LaPiere (1934). In the early 1930s, LaPiere embarked on a sightseeing trip across the United States with a young Chinese couple. Because prejudice against Asians was commonplace among Americans at that time, he was apprehensive about how his Chinese friends would be treated. At each hotel, campground, and restaurant they entered, LaPiere worried that his friends would confront anti-Asian prejudice and that they would be refused service. Much to his surprise, this almost never happened. Of the 251 establishments he and his friends visited, only one refused to serve them.

Struck by this apparent lack of prejudice, LaPiere decided to explore people's attitudes toward Asians in a different way. After his trip, he wrote a letter to each establishment he and his friends had visited, asking if it would serve a Chinese visitor. Of the many establishments who replied, only one said it would. More than 90 percent said they definitely would not; the rest said they were undecided. People's attitudes—as expressed in their response to LaPiere's written inquiry—were in stark contrast to their actual behaviour toward LaPiere's Chinese friends.

LaPiere's study was not, of course, a controlled experiment. As LaPiere acknowledged, there are several reasons why his results may not show consistency between people's attitudes and behaviour. For example, he had no way of knowing whether the proprietors who answered his letter were the same people who had served him and his friends. Further, people's attitudes could have changed in the months that passed between the time they served the Chinese couple and the time they received the letter. Nonetheless, the lack of correspondence between people's attitudes and what they actually did was so striking that we might question the assumption that behaviour routinely follows from attitudes. Indeed, when Allan Wicker (1969) reviewed dozens of more methodologically sound studies, he reached the same conclusion: People's attitudes are poor predictors of their behaviour. In subsequent research, social psychologists have demonstrated that under certain circumstances, attitudes can predict behaviours quite well (DeBono & Snyder, 1995; Fazio, 1990; Zanna & Fazio, 1982). What are those conditions? It turns out that one important factor is whether our behaviour is spontaneous or planned.

PREDICTING SPONTANEOUS BEHAVIOURS

Sometimes we act spontaneously, giving little forethought to what we are about to do. When LaPiere and his Chinese friends entered a restaurant, the manager did not have a lot of time to reflect on whether to serve them; he or she had to make a snap decision. Similarly, when someone approaches us at a shopping mall and asks us to sign a petition in favour of a change in the local zoning laws, we usually don't stop to deliberate for 10 minutes but instead decide whether to sign the petition on the spot.

Attitudes will predict spontaneous behaviours only when they are highly accessible to people (Fazio, 1990, 2000; Kallgren & Wood, 1986). As you will recall, accessibility refers to the strength of the association between an object and your attitude toward that object. When accessibility is high, your attitude comes to mind whenever you see the object. When accessibility is low, your attitude comes to mind more slowly. It follows that highly accessible attitudes will be more likely to predict spontaneous behaviours, because people are more likely to be thinking about their attitude when they are called on to act.

Russell Fazio, Martha Powell, and Carol Williams (1989) demonstrated the role of accessibility in a study of people's attitudes and behaviours toward consumer items. People first rated their attitudes toward several products, such as different brands of gum and candy bars. The researchers assessed the accessibility of these attitudes by measuring how long it took people to respond to the attitude questions. People's actual behaviour was measured by placing 10 of the products on a table (in 2 rows of 5) and telling them that they could choose 5 to take home as a reward for being in the study. To what extent did people's attitudes toward the products determine which ones they chose?

◀ It is commonly assumed that people's attitudes (e.g., toward a social issue) determine their behaviour (e.g., signing a petition supporting that issue). This is not always true, however. If the behaviour is spontaneous, it depends on how accessible people's attitudes are. If the behaviour is deliberate, it depends on their behavioural intentions.

As predicted, it depended on the accessibility of their attitudes. Attitude–behaviour consistency was high among people with accessible attitudes and relatively low among people with inaccessible attitudes. That is, people acted in accordance with their attitudes only if their attitudes came quickly to mind when they were making their choice. What about people with inaccessible attitudes—what determined which products they chose? Interestingly, they were more influenced by an arbitrary aspect of the situation: which products happened to be in the first row on the table in front of them. The closer an item was, the more likely they were to choose it. This is consistent with the idea that when attitudes are inaccessible, people are more influenced by situational variables—in this case, how noticeable and within reach the products were.

PREDICTING DELIBERATIVE BEHAVIOURS

Sometimes behaviour is not spontaneous but deliberative and planned. Most of us give a good deal of thought about where to go to university, whether to accept a new job, or where to spend our vacation. Under these conditions, the immediate accessibility of our attitude is not as important. Given enough time to think about an issue, even people with inaccessible attitudes can bring to mind how they feel. The best-known theory of how attitudes predict deliberative behaviours is Icek Ajzen and Martin Fishbein's **theory of planned behavior** (Ajzen, 1985, 1996; Ajzen & Fishbein, 1980; Ajzen & Sexton, 1999; Fishbein & Ajzen, 1975). According to this theory, when people have time to contemplate how they are going to behave, the best predictor of their behaviour is their intention, which is in turn determined by three things: their attitudes toward the specific behaviour, their subjective norms, and their perceived behavioural control (see Figure 7.2). Let's consider each of these three in turn. First, specific attitudes. What is important here is not people's general attitude about something but their specific attitude toward the behaviour they are considering. According to the theory of planned behaviour, only specific attitudes toward the behaviour in question can be expected to predict that behaviour.

For example, in a study of married women's use of birth control pills, Andrew Davidson and James Jaccard (1979) asked a series of attitude questions, ranging from the general (the women's attitude toward birth control) to the specific (their attitude toward

Theory of planned behaviour

a theory that the best predictors of a person's planned, deliberate behaviours are the person's attitudes toward specific behaviours, subjective norms, and perceived behavioural control

▶ **Figure 7.2**

THE THEORY OF PLANNED BEHAVIOUR.

According to this theory, the best predictors of people's planned, deliberative behaviours are their behavioural intentions. The best predictors of their intentions are their attitudes toward the specific behaviour, their subjective norms, and their perceived control of the behaviour.

(Adapted from Ajzen, 1985)

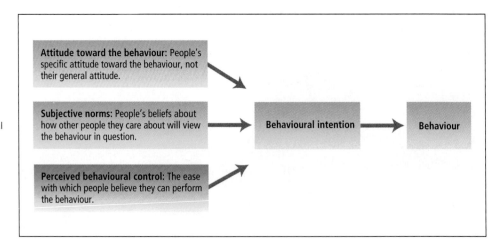

using birth control pills during the next two years; see Table 7.1). Two years later, the women were asked whether they had used birth control pills at any time since the last interview. As seen in Table 7.1, the women's general attitude toward birth control did not predict their use of birth control. This general attitude did not take into account other factors that could have influenced their decision, such as the women's concern about the long-term effects of the pill and their attitude toward other forms of birth control. The more specific the question was about the act of using birth control pills, the better this attitude predicted their actual behaviour.

This may be one reason LaPiere (1934) found in his study such inconsistency between people's attitudes and behaviours. His question to the proprietors—whether they would serve "members of the Chinese race"—was stated very generally. Had he asked a much more specific question—such as whether they would serve an educated, well-dressed, well-to-do Chinese couple accompanied by a white American professor—they might have given an answer that was more in line with their behaviour.

In addition to measuring attitudes toward the behaviour, we also need to measure people's **subjective norms**—their beliefs about how those they care about will view the behaviour in question (see Figure 7.2). To predict someone's intentions, it can be as important to know these beliefs as to know his or her attitudes. For example, suppose we want to predict whether Kristen intends to go to a heavy metal concert, and we know that she has a negative attitude toward this behaviour—she can't stand heavy metal music. We would probably say she won't go. Suppose we also know, though, that Kristen's best friend, Malcolm, really wants her to go. Knowing this subjective norm—her belief about how a close friend views her behaviour—we might make a different prediction.

Finally, as seen in Figure 7.2, people's intentions are influenced by perceived behavioural control, which is the ease with which people believe they can perform the behaviour. If people think it is difficult to perform the behaviour, such as sticking to a gruelling exercise regimen, they will not form a strong intention to do so. If people think it is easy to perform the behaviour, such as remembering to buy milk on the way home from work, they are more likely to form a strong intention to do so.

Subjective norms
people's beliefs about how those they care about will view the behaviour in question

---

TABLE 7.1

Specific attitudes are better predictors of behaviour

Different groups of women were asked about their attitudes toward birth control. The more specific the question, the better it predicted their actual use of birth control. Note: If a correlation is close to 0, it means that there is no relationship between the two variables. The closer the correlation is to 1, the stronger the relationship between attitudes and behaviour. (Adapted from Davidson & Jaccard, 1979)

Attitude Measure	Attitude–Behaviour Correlation
Attitude toward birth control	.08
Attitude toward birth control pills	.32
Attitude toward using birth control pills	.53
Attitude toward using birth control pills during the next two years	.57

A considerable amount of research supports the idea that asking people about these determinants of their intentions—attitudes toward specific behaviours, subjective norms, and perceived behavioural control—increases the ability to predict their planned, deliberative behaviours. For example, Mummery and Wankel (1999) used the theory of planned behaviour to predict whether an intensive cycle of intensive training would be completed by 116 competitive swimmers (ages 11 to 18 years) from swimming clubs across Canada. Attitudes toward the behaviour were assessed with adjective pairs similar to those in Try It! on page 224 (e.g., good–bad, important–unimportant, dull–exciting, pleasant–unpleasant). Subjective norms were assessed by agreement with statements such as "Most of the people important in my life think that I should complete all of the assigned training during the upcoming training cycle." Consistent with the theory of planned behaviour, swimmers who had positive attitudes toward the training cycle, believed that important people in their life wanted them to complete it, and believed that they were capable of doing so, were most likely to report that they intended to complete the upcoming cycle of training. Importantly, swimmers with these intentions also were the most likely to actually complete their training.

The theory of planned behaviour also has proven successful in predicting other behaviours, such as smoking among Quebec high-school students (Hill et al., 1997); exercise among Alberta women and men receiving treatment for cancer (Courneya & Friedenreich, 1997, 1999); exercise, maintaining a low-fat diet, and smoking among Quebec men (Nguyen et al., 1996); as well as participation in exercise classes for the elderly offered at the University of Western Ontario (Estabrooks & Carron, 1999).

The variables of attitudes, subjective norms, and perceived behavioural control also have proven useful in predicting antinuclear activism among students at the University of Ottawa (Horvarth, 1996); alcohol consumption among students at the University of Western Ontario (Wall, Hinson, & McKee, 1998); engaging in AIDS preventive behaviours among first-year university students across Canada (Hawa, Munro, & Doherty-Poirier, 1998); and intentions to use condoms in three cultural groups: the Latin American community in Montreal, the English-speaking Caribbean community in Toronto, and the South Asian community in Vancouver (Godin, Maticka-Tyndale, Adrien, Manson-Singer, Williams, & Cappon, 1996). Thus, this theory applies to a wide range of behaviour.

Before leaving this topic, we should mention that recent evidence suggests that, at least in the domain of health and exercise behaviours, the variables of attitudes and perceived behavioural control are more important than subjective norms in predicting behavioural intentions. This was the conclusion reached by researchers at the University of Western Ontario who conducted a meta analysis of studies on the theory of planned behaviour as applied to exercise (Hausenblas, Carron, & Mack, 1997). (As we mentioned in Chapter 2, a meta analysis is a statistical technique that allows you to combine the results across two or more studies and come up with a meaningful statistical summary.) It was also the conclusion of Gaston Godin (Laval University) and Gerjo Kok (University of Limburg, The Netherlands), based on their meta analysis of 56 studies on health-related behaviours (e.g., smoking, exercise, diet, HIV/AIDS prevention, screening for cancer; Godin & Kok, 1996).

Thus, when it comes to health and exercise behaviours, it may be more important to have positive attitudes and believe that you are able to perform the necessary behaviours than to feel that your friends and family want you to eat well and be fit.

ATTITUDE–BEHAVIOUR CONSISTENCY: IMPLICATIONS FOR SAFE SEX

There is one area in which people's attitudes are often inconsistent with their behaviour, even though the consequences can be fatal. The inconsistency takes the form of their having positive attitudes toward using condoms, expressing intentions to use condoms, but then failing to actually use them in sexual encounters (Hynie & Lydon, 1996). For example, in a study by Herold and Mewhinney (1993), nearly 100 percent of the patrons of various dating bars in southern Ontario agreed with statements such as "If I were to have sex with someone I just met, I would have no objections if my partner suggested that we use a condom." However, these favourable attitudes toward condom use did not translate into safe sex practices. Only 56 percent of the people at the bar who engaged in casual sex had used a condom in their most recent sexual encounter. Even more frightening, a mere 29 percent of the women and men who had engaged in casual sex in the past year reported that they had always used a condom.

Why would people with positive attitudes toward condom use risk their lives by not using them? Perhaps the theory of planned behaviour can provide some clues. As you will recall from the previous section, according to this theory, attitudes are not the only predictor of behaviour. Subjective norms, perceived behavioural control, and behavioural intentions also play a role. Can these variables help us understand why people so often fail to use condoms, despite having positive attitudes toward condom use? Let's take a look at some studies.

Subjective Norms People's beliefs about how others view the behaviour in question are an important determinant of their behaviour. According to one study, 65 percent of the students at a high school in Nova Scotia believe that their sexually active friends use condoms (Richardson et al., 1997). Such beliefs should promote condom use. Indeed, there is evidence that whether university students use condoms depends on the norms for sexual behaviour that operate among their friends (Winslow, Franzini, & Hwang, 1992). However, even if one's friends generally advocate condom use, certain situations may invoke a different norm. For example, the "break loose" university spring breaks have a reputation for providing opportunities for casual sex (Maticka-Tyndale, Herold, & Mewhinney, 1998, 2001). In one study, students from various universities in eastern Ontario on "break loose" vacations in Daytona Beach, Florida, reported that it was more acceptable to have casual sex while on such vacations than while at home (Mewhinney, Herold, & Maticka-Tyndale, 1995). Unfortunately, the norm of permissive sexuality that evolves in such settings is accompanied by a low rate of condom use (Eiser & Ford, 1995).

More importantly, our beliefs about how our sexual partner feels about condoms exert a powerful influence on whether condoms are used. If we anticipate a negative reaction from our partner, we are less likely to end up using condoms. For example, some of the English- and French-speaking university students in Montreal who were interviewed by Maticka-Tyndale (1992) worried that if they suggested using a condom, their partner might not feel trusted. In addition, women were concerned that if they provided condoms, they would be perceived as someone who engages in casual sex—something that "nice" women don't do. Indeed, Hynie and Lydon (1995) found that McGill University students rated a woman more negatively when she provided a condom than when her

▼ If people fear a negative reaction, they are less likely to raise the issue of condom use with a potential sexual partner.

GET THE FACTS
947-9222   1-800-432-1957
The Facts of Life Line

(male) sexual partner did. Moreover, they also assumed that her partner would feel negatively toward her—more so than if he provided the condom or if they did not use any protection. Thus, if people anticipate that their peer group, or more importantly their sexual partner, would not approve of condom use, they are more likely to engage in unprotected sex.

Perceived Behavioural Control If people think it is difficult to perform a behaviour, they will not form strong intentions to do so. What might be so difficult about using condoms? At first glance, it might seem like an easy thing to do. However, that is actu-ally not the case. The first obstacle that some people face is discomfort or embarrassment about purchasing condoms. For example, a study conducted with sexually active students at the University of British Columbia found that those who were embarrassed about buying condoms bought them less often than did those who were not embarrassed (Dahl, Gorn, & Weinberg, 1998). Perhaps of greater importance, a series of studies conducted at McGill University suggests that people may not know how to broach the topic of condom use during a sexual encounter (Hynie et al., 1998; Hynie & Lydon, 1996). In one of these studies, Hynie and colleagues (1998) asked participants to read a story involving two students, Anne-Marie and Eric. According to the story, one night after watching a late-night movie at Anne-Marie's apartment, they made their way to her bedroom. The participants were asked to imagine that Anne-Marie and Eric decide to have sex, and were required to continue the story, describing the couple's interactions in as much detail as possible. Only half of the participants made reference to the use of a condom in their stories. Some participants mentioned a condom, but it didn't actually get used. Based on these findings, Hynie and colleagues concluded that the use of condoms has not been incorporated into people's sexual scripts. In other words, young women and men don't really know when and how to approach the issue of condom use in sexual situations.

Indeed, in subsequent research in which they interviewed women in the Montreal area, Hynie and Lydon (1996) found that some of the respondents had engaged in unsafe sex because they felt too uncomfortable to bring up the topic of condoms and too unassertive to insist that a condom be used.

Behavioural Intentions People will not use condoms unless they intend to do so. What factors might affect people's intentions to use condoms? Researchers at the University of Waterloo (MacDonald, Zanna, & Fong, 1996) have found that for both women and men, alcohol intoxication is associated with lower intentions to use condoms—even among those who have positive attitudes toward condom use. MacDonald and colleagues explain that when people are intoxicated, their ability to process information is impaired, such that they are able to focus only on the most immediate aspects of the situation (i.e., short-term pleasure) rather than on the long-term consequences of their actions. Subsequent studies by these investigators reveal that alcohol is especially likely to lower intentions to use condoms when there are cues in the environment that promote risky behaviour (e.g., sexual arousal, a willing partner) (MacDonald et al., 2000). These findings are alarming, given that alcohol is present in many of the settings in which people are likely to encounter cues that promote casual sex (e.g., bars, parties, vacations). Incidentally, in the "break loose" studies, when the researchers had assistants travel to Daytona Beach to interview students about their casual sex experiences, the interviews had to be conducted before 4:00 p.m. to ensure that participants would be sober (Maticka-Tyndale, Herold, & Mewhinney, 1998, 2001).

More recently, at Queen's University, Tara MacDonald and her colleagues have identified another factor that can influence people's intentions to use condoms, namely their mood (MacDonald & Martineau, 2002). These researchers conducted a study in which they put female students in a good or bad mood. All participants then saw a videotape in which an attractive man and woman, Mike and Rebecca, return to Rebecca's apartment after going out on a date. They become physically intimate and reach the point where they are both interested in having sex. However, neither of them has a condom and there aren't any stores close by. Participants who were in a bad mood and who were low in self-esteem were most likely to report that they would go ahead and have sex anyway. In contrast, those who were in a good mood reported much lower intentions to have unprotected sex in this situation. This held true regardless of whether the participants were high or low in self-esteem. MacDonald and Martineau suggest that when we are in a good mood, we may be more likely to focus on the risks associated with unprotected sex. On the other hand, if we are in a bad mood, particularly if we also tend to be low in self-esteem, we may be more likely to focus on the risk of rejection from a sexual partner. As they discovered, this differential focus can influence whether people intend to engage in safe sex.

In summary, even the most positive of attitudes toward condom use do not guarantee that people will practise safe sex. The theory of planned behaviour would suggest that other variables must be taken into account as well, including subjective norms, perceived behavioural control, and behavioural intentions. Research on subjective norms suggests that when people are in an environment in which unprotected sexual activity is condoned (e.g., "break loose" vacations) or if they anticipate a negative reaction from their partner, they will be less likely to use condoms. Studies relevant to the behavioural control variable suggest that people may not be comfortable purchasing condoms or bringing up the issue of condom use with their partner. The more difficult they find it to perform these behaviours, the less likely it is that condoms will be used. Finally, when people's intentions to use condoms are undermined (e.g., due to intoxication or a bad mood), they will be less likely to practise safe sex. In short, condom use is a highly complex behaviour that cannot be predicted solely on the basis of people's attitudes.

Attitude Change

Attitudes do sometimes change. For example, after the terrorist attacks in the United States on September 11, 2001, Canadians expressed extremely positive attitudes toward Americans. As Chris Baker, vice-president of Environics Research explains, "In the aftermath of September 11, many Canadians set aside whatever animosity and grievances they had to the United States and rallied around this notion that we are all Americans now." However, in the year that followed, many Canadians became disgruntled with U.S. trade tactics and with President George W. Bush's war on terrorism. As a result, attitudes toward Americans took a definite turn for the worse. In fact, in just one year (from September 2001 to September 2002), the number of Canadians who held unfavourable views of Americans doubled from 18 to 36 percent (Samyn, 2002). No doubt, by the time this textbook is printed, attitudes will have changed again.

When attitudes change, they often do so in response to social influence. Our attitudes toward everything from our neighbours to the south to a brand of laundry detergent can be influenced by what other people do or say. This is why attitudes are of such interest to social psychologists: Even something as personal and internal as an attitude is a highly social phenomenon, influenced by the imagined or actual behaviour of other people.

PERSUASIVE COMMUNICATIONS AND ATTITUDE CHANGE

Suppose the Canadian Cancer Society has given you a five-figure budget to come up with an anti-smoking campaign that could be used nationwide. You have a lot of decisions ahead of you. Should you pack your public service announcement with facts and figures? Or should you take a more emotional approach in your message, including frightening visual images of diseased lungs? Should you hire a famous movie star to deliver your message, or a Nobel Prize–winning medical researcher? Should you take a friendly tone and acknowledge that it is hard to quit smoking, or should you take a hard line and tell smokers to (as the Nike ads put it) "just do it"? You can see the point—it's not easy to figure out how to construct a truly **persuasive communication**, one that advocates a particular side of an issue.

Luckily, social psychologists have conducted many studies over the past 50 years on what makes a persuasive communication effective, beginning with Carl Hovland and his colleagues (Hovland, Janis, & Kelley, 1953). These researchers conducted many experiments on the conditions under which people are most likely to be influenced by persuasive communications. In essence, they studied "who says what to whom," looking at the *source of the communication* (e.g., how expert or attractive the speaker is); the *communication itself* (e.g., the quality of the arguments; whether the speaker presents both sides of the issue);

Persuasive communication

communication (e.g., a speech or television ad) advocating a particular side of an issue

▶ To sell a product, it is effective to have a credible, trustworthy celebrity endorsement.

and the *nature of the audience* (e.g., which kinds of appeals work with hostile versus friendly audiences). Because these researchers were at Yale University, this approach to the study of persuasive communications is known as the **Yale Attitude Change Approach**.

This approach yielded a great deal of useful information on how people change their attitudes in response to persuasive communications; some of this information is summarized in Figure 7.3. For example, regarding the source of the communication, research has shown that speakers who are credible, trustworthy, attractive, or likeable are more persuasive than those who are not. In a study on the effects of speaker credibility, Ross, McFarland, Conway, and Zanna (1983) asked students at the University of Waterloo to

Yale Attitude Change Approach

the study of the conditions under which people are most likely to change their attitudes in response to persuasive messages; researchers in this tradition focus on "who said what to whom"—that is, on the source of the communication, the nature of the communication, and the nature of the audience

◀ **Figure 7.3**

THE YALE ATTITUDE CHANGE APPROACH.

The Yale Attitude Change Approach

The effectiveness of persuasive communications depends on who says what to whom.

Who: The Source of the Communication

- Credible speakers (e.g., those with obvious expertise) persuade people more than speakers lacking in credibility (Hovland & Weiss, 1951; Petty, Wegener, & Fabrigar, 1997).
- Attractive speakers (whether due to physical or personality attributes) persuade people more than unattractive speakers do (Eagly & Chaiken, 1975; Petty, Wegener, & Fabrigar, 1997).

What: The Nature of the Communication

- People are more persuaded by messages that do not seem to be designed to influence them (Petty & Cacioppo, 1986; Walster & Festinger, 1962).
- Is it best to present a one-sided communication (one that presents only arguments favouring your position) or a two-sided communication (one that presents arguments for and against your position)? In general, two-sided messages work better, if you are sure to refute the arguments on the other side (Allen, 1991; Allen et al., 1990; Crowley & Hoyer, 1994; Lumsdaine & Janis, 1953).
- Is it best to give your speech before or after someone arguing for the other side? If the speeches are to be given

back to back and there will be a delay before people have to make up their minds, it is best to go first. Under these conditions, there is likely to be a *primacy effect,* wherein people are more influenced by what they hear first. If there is a delay between the speeches and people will make up their minds right after hearing the second one, it is best to go last. Under these conditions, there is likely to be a *recency effect,* wherein people remember the second speech better than the first one (Haugtvedt & Wegener, 1994; Miller & Campbell, 1959).

To Whom: The Nature of the Audience

- An audience that is distracted during the persuasive communication will often be persuaded more than one that is not (Festinger & Maccoby, 1964; Petty & Cacioppo, 1986).
- People low in intelligence tend to be more easily influenced than people high in intelligence, and people with moderate self-esteem tend to be more easily influenced than people with low or high self-esteem (Rhodes & Wood, 1992).
- People are particularly susceptible to attitude change during the impressionable ages of 18 to 25. Beyond those ages, people's attitudes are more stable and resistant to change (Krosnick & Alwin, 1989; Sears, 1981).

listen to a tape-recorded speech in which it was argued that vigorous exercise is actually harmful. Participants in the credible condition were told that the speaker was Dr. James Rundle, a world authority on the effects of exercise; those in the non-credible condition were told that the speech was delivered by a local representative of the Fat Is Beautiful organization. As you might expect, participants were more influenced by the message when it was attributed to a credible source.

People also are more likely to be persuaded when they trust or like the speaker. Speakers will be trusted and liked if it seems as though they are not simply telling the audience what it wants to hear or if they are arguing against their own self-interests. For example, in one study, students at Wilfrid Laurier University were asked to read a pro-environmental speech (opposing the harvesting of trees) supposedly delivered by a politician from northern Ontario (Pancer et al., 1992). Participants had a more positive impression of the politician if they were told that the audience was a group of people in the logging industry than if they were told that the audience was a pro-environmental group. Characteristics of the message that are important, as well as characteristics of the audience that increase the likelihood of persuasion, are shown in Figure 7.3.

Research inspired by the Yale Attitude Change Approach has been important in identifying the determinants of effective persuasion. However, it has not been clear which aspects of persuasive communications are most important—that is, when one factor should be emphasized over another. For example, let's return to that job you have with the Canadian Cancer Society—they want to see their ad next month! If you were to read the many Yale Attitude Change studies, you would find lots of useful information about who should say what to whom in order to construct a persuasive communication. However, you might also find yourself saying, "Gee there's an awful lot of information here, and I'm not sure where I should place the most emphasis. Should I worry most about who delivers the ads? Or should I worry more about the content of the message itself?"

The Central and Peripheral Routes to Persuasion

If you asked these questions, you would be in good company. Some well-known attitude researchers have wondered the same thing. When is it best to stress factors central to the communication—such as the strength of the arguments—and when is it best to stress factors peripheral to the logic of the arguments—such as the credibility or attractiveness of the person delivering the speech? This question has been answered by two influential theories of persuasive communication: Shelly Chaiken's **heuristic-systematic persuasion model** (Chaiken, 1987; Chaiken, Liberman, & Eagly, 1989; Chaiken, Wood, & Eagly, 1996; Chen & Chaiken, 1999), and Richard Petty and John Cacioppo's **elaboration likelihood model** (Petty & Cacioppo, 1986; Petty & Wegener, 1999). These theories specify when people will be influenced by what the speech says (i.e., the logic of the arguments) and when they will be influenced by more superficial characteristics (e.g., who gives the speech or how long it is).

Both theories state that under certain conditions people are motivated to pay attention to the facts in a communication. Thus they will be most persuaded when these facts are logically compelling. That is, sometimes people elaborate on what they hear, carefully thinking about and processing the content of the communication. Chaiken (1980)

Heuristic-systematic model of persuasion

the theory that there are two ways in which persuasive communications can cause attitude change; people either process the merits of the arguments known as systematic processing or use mental shortcuts (heuristics), such as "Experts are always right," known as heuristic processing

Elaboration likelihood model

the theory that there are two ways in which persuasive communications can cause attitude change; the *central route* occurs when people are motivated and have the ability to pay attention to the arguments in the communication, and the *peripheral route* occurs when people do not pay attention to the arguments but are instead swayed by surface characteristics (e.g., who gave the speech)

calls this *systematic processing*; Petty and Cacioppo (1986) call this the *central route to persuasion*. Under other conditions, people are not motivated to pay attention to the facts; instead, they notice only the surface characteristics of the message, such as how long it is and who is delivering it. Here, people will not be swayed by the logic of the arguments, because they are not paying close attention to what the communicator says. Instead, they are persuaded if the surface characteristics of the message—such as the fact that it is long or is delivered by an expert or attractive communicator—make it seem like a reasonable one. Chaiken (1980) calls this *heuristic processing* because attitudes are based on simple rules or cognitive heuristics. (Recall from Chapter 3 that heuristics are defined as mental shortcuts people use to make judgments quickly and efficiently; in the context of attitudes, a heuristic can be viewed as a simple decision rule people use to decide what their attitude is, without having to spend a lot of time analyzing every little fact about the matter.) Petty and Cacioppo (1986) call this the *peripheral route to persuasion*, because people are swayed by things peripheral to the message itself.

What are the conditions under which people take the central versus the peripheral route to persuasion? The key, according to Petty, Cacioppo, and Chaiken, is whether people have the *motivation* and *ability* to pay attention to the facts. To the extent that people are truly interested in the topic and thus motivated to pay close attention to the arguments, they are more likely to take the central route. Similarly, if people have the ability to pay attention—for example, if nothing is distracting them—they will also take the central route (see Figure 7.4).

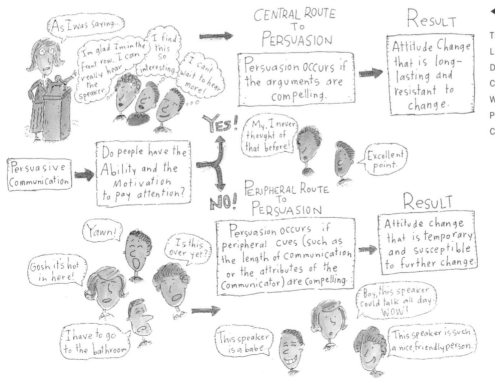

◀ Figure 7.4

THE ELABORATION LIKELIHOOD MODEL DESCRIBES HOW PEOPLE CHANGE THEIR ATTITUDES WHEN THEY HEAR PERSUASIVE COMMUNICATIONS.

The Motivation to Pay Attention to the Arguments   One determinant of whether people are motivated to pay attention to a communication is the personal relevance of the topic—namely, the extent to which a topic has important consequences for a person's well-being. For example, consider the issue of whether Canada Pension Plan benefits should be reduced. How personally relevant is this to you? If you are a 72-year-old whose sole income is from Canada Pension Plan, this issue is obviously extremely relevant; if you are a 20-year-old from a well-to-do family, the issue has little personal relevance.

The more personally relevant an issue is, the more willing people are to pay attention to the arguments in a speech, and thus the more likely they are to take the central route to persuasion. Shelly Chaiken (1980) demonstrated this point by asking students at the University of Toronto to read a transcript of a speech, supposedly made by an administrator at their university, advocating switching from a two-semester system to a trimester system. Half the students were told that the speech had been presented to a university committee in charge of this issue, and that if the committee approved of this policy, it would be implemented the next year; thus for these students the issue was personally relevant. The other participants were told that if approved, this new policy would not be implemented for five years. For these participants the issue was not relevant because they would have completed their studies by then.

Chaiken varied the strength of the arguments (one versus five) that were presented in the speech and the likeability of the speaker. To create feelings of liking, some participants read an excerpt from an interview allegedly conducted with the administrator in which he praised the students and faculty at the University of Toronto and mentioned that he considered them superior to their counterparts at the University of British Columbia, where he had previously held a similar position. He also raved about living in Toronto and described the city as a much more desirable place to live than Vancouver. Needless to say, the University of Toronto students who were in this condition liked him a lot! In the unlikeable condition, the administrator described the students and faculty at the University of Toronto as inferior to the students and faculty at the University of British Columbia. He also extolled the virtues of living in Vancouver, while derogating Toronto. Not surprisingly, participants in this condition did not find much to like about him.

Chaiken predicted that participants for whom the issue of a trimester system was personally relevant would be more persuaded by five arguments in favour of a trimester system from an unlikeable administrator than by one argument from a likeable administrator. In other words, these participants were expected to engage in systematic processing and, therefore, be persuaded by the content of the message. In contrast, participants for whom the issue was not personally relevant were expected to engage in heuristic processing—to be swayed by the likeability of the speaker more than the contents of the message. These participants were expected to show greater attitude change in response to one argument from a likeable source than five arguments from an unlikeable source. As shown in Figure 7.5, the pattern of findings was consistent with this hypothesis.

According to Gelinas-Chebat and Chebat (1992), even subtle cues such as the intensity of a speaker's voice might affect persuasion when relevance is low, because such cues could affect whether a speaker is perceived as prestigious or persuasive. To test this idea,

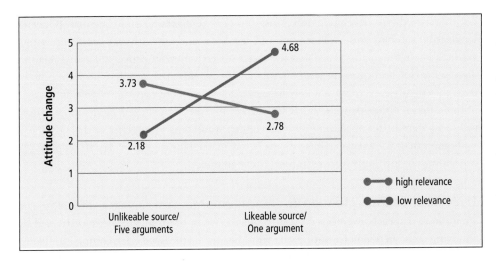

◀ **Figure 7.5**

EFFECTS OF PERSONAL
RELEVANCE ON TYPE OF
ATTITUDE CHANGE.

When the issue was highly
relevant, participants were more
likely to be persuaded by five
arguments in favour of a
trimester system from an
unlikeable source than by one
argument from a likeable source.
These participants engaged in
systematic information
processing (i.e., they were
persuaded by the quality of the
arguments). When the issue was
not very relevant, participants
were swayed by the likeability of
the speaker, rather than by the
quality of the arguments. These
participants engaged in heuristic
information processing.

(Adapted from Chaiken, 1980)

they asked business administration students at the University of Quebec at Montreal to listen to a tape-recorded speech containing arguments about why they should visit a particular bank. In the high-relevance condition, the speaker described special loans that were being offered to students. In the low-relevance condition, participants were offered an ATM card. Participants in the high-relevance condition rated the speech higher in terms of clarity, usefulness, and interest than did participants in the low-relevance condition. Participants in the low-relevance condition were more influenced by characteristics of the speaker's voice. Specifically, these participants were most persuaded by the message if the speaker's voice was low in intensity and intonation—voice qualities that give the impression one is not being pressured or coerced.

These findings reflect a general rule: When an issue is personally relevant, people will pay attention to the arguments in a speech and will be persuaded to the extent that the arguments are sound—the "proof" of the speech, in Aristotle's words. When an issue is of low personal relevance, people will not pay as close attention to the arguments. Instead, they will take a mental shortcut, following such peripheral rules as "Prestigious speakers can be trusted" or "Length implies strong arguments" (Chaiken, 1987; Chaiken & Maheswaran, 1994; Chen & Chaiken, 1999; Fabrigar et al., 1998; Howard, 1997; Petty & Cacioppo, 1986; Petty & Wegener, 1999).

Finally, we should point out that in addition to the personal relevance of a topic, people's motivation to pay attention to a message depends on their personality. Some people enjoy thinking things through more than others do; they are said to be high in the **need for cognition** (Cacioppo et al., 1996). This is a personality variable that reflects the extent to which people engage in and enjoy effortful cognitive activities. People high in the need for cognition are more likely to form attitudes by paying close attention to relevant arguments (i.e., via the central route), whereas people low in the need for cognition are more likely to rely on peripheral cues, such as how attractive or credible the speaker is.

Shestowsky, Wegener, and Fabrigar (1998) reasoned that if people high in the need for cognition base their attitudes on the strength of arguments, their attitudes should be more resistant to change than those of people who are low in the need for cognition. To

Need for cognition
a personality variable
reflecting the extent to which
people engage in and enjoy
effortful cognitive activities

test this hypothesis, they presented American (Yale University) and Canadian (Queen's University) students with a description of a legal case and asked them to come up with a verdict. Then, they paired high and low need-for-cognition students, and asked them to discuss the case and come up with a joint verdict. As expected, people who were high in need for cognition were more likely to persuade their low in need for cognition partner of their views, rather than the other way around. They argued their points more effectively and were better at coming up with counterarguments in response to their partner's statements than were participants who were low in need for cognition. Try It! on page 243 can show you how high you are in need for cognition.

The Ability to Pay Attention to the Arguments Sometimes it is difficult to pay attention to a speech, even if we want to. Maybe we're tired; maybe we're distracted by annoying construction noise outside the window; maybe the issue is too complex and hard to evaluate. Under such circumstances, we are unable to pay close attention to the arguments and thus are swayed more by peripheral cues (Petty & Brock, 1981; Petty, Wells, & Brock, 1976).

Hafer, Reynolds, and Obertynski (1996) investigated whether people will be swayed by peripheral cues when it is difficult to evaluate the message because it is delivered using complicated, jargon-laden language. In this study, participants were presented with arguments in favour of plea bargaining (an issue on which attitudes are generally negative). At the time of their study, a highly publicized plea bargain had just been negotiated: Karla Holmolka's sentence was reduced to manslaughter in the sexual abuse and murder of two teenage girls in exchange for testimony against her former husband, Paul Bernardo. This was a highly involving issue for the participants, who were students at Brock University in St. Catharine's, Ontario—the home of the murder victims.

The arguments presented varied in terms of comprehensibility (easy-to-understand versus difficult-to-understand language) and strength (strong versus weak). Here is an example of a weak, difficult-to-understand argument: "Negotiated dispositions in a properly constructed system of plea bargaining will approximate the probable results of a trial." Here is the easy-to-understand version of the same argument: "Deals in a properly set up plea bargaining system will be similar to the results of a trial."

To assess whether participants would rely on peripheral cues when the language was difficult to understand, researchers also varied the status of the speaker presenting the arguments. In the high-status condition, the speech was attributed to an eminent judge with special expertise in the area of plea bargaining. In the low-status condition, the speech was attributed to a second-year law student.

As expected, when the arguments were easy to understand, people's attitudes toward plea bargaining were more positive when strong, rather than weak, arguments were presented. In other words, persuasion occurred via the central route. Also consistent with central route processing, under these conditions, attitudes were not influenced by the status of the speaker.

In contrast, when the arguments were difficult to understand, attitudes were not affected by argument strength, but rather by the status of the speaker. Specifically, attitudes toward plea bargaining were more positive when the speaker was portrayed as high, rather than low, status. Thus, under these circumstances, persuasion occurred via the peripheral route.

The Need for Cognition

Instructions: For each of the statements below, indicate to what extent the statement is characteristic of you. Use the following scale:

   1 = extremely uncharacteristic of you (not at all like you)
   2 = somewhat uncharacteristic
   3 = uncertain
   4 = somewhat characteristic
   5 = extremely characteristic of you (very much like you)

1. I would prefer complex to simple problems. _____
2. I like to have the responsibility of handling a situation that requires a lot of thinking. _____
3. Thinking is not my idea of fun. _____
4. I would rather do something that requires little thought than something that is sure to challenge my thinking abilities. _____
5. I try to anticipate and avoid situations where there is a chance I will have to think in depth about something. _____
6. I find satisfaction in deliberating hard and for long hours. _____
7. I only think as hard as I have to. _____
8. I prefer thinking about small, daily projects to thinking about long-term ones. _____
9. I like tasks that require little thought once I've learned them. _____
10. The idea of relying on thought to make my way to the top appeals to me. _____
11. I really enjoy a task that involves coming up with new solutions to problems. _____
12. Learning new ways to think doesn't excite me very much. _____
13. I prefer my life to be filled with puzzles that I must solve. _____
14. The notion of thinking abstractly is appealing to me. _____
15. I would prefer a task that is intellectual, difficult, and important to one that is somewhat important but does not require much thought. _____
16. I feel relief rather than satisfaction after completing a task that required a lot of mental effort. _____
17. It's enough for me that something gets the job done; I don't care how or why it works. _____
18. I usually end up deliberating about issues even when they do not affect me personally. _____

This scale measures the need for cognition, which is a personality variable reflecting the extent to which people engage in and enjoy effortful cognitive activities (Cacioppo et al., 1996). As noted in the text, people high in the need for cognition are more likely to form their attitudes by paying close attention to relevant arguments (i.e., via the central route), whereas people low in the need for cognition are more likely to rely on peripheral cues, such as how attract-ive or credible a speaker is. Here are some other findings: (1) people who are high in the need for cognition are slightly high-er in verbal intelligence, but no higher in abstract reasoning (Cacioppo et al., 1996); and (2) there are no gender differences in the need for cognition (Cacioppo et al., 1996).

Scoring: First, reverse your responses to items 3, 4, 5, 7, 8, 9, 12, 16, and 17. Do so as follows: If you gave a 1 to these questions, change it to a 5; if you gave a 2, change it to a 4; if you gave a 3, leave it the same; if you gave a 4, change it to a 2; if you gave a 5, change it to a 1. Then, add up your answers to all 18 questions.

Emotion Influences the Route to Persuasion Suppose things are really going your way one day, and you're feeling great. You pick up a copy of the student newspaper and glance at an editorial written by the president of the student council about a proposed increase in student fees. Are you likely to pore over every word in the editorial and carefully analyze the merits of each and every argument? Or will you give it a cursory glance and think, "Hey, whatever she says is fine with me." What if you are feeling kind of sad that day? Will you read the editorial carefully, or just take the author's word for it?

It turns out that when people are in good moods, they want to continue feeling that way. Therefore they avoid activities—such as going to the effort to read an article about an unpleasant topic—that are likely to spoil their moods (Isen, 1987; Wegener & Petty, 1996). Thus, if you are feeling great, you are likely to glance at the newspaper editorial and take the author's word for it, without going to the effort to think carefully about all of his or her arguments—in short, to take the peripheral route to persuasion. But if you are in a sad or neutral mood, you are more likely to take the central route, analyzing each argument in detail.

To illustrate this point, consider a study by Herbert Bless, Gerd Bohner, Norbert Schwarz, and Fritz Strack (1990), who put university students in temporarily good or bad moods by having them write about happy or sad events in their lives. Then, as part of what was supposedly another study, the researchers asked the participants to listen to a speech arguing that student fees at their university should be increased. In one condition the speech contained strong, well-reasoned arguments, whereas in another condition the speech contained weak, poorly reasoned arguments. The results were clear. People in a sad mood paid close attention to the arguments and thus changed their attitudes when the arguments were strong, but not when the arguments were weak (see left-hand side of Figure 7.6). People in a good mood paid relatively little attention to the strength of the arguments. They seemed

▶ How do people's moods influence the way in which their attitudes change? People who are in good moods often do not want to pay close attention to the content of persuasive communications, and thus change their attitudes via the peripheral route.

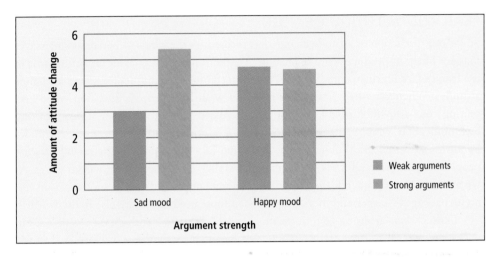

◀ Figure 7.6

EFFECTS OF MOOD ON
ATTITUDE CHANGE.

People in a sad mood paid
attention to a speech, and thus
were more convinced when the
arguments were strong (see left-
hand side of figure). People in a
happy mood paid less attention
to the speech, and thus were
equally convinced by weak and
strong arguments (see right-hand
side of figure).

(Adapted from Bless et al., 1990)

to take the speaker's word for it regardless of how strong the arguments were, and thus they were no more convinced when the arguments were strong than when the arguments were weak (see right-hand side of Figure 7.6). Other studies have shown that people in good moods are more likely to rely on peripheral cues, such as agreeing with speakers who are experts (Sinclair, Mark, & Clore, 1994; Worth & Mackie, 1987). This is especially likely to be true if people think that paying attention to the message will ruin their good mood (Wegener, Petty, & Smith, 1995).

Now that you know a persuasive communication can change people's attitudes in either of two ways—via the central or the peripheral route—you may be wondering what difference it makes. For example, does it really matter whether it was the strength of the arguments or the status of the speaker that changed the Brock University students' attitudes toward plea bargaining? Given the bottom line—they changed their attitudes—why should any of us care how they got to that point?

If we are interested in creating long-lasting attitude change, we should care a lot. People who base their attitudes on a careful analysis of the arguments are more likely to maintain this attitude over time, more likely to behave consistently with this attitude, and are more resistant to counter-persuasion than people who base their attitudes on peripheral cues (Chaiken, 1980; Mackie, 1987; Petty, Haugvedt, & Smith, 1995; Petty & Wegener, 1998). For example, Perlini and Ward (2000) attempted to increase knowledge of AIDS among students attending high schools in Sault Ste. Marie by providing them with scripts describing characters who either had AIDS or were medical experts on AIDS. The purpose of these scripts was to educate the participants concerning how AIDS can be prevented, how it is contracted, and so on. The participants then acted out these various scripts in a role-play situation. Other participants received the same information about AIDS, but it was delivered via a lecture or videotape. The researchers reasoned that the active participation required by the role-play exercise would invoke the central route to persuasion. And, indeed, four weeks later, the role-play participants showed more positive attitudes toward AIDS prevention than did participants in the other groups. Those in the role-play condition also showed the greatest improvement in knowledge of AIDS prevention.

FEAR AND ATTITUDE CHANGE

So far our discussion of attitude change has focused on the kinds of persuasive messages that are likely to produce attitude change. Another approach to changing attitudes is to use fear. In fact, scaring people is one of the most common techniques for trying to change attitudes. When we asked you earlier how you would get people's attention when presenting your anti-smoking ad, it might have crossed your mind to use a **fear-arousing communication**, which is a persuasive message that attempts to change people's attitudes by arousing their fears. Public service ads often take this approach by trying to scare people into practising safer sex, wearing their seat belts, and staying away from drugs. As we mentioned in Chapter 1, the Canadian government places frightening images on cigarette packages—larger and more graphic than those used anywhere else in the world.

Do such fear-arousing communications work? It turns out that fear can work, but only if a moderate amount of fear is created and if people believe that listening to the message will teach them how to reduce this fear (Petty, 1995; Rogers, 1983). Consider a study by Howard Leventhal and his colleagues (Leventhal, Watts, & Pagano, 1967), who showed a group of smokers a graphic film depicting lung cancer and gave them pamphlets with specific instructions about how to quit smoking. These people reduced their smoking significantly more than did people who were shown only the film or only the pamphlet. Why? Seeing the film made people scared, and giving them the pamphlet reassured them that there was a way to reduce this fear—by following the instructions on how to quit. Seeing only the pamphlet didn't work very well, because little fear was motivating people to read it carefully. Seeing only the film didn't work very well either, because people were likely to tune out a message that raised fear but did not give information about how to reduce it. This may explain why some attempts to frighten people into changing their attitudes and behaviour have not been very successful: They succeed in scaring people but do not provide specific recommendations for people to follow (Becker & Josephs, 1988; DeJong & Winsten, 1989; Job, 1988; Soames, 1988).

Fear-arousing appeals will also fail if they are too strong, such that people feel very threatened. If people are scared to death, they will become defensive, will deny the importance of the threat, and will be unable to think rationally about the issue (Baron et al., 1992; Janis & Feshbach, 1953; Jepson & Chaiken, 1990; Liberman & Chaiken, 1992). According to Michael Conway at Concordia University and Laurette Dubé at McGill University (2002), humour can be an effective tool for reducing distress among people who find fear messages especially threatening. In a series of studies, they found that among those who were most threatened by fear messages, the use of humour resulted in greater attitude change and intentions to enact the desired behaviours (using sunscreen to avoid skin cancer and using condoms to avoid AIDS) than did nonhumorous messages.

So, if you have decided to arouse people's fear in your ad for the Canadian Cancer Society, keep these points in mind. First, try to create enough fear to motivate people to pay attention to your arguments but not so much fear that people will tune out or distort what you say. You may even want to throw in a bit of humour for the benefit of those who find fear-inducing messages especially distressing. Second, include some specific recommendations about how to stop smoking, so people will be reassured that paying close attention to your arguments will help them reduce their fear.

Fear-arousing communication

a persuasive message that attempts to change people's attitudes by arousing their fears

▼ This ad is clearly trying to scare people into changing their attitudes and behaviour. Based on research on fear-arousing communications, do you think this ad would work?

IT HAD EVERY SAFETY FEATURE IN THE WORLD. EXCEPT A DESIGNATED DRIVER.

SOMETIMES DRINKING RESPONSIBLY MEANS NOT DRINKING AT ALL. DESIGNATE A DRIVER.

JOSEPH E. SEAGRAM & SONS, INC.
Those who appreciate quality enjoy it responsibly

ADVERTISING AND ATTITUDE CHANGE

We began this chapter with a discussion of daily assaults on our attitudes by advertisers. The world of advertising is rich with examples of the principles of attitude and behaviour change we have been discussing. But is there evidence that advertising really works? Most of the research we have discussed was conducted in the laboratory with university students. What about changes in attitudes and behaviour in the real world? If we see an ad campaign for Scrubadub detergent, are we really more likely to buy Scrubadub when we go to the store? Or are companies wasting the billions of dollars a year they spend on advertising?

A curious thing about advertising is that most people think it works on everyone but themselves (Wilson & Brekke, 1994). A typical comment is "Sure, it influences most people, but not me. Seeing those ads for Scrubadub doesn't influence me at all." Contrary to such beliefs, substantial evidence indicates that advertising works; when a product is advertised, sales tend to increase (Ryan, 1991; Wells, 1997).

Tailoring Advertisements to People's Attitudes Which types of ads work the best? Several studies have shown that it is best to fight fire with fire. If an attitude is cognitively based, try to change it with rational arguments; if it is affectively based, try to change it using emotion (Edwards, 1990; Edwards & von Hippel, 1995; Fabrigar & Petty, 1999; Shavitt, 1989; Snyder & DeBono, 1989). For example, in one study Sharon Shavitt (1990) gave people advertisements for different kinds of consumer products. Some of the items were ones Shavitt called utilitarian products, such as air conditioners and coffee. People's attitudes toward such products tend to be based on an appraisal of the utilitarian aspects of the products (e.g., how energy-efficient an air conditioner is), and thus are cognitively based. The other items were ones Shavitt called social identity products, such as perfume and greeting cards. People's attitudes toward these types of products are based more on their values and concerns about their social identity, and so are more affectively based.

As seen in Figure 7.7, people reacted most favourably to the ads that matched the type of attitude they had. If people's attitudes were cognitively based (e.g., toward air conditioners or coffee), the ads that focused on the utilitarian aspects of these products were most successful. If people's attitudes were more affectively based (e.g., toward perfume or greeting cards), the ads that focused on values and social identity concerns were most successful. Thus, if you ever get a job in advertising, the moral is to know what type of attitude most people have toward your product, then tailor your advertising accordingly.

Many advertisements try to make people's attitudes more affectively based by associating the product with important emotions and values (see our earlier discussion of classical conditioning). Consider, for example, advertisements for long-distance telephone service. This topic does not, for most of us, evoke deep-rooted emotional feelings—until, that is, we see an ad in which a man calls his long-lost brother to tell him he loves and misses him, or an ad in which a man calls his mother to tell her he has just bought her a plane ticket so she can visit him. There is nothing logically compelling about these ads. After all, there is no reason to believe that using Bell service will magically make you closer to your family than using Sprint Canada. However, by associating positive emotions with a product, an advertiser can turn a bland product into one that evokes feelings of nostalgia, love, warmth, and general goodwill.

Do you dream in color?

We do.

Dream this: a unique combination of suction, sealing and filtration that actually helps clean the air you breathe as it cleans your home. Available in a rainbow of colors; that's the beautiful reality of the Miele vacuum cleaner. For the authorized Miele dealer nearest you, call 800-694-4868.

Miele®

Anything else is a compromise.
http://www.mieleusa.com

Proud sponsor of the Clean Air Challenge®.

▲ Advertisers often try to make people's attitudes more affectively based. Whereas most people base their attitudes toward vacuum cleaners on their beliefs about how well they suck up dirt, this ad attempts to get people to base their attitude on style and colour—more affective concerns.

▶ **Figure 7.7**

EFFECTS OF AFFECTIVE AND COGNITIVE INFORMATION ON AFFECTIVELY AND COGNITIVELY BASED ATTITUDES.

When people had cognitively based attitudes (e.g., toward air conditioners and coffee), cognitively based advertisements that stressed the utilitarian aspects of the products worked best. When people had more affectively based attitudes (e.g., toward perfume and greeting cards), affectively based advertisements that stressed values and social identity worked best. The higher the number, the more favourable the thoughts people listed about the products after reading the advertisements.

(Adapted from Shavitt, 1990)

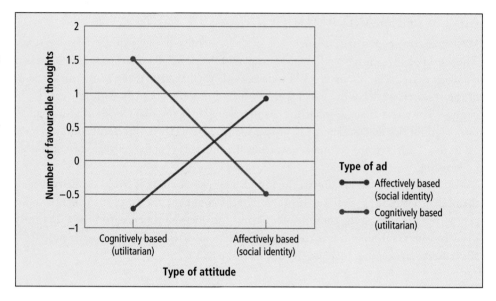

If people's attitudes are cognitively based, then advertisers need to deal with an additional issue—namely, the personal relevance of their product. Consider, for example, the problem of heartburn. This is not a topic that evokes strong emotions and values in most people. Thus, it is more cognitively based. To people who suffer from frequent heartburn, however, it clearly is of direct personal relevance. In this case, the best way to change people's attitudes is to use logical, fact-based arguments: Convince people that your product will reduce heartburn the best, and people will buy it (Chaiken, 1987; Petty & Cacioppo, 1986).

What if you are dealing with a cognitively based attitude that is not of direct per-sonal relevance to people? Here the trick is to *make* your product personally relevant. Let's take a look at some actual ad campaigns to see how this is done. Consider the case of Gerald Lambert, who, in the early part of this century, inherited a company that made a surgical antiseptic used to treat throat infections: Listerine. Seeking a wider market for his product, Lambert decided to promote it as a mouthwash. The only problem was that no one at the time used a mouthwash or even knew what one was. And so, having invented the cure, Lambert invented the disease. Look at the ad that follows, which appeared in countless magazines over the years.

Even though today we would find this ad incredibly sexist, at the time most people did not find it offensive. Instead, the ad successfully played on people's fears about social rejection and failure. The phrase "She was often a bridesmaid but never a bride" became one of the most famous in the history of advertising. In a few cleverly chosen, manipulative words, it succeeded in making a problem—*halitosis*—personally relevant to millions of people. Listerine became a best-selling product that has since earned a fortune. Incidentally, you might think that *halitosis* is the official medical term for bad breath. In fact, it is nothing more than a fancy, medical-sounding term invented by Gerald Lambert and his advertising team to sound like a dreadful disease.

Gerald Lambert's success at playing to people's fears and sense of shame was not lost on other advertisers. Similar ads have been designed to create new markets for many new

She bags the *bouquets* but never a *Beau*

You never have it? – *what colossal conceit.*

End halitosis with LISTERINE

◀ This ad is one of the most famous in the history of advertising. Although today it is easy to see how sexist and offensive it is, when it appeared in 1936 it succeeded in making a problem (bad breath) personally relevant by playing to people's fears and insecurities about personal relationships. Can you think of any contemporary ads that try to raise similar fears?

products, most having to do with personal hygiene or health: underarm deodorants, deodorant soaps, vitamin supplements, oat bran, fish oil, and more. These campaigns work by convincing people that they have problems of great personal relevance and that the advertised product can solve these problems.

Negative Advertising: Does It Work? Another approach that has been taken to advertise everything from household products to politicians is to slam the competition. How effective is this kind of advertising? At least where politics are concerned, apparently not very effective. Neil Roese and Gerald Sande (1993) presented University of Manitoba students with transcripts of a debate that supposedly took place between two political candidates. They varied whether a candidate insulted his opponent and the kinds of insults that were used (e.g., something that the opponent could control, such as his policies, versus something that he could not control, such as a weakness in his family). The researchers found that candidates who insulted their opponent were rated more negatively and garnered fewer votes than candidates who were not insulting, especially when the insults focused on aspects of the opponent's life that were beyond his control.

Do these findings extend to real-world politics? The 1993 Canadian federal election provided an opportunity to find out (Haddock & Zanna, 1997). During this campaign, the Progressive Conservative party briefly aired a commercial in which images of Jean

WHEN PERSUASION ATTEMPTS BOOMERANG: REACTANCE THEORY

It is important not to use too heavy a hand when trying to immunize people against assaults on their attitudes. Suppose you want to ensure that your child never smokes. "Might as well err on the side of giving too strong a message," you might think, absolutely forbidding your child to even look at a pack of cigarettes. "What's the harm?" you figure. "At least this way, my child will get the point about how serious a matter this is."

Actually, there is harm to administering strong prohibitions—the stronger they are, the more likely they will boomerang, causing an increase in interest in the prohibited activity. According to **reactance theory** (Brehm, 1966; Brehm & Brehm, 1981), people do not like to feel that their freedom to do or think whatever they want is being threatened. When they feel that their freedom is threatened, an unpleasant state of reactance is aroused, and people can reduce this reactance by performing the threatened behaviour (e.g., smoking).

For example, James Pennebaker and Deborah Sanders (1976) placed one of two signs in the bathrooms on a university campus, in an attempt to get people to stop writing graffiti on the walls of bathrooms. One sign read, "Do not write on these walls under any circumstances." The other gave a milder prohibition: "Please don't write on these walls." The researchers returned two weeks later and observed how much graffiti had been written since they posted the signs. As they predicted, significantly more people wrote graffiti in the bathrooms with the "Do not write" sign than with the "Please don't write" sign. Similarly, people who receive strong admonitions against smoking, taking drugs, or getting their nose pierced become more likely to perform these behaviours, in order to restore their sense of personal freedom and choice (Bushman & Stack, 1996; Graybar et al., 1989).

Reactance theory

the idea that when people feel their freedom to perform a certain behaviour is threatened, an unpleasant state of reactance is aroused; people can reduce this reactance by performing the threatened behaviour

SUMMARY

An **attitude** is a person's enduring evaluation of a person, object, or idea. All attitudes have affective, cognitive, and behavioural components. A **cognitively based attitude** is based mostly on people's beliefs about the properties of the attitude object. An **affectively based attitude** is based more on people's emotions and values; it can be created through **classical conditioning** or **operant conditioning**. A **behaviourally based attitude** is based on people's actions toward the attitude object. Attitudes vary in terms of whether they are more likely to be based on affect, cognition, or behaviour. When people hold negative attitudes toward a group (e.g., homosexuals), those attitudes are likely to be based on a particular kind of cognition—namely, the belief that members of that group threaten one's cherished values. When people hold positive attitudes toward a group, those attitudes are likely to be based on affect. Attitudes toward issues such as capital punishment tend to be based on affect as well.

Attitudes also differ in their strength. Research on attitude ambivalence shows that attitudes are likely to be strong if they are either positive or negative, rather than a mixture of both. Attitudes are also likely to be strong if they are highly accessible, if it is easy to generate arguments in support of them (i.e., subjective experience), and if we recall personal behaviours we have performed that are relevant to those attitudes. Strong attitudes are not as easily changed as weak attitudes.

When do people behave in line with their attitudes? To answer this question, we need to distinguish between behaviours that are spontaneous versus those that are more planned and deliberative. Attitudes predict spontaneous behaviours only when the attitudes are relatively accessible. When attitudes are inaccessible, behaviour is more likely to be influenced by situational and social factors. The **theory of planned behaviour** specifies how we can predict people's planned and deliberative behaviours. Here it is necessary to know people's attitudes toward the specific act in question, their **subjective norms** (their beliefs about how others view the behaviour in question), and whether they believe that it is easy or difficult to perform the behaviour. Knowing these three things allows us to predict people's behavioural intentions, which are highly correlated with their actual behaviours.

The theory of planned behaviour is useful in understanding an area in which people's attitudes and behaviour are often inconsistent—namely, practising safe sex. Although people tend to express positive attitudes toward using condoms, they often fail to do so. Why? One reason has to do with subjective norms—if people are in a situation where they believe their peers are not using condoms, or if they believe their partner would disapprove of condom use, they probably will not use them. Another reason pertains to perceived behavioural control: If people find it embarrassing to buy condoms or to bring up the topic of condom use with their partner, it is unlikely that condoms will be used. Finally, condoms also will not be used if people's intentions to use them are undermined (e.g., due to excessive alcohol consumption).

The latter part of the chapter focused on attitude change. One way attitudes change is when people receive a **persuasive communication**. According to the **Yale Attitude Change Approach,** the persuasiveness of a communication depends on aspects of the communicator, or source of the message; aspects of the message itself (e.g., its content); and aspects of the audience. The **heuristic-systematic model of persuasion** and the **elaboration likelihood model** specify when people are persuaded more by the strength of the arguments in the communication and when they are persuaded more by surface characteristics, such as the attractiveness of the speaker. People will take the *central route to persuasion* when they have both the ability and the motivation to pay close attention to the arguments. People will take the *peripheral route to persuasion* when they either do not want to or cannot pay close attention to the arguments. Under these conditions, they are persuaded by such peripheral cues as the attractiveness of the speaker or the length of the speech. Finally, when people are in a positive mood, persuasion is likely to occur via the peripheral route; they are less likely to analyze a message carefully then than when they are in a negative mood. Importantly, attitude change is longer lasting and more resistant to attack when it occurs via the central route.

A common tactic for changing attitudes is the use of fear. **Fear-arousing communication** can cause lasting attitude change if a moderate amount of fear is aroused and if specific recommendations are provided for performing the desired behaviours.

The effectiveness of persuasive communications also depends on the type of attitude people have. Appeals to emotion work best if the attitude is based on affect; appeals to utilitarian features work best if the attitude is based on cognition. Under controlled laboratory conditions, **subliminal messages** can have subtle effects on people's preferences, but there is no evidence that subliminal messages have been used successfully in real-world marketing campaigns.

It is possible to make people resistant to attacks on their attitudes. **Attitude inoculation** is the technique whereby people are exposed to small doses of arguments against their position, making it easier for them to refute these arguments when they hear them later. Attempts to manage people's attitudes, however, should not be used with too heavy a hand. According to **reactance theory,** strongly prohibiting people from engaging in certain behaviours can actually cause them to engage in that activity as a means of asserting their autonomy.

IF YOU ARE INTERESTED

Ajzen, I. (1988). *Attitudes, personality, and behavior.* Chicago, IL: Dorsey Press. An in-depth discussion of the relation between attitudes and behaviours, with an emphasis on the theory of reasoned action.

Burgess, Anthony (1963). *A clockwork orange.* A nightmarish look at the future filled with out-of-control adolescents and harrowing techniques of mind control.

Eagly, A., & Chaiken, S. (1993). *The psychology of attitudes.* Fort Worth, TX: Harcourt Brace Jovanovich. An extremely thorough and insightful look at current social psychological research on attitudes.

Huxley, Aldous (1946). *Brave new world.* A classic portrayal of mind control in a futuristic society. It is interesting to draw parallels between Huxley's view of the future and modern techniques of attitude change.

Olson, J. M., & Zanna, M. P. (1993). Attitudes and attitude change. *Annual Review of Psychology, 44,* 117–154. A comprehensive, incisive review of theory and research on attitudes and attitude change, written by two leading researchers in this area. James Olson is at the University of Western Ontario and Mark Zanna is at the University of Waterloo.

Petty, R. E., & Cacioppo, J. T. (1986). *Communication and persuasion: Central and peripheral routes to attitude change.* New York: Springer-Verlag. A comprehensive discussion of the elaboration likelihood model of attitude change.

Pratkanis, A. R., & Aronson, E. (1991). *Age of propaganda: The everyday use and abuse of persuasion.* New York: Freeman. An engaging account of how our attitudes are shaped by the mass media.

Riefenstahl, L. (Director). (1935). *Triumph of the will* [Documentary film]. A film commissioned by Adolph Hitler to disseminate Nazi propaganda. It is interesting to view this film in light of research on attitude change and persuasion, to see how the film tries to change people's attitudes.

Zanna, M. P., Olson, J M., & Herman, C. P. (1987). *Social influence: The Ontario Symposium* (Vol. 5). Hillsdale, NJ: Lawrence Erlbaum. A valuable collection of papers presented by prominent social psychologists at the University of Waterloo in 1984 as part of the Ontario Symposium series. Part I of this volume, Communication and Persuasion, is especially relevant to this chapter.

WEBLINKS

www.as.wvu.edu/~sbb/comm221/primer.htm

Primer of Practical Persuasion and Influence

An interesting and informative tutorial on influence from a communications perspective.

www.propagandacritic.com

Propaganda

This site discusses propaganda in detail and provides many examples of propaganda campaigns from the recent past.

www.adbusters.org

Adbusters

This magazine wants folks to get mad about corporate disinformation, injustices in the global economy, and any industry that pollutes our physical or mental commons.

www.cob.ohio-state.edu/scp

Society for Consumer Psychology

The Society represents the interests of behavioural scientists in the fields of psychology, marketing, advertising, communication, consumer behaviour, and other related areas.

CHAPTER 8

Conformity
influencing behaviour

THE JUDGMENT ISSUED BY THE HONOURABLE MR. JUSTICE MACAULAY ON May 10, 1999, begins with the statement "Reena Virk died on November 14, 1997 after a vicious beating" (*Her Majesty the Queen v. Warren Paul Glowatski*, 1999). Justice Macaulay presided over the trial of Warren Glowatski, who was charged with second-degree murder. The transcript documents the events that led up to the tragic death of this 14-year-old girl. During an exchange with Reena Virk, a student at her school extinguished a lit cigarette on her forehead. Other friends of this student joined in and began beating Virk. One girl testified that she had grabbed a lighter and tried to set Virk's hair on fire; others began punching and kicking Virk in the head and face. According to a pathologist's report, Virk's head injuries alone were severe enough to be life threatening. She also suffered massive internal injuries. The pathologist considered the force of these injuries to be comparable to crush injuries that would result from being run over by a car. The unconscious Virk was dragged by Kelly Ellard and Warren Glowatski to the Gorge waterway not far from downtown Victoria, where she was drowned. According to some reports, Ellard smoked a cigarette as she stood with one foot on Virk's head, holding it underwater. Ellard and Glowatski were charged with second-degree murder. (Note that on February 5, 2003 the British Columbia Court of Appeal ordered a new trial for Kelly Ellard; Warren Glowatski also had appealed, but the Appeal Court upheld his conviction.) Six other girls involved in the beating were given sentences ranging from a 60-day conditional sentence to one year in jail.

Canadians were horrified by Reena Virk's death. How could ordinary high-school students in Victoria, B.C., engage in such brutal, savage acts against a defenceless 14-year-old? Why did some students participate in the beatings, rather than attempt to stop this tragedy?

Sadly, as we shall see, the need to conform to a group probably played a role in Reena Virk's murder. Under what conditions and for what reasons are we likely to fall under the influence of others? This is the key question to be addressed in this chapter.

▶ Reena Virk, a B.C. teenager, was first savagely beaten by her schoolmates and then drowned by two other teenagers. She died on November 14, 1997.

Conformity: When and Why

Think for a moment about the word **conformity**, which we can define as a change in behaviour due to the real or imagined influence of others (Kiesler & Kiesler, 1969). Which of the following two quotations do you find more appealing? Which one best describes your immediate reaction to the word *conformity*? Thomas Fuller: "Do as most do, and [people] will speak well of thee," or Mark Twain: "It were not best that we should all think alike; it is difference of opinion that makes horse races."

We wouldn't be surprised if you preferred the Mark Twain quotation. North American culture stresses the importance of not conforming (Hofstede, 1986; Markus, Kitayama, & Heiman, 1996). This is part of being in an individualistic culture—one that emphasizes being independent, thinking for yourself, and standing up for yourself. We want to be perceived as people who make up our own minds—not as spineless, weak conformists, not as puppets but players. As a result, we may maintain the belief that our behaviour is not influenced by others, even when reality suggests otherwise. This phenomenon was illustrated in research by Jacquie Vorauer and Dale Miller (1997). In one of their studies, students at the University of Manitoba were asked to rate how satisfied they felt with their intellectual abilities. Before making their ratings, they were allowed to see the same ratings supposedly given by another student. Were participants influenced by the other student's responses? Yes, they were. Specifically, if the other student provided a positive self-assessment, participants also evaluated themselves positively—more so than if the other student had provided a negative self-assessment. Most important, participants were not aware that they had been influenced by the other student's responses. Thus, we probably conform a lot more than we actually realize (or want to admit).

People do conform—sometimes in extreme and surprising ways, as suggested by the deaths of 74 Solar Temple cult members (discussed in Chapter 6). But, you might argue, this is an unusual case; surely most people do not conform to this extent. Perhaps the followers of Luc Jouret and Joseph Di Mambro were disturbed people who were somehow predisposed to do what charismatic leaders told them to do. There is, however, another more chilling possibility. Maybe most of us would have acted the same way, had we been exposed to the same, long-standing conformity pressures. According to this view, almost anyone would have conformed had he or she been put in these same extreme situations.

Conformity

a change in behaviour due to the real or imagined influence of other people

◀ North American culture values independence and autonomy, not conformity. In this cartoon, the people with the picket signs reflect this view. However, the truth is, we frequently conform to others' behaviour and attitudes. For example, the demonstrator on the right is there because all of his friends are there.

If this statement is true, we should be able to find other situations in which people, put under strong social pressures, conform to surprising degrees. Unfortunately, we do not have to look very far to find such instances. We opened this chapter with the deeply disturbing story of Reena Virk, who died at the hands of a group of high-school students. Once one of the students began attacking Virk, others went along. In Chapter 6, we described the chilling story of Shidane Arone, who was tortured to death by Canadian peacekeepers in Somalia. In that situation as well, one soldier began beating the boy and others joined in. And, of course, the Holocaust provides countless horrific examples of conformity at its worst.

The examples we have seen so far are all cases of "bad" conformity: Human beings lost their lives as a result of people going along with others. However, conformity is not simply "good" or "bad" in and of itself. Rather than labelling conformity as good or bad, the social psychologist is interested in *why* people conform. Knowing why and when people are influenced by others will help us understand if a given act of conformity in our own lives is wise or foolish.

To return to the example of the Solar Temple cult, some members probably conformed because they did not know what to do in a confusing or unusual situation; the behaviour of the people around them served as a cue as to how to respond, and so they decided to act in a similar manner. Other people probably conformed because they did not wish to be ridiculed or punished for being different from everybody else; they chose to act the way the group expected them to so they wouldn't be rejected or thought less of by group members.

Let's see how each of these reasons for conforming operates.

Informational Social Influence: The Need to Know What's "Right"

One of the important things we get from interacting with other people is information. You won't be surprised to hear that sometimes people don't know what to do in a situation, or even what is happening. Unfortunately, life, unlike our clothing, does not come with labels attached, telling us what is going on and how we should respond. Instead, the social world is frequently ambiguous and ill defined.

For example, how should you address your psychology professor—as Dr. Berman, Professor Berman, Ms. Berman, or Patricia? How should you vote on a proposal to increase your tuition in order to increase student services? Is the scream you just heard coming from a person joking with friends or from the victim of a mugging?

In these and many other everyday situations, we feel uncertain about what to think or how to act. We simply don't know enough to make a good or accurate choice. Luckily, we have a powerful and useful source of knowledge available to us—the behaviour of other people. Asking others what they think or watching what they do helps us reach a definition of the situation (Kelley, 1955; Thomas, 1928). When we subsequently act like everyone else, we are conforming, but not because we are weak, spineless individuals with no self-reliance. Instead, the influence of other people leads us to conform because we see them as a source of information to guide our behaviour. This is called **informational social influence** (Cialdini, 1993; Cialdini, Kallgren, & Reno, 1991; Cialdini & Trost, 1998; Deutsch & Gerard, 1955).

Informational social influence

conforming because we believe that others' interpretation of an ambiguous situation is more correct than ours and will help us choose an appropriate course of action

As an illustration of how other people can be a source of information, imagine you are a participant in the following experiment by Muzafer Sherif (1936). In the first phase of the study, you are seated alone in a dark room and asked to focus your attention on a dot of light 5 metres away. The experimenter asks you to estimate in centimetres how far the light moves. You stare earnestly at the light, and yes, it moves a little. You say, "About 5 centimetres," though it is not easy to tell exactly. The light disappears and then comes back; you are asked to judge again. The light seems to move a little more, and you say, "10 centimetres." After several of these trials, the light seems to move about the same amount each time—about 5 to 10 centimetres.

Now, the interesting thing about this task is that the light was not actually moving at all. It looked as if it was moving because of a visual illusion called the autokinetic effect. If you stare at a bright light in a uniformly dark environment (e.g., a star on a dark night), the light will appear to waver. This occurs because you have no stable reference point to anchor the position of the light. The distance that the light appears to move varies from person to person but becomes consistent for each person over time. In Sherif's (1936) experiment, the participants all arrived at their own, stable estimates during the first phase of the study, but these estimates differed from person to person. Some people thought the light was moving only 2.5 centimetres or so, whereas others thought it was moving as much as 25 centimetres.

Sherif chose to use the autokinetic effect because he wanted a situation that would be ambiguous—where the correct definition of the situation would be unclear to his participants. In the second phase of the experiment, a few days later, the participants were paired with two other people, each of whom had had the same prior experience alone with the light. Now the situation became a truly social one, as all three made their judgments out loud. Remember, the autokinetic effect is experienced differently by different people; some see a lot of movement, some not much at all. After hearing their partners give judgments that were different from their own, what did people do?

Over the course of several trials, people reached a common estimate, and each member of the group conformed to that estimate. These results indicate that people were using each other as a source of information, coming to believe that the group estimate was the correct one (see Figure 8.1).

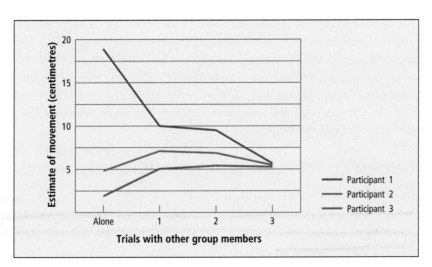

◀ Figure 8.1

ONE GROUP'S JUDGMENTS IN SHERIF'S (1936) AUTOKINETIC STUDIES.

People estimated how far a point of light appeared to move in a dark room. When they saw the light by themselves, their estimates varied widely. When they were brought together in groups and heard other people announce their estimates, they conformed to the group's estimate of how much the light moved.

(Adapted from Sherif, 1936)

Private acceptance
conforming to other people's behaviour out of a genuine belief that what they are doing or saying is right

Public compliance
conforming to other people's behaviour publicly, without necessarily believing in what they are doing or saying

An important feature of informational social influence is that it can lead to **private acceptance**, whereby people conform to the behaviour of others because they genuinely believe that these other people are correct. It might seem equally plausible that people publicly conformed to the group but privately maintained the belief that the light was moving only a small amount. For example, maybe someone privately believed that the light was moving 25 centimetres, but announced that it had moved 7.5 centimetres (the group estimate) to avoid looking silly or foolish. This would be a case of **public compliance**, where a person conforms publicly without necessarily believing in what the group is saying or doing. Sherif cast doubt on this interpretation, however, by asking people to judge the lights once more by themselves, after participating in groups. Even though they no longer had to worry about looking silly in front of other participants, they continued to give the answer the group had given earlier. These results suggest that people were relying on each other to define reality and came to privately accept the group estimate.

In everyday life, of course, we are rarely asked to judge how much a stationary light is moving. However, there are many everyday situations in which we rely on other people to help us define what is going on. Think about the first time you were at the symphony or at a jazz concert. You knew that applause was going to figure in sometime, but exactly when? After a solo? Only at the end of a piece? What about standing ovations, or shouting for an encore? No doubt, you looked to others in the audience to help you learn the appropriate way of showing approval in each setting. That the audience's behaviour can be affected through conformity is not unknown in the performing arts. Davies (1988) describes the use of the claque (hired applause) in early nineteenth-century opera:

> An opera audience must contain people who know the work intimately. Nobody will dare to applaud if they don't know where, and when, and why. They might make an embarrassing mistake [and] look foolish. . . . [A] *claque* is a small body of experts . . . you must have your *bisseurs* who call out loud for encores; your *rieurs* who laugh at the right places . . . your *pleureurs* who sob when sobs are needed. . . . And all of this must be carefully organized—yes, orchestrated—by the *capo di claque* (Davies, 1988).

Using other people to define social reality can also have a significant impact on our emotions, as we saw in Chapter 5 (Schachter, 1959; Schachter & Singer, 1962). For example, you might be feeling quite calm about your upcoming midterm until you run into a group of acquaintances from the class, all of whom are extremely tense and stressed-out about the exam. After talking with them, you feel a little disturbed, too—are you being too complacent about this test? "Maybe they're right," you think. Like the research participants in Sherif's experiment, you may find yourself relying on other people to help you reach a definition of the situation: "Maybe I'm being way too calm about this midterm . . . I'd better study some more tonight."

WHEN WILL PEOPLE CONFORM TO INFORMATIONAL SOCIAL INFLUENCE?

What kinds of situations are most likely to produce conformity because of informational social influence? We will discuss three: ambiguous situations, crises, and situations in which an expert is present.

When the Situation Is Ambiguous You may have had the experience of hearing a fire alarm in a building. What did you do? If you are like most people, you turned to the people around you to see if the situation was an emergency. If other people seemed unconcerned and weren't making moves to leave the building, you probably decided that there wasn't a need to evacuate. On the other hand, if other people started rushing toward the emergency exit doors, your behaviour would probably be quite different. When you are unsure of the correct response, the appropriate behaviour, or the right idea, you will be most open to influence from others. The more uncertain you are, the more you will rely on others (Baron, Vandello, & Brunsman, 1996; Tesser, Campbell, & Mickler, 1983).

When Shidane Arone entered the compound of the Canadian peacekeepers in Somalia, the soldiers experienced considerable ambiguity about how to handle such a situation. One of the commanding officers had given an order that the soldiers should "abuse" intruders. During the court martial, the defence argued that the officer's instruction was that physical force could be used to capture intruders and that the term "abuse" did not imply that torture was acceptable. Regardless of what was intended, it seems that soldiers did not have a clear sense of what should be done if they caught someone entering their compound. More generally, reports on the Somalia affair suggest that the peacekeepers had not been well prepared for their mission. In such situations, when ambiguity abounds, people are especially likely to be influenced by the actions of those around them. And, tragically, such actions cost Shidane Arone his life.

When the Situation Is a Crisis When the situation is a crisis, we usually do not have time to stop and think about exactly which course of action we should take. We need to act, and act now. If we feel scared and panicky, and are uncertain what to do, it is only natural for us to see how other people are responding—and to do likewise. Unfortunately, the people we imitate may also feel scared and panicky, and not behave rationally.

Consider what happened on Halloween Night in 1938. Orson Welles, the gifted actor and film director, and the Mercury Theater broadcast a radio play based loosely on H. G. Wells' science fiction fantasy *The War of the Worlds*. (Remember, this was the era before television; radio was a source of entertainment, with music, comedy, and drama programs, and the only source for fast-breaking news.) That night, Welles and his fellow actors put on a radio drama of a cataclysm—the invasion of Earth by hostile Martians— that was so realistic and effective that at least 1 million American listeners became frightened and several thousand were panic-stricken (Cantril, 1940). The result was a **contagion**, the rapid transmission of emotions or behaviour through a crowd—in this case, the listening audience. Why were so many Americans convinced that what they had heard was a real news report of an actual invasion by aliens? One reason is that the play parodied existing radio news shows very well, and many listeners missed the beginning of the broadcast (when it was clearly labelled as a play) because they had been listening to the nation's number-one-rated show, *Charlie McCarthy,* on another station. Another culprit, however, was informational social influence. Many people were listening with friends and family, and naturally turned to each other, out of uncertainty, to see whether they should believe what they had heard. Seeing looks of concern and worry on their loved ones' faces added to the panic people were beginning to feel. "We all kissed one another and felt we would all die," reported one listener (Cantril, 1940).

Contagion

the rapid transmission of emotions or behaviour through a crowd

▶ The *New York Times* headlined the *War of the Worlds* incident. Partly because of informational social influence, many listeners believed that a fictional radio broadcast about an invasion by Martians was true.

New York Times

Copyright, 1938, by The New York Times Company.

NEW YORK

Radio Listeners in Panic, Taking War Drama as Fact

Many Flee Homes to Escape 'Gas Raid From Mars'—Phone Calls Swamp Police at Broadcast of Wells Fantasy

A wave of mass hysteria seized thousands of radio listeners throughout the nation between 8:15 and 9:30 o'clock last night when a broadcast of a dramatization of H. G. Wells's fantasy, "The War of the Worlds," led thousands to believe that an interplanetary conflict had started with invading Martians spreading wide death and destruction . . . Jersey . . . York . . .

and radio stations here and in other cities of the United States and Canada seeking advice on protective measures against the raids.

The program was produced by Mr. Welles and the Mercury Theatre on the Air over station WABC and the Columbia Broadcasting System's coast-to-coast network, from 8 to 9 o'clock.

Closer to home, Luc Jouret, a leader of the Solar Temple cult, apparently was convinced that the world was coming to an end and managed to persuade his followers that this was true. Needless to say, this constituted a crisis for those who accepted this belief, and they turned to him for guidance. Sadly, they believed him when he said that death by fire was the correct course of action so they could be reborn on the star Sirius. Such instances of mind control or "brainwashing" can actually be extreme cases of informational social influence. When people believe that they are in a crisis situation, they are more likely to succumb to these forms of influence.

When Other People Are Experts Typically, the more expertise or knowledge a person has, the more valuable he or she will be as a guide in an ambiguous or crisis situation (Allison, 1992; Bickman, 1974; Cialdini & Trost, 1998). For example, a passenger who sees smoke coming out of an airplane engine will probably look around for the flight attendants to check their reaction; they have more expertise than the vacationer in the next seat. However, experts are not always reliable sources of information. Imagine the fear felt by the young man who was listening to *The War of the Worlds* and called his local police department for an explanation—only to discover that the police also thought the events described on the radio were actually happening.

However, you may be thinking, *The War of the Worlds* incident occurred in 1938. Surely people are less gullible now. Or are they? It wasn't very long ago that all of us faced a rather ambiguous situation: the arrival of a new millennium. This situation was highly ambiguous; it was unclear whether computers would crash, and along with them, banks, airplanes, and stock markets—the list of possible disasters went on and on. People turned to the experts, who recommended various strategies for dealing with Y2K. Countless dollars were spent installing programs to make computers Y2K-proof. And what happened when January 1, 2000, arrived? Very little. It turned out that the Y2K problem had been vastly overblown. (In Try It!, below, you can explore how the informational social influence variables of ambiguity, crisis, and expertise have operated in your life and in your friends' lives.) The role of experts in exerting informational social influence was examined in a study of students in a military college who were training to become Canadian Armed Forces officers. Serge Guimond (1999) found that students who were in the social sciences became more liberal in their views over their three years in college (e.g., became less blaming of the victims of poverty and unemployment), whereas engineering students became more conservative. Guimond concluded that the students' attitudes had changed as a result of informational social influence—in this case, the information they learned from their professors in these courses.

WHEN INFORMATIONAL CONFORMITY BACKFIRES

The War of the Worlds incident, and more recently the Y2K incident, reminds us that using other people as a source of information can be dangerous. If other people are

Informational Social Influence and Emergencies

One of the most interesting examples of informational social influence in action is the behaviour of bystanders in emergencies. An emergency is by definition a crisis situation. In many respects, it is an ambiguous situation as well. Sometimes there are "experts" present, but sometimes there aren't. In an emergency, the bystander is thinking, "What's happening? Is help needed? What should I do? What's everybody else doing?"

As you'll recall from the story told by Robin Akert on page xxviii, trying to decide if an emergency is really happening and if your help is really needed can be very difficult. Bystanders often rely on informational social influence to help them figure out what to do. Other people's behaviour is a source of important information in an unusual situation; unfortunately, as we saw in Akert's story, if other people are acting as if nothing is wrong, you could be misled by their behaviour and also interpret the situation as a non-emergency. In that case, informational social influence has backfired.

In order to explore informational social influence, gather some stories about people's reactions to emergencies when they were bystanders (not victims). Think

about your own experiences, and ask your friends to tell you about emergencies they have been in. As you recollect your own experience, or talk to your friends about their experiences, note how informational social influence played a role:

1. How did you (and your friends) decide that an emergency was really occurring? Did you glance at other passersby, and watch their response? Did you talk to other people to help you figure out what was going on?

2. Once you decided it was an emergency, how did you decide what to do? Did you do what other people were doing; did you show (or tell) them what to do?

3. Were there any experts present, people who knew more about the situation or how to offer assistance? Did you do what the experts told you to do? If you were in the role of expert (or were at least knowledgeable) at the scene of the emergency, did people follow your lead?

The issues raised by these questions are all examples of informational social influence in action.

misinformed, we will adopt their mistakes and misinterpretations. Depending on others to help us reach a definition of the situation can sometimes lead to an inaccurate definition indeed.

What is particularly interesting about modern cases such as the Y2K scare is the powerful role the mass media play in their dissemination. Through television, radio, newspapers, and magazines, information is spread quickly and efficiently to all segments of the population. Consider, for example, the "Coca-colic" epidemic that occurred in June 1999. It all began when 42 schoolchildren in Belgium complained of nausea, stomach cramps, and headaches after drinking Coca-Cola. Once this story hit the news, these mysterious symptoms began to afflict other Coke drinkers across Belgium and spread to France. As a result, rather extreme actions were taken. Belgium, France, and Luxembourg ordered the removal of more than 65 million cans of Coca-Cola products. Other European countries, as well as Saudi Arabia, banned the sale of all Coca-Cola products coming from Belgium. As it turns out, hospital tests failed to find a medical basis for these symptoms. It appears that the "Coca-colic" epidemic was another example of informational conformity gone awry.

Luckily, the mass media also have the power to introduce more accurate or logical explanations for ambiguous events. In the case of Y2K, as you may recall, the Canadian Bankers Association aired commercials in which it tried to reassure a worried public that it had taken steps to prepare for the Y2K problem and that people's money was safe. As proof, it was pointed out that credit cards with an "00" expiry date were working just fine. It is not known whether the public found these commercials reassuring, but one of your authors (Beverley Fehr) recalls thinking, "I have a credit card with an '00' expiry date, and he's right—it's working just fine."

RESISTING INFORMATIONAL SOCIAL INFLUENCE

As we have seen, relying on others to help us define what is happening can be an excellent idea—or it can be a tragedy in the making. How can we tell in which cases other people are a good source of information and in which cases we should resist other people's definition of a situation?

First, it is important to remember that it is possible to resist illegitimate or inaccurate informational social influence. Some Solar Temple cult members refused to take their own lives, not every student on the scene participated in the fatal attack on Reena Virk, and not every soldier in the Canadian Airborne Regiment participated in the beating death of Shidane Arone. Similarly, during *The War of the Worlds* broadcast, not all listeners panicked (Cantril, 1940). Some engaged in rational problem solving: they checked other stations on the radio dial and discovered that no other station was broadcasting the same news. Instead of relying on others and being caught up in the contagion and mass panic, they searched for and found information on their own.

One reason that the decision about whether to conform is so important is that it influences how people define reality. If you decide to accept other people's definition of the situation, you will come to see the world as they do. If you decide to reject other people's definition of the situation, you will come to see the world differently from the way they do. This basic fact has been demonstrated in an interesting program of research conducted at the University of Waterloo (Griffin & Buehler, 1993; Buehler & Griffin, 1994).

In one study, Roger Buehler and Dale Griffin (1994) asked students to read newspaper reports of a real, highly controversial incident in which an African-Canadian teenager driving a stolen car was shot and killed by white police officers. Many of the details of the situation were ambiguous, such as how much the youth had threatened the officers and how much the officers had feared for their lives.

Buehler and Griffin first asked participants how they interpreted the situation: How fast was the victim's car going? Was the victim trying to ram the police car? Did he realize that his pursuers were the police? What were the police officers thinking and feeling? Each participant was then told that other participants believed that the police were 75 percent responsible and the victim was 25 percent responsible. After indicating whether they agreed with this assessment, the participants were again asked how they interpreted the situation (because their original responses had supposedly been lost in a computer crash). The question was, did participants now interpret the situation differently, depending on whether they agreed with other people's assessments?

The first result of interest was that not everyone conformed to other people's views. As you might expect, those who did conform to the group's opinion started out with a more police-blaming construal of the situation than those who did not. More importantly, people's decision about whether to conform influenced their definition of the situation. As shown in Figure 8.2, people who agreed that the police were responsible changed their interpretations to be consistent with the group; they now believed that the victim had not threatened the police and that police had not feared for their lives. What about the people who did not conform? Interestingly, they also changed their interpretations, but in the opposite direction—they now believed that the victim's car was about to ram the police and that the police were in fear for their lives. It is remarkable that once we have formed an opinion of a situation, we may interpret that same situation quite differently a mere 10 minutes later to bolster our decision to go along with, or deviate from, the majority opinion.

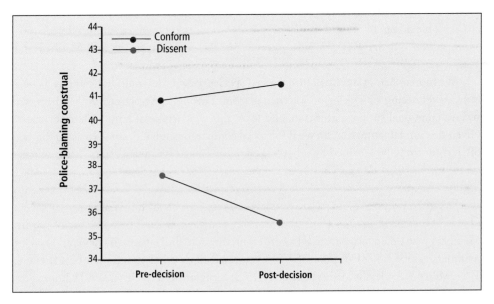

◀ Figure 8.2

PREDECISION AND POST-DECISION CONSTRUALS BY CONFORMITY DECISION.

(Buehler & Griffin, 1994)

Decisions about whether to conform to informational influence, then, will affect not only people's behaviour but also their interpretation of reality. Thus it is important to consider carefully whether other people's reactions to a situation are any more legitimate than your own. Do other people know any more about what is going on than you do? Is there an expert handy, someone who should know more? Do the actions of other people or experts seem sensible? If you behave the way they do, will it go against your common sense, or against your internal moral compass that tells you what is right and wrong? By knowing how informational social influence works in daily life, you are in a better position to know when it is useful and when it is not.

Normative Social Influence: The Need to Be Accepted

In Rio de Janeiro, Brazil, teenage boys and girls engage in a highly dangerous, reckless game: They "surf" on the tops of trains, standing with arms outstretched as the trains speed along. Despite the fact that an average of 150 teenagers die each year from this activity and 400 more are injured by falling off the trains or hitting the 3000-volt electric cable, the surfing continues (Arnett, 1995). Closer to home, in Toronto, teens flock to all-night raves where they buy drugs such as Ecstasy from strangers. Between 2 and 3 a.m., emergency departments in hospitals have come to expect teens who are experiencing "bad trips" from having taken the drug. Tragically, in 1999, nine Ontario teenagers died as a result of having taken tainted Ecstasy. By August 2000, Ecstasy had already claimed the lives of another nine teenagers in that province. Nevertheless, taking high-risk drugs at raves remains an extremely popular activity for youths in many Canadian cities.

Why do these young people engage in such risky behaviour? Why does anyone follow the group's lead when the resulting behaviour is less than sensible and may even be dangerous? We doubt that these teenagers risk their lives due to informational conformity—it is difficult to argue that a teenager at a rave would say, "Gee, I don't know what to do. A stranger wants to sell me drugs that might kill me. I guess it must be a good idea; I see other people doing it." This example tells us that there is another reason for why we conform, aside from the need for information: We also conform so we will be liked and accepted by other people. This is known as **normative social influence**.

We human beings are by nature a social species. Few of us could live happily as hermits, never seeing or talking to another person. Through interactions with others, we receive emotional support, affection, and love, and we partake of enjoyable experiences. Given this fundamental human need for social companionship, it is not surprising that we often conform to be accepted by others. Conformity for normative reasons occurs in situations where we go along with others, not because we are using them as a source of information but rather because we don't want to attract attention, be made fun of, get into trouble, or be rejected. Groups have certain expectations about how the group members should behave, and members in good standing conform to these rules, or **social norms**. Members who do not are perceived as different, difficult, and eventually deviant. Deviant members can be ridiculed, punished, or even rejected by other group members (Levine, 1989; Miller & Anderson, 1979; Schachter, 1951; Kruglanski & Webster, 1991). For example, University of Western Ontario researchers Leslie Janes and James Olson (2000)

Normative social influence

the influence of other people that leads us to conform in order to be liked and accepted by them; this type of conformity results in public compliance with the group's beliefs and behaviours, but not necessarily with private acceptance of the group's beliefs and behaviours

Social norms

the implicit or explicit rules a group has for the acceptable behaviours, values, and beliefs of its members

recently conducted a series of studies on what they call "jeer pressure." Participants observed someone either ridiculing another person or engaging in self-ridicule. Those who observed someone else being ridiculed later showed the greatest conformity to their peers. Why might this be? According to Janes and Olson, groups use ridicule as a means of punishing group members who fail to comply with the group's norms. Thus, when we observe someone else being ridiculed, we will be especially likely to conform to the group's norms in order to avoid being the next target.

Normative social influence is another reason why soldiers in Canada's Airborne Regiment participated in the brutal beating death of Shidane Arone, and why high-school students in Victoria participated in the brutal beating death of Reena Virk. In the case of Virk, fears of being rejected or punished by the group didn't end there. Later, when giving statements to the police and testifying in court, some of the students lied because they were afraid of the consequences of "ratting" on their friends.

CONFORMITY AND SOCIAL APPROVAL: THE ASCH LINE JUDGMENT STUDIES

You probably don't find it too surprising that people sometimes conform in order to be liked and accepted by others. After all, if the group is important to us and it is a matter of wearing the right kind of clothing or using the right "cool" words, why not go along? But surely we won't conform when we are certain of what the correct way of behaving is and the pressures are coming from a group that we don't care all that much about. Or will we? To find out, Solomon Asch (1951, 1956) conducted a series of classic studies exploring the parameters of normative social influence. Asch initiated this program of research because he believed that there are limits to how much people will conform. Naturally, people conformed in the Sherif studies, he reasoned, given that the situation was highly ambiguous—trying to guess how much a light was moving. Asch believed, however, that when a situation was completely unambiguous, people would act like rational, objective problem-solvers. When the group said or did something that contradicted an obvious truth, surely people would reject social pressures and decide for themselves what was going on.

To test his hypothesis, Asch conducted the following study. Had you been a participant, you would have been told that this was an experiment on perceptual judgment and that you would be taking part with seven other students. Here's the scenario. The experimenter shows everyone two cards, one with a single line, the other with three lines labelled 1, 2, and 3. He asks each of you to judge and then announce aloud which of the three lines on the second card is closest in length to the line on the first card (see Figure 8.3).

It is crystal-clear that the correct answer is the second line. Not surprisingly, each participant says, "Line 2." Your turn comes next to last, and of course you say, "Line 2" as well. The last participant concurs. The experimenter then presents a new set of cards and asks the group to again make their judgments and announce them out loud. Again, the answer is obvious, and everyone gives the correct answer. At this point, you are probably thinking to yourself, "What a boring experiment! How many times will we have to judge these silly lines? I wonder what's for dinner tonight."

As your mind starts to wander, something surprising happens. The experimenter presents the third set of lines, and again the answer is obvious—line 3 is clearly the closest in length to the target line. But the first participant announces that the correct answer

▶ **Figure 8.3**

THE JUDGMENT TASK IN
ASCH'S LINE STUDIES.

In a study of normative social
influence, participants judged
which of the three comparison
lines on the right was closest in
length to the standard line on
the left. The correct answer was
obvious (as it is here). However,
members of the group (actually
confederates) said the wrong
answer out loud. Now the
participant was in a dilemma:
Should he say the right answer
and go against the whole group,
or should he conform to their
behaviour and give the
obviously wrong answer?

(Adapted from Asch, 1956)

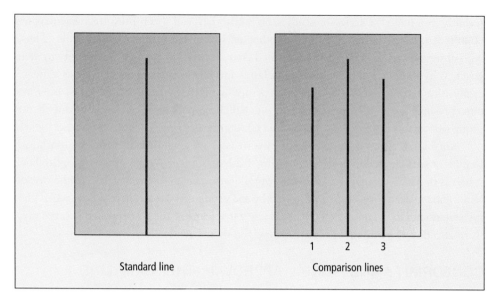

Standard line   Comparison lines

is line 1! "Geez, this guy must be so bored that he fell asleep," you think. Then the second person announces that he also believes that line 1 is the correct answer. The third, fourth, fifth, and sixth participants concur; then it is your turn to judge. By now startled, you are probably looking at the lines very closely to see if you missed something. But no, line 3 is clearly the correct answer. What will you do? Will you bravely blurt out, "Line 3," or will you go along with the group and give the obviously incorrect answer, "Line 1"?

As you can see, Asch set up a situation to see if people would conform even when the right answer was cut and dried. The other participants were actually accomplices of the experimenter, instructed to give the wrong answer on 12 of the 18 trials. Contrary to what Asch thought would happen, a surprising amount of conformity occurred: 66 percent of the

▶ Participants in an Asch line study. The real participant is seated in the middle. He is surrounded by experimenter's accomplices who have just given the wrong answer on the line task.

participants conformed on at least one trial. On average, people conformed on about one-third of the 12 trials on which the accomplices gave the incorrect answer (see Figure 8.4).

Why did people conform so much of the time? One possibility is that people genuinely had a hard time with the task and thus assumed that other people were better judges of the length of lines than they were. If so, this would be another case of informational social influence, as we saw in the Sherif study. This interpretation doesn't make much sense, however, because the correct answers were obvious—so much so that when people in a control group made the judgments by themselves, they were accurate more than 99 percent of the time. Instead, normative pressures came into play. Even though the other participants were strangers, the fear of being the lone dissenter was very strong, causing people to conform, at least occasionally. One participant, for example, had this to say about why he conformed: "Here was a group; they had a definite idea; my idea disagreed; I didn't want particularly to make a fool of myself. . . . I felt I was definitely right . . . [but] they might think I was peculiar" (Asch, 1955).

These are classic normative reasons for conforming. People know that what they are doing is wrong but go along anyway so as not to feel peculiar or look like a fool. These reasons illustrate an important fact about normative pressures: In contrast to informational social influence, normative pressures usually result in public compliance without private acceptance—that is, people go along with the group even if they do not believe in what they are doing or think it is wrong (Cialdini, Reno, & Kallgren, 1990, 1991; Cialdini & Trost, 1998; Deutsch & Gerard, 1955; Sorrels & Kelley, 1984).

What is especially surprising about Asch's results is that people were concerned about looking foolish in front of complete strangers. It is not as if the participants were in danger of being ostracized by a group that was important to them. Nor was there any risk of open punishment or disapproval for failing to conform, or of losing the esteem of people they really cared about, such as friends and family members. Yet decades of research indicate that conformity for normative reasons can occur simply because we do not want to

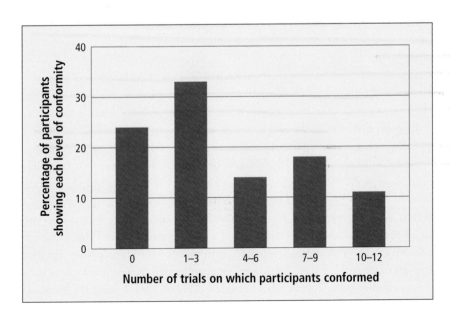

◀ Figure 8.4

RESULTS OF THE ASCH LINE JUDGMENT STUDY.

Participants in the Asch line study showed a surprisingly high level of conformity, given how obvious it was that the group was wrong in their judgments. Seventy-six percent of the participants conformed on at least one trial; only 24 percent of participants never conformed at all (see the bar labelled zero). Most participants conformed on 1 to 3 of the 12 trials where the group gave the wrong answer. However, a sizable number of participants conformed to the group's response nearly every time it gave the wrong answer (see the two bars on the right).

(Adapted from Asch, 1957)

risk social disapproval, even from complete strangers we will never see again (Crutchfield, 1955; Tanford & Penrod, 1984). As Moscovici (1985) comments, the Asch studies are "one of the most dramatic illustrations of conformity, of blindly going along with the group, even when the individual realizes that by doing so he turns his back on reality and truth."

Asch (1957) did a variation of his study that demonstrates the power of social disapproval in shaping a person's behaviour. The confederates gave the wrong answer 12 out of 18 times, as before, but this time the participants wrote their answers on a piece of paper, instead of saying them out loud. Now people did not have to worry about what the group thought of them, because the group would never find out what their answers were. Conformity dropped dramatically, occurring on an average of only 1.5 of the 12 trials.

Normative social influence most closely reflects the negative stereotype of conformity we referred to earlier. At times, conforming for normative reasons can be spineless and weak; it can have negative consequences. Even in a dangerous situation, like that faced by teenagers taking Ecstasy at raves, you might go ahead and conform because normative social pressures can be difficult to resist. The desire to be accepted is part of human nature, but it can have deadly consequences.

WHEN WILL PEOPLE CONFORM TO NORMATIVE SOCIAL INFLUENCE?

Although conformity is commonplace, we are not lemmings who always do what everyone else is doing. And we certainly do not agree on all issues, such as abortion or affirmative action. (One need only tune in to a radio talk show to appreciate how much people disagree on topics such as these.) Exactly when are people most likely to conform to normative pressures?

Social impact theory

the theory that conforming to social influence depends on the strength, immediacy, and number of other people in a group

The answer to this question is provided by Bibb Latané's (1981) **social impact theory**. According to this theory, the likelihood that you will respond to social influence from other people depends on three variables: (a) strength, referring to how important the group of people is to you; (b) immediacy, referring to how close the group is to you in space and time during the influence attempt; and (c) number, referring to how many people are in the group.

Social impact theory predicts that conformity will increase as strength and immediacy increase. Clearly, the more important a group is to us, and the more we are in its presence, the more likely we will be to conform to its normative pressures. Number, however, operates in a different manner. As the size of the group increases, each additional person has less of an influencing effect—going from 3 to 4 people makes more of a difference than going from 53 to 54 people. It is like the law of diminishing returns in economics, where increasing one's total wealth by $1 seems much greater if we have only $1 to start with than if we have $1000. Similarly, if we feel pressure from a group to conform, adding another person to the majority makes much more of a difference if the group consists of 3 rather than 15 people. Latané (1981) constructed a mathematical model that captures these hypothesized effects of strength, immediacy, and number, and has applied this formula to the results of many conformity studies. The formula has done a good job of predicting the actual amount of conformity that occurred (Latané, 1981; Latané & L'Herrou, 1996; Latané, Nowak, & Liu, 1994; Nowak & Latané, 1994).

For example, gay men who lived in communities that were highly involved in AIDS-awareness activities (where strength, immediacy, and number would all be high) reported feeling more social pressure to avoid risky sexual behaviour and stronger intentions to do so than did men who lived in less involved communities (Fishbein et al., 1993). Similarly, as mentioned in Chapter 7, whether or not people use condoms depends, at least in part, on the norms for sexual behaviour that operate in their group of friends (Winslow, Franzini, & Hwang, 1992). (Try It!, below, gives you a chance to observe and experience normative pressures in action.)

Social impact theory covers conformity to all kinds of social influence. For present purposes, let's see in more detail what it says about the conditions under which people will conform to normative social pressures.

When the Group Size Is Three or More ~~As we just saw, conformity increases as the number of people in the group increases—up to a point.~~ Imagine you are a participant

Fashion: Normative Social Influence in Action

You can observe social impact theory in action by focusing on fashion—specifically, the clothes and accessories that you and your group of friends wear, as well as the "look" of other groups on campus. You can also observe what happens when you break those normative rules for fashion; for example, by dressing in a way that deviates from your group.

When you are with a group of friends and acquaintances, note carefully how everyone is dressed. Pretend you are from another culture and not acquainted with the norms of this group; this will help you notice details you might otherwise overlook. For example, what kinds of pants, shoes, shirts, jewellery, and so on are worn by this group? Are there similarities in their haircuts? Can you discover their fashion "rules"?

Next, spend some time on campus "people-watching"; specifically, observe what other groups of people are wearing. Can you discern different subgroups on your campus, defined by their style of dress? If so, there are different types of normative conformity operating on your campus; groups of friends are dressing according to the rules of their subgroup and not according to the rules of the campus as a whole.

Finally, if you are brave, break the fashion rules of your normative group. You can do this subtly or you can be very obvious! (However, do be sensible; don't get yourself arrested!) For example, if you're male, you could wear a skirt around campus. That would definitely attract attention; you will be not conforming to normative influence in a very major way! If you're female, you'll have to get more creative to break the normative rules (since women's fashion includes pants, blazers, and other typically male clothing). You could wear a large, green garbage bag (with holes cut out for your head and arms) over your clothing. In either case, simply walk around campus as usual—as if you don't notice you are wearing anything strange. The interesting part will be how people react to you. What will your friends say? Will strangers stare at you?

Your group of friends (as well as the students at your school in general) may well have the qualities that social impact theory discusses: the group is important to you; the group size is more than three; and the group is unanimous (which is the case if your group of friends or your university or college has definite fashion norms). If you stop conforming to this normative social influence, the other group members will exert some kind of pressure on you, trying to get you to return to conformity.

in Solomon Asch's study, where you judged the length of lines. If there are only you and one other participant, and the latter gives a blatantly wrong answer about the length of the lines, will you be less likely to cave in and conform to that person's response than if there are five other participants all giving the wrong answer? What if there are 15 people in the majority? Asch (1955) studied this question, and, as we can see in Figure 8.5, conformity increased as the number of people in the group increased, but only up to a point.

Asch's (1955) initial research and that of later researchers has established that in this kind of group situation, conformity does not increase much after the group size reaches four or five other people (Gerard, Wilhelmy, & Conolley, 1968; McGuire, 1968; Rosenberg, 1961)—just as social impact theory suggests.

Finally, we should note that research conducted at the University of British Columbia by Campbell and Fairey (1989) suggests that the effects of group size depend on the kind of social influence that is operating. According to these researchers, in situations where the group is clearly wrong, conformity will be motivated by normative influence; the participants will conform in order to be accepted by the group. Under these conditions, the size of the group matters. A participant may not feel much pressure to conform when the first person gives an incorrect response. However, conformity pressure will mount as each additional group member also gives the same incorrect response.

In contrast, in situations where the group is making a judgment that may be correct, participants will turn to the group as a source of information. Under these conditions, group size is less likely to matter. Once the first group member has given his or her response, it adds very little information if two, three, or four group members also provide the same response.

Thus, the size of a group is most likely to affect conformity under the conditions we have been discussing here—namely, when normative social influence is operating. And as we have seen, it does not take an extremely large group to create normative social influence. As Mark Twain wrote in *The Adventures of Huckleberry Finn*, "Hain't we got all the fools in town on our side? And ain't that a big enough majority in any town?"

▶ **Figure 8.5**

EFFECTS OF GROUP SIZE ON CONFORMITY.

Asch varied the size of the unanimous majority and found that once the majority numbered four people, adding more people had little influence on conformity.

(Adapted from Asch, 1955)

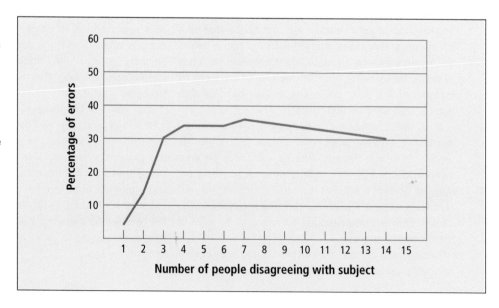

When the Group Is Important Another tenet of social impact theory is that the strength of the group—defined as how important the group is to us—makes a difference. Normative pressures are much stronger when they come from people whose friendship, love, and respect we cherish, because there is a large cost to losing this love and respect. Thus, groups to which we are highly attracted and with which we strongly identify will exert more normative influence on us than groups to which we have little or no attachment (Abrams et al., 1990; Clark & Maass, 1988; Hogg, 1992; Nowak, Szamrej, & Latané, 1990). These processes were examined in a recent, fascinating study by Tafarodi and colleagues (2002). These researchers reasoned that members of bicultural visible-minority groups (e.g., people who are second-generation Canadians or came to Canada as young children) might feel that they are not fully accepted as a member of the majority group because of their physical distinctiveness. As a result, such people might be especially motivated to conform to the majority group in terms of dress, speech, or behaviour. This hypothesis was tested among Chinese women (who were either born in Canada or had come to Canada as young children) attending the University of Toronto. The women were asked to participate in a study on esthetic judgment and were told they would be required to rate how much they liked various pieces of art (presented on a computer screen). The computer "happened" to display various sets of ratings of each painting, including those supposedly given by Chinese Canadians and European Canadians. Half of the participants completed their ratings in view of a mirror (intended to remind them of their visible-minority status); the other half completed the ratings without a mirror. Tafarodi and colleagues reasoned that those participants who were reminded of their distinctive appearance (relative to the majority group) would be most likely to conform to the ratings of the majority (i.e., European Canadians). And that is exactly what happened. Thus, when we are attracted to a group and are reminded that we don't quite fit in, we will be especially motivated to conform.

When the Group Is Unanimous Normative social influence is most powerfully felt when everyone in the group says or believes the same thing—for example, when your group of friends all believe that *Lord of the Rings* was the greatest movie ever made. Resisting such unanimous social influence is difficult or even impossible—unless you have an ally. If another person disagrees with the group—say, by nominating *My Big Fat Greek Wedding* as the best movie ever—this behaviour will help you to buck the tide as well.

To illustrate the importance of having an ally, Asch (1955) conducted another version of his conformity experiment. In this variation, he had six of the seven confederates give the wrong answer, whereas one confederate gave the right answer on every trial. Now the participant was not alone. Having even one ally dramatically helped him or her resist normative pressures. People conformed on an average of only 6 percent of the trials in this study, compared to 32 percent in the version where all of the confederates gave the wrong answer. Several other studies have found that observing another person resist normative social influence emboldens the individual to do the same (Allen & Levine, 1969; Morris & Miller, 1975; Nemeth & Chiles, 1988).

This effect of allies produces some interesting anomalies in everyday life—people who hold unpopular beliefs are able to maintain them in the face of group pressure if they

▶ If you can get a few allies to agree with you, it's easier to buck the majority and believe some rather strange things. Ernst Zundel, a German Holocaust denier based in Canada, tries through his books and Web site to get people to believe that the Holocaust never happened, despite the massive amount of documented evidence to the contrary.

can convince at least a few others to agree with them. For example, a man in Lancaster, California, believes that the earth is flat—despite proof from scientific experiments over a few centuries that it is not. It is difficult to hold such an unpopular (and wrongheaded!) view; not surprisingly, this man has actively recruited followers, and attempts to convince others of his views through his *Flat Earth Newsletter*.

When People Are a Certain Type Is a certain sort of person more likely than another to conform to normative pressures? Research in this area has focused on two aspects of the individual: personality and gender. It seems reasonable to propose that some people are just conforming types, while others' personalities make them highly resistant to normative pressures. Unfortunately, the relationship between personality traits and conforming behaviour is not always very clear-cut. Some researchers have found that people who are low in self-esteem or who have a strong need for approval from others are more likely to conform (Asch, 1956; Crutchfield, 1955; Snyder & Ickes, 1985). Others have found the relation between personality and conformity to be weak or nonexistent (Marlowe & Gergen, 1970). You may recall from Chapter 1 that a fundamental principle of social psychology is that the social situation is often more important than personality in understanding how someone behaves. It appears that this principle applies to conformity as well—in some situations people conform, and in other situations they don't—regardless of what type of person they are.

The second individual variable that has been studied is gender. Is it the case that women and men differ in how readily they conform to social pressures? For many years, the prevailing wisdom has been to answer this question in the affirmative: Women are more conforming than men (Crutchfield, 1955). When your authors studied social psychology in university, this finding was presented as a fact. Recent reviews of the literature, however, have shown that matters are not so simple. In the past few years, researchers have taken an objective look at this question by conducting meta analyses. Alice Eagly and Linda Carli (1981), for example, performed a meta analysis of 145 studies on influenceability that included more than 21 000 participants. Consistent with previous reviews of this literature, they found that, on average, men are less easily influenced than women. However, they also found the size of the difference to be very small.

Not only are sex differences in influenceability small, but they depend on the type of conformity pressures impinging on people. Gender differences are especially likely to be found in group-pressure situations, where an audience can directly observe how much you conform (e.g., the Asch study where everyone can tell whether you give the same answer as the other participants). When faced with this kind of social pressure, women are more likely to conform than men. In situations where conformity is private (e.g., as in the Asch study where participants privately recorded their answers), sex differences in influenceability virtually disappear. Eagly (1987) suggests that this pattern of results stems from the social roles men and women are taught in our society. Women are taught to be more agreeable and supportive, whereas men are taught to be more independent in the face of direct social pressures. And, Eagly suggests, both women and men are more likely to exhibit such gender-consistent behaviours in public situations, where everyone can see how they respond (e.g., the Asch-type conformity study). But remember that the size of these differences is small.

One other finding in this area is surprising and controversial. Eagly and Carli (1981) took note of the gender of the researchers who conducted conformity studies and found that male researchers were more likely than female researchers to find that women conformed more than men. Though the reason for this finding is not yet clear, Eagly and Carli (1981) suggest one possibility: Researchers may be more likely to use experimental materials and situations that are familiar to their own gender. Male researchers, for example, may be more likely than female researchers to study how people conform to persuasive messages about sports. As we saw earlier, people are more likely to conform when confronted with an unfamiliar, ambiguous situation; thus, women may be more likely to conform in the unfamiliar situations designed by male experimenters. A study by Sistrunk and McDavid (1971) speaks to this issue. These researchers constructed a questionnaire in which some topics were more familiar to men (e.g., mechanics), some were more familiar to women (e.g., fashion), and others were gender neutral. Interestingly, women conformed more than men on the masculine items, men conformed more than women on the feminine items, and women and men conformed equally on the gender-neutral items. The same pattern of findings was obtained in a similar study conducted with University of Saskatchewan students (Maupin & Fisher, 1989).

To summarize, there appears to be a small tendency for women to be more easily influenced, especially in group-pressure situations. Further, the already small magnitude of this difference may be exaggerated in studies conducted by male researchers, who are more likely than female researchers to find that women are more easily influenced than men.

When the Group's Culture Is Collectivist In North America, we use the expression "The squeaky wheel gets the grease." In Japan, you would be more likely to hear "The nail that stands out gets pounded down" (Markus & Kitayama, 1991). Is it the case, as these quotations suggest, that the society in which one is raised affects the frequency of normative social influence? Perhaps not surprisingly, the answer is yes. Rod Bond and Peter Smith (1996) conducted a meta analysis of 133 Asch line judgment studies conducted in 17 countries. Participants in collectivist cultures showed higher rates of conformity on the line task than did participants in individualist cultures. In fact, in individualist countries, including Canada (Lalancette & Standing, 1990), the rate of conformity in Asch-type studies has been declining. In contrast, in collectivist cultures, conformity is a valued trait, not a negative one as in North America. Because emphasis is on the group and not the individual, people in such cultures value normative social influence because it promotes harmony and supportive relationships in the group (Guisinger & Blatt, 1994; Kim et al., 1994; Markus, Kitayama, & Heiman, 1996).

J. W. Berry (1967; Kim & Berry, 1993) explored the issue of conformity as a cultural value by comparing two cultures that had very different strategies for accumulating food. He hypothesized that societies that relied on hunting or fishing would value independence, assertiveness, and adventurousness in their members—traits that were needed to find and bring home food—whereas societies that were primarily agricultural would value cooperativeness, conformity, and acquiescence—traits that made close living and interdependent farming more successful. Berry compared the Inuit of Baffin Island in Canada, a hunting and fishing society, to the Temne of Sierra Leone, Africa, a farming society, on an Asch-type conformity task. The Temne showed a significant tendency to accept the suggestions of the group, while the Inuit almost completely disregarded them. As one Temne put it, "When the Temne people choose a thing, we must all agree with the decision—this is what we call cooperation"; in contrast, the few times the Inuit did conform to the group's wrong answer, they did so with "a quiet, knowing smile."

RESISTING NORMATIVE SOCIAL INFLUENCE

Whereas normative social influence is often useful and appropriate, there are times when it is not. What can we do to resist inappropriate normative social influence? The best way to prevent ourselves from following the wrong social norm is to become more aware of what we are doing. If we stop and think carefully about whether the norm that seems to be operating is really the right one to follow, we will be more likely to recognize the times when it is not.

If becoming aware of normative influence is the first step to resistance, taking action is the second. Why do we fail to take action? Because of the possible ridicule, embarrassment, or rejection we may experience. Think for a moment about the norms that operate in your group of friends. Some friends have an egalitarian norm for making group decisions. For example, when choosing a movie such groups will ensure that everyone gets to state a preference; the choice is then discussed until agreement is reached. Think about what would happen if, in a group with this kind of norm, you stated at the outset that you only wanted to see the movie *Being John Malkovich* and weren't going with them otherwise. Your friends would be surprised by your behaviour; they would also be annoyed with you, or even angry. If you continued to disregard the friendship norms of the group by failing to conform to them, two things would most likely occur. First, the group members would attempt to bring you "back into the fold," chiefly through increased communication with you. Teasing comments and long discussions would ensue as your friends tried to figure out why you were acting so strangely and also tried to get you to conform to their expectations (Garfinkle, 1967). If these discussions didn't work, your friends would most likely curtail communication with you (Festinger & Thibaut, 1951; Gerard, 1953). At this point, in effect, you would be rejected.

Stanley Schachter (1951) demonstrated how the group responds to an individual who ignores their normative influence. He asked groups of university students to read and discuss a case history of "Johnny Rocco," a juvenile delinquent. Most of the students took a middle-of-the-road position about the case, believing that Rocco should receive a judicious mixture of love and discipline. Unbeknownst to the participants, however, Schachter had planted an accomplice in the group, who was instructed to disagree with the group's recommendations. He consistently argued that Rocco should receive the harshest amount of punishment, regardless of what the other group members argued.

How was the deviant treated? He received the most comments and questions from the real participants throughout the discussion, until near the end, when communication with him dropped sharply. The group had tried to convince the deviant to agree with them; when it appeared that wouldn't work, they ignored him. In addition, they punished the deviant. After the discussion, they were asked to nominate one group member who should be eliminated from further discussions if the size of the group had to be reduced. They nominated the deviant. They were also asked to assign group members to various tasks in future discussions. You guessed it—they assigned the unimportant or boring jobs, such as taking notes, to the deviant.

Are the findings of Schacter's 1951 study relevant today? Consider the case of Master Seaman Biden, a military police officer with 20 years of service in the Canadian Forces. He was injected with the anthrax vaccine during the Gulf War and subsequently experienced medical problems. When he learned that the vaccine was out of date and that the Michigan manufacturer of the drug had been charged by the U.S. government for numerous health violations, he wrote a letter to his Member of Parliament. Subsequently, Biden received a scathing letter from his commanding officer because members of the military are expected not to voice complaints publicly. He was ordered to stop talking to the media and was ostracized at work. He told an *Ottawa Citizen* reporter that he was assigned menial jobs that were usually done by junior privates: "He cleaned rifles while junior officers sat idle, sipping coffee" (Blanchfield, 2000). The parallels between Biden's experience and the way in which participants in Schacter's 1951 study treated a deviant group member are striking.

As we have seen, social groups are well versed in how to bring a nonconformist into line. No wonder we respond as often as we do to normative pressures! (You can find out what it's like to resist normative social influence in Try It! on page 282.) How can we find the courage to resist normotive pressure? Fortunately, there are some strategies that work. For example, we know that having an ally helps us resist normative pressures. Thus, if you are in a situation where you don't want to go along with the crowd but you fear the repercussions if you don't, try to find another person (or better yet, a group) who thinks the way you do.

In addition, the very act of conforming to normative influence most of the time earns you the right to deviate occasionally without serious consequences. This interesting observation was made by Edwin Hollander (1958, 1960), who stated that conforming to a

▼ Krista Piche paid a high price for not conforming to the military code of silence after being sexually assaulted by a petty officer. She filed a complaint, despite being advised by a medical warrant officer not to do so. Military brass responded by forcing her to work alongside the man who had assaulted her and repeatedly denied her requests for a transfer. Although a career with the military had been her lifelong dream, these consequences of nonconformity made her life so unbearable that she eventually left the military.

Unveiling Normative Social Influence by Breaking the Rules

Every day, you talk to a lot of people—friends, professors, co-workers, and strangers, too. When you have a conversation (whether long or short), you follow certain interaction "rules" that operate in North American culture. These rules for conversation include nonverbal forms of behaviour that we consider "normal" as well as "polite." You can find out how powerful these norms are by breaking them and noting how people respond to you; their response is normative social influence in action.

For example, in conversation, we stand a certain distance from each other—not too far and not too close. About two-thirds of a metre to a metre is typical in our culture. In addition, we maintain a good amount of eye contact when we are listening to the other person; in comparison, when we're talking, we look away from the person more often.

What happens if you break these normative rules? For example, have a conversation with a friend and stand either too close or too far away (e.g., 30 centimetres or 2 metres). Have a typical, normal conversation with your friend, changing only the spacing you normally use with this person. Note how he or she responds. If you're too close, your friend will probably back away; if you contin-ue to keep the distance small, he or she may act uncomfortable and even terminate your conversation sooner than usual. If you're too far away, your friend will probably come closer; if you back up, he or she may think you are in a strange mood. In either case, your friend's response will probably include the following: looking at you a lot; having a puzzled look on his or her face; acting uncomfortable or confused; talking less than normal or ending the conversation, and so on.

You have acted in a non-normative way, and your conversational partner is, first, trying to figure out what is going on, and, second, responding so as to get you to stop acting oddly. From this one brief exercise, you will get the idea of what would happen if you behaved "oddly" all the time—people would try to make you change, and then they would probably start avoiding or ignoring you.

When you're done, please "debrief" your friend, telling him or her about the exercise, so that your behaviour is understood. Let your friend see what it's like to alter interpersonal distance by talking to you too close or too far away.

Idiosyncrasy credits

the credits a person earns, over time, by conforming to group norms; if enough idiosyncrasy credits are earned, the person can, on occasion, behave deviantly without retribution from the group

group over time earns you **idiosyncrasy credits,** much like putting money in the bank. Thus, your past conformity allows you, at some point in the future, to deviate from the group (or act idiosyncratically) without getting into too much trouble. If you refuse to drive your friends (and yourself) home because you've had a few drinks, for example, they may not become upset with you if you have followed their friendship norms in other areas in the past, because you've earned the right to be different, to deviate from their normative rules in this area. Thus, resisting normative influence may not be as difficult (or scary) as you might think, if you have earned idiosyncrasy credits with the group.

SOCIAL INFLUENCE IN EVERYDAY LIFE

Social influence operates on many levels in our daily lives. The clothes we wear are but one example. While few of us are slaves to fashion, we nonetheless tend to wear what is considered appropriate and stylish at a given time. Men wore wide ties in the 1970s, then they wore narrow ties in the 1980s, and undoubtedly they'll be wearing wide ties again at some point. Similarly, women's hemlines have gone up and down over the past century.

◀ On the left, the "zoot suit" look in 1942. The jacket had 15 centimetres of shoulder pads, and the balloon trousers were hitched chest-high. On the right, the current fashion trend for teenagers—baggy pants and oversized shirts and sweaters—is the "in" look in some regions of the country.

Social influence is at work whenever you notice a "look" shared by people in a certain group. The young women in bobby socks and the young men in "zoot suits" of the 1940s had such a look. No doubt 20 years from now current fashions will look dated and silly, and none of us will conform to them.

Social Influence and Women's Body Image

A more sinister form of social influence involves people's attempts to conform to cultural definitions of an attractive body. Though many, if not most, world societies consider plumpness in females attractive, Western culture, and particularly North American culture, currently values thinness in the female form (Jackson, 1992; Lamb et al., 1993; Singh, 1993; Stice & Shaw, 1994; Thompson & Heinberg, 1999).

For example, at Simon Fraser University, Judith Anderson and colleagues (1992) analyzed what people in 54 cultures considered to be the ideal female body. The researchers also analyzed how reliable the food supply was in each culture. They hypothesized that in societies where food was frequently scarce, a heavy body would be considered the most beautiful—for these would be women who had enough to eat and therefore were healthy and fertile. As you can see in Figure 8.6, on page 284, their hypothesis was supported. Heavy women were preferred over slender or moderate ones in cultures with unreliable food supplies. Furthermore, heavy-to-moderate bodies were preferred by the vast majority in all cultures except those with very reliable food supplies. Only in cultures with very reliable food supplies (such as the United States) did the majority prefer moderate-to-slender female bodies.

Have North Americans always considered thinness to be the ideal standard for the female body? Analyses of photographs of women in magazines such as *Ladies' Home Journal* and *Vogue* show a startling series of changes in the cultural definition of female bodily attractiveness during the twentieth century (Silverstein et al., 1986). At the turn of the century, an attractive woman was voluptuous and heavy; by the "flapper" period of the 1920s, the correct look for women was rail-thin and flat chested. The ideal body type changed again in the 1940s, when Second World War "pinup girls," such as Betty Grable,

In other research, Pope and colleagues (2000) asked men in the United States, France, and Austria to alter a computer image of a male body in terms of fat and muscle until it reflected, first, their own bodies; second, the body they'd like to have; and finally, the body they thought women would find most attractive. The men were quite accurate in the depiction of their own bodies. However, men in all three countries chose an ideal body that had on average 12.5 more kilograms of muscle than their own. This ideal standard was also the body they chose for what they thought women would find attractive. (In fact, when women participants did the task, they chose a very normal, typical-looking male body as their ideal.)

All of these data suggest that informational and normative social influence may be operating on men, as well as on women. Indeed, as we mentioned in Chapter 2, men, especially those who read fitness magazines (which, of course, portray very muscular bodies), are engaging in dangerous behaviour such as crash diets and anabolic steroid use (Morry & Staska, 2001; Spitzberg & Rhea, 1999).

Minority Influence: When the Few Influence the Many

We shouldn't end our discussion of social influence by leaving the impression that the individual never has an effect on the group. As Serge Moscovici (1985, 1994) says, if groups really did succeed in silencing nonconformists, rejecting deviants, and persuading everyone to go along with the majority point of view, then how could change ever be introduced into the system? We would all be like robots, marching along with everyone else in monotonous synchrony, never able to adapt to changing reality.

Instead, Moscovici (1985, 1994) argues, the individual, or the minority of group members, can influence the behaviour or beliefs of the majority. This is called **minority influence**. The key is consistency. People with minority views must express the same view over time, and different members of the minority must agree with each other. If a person in the minority wavers between two different viewpoints or if two individuals express different minority views, the majority will dismiss them as people who have peculiar and groundless opinions. If, however, the minority expresses a consistent, unwavering view, the majority is likely to take notice and may even adopt the minority view (Moscovici & Nemeth, 1974).

In a meta analysis of nearly 100 studies, Wendy Wood and colleagues (1994) described how minority influence operates. People in the majority can cause other group members to conform through normative influence. People in the minority can rarely influence others through normative means—the majority has little concern for how the minority views them. In fact, majority group members may be loath to agree publicly with the minority; they don't want anyone to think they agree with those unusual, strange views of the minority. Minorities therefore exert their influence on the group via the other principal method—informational social influence. The minority introduces new, unexpected information to the group and causes the group to examine the issues more carefully. Such careful examination may cause the majority to realize that the minority view has merit, leading the group to adopt all or part of the minority's view. In short, majorities often cause public compliance because of normative social influence, whereas minorities often cause private acceptance because of informational social influence.

Minority influence

the case where a minority of group members influences the behaviour or beliefs of the majority

Compliance: Requests to Change Your Behaviour

We have discussed two main reasons why people conform: because other people serve as a useful source of information (informational social influence) and because of pressures to follow social norms (normative social influence). In the remainder of this chapter, we will see how these reasons for conformity apply to some familiar situations in which you might be asked to do something you really do not want to do. Some of these situations are quite common, such as a salesperson pressuring you into subscribing to some magazines or a charity trying to get you to donate money to its cause. Others are less common but more frightening, such as an authority figure asking you to do something that is against your morals. When and why will people conform in these situations?

We will begin with the case of **compliance**—that is, a change in behaviour due to a direct request from another person. We can hardly make it through a day without a request from someone asking us to do something we would rather not do, be it a letter from a charity asking for money, a telephone call (invariably during dinner) from someone selling time-share vacation property, or a friend wanting to borrow $25. Social psychologists have studied when and why people are likely to comply with these kinds of requests.

Compliance
a change in behaviour due to a direct request from another person

THE DOOR-IN-THE-FACE TECHNIQUE

Suppose you have agreed to go door to door and ask people to donate money to the Canadian Heart Association. Here is a good way to get people to give. First, ask people to donate a large amount of money, with the full expectation that they will refuse. When someone answers the door, you might say, "Hello, I'm asking for donations to the Canadian Heart Association. Do you think you could donate $500?" Once people refuse, you immediately retreat to a more reasonable request: "Well, okay, but do you think you could donate $5?" This approach is called the **door-in-the-face technique**, because the first request is purposefully so large that people will want to slam the door shut. Several studies show that it works well in getting people to agree to the second, more reasonable request (Cialdini & Trost, 1998; Patch, Hoang, & Stahelski, 1997; Reeves et al., 1991; Wang, Brownstein, & Katzev, 1989).

For example, Robert Cialdini and colleagues (1975) decided to see if they could get students to volunteer to chaperone problem adolescents on a two-hour trip to the zoo. When they approached students on a university campus, only 17 percent agreed to this request. In another condition, before asking people to go on the zoo trip, the experimenter made a very large request. The students were asked if they would be willing to work as unpaid counsellors at a juvenile detention centre. The experimenter went on to explain that the position would require two hours of their time per week and that they would have to make a commitment for a minimum of two years. Not surprisingly, no one agreed to such a large request. When students refused, the experimenter said, "Well, we also have another program you might be interested in," and went on to ask if they would chaperone the zoo trip. These students were three times more likely to agree to go on the zoo trip than were the students asked this smaller request alone (see left-hand side of Figure 8.7 on page 288).

Door-in-the-face technique
a technique to get people to comply with a request, whereby people are presented first with a large request, which they are expected to refuse, and then with a smaller, more reasonable request, to which it is hoped they will acquiesce

▶ Figure 8.7

TWO WAYS TO INCREASE
COMPLIANCE WITH A
REQUEST.

Both the door-in-the-face
technique and the foot-in-the-
door technique increase
compliance to a moderate
request. Which technique is
likely to lead to the most long-
term compliance, whereby
people agree to repeated
moderate requests? See the
text for the answer.

(Adapted from Cialdini et al.,
1975; Freedman & Fraser, 1966)

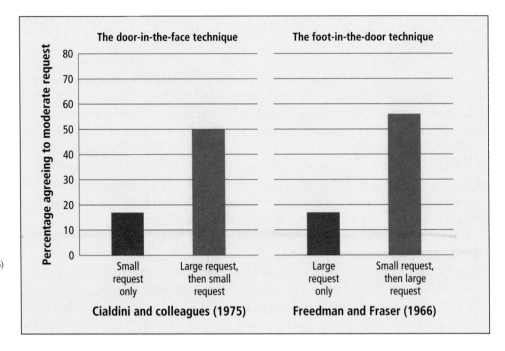

Reciprocity norm

a social norm stating that
receiving anything positive
from another person
requires you to reciprocate
(or behave similarly) in
response

Why does the door-in-the-face technique work? The answer lies in the **reciprocity norm,** which says that if people do something nice for us, we should reciprocate by doing something nice for them (Cialdini & Trost, 1998; Cialdini, Green, & Rusch, 1992; Uehara, 1995; Whatley et al., 1999). Salespeople and charities often capitalize on this tendency for people to follow the reciprocity norm mindlessly. They give us a small gift, such as greeting cards, personalized address labels, or free food to taste in the grocery store. Their plan is to make us feel obligated to reciprocate by buying their product or giving money to their cause (Church, 1993; James & Bolstein, 1992). To illustrate how strong the reciprocity norm is—and how mindlessly people follow it—one researcher chose some names at random out of the telephone book and sent each person a Christmas card, signed with his name (Kunz & Woolcott, 1976). Most people sent a card back to him, even though he was a complete stranger!

In the case of the door-in-the-face technique, the reciprocity norm is invoked when the person backs down from an extreme request to a smaller one. This puts pressure on us to reciprocate by moderating our position too—from an outright "no" to a "well, okay, I guess so." We feel as if the requester is doing us a favour by changing his or her position, trying to meet us halfway; because of the reciprocity norm, we then feel obligated to return the favour and appear reasonable, too.

One disadvantage of the door-in-the-face technique is that it is likely to be short-lived. Once people have agreed to the smaller request, they have met their obligation by meeting the requester halfway; therefore, they will not be more likely to agree to subsequent requests. Suppose, for example, that your goal is to get people to donate money to the Canadian Heart Association on a regular basis. Once you have retreated from your request for $500 to a more reasonable request for $5 and your neighbour has met you

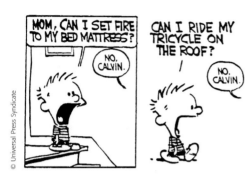

◀ Calvin tries the door-in-the-face technique.

halfway by agreeing, his or her obligation is over. If you ask for another $5 next month, he or she may well feel exploited, thinking, "This person sure is pushy. You'd think I'd get a break after being so reasonable last time." So what should you do if you want long-term compliance?

THE FOOT-IN-THE-DOOR TECHNIQUE

Before answering the question as to what you should do if you want long-term compliance, put yourself in the following situation. You are participating in a study in order to fulfil your Introductory Psychology research requirement. At the end of the study, the experimenter asks if you would mind spending 5 or 10 minutes rating some materials for her next study. You agree to help her out. Then, she makes another request: Would you volunteer to spend a few extra hours participating in research—over and above the hours required for your research requirement—so that some graduate students can complete their studies?

This is a situation in which some University of Western Ontario students found themselves a few years ago (Gorassini & Olson, 1995). They were participants in a study on the **foot-in-the-door technique**, a compliance technique in which people are presented first with a small request, to which they are expected to acquiesce, followed by a larger request, to which it is hoped they will also acquiesce. The expression *foot-in-the-door* comes from salespeople who discovered that they were more likely to make a sale if they could get the customer to agree to an initial, smaller request, such as letting them into the house to display their products. This technique is thus the opposite of the door-in-the-face method. Does this technique work? According to the personal experience of one of your authors (Beverley Fehr), this technique is quite effective—even when used on a social psychologist who is familiar with it! Here is the story:

> I was a new assistant professor at the University of Winnipeg, teaching psychology courses for the first time. In October of that year, my department chair approached me and made a request: Would I agree to teach the Social Psychology class of a colleague who had become ill? It would only involve a class or two. . . . I was extremely busy preparing lectures for my own classes, but I reluctantly agreed. After all, it was only a class or two. . . . At the end of that week, my department chair made another request: Would I be kind enough to teach my colleague's class for another week while things got sorted out? Again,

Foot-in-the-door technique
a technique to get people to comply with a request, whereby people are presented first with a small request, to which they are expected to acquiesce, followed by a larger request, to which it is hoped they will also acquiesce

© Universal Press Syndicate

I reluctantly agreed. Before I knew it, I had taught the rest of the course, and in December I found myself making up the final exam and grading it!

I am convinced that if my department chair had come to me at the outset and presented only the large request ("Would you teach someone else's class for the rest of the semester and compose the final exam and grade it?"), I would have explained that I already had more than a full schedule teaching my own classes for the first time, and therefore, unfortunately, I would have to decline.

The effectiveness of the foot-in-the-door technique is not limited to the personal experience of your authors. In a classic study, Jonathan Freedman and Scott Fraser (1966) tested whether homeowners would agree to put up a large, obtrusive sign in their front yards that said "Drive Carefully." When someone came to their door and asked the homeowners to do this, only 17 percent agreed. But what if they had agreed earlier to a smaller request? The researchers first asked a different group of homeowners to sign a petition indicating that they were in favour of safe driving. Just about everyone agreed to this innocuous request. Two weeks later, a different individual approached these homeowners and asked them to put the sign in their front yard. Though the sign was just as big and obtrusive to these people as to those in the control group, who had not been contacted earlier, they were more than three times more likely to agree to put it in their front yard (see right-hand side of Figure 8.7 on page 288).

A recent meta analysis confirms the effectiveness of the foot-in-the-door technique (Burger, 1999). Interestingly, it works for a very different reason than does the door-in-the-face technique. Instead of invoking a reciprocity norm, it triggers a change in self-perception. By agreeing to the small request, people come to view themselves as the kind of person who helps others. Once this self-image is in place, it makes people more likely to agree to the second, larger request, even when it comes later. Thus, if you are collecting money for the Canadian Heart Association and want your neighbours to donate on a long-term basis, first ask them for a small amount, such as 50 cents or $1. If they agree, they will come to view themselves as the kind of people who give to this worthy cause, increasing the likelihood that future donations will be forthcoming (Burger, 1986; Cialdini, 1993; Cialdini, Trost, & Newsom, 1995; Dillard, 1991; Dolin & Booth-Butterfield, 1995).

LOWBALLING

Lowballing

an unscrupulous strategy whereby a salesperson induces a customer to agree to purchase a product at a very low cost, then subsequently raises the price; frequently, the customer will still make the purchase at the inflated price

Another technique for inducing compliance is called **lowballing** (Cialdini et al., 1978; Weyant, 1996). Robert Cialdini, a distinguished social psychologist, temporarily joined the sales force of an automobile dealership to observe this technique closely. Here's how it works: You enter an automobile showroom, intent on buying a particular car. Having already priced it at several dealerships, you know you can purchase it for about $22 000. You are approached by a personable, middle-aged man, who tells you he can sell you one for $20 000. Excited by the bargain, you agree to the deal and, at the salesperson's request, write out a cheque for the down payment.

Meanwhile, you rub your hands in glee as you imagine yourself driving home in your shiny new bargain. But alas, 10 minutes later the salesperson returns, looking forlorn. He tells you that in his zeal to give you a good deal, he made an error in calculation and the

◀ Car salespeople frequently use a high-pressure technique whereby they make the customer feel as if he or she has entered into an irrevocable agreement.

sales manager caught it. The price of the car actually comes to $22 499. You are disappointed. Moreover, you are pretty sure you can get it a bit cheaper elsewhere. The decision to buy is not irrevocable. Yet, research by Cialdini and colleagues (1978) suggests, far more people will go ahead with the deal than if the original asking price had been $22 499, even though the reason for purchasing the car from this particular dealer—the bargain price—no longer exists. Why?

There are at least three reasons that lowballing works. First, while the customer's decision to buy is certainly reversible, a commitment of sorts does exist, due to the act of signing a cheque for a down payment. This creates the illusion of irrevocability, even though, if the car buyer really thought about it, he or she would quickly realize it is a nonbinding contract. However, in the razzle-dazzle world of high-pressure sales, even temporary illusion can have powerful consequences. Second, this commitment triggered the anticipation of an exciting event: driving out with a new car. To thwart the anticipated event (by not going ahead with the deal) would produce disappointment. Third, although the final price is substantially higher than the customer thought it would be, it is probably only slightly higher than the price at another dealership. Under these circumstances, the customer in effect says, "Oh, what the heck. I'm already here, I've already filled out the forms, I've already written out the cheque—why wait?" And off he or she goes, in a shiny, new car.

Obedience to Authority

The kinds of compliance we have just discussed can be annoying; a skillful salesperson, for example, can make us buy something we don't really need. Rarely, however, do such instances of everyday compliance have life-or-death consequences. Yet, unfortunately,

Obedience

conformity in response to the commands of an authority figure

another kind of social influence can be extremely serious and even tragic—**obedience,** or conformity in response to the commands of an authority figure, to hurt or kill a fellow human being. Consider the My Lai massacre in Vietnam. On the morning of March 16, 1968, in the midst of the Vietnam War, a company of American soldiers boarded helicopters that would take them to the village of My Lai. One of the helicopter pilots radioed that he saw Vietcong soldiers below, and so the American soldiers jumped off the helicopters with rifles firing. They soon realized the pilot was wrong: There were no enemy soldiers. Instead, the soldiers found several villagers—all women, children, and elderly men—cooking their breakfast over small fires. Inexplicably, the leader of the platoon, Lieutenant William Calley, ordered one of the soldiers to kill the villagers. Other soldiers began firing, and the carnage spread. The Americans rounded up and systematically murdered all the villagers of My Lai. They shoved women and children into a ravine and shot them; they threw hand grenades into huts of cowering villagers. Though no one knows the exact number of deaths, the estimates range from 450 to 500 people (Hersch, 1970; Time, 1969).

Why did the soldiers obey Lieutenant Calley's order to kill the innocent villagers? We suspect that all of the reasons people conform combined to produce this atrocity. The behaviour of the other soldiers made the killing seem like the right thing to do (informational influence); the soldiers wanted to avoid rejection and ridicule from their peers (normative influence); and the soldiers followed the obedience to authority social norm too readily, without questioning or taking personal responsibility for what they were doing (mindless conformity). It was the power of these conformity pressures, not personality defects in the American soldiers, that led to the tragedy. This makes the incident all the more frightening because it implies that similar incidents can occur with any group of soldiers if similar conformity pressures are present.

The twentieth century was marked by repeated atrocities and genocides—in Germany, Ukraine, Rwanda, Cambodia, Bosnia, Afghanistan, among others. Thus, one

▶ Under strong social pressure, individuals will conform to the group, even when this means doing something immoral. During the Vietnam War, American soldiers massacred several hundred Vietnamese civilians—old men, women, and children—in the village of My Lai. This award-winning photograph of some of the victims chilled the nation. Why did the soldiers commit this atrocity? As you read this chapter, you will see how the social influence pressures of conformity and obedience can cause decent people to comment indecent acts.

of the most important questions facing the world's inhabitants is, where does obedience end and personal responsibility begin? The philosopher Hannah Arendt (1965) argues that most participants in the Holocaust were not sadists or psychopaths who enjoyed the mass murder of innocent people, but ordinary citizens subjected to complex and powerful social pressures. She covered the trial of Adolf Eichmann, the Nazi official responsible for the transportation of Jews to the death camps, and concluded that he was not the monster that many people made him out to be, but a commonplace bureaucrat like any other bureaucrat, who did what he was told without questioning his orders (Miller, 1995).

Our point is not that the soldiers at My Lai, Adolf Eichmann, or, closer to home, the Canadian peacekeepers who killed Shidane Arone in Somalia be excused for the crimes they committed. The point is that it is too easy to explain their behaviour as the acts of madmen. It is more fruitful—and indeed more frightening—to view their behaviour as the acts of ordinary people exposed to extraordinary social influence. But how do we know whether this interpretation is correct? How can we be sure that it was social influence and not the work of evil people that produced these atrocities? The way to find out is to study social pressure in the laboratory under controlled conditions. We could take a sample of ordinary citizens, subject them to various kinds of social influence, and see to what extent they will conform and obey. Can an experimenter influence ordinary people to commit immoral acts, such as inflicting severe pain on an innocent bystander? Stanley Milgram (1963, 1974, 1976) decided to find out, in what has become the most famous series of studies in social psychology.

Imagine you were a participant in one of Milgram's studies. You answer an ad in the paper asking for participants in a study on memory and learning. When you arrive at the laboratory, you meet another participant, a 47-year-old, somewhat overweight, pleasant-looking fellow. The experimenter explains that one of you will play the role of a teacher and the other that of a learner. You draw a slip of paper out of a hat and discover that you

◀ Victims of the Holocaust, Nordhausen, April 1945. According to social psychologists, most of the German guards and citizens who participated in the Holocaust were not madmen but ordinary people exposed to extraordinary social influences.

will be the teacher. It turns out that your job is to teach the other participant a list of word pairs (e.g., blue–box, nice–day) and then test him on the list. The experimenter instructs you to deliver an electric shock to the learner whenever he makes a mistake, because the purpose of the study is to examine the effects of punishment on learning.

You watch as the other participant—the learner—is strapped into a chair in an adjacent room and electrodes are attached to his arm. You are seated in front of a shock generator whose 30 switches deliver varying levels of shock in 15-volt increments, from 15 to 450 volts. There are labels accompanying these switches, from "Slight Shock," to "Danger: Severe Shock," to an ominous "XXX" beside the highest levels (see the photos on the following page). The experimenter tells you that the first time the learner makes a mistake, you should give him a shock of 15 volts—the smallest amount—and then increase the amount by 15 volts for each subsequent mistake he makes. So you will know what the shocks feel like, the experimenter gives you a sample shock of 45 volts, which is rather painful.

You read the list of word pairs to the learner and then begin the testing phase. After announcing the first word of a pair, you give four possible answers; the learner responds by pressing one of four switches, which illuminates a light on the answer box in front of you. Everything begins smoothly, as the learner gets the first few answers right. Then he gets some wrong, and, as instructed, you deliver the shocks. At this point, you are probably becoming concerned about the number and severity of the shocks you will have to give. When you get to the 75-volt level, the learner, whom you can hear over an intercom, emits a painful "Ugh!" Perhaps you pause and ask the experimenter what you should do. "Please continue," he responds. As the learner continues to make mistakes, you deliver a few more shocks. The learner protests, shouting, "Ugh! That's all! Get me out of here!" You look at the experimenter with grave concern. He tells you, "It is absolutely essential that you continue" (see Figure 8.8 on page 295).

What would you do? How many people do you think would continue to obey the experimenter and increase the level of shock until they had delivered the maximum amount—450 volts?

When this question was posed to psychology majors at Yale University, they estimated that only about 1 percent of the population would go to this extreme. A sample of middle-class adults and a panel of psychiatrists made similar predictions. However, from our discussion of conformity thus far, you are probably not as optimistic. Whereas no one

▶ Left: The shock generator used in the Milgram experiments. Right: The learner (an accomplice of the experimenter) is strapped into the chair, and electrodes are attached to his arm.

(Adapted from Milgram, 1974)

Transcript of Learner's Protests in Milgram's Obedience Experiment

75 volts Ugh!
90 volts Ugh!
105 volts Ugh! (louder)
120 volts Ugh! Hey this really hurts.
135 volts Ugh!!
150 volts Ugh!!! Experimenter! That's all. Get me out of here. I told you I had heart trouble. My heart's starting to bother me now. Get me out of here, please. My heart's starting to bother me. I refuse to go on. Let me out.
165 volts Ugh! Let me out! (shouting)
180 volts Ugh! I can't stand the pain. Let me out of here! (shouting)
195 volts Ugh! Let me out of here. Let me out of here. My heart's bothering me. Let me out of here! You have no right to keep me here! Let me out! Let me out of here! Let me out! Let me out of here! My heart's bothering me. Let me out! Let me out!
210 volts Ugh!! Experimenter! Get me out of here. I've had enough. I won't be in the experiment any more.
225 volts Ugh!
240 volts Ugh!
255 volts Ugh! Get me out of here.
270 volts (Agonized scream) Let me out of here. Let me out of here. Let me out of here. Let me out. Do you hear? Let me out of here.
285 volts (Agonized scream)
300 volts (Agonized scream) I absolutely refuse to answer any more. Get me out of here. You can't hold me here. Get me out. Get me out of here.
315 volts (Intensely agonized scream) I told you I refuse to answer. I'm no longer part of this experiment.
330 volts (Intense and prolonged agonized scream) Let me out of here. Let me out of here. My heart's bothering me. Let me out, I tell you. (Hysterically) Let me out of here. Let me out of here. You have no right to hold me here. Let me out! Let me out! Let me out of here! Let me out!

Instructions Used by Experimenter to Achieve Obedience

Prod 1: Please continue, or Please go on.

Prod 2: The experiment requires that you continue.

Prod 3: It is absolutely essential that you continue.

Prod 4: You have no other choice; you must go on.

The prods were always made in sequence. Only if prod 1 had been unsuccessful could prod 2 be used. If the subject refused to obey the experimenter after prod 4, the experiment was terminated. The experimenter's tone of voice was at all times firm, but not impolite. The sequence was begun anew on each occasion that the participant balked or showed reluctance to follow orders.

Special prods: If the participant asked whether the learner was likely to suffer permanent physical injury, the experimenter said: Although the shocks may be painful, there is no permanent tissue damage, so please go on. [Followed by prods 2, 3, and 4 if necessary.]

If the participant said that the learner did not want to go on, the experimenter replied: Whether the learner likes it or not, you must go on until he has learned all the word pairs correctly. So please go on. [Followed by prods 2, 3, and 4 if necessary.]

◀ **Figure 8.8**

TRANSCRIPT OF THE LEARNER'S PROTESTS IN MILGRAM'S OBEDIENCE STUDY.

Transcript of the prods used by the experimenter to get people to continue giving shocks.

(Adapted from Milgram, 1963, 1974)

would have believed that such travesties as the Holocaust or My Lai could have occurred, they did. Like the people who committed these horrific acts, most of Milgram's participants succumbed to the pressure of an authority figure. The average maximum amount of shock delivered was 360 volts, and 62.5 percent of the participants delivered the 450-volt shock—the maximum amount. A full 80 percent of the participants continued giving the shocks even after the learner, who earlier had mentioned that he had a heart condition, screamed, "Let me out of here! Let me out of here! My heart's bothering me. Let me out of here! . . . Get me out of here! I've had enough. I won't be in the experiment any more" (Milgram, 1974).

It is important to note that the learner was actually an accomplice of the experimenter and play-acted his role; he did not receive any actual shocks. It is equally important to note that the study was very convincingly done, so that people believed they really were shocking the learner. Here is Milgram's description of one participant's response to the teacher role:

> I observed a mature and initially poised businessman enter the laboratory smiling and confident. Within 20 minutes he was reduced to a twitching, stuttering wreck, who was rapidly approaching a point of nervous collapse. He constantly pulled on his earlobe, and twisted his hands. At one point he pushed his fist into his forehead and muttered, "Oh God, let's stop it." And yet he continued to respond to every word of the experimenter, and obeyed to the end (Milgram, 1963).

Why did so many research participants (who ranged in age from their twenties to their fifties and included blue-collar, white-collar, and professional workers) conform to the wishes of the experimenter, to the point where they (at least in their own minds) were inflicting great pain on another human being? Why were the students, middle-class adults, and psychiatrists so wrong in their predictions about what people would do? Each of the reasons that explain why people conform combined in a dangerous way, causing Milgram's participants to obey—just as the soldiers did at My Lai. Let's take a close look at how this worked in the Milgram experiments.

THE ROLE OF NORMATIVE SOCIAL INFLUENCE

First, it is clear that normative pressures made it difficult for people to refuse to continue. As we have seen, if someone really wants us to do something, it can be difficult to say no. This is particularly true when the person is in a position of authority over us. Milgram's participants probably believed that if they refused to continue, the experimenter would be disappointed, hurt, or maybe even angry—all of which put pressure on them to continue. It is important to note that this study, unlike the Asch study, was set up so the experimenter actively attempted to get people to conform, giving such stern commands as "It is absolutely essential that you continue." When an authority figure is so insistent that we obey, it is difficult to say no (Blass, 1993, 1996; Hamilton, Sanders, & McKearney, 1995; Miller, 1986).

The fact that normative pressures were present in the Milgram experiments is clear from a variation of the study he conducted. This time there were three teachers, two of whom were confederates of the experimenter. One confederate was instructed to read the list of word pairs; the other was instructed to tell the learner whether his response was correct. The (real) participant's job was to deliver the shocks, increasing their severity with each error, as in the original experiment. At 150 volts, when the learner gave his first vehement protest, the first confederate refused to continue despite the experimenter's command that he do so. At 210 volts, the second confederate refused to continue. The result? Seeing their peers disobey made it much easier for the actual participant to disobey as well. In this experiment, only 10 percent of the participants gave the maximum level of shock (see Figure 8.9). This result is similar to Asch's finding that people did not conform nearly as much when one accomplice bucked the majority and consistently gave the correct answer.

THE ROLE OF INFORMATIONAL SOCIAL INFLUENCE

Despite the power of the normative pressures in Milgram's original study, they are not the sole reason people complied. The experimenter was authoritative and insistent, but he did not point a gun at participants and tell them to "conform or else." The participants were free to get up and leave any time they wanted to. Why didn't they, especially when the experimenter was a stranger they had never met before and probably would never see again?

As we saw earlier, when people are in a confusing situation and unsure of what they should do, they use other people to reach a definition of the situation. Informational social influence is especially powerful when the situation is ambiguous, when it is a crisis, and when the other people in the situation have some expertise. The situation faced by Milgram's participants was clearly confusing, unfamiliar, and upsetting. It all seemed straightforward enough when the experimenter explained it to them, but then it turned into something else altogether. The learner cried out in pain, but the experimenter told the participant that while the shocks were painful they did not cause any permanent tissue damage. The participant didn't want to hurt anyone, but he or she had agreed to be in the study and to follow directions. When in such a state of conflict, it was only natural

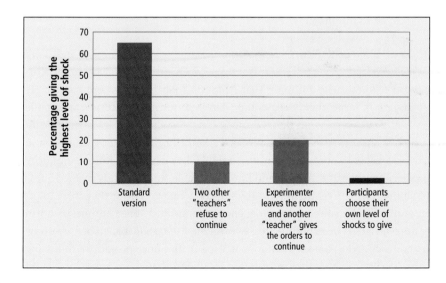

◀ Figure 8.9

THE RESULTS OF DIFFERENT VERSIONS OF THE MILGRAM EXPERIMENT.

Obedience is highest in the standard version, where the participant is ordered to deliver increasing levels of shock to another person (left panel). Obedience drops when other participants model disobedience or when the authority figure is not present (two middle panels). Finally, when no orders are given to increase the shocks, almost no participants do so (right panel). The contrast in behaviour between the far-left and far-right panels indicates just how powerful the social norm of obedience is.

(Adapted from Milgram, 1974)

for the participants to use an expert—the experimenter—to help them decide what they should do (Darley, 1995; Krakow & Blass, 1995; Meeus & Raaijmakers, 1995).

Another version of the experiment that Milgram performed supports the idea that informational influence was operative. This version was identical to the original one except for two critical changes. First, the experimenter never said which shock levels were to be given, leaving this decision up to the teacher (the real participant). Second, the situation was arranged so the experimenter was "unexpectedly" called away from the experiment. The participant was instructed to continue on, and another "teacher"—actually, a confederate, who was supposedly there to record how long it took the learner to respond—said that he had just thought of a good system: How about if they increased the level of shock each time the learner made a mistake? He insisted that the real participant follow this procedure.

Note that in this situation, the expertise of the person giving the commands has been removed. And in this situation, people were much less likely to use the non-expert as a source of information about how they should respond. As seen in Figure 8.9, in this version compliance dropped from 65 percent giving the maximum amount of shock to only 20 percent. (The fact that 20 percent still complied suggests that some people were so uncertain about what to do that they used even a non-expert as a guide.)

An additional variation conducted by Milgram underscores the importance of authority figures as experts in eliciting such conformity and obedience. In this variation, two experimenters gave the real participants their orders. At 150 volts, when the learner first cried out that he wanted to stop, the two experimenters began to disagree about whether they should continue the study. At this point, 100 percent of the participant–teachers stopped responding. Note that nothing the victim ever did caused all the participants to stop obeying; however, when the authorities' definition of the situation became unclear, the participants broke out of their conforming role.

OTHER REASONS WHY WE OBEY

Both normative and informational social influences were very strong in Milgram's experiments. However, there are additional reasons that must be considered in order to explain fully why people acted so inhumanely.

Conforming to the Wrong Norm
Sometimes we are on automatic pilot and don't realize that the social norm we are following is inappropriate or not applicable to the situation we are in. We don't mean to imply that Milgram's participants were completely mindless, or unaware of what they were doing. All were terribly concerned about the plight of the victim. The problem was that they were caught in a web of conflicting norms, and it was difficult to determine which one to follow. At the beginning of the experiment, it was perfectly reasonable to obey the norm that says, "Obey expert, legitimate authority figures." The experimenter was confident and knowledgeable, and the study seemed a reasonable test of an interesting hypothesis. So, why not cooperate and do as they were told?

However, gradually the rules of the game changed, and this "obey authority" norm was no longer appropriate. The experimenter, who seemed so reasonable before, was now asking people to inflict great pain on a fellow participant. But once people are following one norm, it can be difficult to switch midstream, realizing that this norm is no longer appropriate and that another norm, "Do not inflict needless harm on a fellow human being," should be followed. We suspect that if halfway through the experiment Milgram's participants had been told to take a 15-minute break and go sit in a room by themselves, rather than continue with the fast-paced experiment, many more would have realized that they should no longer follow the "obey authority" norm and would have refused to continue.

Self-Justification   Second, it is important to remember that the experimenter asked people to increase the shocks in very small increments. The participants did not go from giving a small shock to giving a potentially lethal one. Instead, at any given point they were faced with the decision about whether to increase the amount of shock they had just given by 15 volts. As we saw in Chapter 6, every time a person makes an important or difficult decision, dissonance is produced, with resultant pressures to reduce it. An effective way of reducing dissonance produced by a difficult decision is to decide that the decision was fully justified. However, because reducing dissonance provides a justification for the preceding action, in some situations it makes a person vulnerable to pressures leading to an escalation of the chosen activity.

Thus, in the Milgram study, once the participants agreed to administer the first shock, it created pressure on them to continue to obey. As the participants administered each successive level of shock, they had to justify it in their minds. Once a particular shock level was justified, it became very difficult for them to find a place where they could draw the line and stop. How could they say, in effect, "Okay, I gave him 200 volts, but not 215— never 215"? Each succeeding justification laid the groundwork for the next shock and would have been dissonant with quitting; 215 volts is not that different from 200, and 230 is not that different from 215. Those who did break off the series did so against enormous internal pressure to continue.

Mika Haritos-Fatouros (1988; Staub, 1989) reports that this incremental approach was used by the Greek military dictatorship of the late 1960s to train torturers. In his interviews with former torturers, Haritos-Fatouros learned that their first contact with political prisoners was to bring them food and "occasionally" give them some blows. Next, they were put on guard while others conducted torture sessions. Next, they would take part in a few group floggings or beatings. The last step, being in charge of a torture ses-

◀ Blind obedience to the "obey authority" norm can be countered by individuals questioning the morality of what the authority is ordering them to do.

sion, "was announced suddenly to the [man] by the commander-in-chief without leaving him any time for reflection" (Haritos-Fatouros, 1988).

It's Not about Aggression   Before leaving our discussion of the Milgram studies, we should mention one other possible interpretation of his results. Did the participants act so inhumanely because there is an evil side to human nature, lurking just below the surface, ready to be expressed on the flimsiest excuse? After all, it was socially acceptable to inflict harm on another person in the Milgram experiment; in fact, participants were ordered to do so. Perhaps this factor allowed the expression of a universal aggressive urge. To test this hypothesis, Milgram conducted another version of his study. Everything was the same except that the experimenter told the participants they could choose any level of shock they wished to give the learner when he made a mistake. Milgram gave people permission to use the highest levels, telling them there was a lot to be learned from all levels of shock. This instruction should have allowed any aggressive urges to be expressed unchecked. Instead, the participants chose to give very mild shocks (see Figure 8.9, on page 297). Only 2.5 percent of the participants gave the maximum amount of shock. Thus, the Milgram studies do not show that people have an evil streak that shines through when the surface is scratched. Instead, these studies demonstrate that social pressures can combine in insidious ways to make humane people act in an inhumane manner. Let us conclude this chapter with the words of Stanley Milgram (1976):

> Even Eichmann was sickened when he toured the concentration camps, but in order to participate in mass murder he had only to sit at a desk and shuffle papers. At the same time the man in the camp who actually dropped Cyclon-B into the gas chambers is able to justify his behaviour on the grounds that he is only following orders from above. Thus there is fragmentation of the total human act; no one man decides to carry out the evil act and is confronted with its consequences. The person who assumes full responsibility for the act has evaporated. Perhaps this is the most common characteristic of socially organized evil in modern society.

SUMMARY

In this chapter, we focused on **conformity**, or how people change their behaviour due to the real (or imagined) influence of others. We found that there are two main reasons people conform: informational and normative social influences.

Informational social influence occurs when people do not know the correct (or best) thing to do or say. This reaction typically occurs in *ambiguous*, *confusing*, or *crisis* situations, where the definition of the situation is unclear. People look to the behaviour of others as an important source of information and use it to choose appropriate courses of action for themselves. *Experts* are powerful

sources of influence, since they typically have the most information about appropriate responses.

Using others as a source of information can backfire, however, as when people panic because others are doing so. **Contagion** occurs when emotions and behaviours spread rapidly throughout a group. You can best resist the inappropriate use of others as a source of information by checking the information you are getting against your internal moral compass.

Normative social influence occurs for a different reason. We change our behaviour to match that of others not because they seem to know better what is going on, but because we want to remain a member of the group, continue to gain the advantages of group membership, and avoid the pain of ridicule and rejection. We conform to the group's **social norms**—implicit or explicit rules for acceptable behaviours, values, and attitudes. Normative social influence can occur even in unambiguous situations; people will conform to others for normative reasons even if they know that what they are doing is wrong. Whereas informational social influence usually results in **private acceptance**, wherein people genuinely believe in what other people are doing or saying, normative social influence usually results in **public compliance** but not private acceptance of other people's ideas and behaviours.

Social impact theory specifies when normative social influence is most likely to occur, by referring to the *strength*, *immediacy*, and *number* of the group members. We are more likely to conform when the group is one we care about, when the group members are unanimous in their thoughts or behaviours, and when the group size is three or more. Failure to respond to normative social influence can be painful. We can resist inappropriate normative pressures by gathering **idiosyncrasy credits** over time, from a group whose membership we value.

Social influence operates on many levels in social life. It influences our eating habits, hobbies, fashion, and so on. Social influence is apparent in societal messages about the ideal body image for women and men, thereby contributing to feelings of dissatisfaction with one's body and negative behaviours such as eating disorders and steroid use.

Minority influence, whereby a minority of group members influence the beliefs and behaviour of the majority, can occur under certain conditions. In order to influence a majority, minority group members must present their views consistently. Minorities influence majori-ties via informational, rather than normative, social influence.

Another form of social influence is **compliance**—conforming in response to requests from others. An effective compliance technique is the **door-in-the-face technique**, where a requester starts out with a big request in order to get people to agree to a second, smaller request. This technique works because of the **reciprocity norm**; when the requester retreats from the larger to the smaller request, it puts pressure on people to reciprocate by agreeing to the smaller request. The **foot-in-the-door technique** is also effective; here the requester starts out with a very small request to get people to agree to a larger request. Another effective compliance technique is **lowballing**, in which a person makes a commitment to an attractive offer. The deal is then changed so the offer is no longer as attractive. Nevertheless, the person tends to go along with this much less attractive deal.

One of the most insidious forms of social influence is **obedience**—conforming to the commands of an authority figure. In Milgram's classic study of obedience, informational and normative pressures combined to cause chilling levels of obedience, to the point where a majority of participants administered what they thought were near-lethal shocks to a fellow human being. In addition, the participants were caught in a web of conflicting social norms, and were asked to increase the level of shocks in small increments. After justifying to themselves that they had delivered one level of shock, it was very difficult for people to decide that a slightly higher level of shock was wrong. Unfortunately, the conditions that produced such extreme antisocial behaviour in Milgram's laboratory have been present in real-life tragedies, such as the Holocaust and the mass murders at My Lai.

IF YOU ARE INTERESTED

Cialdini, R. B. (1993). *Influence: Science and practice* (3rd ed.). New York: HarperCollins. An extremely readable and entertaining account of research on conformity, with applications to everyday life.

Conroy, Pat (1980). *The lords of discipline.* A story of conformity and disobedience set in a military academy. The main character ultimately defies social norms, and puts his life on the line, to protect the lone African-American cadet from the white students' violence.

Elliot, Stephan (Director). (1994). *The adventures of Priscilla, queen of the desert* [Film]. A hilarious and heartwarming tale of three male transvestite entertainers who take their show on the road in the Australian outback. Needless to say, the townspeople have never seen such nonconformity. Remade in the United States as *To Wong Foo, with love, Julie Newmar,* starring Patrick Swayze and Wesley Snipes.

Keneally, Thomas (1982). *Schindler's list.* The compelling, true story of how one man protected and saved 1000 Polish Jews from certain death in Hitler's concentration camps. In particular, it traces his metamorphosis from a self-centred, opportunistic businessman to a compassionate humanitarian who bravely disobeyed the Third Reich. The film based on this work won the Academy Award for Best Picture.

Lumet, Sydney (1957). *12 angry men* [Film]. A gripping account of jury deliberations, this film stars Henry Fonda as the lone dissenter on the jury, desperately trying to convince his peers that their judgment of guilty in a murder case is wrong.

Milgram, S. (1974). *Obedience to authority: An experimental view.* New York: Harper & Row. A detailed description of the most famous studies in social psychology: those in which people were induced to deliver what they believed were lethal shocks to a fellow human being. Nearly 20 years after it was published, Milgram's book remains a poignant and insightful account of obedience to authority.

Salinger, J. D. (1951). *The catcher in the rye.* The classic "coming of age" novel, still a delight no matter how old you are. Follow teenager Holden Caulfield for a few days as he discourses on "the phonies" and other less-than-attractive aspects of adult conformity.

Scorsese, Martin (Director). (1993). *The age of innocence* [Film]. The tale of star-crossed lovers (Daniel Day-Lewis and Michelle Pfeiffer) caught up in the constricting and unforgiving social norms of upper-class New York in the 1870s. Based on a novel by Edith Wharton.

Sherif, M. (1936). *The psychology of social norms.* New York: Harper. An entertaining account of Sherif's study of informational social influence, wherein people judged how much a light was moving. It is still worth reading today.

Turner, J. C. (1991). *Social influence.* Pacific Grove, CA: Brooks/Cole. An in-depth account of social psychological research on social influence and conformity.

Wharton, Edith (1905). *House of mirth.* A huge bestseller upon its publication, this novel chronicles the elaborate and suffocating conformity of late nineteenth-century New York society, and how one young woman is destroyed by it.

Zanna, M. P., Olson, J. M., & Herman, C. P. (1987). *Social influence: The Ontario Symposium* (Vol. 5). Hillsdale, NJ: Lawrence Erlbaum. A collection of papers, by prominent social psychologists, presented at the University of Waterloo as part of the 1984 Ontario Symposium series. The chapters in Part II of this volume, Compliance and Conformity, are especially relevant to this chapter.

WEBLINKS

www.ex.ac.uk/~PWebley/psy1002/asch.html
The Asch Conformity Effect
This site provides a brief discussion and summary of follow-up research on the Asch conformity studies.

www.science.wayne.edu/~wpoff/cor/grp/influenc.html
Influence
This site provides a concise but thorough overview of social psychological principles and research on influence.

Group Processes
influence in social groups

IN 1998, CANADIAN MILITARY OFFICIALS MADE A DECISION TO vaccinate Canadian soldiers against anthrax, a deadly biological weapon, before being deployed to the Gulf War. One soldier who had served in the military for 26 years, Sergeant Michael Kipling, refused to be vaccinated. He had serious concerns about health risks associated with the drug. For his disobedience, Kipling was court martialled.

During the court martial, several facts came to light. One fact was that the anthrax vaccine was not licensed for use in Canada, and therefore Health Canada had recommended that the military seek informed consent from soldiers before administering the drug. Another fact was that the military's legal advisers had made a similar recommendation. However, Canada's highest military commanders decided to ignore the advice of Health Canada and that of their own lawyers, and imposed the vaccine on soldiers without their consent.

What were the consequences of making this decision? One consequence is the debate raging over whether the medical symptoms experienced by half of the 4500 Canadians involved in the Gulf War are the result of the anthrax vaccine. Louise Richard, for example, was a healthy, athletic military nurse when she left for the Gulf in 1991. Now she is too ill to work. She suffers from fatigue, depression, memory loss, gastrointestinal problems, and excessive bleeding. She also has lost all of her hair and has started to lose her teeth. Military officials blame the medical symptoms experienced by Gulf War veterans on stress and possible exposure to chemical warfare. People like Michael Kipling and Louise Richard believe that the anthrax vaccine is to blame.

There was yet another, very serious, consequence of this decision. According to Canada's chief military judge, Colonel Guy Brais, who presided over Michael Kipling's court martial, the military's decision to impose the vaccine violated the human rights of soldiers such as Kipling. In his decision, Judge Brais agreed with the defence that the vaccine Kipling had been ordered to take could have been unsafe, and that his common law and

▶ Louise Richard before and after her tour of duty in the Gulf War. She believes that the anthrax vaccine is responsible for her mysterious illnesses.

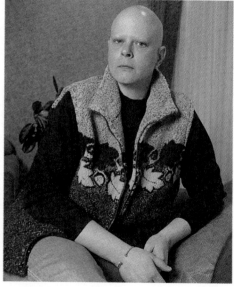

Charter rights were therefore violated. In his words, "The government . . . could never be justified to impose inoculation of soldiers with unsafe and dangerous vaccines" (Edmonds, 2000).

Why would military officials ignore the advice of Health Canada and their own lawyers, and impose a potentially unsafe vaccine on Canadian soldiers? Surely Canada's top military commanders wouldn't be prepared to place Canadian soldiers at risk? And surely they wouldn't want to administer a possibly dangerous substance without obtaining informed consent from the soldiers? Or would they?

In this chapter, we will focus on how people interact in groups, and how groups can end up making decisions that have tragic consequences.

Definitions: What Is a Group?

A **group** is defined as a collection of two or more people who interact with each other and are interdependent, in the sense that their needs and goals cause them to rely on one another (Cartwright & Zander, 1968; Lewin, 1948). Thus, groups are more than a bunch of people who happen to be occupying the same space. Rather, groups are people who have assembled together for a common purpose, such as citizens meeting to solve a community problem, or people who have gathered to blow off steam at a party.

Stop for a moment to think of the number of groups to which you belong. Don't forget to include your family, campus groups, community groups (such as churches or synagogues), sports teams, and more temporary groups (such as your classmates in a small seminar). All of these count as groups because you interact with the other group members and you are interdependent, in the sense that you influence them and they influence you.

Groups

a collection of two or more people who interact with each other and are interdependent, in the sense that their needs and goals cause them to rely on each other

WHY DO PEOPLE JOIN GROUPS?

Why do people join groups? Forming relationships with other people fulfills a number of basic human needs. So basic, in fact, that there may be an innate need to belong to social

◀ This group of five people interacts with each other. Each person's needs and goals cause them to influence each other.

groups. Roy Baumeister and Mark Leary (1995) argue that in our evolutionary past, there was a substantial survival advantage to establishing bonds with other people. People who bonded together were better able to hunt for and grow food, find mates, and care for children. Consequently, the need to belong has become innate and is present in all societies. Consistent with this view, people in all cultures are motivated to form relationships with other people and to resist the dissolution of these relationships (Gardner, Pickett, & Brewer, 2000; Manstead, 1997).

Not surprisingly, perhaps, groups become an important part of our identity, helping us to define who we are (Dion, 2000; Tropp & Wright, 2001). Research by James Cameron (1999) suggests that the groups to which we belong even play an important role in defining who we expect to be in the future. He assessed belongingness to a group by asking students at Mount Allison University how much they agreed with statements such as "In a group of Mount Allison students, I really feel that I belong." Feeling a part of the university was associated with positive self-esteem and well-being. Moreover, students who had a sense of belonging also believed that being a Mount Allison student would help them become the self they aspired to be in the future.

Group membership also plays an important role in motivating people to become involved in social change. For example, Patrick O'Neill (2000) examined collective action among a variety of groups, including board members of a transition house for battered women in Nova Scotia, peace activists in Vancouver, and members of a lower-class Montreal neighbourhood protesting the establishment of a toxic waste dump in their community. Across groups, O'Neill found that those who identified most strongly with their group were most likely to engage in social action. As discussed next, groups also help establish social norms, the explicit or implicit rules defining what is acceptable behaviour.

Social Norms   As we saw in Chapter 8, a powerful determinant of our behaviour is *social norms*. If you belong to a political party, you can probably think of social norms present in your group, such as whether you participate in protest marches and how you are supposed to feel about rival political parties. These norms may not be shared by the members of other groups to which you belong, such as your church or synagogue. Social norms are powerful determinants of our behaviour, as shown by what happens if people violate them too often: They are shunned by other group members and, in extreme cases, pressured to leave the group (Schacter, 1951; see Chapter 8).

Social roles

shared expectations in a group about how particular people are supposed to behave

Social Roles   Most groups also have well-defined **social roles**, which are shared expectations about how particular people are supposed to behave. Whereas norms specify how all group members should behave, roles specify how people who occupy certain positions in the group should behave. A boss and an employee in a business occupy different roles and are expected to act in different ways in that setting. Like social norms, roles can be very helpful, because people know what to expect from each other. When members of a group follow a set of clearly defined roles, they tend to be satisfied and perform well (Bastien & Hostager, 1988; Barley & Bechky, 1994).

There are, however, two potential costs to social roles. First, people can get so "into" a role that their personal identities and personalities are lost. Suppose, for example, that you agreed to take part in a two-week psychology experiment in which you were randomly assigned to play the role of either a prison guard or a prisoner in a simulated prison. You might think that the role you were assigned to play would not be very important; after all, everyone knows it is only an experiment and that people are just pretending to be guards or prisoners. Philip Zimbardo and his colleagues, however, had a different hypothesis. They believed that social roles can be so powerful that they "take over" our personal identities, and we become the role we are playing. To see if this is true, Zimbardo and colleagues conducted an unusual study. They built a mock prison in the basement of the psychology department at Stanford University and paid students to play the role of guard or prisoner (Haney, Banks, & Zimbardo, 1973). The role students played was determined by the flip of a coin. The guards were outfitted with a uniform of khaki shirts and pants, a whistle, a police nightstick, and reflecting sunglasses; the prisoners were outfitted with a loose-fitting smock with an identification number stamped on it, rubber sandals, a cap made from a nylon stocking, and a locked chain attached to one ankle.

The researchers planned to observe the students for two weeks, to see whether they began to act like real prison guards and prisoners. As it turned out, the students quickly assumed these roles—so much so that the researchers had to end the experiment after only six days. Many of the guards became quite abusive, thinking of creative ways of verbally harassing and humiliating the "prisoners." The prisoners became passive, helpless, and withdrawn. Some prisoners, in fact, became so anxious and depressed that they had to be released from the study earlier than others. Remember, everyone knew they were in a psychology experiment and that the "prison" was only make-believe. However, people got "into" their roles so much that their personal identities and sense of decency somehow were lost.

The second drawback of social roles is that there is a cost to acting inconsistently with the expectations associated with those roles. For example, part of the role of being a man

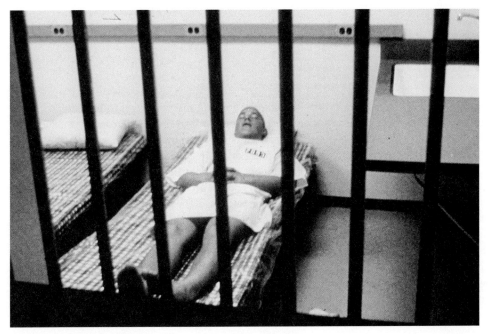

◀ Philip Zimbardo and his colleagues randomly assigned students to play the role of prisoner or guard in a mock prison. The students assumed these roles all too well. Those playing the role of guard became quite aggressive, whereas those playing the role of prisoner became passive, helpless, and withdrawn. People got "into" their roles so much that their personal identities and sense of decency somehow were lost.

in our society involves not wearing female attire, or even carrying a purse. In an essay titled "The Handbag," Alan Neal, host of the CBC Radio One show *The Other Story*, confides how uncomfortable it is for a man to hold a woman's purse, even briefly.

> It doesn't matter that I think of myself as being an enlightened, egalitarian male. There is something about being handed a woman's handbag in a mall that completely destroys me. In all honesty, I would prefer to be handed a squirming ferret by the tail. Because there is no manly way to hold a purse. You hold it by the little hand straps and your wrist automatically bends. Trying to sling it off the shoulder conjures up images of bra straps or spaghetti straps. The only strap I've ever worn was not exactly for public viewing (Neal, 2000).

Neal's obvious discomfort at deviating from the male role, though humorously described, derives from a very real intuition of what others will think of him if they see him carrying a purse in public. The Try It! exercise, below, describes a way you can experience role violation for yourself.

Gender Roles   Role expectations are especially problematic when they are arbitrary or unfair, such as societal expectations based on people's gender. In many cultures, women are expected to assume the role of wife and mother, with only limited opportunities to pursue other careers. In 1973, Ann Beuf conducted a study to determine whether the women's movement had influenced children's conceptions of occupational stereotypes in the direction of greater equality (Beuf, 1974). She asked American children between the ages of three and six, "What do you want to be when you grow up?" More than 70

Role Violation

Pick a behaviour that is part of gender roles in your culture and deliberately violate it. For example, if you are a male in Canada, you might decide to put on makeup or carry a purse to your next class. If you are female, you might decide to dress like a male for a formal occasion, by wearing a jacket and tie.

Keep a journal describing how others react to you. More than likely, you will encounter a good deal of social disapproval, such as people staring at you or questioning your behaviour. For this reason, you want to avoid role violations that are too extreme—consider what happened to Larry Goodwin after wearing women's clothing (see the photo on page 309).

The social pressure that is brought to bear on people who do not conform explains why it can be so difficult to break out of the roles to which we are assigned, even when those roles are arbitrary. Of course, there is safety in numbers; when enough people violate role expectations, others do not act nearly so negatively, and thus the roles begin to change. For example, it is now much more acceptable for men to wear earrings than it was 20 years ago. To illustrate this safety in numbers, enlist the help of several same-sex friends and violate the same role expectation together. Again, note carefully how people react to you. Did you encounter more or less social disapproval in the group than you did as an individual?

People are often punished for violating the expectations associated with their roles, even when such expectations are arbitrary. A man who wears women's clothing, for example, is likely to encounter a good deal of criticism. The man in this picture, Larry Goodwin, is a 51-year-old, heterosexual man who has been married for 29 years and has 2 children. The only part of the traditional male role he violates is that he loves to wear women's clothing. He has paid dearly for this role violation—his house has been vandalized, he has been arrested, and he nearly lost his job (Grove, 1997).

percent of the children chose stereotypical careers for themselves (e.g., police officer for boys; nurse for girls). She then asked another question that turned out to be quite revealing: "If you were a boy (girl), what would you be when you grow up?" Girls suddenly envisioned a world in which anything was possible. In fact, one girl believed that if she were a boy, she could fly like a bird. In sharp contrast, boys perceived that their opportunities would be severely restricted. One boy sighed heavily when asked the question and finally replied, "Oh, if I were a girl I'd have to grow up to be nothing."

More recently, Lupaschuk and Yewchuk (1998) asked children in grades 4 to 12, residing in a rural community in Alberta, what their lives would be like if they woke up the next day and discovered they were the other sex. The results showed that the occupational aspirations of boys and girls continue to be dominated by gender-role stereotyping. For example, a male junior high student remarked that if he were a girl, "People would expect me to do women's work like clean house or be a secretary." The researchers concluded that women are still constrained by expectations that they will pursue traditional occupations, and that child care and housework remain their responsibility. Thus, the roles that people play, and the expectations that come with those roles, can have powerful effects on people's feelings and behaviour (Wood et al., 1997).

THE COMPOSITION OF GROUPS

What do the groups to which you belong have in common? They probably vary in size from two or three members to several dozen members. Most social groups, however, range in size from two to six members (Desportes & Lemaine, 1998; Levine & Moreland,

1998). This is due in part to our definition of social groups as involving interaction between members. If groups become too large, you cannot interact with all of the members; for example, the college or university you attend is not a social group, because you are unlikely to meet and interact with every student there.

Another important feature of groups is that the members tend to be alike in age, sex, beliefs, and opinions (George, 1990; Levine & Moreland, 1998; Magaro & Ashbrook, 1985). The reason is twofold: First, groups tend to attract people who are similar to one another to begin with. Second, group members also become more similar to one another over time (Moreland, 1987).

Group cohesiveness

qualities of a group that bind members together and promote liking between members

Group Cohesiveness

Another important aspect of group composition is how tightly knit the group is. **Group cohesiveness** is defined as qualities of a group that bind members together and promote liking among them (Dion, 2000; Hogg, 1993; Prentice, Miller & Lightdale, 1994). If a group has formed primarily for social reasons, such as a group of friends who like to go to the movies together on weekends, then the more cohesive the group is, the better. This is pretty obvious; would you rather spend your free time with a bunch of people who don't care for each other or a tightly knit bunch of people who feel committed to each other? As might be expected, the more cohesive a group is, the more its members are likely to stay in the group, take part in group activities, and try to recruit like-minded members (Levine & Moreland, 1998; Sprink & Carron, 1994). One drawback of group cohesiveness, however, is that the group members' concern with maintaining good relations can get in the way of finding good solutions to a problem. We will return to this issue later in the chapter, when we discuss group decision making.

How Groups Influence the Behaviour of Individuals

Now that we know why people join groups and some things about group composition, it is interesting to consider the effects that groups have on individuals. Do you act differently when other people are around? Simply being in the presence of other people can have a variety of effects on our behaviour. We will begin by looking at how a group affects your performance on something with which you are very familiar: taking a test in a class.

SOCIAL FACILITATION: WHEN THE PRESENCE OF OTHERS ENERGIZES US

It is time for the final exam in your psychology class. You have spent countless hours studying the material, and you feel ready. When you arrive, you see that the exam is scheduled in a tiny, packed room. You squeeze into an empty desk, elbow to elbow with your classmates. The professor arrives and says that if any students are bothered by the close quarters, they can take the test by themselves in one of several smaller rooms down the hall. What should you do?

The question is whether the mere presence of others will affect your performance (Geen, 1989; Guerin, 1993; Kent, 1994; Sanna, 1992). The mere presence of other people can take one of two forms: (a) performing a task with others who are doing the same thing you are, or (b) performing a task in front of an audience that is not doing anything except observing you. The point is that in either case, you are not interacting with these other people—they're just present in the same room, constituting a nonsocial group. Does their presence make a difference? If you take your exam in the crowded room, will you feel nervous and have trouble recalling the material? Or will the presence of classmates motivate you to do even better than if you took the test alone?

To answer this question, we need to talk about insects—cockroaches, in fact. Believe it or not, a classic study using cockroaches as research participants suggests an answer to the question of how you should take your psychology test. Zajonc, Heingartner, and Herman (1969) built a contraption to see how cockroaches' behaviour was influenced by the presence of their peers. The researchers placed a bright light (which cockroaches dislike) at the end of a runway and timed how long it took a roach to escape the light by running to the other end, where it could scurry into a darkened box (see the left-hand side of Figure 9.1). The question was, did roaches perform this simple feat faster when they were by themselves or when they were in the presence of other cockroaches?

You might be wondering how the researchers managed to persuade other cockroaches to be spectators. They did so by placing extra roaches in clear plastic boxes next to the runway. These roaches were in the bleachers, so to speak, observing the solitary cockroach do its thing (see Figure 9.1). As it happened, the individual cockroaches performed the task faster when they were in the presence of other roaches than when they were by themselves.

Now, we would not give advice, based on one study that used cockroaches, on how you should take your psychology test. But the story does not end here. There have been dozens of studies on the effects of the mere presence of other people, involving human beings as well as other species such as ants and birds (e.g., Bond & Titus, 1983; Guerin, 1986; Rajecki, Kidd, & Ivins, 1976; Zajonc & Sales, 1966). There is a remarkable consistency to the findings of these studies. As long as the task is a relatively simple, well-learned

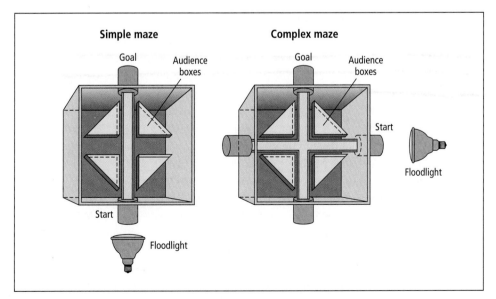

◀ **Figure 9.1**

COCKROACHES AND SOCIAL FACILITATION.

In the maze on the left, cockroaches had a simple task: to go from the starting point down the runway to the darkened box. They performed this feat faster when other roaches were watching than when they were alone. In the maze on the right, the cockroaches had a more difficult task. It took them longer to solve this maze when other roaches were watching than when they were alone.

(Adapted from Zajonc, Heingartner, & Herman, 1969)

one—as escaping a light is for cockroaches—the mere presence of others improves performance. For example, in one of the first social psychology experiments ever done, Norman Triplett (1898) asked children to wind up fishing line on a reel, either by themselves or in the presence of other children. They did so faster when in the presence of other children.

Simple versus Difficult Tasks

Before concluding that you should stay in the crowded classroom to take your exam, we need to consider another set of findings. Remember that we said the presence of others enhances performance on simple, well-learned tasks. Escaping a light is old hat for a cockroach, and winding fishing line on a reel is not difficult, even for a child. What happens when we give people a more difficult task to do and place them in the presence of others? To find out, Zajonc and colleagues (1969) included another condition in the cockroach experiment. This time, the cockroaches had to solve a maze that had several runways, only one of which led to the darkened box (see the right-hand side of Figure 9.1). When working on this more difficult task, the opposite pattern of results occurred: The roaches took longer to solve it when other roaches were present than when they were alone. Many other studies have also found that people and animals do worse in the presence of others when the task is difficult (e.g., Bond & Titus, 1983; Geen, 1989).

Arousal and the Dominant Response

In an influential article published in 1965, Robert Zajonc offered an elegant theoretical explanation for why the presence of others facilitates a well-learned or dominant response but inhibits a less practised or new response. His argument has two steps. First, the presence of others increases physiological arousal (i.e., our bodies become more energized), and second, when such arousal exists, it is easier to do something that is simple (called the dominant response) but harder to do something complex or learn something new. Consider, for example, something that is second nature to you, such as riding a bicycle or writing your name. Arousal, caused by the presence of other people watching you, should make it even easier to perform these well-learned behaviours. But let's say you have to do something more complex, such as learning a new sport or working on a difficult math problem. Now arousal will lead you to feel flustered and do less well than if you were alone. This phenomenon became known as **social facilitation**, which is the tendency for people to do better on simple tasks and worse on complex tasks, when they are in the presence of others and their individual performance can be evaluated.

Suppose, for example, that you decide to stop at a local pool hall and shoot a few racks. Will you perform better or worse if people are watching you wield your pool cue? As we have seen, it should depend on whether shooting pool is a simple or complex task for you. This is what James Michaels and colleagues (1982) found in a field study conducted in the pool hall of a university student union. A team of four students observed several different players from a distance, until they found ones who were experienced (defined as those who made at least two-thirds of their shots) or novices (defined as those who made no more than one-third of their shots). They then casually approached the table and watched people play.

Imagine that you are one of the players. There you are, shooting a little pool, when suddenly you notice four strangers standing around watching you. What will happen to

Social facilitation

the tendency for people to do better on simple tasks and worse on complex tasks, when they are in the presence of others and their individual performance can be evaluated

◀ If this boy has learned his songs well, the presence of an audience will enhance his performance.

your performance? The prediction made by social facilitation theory is clear. If you have played so much pool that you would feel comfortable challenging Cliff Thorburn or Minnesota Fats, the arousal caused by the presence of others should improve your game. If you are a novice and feel as if you are all thumbs, the arousal caused by the presence of others should make your game go to pieces. This is exactly what Michaels and colleagues (1982) found. The novices made significantly fewer of their shots when they were observed, whereas the experts made significantly more of their shots.

Why the Presence of Others Causes Arousal Why does the presence of others lead to arousal? Researchers have developed three theories to explain the role of arousal in social facilitation. Other people cause us to become particularly alert and vigilant; they make us apprehensive about how we're being evaluated; and they distract us from the task at hand.

The first explanation suggests that the presence of other people makes us more alert. When we are by ourselves reading a book, we don't have to pay attention to anything but the book; we don't have to worry that the lamp will ask us a question. When someone else is in the room, however, we have to be alert to the possibility that he or she will do something that requires us to respond. Because people are less predictable than lamps, we are in a state of greater alertness in their presence. This alertness, or vigilance, causes mild arousal. The beauty of this explanation (which is the one preferred by Robert Zajonc [1980]) is that it explains both the animal and the human studies. A solitary cockroach need not worry about what the cockroach in the next room is doing. However, it needs to be alert when in the presence of another member of its species—and the same goes for human beings.

The second explanation focuses on the fact that people are not cockroaches and are often concerned about how other people are evaluating them. When other people can see how you are doing, the stakes are raised: You feel as if the other people are evaluating you and will feel embarrassed if you do poorly and pleased if you do well. This concern about being judged, called *evaluation apprehension*, can cause mild arousal. According to this view, then, it is not the mere presence of others, but the presence of others who are evaluating us that causes arousal and subsequent social facilitation (Blascovich et al., 1999; Bond, Atoum, & VanLeeuwen, 1996; Cottrell, 1968).

The third explanation centres on how distracting other people can be (Baron, 1986; Huguet et al., 1999; Sanders, 1983). It is similar to Robert Zajonc's (1980) notion that we need to be alert when in the presence of others, except that it focuses on the idea that any source of distraction—be it the presence of other people or noise from the party going on in the apartment upstairs—will put us in a state of conflict, because it is difficult to concentrate on what we are doing. Trying to pay attention to two things at once produces arousal, as anyone knows who has ever tried to read the newspaper while a two-year-old clamours for attention. Consistent with this interpretation, Robert Baron (1986) found that nonsocial sources of distraction, such as a flashing light, cause the same kinds of social facilitation effects as does the presence of other people.

We have summarized research on social facilitation in the top half of Figure 9.2. (We will discuss the bottom half of the figure in a moment.) This figure illustrates that there is more than one reason that the presence of other people is arousing. The consequences of this arousal, however, are the same. When an individual is around other people, that individual does better on tasks that are simple and well learned, but worse on tasks that are complex and require them to learn something new.

We can now conclude that you should take your psychology exam in the presence of your classmates, assuming you know the material well, so that it is relatively simple for you to recall it. The arousal produced by being elbow to elbow with your classmates should improve your performance. We can also conclude, however, that when you study for an exam—that is, when you learn new material—you should do so by yourself, and

▶ **Figure 9.2**

SOCIAL FACILITATION AND SOCIAL LOAFING.

The presence of others can lead to social facilitation or social loafing. The important variables that distinguish the two are evaluation, arousal, and the complexity of the task.

(Adapted from Cottrell et al., 1968)

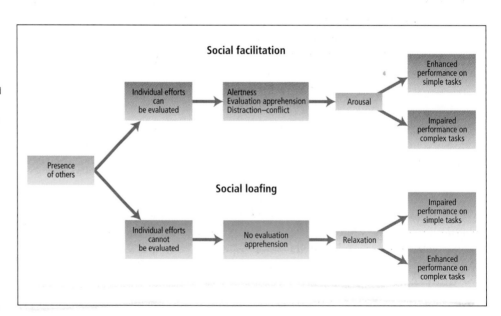

not in the presence of others. In this situation, the arousal caused by others will make it more difficult to concentrate on the new material.

SOCIAL LOAFING: WHEN THE PRESENCE OF OTHERS RELAXES US

When you take your psychology exam, your individual efforts will be evaluated (you will be graded on the test). This is typical of the research on social facilitation we have reviewed. People are working on something (either alone or in the presence of others), and their individual efforts are easily observed and evaluated. Often when you are in the presence of others, however, your efforts cannot be distinguished from those of the people around you. Such is the case when you clap after a concert (no one can tell how loudly you are clapping) or when you play an instrument in a band (your instrument blends in with all the others).

These situations are just the opposite of the kinds of social facilitation settings we have just considered. In social facilitation, the presence of others puts the spotlight on you, making you aroused. However, if being with other people means we can merge into a group, becoming less noticeable than when we are alone, we should become relaxed. Will this relaxation produced by becoming lost in the crowd lead to better or worse performance? Once again, the answer depends on whether we are working on a simple or a complex task.

Let's first consider simple tasks, such as trying to pull as hard as we can on a rope. The question of how working with others would influence performance on such a task was first studied in the 1880s by a French agricultural engineer, Max Ringelmann (1913). He found that when a group of men pulled on a rope, each individual exerted less effort than when he did it alone. A hundred years later, social psychologists Bibb Latané, Kipling Williams, and Stephen Harkins (1979) called this **social loafing**, which is the tendency for people to do worse on simple tasks but better on complex tasks, when they are in the presence of others and their individual performance cannot be evaluated. "Many hands make light work," as the proverb says, and social loafing in groups has since been found for a variety of simple tasks, such as clapping your hands, cheering loudly, and thinking of as many uses for an object as you can (Hoeksema-van Orden, Gaillard, & Buunk, 1998; Karau & Williams, 1995; Shepperd, 1995; Williams, Harkins, & Latané, 1981).

Pulling on a rope or cheering loudly are pretty simple tasks. What happens on complex tasks when our performance is lost in the crowd? Recall that when our performance in a group cannot be identified, we become more relaxed. Recall also this chapter's earlier discussion of the effects of arousal on performance: Arousal enhances performance on simple tasks but impairs performance on complex tasks. By the same reasoning, becoming relaxed should impair performance on simple tasks—as we have just seen—but improve performance on complex tasks. The idea is that when people are not worried about being evaluated, they are more relaxed and should thus be less likely to "tense up" on a difficult task, and do it better as a result (see bottom panel of Figure 9.3).

To test this idea, Jeffrey Jackson and Kipling Williams (1985) asked participants to work on mazes that appeared on a computer screen. The mazes were either simple or complex. Another participant worked on identical mazes on another computer in the

Social loafing

the tendency for people to do worse on simple tasks but better on complex tasks, when they are in the presence of others and their individual performance cannot be evaluated

same room. The researchers either said they would evaluate each person's individual performance (causing evaluation apprehension) or stated that a computer would average the two participants' scores and no one would ever know how well any one person performed (reducing evaluation apprehension). The results were just as predicted. When people thought their score was being averaged with another person's, they were more relaxed, and this relaxation led to better performance (i.e., less time) on the difficult mazes (see the right-hand side of Figure 9.3) but worse performance (i.e., more time) on the easy mazes (see the left-hand side of Figure 9.3).

Research by Cooper, Gallupe, Pollard, and Cadsby (1998) conducted at Queen's University suggests that similar processes may affect the quality of ideas generated by a group. They note that one problem with the use of techniques such as brainstorming is that people worry that others may evaluate their ideas negatively—even though the point of brainstorming is to express whatever ideas come to mind without fear of criticism. These researchers proposed that computers might provide an important vehicle for improving the quality of a group's ideas; computers allow for interaction between people, yet participants can remain anonymous, thereby reducing their researchers evaluation apprehension. Indeed, the researchers found that participants in anonymous, electronic groups found it easier to generate ideas and reported lower evaluation apprehension than did those in non-anonymous (electronic or in-person) discussion groups.

Cooper and colleagues found participants in anonymous electronic discussion groups also generated the greatest number of controversial ideas. This is supposed to be one of the benefits of brainstorming. However, there was an unexpected twist to these findings—it turned out that the kind of controversy generated under these conditions was not very desirable. In fact, some of the ideas generated by the anonymous, electronic groups were highly offensive. For example, for the discussion topic "How to reduce the spread of AIDS," participants generated ideas such as "Burn AIDS carriers at the stake like witches" and "Set a trap encouraging gays to come out of the closet and then eliminate them." The researchers

▶ **Figure 9.3**

SOCIAL LOAFING.

When students worked on easy mazes, those who thought their individual performance would not be evaluated did worse (they took more time to complete them, as seen on the left-hand side of the graph). When students worked on difficult mazes, those who thought their individual performance would not be evaluated did better (they took less time to complete them, as seen on the right-hand side of the graph).

(Adapted from Jackson & Williams, 1985)

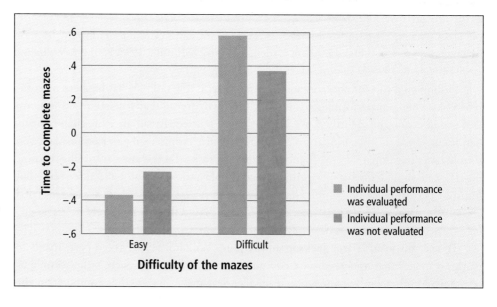

observed that if one group member generated an inappropriate idea, it could set off a vicious cycle of group members attempting to outdo one another. Those who were offended by these responses simply stopped contributing ideas. The researchers concluded that the use of computers can have benefits such as allowing for interaction while preserving anonymity (thereby lowering evaluation apprehension), but that safeguards may be necessary to ensure that the generation of controversial ideas does not spiral out of control.

Gender and Cultural Differences in Social Loafing: Who Slacks Off the Most? Marie and Hans are working with several classmates on a class project, and no one can assess their individual contributions. Who is more likely to slack off and let the others do most of the work—Hans or Marie? If you said Hans, you are probably right. Karau and Williams (1993) reviewed more than 150 studies of social loafing and found that the tendency to loaf is stronger in men than in women. Why? Women tend to focus on the collective, caring more about the welfare of others in groups. Men are more likely to be individualistic, focusing more on their own performance and less on the group (Cross & Madson, 1997; Eagly, 1987; Wood, 1987). This different emphasis on collectivism versus individualism, as you may recall from Chapter 5, also exists across cultures. Many Asian societies stress collectivism, whereas many Western societies stress individualism. Consequently, there are also cultural differences in social loafing. Karau and Williams (1993) found that the tendency to loaf is stronger in Western cultures than in Asian cultures. It is important not to exaggerate these differences; there is evidence that women and men and members of Asian and Western cultures engage in social loafing when in groups (e.g., Chang & Chen, 1995). Nonetheless, social loafing is stronger in men and members of Western cultures.

To summarize, you need to know two things to predict whether the presence of others will help or hinder your performance—whether your individual efforts can be evaluated and whether the task is simple or complex. If your performance can be evaluated, the presence of others will make you alert and aroused. This will lead to social facilitation effects, where people do better on simple tasks but worse on complex tasks (see top of Figure 9.2 on page 314). If your efforts cannot be evaluated (i.e., you are one cog in a machine), you are likely to become more relaxed. This leads to social loafing effects, where people do worse on simple tasks but better on complex tasks (see bottom of Figure 9.2).

These findings have numerous implications for the way in which groups should be organized. If you are a manager who wants your employees to work on a relatively simple problem, a little evaluation apprehension is not such a bad thing—it should improve performance. You shouldn't place your employees in groups where their individual performance cannot be observed, because social loafing (lowered performance on simple tasks) is likely to result. On the other hand, if you want your employees to work on a difficult, complex task, then lowering their evaluation apprehension—by placing them in groups in which their individual performance cannot be observed—is likely to result in better performance.

▼ A review of more than 150 studies of social loafing found that the tendency to loaf is greater in men than in women.

DEINDIVIDUATION: GETTING LOST IN THE CROWD

So far, we have discussed the ways in which a group affects how hard people work and how successfully they learn new things. However, as was demonstrated by the Queen's

Deindividuation

the loosening of normal
constraints on behaviour
when people are in a group,
leading to an increase in
impulsive and deviant acts

University study on brainstorming in anonymous electronic discussion groups (Cooper et al., 1998), being in a group can also cause **deindividuation**, which is the loosening of normal constraints on behaviour, leading to an increase in impulsive and deviant acts. In other words, getting lost in a crowd can lead to an unleashing of behaviours that we would never dream of doing by ourselves.

Throughout history, there have been many examples of groups of people committing horrendous acts that no individual would do on his or her own. In previous chapters we discussed the chilling murder of a young Somalian boy at the hands of Canadian peace-keepers. We also described the My Lai incident during the Vietnam War, in which a group of American soldiers systematically murdered hundreds of defenceless women, children, and elderly men. In Europe, mobs of soccer fans sometimes attack and bludgeon each other. One example of this kind of violence is the Euro 2000 soccer tournament that took place in Belgium in June 2000. Despite organizers' attempts to separate them, English and German fans threw tables and chairs at one another, attacked police officers with bottles, smashed windows, and generally left a trail of destruction. Belgian authorities detained nearly 500 unruly fans. Closer to home, when Russell and Arms (1998) asked male hockey fans in Alberta about the factors that would predispose them to join a fight in the stands, one of the most important variables was the number of other males who accompanied them to the game. The greater the number of male friends with whom they attended the game, the greater the probability of their becoming involved in a fight. To give one last example, the United States has a shameful history of whites lynching African Americans. Brian Mullen (1986) content-analyzed newspaper accounts of 60 lynchings committed in the United States between 1899 and 1946, and discovered an interesting fact: The more people there were in the mob, the greater the savagery and viciousness with which they killed their victims.

The people who participated in lynchings in the United States often did so cloaked in the anonymity of white robes. This combination of anonymity and being in a group can lead to deadly actions. For example, Robert Watson (1973) studied 24 cultures and found that warriors who hid their identities before going into battle—for example, by using face and body paint—were significantly more likely to kill, torture, or mutilate captive prisoners than were warriors who did not hide their identities.

A chilling example of this phenomenon occurred on November 14, 1999, when 15-year-old Matti Baranovski and his friends were approached in a Toronto park by a group of youths looking for a fight. One of the youths wore ski goggles; another covered the lower half of his face with a blue bandana. Still others wore masks or balaclavas to disguise themselves. The youths approached Matti's friends, took their cigarettes, and searched their wallets for money. When Matti questioned what they were doing, they turned on him, viciously punching and kicking him in the head and body. The last kick in the face broke his neck, and Matti died from these injuries. Sadly, this ordeal is not over for Matti's friends and family. On February 25, 2003, his mother appeared in a Toronto court as the trial began for three of the men accused of Matti's murder.

In trying to understand why such violence can occur, some analysts pointed to the fact that the attackers were in a group and, moreover, they were wearing disguises. As noted in one newspaper story, "Disguises tend to make those wearing them capable of far more terrible acts of violence than would normally occur" (Simmie, 1999).

◀ When people can lose their identity in a group, they are more likely to commit impulsive and deviant acts. Matti Baranovski, a Toronto teen, was brutally beaten to death in November 1999 by a group of youths wearing balaclavas, masks, goggles, and other disguises. Here, his grieving mother lays a wreath on the casket at his funeral.

Most of us do not encounter lynch mobs, wars, and masked attackers on a day-to-day basis. It is not as uncommon, however, to be asked to wear uniforms that make us look like everyone else in the vicinity, an arrangement that also might make us feel less accountable for our actions and hence more aggressive. Does wearing a uniform, such as on a sports team, increase aggressiveness? A study by Rehm, Steinleitner, and Lilli (1987) indicates that it does. They randomly assigned fifth-graders in German schools to various five-person teams, then watched the teams play handball against each other. All of the members of one team wore orange shirts and all of the members of the other team wore their normal street clothes. The children who wore the orange shirts (and were thus harder to tell apart) played the game significantly more aggressively than did the children who wore their everyday clothing (and were thus easier to identify).

Even the colour of a uniform can make a difference. Mark Frank and Thomas Gilovich (1988) noted that in virtually all cultures, the colour black is associated with evil and death. They examined penalty records and recorded the colour of uniforms worn by teams in the National Hockey League and the National Football League from 1970 to 1986. Interestingly, teams that wore black uniforms ranked near the top of their leagues in terms of penalties. Moreover, if a team switched to a non-black uniform, there was an immediate decrease in the number of penalties. These researchers also conducted an experiment in which participants played a game wearing either white or black uniforms. Those who wore black uniforms showed greater aggressiveness than did those who wore white uniforms.

Exactly what is it about deindividuation that leads to impulsive (and often violent) acts? Research by Steven Prentice-Dunn and Ronald Rogers (1989) and Ed Diener (1980) points to two factors. First, the presence of others (or the wearing of uniforms and disguises) makes people feel less accountable for their actions, because it reduces the likelihood that any individual will be singled out and blamed (Zimbardo, 1970). Second, the presence of others lowers self-awareness, thereby shifting people's attention away from their moral standards. As discussed in Chapter 5, it is difficult to focus inward on ourselves and outward on the world around us at the same time; thus, at any given point we vary as to how self-aware we are (Carver & Scheier, 1981; Duval & Wicklund, 1972). One consequence of focusing on ourselves is that we are reminded of our moral standards, making us less likely to behave in some deviant or antisocial manner (e.g., "I believe that hurting other people is wrong; I'm not going to throw a chair at this soccer fan—even if he is cheering for the "wrong" team). If we are focusing on our environment, however, self-awareness will be low and we will be more likely to forget our moral standards and act impulsively.

Group Decisions: Are Two (or More) Heads Better than One?

We have just seen that the presence of other people influences individual behaviour in a number of interesting ways. We turn now to one of the major functions of groups: to make decisions. In the Canadian judicial system, many verdicts are determined by groups of individuals (juries), rather than single individuals (see Social Psychology in Action 3: Social Psychology and the Law for a discussion of jury decision making). The Supreme Court is made up of nine justices—not one single, sage member of the judiciary. Similarly, governmental and corporate decisions are often made by groups of people who meet to discuss the issues, and all Canadian prime ministers have a Cabinet and the Privy Council to advise them.

Is it true that two (or more) heads are better than one? Most of us assume that the answer to this question is yes. A lone individual may be subject to all sorts of whims and biases, whereas several people together can exchange ideas, catch each other's errors, and reach better decisions. We have all taken part in group decisions in which we listened to someone else and thought to ourselves, "Hmm, that's a really good point—I would never have thought of that." In general, groups will do better than individuals if they rely on the person with the most expertise (Davis & Harless, 1996) and are stimulated by each other's comments.

Sometimes, though, two heads are not better than one. Several factors, as we will see, can cause groups to actually make worse decisions than individuals.

PROCESS LOSS: WHEN GROUP INTERACTIONS INHIBIT GOOD PROBLEM SOLVING

One problem is that a group will do well only if the most talented member can convince the others that she or he is right—which is not always easy, given that many of us bear a strong resemblance to mules when it comes to admitting that we are wrong (Henry, 1995; Laughlin, 1980; Maier & Solem, 1952). You undoubtedly know what it's like to try to convince a group to follow your idea, be faced with opposition and disbelief, and then have to sit there and watch the group make the wrong decision. Ivan Steiner (1972) called this phenomenon **process loss**, defined as any aspect of group interaction that inhibits good

Process loss

any aspect of group interaction that inhibits good problem solving problem solving. Process loss can occur for a number of reasons. Groups might not try hard enough to find out who the most competent member is and instead rely on somebody who really doesn't know what he or she is talking about. The most competent member might find it difficult to disagree with everyone else in the group (recall our discussion of normative conformity pressures in Chapter 8). Other causes of process loss involve communication problems within the group—in some groups, people don't listen to each other; in others, one person is allowed to dominate the discussion while the others tune out (Watson, Johnson, Kumar, & Critelli, 1998).

Failure to Share Unique Information
Another example of process loss is the tendency for groups to focus on what its members already know in common, failing to discuss information that some members have but others do not. In any group, members share some common knowledge but also have unique information not known by the other members. Consider a medical team trying to decide on the course of treatment of a person with abdominal pain. All members share some knowledge, such as the fact that the patient is a male in his fifties with a history of digestive problems. Some members of the team, however, know things the other members do not. The doctor who first examined the patient in the emergency room may be the only one who knows that the patient had mussels for dinner that night, whereas one of the attending physicians may be the only one to have seen the results of a blood test showing that the patient has an abnormally high white blood cell count. Obviously, to make the most informed decision, the group needs to pool all of the information and use it to decide on the best course of treatment.

As obvious as this is, there is a funny thing about groups: They tend to focus on the information they share and ignore unique information known only to some members of the group. In one study, for example, participants met in groups of four to discuss which candidate for student body president was the most qualified (Stasser & Titus, 1985). In the shared information condition, each participant was given the same packet of information to read: data indicating that candidate *A* was the best choice for office. As seen at the top of Figure 9.4, all participants in this condition knew that candidate *A* had eight positive qualities and four negative qualities, making him superior to the other candidates. Not surprisingly, when this group met to discuss the candidates, almost all of the members chose candidate *A*.

In the unshared information condition, each participant received a different packet of information. As seen at the bottom of Figure 9.4, each person knew that candidate *A* had two positive qualities and four negative qualities. However, the two positive qualities cited in each person's packet were unique—different from those listed in other participants' packets. Everyone learned that candidate *A* had the same four negative qualities; thus, if the participants shared the information in their packets, they would learn that candidate *A* had a total of eight positive qualities and four negative qualities—just as people in the shared information condition knew. Most of the groups in the unshared information condition never realized that candidate *A* had more good than bad qualities, because they focused on the information they shared rather than on the information they did not share. As a result, few of these groups chose candidate *A*.

Subsequent research has focused on ways to get groups to concentrate more on unshared information. Janice Kelly and Steven Karau (1999) found that groups are more

▶ **Figure 9.4**

WHEN PEOPLE ARE IN
GROUPS, DO THEY SHARE
INFORMATION THAT ONLY
THEY KNOW?

Participants in a study met to
discuss candidates for an
election. In the shared
information condition (top half
of figure), each person was
given the same positive and
negative facts about the
candidates. Candidate A was
clearly the superior candidate,
and most groups preferred him.
In the unshared information
condition (bottom half of
figure), each person was given
the same four negative facts
about candidate A, as well as
two unique positive facts. In
discussion, these people
focused on the information they
all shared and failed to
mention the unique
information; these groups no
longer saw candidate A as
superior.

(Adapted from Stasser & Titus,
1985.)

likely to focus on unshared information if it is especially diagnostic. In our medical example, the doctor who knows the blood test results is likely to volunteer this information,
and the group will probably pay attention to it, because this information is clearly relevant
to the decision. The doctor who knows that the patient ate mussels is less likely to volunteer this information, and if he or she does, the group is less likely to pay attention to it,
because it doesn't seem very relevant. The problem is that facts that don't seem relevant
at first can be highly diagnostic when considered in combination with other unshared
facts. Suppose another doctor on the team had just treated a patient for food poisoning
from mussels she ate at Joe's Seafood Palace. If the first doctor fails to mention that the
male patient with stomach pain had also eaten mussels at Joe's, the team will be less
likely to put two and two together and realize that he, too, has food poisoning.

Unshared information is also more likely to be brought up later, over time, suggesting that group discussions should last long enough to get beyond what everybody already
knows (Larson et al., 1998; Larson, Foster-Fishman, & Franz, 1998). Another approach is
to assign different group members to specific areas of expertise so they know that they
alone are responsible for certain types of information. If only one doctor's job is to monitor the blood tests, he or she is more likely to bring up this information, and other members are more likely to pay attention to it (Stasser, Stewart, & Wittenbaum, 1995; Stewart
& Stasser, 1995).

This last lesson has been learned by many couples, who know to rely on each other's
memories for different kinds of information. One member of a couple might be responsible for remembering social engagements, while the other might be responsible for
remembering when to pay the bills (Wegner, Erber & Raymond, 1991). Daniel Wegner
and his colleagues have termed this **transactive memory**, which is the combined memory

Transactive memory

the combined memory of
two people that is more
efficient than the memory of
either individual

of two people that is more efficient than the memory of either individual (Wegner, 1995). By learning to specialize their memories and knowing what their partner is responsible for, couples often do quite well in remembering important information. The same can be true of groups of strangers, if they develop a system whereby different people are remembering different parts of a task (Liang, Moreland, & Argote, 1995; Moreland, 1999; Moreland, Argote, & Krishnan, 1996). In sum, the tendency for groups to fail to share important information known to only some of the members can be overcome if people learn who is responsible for what kinds of information and take the time to discuss these unshared data (Stasser, 2000).

Groupthink: Many Heads, One Mind A possible limitation of research on group problem solving is that most studies use people who have never met before and give people tasks that are unfamiliar and sometimes trivial. Would groups do better if their members were used to working with each other and if they were dealing with important, real-world problems? Our opening example of the Canadian military's decision to administer the anthrax vaccine suggests not. Let's see why.

Using real-world events, Irving Janis (1972, 1982) developed an influential theory of group decision making that he called **groupthink**, defined as a kind of thinking in which maintaining group cohesiveness and solidarity is more important than considering the facts in a realistic manner. According to Janis's theory, groupthink is most likely to occur when certain preconditions are met, such as when the group is highly cohesive, isolated from contrary opinions, and ruled by a directive leader who makes his or her wishes known. When these preconditions of groupthink are met, several symptoms appear; these are outlined in Figure 9.5. The group begins to feel it is invulnerable and can do no wrong. People do not voice contrary views (self-censorship), because they are afraid of

Groupthink
a kind of thinking in which maintaining group cohesiveness and solidarity is more important than considering the facts in a realistic manner

▼ **Figure 9.5**

GROUPTHINK: ANTECEDENTS, SYMPTOMS, AND CONSEQUENCES

Under some conditions, maintaining group cohesiveness and solidarity is more important to a group than considering the facts in a realistic manner (see antecedents). When this happens, certain symptoms of groupthink occur, such as the illusion of invulnerability (see symptoms). These symptoms lead to defective decision making.

(Adapted from Janis, 1982)

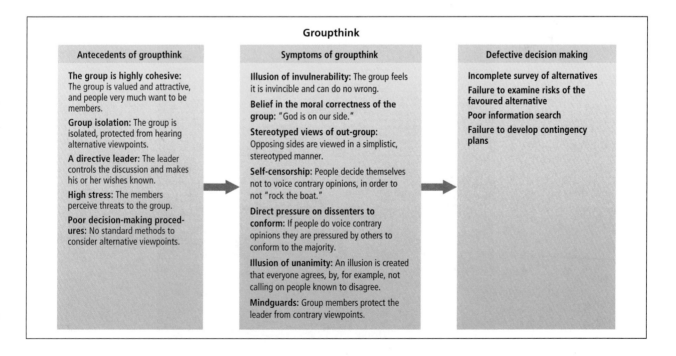

Groupthink		
Antecedents of groupthink	**Symptoms of groupthink**	**Defective decision making**
The group is highly cohesive: The group is valued and attractive, and people very much want to be members. **Group isolation:** The group is isolated, protected from hearing alternative viewpoints. **A directive leader:** The leader controls the discussion and makes his or her wishes known. **High stress:** The members perceive threats to the group. **Poor decision-making procedures:** No standard methods to consider alternative viewpoints.	**Illusion of invulnerability:** The group feels it is invincible and can do no wrong. **Belief in the moral correctness of the group:** "God is on our side." **Stereotyped views of out-group:** Opposing sides are viewed in a simplistic, stereotyped manner. **Self-censorship:** People decide themselves not to voice contrary opinions, in order to not "rock the boat." **Direct pressure on dissenters to conform:** If people do voice contrary opinions they are pressured by others to conform to the majority. **Illusion of unanimity:** An illusion is created that everyone agrees, by, for example, not calling on people known to disagree. **Mindguards:** Group members protect the leader from contrary viewpoints.	**Incomplete survey of alternatives** **Failure to examine risks of the favoured alternative** **Poor information search** **Failure to develop contingency plans**

ruining the high morale, or *esprit de corps,* of the group, or because they are afraid of being criticized by others. If anyone does voice a contrary viewpoint, the rest of the group is quick to criticize that person, pressuring him or her to conform to the majority view.

The perilous state of groupthink causes people to implement an inferior decision-making process (see Figure 9.5). The group does not consider the full range of alternatives, does not develop contingency plans, and does not adequately consider the risks of its preferred choice. Groupthink may well have been behind the decision of the military leaders to go ahead with the anthrax vaccine despite the fact that Health Canada had not approved it and military lawyers had advised against it. Can you think of other decisions that were plagued by groupthink? One example is the fateful decision by NASA to go ahead with the launching of the space shuttle *Challenger*, despite the objections of engineers who said that the freezing temperatures presented a severe danger to the rubber O-ring seals (the ones that eventually failed during the launch, causing the rocket to explode and kill all aboard).

The failure to ratify the Meech Lake Accord may be another example of groupthink. In June 1990, Canada's then prime minister, Brian Mulroney, and the provincial premiers met behind closed doors for seven days to make a decision regarding constitutional reform. The conditions were ripe for groupthink: The politicians met in isolation—away from the media, their constituents, and their advisers. The meetings took place shortly before the Accord would have to be ratified, leaving little time to discuss alternatives. Mulroney was a persuasive, directive leader who managed to convince the premiers that the Meech Lake Accord was the answer to Canada's unity problems, and that failure to sign the Accord would place the country in political and economic peril. His goal in these discussions was to ensure that dissenters conformed. This was the context of his infamous quip that one simply needed to know when to roll the dice and the Meech Lake Accord would be a done deal. Under these conditions, the group reached consensus—a consensus that unravelled

▶ The decision to launch the space shuttle *Challenger*, which tragically exploded due to defective O-ring seals, appears to have been the result of groupthink on the part of NASA officials, who disregarded engineers' concerns about the quality of the seals.

as soon as the premiers emerged from their cloistered environment and returned to their provinces. The Meech Lake Accord faced a sudden death when several provinces refused to endorse it.

Since Janis proposed his theory, it has been put to the test by a number of researchers. Some studies have found that group cohesiveness by itself does not increase groupthink (Adlag & Fuller, 1993; Mohamed & Wiebe, 1996; Tetlock et al., 1992). However, there is evidence that group cohesiveness increases groupthink when it is accompanied by the other risk factors identified by Janis, such as the presence of a directive leader or high stress (see Figure 9.5; Esser, 1998; Hogg & Hains, 1998; Mullen et al., 1994; Turner et al., 1992; Schafer & Crichlow, 1996). Research conducted at the University of Western Ontario suggests that variables such as group cohesion and the influence of the group leader may operate differently, depending on the personalities of the group members (Hodson & Sorrentino, 1997).

How can groupthink be avoided? A wise leader can take several steps to ensure that his or her group is immune to this style of decision making. The leader should not take a directive role, but should remain impartial. He or she should invite outside opinions from people who are not members of the group and who are thus less concerned with maintaining group cohesiveness. He or she should divide the group into subgroups that first meet separately and then meet together to discuss their different recommendations. The leader might also take a secret ballot or ask group members to write down their opinions anonymously; doing so would ensure that people give their true opinions, uncensored by a fear of recrimination from the group (Flowers, 1977; McCauley, 1989; Zimbardo & Andersen, 1993).

GROUP POLARIZATION: GOING TO EXTREMES

Maybe you are willing to grant that groups sometimes make poor decisions. Surely, though, groups will usually make less risky decisions than a lone individual will—one individual might be willing to bet the ranch on a risky proposition, but if others help make the decision they will interject reason and moderation. Or will they? The question of whether groups or individuals make more risky decisions has been examined in numerous studies. Participants are typically given the Choice Dilemmas Questionnaire (CDQ), a series of stories that present a dilemma for the main character and ask the reader to choose how much probability of success there would have to be before the reader would recommend the risky alternative (Kogan & Wallach, 1964). An example of a CDQ item about a chess player appears in Try It! on page 326. People choose their answers alone and then meet in a group to discuss the options, arriving at a unanimous group decision for each dilemma.

Many of the initial studies found, surprisingly, that groups make riskier decisions than individuals do. For example, when deciding alone, people said the chess player should make the risky gambit only if there was at least a 30 percent chance of success. But after discussing the problem with others in a group, people said the chess player should go for it even if there was only a 10 percent chance of success (Wallach, Kogan, & Bem, 1962). Findings such as these became known as the *risky shift*. Yet with increased research, it became clear that such shifts were not the full story. It turns out that groups tend to make decisions that are more extreme in the same direction as the individual's initial

Choice Dilemmas Questionnaire

You will need four or five friends to complete this exercise. First, copy the questionnaire in the table below and give it to each of your friends to complete by themselves, without talking to each other. Do not tell your friends that they will be discussing the questionnaire with the others. Then bring everyone together and ask them to discuss the dilemma and arrive at a unanimous decision. They should try to reach consensus such that every member of the group agrees at least partially with the final decision. Finally, compare people's initial decisions (made alone) with the group decision. Who made the riskier decisions on average: people deciding by themselves, or the group?

As discussed in the text, groups tend to make riskier decisions than individuals on problems such as these. In one study, for example, individuals recommended that the chess player make the risky move only if there was at least a 30 percent chance of success. After discussing the problem with others in a group, however, they recommended that the chess player make the move even if there was only a 10 percent chance of success. Did you find the same thing? Why or why not? If the group did make a riskier decision, was it due more to the persuasive arguments interpretation discussed in the text, the social comparison interpretation, or both? (Adapted from Wallach, Kogan, & Bem, 1962)

The Choice Dilemmas Questionnaire

A low-ranked participant in a national chess tournament, playing an early match against a highly favoured opponent, has the choice of attempting or not attempting a deceptive but risky manoeuvre that might lead to quick victory if it is successful or almost certain defeat if it fails. Please indicate the lowest probability of success that you would accept before recommending that the chess player play the risky move.

_____	1 chance in 10 of succeeding
_____	3 chances in 10 of succeeding
_____	5 chances in 10 of succeeding
_____	7 chances in 10 of succeeding
_____	9 chances in 10 of succeeding
_____	I would not recommend taking the chance.

predispositions, which happened to be risky in the case of the chess problem. What happens if people are initially inclined to be conservative? In cases such as these, groups tend to make even more conservative decisions than individuals do.

Consider this problem: Domenic, a young married man with two children, has a secure but low-paying job and no savings. Someone gives him a tip about a stock that will triple in value if the company's new product is successful but that will plummet if the new product fails. Should Domenic sell his life insurance policy and invest in the company? Most people recommend a safe course of action here: Domenic should buy the stock only if the new product is certain to succeed. When they talk it over in a group, they become even more conservative, deciding that the new product would have to have a nearly 100 percent chance of success before they would recommend that Domenic buy stock in the company.

The finding that groups make more extreme decisions in the direction of people's initial inclinations has become known as **group polarization**, defined as the tendency for

Group polarization

the tendency for groups to make decisions that are more extreme than the initial inclinations of their members

groups to make decisions that are more extreme than the initial inclination of their members—toward greater risk if people's initial tendency is to be risky and toward greater caution if people's initial tendency is to be cautious (Brown, 1965; Friedkin, 1999; Myers & Arenson, 1972; Teger & Pruitt, 1967). Group polarization occurs for two main reasons. According to the *persuasive arguments* interpretation, all individuals bring to the group a set of arguments—some of which other individuals have not considered—supporting their initial recommendation. For example, one person might stress that cashing in the life insurance policy is an unfair risk to Roger's children, should he die prematurely. Another person might not have considered this possibility; thus, she becomes more conservative as well. The result is that group members end up with a greater number of arguments in support of their position than they initially started out with. A series of studies by Eugene Burnstein and Amiram Vinokur (1977) supports this interpretation of group polarization, whereby each member presents arguments that other members had not considered (Burnstein & Sentis, 1981).

According to the *social comparison* interpretation, when people discuss an issue in a group they first check how everyone else feels. What does the group value—being risky or being cautious? In order to be liked, many people then take a position that is similar to everyone else's but a little more extreme. In this way, the individual supports the group's values and also presents himself or herself in a positive light—a person in the vanguard, an impressive thinker. Both the persuasive arguments and the social comparison interpretations of group polarization have received support (Blaskovich, Ginsburg, & Veach, 1975; Brown, 1986; Burnstein & Sentis, 1981; Isenberg, 1986; Zuber, Crott, & Werner, 1992).

LEADERSHIP IN GROUPS

A critical question we have not yet considered is the role of the leader in group decision making. The question of what makes a great leader has intrigued psychologists, historians, and political scientists for some time (Bass, 1990, 1997; Billsberry, 1996; Burns, 1978; Chemers, 2000; Fiedler, 1967; Hollander, 1985; Klenke, 1996; Simonton, 1987). One of the best-known answers to this question is the **great person theory**, which maintains that certain key personality traits make a person a good leader, regardless of the nature of the situation facing the leader.

If the great person theory is true, we ought to be able to isolate the key aspects of personality that make someone a great leader. Is it a combination of intelligence, charisma, and courage? Is it better to be introverted or extroverted? Should we add a dollop of ruthlessness to the mix as well, as Niccoló Machiavelli suggested in 1513, in his famous treatise on leadership, *The Prince*? Or do highly moral people make the best leaders?

Leadership and Personality The relationships between specific personal characteristics and leadership are summarized in the text accompanying the photos on the next page. Some modest relationships have been found; for example, leaders tend to be slightly more intelligent than non-leaders, more driven by the desire for power, more charismatic, more socially skilled, more adaptive and flexible and more confident in their leadership abilities (Albright & Forziati, 1995; Chemers, Watson, & May, 2000; Whitney, Sagrestano, & Maslach, 1994; Zaccaro, Foti, & Kenny, 1991). What is most telling from the summary,

Great person theory
the theory that certain key personality traits make a person a good leader, regardless of the nature of the situation facing the leader

however, is the absence of strong relationships. In addition, surprisingly few personality characteristics correlate with leadership effectiveness. For example, Bradley and colleagues (2002) followed Canadian Forces officer candidates over a five-year period and found little relation between personality variables and leadership ability. Only one trait emerged as particularly useful in predicting who would make a good leader, and that was dominance. Why might that be? In their words, "Military operations are not the place for insecure people."

University of British Columbia social psychologist Peter Suedfeld and his colleagues (Ballard & Suedfeld, 1988; Suedfeld, Conway III, & Eichorn, 2001) have identified another correlate of leadership effectiveness, namely integrative complexity—the ability to recognize more than one perspective on an issue and to be able to integrate these various perspectives. These researchers have found substantial correlation between integrative complexity and greatness among Canadian prime ministers and other prominent leaders.

In the United States, Simonton (1987, 1992) gathered information on 100 personal attributes of all U.S. presidents, such as their family backgrounds, educational experiences, occupations, and personalities. Only three of these variables—height, family size, and the number of books a president published before taking office—correlated with how effective the presidents were in office (as rated by historians). Presidents who were tall, came from small families, and had published many books were more likely to be great leaders. The other 97 characteristics, including personality traits, were not related to leadership effectiveness at all.

We should point out that different ways of analyzing these markers of presidential greatness can produce different results. Stewart McCann (1992) at the University College of Cape Breton analyzed the same data Simonton did, using slightly different statistical techniques. His conclusion was that personological factors do predict greatness—more so than Simonton's analysis would suggest. The variables that emerged as important in McCann's analysis were IQ, height, attractiveness, tidiness, and achievement drive. Specifically, great presidents tend to be smart, tall, not good-looking, messy, and achievement-oriented. However, even this list is rather short.

Leadership: The Right Person in the Right Situation

As you undoubtedly know by now, one of the most important tenets of social psychology is that to understand social behaviour, it is not enough to consider personality traits alone—we must take the social situation into account as well. The inadequacy of the great person theory does not mean that personal characteristics are irrelevant to good leadership. Instead, being good social psychologists, we should consider both the nature of the leader and the situation in which the leading takes place. This view of leadership states that it is not enough to be a great person; you have to be the right person at the right time in the right situation. For example, in McCann's analysis of U.S. presidents, the spirit of the times were found to make a difference. A president was more likely to be considered great if the American public was in a phase of idealism and trying to improve society than if they were in a phase of materialism and self-centred gratification.

Earlier, we discussed research by Peter Suedfeld and colleagues (Ballard & Suedfeld, 1988; Suedfeld, Conway III, & Eichorn, 2001) showing that prime ministerial greatness was strongly correlated with the trait of integrative complexity. However, it turns out that

Leadership and Personality Characteristics

Some modest relationships between personological characteristics and leadership performance have been found, but in general it is difficult to predict how good a leader will be from his or her personal attributes alone.

Intelligence — Supreme Court Chief Justice Beverley McLachlin

There is a modest but positive relationship between intelligence and leadership effectiveness (Simonton, 1985; Stogdill, 1974). Supreme Court Chief Justice Beverley McLachlin graduated with a gold medal from the University of Alberta and is described as having an "unquenchable intellectual curiosity."

Morality — Queen Victoria of Great Britain

An examination of historical records showed that in a sample of 600 monarchs, the ones who became the most eminent were those who were either highly moral or highly immoral (Simonton, 1984). This suggests that there are two roads to eminence: having great moral virtue or having Machiavellian deviousness. Queen Victoria of England stood for moral propriety and good manners, to the point that her name came to stand for restraint, politeness, and decorum.

Motivation — Colonel Mu'ammar al-Qaddafi of Libya

Leaders who have a strong power motive (self-direction, a concern for prestige, abundant energy) are somewhat more likely to be effective (McClelland, 1975; Sorrentino & Field, 1986; Winter, 1987). Colonel Qaddafi is generally considered to be a leader with a great need for power. He has managed to remain leader of Libya for a number of years—though whether he is an effective leader is quite another matter.

Height — Abraham Lincoln, sixteenth U.S. president

There is a modest correlation between a man's height and the likelihood that he will become the leader of a group (Stogdill, 1974). In the United States, the taller candidate has won every presidential election but two: Richard Nixon versus George McGovern in 1972 and Jimmy Carter versus Gerald Ford in 1976. In 1992, Bill Clinton had a quarter-inch height advantage over George Bush. In 1996, Clinton had a half-inch advantage over Robert Dole. Once in office, tall presidents, such as Abraham Lincoln, are more likely to be great leaders, as rated by historians (Simonton, 1987, 1992).

Personality Traits — Pierre Elliott Trudeau, former prime minister of Canada

The great charisma of Pierre Elliott Trudeau contributed to his rise to prime minister of Canada in 1967. Trudeau was also the Canadian prime minister with the highest integrative complexity (Suedfeld, Conway III, & Eichorn, 2001). However, overall, there is surprisingly little evidence that traits such as charisma, dominance, and self-confidence predict who will become a leader.

even this relationship varies, depending on the situation. For example, Canadian prime ministers are more likely to be considered great if the country faced particularly difficult times, such as a war, while they were in power. The one exception is an economic crisis—prime ministers who have had to deal with economic hard times are not perceived as particularly successful or effective (Ballard & Suedfeld, 1988; Suedfeld, Conway III, & Eichorn, 2001). Another situational factor that influences leadership greatness is whether a leader is in a crisis situation. Generally, when people are under stress, their level of integrative complexity decreases—it is harder to see other points of view, integrate them, and come up with complex solutions in crisis mode. Suedfeld and colleagues made the surprising discovery that truly great leaders show just the opposite pattern—they increase in integrative complexity during a crisis and then return to their usual level of complexity afterwards. Consider, for example, Lester B. Pearson, Canada's prime minister from 1963 to 1968. During the Suez invasion in 1956, he was a minister in the Canadian government and managed to negotiate an end to the fighting—an achievement that earned him the 1957 Nobel Peace Prize. Moreover, he came up with the idea of United Nations peacekeeping and was instrumental in bringing it to fruition. Interestingly, Pearson's integrative complexity (as coded from speeches he made during that time) increased during the Suez crisis and then returned to its usual (still high) level once the crisis had ended. Thus, once again, situational factors—in this case, a crisis situation—influenced how the qualities of a leader were manifest.

Several theories of leadership focus on characteristics of the leader, his or her followers, and the situation (e.g., Dienesch & Liden, 1986; Hollander, 1958; House, 1971). The best-known theory of this type is Fred Fiedler's (1967, 1978) **contingency theory of leadership**. According to Fiedler, there are two kinds of leaders: those who are task-oriented and those who are relationship-oriented. The **task-oriented leader** is concerned more with getting the job done than with the feelings of and relationships between the workers. The **relationship-oriented leader** is concerned primarily with the feelings of and relationships between the workers.

The crux of Fiedler's contingency theory is that neither type of leader is *always* more effective than the other; it depends on the nature of the situation—specifically, on the amount of control and influence a leader has over the group. In "high-control" work situations, the leader has excellent interpersonal relationships with subordinates, his or her position in the company is clearly perceived as powerful, and the work to be done by the group is structured and well defined. In "low-control" work situations, the opposite holds—the leader has poor relationships with subordinates and the work to be done is not clearly defined.

As seen in Figure 9.6, task-oriented leaders are most effective in situations that are either very high or very low in control. When situational control is very high, people are happy, everything is running smoothly, and there is no need to worry about people's feelings and relationships. The leader who pays attention only to the task will get the most accomplished. When situational control is very low, the task-oriented leader is best at taking charge and imposing some order on a confusing, ill-defined work environment. Relationship-oriented leaders, however, are most effective in situations that are moderate in control. Under these conditions, the wheels are turning fairly smoothly but some attention to the squeakiness caused by poor relationships and hurt feelings is needed. The leader who can soothe such feelings will be most successful.

Contingency theory of leadership

the theory that leadership effectiveness depends both on how task-oriented or relationship-oriented the leader is and on the amount of control and influence the leader has over the group

Task-oriented leader

a leader who is concerned more with getting the job done than with the feelings of and relationships between the workers

Relationship-oriented leader

a leader who is concerned primarily with the feelings of and relationships between the workers

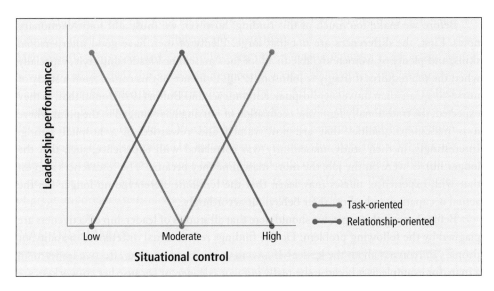

FIEDLER'S CONTINGENCY
THEORY OF LEADERSHIP.

According to Fiedler, task-
oriented leaders perform best
when situational control is
high or low, whereas
relationship-oriented leaders
perform best when situational
control is moderate.

Fiedler's contingency theory has been tested with numerous groups of leaders, including business managers, college administrators, military commanders, and postmasters. These studies have generally been supportive, conforming well to the pattern shown in Figure 9.6 (Chemers, 2000; Peters, Hartke, & Pohlmann, 1985; Schriesheim, Tepper, & Tetrault, 1994; Strube & Garcia, 1981).

Gender and Leadership When we described the task-oriented and relationship-oriented types of leaders, did they remind you of anyone? Be honest. Did it seem that men are more likely to be task-oriented, whereas women are more likely to be relationship-oriented? If so, you have plenty of company: Stereotypes about the leadership styles of women and men abound. Women are thought to care more about the feelings of their co-workers, to be more interpersonally skilled than men, and thus to be more relationship-oriented. Men are often characterized as controlling, Machiavellian leaders who don't even notice what their co-workers are feeling, much less care about those feelings (Deaux & LaFrance, 1998; Klenke, 1996). Is there any truth to these stereotypes?

To find out, Alice Eagly and her colleagues examined hundreds of studies to answer questions about the leadership styles of women versus men (Carli & Eagly, 1999; Eagly & Johnson, 1990; Eagly & Karau, 1991; Eagly, Karau, & Makhijani, 1995; Eagly, Makhijani, & Klonsky, 1992). Consistent with the stereotype, women do tend to lead more democratically than men, possibly because women tend to have better interpersonal skills, allowing them to seek input from group members when making a decision and to gracefully disregard this input when necessary (Eagly & Johnson, 1990).

Does this mean that women make better leaders than men? As we would expect from the contingency theory of leadership, it depends on the nature of the situation. Eagly, Karau, and Makhijani (1995) found that women tend to be better leaders (as measured by both objective measures of performance and ratings of co-workers) in jobs that require interpersonal skills, such as jobs in educational settings. Men tend to be better leaders in jobs that require the ability to direct and control people, such as jobs in the military.

 **The Prisoner's Dilemma**

	Your Options	
Your Friend's Options	Option X	Option Y
Option X	You win $3 / Your friend wins $3	You win $6 / Your friend loses $6
Option Y	You lose $6 / Your friend wins $6	You lose $1 / Your friend loses $1

Instructions: Play this version of a Prisoner's Dilemma game with a friend. First, show the table above to the friend and explain how the game works. On each trial of the game, you and your friend can choose option *X* or option *Y*, without knowing what the other will choose. You should each write your choice on folded pieces of paper that are opened at the same time. The numbers in the table represent imaginary money that you and your friend win or lose on each trial. For example, if you choose option *X* on the first trial and your friend chooses option *Y*, you lose an imaginary $6 and your friend wins an imaginary $6. If both of you choose option *Y*, you both lose an imaginary $1. Play the game for 10 trials and keep track of how much each of you wins or loses. Did you and your friend choose the cooperative option (option *X*) or the competitive option (option *Y*) more often? Why? Did a pattern of trust or mistrust develop over the course of the game?

do not, and this lack of trust leads to an escalating series of competitive moves, so that in the end no one wins. Two countries locked in an arms race may feel that they cannot afford to disarm, out of fear that the other side will take advantage of their weakened position. The result is that both sides add furiously to their stockpile of weapons, neither side gaining superiority over the other and both spending money they could better use to solve domestic problems (Deustch, 1973). Such an escalation of conflict is also seen all too often among couples who are divorcing. Sometimes the goal seems to be to hurt the other person rather than to further one's own needs (or the children's needs). In the end, both suffer because, metaphorically speaking, both partners choose option *Y* too often.

Increasing Cooperation in the Prisoner's Dilemma Such escalating conflict, though common, is not inevitable. Many studies have found that when people play a Prisoner's Dilemma game they will, under certain conditions, adopt the more cooperative response (option *X*), ensuring that both sides end up with a positive outcome. Not surprisingly, if people are playing the game with a friend or if they expect to interact with their partner in the future, they are more likely to adopt a cooperative strategy that maximizes both their own profits and those of their partner (Pruitt & Kimmel, 1977).

SUMMARY

A **group** consists of two or
each other and are interdep
needs and goals cause th
Groups have a number of
an innate need to belong th
with other people. Group
who are similar to one an
have *social norms* that peopl
have well-defined **social ro**
how people are supposed to
assume in groups, and the
those roles, are powerful de
and behaviours in groups.
of a group that bind memt
ing between members, is a
groups that influences the

Simply being in the p
number of interesting effe
efforts on a task can be ev
others leads to **social facil**
enhanced on simple tasks b
When their individual eff
mere presence of othe
Performance is impaired or
complex tasks. Finally, th
lead to **deindividuation**, w
constraints on behaviour w
ing to an increase in impul

One of the major func
sions. Are groups better
making decisions? It turn
decisions than individuals
ideas and listening to the
Often, however, **process l**
expert individual is unable
Further, groups often focu
in common and fail to shar
ter problem can be avoided
vidual members have bee
expertise. Many couples
responsible for remembe
responsible for. Consequ
transactive memory, whic

Total amount of money

use t
Bolt
a sta
decac
nucle

Effe
1962
ing t
adve
and l
an in
as th
(com
chose
the 2

nicat
coop
incre
comi
threa
(no t
its di

trust
foun

Even playing the game with a smaller, rather than a larger, group increases the chances of cooperation, as demonstrated in a recent study by Gerard Seijts of the University of Manitoba and Gary Latham of the University of Toronto (Seijts & Latham, 2000). Participants in this study were told that they could invest money in either a personal account or a joint account. Any money placed in the joint account would be doubled and divided equally among the group members. This is a classic dilemma, because you can make the most money if you put your money in a personal account and then benefit from the money others have put into the joint account. However, if everyone in the group adopts this strategy, it will not be very profitable. The greatest earnings result when the group adopts a cooperative strategy and everyone invests all of their money in the joint account. Seijts and Latham found that participants in three-person groups were more cooperative than participants in seven-person groups, and, as a result, made more money. Members of seven-person groups were more likely to set out with the intent of maximizing their own gains, rather than those of the group.

In situations where only two parties are involved, cooperation can be increased by communicating that you can be trusted not to exploit your opponent. You might do so by choosing option *X* and sticking with it as the game goes on, thereby showing your partner that you are not trying to exploit her. The problem is that you become an easy mark, and your partner knows she can nail you at any time by choosing option *Y*.

To increase cooperation, you can also try the **tit-for-tat strategy**, which is a way of encouraging cooperation by at first acting cooperatively but then always responding the way your opponent did (cooperatively or competitively) on the previous trial. This strategy communicates a willingness to cooperate and an unwillingness to sit back and be exploited if the partner does not cooperate. The tit-for-tat strategy is usually successful in getting the other person to respond with the cooperative, trusting response (Axelrod, 1984; Komorita, Parks, & Hulbert, 1992; Messick & Liebrand, 1995; Pruitt, 1998; Sheldon, 1999). The analogy to the arms race would be to match not only any military buildup made by an unfriendly nation but also any conciliatory gesture, such as a ban on nuclear testing.

USING THREATS TO RESOLVE CONFLICT

When caught in a conflict, many of us are tempted to use threats to get the other party to cave in to our wishes, believing that we should "walk softly and carry a big stick." Parents commonly use threats to get their children to behave, and teachers often threaten their students with demerits or a visit to the principal. At the time of writing this book, the United States is threatening Iraq with war if Iraq does not comply with weapons inspections.

A classic series of studies by Morton Deutsch and Robert Krauss (1960, 1962) indicates that threats are not an effective means of reducing conflict. These researchers developed a game in which two participants imagined they were in charge of trucking companies named Acme and Bolt. The goal of each company was to transport merchandise as quickly as possible to a destination. The participants were paid 60 cents for each "trip," but had 1 cent subtracted for every second it took them to make the trip. The most direct route for each company was over a one-lane road on which only one truck could travel at a time. This placed the two companies in direct conflict, as seen in Figure 9.7. If

Tit-for-tat strategy
a means of encouraging cooperation by at first acting cooperatively but then always responding the way your opponent did (cooperatively or competitively) on the previous trial

▶ If the right strategies are used, negotiation can lead to successful resolution of conflict. Here, Toby Anderson (left), chief negotiator for the Labrador Inuit Association, signs the documents of the Labrador Inuit Land Claims, May 10, 1999. Bob Warren (centre), chief negotiator for Newfoundland Labrador, and Jim MacKenzie (right), chief negotiator for the Government of Canada look on.

IF YOU ARE INTERESTED

Dion, K. L. (2000). Group cohesion: From "field of forces" to multidimensional construct. *Group Dynamics: Theory, Research and Practice*, 4: 7–26. A comprehensive review of theorizing and research on group cohesiveness written by a prominent University of Toronto social psychologist. The review ends with the author's assessment of which approaches to studying group cohesiveness hold the greatest promise for understanding this important concept.

Golding, William (1962). *Lord of the flies.* After their plane crashes on a deserted island, a group of middle-class English boys must fend for themselves. The society they establish—with its norms, rules, and rejections of deviates—is thought provoking and frightening.

Janis, I. (1982). *Groupthink: Psychological studies of policy decisions and fiascoes* (2nd ed.). Boston: Houghton Mifflin. Janis argues persuasively that many important policy decisions, from U.S. President Kennedy's decision to invade Cuba to the escalation of the Vietnam War, were flawed by groupthink, wherein maintaining group cohesiveness and solidarity was more important than considering the facts in a realistic manner.

Kasdan, Lawrence (Director). (1983). *The big chill* [Film]. Seven college housemates meet again at the funeral of a close friend who has committed suicide. A poignant and often funny look at group dynamics.

Levine, J. M. & Moreland, R. L. (1998). Small groups. In D. Gilbert, S. Fiske, & G. Lindzey (Eds.), *Handbook of social psychology* (4th ed., Vol. 2, pp. 415–469). New York: McGraw-Hill. A review of research on small groups by two of the best-known experts in the field.

Malcolm X & Haley, Alex (1965). *The autobiography of Malcolm X.* The autobiographical account of the life of Malcolm X, from his early days in Detroit to his electric leadership role in the Nation of Islam. Malcolm X's life story raises many fascinating questions about the origins and causes of leadership. Made into a movie in 1992, directed by Spike Lee.

Pruitt, D. G. (1998). Social conflict. In D. Gilbert, S. Fiske, & G. Lindzey (Eds.), *Handbook of social psychology* (4th ed., Vol. 2, pp. 470–503). New York: McGraw-Hill. An incisive review of research on conflict, including such topics as social dilemmas, negotiation, broader conflict, and conflict resolution.

Suedfeld, P., Conway III, L. G., & Eichorn, D. (2001). Studying Canadian leaders at a distance. In O. Feldman & L. O. Valenty (Eds.), *Profiling political leaders: Cross-cultural studies of personality and behavior* (pp. 3–19). Westport, CT: Prager Publishers/Greenwood Publishing Group, Inc. Written by University of British Columbia psychologists, this article presents a fascinating analysis of the relation between integrative complexity and greatness among Canadian prime ministers. We learn which prime ministers have scored particularly high on this dimension and which have scored particularly low. Moreover, the authors document changes in the integrative complexity of various prime ministers in response to crises, highlighting who was able to muster his or her cognitive resources and rise to a challenge and who was more likely to lose integrative complexity in the face of stress.

Witte, E., & David, J. H. (1996). *Understanding group behavior* (Volumes 1 and 2). Mahwah, NJ: Erlbaum. A collection of chapters on small groups by experts in the field.

WEBLINKS

www.vcu.edu/hasweb/group/gdynamic.htm

Group Dynamics

This site provides links to various articles, activities, journals, and associations dealing with group dynamics.

www.trinity.edu/~mkearl/socpsy-8.html

Collective Behavior and the Social Psychologies of Social Institutions

This site examines the influence of larger, societal influences on social behaviour. For example, the site includes a survey examining whether people attributed their attitudes on various issues to personal experience, friends/family, media, religion, and so on. The results indicate that people attribute many of their attitudes to societal influences such as media and religion.

www.u.arizona.edu/~jearl/cbsm.html

Collective Behavior and Social Movements

This is the home page of the Collective Behavior and Social Movements section of the American Sociological Association. The purpose of this section is to foster the study of emergent and extra-institutional social forms and behaviour, particularly crowds and social movements.

http://chadwick.jlmc.iastate.edu/theory/grpthink.html

Groupthink

This site provides a summary of groupthink and includes advice on groupthink prevention.

www.people.cornell.edu/pages/jak20/dilemma.html

Links to Game Theory and Social Dilemma Sites

This site provides links to several topics related to social dilemmas.

CHAPTER 10

Interpersonal Attraction
from first impressions to close relationships

Chapter Outline

"THEN I MET NINA . . ." THESE FOUR LITTLE WORDS CHANGED A MAN'S LIFE. A few years ago, Bradley Bird, a Canadian newspaper writer in his early forties, was on a trip, covering a series of sad, dark events—the experiences of Chechen refugees and conflict in Kosovo and Kurdish Turkey. As he wearily boarded a bus in Georgia (near Russia), bracing himself for the 20-hour ride to northeast Turkey for one last story, a woman took the seat beside him. She was a tall, attractive, raven-haired woman in her thirties. As the bus headed into the night, the woman turned to him and asked his name. As Bradley recalls, "I looked at her seriously for the first time and was pleased to see a face as lovely as I'd ever beheld, with dark mysterious eyes, a perfect nose, and full red lips" (Bird, 2001). The woman's name was Nina. To Bradley's surprise, he found himself asking her if there was a man in her life. She answered no. He surprised himself still more by saying, "You need me, and I need you." Because she said she spoke only a little English, he repeated it to make sure she understood. She smiled and they gazed into each other's eyes. It was midnight and the driver turned off the interior lights. Her arm brushed against his in the darkness. "The sensation was incredible," Bradley exclaims, "electric, and I couldn't stop myself, I gave her arm a gentle squeeze." Nina reciprocated.

At first they tried to hide their feelings from the other passengers, but by 12 hours into the ride, they were unable to contain their joy. Bradley informed the driver that his plans had changed and he would now stay on the bus an additional 13 hours so he could have more time with Nina. The driver and passengers began to celebrate with them. An older, heavy man brought out a bottle of vodka to mark the occasion. Bradley reports that by then he and Nina were inseparable and began to make plans for her to come to Canada. He begged to accompany her to Sophia, Bulgaria, where she was going to visit her sister, but she refused. So, he got off the bus in Istanbul, and instead of flying home as scheduled, waited there for three weeks, hoping to catch Nina on her way back to Georgia. During that time he tried to reach her at her sister's, but the phone number she had given him didn't work. Reluctantly, he returned home and mailed her the documents she would need to get a visa. It was May.

Nina wrote back, assuring Bradley of her desire to be with him. She also told him he would have to return to Turkey and plead her case to the Canadian Embassy there. By this time, it was August, and Bradley had accepted a teaching position. What to do now? The answer was clear. Bradley promptly quit his job and spent the next few months trying to reach Nina to make arrangements for them to meet in Turkey. The phone lines were always busy or not working. In December, he decided he simply had to take action. He booked a flight to Turkey and two return tickets to Canada. He managed to track down Nina's sister in Bulgaria and asked her to let Nina know that he was coming. "Oh, Bradley," she said, "Nina is back with her husband. Her daughter insisted on it." With those words, Bradley's dream of a life with Nina was shattered. But Bradley Bird isn't bitter. In his words: "I will always be grateful to Nina for giving me 33 of the happiest hours of my adult life" (Bird, 2001).

As Bradley Bird's experience illustrates, the need to love and be loved is one of the most basic, fundamental human needs. Despite all of the warning signs—the fact that he had just met this woman and knew nothing about her, and had been given the wrong phone number for her sister in Bulgaria—Bradley just couldn't help himself. He fell in love

◀ A trip to Istanbul proved to be a heartbreaker for writer Bradley Bird.

with the mysterious Nina, and it changed his life. Instead of returning home after a gruelling trip, he spent three weeks waiting in Istanbul on the faint chance that he would catch Nina on her way back to Georgia. Not only that, he gave up the job he had just landed in hopes of being able to bring Nina to Canada. And this man in his forties, who had experienced other relationships (he was once married), describes the bus ride with Nina as the happiest 33 hours of his adult life!

What, exactly, is love, and why are we so motivated to seek it? Or perhaps the question should be, why are we so motivated to seek it even when it comes at a high cost? Research conducted by Susan Boon and Karen Pasveer (1999) at the University of Calgary suggests that people are well aware of the risks associated with relationships. One of their participants, a 26-year-old woman, wrote:

> Some of my friends who aren't in relationships are dying to get into one. I don't understand why because most of the time it's more hurtful than it is an enjoyable experience. I told them, "Enjoy being single because it's more fun and I think it's a lot less hassle." Getting into a relationship . . . falling for somebody, and you're bound to set yourself up for a lot of hurt . . . and misery.

Despite the hurt and misery, most people are highly motivated to find love. Why? This is one of the basic questions to be addressed in this chapter. We will discuss the antecedents of attraction, from the initial liking of two people meeting for the first time, to the love that develops in close relationships. We will also discuss how people maintain relationships once they have been formed, as well as the processes whereby relationships end. As we discuss this research, you may want to think about how you can put these social psychological findings to good use in your own life—although we can't guarantee that a thorough reading of this chapter will save you from completely rearranging your life because of a chance meeting with a gorgeous, mysterious stranger on a bus.

Major Antecedents of Attraction

As Ellen Berscheid (1985; Berscheid & Reis, 1998) has noted, we human beings, the most social of social animals, have survived as a species largely because of our ability to know whether another creature or human being is good or bad for us. "Matters of interpersonal attraction are quite literally of life and death importance, not just to the individual but to all of humankind" (Berscheid, 1985). What factors cause one person to be attracted to another? Let's find out.

THE PERSON NEXT DOOR: THE PROPINQUITY EFFECT

There are approximately 5 billion people in the world. In your lifetime, however, you will have the opportunity to meet and interact with only a minuscule percentage of that population. Thus, it will not surprise you to learn that one of the simplest determinants of interpersonal attraction is proximity—sometimes called *propinquity*. The people who, by chance, you see and interact with most often are most likely to become your friends and lovers (Berscheid & Reis, 1998; Fehr, 1996; Moreland & Beach, 1992; Newcomb, 1961; Segal, 1974). This includes people in your city, your neighbourhood, and on your street. Now, this might seem obvious. However, the striking thing about proximity and attraction, or the **propinquity effect**, as social psychologists call it, is that it works on a micro level.

For example, consider a classic study conducted in a housing complex for married students at MIT. Leon Festinger, Stanley Schachter, and Kurt Back (1950) tracked friendship formation among the couples in the various apartment buildings. For example, one section of the complex, Westgate West, was composed of 17 two-storey buildings, each having 10 apartments. The residents had been assigned to their apartments at random, as

Propinquity effect

the finding that the more we see and interact with people, the more likely they are to become our friends

◀ Close friendships are often formed in university, in part because of propinquity.

vacancies opened up, and nearly all of them were strangers when they moved in. The researchers asked the residents to name their three closest friends in the housing project. Just as the propinquity effect would predict, 65 percent of the residents mentioned people who lived in the same building, even though the other buildings were not far away. Even more striking was the pattern of friendships within a building. Each Westgate West building was designed as shown in the drawing in Figure 10.1. The researchers found that 41 percent of the next-door neighbours indicated they were close friends, 22 percent of those who lived two doors apart did so, and only 10 percent of those who lived on opposite ends of the hall did so.

Festinger and colleagues (1950) demonstrated that attraction and propinquity rely not only on actual physical distance but also on the more psychological, functional distance. Functional distance is defined as certain aspects of architectural design that make it likely that some people will come into contact with each other more often than with others. For example, consider the friendship choices of the residents of apartments 1 and 5 (see Figure 10.1). Couples living at the foot of the stairs, and in one case near the mailboxes, saw a great deal of upstairs residents. Sure enough, apartment dwellers in apartments 1 and 5 throughout the complex had more friends upstairs than did dwellers in the other first-floor apartments. (You can map out propinquity effects in your life with Try It! on page 349.)

Mere exposure effect

the finding that the more exposure we have to a stimulus, the more apt we are to like it

The propinquity effect works because of familiarity, or the **mere exposure effect**: The more exposure we have to a stimulus, the more apt we are to like it. We see certain people a lot, and the more familiar they become, the more friendship blooms. Of course, if the person in question is an obnoxious jerk, then, not surprisingly, the more exposure you have to him or her, the greater your dislike (Swap, 1977). However, in the absence of such negative qualities, familiarity breeds attraction and liking (Bornstein, 1989; Bornstein & D'Agostino, 1992; Griffin & Sparks, 1990; Moreland & Zajonc, 1982; Zajonc, 1968).

▼ **Figure 10.1**

THE FLOOR PLAN OF A WESTGATE WEST BUILDING.

All of the buildings in the housing complex had the same floor plan.

(Adapted from Festinger, Schachter, & Back, 1950)

A good example of the propinquity and mere exposure effects is your classroom. All semester long, you see the same people. Does this increase your liking for them? Richard Moreland and Scott Beach (1992) tested this hypothesis by planting female research confederates in a large university classroom. The women did not interact with the professor or the other students; they simply walked in and sat quietly in the first row, where everyone could see them. The confederates differed in how many classes they attended, from 15 meetings down to the control condition of zero. At the end of the semester, the students

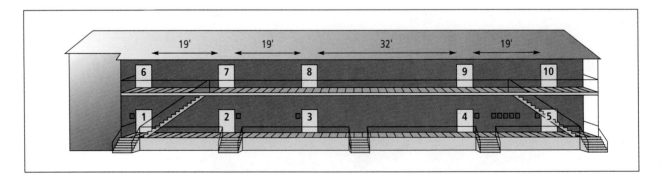

Mapping the Propinquity Effect in Your Life

In this exercise you will examine the relationship between who your friends and acquaintances are and the place(s) where you spend time regularly. Does propinquity explain who your friends are?

First, pick a physical space to focus on. You could choose your dormitory, apartment building, or the building in which you work. (We'll use a dormitory as an example.) Draw a rough floor plan of your dormitory. Include the location of all dorm room doors, the stairs or elevator, the rest room, living room, and so on. Mark your room with a large X. (You can decide whether you need to draw just your floor or more of the building.)

Second, think about who your *close* friends are on the floor. Mark their dorm rooms with the number 1. Next, think about who your friends are; mark their rooms with the number 2. Finally, think about your acquaintances—people you say hello to or chat with briefly now and then. Mark their rooms with the number 3.

Now, examine the pattern of friendships on your map. Are your friends clustered near your room in physical space? Are the dorm rooms with numbers 1 and 2 among the closest to your room in physical space? Are they physically closer to your room than the ones with number 3? And what about the dorm rooms that didn't get a number (meaning that you don't really know these people or interact with them)—are these rooms the farthest from yours?

Finally, examine your propinquity map for the presence of functional distance. Do aspects of the architectural design of your dorm make you more likely to cross paths with some dorm members than others? For example, the location of the rest room, kitchen, living room, stairs or elevator, and mailboxes can play an important role in propinquity and friendship formation. These are all places you go to frequently; when walking to and from them, you pass some people's dorm rooms and not others'. Are the people who live along your path the ones you know best? If so, propinquity has played an important role in determining the people with whom you have formed relationships!

in the class were shown slides of the women, whom they rated on several measures of liking and attractiveness. As you can see in Figure 10.2, mere exposure had a definite effect on liking. Even though they had never interacted, the students liked the woman more, the more often they had seen her in class.

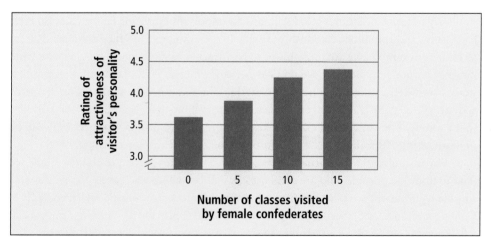

◀ Figure 10.2

THE EFFECTS THAT MERE EXPOSURE IN THE CLASS-ROOM HAS ON ATTRACTION.

The more often students saw a female confederate in their classroom, the more positively they rated her personality, even though they had never interacted with her.

(Adapted from Moreland & Beach, 1992)

Before leaving this topic, we should note that familiarity can occur in a new way today—we can get to know each other through electronic mail and computer chat rooms. Computer-mediated communication offers a new twist on the propinquity effect; the fact that someone is thousands of kilometres away no longer means you can't meet him or her. Are computer-based relationships the same as ones formed in everyday life? Do computer relationships survive when they move from the computer screen to face-to-face interactions? Although it is too early to offer definitive answers to these questions, McKenna and Bargh (2000) have found that two people like each other more if their first encounter is an interaction in an Internet chat room, rather than a face-to-face meeting. They also like each other more on a second, face-to-face meeting if their first meeting was on the Internet. Whether this greater initial liking translates into a satisfying, long-term relationship is a fascinating question for future research.

SIMILARITY

Though propinquity does affect friendship choices, it is also the case that we don't become good friends with everyone who is near us in physical space. What about the match between our interests, background, attitudes, and values and those of the other person? Are we more attracted to people who are like us (the concept of **similarity**), or are we more attracted to people who are our opposites (the concept of **complementarity**)? Folk wisdom may suggest that "opposites attract," but research evidence proves that it is similarity, not complementarity, that draws people together (Berscheid & Reis, 1998).

For example, dozens of tightly controlled experiments have shown that if all you know about a person (whom you've never met) is his or her opinions on several issues, the more similar those opinions are to yours, the more you will like him or her (Byrne & Nelson, 1965). And what happens when you do meet? In a classic study, Theodore Newcomb (1961) randomly assigned male students at the University of Michigan to be roommates in a particular dormitory at the start of the school year. Would similarity predict friendship formation? The answer was yes. Men became friends with those who were demographically similar (e.g., shared a rural background), as well as with those who were similar in attitudes and values (e.g., were also engineering majors or also held liberal political views).

Since Newcomb conducted this research, dozens of studies have demonstrated that similarity in terms of attitudes and values is an important predictor of attraction in both friendships and romantic relationships (Fehr, 1996). Similarity in other domains matters as well. For example, we are more likely to be attracted to someone who enjoys the same kinds of leisure activities that we do (Werner & Parmelee, 1979). In fact, according to a study conducted at the University of Waterloo, for some people similarity in terms of activity preferences is a stronger predictor of attraction than is similarity of attitudes (Jamieson, Lydon, & Zanna, 1987). We also are attracted to people who are similar to us in terms of interpersonal style and communication skills (Burleson & Samter, 1996).

Why is similarity so important in attraction? There are several possibilities. First, we tend to think that people who are similar to us will be inclined to like us. Given this reasonable assumption, we take the first steps and initiate a relationship (Berscheid, 1985; Condon & Crano, 1988). Second, people who are similar provide us with important social validation for our characteristics and beliefs—that is, they provide us with the feeling that

Similarity

attraction to people who are like us

Complementarity

attraction to people who are opposite to us

▼ Similarity is one of the major determinants of attraction.

we are right (Byrne & Clore, 1970). In contrast, when someone disagrees with us on important issues, we tend not to like the person (Rosenbaum, 1986). In addition to feeling validated, recent research suggests that we are more likely to feel understood by those who are similar to us. Specifically, Murray, Holmes, Bellavia, and Griffin (2002) found that students in dating relationships and married couples living in the Kitchener-Waterloo area overestimated the degree of similarity between themselves and their partner. The greater the similarity they perceived, the more understood they felt by their partner. Feelings of understanding, in turn, predicted relationship satisfaction.

Finally, the rewards-of-interaction explanation offers another reason why similarity leads to attraction (Berscheid & Hatfield, 1978; Burleson, 1994). According to this explanation, if a person feels the same way we do on important issues, we assume it would be enjoyable to spend time with him or her. Conversely, it is not very pleasant to interact with someone who disagrees with us on everything.

Thus, the desire to be liked, understood, and validated, as well as the desire to have enjoyable interactions, plays a role in boosting the attractiveness of a like-minded person and diminishing the attractiveness of someone who is dissimilar (Byrne, Clore, & Smeaton, 1986; Cate & Lloyd, 1992; Dryer & Horowitz, 1997; Fehr, 1996; Holtz, 1997).

RECIPROCAL LIKING

Most of us like to be liked. Not surprisingly, **reciprocal liking**—liking someone who likes us in return—is one of the prime determinants of interpersonal attraction. Liking is so powerful it can even make up for the absence of similarity. For example, in one experiment, when a young woman expressed interest in male research participants simply by maintaining eye contact, leaning toward them, and listening attentively, the men expressed great liking for her despite the fact that they knew she disagreed with them on important issues (Gold, Ryckman, & Mosley, 1984). Whether the clues are nonverbal or verbal, perhaps the most crucial determinant of whether we will like someone is the extent to which we believe that person likes us (Berscheid & Walster, 1978; Condon & Crano, 1988; Kenny, 1994; Kubitscheck & Hallinan, 1998; Secord & Backman, 1964).

Interestingly, reciprocal liking can come about because of a self-fulfilling prophecy (see Chapter 3), as demonstrated in an experiment by Rebecca Curtis and Kim Miller (1986). University students who did not know one another took part in the study in pairs. The researchers led some students to believe that they were liked by the student with whom they would be paired. Other students were led to believe that they were disliked by their partner for the study. The pairs of students were then given an opportunity to have a conversation. Just as predicted, those individuals who thought they were liked behaved in more likeable ways with their partner; they disclosed more about themselves, disagreed less about the topic under discussion, and generally behaved in a warmer, more pleasant manner than did those individuals who thought they were disliked. As a result, their partners ended up liking them—more so than did the partners of students who believed they were disliked (see Figure 10.3).

We should note that reciprocal liking effects can only occur if you like yourself in the first place. People with negative self-concepts tend to be skeptical that others actually do like them and therefore do not necessarily reciprocate liking (Swann, Stein-Seroussi, & McNulty, 1992).

Reciprocal liking
when you like someone and that person also likes you

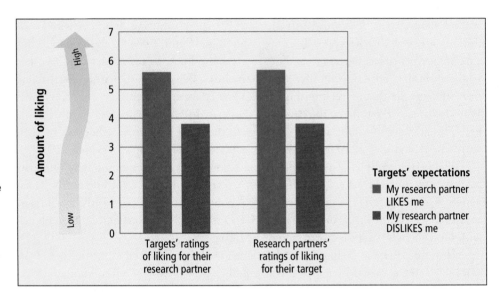

▶ **Figure 10.3**

LIKING AND BEING LIKED.

Research participants were
given false feedback that their
research partner either did or
did not like them. They liked
their partner more if they had
been told beforehand that their
partner liked them (see left-
hand side of figure), and their
partners responded in kind (see
right-hand side of figure).
Beliefs did indeed create
reality.

(Adapted from Curtis & Miller,
1986)

THE EFFECTS OF PHYSICAL ATTRACTIVENESS ON LIKING

Propinquity, similarity, and reciprocal liking are not the only determinants of who we will come to like. We also are affected by people's looks—their physical attractiveness. How important is physical appearance to our first impressions of people? A classic study by Walster (Hatfield) and her colleagues revealed a surprising answer (Walster [Hatfield], Aronson, Abrahams, & Rottman, 1966). These researchers matched 752 incoming students at the University of Minnesota for a blind date at a dance during orientation week. The students had previously taken a battery of personality and aptitude tests; however, the researchers paired them up at random. On the night of the dance, the couples spent a few hours together dancing and chatting. They then evaluated their date and indicated whether they would like to date that person again. Of the many possible characteristics that could have determined whether they liked each other—such as their partner's intelligence, independence, sensitivity, or sincerity—the overriding determinant was physical attractiveness. What's more, there was no great difference between men and women on this score.

The powerful role that physical appearance plays in attraction is not limited to heterosexual relationships. Paul Sergios and James Cody (1985) conducted a replication of the "blind date" study described above, with gay men as the research participants. The gay men responded just as the heterosexual men and women had in the earlier study: the physical attractiveness of their dates was the strongest predictor of their liking for them.

The findings of Walster (Hatfield) and colleagues' study, and subsequent replications, raise a perplexing issue: When people are asked about the qualities they desire in a dating partner or a mate, physical attractiveness is not at the top of the list (Buss & Barnes, 1986). Yet when it comes to people's actual behaviour (what people do, rather than what they say), appearance seems to be the only thing that matters—at least in first-impression situations. Are people unaware of the importance they place on looks, or are they simply unwilling to admit that they so highly value such a superficial characteristic? To find out, Hadjistavropoulos and Genest (1994) designed a clever study. They presented female students at the University of Saskatchewan with photographs of men varying in physical attractiveness, along with descriptions of their (supposed) personality traits. Participants were asked to rate the men in terms of their desirability as a dating partner. The researchers found that attractive men received higher ratings than did unattractive men. Moreover, attractiveness was the best predictor of desirability—more so than personality information. So far this sounds just like the other studies we have been describing. But here's the interesting twist: Some of the participants were connected to an impressive-looking apparatus that they were told was a highly accurate lie detector. The researchers reasoned that if people aren't aware of the emphasis they place on looks, lie detector participants should give the same responses as participants who were not connected to a lie detector. If, on the other hand, people are aware that they base their evaluations of people on looks but feel they shouldn't admit it, then those who are attached to a lie detector should be more likely to "confess" to this than those who are not. And that is exactly what happened. The findings suggest that we are aware of the value we place on looks—but as long as we can get away with it, we won't admit it.

Before leaving this topic we should note that although both sexes value attractiveness, there is a tendency for men, more so than women, to place greater emphasis on looks (Buss, 1989; Buss & Barnes, 1986; Feingold, 1990). For example, in a recent study by Lundy, Tan, and Cunningham (1998), students at Lakehead University were shown photographs of attractive and unattractive opposite-sex persons, and were asked to rate their desirability for sexual intercourse, as a dating partner, for a serious relationship, for marriage, and for marriage with children. Men's ratings of desirability were more influenced by the physical attractiveness of the opposite-sex person (especially for the nonmarital kinds of relationships) than were women's ratings. (Later, when we discuss evolutionary theories of love, we will consider some reasons for this gender difference.)

What Is Attractive?
From early childhood on, the media tell us what is beautiful, and they tell us that this specific definition of beauty is associated with goodness. For example, illustrators of most traditional children's books, as well as the people who draw the characters in Disney movies, have taught us that the heroines—as well as the princes who woo and win them—all look alike. They all have regular features—small, pert noses; big eyes; shapely lips; blemish-free complexions—and slim, athletic bodies—pretty much like Barbie and Ken dolls.

Bombarded as we are with media depictions of attractiveness, it is not surprising to learn that we share a set of criteria for defining beauty (Tseëlon, 1995). Look at the photographs on page 354 of models and actors who are considered attractive in Western culture. Can you describe the facial characteristics that have earned them this label? Michael Cunningham (1986) designed a creative study to determine these standards of beauty. He asked male university students to rate the attractiveness of 50 photographs of women, taken from a college yearbook and from an international beauty pageant program. Cunningham then carefully measured the relative size of the facial features in each photograph. He found that high attractiveness ratings were given to faces with large eyes, a small nose, a small chin, prominent cheekbones and narrow cheeks, high eyebrows, large pupils, and a big smile. Cunningham and his colleagues also examined women's ratings of male beauty in the same manner. They found that higher attractiveness ratings of men were associated with large eyes, prominent cheekbones, a large chin, and a big smile (Cunningham, Barbee, & Pike, 1990).

There is some overlap in the men's and women's ratings. Both sexes admire large eyes in the opposite sex, and these are considered to be a "babyface" feature, for newborn mammals have very large eyes for the size of their faces. Babyface features are thought to be attractive because they elicit feelings of warmth and nurturance in perceivers—take, for example, our response to babies, kittens, and puppies (e.g., Berry, 1995; McArthur & Berry, 1987; Zebrowitz, 1997; Zebrowitz & Montepare, 1992). Both sexes also admire

▼ Research has found that we share some standards of beauty. In females, large eyes, prominent cheekbones and narrow cheeks, high eyebrows, and a small chin were associated with beauty; in males, large eyes, prominent cheekbones, and a large chin were rated as most beautiful. Today's popular models and film stars—such as Brad Pitt, Michelle Pfeiffer, Denzel Washington, Naomi Campbell, Jimmy Smits, and Lucy Liu—fit these criteria.

prominent cheekbones in the opposite sex, an adult feature that is found only in the faces of those who are sexually mature. Note that the female face that is considered beautiful has more babyface features (small nose, small chin) than the handsome male face, suggesting that beauty in the female, more so than in the male, is associated with childlike qualities.

Cultural Standards of Beauty

Are people's perceptions of what is beautiful or handsome similar across cultures? According to a recent review of this literature by University of Toronto social psychologist Karen Dion (Dion, 2002), the answer is a surprising yes (see also Cunningham et al., 1995; Jones & Hill, 1993; McArthur & Berry, 1987; Perrett, May, & Yoshikawa, 1994). Though racial and ethnic groups do vary in specific facial features, people from disparate cultures agree with each other on what is physically attractive in the human face. Researchers in this area have asked participants from various countries, ethnicities, and racial groups to rate the physical attractiveness of photographed faces of people who also represent various countries, ethnicities, and racial groups. The participants' ratings agree to a remarkable extent—a conclusion reinforced by the results of a recent meta analysis conducted by Judith Langlois and colleagues (2000). While there is variation in people's judgments, across large groups a consensus emerges. Perceivers think that some faces are just better looking than others, regardless of cultural background (Berscheid & Reis, 1998).

The results showing cross-cultural agreement on physical attractiveness led Judith Langlois and Lori Roggman (1990; Langlois, Roggman, & Musselman, 1994) to wonder whether there are universal dimensions of faces that are attractive to the species. They hypothesized that attractive faces for both sexes are those whose features are the arithmetic mean—or average—for the species, not the extremes. These researchers have used computer technology to merge up to 32 photographs of faces into a single face that is the exact mathematical average of the facial features of the original people's photographs. The photographs on page 356 show the result of the merging of two photographs of women. Interestingly, in studies conducted by Langlois and her colleagues, research participants judge the composite photograph (the arithmetic average of all the faces) as more attractive than the individual photographs that make up the composite. This is the case for both male and female photographs. The face composites produce what the researchers call a typical or "familiar" face. Individual variation in facial features is melted away in the composite; what is left is a good-looking human being, whose face has a familiar and highly pleasing aspect to it.

Do these results mean that "average" faces are the *most* attractive? Not necessarily. Langlois and her colleagues found that the "average" composite face was perceived as more attractive than all of the faces that made it up. However, that does not mean that these composite "average" faces had all of the physical qualities that people cross-culturally agree are *highly* attractive. To explore this issue, D. I. Perrett and colleagues (1994) created two types of composite faces: One composite was made up of 60 individual photographs and was called the "average attractive" composite. The other composite was composed of the 15 photos from the original 60 that had received the highest ratings of attractiveness on a pretest. This composite was called the "high attractive" composite. The researchers made these two kinds of composites using photographs of Caucasian and

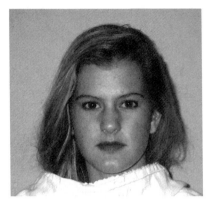 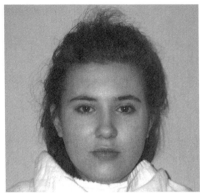 

▲ Physical attractiveness of composite faces. Langlois and Roggman (1990) created composites of faces using a computer. Pictured here is the first step in the process. The two women's photos on the left are merged to create the "composite person" on the right. This composite person has facial features that are the mathematical average of the facial features of the two original women. The final step of the process occurs when 32 individuals' faces have been merged to create one face, the average of all of the prior 32 faces. Perceivers rate the 32-photograph composite face as more physically attractive than any of the individual faces that create it.
(From Langlois, Roggman, & Musselman, 1994)

Japanese women and men. They then asked research participants in Great Britain and Japan to rate all of the composite faces for attractiveness. They found, first, that the "high attractive" composites were rated as being significantly more attractive than the "average attractive" composites. Second, the Japanese and British participants showed the same pattern when judging the faces, reinforcing the idea that similar perceptions of facial attractiveness exist cross-culturally.

You may be wondering: What did these "high attractive" composite faces look like? Their facial shapes, whether Japanese or Caucasian, matched the profile of attractiveness for women and men identified by Michael Cunningham and colleagues discussed earlier (Cunningham, 1986; Cunningham, Barbee, & Pike, 1995). For example, the Japanese and Caucasian "high attractive" female composites had higher cheekbones, a thinner jaw, and larger eyes relative to the size of the face than the "average attractive" composites did. Thus, the "average" composite face is attractive to us because it has lost some of the atypical or unfamiliar variation that makes up individual faces. However, the most attractive composite face is one that started out above average and only became more so as variation was smoothed over.

Assumptions about Attractive People   Most people assume that physical attractiveness is highly correlated with other desirable traits. The results of many studies indicate that beauty constitutes a powerful stereotype—what Karen Dion, Ellen Berscheid, and Elaine Walster (Hatfield) (1972) have called the "what is beautiful is good" stereotype (Ashmore, Solomon, & Longo, 1996; Brigham, 1980; Hatfield & Sprecher, 1986a).

Most research on the "what is beautiful is good" stereotype has been conducted with young people—usually university students. Recently, Perlini, Bertolissi, and Lind (1999) replicated the original Dion, Berscheid, and Walster study, with a twist. They showed photographs of attractive and unattractive younger and older women to first-year university students and senior citizens living in Sault Ste. Marie, Ontario. The researchers found that participants attributed more positive qualities to attractive women—regardless of their age. There was, however, one exception. Older men attributed more positive qualities to attractive young women than to attractive older women. Thus, it appears that the "what is beautiful is good" stereotype applies to older people as well. The exception is older men, for whom the stereotype seems to be "what is beautiful *and younger* is good"—at least with regard to their perceptions of women.

Luckily for those of us who do not look like supermodels, the stereotype is relatively narrow, affecting people's judgments about an individual only in specific areas. Meta analyses conducted by Alice Eagly and her colleagues (1991) and by Alan Feingold (1992a) have revealed that physical attractiveness has the largest effect on both men's and women's attributions when they are making judgments about social competence: The beautiful are thought to be more sociable, extroverted, and popular than the less attractive. They are also seen as more sexual, more happy, and more assertive.

Interestingly, the stereotype that the beautiful are particularly gifted in the area of social competence has some research support; highly attractive people do develop good social interaction skills and report having more satisfying interactions with others than do the less attractive (Berscheid & Reis, 1998; Feingold, 1992a; Reis, Nezlek, & Wheeler, 1980; Reis et al., 1982). An analysis of national survey data gathered by the Institute for Social Research at York University also revealed that attractiveness and income are positively correlated—at least for men (Roszell, Kennedy & Grabb, 1989). Thus, there appears to be a kernel of truth in the "what is beautiful is good" stereotype. The reason is that beautiful people, from a young age, receive a great deal of social attention that helps them develop good social skills (which, in turn, may lead to other positive outcomes, such as interpersonal and occupational success). You probably recognize the self-fulfilling prophecy at work here, a concept we discussed in Chapter 3. The way we treat people affects how they behave and, ultimately, how they perceive themselves.

Can a "regular" person be made to act like a "beautiful" one through the self-fulfilling prophecy? Mark Snyder, Elizabeth Decker Tanke, and Ellen Berscheid (1977) decided to find out. They gave male university students a packet of information about another research participant, including her photograph. The photograph was of either an attractive woman or an unattractive woman. The purpose of the photograph was to invoke the men's stereotype that "what is beautiful is good"—that the woman would be more warm, likeable, poised, and fun to talk to if she was physically attractive than if she was unattractive. The men then had a telephone conversation with a woman, who they were told was the woman in the photograph. (They actually spoke with another woman.) The important question is this: Did the men's beliefs create reality? Yes. The men who thought they were talking to an attractive woman responded to her in a warmer, more sociable manner than did the men who thought they were talking to an unattractive woman. Not only that, but the men's behaviour influenced how the women themselves responded. When observers later listened to a tape recording of the women's half of the conversation, they rated the women whose male partners thought they were physically attractive as more attractive, confident, animated, and warm than the women whose male partners thought they were unattractive. In short, if a man thought he was talking to an attractive woman, he spoke to her in a way that brought out her best and most sparkling qualities.

This study was later replicated with the roles switched. Andersen and Bem (1981) showed female participants a photograph of an attractive or an unattractive man; the women then had a phone conversation with him. The men on the other end of the line were unaware of the women's belief about them. Just as in the Snyder, Tanke, and Berscheid (1977) study, the women acted on their stereotype of beauty, and the unknowing men responded accordingly.

Cultural Differences You might have wondered whether the "what is beautiful is good" stereotype operates across cultures. The answer appears to be yes. Ladd Wheeler and Youngmee Kim (1997) asked students in Seoul, South Korea, to rate a number of yearbook photographs that varied in physical attractiveness. They found that the Korean male and female participants thought the more physically attractive people would also be more socially skilled, friendly, and well-adjusted—the same group of traits that North American participants thought went with physical attractiveness (see Table 10.1).

TABLE 10.1

How culture affects the "what is beautiful is good" stereotype

The "what is beautiful is good" stereotype has been explored in two types of cultures: an "individualist" culture (North America) and a "collectivist" culture (Asia). Male and female research participants in the United States and Canada and in South Korea rated photographs of people with varying degrees of physical attractiveness. Their responses indicated that some of the traits that make up the stereotype are the same across cultures, while other traits that are associated with the stereotype are different in the two types of culture:

Traits that are shared in the Korean, U.S., and Canadian stereotype of "what is beautiful is good"

sociable	extroverted
likeable	happy
popular	well-adjusted
friendly	mature
poised	sexually warm and responsive

Additional traits that are present in the U.S. and Canadian stereotype

strong

dominant

assertive

Additional traits that are present in the Korean stereotype

sensitive	empathic
generous	honest
trustworthy	

The basic elements of the "what is beautiful is good" stereotype are shared across cultures; these traits involve social skills and competence. However, individualist and collectivist cultures add other elements to the stereotype, reflecting what is valued in each. The United States and Canada are individualist cultures, where independence and self-reliance are valued; the "beautiful" stereotype incorporates these traits of personal strength. Korea is a collectivist culture, where harmony in group relations is valued; the "beautiful" stereotype in that culture reflects traits involving integrity and concern for others. Thus, in both cultures, the physically attractive, more so than the less physically attractive, are seen as having the characteristics valued in that culture.

Source: Adapted from Eagly et al., 1991; Feingold, 1992a; Wheeler & Kim, 1997.

However, Korean and North American students differed in some of the other traits they assigned to the beautiful; these differences highlight what is considered important and valuable in each culture (Markus, Kitayama, & Heiman, 1996; Triandis, 1995). For the North American students, who live in individualist cultures that value independence, individuality, and self-reliance, the "beautiful" stereotype included traits of personal strength (see Table 10.1). These traits were not part of the Korean "beautiful" stereotype. Instead, for the Korean students, who live in a collectivist culture that values harmonious group relations, the "beautiful" stereotype included traits of integrity and concern for others—traits that were not part of the North American stereotype (see Table 10.1). Based on her review of this and other studies on this topic, Karen Dion concluded that physical attractiveness stereotyping occurs cross-culturally, although more so in individualistic societies, where greater weight is placed on qualities of the individual, including his or her appearance. In addition, as we have already discussed, some of the qualities attributed to beautiful people vary by culture (Dion, 2002).

In summary, we have discussed four major determinants of attraction: propinquity, similarity, reciprocal liking, and physical attractiveness. We are likely to be attracted to people whose paths we frequently cross, who are similar to us, who seem to like us, and who are good looking.

▲ In Western cultures, where independence is valued, the "beautiful" stereotype includes traits of personal strength. In more collectivistic Asian cultures, beautiful people are assumed to have traits such as integrity and concern for others.

Forming Close Relationships: Defining Love

After getting to this point in the chapter, you should be in a pretty good position to make a favourable first impression the next time you meet someone. Suppose you want Claudia to like you. You should hang around her so you become familiar, emphasize your similarity to her, and find ways of showing that you like her. It also wouldn't hurt to look your best. But what if you want to do more than make a good impression? What if you want to have a close friendship or a romantic relationship?

Until recently, social psychologists had little to say in answer to this question; research on interpersonal attraction focused almost exclusively on first impressions. Why? Primarily because long-term, close relationships are much more difficult to study scientifically than first impressions. As we saw in Chapter 2, random assignment to different conditions is the hallmark of an experiment. When studying first impressions, a researcher can randomly assign you to a get-acquainted session with someone who is similar or dissimilar to you. However, a researcher can't randomly assign you to the similar or dissimilar "lover" condition and make you have a relationship! In addition, psychologists face a daunting task when trying to measure such complex feelings as love and passion. However, as we will see, important strides have been made toward our understanding of close relationships.

WHAT IS LOVE?

In the opening of this chapter, we described Bradley Bird's falling-in-love experience. But what, exactly, is love? For centuries, philosophers, poets, and novelists have grappled with this question. More recently, social psychologists have attempted to provide a scientific answer.

One of the first social psychologists to attempt a scientific analysis of love was Zick Rubin (1970, 1973). He defined love as feelings of intimacy, attachment, and passion, and argued that love is a feeling distinct from liking. Subsequently, social psychologists attempted to dive deeper into the study of love and reached a conclusion that you may already have discovered. There probably isn't a single, simple definition of love because love comes in many forms.

Companionate versus Passionate Love

Companionate versus Passionate Love If you have ever been in love, think back to how you felt about your sweetheart when you first got to know him or her. You probably felt a combination of giddiness, longing, joy, and anxiety—the kinds of feelings that Bradley Bird experienced when he met Nina. The ancient Greeks considered this strange, bewildering set of feelings to be a form of madness, causing all sorts of irrational and obsessional acts. Though times have changed, we are all familiar with the torment—and exhilaration—that comes with falling in love. Now think about how you feel toward your mother, or your brother, or a very close friend. You might also use the word *love* to describe how you feel about these important people in your life, but in this case the feelings are probably quite different from the feelings you have for your sweetheart. Ellen Berscheid and Elaine Walster (Hatfield) (1974; Berscheid & Walster (Hatfield), 1978) attempted to capture this distinction when they proposed that there are two major kinds of love: companionate love and passionate love. **Companionate love** is defined as the feelings of intimacy and affection we feel toward someone with whom our lives are deeply intertwined. People can experience companionate love in nonsexual relationships, such as close friendships or familial relationships, or in sexual relationships, where they experience feelings of intimacy but not a great deal of heat and passion.

   Passionate love involves an intense longing for another person. When things are going well—the other person loves us, too—we feel great fulfillment and ecstasy. When things are not going well, we feel great sadness and despair. This kind of love is characterized by obsessive thoughts about the loved one, as well as heightened physiological arousal wherein we actually feel shortness of breath and a thumping heart when we are in our loved one's presence (Regan, 1998; Regan & Berscheid, 1999).

   Elaine Hatfield and Susan Sprecher (1986b) developed a questionnaire to measure passionate love. Passionate love, as measured by this scale, consists of strong, uncontrollable

Companionate love

the feelings of intimacy and affection we feel for another person about whom we care deeply

Passionate love

the feelings of intense longing, accompanied by physiological arousal, we feel for another person; when our love is reciprocated, we feel great fulfillment and ecstasy, but when it is not, we feel sadness and despair

▼ Does passionate love develop into companionate love in a long-term relationship?

thoughts; intense feelings; and overt acts toward the target of one's affection. Find out if you are experiencing (or have experienced) passionate love, by filling out the questionnaire in Try It!, below.

Triangular Theory of Love Other researchers are not satisfied with a simple dichotomy of two kinds of love. Robert Sternberg (1986, 1988, 1997; Sternberg & Beall, 1991), for example, presents a **triangular theory of love**, which depicts love as comprising three basic

Triangular theory of love
the idea that different kinds of love comprise varying degrees of three components: intimacy, passion, and commitment

The Passionate Love Scale

These items ask you to describe how you feel when you are passionately in love. Think of the person you love most passionately right now. If you are not in love right now, think of the last person you loved passionately. If you have never been in love, think of the person whom you came closest to caring for in that way. Choose your answer by remembering how you felt at the time when your feelings were the most intense.

For each of the 15 items, choose the number between 1 and 9 that most accurately describes your feelings. The answer scale ranges from 1 "not at all true" to 9 "definitely true." Write the number you choose next to each item.

1	2	3	4	5	6	7	8	9
Not at all true				Moderately true			Definitely true	

1. I would feel deep despair if _____ left me.
2. Sometimes I feel I can't control my thoughts; they are obsessively on _____.
3. I feel happy when I am doing something to make _____ happy.
4. I would rather be with _____ than anyone else.
5. I'd get jealous if I thought _____ were falling in love with someone else.
6. I yearn to know all about _____.
7. I want _____—physically, emotionally, and mentally.
8. I have an endless appetite for affection from _____.
9. For me, _____ is the perfect romantic partner.
10. I sense my body responding when _____ touches me.
11. _____ always seems to be on my mind.
12. I want _____ to know me—my thoughts, my fears, and my hopes.
13. I eagerly look for signs indicating _____'s desire for me.
14. I possess a powerful attraction for _____.
15. I get extremely depressed when things don't go right in my relationship with _____.

Scoring: Add up your scores for the 15 items. The total score can range from a minimum of 15 to a maximum of 135. The higher your score, the more your feelings for the person reflect passionate love; the items to which you gave a particularly high score reflect those components of passionate love that you experience most strongly.

Source: Adapted from Hatfield and Sprecher, 1986b.

ingredients: intimacy, passion, and commitment. Intimacy refers to feelings of being close to and bonded with a partner. Passion refers to the "hot" parts of a relationship—feelings of arousal and sexual attraction. Commitment consists of two decisions—the short-term one to love your partner, and the long-term one to maintain that love and stay with your partner. These three ingredients—intimacy, passion, and commitment—can be combined in varying degrees to form different kinds of love (see Figure 10.4). Love can consist of one component alone or of any combination of these three parts. For example, you may feel a great deal of passion or physical attraction (infatuation love) but not know the person well enough to experience intimacy and not be ready to make any kind of commitment. As the relationship develops, it might blossom into romantic love, characterized by passion and intimacy, and maybe even consummate love—the blending of all three components. Sternberg uses the term *companionate love* in the same way we explained earlier, to describe love characterized by intimacy and commitment but not passion (Aron & Westbay, 1996; Hassebrauck & Buhl, 1996; Lemieux & Hale, 1999).

Love styles

the basic theories people have about love that guide their behaviour in relationships

Love Styles Another approach to defining love has focused on **love styles**. According to John Lee (1973, 1988), a sociologist at the University of Toronto, love takes at least six different forms (listed below). Lee's theory was developed further in an extensive program of research by Clyde Hendrick and Susan Hendrick (1986, 1992), who constructed scales to measure each of these styles. What's your style? See if one of the following descriptions matches your approach to love and relationships.

- *Eros* is a passionate, physical love, in which the partner's physical appearance is highly important. The Eros lover gets involved very quickly. A sample item from the Love Attitudes Scale (Hendrick & Hendrick, 1986) to measure this love style is "My partner and I were attracted to each other immediately after we first met."

▶ **Figure 10.4**

THE TRIANGLE OF LOVE.

According to the triangular theory of love, there are seven different forms of love, each made up of varying degrees of intimacy, passion, and commitment.

(Adapted from Sternberg, 1988)

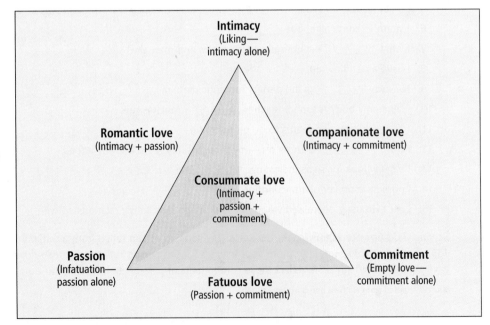

- *Ludus* is love played as a game, never taken too seriously. Very playful in their approach to love, ludic lovers don't mean to cause harm but they often do, sometimes with multiple partners (e.g., "I enjoy playing the 'game of love' with my partner and a number of other partners").

- *Storge* is a slow-growing love, evolving out of affection and friendship (e.g., "Our love is the best kind because it grew out of a long friendship"). Similarity between partners is extremely important.

- *Pragma* is pragmatic love—commonsensical, realistic, feet on the ground. Pragmic lovers know what they're looking for in a relationship and have "conditions" that must be met (e.g., "I considered what my partner was going to become in life before I committed myself to him/her").

- *Mania* is the highly emotional, roller-coaster ride of love. Manic lovers obsess about their partners, vacillate between elation and despair, and are highly dependent on their partners (e.g., "When my partner doesn't pay attention to me, I feel sick all over").

- *Agape* is a selfless, giving, and altruistic love. Agapic lovers think not of themselves but of their partners and what they can do for them (e.g., "I would rather suffer than let my partner suffer"). Their love style is more spiritual than physical.

Hendrick and Hendrick have found that dating and married couples show considerable similarity in their love styles. In addition, couples whose romantic relationships last are higher on Eros (romantic/passionate love) and lower on Ludus (game-playing love) than couples who break up (Hendrick, Hendrick, & Adler, 1988).

Ordinary People's Definition of Love   So far we have been discussing social psychologists' answers to the question, "What is love?" Beverley Fehr (1988, 1994; Fehr & Russell, 1991) has been interested in how ordinary people define love. This is an important issue because the way in which people define love can determine how they act in their close relationships (e.g., deciding whether they are truly "in love," or whether they are experiencing the kind of love that leads to commitment). In an initial set of studies, Fehr (1988) asked students at the University of British Columbia to define love (specifically, participants were asked to list the features or characteristics of the concept of love). The definitions of love that were generated included both companionate features (e.g., warmth, intimacy, caring) and passionate features (e.g., heart rate increases, sexual attraction, thinking about the other person all the time). In follow-up research, other participants were shown these features and asked to rate which were most prototypical, or important, in defining love. As shown in Table 10.2, contrary to the stereotype that university students would view love only in passionate terms, Fehr found that companionate love was seen as capturing the meaning of love, more so than passionate love. Moreover, participants reported that they relied on the level of companionate love, rather than the level of passionate love, when deciding whether a relationship was progressing or deteriorating.

These studies have been replicated by researchers on the east coast of Canada (Button & Collier, 1991) and on the west coast of the United States (Luby & Aron, 1990; Aron & Westbay, 1996). Participants in these studies have shown remarkable agreement on the

TABLE 10.2

Ratings of features of love

Highest Ratings		Lowest Ratings	
Trust	7.50	Think about the other all the time	4.45
Caring	7.28	Energy	4.28
Honesty	7.17	Heart rate increases	4.26
Friendship	7.08	Euphoria	4.12
Respect	7.01	Gazing at the other	4.10
Concern for the other's well-being	7.00	See only the other's good qualities	3.45
Loyalty	7.00	Butterflies in stomach	3.41
Commitment	6.91	Uncertainty	2.88
Accept other the way s/he is	6.82	Dependency	2.81
Supportiveness	6.78	Scary	2.28

Note: Ratings were made on a scale where 1 = extremely poor feature of love, and 8 = extremely good feature of love.

The features of love to which students at the University of British Columbia assigned the highest ratings portray companionate love; the features that received the lowest ratings portray passionate love.

Source: Fehr, 1988.

features of love. The companionate features of love are especially likely to be mentioned, and also consistently receive the highest importance ratings. These findings suggest that, at least within North America, people tend to agree on the meaning of love (Fehr, 1993).

Fehr and Russell (1991) examined ordinary people's conceptions of love from a slightly different angle by asking students at the University of British Columbia and at the University of Winnipeg to list different types of love. They found that the kinds of love listed could be grouped into companionate kinds of love (e.g., friendship love, familial love, maternal love) and passionate kinds of love (romantic love, passionate love, infatuation, sexual love). Once again, the companionate kinds of love were regarded as capturing the true meaning of love. Thus, ordinary people's view of love fits nicely with Berscheid and Hatfield's (Walster's) companionate/passionate distinction (Fehr, 2001). Love is seen as including both companionate and passionate aspects, although the companionate aspect is considered to be the essence of love.

GENDER AND LOVE

Who is all mushy and romantic when it comes to love? Who is practical and solid? If you are like many people, you will answer "women" to the first question and "men" to the second. But think back to our opening story of Bradley Bird and you may come up with a different answer—one that is more consistent with the results of social psychological research. Indeed, when social psychologists began to conduct research on this question, they found that men fall in love more quickly than women and are more likely to endorse romantic beliefs such as "True love lasts forever" (Sprecher & Metts, 1989; Rubin, Peplau, & Hill, 1981). Men are also more likely than women to report having experienced love at first sight—as Bradley Bird can attest. In contrast, women hold a more practical, friendship-based orientation to love (essentially, a companionate view of love). One of the first studies to report this finding was conducted by Kenneth Dion and Karen Dion (1973) at the University of Toronto. Similarly, when Hendrick and Hendrick (1986; Hendrick et al., 1984) began their program of research on love styles, women usually scored higher than men on the Storge (friendship love) and Pragma (practical love) styles. These gender differences continue to be found; women score higher than men on Storge and Pragma, even among culturally diverse participants (Dion & Dion, 1993; we will discuss this research in greater detail in the section on Culture and Love below).

On the other hand, researchers are beginning to realize that there also are similarities in women's and men's definitions and experience of love (Hendrick & Hendrick, 1995). In a recent set of studies conducted at the University of Winnipeg, Beverley Fehr and Ross Broughton (2001) obtained the classic finding—namely, that men's view of love was more romantic and passionate than women's; women's ratings of friendship love were higher than men's. However, some additional, interesting findings emerged. These researchers measured several kinds of companionate love (e.g., familial love, sisterly love, affection), rather than just friendship love, as is usually done. It turned out that men rated these other kinds of companionate love just as high as women did. Moreover, Fehr and Broughton found that even though men rated romantic, passionate kinds of love higher than did women, both sexes gave these kinds of love the lowest ratings and the companionate kinds of love the highest ratings. They concluded that women's and men's views of love are actually more similar than had been thought.

CULTURE AND LOVE

Though love is certainly a human emotion experienced everywhere on the planet, culture does play a role in how people label their experiences and in what they expect (and tolerate) in close relationships. For example, Japanese describe *amae* as an extremely positive emotional state in which one is a totally passive love object, indulged and taken care of by one's romantic partner, much like a mother–infant relationship. There is no equivalent word for *amae* in English or any other Western language; the closest in meaning is the word *dependency*, an emotional state that is considered by Western cultures to be unhealthy in adult relationships (Dion & Dion, 1993; Doi, 1988).

The Chinese have an important relationship concept, *gan qing,* which differs from the Western view of romantic love. *Gan qing* is achieved by helping and working for another person; for example, a "romantic" act would be fixing someone's bicycle or helping them learn new material (Gao, 1996). Another way of conceptualizing love is expressed by the Korean concept of *jung.* Much more than "love," *jung* is what ties two people together. Though couples in new relationships feel strong love for each other, they have not yet developed strong *jung*—that takes time and many mutual experiences. Interestingly, *jung* can develop in negative relationships, too—for example, between business rivals who dislike each other. *Jung* may unknowingly grow between them over time, with the result that they will feel that a strange connection exists (Lim & Choi, 1996).

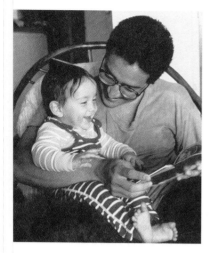

▲ Attachment theory predicts that the attachment style we learn as infants stays with us throughout life, and generalizes to our relationships with other people.

Fearful avoidant style

a type of avoidant attachment in which close relationships are avoided due to mistrust and fears of being hurt

Dismissive avoidant style

a type of avoidant attachment in which the person is self-sufficient and claims not to need close relationships

among a sample of French-Canadian cohabiting and married couples. They found that when difficulties arose, secure participants reported using active, task-centred coping strategies that were aimed at solving problems. These strategies were associated with marital well-being. Anxious/ambivalent participants used passive, emotion-focused coping strategies—strategies that were associated with marital distress. Finally, as you might expect, avoidant participants tended to use passive, avoidant strategies.

In an important conceptual development, Kim Bartholomew, a social psychologist at Simon Fraser University, proposed that there are actually two kinds of avoidant attachment (Bartholomew, 1990; Bartholomew & Horowitz, 1991). People with a **fearful avoidant style** consciously desire intimate relationships, but avoid them because they are afraid to trust others and worry that they will be hurt if they allow themselves to become too close to another person. People with a **dismissive avoidant style** claim that they do not need close relationships, but rather prefer to be independent and self-sufficient. Bartholomew developed what has become the most widely used attachment scale to assess secure attachment, preoccupied attachment (similar to anxious/ambivalent attachment discussed earlier), and these two avoidant types (Bartholomew & Horowitz, 1991; see Table 10.3). Many studies have confirmed this four-category model. For example, people with a fearful avoidant style have a negative view of themselves and of other people, whereas people with a dismissive avoidant style have a positive view of themselves, but a negative view of others (Bartholomew & Horowitz, 1991). People with a fearful style also report greater distress when a romantic relationship ends than do those with a dismissive style (Sprecher et al., 1998).

TABLE 10.3

Measuring attachment styles

Secure style	47%	It is relatively easy for me to become emotionally close to others. I am comfortable depending on others and having others depend on me. I don't worry about being alone or having others not accept me.
Preoccupied (Anxious) style	14%	I want to be completely emotionally intimate with others, but I often find that others are reluctant to get as close as I would like. I am uncomfortable being without close relationships, but I sometimes worry that others don't value me as much as I value them.
Dissmissing Avoidant style	18%	I am comfortable without close emotional relationships. It is very important for me to feel independent and self-sufficient, and I prefer not to depend on others or have them depend on me.
Fearful Avoidant style	21%	I am somewhat uncomfortable getting close to others. I want emotionally close relationships, but I find it difficult to trust others completely, or to depend on them. I sometimes worry that I will be hurt if I allow myself to become too close to others.

Note: The percentages in each category are based on a sample of Introductory Psychology students.

Source: Adapted from Bartholomew & Horowitz, 1991.

A fundamental premise of attachment theory is that based on their interactions with their primary caregiver, people develop expectations about relationships—in particular, about whether others will be available and responsive to their needs. Do people with different attachment styles have different expectations for relationships? To find out, Baldwin, Fehr, Keedian, Seidel, and Thomson (1993) conducted a study in which they presented students at the University of Winnipeg with sentence fragments such as, "If I trust my partner, my partner will . . ." Participants with a secure attachment style showed faster reaction times to the word *care* than those with an avoidant style. In contrast, the reaction times of avoidant participants were faster than those of securely attached participants when the sentence was completed with the word *hurt*. Given these kinds of expectations for relationships, it is not surprising that securely attached individuals have the most satisfying, enduring relationships, whereas avoidant individuals are the most likely to report never having been in a loving, romantic relationship.

Multiple Attachment Representations Please reread the attachment descriptions in Table 10.3. For each description, try to think of a relationship (with a romantic partner, friend, or parent) in which you felt that way. When students at the University of Winnipeg were asked to do so, most of them were able to think of relationships that matched each style (Baldwin et al., 1996). Indeed, researchers are now beginning to acknowledge that rather than possessing one single attachment style that applies to all of our relationships, we can have different kinds of attachment to different people in our lives. For example, Ross and Spinner (2001) recently asked students at the University of New Brunswick and adults from the community to fill out the Bartholomew and Horowitz (1991) scale for four specific relationships (e.g., mother, father, friend). The researchers found that relationship-specific attachment ratings can be quite different from people's reports of their general attachment style. As the authors explain, "Knowing, for example, that an individual is securely attached to his or her mother tells us relatively little about whether that individual is also securely attached in other relationships" (Ross & Spinner, 2001).

A similar conclusion was reached by McGill University researchers Tamarha Pierce and John Lydon (2001). In a series of studies, they found that people's overall attachment style is correlated with, but distinct from, their attachment in specific relationships (mother, father, best friend, and romantic partner). Interestingly, these researchers found that, over time, attachment to specific partners changed in the direction of global, overall attachment, rather than vice versa. In other words, if you are generally secure, your attachment in specific relationships will tend to become secure, whereas the attachment you experience in any particular relationship is less likely to change your overall style.

Attachment Styles: Stable Personality Traits or Flexible Schemas? Findings such as these have led researchers such as Mark Baldwin and Beverley Fehr (1995; Baldwin et al., 1996) to suggest that attachment styles might best be conceptualized as schemas, rather than as stable personality traits. (As you will recall from Chapter 3, schemas are mental structures that people use to organize information—in this case, relational information.) Baldwin and Fehr argue that when we are asked to report on our attachment style, we are, in effect, reporting on which attachment schemas are most chronically accessible for us—in other words, we describe those attachment experiences that are at the forefront of our minds. If attachment styles function as schemas, it should be possible to prime (or make temporarily more accessible) a particular style and observe its effects on information processing. Baldwin and colleagues (1996) attempted to do just that. In one of their studies, University of Winnipeg students were asked to write down the names of people in their lives who matched each of three attachment styles (secure, anxious/ambivalent, avoidant). Then, a few days later, they participated in a seemingly unrelated experiment on how well they could visualize, or picture, other people. One of the people they were asked to visualize was taken from the list of attachment figures generated a few days earlier. Because this exercise didn't take very long, they were asked if they would be willing to participate in another short study on the adequacy of information used by dating services to match potential partners. They were given three "screening sheets," supposedly prepared for clients of a dating service. The screening sheets listed the clients' hobbies, interests, and their answers to the question "How would you describe yourself as a relationship partner?" The responses were designed to reflect either a secure, avoidant, or anxious/ambivalent attachment style. For example, for the anxious/ambivalent style, one response was this: "Few people are as willing and able as I am to commit themselves to a long-term relationship."

The critical question was whether participants would show differential attraction to these "clients" as a function of the attachment style that had been primed earlier (i.e., the person they had been visualizing). The answer is yes. Consistent with the research on similarity and attraction discussed earlier in this chapter, participants tended to be attracted to potential partners whose attachment style matched the style of the relationship they had been visualizing. For example, participants who had visualized a secure relationship were most likely to be attracted to a securely attached potential partner. Those who imagined a relationship that made them feel avoidant were more likely to be attracted to an avoidant potential partner, and so on. Thus, this study demonstrated that attachment styles function as schemas—they can be primed and their effects on information processing can be observed.

As we discussed in Chapter 3, schemas are resistant to change, but not impossible to change. In the context of attachment theory, this is good news, because it implies that people can learn new and healthier ways of relating to others than they experienced in infancy (Kirkpatrick & Hazan, 1994; Kojetin, 1993). Indeed, there is mounting evidence that even if people had unhappy relationships with their parents, they are not doomed to a lifetime of unhappy relationships.

SOCIAL EXCHANGE THEORIES

Social exchange theory
the theory holding that how people feel about a relationship depends on their perceptions of the rewards and costs of the relationship, the kind of relationship they deserve, and their chances of having a better relationship with someone else

Social exchange and equity theories are based on the simple notion that relationships operate on an economic model of costs and benefits, much the way that the marketplace operates (Blau, 1964; Homans, 1961; Kelley & Thibaut, 1978; Thibaut & Kelley, 1959). **Social exchange theory** states that how people feel about their relationships will depend on their perception of the rewards they receive from the relationship and their perception of the costs they incur, as well as their perception of what kind of relationship they deserve and the probability that they could have a better relationship with someone else. In other words, we buy the best relationship we can get, one that gives us the most value for our emotional dollar. The basic concepts of social exchange theory are reward, cost, outcome, comparison level, and comparison level for alternatives (Thibaut & Kelley, 1959).

Rewards are the positive, gratifying aspects of the relationship that make it worthwhile and reinforcing. They include the positive personal characteristics and behaviour of our relationship partner (e.g., similarity, attractiveness, sense of humour) and our ability to acquire external resources by virtue of knowing this person (e.g., gaining access to money, status, activities, or other interesting people; Lott & Lott, 1974). Costs are, obviously, the other side of the coin, and all friendships and romantic relationships have some costs attached to them (e.g., putting up with those annoying habits and characteristics of the other person). The outcome of the relationship is based on a calculation of the **reward/cost ratio**—you can think of it as a mathematical formula in which outcome equals rewards minus costs. (If you come up with a negative number, your relationship is not in good shape.)

How satisfied you are with your relationship depends on another variable—your **comparison level**, or what you expect the outcome of your relationship to be in terms of costs and rewards (Kelley & Thibaut, 1978; Thibaut & Kelley, 1959). Over time, you have amassed a long history of relationships with other people, and this history has led you to have certain expectations as to what your current and future relationships should be like. Some people have a high comparison level, expecting to receive many rewards and few costs in their relationships. If a given relationship doesn't match this expected comparison level, they will be unhappy and unsatisfied. In contrast, people who have a low comparison level would be happy in the same relationship, because they expect relationships to be difficult and costly.

Finally, your satisfaction with a relationship also depends on your perception of the likelihood that you could replace it with a better one—or your **comparison level for alternatives**. There are a lot of people out there. Could a relationship with a different person (or even being alone) give you a better outcome, or greater rewards for fewer costs, than your current relationship? People who have a high comparison level for alternatives, perhaps because they believe the world is full of fabulous people dying to meet them or because they are not afraid to be on their own, are more likely to get out of a relationship. People with a low comparison level for alternatives will be more likely to stay in a costly relationship, because to them, what they have is not great but is better than what they think they could find elsewhere.

Social exchange theory has received a great deal of empirical support; friends and romantic couples do pay attention to the costs and rewards in their relationships, and these affect how people feel about a relationship. There also is evidence that people are more likely to end a relationship when they perceive that attractive alternatives are available (Attridge & Berscheid, 1994; Bui, Peplau, & Hill, 1996; Drigotas, Safstrom, & Gentilia, 1999; Rusbult, 1983; Rusbult & Van Lange, 1996; South & Lloyd, 1995).

Equity Theory
Some researchers have criticized social exchange theory for ignoring an essential variable in relationships—the notion of fairness. Proponents of **equity theory** argue that people are not just out to get the most rewards for the least cost; they are also concerned about equity in their relationships, wherein the rewards and costs they experience and the contributions they make to the relationship are comparable to the rewards, costs, and contributions of the other person (Homans, 1961; Walster, Walster, & Berscheid, 1978). These theorists describe equitable relationships as the most happy and stable type. In comparison, inequitable relationships result in one person feeling overbenefited

Reward/cost ratio
in social exchange theory, the notion that there is a balance between the rewards that come from a relationship and the personal cost of maintaining the relationship. If the ratio is not favourable, the result is dissatisfaction with the relationship.

Comparison level
people's expectations about the level of rewards and costs they deserve in a relationship

Comparison level for alternatives
people's expectations about the level of rewards and punishments they would receive in an alternative relationship

Equity theory
the theory holding that people are happiest with relationships in which the rewards and costs that a person experiences and the contributions that he or she makes to the relationship are roughly equal to the rewards, costs, and contributions of the other person

(getting a lot of rewards, incurring few costs, devoting little time or energy to the relationship) or underbenefited (getting few rewards, incurring a lot of costs, devoting a lot of time and energy to the relationship).

According to equity theory, both underbenefited and overbenefited partners should feel uneasy about this state of affairs, and both should be motivated to restore equity to the relationship. This makes sense for the underbenefited person (who wants to continue feeling miserable?), but why should the overbenefited individual want to give up what social exchange theory indicates is a cushy deal—lots of rewards for little cost and little work? Hatfield and Walster (1978) argue that equity is all about fairness; people will eventually feel uncomfortable or even guilty if they get more than they deserve in a relationship. However, let's face facts—being overbenefited just doesn't feel as bad as being underbenefited, and research has, in fact, borne out that inequity is perceived as more of a problem by the underbenefited individual (Buunk & Prins, 1998; Clark & Chrisman, 1994; Hatfield et al., 1982; Sprecher & Schwartz, 1994; Sprecher, 1998; Traupmann et al., 1981; Van Yperen & Buunk, 1994).

In summary, social psychologists have come up with a number of answers to the important question, "Why do we love?" According to evolutionary theories, we love in order to increase our chances of reproduction, thereby ensuring the survival of our species. According to attachment theory, we learned lessons about how worthy we are of love from our primary caregiver and those lessons determine whether we seek loving relationships, as well as the quality of those relationships. Finally, according to social exchange theories, we love because of the benefits we receive from relationship partners.

Maintaining Close Relationships

So far we have been discussing theories and research on attraction. However, initial attraction is only the first chapter in the story of a relationship. Granted, some relationships read a lot like short stories—they may consist of only one chapter. However, other relationships may evolve into novels, with many chapters. As we mentioned earlier, social psychologists have tended to focus on attraction. However, they also have something to say about the process of maintaining a relationship. As you might imagine, some of the principles of attraction continue to apply, but other variables come into play as well.

SOCIAL EXCHANGE IN LONG-TERM RELATIONSHIPS

According to social exchange theory, we will be happy in a relationship as long as the rewards continue to outweigh the costs. More specifically, the reward/cost ratio must exceed our comparison level (the level of rewards and costs that we feel we deserve in a relationship). Social exchange theories also predict that we will remain in a relationship if we don't think that we have other, attractive alternatives available to us. Indeed, research has shown ample support for social exchange theory in intimate relationships (Rusbult, 1993; Rusbult & Van Lange, 1996; Rusbult, Yovetich, & Verette, 1996; Yovetich & Rusbult, 1994).

However, rewards, costs, and alternatives do not tell the whole story. As you may have observed, many people do not leave their partners, even when they are dissatisfied and their alternatives look bright. Caryl Rusbult and her colleagues would agree; they say we need to consider at least one additional factor to understand close relationships: a person's level of investment in the relationship (Kelley, 1983; Rusbult, 1980, 1983, 1991; Rusbult, Martz, & Agnew, 1998). In her **investment model** of close relationships, Rusbult defines investments as anything people have put into a relationship that will be lost if they leave it. Examples include tangible things, such as financial resources and possessions (e.g., a house), as well as intangible things, such as the emotional welfare of one's children, or time and emotional energy spent building the relationship. As seen in Figure 10.5, the greater the investment individuals have in a relationship, the less likely they are to leave, even if satisfaction is low and alternatives are available. In short, to predict whether people will stay in an intimate relationship, we need to know (a) how satisfied they are with the relationship (that is, the level of rewards minus costs), (b) whether they believe that attractive alternatives are available, and (c) the extent of their investment in the relationship.

To test this model, Rusbult (1983) asked students involved in heterosexual dating relationships to fill out questionnaires for seven months. Every three weeks or so, people answered questions about each of the components of the model shown in Figure 10.5. Rusbult also kept track of whether the students stayed in the relationships or broke up with their partner. As you can see in Figure 10.6, people's satisfaction, alternatives, and investments all predicted how committed they were to the relationship and whether it lasted. Subsequent studies have found similar results for married couples of diverse ages, for lesbian and gay couples, for close friends, and for residents of the United States, the Netherlands, and Taiwan (Kurdek, 1992; Lin & Rusbult, 1995; Rusbult, 1991; Rusbult & Buunk, 1993).

Rusbult also has applied her investment model to the study of destructive relationships. She and John Martz (1995) interviewed women who had sought refuge at a shelter for battered women, asking them about their abusive romantic relationships and marriages. As the theory would predict, the researchers found that feelings of commitment to the abusive relationship were greater among women who had poorer economic alternatives to the relationship, who were more heavily invested in the relationship (e.g., were

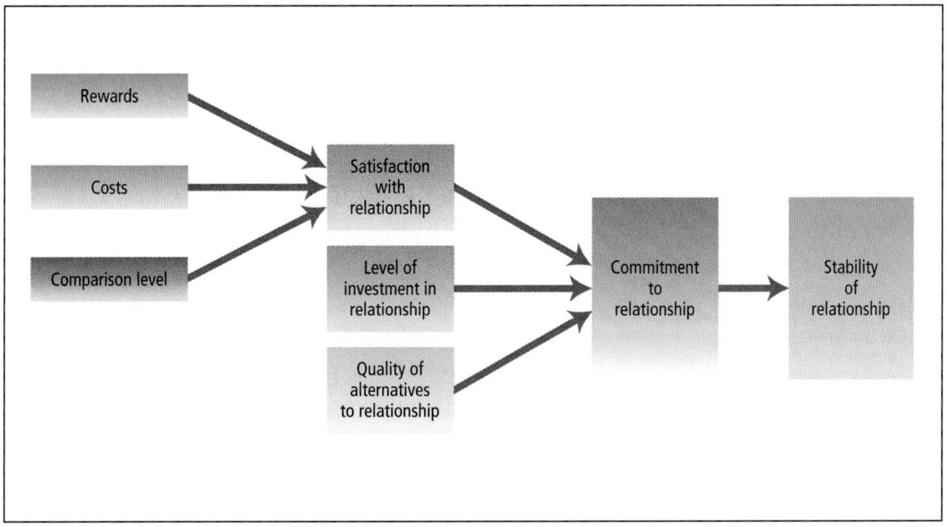

Investment model
the theory holding that people's commitment to a relationship depends on their satisfaction with the relationship in terms of rewards, costs, and comparison level; their comparison level for alternatives; and how much they have invested in the relationship that would be lost by leaving it

▼ **Figure 10.5**

THE INVESTMENT MODEL OF COMMITMENT.

People's commitment to a relationship depends on three variables: how satisfied they are (i.e., rewards minus costs), how much they feel they have invested in the relationship, and whether they have good alternatives to this relationship. These commitment variables in turn predict how stable the relationship will be. For example, a woman who feels that the costs exceed the rewards in her relationship would have low satisfaction. If she also felt she had little invested in the relationship, and a very attractive person was expressing interest in her, she would have a low level of commitment. The end result is low stability; most likely, she will break up with her current partner.

(Adapted from Rusbult, 1983)

▶ Figure 10.6

A TEST OF THE INVESTMENT MODEL.

This study examined the extent to which university students' satisfaction (defined as rewards minus costs) with a relationship, their comparison level for alternatives, and their investment in the relationship predicted their commitment to the relationship and their decision about whether to break up with their partner. The higher the number, the more each variable predicted commitment and breakup, independently of the two other variables. All three variables were good predictors of how committed people were and whether they broke up.

(Adapted from Rusbult, 1983)

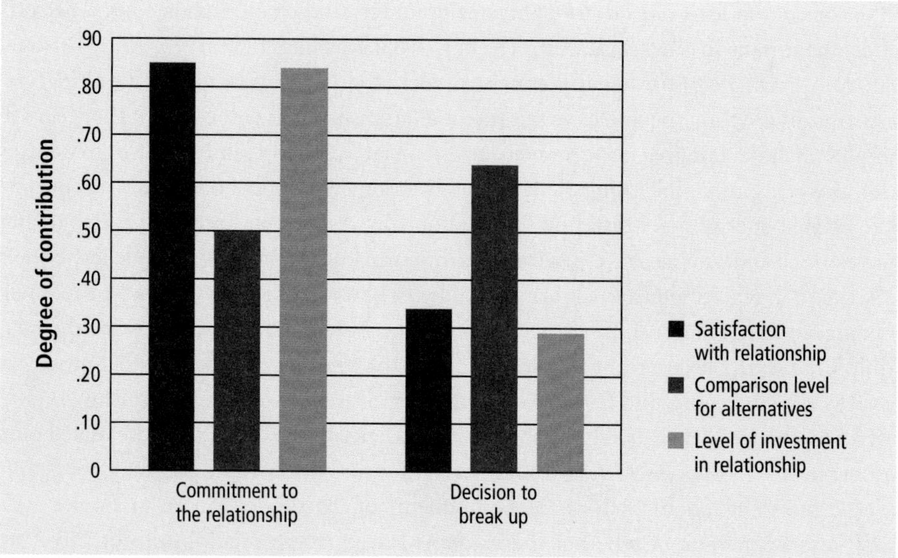

married, had children), and who were less dissatisfied with the relationship (e.g., reported receiving less severe forms of abuse). Thus, when it comes to long-term relationships, commitment is based on more than just the amount of rewards and punishments doled out (i.e., the level of satisfaction); it also depends on the quality of alternatives available and how heavily the individual has invested in the current relationship.

EXCHANGE AND EQUITY IN LONG-TERM RELATIONSHIPS

Earlier, we discussed another social exchange theory that takes into account people's perceptions of fairness—whether they believe that their outcomes are comparable to those of their partner. Does equity theory operate in long-term relationships the same way it does in new or less intimate relationships? Not exactly. Elaine Hatfield and Richard Rapson (1993) note that in casual relationships we trade "in kind"—you lend someone your class notes; he buys you a beer. However, in intimate relationships we trade very different resources, and it can be difficult to determine if equity has been achieved. As Hatfield and Rapson (1993) put it, does "dinner at an expensive restaurant on Monday balance out three nights of neglect due to a heavy workload?" In other words, long-term, intimate relationships seem to be governed by a looser, give-and-take notion of equity, rather than a rigid, tit-for-tat strategy (Kollack, Blumstein, & Schwartz, 1994).

According to Margaret Clark and Judson Mills, interactions between new acquaintances are governed by equity concerns and are called **exchange relationships**. In exchange relationships, people keep track of who is contributing what, and feel taken advantage of when they feel they are putting more into the relationship than they are getting out of it. On the other hand, interactions between close friends, family members, and romantic partners are governed less by an equity norm and more by a desire to help each other in times of need (Clark, 1984, 1986; Clark & Mills, 1979, 1993; Clark & Pataki, 1995; Mills & Clark, 1982, 1994). In these **communal relationships**, people give in response to the other's needs, regardless of whether they are repaid. A good example of a communal

Exchange relationships
relationships governed by the need for equity (i.e., for a comparable ratio of rewards and costs)

Communal relationships
relationships in which people's primary concern is being responsive to the other person's needs

▲ Close relationships can have either exchange or communal properties. Family relationships are typically communal; acquaintanceships are typically based on exchange, though they can become communal if they grow into friendships.

relationship is parenting. As a friend of ours recently put it, "You spend years catering to your child's every need—changing diapers, sitting up with her in the middle of the night when she is throwing up, coaching her soccer team—knowing full well that sooner or later, she will reach an age when she will prefer to spend her time with anyone but you!"

In a series of experiments, Margaret Clark and her colleagues varied whether people desired an exchange or a communal relationship with another person, and then observed the extent to which they were concerned with equity in the relationship. In these experiments, participants interacted with an interesting person and were told either that this person was new to the area and wanted to meet new people (thereby increasing their interest in establishing a communal relationship with the person), or that the other person was married and visiting the area for only a brief time (thereby making them more inclined to favour an exchange relationship with the person). As predicted, people in the exchange condition operated according to the equity norm, as summarized in Figure 10.7. People in the communal condition, thinking there was a chance for a long-term relationship, were relatively unconcerned with a tit-for-tat accounting of who was contributing what (Clark, 1984; Clark & Mills, 1979; Clark & Waddell, 1985; Williamson & Clark, 1989, 1992). These results are not limited to exchange and communal relationships created in the laboratory. Other studies show that ongoing friendships are more communal than relationships between strangers (Clark, Mills, & Corcoran, 1989).

Are people in communal relationships completely unconcerned with equity? No. As we saw earlier, people do feel distressed if they believe that their intimate relationships are inequitable (Walster, Walster, & Berscheid, 1978). However, equity takes on a somewhat different form in communal relationships than it does in less intimate ones. In communal relationships, the partners are more relaxed about what constitutes equity at any given time; they believe that things will eventually balance out and a rough kind of equity will be achieved over time. If this is not the case—if they come to feel that there is a chronic imbalance—the relationship may end.

▶ **Figure 10.7**

EXCHANGE VERSUS
COMMUNAL RELATIONSHIPS.

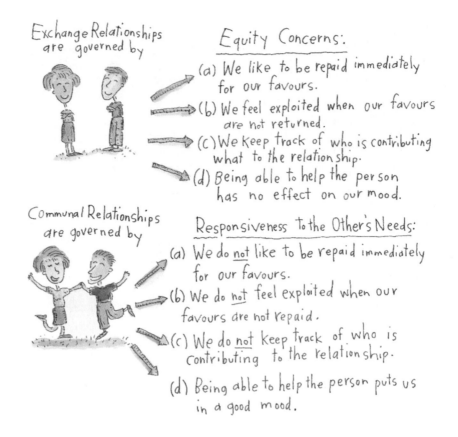

Exchange Relationships are governed by

Equity Concerns:
(a) We like to be repaid immediately for our favours.
(b) We feel exploited when our favours are not returned.
(c) We keep track of who is contributing what to the relationship.
(d) Being able to help the person has no effect on our mood.

Communal Relationships are governed by

Responsiveness to the Other's Needs:
(a) We do <u>not</u> like to be repaid immediately for our favours.
(b) We do <u>not</u> feel exploited when our favours are not repaid.
(c) We do <u>not</u> keep track of who is contributing to the relationship.
(d) Being able to help the person puts us in a good mood.

THE ROLE OF ADVERSITY IN MAINTAINING RELATIONSHIPS

Think about a time when you and a romantic partner or a friend went through a difficult period in your relationship. Did this strengthen your relationship, or did it cause the relationship to deteriorate? According to John Lydon and his colleagues (Lydon, 1999; Lydon, Meana, Sepinwall, Richards, & Mayman, 1999; Lydon & Zanna, 1990), whether adversity has a positive or negative effect on a relationship depends on two factors: the level of adversity, and the level of commitment to the relationship. According to Lydon's **commitment calibration hypothesis**, if the level of adversity is lower than the level of commitment, the relationship will not be threatened and therefore it will not be necessary to engage in efforts to maintain the relationship. Thus, a minor problem in a highly committed relationship is likely to have little effect on the relationship.

However, what if the level of adversity is greater than the level of commitment? This is another situation in which people will not engage in much relationship maintenance—but for a very different reason. Specifically, there is little incentive to "hang in there" if the difficulties you are experiencing surpass your level of commitment to the relationship. So, when do people take steps to preserve their relationship? As you might have guessed by now, they do so when the level of adversity matches the level of commitment. To test this idea, Lydon and colleagues (1999) designed an ingenious experiment. Participants were romantically involved (dating, cohabiting, married) adults who were alumni of or graduate students at McGill University. They were told that the purpose of the study was to test

Commitment calibration hypothesis

the idea that the outcome of adversity on a relationship depends on the level of commitment. If the level of adversity is lower than the level of commitment, the relationship is not challenged. If the level of adversity is higher than the level of commitment, the relationship ends. However, if the level of adversity is equal to the level of commitment, the relationship will be strengthened.

how well computers do at matching people for romantic relationships. In the first session, participants posed for a photograph and filled out a questionnaire about themselves that would be placed in their "portfolio." They then returned to a second session, in which the researchers introduced either a moderate or high level of adversity. In the high-adversity condition, they tried to create a situation that would be highly threatening to a relationship.

Imagine that you were a participant in this study. Because you are a nice person, you have agreed to participate in a psychology study on whether computers can do a good job of matching romantic partners. In the first session, your portfolio is created—no big deal. When you arrive for your second session, a research assistant tells you that in this session you will be evaluating another person's portfolio. You are given a photograph of an extremely attractive opposite-sex person. The information in the person's portfolio indicates that this person is currently not romantically involved. Then the bombshell is dropped. The research assistant mentions that this person has seen the portfolios of participants in the previous session and, lo and behold, has chosen you as the best match for himself/herself! You are then asked how attracted you are to this person.

Based on the commitment calibration hypothesis, Lydon and colleagues expected that participants with only low or moderate commitment to their romantic relationship would not try to protect their relationship in this high-adversity situation. They would find the person in the portfolio highly attractive and would say so. However, participants who were highly committed to their relationships were expected to engage in relationship maintenance efforts—in this case, by convincing themselves that they really were not very attracted to this person. And that is exactly what was found. Participants who were highly committed to their relationships reported that they were not too attracted to this gorgeous, available person who wanted them—less so than participants who were moderate or low in commitment.

And what about the moderate-adversity condition? Participants in this condition also were shown the portfolio of an attractive opposite-sex person, but were simply told that they would be evaluating this person. The researchers reasoned that this situation would be only moderately threatening to a relationship. As expected, in this condition it was the participants who were moderately committed who reported that they were not particularly attracted to the other person—less so than those who were high or low in commitment.

The authors conclude that people will take active steps to shore up a relationship only when the level of adversity is equal to the level of commitment. If the level of adversity is higher or lower than the level of commitment, efforts will not be taken to maintain or preserve the relationship. In the former case, the relationship won't be threatened and therefore won't be in need of maintenance. In the latter case, there isn't enough commitment there to motivate relationship maintenance attempts. The bottom line is that adversity can have a positive effect on relationship maintenance, but only if it comes in just the right amount.

THE ROLE OF POSITIVE ILLUSIONS

Once a relationship has begun, there are inevitable conflicts and disappointments. During these times, we may experience doubts about our choice of partner and question whether

Positive illusions

idealization of our romantic
relationships and partners in
order to maintain the
relationship

ours really is a good relationship. Recent research conducted at the University of Waterloo suggests that under these circumstances we maintain our relationships by indulging in **positive illusions**—that is, fantasies in which we convince ourselves that we have the most wonderful partner and the most wonderful relationship in the world, regardless of the facts. This process of idealization has been explored in several studies by Sandra Murray, John Holmes, and their colleagues.

In one of their first studies, Murray and Holmes (1993) investigated whether people deal with doubts and uncertainties by weaving stories in which their partner's flaws are reinterpreted as virtues. In attempting to test this hypothesis, the researchers faced a challenge: How does one get people to have doubts about their partner? Here's how Murray and Holmes did it. Students in dating relationships were asked whether their partner tended to initiate conflicts. As expected, most participants reported that they did not have the kind of partner who started fights. Those in the experimental group then read a fake *Psychology Today* article in which it was argued that engaging in conflict can be healthy for a relationship. This information was intended to threaten participants' views of their partners. (Participants in the control group read an unrelated story.) Later, when asked again whether their partner initiated conflict, participants in the experimental group (but not in the control group) changed their tune. They now reported that they, in fact, had partners who quite enjoyed a good fight! The researchers suggest that by taking this kind of poetic licence, these participants were able to maintain a positive view of their partner and their relationship.

In a follow-up study, Murray and Holmes (1993) asked a new group of participants to list similarities between themselves and their dating partner. Most people listed many similarities and few differences. Participants in the experimental group then read a bogus *Psychology Today* article arguing that awareness of differences promotes intimacy. (Those in the control group read a neutral story.) Later, those in the experimental group (but not in the control group) altered their previous responses—they were now able to think of many differences and comparatively few similarities!

More recently, Murray and Holmes (1999) have identified another way in which we maintain our relationships—namely, by finding redeeming features in our partner's faults. Specifically, when they asked students at the University of Waterloo to write out their dating partner's faults, approximately half of their participants engaged in "yes, but" refutations. For example, one woman reported that her partner had a tendency to overreact to situations, but then added that she had come to realize he did so only to protect her.

The creative storytelling that people in these studies engaged in suggests that we are highly motivated to maintain positive perceptions of our partners and our relationships—regardless of the facts. Do we actually hold idealistic, rather than realistic, views of our partner? The answer to this question is yes (Murray et al., 2000; Murray, Holmes, and Griffin, 1996a). For example, Murray, Holmes, and Griffin (1996a) asked dating and married couples to rate their own attributes, their partner's attributes, and attributes of an ideal partner. Take, for example, the case of Lucia and Mario. If Lucia's perception of Mario is accurate (based on reality), the way in which she rates him (in terms of intelligence, humour, and consideration) should be very similar to how Mario rates himself on these attributes. If, however, Lucia holds an idealistic view of Mario, she should rate him more positively than he rates himself. And that is exactly what these researchers found. In fact, participants' ratings of their partner closely resembled their ratings of an ideal partner.

The assumption in this research has been that people view their partner in highly positive ways as a means of maintaining their relationships. Is it actually beneficial to see our partners in idealistic ways? Wouldn't relationships be better off if we perceived our partners as they really are? Apparently not. In fact, it would seem that the rosier the glasses through which we view our partners, the better. Murray and Holmes have consistently found that the more that people idealize their partners (and the more that their partner idealizes them), the greater their satisfaction with the relationship (Murray & Holmes, 1997, 1999; Murray et al, 2000; Murray, Holmes, & Griffin, 1996a). Moreover, doing so has survival value; relationships in which partners idealize one another are those most likely to endure. For example, Murray, Holmes, and Griffin (1996b) conducted a longitudinal study in which they measured idealization and satisfaction among dating couples several times over a one-year period. The researchers found that couples who idealized each other at the outset experienced the greatest increases in satisfaction over the course of the year and the greatest decreases in conflicts and doubts. These couples also were more likely to be together a year later than were couples who did not idealize one another. Perhaps most astonishing was the finding that, over time, people began to live up to the idealized image their partner had of them. Stated differently, individuals who idealized their partners ultimately created the partners they wished for. Thus, in the world of close relationships, dreams can actually come true!

Ending Close Relationships

As you may have experienced, some relationships are more likely to resemble nightmares, rather than dreams, come true. In Canada, just over one-third of marriages end in divorce (Statistics Canada, 1999). The dissolution of other kinds of relationships is not publicly recorded. However, in longitudinal studies of dating relationships, a typical finding is that half of the couples break up within a few years, with gay and lesbian relationships showing some of the highest rates of dissolution (Sprecher, 1994; Sprecher & Fehr, 1998). And even though people tend not to break up with friends formally, the loss of friendships is a common experience (Fehr, 1996). After several years of studying what love is and how it blooms, social psychologists are now beginning to explore the end of the story—how it dies.

WHY RELATIONSHIPS END

As you might expect, the reasons that relationships end are complex and multifaceted. Moreover, different kinds of relationships end for different reasons. For example, common reasons given for the dissolution of marriage are financial difficulties, unemployment, alcoholism, sexual infidelity, low religiosity, and premarital pregnancy (White, 1990; Sprecher & Fehr, 1998). Not all of these reasons would apply to dating relationships or friendships. However, there also are some important commonalities across relationships.

One place to look for clues is among the predictors of attraction. If the factors that caused you to be attracted to someone are no longer present, the relationship is likely to be in trouble. For example, at the beginning of this chapter we identified similarity as an

important predictor of attraction. As you might expect, if spouses, friends, or dating partners become dissimilar, the relationship is vulnerable to dissolution (Fehr, 1996; Sprecher
& Fehr, 1998). Statements such as "We grew apart" or "We seemed to be going in different directions" reflect the role of dissimilarity in the breakup of relationships. In a fascinating study, Diane Felmlee (1995) asked 300 university students to focus on a romantic
relationship that had ended, and to list the qualities that had first attracted them to the
person and the characteristics they ended up disliking most about the person. Felmlee
found that 30 percent of these breakups were examples of "fatal attractions." The qualities that were initially so attractive (e.g., "He's so unusual and different," "She's so exciting and unpredictable") became the very reasons why the relationship ended (e.g., "He
and I have nothing in common," "I can never count on her"). "Fatal attractions" were
most likely to occur for qualities on which the partners were dissimilar.

The theories of attraction discussed earlier also shed light on the issue of why relationships end. For example, as mentioned earlier, social exchange theorists find that
relationships are likely to end when rewards are low and costs are high (in other words,
when the relationship is low in satisfaction), when attractive alternatives are available to one
or both partners, and when the partners have invested little in the relationship (Rusbult,
1983; Rusbult, Martz, & Agnew, 1998). Equity also plays a role in the ending of relationships. People are likely to end relationships that they feel are inequitable—particularly if
they are feeling underbenefited.

Finally, there is another reason that relationships end—a reason few of us are willing to
admit—and that is sheer boredom. According to Aron and Aron (1986, 1997), as another
person becomes familiar to us, there is less that is new and exciting for us to discover about
him or her. Marriage or cohabiting relationships may be especially susceptible to boredom.
The day-to-day routine of living together may lead people to feel that they are in a rut and
are missing out on excitement and passion (Baumeister & Bratslavsky, 1999; Fincham &
Bradbury, 1993). John La Gaipa, who has conducted extensive research on friendship at the
University of Windsor, maintains that friendships also dissolve because of boredom, but that
this is not a socially acceptable basis for terminating a friendship. Thus, when asked why a
friendship ended, we are likely to mention reasons such as disloyalty or betrayals of trust (La
Gaipa, 1982). We suspect that people who terminate a marriage would be especially likely to
offer such reasons—even if the culprit was sheer boredom.

THE PROCESS OF BREAKING UP

As the words of a 1970s hit put it, "They say that breaking up is hard to do. . . ." Indeed,
the breakup of a relationship is one of life's more painful experiences. The pain is greatest for the person who is being rejected. However, if you have ever broken up with someone, you may be all too aware that it is no fun telling someone that you no longer wish to
have a relationship with him or her. Thus, it probably does not come as a surprise that
people tend to use passive, avoidance strategies when terminating a relationship.

Baxter (1982) asked people about the strategies they would use to end either a romantic relationship or a friendship. She identified four major strategies from these accounts:
withdrawal/avoidance, positive tone (e.g., trying to prevent "hard feelings"), manipulative

strategies (e.g., getting a third party to communicate the bad news), and open confrontation. For both types of relationships, people reported that they would be most likely to use positive tone strategies. They also said they would use withdrawal/avoidance strategies, especially for friendship terminations. Open confrontation was a more likely strategy for ending romantic relationships. Other research has shown that passive strategies such as withdrawal or avoidance are especially likely to be used in friendships, where people opt to let the relationship "fade away" (Fehr, 1996). In contrast, dating or marital relationships are less likely to simply "fade away"—especially if one partner still wants the relationship to continue. Thus, more direct methods of termination are generally necessary for these sorts of terminations (Baxter, 1985).

THE EXPERIENCE OF BREAKING UP

Can we predict how people will feel when their relationship ends? One key is the role they play in the decision to end the relationship (Helgeson, 1994; Lloyd & Cate, 1985). For example, Robin Akert (1998) asked 344 university students to focus on their most important former romantic relationship. One question asked to what extent they, as compared to their partner, had been responsible for the decision to break up. Participants who indicated a high level of responsibility for the decision were labelled *breakers*, those who reported a low level of responsibility were labelled *breakees*, and those who shared the decision making with their partners about equally were labelled *mutuals*.

Akert found that the role people played in the decision to end the relationship was the single most powerful predictor of their breakup experiences. Not surprisingly, breakees were miserable—they reported high levels of loneliness, depression, unhappiness, and anger, and virtually all reported experiencing physical disorders (e.g., upset stomach, trouble sleeping) in the weeks after the breakup. Breakers experienced the lowest levels of upset, pain, and stress, although they were not exempt from negative effects. In particular, they tended to experience guilt and unhappiness. Mutuals were not as upset or hurt as breakees, but they suffered more than breakers. Thus, it appears that a mutual conclusion to a romantic relationship can be a more stressful experience than a unilateral decision to end it.

The degree of distress experienced after a breakup is influenced by other factors as well. For example, Sprecher, Felmlee, Metts, Fehr, and Vanni (1998) examined a number of predictors of distress following the breakup of a romantic relationship. Consistent with Akert's findings, responsibility for the breakup was associated with less distress. In addition, as you might expect based on our earlier discussion of social exchange theory, the higher one's level of satisfaction and commitment, the greater the distress when the relationship ended. Also consistent with social exchange theory, participants experienced less distress if they were interested in an alternative relationship (and more distress if attractive alternatives were available to their former partner).

The good news is that the participants reported that they felt significantly less distressed currently than they had immediately after the breakup. Thus, if by some unfortunate circumstance your heart has been broken, take comfort in the fact that time really does heal all wounds.

SUMMARY

In the first part of this chapter, we discussed the variables that cause initial attraction between two people. One such variable is physical proximity, or the **propinquity effect**. People you come into contact with the most are the most likely to become your friends and lovers. This occurs because of the **mere exposure effect**; in general, exposure to any stimulus produces liking for it. **Similarity** between people, whether in attitudes, demographic characteristics, values, or activity preferences, is also a powerful cause of attraction and liking. How people behave toward us is also of importance. In general, we like others who behave as if they like us. In other words, **reciprocal liking** is another determinant of attraction. Though most people are reluctant to admit it, **physical attractiveness** also plays an important role in liking. Physical attractiveness of the face has a cross-cultural component; people from different cultures rate photographs quite similarly. The "what is beautiful is good" stereotype indicates that people assume that physical attractiveness is associated with other desirable traits.

In the second part of this chapter, we examined the causes of attraction (or love) in close relationships. Social psychologists have offered several definitions of love. One important distinction is between **companionate love**—feelings of intimacy and affection for those with whom our lives are intertwined—and **passionate love**—feelings of intense longing and arousal. Ordinary people's definition of love includes both companionate and passionate components, although the companionate aspect is seen as the true meaning of love. The **triangular theory of love** distinguishes among three components of love: intimacy, passion, and commitment. According to research on **love styles,** love takes six different forms, known as eros, ludus, storge, pragma, mania, and agape.

Though love is universal, there are gender and cultural differences in the definition and experience of love. Men hold a more romantic, passionate view of love than do women, although recent research suggests that both women and men place the greatest emphasis on companionate love. People who live in individualist cultures are more likely to emphasize passionate love than are people who live in collectivist cultures, where companionate love is valued.

A number of theories have been proposed to explain *why* human beings are so motivated to seek love. The **evolutionary approach** to love states that men and women are attracted to different characteristics in each other because this maximizes reproductive success. This view maintains that when choosing a marriage partner, women care more about men's resources and men care more about women's appearance.

The **theory of attachment** points to people's past relationships, specifically with their primary caregiver, as a significant determinant of the quality of their close relationships as adults. Infants can be classified as having one of three types of attachment relationships: **secure, anxious/ambivalent,** and **avoidant.** The avoidant style can be further divided into **dismissive avoidant** and **fearful avoidant.** People who report having been securely attached as infants have the most intimate and satisfying relationships. Recent research suggests that people have different attachment patterns in different relationships, rather than an overall attachment style. Accordingly, it is suggested that **attachment styles** are best thought of as schemas, rather than as stable personality traits.

Social exchange theory argues that how people feel about their relationships depends on their assessment of the rewards and costs of the relationship. In order to determine whether people will stay in a relationship, we also need to know their **comparison level**—the outcomes they have come to expect in relationships—and their **comparison level for alternatives**—their expectations about how happy they would be in other relationships or alone. There are, however, exceptions to the rule of social exchange. **Equity theory** states that we are happiest when relationships are fair—when what we contribute is comparable to what our partner contributes.

We also discussed how people maintain intimate relationships. Social exchange theories of close relationships, such as the **investment model**, say that to predict whether a relationship will last, we need to know each person's level of satisfaction, comparison level for alternatives, and how much has been invested in the relationship. The notion of equity is different in long-term versus short-term relationships. Short-term relationships are usually **exchange relationships**, in which people are concerned about a fair distribution of rewards and costs. Long-term, intimate relationships are usually **communal relationships,** in which people are less concerned with an immediate accounting of who is contributing what and are more concerned with helping their partner when he or she is in need.

According to the **commitment calibration hypothesis,** adversity can strengthen a relationship, but only if the level of adversity is equal to the level of commitment. **Positive illusions** also play a role in relationship maintenance. The more we idealize our partner, the greater our satisfaction with a relationship and the more likely the relationship will endure.

Unfortunately, intimate relationships end. There are a number of reasons why, including dissimilarity between the partners. Relationships also end when costs are greater than rewards (i.e., when the relationship is no longer satisfying), when attractive alternatives are available, and when investments are low. If we believe that our **reward/cost ratio** is not comparable to our partner's, the relationship is inequitable and vulnerable to dissolution—especially if we believe that our partner is getting a better deal than we are (i.e., we feel underbenefited rather than overbenefited). People tend to use passive strategies when ending relationships, although these strategies may not be effective for ending romantic relationships. While the experience of breaking up is never pleasant, a powerful variable that predicts how a person will weather the breakup is the role he or she plays in the decision to terminate the relationship.

IF YOU ARE INTERESTED

Allen, Woody (Director). (1997). *Annie Hall* [Film]. Woody Allen's witty, wacky, and perceptive take on falling in love in New York City, starring Diane Keaton. Winner of the 1977 Academy Award for Best Picture.

Avnet, Jon (Director). (1991). *Fried green tomatoes* [Film]. A touching story of the meaning and power of friendship in three women's lives. The film is based on the novel by Fannie Flagg.

Brehm, S. S., Miller, R. S., Perlman, D., & Campbell, S. M. (2002). *Intimate relationships* (3rd ed.). New York: McGraw-Hill. A comprehensive, readable overview of the entire field of interpersonal attraction, from first impressions to intimate relationships. One of the authors, Daniel Perlman, is at the University of British Columbia.

Buss, D. M. (1998). The psychology of human mate selection: Exploring the complexity of the strategic repertoire. In C. Crawford & D. C. Krebs (Eds.), *Handbook of evolutionary psychology.* Mahwah, NJ: Erlbaum (pp. 405–429). A leading researcher examines mate selection from an evolutionary perspective. Who we choose as long-term and short-term mates, and gender and cultural differences in those choices, are analyzed in light of evolutionary theory.

Curtiz, Michael (Director). (1942). *Casablanca* [Film]. This all-time classic film was awarded the Oscar for Best Picture. Rick, Elsa, and Victor Laslo are featured in the story of a love triangle set amid pre–Second World War intrigue and treachery. It doesn't get any better than this.

Dion, K. K., & Dion, K. L. (2001). Gender and relationships. In R. K. Unger (Ed.), *Handbook of the psychology of women and gender.* New York: John Wiley and Sons (pp. 256–271). This chapter, written by two prominent social psychologists at the University of Toronto, presents a state-of-the-art review and analysis of gender differences in close relationships. In the first section, the authors discuss how major theories of close relationships (many of which are discussed in this chapter) explain gender differences. The second section examines research on gender differences and focuses on topics such as romanticism, long-distance relationships, and cross-sex friendships. The final section deals with gender, culture, and relationships.

Fehr, B. (1996). *Friendship processes.* Thousand Oaks, CA: Sage. A University of Winnipeg social psychologist documents the life course of friendships: how they are formed, maintained, and terminated. Theories of friendship and gender differences in friendship are discussed as well.

Goodwin, R. (1999). *Personal relationships across cultures.* New York: Routledge. An engaging analysis of relationship processes in different cultures. In addition to topics discussed in this chapter (e.g., love, attraction), the author examines phenomena such as arranged marriages, the role of family networks in mate selection, and so on.

Hatfield, E., & Rapson, R. L. (1993). *Love, sex, and intimacy: Their psychology, biology, and history.* New York: HarperCollins. A fascinating look at love and intimacy, including both current scientific studies and historical comparisons among concepts of love in other eras and cultures.

Hendrick, C., & Hendrick, S. S. (Eds.). (2000). *Close relationships*. Thousand Oaks, CA: Sage. This comprehensive handbook summarizes state-of-the-art research on close relationships, with a focus on dating/marital relationships and friendships. Topics include intimacy, communication, sexuality, as well as the "darker" topics of aggression, jealousy, and depression.

Hytner, Nicholas (Director). (1998). *The object of my affection* [Film]. A romantic comedy about friends and lovers: a gay man, whose lover has dumped him, and his best friend, a single woman who's pregnant and wants him to be the surrogate dad. The novel is by Stephen McCauley.

Márquez, Gabriel García (1989). *Love in the time of cholera*. A magical tale of a man's unrequited but intrepid love, which, after 51 years of waiting, is richly rewarded.

Tyler, Anne (1986). *The accidental tourist*. A compassionate, compelling, and extremely funny tale of two apparently mismatched people who fall in love.

WEBLINKS

www.isspr.org/iarr

International Association for Relationship Research

An organization of researchers who focus on friendships and love relationships. Includes reviews of recent journal articles, links to researchers, and contents of recent conventions.

www.psychology.sunysb.edu/attachment

Attachment Theory and Research

This is a comprehensive site on developmental research on attachment theory.

www.freshy.com/personality/love.html

Love Type Test

This site lets you take a personality test based on Sternberg's (1986) Triangular Theory of Love.

Prosocial Behaviour
why do people help?

WE DESCRIBED IN CHAPTER 2 THE BRUTAL STABBING DEATH OF KITTY Genovese. Neighbours heard her screams for help. Many even watched the assault through their windows. Yet, no one intervened. No one even called the police. This tragic event that took place more than 30 years ago in New York City may seem far removed from our lives today. But is it?

Consider, for example, the following article that appeared in newspapers in 1998:

> Denver—People watched from the safety of their high-rise apartments before dawn yesterday as four men beat a 27-year-old taxi driver to death and dumped his body in the trunk of the cab. According to Detective Virginia Lopez, "Eyewitnesses saw him being beaten and dragged by his feet and thrown in the trunk but no one called 911." People continued to watch while police officers searched for the driver. No one told the police that the body was in the trunk. Detective Lopez pointed out that the man might have lived if police had been able to locate him sooner (Associated Press, 1998).

But, you may be thinking, events such as these wouldn't happen in Canada. Read on.

> January 20, 2000. As Montrealers were making their way to work, they passed a man lying on the sidewalk, arms outstretched, crying and begging for help. It was –41 degrees Celsius. The man was Gino Laplante. He was 38 years old and suffered from psychiatric problems. Because he was lying in the middle of the sidewalk, people had to walk around him to avoid stepping on him. Anne Lavictoire was one of those people. However, unlike the others, she decided to go back to see if she could help. She discovered that Gino's hands were already frozen. She called an ambulance and tried to keep him warm. It took 15 or 20 minutes for an ambulance to arrive. By then, it was too late. Gino Laplante had frozen to death on a sidewalk in Montreal on a cold Thursday morning.

> December 6, 2002. A Port Coquitlam teenager, Breann Voth, was on her way to catch the morning bus when she was murdered. Investigation into this death has revealed that Breann's cries for help were heard in at least 15 households. Yet, no one called the police. Her nude body was found later that morning on the banks of the Coquitlam River.

Based on these events, what is your view of human nature? Are human beings inclined to respond when they see another person in need? Can people be counted on to help?

Now consider the following stories:

> Jake Rupert, a reporter for the *Ottawa Citizen,* was moved to tears as he watched the 400-metre snowshoe final at the Canadian Special Olympics 2000 Winter Games. There were only 50 metres left to go when the front runner fell down. As he struggled to get up, 20-year-old John Rokosh and another athlete caught up to him. They stopped, helped him up, and then the three of them finished the race. John Rokosh came in third. And what was Rokosh's response when the reporter asked him why he didn't just keep going? "Because that wouldn't be fair, silly" (Sinclair, 2000).

◀ Rocky Flett (left) and John Rokosh (right) are two of many people who exhibit prosocial behaviour. What makes some people help others even at considerable cost to themselves?

A 13-year-old Winnipeg boy, Rocky Flett, was on his way to a grocery store in February 2000, when he heard the cries of young children coming from a house. He could smell smoke. Rocky Flett rushed into the house and rescued three children. An adult in the house had collapsed on the stairs due to smoke inhalation. Rocky ran to a neighbour's house and got help rescuing the adult. When asked why he ran into a burning building three times, Rocky's response was, "I didn't stop to think. I just did it."

John Rokosh and Rocky Flett were two of the six winners of the Year 2000 Canada Day People Who Make a Difference Awards sponsored by the *Winnipeg Free Press*.

Based on reading these stories, what is your view of human nature now? Are human beings inclined to respond when they see another person in need? Can people be counted on to help?

Basic Motives Underlying Prosocial Behaviour

Why is it that sometimes people perform acts of great self-sacrifice and heroism, whereas at other times they act in uncaring, heartless ways, ignoring the desperate pleas of those in need? In this chapter, we will consider the major determinants of **prosocial behaviour**, which we define as any act performed with the goal of benefiting another person. We will be particularly concerned with prosocial behaviour motivated by **altruism**, which is the desire to help another person even if it involves a cost to the helper. Someone might act in a prosocial manner out of self-interest—he or she hopes to get something in return. Altruism is helping purely out of the desire to benefit someone else, with no benefit (and often a cost) to oneself. John Rokosh stopped to help an athlete with whom he was competing, thereby forfeiting his chances of coming in first. Rocky Flett risked his life by rescuing three children and an adult from a burning house.

Prosocial behaviour

any act performed with the goal of benefiting another person

Altruism

the desire to help another person even if involves a cost to the helper

We will begin by considering the basic origins of prosocial behaviour and altruism: Why do people help others? Few questions have intrigued observers of the human condition as much as this one. Is the willingness to help a basic impulse with genetic roots? Is it something that must be taught and nurtured in childhood? Is there a pure motive for helping, such that people are willing to aid their fellow human beings even when they have nothing to gain? Or are people willing to help only when there is something in it for them? Let's see how psychologists have addressed these centuries-old questions.

EVOLUTIONARY PSYCHOLOGY: INSTINCTS AND GENES

According to Charles Darwin's (1859) theory of evolution, natural selection favours genes that promote the survival of the individual. Any gene that furthers our survival and increases the probability that we will produce offspring is likely to be passed on from generation to generation. Genes that lower our chances of survival, such as those that cause life-threatening diseases, reduce the chances that we will produce offspring and thus are less likely to be passed on. Several psychologists have pursued these ideas, spawning the field of evolutionary psychology, which, as you may recall from previous chapters, is the attempt to explain social behaviour in terms of genetic factors that evolved over time according to the principles of natural selection (Buss, 1996, 1999; Buss & Kenrick, 1998; Ketelaar & Ellis, 2000; Simpson & Kenrick, 1997; Wright, 1994).

Darwin realized early on that a potential problem exists with evolutionary theory. How can it explain altruism? If people's overriding goal is to ensure their own survival, why would they ever help others at a cost to themselves? It would seem that over the centuries, altruistic behaviour would disappear, because people who acted that way would, by putting themselves at risk, produce fewer offspring than would people who acted selfishly. Genes promoting selfish behaviour would be more likely to be passed on—or would they?

Kin Selection One way that evolutionary psychologists attempt to resolve this dilemma is with the notion of **kin selection**, the idea that behaviours that help a genetic relative are favoured by natural selection (Hamilton, 1964; Meyer, 1999). People can increase the chances that their genes will be passed along not only by having their own children, but also by ensuring that their genetic relatives have children. Because a person's blood relatives share some of his or her genes, the more that person ensures his or her survival, the greater the chance that his or her genes will flourish in future generations. Thus, natural selection should favour altruistic acts directed toward genetic relatives.

There is support for this notion in the animal kingdom, particularly among social insects. Les Greenberg (1979), for example, released bees near a nest protected by guard bees, and observed which ones the guards admitted to the nest and which ones they rebuffed. He had bred the intruders to be of varying genetic similarity to the guards. Some were siblings, some were cousins, and some were more distant relatives. (The guards could tell how related they were to the bees by their odours.) Consistent with the idea of kin selection, the guard bees were much more likely to admit bees that were close relatives, essentially telling their distant relatives that there was no more room at the inn.

There is some evidence that kin selection operates in human beings as well. According to Burnstein, Crandall, and Kitayama (1994), people are especially likely to

Kin selection

the idea that behaviour that helps a genetic relative is favoured by natural selection

◀ According to evolutionary psychology, prosocial behaviour occurs in part because of kin selection, such as this young woman helping her little brother.

help others who are most related to them when this help increases the likelihood that that person will have children. In one study, for example, people reported that they would be more likely to help genetic relatives than non-relatives in life-and-death situations, such as a house fire. People did not report that they would be more likely to help genetic relatives when the situation was non-life threatening. Interestingly, both males and females, as well as American and Japanese participants, followed this rule of kin selection in life-threatening situations.

Of course, in this study people only reported what they would do; this doesn't prove that in a real fire they would indeed be more likely to save their sibling than their cousin. There is some anecdotal evidence from real emergencies, however, that is consistent with these results. Sime (1983) interviewed survivors of a fire at a vacation complex in 1973, and found that when people became aware that there was a fire, they were much more likely to search for family members before exiting the building than they were to search for friends.

Evolutionary psychologists do not mean to imply that people consciously weigh the biological importance of their behaviour before deciding whether to help. It is not as if people crassly compute the likelihood that their genes will be passed on before deciding whether to help someone push her or his car out of a ditch. According to evolutionary theory, however, the genes of people who follow this "biological importance" rule are more likely to survive than the genes of people who do not. Thus, over the millennia, kin selection became ingrained in human behaviour.

One problem with this explanation of prosocial behaviour, however, is that it has difficulty explaining why complete strangers sometimes help each other, even when there is no reason for them to assume that they share some of the same genes. For example, it seems absurd to say that 13-year-old Rocky Flett somehow calculated how genetically similar the occupants of the burning house were to him before deciding to save their lives. And, in the days following September 11, 2001, people in many Canadian cities lined up for hours to donate blood to help the victims of the terrorist attacks in New York and Washington—victims who were complete strangers to them. Clearly, other factors must be considered in order to explain why people help under such conditions. We turn to these next.

Norm of reciprocity

the expectation that helping others will increase the likelihood that they will help us in the future

The Reciprocity Norm To explain altruism, evolutionary psychologists also point to the **norm of reciprocity**, which is the expectation that helping others will increase the likelihood that they will help us in the future. The idea is that as human beings were evolving, a group of completely selfish individuals, each living in his or her own cave, would have found it more difficult to survive than a group who had learned to cooperate with one another. Of course, if people cooperated too readily, they might have been exploited by an adversary who never helped in return. Those who were most likely to survive, the argument goes, were people who developed an understanding with their neighbours about reciprocity: "I will help you now, with the agreement that when I need help, you will return the favour." Because of its survival value, such a norm of reciprocity may have become genetically based (Baron, 1997; Cosmides & Tooby, 1992; de Waal, 1996; Shackelford & Buss, 1996; Trivers, 1971). Try It!, below, describes a way you can use the reciprocity norm to collect money for charity.

According to William Brown and Chris Moore (2000) at Dalhousie University, from an evolutionary perspective it would also be adaptive to be able to detect pure altruists from those who are cheaters (free riders who have no plans of reciprocating helpful acts in the future). In a series of studies using hypothetical scenarios, they demonstrated that people are remarkably adept at discriminating true acts of altruism.

The Reciprocity Norm

As noted in this chapter and in Chapter 8, the reciprocity norm is powerful. If you help people in some way, they will probably feel obligated to help you in the future. This exercise is designed to take advantage of the reciprocity norm to help you collect money for a good cause. Follow the procedures and see if it works for you.

1. Choose a charity or cause for which you would like to collect money.

2. Make a list of 10 to 15 friends and acquaintances you are willing to ask to give money to this charity.

3. Go down the list and flip a coin for each name. If the coin comes up tails, assign them to the "favour" condition. If it comes up heads, assign them to the "no favour" condition.

4. Find a way to do a small favour for each person in the favour condition. For example, if you're going to the pop machine, offer to buy a pop for your friend. If you have a car, give him or her a ride somewhere. The exact favour doesn't matter, and doesn't have to be

the same for each person in your favour condition. The key is that it be a little out of the ordinary, so your friend feels obligated to you.

5. A day later, ask everyone on your list if they can make a donation to your charity. Keep track of how much each person gives. Chances are, people in your favour condition will give more, on average, than people in your no favour condition.

A word of warning: This technique can backfire if your friends perceive your favour as an attempt to manipulate them. That is why it is important to allow a day or so to pass between the time you help them and the time you ask them for a donation; if you ask them right after the favour, they are likely to feel that you helped only to get them to give money—and to resent this intrusion. Also, when you ask them for a donation, do not say anything about your earlier favour. After you have done this exercise, discuss it with your friends and explain why you did what you did.

Learning Social Norms A third way in which evolutionary theory can explain altruism has been offered by Nobel laureate Herbert Simon (1990). He argues that it is highly adaptive for individuals to learn social norms from other members of a society. Over the centuries, a culture learns such things as which foods are poisonous and how best to cooperate with each other, and the person who learns these rules is more likely to survive than the person who does not. Consequently, through natural selection, the ability to learn social norms has become part of our genetic makeup. One norm that people learn is the value of helping others; this is considered to be a valuable norm in virtually all societies. In short, people are genetically programmed to learn social norms, and one of these norms is altruism (Hoffman, 1981).

In sum, evolutionary psychologists believe that people help others because of three factors that have become ingrained in our genes: kin selection, the norm of reciprocity, and the ability to learn and follow social norms. Evolutionary psychology is a challenging and creative approach to understanding prosocial behaviour, though it is important to note that not all psychologists accept its claims. Many are skeptical of the idea that all social behaviours can be traced to our ancestral roots and became instilled in our genes because of their survival value (Batson, 1998; Caporael & Brewer, 2000; Gangestad, 1989; Gould, 1997; Wood & Eagly, 2000). For example, just because people are more likely to save family members than strangers from a fire does not necessarily mean that they are genetically programmed to help genetic relatives. It may simply be that they cannot bear the thought of losing a loved one and so go to greater lengths to save the ones they love than people they have never met. We turn now to other possible motives behind prosocial behaviour that do not necessarily originate in people's genes.

SOCIAL EXCHANGE: THE COSTS AND REWARDS OF HELPING

Though some social psychologists disagree with evolutionary approaches to prosocial behaviour, they do agree that altruistic behaviour can be based on self-interest. In fact, a theory in social psychology—social exchange theory—argues that much of what we do stems from the desire to maximize our rewards and minimize our costs (Homans, 1961; Lawler & Thye, 1999; Thibaut & Kelley, 1959; see Chapter 10 for a more in-depth description of social exchange theory). When it comes to helping, social exchange theory would argue that people help only when the benefits outweigh the costs. Thus, true altruism, in which people help even when doing so is costly, does not exist, according to this theory. People help when it is in their interests to do so, but not when the costs outweigh the benefits.

What might be the benefits of helping? There are actually a number of them. For example, considerable evidence indicates that people are aroused and disturbed when they see another person suffer, and that they help at least in part to relieve their own distress (Dovidio, 1984; Dovidio et al., 1991). Thus, it is rewarding to have our distress alleviated. By helping others, we can also gain such rewards as social approval from others and increased feelings of self-worth. Finally, as we saw with the norm of reciprocity, helping someone is an investment in the future, the social exchange being that, someday, someone will help you when you need it. If this sounds a bit far-fetched or even naive, think about how deeply this idea permeates our society on both a secular and a religious level. Being a good person and treating others with compassion (and receiving such

▶ Helping behaviour is common in virtually all species of animals. Sometimes, helping behaviour even crosses species lines. In August 1996, a three-year-old boy fell into a pit containing seven gorillas at the Brookfield, Illinois, zoo. Binti, a seven-year-old gorilla, immediately picked up the boy. After cradling him in her arms, she placed the boy near a door where zookeepers could get to him. Why did she help? Evolutionary psychologists would argue that prosocial behaviour is selected for and thus becomes part of the genetic makeup of members of many species. Social exchange theorists would argue that Binti had been rewarded for helping in the past. In fact, because she had been rejected by her mother, she had received training in parenting skills from zookeepers and had been rewarded for caring for a doll (Bils & Singer, 1996).

treatment in return) is the hallmark of a civilized society, part of what early philosophers called the "social contract." Few of us would want to live in a "dog-eat-dog" world; we need to believe that kindness will be reciprocated, at least some of the time.

Recall that social exchange theory suggests we will help only when the benefits outweigh the costs. Needless to say, many forms of helping do come at a cost. Helping is costly when it would put us in physical danger, result in pain or embarrassment, take too much time (Dovidio et al., 1991; Piliavin, Piliavin, & Rodin, 1975), or, as in the case of Gino LaPlante, when we are rushing to work in –41-degree Celsius weather. Not surprisingly, under such conditions, people are less likely to help.

If you are like many of our students, you may be experiencing discomfort over this view of helping behaviour, finding it to be a rather cynical portrayal of human nature. Is true altruism, motivated only by the desire to help someone else, really such a mythical act? Must we trace all prosocial behaviour to the self-interest of the helper? Such a view seems to demean prosocial behaviour. When someone behaves generously, as by saving another person's life or donating a huge sum to charity, should we view it as a mere act of self-interest undeserving of our esteem?

Well, a social exchange theorist might reply, there are many ways in which people can obtain gratification, and we should be thankful that one way is by helping others. After all, wealthy people could decide to get pleasure only from lavish vacations, expensive cars, and gourmet meals at fancy restaurants. We should applaud their decision to give money to the disadvantaged, even if, ultimately, it is just another way for them to obtain gratification. Still, many people are dissatisfied with the argument that all helping stems from self-interest. How can it explain why people go so far as to risk their lives for others, as Rocky Flett did when he entered a burning house or, as we described in Chapter 1, as Derek Kennedy did when he rescued people from drowning in Nova Scotia Harbour? According to some social psychologists, people do have hearts of gold and sometimes help only for the sake of helping—as we shall see now.

EMPATHY AND ALTRUISM: THE PURE MOTIVE FOR HELPING

C. Daniel Batson (1991) is the strongest proponent of the idea that people often help purely out of the goodness of their hearts. Batson acknowledges that people sometimes help others for selfish reasons. However, he argues that people's motives also are sometimes purely altruistic, in that their only goal is to help the other person, even if doing so involves some cost. Pure altruism is likely to come into play, he maintains, when we feel **empathy** for the person in need of help, defined as the ability to put ourselves in the shoes of another person, experiencing events and emotions the way that person experiences them. Suppose, for example, that you are at the grocery store and see a man holding a baby and a bag full of diapers, toys, and rattles. As the man reaches for a box of Cheerios, he loses his grip on the bag and all of its contents spill on the floor. Will you stop and help him pick up his things? According to Batson, it depends first on whether you feel empathy for him. If you do, you will help, regardless of what you have to gain. Your goal will be to relieve the other person's distress, not to gain something for yourself. This is the crux of Batson's **empathy-altruism hypothesis**. A study conducted with children in British Columbia found support for this hypothesis. Children who were able to put themselves in another person's shoes were more likely to behave in prosocial ways toward that person (e.g., helping an experimenter who dropped a box of paper clips, letting a friend have a turn at an enjoyable game). In fact, empathy was related to helping even among children as young as five years of age (Roberts & Strayer, 1996).

What if you do not feel empathy? If, for whatever reason, you do not share the man's distress, then, Batson says, social exchange concerns come into play. What's in it for you? If there is something to be gained, such as obtaining approval from the man or from onlookers, you will help the man pick up his things. If you will not profit from helping, you will go on your way without stopping. Batson's empathy-altruism hypothesis is summarized in Figure 11.1.

Batson and his colleagues would be the first to acknowledge that it can be very difficult to isolate the exact causes of complex social behaviours, and indeed, this has been the subject of lively debate (e.g., Cialdini et al., 1997; Hornstein, 1991; Martz, 1991; Smith, Keating, & Stotland, 1989; Sorrentino, 1991). If you saw a woman in the store help the man pick up his possessions, how could you tell whether she was acting out of empathic concern or to gain some sort of social reward? Consider a famous story about Abraham Lincoln. One day while riding in a coach, Lincoln and a fellow passenger were debating the very question we are considering: Is helping ever truly altruistic? Lincoln argued that helping always stems from self-interest, whereas the other passenger took the view that true altruism exists. Suddenly the men were interrupted by the screeching whine of a sow, who was trying to save her piglets from drowning in a creek. Lincoln promptly called out, "Driver, can't you stop for just a moment?" He jumped out of the coach, ran to the creek, and lifted the piglets to the safety of the bank. When he returned, his companion said, "Now, Abe, where does selfishness come in on this little episode?" "Why, bless your soul, Ed," Lincoln replied. "That was the very essence of selfishness. I should have had no peace of mind all day had I gone on and left that suffering old sow worrying over those pigs. I did it to get peace of mind, don't you see?" (Sharp, 1928).

As this example shows, an act that seems truly altruistic is sometimes motivated by self-interest. How, then, can we tell which is which? Batson and colleagues have devised

Empathy

the ability to experience events and emotions (e.g., joy and sadness) the way another person experiences them

Empathy-altruism hypothesis

the idea that when we feel empathy for a person, we will attempt to help him or her purely for altruistic reasons, regardless of what we have to gain

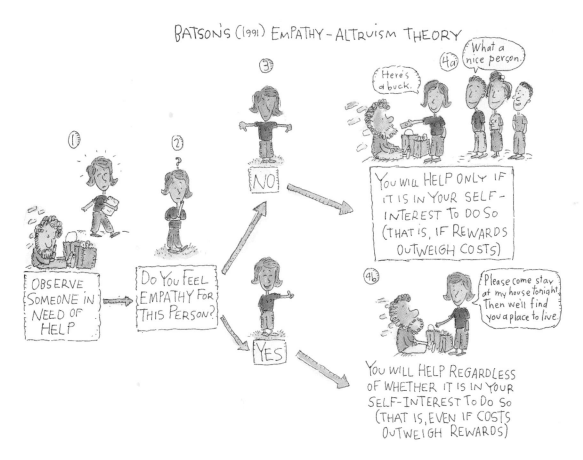

▲ **Figure 11.1**

BATSON'S (1991) EMPATHY-
ALTRUISM THEORY.

a series of clever experiments to unravel people's motives (e.g., Batson, 1998; Batson & Ahmad, in press; Batson & Shaw, 1991; Batson et al., 1996; Batson & Moran, 1999; Batson & Weeks, 1996; Toi & Batson, 1982). Imagine you were one of the participants (an Introductory Psychology student) in a study by Miho Toi and Daniel Batson (1982). You are asked to evaluate some tapes of new programs, one of which is called *News from the Personal Side,* for your university's radio station. There are many different pilot tapes for this program, and you are told that only one person will be listening to each tape. The one you hear is an interview with a student named Carol Marcy. She describes a bad automobile accident and explains that because she is still in a wheelchair, it has been very difficult to keep up with her course work. Carol goes on to mention that she will have to drop her Introductory Psychology class unless she can find a student from whom she can borrow lecture notes.

After you listen to the tape, the experimenter hands you an envelope marked "To the student listening to the Carol Marcy pilot tape," and says that the professor supervising the research asked her to give it to you. The envelope contains a note from the professor, saying that he was wondering if the student who listened to Carol's tape would be willing to meet with her and share his or her Introductory Psychology lecture notes.

As you have no doubt gathered, the point of the study was to look at the conditions under which people agreed to help Carol. Toi and Batson (1982) pitted two motives

Calvin and Hobbes   by Bill Watterson

◀ Calvin seems to be an advocate of social exchange theory.

against each other: self-interest and empathy. First, they varied how much empathy people felt toward Carol by telling different participants to adopt different perspectives when listening to the tape. In the high-empathy condition, people were told to try to imagine how Carol felt about what had happened to her and how it had changed her life. In the low-empathy condition, people were told to try to be objective and to not be concerned with how Carol felt. These instructions had the expected effect on people's feelings: Those in the high-empathy condition reported feeling more empathy with Carol than did people in the low-empathy condition.

Second, Toi and Batson varied how costly it would be *not* to help Carol. In one condition, participants learned that Carol would start coming back to class the following week and happened to be in the same Introductory Psychology section as they were; thus, they would see her every time they went to class and would be reminded of her need for help. This was the high-cost condition, because it would be unpleasant to refuse to help Carol and then run into her every week in class. In the low-cost condition, people learned that Carol would be studying at home and would not be coming to class; thus, they would never have to face her in her wheelchair and feel guilty about not helping her out.

When deciding whether to help Carol, did people take into account the costs involved? According to the empathy-altruism hypothesis, people should have been motivated by genuine altruistic concern, and should have helped regardless of the costs—if empathy was high (see Figure 11.1 on page 396). As you can see in the right-hand side of Figure 11.2, this prediction was confirmed. In the high-empathy condition, about as many

▼ **Figure 11.2**

ALTRUISM VERSUS SELF-INTEREST.

Under what conditions did people agree to help Carol with the work she missed in her Introductory Psychology class? When empathy was high, people helped regardless of the costs and rewards (i.e., regardless of whether they would encounter her in their psychology class). When empathy was low, people were more concerned with the rewards and costs for them—they helped only if they would encounter Carol in their psychology class and thus feel guilty about not helping.

(Adapted from Toi & Batson, 1982)

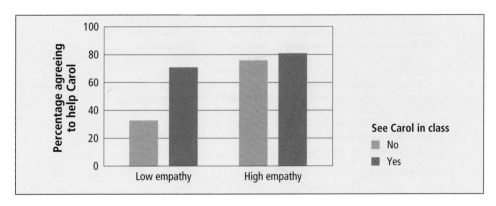

people agreed to help when they thought they would see Carol in class as when they thought they would not see her in class. This suggests that people had Carol's interests in mind, not their own. In the low-empathy condition, however, many more people agreed to help when they thought they would see Carol in class than when they thought they would not see her in class (see the left-hand side of Figure 11.2). This suggests that when empathy was low, social exchange concerns came into play, in that people based their decision to help on the costs and benefits to themselves. They helped when it was in their interests to do so (i.e., when they would see Carol in her wheelchair and feel guilty for not helping) but not otherwise (i.e., when they thought they would never see her again).

The Toi and Batson (1982) study and others (Batson, 1998; Piliavin & Charng, 1990) suggest that when we feel empathy for another person, our motives do seem to be pure, causing us to help even when we have nothing to gain by doing so.

In a recent, interesting twist on this issue, researchers at the University of Waterloo hypothesized that people are most likely to help if the helpful act allows them to see themselves as altruistic—but not unconditionally so (Holmes, Miller, & Lerner, 2002). In other words, we will be helpful if we can "cover up" our altruism with a social exchange interpretation, making it look as though there was something in it for us. Why would we be motivated to do so? According to Holmes and colleagues, if we saw ourselves as pure altruists, we would feel compelled to help each and every time a need arose. Because none of us is able to offer unending help, we would be doomed to feelings of failure and despair. If we can instead construe helping situations in exchange terms, we can happily help in a given situation without feeling that we have now committed ourselves to helping forevermore. To test this line of thinking, the researchers approached people on their

▶ This touching story of early hominid prosocial behaviour is intriguing to think about in terms of different theories of prosocial behaviour. Evolutionary psychologists might argue that the caregivers helped the dwarf because he was a relative, and that people are programmed to help those who share their genes (kin selection). Social exchange theory would maintain that the dwarf's caregivers received sufficient rewards from their actions so as to outweigh the costs of caring for him. The empathy-altruism hypothesis would hold that the caregivers helped out of strong feelings of empathy and compassion for him—an interpretation supported by the article's final paragraph.

Study: Cavemen helped disabled

United Press International
NEW YORK—The skeleton of a dwarf who died about 12,000 years ago indicates that cave people cared for physically disabled members of their communities, a researcher said yesterday.

The skeleton of the 3-foot-high youth was initially discovered in 1963 in a cave in southern Italy but was lost to anthropologists until American researcher David W. Frayer reexamined the remains and reported his findings in the British journal Nature.

Frayer, a professor of anthropology at the University of Kansas at Lawrence, said in a telephone interview that the youth "couldn't have taken part in normal hunting of food or gathering activities so

he was obviously cared for by others."

Archaeologists have found the remains of other handicapped individuals who lived during the same time period, but their disabilities occurred when they were adults, Frayer said.

"This is the first time we've found someone who was disabled since birth . . . .", Frayer said. He said there was no indication that the dwarf, who was about 17 at the time of his death, had suffered from malnutrition or neglect.

He was one of six individuals buried in the floor of a cave and was found in a dual grave in the arms of a woman, about 40 years old.

campus and asked them for either a straight-out charitable donation or to purchase candles in support of a particular charity. The charity was described as either high or low in need. In which condition did people donate the most money? As expected, they were most generous in the condition where they received something in exchange for helping (i.e., candles)—and when the need was high. This latter statement is important because it shows that people were not simply motivated by strict exchange ("I give you money; you give me a candle"), but rather helped in response to a need. The way Holmes and colleagues put it, the candles didn't provide an incentive, but rather an excuse, for giving.

In summary, we have discussed three basic motives underlying prosocial behaviour: the idea that helping is an instinctive reaction to promote the welfare of those genetically similar to us (evolutionary psychology); that the rewards of helping often outweigh the costs, making it in people's self-interest to help (social exchange theory); and that, under some conditions, powerful feelings of empathy and compassion for the victim prompt selfless giving (the empathy-altruism hypothesis). Each of these approaches has vocal proponents and vociferous critics.

Personal Determinants of Prosocial Behaviour: Why Do Some People Help More than Others?

Whatever the nature of people's basic motives, such motives are not the sole determinants of whether people help, for many personal and situational factors can suppress or trigger these motives. If basic human motives were all there was to it, how could we explain the fact that some people are much more helpful than others? Clearly, we need to consider the personal determinants of prosocial behaviour that distinguish the helpful person from the selfish one.

INDIVIDUAL DIFFERENCES: THE ALTRUISTIC PERSONALITY

When you read the examples at the beginning of this chapter, did you think about the different personalities of the people involved? It is natural to assume that people such as John Rokosh, who helped an athlete with whom he was competing; Rocky Flett, who rescued children from a burning house; and Derek Kennedy (introduced in Chapter 1), who rescued drowning people in Nova Scotia Harbour, are cut from a different cloth—selfless, caring people who would never dream of ignoring someone's pleas for help. Similarly, there are Mother Teresas who devote their lives to others, and Adolf Hitlers who are bent on destruction and mayhem. And, of course, there are many people between these extremes of sainthood and wickedness. Psychologists have been quite interested in the nature of the **altruistic personality**, which are those aspects of a person's makeup that cause him or her to help others in a wide variety of situations (Eisenberg et al., 1999; Oliner & Oliner, 1988; Penner et al., 1995; Penner & Finkelstein, 1998).

As we saw in Chapter 1, however, personality is not the sole determinant of how people behave. According to social psychologists, to understand human behaviour—such as how helpful people will be in a given situation—we need to consider the situational pressures impinging on them, as well as their personalities. Predicting how helpful

Altruistic personality
aspects of a person's makeup that cause him or her to help others in a wide variety of situations

people will be is no exception to the rule. Consider, for example, a classic study by Hugh Hartshorne and Mark May (1929). They observed how helpful 10 000 elementary and high-school students were in a variety of situations, including the students' willingness to find stories and pictures to give to hospitalized children, to donate money to charity, and to give small gifts to needy children. The researchers assumed that they were measuring the extent to which people had an altruistic personality.

Surprisingly, the extent to which the children were prosocial in one situation (e.g., finding many stories and pictures for the hospitalized children) was not highly related to how prosocial they were in another. The average correlation between helping in one situation and helping in another was only .23. This means that if you knew how helpful a child was in one situation, you could not predict with much confidence how helpful he would be in another. Moreover, researchers who have studied both children and adults have not found much evidence that people with high scores on personality tests of altruism are more likely to help than those with lower scores (Magoo & Khanna, 1991; Piliavin & Charng, 1990). Clearly, personality is not a major determinant of whether people will help, at least in many situations. However, as we will see, there are other personal factors that are more strongly linked to helping.

THE EFFECTS OF MOOD ON PROSOCIAL BEHAVIOUR

Sometimes we feel up and sometimes we feel down; believe it or not, these transitory emotional states are a key determinant of prosocial behaviour. For example, imagine you are at your local shopping mall. As you walk from one store to another, a fellow in front of you suddenly drops a manila folder, and papers flutter in all directions. He looks around in dismay, then bends down and starts picking up the papers. Would you stop and help him? What do you think the average shopper would do? As it turns out, what the average shopper would do may largely depend on the kind of mood she or he is in at the time.

Effects of Positive Moods: Feel Good, Do Good
Alice Isen and Paul Levin (1972) explored the effect of good moods on prosocial behaviour in shopping malls in San Francisco and Philadelphia. They boosted the mood of shoppers in a simple way—namely, by leaving a dime in the coin-return slot of a pay telephone at the mall and waiting for someone to find it. As the lucky shoppers left the phone with their newly found dime, an assistant of Isen and Levine played the role of the man with the manila folder. He purposefully dropped the folder a few feet in front of the shopper, to see whether the shopper would stop and help him pick up his papers. It turned out that finding the dime had a dramatic effect on helping. Only 4 percent of the people who did not find a dime helped the man pick up his papers. In comparison, 84 percent of the people who found a dime helped.

Researchers have found this "feel good, do good" effect in diverse situations, and have shown that it is not limited to the little boost we get when we find some money. People are more likely to help others when they are in a good mood for a number of reasons, including doing well on a test, receiving a gift, thinking happy thoughts, and listening to pleasant music. And when people are in a good mood, they are more helpful in many ways, including contributing money to charity, helping someone find a lost contact lens, tutoring another student, donating blood, and helping co-workers on the job

(Carlson, Charlin, & Miller, 1988; George & Brief, 1992; Isen, 1999; Salovey, Mayer, & Rosenhan, 1991). See Try It!, below, for a way of doing your own test of the "feel good, do good" hypothesis.

What is it about being in a good mood that makes people more altruistic? It turns out that good moods can increase helping for three reasons. First, good moods make us look on the bright side of life. If you saw the man drop his manila folder full of papers, you could view this incident in at least two ways. "What a klutz," you might think. "Let him clean up his own mess." Or you might have more sympathy for him, thinking, "Oh, that's too bad. The poor guy, he was probably in a big hurry." When we are in a good mood, we tend to see the good side of other people, giving them the benefit of the doubt. A victim who might normally seem clumsy or annoying will, when we are feeling cheerful, seem like a decent, needy person who is worthy of our help (Carlson, Charlin, & Miller, 1988; Forgas & Bower, 1987).

Second, "feel good, do good" occurs because it is an excellent way of prolonging our good mood. If we see someone in need of help, then being a Good Samaritan will spawn even more good feelings, and we can walk away continuing to feel like a million bucks. In comparison, not helping when we know we should is a surefire "downer," deflating our good mood (Clark & Isen, 1982; Isen, 1987; Williamson & Clark, 1989).

Mood and Helping Behaviour

Do people's moods influence how willing they are to help others? Try the experiment described below to find out.

Robert Baron (1997) predicted that people would be in better moods when they are around pleasant fragrances, and that this improved mood would make them more helpful. Consistent with his prediction, shoppers were more likely to help a stranger (by giving change for a dollar) when they were approached in locations with pleasant smells than when they were approached in locations with neutral smells. See if you can replicate this effect at a shopping mall in your area. Pick locations in the mall that have pleasant aromas or neutral aromas. For his pleasant aroma conditions, Baron (1997) used locations near a cookie store, a bakery, and a gourmet coffee café. The areas with neutral smells should be as identical as possible in all other respects; for example, Baron (1997) picked locations that were similar in the volume of pedestrians, lighting, and proximity to mall exits, such as areas outside clothing stores.

At each location, approach an individual who is by himself or herself. Take out a loonie and ask the passerby for change. If the person stops and gives you change, count it as helping. If he or she ignores you or says he or she does not have any change, count it as not helping. Did you replicate Baron's (1997) results? He found that 57 percent of people helped in the locations with pleasant aromas, whereas only 19 percent of people helped in the locations with neutral aromas.

Note: Before conducting this study you might want to seek the permission of the manager of the mall. The manager of the mall in which Baron (1997) conducted his study requested that the researchers only approach persons of the same gender as themselves, because of a concern that cross-gender requests for change would be perceived as "pick-up" attempts. You might want to follow this procedure as well.

Finally, good moods increase self-attention. Sometimes we are particularly attuned to our internal worlds, and sometimes we are not. Good moods increase the amount of attention we pay to ourselves, and this factor in turn makes us more likely to behave according to our values and ideals. Because most of us value altruism and because good moods increase our attention to this value, good moods increase helping behaviour (Berkowitz, 1987; Carlson, Charlin, & Miller, 1988; Salovey & Rodin, 1985).

Negative-State Relief: Feel Bad, Do Good What about when we are in a bad mood? Suppose that when you saw the fellow in the mall drop his folder, you were feeling down in the dumps—would this influence the likelihood that you would help the man? One kind of bad mood clearly leads to an increase in helping—feeling guilty (Baumeister, Stillwell, & Heatherton, 1994; Estrada-Hollenbeck & Heatherton, 1998). When people have done something that has made them feel guilty, helping another person balances things out, reducing their guilty feelings. For example, Mary Harris and her colleagues (1975) found that churchgoers were more likely to donate money to charities before attending confession than afterwards, presumably because confessing to a priest reduced their guilt. Thus, if you just realized you had forgotten your best friend's birthday and you felt guilty about it, you would be more likely to help the fellow in the mall.

But suppose you just had a fight with a friend or just found out you did poorly on a test, and you were feeling sad and blue. Given that feeling happy leads to greater helping, it might seem that feeling sad will decrease helping. Surprisingly, however, sadness can also lead to an increase in helping, at least under certain conditions (Carlson & Miller, 1987; Salovey et al., 1991). When people are sad, they are motivated to engage in activities that make them feel better (Wegener & Petty, 1994).

The idea that people help in order to alleviate their own sadness and distress is called the **negative-state relief hypothesis**, developed by Robert Cialdini (Cialdini, Darby, & Vincent, 1973; Cialdini & Fultz, 1990; Cialdini et al., 1987). It is an example of the social exchange theory approach to helping that we discussed earlier. People help someone else with the goal of helping themselves—namely, to relieve their own sadness and distress. For example, if we are feeling down, we are more likely to donate money to a charity. The warm glow of helping the charity lifts us out of the doldrums (Cialdini, Darby, & Vincent, 1973).

Negative-state relief hypothesis

the idea that people help in order to alleviate their own sadness and distress

GENDER DIFFERENCES IN PROSOCIAL BEHAVIOUR

Consider how helpful you think people would be in these two situations: (a) passing by a house, hearing the cries of young children, and smelling smoke, and (b) being asked by an elderly neighbour for a ride to the nearest grocery store. Who is most likely to help in the first situation, and who is most likely to help in the second?

According to a review by Alice Eagly and Maureen Crowley (1986; Eagly, 1987), the answer is males in the first situation and females in the second situation. In Western cultures, part of the male sex role is to be chivalrous and heroic, whereas part of the female sex role is to be nurturant and caring, valuing close, long-term relationships. As a result, we might expect men to help more in situations that call for brief chivalrous and heroic acts, and women to help more in long-term relationships that involve less danger but more commitment, such as volunteering at a nursing home.

◀ Whereas men are more likely to perform chivalrous and heroic acts, women are more likely to be helpful in long-term relationships that involve greater commitment.

In a review of more than 170 studies on helping behaviour, Eagly and Crowley (1986) found that men are indeed more likely to help in chivalrous, heroic ways. In Canada, the Governor General awards the Medal of Bravery for "acts of bravery in hazardous circumstances." Consistent with Eagly and Crowley's findings, the recipients of these awards tend to be men. For example, in 1999, 14 Medals of Bravery were awarded to men, compared to only 3 to women. In 2000, the number of women who received awards was higher (6 women; 14 men), but men still outnumbered women by more than 2:1. And, as you will recall, we opened the chapter with the story of Rocky Flett, the 13-year-old who was one of the six recipients of the Canada Day People Who Make a Difference Award because of his heroic rescue of three children from a burning house.

Now consider another recipient of this award—Nicole Bouchard, a Winnipeg teacher. Nicole was recognized not for a daring rescue, but for the caring and compassion she extends to her grades 9 and 10 students. The student who nominated her did so "because she cares deeply about her students. There may be that person who doesn't have anyone caring for them but her. . . . [and that] may make the difference between life and death."

Research confirms that helping that involves nurturance and commitment is more likely to be performed by women than by men (Belansky & Boggiano, 1994; Otten, Penner, & Waugh, 1988; Smith, Wheeler, & Diener, 1975). For example, a cross-cultural survey of adolescents found that in each of the seven countries studied, more girls than boys did volunteer work in their communities (Flanagan et al., 1998). Similarly, an analysis of volunteering among Canadians (ages 15 to 65+) found that women were more likely than men to engage in both formal and informal volunteering (Ekos Research Associates and Canadian Policy Research Networks, 1999).

CULTURAL DIFFERENCES IN PROSOCIAL BEHAVIOUR

In all cultures people are more likely to help someone they define as a member of their **in-group,** the group with which an individual identifies and of which he or she feels a member. People everywhere are less likely to help someone they perceive to be a member of an **out-group,** a group with which the individual does not identify (Brewer & Brown, 1998; see Chapter 13). However, cultural factors come into play in determining how strongly people draw the line between in-groups and out-groups. In previous chapters, we noted that people who grow up in Western cultures tend to be individualist and have an independent view of the self, whereas people who grow up in many non-Western cultures tend to be collectivist and have an interdependent view of the self. Because people with an interdependent view of the self are more likely to define themselves in terms of their social relationships and have more of a sense of "connectedness" to others, greater importance is attached to the needs of the in-group. Consequently, members of these cultures are more likely to help in-group members than are members of individualist cultures (Leung & Bond, 1984; Miller, Bersoff, & Harwood, 1990; Moghaddam, Taylor, & Wright, 1993). However, because the line between "us" and "them" is more firmly drawn in interdependent cultures, people in these cultures are less likely to help members of out-groups than are people in individualist cultures (L'Armand & Pepitone, 1975; Leung & Bond, 1984; Triandis, 1994). McCrae and colleagues suggest this is the reason Chinese people score lower than Canadians on scales that assess the altruistic personality type (McCrae et al., 1998). Indeed, when Osamu Iwata (1992) compared the altruistic intentions of Canadian and Japanese students by type of relationship, Canadians expressed greater altruism toward "a person one happens to see occasionally but with whom he or she has no relation." However, Canadians and Japanese students did not differ when altruism was directed toward a person with whom one has "personal and close relations." Thus, to be helped by other people, it is important that they view you as a member of their in-group—as "one of them"—and this is especially true in interdependent cultures (Ting & Piliavin, 2000).

Before leaving this topic, we should point out that cultural norms about taking credit for helping others may also contribute to the perception that people from Asian cultures are less altruistic, overall, than people from Western cultures. According to Lee, Cameron, Xu, Fu, and Board (1997), in Asian cultures children are taught to be modest and self-effacing—and this includes not seeking recognition for helpful acts. These researchers presented scenarios about helping to children (ages 7 to 11) in Canada and China. For example, one of the scenarios described a girl, Kelly, who knew that her friend Anne had lost the money she needed for a class trip. Kelly secretly put some of her own money in Anne's pocket so Anne could go on the trip. Later, a teacher asked Kelly if she knew who had given the money to Anne. Canadian children believed that Kelly should acknowledge this helpful act (thereby garnering the praise of the teacher); Chinese children believed that Kelly should not admit that she had done so because "begging" for praise would violate norms of modesty. More recently, these researchers replicated this study with adults (university students, elementary school teachers, and parents) in Canada and China, and got exactly the same results (Fu et al., 2001).

In-group
the group with which an individual identifies and of which he or she feels a member

Out-group
a group with which the individual does not identify

Situational Determinants of Prosocial Behaviour: When Will People Help?

In the previous section, we considered several personal determinants of prosocial behaviour: personality, moods, gender, and culture. This does not mean, however, that to predict how altruistically people will act, all you need to know is their standing on these variables. Though each contributes a piece to the puzzle of why people help others, they do not complete the picture. To understand more fully why people help, we need to consider the social situation in which they find themselves.

ENVIRONMENT: RURAL VERSUS URBAN

Suppose you are riding your bike one day and, as you turn a corner, your front wheel suddenly drops into a pothole, sending you tumbling over the handlebars. You sit there stunned for a moment, then notice a sharp pain in your shin. Sure enough, you have broken your leg and there is no way you can get up and get help by yourself. You look around, hoping to see someone who will help you out. Now consider this question: Where would you rather have this accident—on the main street of a small, rural town, or in the downtown area of a large city? In which place would passersby be more likely to offer you help?

If you said the small town, you are right. Several researchers have compared the likelihood that people will help in rural versus urban areas, and have consistently found that people in rural areas help more (Korte, 1980; Steblay, 1987). Paul Amato (1983), for example, staged an incident in which a man limped down the street and then suddenly fell down with a cry of pain in front of a pedestrian approaching from the opposite direction. The man lifted the leg of his pants, revealing a heavily bandaged shin that was bleeding profusely (with theatrical blood that looked real). In small towns, about half of the pedestrians for whom this incident was staged offered the man help. In large cities, however, only 15 percent of pedestrians stopped and helped. People in small towns have been found to assist more in a multitude of ways, including helping a stranger who has had an accident, helping a lost child, giving directions, participating in a survey, and returning a lost letter. The finding that help is more likely to be offered in small towns than in large cities has been reported in several countries, including Canada, the United States, Israel, Australia, Turkey, Great Britain, and the Sudan (Hedge & Yousif, 1992; Steblay, 1987).

Why are our chances of being helped greater in small towns? One possibility is that the experience of growing up in a small town enhances the altruistic personality, whereas growing up in a big city diminishes the altruistic personality. According to this view, you would be more likely to be helped by someone who grew up in a small town, even if that person were visiting a big city. The key is the values the small-town resident has internalized, not his or her immediate surroundings. Alternatively, it might be people's immediate surroundings that are the key, not their personalities. Stanley Milgram (1970), for example, proposed an **urban-overload hypothesis**, which holds that people living in cities are constantly being bombarded with stimulation and that they keep to themselves in order to avoid being overloaded by it. According to this argument, if you put urban dwellers in a calmer, less stimulating environment, they would be as likely as anyone else to reach out to others.

Urban-overload hypothesis

the theory that people living in cities are constantly being bombarded with stimulation and that they keep to themselves in order to avoid being overloaded by it

Interestingly, the evidence supports the urban-overload hypothesis more than it does the idea that living in cities makes people less altruistic by nature. When an opportunity for helping arises, it matters more whether the incident occurs in a rural or urban area than which kind of person happens to be there (Steblay, 1987). Further, Robert Levine and his colleagues (1994) found, in field studies conducted in 36 cities in the United States, that population density (the number of people per square kilometre) was more related to helping than was population size. The greater the density of people, the less likely people were to help. This makes sense, according to the urban-overload hypothesis: There should be more stimulation in a small area packed with a lot of people than in a large area where the same number of people are spread out. In short, it would be better to have a city slicker witness your bicycle accident in a small town than to have a small-town person witness it in a big, crowded city. The hustle and bustle in cities can be so overwhelming that even caring, altruistic people turn inward, responding less to those around them.

BYSTANDER INTERVENTION: THE LATANÉ AND DARLEY MODEL

Remember Kitty Genovese? We have just seen one reason why her neighbours may have turned a deaf ear to her cries for help: The murder took place in New York City, one of the most populated areas in the world. Perhaps her neighbours were so overloaded with urban stimulation that they dismissed Genovese's cries as one small addition to the surrounding din. Though it is true that people help less in urban environments, this explanation is not the only one as to why Genovese's neighbours failed to help. Her desperate cries surely must have risen above the everyday noises of garbage trucks and car horns. And, conversely, there have been cases in which people ignored the pleas of their neighbours in small towns. In Fredericksburg, Virginia, a convenience store clerk was beaten in front of customers who did nothing to help, even after the assailant had fled and the clerk lay bleeding on the floor (Hsu, 1995). Fredericksburg has only 20 000 residents.

Bibb Latané and John Darley (1970) are two social psychologists who taught at universities in New York at the time of the Genovese murder. As we discussed in Chapter 2,

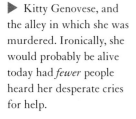

▶ Kitty Genovese, and the alley in which she was murdered. Ironically, she would probably be alive today had *fewer* people heard her desperate cries for help.

they too were unconvinced that the only reason her neighbours failed to help was the stresses and stimulation of urban life. They focused on the fact that many people heard her cries. Paradoxically, they thought, it might be that the greater the number of bystanders who observe an emergency, the less likely it is that any one of them will help. As Bibb Latané (1987) put it, "We came up with the insight that perhaps what made the Genovese case so fascinating was itself what made it happen—namely, that not just one or two, but 38 people had watched and done nothing."

How can this be? Surely, the more people who witness an emergency—such as your hypothetical bicycle accident—the greater one's chance of receiving help. In a series of now classic experiments, Latané and Darley (1970) found that just the opposite was true. In terms of receiving help, there is no safety in numbers. Think back to the seizure experiment we discussed in Chapter 2. In this study, people sat in individual cubicles, participating in a group discussion of university life (over an intercom system) with students in other cubicles. One of the other students suddenly had a seizure, crying out, "I could really—er—use some help so if somebody would—er—give me a little h—help—uh—er—er—er—er—c—could somebody—er—er—help—er—uh—uh—uh (choking sounds). . . . I'm gonna die—er—er—I'm . . . gonna die—er—help—er—er—seizure—er (chokes, then quiet)" (Darley & Latané, 1968). There was actually only one real participant in the study. The other "participants," including the one who had the seizure, were prerecorded voices. The point of the study was to see whether the real participant tried to help the seizure victim, by trying to find him or by summoning the experimenter, or whether, like Kitty Genovese's neighbours, he or she simply sat there and did nothing.

As Latané and Darley anticipated, the answer depended on how many people the participant thought witnessed the emergency. When people believed they were the only ones listening to the student have the seizure, most of them (85 percent) helped within 60 seconds. By two-and-a-half minutes, 100 percent of the people who thought they were the only bystander had offered assistance (see Figure 11.3). In comparison, when the research participants believed there was one other student listening, fewer people

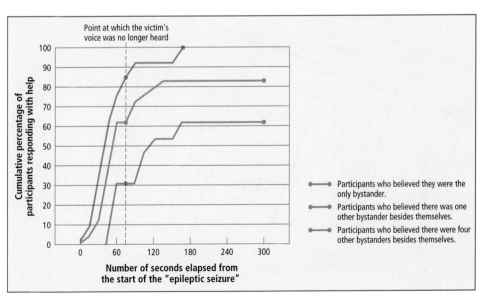

▼ Figure 11.3

BYSTANDER INTERVENTION: THE PRESENCE OF BYSTANDERS REDUCES HELPING.

When people believed that they were the only one witnessing a student having a seizure—when they were the lone bystander—most of them helped him immediately, and all did so within a few minutes. When they believed that someone else was listening as well—that there were two bystanders—they were less likely to help and did so more slowly. And when they believed that four others were listening—that there were five bystanders—they were even less likely to help.

(Adapted from Darley & Latané, 1968)

helped—only 62 percent within 60 seconds. As you can see in Figure 11.3, helping occurred more slowly when there were two bystanders, and never reached 100 percent, even after six minutes, at which point the experiment was terminated. Finally, when the participants believed there were four other students listening in addition to themselves, the percentage of people who helped dropped even more dramatically. Only 31 percent helped in the first 60 seconds, and after six minutes only 62 percent had offered help. Dozens of other studies, conducted both in the laboratory and in the field, have found the same thing. The greater the number of bystanders who witness an emergency, the less likely any one of them is to help the victim—a phenomenon called the **bystander effect**.

Bystander effect

the finding that the greater the number of bystanders who witness an emergency, the less likely it is that any one of them will help

Why is it that people are less likely to help when other bystanders are present? Latané and Darley (1970) developed a step-by-step description of how people decide whether to intervene in an emergency (see Figure 11.4). Part of this description, as we will see, is an explanation of how the number of bystanders can make a difference. But let's begin with the first step: whether people notice that someone needs help.

Noticing an Event Sometimes it is clear that an emergency has occurred, as in the seizure experiment where it was obvious that the other student was in danger. Other times, however, it is not as clear. If you are late for an appointment and are hurrying down

▼ **Figure 11.4**

BYSTANDER INTERVENTION DECISION TREE: FIVE STEPS TO HELPING IN AN EMERGENCY.

Latané and Darley (1970) showed that people go through five decision-making steps before they help someone in an emergency. If bystanders fail to take any one of the five steps, they will not help. Each step, as well as the possible reasons why people decide not to intervene, is outlined above.

(Adapted from Latané & Darley, 1970)

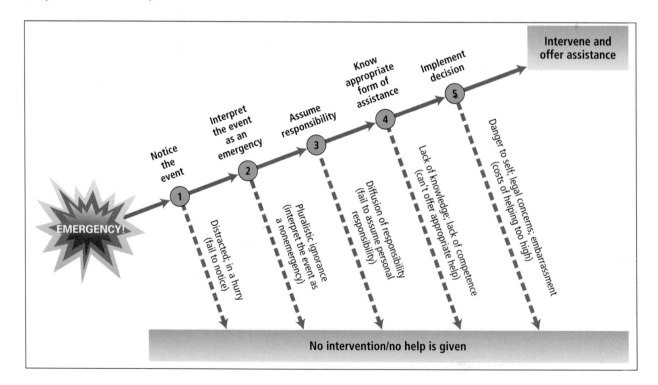

a crowded street, you might not notice that someone has collapsed in the doorway of a nearby building. Obviously, if people don't notice that an emergency has occurred, they will not intervene and offer to help.

What determines whether people notice an emergency? John Darley and Daniel Batson (1973) demonstrated that something as seemingly trivial as how much of a hurry people are in can make more of a difference than what kind of person they are. These researchers conducted a study that mirrored the parable of the Good Samaritan, wherein many passersby failed to stop to help a man lying unconscious on the side of the road. The research participants were people we might think would be extremely altruistic—seminary students preparing to devote their lives to the ministry. The students were asked to walk to another building, where the researchers would record them making a brief speech. Some were told that they were late and should hurry to keep their appointment. Others were told that there was no rush, because the assistant in the other building was a few minutes behind schedule. As they walked to the other building, each of the students passed a man who was slumped in a doorway. The man (an accomplice of the experimenters) coughed and groaned as each student walked by. Did the seminary students stop and offer to help him? If they were not in a hurry, most of them (63 percent) did. If they were hurrying to keep their appointment, however, very few of them (10 percent) did. Many of the students who were in a hurry did not even notice the man.

It is perhaps unsurprising that when people are in a rush, they pay less attention to what's going on around them, making them less likely to help someone in need. What is surprising is that such a seemingly trivial matter as how much of a hurry we are in can overpower the kind of people we are. Darley and Batson (1973) tested the seminary students on a variety of personality measures that assessed how religious they were. They also varied the topic of the speech. Specifically, some students were asked to speak on the parable of the Good Samaritan—surely, seminary students speaking on this topic would be especially likely to stop and help a man slumped in a doorway, given the similarity of this incident to the parable. However, if the students were in a hurry, they were unlikely to help, even if they were very religious individuals about to give a speech about the Good Samaritan. Before leaving this study, we should note that Darley and Batson did find one variable that made a difference—namely, whether the students saw religion as a quest (an open-minded search for truth) versus a set of traditions. Those who viewed religion as a quest were no more likely to stop, but those who did stop were more responsive to the man's needs than those who viewed religion as a set of traditions.

Interpreting the Event as an Emergency Just because people notice someone slumped in a doorway does not mean they will help. The next determinant of helping is whether the bystander interprets the event as an emergency—in other words, as a situation where help is needed (see Figure 11.4). Is the person in the doorway drunk, or seriously ill? If we see white smoke coming out of a vent, is it something innocuous, such as mist from an air conditioner, or a sign that the building is on fire? Is that couple having a particularly loud argument, or is one partner about to beat up the other? If people assume that nothing is wrong when an emergency is taking place, obviously they will not help.

Interestingly, when other bystanders are present, people are more likely to assume that an emergency is something innocuous. To understand why, think back to our discussion of informational social influence in Chapter 8. This type of social influence occurs when we use other people to help us define reality. When we are uncertain about what's going on, such as whether the smoke we see is a sign of a fire, one of the first things we do is look around to see how other people are responding. If other people look up, shrug, and go about their business, we are likely to assume that there is nothing to worry about. If other people look panic-stricken and yell, "Fire!" we immediately assume that the building is indeed on fire. As we saw in Chapter 8, it's often a good strategy to use other people as a source of information when we are uncertain about what's going on. The danger in doing so, however, is that sometimes no one is sure what is happening. Since an emergency is often a sudden and confusing event, bystanders tend to freeze, watching and listening with blank expressions as they try to figure out what's taking place. When they glance at each other, they see an apparent lack of concern on the part of other bystanders. This results in a state of **pluralistic ignorance**, the phenomenon whereby bystanders assume that nothing is wrong in an emergency because no one else looks concerned.

Pluralistic ignorance was demonstrated in another classic experiment by Latané and Darley (1970). Imagine that you have agreed to take part in a study of people's attitudes toward the problems of urban life, and you arrive at the appointed time. A sign instructs you to fill out a questionnaire while you are waiting for the study to begin. You take a copy of the questionnaire, sit down, and work on it for a few minutes. Then something odd happens: White smoke starts coming into the room through a small vent in the wall. Before long, the room is so filled with smoke you can barely see the questionnaire. What will you do?

In fact, there was no real danger—the experimenters were pumping smoke into the room to see how people would respond to this potential emergency. Not surprisingly, when people were by themselves, most of them took action. Within two minutes, 50 percent of the participants left the room and found the experimenter down the hall, reporting that there was a potential fire in the building; by six minutes, 75 percent of the participants left the room to alert the experimenter. But what would happen if people were not alone? Given that 75 percent of the participants who were by themselves reported the smoke, it

Pluralistic ignorance

the phenomenon whereby bystanders assume that nothing is wrong in an emergency because no one else looks concerned

▶ Emergency situations can be confusing. Does this man need help? Have the bystanders failed to notice him, or has the behaviour of the others led each of them to interpret the situation as a non-emergency—an example of pluralistic ignorance?

would seem that the larger the group, the greater the likelihood that someone would report the smoke. In fact, this can be figured mathematically: If there is a 75 percent chance that any one person will report the smoke, there is a 98 percent chance that at least one person in a three-person group will do so.

To find out whether more bystanders would increase the chances of helping, Latané and Darley (1970) included a condition in which three participants took part at the same time. Everything was identical except that three people sat in the room as the smoke began to seep in. Surprisingly, in only 12 percent of the three-person groups did someone report the smoke within two minutes, and in only 38 percent of the groups did someone report the smoke within six minutes. In the remaining groups, the participants sat there filling out questionnaires even when they had to wave away the smoke with their hands to see what they were writing. What went wrong?

Because it was not clear that the smoke constituted an emergency, the participants used each other as a source of information. If the people next to you glance at the smoke and then go on filling out their questionnaires, you will feel reassured that nothing is wrong; otherwise, why would they be acting so unconcerned? The problem is that they are probably looking at you out of the corner of their eyes and, seeing that you appear to be not overly concerned, they too are reassured that everything is okay. Group members gain false reassurance from each other whenever each person assumes that the others know more about what's going on than he or she does. This is particularly likely to happen when the event is ambiguous. If an event is clearly an emergency, as in the case of the attack on Kitty Genovese, we do not need to rely on other people to interpret it for us; however, the more ambiguous an event is, the more likely people are to look to each other to define what's going on. As a result, it is in ambiguous situations, such as seeing smoke coming from a vent, that people in groups will be in a state of pluralistic ignorance, convincing each other that nothing is wrong (Clark & Word, 1972; Solomon, Solomon, & Stone, 1978).

Assuming Responsibility Let's say that as a potential help-giver, you have successfully navigated the first two steps in the decision tree (see Figure 11.4 on page 408): You have noticed something odd, and you have correctly interpreted it as an emergency in which help is needed. What's next? Now you must decide that you will help. After hearing Kitty Genovese cry out, "Oh my God, he stabbed me! Please help me! Please help me!" (Rosenthal, 1964), Genovese's neighbours must have believed that something terrible was happening and that she was desperately in need of assistance. That they did nothing indicates that even if we interpret an event as an emergency, we have to decide that it is our responsibility—not someone else's—to do something about it. When dealing with issues of personal responsibility, the number of bystanders is again a crucial variable, but for different reasons. Consider the condition in the Latané and Darley (1968) seizure experiment, where each participant believed he or she was the only one listening to the student while he had a seizure. The responsibility rested on their shoulders. If they didn't help, no one would, and the student might die. As a result, in this condition most people helped almost immediately, and all helped within a few minutes.

However, what happens when there are many witnesses? **A diffusion of responsibility** occurs, whereby each bystander's sense of responsibility to help decreases as the

Diffusion of responsibility each bystander's sense of responsibility to help decreases as the number of witnesses increases

number of witnesses increases. Because other people are present, no individual bystander feels a strong sense that it is his or her personal responsibility to take action. Recall from our earlier discussion that helping often entails costs; we can place ourselves in danger, and we can look foolish by overreacting or doing the wrong thing. Why should we risk these costs when many other people who can help are present? The problem is that everyone is likely to feel this way, making all of the bystanders less likely to help. This is particularly true if people cannot tell whether someone else has already intervened. When participants in the seizure experiment believed that other students were witnesses as well, they couldn't tell whether another student had already helped because the intercom system transmitted only the voice of the student having the seizure. Each student probably assumed that he or she did not have to help, because surely someone else had already done so.

Similarly, Kitty Genovese's neighbours had no way of knowing whether someone else had called the police. Most likely, they assumed that there was no need to do so because someone else had already made the call. Tragically, everyone assumed it was somebody else's responsibility to take action, thereby leaving Genovese to fight her assailant alone. The sad irony of Genovese's murder is that she probably would be alive today had *fewer* people heard her cries for help. And if fewer people had witnessed the cab driver in Denver who was beaten to death in March 1998, he might have lived to enjoy the wedding that he and his fiancée had planned.

Diffusion of responsibility occurs in non-emergency forms of helping as well. A recent study by Markey (2000) examined whether people would be less likely to help each other in an Internet chat group as the number of people in the chat room increased. The researchers entered chat groups in Yahoo! Chat, in which 2 to 19 people were discussing a wide variety of topics. The researchers posed as either a male or female participant and typed the following request for help: "Can anyone tell me how to look at someone's pro-file?" (A profile is a brief biographical description that each person in the chat group pro-vides.) The message was addressed to either the group as a whole or to one randomly selected person in the chat room. Then the researchers timed how long it took for some-one in the group to respond to the request for help.

When the request was addressed to the group as a whole, Latané and Darley's results were replicated closely: The greater the number of people in the chat room, the longer it took for anyone to respond to the request for help. Interestingly, however, when the request was directed to a specific person, that person responded quickly, regardless of the size of the group. These results suggest that diffusion of responsibility was operating. When a general request for help is made, a large group makes people feel that they, per-sonally, are not responsible. When addressed by name, however, people are more likely to feel that the responsibility is theirs to help, even when many others are present. The impli-cation is clear: If you do have that bicycle accident and there are many people present, do not yell out, "Will someone help me?" Single out one person—"Hey, you in the blue shirt and sunglasses, could you please call 911?"—and you will probably receive help more quickly.

Knowing How to Help Even if a person has made it this far in the helping sequence—noticing an event has occurred, interpreting it as an emergency, and taking responsibil-ity—an additional condition must still be met: The person must decide what form of help

~~is appropriate. Suppose, for example, that on a hot, summer day you see a woman collapse in the street and you decide she is gravely ill. No one else seems to be helping, so you decide it is up to you. But what should you do? Has the woman had a heart attack? Or is she suffering from heat stroke?~~ Should you call an ambulance, administer CPR, or try to get her out of the sun? If people don't know what form of assistance to give, obviously they will be unable to help.

Deciding to Implement the Help ~~Finally, even if you know exactly what kind of help is appropriate, there are reasons why you might decide not to intervene. For one thing, you might not be qualified to deliver the right kind of help. It may be clear, for instance, that the woman has had a heart attack and is in desperate need of CPR, but if you don't know how to administer CPR, you'll be unable to help her.~~ Or you might be afraid of making a fool of yourself. It can be embarrassing to intervene, only to discover that a situation actually wasn't an emergency.

~~Even some forms of helping might be embarrassing.~~ For example, in South Africa, Edwards (1975) conducted a study in which a female confederate "accidentally" dropped either her purse or a box of tampons while walking down a street. Nearly everyone (95 percent) who saw the woman drop her purse returned it. In comparison, 59 percent of bystanders returned the tampons. One potential helper was about to return the tampons, but quickly dropped the box when he realized what it contained! This study was replicated in Canada by James McDonald and Stuart McKelvie (1992) at Bishop's University. In their study, a male confederate dropped either a mitten or a box of condoms while walking through a shopping mall. Nearly half (47 percent) of the people who saw him drop the mitten retrieved it. As for the condoms? Only 17 percent of bystanders returned them. One man "helped" by kicking the condoms along the floor of the mall until they caught up with the confederate! Thus, embarrassment can make people less likely to help.

Another cost of helping is fear of doing the wrong thing and making matters worse, or even of placing yourself in danger by trying to help. Norbert Reinhart, owner of an Alberta oil company, knows what it is like to risk your life to help another person. In June 1999, one of his employees, Ed Leonard, was captured by guerillas while drilling for oil in Colombia. When it became apparent that efforts to free Leonard would not reach a quick resolution, Reinhart offered to take his place. At that point, Reinhart had never even met Leonard. This tremendous act of helping came at a great personal cost to Reinhart. He spent more than three months in captivity in the Colombian mountains, fearing for his life, before finally being released.

In sum, five steps have to be taken before people will intervene in an emergency. They have to notice the event, interpret it as an emergency, decide it is their responsibility to help, know how to help, and decide to act. If people fail to take any one of these steps, they will not intervene. Given how difficult it can be to take all five steps, it is not surprising that incidents such as the Kitty Genovese murder can occur.

THE NATURE OF THE RELATIONSHIP: COMMUNAL VERSUS EXCHANGE RELATIONSHIPS

A great deal of research on prosocial behaviour has looked at helping between strangers, such as Latané and Darley's research on bystander intervention. Although this research is very important, most helping in everyday life occurs between people who know each other well: family members, lovers, close friends. What determines whether people help in these kinds of relationships? It turns out that when the person in need of help is someone close to us, we may focus on the long-term benefits of helping rather than on the immediate benefits (Salovey et al., 1991).

Consider the mother of a three-year-old. One Saturday morning, she sits down with a cup of coffee to read the newspaper. She wants nothing more than a moment's peace while she catches up on the news. Her daughter, however, has other ideas. The child asks her mother to read *Barney's Birthday Party* for the fiftieth time. Reading to the child has few short-term benefits in this situation. The coffee gets cold, the newspaper goes unread, and the moment's peace disappears. However, even when there are no short-term benefits, prosocial behaviour can reap large long-term rewards. Parents who sit around sipping coffee and reading the newspaper while ignoring their children are less likely to obtain the long-term satisfaction of having a good relationship with their children and seeing them flourish. Thus, parents might read to their children with this long-term goal in mind, enduring the short-term annoyance of being interrupted and having to read about Barney's festivities yet again.

Even more fundamentally, in some types of relationships people may not be concerned at all with the rewards they receive. In Chapter 10, we distinguished between communal and exchange relationships. Communal relationships are those in which people's primary concern is the welfare of the other person (e.g., a child), whereas exchange relationships are those governed by concerns about equity—that what you put into the relationship equals what you get out of it. When it comes to helping, Margaret Clark and Judson Mills (1993) argue, people in communal relationships are less concerned with the benefits they will receive by helping, and more concerned with simply satisfying

▶ In communal relationships, such as those between parents and their children, people are concerned less with who gets what and more with how much help the other person needs.

the needs of the other person. In support of this argument, Clark and colleagues have found that people in communal relationships pay less attention to who is getting what than do people in exchange relationships (Clark, 1984; Clark & Grote, 1998; Clark, Mills, & Corcoran, 1989).

Consider a study in which the researchers measured how often people in different relationships looked at some lights that meant different things in different conditions (Clark, Mills, & Corcoran, 1989). In one condition, people thought that the lights would change when their partner in another room needed help on a task. Participants were not in a position to help their partner on the task, but the idea was that the more concerned they were with their partner's needs, the more they would look at the lights. In another condition, people thought that the lights would change whenever their partner in the other room did especially well on a task they were both working on and for which they would be rewarded. The idea here was that people who were concerned about exchange and equity should be especially likely to look at these lights, to keep track of what they "owed" their partner for helping them get the reward.

As seen in Figure 11.5, the number of times people looked at the lights in each condition depended on whether they were in a communal relationship (their partner was a friend) or an exchange relationship (their partner was a stranger). In communal relationships, people were much more concerned with the needs of their partner (whether this person needed help on the task) than with whether they "owed" their partner (whether this person did well on the task). Keep in mind that people did not think they could go help their partner; they simply seemed concerned with whether the person was in need. In exchange relationships, people were relatively unconcerned with whether their partner needed help. Instead, they were concerned with how well their partner was doing on the task, presumably to keep track of what they owed their partner in return.

In short, helping in exchange relationships appears to be governed by rules and norms that differ from those governing helping in communal relationships. In exchange relationships, people are concerned more with who is getting what, and they become upset if the scales are tipped too far toward one person ("It seems as if I'm always doing favours for Bob, but he never helps me in return"). In communal relationships, people are concerned less with who gets what and more with how much help the other person needs ("My daughter really needs my help right now").

▼ Figure 11.5

KEEPING TRACK IN RELATIONSHIPS.

In communal relationships, people looked at the light the most when it signified how much help their partner needed. In exchange relationships, people looked at the light the most when it signified how well their partner did on a joint task, presumably to keep track of what they "owed" their partner in return.

(Adapted from Clark, Mills, & Corcoran, 1989)

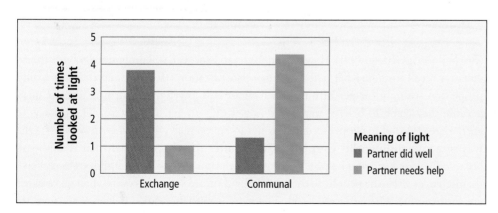

How Can Helping Be Increased?

Most religions stress some version of the Golden Rule, urging us to do unto others as we would have others do unto us. There are many saintly people in the world who succeed in following this rule, devoting their lives to the welfare of others. We would all be better off, however, if prosocial behaviour was more common than it is. How can we get people, when faced with an emergency, to act more like Rocky Flett and less like Kitty Genovese's neighbours?

Before addressing this question, we should point out that people do not always *want* to be helped. Imagine that you are sitting at a computer terminal at the library and are struggling to get to a particular Web site. You can't figure out why the address you're trying doesn't seem to be working, and are becoming increasingly frustrated as the computer responds with annoying beeps and incomprehensible messages. A confident-looking guy strides into the room and peers over your shoulder for a few minutes. "Boy," he says, "you sure have a lot to learn. Step aside and let me show you how this works." How would you react? You might feel some gratitude at receiving this guy's help; after all, you will now learn how to get to the Web site. More than likely, however, you will also feel some resentment. His offer of help comes with a message: "You are too stupid to figure this out for yourself." Receiving help can make us feel inadequate and dependent. As a result, people do not always react positively when someone offers them aid. People do not want to appear incompetent, so they often decide to suffer in silence—even if doing so lowers their chances of successfully completing a task (Nadler & Fisher, 1986; Schneider et al., 1996).

Nonetheless, it seems clear that the world would be a better place if more people helped their fellow human beings. How can we increase everyday acts of kindness, such as looking out for an elderly neighbour or volunteering to read to kids at the local school? One answer is to cultivate helping behaviour early on. In addition, as we shall see, if we simply make people aware of the barriers to helping, they are more likely to engage in prosocial behaviours.

INSTILLING HELPFULNESS WITH REWARDS AND MODELS

Developmental psychologists have discovered that prosocial behaviour occurs early in life. Even children as young as 18 months frequently help others, such as assisting a parent with household tasks or trying to make a crying infant feel better (Rheingold, 1982; Zahn-Waxler, Radke-Yarrow, & King, 1979). One powerful way to encourage prosocial behaviour is for parents and others to reward such acts with praise, smiles, and hugs. Several studies suggest that these kinds of rewards increase prosocial behaviour in children (Fischer, 1963; Grusec, 1991). Rewards should not, however, be emphasized too much. As you may recall from our discussion of the overjustification effect in Chapter 5, rewarding people too strongly for performing a behaviour can lower their intrinsic interest in it, because they come to believe they are doing it only to get the reward. The trick is to encourage children to act prosocially but not to be too heavy-handed with rewards. One way of accomplishing this is to tell children, after they have helped, that they did so because they are kind and helpful people. Such comments encourage children to perceive themselves as altruistic people, so they will help in future situations even when no rewards are forthcoming (Grusec et al., 1979). The same is true for adults: Believing that we are

◀ Adult approval serves as a powerful reward for children when they behave prosocially.

helping someone in order to get a reward diminishes our view of ourselves as altruistic, selfless people (Batson et al., 1978; Uranowitz, 1975).

Another way for parents to increase prosocial behaviour in their children is to behave prosocially themselves. Children often model behaviours they observe in others, including prosocial behaviours (Batson, 1998; Dodge, 1984; Mussen & Eisenberg-Berg, 1977). Children who observe their parents helping others (e.g., volunteering to help the homeless) learn that helping others is a valued act. Interviews with people who have gone to great lengths to help others—such as Christians who helped Jews escape from Nazi Germany during the Second World War—indicate that their parents were also dedicated helpers (London, 1970; Rosenhan, 1970).

Closer to home, S. Mark Pancer and Michael Pratt (1999) found that Canadian youth who spend time volunteering are likely to have parents who have instilled values of kindness and helping, and who model those behaviours. The response of one 17-year-old girl who participated in this research is illustrative. This girl's sister had been in an accident and therefore was temporarily unable to continue her after-school position working with a high-needs handicapped child.

> And so my mom and my sister convinced me to work hours for her. . . .
>
> And this child, you really have to care for her to work with her.
>
> She's a really sad case. . . . You have to not lose patience with her. . . .
>
> My mom's a really caring person and she has a really strong bond
>
> with this little girl. She and my sister *should* be able to rely on me
>
> to help out on this.

▶ Children are good imitators and learn prosocial behaviour from observing other people (e.g., their parents) behaving prosocially.

◀ Children are good imitators and learn prosocial behaviour from observing other people (e.g., their parents) behaving prosocially.

~~Children also imitate adults other than their parents.~~ Teachers, relatives, and even television characters can serve as models for children. J. Philippe Rushton (1975) demonstrated this fact in an interesting study of British elementary school children. The children played a bowling game in which they won tokens, which could be exchanged for prizes or donated to a needy child named Bobby as part of a "Save the Children" fund. Before playing the game, the children watched an adult—who was said to be a future teacher at their school—play the game. In one condition, the adult kept all of the tokens, refusing to donate any to Bobby. In another condition, the adult put half of her tokens in a jar for Bobby. All of the children then played the game by themselves, and the researchers kept track of how many tokens the kids donated to Bobby.

The children who watched the generous adult were much more likely to follow suit, donating some of their tokens. It is not clear, however, whether they did so because they had learned to be more altruistic, or because they simply felt pressure to give away some of their tokens. It's similar to the situation when someone passes the hat at the office to buy a birthday present for a colleague. Sometimes we throw in a few dollars because everyone else is doing so, not because we are feeling particularly altruistic.

Rushton (1975) conducted a second phase of his experiment to address this question. Two months after the first session, a different experimenter took the children to a room and left them to play the bowling game again. This time, they could choose to donate some of their tokens to a different charity—namely, a fund for starving Asian children. They did not observe any adults giving or not giving to this fund, nor were there any adults present to observe what they did. Nonetheless, the kids who had seen the adult give tokens to Bobby two months earlier donated more tokens to this new charity than did kids who had seen the adult keep all of the tokens. The children who had seen the generous adult seemed to have become genuinely altruistic, causing them to donate more tokens several weeks later in a new situation even when no models were present. The lesson for parents is clear: If you want your children to be altruistic, act in altruistic ways yourself.

INCREASING AWARENESS OF THE BARRIERS TO HELPING

Finally, there is evidence that simply being aware of the barriers to helping can increase people's chances of overcoming those barriers. A few years ago at Cornell University, several students intervened to prevent another student from committing suicide. As is often the case with emergencies, the situation was a very confusing one, and at first the bystanders were not sure what was happening or what they should do. The student who led the intervention said she was reminded of a lecture she had heard on bystander intervention in her Introductory Psychology class a few days earlier and had realized that if she didn't act, no one might (Savistky, 1998). Consider also a recent incident at Vassar College, where some students looked outside their dormitory and saw a student being attacked by a mugger. Like Kitty Genovese's neighbours, most of them did nothing, probably because they assumed that someone else had already called the police. One of the students, however, immediately called the campus police because she was struck by how similar the situation was to the studies on bystander intervention she had read about in her Social Psychology course—even though she had taken the course more than a year earlier (Coats, 1998)

As encouraging as these incidents are, it is difficult to know whether the people who intervened were really spurred on by what they had learned in their psychology classes. Perhaps they were especially helpful people who decided to intervene and were then reminded of bystander intervention research. Fortunately, there is systematic research on whether learning about this research makes people more likely to help. Arthur Beaman and his colleagues (1978) randomly assigned students to listen to a lecture on Latané and Darley's (1970) bystander intervention research or to a lecture on an unrelated topic. Two weeks later, all of the students participated in what they thought was a completely unrelated sociology study, during which they encountered a student lying on the floor. Was he in need of help? Had he fallen and injured himself, or was he simply a student who had fallen asleep after pulling an all-nighter? As we have seen, when in an ambiguous situation such as this, people look to see how other people are reacting. Because an accomplice of the experimenter (posing as another participant) purposefully acted unconcerned, the natural thing for participants to do was assume that nothing was wrong. This is exactly what most of Beaman's participants did, if they had not heard the lecture about bystander intervention research; in this condition, only 25 percent of them stopped to help the student. However, if the participants had heard the lecture about bystander intervention, 43 percent stopped to help the student. Thus, knowing how we can unwittingly be influenced by others can by itself help us overcome this type of social influence. We can only hope that knowing about other barriers to prosocial behaviour will also make them easier to overcome.

We conclude with the reminder that we should not impose help on everyone we meet, whether the person wants it or not. Research on reactions to help indicates that under certain conditions, receiving help can have damaging effects on a person's self-esteem. The goal is to make the help supportive, highlighting your concern for the recipient rather than using the helping encounter to communicate your superior knowledge and skill. If you would like to learn more about the conditions under which people help others, in an experiment of your own design, see Try It!, below.

The Lost Letter Technique

Here is a way you can test many of the hypotheses about helping behaviour you have read about in this chapter—as well as hypotheses of your own.

An interesting way to study prosocial behaviour is to leave some stamped letters lying on the ground and see whether people pick them up and mail them. This procedure, called the lost letter technique, was invented by Stanley Milgram (1969). He found that people were more likely to mail letters addressed to organizations they supported; for example, 72 percent of letters addressed to "Medical Research Associates" were mailed, whereas only 25 percent of letters addressed to "Friends of the Nazi Party" were mailed. (All were addressed to the same post office box, so that Milgram could count how many were returned.)

Use the lost letter technique to test some of the hypotheses about helping behaviour we have discussed in this chapter, or hypotheses that you come up with on your own. Put your address on the letters so you can count how many are returned, but vary where you put the letters or to whom they are addressed. For example, drop some letters in a small town and some in an urban area to see whether people in small towns are more likely to mail them (be sure to mark the envelopes in some way that will let you know where they were dropped; e.g., put a small pencil mark on the back of the ones dropped in small towns). Studies by Bridges and Coady (1996) and Hansson and Slade (1977) found that people living in small towns are more likely to mail the letters. Or you might vary the ethnicity of the name of the person on the address, to see if people are more likely to help members of some ethnic groups than others. Be creative!

After deciding what you want to vary (e.g., the ethnicity or gender of the addressee), be careful to place envelopes of both types (e.g., those addressed to males and females) in similar locations. It is best to use a fairly large number of letters (e.g., a minimum of 15 to 20 in each condition) to get reliable results. Obviously, you should not leave more than one letter in the same location. You might want to team up with some classmates on this project, so that you can split the cost of the stamps.

SUMMARY

For centuries people have debated the determinants of **prosocial behaviour**—that is, acts performed with the goal of benefiting another person. People have been particularly intrigued with the causes of **altruism**, which is the desire to help another person even if it involves cost to the helper. According to the evolutionary psychology explanation, prosocial behaviour has genetic roots because it has been selected for in three ways: (a) people further the survival of their genes by helping genetic relatives (**kin selection**); (b) there is a survival advantage to the

following the **norm of reciprocity**, whereby people help strangers in the hope that they will receive help when they need it; and (c) there is a survival advantage to the ability to learn and follow social norms of all kinds, including altruism.

Social exchange theory views helping behaviour as a weighing of rewards and costs; helping occurs due to self-interest—that is, in situations where the rewards for helping are greater than the costs. Rewards include recognition, praise, and the relief of personal distress.

Neither of these theories sees helping behaviour as a form of altruism; self-gain is always involved. In comparison, the **empathy-altruism hypothesis** suggests that people do sometimes behave in truly altruistic ways, namely when they experience **empathy** for those in need.

Prosocial behaviour is multidetermined, and both personal and situational factors can override or facilitate basic motives to help. Personal determinants of helping include the **altruistic personality**, the idea that some people are more helpful than others. Gender is another personal factor that comes into play. Though one sex is not more altruistic than the other, the ways in which men and women help often differ, with men more likely to help in heroic, chivalrous ways and women more likely to help in nurturant ways that involve a long-term commitment. People's cultural background also matters. Compared to members of individualist cultures, members of interdependent cultures are more likely to help people they view as members of their **in-group** but are less likely to help people they view as members of an **out-group**.

Mood also affects helping. Interestingly, being in either a good or a bad mood—compared to being in a neutral mood—can increase helping. Good moods increase helping for several reasons, including the fact that they allow us to see the good side of other people, making us more willing to help them. Bad moods can also increase helping. According to the **negative-state relief hypothesis**, helping someone makes us feel good, lifting us out of the doldrums.

Situational determinants of prosocial behaviour include rural versus urban environments, with helping behaviour more likely to occur in rural settings. One reason for this is the **urban-overload hypothesis**, which states that cities bombard people with so much stimulation that they keep to themselves to avoid being overloaded. The **bystander effect** specifies the impact of the number of bystanders on whether help is given: the fewer the bystanders, the better. The bystander decision tree indicates that a potential helper must make five decisions before providing help: notice the event, interpret the event as an emergency (here **pluralistic ignorance** can occur, whereby everyone assumes nothing is wrong, because no one else looks concerned), assume personal responsibility (here a **diffusion of responsibility** created by several bystanders may lead us to think it's not our responsibility to act), know how to help, and implement the help. In addition, the nature of the relationship between the helper and the person in need is important. In exchange relationships, people are concerned with equity and they keep track of who is contributing what to the relationship. In communal relationships, people are concerned less with who gets what and more with how much help the other person needs.

How can helping be increased? One way is for parents to reward their children for helping. Rewards must be used carefully, however, or they will undermine the child's intrinsic interest in helping, causing an overjustification effect. Children also are more likely to be helpful when they observe adults engaging in helpful behaviours. Finally, research has indicated that teaching people about the determinants of prosocial behaviour makes them more aware of why they sometimes don't help, with the happy result that they help more in the future.

IF YOU ARE INTERESTED

Attenborough, Richard (Director). (1982). *Gandhi* [Film]. An award-winning film about the life of Mahatma Gandhi, the Indian leader who captured the minds and hearts of the world by leading a persistent, peaceful revolt against the British Empire. Gandhi became an international symbol of selflessness and nonviolence. His life raises many interesting questions about the causes of altruism.

Batson, C. D. (1998). Altruism and prosocial behavior. In D. Gilbert, S. Fiske, & G. Lindzey (Eds.), *The handbook of social psychology* (4th ed., Vol. 2, pp. 282–316). New York: McGraw-Hill. A thorough review of all aspects of prosocial behaviour.

Clark, M. S. (1991). *Prosocial behavior: Review of personality and social psychology* (Vol. 12). Newbury Park, CA: Sage. A resource containing chapters by top researchers in the field of prosocial behaviour, many of whom were cited in this chapter. Topics include the development of altruism, the debate about whether people are ever truly altruistic or are always concerned with their self-interest, the effects of mood on helping, and the consequences of helping.

DeWaal, F. (1996). *Good natured: The origins of right and wrong in humans and other animals*. Cambridge, MA: Harvard University Press. A fascinating look at morality and prosocial behaviour among animals. One does not have to be human, DeWaal argues, to be humane.

Latané, B., & Darley, J. M. (1970). *The unresponsive bystander: Why doesn't he help?* Englewood Cliffs, NJ: Prentice Hall. A classic look at why bystanders often fail to help victims in emergencies, including an in-depth discussion of the "seizure" and "smoke" studies described in this chapter.

Pancer, M. S., & Pratt, M. W. (1992). Social and family determinants of community service involvement in Canadian youth. In M. Yates & J. Youniss (Eds.), *Roots of civic identity* (pp. 32–55). Cambridge, UK: Cambridge University Press. This chapter begins with a fascinating look at the history of volunteering in Canada and chronicles the authors' own research on the frequency and determinants of community service involvement among contemporary Canadian youth.

Spacapan, S., & Oskamp, S. (1992). *Helping and being helped: Naturalistic studies*. Newbury Park, CA: Sage. This book contains chapters by researchers investigating helping in everyday life, including self-help groups, spousal caregiving, organ donation, and AIDS volunteerism.

Spielberg, Stephen (Director). (1994). *Schindler's list* [Film]. The true story of how a German profiteer saved the lives of hundreds of Jews during the Second World War. Whereas Oskar Schindler's original motivation stemmed from a capitalistic need for cheap labour, his actions went far beyond his original intentions, raising intriguing questions about the origins of altruism.

Wolpert, Stanley. (1962). *Nine hours to Rama*. A fictionalized account of the life of Mahatma Gandhi.

WEBLINKS

www.volunteer.ca

Volunteerism Canada

This site provides information on volunteerism in Canada.

www.giraffe.org

Sticking Your Neck Out

This site is about an organization that promotes prosocial behaviour, and provides a wealth of educational information.

www.apa.org/pubinfo/altruism.html

What Makes Kids Care?

This article from the APA site discusses how to teach gentleness and caring to children.

http://129.128.19.162/docs/bystajhs.html

Bystander Intervention

This article considers what aspects of situations encourage or discourage prosocial acts, discussing reactions to illegal acts, the impact of mood, characteristics of victims and rescuers, victim reactions, and the ambiguities and legal implications of bystander intervention.

CHAPTER 12

Aggression
why we hurt other people

Chapter Outline

IN 1986, PIERRE LEBRUN BEGAN DRIVING BUSES FOR OC TRANSPO, Ottawa's transit company. All went well for more than a decade. Then, in August 1997, he began complaining that co-workers were making fun of his stuttering. Later that month, he got into a fistfight with one of his co-workers and was fired. His union managed to get him reinstated, but he continued to file complaints and eventually left his job. After a trip to Las Vegas in March 1999, there was little left of his severance pay. Upon returning to Ottawa, Pierre Lebrun made a list of the four co-workers he most despised, and on April 6, 1999, he drove to the transit garage with a Remington 760 pump-action shotgun in his car. It was 2:30 p.m. when he walked into the garage, yelling, "It's Judgment Day!" and started firing. He fatally shot two transit workers as others scrambled for cover. Next, he entered a small office and killed two more people. Another two employees were wounded. Pierre Lebrun's last act was to turn his gun on himself and pull the trigger.

Sadly, the Pierre Lebrun case isn't an isolated one. On October 15, 2002, Richard Anderson, a 55-year-old provincial government employee in Kamloops, B.C., received a disciplinary letter concerning his job performance. He met with a counsellor, then left work, only to return a few hours later with a handgun. Anderson shot and killed two of his co-workers before turning the gun on himself. The entire incident took two minutes.

Now, on to another story . . . Flight attendants and other airline workers are increasingly becoming the targets of aggression from passengers. As a result, July 6, 2000, was declared a Day of Action Against Air Rage. Ironically, the very next day Winnipeg police were called to the airport—the second time in a week—to apprehend a passenger who began hitting and spitting on a male flight attendant halfway through the flight. Such incidents are becoming increasingly common. During an eight-month period (January to September 1998), Pearson International Airport dealt with nearly 200 incidents of unruly

▶ The alarming increase of air rage incidents, including physical attacks on airline workers, prompted this advertisement by the Skyrage Foundation.

behaviour from passengers. In 111 of those incidents, police had to be called to meet the aircraft. In 34 cases, passengers had to be removed from the aircraft before departure, and in 53 cases, passengers were prevented from boarding the aircraft because of their aggressiveness (Dotto, 2000). According to Denise Hill, president of the airline division of the Canadian Union of Public Employees, in recent years there has been an increase in flight attendants being yelled at, grabbed, kicked, and bitten. In an interview with *Equinox,* she commented, "At first we thought it was just verbal abuse, but physical violence is on the increase, too."

In the aftermath of events such as Pierre Lebrun's or Richard Anderson's shooting rampages and publicized incidents of air rage, there is no shortage of explanations. Many people attributed Lebrun's actions to a retribution motive—wanting to "get even" with the co-workers who had mocked him. The police inspector in charge of the investigation described him as a "disturbed individual." Situational factors such as losing his job and subsequently losing his money in Las Vegas also may have played a role. As for air rage, incidents of this kind of aggression have been attributed to alcohol intoxication, not allowing people to smoke on airplanes, the loss of control that sets in once a person boards an aircraft, and so on.

In this chapter, we begin with the fundamental question, "What is aggression?" and then move on to another fundamental question, "What causes it?" Are human beings instinctively aggressive? Can situational factors cause "normal people" to commit violence? Can aggression be prevented or reduced? These are social psychological questions of the utmost importance. Needless to say, we don't have all the answers. By the time you reach the end of this chapter, however, we hope you will have gained some insight into the issues. But first, let's be sure we know what we mean by the term.

What Is Aggression?

Social psychologists define **aggression** as intentional behaviour aimed at causing either physical or psychological pain. It is not to be confused with assertiveness—even though people often loosely refer to others as "aggressive" if they stand up for their rights, write letters to the editor complaining about real or imagined injustices, work extra hard, display a great deal of ambition, or are real "go-getters." Similarly, in a sexist society, a woman who simply speaks her mind or picks up the phone and makes the first move by inviting a male acquaintance to dinner might be called aggressive by some. Our definition is clear: Aggression is an intentional action aimed at doing harm or causing pain. The action might be physical or verbal; it might succeed in its goal or not. It is still aggression. Thus, if someone throws a beer bottle at your head, and you duck so the bottle misses, the throwing was still an aggressive act. The important thing is the intention. By the same token, if a drunk driver unintentionally runs you down while you're attempting to cross the street, that is not an act of aggression, even though the damage would be far greater than that caused by a flying beer bottle.

It is also useful to distinguish between hostile aggression and instrumental aggression (Berkowitz, 1993). **Hostile aggression** is an act of aggression stemming from feelings of anger and aimed at inflicting pain or injury. With **instrumental aggression**, there is an intention to hurt the other person, but the hurting takes place as a means to some goal other

Aggression
intentional behaviour aimed at causing either physical or psychological pain

Hostile aggression
an act of aggression stemming from feelings of anger and aimed at inflicting pain

Instrumental aggression
aggression as a means to some goal other than causing pain

than causing pain. For example, in a professional football game, a defensive lineman will usually do whatever it takes to thwart his opponent (the blocker) and tackle the ball carrier. This typically includes intentionally inflicting pain on his opponent if doing so is useful in helping him get the blocker out of the way so he can get to the ball carrier. This is instrumental aggression. On the other hand, if he believes his opponent has been playing dirty, he might become angry and go out of his way to hurt the other player, even if doing so does not increase his opportunity to tackle the ball carrier. This is hostile aggression.

IS AGGRESSION INBORN, OR IS IT LEARNED?

Scientists, philosophers, and other serious thinkers are not in complete agreement with one another about whether aggression is an inborn, instinctive phenomenon or is learned (Baron & Richardson, 1994; Berkowitz, 1993; Geen, 1998). This controversy is not new; it has been raging for centuries. For example, Thomas Hobbes, in his classic work *Leviathan* (first published in 1651), took the view that we human beings, in our natural state, are brutes and that only by enforcing the law and order of society could we curb what to Hobbes was a natural instinct toward aggression. On the other hand, Jean-Jacques Rousseau's concept of the noble savage (a theory he developed in 1762) suggested that we human beings, in our natural state, are gentle creatures and that it is a restrictive society that forces us to become hostile and aggressive.

Hobbes's more pessimistic view was elaborated on in the twentieth century by Sigmund Freud (1930), who theorized that human beings are born with an instinct toward life, which he called **Eros**, and an equally powerful death instinct, **Thanatos**, which leads to aggressive actions. Freud believed that aggressive energy must come out somehow, lest it continue to build up and produce illness. The analogy is one of water pressure building up in a container: Unless aggression is allowed to drain off, it will produce some sort of explosion. According to Freud, society performs an essential function in regulating this instinct and in helping people to sublimate it—turning the destructive energy into acceptable or useful behaviour.

IS AGGRESSION INSTINCTUAL? SITUATIONAL? OPTIONAL?

As elegant as it is, Freud's theory has never been proved scientifically, in part because it is difficult or unethical to experiment on these factors using humans. Accordingly, much of the evidence on whether aggression is instinctive in human beings is based on the observation of and experimentation with species other than humans. The idea behind this research is that if one can succeed in demonstrating that certain so-called instinctive aggressive behaviours in the lower animals are not rigidly preprogrammed, then surely aggression is not rigidly preprogrammed in human beings. For example, consider the prevalent belief about cats and rats. Popular wisdom says that cats will instinctively stalk and kill rats. Biologist Zing Yang Kuo (1961) attempted to demonstrate that this was a myth: He raised a kitten in the same cage with a rat. What did he find? Not only did the cat refrain from attacking the rat, but the two became close companions. Moreover, when given the opportunity, the cat refused either to chase or to kill other rats; thus, the benign behaviour was not confined to his buddy, but generalized to rats the cat had never encountered before.

Eros

the instinct toward life, posited by Freud

Thanatos

according to Freud, an instinctual drive toward death, leading to aggressive actions

While this experiment is charming, it fails to prove that aggressive behaviour is not instinctive; it merely demonstrates that the aggressive instinct can be inhibited by early experience. What if an organism grows up without any experience with other organisms? Will it or won't it show normal aggressive tendencies? Irenaus Eibl-Eibesfeldt (1963) showed that rats raised in isolation (i.e., without any experience in fighting other rats) will attack a fellow rat when one is introduced into the cage; moreover, the isolated rat uses the same pattern of threat and attack used by experienced rats. Thus, although aggressive behaviour can be modified by experience (as shown by Kuo's experiment), Eibl-Eibesfeldt showed that aggression apparently does not need to be learned. On the other hand, one should not conclude from this study that aggression is necessarily instinctive, for, as John Paul Scott (1958) pointed out, the stimulus in Eibl-Eibesfeldt's experiment came from the outside—that is, the sight of a new rat stimulated the isolated rat to fight. There was no physiological evidence of spontaneous stimulation for fighting that arose from within the body alone, leading Scott to conclude that there is no inborn need for fighting.

Scott's conclusion was called into question by the Nobel Prize–winning ethologist Konrad Lorenz (1966), who observed the behaviour of cichlids—highly aggressive tropical fish. Male cichlids will attack other males of the same species to establish and defend their territory. In its natural environment, the male cichlid does not attack female cichlids; nor does it attack males of a different species—it attacks only males of its own species. What happens if all other male cichlids are removed from an aquarium, leaving only one male alone with no appropriate target? The cichlid will attack males of other species—males it previously ignored. Moreover, if all other males are removed, the male cichlid will eventually attack and kill females.

What are we to conclude about the innateness of aggression? According to Lore and Schultz (1993), the universality of aggression among vertebrates strongly suggests that aggressiveness has evolved and has been maintained because it has survival value. However, it is also the case that nearly all organisms also have evolved strong inhibitory mechanisms that enable them to suppress aggression when it is in their best interests to do so. Thus, even in the most violence-prone species, aggression is an optional strategy; whether it is expressed is determined by the animal's previous social experiences as well as by the specific social context in which the animal finds itself.

AGGRESSIVENESS ACROSS CULTURES

Social psychologists are in general agreement with the interpretation of the animal research offered by Lore and Schultz. Moreover, where humans are concerned, because of the complexity and importance of our social interactions, the social situation takes on even greater importance than it does among the lower organisms (Bandura, 1973; Berkowitz, 1968, 1993; Lysak, Rule, & Dobbs, 1989). Indeed, there is a lot of support for the view, taken by most social psychologists, that for humankind, innate patterns of behaviour are infinitely modifiable and flexible. Consider, for example, how widely human cultures vary in their degree of aggressiveness. European history, when condensed, consists of one major war after another; in contrast, the Lepchas of Sikkim, the Pygmies of Central Africa, and the Arapesh of New Guinea live in apparent peace and harmony—with acts of aggression being extremely rare (Baron & Richardson, 1994).

Evidence of cross-cultural variability in violence also comes from a study by Archer and McDaniel (1995), in which teenagers from 11 countries were asked to read stories involving conflict among people. The participants were asked to describe how they thought the characters in the stories would resolve the issue. Their responses were coded for the presence of violence (e.g., threatening another person with a weapon, use of physical coercion, injury or death of another person). Teenagers in New Zealand produced the most violent responses. The United States ranked fourth and Canada ranked seventh. Koreans generated the least violent responses to these stories.

Even within a given culture, changing social conditions can lead to striking changes in aggressive behaviour. For example, for hundreds of years the Iroquois lived in benign peacefulness; they simply did not engage in aggressive behaviour against other tribes. But in the seventeenth century, barter with the newly arrived Europeans brought the Iroquois into direct competition with the neighbouring Huron over furs, which dramatically increased in value because they could now be traded for manufactured goods. A series of skirmishes with the Huron ensued, and within a short time the Iroquois developed into ferocious warriors. It would be hard to argue that they were spectacular warriors because of uncontrollable aggressive instincts; rather, their aggressiveness almost certainly came about because a social change produced increases in competition (Hunt, 1940).

To give another example, in the United States, marked regional differences exist both in aggressive behaviour and in the kinds of events that trigger violence. For instance, homicide rates for white southern males are substantially higher than those for white northern males, especially in rural areas (Nisbett, 1993). Due to a "culture of honour" in the Deep South, southerners are more inclined to endorse violence for protection and in response to insults. Although this concept may not apply to Canada, Wells, Graham, and West (1998) suggest that a code of male honour exists in a particular Canadian subculture, namely among security staff (bouncers) who work in bars. These researchers observed that bouncers (working in various bars in London, Ontario) were most likely to engage in

▶ In a "culture of honour," a real or imagined insult frequently results in violence. Recent research suggests that a culture of honour exists among bouncers.

excessive aggression against bar patrons when they perceived that their authority or masculinity was being threatened. More recent research by these investigators (Graham & Wells, 2001a, 2001b; Graham, West & Wells, 2000) suggests that this code of male honour also applies to bar patrons. Trained observers recorded instances of aggression in various bars in London, Ontario, over a seven-month period. Analyses of these incidents revealed a "macho subculture" in which males bullied one another or made threatening comments in response to little or no provocation. For example, in one incident, a group of males gathered around two men embroiled in a confrontation. The situation deteriorated to the point where two of the onlookers started fighting with each other, while the others placed bets on who would win.

Taking these findings into account, we would conclude that although an instinctual component of aggression is almost certainly present in human beings, aggression is not caused entirely by instinct. As we will see, events in the brain are linked to aggressive behaviour. More importantly, from a social psychological perspective there are clear examples of situational and social events that can produce aggressive behaviour. We know that in human beings such behaviour also can be modified by situational and social factors. In short, aggressive behaviour can be changed.

Neural and Chemical Influences on Aggression

Aggressive behaviour in human beings, as well as in lower animals, is associated with an area in the core of the brain called the **amygdala**. When the amygdala is stimulated, docile organisms become violent; similarly, when neural activity in that area is blocked, violent organisms become docile (Moyer, 1976). However, it should be noted that there is flexibility here also: The impact of neural mechanisms can be modified by social factors, even in sub-humans. For example, if a male monkey is in the presence of other, less dominant monkeys he will indeed attack the other monkeys when the amygdala is stimulated. But if the amygdala is stimulated while the monkey is in the presence of more dominant monkeys, he will not attack, but instead will run away.

Amygdala

an area in the core of the brain that is associated with aggressive behaviour

TESTOSTERONE

Certain chemicals have been shown to influence aggression. For example, the injection of **testosterone**, a male sex hormone, will increase aggression in animals (Moyer, 1983). Among human beings, there is a parallel finding. James Dabbs and his colleagues (1988, 1995) have also found that naturally occurring testosterone levels are significantly higher among prisoners convicted of violent crimes than among those convicted of nonviolent crimes. Also, once incarcerated, prisoners with higher testosterone levels violate more prison rules—especially those involving overt confrontation. Dabbs and his colleagues have also found that juvenile delinquents have higher testosterone levels than do university students (Banks & Dabbs, 1996).

In research conducted with non-criminal populations, the link between testosterone and aggression may not be as strong. For example, in a longitudinal program of research conducted with lower-class 12- and 13-year-old boys in Quebec, Richard Tremblay and

Testosterone

a hormone associated with aggression

his colleagues (1998) found that testosterone was not strongly related to physical aggression but was associated with social dominance. What are we to conclude? Recently, researchers at Queen's University conducted a meta analysis of 45 studies and found that, overall, a weak, positive correlation exists between testosterone and aggression (the average correlation was .14; recall that correlations range from 0—no relation—to 1—a perfect correlation) (Brook, Starzyk, & Quinsey, 2001). Thus, although testosterone may be a factor in some cases of aggression, there are many other causes. As we shall see, situational factors play a powerful role.

If testosterone level affects aggressiveness—at least to some degree—does that mean men are more aggressive than women? Apparently so; in a classic survey of research on children, Eleanor Maccoby and Carol Jacklin (1974) demonstrated that boys appear to be more aggressive than girls. For example, in one study, the investigators closely observed children at play in a variety of different cultures, including the United States, Switzerland, and Ethiopia. There was far more "nonplayful" pushing, shoving, and hitting among boys than among girls (for a review of this literature, see Deaux & LaFrance, 1998).

What about adults? Generally speaking, men are much more aggressive than women. For example, among adults worldwide, the great majority of persons arrested for criminal offences of all kinds are men. Further, when women are arrested it is usually for property crimes (forgery, fraud, larceny), rather than for violent crimes (murder, aggravated assault). Are these differences due to biological differences or to social learning differences? We cannot be sure. In Canada, female youth violent crime has increased 81 percent from 1989 to 1999, compared to a 30 percent increase in male youth violent crime. This statistic might indicate the influence of social learning (e.g., the loosening of restrictions on girls to behave in "feminine" ways). However, during this period, the male youth violent crime rate was still almost three times that of the female rate, which might suggest a biological difference (Statistics Canada, 1999).

It is important to point out that gender differences in aggression also vary, depending on the situation. For example, a meta analysis of 64 separate experiments found that although men are much more aggressive than women under ordinary circumstances, the gender difference becomes much smaller when women and men are provoked (Bettencourt & Miller, 1996). In fact, a recent study conducted at McGill University found that women were just as aggressive as men when subjected to strong provocation from a confederate (Hoaken & Pihl, 2000).

The conclusion that men are more aggressive than women also must be modified when we consider another situational factor, namely the target of aggression. It is well established that men's aggression is generally directed at other men (friends or strangers). Men's aggression is also more likely to take place in bars or other public places, more likely to involve alcohol consumption, and tends to have less of an emotional impact. Women's aggression, on the other hand, is much more likely to be directed at a romantic partner, is less likely to involve alcohol, and tends to have a highly negative emotional impact (Graham & Wells, 2001a, 2001b). A recent meta analysis of well over 100 studies confirms that women are more likely than men to be physically aggressive toward their partners (Archer, 2000; for examples of other Canadian studies that have found this gender difference, see Kwong, Bartholomew, & Dutton, 1999; Sharpe & Taylor, 1999).

However, there are some important qualifiers. First, physical aggression is most likely to be reported among younger women in dating relationships. Second, women's physical aggression does less damage than men's physical aggression; women are much more likely to suffer serious injuries at the hands of their male partner than the other way around. In fact, women are at far greater risk of being murdered by their partners than are men.

Therefore, which gender is most aggressive depends on a variety of situational factors. It also depends on culture. Earlier we described a study by Archer and McDaniel (1995) in which the violence of teenagers' responses to conflict scenarios was assessed in 11 countries. When the researchers compared the responses of male and female participants, they found that young men showed a greater tendency toward violent solutions to conflict than did young women. However, culture also played a major role. For example, women from Australia and New Zealand produced more violent responses than did men from Sweden and Korea.

One final note before leaving this topic: Regardless of whether gender differences in aggression are due to biological factors or to social factors, such behaviour is unacceptable. Moreover, it can be altered by a social intervention—as we shall see.

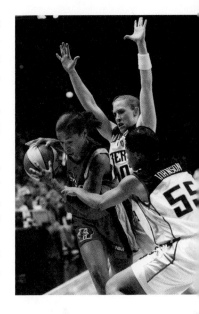

▲ Testosterone levels do affect aggressiveness, but the research on gender differences is more complicated than it might seem on the surface.

ALCOHOL

As most socially active university students know, alcohol tends to lower inhibitions against committing behaviour frowned on by society, including acts of aggression (Desmond, 1987; Taylor & Leonard, 1983). The linkage between the consumption of alcoholic beverages and aggressive behaviour is a common observation (White, 1997; Yudko et al., 1997). For example, we are well aware that fights frequently break out in bars and nightclubs. The exact role that alcohol plays in such acts of aggression has been investigated by researchers at the Centre for Addiction and Mental Health in London, Ontario (Graham & Wells, 2001a, 2001b; Graham, West, & Wells, 2000). As mentioned earlier in our discussion of the male culture of honour, in this research observers recorded incidents of aggression (physical and nonphysical) in various bars in London, Ontario. And, as mentioned in our discussion of gender differences, men were much more likely than women to be involved in incidents of barroom aggression. As for the role of alcohol, the findings were clear: The more people drank, the more likely they were to engage in aggression, especially severe forms of physical aggression (e.g., punching, kicking, brawling).

Unfortunately, these effects are not limited to the bar. Intoxication also has been implicated as a factor in cases of air rage. And crime statistics reveal that more than half of the individuals who have committed violent crimes were drinking heavily at the time (Murdoch, Pihl, & Ross, 1990; Pihl & Peterson, 1995).

Finally, family violence also is associated with the abuse of alcohol (Holtzworth-Munroe et al., 1997). Consider, for example, the following statistic: If a spouse drinks heavily, the rate of marital violence is six times higher than if a spouse drinks moderately or not at all (Statistics Canada, 2000). Marital violence is between four and six times more likely if the husband is an alcoholic than if the husband is not an alcoholic (O'Farrell & Murphy, 1995). Analysis of data gathered as part of the 1993 Statistics Canada Violence Against Women survey shows that violent men drink more often, and more heavily, than nonviolent men (Johnson, 2001).

Thus, it is clear that excessive alcohol consumption is associated with relationship violence. Parallel to the findings for barroom aggression, not only is violence more likely to occur when alcohol is involved, but it also tends to be more severe (Johnson, 2001; Wekerle & Wall, 2002; Wells, Graham & West, 2000).

Sadly, it appears that the stage for alcohol-related aggression is set early on. York University psychologist Debra Pepler and her colleagues (2002) recently conducted a large-scale study of alcohol use and aggression in a sample of nearly 1000 early adolescents. The vast majority was middle class and living in two-parent homes. The researchers discovered that by grade six, approximately 10 percent of boys and 4 percent of girls reported alcohol use (e.g., getting drunk, buying or stealing beer or wine). By grade eight, these percentages had increased such that close to 35 percent of boys and 25 percent of girls reported alcohol use. When Pepler and colleagues examined the relation between bullying other children and alcohol use, the results were shocking: "both boys and girls who bullied others were almost five times more likely to report alcohol use than boys and girls who did not report bullying." These researchers also examined the relation between alcohol and dating violence among those adolescents who had dating experience. Unfortunately, the results mirrored those found for bullying: Dating aggression was up to five times more likely among adolescents who used alcohol compared to those who did not. Pepler and colleagues conclude that interventions aimed at reducing relationship violence and substance abuse must be introduced well before high school, given how early these detrimental patterns are established.

You may have noticed that the data we have been presenting are correlational, and, as you well know by now, one cannot draw causal conclusions from correlational data. For example, in the case of domestic violence, it has been suggested that some men may consume alcohol prior to behaving violently so they can later use their intoxication to excuse their behaviour (Dutton, 1995). Thus, in these situations, alcohol may be contributing to violence but only in an indirect way.

Is there any evidence that alcohol also increases aggression in a direct manner? In other words, can we be sure that alcohol is a direct cause of aggression? Obviously, it is not ethical to administer large amounts of alcohol to research participants and then observe whether they behave violently toward their loved ones. However, researchers have administered alcohol to people to see if they behave more aggressively in laboratory situations. These studies show that when individuals ingest enough alcohol to make them legally drunk, they tend to respond more violently to provocations than do those who have ingested little or no alcohol. For example, research conducted with students at McGill University has found that intoxicated men who are provoked administer stronger shocks to a fictitious opponent than participants who are not intoxicated (Hoaken & Pihl, 2000; Pihl et al., 1995).

MacDonald, Zanna, and Holmes (2000) examined these effects in a way that is more directly relevant to close relationships. In their study, male students at the University of Waterloo who were dating or married were asked to describe a conflict in their relationship. Then, one-third of the participants was given enough vodka to bring their blood alcohol level to Ontario's legal limit of .08. Another one-third received a placebo (a drink that smelled of alcohol but contained only a minuscule amount), while the remaining one-third did not receive drinks of any kind. The participants were then asked to evaluate the conflict they had previously described, with rather disturbing results: Intoxicated partici-pants reported more negative emotions when thinking about the conflict and had more negative perceptions of their partner's feelings than did the other two groups (who did not differ from each other). The researchers conclude that, "alcohol can play a causal role in exacerbating relationship conflict."

In short, it appears that whenever people are intoxicated, the stage is set for aggression. This does not mean that people who have ingested alcohol necessarily go around picking fights. However, alcohol consumption does increase the likelihood of aggressive behaviour. An extensive program of research conducted at McGill University by Pihl and colleagues suggests that alcohol can contribute to aggression in a variety of ways (Pihl & Hoaken, 2002; Pihl & Peterson, 1995; Pihl, Peterson, & Lau, 1993). Alcohol can reduce our inhibi-tions such that we are more likely to perform behaviour we would normally keep in check. Alcohol also can lower our threshold for aggressive behaviour. In other words, we have a "shorter fuse" when under the influence of alcohol. Finally, alcohol may interfere with our ability to consider the consequences of our actions—or make us less concerned with those consequences. The bottom line is that after ingesting alcohol, people who are subjected to social pressure to aggress, or who are frustrated or provoked (or perceive provocation), will experience fewer restraints or inhibitions against committing violent acts.

© The New Yorker Collection, 1975, Dana Fradon. From cartoonbank.com. All Rights Reserved

▲ "Oh, that wasn't me talking. It was the alcohol talking."

Situational Causes of Aggression

As social psychologists, we are particularly interested in the kinds of situational factors that produce aggressive behaviour. As we will see, certain situations are conducive to aggression—so conducive that even the most docile, laid-back person among us might resort to aggressive behaviour. What might some of these situations be?

PAIN AND DISCOMFORT AS A CAUSE OF AGGRESSION

If an animal experiences pain and cannot flee the scene, it will almost invariably attack; this is true of rats, mice, hamsters, foxes, monkeys, crayfish, snakes, raccoons, alligators, and a host of others (Azrin, 1967; Hutchinson, 1983). Such animals will attack members of their own species, members of different species, or anything else in sight, including stuffed dolls and tennis balls. Do you think this is true of human beings as well? Most of us have experienced becoming irritable when subjected to a sharp, unexpected pain (e.g., when we stub our toe) and hence being prone to lash out at the nearest available tar-get. Indeed, when Russell and Fehr (1994) asked students at the University of British Columbia to describe an experience of anger, physical pain was among the causes men-tioned. Most of us probably can relate to the student who wrote that he experienced intense anger when he bashed his kneecap on the edge of a swimming pool. In a series of experiments, Leonard Berkowitz (1983, 1988) showed that students who underwent the pain of having their hand immersed in very cold water showed a sharp increase in their likelihood to aggress against other students.

By the same token, it has long been speculated that other forms of bodily discomfort, such as heat, humidity, air pollution, and offensive odours, might act to lower the thresh-old for aggressive behaviour (Stoff & Cairns, 1996). Indeed, research conducted in the

United States has found that the hotter it is on a given day, the greater the likelihood that riots and violent crimes will occur (Anderson & Anderson, 1984; Anderson, Bushman, & Groom, 1997; Carlsmith & Anderson, 1979; Cotton, 1981, 1986; Harries & Stadler, 1988; Rotton & Frey, 1985). In the desert city of Phoenix, Arizona, drivers without air-conditioned cars are more likely to honk their horns in traffic jams than are drivers with air-conditioned cars (Kenrick & MacFarlane, 1986) And, believe it or not, it has been shown that in major league baseball games, significantly more batters are hit by pitched balls when the temperature is above 32 degrees Celsius than when it is below that temperature (Reifman, Larrick, & Fein, 1988). See Try It!, below, to conduct your own observational research on heat and aggression.

As you know by now, one has to be cautious about interpreting events that take place in natural settings. For example, the scientist in you might be tempted to ask whether increases in aggression are due to the temperature itself or merely to the fact that more people are apt to be outside (getting in each other's way!) on hot days than on cool or rainy days. Fortunately, we can test this by conducting laboratory experiments. For example, in one such experiment, Griffitt and Veitch (1971) administered a test to students, some of whom took it in a room with normal temperature, others of whom took it in a room where the temperature was allowed to soar to 32 degrees Celsius. The students in the hot room not only reported feeling more aggressive but also expressed more hostility to a stranger. In an investigation along the same lines, Rule, Taylor, and Dobbs (1987) presented students at the University of Alberta with ambiguous stories that could end with aggression or nonaggression. Here's an example of one of the stories:

> Todd was on his way home from work one evening when he had to brake quickly for a yellow light. The person in the car behind him . . . crashed into the back of Todd's car, causing a lot of damage to both vehicles. Fortunately, there were no injuries. Todd got out of his car and surveyed the damage. He then walked over to the other car.

The researchers found that participants who read these stories in an uncomfortably hot room (32 degrees Celsius) were more likely to complete the stories with aggression

Heat, Humidity, and Aggression

The next time you find yourself caught in a traffic jam, try doing a simple, natural replication of the Kenrick and MacFarlane (1986) experiment. Consider the following hypothesis: The greater the heat and humidity, the greater the aggression.

- Take notes on how much aggression you notice (in the form of horn-honking).

- Note the heat and humidity that day.
- The next two or three times you get caught in a traffic jam, do the same thing.

Can you discern a relationship between heat/humidity and horn honking?

and frustration responses than were participants who performed the task at room temperature (21 degrees Celsius).

FRUSTRATION AS A CAUSE OF AGGRESSION

Imagine that your friend Alain is driving you to the airport so you can take a plane home for the Christmas holidays. Alain is starting out a bit later than you feel comfortable with, but when you mention it, he accuses you of being overly anxious and assures you that he knows the route well and that you will arrive there with a good 30 minutes to spare. Halfway to your destination, Alain's car grinds to a halt in bumper-to-bumper traffic. You glance at your watch. Once again, Alain assures you that there is plenty of time—but this time you detect less confidence in his tone. After a few minutes, you notice that your palms are sweating and you are beginning to wring your hands. A few minutes later, you open the car door and survey the road ahead. There is nothing but gridlock as far as the eye can see. You get back in the car, slam the door, and glare at Alain. He smiles lamely and says, "How was I supposed to know there would be so much traffic?" Should he be prepared to duck?

As the above scenario suggests, frustration is a major cause of aggression. Frustration occurs when a person is thwarted on the way to an expected goal or gratification. All of us have experienced some degree of frustration from time to time; indeed, it's unlikely we can get through a week without experiencing it. According to **frustration-aggression theory**, people's perception that they are being prevented from obtaining a goal will increase the probability of an aggressive response (Dollard et al., 1939). As we shall see in a moment, this is not meant to imply that frustration always leads to aggression—but it frequently does. In a classic experiment by Barker, Dembo, and Lewin (1941), young children were shown a roomful of attractive toys that were kept out of their reach. The children stood outside a wire screen looking at the toys—fully expecting to play with them because they had been allowed to earlier—but were unable to reach them. After a

Frustration-aggression theory
the theory that frustration—the perception that you are being prevented from obtaining a goal—will increase the probability of an aggressive response

◀ Feelings of frustration can occur when we are blocked or delayed as we strive to reach a goal. For example, being stuck in a traffic jam can elicit aggressive responses, ranging from pointless honking to fistfights or even shootings.

painfully long wait, the children were finally allowed to play with the toys. In a control condition, a different group of children was allowed to play with the toys directly, without first being frustrated. This second group of children played joyfully with the toys. However, the frustrated group, when finally given access to the toys, was extremely destructive: These children tended to smash the toys, throw them against the wall, and step on them.

Several factors can increase frustration and, accordingly, will increase the probability that some form of aggression will occur. One such factor involves your closeness to the goal or the object of your desire. The closer the goal, the greater the expectation of pleasure that is thwarted; the greater the expectation, the more likely the aggression. This was demonstrated in a field experiment by Mary Harris (1974), who instructed confederates to cut in line in front of people who were waiting in a variety of places—for movie tickets, outside crowded restaurants, or at the checkout counter of a supermarket. On some occasions, the confederates cut in front of the second person in line; on other occasions, they cut in front of the twelfth person in line. The results were clear: The responses of the people standing behind the intruders were much more aggressive when the confederate cut in to the second place in line.

Aggression also increases when the frustration is unexpected. James Kulik and Roger Brown (1979) hired students to telephone strangers and ask for donations to a charity. The students were hired on a commission basis—that is, they received a small fraction of each dollar pledged. Some of the students were led to expect a high rate of contributions; others were led to expect far less success. The experiment was rigged so none of the potential donors agreed to make a contribution. The experimenters found that the callers with high expectations directed more verbal aggression toward the non-donors, speaking more harshly and slamming down the phone with more force than the callers with low expectations.

As we have already mentioned, frustration does not always produce aggression. Rather, it seems to produce anger or annoyance and a readiness to aggress if other things about the situation are conducive to aggressive behaviour (Berkowitz, 1978, 1988, 1989, 1993; Gustafson, 1989). For example, the size and strength of the person responsible for your frustration—as well as that person's ability to retaliate—will influence whether you react with aggression. It is undoubtedly easier to slam the phone down on a reluctant donor who is kilometres away and has no idea who you are, than to take out your anger against your frustrator if he turns out to be a defensive lineman for the Edmonton Eskimos and is staring you in the face. Similarly, if the frustration is understandable, legitimate, and unintentional, the tendency to aggress will be reduced. For example, in an experiment by Burnstein and Worchel (1962), when a confederate "unwittingly" sabotaged the problem solving of his groupmates because his hearing aid stopped working, the resulting frustration did not lead to a measurable degree of aggression.

We should also point out that frustration is not the same as deprivation. Children who simply don't have toys do not aggress more than children who do have toys. In the experiment by Barker and his colleagues discussed above, frustration and aggression occurred because the children had every reason to *expect* to play with the toys, and their reasonable expectation was thwarted; this thwarting was what caused the children to behave destructively. Thus, what causes aggression is not deprivation but **relative deprivation**: the perception that you (or your group) have less than you deserve, less than what

Relative deprivation

the perception that you (or your group) have less than you deserve, less than you have been led to expect, or less than people similar to you have

you have been led to expect, or less than what people similar to you have. In accord with this distinction, the Reverend Jesse Jackson (1981), with great insight, pointed out that the race riots that occurred in the United States in 1967 and 1968 took place "in the middle of rising expectations and the increased, though inadequate, social spending." In short, Jackson was suggesting that thwarted expectations were largely responsible for the frustration and aggression.

A similar phenomenon occurred when the Berlin Wall came down and East Germans began to expect higher employment rates and wages. When these changes did not immediately materialize, high levels of anger and frustration ensued. Primo Levi (1986), a survivor of Auschwitz, contends that even in concentration camps the few instances of rebellion were performed not by the inmates at the bottom of the camp totem pole—the suffering victims of unrelenting horror—but "by prisoners who were privileged in some way."

Feelings of relative deprivation also have been created in the laboratory (Wright, 1997; Wright, Taylor, & Moghaddam, 1990). In one experiment (Wright, Taylor, & Moghaddam, 1990), students at McGill University were told that everyone would begin as a member of a low-status group, but that there would be an opportunity to become a member of a high-status group depending on how they performed on a decision-making task. The many benefits of being in the high-status group were described—among them, the chance to win $100. After completing the decision-making task, some participants were told that the high-status group had decided to accept only those who scored at least 8.5, and that their mark was only 6. Other participants were told that they had just missed the cutoff with their mark of 8.2. All participants were then given various options for responding to the high-status group's decision not to accept them.

Participants who almost made it into the high-status group responded differently than those who were told they were far from being accepted. Specifically, those who nearly made it were most likely to write a letter of protest demanding that the high-status group reverse its decision (even though they were told that the decision was final and that the high-status group disapproved of protest action). These participants also perceived greater injustice in the situation than did those who were far from being accepted. In contrast, those who were far from being accepted into the high-status group were more likely to passively accept their fate of having to remain in the low-status group for the remainder of the experiment.

DIRECT PROVOCATION AND RECIPROCATION

Imagine being in the following situation: You're sitting down to lunch in the cafeteria, quietly minding your own business. While you're eating, you notice two guys whispering to each other and occasionally glancing in your direction. One of the guys picks up his lunch tray and walks toward you. He dumps his tray in the garbage next to you, dropping leftovers all over you.

How do you respond? This was one of the scenarios presented to male high-school students in Nova Scotia in a study by Van Oostrum and Horvath (1997). The researchers found that the participants' response to situations such as this one depended on whether they interpreted the other student's behaviour as intentional. Those who attributed hostile intentions (i.e., believed that the student spilled the tray "to be mean") reported that they would respond with aggression—more so than did students who interpreted the event as an accident or who believed that the other student's motives were ambiguous. Interestingly, the participants who reported the greatest use of aggression in their everyday lives were also the most likely to attribute hostile intent in the scenarios.

Thus, one obvious cause of aggression stems from the urge to reciprocate after being provoked by aggressive behaviour from another person. While the Christian plea to "turn the other cheek" is wonderful advice, it does not appear to be the typical reaction of most human beings. This has been illustrated in countless experiments in and out of the laboratory. Typical of this line of research is an experiment by Robert Baron (1988), in which subjects prepared an advertisement for a new product; their ad was then evaluated and criticized by an accomplice of the experimenter. In one condition, the criticism, while strong, was done in a gentle and considerate manner ("I think there's a lot of room for improvement"); in the other condition, the criticism was given in an insulting manner ("I don't think you could be original if you tried"). When provided with an opportunity to retaliate, subjects who were treated harshly were far more likely to do so than were those in the "gentle" condition.

It is understandable that we will want to retaliate if someone deliberately provokes us. However, unfortunately, this can become an excuse for treating others in abusive, violent ways. As we saw in Chapter 4, people are more likely to see domestic violence as justified if the wife is perceived as having provoked her husband—even if the husband's reaction is way out of proportion to the provocation (Kristiansen & Giulietti, 1990; Perrott, Miller, & Delaney, 1997).

Before leaving this topic, it is important to point out that, when provoked, people do not always reciprocate. One determinant of reciprocation is the intentionality of the provocation; if we are convinced it was unintentional, most of us will not reciprocate (Kremer & Stephens, 1983). Similarly, if there are mitigating circumstances, and we are aware of them, counter-aggression will not occur. This was demonstrated in an experiment conducted at the University of Alberta by Johnson and Rule (1986). In the first phase of the experiment, male research participants prepared an essay that subsequently received an insulting evaluation, supposedly from another student with whom they had been paired for the experiment. Before receiving the insult, half of the participants read a speech allegedly written by the other student, in which he mentioned that he was upset

Insults and Aggression

Think about the last time you were insulted.

- Who insulted you?
- What were the circumstances?
- Did you take it personally or not?

- How did you respond?

How does your behaviour relate to the material you have just finished reading?

because he had just received an unfair grade on a chemistry exam. The other participants read the speech after they had been insulted. Later, as part of a so-called learning experiment, all participants were given an opportunity to deliver loud bursts of noise to their research partner whenever he made an error. Students who knew about the mitigating circumstances before being insulted delivered less intense bursts of noise than did those who learned about the circumstances *after* they had been insulted. How can we account for this difference? Apparently, at the time of the insult, the informed students simply did not take it personally and therefore had no strong need to retaliate. This interpretation is bolstered by evidence of their physiological arousal. At the time of the insult, the heartbeat of the insulted students did not increase as rapidly if they knew beforehand about their research partner's unhappy state of mind.

SOCIAL EXCLUSION

It is becoming an all-too-common theme: A high-school student shows up at school one day with a gun and goes on a killing rampage (we will discuss some of these incidents in greater detail later in the chapter). Analyses of these tragedies often paint a picture of the killers as socially isolated individuals who experienced rejection from their peers. They then deal with the pain of rejection by mounting a lethal attack on those whose acceptance they craved most.

Is there validity to these kinds of analyses? Does social exclusion actually lead to aggressive behaviour? Recently, Jean Twenge and colleagues (2001) decided to find out. Imagine you were a participant in one of their studies. You arrive at a laboratory along with four or five other students. First, you spend 15 minutes chatting as part of a getting-acquainted exercise. Then, you are informed that the actual experiment involves working in groups on a task. You and the other students are asked to "name the two people (out of those you met today) you would most like to work with." You eagerly write down the names of the two people you enjoyed most during the getting-acquainted discussion. The experimenter then collects the names and tells you she will be back shortly to announce the group assignments. To your horror, when she returns she says, "I hate to tell you this, but no one chose you as someone they wanted to work with." How do you react?

If you are like the actual participants in this study, you react with aggression. The rest of the experiment was set up so participants were given an opportunity to deliver loud bursts of white noise to a confederate who insulted them. Those participants who had been rejected earlier were much more aggressive toward the confederate (gave longer and louder bursts of noise) than those who were told they had been accepted by the group. Quite remarkably, the experience of being excluded from a group of strangers in a laboratory provoked considerable levels of aggression in this study (and other similar studies conducted by these researchers; Twenge et al., 2001). It is perhaps little wonder that those who experience the sting of rejection from classmates on a daily basis end up reacting with extreme aggression.

AGGRESSIVE OBJECTS AS A CAUSE OF AGGRESSION

Is it conceivable that the mere presence of an **aggressive stimulus**—an object associated with aggressive responses (e.g., a gun) might increase the probability of aggression? In a

Aggressive stimulus
an object that is associated with aggressive response (e.g., a gun) and whose mere presence can increase the probability of aggression

classic experiment by Leonard Berkowitz and Anthony LePage (1967), university students were made angry. Some of them were made angry in a room in which a gun was left lying around (ostensibly from a previous experiment), and others were made angry in a room in which a neutral object (a badminton racket) was substituted for the gun. Participants were then given the opportunity to administer electric shocks to a fellow student. Those individuals who had been made angry in the presence of the gun administered more intense electric shocks than did those made angry in the presence of the badminton racket.

The results are illustrated in Figure 12.1. The basic findings, replicated in the United States and Europe (Frodi, 1975; Turner & Leyens, 1992; Turner & Simons, 1974; Turner et al., 1977), are provocative, and point to a conclusion opposite to a familiar slogan often used by opponents of gun control: "Guns don't kill; people do." Guns *do* kill. As Leonard Berkowitz (1981) puts it, "An angry person can pull the trigger of his gun if he wants to commit violence; but the trigger can also pull the finger or otherwise elicit aggressive reactions from him, if he is ready to aggress and does not have strong inhibitions against such behaviour."

Consider Seattle, Washington, and Vancouver, British Columbia. They are virtually twin cities in a lot of ways; they have similar climates, populations, economies, general crime rates, and rates of physical assault. They differ, however, in two respects: (a) Vancouver severely restricts handgun ownership, while Seattle does not, and (b) the murder rate in Seattle is more than twice as high as that in Vancouver (Sloan et al., 1988). Is the one the cause of the other? We cannot be sure. However, the laboratory experiments discussed above strongly suggest that the ubiquitous presence of that aggressive stimulus in the United States might be a factor. This speculation receives additional support from Dane Archer and Rosemary Gartner (1984), who, in a cross-national study of violence, found that the homicide rate in countries all over the world is highly correlated with the

▶ Figure 12.1

THE TRIGGER CAN PULL THE FINGER.

Aggressive cues, such as weapons, tend to increase levels of aggression.

(Adapted from Berkowitz & LePage, 1967)

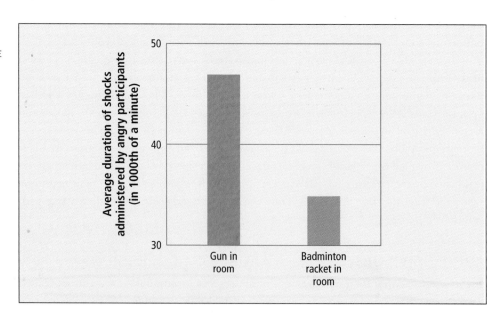

availability of handguns. Britain, for example, where handguns are banned, has one-quarter the population of the United States and one-sixteenth as many homicides.

Before leaving this topic, we should note that the effects we have been discussing apply to any aggressive stimulus—not just to guns. In a study by Wendy Josephson (1987), it was found that even neutral objects can come to be associated with aggression, via classical conditioning. Some of the participants (young boys) were shown a violent television segment in which snipers communicated via walkie-talkies. Later, they played a game of floor hockey while observers recorded instances of aggression by speaking into either a walkie-talkie or a tape recorder. Participants showed greater aggression when the observers used walkie-talkies than when they used tape recorders. Thus, the walkie-talkie had become a violence-related cue, just from having been associated with the violence in the television show the participants had seen earlier.

IMITATION AND AGGRESSION

A major cause of aggression has its roots in social learning. Children frequently learn to solve conflicts aggressively by imitating adults and their peers, especially when they see that the aggression is rewarded. For example, in high-contact sports (e.g., football and hockey) it is frequently the case that the more aggressive players achieve the greatest fame (and the highest salaries) and the more aggressive teams win more games. In these sports, it usually doesn't pay to be a gentle soul—or, as famed baseball manager Leo Durocher once said, "Nice guys finish last!" The data are consistent with this observation. For instance, in one study it was found that among hockey players, those most frequently sent to the penalty box for overly aggressive play tended to be the ones who scored the most goals (McCarthy & Kelly, 1978). What lessons are children learning from observing aggression among athletes and other adults?

In a classic series of experiments, Albert Bandura and his associates (1961, 1963) demonstrated the power of **social learning theory**—a theory holding that we learn social behaviour (e.g., aggression) by observing others and imitating them. The basic procedure in the Bandura experiments was to have an adult knock around a plastic, air-filled "Bobo" doll (the kind that bounces back after it's been knocked down). The adult would smack the doll around with the palm of his or her hand, strike it with a mallet, kick it, and yell aggressive things at it. Children were then allowed to play with the doll. In these experiments, the children imitated the aggressive models and treated the doll in an abusive manner. Children in a control condition, who did not see the aggressive adult in action, almost never unleashed any aggression against the hapless doll. Moreover, the children who watched the aggressive adult used identical actions and identical aggressive words to those of the adult. In addition, many went beyond mere imitation—they also engaged in novel forms of aggressive behaviour.

Given findings such as these, it probably comes as no surprise that a number of studies have found that a large percentage of physically abusive people were themselves abused by their parents when they were kids (Dutton & Hart, 1992a, 1992b; Silver, Dublin, & Lourie, 1969; Strauss & Gelles, 1980). When children experience aggressive treatment at the hands of their parents, they learn that violence is the way to respond to conflict or anger. People may also imitate acts of violence performed by their peers.

Social learning theory the theory that we learn social behaviour (e.g., aggression) by observing others and imitating them

▶ It is clear from the studies of Bandura and colleagues (1961, 1963) that children learn aggressive behaviour through imitation and modelling.

In April 1999, the shooting rampage of two students at Columbine High School in Littleton, Colorado, made news headlines around the world. Eric Harris and Dylan Klebold shot and killed 13 people at their high school before fatally shooting themselves. Later that month, a 14-year-old boy (who cannot be named because he is a minor) attending W. R. Meyers High School in Taber, Alberta, opened fire, killing one student and wounding another. Although it cannot be proven, it was widely speculated that the Tabor tragedy was an imitation of the Columbine massacre. Police feared there would be other copycat killings. Thus, in early May of that year, when a 20-year-old man and a 14-year-old boy in Brandon, Manitoba, made death threats against students and staff at two schools in that city, police were quick to lay charges. That was not an isolated case—similar threats increased dramatically across the country following the Taber shootings. Moreover, according to Kevin Cameron, the social worker who led the crisis unit team sent to Taber, critical periods, such as the anniversary of the shootings, are associated with increased threats for at least three to five years afterwards (Cameron, 2000). Indeed, on the one-year anniversary of the Columbine shootings, four students and one staff member at Cairine Wilson High School in Orleans, Ontario, were wounded when they were attacked by a knife-wielding student.

THE EFFECTS OF WATCHING MEDIA VIOLENCE

The classic experiments by Albert Bandura and his colleagues make it clear that observing other people behaving aggressively can increase the aggressive behaviour of the viewer. This raises the obvious question: Does watching violence on TV make people more violent? Let's take a close look at the data.

Effects on Children
There is no doubt that television plays an important role in the socialization of children (Huston & Wright, 1996). There is also no doubt that TV

◀ Studen
Pearson Hi
Calgary, sob
old student v
death at schoo

remains steeped in violence. According to one study (Seppa, 1997), 58 percent of all TV programs contain violence—and of those, 78 percent include no remorse, criticism, or penalty for that violence. Indeed, some 40 percent of recent violent incidents seen on TV are initiated by characters portrayed as heroes or other attractive role models for children (Cantor, 1994; Kunkel et al., 1995).

Exactly what do children learn from watching violence on TV? A number of long-term studies indicate that the more violence individuals watch on TV as children, the more violence they exhibit years later as teenagers and young adults. For example, in an impressive longitudinal program of research, Eron and Huesmann and their colleagues (Eron, 1982, 1987; Eron et al., 1996; Huesmann, 1982; Huesmann & Miller, 1994) assessed television viewing habits of nearly 900 eight-year-old children. The children were asked to report which shows they watched on TV and how frequently they watched them; the shows were independently rated by judges as to how violent they were. Then, the general aggressiveness of the children was independently rated by their teachers and class-mates. The researchers found a small, but significant, correlation between the amount of violent TV watched and the children's aggressiveness. More striking was the finding that the impact of watching violent television accumulated over time. Ten years later, when the original research participants were 18 years of age, the correlation between television violence and aggression was stronger than it had been at age 8! While these are powerful data, they do not definitively prove that watching a lot of violence on TV causes children to become violent teenagers. After all, it is at least conceivable that the aggressive kids were born with a tendency to enjoy violence and that this enjoyment manifested itself in both their aggressive behaviour and their liking for watching violence on TV. In order to demonstrate conclusively that watching violence on TV actually causes violent behaviour, the relationship must be shown experimentally.

Because this is an issue of great importance to society, it has been well researched. The overwhelming thrust of the experimental evidence demonstrates that watching violence does indeed increase the frequency of aggressive behaviour in children (for reviews of the literature, see Donnerstein, Slaby, & Eron, 1994; Eron et al., 1996; Geen, 1994, 1998; Huesmann & Miller, 1994; Hughes & Hasbrouck, 1996). As mentioned in Chapter 2, this was also the conclusion reached by Wendy Wood and her colleagues based on a meta analysis of studies of TV violence (Wood, Wong, & Chachere, 1991). Here are a few examples of the kinds of experiments on which this conclusion is based. In an early experiment on this issue, Robert Liebert and Robert Baron (1972) exposed a group of children to an extremely violent TV episode of a police drama. In a control condition, a similar group of children was exposed to an exciting but nonviolent TV sporting event for the same length of time. Each child was then allowed to play in another room with a group of other children. Those who had watched the violent police drama showed far more aggression against their playmates than did those who had watched the sporting event. The results of this experiment are depicted in Figure 12.2.

To give another example, in Chapter 2 we referred to an experiment by Josephson (1987), who found that watching TV violence has the greatest impact on youngsters who are somewhat prone to violence to begin with. In this experiment, nearly 400 boys from various Winnipeg schools were exposed to either a film depicting a great deal of police violence or an exciting, nonviolent film about bike racing. The boys then played a game of floor hockey. Watching the violent film had the effect of increasing the number of aggressive acts committed during the hockey game—primarily by those boys who had previously been rated as highly aggressive by their teachers. These boys hit others with their sticks, threw elbows, and yelled aggressive things at their opponents to a much greater extent than was seen in either the boys rated as nonaggressive who had also watched the violent film or the boys rated as aggressive who had watched the nonviolent

▶ **Figure 12.2**

TV VIOLENCE AND AGGRESSION.

Being exposed to violence on TV increases aggressive behaviour in children.

(Adapted from Liebert & Baron, 1972)

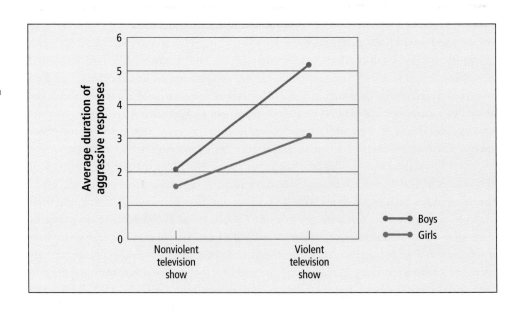

film. Thus, it may be that watching media violence in effect serves to give aggressive children "permission" to express their aggression. Josephson's experiment suggests that children who do not have aggressive tendencies to begin with do not necessarily act aggressively—at least, not on the basis of seeing only one violent film.

That last phrase is an important one, because it may be that even children who are not prone to aggression will become more aggressive if exposed to a steady diet of violent films over a long period. Indeed, that is exactly what was found in a set of experiments performed in Belgium by Phillippe Leyens and his colleagues (1975; Parke et al., 1977).

Finally, before leaving this topic we should note that the kinds of effects we have been discussing extend to violence portrayed in the media more generally—not just in television programming. The Columbine High School killings raised the disturbing question of whether violent entertainment, such as violent video games, can contribute to aggression. Apparently Harris and Klebold enjoyed playing a bloody, extremely violent video game licensed by the U.S. military to train soldiers how to kill. For a class project, Harris and Klebold produced a videotape that was an eerie rendition of the killings they subsequently carried out. Their videotape, modelled after the video game, featured the two of them wearing trench coats, carrying guns, and killing school athletes.

Does playing violent video games actually produce violent behaviour? Recent research by Craig Anderson and his colleagues (Anderson & Dill, 2000; Bartholow & Anderson, 2002) suggests that it does. In an initial, correlational investigation, these researchers found that playing violent video games was associated with aggression and delinquency (Anderson & Dill, 2000). This was followed by several laboratory experiments with university students. These experiments confirmed that exposure to violent video games does, in fact, increase aggressive thoughts and behaviours (Anderson & Dill, 2000; Bartholow & Anderson, 2002). (If this isn't enough to persuade you to curb time spent playing video games, we might note that Anderson and Dill also found that the more time the participants spent playing video games—violent or not—the lower their grades!).

What about Adults? Thus far, in discussing the effects of media violence we have focused much of our attention on children, and for good reason. Youngsters are by definition much more malleable than adults are—that is, it is generally assumed that their attitudes and behaviour can be more deeply influenced by the things they view. However, the effect of media violence on violent behaviour may not be limited to children or adolescents. On numerous occasions, adult violence seems to be a case of life imitating art. For example, a few years ago a man drove his truck through the window of a crowded cafeteria in Killeen, Texas, and began shooting people at random. By the time the police arrived, he had killed 22 people, making this the most destructive shooting spree in American history. He then turned the gun on himself. In his pocket, police found a ticket stub to *The Fisher King*, a film that depicts a deranged man firing a shotgun into a crowded bar, killing several people.

Did seeing the film cause the violent act? We cannot be sure. However, we do know that violence in the media can and does have a profound impact on the behaviour of adults. Several years ago, David Phillips (1983, 1986) scrutinized the daily homicide rates in the United States and found that they almost always increased during the week following a heavyweight boxing match. Moreover, the more publicity surrounding the fight, the greater the subsequent increase in homicides. Still more striking, the race of prizefight losers was related to the race of victims of murders after the fights. After white boxers lost fights, there was a corresponding increase in murders of white men but not of black men; after black boxers lost fights, there was a corresponding increase in murders of black men but not of white men. Phillips' results are convincing; they are far too consistent to be dismissed as merely a fluke.

Again, this should not be construed as indicating that all people or even a sizable percentage of people are motivated to commit violence through watching media violence. However, the fact that some people are influenced—and that the results can be tragic—cannot be denied.

The Numbing Effect of TV Violence

It seems that repeated exposure to difficult or unpleasant events tends to have a numbing effect on our sensitivity to those events. One of the authors of this book, Elliot Aronson, offers the following personal example:

> Several years ago, I moved to Manhattan for a few months. Soon after my arrival, I was walking down Fifth Avenue with a friend who is a native New Yorker. I was struck and touched by the great number of obviously homeless people, living in cardboard boxes, carrying their meagre possessions in paper bags or wheeling them around in broken-down supermarket shopping carts. I was both deeply moved and appalled. All during our walk, I kept reaching into my pockets and dropping coins into the hands of those unfortunate souls. My friend was appalled at my behaviour. "You'll have to learn to ignore these people," my friend said. "Never," I replied, indignantly and self-righteously. Yet sure enough, within a few weeks I found myself walking down the streets of Manhattan staring straight ahead and keeping my hands out of my pockets. Amazingly, I had become so accustomed to the sight that, for all intents and purposes, I had become virtually indifferent to it.

Is it possible that by a similar process, being constantly exposed to violence on TV tends to make people more tolerant of real violence? There is good evidence that this is so. In one experiment, Victor Cline and his associates (1973) measured the physiological responses of several young men while they were watching a rather brutal and bloody boxing match. Those who watched a lot of TV in their daily lives seemed relatively indifferent to the mayhem in the ring—that is, they showed little physiological evidence of excitement or anxiety. They treated the violence in a lackadaisical manner. On the other hand, those who typically watched relatively little TV underwent major physiological arousal. The violence really got to them.

In a related vein, Margaret Hanratty Thomas and her colleagues (1977) demonstrated that viewing television violence can subsequently numb people's reactions when they are faced with real-life aggression. Participants in this study watched either a violent police drama or an exciting but nonviolent volleyball game. After a short break, they observed a verbally and physically aggressive interaction between two preschoolers. Those who had watched the police show responded less emotionally (as measured by changes in galvanic skin response) than did those who had watched the volleyball game. It seems that viewing the initial violence served to desensitize them to further acts of

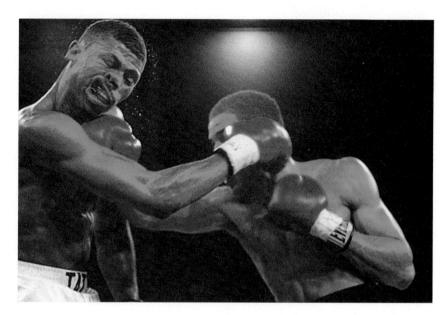

Do violent sporting events increase homicide rates?

violence—they were not upset by an incident that by all rights should have upset them. While such a reaction may psychologically protect us from upset, it may also have the unintended effect of increasing our indifference to victims of violence and perhaps rendering us more accepting of violence as a necessary aspect of modern life. In a follow-up experiment, Thomas (1982) took this reasoning a step further. She demonstrated that students exposed to a great deal of TV violence not only showed physiological evidence of greater acceptance of violence but also, when subsequently given the opportunity to administer electric shocks to a fellow student, delivered more powerful electric shocks than did those in the control condition.

Why Does Media Violence Affect Viewers' Aggression? As suggested throughout this section, there are four distinct reasons that explain why exposure to violence via the media might increase aggression:

1. **"If they can do it, so can I."** When people watch characters on TV expressing violence, it might simply weaken their previously learned inhibitions against violent behaviour.

2. **"Oh, so that's how you do it!"** When people watch characters on TV expressing violence, it might trigger imitation, providing them with ideas as to how they might go about it.

3. **"I think it must be aggressive feelings that I'm experiencing."** Watching violence makes feelings of anger more easily available and makes an aggressive response more likely simply through priming. Thus, exposing children to an endless supply of violence on TV, in films, and in video games makes it more likely that aggression will come to mind as a response to situations. In this regard we might mention that it has been estimated that the average 12-year-old has witnessed more than 100 000 acts of violence on television (Signorielli, Gerbner, & Morgan, 1995).

4. **"Ho-hum, another brutal beating—what's on the other channel?"** Watching a lot of violence seems to reduce both our sense of horror about violence and our sympathy for the victims, thereby making it easier for us to live with violence and perhaps easier for us to act aggressively.

VIOLENT PORNOGRAPHY AND SEXUAL AGGRESSION

If viewing aggression in films and on television contributes to aggressiveness, doesn't it follow that viewing pornographic material could increase the incidence of sexual aggression? Many people think so. For example, Lavoie, Robitaille, and Hébert (2000) conducted discussion groups with youths who frequented a teen drop-in centre in Quebec City. Both males and females perceived pornography as a cause of sexual violence in relationships. As we will see, research confirms these perceptions. For example, Sommers and Check (1987) found that women living in shelters or attending counselling groups for battered women in the Toronto area reported much greater consumption of pornographic material by their partner than did a comparison group of women who were not battered. (The battered women experienced higher levels of verbal aggression, physical aggression, and sexual aggression from their partners than did the control group.) In addition, 39 percent of the battered women (versus 3 percent of the control group) answered "yes" to the question, "Has your partner ever upset you by trying to get you to do what he'd seen in pornographic pictures, movies, or books?" Similarly, in Lavoie and colleagues' study of Quebec City teenagers, participants reported that it was not uncommon for them or their partners to imitate acts of sexual violence observed in pornographic movies or magazines.

The findings from carefully controlled laboratory studies show that exposure to violent pornography promotes greater acceptance of sexual violence toward women (Donnerstein, 1980; Donnerstein & Berkowitz, 1981; Donnerstein & Linz, 1994; Malamuth, 1981, 1986; Malamuth & Brière, 1986; Malamuth et al., 1995; Dean &

▶ Because of ethical concerns, little research has been conducted on the effects of showing children erotic films; however, research does show that viewing violent content can have lasting ill effects.

"AT LAST, A MOVIE WITHOUT ALL THOSE FILTHY SEX SCENES!"

Malamuth, 1997). For example, Neil Malamuth and James Check (1981) asked students at the University of Manitoba to watch a movie shown at a campus theatre, supposedly as part of a study on the evaluation of movies. The participants saw either a movie that contained sexual violence against women or a nonviolent movie that portrayed a positive, caring relationship. Several days later, the students were asked to complete a Sexual Attitudes Survey in their psychology class. The researchers found that male students who had viewed the movie containing sexual violence were more accepting of violence against women than were those who had seen the nonviolent movie.

In a similar study (Malamuth, 1981), male students at the University of Manitoba viewed one of two erotic films. One version portrayed two mutually consenting adults engaged in lovemaking; the other version portrayed a rape incident. After viewing the film, the men were asked to engage in sexual fantasy. Those men who had watched the rape version of the film created more violent sexual fantasies than did those who had watched the mutual consent version. Other studies have found that prolonged exposure to depictions of sexual violence against women (so-called "slasher" films) makes viewers more accepting of this kind of violence and less sympathetic toward the victim (Linz, Donnerstein, & Penrod, 1984, 1988; Zillmann & Bryant, 1984).

We have seen that exposure to sexual violence is associated with greater acceptance of violence toward women and with more violent fantasies. But do laboratory studies show that men who view violent pornography actually behave aggressively toward women? Sadly, the answer is yes. In one experiment (Donnerstein & Berkowitz, 1981), male participants were angered by a female accomplice. They were then shown one of three films—an aggressive-erotic one involving rape, a purely erotic one without violence, or a film depicting non-erotic violence against women. After viewing one of these films, the men took part in a supposedly unrelated experiment that involved teaching the female accomplice by means of administering electric shocks to her whenever she gave incorrect answers. They were also allowed to choose whatever level of shock they wished to use. (Needless to say, as with other experiments using this procedure, no shocks were actually received.) The men who had earlier seen the violent pornographic film subsequently administered the most intense shocks; those who had seen the erotic, nonviolent film administered the lowest level of shocks. There is also evidence showing that those who view violent pornographic films will administer more intense shocks to a female confederate than to a male confederate (Donnerstein, 1980).

Unfortunately, these are not isolated findings. Researchers at the Canadian National Foundation for Family Research and Education recently conducted a meta analysis of 46 American and Canadian studies on the effects of pornography and reached the following conclusion:

> Exposure to pornographic material puts one at increased risk for developing sexually deviant tendencies, committing sexual offenses, experiencing difficulties in one's intimate relationships, and accepting the rape myth (Paolucci-Oddone, Genius, and Violato, 2000).

This is a deeply disturbing conclusion given that violence is a prevalent theme in pornographic materials. For example, an analysis of adults-only fiction paperback books found that almost one-third of all sex episodes involved the use of force (physical, mental, or blackmail) by a male to make a female engage in unwanted sex (Smith, 1976).

 **The Incidence of Violence in Intimate Relationships**

Violence in intimate relationships is usually assessed using the Conflict Tactics scale (or variations of it), in which people report whether their partner has used any of the following types of violence:

- threatened to hit
- threw something
- pushed, grabbed, or shoved
- slapped
- kicked, bit, or hit
- hit with something
- beat

- choked
- used or threatened to use a gun or knife
- sexual assault

To see how knowledgeable you are about the incidence of spousal violence (including in common-law relationships) in Canada, answer the following questions:

1. Which of these kinds of violence do you think is most common in marriages?

2. Which of these kinds of violence is more likely to be experienced by women?

3. Which of these kinds of violence is more likely to be experienced by men?

ANSWERS

Note: The percentages we report below are based on Statistics Canada (1999) information gathered on 26 000 Canadians. Respondents were asked whether violence with a current partner occurred in the past five years. In cases where a marriage had ended in the past five years, respondents reported on violence that had occurred with their former spouse. The rates of violence reported for these marriages that had ended were considerably higher than the rates of violence reported for marriages that were currently intact.

1. The most prevalent kinds of spousal violence are "threatened to hit" (54 percent of those who reported violence from a spouse), "pushed, grabbed, or shoved" (52 percent), and "slapped" (41 percent).

2. Women were most likely to report being pushed, grabbed, or shoved (72 percent of women versus 34 percent of men). They were also much more likely than men to report the more severe forms of violence. For example, they were much more likely than men to report being beaten (13 percent versus 4 percent), choked (10 percent versus zero percent), or sexually assaulted by their spouse (8 percent versus zero percent).

3. Men were most likely to report that their spouse had thrown something at them (54 percent of men versus 35 percent of women). They also were twice as likely as women to report being kicked, bitten, or hit (41 percent versus 19 percent), and were more likely to report that they had been slapped (51 percent versus 30 percent).

How to Reduce Aggression

Throughout history, beleaguered parents have attempted to curb the aggressive behaviour of their children. One of the prime techniques is punishment. After all, as the old saying goes, "Spare the rod and spoil the child." How well does punishment work? Let's consider the data.

DOES PUNISHING AGGRESSION REDUCE AGGRESSIVE BEHAVIOUR?

Punishment is a complex event, especially as it relates to aggression. On the one hand, you might guess that punishing any behaviour, including aggression, would reduce its frequency. On the other hand, because severe punishment itself usually takes the form of an aggressive act, the punishers are actually modelling aggressive behaviour for the person whose aggressive behaviour they are trying to stamp out, and might induce that person to imitate the action. This seems to be true—for children. As we have seen earlier in this chapter, children who grow up with punitive, aggressive parents tend to be prone toward violence when they grow up (Vissing et al., 1991).

Moreover, as we saw in Chapter 6, several experiments with preschoolers have demonstrated that the threat of relatively severe punishment for committing a transgression has little impact on diminishing the attractiveness of the transgression. On the other hand, the threat of mild punishment—of a degree just powerful enough to get the child to cease the undesired activity temporarily—can induce the child to try to justify his or her restraint and thereby produce a diminution in the attractiveness of the action (Aronson & Carlsmith, 1963; Freedman, 1965). Dan Olweus (1994, 1995a, 1995b, 1995c, 1996, 1997) has applied these ideas in the Norwegian and Swedish school systems in hopes of curbing bullying. Olweus was able to reduce the occurrence of bullying behaviour among fourth through seventh graders by as much as 50 percent, by training teachers and administrators to be vigilant to the problem and to make moderate and swift interventions. The intervention strategy was effective both immediately and over the long haul. Unfortunately, the results were not quite so positive when the Norwegian intervention program was adapted for use in Toronto schools, in part because a more modest version of the program was instituted (Pepler et al., 1994). (In Norway, the anti-bullying intervention was a large-scale national program funded by the Ministry of Education, whereas in Toronto, schools attempted to implement the program with limited resources and expertise.) Overall, this research indicates that children, who have not yet formed their values, are more apt to develop a distaste for aggression if the punishment for aggressive actions is swift and not severe enough to make it unnecessary for the children to justify their restraint.

◀ If a parent wants to curb the aggression of his or her child, threats of severe punishment will have only a temporary effect.

Using Punishment on Violent Adults How should society use punishment as a deterrent with adults who manifest a tendency to commit aggressive acts? Here, a slightly different picture emerges. The criminal justice system of most cultures administers harsh punishments as a means of deterring violent crimes. Does the implicit threat of harsh punishments for crimes such as murder, manslaughter, and rape diminish the occurrence of such crimes? Do people who are about to commit such crimes say to themselves, "I'd better think twice about this, because if I get caught, I'll be severely punished"? Here, the scientific evidence is mixed. Under ideal conditions, laboratory experiments indicate that punishment can act as a deterrent (Bower & Hilgard, 1981). By "ideal conditions" we mean that the punishment must be both prompt and certain; that is, it must come close on the heels of the commission of the violent act, and the chances of escaping punishment must be virtually nonexistent. Needless to say, these ideal conditions are almost never met in the real world. In most North American cities, the probability that a person who has committed a violent crime will be apprehended, charged, tried, and convicted is not high. Moreover, promptness is rarely possible—punishment is typically delayed by months or even years. Consequently, in the real world of the criminal justice system, severe punishment is unlikely to have the kind of deterrent effect it does in the laboratory.

Given these realities, you will not be surprised to learn that severe punishment does not seem to deter violent crimes. The United States—where many states invoke the death penalty for murder—has a much higher rate of homicide than many industrial countries (see Figure 12.3). Moreover, the American states that have abolished the death penalty have not experienced the increase in capital crimes that some experts predicted (Archer & Gartner, 1984; Nathanson, 1987). Ruth Peterson and William Bailey (1988) examined a period in the United States just after a national hiatus on the death penalty, resulting from the Supreme Court ruling that it constituted cruel and unusual punishment. When the Supreme Court reversed itself in 1976, there was no indication that the return to capital punishment produced a decrease in homicides.

▼ Figure 12.3

HOMICIDE IN INDUSTRIAL SOCIETIES.

The homicide rate in the United States far outstrips that of other industrial countries.

(Adapted from Archer & Gartner, 1984)

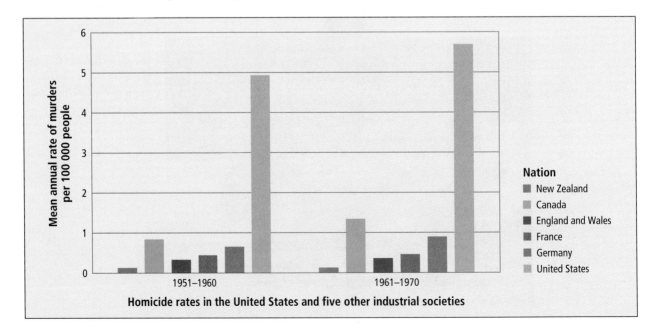

A study by the National Academy of Sciences (see Berkowitz, 1993) demonstrated that consistency and certainty of punishment were far more effective deterrents of violent behaviour than was severe punishment. In fact, the evidence suggests that mild punishment, consistently meted out, can be quite effective in reducing violent behaviour. This was demonstrated in a simple but powerful field experiment on reducing domestic violence conducted by the Minneapolis Police Department (Sherman & Berk, 1984; Cohen, 1987). In this experiment, police officers were randomly assigned to one of three conditions. In the first condition, they performed brief, on-the-spot counselling when called to intervene in a domestic violence situation; in the second condition, they asked the perpetrator to leave the scene for eight hours; in the third condition, they arrested the perpetrator. Police reports were then carefully monitored over the next six months. The results indicated that during those months, 19 percent of the perpetrators given counselling and 24 percent of those asked to leave the premises repeated their aggressive actions, whereas only 10 percent of those placed under arrest (and made to spend a night or two in jail) repeated their actions. These data show that when law enforcement officers demonstrate that they are taking the offence seriously by hauling the perpetrator off to jail, domestic violence is diminished. The findings led the Minneapolis Police Department to revamp its policies regarding the arrest of perpetrators of domestic violence, a move that has attracted considerable attention. Similar programs have been instituted in other American cities, with mixed success (Langer, 1986; Sherman, 1992). More detailed research is needed to determine the ideal conditions for long-term results (Berk, Fenstermaker, & Newton, 1988; Berk et al., 1992). One important point that has emerged from research on the Minneapolis project, however, is that arrest is only effective for perpetrators who have something to lose by being arrested (Dutton, 1995). A person who is employed, for example, may be worried about how to explain his absence from work due to jail time; an arrest for domestic assault may create embarrassment or rejection for someone whose social circle consists of people who disapprove of the use of violence in relationships; and so on.

Closer to home, in 1990, Manitoba instituted a Family Violence Court to deal specifically with family violence cases, and in 1997, Ontario established similar courts. These specialized courts are part of an overall response to family violence that includes a zero-tolerance policy for arrest, early intervention in domestic abuse situations, the use of Crown attorneys with expertise in family violence issues (e.g., sensitivity to victims' reluctance to testify, ensuring that the legal process does not revictimize victims of violence), and treatment programs for offenders and victims of family violence. The message being sent from these courts is that family violence is a serious crime with immediate, serious consequences.

The establishment of family violence courts has had several effects. The first has been a dramatic increase in the number of arrests and convictions. Importantly, the high rate of convictions has been coupled with an emphasis on rehabilitation. For example, most offenders are required to participate in treatment groups. It is too early to tell whether these initiatives will have long-term benefits, or whether these courts have been effective in communicating that family violence is unacceptable. However, it is encouraging that the rate of spousal assault has declined in the past five years (Statistics Canada, 2000).

CATHARSIS AND AGGRESSION

It is generally believed that one way for an individual to reduce feelings of aggression is to do something aggressive. "Get it out of your system" has been common advice for a great many years. So, if you are feeling angry (the belief goes), don't try to ignore it, but instead yell, scream, curse, throw some crockery at the wall—and then you'll be rid of it and it won't fester and grow into something truly uncontrollable. This common belief, held even among some professional psychologists, is based on an oversimplification of the psychoanalytic notion of **catharsis** (see Freud, 1933; Dollard, et al., 1939). As we mentioned earlier in this chapter, Freud believed that unless people were allowed to express their aggression in relatively harmless ways, the aggressive energy would be dammed up, pressure would build, and the energy would seek an outlet, either exploding into acts of extreme violence or manifesting itself as symptoms of mental illness. Freud was a brilliant and complex thinker who invariably stopped short of giving simplistic advice. Alas, as the simplified version of his theory of catharsis got into the hands of famed advice columnist Ann Landers, she translated it into the pronouncement, "Youngsters should be taught to vent their anger." The idea behind this advice is that blowing off steam will not only make angry people feel better but also serve to make them less likely to engage in subsequent acts of destructive violence. Does this square with the data?

Consider a recent study by Bushman, Baumeister, and Stack (1999). They asked university students to read an article, supposedly published in *Science,* titled "Research Shows That Hitting Inanimate Objects Is an Effective Way to Vent Anger." In the article, a Harvard psychologist claimed that people who vent their anger by hitting a punching bag subsequently behave less aggressively toward others. Other participants read the same article, except that the word "Effective" was changed to "Ineffective" in the title, and the article stated that venting one's anger did *not* reduce aggression. Later, who was most likely to want to hit a punching bag after being insulted by a confederate? As you probably guessed, it was the participants who read the pro-catharsis article.

This study confirms that people can be convinced that catharsis reduces aggression, but the critical question is this: Does hitting a punching bag actually make you less aggressive? To answer this question, the researchers conducted a second study. First, participants read either the pro-catharsis or the anti-catharsis message from the first study (a control group did not receive any catharsis message). They were then insulted by a confederate. Some participants were given a chance to vent their anger by hitting a punching bag; other participants were not. Later, all participants were given an opportunity to deliver bursts of noise either to the person who insulted them or to a different person. It turned out that the most aggressive participants (those who delivered the longest and loudest blasts of noise) were those who had read the pro-catharsis message and had hit the punching bag. Moreover, they were equally aggressive, regardless of whether the target was the person who had angered them or an innocent person. Thus, it appears that venting anger actually increases anger, rather than reducing it.

Similar findings have been obtained in studies examining whether participating in aggressive sports has a cathartic effect. For example, Patterson (1974) measured the hostility of high-school football players, rating them both one week before and one week after the football season. If it were true that the intense competitiveness and aggressive behaviour that are part of playing football serve to reduce the tension caused by pent-up

Catharsis

the notion that "blowing off steam"—by performing an aggressive act, watching others engage in aggressive behaviour, or engaging in a fantasy of aggression— relieves built-up aggressive energies and hence reduces the likelihood of further aggressive behaviour

◀ Fans watching aggressive sports do not become less aggressive—contrary to the idea of catharsis.

aggression, the players would be expected to exhibit a decline in hostility over the course of the season. Instead, the results showed a significant *increase* in feelings of hostility. This is not to say that people do not get pleasure from these games; they do. However, engaging in these games does not decrease participants' aggressive feelings—if anything, it increases them.

Some people believe in another variation of the catharsis hypothesis, namely that watching competitive and aggressive games is a safe way to get rid of our aggressive impulses. Gordon Russell (1983), a sports psychologist at the University of Lethbridge, tested this proposition by measuring the hostility of spectators at an especially violent hockey game. As the game progressed, the spectators became increasingly belligerent; toward the end of the final period, their level of hostility was enormous and did not return to the pre-game level until several hours after the game was over. Similar results have been found among spectators at football games and wrestling matches (Arms, Russell, & Sandilands, 1979; Goldstein & Arms, 1971; Branscombe & Wann, 1992). Thus, as with participating in an aggressive sport, watching one serves to increase, rather than reduce, aggressive behaviour.

Blaming the Victim of Our Aggression On the surface, catharsis appears to be a reasonable idea, in a limited way. That is, when somebody angers us, venting our hostility against that person does indeed seem to relieve tension and make us feel better. However, "feeling better" should not be confused with a reduction in our hostility. Aggressing the first time can reduce your inhibitions against committing other such actions; in a sense, the aggression is legitimized, making it easier to carry out such assaults. Further, and more importantly, the main thrust of the research on this issue indicates that committing an overt act of aggression against a person changes one's feelings about that person—in a negative direction—thereby increasing the probability of future aggression against that person.

Does this material begin to sound familiar? It should. As we have seen in Chapter 6, when one person does harm to another person, it sets in motion cognitive processes aimed at justifying the act of cruelty. Specifically, when you hurt another person you experience cognitive dissonance. The cognition "I have hurt Charlie" is dissonant with the cognition "I am a decent, reasonable person." A good way for you to reduce dissonance is somehow to convince yourself that hurting Charlie was not an indecent, unreasonable, bad thing to do. You can accomplish this by convincing yourself that Charlie is a terrible human being who deserved to be hurt. This would especially hold if the target was an innocent victim of your aggression. In Chapter 6, we discussed experiments in which participants inflicted either psychological or physical harm on an innocent person who had done them no prior harm. The participants then proceeded to derogate their victims, convincing themselves that the victims were not nice people and therefore deserved what they got. This reduces dissonance, all right—and it also sets the stage for further aggression, because once a person has succeeded in derogating someone, it makes it easier for him or her to do further harm to the victim in the future.

What happens if the victim isn't totally innocent? That is, imagine that the victim has done something that hurts or disturbs you and is therefore deserving of your retaliation. This situation was examined nearly 40 years ago by Michael Kahn (1966). In Kahn's experiment, a young man posing as a medical technician taking some physiological measurements from university students made derogatory remarks about them. In one condition, the participants were allowed to vent their hostility by expressing their feelings about the technician to his employer—an action that looked as though it would get the technician into serious trouble, perhaps even cost him his job. In another condition, the participants were not given the opportunity to express any aggression against the person who had aroused their anger. Those who were allowed to express their aggression subsequently felt greater dislike and hostility for the technician than did those who were inhibited from expressing their aggression. In other words, expressing aggression did not inhibit the tendency to aggress; rather, it tended to increase it—even when the target was not an innocent victim.

These results suggest that when people are made angry, they frequently engage in overkill. In this case, costing the technician his job is much more devastating than the minor insult delivered by the technician. The overkill produces dissonance in much the same way that hurting an innocent person produces dissonance. That is, if there is a major discrepancy between what the person did to you and the force of your retaliation, you must justify that discrepancy by derogating the object of your wrath.

If our reasoning is correct, it might help explain why it is that when two nations are at war, a relatively small percentage of the members of the victorious nation feel much sympathy for the innocent victims of the nation's actions. For example, near the end of the Second World War, American planes dropped atom bombs on Hiroshima and Nagasaki. More than 100 000 civilians—including many children—were killed, and countless thousands suffered severe injuries. Shortly thereafter, a poll of the American people indicated that less than 5 percent felt that those weapons should not have been used, whereas 23 percent felt that many more of them should have been used before giving Japan the opportunity to surrender. Why would so many Americans favour the wanton death and destruction of innocent victims? Our guess is that in the course of the war, a sizable

proportion of Americans adopted increasingly derogatory attitudes toward the Japanese that made it easier to accept the fact that Americans were causing them a great deal of misery. The more misery the Americans inflicted on them, the more the Americans derogated them—leading to an endless spiral of aggression and the justification of aggression, even to the point of favouring a delay in ending the war so that still more destruction might be inflicted.

Does this sound like ancient history? Think back to Chapter 1, where we described Canada's involvement in launching air attacks on Serbia in March 1999. More than 5000 people were killed as a result of the bombings; most of them were civilians. How did Canadians react? One prominent Canadian, Prime Minister Jean Chrétien, proudly announced that Canada and its NATO allies had "carried the day," and congratulated the Canadian troops for their efforts. In a speech to the House of Commons on June 10, 1999, the day the bombings stopped, Chrétien repeatedly mentioned that it was a great day—a great day for the stability and security of Europe and a great day for Canada. Please note that we are not raising the question here of whether the war was just or necessary. The only question we are raising is this: What percentage of Canadians do you suppose paused for a few moments to feel sadness or regret about the civilians killed in that war? To give an even more recent example, what percentage of Canadians do you suppose paused to feel sadness about the civilian lives lost when Canada assisted the United States in its attempt to weed out terrorists in Afghanistan? Polls conducted in the United States show that there is little sympathy for the innocent victims in such situations. We suspect the same holds true for Canada. You now have the tools to begin to understand the mechanics of how that phenomenon comes about.

Interestingly, when a nation is at war, the impact of that situation extends even beyond feelings of hostility toward the enemy. Specifically, being at war makes the population—even the noncombatants—more prone to commit aggressive actions against one another.

▲ When two nations are at war, their people tend to feel little sympathy for the enemy nation. During the Second World War, for example, Americans tended to derogate Japanese by depicting them as less than human (as in the magazine cover on the left). This helped justify the destruction inflicted on Nagasaki (right) and Hiroshima.

Dane Archer and Rosemary Gartner (1976, 1984) compared the crime rates for 110 countries since 1900 (see Figure 12.4). They found that compared with similar nations that remained at peace, countries that fought wars exhibited substantial post-war increases in their homicide rates. This should not be surprising; it is consistent with everything we have been saying about the social causes of aggression. In a sense, when a nation is at war it's like one big, violent TV drama. Thus, just as with overexposure to TV violence, the fact that a nation is at war (a) weakens the population's inhibitions against aggression, (b) leads to imitation of aggression, (c) makes aggressive responses more available, and (d) numbs our senses to the horror of cruelty and destruction, making us less sympathetic toward the victims. In addition, being at war serves to legitimize to the population the use of violent solutions to address difficult problems.

WHAT ARE WE SUPPOSED TO DO WITH OUR ANGER?

If violence leads to self-justification, which in turn breeds more violence, then if we are feeling angry with someone, what are we to do with our angry feelings—stifle them? Surely, Sigmund Freud and Ann Landers were not totally wrong when they indicated that stifled anger might be harmful to the individual. Indeed, recent research suggests that stifling powerful emotions can lead to physical illness (Pennebaker, 1990). However, if it is harmful to keep our feelings bottled up and harmful to express them, what are we supposed to do with them? This dilemma isn't as difficult as it might seem.

Venting versus Self-Awareness We would suggest that there is an important difference between being angry and expressing that anger in a violent and destructive manner. To experience anger in appropriate circumstances is normal and usually harmless. It is certainly possible to express that anger in a nonviolent manner—for example, by making a clear and simple statement indicating that you are feeling angry and why. Indeed, such a statement in itself is a vehicle for self-assertion and probably serves to relieve tension and to make the angered person feel better. At the same time, because no actual harm

▶ **Figure 12.4**

THE EFFECTS OF WAR ON COMBATANTS VERSUS NONCOMBATANTS.

Immediately after a war, combatant countries are more likely to show an increase in violent crimes than countries not involved in a war. How would you explain this?

(Adapted from Archer & Gartner, 1976)

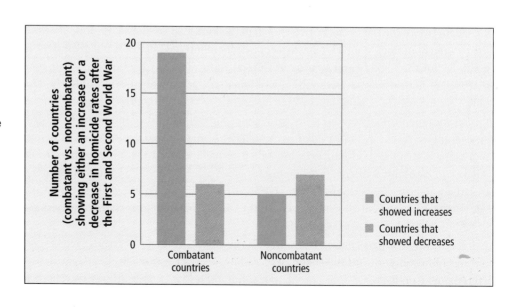

befalls the target of your anger, such a response does not set in motion the cognitive processes that would lead you to justify your behaviour by ridiculing or derogating the target person. The person with whom you are angry also is more likely to react in a constructive manner. For example, in a study conducted at the University of Winnipeg, Fehr, Baldwin, Collins, Patterson, and Benditt (1999) found that if participants were angry at their partner, they expected that their partner would react more positively if they, themselves, expressed their anger in positive, constructive ways (e.g., talking it over, expressing hurt feelings). On the other hand, participants expected that if they expressed anger in negative ways (e.g., with direct or indirect aggression), their partner would be likely to respond in kind.

When feelings of anger are expressed in a clear, open, nonpunitive manner, the result can be greater mutual understanding and a strengthening of the relationship. It almost seems too simple. Yet we have found such behaviour to be a reasonable option that will have more beneficial effects than, on the one hand, shouting, name-calling, and throwing crockery, or on the other hand, suffering in silence as you grin and bear it.

While it is probably best to reveal your anger to the person who caused it, you may also derive some benefit from sharing your anger with a third party. Although he did not work specifically with anger, the research of James Pennebaker (1990) indicates that when we are experiencing emotional stress, it is helpful to reveal that emotion to another person. In Pennebaker's experiments with people undergoing a wide range of traumatic events, those who were induced to reveal the details of the event, as well as their feelings at the time they were experiencing the event, felt healthier and suffered fewer physical illnesses six months later than either people who were allowed to suffer in silence or those who were induced to talk about the details of the events but not the underlying feelings.

Pennebaker suggests that the beneficial effects of "opening up" are due not simply to the venting of feeling, but primarily to the insights and self-awareness that usually accompany such self-disclosure. Some independent corroboration of this suggestion comes from a rather different experiment by Leonard Berkowitz and Bartholmeu Troccoli (1990). In this experiment, young women listened to another woman talk about herself as part of a job interview. Half of the listeners did so while extending their nondominant arm, unsupported (causing discomfort and mild pain), while the others listened with their arms resting comfortably on the table. In each condition, half of the participants were asked to rate their feelings while they were listening to the job interview. According to the researchers, this procedure provided those participants with a vehicle for understanding their discomfort and a way to gain insight into it. The results were striking: Those who experienced pain and discomfort during the interview, but were not given the opportunity to process it, experienced the most negative feelings toward the interviewee—and the more unpleasant the experience was for them, the more negatively they felt toward the interviewee. On the other hand, the participants who were given the opportunity to process their pain were more likely to be aware of the cause of their negative feelings, and as a result were less likely to have those negative feelings "spill over" to their evaluation of the interviewee.

Defusing Anger through Apology
An effective way to reduce aggression in another person is to take some action aimed at diminishing the anger and annoyance that caused it. Suppose you are scheduled to be at your friend's house at 7:30 p.m. in order to

drive her to a concert scheduled to start at 8:00. The concert is an exciting one for her—it involves one of her favourite soloists—and she has been looking forward to it for several weeks. You rush out of your house with just barely enough time to get there, but after driving for a few minutes you discover that you have a flat tire. By the time you change the tire and get to her house, you are already 20 minutes late for the concert. Imagine her response if you (a) casually walk in, grin at her, and say, "Oh well, it probably wouldn't have been an interesting concert anyway. Lighten up; it's not such a big deal. Where's your sense of humour?" or (b) run in with a sad and anguished look on your face, show her your greasy and dirty hands, tell her you left your house in time to make it but unaccountably got this flat tire, apologize sincerely and profusely, and vow to find a way to make it up to her.

Our guess is that your friend would be prone toward aggression in the first instance but not in the second. This guess is supported by the results of several experiments (Baron, 1988, 1990; Ohbuchi & Sato, 1994; Weiner et al., 1987). Typical of these experiments is one by Ohbuchi, Kameda, and Agarie (1989) in which university students performed poorly on a complex task because of errors made by the experimenter's assistant while presenting the materials. In three conditions, the assistant (a) apologized publicly, (b) apologized privately, or (c) did not apologize at all. In a fourth condition, the senior experimenter removed the harm by indicating that he surmised there was an administrative blunder and therefore did not hold the students responsible for their poor performance. The results were clear: The students liked the assistant better and showed far less tendency to aggress against him if he apologized than if he didn't apologize, even if the harm was subsequently removed by the experimenter. Moreover, whether the apology was public or private made little difference; any apology—sincerely given, and in which the perpetrator took full responsibility—proved to be an effective way to reduce aggression.

Thus, one way to reduce aggression is for the individual who caused the frustration to take responsibility for the action, apologize for it, and indicate that it is unlikely to happen again. With this in mind, one of the authors of this book (Elliot Aronson) has occasionally speculated about the great advantages that might be gained by equipping automobiles with "apology" signals. Picture the scene: You are lost in thought as you drive home from an especially interesting social psychology class and suddenly realize that you are supposed to be in the next lane. You turn quickly, and in doing so inadvertently cut off the driver behind you. What happens? In most urban centres, the offended driver will honk his or her horn angrily at you, or open the window and give you that near-universal one-fingered gesture of anger and contempt. Because nobody likes to be the recipient of such abuse, you might be tempted to honk back—and the escalating anger and aggression could be unpleasant. Such escalation might be avoided, though, if in addition to the horn (which throughout the world is most often used as an instrument of aggression), every car were equipped with an apology signal—perhaps, at the push of a button, a little flag could pop up, saying, "Whoops! Sorry!" In the foregoing scenario, had you pushed such a button as soon as you became aware of your transgression, doing so might well have defused the cycle of anger and retaliation that is all too frequently a part of the driving experience. (We might note in passing that companies in various countries are currently in the process of developing written signs or a system of coloured lights that could be used in vehicles to communicate apologies. However, in the United States such devices are currently illegal because of fears that reading such signs could distract drivers from paying attention to the road.)

The Modelling of Nonaggressive Behaviour

We have seen that children will be more aggressive (toward dolls as well as other children) if they witness examples of aggressive behaviour in similar situations. What if we were to turn that inside out and expose children to nonaggressive models—to people who, when provoked, expressed themselves in a restrained, rational, pleasant manner? This has been tested in several experiments (Baron, 1972; Donnerstein & Donnerstein, 1976; Vidyasagar & Mishra, 1993) and found to work. In those experiments, children were first allowed to witness the behaviour of youngsters who behaved nonaggressively when provoked; when the children were subsequently placed in a situation in which they themselves were provoked, they showed a much lower frequency of aggressive responses than did children who were not exposed to the nonaggressive models.

Training in Communication and Problem-Solving Skills

It is impossible to go through life—or, in some circumstances, to get through the day—without experiencing frustration, annoyance, anger, or conflict. As we indicated earlier, there is nothing wrong with anger; it is part of being human. What causes the problem is the expression of anger in violent ways. Yet we are not born with the knowledge of how to express anger or annoyance in constructive, nonviolent, nondisruptive ways. Indeed, as we have seen, it seems almost natural to lash out when we are angry. As Hans Toch (1980) has indicated, in most societies it is precisely the people who lack proper social skills who are most prone to violent solutions to interpersonal problems. Thus, one way to reduce violence is to teach people how to communicate anger or criticism in constructive ways, how to negotiate and compromise when conflicts arise, how to be more sensitive to the needs and desires of others, and so on. There is some evidence that such formal training can be an effective means of reducing aggression (see Studer, 1996).

For example, in an experiment by Joel Davitz (1952), children were allowed to play in groups of four. Some of these groups were taught constructive ways to relate to each other and were rewarded for such behaviour; others were not so instructed but were rewarded for aggressive or competitive behaviour. Next, the youngsters were deliberately frustrated. This was accomplished by building up the expectation that they would be shown a series of entertaining movies and be allowed to have fun. The experimenter began to show a movie and to hand out candy bars, but then he abruptly terminated the movie at the point of highest interest and took the candy bars away. Now the children were allowed to play freely. As you have learned, this was a setup for the occurrence of aggressive behaviour. However, those children who had been trained for constructive behaviour displayed far more constructive activity and far less aggressive behaviour than did those in the other group. A great many elementary and secondary schools are now specifically training students to employ these nonaggressive strategies for resolving conflict (Eargle, Guerra, & Tolan, 1994; Ester, 1995).

Building Empathy

Picture the following scene: A long line of cars is stopped at a traffic light at a busy intersection; the light turns green; the lead car hesitates for 10 seconds.

▲ Mahatma Gandhi was effective in bringing about the independence of India from the British Empire, using and modelling nonviolent resistance. Being nonviolent in the face of violence is difficult, but effective.

What happens? Almost inevitably, there will be an eruption of honking horns. We're talking not about one little jab of the horn (which might be a way of informing the lead car that the light has changed) but about loud and persistent honking. In a controlled experiment, Robert Baron (1976) found that when the lead car failed to move after the light turned green, almost 90 percent of the drivers of the second car honked their horn in a relentless, aggressive manner (see Figure 12.5). As part of the same experiment, a pedestrian crossed the street between the first and second cars while the light was still red and was out of the intersection by the time the light turned green. As you might imagine, this did not have an effect on the behaviour of the drivers of the next car in line—almost 90 percent honked their horn when the light turned green. However, in another condition the pedestrian was on crutches, but managed to hobble across the street before the light turned green. Interestingly, in this condition the percentage of drivers who honked their horn dropped to 57 percent. Why? Apparently, seeing a person on crutches evoked feelings of **empathy**—the ability to put oneself in the shoes of another person and vicariously experience some of the same feelings that person is experiencing. In this instance, once evoked, the feeling of empathy infused the consciousness of the potential horn-honkers and decreased their urge to be aggressive.

Empathy is an important human phenomenon. As Feshbach and Feshbach (1969, 1971, 1978) have observed, most people find it difficult to inflict pain on another human being unless they can find some way to dehumanize their victim. Thus, as we mentioned in Chapter 6, when Canadian soldiers were on a peacekeeping mission to Somalia, they referred to Somalians as "gimmes," "smufties," or "nignogs." We see this as a dehumanizing rationalization for acts of cruelty such as the torture and killing of Shidane Arone; it's easier to commit violent acts against a "gimme" or a "nignog" than against a fellow human being. But as you know, this kind of rationalization not only makes it possible for us to aggress against another person but also guarantees we will *continue* to aggress against him or her. Once we succeed in convincing ourselves that our enemy is not really a human being at all but just a "nignog," it lowers our inhibitions for committing all kinds of atrocities.

Empathy

the ability to put oneself in the shoes of another person—to experience events and emotions (e.g., joy and sadness) the way that person experiences them

---

▶ **Figure 12.5**

THE EFFECT OF EMPATHY ON AGGRESSION.

When we are feeling empathy, in this case brought on by seeing a person on crutches, we are less likely to behave aggressively.

(Adapted from Baron, 1976)

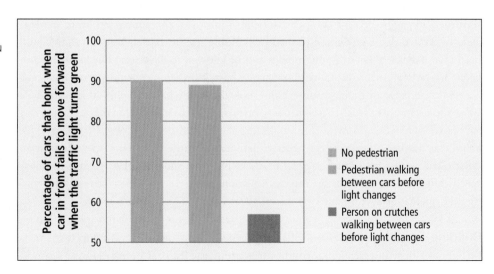

An understanding of the process of dehumanization is the first step toward reversing it. Specifically, if it is true that most individuals must dehumanize their victims in order to commit an extreme act of aggression, then by building empathy among people, aggressive acts will become more difficult to commit. In their groundbreaking research, Feshbach and Feshbach (1969) found a negative correlation between empathy and aggression in children: The more empathy a child has, the less the child resorts to aggressive actions. Deborah Richardson and her colleagues (1994) demonstrated a direct causal link between empathy and aggression, showing that specifically training students to take the perspective of the other person directly inhibited their aggressive behaviour toward that person. In a related vein, Ken-ichi Ohbuchi (1988) had Japanese students deliver electric shocks to another student as part of a learning experiment. In one condition, the victims first disclosed something personal about themselves; in the other condition, they were not afforded this opportunity. Participants administered less severe shocks when the victim disclosed information about himself or herself.

Teaching Empathy in Schools "What would the world look like to you if you were as small as a cat?" "What birthday presents would make each member of your family happiest?" These questions form the basis of exercises designed by Norma Feshbach, who has pioneered the teaching of empathy in elementary schools. Thinking hard about the answers to such questions expands children's ability to put themselves in another's situation. This empathy-building program also involves role playing, analyzing videotapes to learn how people look and sound when they express different feelings, and so on. Not only do children learn empathy, but this program also has several positive "side effects." At the end of the program, children show higher self-esteem, higher academic achievement, and lower aggression compared to those who have not participated in it (Feshbach, 1989, 1997; Feshbach & Cohen, 1988).

SUMMARY

We define **aggression** as intentional behaviour aimed at doing harm or causing physical or psychological pain to another person. **Hostile aggression** involves having the goal of inflicting pain; **instrumental aggression** involves inflicting pain on the way to some other goal.

Over the centuries, there has been a great deal of disagreement among scholars over whether aggressiveness is primarily instinctive or learned. Sigmund Freud theorized that human beings are born with an instinct toward life, called **Eros**, and a death instinct, **Thanatos**, which leads to aggressive actions. In Freud's view, aggressive energy must be released to avoid buildup that might result in an explosion.

Because aggressiveness has had survival value, most contemporary social psychologists accept the proposition

that it is part of our evolutionary heritage. At the same time, we know that human beings have developed exquisite mechanisms for controlling their aggressive impulses and that human behaviour is flexible and adaptable to changes in the environment. Thus, whether aggression is actually expressed depends on a complex interplay between our biological propensities and the social situation in which we find ourselves.

There are many causes of aggression, ranging from the neurological and chemical to the social. The area in the core of the brain called the **amygdala** is thought to control aggression. It is reasonably clear that the hormone **testosterone** is correlated with aggressive behaviour—for example, prisoners convicted of violent crimes tend to have higher levels of testosterone than do those convicted

CHAPTER 13

Prejudice
causes and cures

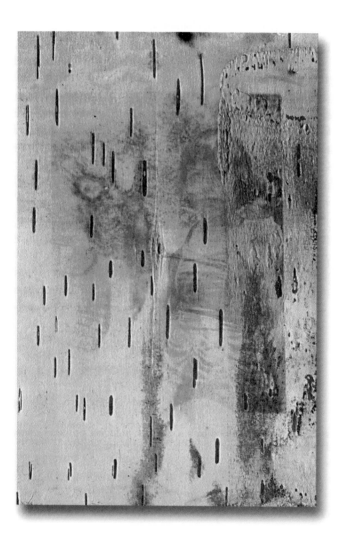

Chapter Outline

Meet Mary Young, the Native Student Adviser at the University of Winnipeg. Mary grew up in Bloodvein First Nation, an Ojibway community in northern Manitoba. When she was growing up, Mary understood that she was a treaty Indian according to the Indian Act, but being an Indian was not part of her identity. She thought of herself as Anishinabe, and she was comfortable with that identity. At the age of 14, she moved to Winnipeg with the dream of being the first person from Bloodvein to graduate from high school. With that move came the startling discovery that the other students thought of her as Indian. Moreover, *Indian* was not a neutral term—it was saturated with negative connotations. Thus, Mary was forced to adopt a new identity (or at least to have a new identity imposed on her), and also learned quickly that this new identity meant she was less acceptable, less deserving, and less worthy than the white students attending her high school.

In reflecting on these experiences, Mary comments, "When I left home at the age of fourteen . . . my goal was to finish high school. I never expected that I would have difficulty with my identity, my cultural background, nor did I think I was going to allow myself to feel ashamed of my family, including my own shame of being an 'Indian.'" In reflecting on this life-shattering experience, Mary wrote the following poem:

AFRAID

I heard
"The Only Good Indian
Is a Dead Indian"
I never heard that on
The reserve
I was fine before I
Came to the city
What is wrong with me
Now?

I have no answer
All I know is that
I am afraid of making
A mistake
I am afraid if I succeed
It will not make any
Difference.

There was a time
Laughing at myself
Came easily
Now all I feel is
Shame
I am afraid to open
My mouth
I know that I am not dead
Does this mean
I am no good?

▲ Mary Young felt the impact of racism in her life when she moved from her First Nations community to Winnipeg to attend high school.

I must be no good
Because I feel ugly
I hate being Indian
Why was I born on the
Reserve anyway?

There is nothing I can do
To change that
I can't change who I am
I'm afraid I am
Not prepared to die
Just yet
So I have to try
Harder
"To Be a Good Indian."

Of all the social behaviours we discuss in this book, prejudice is perhaps the most widespread and certainly among the most dangerous. Prejudice touches nearly everyone's life. We are all victims or potential victims of stereotyping and discrimination, for no other reason than our membership in an identifiable group—whether it be ethnic, religious, gender, national origin, sexual preference, obesity, or disability. However, some people are more strongly victimized than others. People who are members of visible minorities report the greatest degree of prejudice and discrimination, and if they are of a minority status in more than one way, they are especially likely to be discriminated against. For example, black immigrants to Canada experience more prejudice and discrimination than do white immigrants, and this experience is compounded for a black person who is Muslim or is female (Dion, 2001; Dion & Dion, 2001). Similarly, researchers at York University found that women of colour feel that both gender and racial stereotypes are applied to them (Patterson, Cameron & Lalonde, 1996).

Granted, many manifestations of prejudice are less frequent and less flagrant than they used to be. However, as the story of Mary Young illustrates, prejudice continues to exact a heavy toll on its victims. In this chapter, we will examine prejudice as a social psychological phenomenon. We will focus on two fundamental questions: "What causes prejudice?" and "How can prejudice be reduced?"

Prejudice: The Ubiquitous Social Phenomenon

The story of Mary Young illustrates that minority groups are often targets of prejudice at the hands of the dominant majority. Needless to say, this aspect of prejudice is extremely powerful and poignant. However, the truth is that prejudice is ubiquitous; in one form or another, it affects all of us. For one thing, prejudice is a two-way street; it frequently flows from the minority group to the majority group, as well as from the majority to the minority. In addition, any group can be a target of prejudice. Let us take one of the most superordinate groups to which you belong—your nationality. Canadians are often stereotyped as the nice, dull, boring "country cousins" of their more adventurous, exciting counterparts to the south (i.e., Americans). Even worse, some nations view Canada as hypocritical—

calling other countries to task on unfair treatment of minority groups while First Nations people in Canada live in poverty.

Your nationality is only one of a number of aspects of your identity that can cause you to be labelled and discriminated against. Racial and ethnic identity is a major focal point for prejudiced attitudes. Canada, for example, views itself as a country that embraces multiculturalism; a country that appreciates the diversity that different racial and ethnic groups contribute to its social fabric. However, all you have to do is ask Canadians about their attitudes toward Aboriginals, Pakistanis, East Asians, or Sihks, and it quickly becomes apparent that diversity is not always celebrated, or even tolerated (Esses & Gardner, 1996; Pruegger & Rogers, 1993). (The Try It! box below raises some interesting issues about the merits of multiculturalism.) In fact, groups such as these are common targets of prejudice. Even particular subgroups of white Canadians are subjected to prejudice, as witnessed by the long-standing popularity of "Newfie" jokes, the tensions between anglophones and francophones in Quebec, and "centre of the universe" comments about Torontonians.

Other aspects of your identity also leave you vulnerable to prejudice—for example, your gender, your sexual preference, and your religion. Your appearance or physical state can arouse prejudice as well; obesity, disabilities, and diseases such as AIDS, for instance, cause people to be perceived negatively by others. Even the labels used to refer to people can invoke prejudice. For example, at the University of Toronto, Kenneth Dion and colleagues have been conducting research on the "Ms." stereotype (see Dion, 1999). In one of their studies (Dion & Schuller, 1991), visitors to the Ontario Science Centre were given a description of a 23-year-old woman. Those who read that she preferred the title "Ms."

 **Multiculturalism: Is It Working?**

In a country such as the United States, members of different nationalities or ethnic groups are expected to assimilate to the majority. The image is one of a "melting pot," as opposed to the image of the "cultural mosaic" often used to describe Canada. In Canada, cultural groups are encouraged to maintain their values and customs while participating in Canadian society. (Canada formally passed a Multiculturalism Act in 1987.) Slogans such as "celebrating differences" reflect our country's multicultural orientation. Recently, some social psychologists have begun to question the merits of this approach. As you may recall from Chapter 10, similarity is one of the best predictors of attraction and liking. Might it actually be counterproductive for intercultural relations to emphasize differences between groups? A recent study of English Canadians, French Canadians, Jews, Indians, Algerians, and Greeks living in Montreal found that the more similar the respondents perceived a group to be to their own group, the greater their willingness to associate with members of that group (Osbeck, Moghaddam, and Perreault, 1997).

These findings raise some intriguing questions (which you may want to discuss with a friend):

1. What are the implications of these findings for Canada's policy of multiculturalism?

2. Is it actually possible to "celebrate differences"?

3. Are there ways in which basic similarities between groups could be highlighted, while allowing for an appreciation of differences?

rated her more negatively (i.e., perceived her as less likeable) than those who read that she preferred a traditional form of address (Miss or Mrs.). And when it comes to racial prejudice, Donakowski and Esses (1996) found that non-Native Canadians expressed more negative attitudes toward Canada's Native peoples when they were referred to as "Native Canadians" or "First Nations people" than when they were referred to as "Aboriginal peoples," "Native Indians," or "Native peoples."

Finally, even your profession or hobbies can lead to your being stereotyped. We are all familiar with the "dumb jock" and "computer nerd" stereotypes. Some people have negative attitudes about blue-collar workers; others, about "MBA types." In fact, Kenneth Dion (1985) found that students at the University of Toronto reported greater prejudice toward people with low-status occupations than they did toward people of a different race or nationality. However, even high-status occupations can be the target of stereotyping and prejudice, as witnessed by the popularity of lawyer jokes (Olson, Maio, & Hobden, 1999). The point is that none of us emerges completely unscathed from the effects of prejudice; it is a problem of and for all humankind.

In addition to being widespread, prejudice is dangerous. Simple dislike of a group can be relentless and can lead to extreme hatred, to thinking of its members as less than human, and to behaviour such as torture, murder, and genocide. However, even when murder or genocide is not the culmination of prejudiced beliefs, the targets of prejudice will suffer in less dramatic ways. In a classic experiment conducted in the United States in the late 1940s, social psychologists Kenneth Clark and Mamie Clark (1947) demonstrated that African-American children—some of them only three years old—were already convinced that it was not particularly desirable to be black. In this experiment, the children were offered a choice between playing with a white doll or a black doll. The great majority of them rejected the black doll, feeling that the white doll was prettier and generally superior.

You may be thinking, "But that was more than 50 years ago and it took place in the United States. Surely these findings are no longer relevant, and surely they wouldn't apply to Canada!" As it turns out, all you have to do is substitute "Native Canadian" for "African American." For example, Corenblum and Annis (1993) presented white and

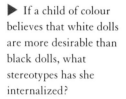

▶ If a child of colour believes that white dolls are more desirable than black dolls, what stereotypes has she internalized?

Native children attending schools in Brandon, Manitoba, with drawings of white and Native boys and girls. When asked which child they would like to play with, Native children were slightly more likely to choose a white child than a Native child. (White children overwhelmingly chose the white child.) Native children also attributed more positive qualities (e.g., friendliness) to a white child than to a Native child. Conversely, they attributed more negative qualities to a Native child (e.g., is bad, gets into fights) than to a white child.

We should note that significant changes have taken place over the past 50 years or so. For example, African-American children have gradually become more content with black dolls than they were in 1947 (Porter, 1971; Porter & Washington, 1979, 1989; Gopaul-McNicol, 1987), and people are less prejudiced toward homosexuals than they used to be (Altemeyer, 2001). However, it would be a mistake to conclude that prejudice has ceased to be a serious problem. One need only be reminded that the research on Native and white children by Corenblum and Annis (1993; Corenblum, Annis, & Young, 1996) was conducted as recently as the 1990s. Yes, prejudice continues to exist, and it does so in countless subtle and not-so-subtle ways.

During the past half-century, social psychologists have contributed greatly to our understanding of the psychological processes underlying prejudice and have begun to identify and demonstrate some possible solutions. What is prejudice? How does it come about? How can it be reduced?

Prejudice, Stereotyping, and Discrimination Defined

Prejudice is an attitude toward a group of people. Attitudes, as discussed in Chapter 7, are made up of three components: an affective or emotional component, representing the type of emotion linked with the attitude (e.g., anger, warmth); a cognitive component, involving the beliefs or thoughts (cognitions) that make up the attitude; and a behavioural component, relating to one's actions—people don't simply hold attitudes; they usually act on them as well.

PREJUDICE: THE AFFECTIVE COMPONENT

The term *prejudice* refers to the general attitude structure and its affective (emotional) component. Though prejudice can involve either positive or negative affect, social psychologists (and people in general) reserve the word *prejudice* for use only when it refers to negative attitudes about others. Specifically, **prejudice** is defined as a hostile or negative attitude toward people in a distinguishable group, based solely on their membership in that group. For example, when we say that an individual is prejudiced against Natives, we mean that he or she feels hostility or disliking toward Native people as a whole.

Prejudice
a hostile or negative attitude toward a distinguishable group of people, based solely on their membership in that group

STEREOTYPES: THE COGNITIVE COMPONENT

Close your eyes for a moment and imagine the appearance and characteristics of the following people: a cheerleader, a Pakistani cabdriver, a Jewish doctor, a black musician. Our guess is that this task was not difficult. We all walk around with images of various "types"

▶ Our attitudes tend to organize the way we process information about the targets of those attitudes.

"It's a cat calendar, so it may not be all that accurate."

Ziegler © 1994 from the New Yorker Collection. All rights reserved.

of people in our heads. The distinguished journalist Walter Lippmann (1922), who was the first to introduce the term *stereotype,* described the distinction between the world out there and stereotypes—"the little pictures we carry around inside our heads." Within a given culture, these pictures tend to be remarkably similar. For example, we would be surprised if your image of the cheerleader was anything but bouncy, full of pep, pretty, nonintellectual, and (of course!) female. We would also be surprised if the Jewish doctor or the Pakistani cabdriver in your head were female—or if the black musician was playing classical music.

It goes without saying that there are male cheerleaders, female doctors, and black classical musicians. Deep down, we know that cabdrivers come in every size, shape, race, and gender. However, we tend to categorize according to what we regard as normative within a culture. In this sense, one can think of a stereotype as a particular kind of schema (see Chapter 3). Stereotyping, however, goes a step beyond simple categorization. A **stereotype** is a generalization about a group of people in which identical characteristics are assigned to virtually all members of the group, regardless of actual variation among the members. Once formed, stereotypes are resistant to change on the basis of new information.

It is important to point out that stereotyping is not necessarily emotional and does not necessarily lead to intentional acts of abuse. Frequently, stereotyping is merely a way to simplify how we look at the world—and we all do it to some extent. For example, Gordon Allport (1954) described stereotyping as "the law of least effort." According to Allport, the world is simply too complicated for us to have a highly differentiated attitude about everything. Instead, we maximize our cognitive time and energy by developing elegant, accurate attitudes about some topics, while relying on simple, sketchy beliefs for others. (This should remind you of the discussion of schemas in Chapter 3.) Given our limited information-processing capacity, it is reasonable for us to take shortcuts and adopt certain rules of thumb in our attempt to understand other people (Fiske, 1989b; Fiske & Depret, 1996; Taylor, 1981; Taylor & Falcone, 1982). To the extent that the resulting stereotype is based on experience and is at all accurate, it can be an adaptive, shorthand way of dealing

Stereotype

a generalization about a group of people in which identical characteristics are assigned to virtually all members of the group, regardless of actual variation among the members

with complex events. On the other hand, if the stereotype blinds us to individual differences within a class of people, it is maladaptive, unfair, and can lead to discrimination. For one insight into where stereotypes might come from, see Try It! on page 474.

DISCRIMINATION: THE BEHAVIOURAL COMPONENT

This brings us to the final component of prejudice—the action component. Stereotypic beliefs often result in unfair treatment. We call this **discrimination**, defined as unjustified negative or harmful action toward the members of a group, simply because of their membership in that group. If you are an elementary school math teacher and you have the stereotypic belief that girls are hopeless at math, you might be less likely to spend as much time in the classroom coaching a girl than you would a boy. If you are a police officer and you have the stereotypic belief that blacks are more violent than whites, this might affect your behaviour toward a specific black man you are trying to arrest.

In one study, Charles Bond and his colleagues (1988) compared the treatment of patients in a psychiatric hospital run by an all-white professional staff. The researchers examined the two most common methods used by staff members to handle patients' violent behaviour: (a) secluding the individual in a time-out room, and (b) restraining the individual in a straitjacket and administering tranquilizing drugs. An examination of hospital records over 85 days revealed that the harsher method—physical and chemical restraint—was used against black patients nearly four times as often as it was against white patients (see left side of Figure 13.1). This was the case despite the virtual lack of differences in the number of violent incidents committed by the black and the white patients. Moreover, this discriminatory treatment occurred even though the black patients, on being admitted to the hospital, had been diagnosed as slightly less violent than the white patients.

This study did uncover an important positive finding. After several weeks, reality managed to overcome the effects of the existing stereotype. The staff eventually noticed that the black and the white patients did not differ in their degree of violent behaviour,

Discrimination

unjustified negative or harmful action toward a member of a group, simply because of his or her membership in that group

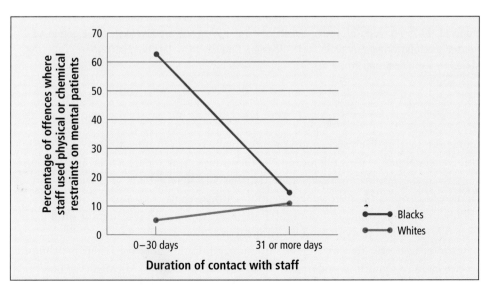

◀ Figure 13.1

USE OF EXTREME MEASURES AGAINST BLACK MENTAL PATIENTS.

During the first 30 days of confinement, there appeared to be an assumption that blacks would be more violent than whites.

(Adapted from Bond, DiCandia, & McKinnon, 1988)

Stereotype Content: Where Does It Come from?

Have you ever wondered where stereotypes come from? Who decides whether positive or negative characteristics apply to a given group? And who decides which particular positive or negative characteristics apply? These are questions that have been addressed in a program of research conducted at the University of British Columbia by Mark Schaller and his colleagues (Schaller & Conway, 1999, 2001; Schaller, Conway, & Tanchuk, 2002; Schaller & O'Brien, 1992). According to these researchers, the traits or characteristics of a group that other people are most likely to talk about are the traits that become part of the stereotype of that group. Moreover, the more these traits are talked about, the more likely it is they will remain part of that group's stereotype over time. In short, it is the traits that have the highest communicability, or "gossip" value, that will become part of the stereotype of a particular group. You may wish to test this hypothesis yourself or with a group of friends. First, list the traits or characteristics you would be most likely to mention if you were talking about the following groups:

- White Canadians (more specifically, white Canadians living in Vancouver)

- Chinese

- East Indian

- First Nations

Now, check whether any of the traits you (or your friends) mentioned are part of the following stereotypes of these groups (as identified by a multicultural group of students at the University of British Columbia; Schaller, Conway III, & Tanchuk, 2002):

- White Canadians: athletic, individualistic, pleasure-loving, straightforward, sportsmanlike

- Chinese: ambitious, loyal to family ties, intelligent, efficient, conservative

- East Indian: very religious, tradition-loving, aggressive, loyal to family ties, physically dirty

- First Nations: poor, physically dirty, lazy, tradition-loving, superstitious

Schaller and colleagues' research suggests that the traits you and others would be most likely to mention would be traits that are part of the stereotype of that group. These researchers also found that positive traits are more likely to become part of the stereotype of the largest groups in a society (in Vancouver, white Canadians, followed by Chinese people), whereas negative traits were more likely to become part of the stereotype of smaller groups (First Nations people). To make matters even worse, they found that negative traits were more likely than positive traits to persist over time. In other words, once a negative trait becomes part of a stereotype of a group, it becomes very difficult to shed it.

Schaller and colleagues conclude that, "In a sense, traits are like viruses: Those that are more highly communicable are more likely to infect the stereotypic beliefs of a population and are less likely to be gotten rid of" (Schaller, Conway III, & Tanchuk, 2002).

and began to treat black and white patients equally (see right side of Figure 13.1). While this is encouraging, the overall meaning of the study is clear and disconcerting: The existing stereotype resulted in undeserved, harsher initial treatment of black patients by trained professionals. At the same time, the fact that reality overcame the stereotype is a tribute to the professionalism of the staff, because, as we shall see, in most cases deeply rooted prejudice, stereotypes, and discrimination are not easy to change.

Closer to home, Stewart Page has examined discriminatory behaviour by landlords in two cities in Ontario (London and Windsor) and in Detroit, Michigan. In one study

(Page, 1998) a caller inquiring about accommodation that had been advertised in a local paper identified himself or herself as homosexual ("I guess it's only fair to tell you that I'm a gay person [or lesbian]") or did not mention his or her sexual orientation. Landlords were more likely to claim that the accommodation was unavailable when the caller claimed to be homosexual than when no mention was made of his or her sexual orientation. In a subsequent study, Page (1999) found that landlords were five times more likely to say that the accommodation was unavailable when the caller mentioned that she or he had AIDS.

What Causes Prejudice?

What makes people prejudiced? Is it "natural" or "unnatural"? Evolutionary psychologists have suggested, as noted in Chapter 11, that animals have a strong tendency to feel more favourably toward genetically similar others and to express fear and loathing toward genetically dissimilar organisms, even if the latter have never done them any harm (Buss & Kenrick, 1998; Rushton, 1989; Trivers, 1985). Thus, prejudice might be built in—an essential part of our biological survival mechanism inducing us to favour our own family, tribe, or race, and to express hostility toward outsiders. On the other hand, it is conceivable that, as humans, we are different from the lower animals; perhaps our natural inclination is to be friendly, open, and cooperative. If this were the case, then prejudice would not come naturally. Rather, the culture (parents, community, media) might, intentionally or unintentionally, instruct us to assign negative qualities and attributes to people who are different from us.

No one knows for sure whether prejudice is a vital and necessary part of our biological makeup. However, most social psychologists would agree that the specifics of prejudice must be learned. How easy is it to learn prejudice? At the University of Waterloo, Meg Rohan and Mark Zanna (1996) took a close look at the folk wisdom that "the apple never falls far from the tree," by examining attitude and value similarity between parents and their adult children. They found that similarity was significantly stronger between children and parents when parents held egalitarian attitudes and values than when parents held prejudice-related attitudes and values. Our guess is that this discrepancy takes place because the culture as a whole is more egalitarian than the bigoted parents. Thus, when children of bigoted parents leave home (e.g., to go off to university), they are more likely to be exposed to competing views.

THE WAY WE THINK: SOCIAL COGNITION

Our first explanation for what causes prejudice is that it is the inevitable by-product of the way we process and organize information—in other words, it is the dark side of human social cognition (as discussed in Chapter 3). Our tendency to categorize and group information together, to form schemas and to use these to interpret new or unusual information, to rely on potentially inaccurate heuristics (shortcuts in mental reasoning), and to depend on what are often faulty memory processes—all of these aspects of social cognition can lead us to form negative stereotypes and to apply them in a discriminatory fashion. Let's examine this dark side of social cognition more closely.

None of us is a 100-percent-reliable accountant when it comes to processing social information we care about; the way the human mind works, we simply do not tally events objectively. Accordingly, individuals who hold specific schemas (stereotypes) about certain groups will process information about those groups differently from the way they process information about other groups. Specifically, information consistent with their notions about these target groups will be given more attention, will be rehearsed (or recalled) more often, and therefore will be remembered better than information that is not consistent with these notions (Bodenhausen, 1988; Bodenhausen & Lichtenstein, 1987; Dovidio, Evans, & Tyler, 1986; Wyer, 1988). These are the familiar effects of *schematic processing* we discussed in Chapter 3.

Information relevant to a particular schema will also be processed more quickly than information unrelated to it. For example, Gardner, MacIntyre, and Lalonde (1995) asked English-speaking students in Quebec to rate the characteristics of various groups (e.g., English Canadians, French Canadians, males, females). Participants were faster when rating the stereotypical characteristics of each group than when rating its non-stereotypical characteristics. For example, when the target group was males, characteristics such as *rugged, impatient,* and *talkative* were rated more quickly than characteristics such as *irreligious, artistic,* and *impolite.*

▼ This cartoon depicts a common stereotype of the Mexican as lazy. Note how your eye focuses on the one sleeping person but tends to ignore the 10 hardworking people. Without intending to, the cartoonist is showing us how powerfully distorting a stereotype can be.

We also tend to "fill in the blanks" with schema-consistent information. In a study by Kunda, Sinclair, and Griffin (1997), students at the University of Waterloo were told that Michael was either a salesperson or an actor, and that his friends described him as very extroverted. They were then asked, "What kinds of behaviours do you suppose they have in mind when they describe him this way?" The researchers found that when told that Michael was a salesperson, participants generated pushy descriptions (e.g., "loud speaking," "monopolized conversation"), whereas when Michael was described as an actor, they generated descriptions such as "life of the party" and "not afraid of the spotlight." In another study by these researchers, participants read about John the lawyer versus John the construction worker, and were asked to generate aggressive behaviour that John might perform. John the lawyer was seen as more likely to argue, whereas John the construction worker was seen as more likely to punch and fight (Kunda, Sinclair, & Griffin, 1997). In other words, given a stereotype label, we fill in the blanks with all kinds of stereotype-consistent information.

Schemas also are highly resistant to change—even in the face of contradictory evidence. This tendency was evident in a study by Taylor and Gardner (1969). Anglophone students listened to a tape recording in which a French-Canadian speaker described himself in ways that were either consistent or inconsistent with English Canadians' stereotype of French Canadians as religious, emotional, talkative, sensitive, and proud. Even if the speaker completely contradicted the stereotype, he was still perceived in stereotypical terms (although less so than when he confirmed the stereotype).

Indeed, it appears that we have a remarkable ability to explain away disconfirming evidence and thereby maintain our stereotypes, as illustrated by the 1951 cartoon (left). While 10 Mexicans are seen in the background working hard, the cartoon focuses on the stereotypical image in the foreground. The cartoon's message is that the lazy individual is the true exemplar of his ethnic group. No matter how many others refute the stereotype, the cartoon is implying, it is still true. (Note that half a century ago, not only was this message considered acceptable, but the cartoon was chosen as one of the best of the year.)

Alan @ 1951 The New Yorker: 25th Annual Album, Harper & Bros

Indeed, research shows that we are quite good at dismissing evidence that might disconfirm our stereotypes. In a study by William Ickes and his colleagues (1982), male university students were led to expect that the person with whom they would be interacting was either friendly or extremely unfriendly. During the interaction, the person behaved in a friendly manner. How was his behaviour interpreted? Those who expected him to be unfriendly interpreted his friendly behaviour as phony—as a temporary, fake response to their own nice behaviour. They were convinced that underneath it all, he really was an unfriendly person. Thus, even behaviour that completely contradicts the stereotype of a group can be reinterpreted in ways that leave our stereotypes intact.

Sometimes, the person we encounter may be so contrary to our stereotype that it is impossible to interpret the person's behaviour in stereotype-consistent terms. What do we do then? According to Ziva Kunda and Kathryn Oleson (1995, 1997), we may simply create a new "subtype" for this deviant member, particularly if we are able to come up with some justification for doing so. For example, in one study, the researchers presented University of Waterloo students with a description of a monogamous homosexual man—thereby contradicting their stereotype of homosexuals as promiscuous. Some participants were given additional, neutral information—namely, that the man was an accountant. The researchers found that this irrelevant information was used as grounds for creating a new subtype, thereby leaving the original stereotype intact. In effect, these participants were saying, "Gay men, in general, are promiscuous. The one exception is gay men who are accountants." Participants who were not provided with this additional information (i.e., about the man's occupation) had little basis on which to create an exception to the rule. Thus, when faced with someone who contradicted their stereotype, these participants were more likely to change their stereotype of homosexuals as promiscuous. In short, one way of hanging on to our stereotype of a group, even when we encounter someone who contradicts the stereotype, is to create a new subcategory of exceptions to the rule.

Sadly, members of stereotyped groups seem to be aware of this tendency, and it places them in a "no win" situation. Consider, for example, the remarks of Sajjad, a student who was interviewed as part of a study on discrimination experienced by Muslim students in Canadian schools (Zine, 2001). Sajjad moved to Canada from Guyana when he was seven years old, and by junior high school he was all too aware that stereotypes are virtually impossible to overcome. In his words, "I'd given up a long time ago trying to impress other people, or trying to prove to other people that I'm a good black person, or I'm a good Indian person. . . . Even if I were to be a good person . . . they have a certain image of coloured people, so it's like, 'Well all coloured people are bad, but he's a good one . . . he's an exception.' "

Social Categorization: Us versus Them We make sense out of the physical world by grouping animals and plants into taxonomies; we make sense out of our social world by grouping people by gender, nationality, and ethnicity (Brewer & Brown, 1998; Rosch & Lloyd, 1978; Taylor, 1981). However, this simple cognitive process has profound implications because the process of classifying people into groups is rarely a neutral one. According to social identity theory (Tajfel, 1982a, 1982b; Turner et al., 1987), other people are seen as either belonging to our group (known as the *in-group*) or to a different group (known as the *out-group*). And, it probably comes as no surprise that we tend to evaluate people in the in-group more positively than those in the out-group.

For example, when researchers at Queen's University assessed the attitudes of more than 3000 Canadians toward 14 different ethnic groups, a clear finding was that participants assigned the most favourable ratings to their own ethnic group (Kalin & Berry, 1996). Believe it or not, we even think that people who look good must be members of our own group! Ronald Johnson (1981), at St. Francis Xavier University, showed supporters of three political parties (Liberal, Progressive Conservative, and the New Democratic Party) photos of people varying in attractiveness and asked them to predict which party these people supported. Members of the Liberal and Progressive Conservative parties (but not the NDP) assumed that the best-looking people were members of their own party, and that the worst-looking people supported one of the other parties!

Unfortunately, the tendency to denigrate out-group members extends well beyond judgments of physical attractiveness. There is considerable evidence that out-group members are often seen as possessing negative traits and are often disliked. Lalonde, Moghaddam, and Taylor (1987) found evidence of this among fans at home games of the McGill University hockey team. The fans rated the opposing teams higher in negative characteristics such as arrogance and aggressiveness than they did their own team. In fact, as each game progressed, the ratings of the two teams increasingly diverged.

This tendency to favour the in-group while denigrating the out-group is so pervasive that people show this bias even under the most minimal conditions. Such effects have been demonstrated by British social psychologist Henri Tajfel and his colleagues, who have created entities they refer to as minimal groups (Tajfel, 1982a, 1982b; Tajfel & Billig, 1974; Tajfel & Turner, 1979). In these experiments, complete strangers are formed into groups using the most trivial criteria imaginable. For example, in one experiment participants watched a coin toss that randomly assigned them to either group *X* or group *W*. In another experiment, participants were first asked to express their opinions about artists they had never heard of and were then randomly assigned to a group that appreciated either the "Klee style" or the "Kandinsky style," ostensibly due to their picture preferences. The striking thing about the Tajfel research is that despite the fact that the participants were strangers prior to the experiment and didn't interact with one another during it, they behaved as if those who shared the same meaningless label were their dear friends or close kin. They liked the members of their own group better; they rated the members of their in-group as more likely than out-group members to have pleasant personalities and to have done better work. Most striking, the participants allocated more money and other rewards to those who shared their label, and did so in a rather hostile, cutthroat manner—that is, when given a clear choice, they preferred to give themselves only $2 if it meant giving the out-group person $1, rather than give themselves $3 if that meant the out-group member received $4 (Brewer, 1979; Hogg & Abrams, 1988; Oakes & Turner, 1980; Mullen, Brown, & Smith, 1992; Reichl, 1997).

According to research conducted with French-speaking Acadians in New Brunswick, the tendency to discriminate against the out-group is even stronger when people have chosen their group rather than have been randomly assigned to it (Perreault & Bourhis, 1999)

Finally, recent research conducted at the University of Alberta shows that an "in-group" can be created simply by photographing people together (Burgess, Enzle, & Morry, 2000). More specifically, these researchers found that pairs of strangers who were

▲ Wearing our school colours is a way of demonstrating that we are members of the in-group.

photographed together were more likely to like one another and to use terms such as "we" and "us" than pairs of strangers who sat next to each other but were not photographed together. (Note that taking a picture of each person separately did not produce this "we" feeling.) Thus, feelings of "us" and "them" can be created under truly minimal conditions.

Why Do We Show the In-group Bias? Why do we show this tendency to favour the in-group and discriminate against the out-group even when group membership is based on something as trivial as the toss of a coin or having a joint photo taken? There is a two-part answer to this question. The first part is that belonging to a group gives us a social identity. The second part is that having a social identity, in turn, contributes to feelings of self-esteem. By perceiving members of our group as possessing positive qualities and members of out-groups as possessing negative qualities, we can boost our own group and our identification with it. And that makes us feel good.

- **Social identity benefits.** If it is true that belonging to a group provides us with a social identity, we would expect that individuals who strongly identify with a group will be more likely to discriminate against an out-group than individuals who only weakly identify with their group. That is exactly what was found in a study by Gagnon and Bourhis (1996). In the study, French-Canadian university students were told they would be making decisions about how to allocate 5 percentage points to be added to other participants' psychology grades. They also were given information that they belonged to Group K or Group W (based on a coin toss). As predicted, those who identified most strongly with their group discriminated most against the other group when awarding grade points. Moreover, the more these participants discriminated, the more they liked being a member of their group.

  Similar findings were obtained in a recent "real-world" study by Serge Guimond (2000). He assessed the attitudes of prospective Canadian military officers at the beginning and the end of a four-year officer training program. He found that the more strongly the majority group (anglophones) identified with the military, the more negative they became in their attitudes toward out-groups (francophones, civilians, and immigrants to Canada). Why would identification with the military be associated with negative attitudes toward out-groups? Guimond suggests that the military reinforces dominant societal attitudes about the superiority of particular groups.

  One implication of findings such as these is that if a person's sense of social identity is threatened, that person might be especially likely to discriminate against an out-group. This prediction was tested in a series of studies by Peter Grant (1992, 1993). Students at the University of Saskatchewan who cared about either a "women's issue" (e.g., women should be encouraged to apply for high-status jobs) or a "men's issue" (e.g., men's roles have become confusing and unclear) discussed these topics in same-sex groups. They were told that later they would also exchange ideas with an opposite-sex group. Before doing so, those in the high-threat condition were informed that the opposite-sex group couldn't care less about their issue and didn't see a need for change in that area. Participants in the low-threat condition were told that the other group thought the issue was important and had come up with some strategies for change. As expected, participants whose identities were threatened (i.e., those who were told the other group didn't care about their issue) rated the other group more negatively than did those whose identities were not threatened.

Similar processes may at least partly account for Native Canadians' prejudice against white Canadians. In a recent study, Corenblum and Stephan (2001) found that the more Canada's Native people identified with their own group, the more likely they were to perceive white people as threatening their values and beliefs. These feelings of threat, in turn, predicted prejudice toward whites.

- **Self-esteem benefits.** Clearly, there is evidence that dividing the world into "us" and "them" gives us a sense of social identity. Why is this important? As we mentioned earlier, it gives people a self-esteem boost if they believe that their group is superior and that other groups are inferior. Evidence of this was found in a study conducted by Louise Lemyre and Phillip Smith (1985). Participants were University of British Columbia students who were simply told that they were in the "red" group or the "blue" group. Some participants were then given an opportunity to discriminate against the out-group (by giving them fewer points), whereas others were not. Those who discriminated against the out-group showed higher self-esteem than did those who were not given the chance to discriminate. We should note that in this study there also was a condition in which participants were not assigned to any group but were allowed to discriminate against one of the groups. These participants did not show an increase in self-esteem. Thus, discriminating against others improves our self-esteem only when our social identity is involved.

  As you might expect, when people's self-esteem is threatened, they are especially likely to denigrate the out-group as a means of restoring their self-esteem. This was demonstrated in a study at the University of Waterloo by Meindl and Lerner (1984). These researchers threatened the self-esteem of some their participants (English-speaking Canadians) by making them feel responsible for an accident in the laboratory. (Other participants were not made to feel responsible for the accident.) Feelings of group identification were manipulated by asking participants to rate various issues related to Quebec either "as a member of the English-speaking majority in Canada" or as "an individual." Participants who experienced a threat to their self-esteem rated French Canadians more negatively on a variety of traits (e.g., aggressiveness) than those whose self-esteem had not been threatened, especially if their identity as an English-speaking Canadian had been made salient.

Given findings such as these, it is sad, but not surprising, that people categorize others as "us" and "them." Doing so provides us with important social identity and self-esteem benefits.

Is there a way to minimize such effects? One way might be to foster feelings of a common identity between groups. Research by Richard Clément and colleagues (Clément, Noels, & Deneault, 2001; Noels & Clément, 1996) is interesting in this regard. They conducted a series of studies with francophone and anglophone students at the University of Ottawa and found that competence in the other group's language promoted feelings of identity with that group. This was true for both French-speaking anglophones and English-speaking francophones. The researchers suggest that, at a very basic level, speaking the same language can help blur the distinction between "us" and "them." The down side of these findings was that the anglophones who showed stronger identification with francophones still retained their own identity (presumably because they were the majority group). However, among francophones (the minority group), increased identification with anglophones was associated with decreased identification with their own group. Thus, for those in a minority position, it may feel as though the only way to minimize the distinction between "us" and "them" is to become one of "them." (Later, in our discussion of social dominance orientation, we will describe other ways of creating common or shared identities between groups).

Another avenue for minimizing discrimination against out-groups is to provide people with alternative routes to self-esteem. A study by Fein and Spencer (1997) suggests that this may be a particularly effective means of reducing discrimination. Based on self-affirmation theory (see Chapter 6), these researchers predicted that if people were affirmed in some way, they would be less likely to need to boost their self-esteem by derogating out-group members. Participants in the self-affirmation condition were asked to write down why certain values were important to them; other participants did not engage in this self-affirmation exercise. Next, all participants saw a video of a woman who was portrayed as Jewish (a group that was negatively stereotyped by the participants). Those who had not been affirmed rated the woman more negatively than did those in the self-affirmation condition. These findings suggest that if we can find some other domain in which to give our self-esteem a boost, we are less likely to need to derogate others in order to feel good about ourselves.

Out-Group Homogeneity. Aside from the in-group bias, there is another consequence of social categorization: the perception of out-group homogeneity (Linville, Fischer, & Salovey, 1989; Quattrone, 1986). In-group members tend to perceive those in the out-group as being more similar to each other (homogeneous) than they really are, as well as more homogeneous than the in-group members. In short, "they" are all alike. George Quattrone and Edward E. Jones (1980) studied this phenomenon using rival universities: Princeton and Rutgers. The rivalry between these universities is based on athletics, academics, and even class-consciousness, with Princeton being private and Rutgers public. Male research participants at the two schools watched videotaped scenes in which three different young men were asked to make a decision—for example, in one videotape an experimenter asked a man whether he wanted to listen to rock music or classical music while he participated in an experiment on auditory perception. The participants were told that the man was either a Princeton or a Rutgers student; thus, for some of them the student in the videotape was an in-group member, and for others he was an out-group member. The participants' job was to predict what the man in the videotape would

Out-group homogeneity
the perception that those in the out-group are more similar (homogeneous) to each other than they really are, as well as more similar than the members of the in-group

choose. After they saw the man make his choice (e.g., rock or classical music), they were asked to predict what percentage of male students at that institution would make the same choice.

Did the predictions vary due to the in-group or out-group status of the target men? As you can see in Figure 13.2, the results support the out-group homogeneity hypothesis: When the target person was an out-group member, the participants believed his choice was more predictive of what his peers would choose than when he was an in-group member (a student at their own school). In other words, if you know something about one out-group member, you are more likely to feel you know something about all of them. Similar results have been found in a wide variety of experiments in the United States, Europe, and Australia (Duck, Hogg, & Terry, 1995; Judd & Park, 1988; Hartstone & Augoustinos, 1995; Ostrom & Sedikides, 1992). In Canada, Hilton, Potvin, and Sachdev (1989) assessed the perceptions that francophone landlords in Montreal held of French Quebecers, English Quebecers, Italians, Asians, and Haitians. And, indeed, members of each out-group were perceived as more homogeneous than members of their own group (i.e., French Quebecers).

WHAT WE BELIEVE: STEREOTYPES

If we have a negative stereotype of a group, we will show prejudice toward members of that group. Right? Although that is often the case, it's actually not that simple. The relation between stereotyping and prejudice is a highly complex one. One of the complexities is that our stereotypes are not activated in every situation. As we will see, whether our stereotypes are turned "on" or "off" has important implications for prejudice. It is also the case that our attitudes toward members of another group are determined not only by our stereotype of that group, but also by our perception of that group's stereotype of *us*.

▶ **Figure 13.2**

JUDGMENTS ABOUT IN-GROUP AND OUT-GROUP MEMBERS.

After watching the target person make a choice between two alternatives, participants were asked to estimate what percentage of students at their school (in-group) and their rival school (out-group) would make the same choice. An out-group homogeneity bias was found: Students' estimates for out-group members were higher (greater similarity) than for in-group members.

(Adapted from Quattrone & Jones, 1980)

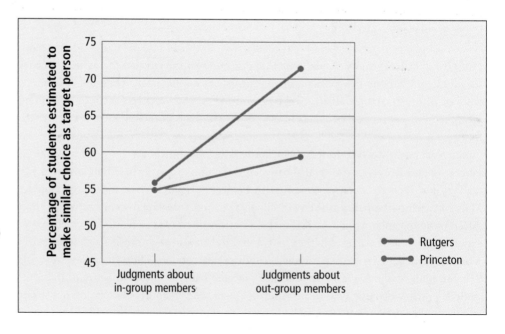

The Activation of Stereotypes Imagine this scenario: You are a member of a group, judging another person's performance. Someone in your group makes an ugly, stereotypical comment about the individual. Will the comment affect your judgment of the performance? "No," you are probably thinking, "I'd disregard it completely." But would you be able to do so? Is it possible that the comment would trigger in your mind all the other negative stereotypes and beliefs about people in that group and affect your judgment about this particular individual—even if you neither believe the stereotype nor consider yourself prejudiced against this group?

Greenberg and Pyszczynski (1985) conducted a study in which participants watched a debate between a black person and a white person. When a confederate made a racist comment about the black debater, participants rated the black debater's performance lower than when no racist remark was made. In other words, this derogatory comment activated other negative, stereotypical beliefs about blacks, so that the participants who heard it rated the same performance as less skilled than did those who had not heard the racist remark.

Similar results were obtained by Henderson-King and Nisbett (1996), who showed that all it took was one negative action by one African American (actually a confederate of the experimenters) to activate the negative stereotypes against blacks and to discourage the participants from wanting to interact with a different African American. These findings suggest that stereotypes in most of us lurk just beneath the surface. It doesn't require much to activate the stereotype, and, once activated, it can have dire consequences for how a particular member of that out-group is perceived and treated.

How does this activation process work? Patricia Devine and her colleagues (Devine, 1989a, 1989b; Zuwerink et al., 1996) have done some fascinating research on how stereotypical beliefs affect cognitive processing. Devine differentiates between automatic processing of information and controlled processing of information. An automatic process is one over which we have no control. For example, even if you score very low on a prejudice scale, you are certainly familiar with certain stereotypes that exist in the culture, such as "Native Canadians are lazy," "Jews are money-hungry," or "Homosexual men are effeminate." These stereotypes are automatically triggered under certain conditions—they just pop into one's mind. However, for people who are not deeply prejudiced, their controlled processes can suppress or override these stereotypes. For example, such a person can say to himself or herself, "Hey, that stereotype isn't fair and it isn't right—Jews are no more money-hungry than non-Jews. Ignore the stereotype about this person's ethnicity." What Devine's theory suggests, therefore, is a two-step model of cognitive processing. The automatic processing brings up information—in this case, stereotypes—but the controlled (or conscious) processing can refute or ignore it (see Figure 13.3).

Not all research has been consistent with this theory, however. For example, in a study that focused on the stereotype of black Canadian men, high-prejudice participants showed evidence of stereotype activation under both automatic and controlled processing conditions, whereas low-prejudice participants did not show stereotype activation under either automatic or controlled conditions (Kawakami, Dion, & Dovidio, 1998). Lepore and Brown (1997) found, consistent with Devine's theory, that both high- and low-prejudice people were aware of the stereotype of blacks. Both groups also automatically activated the negative stereotype of blacks when negative stereotype words such as *hostile*

EVERYONE SAYS THAT TORONTONIANS HAVE A SUPERIORITY COMPLEX.

WE PREFER TO CALL IT A SHOPPING, DINING AND ENTERTAINMENT COMPLEX.

Actually it's a 285 store complex at the corner of Yonge and Dundas. To find out more, call (416) 598-8700 or visit our website at www.torontoeatoncentre.com. And if you show this ad with $150 (excluding taxes) of receipts from any retailer in the Toronto Eaton Centre, you'll receive a *free gift*. Visit our Customer CARE desk for more details.

*One gift per person. While supplies last. Does not include downtown stores. Offer expires March 30, 2000.

THE CENTRE OF THE UNIVERSE IS IN TORONTO
THE EATON CENTRE

▲ No one can escape being stereotyped. Do you agree or disagree with this notion of Toronto?

either a white manager or a black manager (both managers were confederates). Half of the participants received a positive evaluation from the manager (e.g., "I was very impressed with this person, I think he has really good interpersonal skills"), whereas the others received a negative evaluation (e.g., "I was not very impressed with this person").

Sinclair and Kunda predicted that participants who received negative feedback from the black manager would activate their (negative) stereotype of blacks. In contrast, the participants who were praised by the black manager were expected to inhibit the black stereotype. How could the researchers tell whether participants activated or inhibited their stereotype of blacks? In the next phase of the experiment, the students were asked if they would participate in a supposedly unrelated study on word completions. The word fragments presented could be completed to form either racial or nonracial words. For example, _ _ A C K could be completed as BLACK or as any number of nonracial words (e.g., SNACK); C R _ _ _ could be completed as CRIME or as a nonracial word such as CREEK. The researchers reasoned that participants who activated their stereotype of blacks would be most likely to use racial word completions, whereas those who inhibited their stereotype of blacks would show the fewest racial word completions.

The results are shown in Figure 13.4. In interpreting these findings, you may wish to think of the participants who were evaluated by a white manager as the control group. These participants give us a sense of how many racial word completions came to mind for participants who were not motivated to activate or inhibit their stereotype of blacks. As you can see in the figure, participants who received negative feedback from a black manager generated more racial words than did those who received negative feedback from a white manager. This is evidence of stereotype activation. In contrast, those who were praised by the black manager pushed the stereotype of blacks right out of their minds—they came up with even fewer racial word completions than did participants who were praised by a white manager. This is evidence of stereotype inhibition. Finally, as you might expect, participants who were criticized by the black manager rated his skill at evaluating them lower than did participants who were praised by a black manager. (White managers who gave negative feedback also were rated as less skilled than white

▶ **Figure 13.4**

NUMBER OF RACIAL COMPLETIONS AS A FUNCTION OF FEEDBACK FAVOURABILITY AND MANAGER RACE.

(Sinclair & Kunda, 1999)

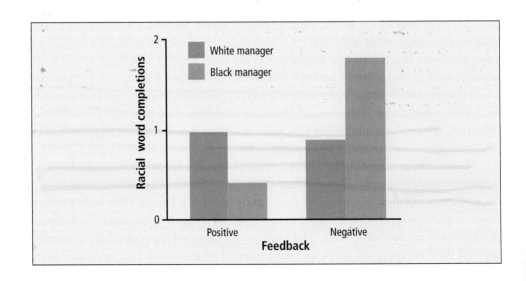

managers who gave positive feedback, but this difference was not nearly as pronounced as it was for black managers.)

In other research, Sinclair and Kunda (2000) demonstrated that similar processes operate when people stereotype women. For example, in one study they asked students at the University of Waterloo to evaluate their course instructors and to indicate the grade they received in each course. Students rated their female instructors as less competent than male professors when they received a low grade in the course—but not when they received a high grade. The researchers sum up this phenomenon as "She's fine if she praised me but incompetent if she criticized me." In contrast, the ratings of male professors did not depend as much on the grades that students received from them.

In short, this research suggests that if we can salvage our self-esteem by activating negative stereotypes about a group, we will do so. However, if a negative stereotype will interfere with a self-esteem boost (e.g., when we are praised by a member of a stereotyped group), we simply push that stereotype out of our minds.

Finally, we should point out that in everyday life, stereotype activation and inhibition can become quite a complex process. Most people belong to multiple groups, which means that a number of stereotypes can apply to the same person. Sinclair and Kunda (1999) suggest that we "pick and choose" which stereotypes to activate or inhibit—once again, depending on what will produce the greatest self-enhancement. For example, in one of their studies they focused on two stereotypes that have opposing implications for competence—the negative stereotype of black people, and the positive stereotype of doctors. As in their earlier study, participants received either a positive or a negative evaluation—from either a white doctor or a black doctor. The researchers predicted that when the black doctor delivered praise, the doctor stereotype would be activated (to bolster their desired positive impression of him) and the black stereotype would be inhibited (to prevent it from interfering with a positive impression of him). When he delivered criticism, just the opposite was expected—namely, that participants would bring the black stereotype to mind and push the doctor stereotype out of their minds. And that is exactly what happened.

Meta-Stereotypes Recently, Jacquie Vorauer and her colleagues (Vorauer, in press; Vorauer, Main, & O'Connell, 1998; Vorauer et al., 2000; Vorauer & Kumhyr, 2001) have raised the intriguing possibility that our level of prejudice depends not solely on whether our stereotype of a particular group is positive or negative, but also on whether we think members of that group have a positive or negative stereotype of us. These researchers have introduced the term **meta-stereotype** to refer to a person's beliefs regarding the stereotype that out-group members hold about their own group. In one of their studies (Vorauer, Main, & O'Connell, 1998), white students at the University of Manitoba were asked to complete the sentence "According to the stereotype that exists in Native Indian society, about ____ % of White Canadians possess this trait" for 76 different traits. The study revealed that white students believed that Native Canadians perceive white Canadians as prejudiced, unfair, selfish, arrogant, wealthy, materialistic, phony, and so on. Overall, there was agreement on the meta-stereotype, although low-prejudice people held more negative meta-stereotypes than did high-prejudice people. In other words, those who were low in prejudice were more likely to think that Native Canadians view white Canadians in negative ways.

Meta-stereotype
a person's beliefs regarding the stereotype that out-group members hold about their own group

In additional studies conducted by Vorauer and colleagues (1998), white students were asked about their expectations regarding an interaction with an Aboriginal person. The researchers found that participants who thought that they personally would be perceived in terms of the meta-stereotype anticipated that they would experience negative emotions during the interaction and would not enjoy it very much. These participants also expressed the greatest amount of prejudice. Perhaps most striking, the participants' sense of whether the out-group member would stereotype them predicted attitudes and reactions more strongly than did their own stereotypes of the out-group. In other words, the participants were more affected by their beliefs about how they would be evaluated than by their own evaluation of the other person.

We have seen that people report greater prejudice when they expect to be perceived in terms of the stereotypes they believe others hold of their group. But does this actually happen? Do other people perceive us in terms of meta-stereotypes? To find out, Vorauer and Kumhyr (2001) had pairs of Aboriginal and white Canadians engage in a getting-acquainted conversation. Afterwards, each person rated their conversation partner in terms of several traits and also made parallel ratings of how they believed their conversation partner perceived them. The results were rather striking—white Canadians who were high in prejudice felt that they were stereotyped by their Aboriginal partner, when, in reality, they were not. Low-prejudice white participants did not feel as though they were stereotyped by their Aboriginal conversation partner, and they were right. Interestingly, neither high-prejudice nor low-prejudice white participants stereotyped their Aboriginal partner. Moreover, the Aboriginal participants did not feel as though they had been the targets of prejudice. This story, however, does not have a happy ending. Additional analyses revealed that Aboriginal participants who were paired with a high-prejudice white participant experienced discomfort during the interaction and took it out on themselves. They reported feeling self-critical, ashamed, and angry with themselves, but did not experience negative feelings toward their white interaction partner. Thus, it appears that the Aboriginal participants failed to recognize that they had been the targets of prejudice, and instead attributed the negativity they had experienced to themselves. These findings suggest that on one level, Aboriginal and white students reacted similarly to the exchange: They were both more preoccupied with drawing conclusions about themselves and how they were viewed than with drawing conclusions about the other person.

THE WAY WE FEEL: AFFECT AND MOOD

So far, we have focused on the cognitive aspect of prejudice—namely, the stereotypes we hold of different groups. As we have seen, under certain conditions stereotyping is indeed related to prejudice. However, as Esses, Haddock, and Zanna (1993) point out, "there is more to prejudice than merely the attribution of stereotypes to groups." Their research suggests that the emotions elicited by a particular group are important in determining our level of prejudice—perhaps even more important than our stereotypes. Before discussing some of their studies, we should note that these researchers suggest that prejudice is also a product of our perception that a particular group promotes or hinders values that we cherish (symbolic beliefs) and a product of our experiences with members of the group (behaviour) (Maio, Esses, & Bell, 1994). As we will see, of all these predictors of prejudice (emotion, stereotypes, symbolic beliefs, and behaviour), the results generally are strongest for emotion.

For example, Haddock, Zanna, and Esses (1993, 1994) assessed the attitudes held by students at the University of Waterloo toward four ethnic groups (English Canadians, French Canadians, Natives Canadians, and Pakistanis) and homosexuals. To find out what best predicted these attitudes, the researchers asked the participants to describe the emotions they experienced when thinking about members of each group, their stereo-typic beliefs (characteristics you would use to describe the group), and their symbolic beliefs (the values that you believe members of the group promote or hinder). Behaviour was assessed by asking participants to describe the frequency of contact and quality of their most recent experiences with members of these groups.

Which of these variables best predicted attitudes (prejudice)? It turns out that all of these variables were related to attitudes. However, overall, the strongest relations were found for emotion. There was some variation, though, depending on the group being rated. Specifically, emotion was the best predictor of attitudes (prejudice) for the groups toward which participants expressed the lowest levels of prejudice (English Canadians and Native Canadians). For these groups, knowing how someone feels about members of the group would allow you to predict his or her level of prejudice with the greatest accu-racy. Symbolic beliefs best predicted attitudes (prejudice) for the groups toward which participants expressed the highest levels of prejudice (Pakistanis and homosexuals). For these groups, prejudice would be predicted most accurately by asking whether the group threatens important beliefs or values. Stereotypes did not strongly predict attitudes toward any of these groups when emotions, symbolic beliefs, and behaviour were taken into account.

Recent research by Corenblum and Stephan (2001) suggests that emotion is also a strong predictor of the prejudice that minority groups feel toward majority groups. In this study, white Canadians and Native Canadians were asked about their stereotypes, sym-bolic beliefs (agreement with statements such as "Natives and white Canadians have many incompatible values"), and emotions—specifically, anxiety about interacting with out-group members. All of these variables, but especially emotion, predicted the level of prejudice that white Canadians felt toward Native Canadians. The same held true when predicting the level of prejudice that Native Canadians felt toward white Canadians. Thus, the more threatened and anxious people expect to feel while interacting with mem-bers of the another group, the greater their prejudice toward that group—regardless of whether their group is in a majority or minority position.

It is important to point out that even though we have been speaking of predictors of prejudice, the research we have been discussing does not actually tell us whether negative emotions *cause* people to be prejudiced toward certain groups, or whether prejudice pro-duces nasty feelings in people. How might we disentangle this? One way would be to change people's emotions and see if that has an effect on their attitudes. Esses and Zanna (1995) did just that. In a series of experiments, they induced either a positive, neutral, or negative mood in their participants. The moods were created in a variety of ways—by having participants listen to music that was supposed to produce certain moods; by hav-ing them describe events in their lives that made them feel extremely happy, unhappy, or neutral; or simply by having them read positive, negative, or neutral statements into a tape

◀ Recent research has suggested that mood affects prejudice; people in a good mood feel more favourably toward other racial or ethnic groups.

recorder. Regardless of how the mood was created, participants in a bad mood described various ethnic groups in more negative terms than did those who were in a good mood or a neutral mood.

Perhaps most striking, there was evidence that even the same characteristic was perceived differently, depending on the participant's mood. For example, in one study participants listed the characteristics of various ethnic groups. Two days later, they received a mood induction, and then were presented with the list of characteristics they had previously generated, with instructions to rate whether each was positive or negative. Mood was found to influence these ratings. For example, some of the participants had originally described Native Canadians as "proud." Later, those who were put in a bad mood rated this as a more negative characteristic than did those who were put in a good mood or a neutral mood (Esses & Zanna, 1995). Similar findings were reported in a study conducted at the University of Western Ontario by Bell and Esses (1997).

Finally, we should note that the role of emotion in predicting attitudes may vary, depending on the situation. For example, Haddock, Zanna, and Esses (1994) examined whether symbolic beliefs (values) can move to the forefront as a predictor of our attitudes. The Oka crisis provided an opportunity to find out. As you may recall, in 1990, Mohawk warriors in Oka, Quebec, erected a roadblock to protest the town's plans to develop a golf course on land that was considered sacred by the Mohawk people. Throughout the two-month standoff, Canadians were bombarded with images of armed Mohawk warriors on one side of a barricade and armed police officers (and eventually the Canadian Armed Forces) on the other side. Haddock and colleagues hypothesized that because the values of the Mohawk were vividly portrayed in Canadian's minds, their attitudes toward Native peoples during the Oka crisis might be most strongly predicted by symbolic beliefs (the values the Mohawk were seen as promoting or hindering). Indeed, in this study, emotion continued to predict attitudes, but the strongest predictor of attitudes was symbolic beliefs (values). (Consistent with other studies in this research program, stereotypic beliefs remained a weak predictor.)

We want to be clear on the point that these researchers are making. They are not saying that stereotyping never produces prejudice. Indeed, earlier in this chapter we presented evidence to the contrary. However, this program of research does suggest that an even stronger determinant of prejudice is how we feel about a group.

This "bottom line" has important implications for interventions aimed at reducing prejudice. If we want to reduce prejudice, it might be best to design interventions that will speak to people's hearts, rather than to their heads. Recently, Esses and Dovidio (2002) attempted to do just that. White participants were shown a videotape of a black man experiencing discrimination in several situations. Some participants were instructed to pay attention to their feelings about each situation; others were told to pay attention to their thoughts. Those who focused on their feelings subsequently expressed more willingness to engage in future contact with blacks than did those who focused on their thoughts. Why might this be? Additional analyses revealed that the focus on feelings about the discriminatory situations did not affect people's stereotypes of blacks, nor their symbolic beliefs. However, it did affect their emotions—they now felt more positive toward blacks, and therefore were more willing to interact with blacks in the future.

THE WAY WE ASSIGN MEANING: ATTRIBUTIONAL BIASES

The human tendency to make attributions for people's behaviour can also serve to perpetuate stereotyping and prejudice. As we saw in Chapter 4, we frequently make self-serving attributions—taking credit for our successes and blaming external factors for our failures. Sadly, when it comes to explaining the behaviour of members of out-groups, we tend to show just the opposite pattern—attributing negative behaviours to internal, dispositional factors and explaining away positive behaviours as due to situational or external factors (e.g., luck). Thomas Pettigrew (1979) has called this the **ultimate attribution error** because we apply these attributional tendencies to entire groups of people.

To use gender stereotypes as an example, Janet Swim and Lawrence Sanna (1996) carefully studied some 58 separate experiments done over the past 20 years and found that if a man was successful on a given task, observers attributed his success to ability; if a woman was successful at that same task, observers attributed her success to hard work. If a man failed on a given task, observers attributed his failure either to bad luck or to lower effort; if a woman failed, observers felt the task was simply too hard for her ability level (see also Deaux & Emsweiler, 1974; Feldman-Sommers & Kiesler, 1974).

Unfortunately, if a stereotype is strong enough, even members of the stereotyped group buy into it. In one experiment, grade four boys attributed their own successful outcomes on a difficult intellectual task to their ability and blamed their failures on bad luck; girls tended to derogate their own successful performance and blamed themselves for failures (Nichols, 1975). The tendency girls have to downplay their own ability may be most prevalent in traditionally male domains—such as mathematics. For example, Stipek and Gralinski (1991) found that junior high-school girls attributed their success on a math exam to luck, while boys attributed their success to ability. Girls also showed fewer feelings of pride than boys, following success on a math exam.

As you might expect, such effects are not limited to gender stereotypes. Corenblum, Annis, and Young (1996) showed white and Native children attending elementary schools in Brandon, Manitoba, videos in which a white child performed better than a Native

Ultimate attribution error
our tendency to make internal, dispositional attributions for the negative behaviours of out-group members and external, situational attributions for their positive behaviours

child, a Native child performed better than a white child, or both children performed equally well. When a white child performed well, both Native and white participants made internal attributions for the child's performance (e.g., being smart); when a white child performed poorly, both Native and white participants made external attributions (e.g., bad luck). Exactly the opposite pattern was observed when making attributions for the performance of the Native children. Good performance was attributed to external factors (e.g., luck, an easy task) by both Native and white children; poor performance was attributed to internal factors (e.g., not being smart). Thus, we tend to explain the behaviour of out-group members in a way that perpetuates our stereotypes of them, thereby fostering prejudice.

THE WAY WE ALLOCATE RESOURCES: REALISTIC CONFLICT THEORY

One of the most obvious sources of conflict and prejudice is competition—for scarce resources, for political power, and for social status. Indeed, it can be said that whatever problems result from the simple in-group versus out-group phenomenon, they will be magnified by real economic, political, or status competition. **Realistic conflict theory** holds that limited resources lead to conflict among groups, and result in prejudice and discrimination (Jackson, 1993; Levine & Campbell, 1972; Sherif, 1966; White, 1977). Thus, prejudiced attitudes tend to increase when times are tense and conflict exists over mutually exclusive goals. In what has become a classic experiment, Muzafer Sherif and his colleagues (1961) tested group conflict theory using the natural environment of a Boy Scout camp. The participants in the camp were normal, well-adjusted, 12-year-old boys who were randomly assigned to one of two groups, the Eagles or the Rattlers. Each group stayed in its own cabin, and the cabins were located quite a distance apart in order to reduce contact between the two groups. The youngsters were placed in situations designed to increase the cohesiveness of their own group. This was done by arranging enjoyable activities, such as hiking and swimming, and by having the groups work on various building projects, preparing group meals, and so on.

After feelings of cohesiveness developed within each group, the researchers set up a series of competitive activities in which the two groups were pitted against each other—for example, in games such as football, baseball, and tug-of-war, where prizes were awarded to the winning team. These competitive games aroused feelings of conflict and tension between the two groups. In addition, the investigators created other situations to further intensify the conflict. For example, a camp party was arranged, but each group was told it started at a different time, thereby ensuring that the Eagles would arrive well before the Rattlers. The refreshments at the party consisted of two different kinds of food: Half of the food was fresh, appealing, and appetizing, while the other half was squashed, ugly, and unappetizing. As one might expect, the early arriving Eagles grabbed most of the appealing refreshments, leaving only the less interesting, less appetizing, squashed, and damaged food for their adversaries. When the Rattlers finally arrived and saw what had happened, they became angry—so angry, in fact, that they began to call the exploitive group rather uncomplimentary names. Because the Eagles believed that they deserved what they got (first come, first served), they resented the name-calling and responded in

Realistic conflict theory the theory that limited resources lead to conflict between groups and result in increased prejudice and discrimination

kind. Name-calling escalated into food-throwing, and within a short time the boys were throwing punches and a full-scale riot ensued.

Following this incident, the investigators tried to reverse the hostility they had promoted. Competitive games were eliminated, and a great deal of nonconflictual social contact was initiated. Once hostility had been aroused, however, simply eliminating the competition did not eliminate the hostility. Indeed, hostility continued to escalate, even when the two groups were engaged in such benign activities as watching movies together. Thus, conflict and competition can lead to long-lasting prejudice. (Eventually, the investigators did manage to reduce the hostility between the two groups; exactly how this was accomplished will be discussed at the end of this chapter.)

Economic and Political Competition Whenever people compete for any scarce resource, the stage is set for prejudice. In his classic study of prejudice in a small U.S. industrial town, John Dollard (1938) was among the first to document the relation between discrimination and economic competition. Though initially there was no discernible prejudice against the new German immigrants to the town, as jobs grew scarce, prejudice flourished. Similarly, in the nineteenth century, when Chinese immigrants in the United States joined the gold rush in California, in direct competition with miners of Anglo-Saxon origin, they were described as "depraved and vicious . . . gross gluttons, . . . bloodthirsty and inhuman" (Jacobs & Landau, 1971). However, only a few years later, when they were willing to accept back-breaking work as labourers on the Transcontinental Railroad—work few white Americans were willing to do—they were regarded as sober, industrious, and law-abiding. With the end of the Civil War came an influx of former soldiers into an already tight job market. This was immediately followed by a dramatic increase in negative attitudes toward the Chinese: The stereotype changed to one characterizing them as criminal, conniving, crafty, and stupid (Jacobs & Landau, 1971).

Closer to home, prejudice toward Natives has increased in Burnt Church, New Brunswick, as a result of the dispute between Native and non-Native fishers over lobster fishing in Miramichi Bay. It is reported that relations between Natives and non-Natives were harmonious until a dispute erupted over access to a scarce resource, namely lobster. White fishers resented Native fishers' position that they were exempt from fishing limits imposed by the federal Fisheries Department, resulting in violent confrontations between the two groups. Relations continue to be strained.

Events such as these suggest that when times are tough and resources are scarce, members of the in-group will feel more threatened by members of the out-group and will therefore show more prejudice, discrimination, and violence toward the latter. How might this hypothesis be tested? We might look for increases in violent acts directed at minority group members during times of economic hardship. Carl Hovland and Robert Sears (1940) did just that, by correlating two sets of very different data: (a) the price of cotton in the southern states from 1882 to 1930, and (b) the number of lynchings of southern African Americans during that same period. During this period, cotton was by far the most important crop in the South; as cotton went, so went the economy. Hovland and Sears (1940) found that as the price of cotton dropped, the number of lynchings increased. In short, as members of the in-group experienced the hardships of an economic depression, they

▶ Conflict over scarce resources—namely lobster—has fuelled racial tension between white and Native fishers in Burnt Church, New Brunswick.

became more hostile toward out-group members, whom they almost certainly perceived as a threat to their livelihood. Other studies conducted in the United States also have found that prejudice is most pronounced when whites and African Americans are in close competition for jobs (Simpson & Yinger, 1958; Vanneman & Pettigrew, 1972).

In Canada, Douglas Palmer (1996) has documented that attitudes toward immigration mirror unemployment rates. For example, between 1975 and 1995, the unemployment rate increased, and so did negative attitudes about immigration. These results are shown in Figure 13.5. Between 1996 and 1998, the unemployment rate dropped, and—you guessed it—so did opposition toward immigration (Palmer, 2000).

The astute reader will have noticed that the research we have been describing is correlational; experimental research designs allow us to make cause-and-effect statements with far more confidence than we can on the basis of correlational research (see Chapter 2). How might we study the relationship between competition and prejudice experimentally?

Esses, Jackson, and Armstrong (1998) devised a way. They conducted a series of experiments to see whether perceived competition for resources causes unfavourable attitudes toward immigrants. Participants in these studies (students at the University of Western Ontario and the University of Manitoba) read one of two editorials on immigration to Canada. In the competition condition, the editorial focused on the scarcity of jobs in Canada and the high rate of participation of skilled immigrants in the job market. In the no-competition condition, the job market was not mentioned. Next, participants were told that because of a natural disaster in the country of Sandir (a fictitious country), a new group of immigrants, the Sandirians, would be arriving in Canada. The researchers described the Sandirians in positive terms: ambitious, hardworking, smart, family-oriented, spiritual, and religious. When participants were later asked about their attitudes toward Sandirians and toward immigration more generally, those who had earlier read the competition article construed the traits of the Sandirians more negatively than did

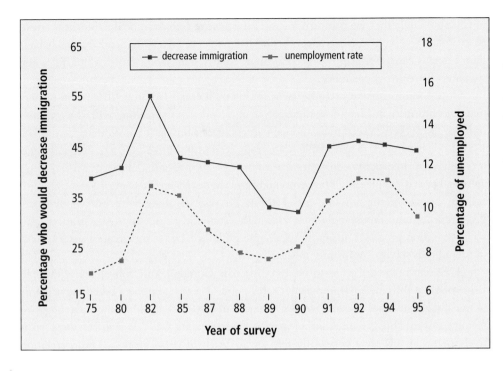

◀ Figure 13.5

UNEMPLOYMENT RATES AND
ATTITUDES TOWARD
IMMIGRATION.

When unemployment increases,
attitudes toward immigration
become more negative; when
unemployment decreases,
attitudes toward immigration
become more positive.

(Palmer, 1996)

those in the no-competition condition (e.g., "Since they are family-oriented, they are probably not too accepting of others outside the family [don't welcome others in]"). Participants in the competition condition also expressed more negative attitudes toward the idea of Sandirian immigration to Canada and toward immigrants in general.

If we are prejudiced against immigrant groups because we fear that they will compete with us for scarce resources such as jobs, this raises the rather ironic possibility that we might actually be more prejudiced toward successful immigrants than toward unsuccessful immigrants. This idea was recently explored in series of studies by Esses and colleagues (see Esses et al., 2001). In this research, participants again read about the Sandirians. This time, some participants read an editorial indicating that the Sandirians were successful even in difficult economic times; other participants read an editorial that did not make reference to the Sandirians' success. Who expressed the most negative attitudes toward Sandirians and toward immigration to Canada in general? You guessed it—those participants who read that the Sandirians excel under conditions of economic hardship. Thus, a quality that we would normally find attractive in a group suddenly becomes unattractive when our own self-interest is at stake.

THE WAY WE CONFORM: NORMATIVE RULES

As we have seen, prejudice is created and maintained by many forces in the social world. Some we can observe operating within the individual, such as the ways we process information and assign meaning to events. Some we can observe operating on whole groups of people, such as the effects of competition, conflict, and frustration. Our final explanation for what causes prejudice also occurs on the group level—conformity to normative standards or rules in the society. Conformity is a frequent part of social life, as we discussed in Chapter 8, whether we conform to gain information (informational conformity) or to fit in and be accepted (normative conformity). Again, a relatively innocuous social behaviour—in this case, conformity—becomes particularly dangerous and debilitating when we enter the realm of prejudice.

How does normative prejudice work? As you'll recall from our discussion of **normative conformity** in Chapter 8, there is a strong tendency to go along with the group in order to fulfill their expectations and gain acceptance. Thus, as Thomas Pettigrew (1958, 1985, 1991) has noted, many people hold prejudiced attitudes and engage in discriminatory behaviour in order to conform to, or fit in with, the prevailing majority view of their culture. It's as if people say, "Hey, everybody else thinks Xs are inferior; if I treat Xs with respect, people might not like me. I think I'll just go along with everybody else." Pettigrew argues convincingly that although economic competition, frustration, and social cognition processes do account for some prejudice, by far the greatest determinant of prejudice is slavish conformity to social norms.

A recent program of research by Christian Crandall and colleagues (Crandall, Eshleman, & O'Brien, 2002) underscores this point. These researchers asked participants to rate a large number of social groups in terms of how acceptable it is to have negative feelings toward this group. Another group of participants was asked to rate how positively or negatively they personally felt toward each of these groups. The correlation between the two groups' ratings was astonishingly high—.96. (Recall that a perfect correlation is 1.00). In other words, "to ask people about the norms regarding prejudice is, in practical terms, the same as asking people how they personally feel" (Crandall, Eshleman, & O'Brien, 2002). The researchers note that although we may start out being hesitant to accept the norms of any given group, over time, as we begin to identify with the group, we internalize its norms and make them our very own.

It probably comes as no surprise that Crandall and colleagues found that one of the prejudices that has become more socially unacceptable is prejudice against racial or ethnic minorities. You probably also have noticed from this chapter that this is the kind of prejudice that social psychologists are most likely to study. Thus, modern social psychologists conducting research on prejudice face a rather formidable challenge—the kinds of attitudes they are most interested in studying are the kinds of attitudes people may be least willing to admit. We turn to this issue next.

"Modern" Prejudice As the norm swings toward tolerance for certain out-groups, many people simply become more careful—outwardly acting unprejudiced, but inwardly maintaining their prejudiced views. This phenomenon is called **modern prejudice** (Dovidio & Gaertner, 1996; Gaertner & Dovidio, 1986; McConahay, 1986). One consequence of modern prejudice is that social psychologists have to be vigilant about subtle indicators of prejudice. For example, in one study, Allen Hart and Marian Morry (1997) showed white students a videotape of a black person and a white person making speeches. Participants attributed more negative characteristics to the black speaker than to the white speaker when performance was poor. On the other hand, when the speakers performed well, participants "bent over backwards" to show that they were not prejudiced and rated the black speaker even more positively than the white speaker. Thus, one subtle manifestation of prejudice can be overly positive reactions to the targets of prejudice—trying too hard to convince others that one really isn't prejudiced at all.

Normative conformity

the tendency to go along with the group in order to fulfill their expectations and gain acceptance

---

Modern prejudice

outwardly acting unprejudiced while inwardly maintaining prejudiced attitudes

◀ According to Pettigrew, the greatest determinant of prejudice is slavish conformity to social norms. Perhaps normative conformity is part of the problem at the Cole Harbour District High School in Dartmouth, Nova Scotia, where racial violence reached a peak in October 1997, forcing the shutdown of the school, multiple expulsions, installation of security cameras, and patrols by RCMP officers. Here, two officers keep watch outside the school as a busload of children leaves the grounds following a riot. Normative conformity may also become part of the solution; student mediators, anti-racism workshops, and other programs have been introduced as the local community bonds together to overcome the school's problems.

Because of modern prejudice, social psychologists also have had to develop scales that assess prejudice in more subtle ways. For example, the Modern Racism Scale is a subtle, indirect measure of racial prejudice (McConahay, 1986). It turns out that people who are reluctant to express blatant prejudice nevertheless are quite willing to agree with statements such as, "Minorities are getting too demanding in their push for special rights." Research conducted in Canada, the United States, and Britain has shown that those who score high on modern prejudice scales are more likely to be prejudiced against blacks than those who score low (Kawakami, Dion, & Dovidio, 1998; Lepore & Brown, 1997). For example, Wittenbrink, Judd, and Park (1997) flashed the word *black* or *white* subliminally on a computer screen—too quickly for the participants (all of whom were white) to be aware of having seen the words. Participants were then required to judge as quickly as possible whether letter strings were words or non-words. The words were positive and negative black and white stereotype words. Participants who scored high on modern prejudice were quicker to identify negative black stereotype words (e.g., violent) as words when primed with the word *black* than those who scored low on modern prejudice. They also were quicker to identify positive white stereotype words (e.g., intelligent) as words when primed with the word *white* (Wittenbrink, Judd, & Park, 1997).

At the University of Ottawa, Francine Tougas and her colleagues have developed a scale—the Neosexism Scale—to assess sexist attitudes in a more subtle manner (Tougas et al., 1995). Parallel to the issue of racism, these researchers reasoned that people who are opposed to equality for women may be reluctant to say so directly, but might find it acceptable to express disagreement with social policies aimed at increasing the status of women. Accordingly, the Neosexism Scale asks respondents to indicate how much they agree with statements such as, "Women will make more progress by being patient and not pushing too hard for change." In a study of male managers working in a Canadian federal agency, Beaton, Tougas, and Joly (1996) found that those who scored high on neosexism were more likely to show a pro-male bias when evaluating women's and men's competence (e.g., they believed that male managers were more competent in general than female managers), and reported less willingness to support women in the workplace than did managers who scored low. These researchers also found that secretaries who scored high on neosexism were opposed to affirmative action programs for women and, like the male managers in the previous study, showed a pro-male bias when evaluating women's and men's competence (Tougas et al., 1999). Finally, a study conducted with students at the University of Windsor found that neosexism was associated with negative attitudes toward the feminist movement and toward lesbians and gay men (Campbell, Schellenberg, & Senn, 1997).

In conclusion, there is reason to believe that prejudiced people may hide their prejudice in order to avoid social disapproval. This raises a rather daunting question: How does one go about trying to reduce prejudice in people who aren't willing to admit that they are prejudiced, or perhaps aren't even aware that they are prejudiced in the first place? Son Hing, Li, and Zanna (2002), at the University of Waterloo, took on this challenge. They focused on a particular kind of modern prejudice known as aversive racism. Aversive racists are people who consciously hold nonprejudiced attitudes but subconsciously hold prejudiced attitudes. How might one identify people who are prejudiced at a subconscious, but not a conscious level? Here's how Son Hing and colleagues did it. First, they selected participants who were low in explicit (conscious) prejudice. (These people gave nonprejudiced responses on a prejudice scale.) To assess implicit prejudice (prejudice at a subconscious level), they used a stereotype activation procedure: Participants first interacted with a Chinese experimenter for five minutes and then were given a word completion task. The words could be completed with either Asian stereotype words or nonstereotype words. For example, a word fragment such as S_Y could be completed as SLY (a negative stereotypic word) or SKY (a nonstereotypic word). The researchers assumed that people who are implicitly prejudiced would be more likely to complete the word fragments with negative Asian stereotype words. Finally, those who scored low on the explicit measure and high on the implicit (stereotype activation) measure, were classified as aversive racists. (Those who scored low on both measures were considered to be unprejudiced).

Son Hing and colleagues reasoned that a hypocrisy induction might be an especially effective tool for reducing prejudice among aversive racists. Recall that in Chapter 7 we discussed research showing that university students who agreed to give a speech to high-school students on the importance of practising safe sex, after having been reminded of their own failure to use condoms, were more likely to purchase condoms afterwards (Aronson, Fried, & Stone, 1991; Stone et al., 1994). The University of Waterloo researchers followed a similar procedure. First, participants were asked to write an essay on why it is important to treat minority students fairly. To give added weight to this task, they were told that excerpts of their essay might be featured in pamphlets to be distributed as part of a Racial Equality Forum. Next, to induce hypocrisy, participants were asked to write about situations in which "you reacted more negatively to an Asian person than you thought you should."

What effect did this have on aversive racists? It turns out that inducing hypocrisy created feelings of guilt and discomfort. But did it affect their behaviour? To find out, the researchers arranged for a confederate to approach the participants after the experiment was over and ask for their help in deciding how funding cuts to student groups should be distributed. It was predicted that aversive racists would relieve the negative feelings caused by the hypocrisy induction by recommending that the Asian Students' Association should be spared major budget cuts. And this is exactly what happened. Aversive racists in the hypocrisy condition recommended a mere 6.5 percent cut to the Asian Students' Association, whereas aversive racists in a control condition (who did not receive the hypocrisy induction) recommended a cut of 26.9 percent. Son Hing and colleagues concluded that the hypocrisy induction made aversive racists become aware of attitudes they typically repress. The disturbing realization that they actually were prejudiced caused them to bend over backwards to act in a nonprejudicial manner.

Individual Differences in Prejudice

As we have mentioned repeatedly throughout this chapter, no one is immune from prejudice. The simple act of classifying people into groups tends to bring with it value judgments about which groups are better than others. However, as you probably have observed, some people do seem to hold more prejudiced attitudes than others. Indeed, research confirms that certain kinds of people are especially likely to hold negative attitudes toward members of out-groups. As we will see, those who are high in just world beliefs, right-wing authoritarianism, religious fundamentalism, and social dominance orientation are more likely to be prejudiced than those who are low in these dimensions.

JUST WORLD BELIEFS

As we discussed in Chapter 4, the tendency to blame victims for their victimization is typically motivated by a desire to see the world as a fair and just place—one in which people get what they deserve and deserve what they get. How does the belief in a just world lead to derogation of a victim? When something bad happens to a person (e.g., the person has difficulty finding a job because of race), we undoubtedly feel sorry for him or her, but at the same time we feel relieved that this thing didn't happen to us. In addition, we also feel scared that such a thing might happen to us in the future. How can we cope with these fears and worries? The best way to protect ourselves from the fear we feel when we hear about someone else's mistreatment is to convince ourselves that the person must have done something to bring it on himself or herself. Therefore, in our own minds, we are safe because we would have behaved differently (Jones & Aronson, 1973). As Melvin Lerner and his colleagues have shown (1980, 1991; Lerner & Grant, 1990), most people, when confronted with evidence of an inequitable outcome that is otherwise difficult to explain, find a way to blame the victim. For example, in one experiment Lerner and colleagues found that if two people worked equally hard on the same task and, by the flip of a coin, one received a sizable reward and the other received nothing, observers—after the fact— tended to reconstruct what happened and convince themselves that the unlucky person must have worked less hard. People who display strong just world beliefs are especially likely to make such attributions. For example, Furnham and Gunter (1984) found that negative attitudes toward the poor and the homeless—including blaming them for their own plight—are more prevalent among individuals with strong just world beliefs.

RIGHT-WING AUTHORITARIANISM

At the University of Manitoba, Bob Altemeyer (1981, 1988, 1996) has identified an individual difference variable—right-wing authoritarianism—that is strongly associated with prejudice. Right-wing authoritarianism is defined in terms of three clusters of attitudes: authoritarian submission (a high degree of submission to authority figures in society), authoritarian aggression (aggression directed toward groups that are seen as legitimate targets by authority figures), and conventionalism (a high degree of conformity to the rules and conventions that are established by authority figures). Right-wing authoritarianism is assessed with items such as "Once our government leaders give us the 'go ahead,' it will be the duty of every patriotic citizen to help stomp out the rot that is poisoning our country from within" (Altemeyer, 1998).

In research conducted at the University of Manitoba over the past three decades, Altemeyer (1981, 1996, 1998) has obtained strong positive correlations between right-wing authoritarianism and racial prejudice. Similarly, at the University of Waterloo, Haddock, Zanna and Esses, (1993) found that high right-wing authoritarians express more negative attitudes than low right-wing authoritarians toward French Canadians, Natives, and Pakistanis. In addition, those who are high in right-wing authoritarianism hold traditional, nonegalitarian attitudes toward women (e.g., believing that women should be subservient to men; Altemeyer, 1996, 1998; Perrott, Miller, & Delaney, 1997) and, therefore, not surprisingly, are prejudiced against feminists (Haddock & Zanna, 1994). Finally, those who are high in right-wing authoritarianism show especially high levels of prejudice toward homosexuals (Altemeyer, 1996, 1998; Altemeyer & Hunsberger, 1992; Haddock, Zanna, & Esses, 1993; Hunsberger, 1996; Whitley, 1999).

Research on right-wing authoritarianism has been conducted with university students, their parents, and other community samples in Canada and the United States. Bob Altemeyer offers the following succinct summary of these studies:

> In North America, research has shown that high RWAs [right-wing authoritarians] dislike Blacks, Hispanics, homosexuals, feminists, Aboriginals, East Indians, Japanese, Chinese, Pakistanis, Filipinos, Africans, Jews and Arabs. One could say that right-wing authoritarians are equal-opportunity bigots, disliking all "different" people regardless of race, creed or color (Altemeyer & Hunsberger, 1992).

Must we leave you with this bleak conclusion, or is there hope that the attitudes of right-wing authoritarians can be changed? Given that right-wing authoritarians are especially prejudiced toward homosexuals, Altemeyer (1988, 2001) has focused on ways of changing attitudes toward this group. And he is finding that even right-wing authoritarians can become less prejudiced. One strategy that has proven effective is to create awareness that attitudes generally have become more positive toward homosexuals (Altemeyer, 2001). When right-wing authoritarians are shown that their attitudes toward homosexuals are much more negative than other people's, they tend to change their attitudes because conforming to social norms is important to them.

Another effective strategy for reducing prejudice is to encourage interaction with members of out-groups (the benefits of contact are discussed more fully at the end of this chapter). Bob Altemeyer decided to find out if right-wing authoritarians would actually change their attitudes if they personally knew a homosexual person. He did so by telling one of his psychology classes at the University of Manitoba that he was a homosexual and actively involved in the gay rights movement. (Bob Altemeyer actually is not gay, although a newspaper article describing this demonstration reported that he was, which apparently came as quite a surprise to his father-in-law!) What effect did this revelation have on the right-wing authoritarians in his class? They subsequently became more positive in their attitudes toward homosexuals as a group (see Altemeyer, 2001). Thus, there is reason to be optimistic that prejudice can be reduced, even among right-wing authoritarians.

RELIGIOUS FUNDAMENTALISM

Research conducted at Wilfrid Laurier University by Bruce Hunsberger (1995, 1996) and at the University of Manitoba (Altemeyer & Hunsberger, 1992, 1993) suggests that religious fundamentalism is another individual difference variable that is related to prejudice. Religious fundamentalism is defined as a belief in the absolute and literal truth of one's religious beliefs. People who are high in fundamentalism also believe that their religion is the "right" one and that forces of evil are constantly threatening to undermine the truth. (Note that the term *fundamentalism* does not refer to a specific religion, but rather applies to any religious beliefs that are seen as portraying the ultimate truth.) Studies conducted with university students and community samples have shown that religious fundamentalism is correlated with racial prejudice as well as with negative attitudes toward homosexuals (Altemeyer & Hunsberger, 1992, 1993). For example, Hunsberger (1996) assessed religious fundamentalism and attitudes toward homosexuals among Muslims, Jews, and Hindus living in Toronto. Within each group, the greater the fundamentalism, the greater the hostility toward homosexuals.

In a series of studies conducted at the University of Western Ontario, Jackson and Esses (1997) found that those who were high in religious fundamentalism blamed homosexuals and single mothers (groups whose behaviour is seen as immoral by religious fundamentalists) for unfortunate situations (e.g., unemployment), whereas groups who were not seen as threatening basic religious values (Native Canadians, students) were not blamed to the same extent. Religious fundamentalists also were more likely to believe that homosexuals and single mothers should not receive any assistance.

It may have crossed your mind that there are similarities between religious fundamentalism and right-wing authoritarianism. Indeed, Altemeyer and Hunsberger (1993) have reached the conclusion that fundamentalism is a religious manifestation of right-wing authoritarianism.

Finally, we want to emphasize that these researchers are not saying that religion *per se* is associated with prejudice, but rather that there is a relation between prejudice and the way in which people hold their religious beliefs. Those who regard their beliefs as absolute truths that must be zealously followed are likely to be prejudiced. However, this is not the case for those who have a flexible, open, and questioning orientation to religion (known as religious quest). In fact, religious quest tends to be negatively correlated with prejudice (Altemeyer & Hunsberger, 1992, 1993).

SOCIAL DOMINANCE ORIENTATION

Recently, social psychologists have begun to examine another individual difference variable that is related to prejudice, namely social dominance orientation (Pratto et al., 1994; Sidanius, Levin, & Pratto, 1996). Individuals who are high on social dominance orientation believe that groups of people are inherently unequal and that it is acceptable for some groups in society to benefit more than others. They prefer to be in the advantaged group, even if it means treating other groups badly. For example, people high in social dominance orientation agree with statements such as, "To get ahead in life, it is sometimes necessary to step on others." Research conducted in Canada, China, Israel, Mexico, New Zealand, Taiwan, and the United States has shown that social dominance is associated with racial prejudice, sexism, and negative attitudes toward homosexuals (Altemeyer, 1998; Pratto et al., 2000; Pratto et al., 1994; Sidanius, Levin, & Pratto, 1996; Whitley, 1999). In addition, research conducted with students in Canadian and American universities (Esses, Jackson, & Armstrong, 1998; Esses et al., 2001) shows that people who are high in social dominance orientation hold negative attitudes toward immigration and are opposed to offering assistance to immigrant groups to help them adjust to a new country. People high in social dominance hold these negative attitudes in part because they believe that any gains made by immigrants occur at their expense.

This latter finding raises an interesting question, namely whether those who are high in social dominance orientation would be less prejudiced if they could be persuaded that they do not necessarily lose out when immigrants get ahead. Esses and colleagues (2001) addressed this question by having participants read an editorial containing statements such as, "It is not the case that when immigrants make gains in employment, it is at the expense of Canadians living here." Did this message have any impact on those who were high in social dominance orientation? Sadly, no. In fact, these sorts of arguments seemed to backfire, such that those who were high in social dominance orientation became even more negative toward immigrants (compared to participants in a control condition). It appears that a challenge to their world view only caused them to bolster their beliefs.

Does this leave any hope that the attitudes of people high in social dominance orientation can be changed? Thanks to the tenacious efforts of Esses and colleagues (2001), there is reason for optimism. In a second attempt to reduce prejudice among those high in social dominance orientation, these researchers constructed editorials that were intended to create a sense of shared identity between the participants and immigrant groups. For example, it was pointed out that most Canadians immigrated to this country and that the participants themselves could probably trace their own ethnic roots. This more indirect approach met with success—those who were high in social dominance orientation later expressed more positive attitudes toward immigrants than those who read a neutral editorial. (Note that those who were low in social dominance orientation were unaffected by the editorials because they weren't prejudiced to begin with.) In discussing these findings, Esses and colleagues refer to a speech delivered by former Minister of Citizen and Immigration Canada Elinor Caplin in which she stated, "My grandparents were immigrants, and so were many of yours. Indeed, apart from our aboriginal population, *all* Canadians are descended from immigrants or refugees" (Caplin, 1999). Simple reminders such as this may actually be quite effective in reducing prejudice toward immigrant groups.

Effects of Stereotyping, Prejudice, and Discrimination

When a member of a majority group mistreats a member of a disadvantaged group, the disadvantaged person is unlikely to perform well, thereby confirming the majority group member's negative stereotype and in turn perpetuating the discrimination. You probably recognize this as our old friend, the self-fulfilling prophecy, once again rearing its head. Moreover, as we will see, research on stereotype threat shows that fears that one will confirm the negative stereotype of one's group also can impede performance. Perhaps most tragic of all, even when the poor performance of disadvantaged groups is clearly the result of discrimination, they may nevertheless blame themselves, rather than placing the blame where it deserves to be placed—on the shoulders of those who are engaging in the discriminatory behaviour.

SELF-FULFILLING PROPHECIES

All other things being equal, if you believe that Amy is stupid and treat her accordingly, chances are that she will not say a lot of clever things in your presence. This is the well-known **self-fulfilling prophecy**, discussed in Chapter 4. How does this come about? If you believe that Amy is stupid, you probably will not ask her interesting questions and you will not listen intently while she is talking; indeed, you might even look out the window or yawn. You behave this way because of a simple expectation: Why waste energy paying attention to Amy if she is unlikely to say anything smart or interesting? This is bound to have an important impact on Amy's behaviour, for if the people she is talking to aren't paying much attention, she will feel uneasy and will probably clam up and not come out with all the poetry and wisdom within her. This in turn serves to confirm the belief you had about her in the first place. The circle is closed; the self-fulfilling prophecy is complete.

The relevance of this phenomenon to stereotyping and discrimination was elegantly demonstrated in an experiment by Carl Word, Mark Zanna, and Joel Cooper (1974). They asked white university undergraduates to interview several job applicants; some of the applicants were whites, and others were African Americans. Unwittingly, the students displayed discomfort and lack of interest when interviewing African-American applicants. For example, they sat farther away, they tended to stammer when talking, and they terminated the interview far sooner than when they were interviewing white applicants. Can you guess how this behaviour might have affected the African-American applicants? To find out, the researchers, in a second experiment, systematically varied the behaviour of the interviewers (actually confederates) so it coincided with the way the real interviewers had treated the African-American or white interviewees in the first experiment. However, in the second experiment, all of the interviewees were white. The researchers videotaped the proceedings and had the applicants rated by independent judges. They found that those applicants who were interviewed the way African Americans had been interviewed in the first experiment were judged to be far more nervous and far less effective than those who were interviewed the way whites had been interviewed in the first experiment. In sum, these experiments demonstrate clearly that when African Americans are interviewed by whites, they are unintentionally placed at a disadvantage and are likely to perform less well than their white counterparts (see Figure 13.6).

On a societal level, the insidiousness of the self-fulfilling prophecy goes even farther. Suppose there is a general belief that a particular group is irredeemably stupid, uneducable, and fit only for menial jobs. Why waste educational resources on them? Hence, they are given inadequate schooling. Thirty years later, what do you find? An entire group

Self-fulfilling prophecy

the case whereby people (a) have an expectation about what another person is like, which (b) influences how they act toward that person, which (c) causes that person to behave in a way consistent with people's original expectations

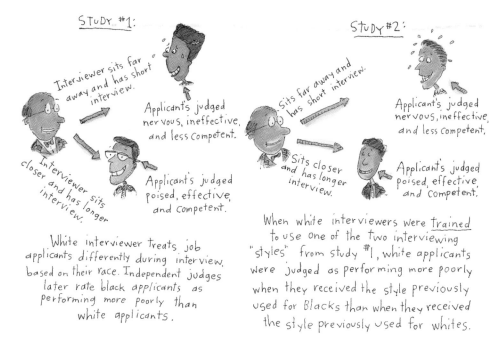

STUDY #1:

Interviewer sits far away and has short interview.

Applicant's judged nervous, ineffective, and less competent.

Interviewer sits closer and has longer interview.

Applicant's judged poised, effective, and competent.

White interviewer treats job applicants differently during interview, based on their race. Independent judges later rate black applicants as performing more poorly than white applicants.

STUDY #2:

Sits far away and has short interview.

Applicant's judged nervous, ineffective, and less competent.

Sits closer and has longer interview.

Applicant's judged poised, effective, and competent.

When white interviewers were trained to use one of the two interviewing "styles" from study #1, white applicants were judged as performing more poorly when they received the style previously used for Blacks than when they received the style previously used for whites.

that with few exceptions is fit only for menial jobs. "See? I was right all the time," says the bigot. "How fortunate that we didn't waste our precious educational resources on such people!" The self-fulfilling prophecy strikes again.

STEREOTYPE THREAT

Claude Steele and Joshua Aronson (Steele, 1997; Steele & Aronson, 1995a, 1995b; Aronson, Quinn, & Spencer, 1998) wondered whether the lower academic performance that has been observed among African-American students in the United States might be attributable to a phenomenon they termed **stereotype threat**. Specifically, when African-American students find themselves in highly evaluative educational situations, most tend to experience apprehension about confirming the existing negative cultural stereotype of "intellectual inferiority." In effect, they are saying, "If I perform poorly on this test, it will reflect poorly on me and on my race." This extra burden of apprehension in turn inter-feres with their ability to perform well in these situations. For example, in one of their experiments, Steele and Aronson administered a difficult verbal test, the GRE, individu-ally to African-American and white students at Stanford University. Half of the students of each race were led to believe that the investigator was interested in measuring their intellectual ability; the other half were led to believe that the investigator was merely try-ing to develop the test itself—and, because the test was not yet valid or reliable, they were assured that their performance would mean nothing in terms of their actual ability.

The results confirmed the researchers' speculations. White students performed equally well regardless of whether they believed the test was being used as a diagnostic tool. The African-American students who believed the test was non-diagnostic of their abilities performed as well as white students; in contrast, the African-American students who were led to believe that the test was measuring their abilities performed less well

Stereotype threat

the apprehension experienced by members of a minority group that they might behave in a manner that confirms an existing cultural stereotype

© 1992 Gary Hallgren

◄ What message is this female student getting about the competence of women? How likely is it that she will want to demonstrate her competence in the future?

than white students. In subsequent experiments in the same series, Steele and Aronson also found that if race is made more salient, the decrement in performance among African Americans is even more pronounced.

The phenomenon of stereotype threat applies to gender as well. As you know, a common stereotype of women is that, compared to men, they are not very good at math. In an experiment by Spencer, Steele, and Quinn (1999), when women were led to believe that men generally performed better on a particular test, they did not perform as well as men; however, in another condition, when women were led to believe that the same test did not generally show gender differences, they performed as well as men. These effects were replicated in Canada by Walsh, Hickey, and Duffy (1999). Male and female university students in Newfoundland were told that they would be taking a math test. The researchers mentioned that on Part A of the test, men typically scored higher than women, and that the purpose of Part B was to compare the performance of Canadian students with American students. (These instructions were reversed for other students, such that they were told that Part A was a comparison with American students, and that on Part B, men usually outperformed women.) Women scored lower than men only on the part of the test where they expected to be outperformed by men. They did as well as men on the part they believed was a comparison of the performance of Canadian and American university students.

As we have seen, if you are a woman and have been reminded of the stereotype that women don't perform well on math tests, you will do more poorly than if the stereotype is not brought to mind. But what if you happen to be an Asian woman and you also are aware of the stereotype that Asians are good at math? Might you perform differently depending on which stereotypes about you are activated? Shih, Pittinsky, and Ambady (1999) raised the intriguing possibility that you might actually perform differently, depending on which identity was activated—your identity as an Asian or your identity as a woman. The researchers conducted a fascinating study in which they administered the Canadian Math Competition test to a group of Asian-American female university students. Some of the women were reminded of their ethnicity before they took the test and others were reminded of their gender (a control group was not reminded of any identity before taking the test). Remarkably, the participants who had been reminded that they were Asian had the highest performance on the test, whereas those who had been reminded that they were women had the lowest performance (the control group scored in between these two groups).

In a follow-up study, Shih and colleagues demonstrated that these effects occur not because a particular identity has been activated, but rather because a stereotype associated with that identity has been activated. They again administered a math test, but this time to a group of Asian female students in Vancouver. They chose Vancouver because they believed that the stereotype that Asians are talented at math is not held as strongly in Canada as it is in the United States. Thus, in this study, being reminded that they were Asian was not expected to activate a stereotype of superior math performance. Indeed, in this study participants who were reminded of being Asian performed worse than a control group (who had not been reminded of any identity). Those who had been reminded of their gender again showed the lowest level of performance.

The researchers point out that being reminded of the stereotypes associated with one's identity usually has negative effects. However, as their first study demonstrated, given the right stereotype, performance may even be improved. This statement must be qualified, however, in light of Shih and colleagues' (2002) most recent findings. Specifically, these researchers found that the math performance of Asian Americans improved only when the stereotype that Asians are good at math was activated in a subtle manner. If Asian-American participants were explicitly reminded of the stereotype that Asians are good at math, their performance actually suffered. Why? The researchers suggest that blatant activation of a positive stereotype can cause people to "choke" under the pressure of living up to the high expectations that others have of their group (see Cheryan & Bodenhausen, 2000, for similar findings).

SELF-BLAMING ATTRIBUTIONS FOR DISCRIMINATION

Can you explain the following paradox? Numerous studies have found that members of disadvantaged groups often report that their group is discriminated against, but that they, personally, have not been the target of discrimination (Dion & Kawakami, 1996; Taylor, Ruggiero, & Louis, 1996; Taylor et al., 1990). For example, in research conducted at Carleton University (Foster & Matheson, 1999) and at the University of Western Ontario (Quinn et al., 1999), women reported greater group than personal discrimination in terms of pay equity, career opportunities, and sexual harassment. In Toronto, the Housing New Canadians Project has examined experiences of discrimination among three immigrant groups—Jamaicans, Poles, and Somalis—and has found that the personal-group discrimination discrepancy is most evident among the two most visible minority groups (because they are black; Dion, 2001). In other words, members of these groups claim that their group overall has encountered greater housing discrimination than they, personally, have experienced. Similarly, members of the East Indian community in Ottawa (Clément, Noels, & Deneault, 2001) and members of Aboriginal and other visible minority groups in Prince George, British Columbia (Michalos & Zumbo, 2001), report greater discrimination against their group than against them personally. Thus, these effects are widespread, and tend to be most pronounced among members of visible minorities.

How can we explain these findings? According to a program of research by Karen Ruggiero and Donald Taylor (1995, 1997; Taylor, Ruggiero, & Louis, 1996), individuals tend to minimize the discrimination they experience and instead blame themselves. In one of their first studies (Ruggiero & Taylor, 1995), female students from various faculties at McGill University took a test that would supposedly predict how successful they would be in their future careers. Moreover, they were told that anyone who performed well on the test would have a chance to win $50. After taking the test, the women were told that it would be graded by a group of male evaluators, and that either 100 percent, 75 percent, 50 percent, 25 percent, or 0 percent of the evaluators were known to discriminate against women. All of the participants received a mark of *F* on the test. They were then asked why they got such a low mark. Was it the quality of their answers? Was it the result of discrimination? Not surprisingly, participants who were told that 100 percent of the male evaluators were known to discriminate against women chalked up their low mark to discrimination. However, if there was any room for ambiguity at all, the women attributed their low grade to themselves (i.e., the quality of their answers) and not to discrimination. Remarkably, as shown in Figure 13.7, women who were told that there was a 75 percent chance they had been discriminated against blamed themselves as much as those who were told there was a 25 percent chance of discrimination.

Why would members of disadvantaged groups blame themselves—even when they are told that there is a 75 percent chance they have been discriminated against? To find out, Ruggiero and Taylor (1997) conducted another study, this time focusing on racial discrimination. Participants were East Asian and black (West Indian) students at McGill University who took the same career success test used in the previous study. This time, however, participants were told that the evaluators were white and that there was a 100 percent, 75 percent, 50 percent, 25 percent, or 0 percent chance that the evaluators discriminated against their ethnic group. Once again, participants attributed their failure to discrimination only when discrimination was 100 percent certain. In all other conditions, participants blamed themselves for their poor performance.

The researchers also assessed the participants' performance self-esteem (feeling good about their achievements), social self-esteem (feeling socially accepted), and perceived control. It turned out that when the victims of discrimination attributed their failure to discrimination (i.e., the 100 percent condition), their social esteem suffered (they experienced feelings of social rejection); however, their performance self-esteem remained intact because they knew that their score was not a valid assessment of their performance. In the other conditions, participants minimized the discrimination and blamed themselves, and this cost them performance self-esteem. However, doing so allowed them to maintain both social self-esteem and feelings of control.

These findings are highly disturbing, because in real-world situations one can rarely be 100 percent certain that one has been discriminated against. The results of this research suggest that, in most cases, victims of discrimination will blame themselves instead—

▶ **Figure 13.7**

SELF-BLAME AND
DISCRIMINATION.

Mean ratings of attribution to
quality of answers and
discrimination by participants in
five probability-for-discrimination
conditions.

(Ruggiero & Taylor, 1995)

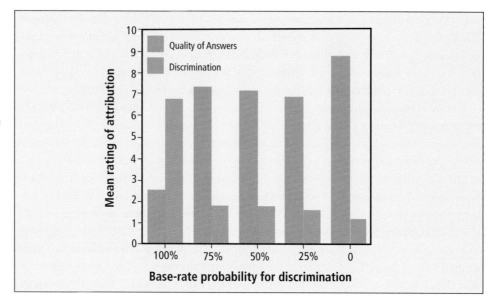

choosing to forfeit a sense of competence in favour of maintaining social acceptance and perceived control. Sadly, as Ruggiero and Taylor point out, this pattern may set up a vicious cycle. If minority group members blame themselves for negative outcomes, majority group members are able to justify their ongoing discrimination.

How Can Prejudice and Discrimination Be Reduced?

Sometimes subtle, sometimes brutally overt—prejudice is indeed ubiquitous. Does this mean that prejudice is an essential aspect of human social interaction and will therefore always be with us? We social psychologists do not take such a pessimistic view. We tend to agree with Henry David Thoreau, who said, "It is never too late to give up our prejudices." People can change. But how? We have offered a few clues throughout this chapter. For example, we have seen that getting people to focus on positive aspects of themselves (self-affirmation) reduces the need to denigrate others in order to get a self-esteem boost. We have also seen that blurring the distinction between "us" and "them" can improve attitudes toward out-groups. We will now focus on several more general strategies for eliminating, or at least reducing, this noxious aspect of human social behaviour.

LEARNING NOT TO HATE

It is obvious that parents and teachers play a crucial role in teaching children to treat others in a nondiscriminatory manner. Earlier we described a study by Rohan and Zanna (1996), showing that children tend to adopt their parents' values regarding issues related to prejudice. The important role that teachers can play was illustrated by the life-altering lesson in prejudice that Jane Elliot (1977), a teacher in Riceville, Iowa, taught her grade three class. Elliot was concerned that her young students were leading too sheltered a life.

The children all lived in rural Iowa, they were all white, and they were all Christian. Elliot felt it was important to give them some direct experience about what stereotyping and discrimination felt like, from both sides. To achieve this end, Elliot divided her class by eye colour. She told her students that blue-eyed people were superior to brown-eyed people—smarter, nicer, more trustworthy, and so on. The brown-eyed youngsters were required to wear special cloth collars around their necks so they would be instantly recognizable as a member of the inferior group. She gave special privileges to the blue-eyed youngsters; for example, they got to play longer at recess, could have second helpings at the cafeteria, and were praised in the classroom. How did the children respond?

In a matter of hours, Elliot succeeded in creating a microcosm of a prejudiced society in her classroom. Just a few hours before the experiment began, the children had been a cooperative, cohesive group; once the seeds of divisiveness were planted, there was trouble. The "superior" blue-eyed kids made fun of the brown-eyed kids, refused to play with them, tattled on them to the teacher, thought up new restrictions and punishments for them, and even started a fistfight in the schoolyard. The "inferior" brown-eyed kids became self-conscious, depressed, and demoralized. They performed poorly on classroom tests that day.

The next day, Elliot switched the stereotypes about eye colour. She said she'd made a dreadful mistake—that brown-eyed people were really the superior ones. She told the brown-eyed kids to put their collars on the blue-eyed kids. They gleefully did so. The tables had turned—and the brown-eyed kids exacted their revenge.

On the morning of the third day, Elliot explained to her students that they had been learning about prejudice and discrimination, and how it feels to be a person of colour. The children discussed the two-day experience and clearly understood its message. In a follow-up, Elliot met with these students at a class reunion when they were in their mid-twenties. Their memories of the exercise were startlingly clear—they reported that the experience had a powerful and lasting impact on their lives. They felt that they were less prejudiced and more aware of discrimination against others because of this childhood experience.

Jane Elliot's eye colour exercise has been used widely in classrooms and other settings (e.g., with prison staff) with the hope that experiencing discrimination firsthand will make people less likely to behave in discriminatory ways. For example, on March 21, 1998, Laidlaw School in Winnipeg implemented a variation of the eye colour exercise. Students whose hands had been marked with black ink were subjected to discrimination, while the other students received special privileges. In the afternoon, the situation was reversed. What impact did this experience have on the students? A grade seven student remarked that she now realized that "Every little comment or joke hurts a person . . . I know being a part (of the marking exercise) is just a small taste of what it's really like, [but] it really makes you think." As a result of this experience and other school activities designed to combat prejudice and racism, students in grades one to nine worked together to compose the following pledge:

Laidlaw School Pledge against Racism

I promise:

I will treat everyone equally because we are all the same inside.

I will stand up for others who are being treated unfairly because I will think how I would feel.

I will stop racist jokes and remarks.

I will not make fun of someone because they are from a different place or because of what they believe in.

I will be blind to the colour of skin.

Finally, an intriguing study by Aboud and Doyle (1996) suggests that children may be quite effective at teaching one another not to be prejudiced. Participants in this study were white students in grades three and four attending various schools in Quebec. First, their attitudes toward whites, blacks, and Chinese Canadians were assessed. Then the researchers paired a high-prejudice child with a low-prejudice child and asked the pairs to discuss their perceptions of different racial groups. Low-prejudice children were more likely than high-prejudice children to point out negative characteristics of whites and similarities across racial groups. For example, if a prejudiced child mentioned that a black classmate or a Chinese classmate had been mean, a low-prejudice child would point out white classmates who had been mean as well. Importantly, these discussions had the effect of reducing prejudice among the high-prejudice children. (Happily, the opposite did not occur; high-prejudice children did not create prejudice among low-prejudice children.) These findings are encouraging, and suggest that peers also may play an important role in teaching one another not to hate.

REVISING STEREOTYPICAL BELIEFS

Earlier, we mentioned that people tend to process information in ways that confirm their stereotypes—even if that information completely contradicts the stereotype. This may have left you feeling unconvinced that people can actually change. What sort of information would actually refute a stereotype? Let's say our next-door neighbour harbours two stereotypes that we find particularly annoying: He believes that professors are lazy and that immigrants are a drain on the welfare system. What would happen if we provided him with evidence that his stereotypes are incorrect? For example, what if we showed him data demonstrating that professors at the local university work a 50-hour week? What if we pointed out that unemployment rates are particularly low among immigrant groups? Would this information affect our neighbour's stereotypes?

Not necessarily. Renée Webber and Jennifer Crocker (1983) show that a great deal depends on how the disconfirming information is presented. According to these researchers, there are three possible models for revising stereotypical beliefs: (a) the **bookkeeping model**, wherein each piece of disconfirming information modifies the stereotype; (b) the **conversion model**, wherein the stereotype radically changes in response to a powerful, salient piece of information; and (c) the **subtyping model**, wherein new subtype or subcategory stereotypes are created to accommodate the disconfirming information, unless one receives information that the disconfirming information applies to a large number of cases. Webber and Crocker conducted several experiments to see which model(s) might be right. They presented participants with information that disconfirmed their stereotypes about two occupational groups: librarians and corporate lawyers. In one

Bookkeeping model
information inconsistent with a stereotype that leads to a modification of the stereotype

Conversion model
information inconsistent with a stereotype that leads to a radical change in the stereotype

Subtyping model
information inconsistent with a stereotype that leads to the creation of a new sub-stereotype to accommodate the information without changing the initial stereotype

◀ Although laws prohibiting Asian immigrants from voting, running for office, or becoming lawyers were overturned in the 1960s, Ujjal Dosanjh, the former premier of British Columbia, was the first Indo-Canadian ever to hold the office of premier in Canada. (He is shown here, hugging his wife after winning at the NDP leadership convention in Vancouver in February 2000.) Might a bigoted person have voted for him? Perhaps—if the bigot characterized him as "the exception that proves the rule."

condition, the participants received information in the bookkeeping style, one disconfirming fact after another. In another condition, the participants received conversion information, a single fact that strongly disconfirmed their stereotype. In the final condition, the participants received information that could lead them to create a subtype of their stereotype. Did these three styles of disconfirming information change people's minds about their stereotypes?

Webber and Crocker found that the bookkeeping information and the subtyping information did weaken the participants' stereotypes, but that the conversion information did not. Why? When many members of the categorized group exhibited the disconfirming traits, participants employed a bookkeeping strategy and gradually modified their beliefs. In other words, to return to our example, if our neighbour found out, on many occasions, that numerous professors worked a 50-hour week, this would slowly but eventually lead him to abandon the notion that professors are lazy. When the disconfirming traits were concentrated among only a few individuals of the group, participants used a subtyping model. Thus, if our neighbour encountered a few hardworking professors, he might create a new subtype, but leave the original stereotype intact. However, if information was provided about many professors who contradicted the stereotype to at least some extent, the original stereotype did change. Finally, the conversion approach just didn't work: one fact about an out-group that was evidence against the stereotype just wasn't enough to change people's minds—even if it was a powerful piece of information.

THE CONTACT HYPOTHESIS

As you have perhaps experienced in your own life, repeated contact with members of an out-group can have a positive effect on stereotypes and prejudice. However, as we shall see, mere contact is not enough; it must be a special kind of contact. Let's take a look at what we mean by "a special kind of contact." In his strikingly prescient masterwork *The Nature of Prejudice,* Gordon Allport (1954) stated the contact hypothesis in this way:

> Prejudice may be reduced by equal status contact between majority and minority groups in the pursuit of common goals. The effect is greatly enhanced if this contact is sanctioned by institutional supports (i.e., by law, custom or local atmosphere), and provided it is of a sort that leads to the perception of common interests and common humanity between members of the two groups.

In other words, Allport is not talking about mere contact; he is clear that contact must be between people who are of equal status and in pursuit of common goals. Four decades of research have substantiated Allport's early claim that these conditions must be met before contact will lead to a decrease in prejudice between groups (Cook, 1985). Let's now turn to a discussion of these conditions.

Remember Muzafer Sherif's (1961) study at the boys' camp—the Eagles and the Rattlers? Stereotyping and prejudice were created by instigating conflict and competition among the boys. As part of the study, Sherif and his colleagues also staged several events to reduce the prejudice they had created. Their findings at the boys' camp tell us a great deal about what contact can and cannot do.

First, the researchers found that once hostility and distrust were established, harmony between the groups could not be restored simply by removing the conflict and the competition. As a matter of fact, all attempts to bring the two groups together in neutral situations served only to increase the hostility and distrust. For example, the children in these groups had trouble with each other even when they were simply watching a movie together.

How did Sherif succeed in reducing their hostility? By placing the two groups of boys in situations in which they experienced **mutual interdependence**—a situation where two or more groups need each other and must depend on each other in order to accomplish a goal that is important to each group. For example, the investigators set up an emergency situation by damaging the water supply system. The only way the system could be repaired was for all of the Rattlers and Eagles to cooperate immediately. On another occasion, the camp truck broke down while the boys were on a camping trip. To get the truck going again, it was necessary to pull it up a steep hill. This could be accomplished only if all of the youngsters pulled together, regardless of whether they were Eagles or Rattlers. Eventually, these sorts of situations brought about a diminution of hostile feelings and negative stereotyping among the campers. In fact, after these cooperative situations were introduced, the number of boys who said their closest friend was in the other group increased dramatically (see Figure 13.8). Thus, two of the key factors in the success of contact are *mutual interdependence* and a *common goal* (Amir, 1969, 1976).

The third condition is *equal status*. At the boys' camp (Sherif et al., 1961), the group members were very much the same in terms of status and power. However, when status is unequal, interactions can easily follow stereotypical patterns—the bosses will act like stereotypical bosses, the employees will act like stereotypical subordinates—and no one will learn new, disconfirming information about the other group (Pettigrew, 1969; Wilder, 1984). The whole point of contact is to allow people to learn that their stereotypes are inaccurate; contact and interaction should lead to disconfirmation of negative, stereotyped beliefs.

Mutual interdependence

a situation in which two or more groups need each other and must depend on each other in order to accomplish a goal that is important to each group

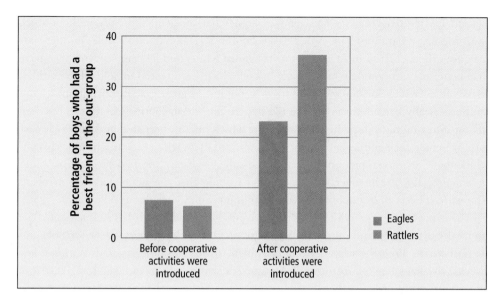

◀ Figure 13.8

INTERGROUP RELATIONS.

Intergroup tensions were eased
only after members engaged in
cooperative activities.

(Adapted from Sherif et al.,
1961)

Fourth, contact must occur in a *friendly, informal setting*, where in-group members
can interact with out-group members on a one-to-one basis (Brewer & Miller, 1984; Cook,
1984; Wilder, 1986). Simply placing two groups in contact in a room where they can
remain segregated will do little to promote their understanding or knowledge of each
other.

Fifth, through friendly, informal interactions *with multiple members* of the out-group,
an individual will learn that his or her beliefs about the out-group are wrong. It is crucial
for the individual to believe that the out-group members he or she comes to know are typical of their group; otherwise, the stereotype can be maintained by labelling one out-group
member as the exception (Wilder, 1984).

Sixth and last, contact is most likely to lead to reduced prejudice when *social norms
that promote and support equality* among groups are operating in the situation (Amir, 1969;
Wilder, 1984). We know the power of social norms; here, they can be harnessed to motivate people to reach out to members of the out-group. For example, if the boss in a work
setting or the professor in a classroom creates and reinforces a norm of acceptance and tolerance, group members will modify their own behaviour to fit the norm.

To conclude, when these six conditions of contact—mutual interdependence; a common goal; equal status; informal, interpersonal contact; multiple contacts; and social
norms of equality—are met, suspicious or even hostile groups will reduce their stereotyping, prejudice, and discriminatory behaviour (Aronson & Bridgeman, 1979; Cook,
1984; Riordan, 1978).

COOPERATION AND INTERDEPENDENCE: THE JIGSAW
CLASSROOM

Let's paint a scenario. Imagine a sixth-grader of Mexican origin, whom we will call
Carlos. Carlos has been attending schools in an underprivileged neighbourhood for his
entire life. Because the schools in his neighbourhood were not well equipped or well

staffed, his first five years of education were somewhat deficient. Suddenly, without much warning or preparation, he is bused to a school in a predominantly white, middle-class neighbourhood. Carlos must now compete against white, middle-class students who have had better preparation than he has had, and who have been reared to hold white middle-class values, which include working hard in pursuit of good grades, raising one's hand enthusiastically whenever the teacher asks a question, and so on. In effect, Carlos has been thrust into a highly competitive situation for which he is unprepared and in which pay-offs are made for abilities he has not yet developed. The white kids might quickly conclude that Carlos is stupid, unmotivated, and sullen—just as they had suspected (Wilder & Shapiro, 1989). Moreover, Carlos might conclude that the white kids are arrogant showoffs. This is an example of the self-fulfilling prophecy we discussed earlier.

Is it possible to get white students and minority students to have equal status, be mutually dependent, and pursue common goals? One of the authors of this textbook got to find out. In 1971, the school system of Austin, Texas, was desegregated. Within a few weeks, the schools were in turmoil. African-American, white, and Mexican-American children were in open conflict; fistfights broke out between the various racial groups in the corridors and schoolyards. The school superintendent invited Elliot Aronson, who was then a professor at the University of Texas, to enter the system with the mandate to do anything within reason to create a more harmonious environment. After spending a few days observing the dynamics of several classrooms, Aronson and his graduate students were strongly reminded of the situation that existed in the Sherif (1961) camp experiment. With the findings of that study in mind, they developed a technique that created an interdependent classroom atmosphere, designed to encourage the students of various racial and ethnic groups to pursue common goals. They called it the **jigsaw classroom**, because it resembled the assembling of a jigsaw puzzle (Aronson, 1992; Aronson & Bridgeman, 1979; Aronson & Gonzalez, 1988; Aronson et al., 1978; Aronson & Patnoe, 1997).

Here is how the jigsaw classroom works: Students are placed in diverse six-person learning groups. The day's lesson is divided into six paragraphs, so that each student has one segment of the written material. For example, if the students are to learn the life of Mother Teresa, her biography is arranged in six parts. Each student has possession of a unique and vital part of the information, which, like the pieces of a jigsaw puzzle, must be put together before anyone can learn the whole picture. The individual must learn his or her own section and teach it to the other members of the group—who do not have any other access to that material. Thus, if Debbie wants to do well on the ensuing exam about the life of Mother Teresa, she must pay close attention to Carlos (who is reciting on Mother Teresa's childhood), to Natalie (who is reciting on Mother Teresa's humanitarian actions), and so on.

Through the jigsaw process, the children begin to pay more attention to each other and to show respect for each other. As you might expect, a child like Carlos would respond to this treatment by simultaneously becoming more relaxed and more engaged; this would inevitably produce an improvement in his ability to communicate. And, the other students would begin to realize that Carlos is a lot smarter than they had thought he was. They begin to like him. Carlos begins to enjoy school more, his academic performance begins to improve, and so does his self-esteem. The vicious circle has been broken.

Jigsaw classroom
a classroom setting designed to reduce prejudice between children by placing them in small, desegregated groups and making each child dependent on the other children in the group to learn the course material and do well in the class

◀ When the classroom is structured so students of various ethnic groups work together cooperatively, prejudice decreases.

The formal data that Aronson and his colleagues gathered from the jigsaw experiments were clear and striking. Compared to students in traditional classrooms, students in jigsaw groups showed a decrease in prejudice and stereotyping, as well as an increase in their liking for their groupmates, both within and across ethnic boundaries. In addition, children in the jigsaw classrooms performed better on objective exams, liked school more, and showed a significantly greater increase in self-esteem than did children in traditional classrooms. Moreover, children in schools where the jigsaw technique was practised developed a greater ability to empathize with others and showed substantial evidence of true integration—that is, in the schoolyard there was far more intermingling among the various races and ethnic groups than in the yards of schools using more traditional classroom techniques (Aronson & Bridgeman, 1979). See Try It! on page 516.

The jigsaw approach was first tested in 1971; since then, several similar cooperative techniques have been developed (Cook, 1985; Johnson & Johnson, 1987, 1989; Meier, 1995; Sharan, 1980; Slavin, 1980, 1996). The striking results described above have been successfully replicated in thousands of classrooms in all regions of the United States, and in other countries as well. What began as a simple experiment in one school system has spread dramatically and has been adopted by a great many schools. Cooperative learning has become a major force within the field of public education and is generally accepted as one of the most effective ways of improving race relations in schools (McConahay, 1981; Deutsch, 1997; Slavin, 1996).

THE EXTENDED CONTACT HYPOTHESIS

We have seen that contact between groups can be highly effective in reducing prejudice. However, it isn't always possible to have members of different groups interact, particularly under the "right" conditions—where both groups have equal status, are mutually dependent on one another, have a common goal, and so on. Fortunately, recent research

Jigsaw-Type Group Study

The next time a quiz is coming up in one of your cours-es, try to organize a handful of your classmates into a jigsaw-type group for purposes of studying for the quiz.

Assign each person a segment of the reading. Each person is responsible for becoming the world's greatest expert on his or her material. Each person will organize the material into a report that she or he will present to the rest of the group. The rest of the group will feel free to ask questions in order to ensure that they fully under-stand the material. At the end of the session, ask the group members the following questions:

1. Compared to studying alone, was this more or less enjoyable?

2. Compared to studying alone, was this more or less efficient?

3. How do you feel about each person in the group—compared to how you felt about him or her prior to the session?

4. Would you like to do this again?

You should realize that this situation is probably a lot less powerful than the jigsaw groups described in this book. Why?

Extended contact hypothesis

the mere knowledge that a member of one's own group has a close relationship with a member of another group can reduce prejudice toward that group

on the **extended contact hypothesis** suggests that prejudice can be reduced simply by informing people that a member of their own group has a close relationship with an out-group member (Wright et al., 1997). Take a moment to think about a racial or ethnic group to which you do not belong. Then ask yourself how many people in your racial or ethnic group are friends with members of that group? Wright and colleagues found that the greater the number of people in our group who have friendships with out-group members, the less prejudiced we are toward that group. These effects have been found for both majority and minority groups.

In a fascinating study, these researchers examined whether they could reduce preju-dice between groups simply by creating some cross-group friendships and making each group aware of these friendships. Specifically, they recreated Sherif and colleagues' (1961) boys' camp study in which conflict was created between the Eagles and Rattlers, except they did so in their laboratory. At the beginning of the four-day study, university students were assigned to either the "blue" group or the "green" group and attempts were made to create conflict and hostility between the groups (these attempts apparently were quite suc-cessful). Then, one member of the blue group and one member of the green group were selected to participate in a supposedly unrelated experiment. This so-called "experiment" was actually a friendship-building exercise. Later, each of these participants was asked to describe the experience to their group. Remarkably, the discovery that one of the group members was now friends with the "enemy" caused the remaining group members of adopt more positive attitudes toward the out-group as a whole. They also became more generous to the out-group when allocating monetary rewards. These results are highly encouraging. To leave you with a take-home message, this research suggests that if you make the effort to become friends with a member of an out-group, it can have rather far-reaching effects. As members of the groups to which you belong learn about this friendship, they will become less prejudiced toward that group. Thus, you, alone, can truly make a difference.

SUMMARY

Prejudice is a widespread phenomenon, present in all walks of life. Social psychologists define **prejudice** as a hostile or negative attitude toward a distinguishable group of people based solely on their group membership. A **stereotype** is the cognitive component of the prejudiced attitude; it is defined as a generalization about a group whereby identical characteristics are assigned to virtually all members, regardless of actual variation among the members. **Discrimination**, the behavioural component of the prejudiced attitude, is defined as unjustified negative or harmful action toward members of a group based on their membership in that group.

As a broad-based and powerful attitude, prejudice has many causes. We discussed five aspects of social life that bring about prejudice: the way we think, the way we feel, the way we assign meaning or make attributions, the way we allocate resources, and the way we conform to social rules.

Social cognition processes (i.e., the way we think) are an important element in the creation and maintenance of stereotypes and prejudice. Categorization of people into groups leads to the formation of in-groups and out-groups. The in-group bias means that we will treat members of our own group more positively than we will members of the out-group, as demonstrated by the research on minimal groups. The perception of **out-group homogeneity** is another consequence of categorization: in-group members perceive out-group members as being more similar to one another than the in-group members are to one another. Stereotypes are widely known in a culture; even if you do not believe them, they can affect your cognitive processing of information about an out-group member. Recent research has shown that stereotypes can be selectively activated or inhibited, depending on motivational factors, most notably self-enhancement. The stereotypes that we believe out-groups hold of us, known as **meta-stereotypes**, also play a role in prejudice—we expect more negative interactions with and show more

prejudice toward members of groups we believe hold negative stereotypes of us.

Our emotions or moods also determine how prejudiced we are. When we are in a good mood, we are likely to evaluate members of out-groups more favourably than when we are in a bad mood. In addition, the attributions we make can serve to perpetuate prejudice. We tend to attribute the negative behaviours of out-group members to internal, dispositional factors and dismiss their positive behaviour as due to external, situational factors. This is known as the **ultimate attribution error**.

Realistic conflict theory states that prejudice is the inevitable by-product of real conflict between groups for limited resources—whether involving economics, power, or status. Competition for resources leads to derogation of and discrimination against the competing out-group. Social learning theory states that we learn the appropriate norms of our culture, including stereotypes and prejudiced attitudes. **Normative conformity**, or the desire to be accepted and "fit in," leads us to go along with stereotyped beliefs and not challenge them. People who are high in **modern prejudice** or neosexism tend to be prejudiced, but aren't willing to admit it because current social norms suggest that these kinds of prejudice are no longer acceptable.

A number of individual difference variables are associated with prejudice. Those who subscribe to just world beliefs and who are high in right-wing authoritarianism, religious fundamentalism, and social dominance are more likely to be prejudiced against out-groups than are those low on these dimensions.

Stereotyping, prejudice, and discrimination can have devastating effects on its victims. Research on **self-fulfilling prophecies** suggests that we may unknowingly create stereotypical behaviour in out-group members through our treatment of them. Members of an out-group also may experience **stereotype threat**—a fear that they might behave in a manner that confirms an existing stereotype about their group. Finally, there is evidence that victims of discrimination may blame themselves for their poor performance as a means of preserving social self-esteem and the perception of control.

Finally, on a societal level, the most important question to be asked is this: How can prejudice be reduced? One approach is to "nip it in the bud" by teaching children not to be prejudiced. Social cognition research has indicated that stereotypes can be revised; the **bookkeeping model** and the **subtyping model** (but not the **conversion model**) describe processes through which negative stereotypes change. An especially effective way of reducing prejudice is through contact—bringing in-group and out-group members together. However, mere contact is not enough and can even exacerbate the existing negative attitudes. Instead, contact situations must include the following conditions: **mutual interdependence**; a common goal; equal status; informal, interpersonal contact; multiple contacts; and social norms of equality. The **jigsaw classroom**, a learning atmosphere in which children must depend on each other and work together to learn and to reach a common goal, has been found to be a powerful way to reduce stereotyping and prejudice among children of different ethnicities. Finally, research on the **extended contact hypothesis** has shown that the mere knowledge that a member of our group is friends with an out-group can reduce prejudice toward that out-group.

IF YOU ARE INTERESTED

Allport, G. (1954). *The nature of prejudice*. Reading, MA: Addison-Wesley. Written the same year as the landmark U.S. Supreme Court decision on desegregation, this classic work remains an exciting and penetrating analysis of the social psychology of prejudice.

Altemeyer, B. (1981). *Right-wing authoritarianism*. Winnipeg, MB: The University of Manitoba Press. This is the first of three groundbreaking books on authoritarianism. The author introduces a new conceptualization of right-wing authoritarianism and describes the development of measures of this construct. He also presents an impressive series of studies spanning more than a decade to support his conceptualization. This is the definitive work on right-wing authoritarianism.

Altemeyer, B. (1988). *Enemies of freedom*. San Francisco, CA: Jossey-Bass. This is the sequel to *Right-wing authoritarianism*. The author documents conceptual and methodological developments in the study of right-wing authoritarianism. The relation between authoritarianism and aggression, religion, and politics is discussed, and possible explanations for authoritarianism are presented.

Altemeyer, B. (1994). Reducing prejudice in right-wing authoritarians. In M. P. Zanna & J. M. Olson (Eds.). *The psychology of prejudice: The Ontario symposium* (Vol. 7, pp. 131–148). Hillsdale, NJ: Erlbaum. In this article, Bob Altemeyer describes research in which he uses a value confrontation technique to lower prejudice among right-wing authoritarians. The results offer promise that right-wing authoritarians are not destined to live a life of bigotry.

Altemeyer, B. (1996). *The authoritarian specter*. Cambridge, MA: Harvard University Press. Topics in this most recent work include authoritarianism and religion, sex and the single authoritarian, and effects of hate literature. The book also describes the author's recent foray into left-wing authoritarianism. The final chapter provides a fascinating look at authoritarianism among North American legislators.

Aronson, E., & Patnoe, S. (1997). *Cooperation in the classroom: The jigsaw method*. New York: Longman. An updated account of the story of the classroom experiment that helped make school desegregation work—and that contributed to the launching of the trend toward cooperative education.

Dion, K. L. (2002). The social psychology of perceived prejudice and discrimination. *Canadian Psychology, 43*, 1–10. Kenneth Dion, a social psychologist at the University of Toronto, was the 2001 recipient of the prestigious D. O. Hebb Award for Distinguished Contributions to Psychology as a Science. This article was written in recognition of this award. In it, Dion documents the many and varied effects of prejudice and discrimination on its victims. A thought-provoking look at the phenomenology of prejudice.

Dion, K. L. (in press). Prejudice, racism, and discrimination. In M. J. Lerner (Ed.). *Comprehensive handbook of psychology*, Vol. 5. New York: John Wiley & Sons. A thorough, state-of-the-art review and analysis of research and theorizing on prejudice and discrimination.

Esses, V. M., Haddock, G., & Zanna, M. P. (1993). Values, stereotypes, and emotions as determinants of intergroup attitudes. In D. M. Mackie & D. L. Hamilton (Eds.). *Affect, cognition, and stereotyping*. San Diego, CA: Academic Press. This chapter offers an insightful summary and analysis of studies conducted at the University of Waterloo and the University of Western Ontario by the authors on emotion, cognition (stereotypes and values), and behaviour as determinants of attitudes toward social groups. This chapter was selected as the 1992 winner of the Otto Klineberg Intercultural and International Relations Award for offering "a substantial advance in our understanding of basic psychological processes underlying racism, stereotyping, and prejudice."

Fiske, S. (1998). Prejudice, stereotyping and discrimination. In D. Gilbert, S. Fiske & G. Lindzey (Eds.). *The handbook of social psychology* (4th ed., Vol. 1). New York: McGraw-Hill. A thorough treatment of stereotyping, its causes and consequences.

McKay, Jeff (Director/Editor). (1994). *Fat Chance* [Documentary]. This video produced by the National Film Board offers a poignant, touching look at the stigma of obesity in our society. The video documents the journey toward self-acceptance of several individuals struggling with obesity.

Pettigrew, T. F., & Meertens, R. W. (1995). Subtle and blatant prejudice in Western Europe. *European Journal of Social Psychology, 25,* 57–75. An excellent analysis of the distinctive difference between blatant and subtle forms of prejudice and how they affect behaviour in different ways.

Taylor, D. M., & Moghaddam, F. M. (1994). *Theories of intergroup relations* (2nd ed.). Westport, CT: Praeger Publishers. This book, written by two McGill University social psychologists, analyzes intergroup relations from an international perspective. Many of the topics covered in this chapter are discussed, including social identity theory, realistic conflict theory, and intergroup contact, to name a few. Of particular interest to Canadian readers are topics such as anglophone–francophone relations and the debate over multiculturalism.

WEBLINKS

www.cpa.ca/cjbsnew/1996/vol28-3.html

Ethnic Relations in a Multicultural Society—Special Issue of the Canadian Journal of Behavioural Science

This site provides access to the full text of this issue, which contains articles dealing with ethnic attitudes, prejudice, and discrimination.

www.crr.ca/EN/Publications/ePubHome.htm

Canadian Race Relations Foundation

The Canadian Race Relations Foundation produces a variety of publications on racism and racial discrimination that can be accessed from this site.

www.adl.org

Anti-defamation League of B'nai B'rith

Founded in 1913, this organization is the premier civil rights/human relations agency fighting anti-Semitism, prejudice, and bigotry.

www.eburg.com/~cole/index.html

Beyond Prejudice

This site discusses ways in which prejudice can be reduced, and myths about prejudicial behaviour.

Social Psychology and Health

LET US INTRODUCE YOU TO ERIKA "KATY" SIMONS, A VIVACIOUS, energetic woman who was born in Amsterdam in 1911. Katy grew up during the Second World War in Holland, where her family offered sanctuary to Jews. Whenever there was a knock on the door, Jews who were staying with them had to be quickly hidden. Katy and her family were well aware that they were placing their lives at risk by offering a safe haven to Jews. "I don't remember if I was ever afraid," she says. "It didn't matter. You just did what you needed to do." For Katy, doing what you needed to do also entailed delivering food and supplies to Jews. She was eventually captured by the Nazis and imprisoned. Katy and the other prisoners took turns sleeping on a single straw mattress and comforted one another by singing and reminiscing. During this time, she didn't know whether her family members also had been captured or if they were even alive. (Her mother eventually managed to have a note smuggled into the prison letting her know that they were fine.) When Katy was released from prison, she immediately resumed her acts of compassion, becoming a courier for the underground resistance movement and providing help to Jews. In April 2002, at the age of 91, Katy Simons was the first Canadian ever to receive the Righteous among the Nations award from the Holocaust memorial centre in Jerusalem. This award is bestowed on non-Jews who risked their lives to save Jews from the Holocaust. Although Katy Simons is honoured to be the recipient of this award, she accepts it with her usual modesty: "It is simple. If you can save a life, you do it" (Elvers, 2002).

The Second World War prevented Katy Simons from following her dream of attending university. Actually, she had hoped to begin university before the war started, but her father died and she was needed at home to help take care of her younger siblings. When she left home, she ended up taking nurse's training in a college in England because she needed to get into a career quickly in order to support herself financially. Although she longed to attend university, it wasn't an option; she never married and needed to keep working to make ends meet. But Katy never let go of her dream. As soon as she retired (by then she was in Canada), she registered for courses at the University of Winnipeg. She was a little worried that the other students might wonder what that "old lady" was doing there, and one day asked a fellow student if the others minded having her in class. "Oh, no!" said the student, "Not at all! You ask the questions I'd be too afraid to ask." Katy then knew that she was welcome.

Shortly after Katy started attending university, she required hip surgery. She recalls not wanting to miss her evening history class, so she managed to obtain special permission to leave the hospital. In her usual unstoppable way, she walked from the hospital to the university—a distance of at least one kilometre. (She did, however, accept a ride back to the hospital from her professor!) Katy became a familiar sight at the university and eventually graduated. Her infectious enthusiasm, humour, and warmth gained her instant popularity among students, staff, and faculty. Her age was never an issue.

The enthusiasm with which Katy embraced her university studies is characteristic of her approach to life. She still finds pleasure in the many activities in her life, which include origami and reciting poetry in any of the four languages she speaks fluently.

As Katy's experiences would suggest, her life has not been easy. Quite the contrary. She suffers from health problems that have reduced her mobility to the point where she

▶ Katy Simons, age 92, maintains her zest for life, despite the difficulties she faces.

had to move into an assisted living apartment. Remarkably, she manages to get around with the use of arm crutches, and she is thankful for the independence she has. When she was interviewed for this textbook, at age 92, she passed by the elevator and insisted on taking two flights of stairs up to the coffee shop in her building! People who know Katy are struck by the fact that her feisty spirit, her pleasant smile, and the sparkle in her eyes have not dimmed with age.

Why has Katy Simons lived such a long and rewarding life? Is her positive outlook on life related to her longevity, or is she simply blessed with good genes and good luck? As we will see, it may be more than a coincidence that Katy is so upbeat and in control of her life and in such good health for someone in her nineties.

This chapter is concerned with the application of social psychology to physical and mental health, which is a flourishing area of research (Cohen & Herbert, 1996; Pennebaker, 1982; Salovey, Rothman, & Rodin, 1998; Taylor, 1995). We will focus on topics on the interface of social psychology and health: how people cope with stress in their lives, the relationship between their coping styles and their physical and mental health, and how we can get people to behave in healthier ways.

Stress and Human Health

A great deal of anecdotal evidence indicates that stress can affect the body in dramatic ways. Consider these examples, reported by the psychologist W. B. Cannon (1942):

- After eating some fruit, a New Zealand woman learns that it came from a forbidden supply reserved for the chief. Horrified, her health deteriorates, and the next day she dies—even though it was a perfectly fine piece of fruit.

- A man in Africa has breakfast with a friend, eats heartily, and goes on his way. A year later, he learns that his friend made the breakfast from a wild hen, a food strictly forbidden in the man's culture. The man immediately begins to tremble, and is dead within 24 hours.

- An Australian man's health deteriorates after a witch doctor casts a spell on him. He recovers only when the witch doctor removes the spell.

These examples probably sound pretty bizarre. But let's fast-forward to the beginning of the twenty-first century, where many similar cases of sudden death occur following a psychological trauma. When people undergo a major upheaval in their lives, such as losing a spouse, declaring bankruptcy, or being forced to resettle in a new culture, their chance of dying increases (Morse, Martin, & Moshonov, 1991). There are many cases of sudden, unexplained deaths of people who are experiencing major life changes, such as among refugees who escaped Southeast Asia and resettled in the United States (Kirschner, Eckner, & Baron, 1986). Or consider the plight of an older person who is institutionalized in a long-term health care facility. In many such institutions in Canada, the residents have little responsibility for or control over their own lives. They cannot choose what to eat, what to wear, or even when to go to the bathroom. Residents in such institutions often become passive and withdrawn, and fade into death as if they have simply given up. This is quite a contrast to the zest shown by Katy Simons as she begins her tenth decade of life!

Stress also takes a toll on its victims in the here and now. According to research conducted at McGill University, Holocaust survivors, particularly those who were adolescents or young adults at the end of the war, continue to experience negative psychological effects such as paranoia and depression—more than 40 years after they were persecuted (Sigal & Weinfeld, 2001). Similarly, the cruelty and abuse some First Nations people suffered in residential schools continue to have traumatic effects on the survivors (Hanson & Hampton, 2000). And, as you know all too well, university life is fraught with stress. A large-scale study of university students across Canada found that psychological distress (e.g., anxiety, depression) was significantly higher among students than in Canada's general population (Adlaf et al., 2001). The good news was that distress declined with each successive year in university. Thus, things will get better as you go along!

As these examples suggest, our physical and psychological health is closely tied to the amount of stress in our lives. As we will see, we need to consider not only the amount of stress in our lives, but also how we deal with that stress (Inglehart, 1991).

EFFECTS OF NEGATIVE LIFE EVENTS

Among the pioneers in research on stress was Hans Selye (1956, 1976), who defined stress as the body's physiological response to threatening events. He focused on how the human body adapts to threats from the environment, regardless of the source of a threat—be it a psychological or physiological trauma. Later researchers have examined what it is about a life event that makes it threatening. Holmes and Rahe (1967), for example, suggested that stress is the degree to which people have to change and readjust their lives in response to an external event. The more change required, the more stress that occurs. For example, if a spouse or partner dies, just about every aspect of a person's life is disrupted, leading to a great deal of stress. This definition of stress applies to happy events in one's life as well, if the event causes a person to change his or her daily routine. Graduating from university is a happy occasion, but it can be stressful because of the major changes it sets in motion in one's life. Similarly, many people look forward to retirement, failing to anticipate the extent of life change that occurs as a result of this transition. For example, a recent study of Bell Canada retirees found that, for many people, retirement brings with it considerable instability and stress (Marshall, Clarke, & Ballantyne, 2001).

To assess such life changes, Holmes and Rahe (1967) developed a measure called the Social Readjustment Rating Scale (see Table SPA1.1). Some events, such as the death of a spouse or partner, have many "life change units," because they involve the most change in people's daily routines. Other events, such as getting a traffic ticket, have relatively few life change units. Here's how the scale works. Participants check all events that have occurred to them in the preceding year and then get a score for the total number of life change units caused by those events. The scores are then correlated with the frequency with which the participants become sick or have physical complaints. Several studies have found that the more life changes people report, the more anxiety they feel and the more likely they are to have been sick (Elliot & Eisdorfer, 1982; Seta, Seta, & Wang, 1990).

These findings probably don't come as much of a surprise; it seems pretty obvious that people who are experiencing a lot of change and upheaval in their lives are more likely to feel anxious and get sick. A closer look, however, reveals that these findings aren't all that straightforward. One problem, as you may have recognized, is that most studies in this area use correlational designs, rather than experimental designs. Just because life changes are correlated with health problems does not mean that the life changes *caused* the health problems (see our discussion in Chapter 2 of correlation and causality). Some researchers have argued persuasively that it is not life changes that cause health problems, but rather that people with certain personality traits, such as the tendency to experience negative moods, are more likely to experience life difficulties and to have health problems (Schroeder & Costa, 1984; Watson & Pennebaker, 1989).

Another problem with inventories such as Holmes and Rahe's is that it focuses on stressors experienced by the middle class and underrepresents stressors experienced by the poor and members of minority groups. Variables such as poverty and racism are potent causes of stress (Clark et al., 1999; Jackson & Inglehart, 1995; Jackson et al, 1996). To understand the relationship between stress and health, we need to understand better such community-level and culture-level variables as poverty and racism.

PERCEIVED STRESS AND HEALTH

A further limitation of simply counting the number of negative life events that people experience—such as whether people have gotten married or lost their job—is that it violates a basic principle of social psychology: Subjective situations have more of an impact on people than do objective situations (Griffin & Ross, 1991). Now, we certainly acknowledge that some situations are objectively bad for one's health, regardless of how one interprets them (Jackson & Inglehart, 1995; Taylor, Repetti, & Seeman, 1997). Still, there are events that seem to have negative effects only on the people who construe them in negative ways. Some people view getting a traffic ticket as a major hassle, whereas others view it as a minor inconvenience. Some people view a major life change such as getting divorced as a liberating escape from an abusive relationship, whereas others view it as a devastating personal failure. As recognized by Richard Lazarus (1966, 1993, 2000) in his pioneering work on stress, it is subjective, not objective, stress that causes problems. An event is stressful for people only if they interpret it as stressful; thus, we can define **stress**

Stress

the negative feelings and beliefs that occur whenever people feel unable to cope with demands from their environment

TABLE SPA1.1

The Social Readjustment Rating Scale

Rank	Life event	Life change units
1	Death of spouse	100
2	Divorce	73
3	Marital separation	65
4	Jail term	63
5	Death of a close family member	63
6	Personal injury or illness	53
7	Marriage	50
8	Fired at work	47
9	Marital reconciliation	45
10	Retirement	45
11	Change in health of a family member	44
12	Pregnancy	40
13	Sex difficulties	39
14	Gain of new family member	39
15	Business readjustment	39
16	Change in financial state	38
17	Death of close friend	37
18	Change to different line of work	36
19	Change in number of arguments with spouse	35
20	Mortgage over $10 000	31
21	Foreclosure of mortgage or loan	30
22	Change in responsibilities at work	29
23	Son or daughter leaving home	29
24	Trouble with in-laws	29
25	Outstanding personal achievement	28
26	Spouse begins or stops work	26
27	Begin or end school	26
28	Change in living conditions	25
29	Revision of personal habits	24
30	Trouble with boss	23
31	Change in work hours or conditions	20
32	Change in residence	20
33	Change in school	20
34	Change in recreation	19
35	Change in church activities	19
36	Change in social activities	18
37	Mortgage or loan less than $10 000	17
38	Change in sleeping habits	16
39	Change in number of family get-togethers	15
40	Change in eating habits	15
41	Vacation	13
42	Christmas	12
43	Minor violations of the law	11

Note: According to Holmes and Rahe (1967), the greater the number of "life change units" you are experiencing right now, the greater the likelihood that you will become physically ill. (Adapted from Holmes & Rahe, 1967.)

▶ Some of these events are happy, yet they cause stress. Which of these situations might cause you to experience stress?

as the negative feelings and beliefs that occur whenever people feel unable to cope with demands from their environment (Lazarus & Folkman, 1984).

Consider, for instance, our opening example of Katy Simons. If she were filling out the Social Readjustment Rating Scale, she would check "personal injury or illness," given that she is experiencing a number of health problems, as well as "begin or end school," and "change in living conditions," to name a few. She would thus receive a large number of life change units. According to the theory, she should be at high risk for further physical problems, due to the stress caused by her hip surgery, completing university, and so on. But as we saw, Katy is not particularly bothered by these events. With her characteristic optimism, she looks on the bright side, welcoming the fact that she is able to get about with crutches. Because she finds these events possible to cope with, they do not fit our definition of stress.

Studies using this subjective definition of stress confirm the idea that it is the life experiences that we perceive as negative that are bad for our health. For example, Lefrançois, Leclerc, Hamel, and Gaulin (2000) administered a French version of the Holmes and Rahe (1967) Social Readjustment Rating Scale (modified to focus on the life changes associated with aging) to elderly people in Quebec. As expected, life changes that were regarded to be negative were associated with the greatest psychological distress.

Stress caused by negative interpretations of events can even affect our immune systems, making us more susceptible to disease. Consider, for example, the common cold. When people are exposed to the virus that causes a cold, 20 to 60 percent of them become sick. Is it possible that stress is one determinant of who will become ill? To find out, Cohen, Tyrrell, and Smith (1991, 1993) asked volunteers to spend a week at a research institute in southern England. As a measure of stress, the participants listed recent events that had had a negative impact on their lives. That is, consistent with our definition of stress, the participants listed only events they perceived to be negative. The researchers then gave participants nasal drops that contained either the virus that causes the common cold, or saline (saltwater). The participants were subsequently quarantined for several days so that they had no contact with other people.

As you can see in Figure SPA1.1, the people who were experiencing a great deal of stress in their lives were more likely to catch a cold from the virus. Among people who reported the least amount of stress, about 27 percent came down with a cold. This rate increased steadily the more stress people reported, topping out at a rate of nearly 50 percent in the group that was experiencing the most stress. This effect of stress was found even when several other factors that influence catching a cold were taken into account, such as the time of year people participated and the participant's age, weight, and gender. This study, along with others like it, shows that the more stress people experience, the lower their immunity to disease (Cohen, 1996; Cohen et al., 1998; Cohen & Herbert, 1996; O'Leary, 1990).

The results from Cohen and colleagues' correlational study have been confirmed by research using experimental designs. For example, there are studies in which people's immune responses are measured before and after undergoing mildly stressful tasks in the laboratory, such as solving mental arithmetic problems continuously for six minutes or giving speeches on short notice. It turns out that even relatively mild stressors such as these can lead to a suppression of the immune system (Cacioppo, 1998; Cacioppo et al., 1998).

The finding that stress has negative effects on people's health raises an important question: What exactly is it that makes people perceive a situation as stressful? One important determinant, as we will now see, is the amount of control they believe they have over the event.

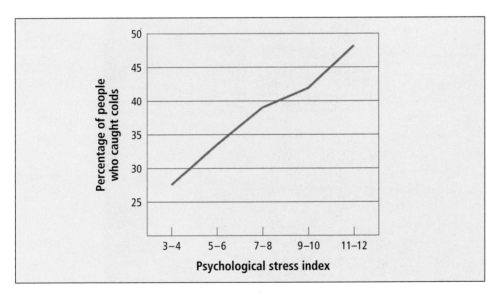

◀ Figure SPA1.1

STRESS AND THE LIKE-LIHOOD OF CATCHING A COLD.

People were first exposed to the virus that causes the common cold, then isolated. The greater the amount of stress they were experiencing, the greater the likelihood that they caught a cold from this virus.

(Adapted from Cohen, Tyrell, & Smith, 1991)

FEELING IN CHARGE: THE IMPORTANCE OF PERCEIVED CONTROL

How much control do you have over your own life? Are you able to decide what to do with each day? When and what to eat? When to study? When to go out with friends? Is it possible that the amount of control you have over your life is related to your health?

Studies with the chronically ill suggest that it is. Shelley Taylor and her colleagues (1984), for example, interviewed women with breast cancer and found that many of them believed they could control whether their cancer returned. Here is how one man described his wife: "She got books, she got pamphlets, she studied, she talked to cancer patients. She found out everything that was happening to her and she fought it. She went to war with it. She calls it 'taking in her covered wagons and surrounding it'" (quoted in Taylor, 1989). The researchers found that women who believed that their cancer was controllable were better adjusted psychologically. Moreover, there is some evidence that people who try to control their cancer and its treatment live slightly longer than those who do not (Taylor, 1989).

It is important to note that the beliefs of at least some of the women about their control over the cancer were probably incorrect. One woman, who worked in a dress shop, said that for years she carried dresses from the racks to the fitting room over her left arm, so that the hangers banged against her left breast. When she developed a tumour in her left breast, she assumed these repeated blows had caused it. From that point on, she put the dresses on a rack and rolled them to the fitting room. According to the experts, blows to the breast are not a cause of cancer. Nonetheless, this woman gained a sense of control by believing she knew the cause of her tumour and by doing something she believed helped. This suggests that **perceived control**, defined as the belief that we can influence our environment in ways that determine whether we experience positive or negative outcomes, is as important as real control (Burger, 1992; Skinner, 1995, 1996).

The benefits of perceived control have been demonstrated in a variety of domains. For example, Helgeson and Fritz (1999) interviewed patients who had undergone a

Perceived control

the belief that we can influence our environment in ways that determine whether we experience positive or negative outcomes

▶ Giving senior citizens a sense of control over their lives has been found to have positive benefits, both physically and psychologically.

coronary angioplasty because of diseased arteries. ~~The people who had a high sense of control over their futures were less likely to experience subsequent heart problems than those with a low sense of control~~.

Such effects are not limited to physical health. A study conducted with clients at sexual assault centres in southern Ontario found that rape victims who believed that they generally had control over outcomes in their lives experienced less depression and showed fewer symptoms of post-traumatic stress six months or more after the event. Rape victims who felt that they had little control were more likely to be suffering from depression and to be experiencing post-traumatic stress (Regehr, Cadell, & Jansen, 1999). In a very different vein, longitudinal research conducted by the Canadian Aging Research Network with elderly residents of Manitoba has found that those who perceive that they have control over difficulties with housework and outdoor work also are more likely to see themselves as having good health—more so than elderly people who perceive less control. Importantly, those who perceive control actually are in better health (Chipperfield, Perry, & Menec, 1999) and tend to live longer (Menec & Chipperfield, 1997).

Of course, studies such as these cannot prove that feelings of control cause good physical or emotional health; for example, it is possible that good physical or emotional health causes one to feel more in control. Indeed, Menec, Chipperfield, and Perry (1999) found that elderly people who believed that they were in good health were also more likely to perceive control over their lives and engage in control-enhancing strategies. To address the question of whether feelings of control have beneficial causal effects, we need to conduct experimental studies in which people are randomly assigned to conditions of "high" versus "low" perceived control. Fortunately, a number of such experimental studies have been conducted (Heckhausen & Schulz, 1995; Rodin, 1986).

Some of the most dramatic effects of perceived control have been found in studies of older people in nursing homes. Many people who end up in nursing homes and hospitals feel that they have lost control of their lives (Raps et al., 1982). People are often placed in long-term care facilities against their wishes, and, once there, have little say in what they do, whom they see, or what they eat. For example, an observational study of residents at a nursing home in Alberta found that patients tended to sit passively and to rely on nursing staff to initiate contact (Intrieri & Morse, 1997).

Ellen Langer and Judith Rodin (1976) believed that it would be beneficial for residents of a nursing home if their feelings of control were increased. To do so, they asked the director of a nursing home in Connecticut to convey to the residents that, contrary to what they might think, they had a lot of responsibility for their own lives. Here is an excerpt of his speech:

> Take a minute to think of the decisions you can and should be making. For example, you have the responsibility of caring for yourselves, of deciding whether or not you want to make this a home you can be proud of and happy in. You should be deciding how you want your rooms to be arranged—whether you want it to be as it is or whether you want the staff to help you rearrange the furniture. You should be deciding how you want to spend your time. . . . If you are unsatisfied with anything here, you have the influence to change it. . . . These are just a few of the things you could and should be deciding and thinking about now and from time to time every day (Langer & Rodin, 1976).

The director went on to say that a movie would be shown on two nights the following week and that the residents should decide which night they wanted to attend. Finally, he gave each resident a gift of a houseplant, emphasizing that it was up to the resident to take care of it.

The director also gave a speech to residents assigned to a comparison group. This speech was different in one crucial way—all references to making decisions and being responsible for oneself were deleted. The director emphasized that he wanted the residents to be happy, but he did not say anything about the control they had over their lives. He said that a movie would be shown on two nights the next week but that the residents would be assigned to see it on one night or the other. He gave plants to these residents as well, but said that the nurses would take care of the plants.

The director's speech might not seem like a major change in the lives of the residents. The people in the induced control group heard one speech about the responsibility they had for their lives and were given one plant to water. That doesn't seem like very strong stuff, does it? The important point to keep in mind is that to an institutionalized person who feels helpless and constrained, even a small boost in control can have a dramatic effect. Langer and Rodin (1976) found that the residents in the induced control group became happier and more active than did residents in the comparison group. Most dramatic of all, the induced control intervention affected the residents' health and mortality (Rodin & Langer, 1977). Eighteen months after the director's speech, 15 percent of the residents in the induced control group had died, compared to 30 percent in the comparison condition (see the left-hand side of Figure SPA1.2).

Richard Schulz (1976) increased feelings of control in residents of nursing homes in a different way. Schulz started a program in a North Carolina nursing home wherein undergraduates visited the residents once a week for two months. In the induced control condition, the residents decided when the visits would occur and how long they would last. In a randomly assigned comparison condition, it was the students, not the residents, who decided when the visits would occur and how long they would last. Thus, the

▼ Figure SPA1.2

PERCEIVED CONTROL AND MORTALITY.

In two studies, elderly residents in nursing homes were made to feel more in control of their lives. In one (Rodin & Langer, 1977), the intervention endured over time so that people continued to feel in control. As seen in the left-hand side of the figure, this intervention had positive effects on mortality rates. Those who received it were more likely to be alive 18 months later than those who did not. In the other study (Schulz & Hanusa, 1978), the intervention was temporary. Being given control and then having it taken away had negative effects on mortality rates, as seen in the right-hand side of the figure.

(Adapted from Rodin & Langer, 1977, and Schulz & Hanusa, 1978.)

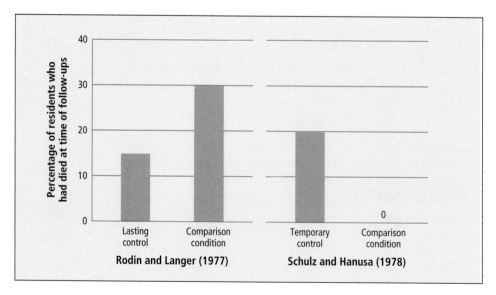

residents received visits in both conditions, but in only one could they control the visits' frequency and duration. This may seem like a minor difference, but again, giving the residents some semblance of control over their lives had dramatic effects. After two months, those in the induced control condition were happier, healthier, more active, and were taking fewer medications than those in the comparison group.

Schulz returned to the nursing home several months later to assess the long-term effects of his intervention, including its effect on mortality rates. Based on the results of the Langer and Rodin (1976) study, we might expect that those residents who could control the students' visits would be healthier and more likely to still be alive than residents who could not. However, there is a crucial difference between the two studies that should affect how long lasting the interventions were. The residents in the Langer and Rodin study were given an enduring sense of control, whereas the residents in the Schulz study were not. Langer and Rodin's participants could continue to choose which days to participate in different activities, continue to take care of their plant, and continue to feel they could make a difference in what happened to them—even after the study ended. By contrast, when Schulz's study was over, the student visits ended. The residents who could control the visits suddenly had that control taken away. The question is, What happens when people are given a sense of control, only to have it taken away? Unfortunately, Schulz's intervention had an unintended effect. Over time, the people in the induced control group did worse (Schulz & Hanusa, 1978). Compared to people in the comparison group, they were more likely to have experienced deteriorating health and zest for life, and they were more likely to have died (see the right-hand side of Figure SPA1.2). This study has sobering implications for the many programs in which volunteers visit residents of nursing homes, prisons, and mental hospitals. These programs might be beneficial in the short run, but do more harm than good after they end.

We close this section with a word of caution. First, the findings we have been describing are culturally specific. There is evidence that the relationship between perceived control and psychological distress is much higher in Western cultures than in Asian cultures (Sastry & Ross, 1998). In Western cultures, where mastery and individualism are prized, people are much more likely to feel distressed when they cannot control their destinies. Asians are less likely to worry about lower control because of their emphasis on collectivism and putting the group ahead of the individual.

Second, even in Western societies, there is a danger in exaggerating the relation between perceived control and physical health. As noted by Susan Sontag (1978, 1988), when a society is plagued by a deadly but poorly understood disease, such as tuberculosis in the nineteenth century and AIDS currently, the illness is often blamed on some kind of human frailty, such as lack of faith, moral weakness, or a broken heart. As a result, people sometimes blame themselves for their illnesses, even to the point where they do not seek effective treatment. Thus, whereas it is beneficial for people to feel that they are in control of their illnesses, the downside of this strategy is that if a person does not get better, he or she may feel a sense of self-blame and failure. Tragically, diseases such as cancer can be fatal no matter how much control a person feels. It only adds to the tragedy if people with serious diseases feel a sense of moral failure, blaming themselves for a disease that was unavoidable.

Fortunately, there are ways to maintain a sense of control even when one's health fails. Suzanne Thompson and her colleagues studied people with serious illnesses such as cancer and AIDS, and found that even if these people felt no control over the disease, many of them believed they could control the *consequences* of the disease (e.g., their emotional reactions and the nature of the physical symptoms related to the disease). These perceptions of control over the consequences were highly related to people's psychological adjustment. The more people felt they could control the consequences, the better adjusted they were, even if they knew they could not control the course of the disease. In short, it is important to feel in control of something—even if it is not the disease itself (Thompson, Nanni, & Levine, 1994; Thompson et al., 1993).

KNOWING YOU CAN DO IT: SELF-EFFICACY

Believing we have control over our lives is one thing. According to Albert Bandura (a highly influential social psychologist who was born in Alberta and studied at the University of British Columbia), we also have to believe that we can actually execute the specific behaviour that will get us what we want (Bandura, 1986, 1997, 1999; Bandura, Pastorelli, Barbaranelli, & Caprara, 1999). Sam might have a general sense that he is in control of his life, but does this mean that he will find it easy to stop smoking? According to Bandura, we have to examine his **self-efficacy**, which is the belief in one's ability to carry out specific actions that produce desired outcomes. If Sam believes that he is able to perform the behaviour that will enable him to quit smoking—throwing away his cigarettes, avoiding situations in which he is most tempted to smoke, distracting himself when he craves a cigarette—then chances are he will succeed. If he has low self-efficacy in this domain—he believes that he can't perform the behaviour necessary to quit—then he is likely to fail.

People's level of self-efficacy has been found to predict a number of important health behaviours, such as the likelihood that one will quit smoking, lose weight, lower one's cholesterol, and exercise regularly (Bandura, 1997; Salovey, Rothman, & Rodin, 1998). For example, a recent study of more than 1000 high-school students in Toronto found that those who were high in self-efficacy (in the area of exercise) were more likely to engage in vigorous physical exercise than those who were low in self-efficacy in this area (Allison, Dwyer, & Makin, 1999). Again, it is not a general sense of control that predicts this behaviour, but the confidence that one can perform the specific behaviour in question. A person might have high self-efficacy in one domain, such as high confidence that she can lose weight, but low self-efficacy in another domain, such as low confidence that she can quit smoking.

Self-efficacy increases the likelihood that people will engage in healthier behaviour in two ways. First, it influences people's persistence and effort at a task. People with low self-efficacy tend to give up easily, whereas people high in self-efficacy set higher goals, try harder, and persist more in the face of failure—thereby increasing the likelihood that they will succeed (Cervone & Peake, 1986; Litt, 1988). Second, self-efficacy influences the way our bodies react while we are working toward our goals. For example, people with high self-efficacy experience less anxiety while working on a difficult task, and their immune system functions more optimally (Wiedenfield et al., 1990; Bandura et al., 1988). In short, self-efficacy operates as a kind of self-fulfilling prophecy. The more you believe that you can accomplish something, such as quitting smoking, the greater the likelihood that you will.

Self-efficacy

the belief in one's ability to carry out specific actions that produce desired outcomes

How can self-efficacy be increased? A study by Blittner, Goldberg, and Merbaum (1978) on smoking cessation suggests one way. The participants were adult smokers who answered an advertisement for a treatment program to quit smoking. After filling out some initial questionnaires, they were randomly assigned to one of three groups. In the self-efficacy condition, people were told that they had been chosen for the study because they "showed that they had strong willpower and great potential to control and conquer their desires and behaviour" and that "it was quite certain that during the course of the treatment they would completely stop smoking" (Blittner, Goldberg, & Merbaum, 1978). These participants then underwent a 14-week program that taught them how to quit, by, for example, starting with the situations in which they found it easiest not to smoke and gradually working up to the situations in which they found it hardest not to smoke.

Participants in the treatment alone condition underwent the same 14-week program as people in the self-efficacy condition, with one important difference: Instead of being told that they had been selected because of their high potential for quitting, they were told that they had been chosen at random for the treatment program. Finally, participants in the no treatment control condition did not receive self-efficacy instructions or take part in the treatment program. They were told that they would be contacted for the study at a later time.

As seen in Figure SPA1.3, the self-efficacy instructions were quite effective. By the end of the treatment period, 67 percent of people in the self-efficacy condition had quit smoking, compared to only 28 percent in the treatment alone group and 6 percent in the no treatment control group. Remember that the only way in which the self-efficacy and treatment alone conditions differed was that the former participants believed that they had high potential for quitting. Believing that we can do something is a powerful determinant of whether we actually succeed.

▼ **Figure SPA1.3**

THE ROLE OF SELF-EFFICACY IN SMOKING CESSATION.

Adult smokers were randomly assigned to one of three conditions. In the self-efficacy condition, people were told that they were selected for the study because they had great potential to quit. They then underwent a 14-week smoking cessation program. People in the treatment alone condition participated in the same program, but were told that they had been randomly selected for it. People in the no treatment control condition did not take part in the program. At the end of the 14-week period, substantially more people in the self-efficacy condition had quit smoking. Believing that one has the ability to carry out beneficial behaviour—having high self-efficacy—is an important determinant of whether people succeed.

(Adapted from Blittner, Goldberg, & Merbaum, 1978)

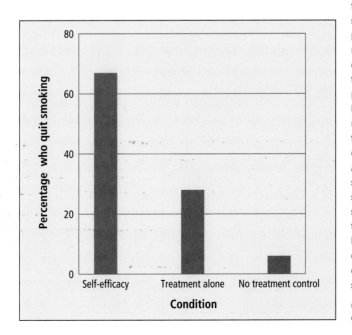

EXPLAINING NEGATIVE EVENTS: LEARNED HELPLESSNESS

What happens when we experience a setback? Despite our belief in ourselves, maybe we failed to quit smoking or to maintain our fitness regimen. Another important determinant of our physical and mental health is how we explain to ourselves why a negative event occurred.

Imagine getting a poor grade on a math exam. Explaining this negative event as due to a stable cause—that is, making a **stable attribution**—is to believe that the cause of the event is due to factors that will not change over time (e.g., your intelligence), as opposed to unstable factors that can change over time (e.g., the amount of effort you put into studying). Explaining this negative event as due to an internal cause—that is, making an **internal attribution**—is to believe that the cause of the event is due to things about you (e.g., your own ability or effort), as opposed to factors that are external to you (e.g., the difficulty of a test). Finally, explaining an event as due to a global cause—that is, making a **global attribution**—is to believe that the cause of an event is due to factors that apply in a large number of situations (e.g., your intelligence, which will influence your performance in many areas), as opposed to believing that the cause is specific and applies in only a limited number of situations (e.g., your math ability, which will affect your performance in math courses but not in other courses). According to **learned helplessness** theory, making stable, internal, and global attributions for negative events leads to hopelessness, depression, reduced effort, and difficulty in learning (see Figure SPA1.4).

In Figure SPA1.4, student 2, for example, believes that the cause of his poor grade on a calculus test is stable (being unintelligent will last forever), internal (something about him is to blame), and global (being unintelligent will affect him in many situations other than calculus classes). This kind of explanation will lead to learned helplessness, thereby producing depression, reduced effort, and the inability to learn new things. Student 1, on the other hand, believes that the cause of her poor grade is unstable (the professor will make the tests easier, and she can study harder next time), external (the professor purposefully made the test hard), and specific (the things that caused her poor calculus grade are unlikely to affect anything else, such as her grade in English). People who explain bad events in this more optimistic way are less likely to be depressed and more likely to do better on a broad range of tasks (Joiner & Wagner, 1995; Peterson & Seligman, 1984; Sweeney, Anderson, & Bailey, 1986).

To return to Figure SPA1.4, we do not know the real reason our hypothetical students did poorly on their calculus test. Instead, learned helplessness theory states that it is

Stable attribution
the belief that the cause of an event is due to factors that will not change over time, as opposed to unstable factors that will change over time

Internal attribution
the belief that the cause of an event is due to things about you, as opposed to factors that are external to you (e.g., the difficulty of a test)

Global attribution
the belief that the cause of an event is due to factors that apply in a large number of situations, as opposed to the belief that the cause is specific and applies in only a limited number of situations

Learned helplessness
the state of pessimism that results from explaining a negative event as due to stable, internal, and global factors

▶ People can experience learned helplessness in a variety of settings, including at work. Fortunately, most bosses do not encourage learned helplessness in the way that Dilbert's boss does.

DILBERT reprinted by permission of United Feature Syndicate, Inc.

THE THEORY OF LEARNED HELPLESSNESS

Unstable, External, Specific Attribution

An F on my calculus test! Oh well, I bet the professor purposefully made the test hard. And I have to admit, I could have studied more.

Increased Effort

Improved Performance

B+

Stable, Internal, Global Attribution

An F on my calculus test! I've been worried that I'm not smart enough to make it in university and now I know it's true.

Learned Helplessness (Depression, Lowered Effort, Poor Learning)

Poor Performance

▲ **Figure SPA1.4**

THE THEORY OF LEARNED HELPLESSNESS.

Explaining a negative event in a pessimistic manner leads to learned helplessness (depression, lowered effort, poor learning).

more important to consider people's perceptions of these causes. The real causes, of course, are not irrelevant. If students lack ability in calculus, they are likely to do poorly on future calculus tests. However, often in life what actually causes our behaviour is not as clear-cut or as fixed. In such situations, people's attributions about the causes of their problems can be very important.

To explore this link between learned helplessness and academic performance, Tim Wilson and Patricia Linville (1982, 1985) conducted a study with first-year students at Duke University. They assumed that many first-year students experience academic difficulties because of a damaging pattern of attributions. Due to the difficulty of adjusting to a new academic and social environment, the first year of university has its rough spots for nearly everyone. The problem is, many first-year students do not realize how common such adjustment problems are and assume that their problems are due to personal predicaments that are unlikely to change—just the kind of attribution that leads to learned helplessness.

Wilson and Linville tried to combat this pessimism by convincing first-year students who were concerned about their academic performance that the causes of poor performance are often temporary. In the treatment condition, the students watched videotaped interviews of four more senior students, each of whom, during the interviews, mentioned that his or her grades had been poor or mediocre during the first year but had improved significantly since then. The students were also given statistics indicating that academic performance is often poor in the first year of university but improves thereafter. The researchers hypothesized that this simple message would help prevent learned helplessness, increasing the students' motivation to try harder and removing needless worries about their abilities. Judging by the students' future performance, this is just what happened. Compared to students in a control group who participated in the study but did not watch the videotaped interviews or see the statistics, students in the treatment condition improved their grades more in the following year and were less likely to drop out (see Figure SPA1.5). Similar results have been found in studies in other countries, such as in Canada and Belgium (Menec et al., 1994; Van Overwalle & De Metsenaere, 1990).

Because people's attributions were not directly measured in the Wilson and Linville (1982) study, we can only infer that the students improved their academic performance because of a beneficial change in their attributions. However, several other studies have directly measured people's attributions and found that those who explain bad events in optimistic ways are less depressed, in better health, and do better in school and in their careers (Burhans & Dweck, 1995; Dweck, 1999; Peterson, Seligman, & Vaillant, 1988; Seligman & Schulman, 1986; Snyder, Irving, & Anderson, 1991). For example, a recent study conducted at the University of Manitoba found that first-year students who felt that they had control over their academic performance reported less anxiety and boredom and actually received better grades than those who perceived less control (Perry, Hladkyj, Pekrun, & Pelletier, 2001). Students who were high in perceived control and who used failure experiences as a motivation to do better in the future, rather than dwelling on the failure, were especially likely to do well.

Recent research by Rempel, Ross, and Holmes (2001) suggests that those who make optimistic attributions for negative events also do better in their close relationships. Married couples living in the Waterloo area were asked to discuss a problem issue in their relationship. The researchers then compared whether couples who were high in trust made different attributions for problem issues in their relationships than couples who

▼ **Figure SPA1.5**

COMBATING LEARNED HELP-LESSNESS IN FIRST-YEAR UNIVERSITY STUDENTS.

In the treatment condition, first-year university students learned that the causes of poor academic performance in the first year can be temporary. This knowledge led to improvements in their grade-point average and made them less likely to drop out.

(Adapted from Wilson & Linville, 1982)

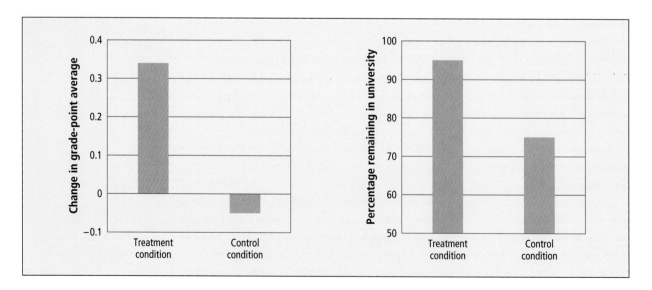

were low in trust. Indeed, high-trust couples were found to make positive, global attributions for their partner's behaviour. Thus, even when discussing a conflict issue, these couples were optimistic—they focused on the enduring, positive aspects of their partner and the relationship. In contrast, low-trust couples showed a pattern of negative, pessimistic attributions. In the words of Rempel and colleagues (2001), "People in low-trust relationships seem to have resigned themselves to the belief that the struggle to find solutions for current problems offers too little chance of return on the required emotional investment." In short, for these couples, learned helplessness has set in.

In summary, we have seen that people's feelings of control and self-efficacy, and the kinds of attributions they make for their performance, are important determinants of their psychological and physical adjustment. People who feel a lack of control and self-efficacy, or explain events in pessimistic terms (i.e., who experience learned helplessness) are more likely to be in poor health and to experience academic, professional, and relationship problems. The power of our minds over our bodies is, of course, limited. However, research shows that perceived control, self-efficacy, and optimistic attributions are beneficial, making it easier for us to cope with the hardships life deals us.

Coping with Stress

Now that we know the causes of perceived stress, it is important to consider how people deal with stress. There has been a great deal of research on **coping styles**, defined as the ways in which people react to stressful events (e.g., Aspinwall & Taylor, 1997; Lazarus & Folkman, 1984; Lehman, Davis, DeLongis, & Wortman, 1993; Pennebaker & Harber, 1993; Salovey, Rothman, & Rodin, 1998; Somerfield & McCrae, 2000). What are these styles and how successful are they? We will examine a few coping styles here, beginning with research on personality traits related to coping.

Coping styles
the ways in which people react to stressful events

PERSONALITY AND COPING STYLES

What is it about some people that seems to make them more resistant to stress? A number of personality variables have been studied, such as optimism. It seems that some people, such as Katy Simons, are by nature optimistic, generally expecting the best out of life, whereas others are sourpusses who always see the dark underside of life. Consistent with research on learned helplessness, there is evidence that optimistic people react better to stress and are healthier than their pessimistic counterparts (Armor & Taylor, 1998; Carver & Scheier, 1998; Carver et al., 2000; Salovey et al., 2000; Scheier & Carver, 1987; Scheier et al., 1990). To get an idea of how optimistic you tend to be, complete the test in the Try It! box on page 538.

Most people have been found to have optimistic outlooks on life. In fact, there is evidence that most people are *unrealistically* optimistic about their lives (Armor & Taylor, 1998; Taylor & Brown, 1988, 1994). As you may recall, in Chapter 4 we discussed research on unrealistic optimism showing that we tend to expect that good events are more likely to happen to us than to our peers, and that negative events are less likely to happen to us than to our peers. This kind of unrealistic optimism would be a problem if it caused people to make serious mistakes about their prospects in life. Obviously, it would not be a good idea to convince ourselves that we will never get lung cancer and therefore smoke

The Life Orientation Test

Please indicate the extent of your agreement with each of the following 10 statements, using the scale below. Be as accurate and honest as you can on all items, and try not to let your answer to one question influence your answer to other questions. There are no right or wrong answers.

0	1	2	3	4
strongly disagree	disagree	neutral	agree	strongly agree

1. In uncertain times, I usually expect the best.
2. It's easy for me to relax.
3. If something can go wrong for me, it will.
4. I'm always optimistic about my future.
5. I enjoy my friends a lot.
6. It's important for me to keep busy.
7. I hardly ever expect things to go my way.
8. I don't get upset too easily.
9. I rarely count on good things happening to me.
10. Overall, I expect more good things to happen to me than bad.

Scoring: First, reverse your answers to questions 3, 7, and 9. That is, for these questions, change a 0 to a 4, a 1 to a 3, a 3 to a 1, and a 4 to a 0. Then, total these reversed scores and the scores you gave to questions 1, 4, and 10. (Ignore questions 2, 5, 6, and 8, because they were filler items.)

This is a measure of dispositional optimism created by Scheier, Carver, and Bridges (1994). According to these researchers, the higher your score, the more optimistic your approach to life. The average score for university students in their study was 14.3, with no significant differences between women and men. Several studies have found that optimistic people cope better with stress and are healthier than their pessimistic counterparts.

Type A versus Type B personality

a personality typology based on how people typically confront challenges in their lives; the Type A person is typically competitive, impatient, hostile, and control-oriented, whereas the Type B person is typically patient, relaxed, and noncompetitive

three packs of cigarettes a day. David Armor and Shelley Taylor (1998) suggest, however, that most people have a healthy balance of optimism and reality monitoring. We manage to put a positive spin on many aspects of our lives, which leads to increased feelings of control and self-efficacy—which, as we have seen, is a good thing. At the same time, Armor and Taylor found that most people are able to keep their optimistic biases in check when they are faced with a real threat and need to take steps to deal with that threat.

Another personality variable that has received a great deal of attention is the **Type A versus Type B personality**, which is a personality typology based on how people typically confront challenges in their lives (Rosenman, 1993). The Type A individual is typically competitive, impatient, hostile, aggressive, and control-oriented, whereas the Type B person is typically patient, relaxed, and noncompetitive. We are all familiar with the Type A pattern; this is the person who honks and yells at other drivers when they don't drive to his

Edward Koren ® 1989 from The New Yorker Collection. All rights reserved.

◀ It is important to try to adopt an optimistic approach to life, because optimists have been found to be healthier and to react better to stress.

or her satisfaction. People with this personality trait appear to deal with stress efficiently and aggressively. Their hard-driving, competitive approach to life pays off in some respects; Type A individuals tend to get good grades in university and to be successful in their careers (Kliewer, Lepore, & Evans, 1990; Ovcharchyn, Johnson, & Petzel, 1981). However, this success comes with some costs. According to research conducted at York University, Type A individuals spend relatively little time on non-work activities (Burke & Greenglass, 1990) and have more difficulty balancing their work and family lives. For example, Esther Greenglass (1991) found that among female professors, being Type A was associated with having high career aspirations and reporting conflict between professional and familial roles. Type A women with children were particularly hard-driven—they spent an average of 86 hours per week working on job-related and household tasks. Further, numerous studies show that Type A individuals are more prone to coronary heart disease, compared to Type B people (Matthews, 1988). Subsequent studies have tried to narrow down what it is about the Type A personality that is most related to heart disease. The most likely culprit is hostility (Matthews, 1988; Salovey, Rothman, & Rodin, 1998; Williams, 1987). Competitiveness and a fast-paced life might not be so bad by themselves, but people who are chronically hostile are more at risk for coronary disease.

Type A personality may partially explain why Stewart McCann (2001) at the University College of Cape Breton found that people who peak early in their careers have shorter lives. This tendency to die young if you peak early was found among American and French presidents, Canadian prime ministers, Nova Scotia premiers, and distinguished psychologists, to name a few. McCann suggests that the higher mortality rate among high achievers may be due to the stress that is associated with high-level performance, perhaps coupled with Type A personality.

What determines whether people have Type A or Type B personalities? A number of factors have been found to be related. You are more likely to be a Type A if you are male, your parents are Type A, and you live in an urban rather than a rural area

▶ People with a Type A personality—those who are impatient, competitive, and hostile—are more likely to get coronary disease than are people who are relaxed, patient, and non-hostile. Former Maple Leafs coach Pat Burns is known for his competitive and impatient personality—a winning combination, in this case.

(Rosenman, 1993). The culture in which you grow up may also play a role. It is well known that a higher incidence of coronary disease exists in many Western cultures than in many Asian cultures, such as Japan. Triandis (1995) suggests that one reason for this disparity is the emphasis on independence and individualism in Western cultures and on interdependence and collectivism in Asian cultures. He points to two ways in which these emphases might be related to heart disease. First, cultures that stress individualism emphasize competitiveness more and thus might encourage personality types more like Type A. Second, people who live in cultures that stress collectivism might have more support from other people when they experience stress, and, as we will see shortly, such social support is a valuable way of making stress more manageable.

Hardiness

a personality trait defined as a combination of self-esteem and a sense of control

Kenneth Dion and his colleagues recently examined the personality variable of **hardiness** in relation to a particular kind of stress, namely the stress of being a victim of prejudice and discrimination (Dion, in press, 2002). Hardiness is a combination of self-esteem and a sense of control that helps people interpret and deal with stressful events in a positive, effective manner. In one study, Dion and colleagues assessed perceptions of discrimination, stress symptoms, and hardiness among members of Toronto's Chinese community (Dion, Dion, & Pak, 1992). They found that discrimination was correlated with psychological stress—but only for those who were low in hardiness. People with hardy personalities reported just as much discrimination, but much less stress.

Why might people who are hardy experience less stress in the face of discrimination? Foster and Dion (2001) wondered whether people who are high in hardiness make different attributions for discrimination than those who are low in hardiness. To find out, they conducted a study on gender discrimination and found that hardy women tended to attribute discrimination to specific, unstable factors rather than to global, stable factors. In other words, the hardy participants, unlike their less hardy counterparts, treated the discrimination they experienced as an isolated event. Dion and colleagues are currently exploring other explanations for why hardy people cope better with stress, as well as the limits of hardiness (Dion, in press, 2002).

Investigations such as these are in the domain of personality psychology, in that they focus on traits that set people apart: What is it about one person that makes her or him more resistant to health problems than another person? The social psychologist takes a different tack: Can we identify ways of coping with stress that everyone can adopt to make it easier to deal with the challenges of life?

"OPENING UP": CONFIDING IN OTHERS

When something traumatic happens to you, is it best to try to bury it as deep as you can and never talk about it, or to open up and discuss your problems with others? Although folk wisdom has long held that it is best to open up, only recently has this assumption been put to the test. James Pennebaker (1990, 1997; Pennebaker & Seagal, 1999) and his colleagues have conducted a number of interesting experiments on the value of confiding in others. Pennebaker and Beale (1986), for example, asked university students to write, for 15 minutes on each of 4 consecutive nights, about a traumatic event that had happened to them. Students in a control condition wrote for the same amount of time about a trivial event. The traumas that people chose to write about were highly personal and in many cases quite tragic, including such events as rape and the death of a sibling.

Writing about these events was upsetting in the short term: People who wrote about traumatic events reported more negative moods and showed greater increases in blood pressure. However, there were long-term benefits. The people who wrote about traumatic events were less likely to visit the student health centre during the next six months, and they reported having fewer illnesses. Similarly, Pennebaker and his colleagues found that first-year university students who wrote about the problems of entering university (Pennebaker, Colder, & Sharp, 1990) and survivors of the Holocaust who disclosed the most about their Second World War experiences improved their health over the next

◀ Research by Pennebaker (1990) on "opening up" shows that there are long-term health benefits to writing or talking about one's personal trauma.

several months (Pennebaker, Barger, & Tiebout, 1989). Other research confirms the importance of "opening up." For example, a study of more than 2000 Ontario nurses found that those who reported having a friend to confide in experienced fewer stress-related health problems, although this relation was more likely to hold for women than for men (Walters et al., 1996).

What is it about "opening up" that leads to better health? Pennebaker argues that actively trying to inhibit or not think about a traumatic event takes a lot of mental and physical energy and is thus itself stressful. Having to constantly fight back thoughts about a trauma exerts a toll on our bodies. Evidence for this was found in a study by Jane Richards and James Gross (1999). In this study, research participants were shown slides of people who had been physically injured. The injuries ranged from very mild to very severe (the latter being upsetting to look at). In addition, biographical information about each injured person was presented orally during the slide show. Half of the research participants were told to watch the slides and listen to the background information; the other half were also told, "If you have any feelings as you watch the slides, please try your best not to let those feelings show." The research participants were surreptitiously videotaped; analyses of these videotapes revealed that those who had been told to suppress their emotions did a very good job of doing so. But at what cost? Richards and Gross found that suppressing negative emotions led participants to have significantly poorer memory for the biographical information and significantly higher blood pressure readings when compared to the participants who were allowed to express whatever emotion they felt. Thus, suppressing emotions such as anger, fear, or sadness interferes with cognitive processing (impaired memory for information encountered at the same time), and takes a toll on our physical health. Trying to suppress negative thoughts can lead to another cognitive difficulty, namely an obsession with those very thoughts, such that people think about them more and more (Wegner, 1994).

Another reason that writing about or confiding in others about a traumatic event is beneficial is that it may help people gain a better understanding of the event, helping them to put it behind them. This idea was explored in a recent, intriguing study by Anita Kelly and colleagues (2001). These researchers had people write about their most personal, private secrets. Participants in the insight group were asked to "focus on making sense out of the secret or gaining new insights into the secret." Those in the catharsis group were asked to "focus on what you are feeling about the secret and getting those feelings out in the open." The results were clear: Those in the insight group experienced more positive emotions two weeks later, and felt that they had come to terms with their secret—more so than those in the catharsis group. For example, one participant in the insight group who wrote about a family member's suicide reported now having a different perspective on this experience:

> it makes me look at life from a different perspective . . . it has been one of the most enlightening experiences of my life. It has made me see the importance of openness and honesty with one's problems.

Finally, another benefit of "opening up" is that it might also elicit emotional support from others—which, as we will now see, can be an important part of the coping process.

SOCIAL SUPPORT: GETTING HELP FROM OTHERS

A number of studies have found that **social support**, defined as the perception that others are responsive and receptive to one's needs, is an important aid in dealing with stress (Helgeson & Cohen, 1996; Hobfoll & Vaux, 1993; Sarason, Sarason, & Pierce, 1990; Stroebe & Stroebe, 1996; Uchino, Uno, & Holt-Lunstead, 1999). For example, Fran Norris and Krzysztof Kaniasty (1996) studied the survivors of two hurricanes: Hurricane Hugo, which struck North Carolina and South Carolina in 1989, and Hurricane Andrew, which struck southern Florida in 1992. Both storms caused wide devastation, killing dozens of people and destroying the homes and property of thousands of others. Norris and Kaniasty (1996) found that the people who coped with these disasters the best were those who felt that they had the most social support, such as having others to talk to and to help solve problems.

Social support also plays an important role in the workplace, particularly for those who are employed in high-stress occupations. For example, a recent study of more than 800 Canadian and American firefighters found that those who received social support at work and from their families were less likely to suffer from post-traumatic stress disorder (Corneil et al., 1999). Similarly, a study of physicians, nurses, and technicians employed at cancer clinics in southern Ontario found that stress was less likely to impair job performance for those health care professionals who perceived that social support was available in their workplace (Stewart & Barling, 1996). Clearly, when we believe that we have someone to lean on, we can deal better with life's problems.

Evidence for the role of social support also comes from cross-cultural studies. People who live in cultures that stress interdependence and collectivism suffer less from stress-related diseases, possibly because it is easier for people in these cultures to obtain social support. People who live in cultures that stress individualism are more often expected to "go it alone" (Bond, 1991; Brislin, 1993).

The problem is that going it alone can take its toll on our health. For example, a recent study of elderly women and men from two different regions in Quebec found that those who were lacking in social support experienced greater psychological distress (e.g., depression, anxiety) than those with adequate social support (Lefrançois et al., 2000). Perhaps more dramatically, the availability of social support has even been found to affect our longevity. James House and his colleagues (1982) assessed the level of social support in a large sample of men and women in the years 1967 to 1969. They found that men with a low level of social support were two to three times more likely to die over the next 12 years than were men with a high level of social support; women with a low level of social support were 1.5 to 2 times more likely to die.

But, you may be saying, how do we know for sure that it was the lack of social support that led to increased mortality? Once again, we need to rely on experiments to be sure. David Spiegel and his colleagues (1989) randomly assigned women with advanced breast cancer to a social support condition or a control condition. People in the social support condition met weekly with doctors and other patients to discuss their problems and fears, whereas people in the control group did not have access to this support system. Social support not only improved women's moods and reduced their fears, but also lengthened their lives by an average of 18 months. More recently, the effects of such support were evaluated among a group of Canadian women who had been widowed in the

Social support

the perception that others are responsive and receptive to one's needs

previous two years (Stewart et al., 2001). These women met weekly in small groups led by a peer (a woman who also was widowed) and a mental health professional. At the end of the 20-week program, the women showed a number of improvements, including increased positive affect and increased hope and confidence.

Does this mean that you should always seek out comfort and advice from others? Not necessarily. According to the **buffering hypothesis**, we are in greatest need of social support when we are under stress (Cohen & Wills, 1985; Koopman et al., 1998; Pierce et al., 1996). When things are going great and we feel in control of our lives, we can go it alone. When times are tough—when we've just broken up with our girlfriend or boyfriend, or our parents have gone off the deep end again—social support helps in two ways. First, it can help us interpret an event as less stressful than we otherwise would. Suppose you've just found out that you have midterms in your psychology and calculus classes on the same day. If you have several friends in these classes who can commiserate with you and help you study, you are likely to find the tests less of a big deal than if you had to cope with them on your own. Second, even if we do interpret an event as stressful, social support can help us cope. Suppose you've just done poorly on a midterm and feel bad about it. It's best to have close friends nearby to help you deal with this and figure out how to do better on the next test (Stroebe & Stroebe, 1996). The moral? The countless pop songs you've heard are right: In times of stress, find a friend to lean on. To get an idea of the amount of social support you feel is available in your life, complete the quiz in the Try It! box on page 545.

Buffering hypothesis
the hypothesis that we need social support only when we are under stress, because it protects us against the detrimental effects of this stress

Prevention: Improving Health Habits

In addition to helping people reduce stress, it would be beneficial to get them to change their health habits more directly—to stop smoking, lose weight, eat a healthier diet, and stop abusing alcohol or other drugs. This is an area in which social psychology can be especially helpful.

North Americans are doing a pretty good job of improving some of their health habits. For instance, the percentage of the Canadian population (ages 15 and over) who

▶ North Americans are making progress in improving some areas of health; for example, more and more people are quitting smoking. However, North Americans are not doing very well in other areas. Many people find it difficult to lose weight and maintain a regular exercise program. How can social psychology help people act in healthier ways?

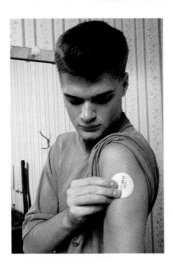

 **Social Support**

This scale is made up of a list of statements, each of which may or may not be true about you. For each statement, circle probably TRUE (T) if the statement is true about you or probably FALSE (F) if the statement is not true about you.

You may find that many of the statements are neither clearly true nor clearly false. In these cases, try to decide quickly whether probably TRUE (T) or probably FALSE (F) is more descriptive of you. Although some questions will be difficult to answer, it is important that you pick one alternative or the other. Remember to circle only one of the alternatives for each statement.

Read each item quickly but carefully before responding. Remember that this is not a test and there are no right or wrong answers.

1. There is at least one person I know whose advice I really trust. T F

2. There is really no one I can trust to give me good financial advice. T F

3. T here is really no one who can give me objective feedback about how I'm handling my problems. T F

4. When I need suggestions for how to deal with a personal problem, I know there is someone I can turn to. T F

5. There is someone whom I feel comfortable going to for advice about sexual problems. T F

6. There is someone I can turn to for advice about handling hassles over household responsibilities. T F

7. I feel that there is no one with whom I can share my most private worries and fears. T F

8. If a family crisis arose, few of my friends would be able to give me good advice about how to handle it. T F

9. There are very few people I trust to help solve my problems. T F

10. There is someone I could turn to for advice about changing my job or finding a new one. T F

Scoring: You get one point each time you answered TRUE to questions 1, 4, 5, 6, and 10 and one point for each time you answered FALSE to questions 2, 3, 7, 8, and 9.

This is a scale that Cohen and Wills (1985) developed to measure what they call *appraisal social support,* or "the perceived availability of someone to talk to about one's problems." One of their findings was that when people were not under stress, those low in social support had no more physical symptoms than those high in social support. However, when people were under stress, those low in social support had more physical symptoms than those high in social support. This is support for the buffering hypothesis talked about in the text: We need social support the most when times are tough. Another finding was that women scored reliably higher than men did on the social support scale. (Adapted from Cohen & Wills, 1985)

were smokers in 2001 dropped to 22 percent (Health Canada, 2002). Also, people are more likely today to avoid high-cholesterol and fatty foods than they were a few years ago, and more women are getting Pap smears to detect cancer. There is definitely room for improvement, however. The number of obese Canadian adults (between ages 20 and 64) grew by 24 percent from 1994–1995 to 2000–2001, according to Statistics Canada's Canadian Community Health Survey (Bhatia, 2002). Furthermore, although Canadian adults report living more active lifestyles, obesity is on the rise: There are 2.8 million obese adults comprising 15 percent of the adult population, up from 13 percent six years earlier. Polls conducted in the United States have found that people drink more alcohol, exercise less, and get fewer hours of sleep than they did five years earlier (*Washington Post Health,* January 9, 1996). Binge drinking on university campuses is occurring at an alarmingly high rate. A study conducted at York University found that students who drink alcohol tend to do so two to three times per week, and on each occasion generally consume five or six standard drinks (e.g., five or six bottles of beer). For male students, this results in an average of 16 drinks per week; for female students, the weekly average is 13 drinks. According to the researchers, this level of alcohol consumption qualifies as "heavy social drinking" (Wall, Hinson, & McKee, 1998). Although most binge drinkers believe that it will be easy to stop after leaving university, many will find it very hard to do so and will develop serious drinking problems. Finally, as we discussed in Chapter 7, people who are at risk for getting AIDS are not taking as many precautions as they should. For example, a study conducted in Ontario found that only 29 percent of young adults who had engaged in casual sex over the past year had always used a condom (Herold & Mewhinney, 1993). How can we persuade people to change their health habits?

MESSAGE FRAMING: STRESSING GAINS VERSUS LOSSES

One approach, as we discussed in Chapter 7 on attitude change, is to present people with persuasive communications urging them to act in healthier ways. As we mentioned in that chapter, the Canadian government has placed graphic photographs of people suffering from lung cancer and other smoking-related diseases on cigarette packages, with the intent of frightening them into quitting, or not starting, smoking. Many public service advertisements take this approach, trying to scare people into applying sunscreen, using condoms, and wearing seat belts.

Is it always best to scare people, emphasizing what they have to lose by acting in unhealthy ways? Suppose, for example, that you were devising a public service ad to

▶ One of the new graphic photos on cigarette packaging. The new packaging, which attempts to use fear to change people's behaviour, was introduced by the Canadian government in an attempt to curb smoking.

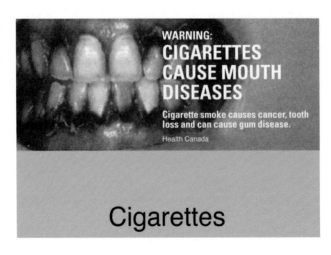

lower fatalities from skin cancer. Your goal is to get people to examine their skin regularly for cancer and to use sunscreen when they are exposed to the sun. You could frame your message in terms of what people have to lose by not performing these behaviours; for example, you might emphasize that most skin cancers are fatal if not detected at an early stage. Or you could frame your message in a more positive way by emphasizing what people have to gain; for example, you could say that skin cancers are curable if detected early and that people can decrease their chances of getting skin cancer by using sunscreen.

It might seem that these different messages would have the same effect; after all, they convey the same information—it is a good idea to examine your skin regularly and use sunscreen. However, Rothman and Salovey (1997) found that framing messages in terms of losses versus gains can make a big difference. When trying to get people to *detect* the presence of a disease, it is best to use a loss frame, emphasizing what they have to lose by avoiding this behaviour (e.g., the costs of not examining one's skin for cancer) (Meyerowitz & Chaiken, 1987; Rothman, 2000; Rothman et al., 1993; Wilson, Purdon, & Wallston, 1988). When trying to get people to engage in behaviour that will *prevent* disease, it is best to use a gain frame, emphasizing what they have to gain by engaging in this behaviour (e.g., using sunscreen) (Christophersen & Gyulay, 1981; Linville, Fischer, & Fischhoff, 1993; Rothman et al., 1999). Alex Rothman and his colleagues (1993), for example, found that framing a message in terms of losses increased women's intentions to examine their skin for cancer (a detection behaviour), whereas framing a message in terms of gains increased women's intentions to use sunscreen (a prevention behaviour; see Figure SPA1.6).

Why does the way in which a message is framed make a difference? Rothman and Salovey (1997) suggest that it changes the way in which people think about their health. A loss frame focuses people's attention on the possibility that they might have a problem that can be dealt with by performing detection behaviour (e.g., examining their skin for cancer or performing breast self-exams). A gain frame focuses people's attention on the

▼ Figure SPA1.6

FRAMING HEALTH MESSAGES IN TERMS OF GAINS OR LOSSES.

Rothman and colleagues (1993) presented women with information trying to get them to avoid skin cancer. Some participants received a message that focused on the positive benefits of being concerned about skin cancer (e.g., "If they are detected early, most of these cancers are curable"). Other participants received a message framed in terms of the negative consequences of not being concerned about skin cancer (e.g., "Unless they are detected and treated early, most of these cancers are not curable"). As seen in the left-hand side of the figure, the loss frame message worked best on detection behaviour (people's intention to perform exams of their skin). As seen in the right-hand side of the figure, the gain frame message worked best with prevention behaviour (requesting a sample of sunscreen).

(Adapted from Rothman et al., 1993)

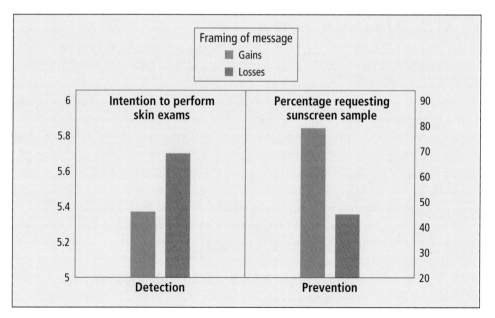

fact that they are in a good state of health and that to stay that way it is best to perform preventive behaviour (e.g., using sunscreen when exposed to the sun and condoms when having sex). So, before designing your public health ad, decide which kind of behaviour you are going to target—a prevention or detection behaviour—and design your ad accordingly.

CHANGING HEALTH-RELEVANT BEHAVIOUR USING DISSONANCE THEORY

Unfortunately, when it comes to changing some intractable, ingrained health habits, public service ads may be of limited success. The problem is that with many health problems there are overwhelming barriers to change. Consider the use of condoms. Most people are aware that AIDS is a serious problem and that using condoms provides some protection against AIDS. Still, a surprisingly small percentage of people use condoms. One reason is that many people find condoms to be inconvenient and unromantic, as well as a reminder of disease—something they don't want to think about when they are having sex. Where sexual behaviour is involved, there is a strong tendency to go into denial—in this case, to decide that although AIDS is a problem, we are not at risk. What can be done to change this potentially fatal attitude?

One of the most important messages of social psychology is that to change people's behaviour, you need to challenge their self-esteem in such a way that it becomes to their advantage—psychologically—to change their behaviour. By doing so, they feel good about themselves, maintaining their self-esteem. Sound familiar? This is a basic tenet of dissonance theory. As we discussed in Chapter 6, Elliot Aronson and his colleagues have recently shown that the principles of dissonance theory can be used to get people to behave in healthier ways, including using condoms more often. To review briefly, Aronson, Fried, and Stone (1991; Stone et al., 1994) asked university students to compose a speech describing the dangers of AIDS and advocating the use of condoms "every single time you have sex." The students gave their speech in front of a video camera, after being informed that the resulting videotape would be played to an audience of high-school students. Giving this speech, alone, was not sufficient to change behaviour. Other students were made mindful of their own failure to use condoms and then delivered the speech advocating condom use. Thus, these students were keenly aware of their own hypocrisy—namely, that they were preaching behaviour to high-school students that they themselves were not practising. Because no one likes to feel like a hypocrite, these participants needed to take steps to fix their damaged self-esteem. A clear way of doing this would be to start practising what they were preaching. This is exactly what Aronson and his colleagues found: Students in the hypocrisy condition showed the greatest willingness to use condoms in the future, and when given the opportunity purchased significantly more condoms for their own use than did students in the non-hypocrisy conditions.

The Aronson and colleagues (1991) condom study is yet another illustration of a familiar point: Sometimes the best way to change people's behaviour is to change their interpretation of themselves and the social situation. No attempt was made to modify the research participants' behaviour (their use of condoms) directly. They were not rewarded for using condoms; nor were they given any information about what would happen if they didn't. Instead, the researchers altered the way in which the participants interpreted their failure to use condoms. We cannot overemphasize this important social psychological message. One of the best ways to solve applied problems is often to change people's interpretation of the situation.

Now that you have read about several of the factors that influence health behaviour, see if you can improve your habits by reading the Try It! box below.

Changing Your Health Habits

Pick a health habit of yours and try to improve it, using the principles we have discussed in this chapter. For example, you might try to lose a few kilograms, exercise more, or cut down on your smoking. We should mention right away that this is not easy. If it were, we would all be svelte, physically fit nonsmokers! We suggest that you start small with a limited goal; try to lose 2.5 kilograms, for example, or increase your exercise by one or two hours a week.

Here are some specific suggestions as to how to change your behaviour:

Increase your feelings of control over your behaviour, particularly your self-efficacy in this domain. One way to do this is to start small. If you are trying to lose weight, for example, begin slowly with some easy-to-control behaviour. You might start by eliminating one food or beverage from your diet that you do not like all that much but that is pretty fattening. Suppose, for example, that you drink a 200-calorie fruit juice five times a week. Replacing the juice with water will save 52 000 calories a year, which is equivalent to 6 kilograms! The idea is to gain mastery over your behaviour slowly, improving your feelings of self-efficacy. When you've mastered one behaviour, try another. You can do it!

If you experience a setback, such as eating two pieces of cake at a birthday party when you really didn't mean to, avoid a damaging pattern of attributions. Do not assume that the setback was due to internal, stable, global causes—this will cause learned helplessness. Remember that almost everyone fails the first time they try to diet or quit smoking. It often takes people several attempts; thus, a setback or two is not due to something unchangeable about you. Keep trying.

Try your own little dissonance experiment, such as the one we discussed by Elliot Aronson and colleagues (1991) on safer sex. There are two steps. First, make a speech to others urging them to adopt the behaviour you are trying to change. For example, tell all of your friends about the dangers of obesity. The more involved and detailed you make your speech and the wider your audience, the better. Second, make a detailed list of times when you did not practise what you preached (e.g., when you gained weight). You might find it easier to quit once you have put yourself through this "hypocrisy" procedure.

It can be stressful to change a well-ingrained habit, and it is at times of stress that social support is most important. Talk with your friends and family about your attempts to change your behaviour. Seek their advice and support. Even better, convince several friends to try these techniques with you. Make it a group project, in which you and your friends support each others' efforts to alter your behaviour.

SUMMARY

We examined the effects of stress on human health, the causes of stress, how people cope with stress, and how to encourage people to change their health habits. Stress has been found to have a number of negative effects, such as impairment of the immune system. **Stress** is best defined as the negative feelings that occur when people feel that they cannot cope with their environment. One key determinant of stress is how much **perceived control** people have over their environment. The less control people believe they have, the more likely it is that the event will cause them physical and psychological problems. For example, the loss of control experienced by many older people in nursing homes can have negative effects on their health and mortality. It is also important for people to have high **self-efficacy** in a particular domain, which is the belief in one's ability to carry out specific actions that produce desired outcomes. In addition, the way in which people explain the causes of negative events is critical to how stressful those events will be. When bad things happen, **learned helplessness** results if people make **stable, internal,** and **global attributions** for those events. Learned helplessness leads to depression, reduced effort, and difficulty in learning new material.

People's **coping styles** refer to the ways in which they react to stressful events. Research on personality traits, such as optimism, the **Type A versus Type B personality,** and **hardiness,** focuses on how people typically deal with stress and how these styles are related to their physical health. Optimistic people tend to react better to stress and to be healthier. Type A individuals—particularly those with high levels of hostility—are more at risk for coronary disease.

Other researchers focus on ways of coping with stress that everyone can adopt. Several studies show that "opening up," which involves writing or talking about one's problems, has long-term health benefits. **Social support**—the perception that other people are responsive to one's needs—is also beneficial. According to the **buffering hypothesis**, social support is especially helpful in times of stress, making people less likely to interpret an event as stressful and helping them cope with stressful events.

It is also important to explore strategies of getting people to act in healthier ways. One strategy is to present people with persuasive communications urging them to adopt better health habits. To be successful, it is important to tailor these messages to the kinds of behaviour you want people to adopt. To get people to perform detection behaviour, such as examining their skin for cancer, it is best to use messages framed in terms of losses (the negative consequences of failing to act). To get people to perform preventive behaviour, such as using sunscreen, it is best to use messages framed in terms of gains (the positive consequences of performing the behaviour). Even more powerful are techniques that arouse dissonance that will be reduced by changing one's health habits, such as making people feel hypocritical about their failure to use condoms.

IF YOU ARE INTERESTED

Flett, G.L., Endler, N.S., & Fairlie, P. (1999). The interaction model of anxiety and the threat of Quebec's separation from Canada. *Journal of Personality and Social Psychology,* 76, 143–150. A fascinating analysis of reactions to the threat of Quebec's separation from Canada. Data were gathered from York University students three hours before the October 1995 Quebec referendum (as well as one week after the vote). The researchers found that participants who tended to be anxious and who perceived the referendum situation as ambiguous and threatening experienced high levels of anxiety prior to the vote.

Goldberger, L., & Breznitz, S. (Eds.). (1993). *Handbook of stress: Theoretical and clinical aspects* (2nd ed.). New York: Free Press. A large collection of chapters on all aspects of stress, written by experts in the field. The topics include basic psychological and biological aspects of stress, the measurement of stress and coping, sociocultural and developmental sources of stress, and treatment for stress.

Haines, Randa (Director). (1991). *The doctor* [Film]. A surgeon discovers what it is like to be on the other side of the health care system when he develops throat cancer. The surgeon develops a close relationship with a terminally ill patient as he struggles with his own mortality. An interesting look at issues of learned helplessness and perceived control and health.

Hanson, I., & Hampton, M. R. (2000). Being Indian: Strengths sustaining First Nations People in Saskatchewan residential schools. *Canadian Journal of Community Mental Health, 19*, 127–142. Elders who were survivors of residential schools in Saskatchewan were interviewed about their experiences and how they coped. From these interviews, the authors identify eight major strategies that the survivors used for coping with the horrific abuse they suffered. It is suggested that these strategies reflect traditional sources of strength for Native peoples and should be incorporated into community health programs aimed at healing the trauma of the residential school experience.

Pennebaker, J. W. (1990). *Opening up: The healing powers of confiding in others*. New York: William Morrow. An insightful, accessible presentation of research on the value of discussing one's problems with other people.

Salovey, P., Rothman, A. J., & Rodin, J. (1998). *Social psychology and health behaviour*. In D. Gilbert, S. Fiske, & G. Lindzey (Eds.), *The handbook of social psychology* (4th ed., Vol. 2, pp. 633–683). New York: McGraw-Hill. A broad, insightful review of the emerging field of health psychology.

Seligman, M. E. P. (1990). *Learned optimism*. New York: Springer-Verlag. An interesting book on optimism and learned helplessness theory, by one of its originators.

Suedfeld, P. (Ed.) (2001). *Light from the ashes: Social science careers of young Holocaust refugees and survivors*. Ann Arbor: University of Michigan Press. In this book, University of British Columbia social psychologist Peter Suedfeld presents a collection of essays written by high-profile social scientists who were Holocaust survivors. The contributors, including Peter Suedfeld, offer poignant, deeply touching accounts of their Holocaust experiences and explore the impact of these experiences on their personal and professional lives. Professor Suedfeld raises the intriguing possibility that success of several might be attributable, at least in part, to the resiliency and coping ability that Holocaust survivors developed because of the trauma they experienced.

Taylor, S. E. (1989). *Positive illusions: Creative self-deception and the healthy mind*. New York: Basic Books. A readable book that examines the relationship between people's illusions about themselves and the social world, and their physical and mental health. Includes an in-depth discussion of many of the issues covered in this module, including perceived control and learned helplessness.

WEBLINKS

http://is.dal.ca/~hlthpsyc/hlthhome.htm

The Health Psychology Section (Canadian Psychological Association)

This is the home page for the Health Psychology Section of the Canadian Psychological Association, and provides links to assorted health psychology sites, conferences, and career opportunities.

http://healthpsych.com

Health Psychology & Rehabilitation

This site offers research, viewpoints, and practical suggestions about the practice of health psychology in medical and rehabilitation settings, and links to many other health psychology resources.

http://userpage.fu-berlin.de/~health/lingua5.htm

Self-Efficacy across Cultures

The paper provided at this site compares perceived levels of self-efficacy across 14 different cultures.

Social Psychology and the Environment

Chapter Outline

"BRITISH COLUMBIA RESIDENTS LAUNCH LAWSUIT OVER AIRPORT NOISE," "Residents protest new runway opening in Toronto area," "Community in Canada angered by barking dogs," "Canadian Native people disturbed by noise from military jets," "Vancouver police checkpoints to inspect noise levels of motorcycles." The list of headlines goes on and on. Airplanes, military jets, traffic noise, motorcycles, barking dogs, concerts—all of these, and more, are making noise people don't want to hear. A few years ago, even a hapless 67-year-old accordion player in player in Bronte, Ontario, was creating too much noise with his summer outdoor concerts, according to some nearby residents who filed complaints with the police. After playing on the same spot for 17 years, Ron Jensen was asked to turn down the volume and move to a new location, or else risk ending up in court and being charged with a noise bylaw violation.

And then there's the case of Robin Ward, a resident of the Rosedale neighbourhood in Toronto. In the fall of 1997, Ward had to quickly find a new home due to the dissolution of his marriage. He fell in love with a house in Rosedale and invested a substantial sum of money in repairs and renovations. While resting on his sofa on a Saturday afternoon in the spring, he was jolted upright by a tremendous, frightening roar. Three people wearing headphones were operating leaf blowers near his house. He rushed outside to confront them, but apparently they couldn't hear a thing he said. This event triggered a series of attempts to force people in the neighbourhood using leaf blowers, lawn mowers, and weed eaters to stop making so much noise. However, Toronto's noise bylaws did not adequately address noise created by such devices. The result? Ward found the noise so unbearable that he moved out of his house (though he still hopes one day to win the battle of the leaf blowers and return to his home).

As is apparent from the headlines, and in the story of Robin Ward, our physical world is becoming an increasingly important source of stress. It is getting more difficult

◀ As the human population increases, the physical world is becoming an increasingly important source of stress. Noise from airplanes, for example, is a common feature of urban life.

to escape the noise caused by such modern conveniences as jetliners, heavy traffic, and, alas, even leaf blowers. And just as our environment exerts stress on us, so we exert stress on our environment. Few problems are as pressing as the damage we are doing to the environment, including toxic waste, overflowing landfills, pollution, global warming, and the destruction of rain forests. In this unit we will consider both of the following questions. To what extent and under what conditions is the environment a source of stress? And how can social influence techniques be used to get people to behave in more environmentally sound ways?

The Environment as a Source of Stress

Ever been stuck in rush-hour traffic, venting your anger and frustration by leaning on your car horn? Ever been bothered by the noise we humans generate from cars, planes, and loud parties? If so, you have found your environment to be a source of stress. But what makes our environments stressful? Why is it that an event—such as loud music—can be enjoyable on some occasions but highly stressful on others? The answer has to do with a basic assumption of social psychology: It is not objective but *subjective* situations that influence people. To understand when our environment will be stressful, then, we need to understand how and why people construe that environment as a threat to their well-being.

In one sense, the environment has always been a source of stress to human beings. We sometimes forget, as we sit in our comfortable, well-heated homes, eating food we purchased at the grocery store, how tenuous our existence has been throughout most of our history. Our ancestors were no strangers to starvation, which was no further away than one bad harvest or unlucky hunting season. Severe winters claimed many victims, as did diseases that spread unchecked due to contaminated drinking water, poor sanitation, and close living quarters.

Now, early in the twenty-first century, we have learned to master most of the harsh environmental hazards that plagued our ancestors (though, tragically, in many areas of the world starvation and preventable diseases are still a major cause of death). The irony is that as human beings have learned how to master the environment, we have created new environmental stressors that our ancestors never had to face.

Consider, for example, the lives of a group of people called the Mabaan, who live in the Republic of Sudan in Africa, near the equator. When studied by Samuel Rosen and his colleagues (1962) in the early 1960s, this culture was relatively untouched by modern civilization. The Mabaan lived in bamboo huts, wore little clothing, and thrived on a diet of grains, fish, and small game. Their environment was quiet and uncrowded, free of many of the stressors associated with modern urban life. There were no sleep-jarring noises from sirens and trucks, no traffic jams to endure at the end of the day, and little fear of crime. Rosen and his colleagues found that, compared to adults in the United States, the Mabaan had less hypertension (high blood pressure), less obesity, and superior hearing.

We cannot be sure, of course, that the absence of modern environmental stressors, such as the problems with urban life, was responsible for the Mabaan's excellent health. Even if it were, we might not want to conclude that living in modern, urban areas is

▼ Just as our environment can exert stress on us, so too can we exert stress on our environment.

always stressful, inevitably causing health problems. As we mentioned, the same objective event, such as loud noise, is experienced as stressful under some conditions and pleasurable under others. When will modern environmental conditions such as noise and crowding be stressful? Social psychologists have conducted numerous studies to find out.

NOISE AS A SOURCE OF STRESS

Samuel Rosen and his colleagues (1962) attributed the superior hearing of the Mabaan in part to the fact that the environment in which they lived was, compared to modern, urban areas, extremely quiet. Are loud noises always psychologically stressful? As you probably know by now, it depends on how people interpret the noise and how much control they feel they have over it. Many people voluntarily go to rock concerts where the music is extremely loud—louder than the sound of a jet flying overhead. Many people thrive on the hustle, bustle, and noise of urban life, as long as they can escape to a quiet corner of their apartment when they choose to do so. (In contrast, Robin Ward did not choose to hear the leaf blowers around his house and could not escape this noise while in his home.)

Noise and Perceived Control As compelling as our examples may be, we cannot be sure that perceived control eliminates the stressful effects of noise, unless we conduct well-controlled experiments. Fortunately, David Glass and Jerome Singer (1972) have performed just such a series of studies. A typical experiment went like this. Participants were given several problems to solve, such as complex addition problems and a proofreading task. While they worked on these problems, they heard loud bursts of noise. The noise was of such things as a mimeograph machine, a typewriter, and two people speaking in Spanish. The noise was played at 108 decibels, about what you would hear if you were operating a riveting machine or were standing near the runway when a large commercial jet took off.

In one condition, the bursts of noise occurred at unpredictable lengths and at unpredictable intervals over the course of the 25-minute session. In a second condition, people heard the same sequence of noises but were given a sense of control over them. The experimenter told participants that they could stop the noise at any point by pressing a button. "Whether or not you press the button is up to you," explained the experimenter. "We'd prefer that you do not, but that's entirely up to you" (Glass & Singer, 1972). A key fact to remember is that *no one* actually pressed the button. Thus, people in this condition heard the same amount of noise as people in the uncontrollable noise condition; the only difference was that they believed they could stop the noise whenever they wanted. Finally, a third condition was included wherein people worked on the problem in peace and quiet. After the 25-minute session was over, people in all conditions worked on new problems without any noise being played.

Interestingly, the noise had little effect on people during the initial 25-minute session. As long as a task was not too complex, people could bear down and ignore unpleasant noises, doing just as well on the problems as people who worked on them in quiet surroundings. A different picture emerged, however, when people worked on problems in the next session, in which everyone could work in peace and quiet. As you can see in Figure SPA2.1, those who had endured the uncontrollable noises made significantly more errors during this session than did people who had not heard noises during the first

▶ Figure SPA2.1

NOISE AND PERCEIVED
CONTROL

People who believed they could
control the noxious noise did
about as well on a subsequent
task as people who heard no
noise at all.

(Adapted from Glass & Singer,
1972)

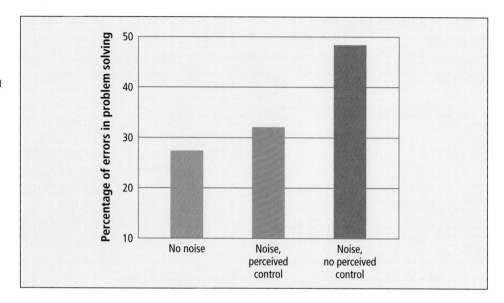

session. And what about the people who heard the noises but believed they could control
them? As Figure SPA2.1 shows, these people did almost as well on the subsequent problems as those who heard no noise at all. When people knew they could turn off the noise
at any point, the noise was much easier to tolerate and did not impair later performance—
even though these people had never actually turned it off.

Why did noise lower performance after it ended, and why did this occur only in the
condition where the noise couldn't be controlled? When people are initially exposed to
uncontrollable, negative events, they often attempt to overcome them as best they can. In
Glass and Singer's (1972) study, people initially were able to overcome the noxious effects
of the noise by bearing down and concentrating as best they could. However, if negative,
uncontrollable events continue despite our best efforts to overcome them, learned helplessness sets in (Abramson, Seligman, & Teasdale, 1978; Wortman & Brehm, 1975). Robin
Ward, for example, tried to confront the leaf blowers, and made many trips to Toronto's
City Hall, hoping to find a noise bylaw that would force them to stop. When he met with
nothing but dead ends, he moved out of his house. As discussed in Social Psychology in
Action 1, learned helplessness occurs when people reach the conclusion that a negative
event is caused by things they can't change.

In a study conducted at the University of Manitoba, Cramer, Nickels, and Gural
(1997) found that participants who were told that there was nothing they could do to
escape bursts of loud noise (78dB) resembling sirens of emergency vehicles did, in fact, feel
more helpless than did those who were told they had some control. Interestingly, among
those who were told that they had some control, helplessness was reduced to the same
extent, regardless of whether participants were told that they had 25 percent, 50 percent,
or 75 percent control. As the researchers put it, "A little control may go far to shield a person from feelings of helplessness, and additional control provides little extra protection."

One consequence of learned helplessness is reduced effort and difficulty in learning
new material. Those participants who could not control the noise in the Glass and Singer
(1972) experiment were able to deal with it and do well on the problems initially, but the

lack of control they experienced eventually took its toll, causing them to do poorly on the second task. In contrast, participants who believed they could control the noise never experienced learned helplessness and thus were able to do well on the second set of problems.

Noise and Urban Life Unfortunately, in modern, urban life, loud noises are often not controllable, and they last a lot longer than the 25-minute sessions in the Glass and Singer (1972) study. Sheldon Cohen and his colleagues have shown that people who are exposed to such real-life noises respond in the way the participants did in the uncontrollable noise condition of Glass and Singer's (1972) studies. For example, these researchers studied children living in a New York City high-rise apartment building located next to a busy highway (Cohen, Glass, & Singer, 1973). The children who lived on the lower floors, and who were thus subjected to the most traffic noise, did more poorly on reading tests than did children living on the upper floors.

In a later study, Cohen and his colleagues (1980, 1981) studied children who attended schools in the air corridor of Los Angeles Airport. More than 300 jets roared over these schools every day, causing an extremely high level of noise. Compared to children who attended quiet schools (matched on the basis of their race, ethnic group, economic background, and social class), the children at the noisy schools had higher blood pressure, were more easily distracted, and were more likely to give up when working on difficult puzzles. These deficits are classic signs of learned helplessness. Many of these problems were still there when the researchers tested the kids again a year later, suggesting that long-term exposure to loud, uncontrollable noise can cause serious problems in children.

More recent studies have also found detrimental effects of noise (Evans, 2000; Evans, Bullinger & Hygge, 1998; Staples, 1996). Due in part to studies such as these, attempts have recently been made to reduce the amount of noise to which people are subjected—

◀ Frequent, unpredictable noises are an unavoidable fact of urban life. Studies have shown that children who are exposed to constant noises have higher blood pressure, are more easily distracted, and are more likely than other children to give up when working on difficult puzzles.

for example, by adding soundproofing materials to schools and devices to jet engines that make them less noisy.

CROWDING AS A SOURCE OF STRESS

As we write, more than 6 billion human beings inhabit the earth—more people than the total number of all human beings who have ever lived before. The world's population is increasing at the rate of 250 000 people every day. At our current rate of growth, the world population will double by the year 2025 and double again at increasingly shorter intervals. Overcrowding can be a source of considerable stress to both animals and human beings. When animals are crowded together, in either their natural environments or the laboratory, they reproduce more slowly, take inadequate care of their young, and become more susceptible to disease (Calhoun, 1973; Christian, 1963).

Studies of crowding in human beings show similar negative effects. As crowding increases in prisons, for example, disciplinary problems, suicides, and overall death rates also increase (Paulus & Dzindolet, 1992; Paulus, McCain, & Cox, 1981). Studies at universities find that students living in crowded dorms (e.g., ones that have long corridors with common bathroom and lounge facilities) are more withdrawn socially and are more likely to show signs of learned helplessness than are students living in less crowded dorms (e.g., ones with smaller suites that have their own bathrooms; Baum & Valins, 1979; Evans, Lepore, & Schroeder, 1996). University of Saskatchewan researchers Debra Morgan and Norma Stewart (1998) found that elderly people suffering from dementia who were moved to a new special care unit where conditions were less crowded (e.g., private rooms compared to the old units with two to four beds per room) showed beneficial effects such as decreases in disruptive behaviour (resisting care, antisocial remarks) and a stable rate of nondisruptive behaviour. In contrast, those who remained in the old units showed an increase in disruptive behaviour and a decrease in nondisruptive behaviour.

What is it about crowding that is so aversive? To answer this question, we must first recognize that the presence of other people is not always unpleasant. Many people love living in large cities. When Saturday night arrives, many of us are ready to join our friends for an evening of fun, feeling that the more people we round up, the merrier. This fact has led researchers to distinguish between two terms. **Density** is a neutral term that refers to the number of people who occupy a given space; a classroom with 20 students has a lower density of people than the same classroom with 50 students. **Crowding** is the subjective feeling of unpleasantness due to the presence of other people; it is the stress we feel when density becomes unpleasant. Under some circumstances, the class with 20 students might feel more crowded than the class with 50 students.

Density
the number of people who occupy a given space

Crowding
the subjective feeling of unpleasantness due to the presence of other people

Crowding and Perceived Control
When will density turn into crowding? One factor, as you might expect, pertains to how people interpret the presence of others, including how much control they feel they have over the crowded conditions (Baron & Rodin, 1978; Schmidt & Keating, 1979; Sherrod & Cohen, 1979). If the presence of others lowers our feelings of control—for example, making us feel it is harder to move around as freely as we would like, or harder to avoid running into people we would just as soon avoid—then we are likely to experience a crowd as stressful. If we feel we have control over the situation—for example, if we know we can leave the crowd at any point and find solace in a quiet spot—then we are unlikely to experience stress.

◀ As the human population explodes, our planet is becoming more and more crowded. Under what conditions will crowding be stressful?

To test this hypothesis, Drury Sherrod (1974) performed a study that was very much like the one Glass and Singer (1972) conducted on the effects of noise. He asked high-school students to work on some problems in a room that was jam-packed with other people. In one condition, he told the students that they were free to leave at any point. "In the past, some people who have been in the experiment have chosen to leave," he said. "Others have not. We would prefer that you do not, but that's entirely up to you" (Sherrod, 1974). Students in a second condition worked under identical crowded conditions but were not given the choice to leave at any point. Finally, students in a third condition worked in uncrowded conditions. After working on the initial set of problems, the participants were moved to uncrowded quarters, where they worked on a series of difficult puzzles.

The results mirrored those of Glass and Singer (1972). First, students who were crowded—regardless of whether they had a sense of control—solved as many problems as did students who were not crowded. Initially, they were able to concentrate, ignoring the fact that they were shoulder to shoulder with other people. However, in the condition where the students thought they could not escape, the lack of control eventually took its toll. As seen in Figure SPA2.2, the students who had no control over the crowded conditions in the first session tried to solve significantly fewer puzzles in the second session, as compared to students in the other conditions. The students who had a sense of perceived control over the crowded conditions worked on almost as many difficult puzzles as the students who had not been crowded at all.

Thus, the effects of noise and crowding appear to be similar. If we feel we have control over these environmental conditions, they do not bother us very much. If we feel we do not have control over them, we can, in the short run, concentrate on our task and ignore the unpleasant effects of these stressors. Eventually, however, they take their toll, impairing our ability to cope.

▶ **Figure SPA2.2**

CROWDING AND PERCEIVED CONTROL.

People who believed that they had control over the crowded conditions tried almost as hard on a subsequent task as people who were not crowded at all.

(Adapted from Sherrod, 1974)

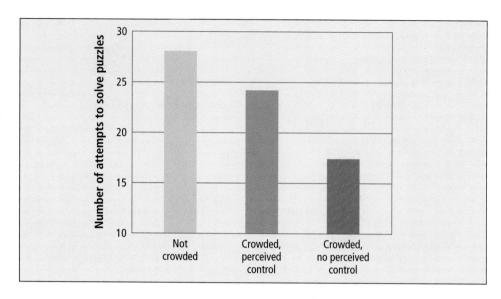

Consequently, it is important for people to feel they can control how crowded and noisy their environments are. It might seem that this is much easier in some parts of the world than in others. If you live in a high-rise in New York City, for example, it would seem to be more difficult to avoid crowded conditions than if you live on a farm on Prince Edward Island. Similarly, homes and apartments are much smaller in Japan than in Canada, and to Canadians, at least, it might seem that it would be more difficult to escape crowded conditions in Japan. Yet even in areas where the density of people is quite high, norms develop to protect people's privacy and to allow them an escape from feelings of being overcrowded. Richard Brislin (1993) notes, for instance, that in Japan and in the slums of Mexico, both of which have a high density of people, norms about visiting people in their homes are different from those in North America. In Mexico, one's home is respected as a sacrosanct place where one can be oneself by and escape the stress of crowded conditions; it is virtually unheard of for an individual to "drop in" to someone else's house (Pandey, 1990). Similarly, the Japanese entertain in their homes much less than North Americans do; they are more likely to invite guests for a meal in a restaurant. The way in which people in different cultures gain control over crowding differs, then, but the need for control appears to be universal (Fuller et al., 1996). To examine whether density or perceived control is most likely to produce feelings of crowding, see Try It! on page 561.

Crowding and Expectations As we have already discussed, the fact that a large number of people are in our environment doesn't necessarily mean that we feel crowded. What is important is how we perceive the situation. For example, we are likely to feel crowded when an environment contains more people than we expect. Vaske, Donnelly, and Petruzzi (1996) interviewed two kinds of visitors to the Columbia Icefields in Jasper National Park—those who saw the glacier on a tour bus and those who explored the glacier on their own. Not surprisingly, visitors who arrived via tour bus encountered many more people on the glacier than did those who were on their own. However, the tour bus people didn't necessarily feel any more crowded than did the others. What determined

When Do People Feel Crowded?

Over a period of a few days, observe people in a variety of situations in which crowding might occur, such as a university or college party, a busy bus stop, a line to enter a movie theatre or dining hall, or a rock concert. In each situation, make the following ratings:

1. What is the density of people in this setting? That is, how many people are there per square metre? Obviously this will be hard to measure exactly, but make a rough estimate.

2. How much control do people have in this situation? Specifically, how easily could they leave and find a less crowded setting, if they so desired? Make your rating based on this scale:

In this situation, people seem to feel:

    1   2   3   4   5   6   7   8   9
very little control   complete control

3. How crowded do people appear to be? Specifically, how negative an experience is it to be in this setting? Make your rating based on this scale:

People seem to find this setting:

    1   2   3   4   5   6   7   8   9
very unpleasant   very pleasant

After sampling several situations, see which predicts your answers to number 3 the best: the density of people (question 1) or how much control people feel (question 2). If you have had a course in statistics, you can compute the correlation coefficient between your answers to questions 1 and 3 and between your answers to questions 2 and 3, to see which one is bigger. If you haven't, just examine the pattern of answers and see whether your answers to question 3 seem to follow more your answers to question 1 or question 2. Based on the research discussed in the text, it is likely that your answers to question 3 depended more on the amount of control people felt (question 2) than on the objective density of people in the situation (question 1).

feelings of crowding by both kinds of visitors was the number of people they *expected* would be on the glacier: If there were more people on the glacier than they had anticipated, the visitors felt crowded. This held true regardless of the visitors' country of origin (Canada, United States, Japan, Germany, or England).

Crowding and Attribution Other factors also determine how aversive people will find crowded conditions. It is well known, for example, that the presence of others makes people physiologically aroused (Zajonc, 1965). As we have seen elsewhere (see Chapter 5), arousal can have intriguing consequences. It can lead to quite different emotions, depending on the attributions people make about the source of their arousal (Schachter & Singer, 1962). Thus, as we might expect, an important determinant of how aversive crowding will be is people's attributions for the arousal caused by crowding. If people attribute their arousal to the presence of the other people, they will interpret it as a sign that the setting is too crowded, and will feel uncomfortable, cramped, and irritated. If they attribute the arousal to another source, they will not feel crowded (Aiello, Thompson, & Brodzinsky, 1983; Schmidt & Keating, 1979). For example, if a student in a class of 300 people attributes her arousal to the stimulating and fascinating lecture she is hearing, she will feel less crowded than if she attributes her arousal to the fact that she feels like a sardine in a can.

Sensory overload

the situation in which we receive more stimulation from the environment than we can pay attention to or process

Crowding and Sensory Overload Finally, crowding will be aversive if it leads to **sensory overload** (Cohen, 1978; Milgram, 1970), which occurs when we receive more stimulation from the environment than we can pay attention to or process. Since other people are a key source of stimulation, one instance in which sensory overload can occur is when so many people are around that we cannot pay attention to everyone. For example, if a committee of 10 people was interviewing you for a job, you'd feel that you had to pay close attention to everything each interviewer said and did. The result? A severe demand would be placed on your attention system—and most likely have negative consequences for you.

TOXIC ENVIRONMENTS AS A SOURCE OF STRESS

Imagine living in an area described as Canada's worst toxic waste site. Imagine, also, hearing that people who live where you do show particularly high rates of cancer. How would this affect you? This is the situation in which residents of Nova Scotia living near the Sydney Tar Ponds find themselves. For nearly a century, emissions and waste products from Sydney's Synco steel plant have been dumped here. The high level of carcinogenic materials present makes this one of Canada's most hazardous toxic sites. To find out how people are affected by living in such an environment, researchers at the University College of Cape Breton recently interviewed junior high-school students attending a school near the Tar Ponds (O'Leary & Covell, 2002). The researchers found that these adolescents reported worrying about environmental issues and about their own health and that of their families—more so than students attending a school 40 kilometres away. Sadly, the adolescents who worried most about health also showed the highest level of depression. (Overall, depression levels were higher among both groups of adolescents than the national average. The researchers suggest that even the students who lived 40 kilometres away may have felt affected by this environmental hazard.)

What did Tar Pond adolescents identify as the greatest problem in their neighbourhood? Not peer pressure or bullying, but pollution. Clearly, even among 12- to 14-year-olds, living in a toxic environment creates stress. A study conducted with two communities in Ontario found that even nonhazardous landfill sites create stress and reduce well-being among residents (Wakefield & Elliott, 2000). These researchers found that the decision-making process (e.g., whether the government allowed public input, divisions in the community over the effects of the site) often created as much stress as the outcome itself.

In sum, as humans have evolved, we have learned to master many environmental hazards—but in the process have produced new ones, such as noise, crowding, and toxic waste. Changes in attitudes and behaviour are urgently needed to avoid environmental catastrophe. Social psychologists have studied a number of techniques involving social influence and social interaction that encourage people to behave in more environmentally sound ways (Oskamp, 1995; Sundstrom et al., 1996).

Using Social Psychology to Change Environmentally Damaging Behaviour

When human beings were hunters and gatherers and lived in small groups, they could get away with discarding their trash wherever they pleased. Now, however, there are more than 6 billion of us (and counting), and we have developed toxic waste that will remain poisonous for centuries, so our environment has become a source of concern (Gilbert, 1990). Pollution in the Los Angeles area is so bad that children who grow up there have lungs that function 10 to 15 percent less efficiently than the lungs of children who grow up in less polluted areas (Basu, 1989).

Closer to home, more than 360 chemical compounds have been identified in the Great Lakes. As a result, various species of fish are suffering from tumours, lesions, and reproductive difficulties. For example, 7 of the 10 most highly valued species of fish in Lake Ontario have nearly disappeared (Great Lakes: Chemical hot spot, 2000). And on land, the discovery of hideous deformities on frogs has been traced to farmers' pesticide use. Researcher Martin Ouellet and a team of Canadian Wildlife Service biologists have examined nearly 30 000 frogs along the St. Lawrence River and have documented abnormalities such as a frog with an eye staring out of its back, a frog with 23 extra toes, frogs with missing eyes and limbs, and frogs whose altered DNA makes them appear male although they are female inside (Jacobs, 1998). Rates of deformity are dramatically higher on agricultural land that has been sprayed with pesticides or other chemicals, compared to land that has not been sprayed for decades. Sadly, these findings also have implications for humans. Research conducted in Canada, the United States, and Finland shows that farmers' children are more likely to have deformities such as missing fingers and toes and abnormal hearts, kidneys, and sexual organs than are children whose parents are not farmers (Jacobs, 1998).

Clearly, it is important to find ways of convincing people to treat the environment better, to avoid problems such as these. This is a classic social psychological question, in that

◀ Pollution and waste hurt not only humans, but also many other species.

"Help!"

it concerns how we can change people's attitudes and behaviour. Let's see what solutions social psychologists have come up with for the planet's pressing environmental problems.

RESOLVING SOCIAL DILEMMAS

The first step is to realize that we are dealing with a classic social dilemma. As we discussed in Chapter 9, a *social dilemma* is a conflict in which the most beneficial action for an individual will, if chosen by most people, have harmful effects on everyone. Of particular relevance to the environment is a variant called the *commons dilemma,* defined as a situation in which everyone takes from a common pool of goods that will replenish itself if used in moderation, but that will disappear if overused. Examples include the use of limited resources such as water and energy. Individuals benefit by using as much as they need, but if everyone does so, shortages often result. As with many social dilemmas, however, so many individuals act in their own self-interest that everyone suffers (Dawes, 1980; Kerr & Kaufman-Gilliland, 1997; Komorita & Parks, 1995; Levine & Moreland, 1998; Pruitt, 1998).

Canada's National Parks face the dilemma of developing these areas in the interest of tourism, but in doing so possibly destroying the very beauty that tourists are coming to see. Edgar Jackson (1987) found that people's views on preservation of land versus development of land for recreational purposes depended on the kinds of recreational activities they engaged in. In a survey conducted with residents of Calgary and Edmonton, he found that people who performed mechanized (e.g., snowmobiling) and consumptive (e.g., fishing) recreational activities more strongly favoured development. Those who preferred activities such as canoeing or hiking more strongly favoured preservation of the environment.

How can we resolve social dilemmas, convincing people to act for the greater good of everyone, rather than purely out of self-interest? Social psychologists have devised some fascinating laboratory games to try to answer this question. For example, imagine you were a participant in a game developed by Orbell, van de Kragt, and Dawes (1988). You arrive for the study and discover that there are six other participants you have never met before. The experimenter gives you and the other participants $6 and says that each of you can keep the money. There is, however, another option. Each person can donate his or her money to the rest of the group, to be divided equally among the six other members. If anyone does so, the experimenter will double the contribution. For example, if you donate your money, it will be doubled to $12 and divided evenly among the six other participants. If other group members donate their money to the pot, it will be doubled and you will get a share.

Think about the dilemma. If everyone (including you) cooperates by donating his or her money to the group, once it is doubled and divided up, your share will be $12—double what you started with. Donating your money is risky, however; if you are the only one who does so, you will end up with nothing, while having increased everyone else's winnings (see Table SPA2.1). Clearly, the most selfish (and safest) course of action is to keep your money, hoping that everyone else donates *theirs.* That way, you would make up to $18—your $6, plus your share of the money everyone else threw into the pot. Of course, if everyone thinks this way, you'll make only $6, because no one will donate any money to the group.

TABLE SPA2.1

Amount of money you stand to win in the Orbell, van de Kragt, and Dawes experiment

You can either keep your $6 or donate it to the six other group members. If you donate it, the money will be doubled, so that each group member will receive $2. Most people who play this game want to keep their money, to maximize their own gains. The more people who keep their money, however, the more everyone loses.

Other people's decisions

Your Decision	6 Keep 0 Give	5 Keep 1 Give	4 Keep 2 Give	3 Keep 3 Give	2 Keep 4 Give	1 Keep 5 Give	0 Keep 6 Give
Keep Your $6	$6	$8	$10	$12	$14	$16	$18
Give Your $6	$0	$2	$4	$6	$8	$10	$12

(Adapted from Orbell, van de Kragt, & Dawes, 1988)

What would you do if you were in the Orbell and colleagues (1988) study? If you were like most of the actual participants, you would keep your $6. After all, as you can see in Table SPA2.1, you will always earn more money by keeping your $6 than by giving it away (i.e., the winnings in the top row of Table SPA2.1 are always higher than the winnings in the bottom row). The only problem with this strategy is that because most people adopted it, everyone suffered. That is, the total pool of money to be divided remained low, because few people donated to the group, which would have allowed the experimenter to double the money. As with many social dilemmas, most people looked out for themselves—as a result, everyone lost.

How can people be convinced to trust their fellow group members, cooperating in such a way that everyone benefits? It is notoriously difficult to resolve social dilemmas, as indicated by the effort required to get people to conserve water when there are droughts, recycle their waste goods, clean up a common area in a dormitory or apartment, or reduce the use of pesticides and thus lower the production and visual appeal of produce. In another condition of their experiment, however, John Orbell and his colleagues (1988) found an intriguing result: Simply allowing the group to talk together for 10 minutes dramatically increased the number of members who donated money to the group—from 38 to 79 percent. The increase in the number of donors led to a larger pool of money to be divided, from an average of $32, to $66. Communication works because it allows each person to find out whether the others are planning to act cooperatively or competitively, as well as to persuade others to act for the common good, e.g., "I'll donate my money if you donate yours" (Bouas & Komorita, 1996; Kerr & Kaufman-Gilliland, 1994).

This finding is encouraging, but it may be limited to small groups that are able to communicate face to face. What happens when an entire community is caught in a social dilemma? When large groups are involved, alternative approaches are needed. One approach is to make people's behaviour as public as possible. If people can take the selfish route privately, undiscovered by their peers, they will often do so. However, if their actions are public, the kinds of normative pressures we discussed in Chapter 8 come into play, making people's behaviour more consistent with group norms. For example, Scott

(1999) found that residents of the Greater Toronto area recycled a higher number of products when they felt social pressure to do so. As one respondent remarked, "[People] feel they have to because their neighbours put out a Blue Box."

CONSERVING WATER

Several years ago, when California experienced severe water shortages, the administrators at one campus of the University of California realized that an enormous amount of water was being wasted by students using the university athletic facilities. The administrators posted signs in the shower rooms of the gymnasiums, exhorting students to conserve water by taking briefer, more efficient showers. The signs appealed to the students' conscience by urging them to take brief showers and to turn off the water while soaping up. The administrators were confident that the signs would be effective because the vast majority of students at this campus were ecology-minded and believed in preserving natural resources. However, systematic observation revealed that less than 15 percent of the students complied with the conservation message on the posted signs.

The administrators were puzzled—perhaps the majority of the students hadn't paid attention to the sign? After all, a sign on the wall is easy to ignore. So administrators made each sign more obtrusive, putting it on a tripod at the entrance to the showers so the students needed to walk around the sign in order to get into the shower room. Though this increased compliance slightly (19 percent turned off the shower while soaping up), it apparently made a great many students angry. The sign was continually being knocked over and kicked around, and a large percentage of students took inordinately *long* showers, apparently as a reaction against being told what to do. The sign was doing more harm than good, which puzzled the administrators even more. It was time to call in the social psychologists.

Elliot Aronson and his students (Dickerson et al., 1992) decided to apply the hypocrisy technique (used in an earlier study to increase condom purchases; see Aronson, Fried and Stone [1991]) to this new situation. The procedure involved intercepting female students who were on their way from the swimming pool to the women's shower room, introducing the experimental manipulations, and then having a research assistant casually follow them into the shower room, where the assistant unobtrusively timed their showers. Research participants in one condition were asked to respond to a brief questionnaire about their water use, a task designed to make them mindful of how they sometimes wasted water while showering. In another condition, research participants made a public commitment, exhorting others to take steps to conserve water. Specifically, these participants were asked to sign their names to a public poster that read, "Take Shorter Showers. Turn Shower Off While Soaping Up. If I Can Do It, So Can YOU!" In the crucial condition—the "hypocrisy" condition—the participants did both; that is, they were made mindful of their own wasteful behaviour and indicated publicly (on the poster) that they were practising water conservation. In short, they were made aware that they were preaching behaviour they themselves were not practising. Just as in the condom study described earlier, participants who were made to feel like hypocrites changed their behaviour so they could feel good about themselves. In this case, they took very brief showers. Indeed, the procedure was so effective that the average time students in this condition spent showering was reduced to 3.5 minutes. The hypocrisy procedure has also been

◀ In a study by Dickerson, Thibodeau, Aronson, & Miller (1992), university students who were made aware that they were advocating conservation behaviour they themselves were not practising changed their behaviour by taking shorter showers.

found to increase other environmentally sound practices, such as recycling (Fried & Aronson, 1995).

Other approaches may be necessary when attempting to increase water conservation on a wider scale. In Great Britain, Van Vugt (2001) adopted a social dilemma approach and hypothesized that people would be more likely to conserve water if they were charged for how much water they actually used (variable tariff) than if they were simply charged a standard fee, regardless of use (fixed tariff). This hypothesis was supported in a nine-month field study (tracking how much water was used in nearly 300 households) as well as in a laboratory study. Thus, if there is a direct relation between how much we use a resource and how much we pay for it, we may be more motivated to reduce our consumption.

CONSERVING ENERGY

Historically, we have felt perfectly content using as much energy as we needed, assuming that the planet had an infinite supply of oil, natural gas, and electric power. Indeed, according to research conducted with geography students at the University of Alberta, people favour the continued exploitation of such resources, with less support for the idea of energy conservation, development of solar power, and so on (Jackson, 1985). As this chapter is being written, the Kyoto Accord is a topic of hot debate. Alberta is one of the provinces most strongly opposed to the energy-conservation measures proposed in the accord. Regardless of one's view on this particular agreement, one thing is clear: There is not an unlimited supply of resources.

Can people be motivated to engage in energy conservation? Let's take private homes as an example. Through simple measures such as increasing ceiling, wall, and floor insulation, plugging air leaks, using more efficient lightbulbs, and properly maintaining furnaces, the typical energy consumer could reduce the amount of energy used to heat, light, and cool his or her home by 50 to 75 percent (Williams & Ross, 1980). The technology needed to increase energy efficiency currently exists and is well within the financial means of most homeowners. This technology would not only save energy, but also save the individual homeowner a great deal of money. Indeed, when McKenzie-Mohr, Nemiroff, Beers, and Desmarais (1995) interviewed residents of British Columbia, they found that both environmental concerns and cost-saving concerns predicted the use of energy-saving devices such as compact fluorescent bulbs and programmable thermostats. Despite the fact that the societal and financial advantages of conservation have been well publicized, the vast majority of homeowners have not taken action. Why? Why have North Americans been slow to act in a manner that is in their economic self-interest? This lack of compliance has puzzled economists and policymakers, because they have failed to see that the issue is partly a social psychological one.

One reason people fail to conserve energy is that they lack information on exactly how much energy they are using and how much money they could be saving by reducing energy consumption. The bill for natural gas and electricity comes only once a month, and is spread over dozens of appliances; thus, the homeowner has no clear idea which of his or her many appliances is using the most energy. It is as if you were buying food in a supermarket where the prices of individual items were unmarked and you were billed only at the end of the month. How would you know what to do to save money on your purchases?

Hutton, Mauser, Filiatrault, and Ahtola (1986) reasoned that if people had explicit information on how much energy was being used, they might be inclined to use less of it. The researchers equipped households in Montreal, Vancouver, and Vacaville, California, with monitors that provided detailed information on how much electricity was being used, the cost of that level of use, and so on. However, in this study, having such a monitor did not have a dramatic impact on energy consumption.

Are there other ways in which people might be persuaded to decrease the amount of energy they use? People's attention is typically directed to the aspects of their environment that are conspicuous and vivid. Elliot Aronson and his colleagues (Aronson, 1990; Aronson & Yates, 1985; Coltrane, Archer, & Aronson, 1986) reasoned that if the issue of energy conservation was made more vivid, people would be more likely to take action. To test this hypothesis, Aronson and his colleagues (Aronson & Gonzales, 1990; Gonzales, Aronson, & Costanzo, 1988) worked with several energy auditors in California. As in many U.S. states, California utility companies offer a free service wherein an auditor will come to people's homes and give them a customized assessment of what needs to be done to make their homes more energy efficient. What a deal! The problem was that less than 20 percent of the individuals requesting audits were actually following the auditors' recommendations.

To increase compliance, the Aronson research team trained the auditors to present their findings in a more vivid manner. For example, let's consider weather stripping. For most people, a small crack under the door didn't seem like a huge drain of energy, so when an auditor told them they should put in some weather stripping, they thought, "Yeah, big deal." Aronson and his colleagues told the auditors to make this statement more vivid, i.e., "If you were to add up all the cracks around and under the doors of your home, you'd have the equivalent of a hole the size of a football in your living room wall. Think for a moment about all the heat that would escape from a hole that size.

That's precisely why I'm recommending that you install weather stripping" (Gonzales, Aronson, & Costanzo, 1988). Similar attempts were made to make other problems more vivid—for example, referring to an attic that lacks insulation as a "naked attic" that is like "facing winter not just without an overcoat, but without any clothing at all" (Gonzales, Aronson, & Costanzo, 1988).

The results were striking. The proportion of homeowners who followed the vivid recommendations jumped to 61 percent. This study demonstrates that people will, in fact, act in a manner that is sensible in terms of environmental goals and their own economic self-interest, but that if old habits are involved, the communication must be one that is vivid enough to break through those established habits.

Frans Siero and his colleagues have demonstrated another simple but powerful way to get people to conserve energy in the workplace (Siero et al., 1996). At one unit of a factory in the Netherlands, the employees were urged to engage in energy-saving behaviour. For example, announcements were placed in the company magazine asking people to close windows during cold weather and to turn off lights when leaving a room. In addition, the employees received weekly feedback on their behaviour; graphs were posted that showed how much they had improved their energy-saving behaviour, such as how often they had turned off the lights. This intervention resulted in modest improvement. By the end of the program, for example, the number of times people left the lights on decreased by 27 percent.

Another unit of the factory took part in an identical program, with one difference. In addition to receiving weekly feedback on their own energy-saving actions, they received feedback about how the other unit was doing. Siero and colleagues (1996) hypothesized that this social comparison information would motivate people to do better than their colleagues in the other unit. As seen in Figure SPA2.3, they were right. By the end of the

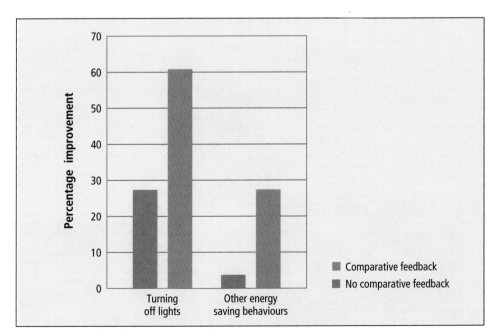

◀ **Figure SPA2.3**

EFFECTS OF COMPARATIVE
FEEDBACK ON ENERGY-
SAVING BEHAVIOUR.

Two units of a factory were urged to conserve energy, and then received feedback about how their unit was doing. Only one of the units, however, received comparative feedback about how they were doing relative to the other unit. As seen in the graph, this second unit improved their behaviour the most, especially by turning off the lights more.

(Adapted from Siero et al., 1996)

program, the number of times people left the lights on had decreased by 61 percent. Clearly, engaging people's competitive spirit can have a significant impact on their behaviour.

REDUCING LITTER

Compared to other environmental problems, littering may not seem to be all that serious. Most people seem to think it isn't a big deal to leave their paper cup at the side of the road instead of in a garbage can. Unfortunately, those paper cups add up. In California, for example, littering has increased steadily over the past 15 years, to the point where $100 million of tax money is spent cleaning it up—every year (Cialdini, Kallgren, & Reno, 1991). Aside from the cost, the material people discard is polluting water systems and endangering wildlife. Littering is another classic social dilemma. Sometimes it's a pain to find a garbage can, and from an individual's point of view, what's one more paper cup added to the side of the road? As with all social dilemmas, the problem is that if everyone thinks this way, everyone suffers. How can we get people to act less selfishly when they have that empty paper cup in hand?

As we saw in Chapter 8, one answer is to remind people of the social norms against littering. Robert Cialdini, Raymond Reno, and Carl Kallgren have pointed out that there are two important kinds of social norms that can influence whether people litter (Cialdini, Kallgren, & Reno, 1991; Cialdini, Reno, & Kallgren, 1990; Kallgren, Reno, & Cialdini, 2000; Reno, Cialdini, & Kallgren, 1993). First, there are **injunctive norms**, which are socially sanctioned behaviours—people's perceptions of what behaviour is approved or disapproved of by others. For example, we may be in an environment where many people are littering but know there is an injunctive norm against littering—most people disapprove of it. Second, there are **descriptive norms**, which are people's perceptions of how people are actually behaving in a given situation, regardless of whether the behaviour is approved or disapproved of by others.

Injunctive norms

people's perceptions of what behaviour is approved or disapproved of by others

Descriptive norms

people's perceptions of how other people actually behave in a given situation, regardless of whether the behaviour is approved or disapproved of by others

▶ Besides being unsightly, litter can cost millions of dollars to clean up. Social psychologists have found that emphasizing various kinds of social norms against littering is an effective way to prevent it.

Focusing people's attention on either of these norms has been found to reduce littering. For example, Reno and colleagues (1993) conducted a field experiment to investigate the power of injunctive norms. As people left a local library and approached their cars in the parking lot, an accomplice walked by them, picked up a fast-food bag that had been discarded on the ground, and put the bag in the trash. In a control condition, no bag was on the ground, and the accomplice simply walked by the library patrons. When the patrons got to their car, they found a pamphlet on their windshield. The question was, How many of these people would litter by throwing the pamphlet on the ground? Reno and colleagues hypothesized that seeing the accomplice pick up the fast-food bag would be a vivid reminder of the injunctive norm—littering is bad, and other people disapprove of it—and hence would lower the subject's own inclination to litter. They were right. In this condition, only 7 percent of the people tossed the pamphlet on the ground, compared to 37 percent in the control condition. If you would like to try to replicate this effect in an experiment of your own, see Try It! below.

What is the best way to communicate descriptive norms against littering? The most straightforward way, it would seem, would be to clean up all of the litter in an environment, to illustrate that "no one litters here." In general, this is true: The less litter there is in an environment, the less likely people are to litter (Huffman et al., 1995; Reiter & Samuel, 1980). There is, however, an interesting exception to this finding. Cialdini and colleagues (1990) figured that seeing one conspicuous piece of litter on the ground, spoiling an otherwise clean environment, would be a better reminder of descriptive norms

 **Reducing Littering Using Injunctive Norms**

See if you can get people to pick up litter by invoking injunctive norms, using the techniques discovered by Raymond Reno and his colleagues (1993). This exercise is easiest to do with a friend. Here's how it works:

Find an environment in which people are likely to litter. For example, at one of our universities the student newspaper often comes with an advertising insert. When people pick up a copy of the newspaper in the psychology building, they often discard the insert on the floor. This exercise is best done with a friend who can observe people unobtrusively to see if they litter.

Next, plant a conspicuous piece of litter in this environment. Reno and colleagues (1993) used a fast-food bag stuffed with trash. Place it in a location that people are sure to see, such as near a doorway.

In one condition, wait until an individual enters the environment and is in full view of the piece of trash you have planted. Then, pick up the trash, throw it away, and go on your way. It is critical that the person realizes it wasn't *your* bag but that you decided to pick it up and throw it away anyway. In a second condition, walk by the trash, glance at it, and continue on your way without picking it up.

The observer should watch to see whether people litter; for example, whether they throw the advertising insert on the floor or put it in a garbage can. As discussed in the text, Reno and colleagues (1993) found that when people saw someone pick up another person's litter, they were much less likely to litter themselves. Did you replicate this effect? Why or why not, do you think?

than seeing a completely clean environment. The single piece of trash sticks out like a sore thumb, reminding people that no one has littered here—except for one thoughtless person. In comparison, if there is no litter on the ground, people might not even think about the descriptive norm. Ironically, then, littering may be more likely to occur in a totally clean environment than in one containing a single piece of litter.

To test this hypothesis, the researchers stuffed students' mailboxes with brochures and then observed, from a hidden vantage point, how many of the students dropped them on the floor (Cialdini, Reno, & Kallgren, 1990). In the first condition, the researchers cleaned up the mailroom so there were no other pieces of litter to be seen. In the second condition, they placed one very noticeable piece of litter on the floor—a hollowed-out piece of watermelon. In the third condition, they not only put the watermelon rind on the floor, but also spread out dozens of discarded brochures. As predicted, the lowest rate of littering occurred in the condition where there was a single piece of trash on the floor (see Figure SPA2.4). The single violation of a descriptive norm highlighted the fact that no one had littered except the one idiot who had dropped the watermelon rind. Now that people's attention was focused on the descriptive norm against littering, virtually none of the students littered. The highest percentage of littering occurred when the floor was littered with many brochures; here it was clear that there was a descriptive norm in favour of littering, and many of the students followed suit.

Clearly, drawing people's attention to both injunctive and descriptive norms can reduce littering. Of the two kinds of norms, Cialdini and colleagues suggest that injunctive norms work better. Descriptive norms work only if everyone cooperates—for example, by keeping an environment relatively free of litter. This method is not perfect, however; if trash starts to accumulate, the descriptive norm becomes "See, lots of people litter here!" and littering will increase. In contrast, reminding people of the injunctive norm works in a wide variety of situations (Reno, Cialdini, & Kallgren, 1993; Kallgren,

▶ **Figure SPA2.4**

DESCRIPTIVE NORMS AND LITTERING.

Who littered the least—people who saw that no one else had littered, people who saw one piece of litter on the floor, or people who saw several pieces of litter? As shown in the figure, it was people who saw one piece of litter. Seeing the single piece of litter was most likely to draw people's attention to the fact that most people had not littered, making participants less likely to litter.

(Adapted from Cialdini, Reno, & Kallgren, 1990)

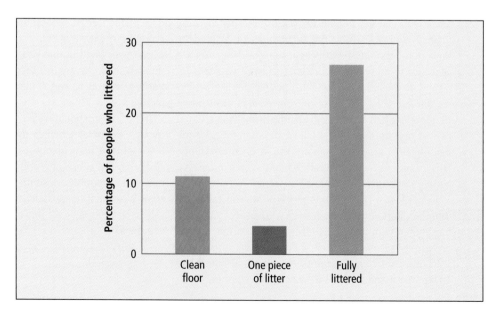

Reno, & Cialdini, 2000). Once we are reminded that "people disapprove of littering," we are less likely to litter in virtually all circumstances.

GETTING PEOPLE TO RECYCLE

Suppose we succeeded in getting people to stop littering. That would be wonderful, because roadsides would look pretty and we wouldn't have to spend millions of dollars in tax money to clean up the trash. However, the problem of what to do with our garbage, once it is collected and thrown away, would remain. Even if we could find a place for it, there is another issue—namely, that many of the things we throw away contain toxic chemicals and dangerous metals.

To reduce the amount of garbage that ends up in landfills, many cities are encouraging their residents to recycle materials such as glass, paper, and aluminum. However, as you know, it can be inconvenient to do so; in some areas you have to load your car with boxes of cans and bottles and drop them off at a recycling centre, which might be several kilometres from your house. Other cities have curbside recycling, whereby a truck picks up recycling materials that you put out on the curb on a designated day. Even then, though, you have to remember to separate your cans, bottles, and newspapers, and find a place to store them until pickup day. We thus have another social dilemma—a behaviour (recycling) that, while good for us all, is effortful and unpleasant for individuals. As you might imagine, several social psychologists have turned their attention to ways of getting people to recycle more.

There have been two general approaches to this problem. First, some psychologists have focused on ways of changing people's attitudes and values in a pro-environment direction, with the assumption that behaviour will follow. This assumption is consistent with social psychological research on attitudes, which has found that under many conditions people's attitudes are good predictors of their behaviour (see Chapter 7). Several

◀ Social psychologists have identified several ways of increasing the likelihood that people will recycle materials such as bottles, cans, and newspapers. One way is to make it as convenient as possible; for example, by offering curbside pickup, as shown in this photo of the recycling service in Toronto.

studies have found that people's attitudes toward recycling, are, in fact, good predictors of their recycling behaviour, suggesting that a mass media campaign that targets people's attitudes is a good way to go (Cheung, Chan, & Wong, 1999; Oskamp et al., 1998; Scott, 1999; Thøgersen, 1996).

Sometimes, though, we might fail to act consistently with our attitudes, despite our best intentions. Perhaps the recycling centre is too far away, or we just can't find the time to sort our trash (even though we know we should). Research conducted with residents of Cornwall, Ontario, found that a major reason why people failed to engage in pro-environmental actions was, "I just can't seem to make the effort to change my habits" (Pelletier et al., 1999). Kurt Lewin (1947), one of the founders of social psychology, made the observation that big social changes can sometimes occur by removing small barriers from people's environments (Ross & Nisbett, 1991). In the context of recycling, it might be better to simply remove some of the hassles involved—such as by instituting curbside recycling—than to try to change people's attitudes toward the environment. Indeed, the results of studies on recycling conducted with residents of Edmonton (Wall, 1995) and four communities in the Greater Toronto area (Scott, 1999), as well as a 1991 Statistics Canada survey on the environment (Berger, 1997), all converge on the same conclusion— namely, that "people will take pro-environmental actions if they have access to a convenient way of doing so" (Berger, 1997). Increasing the number of recycling bins in a

Changing Environmentally Damaging Behaviour

Use the techniques discussed in this chapter to change people's behaviour in ways that help the environment. Here's how to proceed:

Choose the behaviour you want to change. You might try to increase the amount that you and your roommates recycle, reduce the amount of energy wasted in your dorm, or increase water conservation.

Choose the technique you will use to change the behaviour. For example, you might use the comparative feedback technique used by Frans Siero and colleagues (1996) to increase energy conservation. Encourage two areas of your dormitory to reduce energy use or to recycle, and give each feedback about how they are doing relative to the other area. (To do this, you will have to have an easy, objective way of measuring people's behaviour, such as the number of times lights are left on at night or the number of cans that are recycled.) Or you might try the hypocrisy technique used by Elliot Aronson and colleagues (1991) to increase water conservation,

whereby you ask people to sign a public poster that encourages recycling and have them fill out a questionnaire that makes them mindful of times they have failed to recycle. Be creative and feel free to use more than one technique.

Measure the success of your intervention. Find an easy way to measure people's behaviour, such as the amount they recycle. Assess their behaviour before and after your intervention. If possible, include a control group of people who do not receive your intervention (randomly assigned, of course). In the absence of such a control group, it will be difficult to gauge the success of your intervention; for example, if people's behaviour changes over time, you won't be able to tell if it is because of your intervention or some other factor (e.g., an article on recycling that happened to appear in the newspaper). By comparing the changes in behaviour in your target group to the control group, you will have a better estimate of the success of your intervention.

community, instituting curbside recycling, and allowing residents to mix materials instead of having to sort them, have all been found to increase people's recycling behaviour (Ludwig, Gray, & Rowell, 1998; Porter, Leeming, & Dwyer, 1995; Schultz, Oskamp, & Mainieri, 1995).

The moral? There are two ways to get people to act in more environmentally sound ways. First, you can try to change people's attitudes in a pro-environmental direction; this will motivate them to act in environmentally friendly ways, even if there are barriers that make it hard to do so (such as having to find a box for your bottles and cans, and then taking it to a recycling centre). It is often easier, however, simply to remove the barriers (such as by instituting curbside recycling and giving people containers). When it is easy to comply, many people will make an effort, even if they do not have strong pro-environmental attitudes. Now that you have read about several ways of changing people's behaviour in ways that help the environment, you are in a position to try them out yourself. See Try It! on page 574.

SUMMARY

We discussed the environment as a source of stress on people. As we human beings continue to populate the earth at an alarming rate, our physical world is becoming a crowded, noisy, and toxic place in which to live. Social psychologists have focused on how people interpret and explain such conditions. One key interpretation is how much perceived control people have over an event. The less control people believe they have, the more likely it is that the event will cause them physical and psychological problems. For example, if people in high-**density** settings feel they have a low level of control (i.e., they believe it is difficult to escape to a less dense setting), they will experience **crowding**, the subjective feeling of unpleasantness due to the presence of other people. People will also experience crowding if an environment contains more people than they had expected. Crowding can be aversive if it leads to **sensory overload**, which occurs when other people place a severe demand on our attention system. In addition, the way in which people explain the causes of negative events is critical to how an event is interpreted, and thus to how stressful it will be.

We also discussed the effects people are having on the environment and the ways in which social influence techniques can be used to get people to behave in more environmentally sound ways. This is not easy because many environmental problems are classic social dilemmas, wherein actions that are beneficial for individuals, if performed by most people, are harmful to everyone. Using proven techniques to change people's attitudes and behaviour, however, social psychologists have had some success in getting people to act in more environmentally sound ways. One technique is to arouse dissonance in people by making them feel that they are not practising what they preach—for example, that even though they believe in water conservation, they are taking long showers. Another is to remind people of both **injunctive** and **descriptive norms** against environmentally damaging acts, such as littering. Focusing people's attention on injunctive norms against littering—the idea that throwing trash on the ground is not a socially accepted behaviour—is especially effective. Finally, removing barriers that make pro-environmental behaviour difficult, such as by instituting curbside recycling and providing people with recycling bins, has been shown to be effective.

I F

Cohe
(198
Yor
hur
duc

Gore
spiri
rela

Kom
Dul
tion
eva

Liebi
(199
ings

W E

www.
Envii
This

TWO DAYS BEFORE CHRISTMAS IN 1981, BARBARA STOPPEL, A BEAUTIFUL 16-year-old girl, was found strangled in the Winnipeg doughnut shop where she worked. Several people reported that they had seen a tall, lanky man wearing a cowboy hat near the doughnut shop around the time she was killed. Police artists composed a sketch of the suspect based on the descriptions offered by these eyewitnesses. The police sketch looked a lot like Thomas Sophonow, a tall, lanky hotel doorman from Vancouver who was in Winnipeg at the time. Moreover, several witnesses testified that they had seen him leaving the doughnut shop around the time that Stoppel was strangled.

On the basis of this evidence, Sophonow was charged with murder. His trial in 1982 resulted in a hung jury (which means jury members were unable to reach a verdict). He was tried a second time in 1983; that jury found him guilty of second-degree murder after only four hours of deliberation. Sophonow appealed the conviction and was tried a third time in 1985. This time, after five days of deliberation (which was a record in Canada), a "problematic" juror was removed, after which the 11 remaining jurors rendered their verdict: guilty of second-degree murder. Sophonow again appealed. In all, he spent four years in prison for a murder he claimed he did not commit. In December 1985, after conducting an extensive examination of this case, the Manitoba Court of Appeal argued that he should not face a fourth trial, and set him free (but did not declare him innocent). Many people, including Winnipeg's Chief of Police, continued to believe that Sophonow was Stoppel's killer.

In 1998, Winnipeg police reopened the case because Sophonow lobbied for DNA testing of gloves that had been found at the scene of the crime. (DNA testing had not been available at the time of his trials.) It is unclear whether this turned out to be useful evidence, because many people, including Sophonow and a Crown attorney, had tried on the gloves in court. However, police did finally reach the conclusion that Sophonow was not Stoppel's killer and announced that they had a new suspect. On June 8, 2000, after more than 18 years of agony, a sobbing Sophonow accepted apologies from the Winnipeg police and the Crown for sending him to prison for a crime he had not committed. However, life has not returned to normal for Sophonow. The following year he had to relive the trauma of his arrest and wrongful conviction during an inquiry into what went wrong. The judge presiding over the inquiry awarded Sophonow $2.6 million in compensation. However, even collecting the compensation has been an uphill battle. In June 2002, more than a year after the inquiry, Sophonow found himself in the middle of a fight between the city of Winnipeg and the province of Manitoba over whose responsibility it is to pay up. Even though this issue has not yet been resolved, a cheque was eventually issued to Mr. Sophonow on February 22, 2003. He decided to accept the settlement so that he could begin to get on with his life.

The case of Thomas Stophonow raises a number of important questions: If he was innocent, why did eyewitnesses say that he was Barbara Stoppel's killer? And why did two juries believe them? How common are such miscarriages of justice? In this chapter, we will discuss the answers to these questions, focusing on the role that social psychological processes play in the legal system.

Let's begin with a brief review of the Canadian justice system. When someone commits a crime and the police arrest a suspect, the Crown attorney's office usually decides whether there is enough evidence to press formal charges (sometimes at a preliminary hearing, a judge decides whether there will be a trial). If there is adequate evidence to press charges, lawyers for the defence and the prosecution gather evidence and negotiate with each other. As a result of these negotiations, the defendant often pleads guilty to a lesser charge. About a quarter of the cases go to trial, during which a jury or a judge decides the defendant's fate. There are also civil trials, in which one party (the plaintiff) brings a complaint against another (the defendant) for violating the former's rights in some way.

All of these steps in the legal process are intensely social psychological. For example, first impressions of the accused and of witnesses have a powerful effect on police investigators and the jury; attributions about what caused the criminal behaviour are made by police, lawyers, jurors, and the judge; prejudiced beliefs and stereotypical ways of thinking affect those attributions; attitude change and persuasion techniques abound in the courtroom, as lawyers for each side argue their case and jurors later debate with one another; and the processes of social cognition affect the jurors' decision making when deciding guilt or innocence. Social psychologists have studied the legal system a great deal in recent years, both because it offers an excellent applied setting in which to examine basic psychological processes and because of its immense importance in daily life. If you, through no fault of your own, are accused of a crime, what do you need to know to convince the system of your innocence?

As we progress through this module, we will from time to time refer back to the Thomas Sophonow case, which vividly illustrates many of the points we want to make. We will begin our discussion with eyewitness testimony, the most troubling aspect of the case. How accurate are people at identifying someone who has committed a crime?

▲ Thomas Sophonow endured three trials and spent four years in jail for a murder he did not commit. His wrongful conviction was due in part to his resemblance to the police sketch circulated at the time. Left: Sophonow in 1983. Centre: Terry Samuel Arnold, the new suspect in the Barbara Stoppel case, bears a striking resemblance to Sophonow. He is currently serving a life sentence in prison for killing a B.C. woman in 1991, and is the suspect in a third murder case. Right: Sophonow at a news conference in June 2000 after receiving an apology from police.

Eyewitness Testimony

In countries such as Canada, the legal system assigns a great deal of significance to eyewitness testimony. If an eyewitness fingers you as the culprit, you are quite likely to be convicted, even if considerable circumstantial evidence indicates you are innocent. Thomas Sophonow was convicted largely because of the testimony of eyewitnesses who claimed that they had seen him near the doughnut shop around the time of the murder. However, there should have been reason to be suspicious of this testimony. Some witnesses admitted that they had come forward because of the rewards that were being offered for information on the case. One witness told a dramatic tale of having chased Sophonow after the murder, finally catching him on a bridge, where a fight ensued between them. This story was never corroborated. Numerous witnesses claimed that with each trial, their initially sketchy memories had become sharper and more accurate. There also should have been skepticism about the clarity with which witnesses could have seen Sophonow, given that the murder occurred between 8:15 and 8:45 on a winter evening. Moreover, witnesses offered conflicting reports of the direction in which he had headed. Despite the lack of physical evidence linking Sophonow to the scene of the crime, the eyewitness testimony that he had been in the vicinity of the doughnut shop was enough to convict him—twice.

Systematic experiments have confirmed that jurors rely heavily on eyewitness testimony when they are deciding whether someone is guilty. Unfortunately, jurors also tend to overestimate the accuracy of eyewitnesses (Ellsworth & Mauro, 1998; Leippe, Manion, & Romanczyk, 1992; R. Lindsay, 1994; Loftus, 1979; Potter & Brewer, 1999; Wells, Lindsay, & Ferguson, 1979). Rod Lindsay and his colleagues (1981) conducted a clever experiment that illustrates both of these points. The researchers first staged the theft of a calculator in front of unsuspecting University of Alberta students, then tested how accurately the students could pick out the "thief" from a set of six photographs. In one condition, it was difficult to identify the thief because he had worn a knit cap pulled over his ears and was in the room for only 12 seconds. In the second condition, the thief had worn the knit cap higher on his head, revealing some of his hair, so it was easier to identify him. In the third condition, the thief had worn no hat and had stayed in the room for 20 seconds, making it very easy to identify him.

The first set of results is as we'd expect: the more visual information available about the thief, the higher the percentage of students who correctly identified him in the photo lineup (see the bottom line in Figure SPA3.1). In the next stage of the experiment, a researcher playing the role of lawyer questioned the students about their eyewitness identifications, just as a real lawyer would cross-examine witnesses in a trial. These question-and-answer sessions were videotaped. A new group of participants, playing the role of jurors, watched the videotapes of these cross-examinations and rated the extent to which they believed the witnesses had correctly identified the thief. As seen by the top line in Figure SPA3.1, the jurors overestimated the accuracy of the witnesses, especially in the condition where the thief was difficult to identify.

How accurate are eyewitnesses to real crimes? Although it is impossible to say exactly what percentage of the time eyewitnesses are accurate, there is reason to believe that they often make mistakes. Researchers have documented many cases of wrongful arrest, and in a remarkably high proportion of these cases the wrong person was convicted because an

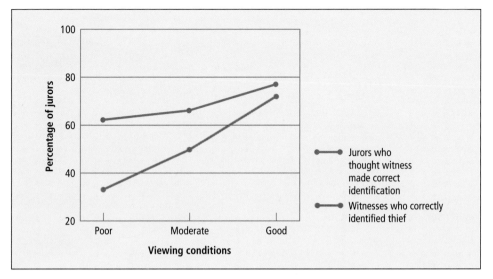

◀ **Figure SPA3.1**

THE ACCURACY OF EYE-
WITNESS IDENTIFICATION.

The accuracy of eyewitness
identification depends on the
viewing conditions at the time
the crime was committed. As in
this study, however, most jurors
believe that witnesses can
correctly identify the criminal
even when viewing conditions are
poor.

(Adapted from Lindsay, Wells, &
Rumpel, 1981)

eyewitness mistakenly identified him or her as the criminal (Brandon & Davies, 1973; Penrod & Cutler, 1999; Span, 1994; Sporer, Koehnken, & Malpass, 1996; Wells, Wright, & Bradfield, 1999, Yarmey, 2001a; see Read, Connolly, & Turtle, 2001 for a review of this literature in the context of Canadian law). For example, Gary Wells and his colleagues (1998) examined 40 cases in which DNA evidence, obtained after the conviction of a suspect, indicated that the suspect was innocent. In 36 of these cases, an eyewitness had falsely identified the suspect as the criminal. Five of these falsely accused people were on death row when they were exonerated. According to University of Guelph psychologist A. Daniel Yarmey, "Mistaken eyewitness identification is responsible for more wrongful convictions than all other causes combined" (Yarmey, 2001a).

WHY ARE EYEWITNESSES OFTEN WRONG?

The problem is that our minds are not like video cameras that can record an event, store it over time, and play it back later, all with perfect accuracy. Memory is much more complicated than that. In order for someone to remember an event, he or she must successfully complete three stages of memory processing: acquisition, storage, and retrieval of the events witnessed.

Acquisition refers to the process whereby people notice and pay attention to information in the environment. Because people cannot perceive everything that is happening around them, they acquire only a subset of the information available in the environment. **Storage** refers to the process by which people store in memory information they have acquired from the environment, whereas **retrieval** refers to the process by which people recall information stored in their memories (see Figure SPA3.2). Eyewitnesses can be inaccurate because of problems at any of these three stages.

Acquisition No one doubts that people accurately perceive a great deal of information about the world around them. Nonetheless, our ability to take in information is limited, particularly when we observe unexpected, complex events. The psychologist Hugo

Acquisition

the process by which people notice and pay attention to information in the environment; people cannot perceive everything that is happening around them, so they acquire only a subset of the information available in the environment

Storage

the process by which people store in memory information they have acquired from the environment

Retrieval

the process by which people recall information stored in their memories

▶ Figure SPA3.2

ACQUISITION, STORAGE,
AND RETRIEVAL.

To be an accurate eyewitness,
people must complete these
three stages of memory
processing. There are sources of
error at each of the three
stages.

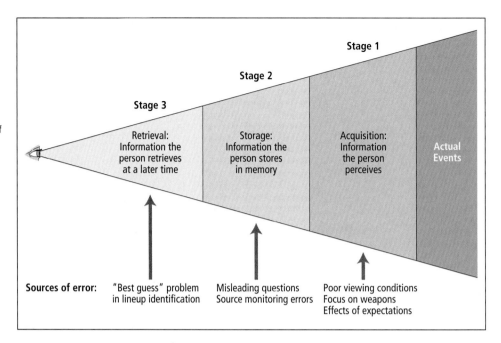

▶ Figure SPA3.2

ACQUISITION, STORAGE, AND RETRIEVAL.

To be an accurate eyewitness, people must complete these three stages of memory processing. There are sources of error at each of the three stages.

Münsterberg (1908), for example, described the following event, which occurred at a scientific meeting attended by psychologists, lawyers, and physicians. In the middle of the meeting, a clown burst into the room, followed closely by a man with a revolver. The two men shouted wildly, grabbed each other, then fell to the ground in a fierce struggle. One of them fired a shot; then both men ran out of the room.

All of the witnesses were asked to write down an exact account of what they had just seen (which was actually an event staged by two actors). Even though the eyewitnesses were educated people with (presumably) good memories, their accounts were surprisingly inaccurate. Most of the witnesses omitted or wrote mistaken accounts of about half of the actions they had observed. Most made errors about how long the incident had occurred—though the two men were in the room for about 20 seconds, the witnesses' estimates ranged from a few seconds to several minutes.

Patricia Tollestrup, John Turtle, and John Yuille (1994) found many similar eyewitness errors in a study of actual criminal cases. They examined records of robbery and fraud cases handled by the RCMP in Vancouver, in which a suspect was caught and then confessed to the crime. Accuracy of both victims' and bystanders' descriptions of the criminal was assessed by comparing the witness's initial description of the criminal to the criminal's actual physical characteristics (for example, were witnesses correct that the criminal had blond hair and a moustache?). Eyewitnesses weren't too bad at remembering some details; 100 percent of bystanders correctly remembered whether the criminal had facial hair (although crime victims correctly remembered this only 60 percent of the time). However, only 48 percent of the bystanders and 38 percent of the victims correctly remembered the suspect's hair colour. Most importantly, neither bystanders nor victims did a very good job of picking the criminal out of a lineup; overall, they correctly identified the criminal only 48 percent of the time.

A number of factors limit the amount of information about a crime that people take in, such as how much time they have to watch an event and the nature of the viewing conditions. As obvious as this may sound, people sometimes forget how these factors limit eyewitness reports of crimes (Read, Connolly, & Turtle, 2001). Crimes usually occur under the very conditions that make acquisition difficult: quickly, unexpectedly, and under poor viewing conditions, such as at night. As we have already mentioned, Barbara Stoppel's murder took place after dark on a winter evening. Presumably, it would have been quite difficult for eyewitnesses to get a good look at the murderer making his getaway.

We should also remember that eyewitnesses who are victims of a crime will be terribly afraid, and this alone can make it difficult to take in everything that is happening. For example, Patricia Tollestrup and her colleagues (1994) found that victims of crimes such as robbery tended to make more mistakes than did bystanders. Another reason victims of crime have a poor memory for a suspect is that they focus their attention mostly on any weapon they see and less on the suspect's features (Christianson, 1992; Pickel, 1998; Shaw & Skolnick, 1999; Williams, Loftus, & Deffenbacher, 1992). If someone points a gun at you and demands your money, your attention is likely to be on the gun rather than on whether the robber has blue or brown eyes. (Note that this is also true for people witnessing crimes—Tollestrup, Turtle, & Yuille [1994] found that 73 percent of eyewitnesses correctly identified the police suspect when no weapon was present during a crime; this figure dropped to 31 percent when a weapon was present.)

Finally, the information people notice and pay attention to is also influenced by what they expect to see. Consider our friend Alan, a social psychologist who is an expert on social perception. One Sunday, Alan was worried because his neighbour, a frail woman in her eighties, did not appear for church. After knocking on her door repeatedly and receiving no response, Alan jimmied open a window and searched her house. Soon his worst fears were realized: The woman was lying dead on the floor of her bedroom.

▲ Eyewitness testimony has a far greater effect on jurors than it should, given that it is often inaccurate. Many cases of wrongful arrest and conviction are due to mistaken identification made by eyewitnesses.

◄ Imagine you are on this corner and suddenly witness a holdup across the street. A thief robs a man of his wallet and is gone in a matter of seconds. How accurate would your description of the thief be?

Shaken, Alan returned to his house and telephoned the police. After spending a great deal of time in the woman's house, a detective came over and asked Alan increasingly detailed questions, such as whether he had noticed any suspicious activity in the past day or two. Alan was confused by this line of questioning and finally burst out, "Why are you asking me these questions? Isn't it obvious that my neighbour died of old age? Shouldn't we be notifying her family?" Now it was the detective's turn to look puzzled. "Aren't you the one who discovered the body?" he asked. Alan said he was. "Well," said the detective, "didn't you notice that her bedroom had been ransacked, that there was broken glass everywhere, and that there was a belt tied around her neck?"

It turned out that Alan's neighbour had been strangled by a man who had come to spray her house for insects. There had been a fierce struggle, and the fact that the woman was murdered could not have been more obvious. However, Alan saw none of the signs. He was worried that his elderly neighbour had passed away. When he discovered that she had in fact died, he was quite upset, and the farthest thing from his mind was that she had been murdered. As a result, he saw what he expected to see, and failed to see the unexpected. When the police later showed him photographs of the crime scene, he felt as though he had never been there. He recognized almost nothing. Alan's experiences are consistent with our discussion in Chapter 3 of how people use theories and schemas. We have many theories about the world and the people in it, and these theories influence what we notice and remember.

Similarly, the information we take in is influenced by how familiar we are with it. Unfamiliar things are more difficult to remember than familiar things. For example, people are better at recognizing faces within their own race, a finding called the **own-race bias**. Whites are better at recognizing white faces than black or Asian faces, blacks are better at recognizing black than white faces, and Asians are better at recognizing Asian than white faces (Anthony, Cooper, & Mullen, 1992; Bothwell, Brigham, & Malpass, 1989; Ng & Lindsay, 1994; Shapiro & Penrod, 1986). According to Daniel Levin (2000), it's actually not the case that we are unable to perceive differences between cross-race faces—the problem is that we don't. Levin explains that when we see cross-race faces, we tend to classify the face in terms of race and stop at that. In contrast, when perceiving faces from our own race, we are more likely to focus on the specific features of the person. In other words, "When a white person looks at another white person's nose, they're likely to think to themselves, 'That's John's nose.' When they look at a black person's nose, they're likely to think, 'That's a black nose.' " In a series of studies, Levin demonstrated that when people are required to move beyond their initial snap judgments and pay attention to individuating information, they are quite capable of discriminating between cross-race faces.

Own-race bias
the finding that people are better at recognizing faces of their own race than those of other races

Storage Many people think that memory is like a collection of photographs. We record a picture of an event, such as the face of a robber, and place it in the memory "album." The picture may not be perfect—after all, few of us have photographic memories. Further, it might fade a bit over time because memories, like real photographs, fade with age. It seems unlikely, however, that the picture can be altered or retouched, such that things are added to or subtracted from the image. If the robber we saw was clean-shaven, surely we will not pencil in a moustache at some later time.

Unfortunately, the way in which our memories work is not so simple. People can become confused about where they heard or saw something, so that memories in one "album" get confused with memories in another. As a result, people can have quite inaccurate recall about what they saw. In the case of Thomas Sophonow, apparently the police (who were under extreme pressure to make an arrest) arranged for a key witness to meet Sophonow "accidentally" at the remand centre where he was being held. And, as mentioned earlier, other witnesses reported that their memory of the killer's appearance started becoming clearer with each trial. Is it possible that actually seeing Sophonow altered the witnesses' memories of the appearance of the tall, lanky man with a cowboy hat that they had seen the night of the murder? The answer to this question is yes.

This answer is based on years of research conducted by Elizabeth Loftus and her colleagues on **reconstructive memory**, defined as the process whereby memories for an event become distorted by information encountered after the event has occurred (Loftus, 1979; Loftus & Hoffman, 1989; McDonald & Hirt, 1997; Weingardt, Toland, & Loftus, 1994). According to Loftus, information we obtain after witnessing an event can change our memories of the event. In one of her studies, she showed students 30 slides depicting different stages of an automobile accident. The contents of one slide varied; some students saw a car stopped at a stop sign, whereas others saw the same car stopped at a yield sign (see the photos on page 586). After the slide show, the students were asked several questions about the car accident they had "witnessed." In one version, the key question was "Did another car pass the red Datsun while it was stopped at the stop sign?" In another version, the question was "Did another car pass the red Datsun while it was stopped at the yield sign?" Thus, for half of the participants the question described the traffic sign as they had in fact seen it. But for the other half, the wording of the question subtly introduced new information—for example, if they had seen a stop sign, the question described it as a yield sign. Would this small change (akin to what might occur when witnesses are being questioned by police investigators or attorneys) have an effect on people's memories of the actual event?

All of the students were shown the two pictures reproduced on the next page and were asked which one they had originally seen. Most people (75 percent) who were asked about the sign they had actually seen chose the correct picture; that is, if they had seen a stop sign and were asked about a stop sign, most of them correctly identified the stop-sign photograph (note that 25 percent made a crucial mistake on what would seem to be an easy question). However, of those who had received the misleading question, only 41 percent chose the correct photograph (Loftus, Miller, & Burns, 1978).

In subsequent experiments, Loftus and her colleagues have found that misleading questions can change people's minds about how fast a car was going, whether broken glass was at the scene of an accident, whether a traffic light was green or red, or whether a robber had a moustache (Loftus, 1979).

In a more recent study along the same lines, Jennifer Tomes and Albert Katz (1997) showed students at the University of Western Ontario crime episodes from various films. For example, one episode, taken from *Talons of the Eagle,* showed a woman at an airport, putting her luggage in a red convertible car. A man in a truck drove up and stole her luggage and coat. The woman screamed at him and he drove away. Later, when questioned about the incident, some participants received incorrect information. For example, one

Reconstructive memory
the process whereby memories for an event become distorted by information encountered after the event has occurred

▶ Students saw one of these pictures and then tried to remember whether they had seen a stop sign or a yield sign. Many of those who heard leading questions about the street sign made mistaken reports about which sign they had seen. (From Loftus, Miller, & Burns, 1978)

question made reference to the assailant's blue truck, when in fact the truck was rust-coloured. In another question, it was mentioned that the woman dropped her purse, even though she had not carried one. When participants were again questioned about the crimes, those who had been exposed to misinformation were more likely to have incorporated it into their memories of the event compared to a control group that had not been exposed to misinformation.

Studies such as these show that the way in which the police and lawyers question witnesses can change the witnesses' reports about what they saw. Needless to say, actually seeing a suspect after the event, as in the Thomas Sophonow case, could have a profound effect on eyewitnesses' reports of what they saw. But, we might ask, do misleading questions alter what is stored in eyewitnesses' memories, or do the questions change only what these people are willing to report, without retouching their memories? Though some controversy exists over the answer to this question (Ayers & Reder, 1998; Belli, 1989; Koriat, Goldsmith, & Panšky, 2000; Loftus & Hoffman, 1989; McCloskey & Zaragoza, 1985; Smith & Ellsworth, 1987), most researchers endorse the following position: Misleading questions cause a problem with **source monitoring**, the process by which people try to identify the source of their memories (Crombag, Wagenaar, & Van Koppen, 1996; Johnson, Hashtroudi, & Lindsay, 1993; D. Lindsay, 1994; Mitchell & Johnson, 2000). People who saw a rust-coloured truck (as in the Tomes and Katz [1997] study discussed above) but received the misleading question about a blue truck now have two pieces of

Source monitoring

the process whereby people try to identify the source of their memories

information in memory: the rust-coloured truck and the blue truck. This is all well and good, as long as they remember where these memories came from: The rust-coloured truck from the crime they saw earlier, and the blue truck from the question they were asked later. The problem is that people often become confused about where they heard or saw something, mistakenly believing that the truck in the crime scene was blue. When information is stored in memory, it is not always well "tagged" as to where it came from. For example, research conducted at Bishop's University found that when participants received information about a crime via a radio broadcast and in written form, there was a tendency to confuse the source of these statements. Most frequently, this took the form of thinking they'd heard something on the radio that they had actually read about (Eberman & McKelvie, 2002). Thus, it is not surprising that we can become confused about the source of our memories.

The implications for legal testimony are sobering. Eyewitnesses who are asked misleading questions often report seeing things that were not really there. In addition, eyewitnesses might be confused as to why a suspect looks familiar. Thomas Sophonow might have looked familiar to eyewitnesses because he happened to resemble the police sketch or because they had seen him in the earlier trials, or, as in the case of one witness, because he had seen Sophonow at the remand centre.

Retrieval Suppose the police have arrested a suspect and want to see if you, the eyewitness, can identify the person. It is common practice for the police to arrange a lineup at the police station, where you will be asked whether one of several people is the perpetrator. Sometimes you will be asked to look through a one-way mirror at an actual lineup of the suspect and some foils (people known not to have committed the crime). Other times you will be asked to examine videotapes of a lineup or photographs of the suspect and the foils. In each case, if a witness identifies a suspect as the culprit, the suspect is likely to be charged and convicted of the crime.

Do lineups result in correct identifications? Research conducted with people living in southern Ontario suggests that lineups have a higher success rate than the alternative of showing eyewitnesses only one person (Yarmey, Yarmey, & Yarmey, 1996). Yarmey and colleagues found that if only one person was shown, and that person was innocent, a mistaken identification was four times more likely than when the same person appeared in a six-person lineup. Errors were especially likely if the innocent person wore clothing similar to that worn by the person who committed the crime. Thus, the use of lineups appears to be better than the alternative of presenting only one person and asking eyewitnesses whether that person committed the crime.

That is not to say, however, that lineups are without problems. Just as there are problems with acquisition and storage of information, so too can there be problems with how people retrieve information from their memories (Ellsworth & Mauro, 1998; Koehnken, Malpass, & Wogalter, 1996). A number of things other than the image of a person that is stored in memory can influence whether eyewitnesses will pick someone out of a lineup. Witnesses often choose the person in a lineup who most resembles the criminal, even if the resemblance is not strong. Suppose, for example, that a 19-year-old woman committed a robbery and the police mistakenly arrest you, a 19-year-old woman, for the crime. They put you in a lineup and ask witnesses to pick out the criminal. Which do you think would be fairer: if the other people in the lineup were a 20-year-old man, a 3-year-old child, and an 80-year-old woman, or if the other people were all 19-year-old women? In the former case, the witnesses might pick you only because you are the one who most resembles the actual criminal (Buckhout, 1974). In the latter case, it is much less likely that the witnesses will mistake you for the criminal, because everyone in the lineup is the same age and sex as the culprit (Wells, 1993; Wells & Luus, 1990). In the Thomas Sophonow case, apparently witnesses were asked by police to identify the man with the cowboy hat they had seen outside the doughnut shop from a photographic lineup. Nine of the photographs had been taken indoors and none of the people wore hats. The tenth photo—the photo of Thomas Sophonow—was larger than the others, was taken outdoors, and showed him wearing a cowboy hat. Apparently, police later admitted that the photo gallery was biased and presented a less biased lineup to the witnesses. However, according to Elizabeth Loftus, who testified at the inquiry into Sophonow's wrongful conviction, it is highly unlikely that the new, fairer lineup would have reversed the damage done by the first one. "That's like trying to squeeze toothpaste back in the tube," she said (Janzen, 2001).

To avoid this "best guess" problem wherein witnesses pick the person who looks most like the suspect, social psychologists recommend that police follow these six steps:

1. **Ensure that everyone in the lineup resembles the witness's description of the suspect.** Doing so will minimize the possibility that the witness will simply choose the person who looks most like the culprit (Wells et al., 1998).

2. **Tell the witnesses that the person suspected of the crime may or may not be in the lineup.** If witnesses believe that the culprit is present, they are much more likely to choose the person who looks most like the culprit, rather than saying that they aren't sure or that the culprit is not present. False identifications are more likely to occur when people believe that the culprit is in the lineup (Gonzalez, Ellsworth, & Pembroke, 1993; Malpass & Devine, 1981; Wells et al., 1998; Wells et al., 2000).

3. **Do not always include the suspect in an initial lineup.** If a witness picks out someone as the culprit from a lineup that includes only foils, you will know the witness is not reliable. For example, in a study conducted at the University of Alberta, 61 percent of the research participants who made an identification from a blank lineup failed to identify the correct person later when he was actually present in a photo lineup. In contrast, of participants who correctly indicated that the suspect was not in the blank lineup, only 31 percent later made a mistaken identification when shown a lineup containing the suspect (Wells, 1984).

4. **Present pictures of people sequentially instead of simultaneously.** Doing so makes it more difficult for witnesses to compare all of the pictures, choosing the one that most resembles the criminal, even when the criminal is not actually in the lineup. For example, in a study conducted at Queen's University, 35 percent of research participants exposed to a simultaneous lineup mistakenly identified an innocent person as the perpetrator, whereas only 18 percent of those exposed to a sequential lineup make a mistaken identification (Lindsay & Wells, 1985; Sporer, 1994).

5. **Present witnesses with photographs of people and sound recordings of their voices.** Witnesses who both see and hear members of a lineup are much more likely to identify the person they saw commit a crime than are people who only see the pictures or

only hear the voice recordings (Melara, DeWitt-Rikards, & O'Brien, 1989). In fact, Yarmey and colleagues (2001) found that people are really quite inaccurate when identifying voices—much less accurate than they think they are. For example, if the voice was unfamiliar to the participants, the false identification rate was 45 percent (Yarmey et al., 2001).

6. **Try to minimize the time between the crime and the identification of suspects.** Studies based on staged crimes (Yarmey, Yarmey, & Yarmey, 1996) and actual crimes reported in RCMP records (Tollestrup, Turtle, & Yuille, 1994) have found that the longer the time that elapses between seeing a suspect and being asked to identify the person from a lineup, the greater the likelihood of error (Read, Connolly, & Turtle, 2001).

JUDGING WHETHER EYEWITNESSES ARE MISTAKEN

Suppose you are a police detective or a member of a jury who is listening to a witness describe a suspect. How can you tell whether the witness's memory is accurate or whether he or she is making one of the many mistakes in memory we have just documented? It might seem that the answer to this question is pretty straightforward: Pay careful attention to how confident the witness is. Suppose the witness stands up in the courtroom, points her finger at the defendant, and says, "That's the man I saw commit the crime. There's absolutely no doubt in my mind—I'd recognize him anywhere." Sounds pretty convincing, doesn't it? Compare this testimony to a witness who says, "Well, gee, I'm really not sure, because it all happened so quickly. If I had to guess, I'd say it was the defendant, but I could be wrong." Which witness would you be more likely to believe? The eyewitness who was more confident, of course. And you would not be alone—there is evidence that confident witness are more likely to be believed by police investigators, judges, and jurors (Read, Connolly, & Turtle, 2001).

"That's him! That's the one! ... I'd recognize that silly little hat anywhere!"

The FarSide® by Gary Larson © 1985 Far Works, Inc. By permission Creators Syndicate. All rights reserved.

◀ Lineups have to be carefully constructed to avoid mistaken identifications.

In the Thomas Sophonow case, however, as we have already mentioned, the eyewitnesses who identified him as the man near the doughnut shop became more confident of their descriptions with each trial. Sophonow testified that on the evening of Barbara Stoppel's murder he had stopped at a store to buy some food. While he was there, he decided to purchase stockings filled with treats to distribute to children who would have to spend Christmas in a hospital. At the second trial, the court heard testimony from a ward clerk at a Winnipeg hospital, who testified that a man fitting Sophonow's description had arrived at her desk between 8:10 and 8:30 p.m. on December 23 with Christmas stockings for sick children. The clerk had told him that her hospital didn't have a children's ward, but gave him directions to three hospitals that did. Employees of those hospitals verified that a tall, slim man had arrived with Christmas stockings. However, none of them was certain that the man had been Sophonow, nor were they certain of the exact date that the stockings had been delivered. Who did the jurors believe? The witnesses who presented their testimony with greater confidence, apparently.

Does Certainty Mean Accuracy?

The only problem—and it is a big one—is that numerous studies have shown that a witness's confidence is not strongly related to his or her accuracy (Bothwell, Deffenbacher, & Brigham, 1987; Luus & Wells, 1994a; Olsson, 2000; Read, Connolly, & Turtle, 2001; Smith, Kassin, & Ellsworth, 1989). We don't mean to say that there is no relation between confidence and accuracy; if witnesses pick a suspect out of a lineup, there is a modest relationship between how confident they are and whether their identification is correct (Sporer et al., 1995). Surprisingly, however, this relationship is not strong, and it is dangerous to assume that because a witness is very confident, he or she must therefore be correct. For example, in the Lindsay and colleagues (1981) experiment we discussed earlier, witnesses who saw the crime under poor viewing conditions (in which the thief wore the cap over his ears) had as much confidence in their identifications as did witnesses who saw the crime under moderate or good viewing conditions, even though the former were considerably less accurate (see Figure SPA3.1 on page 581).

Similar results were obtained at the University of Alberta by Wells, Lindsay, and Ferguson (1978) who conducted a study along the lines of the Lindsay and colleagues (1981) study described earlier. Specifically, these researchers staged the theft of a calculator from a research laboratory. Research participants were asked to identify the thief from a photo lineup as well as to indicate how certain they were that they had identified the correct person. The correlation between participants' confidence that they had made a correct identification and the accuracy of their identifications was only .29 (recall that a perfect correlation is 1.00). Participants also were cross-examined (asked questions about the event). Other research participants, serving as jurors, observed the cross-examinations. It turned out that jurors were more likely to believe confident, rather than unconfident, witnesses—a disturbing finding, given the weak relation between accuracy and confidence.

Signs of Accurate Testimony

How, then, can we tell whether a witness's testimony is correct? It is by no means easy, but research by David Dunning and Lisa Beth Stern (1994; Stern & Dunning, 1994) suggests some answers. They showed participants a film in which a man stole some money from a woman's wallet, asked participants to pick the man out of a photo lineup, and then asked participants to describe how they had made up their minds. Dunning and Stern found some interesting differences between the reports of people who accurately identified the man and the reports of people who did not. Accurate witnesses tended to say that they didn't really know how they recognized the man, that his face just "popped out" at them. Inaccurate witnesses tended to say that they used a process of elimination whereby they deliberately compared one face to another. Ironically, taking more time and thinking more carefully about the pictures was associated with making more mistakes. We should thus be more willing to believe a witness who says, "I knew it was the defendant as soon as I saw him in the lineup" than one who says, "I compared everyone in the lineup, thought about it, and decided it was the defendant."

The research by Dunning and Stern, while intriguing, leaves unanswered an important question: Did taking more time on the identification task make people less accurate, or did people who were less accurate to begin with simply take more time? Maybe some people did not pay close attention to the film of the robbery and thus had difficulty recognizing the robber in the lineup. Consequently, they had to spend more time thinking about it and comparing the faces, such that inaccuracy caused a longer decision time. Alternatively, there might have been something about making identifications thoughtfully and deliberately that impaired accuracy.

The Problem with Verbalization   Some fascinating studies by Schooler and Engstler-Schooler (1990) support this second possibility and suggest that trying to put an image of a face into words can cause problems. They showed students a film of a bank robbery and asked some of the students to write detailed descriptions of the robber's face (the verbalization condition). The others spent the same amount of time completing an unrelated task (the no verbalization condition). All students then tried to pick out the robber from a photo lineup of eight faces. It might seem that writing a description of the robber would be a good memory aid and make people more accurate. In fact, the reverse was true. Only 38 percent of the people in the verbalization condition correctly identified the robber, compared to 64 percent of the people in the no verbalization condition.

Schooler and Engstler-Schooler (1990; see also Dodson, Johnson, & Schooler, 1997; Schooler, Fiore, & Brandimonte, 1997) suggest that trying to put a face into words is difficult and impairs memory for that face. Using the word "squinty" to describe a robber's eyes, for example, might be a general description of what his eyes looked like, but probably does not capture the subtle contours of his eyes, eyelids, eyelashes, eyebrows, and upper cheeks. When you see the photo lineup, you look for eyes that are squinty, and doing so interferes with your attention to the finer details of the faces. If you ever witness a crime, then, you should not try to put into words what the criminal looked like. And if you hear someone say she or he wrote down a description of the criminal and then deliberated long and hard before deciding whether the person was present at a lineup, you might doubt the accuracy of the witness's identification.

By now we have seen several factors that make eyewitness testimony inaccurate, leading to all too many false identifications. Perhaps the legal system in Canada should rely less on eyewitness testimony than it now does. This might mean that some guilty people go free, but it would avoid many false convictions. To see how accurate you and your friends are at eyewitness testimony, and to illustrate some of the pitfalls we have discussed, tackle Try It! on page 592.

The Accuracy of Eyewitness Testimony

Try this demonstration with a group of friends whom you know will be gathered in one place, such as a dorm room or an apartment. The idea is to stage an "incident," in which someone comes into the room suddenly, acts in a strange manner, and then leaves. Your friends will then be asked to recall as much as they can about this person, to see if they are good eyewitnesses. Here are some specific instructions about how you might do this.

1. Take one friend, whom we will call the actor, into your confidence before you do this exercise. Ideally, the actor should be a stranger to the people who will be the eyewitnesses. The actor should suddenly rush into the room where you and your other friends are gathered and act in a strange (but nonthreatening) manner. For example, the actor could hand someone a flower and say, "The flower man cometh!" Or, he or she could go up to each person and say something unexpected, such as, "Meet me in Moscow at New Year's." Ask the actor to hold something in his or her hand during this episode, such as a pencil, shoelace, or banana. Important note: The actor should not act in a violent or threatening way, or make the eyewitnesses uncomfortable. The goal is to act in unexpected and surprising ways, not to frighten people. After a few minutes, the actor should leave the room.

2. Inform your friends that you staged this event as a demonstration of eyewitness testimony and that if they are willing, they should try to remember, in as much detail as possible, what occurred. Ask them to write down answers to these questions:

   a. What did the actor look like? Write down a detailed description.

   b. What did the actor say? Write down his or her words as best you can remember.

   c. How much time passed between the time the actor entered the room and the time he or she left?

   d. Did the actor touch anyone? If yes, whom?

   e. What was the actor holding in his or her hand?

3. After everyone has answered these questions, ask them to read their answers out loud. How much did they agree? How accurate were people's answers? Discuss with your friends why they were correct or incorrect in their descriptions.

Note: This demonstration will work best if you have access to a video camera and can record the actor's actions. That way, you can play the tape to assess the accuracy of the eyewitnesses' descriptions. If you cannot videotape it, keep track of how much time elapsed so you can judge the accuracy of people's time estimates.

JUDGING WHETHER EYEWITNESSES ARE LYING

There is yet another reason eyewitness testimony can be inaccurate. Even if witnesses have very accurate memories for what they saw, they might deliberately lie when on the witness stand. In the Thomas Sophonow case, some witnesses admitted that they testified because they wanted a reward. The man who told the wild tale of chasing and catching Sophonow was found to be lying. The Crown also relied on jailhouse informants who claimed that Sophonow had confessed to them that he was Barbara Stoppel's killer. Deals had been struck with these informants in exchange for their testimony. Why couldn't two different sets of jurors see through these stories?

Sadly, the Sophonow case is not unique in this regard. In other cases of wrongful conviction, such as those of David Milgaard and Donald Marshall, police and jury members believed the false stories of the acquaintances who testified against them. Sometimes, the truth is never established. Consider, for example, the controversy over the guilt or innocence of O.J. Simpson. Was he lying when he denied murdering Nicole Simpson and Ronald Goldman? What about the testimony of Mark Fuhrman, the police detective who discovered the bloody glove at O.J. Simpson's house? Some people believe that Fuhrman was lying and that he planted the glove at the estate. Others believe that while he may well be a racist, he was telling the truth about finding the glove. How can we tell whether witnesses such as these are lying or telling the truth?

Several studies have tested people's ability to detect deception (Bond & Atoum, 2000; DePaulo & Friedman, 1998; Ekman, 1992; Ekman, O'Sullivan, & Frank, 1999; Gordon & Miller, 2000). When people watch videotapes of actors who are either lying or telling the truth, their ability to tell who is lying is only slightly better than chance guessing (DePaulo, 1994; DePaulo, Stone, & Lassiter, 1985). But surely some people must be very good at detecting deception; after all, some jobs require exactly that skill. For example, law enforcement officials, most of whom have spent years with suspects who concoct stories professing their innocence, may be much more skilled than the average person at seeing through these stories to the underlying truth. Unfortunately, research suggests otherwise. For example, Bella DePaulo and Roger Pfeiffer (1986) tested the ability of experienced law enforcement officers—including members of the U.S. Customs Service, the Secret Service, the armed forces, police detectives, and judges—to detect deception. In general, these officials were no better at telling whether someone was lying than were untrained university students. The problem is that both untrained people and experts tend to think that there are reliable cues to deception, such as whether a person refuses to look you in the eye (Akehurst et al., 1996). Unlike Pinocchio with his lengthening nose, human beings do not show obvious signs of lying that are the same for every person in every situation. If people are lying, they often get away with it, regardless of whether they are talking to law enforcement experts, friends, or strangers (DePaulo & Friedman, 1998; Kashy & DePaulo, 1996).

If people are poor lie detectors, perhaps machines can do better. You've probably heard of a **polygraph**, a machine that measures people's physiological responses, such as their heart rate and breathing rate. Polygraph operators attempt to tell if someone is lying by observing how that person responds physiologically while answering questions. In one version, called the control question test, the operator asks people both relevant questions about a crime (e.g., "Did you steal money from the cash register of the restaurant?") and control questions that are known to produce truthful responses (e.g., "Have you ever stolen anything in your whole life?"). The assumption is that when people lie they become anxious, and that this anxiety can be detected by increases in heart rate, breathing rate, and so on. Thus, the operator sees whether you have more of a physiological response to the relevant question than to the control question.

Another version is called the guilty knowledge test. Here, people answer multiple choice questions about specific aspects of a crime, the answers to which are known only by the police and the culprit. For example, you might be asked, "Was the amount stolen from the cash register $10, $23, $34, $54, or $110?" The idea is that only the criminal would know the correct answer and thus be anxious when that answer is read. For example, the thief who knows that he stole $23 will probably be more anxious when this amount is read than will an innocent person who does not know how much money was stolen.

Polygraph
a machine that measures people's physiological responses (e.g., heart rate); polygraph operators attempt to tell if someone is lying by observing how that person responds physiologically while answering questions

There's a great deal of controversy over the accuracy of polygraph tests. How well do they actually work? The first thing to realize is that they are only as good as the person operating and interpreting the test. With several responses being measured, it is not always easy to tell whether a person has had more of a physiological response to one question than to another. One disturbing finding is that operators often disagree with one another, suggesting that the test is by no means infallible (Ellsworth & Mauro, 1998).

When the test is administered under optimal conditions by an experienced examiner, it does reveal whether someone is lying or telling the truth at levels better than chance. But even then it is not perfect (Ellsworth & Mauro, 1998; Iacono & Patrick, 1999; Saxe, 1994; Saxe, Dougherty, & Cross, 1985). The error rates vary somewhat, depending on the technique used to administer the test. Some studies have found that false negatives, in which liars are found to be telling the truth, are the most common kind of error (Honts, 1994). Research conducted with inmates in a British Columbia prison found that there was a tendency for the test to mistakenly classify as liars those who were actually telling the truth (Patrick & Iacono, 1989). A review by Paul Ekman (1992), averaging across all the different techniques, estimates that the polygraph typically misidentifies about 15 percent of liars as truth-tellers (false negatives) and about 15 percent of truth-tellers as liars (false positives).

Because of the rate of error, Canada does not allow the results of polygraph tests to be used in court. In Thomas Sophonow's third trial, his defence lawyer attempted to have him take a lie detector test in court, but the judge refused. Incidentally, we might note that after Sophonow was acquitted, he took a lie detector test when he was interviewed on the television program *W-5* in 1986, and passed with flying colours.

To see how well you and your friends can tell whether someone is lying, do Try It! on page 595. How did you do? It would be nice if there were a foolproof method of telling whether someone is lying. Controversial cases such as the O.J. Simpson trial could be

▶ Although polygraphs can detect whether someone is lying at levels better than chance, they are by no means infallible. Because of the rate of error, Canada does not allow the results of polygraph tests to be used in court.

easily resolved, and David Milgaard, Donald Marshall, and Thomas Sophonow—to name a few—would not have had to spend years in prison for crimes they did not commit. Many psychologists doubt, though, that such a test will ever be developed; the nuances of human behaviour are too rich and complex to allow foolproof tests of honesty.

CAN EYEWITNESS TESTIMONY BE IMPROVED?

We have seen a number of ways in which eyewitness testimony can go wrong. Given how important such testimony is in criminal trials, are there ways to improve it? Two general approaches have been tried, but unfortunately neither has proven to be very successful.

The first involves hypnosis. You may have seen movies in which a witness to a terrible crime has no memory of what occurred—until he or she is put under hypnosis. Then, while in a trance-like state, the person is able to describe the murderer in great detail.

Lie Detection

The purpose of this exercise, which should be done with a group of friends, is to see how well people can tell if someone is lying. Ask for a volunteer to be the speaker and the others to be the audience. The speaker's job will be to lie about how much he or she likes five high-school acquaintances, and to tell the truth about how much he or she likes five other high-school acquaintances. The audience's job is to try to guess when the speaker is telling the truth and when he or she is lying. Here are some specific instructions:

Instructions for the speaker: Make a list of 10 people you knew in high school and think about how much you liked each person. Randomly choose five people and put a *T* next to their names. These are the people about whom you will be truthful. Put an *L* next to the other names. These are the people about whom you will lie. Take a few minutes to think about what you will say. When you are ready, describe your feelings toward each person (truthfully or not) to the audience. Give a few sentences about each person.

Instructions for the audience: The speaker will be describing her or his feelings toward 10 high-school acquaintances. He or she will be telling the truth about half of the people and lying about the other half. Listen carefully and try to guess when the speaker is telling the truth and when he or she is lying. You may use any cues you want to make your decision. Make a list from 1 to 10, and put "Truth" or "Lie" next to the name of each person the speaker describes.

Scoring: The speaker, when done, should reveal when he or she was telling the truth versus lying. The audience members should tally how often they were right. People should be correct half of the time just by guessing; scores that are substantially above 50 percent may indicate that you are good at detecting deception. Trade notes about what kinds of cues you paid attention to in the speaker. What did he or she do that made you think he or she was telling a lie?

Variation: Here is an interesting variation you can try: Have half of the audience sit with their backs to the speaker so they can hear but not see him or her. The other half of the audience should sit facing the speaker. Which group was better at detecting when the speaker was lying? Bella DePaulo, Dan Lassiter, and Julie Stone (1983) found that people who were instructed to pay special attention to a speaker's tone of voice did better at lie detection than did people instructed to pay attention to how the speaker looked. When people can see a speaker, they tend to focus on facial cues that they think are good indications of lying, but which, in fact, are not. Thus, the group of people who cannot see the speaker might rely more on tone of voice, and may be more accurate.

Unfortunately, this is a case in which the movies do not reflect real life. University of Toronto psychologist Marilyn Smith (1983) conducted a careful review and analysis of the literature and concluded that there is no hard evidence that people's memories improve when they are hypnotized. Subsequent research supports this conclusion (Ellsworth & Mauro, 1998; Erdelyi, 1994; Kebbell & Wagstaff, 1998; see review by Read, Connolly, & Turtle, 2001). In fact, there is some evidence that when people are under hypnosis they are more susceptible to suggestion, coming to believe that they saw things that they did not (Sanders & Simmons, 1983; Sheehan & Tilden, 1984; Wagstaff, 1989). Even worse, people tend to become more confident in their memories after they have been hypnotized, even if they are no more accurate (Spiegel & Spiegel, 1987). This is dangerous because, as we saw earlier, juries often interpret a witness's confidence as a sign of how accurate a witness is, even though confidence is not very related to accuracy.

The second way people have tried to increase eyewitness accuracy is with the use of the **cognitive interview** (Geiselman & Fischer, 1989). With this technique, a trained interviewer tries to improve an eyewitness's memories by focusing the individual's attention on the details and context of the event. This is done chiefly by asking the person to recall the event several times from different starting points (e.g., from the beginning of the event and from the middle of the event) and by asking the person to create a mental image of the scene. Some research using this technique looked promising, finding that it improved people's memories by as much as 35 percent (Brock, Fisher, & Cutler, 1999). Other research, however, has been more sobering, finding that the cognitive interview may increase errors and confabulations of memory, especially when used with children (Finger & Pezdek, 1999; Memom & Stevenage, 1996; Roberts, 1996). One reason for this is that repeatedly imagining an event has been found to increase source monitoring errors, whereby people become confused about whether they actually witnessed an event or simply imagined it later (Johnson et al., 1979).

Thus, so far there is no tried-and-true way to improve eyewitnesses' memories—other than by trying to avoid the pitfalls we have discussed in this chapter.

Cognitive interview

a technique whereby a trained interviewer tries to improve eyewitnesses' memories by focusing their attention on the details and context of the event

▶ Sometimes people are hypnotized as a way of improving their memory of a crime. Unfortunately, there is no evidence that hypnosis improves the accuracy of eyewitnesses' memories.

The Recovered Memory Debate Another form of eyewitness memory has received a great deal of attention: the case in which a person recalls having been the victim of a crime after many years of being consciously unaware of that fact. Understandably, there is a great deal of controversy over the accuracy of **recovered memories**, recollections of past events, such as sexual abuse, that have been forgotten or repressed (Pezdek & Banks, 1996; Pope, 1996; Schooler & Eich, 2000).

For example, in 1992, John Popowich, a Saskatoon police officer, was charged with sexually assaulting children at a daycare centre. The children claimed that he and other adults had forced them to drink blood, perform sexual acts, and watch people having their eyes plucked out. These charges came at a time when recovered memory syndrome was receiving a lot of attention in the media and the courts; as a result, the children's testimony was believed. After a 10-year fight that took a tremendous toll on his personal and professional life, Popowich managed to establish his innocence. In the summer of 2002, Saskatchewan's justice minister issued an apology to Popowich for his wrongful conviction and agreed to pay $1.3 million in compensation (Millin, 2002).

There are those who argue strongly that it is quite common for people to repress traumatic events, such that they have no memory of them until these events can be "recovered," usually with the help of a therapist (Bass & Davis, 1994). On the other side of the issue are academic psychologists who argue that the accuracy of recovered memories cannot be accepted on faith (e.g., Loftus & Ketcham, 1994; Schacter, 1995, 1996; Schooler, 1999). These psychologists acknowledge that sexual abuse and other childhood traumas are a terrible problem and more common than we would like to think. They further agree that claims of sexual abuse should be taken very seriously and fully investigated, and that when sufficient evidence of guilt exists, the person responsible for the abuse should be prosecuted.

But here's the problem: What is sufficient evidence? Unfortunately, there is evidence from numerous laboratory studies and from everyday life that people can acquire vivid memories of events that never actually occurred (Loftus, 1993; Schooler & Eich, 2000). Unfortunately, it is very difficult to distinguish between accurate memories and false ones, in the absence of any corroborating evidence. For this reason, claims of abuse cannot be taken on faith alone.

Are there other kinds of evidence that can be used by the legal system that might be less susceptible to the kinds of inaccuracies that plague eyewitness testimony? We turn to this issue next.

Recovered memories
recollections of an event, such as sexual abuse, that had been forgotten or repressed

Other Kinds of Evidence

There are a number of other kinds of evidence that police investigators, judges, and juries can rely on in reaching decisions about the guilt or innocence of people accused of crimes. They can turn to experts for information (e.g., about an accused's mental state). They also can rely on physical evidence such as fingerprints or DNA tests conducted on hair samples or blood. Legal professionals and juries also can base their verdicts on statistical evidence—the probability that the accused committed the crime. As we shall see, juries find some of these kinds of evidence more persuasive than others.

EXPERT TESTIMONY

There are a number of thorny issues surrounding the use of expert testimony in court (Pfeifer, 1997). For example, research conducted at York University suggests that jurors may not always understand judges' instructions about the kinds of evidence that are permissible from an expert witness and the kinds of evidence that should be disregarded (Schuller & Paglia, 1999; see Schuller & Yarmey, 2001 for a review). It is important that jurors know how to properly evaluate expert testimony, because research has shown that jurors are influenced by such information. For example, in one study, students at York University and visitors to the Ontario Science Centre were presented with a transcript of a homicide case (based on an actual case) in which an abused woman shot and killed her husband (Schuller & Hastings, 1996). Participants in the expert testimony condition read that a psychologist had testified that the woman's behaviour should be understood in terms of battered wife syndrome. The psychologist explained that battered wife syndrome resembles post-traumatic stress disorder in terms of its emotional and psychological consequences. (Participants in the control condition were not exposed to any expert testimony.) Did expert testimony have an effect on the mock jurors' verdicts? The answer is yes. Participants who received expert testimony were more likely to conclude that the woman acted out of self-defence than were participants who did not hear expert testimony. Importantly, those who received expert testimony also rendered a more lenient verdict.

In Canada, the courts have shown a tendency to move away from expert testimony (Peters, 2001; Yarmey, 2001b; although see Saunders, 2001 for a different opinion). Why is this the case? According to Martin Peters, a Toronto criminal lawyer, some judges believe that much of what experts—in particular, psychological experts—have to offer is common sense. In other words, jury members are assumed to already know whatever a psychologist might have to offer. Other judges are concerned that jury members will rely too heavily on what the experts say, rather than critically evaluate information themselves (Peters, 2001). Not surprisingly, psychologists argue that they do have something to offer the legal system. As A. Daniel Yarmey (2001b) points out, research on the accuracy of eyewitness testimony and on identification of suspects from lineups has revealed important information that is not part of common sense knowledge. Given that wrongful convictions are generally due to mistaken eyewitness identification, experts can provide the kind of information that would enable jurors to properly evaluate such evidence. Fortunately, some judges agree. According to the Honourable Mr. Justice Jamie W. S. Saunders of the Nova Scotia Court of Appeal, expert testimony does have a place in Canadian courts, providing certain guidelines are followed (e.g., experts must be independent and objective).

PHYSICAL EVIDENCE

When crimes occur, forensic experts might scrutinize the scene for footprints, fingerprints, or samples of hair or fibres. In addition, in recent years DNA testing has become much more accurate, and courts increasingly rely on this kind of evidence. For example, when Larry Fisher was tried for the murder of Gail Miller (the murder for which David Milgaard had been wrongfully convicted), DNA testing proved that he had raped Miller. The jury then used this information to infer that he had killed her as well. The same kind of evidence that was used to convict Larry Fisher was used to exonerate Guy Paul Morin,

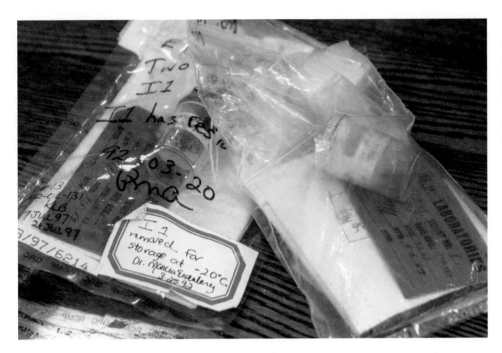

A vial of melted snow containing semen samples found at the scene where Gail Miller was murdered in 1969 was the source of DNA evidence used to exonerate David Milgaard and convict Larry Fisher.

who was wrongfully convicted of sexually assaulting and killing a nine-year-old girl in 1986. In 1995, he was eventually exonerated on the basis of DNA evidence.

However, what about other kinds of physical evidence that might not be as conclusive as DNA testing? Research conducted by Elizabeth Loftus (1974, 1983) suggests that other kinds of physical evidence tend not to be very persuasive. For example, in one study, Loftus (1974) presented research participants with a description of a robbery of a grocery store and the murder of its owner. Participants in the physical evidence condition read that the defendant had been found with large sums of cash and that traces of the cleaning solution used on the store's floor had been found on his shoes. Those in the eyewitness testimony condition read that a store clerk had identified the defendant as the killer. Participants in a third condition received both physical and eyewitness evidence, but the eyewitness testimony was discredited. Specifically, participants were told that the eyewitness had poor vision. It turned out that physical evidence alone was not very convincing to these mock jurors—only 18 percent of them rendered a guilty verdict. In sharp contrast, 72 percent of participants who received eyewitness testimony believed that the defendant was guilty. Perhaps most disturbing, 68 percent of participants who received eyewitness testimony that was later discredited nevertheless considered the defendant to be guilty.

In the Thomas Sophonow case, physical evidence was presented at the third trial that made it unlikely that he could have been at the doughnut shop at the time of Barbara Stoppel's murder. Sophonow testified that he had telephoned his mother in Vancouver (before delivering the Christmas stockings to hospitals). Telephone records confirmed that he had placed the call at 7:56 p.m. from a location that would have made it difficult to reach the doughnut shop by the time the murder took place (between 8:15 and 8:45 p.m.). However, consistent with Loftus's research, jurors obviously did not find this evidence very convincing, choosing instead to believe the reports of people who claimed to have seen Sophonow at the scene of the crime.

STATISTICAL EVIDENCE

Consider a hypothetical case that legal scholars have frequently debated. A bus hits and kills a dog. Although it is not known to which company the bus belongs, 80 percent of the buses on the route where the dog was killed are owned by the Blue Bus company. The key question is this: Should the Blue Bus company be held liable for this accident based on this statistical information alone? According to civil law, which applies to cases such as this, the Blue Bus company should be held responsible if it is "more likely than not" that a Blue Bus killed the dog.

Gary Wells (1992) presented this case to students at the University of Alberta. He found that participants who were told that 80 percent of the buses on the route were owned by the Blue Bus company were extremely reluctant to assign guilt to the Blue Bus company on this basis; only 8 percent of them held the Blue Bus company liable. In another condition, participants were told that a weigh station attendant had seen a Blue Bus on that road earlier that day, but that his reports tended to be only 80 percent accurate. Remarkably, in this case, 67 percent of participants assigned responsibility for the accident to the Blue Bus company. Thus, even though the probabilities were the same in each condition (80 percent), participants were much more swayed by eyewitness testimony than by statistical evidence (i.e., 67 percent versus 8 percent convictions). Interestingly, when Wells presented the Blue Bus case to experienced judges, he found that they were no more likely than university students to assign guilt based on statistical evidence alone.

Might there be conditions under which people would willingly place more weight on statistical evidence? Edward Wright and colleagues (1996) designed a study to answer this question. They presented the Blue Bus case to students at St. Francis Xavier University, varying the amount of time participants had before presenting their verdict, to see whether having a lot of time to think about this kind of evidence might cause people to rely on it more. Some participants were also given the opportunity to discuss the evidence with others to see if group discussion might increase reliance on statistical evidence. However, neither extended decision-making time nor group discussion made participants more likely to assign guilt to the Blue Bus company (Wright et al., 1996).

Thus, it appears that when considering different kinds of evidence, juries and judges tend to be persuaded by the kind of evidence that is most likely to be unreliable—the reports of other people. If eyewitnesses claim that they saw the person (or bus) in question, juries are likely to render a guilty verdict based on that testimony. The testimony of an expert witness—another kind of report from a person—is likely to be persuasive as well. Physical evidence and especially statistical evidence apparently are not very persuasive at all. In short, it seems that what is most likely to convince us of something is hearing another person say that it is so.

Juries: Group Processes in Action

Juries are of particular interest to social psychologists because the way they reach verdicts is directly relevant to social psychological research on group processes and social interaction.

The right to be tried by a jury of one's peers has a long tradition in Canadian law. Trial by jury was an established institution in England at the beginning of the seventeenth century, and this tradition was adopted by Canada in 1867. Despite this tradition, the jury system has often come under attack. We have already discussed several cases in which juries in Canada have reached the wrong decision and convicted innocent people. The jury system also has been criticized on grounds that jurors may lack the ability to understand complex evidence and reach a dispassionate verdict. Research conducted at Simon Fraser University by Rose and Ogloff (2001) has demonstrated that jury members' comprehension of the instructions given to them by judges is remarkably low. For example, one of their studies revealed that participants acting as mock jurors understood just over 60 percent of what they had been told. Given that the fate of people's lives rests in jurors' hands, one would hope that jurors would clearly comprehend instructions from the judge. Stephen Adler (1994), for example, suggests that in some cases (e.g., complex civil suits) we dispense with juries altogether. As noted by a former dean of the Harvard Law School, "Why should anyone think that 12 persons brought in from the street, selected in various ways for their lack of general ability, should have any special capacity for deciding controversies between persons?" (Kalven & Zeisel, 1966). The jury system has its staunch supporters, of course, and few people argue that it should be abolished altogether. The point is that it is not a perfect system and that, based on research in social psychology, there are ways we might expect it to go wrong. Problems can arise at each of three phases of a jury trial: the way in which jurors use information they obtain before the trial begins; the way in which they process information during the trial; and the way in which they deliberate in the jury room after all of the evidence has been presented.

EFFECTS OF PRETRIAL PUBLICITY

The murder of Barbara Stoppel received considerable attention in the media, and it is therefore possible that the jury, before the trial began, was biased by what its members had read in the newspapers. The police sketch of the suspect was widely circulated because police were under extreme pressure to make an arrest. Similarly, the jurors in the O.J. Simpson murder trial probably had heard a lot about this case before the trial, given the amount of media attention it received. What are the effects of such pretrial publicity?

Even when the information reported by the media is accurate, it is often stacked against a suspect for a simple reason: The press gets much of its information from the police and the Crown prosecutor, who are interested in presenting as strong a case as they can against the suspect (Imrich, Mullin, & Linz, 1995). Thus, it's not surprising that the more people hear about a case in the media, the more they believe that the suspect is guilty (Kerr, 1995; Moran & Cutler, 1991; Otto, Penrod, & Dexter, 1994; Steblay et al., 1999).

Kramer, Kerr, and Carroll (1990) showed that emotional publicity that arouses public passions, such as lurid details about a murder, is particularly biasing. They contacted people who had just finished serving on juries in Michigan and asked them to watch a videotaped trial of a man accused of robbing a supermarket. Before the jurors viewed the trial, the researchers exposed them to emotional publicity (reports that a car matching the one used in the robbery struck and killed a seven-year-old girl after the robbery), factual publicity (a report that the suspect had an extensive prior criminal record), or no publicity. After watching the trial and deliberating in 12-member mock juries, the participants rated whether they would vote to convict the suspect. The emotional publicity biased jurors the most, significantly increasing the percentage of jurors who gave guilty verdicts—even though the jurors knew they were not supposed to be influenced by any information they had learned before viewing the trial.

Judges and lawyers have a variety of strategies they use to try to remedy this problem. First, lawyers are allowed to question prospective jurors before the trial. The lawyers ask people whether they have heard anything about the case, and, if so, whether they feel they can render an unbiased verdict. One problem with this approach, however, is that people are often unaware that they have been biased by pretrial publicity (Ogloff & Vidmar, 1994). In the Kramer and colleagues (1990) study we just reviewed, for example, the researchers removed from the study any jurors who said that because of the pretrial publicity they could not form an unbiased opinion. Nonetheless, the emotional publicity still influenced the verdicts given by the remaining jurors.

Second, judges can instruct jurors to disregard what they have heard in the media. Several studies have shown, however, that these instructions do little to erase the effects of pretrial publicity and may even *increase* the likelihood that jurors use it (Fein, McCloskey, & Tomlinson, 1997; Kramer, Kerr, & Carroll, 1990; Shaw & Skolnick, 1995). One reason this can happen is that it's very difficult to erase something from our minds once we have heard it. In fact, as mentioned in Chapter 3, the more we try not to think about something, the more that very thing keeps popping into consciousness (Wegner, 1989, 1992, 1994).

Another problem with pretrial publicity is that linking a person's name with incriminating events can cause negative impressions of the person, even if the media explicitly deny any such connection. Daniel Wegner and colleagues (1981) found that when research participants read a headline denying any wrongdoing on someone's part—such as "Bob Talbert not linked with Mafia"—they had a more negative impression of the person than did participants who read an innocuous headline—such as "Bob Talbert arrives in city." The mere mention of Bob Talbert and the Mafia in the same headline was enough to plant seeds of doubt in readers, despite the headline's explicit denial of a connection.

Thus, media reports can have unintended negative effects, and, once there, those effects are hard to erase. A recent study found that pretrial publicity had the strongest effect when mock jurors (University of Toronto students) were asked to pronounce a verdict right after hearing the publicity (Freedman, Martin, & Mota, 1998). After participants actually viewed a videotape of the trial, their decisions were more likely to be influenced by the evidence presented in the trial. One can only hope that the same holds true in actual trials. Obviously, the best solution is to include only jurors who have heard nothing about the case.

HOW JURORS PROCESS INFORMATION DURING THE TRIAL

How do individual jurors think about the evidence they hear during a trial? As we saw in Chapter 3, people often construct theories and schemas to interpret the world around them, and the same is true of jurors. Nancy Pennington and Reid Hastie (1990, 1992, 1993; Hastie & Pennington, 1991, 1995, 2000) suggest that jurors decide on one story that best explains all of the evidence; they then try to fit this story to the possible verdicts they are allowed to render. If one of those verdicts fits well with their preferred story, they are likely to vote to convict on that charge.

This explanation has important implications for how lawyers present their cases. Lawyers typically present the evidence in one of two ways. In the first, called the *story order,* they present the evidence in the sequence that events occurred, corresponding as closely as possible to the story they want the jurors to believe. In the second, called the *witness order,* they present witnesses in the sequence they think will have the greatest impact, even if this means that events are described out of order. For example, a lawyer might save his or her best witness for last, so the trial ends on a dramatic, memorable note, even if this witness describes events that occurred early in the alleged crime.

If you were a lawyer, in which order would you present the evidence? You probably can guess which order Pennington and Hastie hypothesized would be most successful. If jurors are ultimately swayed by the story they think best explains the sequence of events, the best strategy should be to present the evidence in story order and not witness order. To test their hypothesis, Pennington and Hastie (1988) asked mock jurors to listen to a simulated murder trial. The researchers varied the order in which the defence attorney and the prosecuting attorney presented their cases. In one condition, both used the story order, whereas in another condition, both used the witness order. In other conditions, one attorney used the story order, whereas the other used the witness order.

The results provided clear and dramatic support for the story order strategy. As seen in Table SPA3.1, when the prosecutor used the story order and the defence used the witness order, the jurors were most likely to believe the prosecutor—78 percent voted to convict the defendant. When the prosecutor used the witness order and the defence used the story order, the tables were turned—only 31 percent voted to convict. Pennington and Hastie (1990) speculate that one reason the conviction rate in felony trials in the United States is so high—approximately 80 percent—is that in real trials prosecutors usually present evidence in story order, whereas defence attorneys usually use witness order. To those of our readers who are budding lawyers, remember this when you are preparing for your first trial!

TABLE SPA3.1

How should lawyers present their cases?

Lawyers can present their cases in a variety of ways. This study found that story order, in which lawyers present the evidence in the order that corresponds most closely to the "story" they want the jurors to believe, works best.

Percentage of people voting to convict the defendant

Prosecution evidence	Defence evidence	
	Story order	Witness order
Story order	59%	78%
Witness order	31%	

(Adapted from Pennington & Hastie, 1988)

DELIBERATIONS IN THE JURY ROOM

You may have noticed that our discussion so far has left out a crucial part of the jury process—the part where the jury retires to the jury room and deliberates before deciding on the verdict. Even if most jurors are inclined to vote to convict, there might be a persuasive minority that changes their fellow jurors' minds. Sometimes this can be a minority of one, as in the classic movie *12 Angry Men*. When this film begins, a jury has just finished listening to the evidence in a murder case and all of the jurors except one vote to convict the defendant. However, over the next 90 minutes, the lone holdout, played by Henry Fonda, persuades his peers that there is reason to doubt that the young Hispanic defendant is guilty. At first, the other jurors pressure Fonda to change his mind (using techniques of normative and informational conformity, as discussed in Chapter 8), but in the end, reason triumphs and the other jurors come to see that Fonda is right.

As entertaining as this movie is, research indicates that it does not reflect the reality of most jury deliberations (Ellsworth & Mauro, 1998; MacCoun, 1989). Harry Kalven, Jr. and Hans Zeisel (1966) interviewed members of more than 200 juries in actual criminal trials. In the vast majority of the cases (97 percent), the jury's final decision was the same as the one favoured by a majority of the jurors on the initial vote. Thus, just as we saw in Chapter 8 on conformity, majority opinion usually carries the day, bringing dissenting jurors into line. In the O.J. Simpson trial, for example, one juror initially voted guilty, but quickly changed her mind. And what happens if a dissenting juror does not succumb to pressure to go along with the majority opinion? In Chapter 8, we found that dissenters may eventually be rejected from the group. This may have been the case in the third Sophonow trial, where jurors were unable to reach a unanimous verdict after five long days of deliberation—apparently because one juror refused to go along with the rest of the group. In a startling move, the judge dismissed this juror because she supposedly had claimed to possess "psychic powers and special gifts." (The juror who was removed maintains that she said no such thing.) Once the problematic juror was removed, it took little time for the remaining 11 members to render their guilty verdict.

▶ In the classic movie *12 Angry Men,* Henry Fonda convinces all of his fellow jurors to change their minds about a defendant's guilt. In real life, however, such cases of a minority in a jury convincing the majority to change the verdict are rare.

If jury deliberation is stacked toward the initial, majority opinion, why not just abandon the deliberation process, letting the jury's initial vote determine a defendant's guilt or innocence? For two reasons, this would not be a good idea. First, forcing juries to reach a unanimous verdict makes them consider the evidence more carefully, rather than simply assuming that their initial impressions of the case were correct (Hastie, Penrod, & Pennington, 1983). Second, even if minorities seldom succeed in persuading the majority to change their minds about guilt or innocence, minorities often do change people's minds about the degree of guilt. In criminal trials, juries usually have some discretion about the type of guilty verdict they can reach. Pennington and Hastie (1990) found that people on a jury who have a minority point of view often convince the majority to change their minds about the specific verdict to render. Thus, while a minority is unlikely to convince a majority to change its verdict from first-degree murder to not guilty, it might well convince the majority to change the verdict to second-degree murder.

Why Do People Obey the Law?

Ultimately, the success of the legal system depends on keeping people out of it. We should, of course, find ways to improve the accuracy of eyewitness testimony and help juries make better decisions. It is even more important, though, to find ways to prevent people from committing crimes in the first place. We thus close this chapter with a discussion of how to get people to obey the law.

DO SEVERE PENALTIES DETER CRIME?

Crime rates have been dropping. For example, 1999 Crime Statistics for Canada recorded a decrease in violent crime for the seventh consecutive year (Statistics Canada, 1999). Analysts have attributed the decrease in crime to the aging of the population (most violent crimes are committed by adolescents and young adults), Canada's healthy economy, and new approaches to preventing and solving crimes. Similar reasons have been given for the decline in violent crime that has been observed in the United States. However, the U.S. Attorney General believes that stiffer penalties for crimes are at least partly responsible ("Juveniles committing fewer violent crimes," 1997). It seems to make perfect sense that the harsher the penalty for a crime, the less likely people would be to commit it. As we have seen many times in this book, however, common sense is not always correct, and in the case of crime and prison sentences, the story is not as straightforward as it might seem.

Let's begin with a theory that says that stiff penalties do prevent crimes. **Deterrence theory** argues that people refrain from criminal activity because of the threat of legal punishment, as long as the punishment is perceived as severe, certain, and swift (Gibbs, 1985; Williams & Hawkins, 1986). Undoubtedly this theory is correct under some circumstances. As we mentioned in Chapter 12, Manitoba and Ontario have set up special family violence courts to ensure that penalties for domestic violence are relatively severe, certain, and swift. Although it is too soon to tell whether these courts are effective in reducing family violence, the early signs are encouraging. (Note that because these courts combine certain, swift punishment with rehabilitation, it is difficult to determine whether reductions in violence are due to punishment, rehabilitation, or both.) Consider another example: Imagine you are heading to Toronto for an important interview one day and

Deterrence theory

the theory that people refrain from criminal activity because of the threat of legal punishment, as long as the punishment is perceived as relatively severe, certain, and swift

become ensnarled in a traffic jam on Highway 401. At last the traffic clears, but unless you hurry, you will be late. "Maybe I'll speed up just a little," you think, as the speedometer creeps up to 125 kilometres per hour. Your decision to exceed the speed limit was probably based on a consideration of the fact that (a) you are unlikely to get caught, and (b) if you do, the penalty won't be too severe. However, suppose you knew that the 401 is always patrolled by the Ontario Provincial Police and that the penalty for speeding is a five-year prison sentence. Chances are, you would not dare to press too hard on the accelerator.

In this example, we have made a couple of important assumptions. First, we assumed that you know the penalties for speeding. Second, we assumed that you have control over your behaviour and that whether you speed is a rational decision that you make after reflecting on the consequences. For many crimes, however, these assumptions do not hold. Surveys have found that many people are ignorant of the penalties for different crimes; obviously, if they do not know what the penalties are, the penalties cannot act as a deterrent. (To see how well you know the penalties for various federal crimes, complete Try It! on page 607) Further, other types of crimes are not based on a rational decision process. Many murders, for example, are impulsive crimes of passion committed by people in highly emotional states, not by people who carefully weigh the pros and cons. In general, severe penalties will only work when people know what the penalties are, believe that they are relatively certain to be caught, and weigh the consequences before deciding whether to commit a crime.

To illustrate these points, let's consider two different kinds of crimes: drunk driving and murder. The decision about whether to drink and drive is one that most of us can control; when we go to a party or a bar and know that we will be driving home afterwards, we can decide how much we will drink. Given that this decision is a fairly rational one—at least, under most circumstances—we would expect that certain, severe penalties would act as a deterrent. Researchers in the United States have found some support for this conclusion by comparing states with different drunk driving laws. (Such research is more difficult to conduct in Canada, given that drunk driving falls under the Canadian Criminal Code. Thus, penalties should be the same from province to province.) These studies have found that increasing the severity of penalties for drunk driving is not related, by itself, to lower alcohol-related, motor vehicle fatalities. However, consistent with deterrence theory, increasing the certainty of being caught for drunk driving—by checking the blood alcohol level of all motorists stopped at sobriety checkpoints—is associated with lower alcohol-related accidents (Evans, Neville, & Graham, 1991; Stuster & Blowers, 1995; Voas, Holder, & Gruenewald, 1999). These results suggest that what acts as a deterrent is not the severity of the penalty itself, but an increase in the certainty of being caught.

Now consider a very different crime and a very different penalty—murder and capital punishment. A majority of Americans support the death penalty for murder, in part because they believe that it acts as a deterrent. (In Canada, capital punishment has been abolished. However, like their American counterparts, Canadians who favour capital punishment tend to believe that it has a deterrent effect; Haddock & Zanna, 1998; Vidmar, 1974.) There is no more severe penalty than death, of course, and if the death penalty prevents even a few murders, it might be worth it—or so the argument goes. To see if this argument is correct, a number of studies have compared the murder rates in American

Are You Aware of the Penalties for Crimes?

Deterrence theory holds that legal penalties will prevent crimes if perceived to be severe, certain, and swift. However, if people are unaware that a crime has a severe penalty, those penalties cannot act as a deterrent. Are you aware, for example, of the penalties specified in the Canadian Criminal Code for the following crimes? Take the following quiz to find out. The answers are printed upside down below.

What Are the Penalties for the Following Crimes?

1. First-degree murder (deliberate, planned murder). Note that first-degree murder charges also apply if someone dies as a result of a crime being committed (e.g., a drunk driver having an accident in which someone is killed).

2. Second-degree murder (deliberate, but unplanned, murder)

3. Manslaughter (causing the death of another person accidentally or due to carelessness)

4. Communication for prostitution

5. Break and enter

6. Drug trafficking

7. Impaired, or over .08, driving

8. False pretence (e.g., forging a cheque)

9. Assisting suicide

10. Sexual assault

ANSWERS

According to the Canadian Criminal Code, the following are the maximum and minimum penalties for the crimes listed above. (Note that if a minimum penalty is not specified, there is no minimum penalty for that crime.)

1. Maximum sentence: Life imprisonment; minimum sentence: 25 years imprisonment without parole

2. Maximum sentence: Life imprisonment; minimum sentence: 10 years imprisonment without parole

3. Maximum sentence: Life imprisonment

4. You may be surprised to learn that prostitution itself is not illegal in Canada, but communicating about it (either verbally or nonverbally) is illegal. The person offering sexual services or the person seeking sexual services can be charged. Maximum sentence: 6 months imprisonment and $2000 fine

5. If a break-and-enter charge applies to a home, the maximum sentence is life imprisonment. If a break-and-enter charge applies to a building, the maximum sentence is 10 years imprisonment.

6. Sentences vary depending on the drug being sold. For cocaine, the maximum sentence is life imprisonment. For steroids, the maximum sentence is three years imprisonment.

7. The maximum penalty for impaired driving is five years imprisonment. If it is a first offence, the minimum penalty is a $300 fine. If it is a second offence, the minimum penalty is 14 days imprisonment.

8. Maximum sentence: 10 years imprisonment

9. Maximum sentence: 14 years imprisonment

10. The maximum penalty for sexual assault is 10 years imprisonment; minimum penalty: 4 years imprisonment. If a firearm is used, the maximum penalty is 14 years imprisonment.

states that have the death penalty with those in states that do not; compared the murder rates in American states before and after they adopted the death penalty; and compared the murder rates in other countries before and after they adopted the death penalty. The results are clear: There is no evidence that the death penalty prevents murders (Archer & Gartner, 1984; Bedau, 1997; Ellsworth & Mauro, 1998; Sorenson et al., 1999).

Opponents of the death penalty point out, as we mentioned, that most murders are crimes of passion that are not preceded by a rational consideration of the consequences.

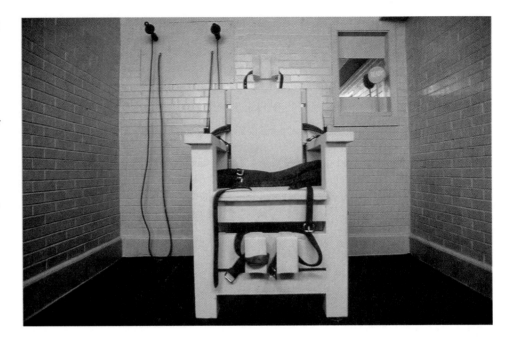

▶ An electric chair, used in some U.S. states to execute serious offenders. Many Canadians are in favour of capital punishment because they believe that it deters other murders. Not only have studies failed to support this claim, but some have found that executions are followed by an *increase* in the murder rate.

Because people are not considering the consequences of their actions, the death penalty does not act as a deterrent. Proponents of the death penalty say that severity of the crime is not enough—as argued by deterrence theory, severe penalties must be applied with certainty and speed. The last of these conditions is almost never met in the United States. The time between a conviction for murder and the execution of the murderer is often many years, because of the slowness of the judicial system and the many avenues of appeal open to prisoners on death row. Were the process speeded up, this argument goes, the death penalty *would* act as a deterrent.

Although this is an empirical question, there is reason to doubt that the death penalty would act as a deterrent, even if it were applied swiftly. We refer to a few studies that have found that executions are followed not by a decrease but by an *increase* in murders (Archer & Gartner, 1984; Bailey & Peterson, 1997; Bowers & Pierce, 1980). This might seem like a bizarre finding; why would the execution of a convicted murderer *increase* the likelihood that someone else would commit a murder? If you recall our discussion on aggression in Chapter 12, the finding makes sense. As we saw, observing someone else commit a violent act weakens people's inhibitions against aggression, leads to imitation of aggression, and numbs their sense of horror over violence. Could it be that observing the government put someone to death lowers other people's inhibitions, making them more likely to commit murders? Though the data are not conclusive, this argument makes eminent social psychological sense—and there is some evidence to support it (Bailey & Peterson, 1997).

PROCEDURAL JUSTICE: PEOPLE'S SENSE OF FAIRNESS

We have just seen that one reason people obey the law is their fear of being caught and punished. An even more important reason, however, is their moral values about what constitutes good behaviour. People will obey a law if they think that it is just, even if they are unlikely to be caught breaking it. For example, many people are honest on their tax returns because they think that cheating is wrong, not because they fear being caught for cheating.

Thus, if you were a lawmaker, you could try to prevent crime in two ways. You could increase the penalties for breaking the law and the probability that people will be caught, or you could try to convince people that the law is just and fair. As we have seen, the former approach is difficult and sometimes ineffective. If we want to prevent people from driving through red lights, we could increase the penalties for doing so and station a police officer at every intersection. However, it would be far simpler to convince people that it is wrong to run red lights, so they comply with the law even when no police officers are around.

What determines whether people think a law is just? One important factor is their perception of the fairness of legal proceedings. **Procedural justice** is defined as people's judgments about the fairness of the procedures used to determine outcomes, such as whether they are innocent or guilty of a crime (Bobocel et al., 1998; Kelley & Thibaut, 1978; Miller & Ratner, 1996; Skarlicki, Ellard, & Kelln, 1998; Thibaut & Walker, 1975; Tyler et al., 1997; Wenzel, 2000). People who feel that they have been treated fairly are more likely to comply with the law than are people who feel that they have been treated unfairly (Tyler, 1990). Consider, for example, what happens when the police are called because of a domestic assault. What determines whether the person accused of assault will repeat this crime in the future? It turns out that one factor is whether suspects feel that they were treated fairly by the police ("Misconceptions about why people obey laws," 1997). As another example, imagine that you receive a traffic ticket one day for failing to stop at a stop sign. You believe that the ticket is unfair because your view of the stop sign was obstructed by branches from a large tree that should have been trimmed by the city. You decide to go to court to protest the ticket. You take photographs of the tree, make careful diagrams of the intersection, and spend hours practising your testimony before your friends. Finally, your day in court arrives. Now, imagine that one of two things occurs. In the first scenario, your ticket is dismissed without a hearing because the officer who gave you the ticket could not appear in court that day. In the second scenario you get to present your case. The judge listens carefully, asks you a number of questions, and compliments you on your photographs and diagrams. After carefully considering all the facts, however, she rules against you, arguing that the stop sign, while obstructed, was still visible. Which outcome would you prefer—the first or the second?

It might seem that people would prefer the first scenario, because here they received a positive outcome—no fine, no points on their driving record, no increase in their insurance rates. Research by Tom Tyler (1990), however, suggests that people prefer the second scenario. Here, even though the outcome was negative, people's sense of procedural justice is high—they had their day in court and were treated with fairness and respect. It is often more important to people to maintain a sense of procedural justice than to receive positive outcomes.

In sum, social psychological research indicates that the Canadian legal system can go wrong in a number of ways. Juries rely heavily on eyewitness testimony, when in fact such testimony is often in error. Moreover, juries are groups of people who try to reach

Procedural justice
people's judgments about the fairness of the procedures used to determine outcomes, such as whether they are innocent or guilty of a crime

consensus by discussing, arguing, and bargaining—bringing into play the kinds of conformity pressures and group processes we discussed in Chapters 8 and 9 that can lead to faulty decisions. By illuminating these problems in their research, however, social psychologists can help initiate change in the legal system—change that will lead to greater fairness and equity and to a greater sense of procedural justice.

SUMMARY

Many social psychological principles predict how people will respond in the legal arena. Because of the limitations of memory, eyewitness testimony is often inaccurate. A number of factors bias the **acquisition**, **storage**, and **retrieval** of what people observe, sometimes leading to the false identification of criminals. For example, research on the **own-race bias** shows that people find it more difficult to recognize members of other races than members of their own race. Research on **reconstructive memory** indicates that errors in **source monitoring** can occur, whereby people become confused about where they saw or heard something. Jurors often place a great deal of faith in eyewitness testimony, even though jurors are not very good at determining when someone is lying. Because the **polygraph** is also an imperfect measure of lie detection, false testimony by eyewitnesses and others sometimes goes undetected. Researchers have tried to develop ways of improving eyewitness testimony, but neither hypnosis nor the **cognitive interview** has been very successful at improving eyewitness accuracy.

There is a great deal of controversy over another form of eyewitness testimony, namely the accuracy of people's memories about their own past traumatic experiences. Although **recovered memories**, the sudden recollection of such events, may be true in some instances, it is also the case that people "remember" events that have never occurred.

Other kinds of evidence are admitted in court as well, including expert testimony, physical evidence, and statistical evidence (information on the probability that the accused committed the crime). People generally do not find physical or statistical evidence convincing, preferring instead to rely on eyewitness testimony, despite its inaccuracies.

Juries are of particular interest to social psychologists because the way they reach verdicts is directly relevant to social psychological research on group processes and social interaction. Jurors are susceptible to the same kinds of biases and social pressures we documented in earlier chapters. They are sometimes biased by pretrial publicity, even when trying to put it out of their minds. During a trial, jurors attempt to make sense of the testimony and often decide on one story that explains all of the evidence. Juries are thus most swayed by lawyers who present the evidence in a way that tells a consistent story. During deliberations, jurors with minority views are often pressured into conforming to the view of the majority; thus, verdicts usually correspond to the initial feelings of the majority of jurors.

It is also important to examine people's perceptions of the legal system, because these perceptions have a lot to do with how likely people are to obey the law. For example, **deterrence theory** holds that people refrain from criminal activity if they view penalties as severe, certain, and swift. Deterrence theory may be correct about crimes that are the result of rational thought, but it is unlikely to apply to crimes of passion that are not rational, such as many murders. There is no evidence that the death penalty deters murder, and there is even some evidence that it leads to an increase in the murder rate. Finally, people are more likely to obey the law if their sense of **procedural justice** is high; that is, if they believe that the procedures used to determine their guilt or innocence are fair.

IF YOU ARE INTERESTED

Anderson, B. with Anderson, D. (1998). *Manufacturing guilt: Wrongful convictions in Canada*. Halifax: Fernwood Books. This book recounts the cases of six wrongful convictions in Canada, including those of Guy Paul Morin, David Milgaard, and Donald Marshall, and takes a critical look at the Canadian justice system.

Bedau, H. A. (Ed.). (1997). *The death penalty in America: Current controversies*. New York: Oxford University Press. An excellent collection of articles about capital punishment, considering such issues as whether the death penalty acts as a deterrent and whether it is applied equally to people of all races. The book includes chapters by both proponents and opponents of the death penalty.

Canadian Psychology (2001). Special section—Expert testimony, *42*, 2. This special issue of *Canadian Psychology* presents different perspectives on the use of expert testimony in legal proceedings, with contributions by psychologists, a lawyer, and a Supreme Court judge.

Colman, A. M. (1991). Crowd psychology in South African murder trials. *American Psychologist, 46*, 1071–1079. The author, a British social psychologist, describes his experiences as an expert witness in the murder trials of several black South Africans. In cases where psychological phenomena such as deindividuation, conformity, and obedience were accepted as extenuating factors by the court, the defendants did not receive the death penalty. Colman provides a deeply moving, thought-provoking analysis of the complex moral and ethical issues involved in providing expert social psychological testimony.

Lumet, Sydney (Director). (1957). *12 angry men* [Film]. A classic film in which a character played by Henry Fonda convinces all of his fellow jurors that a defendant accused of murder is innocent. As discussed in the chapter, the film is an interesting depiction of jury decision making, but does not reflect everyday life. In real life, a lone juror seldom succeeds in changing the minds of the other 11 jurors.

Roesch, R., Hart, S. D., & Ogloff, J. R. P. (Eds). (1999). *Psychology and the law: The state of the discipline*. New York: Kluwer Academic/Plenum. A collection of chapters about law and psychology by leading researchers in the field. Topics include eyewitness testimony, jury decision making, predicting violence in mentally disordered populations, and issues concerning children and the law. Several chapters were contributed by Canadian psychologists, including by the editors, who are all at Simon Fraser University.

Ross, D. F., Read, D. J., & Toiglia, M. P. (Eds.). (1994). *Adult eyewitness testimony: Current trends and developments*. New York: Cambridge University Press. A collection of chapters about eyewitness testimony from leading researchers in the field. They cover such topics as what factors influence the accuracy of eyewitness testimony, how to construct unbiased lineups, and how to tell whether an eyewitness is accurate.

Schuller, R. A. & Ogloff, J. R. P. (Eds.). (2001). *Introduction to psychology and law: Canadian perspectives*. Toronto: University of Toronto Press. A state-of-the-art synopsis of research on psychology and the law, particularly as it applies to the Canadian legal system. Regina Schuller is a professor of psychology at York University; James Ogloff is a professor and the director of the program in law and forensic psychology at Simon Fraser University. Individual chapters were written by prominent Canadian scholars of psychology and the law. A must-read for any student interested in psychology and law.

Spanos, N. P. (1996). *Multiple identities and false memories*. Washington, DC: American Psychological Association Press. This book, written by a Carleton University psychologist, illustrates the extreme ways in which memories for events can become distorted. Section II of the book, Creating False Memories, is especially relevant to this chapter.

Tyler, T. R. (1990). *Why people obey the law*. New Haven: Yale University Press. An interesting look at why people obey laws, with an emphasis on people's sense of procedural justice.

Williams, Stephen (Director). (1999). *Hardtime: The David Milgaard story* [Docudrama]. This acclaimed CTV film, winner of six 1999 Gemini awards, depicts the tragic, moving story of the wrongful conviction of David Milgaard, who spent 23 years in prison for a murder he did not commit. The film also documents the long, difficult fight to prove Milgaard's innocence.

WEBLINKS

www.acjnet.org

Access to Justice Network

This site contains very useful links to Canadian law and justice resource material, including legislation, organizations, databases, and discussions.

www.atkinson.yorku.ca/~sarmac/index.htm#Menu

The Society for Applied Research in Memory and Cognition (SARMAC)

This site contains abstracts of SARMAC conference papers and links to journals, including studies dealing with eyewitness testimony.

www.skeptic.com/02.3.hochman-fms.html

Recovered Memory Therapy and False Memory Syndrome

This site discusses recovered memory therapy and false memory syndrome.

www.brown.edu/Departments/Taubman_Center/Recovmem/Archive.html

The Recovered Memory Project

An in-depth look at the operation of recovered memory in legal proceedings and case studies. Includes links to other studies and criticisms of theories of recovered memory, including ideas about "false memory syndrome."

GLOSSARY

Note: Chapter numbers are specified below in brackets.

Accessibility the extent to which schemas and concepts are at the forefront of people's minds and are therefore likely to be used when making judgments about the social world [3]

Acquisition the process by which people notice and pay attention to information in the environment; people cannot perceive everything that is happening around them, so they acquire only a subset of the information available in the environment [SPA3]

Actor/observer difference the tendency to see other people's behaviour as dispositionally caused, while focusing more on the role of situational factors when explaining one's own behaviour [4]

Affect blend a facial expression in which one part of the face is registering one emotion and another part of the face is registering a different emotion [4]

Affectively based attitude an attitude based primarily on people's feelings and values pertaining to the attitude object [7]

Aggression intentional behaviour aimed at causing either physical or psychological pain [12]

Aggressive stimulus an object that is associated with aggressive responses (e.g., a gun) and whose mere presence can increase the probability of aggression [12]

Altruism the desire to help another person even if involves a cost to the helper [11]

Altruistic personality aspects of a person's makeup that cause him or her to help others in a wide variety of situations [11]

Amygdala an area in the core of the brain that is associated with aggressive behaviour [12]

Anchoring and adjustment heuristic a mental shortcut that involves using a number or value as a starting point, and then adjusting one's answer away from this anchor; people often do not adjust their answer sufficiently [3]

Anxious/ambivalent attachment style an attachment style characterized by a concern that others will not reciprocate one's desire for intimacy, resulting in higher-than-average levels of anxiety [10]

Applied research studies designed specifically to solve a particular social problem; building a theory of behaviour is usually secondary to solving the specific problem [2]

Archival analysis a form of the observational method, whereby the researcher examines the accumulated documents, or archives, of a culture (e.g., diaries, novels, magazines, and newspapers) [2]

Attachment styles the expectations people develop about relationships with others, based on the relationship they had with their primary caregiver when they were infants [10]

Attitude an evaluation of a person, object, or idea [7]

Attitude accessibility the strength of the association between an object and a person's evaluation of that object; accessibility is measured by the speed with which people can report how they feel about an issue or object [7]

Attitude inoculation the process of making people immune to attempts to change their attitudes by initially exposing them to small doses of the arguments against their position [7]

Attribution theory a description of the way in which people explain the causes of their own and other people's behaviour [4]

Autobiographical memories memories about one's own past thoughts, feelings, and behaviours [5]

Automatic processing thinking that is non-conscious, unintentional, involuntary, and effortless [3]

Availability how easy or difficult it is for someone to bring a schema or concept to mind [3]

Availability heuristic a mental rule of thumb whereby people base a judgment on the ease with which they can bring something to mind [3]

Avoidant attachment style an attachment style characterized by a suppression of attachment needs, because attempts to be intimate have been rebuffed; people with this style find it difficult to develop intimate relationships [10]

Base rate information information about the frequency of members of different categories in the population [3]

Basic research studies that are designed to find the best answer as to why people behave the way they do and that are conducted purely for reasons of intellectual curiosity [2]

Behaviourally based attitude an attitude based primarily on observations of how one behaves toward an attitude object [7]

Behaviourism a school of psychology maintaining that to understand human behaviour, one need only consider the reinforcing properties of the environment—that is, how positive and negative events in the environment are associated with specific behaviours [1]

Belief in a just world a form of defensive attribution wherein people assume that bad things happen to bad people and that good things happen to good people [4]

Biased sampling making generalizations from samples of information that are known to be biased [3]

Bookkeeping model information inconsistent with a stereotype that leads to a modification of the stereotype [13]

Buffering hypothesis the hypothesis that we need social support only when we are under stress, because it protects us against the detrimental effects of this stress [SPA1]

Bystander effect the finding that the greater the number of bystanders who witness an emergency, the less likely it is that any one of them will help [11]

Catharsis the notion that "blowing off steam"—by performing an aggressive act, watching others engage in aggressive behaviour, or engaging in a fantasy of aggression—relieves built-up aggressive energies and hence reduces the likelihood of further aggressive behaviour [12]

Causal theories theories about the causes of one's own feelings and behaviours; often we learn such theories from our culture (e.g., "absence makes the heart grow fonder") [5]

Classical conditioning the case whereby a stimulus that elicits an emotional response is repeatedly experienced along with a neutral stimulus that does not, until the neutral stimulus takes on the emotional properties of the first stimulus [7]

Cognitive dissonance a feeling of discomfort caused by the realization that one's behaviour is inconsistent with one's attitudes or that one holds two conflicting attitudes [6]

Cognitive interview a technique whereby a trained interviewer tries to improve eyewitnesses' memories by focusing their attention on the details and context of the event [SPA3]

Cognitively based attitude an attitude based primarily on a person's beliefs about the properties of an attitude object [7]

Commitment calibration hypothesis the idea that the outcome of adversity on a relationship depends on the level of commitment. If the level of adversity is lower than the level of commitment, the relationship is not challenged. If the level of adversity is higher than the level of commitment, the relationship ends. However, if the level of adversity is equal to the level of commitment, the relationship will be strengthened. [10]

Communal relationships relationships in which people's primary concern is being responsive to the other person's needs [10]

Companionate love the feelings of intimacy and affection we feel for another person about whom we care deeply [10]

Comparison level people's expectations about the level of rewards and costs they deserve in a relationship [10]

Comparison level for alternatives people's expectations about the level of rewards and punishments they would receive in an alternative relationship [10]

Complementarity attraction to people who are opposite to us [10]

Compliance a change in behaviour due to a direct request from another person [8]

Conformity a change in behaviour due to the real or imagined influence of other people [8]

Consensus information information about the extent to which other people behave the same way as the actor does toward the same stimulus [4]

Consistency information information about the extent to which the behaviour between one actor and one stimulus is the same across time and circumstances [4]

Construal the way in which people perceive, comprehend, and interpret the social world [1]

Contagion the rapid transmission of emotions or behaviour through a crowd [8]

Contingency theory of leadership the theory that leadership effectiveness depends both on how task-oriented or relationship-oriented the leader is and on the amount of control and influence the leader has over the group [9]

Controlled processing thinking that is conscious, intentional, voluntary, and effortful [3]

Conversion model information inconsistent with a stereotype that leads to a radical change in the stereotype [13]

Coping styles the ways in which people react to stressful events [SPA1]

Correlation coefficient a statistical technique that assesses how well you can predict one variable based on another; for example, how well you can predict people's weight from their height [2]

Correlational method the technique whereby researchers systematically measure two or more variables, and assess the relation between them (i.e., how much one can be predicted from the other) [2]

Counter-attitudinal advocacy the process that occurs when a person states an opinion or attitude that runs counter to his or her private belief or attitude [6]

Counterfactual thinking mentally changing some aspect of the past as a way of imagining what might have been [3]

Covariation model a theory stating that in order to form an attribution about what caused a person's behaviour, we systematically note the pattern between the presence (or absence) of possible causal factors and whether or not the behaviour occurs [4]

Cover story a description of the purpose of a study, given to participants, that is different from its true purpose; cover stories are used to maintain psychological realism [2]

Crowding the subjective feeling of unpleasantness due to the presence of other people [SPA2]

Debriefing the process of explaining to the participants, at the end of the experiment, the purpose of the study and exactly what transpired [2]

Deception the procedure whereby participants are misled about the true purpose of a study or the events that will actually transpire [2]

Decode to interpret the meaning of the nonverbal behaviour other people express, such as deciding that a pat on the back was an expression of condescension and not kindness [4]

Defensive attributions explanations for behaviour that avoid feelings of vulnerability and mortality [4]

Deindividuation the loosening of normal constraints on behaviour when people are in a group, leading to an increase in impulsive and deviant acts [9]

Density the number of people who occupy a given space [SPA2]

Dependent variable the variable a researcher measures to see if it is influenced by the independent variable; the researcher hypothesizes that the dependent variable will depend on the level of the independent variable [2]

Descriptive norms people's perceptions of how other people actually behave in a given situation, regardless of whether the behaviour is approved or disapproved of by others [SPA2]

Deterrence theory the theory that people refrain from criminal activity because of the threat of legal punishment, as long as the punishment is perceived as relatively severe, certain, and swift [SPA3]

Diffusion of responsibility each bystander's sense of responsibility to help decreases as the number of witnesses increases [11]

Discrimination unjustified negative or harmful action toward a member of a group, simply because of his or her membership in that group [13]

Dismissive avoidant style a type of avoidant attachment in which the person is self-sufficient and claims not to need close relationships [10]

Display rules culturally determined rules about which nonverbal behaviours are appropriate to display [4]

Distinctiveness information information about the extent to which one particular actor behaves in the same way to different stimuli [4]

Door-in-the-face technique a technique to get people to comply with a request, whereby people are presented first with a large request, which they are expected to refuse, and then with a smaller, more reasonable request, to which it is hoped they will acquiesce [8]

Downward social comparison the process whereby we compare ourselves to people who are worse than we are on a particular trait or ability [5]

Elaboration likelihood model the theory that there are two ways in which persuasive communications can cause attitude change; the *central route* occurs when people are motivated and have the ability to pay attention to the arguments in the communication, and the *peripheral route* occurs when people do not pay attention to the arguments but are instead swayed by surface characteristics (e.g., who gave the speech) [7]

Emblems nonverbal gestures that have well-understood definitions within a given culture; they usually have direct verbal translations, such as the "okay" sign [4]

Empathy the ability to experience events and emotions (e.g., joy and sadness) the way another person experiences them [11, 12]

Empathy-altruism hypothesis the idea that when we feel empathy for a person, we will attempt to help him or her purely for altruistic reasons, regardless of what we have to gain [11]

Encode to express or emit nonverbal behaviour, such as smiling or patting someone on the back [4]

Equity theory the theory holding that people are happiest with relationships in which the rewards and costs that a person experiences and the contributions that he or she makes to the relationship are roughly equal to the rewards, costs, and contributions of the other person [10]

Eros the instinct toward life, posited by Freud [12]

Evolutionary approach an approach derived from evolutionary biology that states that men and women are attracted to different characteristics in each other (men are attracted by women's appearance; women are attracted by men's resources) because this maximizes their reproductive success [10]

Evolutionary psychology the attempt to explain social behaviour in terms of genetic factors that evolved over time according to the principles of natural selection [1]

Exchange relationships relationships governed by the need for equity (i.e., for a comparable ratio of rewards and costs) [10]

Experimental method the method in which the researcher randomly assigns participants to different conditions and ensures that these conditions are identical except for the independent variable (the one thought to have a causal effect on people's responses) [2]

Extended contact hypothesis the mere knowledge that a member of one's own group has a close relationship with a member of another group can reduce prejudice toward that group [13]

External attribution the inference that a person is behaving a certain way because of something about the situation he or she is in; the assumption is that most people would respond the same way in that situation [4]

External justification a person's reason or explanation for dissonant behaviour that resides outside the individual (e.g., in order to receive a large reward or avoid a severe punishment) [6]

External validity the extent to which the results of a study can be generalized to other situations and to other people [2]

Extrinsic motivation the desire to engage in an activity because of external rewards or pressures, not because we enjoy the task or find it interesting [5]

Fear-arousing communication a persuasive message that attempts to change people's attitudes by arousing their fears [7]

Fearful avoidant style a type of avoidant attachment in which close relationships are avoided due to mistrust and fears of being hurt [10]

Field experiments experiments conducted in natural settings, rather than in the laboratory [2]

Foot-in-the-door technique a technique to get people to comply with a request, whereby people are presented first with a small request, to which they are expected to acquiesce, followed by a larger request, to which it is hoped they will also acquiesce [8]

Frustration-aggression theory the theory that frustration—the perception that you are being prevented from obtaining a goal—will increase the probability of an aggressive response [12]

Fundamental attribution error the tendency to overestimate the extent to which people's behaviour is due to internal, dispositional factors and to underestimate the role of situational factors [1, 4]

Gestalt psychology a school of psychology stressing the importance of studying the subjective way in which an object appears in people's minds, rather than the objective, physical attributes of the object [1]

Global attribution the belief that the cause of an event is due to factors that apply in a large number of situations, as opposed to the belief that the cause is specific and applies in only a limited number of situations [SPA1]

Great person theory the theory that certain key personality traits make a person a good leader, regardless of the nature of the situation facing the leader [9]

Group cohesiveness qualities of a group that bind members together and promote liking between members [9]

Group polarization the tendency for groups to make decisions that are more extreme than the initial inclinations of their members [9]

Groups a collection of two or more people who interact with each other and are interdependent, in the sense that their needs and goals cause them to rely on each other [9]

Groupthink a kind of thinking in which maintaining group cohesiveness and solidarity is more important than considering the facts in a realistic manner [9]

Hardiness a personality trait defined as a combination of self-esteem and a sense of control [SPA1]

Heuristic-systematic model of persuasion the theory that there are two ways in which persuasive communications can cause attitude change; people either process the merits of the arguments, known as *systematic processing*, or use mental shortcuts (heuristics), such as "Experts are always right," known as *heuristic processing* [7]

Hostile aggression an act of aggression stemming from feelings of anger and aimed at inflicting pain [12]

Idiosyncrasy credits the credits a person earns, over time, by conforming to group norms; if enough idiosyncrasy credits are earned, the person can, on occasion, behave deviantly without retribution from the group [8]

Implicit personality theory a type of schema people use to group various kinds of personality traits together; for example, many people believe that if someone is kind, he or she is generous as well [4]

Impression management our conscious or unconscious orchestration of a carefully designed presentation of self so as to create a certain impression that fits our goals or needs in a social interaction [5]

Independent variable the variable a researcher changes or varies to see if it has an effect on some other variable [2]

Independent view of the self defining oneself in terms of one's own internal thoughts, feelings, and actions, and not in terms of the thoughts, feelings, and actions of other people [5]

Individual differences the aspects of people's personalities that make them different from other people [1]

Informational social influence conforming because we believe that others' interpretation of an ambiguous situation is more correct than ours and will help us choose an appropriate course of action [8]

Informed consent the procedure whereby researchers explain the nature of the experiment to participants before it begins, and obtain their consent to participate [2]

In-group the group with which an individual identifies and of which he or she feels a member [11]

Injunctive norms people's perceptions of what behaviour is approved or disapproved of by others [SPA2]

Instrumental aggression aggression as a means to some goal other than causing pain [12]

Insufficient punishment the dissonance aroused when individuals lack sufficient external justification for having resisted a desired activity or object, usually resulting in individuals devaluing the forbidden activity or object [6]

Integrative solution a solution to a conflict whereby the parties make trade-offs on issues according to their different interests; each side concedes the most on issues that are unimportant to it but that are important to the other side [9]

Interdependent view of the self defining oneself in terms of one's relationships to other people; recognizing that one's behaviour is often determined by the thoughts, feelings, and actions of others [5]

Interjudge reliability the level of agreement between two or more people who independently observe and code a set of data; by showing that two or more judges independently come up with the same observations, researchers ensure that the observations are not the subjective, impressions of one individual [2]

Internal attribution the inference that a person is behaving in a certain way because of something about him or her,

such as his or her attitude, character, or personality [4, SPA1]

Internal justification the reduction of dissonance by changing something about oneself (e.g., one's attitude or behaviour) [6]

Internal validity ensuring that nothing other than the independent variable can affect the dependent variable; this is accomplished by controlling all extraneous variables and by randomly assigning people to different experimental conditions [2]

Intrinsic motivation the desire to engage in an activity because we enjoy it or find it interesting, not because of external rewards or pressures [5]

Introspection the process whereby people look inward and examine their own thoughts, feelings, and motives [5]

Investment model the theory holding that people's commitment to a relationship depends on their satisfaction with the relationship in terms of rewards, costs, and comparison level; their comparison level for alternatives; and how much they have invested in the relationship that would be lost by leaving it [10]

Jigsaw classroom a classroom setting designed to reduce prejudice between children by placing them in small, desegregated groups and making each child dependent on the other children in the group to learn the course material and do well in the class [13]

Judgmental heuristics mental shortcuts people use to make judgments quickly and efficiently [3]

Justification of effort the tendency for individuals to increase their liking for something they have worked hard to attain [6]

Kin selection the idea that behaviour that helps a genetic relative is favoured by natural selection [11]

Learned helplessness the state of pessimism that results from explaining a negative event as due to stable, internal, and global factors [SPA1]

Looking-glass self the idea that we see ourselves through the eyes of other people and incorporate their views into our self-concept [5]

Love styles the basic theories people have about love that guide their behaviour in relationships [10]

Lowballing an unscrupulous strategy whereby a salesperson induces a customer to agree to purchase a product at a very low cost, then subsequently raises the price; frequently, the customer will still make the purchase at the inflated price [8]

Mere exposure effect the finding that the more exposure we have to a stimulus, the more apt we are to like it [10]

Meta analysis a statistical technique that averages the results of two or more studies to see if the effect of an independent variable is reliable [2]

Meta-stereotype a person's beliefs regarding the stereotype that out-group members hold about their own group [13]

Minority influence the case where a minority of group members influences the behaviour or beliefs of the majority [8]

Misattribution of arousal the process whereby people make mistaken inferences about what is causing them to feel the way they do [5]

Modern prejudice outwardly acting unprejudiced while inwardly maintaining prejudiced attitudes [13]

Mundane realism the extent to which an experiment is similar to real-life situations [2]

Mutual interdependence a situation in which two or more groups need each other and must depend on each other in order to accomplish a goal that is important to each group [13]

Need for cognition a personality variable reflecting the extent to which people engage in and enjoy effortful cognitive activities [7]

Negative-state relief hypothesis the idea that people help in order to alleviate their own sadness and distress [11]

Negotiation a form of communication between opposing sides in a conflict, in which offers and counteroffers are made and a solution occurs only when both parties agree [9]

Nonverbal communication the way in which people communicate, intentionally or unintentionally, without words; nonverbal cues include facial expressions, tones of voice, gestures, body position and movement, the use of touch, and eye gaze [4]

Norm of reciprocity the expectation that helping others will increase the likelihood that they will help us in the future [11]

Normative conformity the tendency to go along with the group in order to fulfil their expectations and gain acceptance [13]

Normative social influence the influence of other people that leads us to conform in order to be liked and accepted by them; this type of conformity results in public compliance with the group's beliefs and behaviours, but not necessarily with private acceptance of the group's beliefs and behaviours [8]

Obedience conformity in response to the commands of an authority figure [8]

Observational method the technique whereby a researcher observes people and systematically records measurements of their behaviour [2]

Operant conditioning the case whereby behaviours that people freely choose to perform increase or decrease in frequency, depending on whether they are followed by positive reinforcement or punishment [7]

Operational definition the precise specification of how variables are measured or manipulated [2]

Out-group a group with which the individual does not identify [11]

Out-group homogeneity the perception that those in the out-group are more similar (homogeneous) to each other than they really are, as well as more similar than the members of the in-group [13]

Overconfidence barrier the barrier that results when people have too much confidence in the accuracy of their judgments; people's judgments are usually not as correct as they thing they are [3]

Overjustification effect the case whereby people view their behaviour as caused by compelling extrinsic reasons, making them underestimate the extent to which their behaviour was caused by intrinsic reasons [5]

Own-race bias the finding that people are better at recognizing faces of their own race than those of other races [SPA3]

Participant observation a form of the observational method whereby the observer interacts with the people being observed, but tries not to alter the situation in any way [2]

Passionate love the feelings of intense longing, accompanied by physiological arousal, we feel for another person; when our love is reciprocated, we feel great fulfilment and ecstasy, but when it is not, we feel sadness and despair [10]

Perceived control the belief that we can influence our environment in ways that determine whether we experience positive or negative outcomes [SPA1]

Perceptual salience information that is the focus of people's attention; people tend to overestimate the causal role of perceptually salient information [4]

Performance-contingent rewards rewards that are based on how well we perform a task [5]

Perseverance effect the finding that people's beliefs about themselves and the social world persist even after the evidence supporting these beliefs is discredited [3]

Persuasive communication communication (e.g., a speech or television ad) advocating a particular side of an issue [7]

Pluralistic ignorance the phenomenon whereby bystanders assume that nothing is wrong in an emergency because no one else looks concerned [11]

Polygraph a machine that measures people's physiological responses (e.g., heart rate); polygraph operators attempt to tell if someone is lying by observing how that person responds physiologically while answering questions [SPA3]

Positive illusions idealization of our romantic relationships and partners in order to maintain the relationship [10]

Postdecision dissonance dissonance that is inevitably aroused after a person makes a decision; such dissonance is typically reduced by enhancing the attractiveness of the chosen alternative and devaluing the rejected alternatives [6]

Prejudice a hostile or negative attitude toward a distinguishable group of people, based solely on their membership in that group [13]

Priming the process by which recent experiences increase a schema's or trait's accessibility [3]

Private acceptance conforming to other people's behaviour out of a genuine belief that what they are doing or saying is right [8]

Probability level (*p*-value) a number, calculated with statistical techniques, that tells researchers how likely it is that the results of their experiment occurred by chance and not because of the independent variable(s); the convention in science, including social psychology, is to consider results significant if the probability level is less than 5 in 100 that the results might be due to chance factors and not the independent variables studied [2]

Procedural justice people's judgments about the fairness of the procedures used to determine outcomes, such as whether they are innocent or guilty of a crime [SPA3]

Process loss any aspect of group interaction that inhibits good problem solving [9]

Propinquity effect the finding that the more we see and interact with people, the more likely they are to become our friends [10]

Prosocial behaviour any act performed with the goal of benefiting another person [11]

Psychological realism the extent to which the psychological processes triggered in an experiment are similar to psychological processes that occur in everyday life; psychological realism can be high in an experiment, even if mundane realism is low [2]

Public compliance conforming to other people's behaviour publicly, without necessarily believing in what they are doing or saying [8]

Random assignment to condition the process whereby all participants have an equal chance of taking part in any condition of an experiment; through random assignment, researchers can be relatively certain that differences in the participants' personalities or backgrounds are distributed evenly across conditions [2]

Random selection a way of ensuring that a sample of people is representative of a population, by giving everyone in the population an equal chance of being selected for the sample [2]

Rationalization trap the potential for dissonance reduction to produce a succession of self-justifications that ultimately result in a chain of stupid or immoral actions [6]

Reactance theory the idea that when people feel their freedom to perform a certain behaviour is threatened, an unpleasant state of reactance is aroused; people can reduce this reactance by performing the threatened behaviour [7]

Realistic conflict theory the theory that limited resources lead to conflict between groups and result in increased prejudice and discrimination [13]

Reciprocal liking when you like someone and that person also likes you [10]

Reciprocity norm a social norm stating that receiving anything positive from another person requires you to reciprocate (or behave similarly) in response [8]

Reconstructive memory the process whereby memories for an event become distorted by information encountered after the event has occurred [SPA3]

Recovered memories recollections of an event, such as sexual abuse, that had been forgotten or repressed [SPA3]

Relative deprivation the perception that you (or your group) have less than you deserve, less than you have been led to expect, or less than people similar to you have [12]

Relationship-oriented leader a leader who is concerned primarily with the feelings of and relationships between the workers [9]

Replication repeating a study, often with different subject populations or in different settings [2]

Representativeness heuristic a mental shortcut whereby people classify something according to how similar it is to a typical case [3]

Retrieval the process by which people recall information stored in their memories [SPA3]

Reward/cost ratio in social exchange theory, the notion that there is a balance between the rewards that come from a relationship and the personal cost of maintaining the relationship. If the ratio is not favourable, the result is dissatisfaction with the relationship. [10]

Schemas mental structures people use to organize their knowledge about the social world around themes or subjects; schemas affect what information we notice, think about, and remember [3]

Secure attachment style an attachment style characterized by trust, a lack of concern with being abandoned, and the view that one is worthy and well liked [10]

Self-affirmation theory a theory suggesting that people will reduce the impact of a dissonance-arousing threat to their self-concept by focusing on and affirming their competence on some dimension unrelated to the threat [6]

Self-awareness the act of thinking about ourselves [5]

Self-awareness theory the idea that when people focus their attention on themselves, they evaluate and compare their behaviour to their internal standards and values [5]

Self-completion theory the theory that when people experience a threat to a valued aspect of their self-concept, or identity, they become highly motivated to seek social recognition of that identity [6]

Self-concept the contents of the self; that is, our knowledge about who we are [5]

Self-discrepancy theory the theory that we become distressed when our sense of who we truly are—our actual self—is discrepant from our personal standards or desired self-conceptions [6]

Self-efficacy the belief in one's ability to carry out specific actions that produce desired outcomes [SPA1]

Self-enhancement a tendency to hold unrealistically positive views about ourselves [6]

Self-esteem people's evaluations of their own self-worth—that is, the extent to which they view themselves as good, competent, and decent [1]

Self-evaluation maintenance theory the theory that one's self-concept can be threatened by another individual's behaviour and that the level of threat is determined by both the closeness of the other individual and the personal relevance of the behaviour [6]

Self-fulfilling prophecy the case whereby people (a) have an expectation about what another person is like, which (b) influences how they act toward that person, which (c) causes that person to behave consistently with people's original expectations [3, 13]

Self-justification the tendency to justify one's actions in order to maintain one's self-esteem [6]

Self-perception theory the theory that when our attitudes and feelings are uncertain or ambiguous, we infer these states by observing our behaviour and the situation in which it occurs [5]

Self-presentation the attempt to present who we are, or who we want people to believe we are, through our words, nonverbal behaviour, and actions [5]

Self-schemas organized knowledge structures about ourselves, based on our past experiences, that help us understand, explain, and predict our own behaviour [5]

Self-serving attributions explanations for one's successes that credit internal, dispositional factors and explanations for one's failures that blame external, situational factors [4]

Self-verification theory a theory suggesting that people have a need to seek confirmation of their self-concept, whether the self-concept is positive or negative; in some circumstances, this tendency can conflict with the desire to uphold a favourable view of oneself [6]

Sensory overload the situation in which we receive more stimulation from the environment than we can pay attention to or process [SPA2]

Similarity attraction to people who are like us [10]

Social cognition how people think about themselves and the social world; more specifically, how people select, interpret, remember, and use social information [1, 3]

Social comparison theory the idea that we learn about our own abilities and attitudes by comparing ourselves to other people [5]

Social dilemma a conflict in which the most beneficial action for an individual, if chosen by most people, will have harmful effects on everyone. [9]

Social exchange theory the theory holding that how people feel about a relationship depends on their perceptions of the rewards and costs of the relationship, the kind of relationship they deserve, and their chances of having a better relationship with someone else [10]

Social facilitation the tendency for people to do better on simple tasks and worse on complex tasks, when they are in the presence of others and their individual performance can be evaluated [9]

Social impact theory the theory that conforming to social influence depends on the strength, immediacy, and number of other people in a group [8]

Social learning theory the theory that we learn social behaviour (e.g., aggression) by observing others and imitating them [12]

Social loafing the tendency for people to do worse on simple tasks but better on complex tasks, when they are in the presence of others and their individual performance cannot be evaluated [9]

Social norms the implicit or explicit rules a group has for the acceptable behaviours, values, and beliefs of its members [8]

Social perception the study of how we form impressions of and make inferences about other people [4]

Social psychology the scientific study of the way in which people's thoughts, feelings, and behaviours are influenced by the real or imagined presence of other people [1]

Social roles shared expectations in a group about how particular people are supposed to behave [9]

Social support the perception that others are responsive and receptive to one's needs [SPA1]

Source monitoring the process whereby people try to identify the source of their memories [SPA3]

Stable attribution the belief that the cause of an event is due to factors that will not change over time, as opposed to unstable factors that will change over time [SPA1]

Stereotype a generalization about a group of people in which identical characteristics are assigned to virtually all members of the group, regardless of actual variation among the members [13]

Stereotype threat the apprehension experienced by members of a minority group that they might behave in a manner that confirms an existing cultural stereotype [13]

Storage the process by which people store in memory information they have acquired from the environment [SPA3]

Stress the negative feelings and beliefs that occur whenever people feel unable to cope with demands from their environment [SPA1]

Subliminal messages words or pictures that are not consciously perceived but that supposedly influence people's judgments, attitudes, and behaviours [7]

Subjective norms people's beliefs about how those they care about will view the behaviour in question [7]

Subtyping model information inconsistent with a stereotype that leads to the creation of a new sub-stereotype to accommodate the information without changing the initial stereotype [13]

Surveys research in which a representative sample of people are asked questions about their attitudes or behaviour [2]

Task-contingent rewards rewards that are given for performing a task, regardless of how well we do that task [5]

Task-oriented leader a leader who is concerned more with getting the job done than with the feelings of and relationships between the workers [9]

Testosterone a hormone associated with aggression [12]

Thanatos according to Freud, an instinctual drive toward death, leading to aggressive actions [12]

Theory an organized set of principles that can be used to explain observed phenomena [2]

Theory of planned behaviour a theory that the best predictors of a person's planned, deliberate behaviours are the person's attitudes toward specific behaviours, subjective norms, and perceived behavioural control [7]

Thought suppression the attempt to avoid thinking about something we would just as soon forget [3]

Tit-for-tat strategy a means of encouraging cooperation by at first acting cooperatively but then always responding the way your opponent did (cooperatively or competitively) on the previous trial [9]

Transactive memory the combined memory of two people that is more efficient than the memory of either individual [9]

Triangular theory of love the idea that different kinds of love comprise varying degrees of three components: intimacy, passion, and commitment [10]

Two-factor theory of emotion the idea that emotional experience is the result of a two-step self-perception process in which people first experience physiological arousal and then seek an appropriate explanation for it [5]

Type A versus Type B personality a personality typology based on how people typically confront challenges in their lives; the Type A person is typically competitive, impatient, hostile, and control-oriented, whereas the Type B person is typically patient, relaxed, and noncompetitive [SPA1]

Ultimate attribution error our tendency to make internal, dispositional attributions for the negative behaviours of out-group members and external, situational attributions for their positive behaviours [13]

Unrealistic optimism a form of defensive attribution wherein people think that good things are more likely to happen to them than to their peers and that bad things are less likely to happen to them than to their peers [4]

Upward social comparison the process whereby we compare ourselves to people who are better than we are on a particular trait or ability [5]

Urban-overload hypothesis the theory that people living in cities are constantly being bombarded with stimulation and that they keep to themselves in order to avoid being over-loaded by it [11]

Yale Attitude Change Approach the study of the conditions under which people are most likely to change their attitudes in response to persuasive messages; researchers in this tradition focus on "who said what to whom"—that is, on the source of the communication, the nature of the communication, and the nature of the audience [7]

REFERENCES

Abelson, R. P., Kinder, D. R., Peters, M. D., & Fiske, S. T. (1982). Affective and semantic components in political person perception. *Journal of Personality and Social Psychology, 42,* 619–630.

Aboud, F. E., & Doyle, A.B. (1996). Does talk of race foster prejudice or tolerance in children? *Canadian Journal of Behavioural Science, 28,* 161–170.

Abrams, D., Wetherell, M., Cochrane, S., Hogg, M.A., & Turner, J. C. (1990). Knowing what to think by knowing who you are: Self-categorization and the nature of norm formation, conformity, and group polarization. *British Journal of Social Psychology, 29,* 97–119.

Abramson, L. Y., Seligman, M. E. P., & Teasdale, J. D. (1978). Learned helplessness in humans: Critique and reformulation. *Journal of Abnormal Psychology, 87,* 49–74.

Adlaf, E. M., Gliksman, L., Demers, A., & Newton-Taylor, B. (2001). The prevalence of elevated psychological distress among Canadian undergraduates: Findings from the 1998 Canadian Campus Survey. *Journal of American College Health, 50,* 67–72.

Adlag, R. J., & Fuller, S. R. (1993). Beyond fiasco: A reappraisal of the groupthink phenomenon and a new model of group decision processes. *Psychological Bulletin, 113,* 533–552.

Adler, J. (1997, Spring/Summer). It's a wise father who knows.... *Newsweek,* p. 73.

Adler, S. J. (1994). *The jury: Trial and error in the American courtroom.* New York: Times Books.

Aiello, J. R., Thompson, D. E., & Brodzinsky, D. M. (1983). How funny is crowding anyway? Effects of room size, group size, and the introduction of humor. *Basic and Applied Social Psychology, 4,* 193–207.

Ainsworth, M. D. S., Blehar, M. C., Waters, E., & Wall, S. (1978). *Patterns of attachment: A psychological study of the strange situation.* Hillsdale, NJ: Erlbaum.

Ajzen, I. (1985). From intentions to actions: A theory of planned behavior. In J. Kuhl & J. Beckmann (Eds.), *Action-control: From cognition to behavior* (pp. 11–39). Heidelberg, Germany: Springer.

Ajzen, I. (1996). The directive influence of attitudes on behavior. In P. M. Gollwitzer & J. A. Bargh (Eds.), *The psychology of action: Linking cognition and motivation to behavior* (pp. 385–403). New York: Guilford.

Ajzen, I., & Fishbein, M. (1980). *Understanding attitudes and predicting social behavior.* Englewood Cliffs, NJ: Prentice Hall.

Ajzen, I., & Sexton, J. (1999). Depth of processing, belief congruence, and attitude-behavior correspondence. In S. Chaiken & Y. Trope (Eds.), *Dual-process theories in social psychology* (pp. 117–138). New York: Guilford Press.

Akehurst, L., Kohnken, G., Vrij, A., & Bull, R. (1996). Lay persons' and police officers' beliefs regarding deceptive behaviour. *Applied Cognitive Psychology, 10,* 461–471.

Akert, R. M. (1993). *The effect of autobiographical memories on the current definition of self.* Unpublished manuscript, Wellesley College.

Akert, R. M. (1998). *Terminating romantic relationships: The role of personal responsibility and gender.* Unpublished manuscript, Wellesley College.

Albright, L., & Forziati, C. (1995). Cross-situational consistency and perceptual accuracy in leadership. *Personality and Social Psychology Bulletin, 21,* 1269–1276.

Allen, M. (1991). Meta-analysis comparing the persuasiveness of one-sided and two-sided messages. *Western Journal of Speech Communication, 55,* 390–404.

Allen, M., Hale, J., Mongeau, P., Berkowits-Stafford, S., Stafford, S., Shanahan, W., Agee, P., Dillon, K., Jackson, R., & Ray, C. (1990). Testing a model of message sidedness: Three replications. *Communication Monographs, 57,* 274–291.

Allen, V. L., & Levine, J. M. (1969). Consensus and conformity. *Journal of Personality and Social Psychology, 5,* 389–399.

Allison, K. R., Dwyer, J. M., & Makin, S. (1999). Self-efficacy and participation in vigorous physical activity by high school students. *Health Education and Behavior, 26,* 12–24.

Allison, P. D. (1992). The cultural evolution of beneficient norms. *Social Forces, 71,* 279–301.

Allison, S. T., & Beggan, J. K. (1994). Estimating popular support for group decision outcomes: An anchoring and adjustment model. *Journal of Social Behavior and Personality, 9,* 617–638.

Allison, S. T., Beggan, J. K., & Midgley, E. H. (1996). The quest for "similar instances" and "simultaneous possibilities": Metaphors in social dilemma research. *Journal of Personality and Social Psychology, 71,* 479–497.

Allison, S. T., Mackie, D. M., Muller, M. M., & Worth, L. T. (1993). Sequential correspondence biases and perceptions of change: The Castro studies revisited. *Personality and Social Psychology Bulletin, 19,* 151–157.

Allport, G. (1954). *The nature of prejudice.* Reading, MA: Addison-Wesley.

Allport, G. W. (1985). The historical background of social psychology. In G. Lindzey & E. Aronson (Eds.), *The handbook of social psychology* (Vol. 1, pp. 1–46). Reading, MA: Addison-Wesley.

Altemeyer, B. (1981). *Right-wing authoritarianism.* Winnipeg, MB: The University of Manitoba Press.

Altemeyer, B. (1988). *Enemies of freedom: Understanding right-wing authoritarianism.* San Francisco, USA: Jossey-Bass Publishers.

Altemeyer, B. (1996). *The authoritarian specter.* Cambridge, MA: Harvard University Press.

Altemeyer, B. (1998). The other "authoritarian personality." In M.P. Zanna (Ed.), *Advances in experimental social psychology* (Volume 30). San Diego, California: Academic Press Limited.

Altemeyer, B. (2001). Changes in attitudes toward homosexuals. *Journal of Homosexuality, 42,* 63–75.

Altemeyer, B., & Hunsberger, B. (1992). Authoritarianism, religious fundamentalism, quest, and prejudice. *The International Journal for the Psychology of Religion, 2,* 113–133.

Altemeyer, B., & Hunsberger, B. (1993). Reply to Gorsuch. *International Journal for the Psychology of Religion, 3,* 33–37.

Amato, P. R. (1983). Helping behavior in urban and rural environments: Field studies based on a taxonomic organization of helping episodes. *Journal of Personality and Social Psychology, 45,* 571–586.

Ambady, N., & Rosenthal, R. (1992). Thin slices of expressive behavior as predictors of interpersonal consequences: A meta-analysis. *Psychological Bulletin, 111,* 256–274.

Ambady, N., & Rosenthal, R. (1993). Half a minute: Predicting teacher evaluations from thin slices of nonverbal behavior and physical attractiveness. *Journal of Personality and Social Psychology*, *64*, 431–441.

Amir, I. (1969). Contact hypothesis in ethnic relations. *Psychological Bulletin, 71,* 319–342.

Amir, Y. (1976). The role of intergroup contact in change of prejudice and ethnic relations. In P. Katz (Ed.), *Towards the elimination of racism.* New York: Pergamon Press.

Andersen, B. L., & Cyranowski, J. M. (1994). Women's sexual self-schema. *Journal of Personality and Social Psychology, 67,* 1079–1100.

Andersen, S. M. (1984). Self-knowledge and social inference: II. The diagnosticity of cognitive/affective and behavioral data. *Journal of Personality and Social Psychology, 46,* 294–307.

Andersen, S. M., & Bem, S. L. (1981). Sex typing and androgyny in dyadic interaction: Individual differences in responsiveness to physical attractiveness. *Journal of Personality and Social Psychology, 41,* 74–86.

Andersen, S. M., & Ross, L. D. (1984). Self-knowledge and social inference: I. The impact of cognitive/affective and behavioral data. *Journal of Personality and Social Psychology, 46,* 280–293.

Anderson, C. A. (1995). Implicit personality theories and empirical data: Biased assimilation, belief perseverance and change, and covariation detection sensitivity. *Social Cognition, 13,* 25–48.

Anderson, C. A. (1999). Attributional style, depression, and loneliness: A cross-cultural comparison of American and Chinese students. *Personality and Social Psychology Bulletin, 25,* 482–499.

Anderson, C. A., & Anderson, D. C. (1984). Ambient temperature and violent crime: Tests of the linear and curvilinear hypotheses. *Journal of Personality and Social Psychology, 46,* 91–97.

Anderson, C. A., & Bushman, B. J. (1997). External validity of "trivial" experiments: The case of laboratory aggression. *Review of General Psychology, 1,* 19–41.

Anderson, C. A., Bushman, B. J., & Groom, R. W. (1997). Hot years and serious and deadly assault: Empirical tests of the heat hypothesis. *Journal of Personality and Social Psychology, 73,* 1213–1223.

Anderson, C. A., & Dill, K. E. (2000). Video games and aggressive thoughts, feelings, and behavior in the laboratory and in life. *Journal of Personality and Social Psychology, 78,* 772–790.

Anderson, C. A., Lepper, M. R., & Ross, L. (1980). The perseverance of social theories: The role of explanation in the persistence of discredited information. *Journal of Personality and Social Psychology, 39,* 1037–1049.

Anderson, C. A., & Lindsay, J. J. (1998). The development, perseverance, and change of naive theories. *Social Cognition, 16,* 8–30.

Anderson, C. A., Lindsay, J. J., & Bushman, B. J. (1999). Research in the psychological laboratory: Truth or triviality? *Current Directions in Psychological Science, 8,* 3–9.

Anderson, C. A., & Sedikides, C. (1990). Thinking about people: Contributions of a typological alternative to associationistic and dimensional models of person perception. *Journal of Personality and Social Psychology, 60,* 203–217.

Anderson, J. L., Crawford, C. B., Nadeau, J., & Lindberg, T. (1992). Was the Duchess of Windsor right? A cross-cultural review of the socioecology of ideals of female body shape. *Ethology and Sociobiology, 13,* 197–227.

Anthony, T., Cooper, C., & Mullen, B. (1992). Cross-racial facial identification: A social cognitive interpretation. *Personality and Social Psychology Bulletin, 18,* 296–301.

Archer, D. (1997b). Unspoken diversity: Cultural differences in gestures. *Qualitative Sociology*, *20*, 79–105.

Archer, D., & Akert, R. M. (1980). The encoding of meaning: A test of three theories of social interaction. *Sociological Inquiry, 50*(3–4), 393–419.

Archer, D., & Akert, R. M. (1984). Problems of context and criterion in nonverbal communication: A new look at the accuracy issue. In M. Cook (Ed.), *Issues in person perception* (pp. 114–144). London and New York: Methuen.

Archer, D., & Akert, R. M. (1998). *The interpretation of behavior: Verbal and nonverbal factors in person perception.* New York: Cambridge University Press.

Archer, D., & Gartner, R. (1976). Violent acts and violent times: A comparative approach to postwar homicide rates. *American Sociological Review, 41,* 937–963.

Archer, D., & Gartner, R. (1984). *Violence and crime in cross-national perspective.* New Haven, CT: Yale University Press.

Archer, D., & McDaniel, P. (1995). Violence and gender: Differences and similarities across societies. In R. B. Ruback & N. A. Weiner (Eds.), *Interpersonal violent behaviors: social and cultural aspects* (pp. 63–88). New York: Springer Publishing.

Archer, J. (2000). Sex differences in aggression between heterosexual partners: A meta-analytic review. *Psychological Bulletin, 126,* 651–680.

Arendt, H. (1965). *Eichmann in Jerusalem: A report on the banality of evil.* New York: Viking.

Argyle, M. (1975). *Bodily communication.* New York: International Universities Press.

Arkin, R. M., & Oleson, K. C. (1998). Self-handicapping. In J. M. Darley & J. Cooper (Eds.), *Attribution and social interaction: The legacy of Edward E. Jones* (pp. 313–341). Washington, DC: American Psychological Association.

Armor, D. A., & Taylor, S. E. (1998). Situated optimism: Specific outcome expectancies and self-regulation. In M. P. Zanna (Ed.), *Advances in experimental social psychology* (Vol. 30, pp. 309–379). San Diego, CA: Academic Press.

Arms, R. L., Russell, G. W., & Sandilands, M. L. (1979). Effects on the hostility of spectators of viewing aggressive sports. *Social Psychology Quarterly, 42,* 275–279.

Arnett, J. (1995). The young and the reckless: Adolescent reckless behavior. *Current Directions in Psychological Science, 4,* (June), 67–71.

Aron, A., & Aron, E. N. (1986). Falling in love: Prospective studies of self-concept change. *Journal of Personality and Social Psychology, 69,* 1102–1112.

Aron, A., & Rodriguez, G. (1992). Scenarios of falling in love among Mexican, Chinese, and Anglo-Americans. In A. Aron (Chair), *Ethnic and cultural differences in love.* Symposium conducted at the Sixth International Conference on Personal Relationships, Orono, ME.

Aron, A., & Westbay, L. (1996). Dimensions of the prototype of love. *Journal of Personality and Social Psychology, 70,* 535–551.

Aron, E. N., & Aron, A. (1997). Sensory processing sensitivity and its relation to introversion and emotionality. *Journal of Personality and Social Psychology, 73,* 345–368.

Aronson, E. (1968). Dissonance theory: Progress and problems. In R. P. Abelson, E. Aronson, W. J. McGuire, T. M. Newcomb, M. J. Rosenberg, and P. H. Tannenbaum (Eds.), *Theories of Cognitive Consistency: A Sourcebook* (pp. 5–27). Chicago: Rand McNally.

Aronson, E. (1969). The theory of cognitive dissonance: A current perspective. In L. Berkowitz (Ed.), *Advances in experimental social psychology* (Vol. 4, pp. 1–34). New York: Academic Press.

Aronson, E. (1990). Applying social psychology to prejudice reduction and energy conservation. *Personality and Social Psychology Bulletin, 16*, 118–132.

Aronson, E. (1992). Stateways can change folkways. In R. Baird & S. Rosenbaum (Eds.), *Bigotry, prejudice and hatred: Definitions, causes and solutions*. Buffalo, NY: Prometheus Books.

Aronson, E. (1997a). The giving away of psychology—and condoms. *APS Observer, 10*, 17–35.

Aronson, E. (1997b). The theory of cognitive dissonance: The evolution and vicissitudes of an idea. In C. McGarty & S. Alexander Haslam (Eds.), *The message of social psychology: Perspectives on mind in society* (pp. 20–35). Oxford, England: Blackwell Publishers, Inc.

Aronson, E. (1998). Dissonance, hypocrisy, and the self-concept. In E. Harmon-Jones & J. S. Mills, *Cognitive dissonance theory: Revival with revisions and controversies*. Washington, DC: American Psychological Association.

Aronson, E., & Bridgeman, D. (1979). Jigsaw groups and the desegregated classroom: In pursuit of common goals. *Personality and Social Psychology Bulletin, 5*, 438–446.

Aronson, E., & Carlsmith, J. M. (1962). Performance expectancy as a determinant of actual performance. *Journal of Abnormal and Social Psychology, 65*, 178–182.

Aronson, E., & Carlsmith, J. M. (1963). Effect of severity of threat in the devaluation of forbidden behavior. *Journal of Abnormal and Social Psychology, 66*, 584–588.

Aronson, E., & Carlsmith, J. M. (1968). Experimentation in social psychology. In G. Lindzey & E. Aronson (Eds.), *The handbook of social psychology* (Vol. 2, pp. 1–79). Reading, MA: Addison-Wesley.

Aronson, E., Chase, T., Helmreich, R., & Ruhnke, R. (1974). A two-factor theory of dissonance reduction: The effect of feeling stupid or feeling awful on opinion change. *International Journal for Research and Communication, 3*, 59–74.

Aronson, E., Ellsworth, P. C., Carlsmith, J. M., & Gonzalez, M. H. (1990). *Methods of research in social psychology* (2nd ed.). New York: McGraw-Hill.

Aronson, E., Fried, C., & Stone, J. (1991). Overcoming denial and increasing the intention to use condoms through the induction of hypocrisy. *American Journal of Public Health, 81*, 1636–1638.

Aronson, E., & Gonzales, M. (1990). The social psychology of energy conservation. In J. Edwards (Ed.), *Social influence processes and prevention*. New York: Plenum.

Aronson, E., & Mettee, D. (1968). Dishonest behavior as a function of differential levels of induced self-esteem. *Journal of Personality and Social Psychology, 9*, 121–127.

Aronson, E., & Mills, J. (1959). The effect of severity of initiation on liking for a group. *Journal of Abnormal and Social Psych-ology, 59*, 177–181.

Aronson, E., & Patnoe, S. (1997). *Cooperation in the classroom: The jigsaw method*. New York: Longman.

Aronson, E., Stephan, C., Sikes, J., Blaney, N., & Snapp, M. (1978). *The jigsaw classroom*. Beverly Hills, CA: Sage.

Aronson, E., Wilson, T. D., & Brewer, M. (1998). Experimental methods. In D. Gilbert, S. Fiske, & G. Lindzey (Eds.), *The handbook of social psychology* (4th ed., Vol. 1, pp. 99–142). New York: Random House.

Aronson, E., & Yates, S. (1985). Social psychological aspects of energy conservation. In D. Hafemeister, H. Kelly, & B. Levi, (Eds.), *Energy sources: Conservation and renewables* (pp. 81–91). New York: American Institute of Physics Press.

Aronson, J., Cohen, J., & Nail, P. (1998). Self-affirmation theory: An update and appraisal. In E. Harmon-Jones & J. S. Mills, *Cognitive dissonance theory: Revival with revisions and controversies*. Washington, DC: American Psychological Association.

Aronson, J. M., Quinn, D., & Spencer, S. (1998). Stereotype threat and the academic underperformance of women and minorities. In J. K. Swim & C. Stangor (Eds.), *Stigma: The target's perspective* (pp. 83–103). San Diego, CA: Academic Press.

Asch, S. E. (1951). Effects of group pressure upon the modification and distortion of judgment. In H. Guetzkow (Ed.), *Groups, leadership, and men*. Pittsburgh, PA: Carnegie Press.

Asch, S. E. (1955). Opinions and social pressure. *Scientific American, 193*, 31–35.

Asch, S. E. (1956). Studies of independence and conformity: A minority of one against a unanimous majority. *Psychological Monographs, 70* (9, Whole No. 416).

Asch, S. E. (1957). An experimental investigation of group influence. In *Symposium on preventive and social psychiatry* (pp. 15–17). Walter Reed Army Institute of Research. Washington, DC: U.S. Government Printing Office.

Ashmore, R. D., Solomon, M. R., & Longo, L. C. (1996). Thinking about fashion models' looks: A multidimensional approach to the structure of perceived physical attractiveness. *Personality and Social Psychology Bulletin, 22*, 1083–1104.

Aspinwall, L. G., & Taylor, S. E. (1993). Effects of social comparison direction, threat, and self-esteem on affect, evaluation, and expected success. *Journal of Personality and Social Psychology, 64*, 708–722.

Aspinwall, L. G., & Taylor, S. E. (1997). A stitch in time: Self-regulation and proactive coping. *Psychological Bulletin, 121*, 417–436.

Associated Press. (1998, March 30). High-rise dwellers watch murder: No one calls 911, Denver police say. *Winnipeg Free Press*, p. C8.

Associated Press. (2000, April 3). Parents led kids to death: Childhood seen as sinful by cult.

Atlas, R. S., & Pepler, D. J. (1998). Observations of bullying in the classroom. *Journal of Educational Research, 92*, 86–99.

Attridge, M. & Berscheid, E. (1994). Entitlement in romantic relationships in the United States: A social exchange perspective. In M. J. Lerner & G. Mikula (Eds.), *Entitlement and the affectional bond: Justice in close relationships* (pp. 117–148). New York: Plenum.

Aune, K. S. & Aune, R. K. (1996). Cultural differences in the self-reported experience and expression of emotions in relationships. *Journal of Cross-Cultural Psychology, 27*, 67–81.

Axelrod, R. (1984). *The evolution of cooperation*. New York: Basic Books.

Ayers, M. S., & Reder, L. M. (1998). A theoretical review of the misinformation effect: Predictions from an activation-based memory model. *Psychonomic Bulletin and Review, 5*, 1–21.

Azrin, N. H. (1967, May). Pain and aggression. *Psychology Today*, pp. 27–33.

Babad, E. (1993). Pygmalion—25 years after interpersonal expectations in the classroom. In P. D. Blank (Ed.), *Interpersonal expectations: Theory, research, and applications* (pp. 125–153). New York: Cambridge University Press.

Bahrick, H. P., Hall, L. K., & Berger, S. A. (1996). Accuracy and distortion in memory for high school grades. *Psychological Science, 7*, 265–271.

Bailey, W. C., & Peterson, R. D. (1997). Murder, capital punishment, and deterrence: A review of the literature. In H. A. Bedau, *The death penalty in America: Current controversies* (pp. 135–161). New York: Oxford University Press.

Baldwin, M. W. (1992). Relational schemas and the processing of social information. *Psychological Bulletin, 112,* 461–484.

Baldwin, M. W., Carrell, S. E., & Lopez, D. F. (1990). Priming relationship schemas: My advisor and the pope are watching me from the back of my mind. *Journal of Experimental Social Psychology, 26,* 435–454.

Baldwin, M. W., & Fehr, B. (1995). On the instability of attachment style ratings. *Personal Relationships, 2,* 247–261.

Baldwin, M. W., Fehr, B., Keedian, E., Seidel, M., & Thomson, D. W. (1993). An exploration of the relational schemata underlying attachment styles: Self-report and lexical decision approaches. *Personality and Social Psychology Bulletin, 19,* 746–754.

Baldwin, M. W., & Holmes, J. O. (1987). Salient private audiences and awareness of the self. *Journal of Personality and Social Psychology, 52,* 1087–1098.

Baldwin, M. W., Keelan, J. P. R., Fehr, B., Enns, V., & Koh-Rangarajoo, E. (1996). Social-cognitive conceptualizations of attachment working models: Availability and accessibility effects. *Journal of Personality and Social Psychology, 71,* 94–109.

Baldwin, M. W., & Main, K. J. (2001). Social anxiety: The cued activation of relational knowledge. *Personality and Social Psychology Bulletin, 27,* 1637–1647.

Baldwin, M. W., & Meunier, J. (1999). The cued activation of attachment relational schemas. *Social Cognition, 17,* 209–227.

Baldwin, M. W., & Sinclair, L. (1996). Self-esteem and "if … then" contingencies of interpersonal acceptance. *Journal of Personality and Social Psychology, 71,* 1130–1141.

Ballard, E. J., & Suedfeld, P. (1988). Performance ratings of Canadian prime ministers: Individual and situational factors. *Political Psychology, 9,* 291–302.

Bandura, A. (1973). *Aggression: A social learning analysis.* Englewood Cliffs, NJ: Prentice Hall.

Bandura, A. (1986). *Social foundations of thought and action.* Englewood Cliffs, NJ: Prentice Hall.

Bandura, A. (1997). *Self-efficacy: The exercise of control.* New York: Freeman.

Bandura, A. (1999). A sociocognitive analysis of substance abuse: An agentic perspective. *Psychological Science, 10,* 214–217.

Bandura, A., Cioffi, D., Taylor, C. B., & Brouillard, M. E. (1988). Perceived self-efficacy in coping with cognitive stressors and opioid activation. *Journal of Personality and Social Psychology, 55,* 479–488.

Bandura, A., Pastorelli, C., Barbaranelli, C., & Caprara, G. V. (1999). Self-efficacy pathways to childhood depression. *Journal of Personality and Social Psychology, 76,* 258–269.

Bandura, A., Ross, D., & Ross, S. (1961). Transmission of aggression through imitation of aggressive models. *Journal of Abnormal and Social Psychology, 63,* 575–582.

Bandura, A., Ross, D., & Ross, S. (1963). Imitation of film-mediated aggressive models. *Journal of Abnormal and Social Psychology, 66,* 3–11.

Banks, T., & Dabbs, J. M., Jr. (1996). Salivary testosterone and cortisol in delinquent and violent urban subculture. *Journal of Social Psychology, 136,* 49–56.

Bargh, J. A. (1990). Auto-motives: Preconscious determinants of social interaction. In E. T. Higgins & R. M. Sorrentino (Eds.), *Handbook of motivation and cognition* (Vol. 2, pp. 93–130). New York: Guilford.

Bargh, J. A. (1994). The four horseman of automaticity: Awareness, intention, efficiency, and control in social cognition. In R. S. Wyer, Jr., & T. K. Srull (Eds.), *Handbook of Social Cognition* (Vol. 1, pp. 1–40). Hillsdale, NJ: Erlbaum.

Bargh, J. A. (1996). Automaticity in social psychology. In E. T. Higgins & A. W. Kruglanski (Eds.), *Social psychology: Handbook of basic principles* (pp. 169–183). New York: Guilford.

Bargh, J. A. (1999). The cognitive monster: The case against the controllability of automatic stereotype effects. In S. Chaiken & Y. Trope (Eds.), *Dual-process theories in social psychology* (pp. 361–382). New York: Guilford Press.

Bargh, J. A., & Chartrand, T. L. (1999). The unbearable automaticity of being. *American Psychologist, 54,* 462–479.

Bargh, J. A., & Pietromonaco, P. (1982). Automatic information processing and social perception: The influence of trait information presented outside of conscious awareness on impression formation. *Journal of Personality and Social Psychology, 43,* 437–449.

Barker, R., Dembo, T., & Lewin, K. (1941). Frustration and aggression: An experiment with young children. *University of Iowa Studies in Child Welfare, 18,* 1–314.

Barley, S. R., & Bechky, B. A. (1994). In the backrooms of science: The work of technicians in science labs. *Work and Occupations, 21,* 85–126.

Baron, J. (1997). The illusion of morality as self-interest: A reason to cooperate in social dilemmas. *Psychological Science, 8,* 330–335.

Baron, R., & Rodin, J. (1978). Personal control as a mediator of crowding. In A. Baum, J. S. Singer, & S. Valins (Eds.), *Advances in environmental psychology* (Vol. 1, pp. 145–190). Hillsdale, NJ: Erlbaum.

Baron, R. A. (1972). Reducing the influence of an aggressive model: The restraining effects of peer censure. *Journal of Experimental Social Psychology, 8,* 266–275.

Baron, R. A. (1976). The reduction of human aggression: A field study on the influence of incompatible responses. *Journal of Applied Social Psychology, 6,* 95–104.

Baron, R. A. (1988). Negative effects of destructive criticism: Impact on conflict, self-efficacy, and task performance. *Journal of Applied Psychology, 73,* 199–207.

Baron, R. A. (1990). Countering the effects of destructive criticism: The relative efficacy of four interventions. *Journal of Applied Psychology, 75,* 235–245.

Baron, R. A., & Richardson, D. R. (1994). *Human aggression* (2nd ed.). New York: Plenum.

Baron, R. S., Inman, M., Kao, C., & Logan, H. (1992). Emotion and superficial social processing. *Motivation and Emotion, 16,* 323–345.

Baron, R. S., Vandello, J. A., & Brunsman, B. (1996). The forgotten variable in conformity research: Impact of task importance on social influence. *Journal of Personality and Social Psychology, 71,* 915–927.

Bartholomew, B. D., & Anderson, C. A. (2002). Effects of violent video games on aggressive behavior: Potential sex differences. *Journal of Experimental Social Psychology, 38,* 283–290.

Bartholomew, K. (1990). Avoidance of intimacy: An attachment perspective. *Journal of Social and Personal Relationships, 7,* 147–178.

Bartholomew, K., & Horowitz, L. M. (1991). Attachment styles among young adults: A test of a four-category model. *Journal of Personality and Social Psychology, 61,* 226–244.

Bartlett, D. C. (1932). *Remembering.* Cambridge: Cambridge University Press.

Bass, B. M. (1990). *Bass and Stogdill's handbook of leadership: Theory, research, and managerial applications* (3rd ed.). New York: Free Press.

Bass, B. M. (1997). Does the transactional-transformational leadership paradigm transcend organizational and national boundaries? *American Psychologist, 52,* 130–139.

Bass, E., & Davis, L. (1994). *The courage to heal: A guide for women survivors of child sexual abuse* (3rd ed.). New York: HarperCollins.

Bassili, J. N. (1995). Response latency and the accessibility of voting intentions: What contributes to accessibility and how it affects vote choice. *Personality and Social Psychology Bulletin, 21,* 686– 695.

Bassili, J. N. (1996). Meta-judgmental versus operative indexes of psychological attributes: The case of measures of attitude strength. *Journal of Personality and Social Psychology, 71,* 637–653.

Bastien, D., & Hostager, T. (1988). Jazz as a process of organizational innovation. *Communication Research, 15,* 582–602.

Basu, J. E. (1989, August). Why no one's safe: Effects of smog on residents in Los Angeles Basin. *American Health,* 64.

Batson, C. D. (1991). *The altruism question: Toward a social-psychological answer.* Hillsdale, NJ: Erlbaum.

Batson, C. D. (1998). Altruism and prosocial behavior. In D. Gilbert, S. Fiske, & G. Lindzey (Eds.), *The handbook of social psychology* (4th ed., Vol. 2, pp. 282–316). New York: McGraw-Hill.

Batson, C. D., & Ahmad, N. (2001). Empathy-induced altruism in a prisoner's dilemma II: What if the target of empathy has defected? *European Journal of Social Psychology, 31,* 25–36.

Batson, C. D., Coke, J. S., Jasnoski, M. L., & Hanson, M. (1978). Buying kindness: Effect of an extrinsic incentive for helping on perceived altruism. *Personality and Social Psychology Bulletin, 4,* 86–91.

Batson, C. D., & Moran, T. (1999). Empathy-induced altruism in a prisoner's dilemma. *European Journal of Social Psychology, 29,* 909–924.

Batson, C. D., & Shaw, L. L. (1991). Evidence for altruism: Toward a pluralism of prosocial motives. *Psychological Inquiry, 2,* 107–122.

Batson, C. D., Sympson, S. C., Hindman, J. L., Decruz, P., Todd, R. M., Weeks, J. L., Jennings, G., & Burris, C. T. (1996). "I've been there, too": Effect on empathy of prior experience with need. *Personality and Social Psychology Bulletin, 22,* 474–482.

Batson, C. D., & Weeks, J. L. (1996). Mood effects of unsuccessful helping: Another test of the empathy-altruism hypothesis. *Personality and Social Psychology Bulletin, 22,* 148–157.

Baum, A., & Valins, S. (1979). Architectural mediation of residential density and control: Crowding and the regulation of social contract. In L. Berkowitz (Ed.), *Advances in experimental social psychology* (Vol. 12, pp. 131–175). New York: Academic Press.

Baumeister, R. (Ed.) (1993). *Self-esteem: The puzzle of low self-regard.* New York: Plenum.

Baumeister, R. F. (1991). *Escaping the self: Alcoholism, spirituality, masochism, and other flights from the burden of selfhood.* New York: Basic Books.

Baumeister, R. F. (1998). The self. In D. T. Gilbert, S. T. Fiske, & G. Lindzey (Eds.), *The handbook of social psychology* (4th ed., Vol. 1, pp. 680–740). New York: McGraw-Hill.

Baumeister, R. F., & Bratslavsky, E. (1999). Passion, intimacy, and time: Passionate love as a function of change in intimacy. *Personality and Social Psychology Review, 3,* 49–67.

Baumeister, R. F., & Leary, M. R. (1995). The need to belong: Desire for interpersonal attachment as a fundamental human motivation. *Psychological Bulletin, 117,* 497–529.

Baumeister, R. F., Muraven, M., & Tice, D. M. (2000). Ego depletion: A resource model of volition, self-regulation, and controlled processing. *Social Cognition, 18,* 130–150.

Baumeister, R. F., & Sommer, K. L. (1997). Patterns in the bizarre: Common themes in satanic ritual abuse, sexual masochism, UFO abductions, fictitious illnesses, and external love. *Journal of Social and Clinical Psychology, 16,* 213–223.

Baumeister, R. F., & Sommer, K. L. (1997). What do men want? Gender differences and two spheres of belongingness: Comment on Cross and Madson (1997). *Psychological Bulletin, 122,* 38–44.

Baumeister, R. F., Stillwell, A. M., & Heatherton, T. F. (1994). Guilt: An interpersonal approach. *Psychological Bulletin, 115,* 243–267.

Baxter, L. A. (1982). Strategies for ending relationships: Two studies. *Western Journal of Speech Communication, 47,* 85–98.

Baxter, L. A. (1985). Accomplishing relationship disengagement. In S. Duck & D. Perlman (Eds.), *Understanding personal relationships* (pp. 243–265). London: Sage.

Bazerman, M., & Neale, M. (1992). *Negotiating rationally.* New York: Free Press.

Beach, S., Tesser, A., Mendolia, M., & Anderson, P. (1996). Self-evaluation maintenance in marriage: Toward a performance ecology of the marital relationship. *Journal of Family Psychology, 10,* 379–396.

Beaman, A. L., Barnes, P. J., Klentz, B., & McQuirk, B. (1978). Increasing helping rates through informational dissemination: Teaching pays. *Personality and Social Psychology Bulletin, 4,* 406–411.

Beaman, A. L., Klentz, B., Diener, E., & Svanum, S. (1979). Objective self-awareness and transgression in children: A field study. *Journal of Personality and Social Psychology, 37,* 1835–1846.

Beaton, A. M., Tougas, F., & Joly, S.(1996). Neosexism among male managers: Is it really a matter of numbers? *Journal of Applied Social Psychology, 26,* 2189–2203.

Becker, M. H., & Josephs, J. G. (1988). AIDS and behavioral change to reduce risk: A review. *American Journal of Public Health, 78,* 394–410.

Bedau, H. A. (Ed.) (1997). *The death penalty in America: Current controversies.* New York: Oxford University Press.

Behrman, M., Winocur, G., & Moscovitch, M. (1992). *Nature, 359,* 636–637.

Belansky, E. S., & Boggiano, A. K. (1994). Predicting helping behaviors: The role of gender and instrumental/expressive self-schemata. *Sex Roles, 30,* 647–661.

Bell, D. W., & Esses, V. (1997). Ambivalence and response amplification toward Native peoples. *Journal of American Social Psychology, 27,* 1063–1084.

Bell, D. W., & Esses, V. M. (2002). Ambivalence and response amplification: A motivational perspective. *Personality and Social Psychology Bulletin, 28,* 1143–1152.

Bell, S. T., Kuriloff, P. J., & Lottes, I. (1994). Understanding attributions of blame in stranger rape and date rape situations: An examination of gender, race, identification, and students' social perceptions of rape victims. *Journal of Applied Social Psych-ology, 24,* 1719–1734.

Belli, R. F. (1989). Influences of misleading postevent information: Misinformation interference and acceptance. *Journal of Experimental Psychology: General, 118,* 72–85.

Bem, D. J. (1972). Self-perception theory. In L. Berkowitz (Ed.), *Advances in experimental social psychology* (Vol. 6, pp. 1–62). New York: Academic Press.

Berger, I. E. (1997). The demographics of recycling and the structure of environmental behavior. *Environment and Behavior, 29,* 515–531.

Berk, R., Campbell, A., Klap, R., & Western, B. (1992). The deterrent effect of arrest in incidents of domestic violence: A Bayesian analysis of four field experiments. *American Sociological Review, 57,* 698–708.

Berk, R., Fenstermaker, S., & Newton, P. (1988). An empirical analysis of police responses to incidents of wife battery. In G. Hotaling, D. Finkelhor, J. Kirkpatrick, & M. Straus (Eds.), *Coping with family violence: Research and policy perspectives,* (pp. 158–168). Newbury Park, CA: Sage.

Berkow, J. H. (1989). *Darwin, sex, and status: Biological approaches to mind and culture.* Toronto: University of Toronto Press.

Berkowitz, L. (1968, September). Impulse, aggression, and the gun. *Psychology Today,* pp. 18–22.

Berkowitz, L. (1978). Whatever happened to the frustration-aggression hypothesis? *American Behavioral Scientist, 21,* 691–708.

Berkowitz, L. (1981, June). How guns control us. *Psychology Today,* pp. 11–12.

Berkowitz, L. (1983). Aversively simulated aggression. *American Psychologist, 38,* 1135–1144.

Berkowitz, L. (1987). Mood, self-awareness, and willingness to help. *Journal of Personality and Social Psychology, 52,* 721–729.

Berkowitz, L. (1988). Frustrations, appraisals, and aversively stimulated aggression. *Aggressive Behavior, 14,* 3–11.

Berkowitz, L. (1989). Frustration-aggression hypothesis: Examination and reformulation. *Psychological Bulletin, 106,* 59–73.

Berkowitz, L. (1993). *Aggression: Its causes, consequences, and control.* New York: McGraw-Hill.

Berkowitz, L., & LePage, A. (1967). Weapons as aggression-eliciting stimuli. *Journal of Personality and Social Psychology, 7,* 202–207.

Berkowitz, L., & Troccoli, B., (1990). Feelings, direction of attention, and expressed evaluations of others. *Cognition and Emotion, 4,* 305–325.

Berry, D. S. (1995). Beyond beauty and after affect: An event perception approach to perceiving faces. In R. A. Eder (Ed.), *Craniofacial anomalies: Psychological perspectives.* New York: Springer-Verlag.

Berry, D. S., & McArthur, L. Z. (1986). Perceiving character in faces: The impact of age-related craniofacial changes in social perception. *Psychological Bulletin, 100,* 3–18.

Berry, J. W. (1967). Independence and conformity in subsistence-level societies. *Journal of Personality and Social Psychology, 7,* 415–418.

Berscheid, E. (1985). Interpersonal attraction. In G. Lindzey & E. Aronson (Eds.), *The handbook of social psychology* (pp. 413–484). New York: McGraw-Hill.

Berscheid, E., & Hatfield, E. (1978). *Interpersonal Attraction,* (2nd ed.) Reading, MA: Addison-Wesley.

Berscheid, E., & Reis, H. T. (1998). Attraction and close relationships. In D. Gilbert, S. Fiske, & G. Lindzey (Eds.), *The handbook of social psychology* (4th ed., Vol. 2, pp. 193–281). New York: McGraw-Hill.

Berscheid, E., & Walster (Hatfield), E. (1974). A little bit about love. In T. L. Huston (Ed.), *Foundations of interpersonal attraction* (pp. 355-381). New York: Academic Press.

Berscheid, E., & Walster (Hatfield), E. (1978). *Interpersonal attraction.* Reading, MA: Addison-Wesley.

Bettencourt, B. A., & Miller, N. (1996). Gender differences in aggression as a function of provocation: A meta-analysis. *Psychological Bulletin, 119,* 422–447.

Beuf, A. (1974). Doctor, lawyer, household drudge. *Journal of Communication, 24,* 142–145.

Bhatia, J. (2002, May 10). Obesity climbs among Canadian adults. Reuters Health. www.billingsclinic.com/HealthNews/reuters/NewsStory0510200217.htm.

Bickman, L. (1974). The social power of a uniform. *Journal of Applied Social Psychology, 4,* 47–61.

Biehl, M., Matsumoto, D., Ekman, P., Hearn, V., Heider, K., Kudoh, T., & Ton, V. (1997). Matsumoto and Ekman's Japanese and Caucasian facial expressions of emotion (JACFEE): Reliability and cross-national differences. *Journal of Nonverbal Behavior, 21,* 3–21.

Biek, M., Wood, W., Chaiken, S. (1996). Working knowledge, cognitive processing, and attitudes: On the determinants of bias. *Personality and Social Psychology Bulletin, 22,* 547–556.

Biernat, M., Crandall, C. S., Young, L. V., Kobrynowicz, D., & Halpin, S. M. (1998). All that you can be: Stereotyping of self and others in a military context. *Journal of Personality and Social Psychology, 75,* 301–317.

Billsberry, J. (Ed.) (1996). *The effective manager: Perspectives and illustrations.* London, England: Sage.

Bils, J., & Singer, S. (1996, August 16). Gorilla saves tot in Brookfield ape pit. *Chicago Tribune,* p. 1.

Bird, B. (2001, January 28). Love as fleeting as a bus ride. *Winnipeg Free Press,* p. B5.

Blairy, S., Herrera, P., & Hess, U. (1999). Mimicry and the judgment of emotional facial expressions. *Journal of Nonverbal Behavior, 23,* 5–41.

Blais, M. R., Sabourin, S., Boucher, C., & Vallerand, R. J. (1990). Toward a motivational model of couple happiness. *Journal of Personality and Social Psychology, 59,* 1021–1031.

Blanchfield, M. (2000, June 21). I will never be able to trust my leaders again. *Ottawa Citizen Online.* www.ottawacitizen.com/national/000227/3666380.html

Blank, P. D. (Ed.). (1993). *Interpersonal expectations: Theory, research, and applications.* New York: Cambridge University Press.

Blascovich, J., Mendes, W. B., Hunter, S. B., & Salomon, K. (1999). Social "facilitation" as challenge and threat. *Journal of Personality and Social Psychology, 77,* 68–77.

Blaskovich, J., Ginsburg, G. P., & Veach, T. L. (1975). A pluralistic explanation of choice shifts on the risk dimension. *Journal of Personality and Social Psychology, 31,* 422–429.

Blass, T. (1993). Psychological perspectives on the perpetrators of the Holocaust: The role of situational pressures, personal dispositions, and their interactions. *Holocaust and Genocide Studies, 7,* 30–50.

Blass, T. (1996). Attribution of responsibility and trust in the Milgram obedience experiment. *Journal of Applied Social Psychology, 26,* 1529–1535.

Blau, P. M. (1964). *Exchange and power in social life.* New York: Wiley.

Bless, H., Bohner, G., Schwarz, N., & Strack, F. (1990). Mood and persuasion: A cognitive response analysis. *Personality and Social Psychology Bulletin, 16,* 331–345.

Blittner, M., Goldberg, J., & Merbaum, M. (1978). Cognitive self-control factors in the reduction of smoking behavior. *Behavior Therapy, 9,* 553–561.

Boadle, A. (1994, Nov. 8). Pictures of Somali beaten to death shock Canadians [Reuters]. http://burn.ucsd.edu/archives/riot-l/1994.Nov/0012.html

Bobocel, D. R., Son Hing, L. S., Davey, L. M., Stanley, D. J., & Zanna, M. P. (1998). Justice-based opposition to social policies: Is it genuine? *Journal of Personality and Social Psychology, 75,* 653–669.

Bochner, S. (1994). Cross-cultural differences in the self-concept: A test of Hofstede's individualism/collectivism distinction. *Journal of Cross-Cultural Psychology, 25,* 273–283.

Bodenhausen, G. V. (1988). Stereotypic biases in social decision making and memory: Testing process models of stereotype use. *Journal of Personality and Social Psychology, 55,* 726–737.

Bodenhausen, G. V., & Lichtenstein, M. (1987). Social stereotypes and information-processing strategies. The impact of task complexity. *Journal of Personality and Social Psychology, 52,* 871–880.

Bond, C., DiCandia, C., & McKinnon, J. R. (1988). Response to violence in a psychiatric setting. *Personality and Social Psychology Bulletin, 14,* 448–458.

Bond, C. F., Atoum, A. O., & VanLeeuwen, M. D. (1996). Social impairment of complex learning in the wake of public embarrassment. *Basic and Applied Social Psychology, 18,* 31–44.

Bond, C. F., & Titus, L. J. (1983). Social facilitation: A meta-analysis of 241 studies. *Psychological Bulletin, 94,* 264–292.

Bond, C. F., Jr., & Atoum, A. O. (2000). International deception. *Personality and Social Psychology Bulletin, 26,* 385–395.

Bond, M. (1991). Chinese values and health: A culture-level examination. *Psychology and Health*, 5, 137–152.

Bond, M. H. (Ed.). (1988). *The cross-cultural challenge to social psychology*. Newbury Park, CA: Sage.

Bond, M. H. (1996). Chinese values. In M. H. Bond (Ed.), *The handbook of Chinese psychology* (pp. 208–226). Hong Kong: Oxford University Press.

Bond, R., & Smith, P. B. (1996). Culture and conformity: A meta-analysis of studies using Asch's (1952b, 1956) Line Judgment task. *Psychological Bulletin, 119*, 111–137.

Boon, S. D., & Pasveer, K. A. (1999). Charting the topography of risky relationship experiences. *Personal Relationships, 6*, 317–336.

Bornstein, R. F. (1989). Exposure and affect: Overview and meta-analysis of research, 1968–1987. *Psychological Bulletin, 106*, 265–289.

Bornstein, R. F., & D'Agostino, P. R. (1992). Stimulus recognition and the mere exposure effect. *Journal of Personality and Social Psychology, 63*, 545–552.

Bornstein, R. F., & Pittman, T. S. (Eds.). (1992). *Perception without awareness: Cognitive, clinical, and social perspectives.* New York: Guilford.

Bothwell, R. K., Brigham, J. C., & Malpass, R. S. (1989). Cross-racial identification. *Personality and Social Psychology Bulletin, 15*, 19–26.

Bothwell, R. K., Deffenbacher, K. A., & Brigham, J. C. (1987). Correlation of eyewitness accuracy and confidence: Optimality hypothesis revisited. *Journal of Applied Psychology, 72*, 691–695.

Bouas, K. S., & Komorita, S. S. (1996). Group discussion and cooperation in social dilemmas. *Personality and Social Psychology Bulletin, 22*, 1144–1150.

Bower, G. H., & Hilgard, E. R. (1981). *Theories of learning* (15th ed.). Englewood Cliffs, NJ: Prentice Hall.

Bowlby, J. (1969). *Attachment and loss: Vol. 1. Attachment.* New York: Basic Books.

Bowlby, J. (1973). *Attachment and loss: Vol. 2. Separation: Anxiety and anger.* New York: Basic Books.

Bowlby, J. (1980). *Attachment and loss: Vol. 3. Loss.* New York: Basic Books.

Bradley, J. P., Nicol, A. A. M., Charbonneau, D., & Meyer, J. P. (2002). Personality correlates of leadership development in Canadian Forces officer candidates. *Canadian Journal of Behavioural Science, 34*, 92–103.

Bradshaw, R. H., Bubier, N. E., & Sullivan, M. (1994). The effects of age and gender on perceived facial attractiveness: A reply to McLellan and McKelvie. *Canadian Journal of Behavioral Science, 26*, 199–204.

Brandon, R., & Davies, C. (1973). *Wrongful imprisonment: Mistaken convictions and their consequences.* London: Allen & Unwin.

Branscombe, N. R., Owen, S., Garstka, T. A., & Coleman, J. (1996). Rape and accident counterfactuals: Who might have done otherwise and would it have changed the outcome? *Journal of Applied Social Psychology, 26*, 1042–1067.

Branscombe, N. R., & Wann, D. L. (1992). Role of identification with a group, arousal, categorization processes, and self-esteem in sports spectator aggression. *Human Relations, 45*, 1013–1033.

Branswell, B. (1998, June 1). Pain and pride. *Maclean's,* p. 21.

Brattesani, K. A., Weinstein, R. S., & Marshall, H. H. (1984). Student perceptions of differential teacher treatment as moderators of teacher expectation effects. *Journal of Educational Psychology, 76*, 236–247.

Breckler, S. J., & Wiggins, E. C. (1989). On defining attitude and attitude theory: Once more with feeling. In A. R. Pratkanis, S. J. Breckler, & A. G. Greenwald (Eds.), *Attitude structure and function* (pp. 407–427). Hillsdale, NJ: Erlbaum.

Brehm, J. W. (1956). Postdecision changes in the desirability of alternatives. *Journal of Abnormal and Social Psychology, 52*, 384–389.

Brehm, J. W. (1966). *A theory of psychological reactance.* New York: Academic Press.

Brehm, S. S., & Brehm, J. W. (1981). *Psychological reactance.* New York: Academic Press.

Brewer, M. B. (1979). In-group bias in the minimal intergroup situation: A cognitive-motivational analysis. *Psychological Bulletin, 86*, 307–324.

Brewer, M. B., & Brown, R. J. (1998). Intergroup relations. In D. Gilbert, S. Fiske, & G. Lindzey (Eds.), *The handbook of social psychology* (4th ed., Vol. 2, pp. 554–594). New York: McGraw-Hill.

Brewer, M. B., & Gardner, W. L. (1996). Who is this "we"? Levels of collective identity and self representations. *Journal of Personality and Social Psychology, 71*, 83–93.

Brewer, M. B., & Miller, N. (1984). Beyond the contact hypothesis: Theoretical perspectives on desegregation. In N. Miller & M. B. Brewer (Eds.), *Groups in contact: The psychology of desegregation* (pp. 281–302). New York: Academic Press.

Bridges, F. S., & Coady, N. P. (1996). Affiliation, urban size, urgency, and cost of responses to lost letters. *Psychological Reports, 79*, 775–780.

Brigham, J. C. (1980). Limiting conditions of the "physical attractiveness stereotype": Attributions about divorce. *Journal of Research in Personality, 14*, 365–375.

Brislin, R. (1993). *Understanding culture's influence on behavior.* Fort Worth, TX: Harcourt Brace.

Brock, P., Fisher, R. P., & Cutler, B. L. (1999). Examining the cognitive interview in a double-test paradigm. *Psychology, Crime and Law, 5*, 29–45.

Brock, T. C., Edelman, S., Edwards, S., & Schuck, J. (1965). Seven studies of performance expectancy as a determinant of actual performance. *Journal of Experimental Social Psychology, 1*, 295–310.

Brook, A. S., Starzyk, K. B., & Quinsey, V. L. (2001). The relationship between testosterone and aggression: a meta-analysis. *Aggression and Violent Behavior, 6*, 579–599.

Brophy, J. E. (1983). Research on the self-fulfilling prophecy and teacher expectations. *Journal of Educational Psychology, 75*, 631–661.

Brown, J. D. (1990). Evaluating one's abilities: Shortcuts and stumbling blocks on the road to self-knowledge. *Journal of Experimental Social Psychology, 26*, 149–167.

Brown, J. D., & Rogers, R. J. (1991). Self-serving attributions: The role of physiological arousal. *Personality and Social Psychology Bulletin, 17*, 501–506.

Brown, R. (1965). *Social psychology.* New York: Free Press.

Brown, R. (1986). *Social psychology: The second edition.* New York: Free Press.

Brown, W. M., & Moore, C. (2000). Is prospective altruist-detection an evolved solution to the adaptive problem of subtle cheating in cooperative ventures? Supportive evidence using the Wason selection task. *Evolution and Human Behavior, 21*, 25–37.

Brunstein, J., & Gollwitzer, P. (1996). Effects of failure on subsequent performance: The importance of self-defining goals. *Journal of Personality and Social Psychology, 70*, 395–407.

Buck, R. (1984). *The communication of emotion.* New York: Guilford Press.

Buckhout, R. (1974). Eyewitness testimony. *Scientific American, 231*, 23–31.

Buckle, L., Gallup, G. G., & Rodd, Z. A. (1996). Marriage as a reproductive contract: Patterns of marriage, divorce and remarriage. *Ethology and Sociobiology, 17*, 363–377.

Buehler, R., & Griffin, D. (1994). Change-of-meaning effects in conformity and dissent: Observing construal processes over time. *Journal of Personality and Social Psychology, 67,* 984–996.

Buehler, R., & McFarland, C. (2001). Intensity bias in affective forecasting: The role of temporal focus. *Personality and Social Psychology Bulletin, 27,* 1480–1493.

Bui, K-V. T., Peplau, L. A., & Hill, C. T. (1996). Testing the Rusbult Model of relationship committment and stability in a 15-year study of hetereosexual couples. *Personality and Social Psychology Bulletin, 22,* 1244–1257.

Burger, J. M. (1981). Motivational biases in the attribution of responsibility for an accident: A meta-analysis of the defensive-attribution hypothesis. *Psychological Bulletin, 90,* 496–512.

Burger, J. M. (1986). Increasing compliance by improving the deal: The that's-not-all technique. *Journal of Personality and Social Psychology, 51,* 277–283.

Burger, J. M. (1992). *Desire for control: Personality, social, and clinical perspectives.* New York: Plenum.

Burger, J. M. (1999). The foot-in-the-door compliance procedure: A multiple-process analysis and review. *Personality and Social Psychology Review, 3,* 303–325.

Burgess, M., Enzle, M. E., & Morry, M. (2000). The social psychological power of photography: Can the image-freezing machine make something out of nothing? *European Journal of Social Psychology, 30,* 595–612.

Burgoon, M. (1993). Interpersonal expectations, expectancy violations, and emotional communication. *Journal of Language and Social Psychology, 12,* 30–48.

Burhans, K. K., & Dweck, C. S. (1995). Helplessness in early childhood: The role of contingent worth. *Child Development, 66,* 1719–1738.

Burke, R.J., & Greenglass, E. R. (1990). Type A Behavior and non-work activities. *Personality and Individual Differences, 11,* 945–952.

Burleson, B. R., & Samter, W. (1996). Similarity in the communication skills of young adults: Foundations of attraction, friendship, and relationship satisfaction. *Communication Reports, 9,* 127–139.

Burns, J. M. (1978). *Leadership.* New York: Harper Torchbooks.

Burnstein, E., Crandall, C., & Kitayama, S. (1994). Some neo-Darwinian decision rules for altruism: Weighing cues for inclusive fitness as a function of the biological importance of the decision. *Journal of Personality and Social Psychology, 67,* 773–789.

Burnstein, E., & Sentis, K. (1981). Attitude polarization in groups. In R. E. Petty, T. M. Ostrom, & T. C. Brock (Eds.), *Cognitive responses in persuasion* (pp. 197–216). Hillsdale, NJ: Erlbaum.

Burnstein, E., & Vinokur, A. (1977). Persuasive argumentation and social comparison as determinants of attitude polarization. *Journal of Experimental Social Psychology, 13,* 315–332.

Burnstein, E., & Worchel, P. (1962). Arbitrariness of frustration and its consequences for aggression in a social situation. *Journal of Personality, 30,* 528–540.

Burt, M. R. (1980). Cultural myths and supports for rape. *Journal of Personality and Social Psychology, 38,* 217–230.

Bushman, B. J., Baumeister, R. F., & Stack, A. D. (1999). Catharsis, aggression, and persuasive influence: Self fulfilling or self-defeating prophecies? *Journal of Personality and Social Psychology, 76,* 367–376.

Bushman, B. J., & Bonacci, A. M. (2002). Violence and sex impair memory for television ads. *Journal of Applied Psychology, 87,* 557–564.

Bushman, B. J., & Stack, A. D. (1996). Forbidden fruit versus tainted fruit: Effects of warning labels on attraction to television violence. *Journal of Experimental Psychology: Applied, 2,* 207–226.

Buss, D. (1994). *The evolution of desire.* New York: Basic Books.

Buss, D. (1996). The evolutionary psychology of human social strategies. In E. T. Higgins & A. W. Kruglanski (Eds.), *Social psychology: Handbook of basic principles* (pp. 3–38). New York: Guilford.

Buss, D. (1996). Sexual conflict: Evolutionary insights into feminism and the "battle of the sexes." In D. Buss & N. Malamuth (Eds.), *Sex, power, conflict: Evolutionary and feminist perspectives* (pp. 296–318). New York: Oxford University Press.

Buss, D. M. (1985). Human mate selection. *American Scientist, 73,* 47–51.

Buss, D. M. (1988a). The evolution of human intrasexual competition. *Journal of Personality and Social Psychology, 54,* 616–628.

Buss, D. M. (1988b). Love acts: The evolutionary biology of love. In R. J. Sternberg & M. L. Barnes (Eds.), *The psychology of love* (pp. 110–118). New Haven, CT: Yale University Press.

Buss, D. M. (1989). Sex differences in human mate preferences: Evolutionary hypotheses tested in 37 cultures. *Behavioral and Brain Sciences, 12,* 1–49.

Buss, D. M. (1999). *Evolutionary psychology: The new science of the mind.* Needham Heights, MA: Allyn & Bacon.

Buss, D. M., Abbott, M., Angleitner, A., Biaggio, A., Blanco-Villasenor, A., Bruchon-Schweitzer, M., Ch'u, H., Czapinski, J., Deraad, B., Ekehammar, B., El Lohamy, N., Fioravanti, M., Georgas, J., Gjerde, P., Guttman, R., Hazan, F., Iwawaki, S., Janakiramaiah, N., Khosroshani, F., Kreitler, S., Lachenicht, L., Lee, M., Liik, K., Little, B., Mika, S., Moadel-Shahid, M., Moane, G., Montero, M., Mundy-Castle, A. C., Niit, T., Nsenduluka, E., Pienkowski, R., Pirttila-Backman, A., Ponce de Leon, J., Rousseau, J., Runco, M., Safir, M. P., Samuels, C., Sanitioso, R., Serpell, R., Smid, N., Spencer, C., Tadinac, M., Todorova, E. N., Troland, K., Van Den Brande, L., Van Heck, G., Van Langenhove, L., & Yang, K. (1990). International preferences in selecting mates: A study of 37 cultures. *Journal of Cross-Cultural Psychology, 21,* 5–47.

Buss, D. M., & Barnes, M. (1986). Preferences in human mate selection. *Journal of Personality and Social Psychology, 50,* 559–570.

Buss, D. M., & Kenrick, D. T. (1998). Evolutionary social psychology. In D. Gilbert, S. Fiske, & G. Lindzey (Eds.), *The handbook of social psychology* (4th ed., Vol. 2, pp. 982–1026). New York: Random House.

Buss, D. M., & Schmitt, D. P. (1993). Sexual strategies theory: An evolutionary perspective on human mating. *Psychological Bulletin, 100,* 204–232.

Butler, D., & Geis, F. L. (1990). Nonverbal affect responses to male and female leaders: Implications for leadership evaluations. *Journal of Personality and Social Psychology, 58,* 48–59.

Button, C. M., & Collier, D. R. (1991, June). A comparison of people's concepts of love and romantic love. Paper presented at the Canadian Psychological Association Conference, Calgary, Alberta.

Buunk, B. P., & Prins, K. S. (1998). Loneliness, exchange orientation, and reciprocity in friendships. *Personal Relationships, 5,* 1–14.

Bybee, J., Luthar, S., Zigler, E., & Merisca, R. (1997). The fantasy, ideal, and ought selves: Content, relationship to mental health, and functions. *Social Cognition, 15,* 37–53.

Byrne, D., & Clore, G. L. (1970). A reinforcement model of evaluative processes. *Personality: An International Journal, 1,* 103–128.

Byrne, D., Clore, G. L., & Smeaton, G. (1986). The attraction hypothesis: Do similar attitudes affect anything? *Journal of Personality and Social Psychology, 51,* 1167–1170.

Byrne, D., & Nelson, D. (1965). Attraction as a linear function of positive reinforcement. *Journal of Personality and Social Psychology, 1,* 659–663.

Cacioppo, J. T. (1998). Somatic responses to psychological stress: The reactivity hypothesis. *Advances in Psychological Science, 2,* 87–112.

Cacioppo, J. T., Berntson, G. G., Malarkey, W. B., Kiecolt-Glaser, J. K., Sheridan, J. F., Poehlmann, K. M., Burleson, M. H., Ernst, J. M., Hawkley, L. C., & Glaser, R. (1998). Autonomic, neuroendocrine, and immune responses to psychological stress: The reactivity hypothesis. *Annals of the New York Academy of Sciences, 840,* 664–673.

Cacioppo, J. T., Marshall-Goodell, B. S., Tassinary, L. G., & Petty, R. E. (1992). Rudimentary determinants of attitudes: Classical conditioning is more effective when prior knowledge about the attitude stimulus is low than high. *Journal of Experimental Social Psychology, 28,* 207–233.

Cacioppo, J. T., Petty, R. E., Feinstein, J., & Jarvis, B. (1996). Dispositional differences in cognitive motivation: The life and times of individuals low versus high in need for cognition. *Psychological Bulletin, 119,* 197–253.

Cadinu, M. R., & Rothbart, M. (1996). Self-anchoring and differentiation processes in minimal group setting. *Journal of Personality and Social Psychology, 70,* 661–677.

Calder, B. J., & Staw, B. M. (1975). Self-perception of intrinsic and extrinsic motivation. *Journal of Personality and Social Psych-ology, 31,* 599–605.

Calhoun, J. B. (1973). Death squared: The explosive growth and demise of a mouse population. *Proceedings of the Royal Society of Medicine, 66,* 80–88.

Cameron, J. E. (1999). Social identity and the pursuit of possible selves: Implications for the psychological well-being of university students. *Group Dynamics: Theory, Research & Practice, 3,* 179–189.

Cameron, J. J., Ross, M., & Holmes, J. G. (2002). Loving the one you hurt: Positive effects of recounting a transgression against an intimate partner. *Journal of Experimental Social Psychology, 38,* 307–314.

Cameron, K. (2000). Student threats in the aftermath of the Taber and Littleton school shootings: How seriously do we take them? *Psynopsis,* Fall, 13.

Campbell, B., Schellenberg, E.G., & Senn, C.Y. (1997). Evaluating measures of contemporary sexism. *Psychology of Women Quarterly, 21,* 89–102.

Campbell, D. T., & Stanley, J. C. (1967). *Experimental and quasi-experimental designs for research.* Chicago: Rand McNally.

Campbell, J. D. (1986). Similarity and uniqueness: The effects of attribute type, relevance, and individual differences in self-esteem and depression. *Journal of Personality and Social Psych-ology, 50,* 281–294.

Campbell, J. D. (1990). Self-esteem and clarity of the self-concept. *Journal of Personality and Social Psychology, 59,* 538–549.

Campbell, J. D., Assanand, S., & DiPaula, A. (2000). Structural features of the self-concept and adjustment. In A. Tesser, R. B. Felson, & J. M. Suls (Eds.). *Psychological perspectives on self and identity* (pp. 67–87). Washington, D.C.: American Psychological Association.

Campbell, J. D., & Fairey, P. J. (1989). Informational and normative routes to conformity: The effect of faction size as a function of norm extremity and attention to the stimulus. *Journal of Personality and Social Psychology, 57,* 457–468.

Campbell, J. D., Fairey, P. J., & Fehr, B. (1986). Better than me or better than thee? Reactions to intrapersonal and interpersonal performance feedback. *Journal of Personality, 54,* 479–493.

Campbell, J. D., & Fehr, B. (1990). Self-esteem and perceptions of conveyed impressions: Is negative affectivity associated with greater realism? *Journal of Personality and Social Psychology, 58,* 122–133.

Campbell, J. D., Trapnell, P. D., Heine, S. J., Katz, I. M., Lavallee, L. F., & Lehman, D. R. (1996). "Self-concept clarity: Measurement, personality correlates, and cultural boundaries": Correction. *Journal of Personality and Social Psychology, 70,* 141–156.

Cannon, W. B. (1942). "Voodoo" death. *American Anthropologist, 44,* 169–181.

Cantor, J. (1994). Confronting children's fright responses to mass media. In D. Zillmann, J. Bryant, & Aletha C. Huston (Eds.), *Media, children, and the family: Social scientific, psychodynamic, and clinical perspectives* (pp. 139–150). Hillsdale, NJ: Erlbaum.

Cantor, N., & Kihlstrom, J. F. (1987). *Personality and social intelligence.* Englewood Cliffs, NJ: Prentice Hall.

Cantril, H. (1940). *The invasion from Mars: A study in the psychology of panic.* New York: Harper & Row.

Caplin, E. (1999, September). *Remarks to the Canadian Club.* www.cic.gc.ca/english/press/speech/canclub-e.html.

Caporael, L. R., & Brewer, M. B. (2000). Metatheories, evolution, and psychology: Once more with feeling. *Psychological Inquiry, 11,* 23–26.

Carli, L. L. (1999). Cognitive reconstruction, hindsight, and reactions to victims and perpetrators. *Personality and Social Psychology Bulletin, 25,* 966–979.

Carli, L. L., & Eagly, A. H. (1999). Gender effects on social influence and emergent leadership. In G. N. Powell (Ed.), *Handbook of gender and work* (pp. 203–222). Thousand Oaks, CA: Sage.

Carlsmith, J. M., & Anderson, C. A. (1979). Ambient temperature and the occurrence of collective violence: A new analysis. *Journal of Personality and Social Psychology, 37,* 337–344.

Carlson, M., Charlin, V., & Miller, N. (1988). Positive mood and helping behavior: A test of six hypotheses. *Journal of Personality and Social Psychology, 55,* 211–229.

Carlson, M., & Miller, N. (1987). Explanation of the relationship between negative mood and helping. *Psychological Bulletin, 102,* 91–108.

Carlston, D. E., & Skowronski, J. J. (1994). Savings in the relearning of trait information as evidence of spontaneous inference generation. *Journal of Personality and Social Psychology, 66,* 840–856.

Carnevale, P. J. (1986). Strategic choice in mediation. *Negotiation Journal, 2,* 41–56.

Carpenter, S. (2000, December). Why do "they all look alike"? *Monitor on Psychology,* pp. 44–45.

Carroll, J. M., & Russell, J. A. (1996). Do facial expressions signal specific emotions? Judging emotion from the face in context. *Journal of Personality and Social Psychology, 70,* 205–218.

Cartwright, D., & Zander, A. (Eds.). (1968). *Group dynamics: Research and theory* (3rd ed.). New York: Harper & Row.

Carver, C. S., Harris, S. D., Lehman, J. M., Durel, L. A., Antoni, M. H., Spencer, S. M., & Pozo-Kaderman, C. (2000). How important is the perception of personal control? Studies of early stage breast cancer patients. *Personality and Social Psychology Bulletin, 26,* 139–149.

Carver, C. S., & Scheier, M. F. (1981). *Attention and self-regulation: A control-theory approach to human behavior.* New York: Springer-Verlag.

Carver, C. S., & Scheier, M. F. (1998). *On the self-regulation of behavior.* New York: Cambridge University Press.

Cate, R. M., & Lloyd, S. A. (1992). *Courtship.* Newbury Park, CA: Sage.

Cervone, D., & Peake, P. (1986). Anchoring, efficacy, and action: The influence of judgmental heuristics on self-efficacy judgments and behavior. *Journal of Personality and Social Psych-ology, 50,* 492–501.

Chaiken, S. (1980). Heuristic versus systematic information processing and the use of source versus message cues in persuasion. *Journal of Personality and Social Psychology, 39,* 752–766.

Chaiken, S. (1987). The heuristic model of persuasion. In M. P. Zanna, J. M. Olson, & C. P. Herman (Eds.), *Social influence: The Ontario Symposium* (Vol. 5, pp. 3–39). Hillsdale, NJ: Erlbaum.

Chaiken, S., & Baldwin, M. W. (1981). Affective–cognitive consistency and the effect of salient behavioral information on the self perception of attitudes. *Journal of Personality and Social Psychology, 41,* 1–12.

Chaiken, S., Liberman, A., & Eagly, A. H. (1989). Heuristic and systematic information processing within and beyond the persuasion context. In J. S. Uleman & J. A. Bargh (Eds.), *Unintended thought* (pp. 212–252). New York: Guilford Press.

Chaiken, S., & Maheswaran, D. (1994). Heuristic processing can bias systematic processing: Effects of source and credibility, argument ambiguity, and task importance on attitude judgment. *Journal of Personality and Social Psychology, 66,* 466–473.

Chaiken, S., Wood, W., & Eagly, A. H. (1996). Principles of persuasion. In E. T. Higgins & A. W. Kruglanski (Eds.), *Social psychology: Handbook of basic principles* (pp. 702–742). New York: Guilford.

Chang, C., & Chen, J. (1995). Effects of different motivation strategies on reducing social loafing. *Chinese Journal of Psychology, 37,* 71–81.

Chapman, G. B., & Bornstein, B. H. (1996). The more you ask for, the more you get: Anchoring in personal injury verdicts. *Applied Cognitive Psychology, 10,* 519–540.

Chassin, L., Presson, C. G., & Sherman, S. J. (1990). Social psychological contributions to the understanding and prevention of adolescent cigarette smoking. *Personality and Social Psychology Bulletin, 16,* 133–151.

Chemers, M. M. (2000). Leadership research and theory: A functional integration. *Group Dynamics: Theory, Research, and Practice, 4,* 27–43.

Chemers, M. M., Watson, C. B., & May, S. T. (2000). Dispositional affect and leadership effectiveness: A comparison of self-esteem, optimism, and efficacy. *Personality and Social Psychology Bulletin, 26,* 267–277.

Chen, S., & Andersen, S. M. (1999). Relationships from the past in the present: Significant-other representations and transference in interpersonal life. In M. P. Zanna (Ed.), *Advances in experimental social psychology* (Vol. 31, pp. 123–190). San Diego, CA: Academic Press.

Chen, S., & Chaiken, S. (1999). The heuristic-systematic model in its broader context. In S. Chaiken & Y. Trope (Eds.), *Dual-process theories in social psychology* (pp. 73–96). New York: Guilford Press.

Cheryan, S. & Bodenhausen, G. V. (2000). When positive stereotypes threaten intellectual performance: The psychological hazards of "model minority" status. *Psychological Science,* Vol 11(5), 399–402.

Cheung, S. F., Chan, D. K., & Wong, Z. S. (1999). Reexamining the theory of planned behavior in understanding wastepaper recycling. *Environment and Behavior, 31,* 587–612.

Chipperfield, J. G., Perry, R. P., & Menec, V. H. (1999). Primary and secondary control-enhancing strategies: Implications for health in later life. *Journal of Aging and Health, 11,* 517–539.

Chiu, C., Morris, M. W., Hong, Y., & Menon, T. (2000). Motivated cultural cognition: The impact of implicit cultural theories on dispositional attribution varies as a function of need for closure. *Journal of Personality and Social Psychology, 78,* 247–259.

Choi, I., & Nisbett, R. E. (1998). Situational salience and cultural differences in the correspondence bias and in the actor-observer bias. *Personality and Social Psychology Bulletin, 24,* 949–960.

Christensen, L. (1988). Deception in psychological research: When is its use justified? *Personality and Social Psychology Bulletin, 14,* 664–675.

Christian, J. J. (1963). The pathology of overpopulation. *Military Medicine, 128,* 571–603.

Christianson, S. (1992). Emotional stress and eyewitness memory: A critical review. *Psychological Bulletin, 112,* 284–309.

Christophersen, E. R., & Gyulay, J. E. (1981). Parental compliance with car seat usage: A positive approach with long term follow-up. *Journal of Pediatric Psychology, 6,* 301–312.

Church, A. H. (1993). Estimating the effects of incentives on mail survey response rates: A meta-analysis. *Public Opinion Quarterly, 57,* 62–79.

Cialdini, R. B. (1993). *Influence: Science and practice.* (3rd ed.). New York: HarperCollins.

Cialdini, R. B., Brown, S. L., Lewis, B. P., Luce, C., & Neuberg, S. L. (1997). Reinterpreting the empathy-altruism relationship: When one into one equals oneness. *Journal of Personality and Social Psychology, 73,* 481–494.

Cialdini, R. B., Cacioppo, J., Basset, R., & Miller, J. (1978). Low-ball procedure for producing compliance: Commitment then cost. *Journal of Personality and Social Psychology, 36,* 463–476.

Cialdini, R. B., Darby, B. L., & Vincent, J. E. (1973). Transgression and altruism: A case for hedonism. *Journal of Experimental Social Psychology, 9,* 502–516.

Cialdini, R. B., & Fultz, J. (1990). Interpreting the negative mood-helping literature via "mega"-analysis: A contrary view, *Psychological Bulletin, 107,* 210–214.

Cialdini, R. B., Green, B. L., & Rusch, A. J. (1992). When tactical pronouncements of change become real change: The case of reciprocal persuasion. *Journal of Personality and Social Psychology, 63,* 30–40.

Cialdini, R. B., Kallgren, C. A., & Reno, R. R. (1991). A focus theory of normative conduct: A theoretical refinement and reevaluation of the role of norms in human behavior. In M. P. Zanna (Ed.), *Advances in experimental social psychology* (Vol. 24, pp. 201–234). San Diego, CA: Academic Press.

Cialdini, R. B., Reno, R. R., & Kallgren, C. A. (1990). A focus theory of normative conduct: Recycling the concept of norms to reduce littering in public places. *Journal of Personality and Social Psychology, 58,* 1015–1026.

Cialdini, R. B., Schaller, M., Houlihan, D., Arps, K., Fultz, J., & Beaman, A. L. (1987). Empathy-based helping: Is it selflessly or selfishly motivated? *Journal of Personality and Social Psychology, 52,* 749–758.

Cialdini, R. B., & Trost, M. R. (1998). Social influence: Social norms, conformity, and compliance. In D. Gilbert, S. Fiske, & G. Lindzey (Eds.), *The handbook of social psychology* (4th ed., Vol. 2, pp. 151–192). New York: McGraw-Hill.

Cialdini, R. B., Trost, M. R., & Newsom, J. T. (1995). Preference for consistency: The development of a valid measure and the discovery of surprising behavioral implications. *Journal of Personality and Social Psychology, 69,* 318–328.

Cialdini, R. B., Vincent, J. E., Lewis, S. K., Catalan, J., Wheeler, D., & Darby, B. L. (1975). Reciprocal concessions procedure for inducing compliance: The door-in-the-face technique. *Journal of Personality and Social Psychology, 31,* 206–215.

Clark, K., & Clark, M. (1947). Racial identification and preference in Negro children. In T. M. Newcomb & E. L. Hartley (Eds.), *Readings in social psychology* (pp. 169–178). New York: Holt.

Clark, M. S. (1984). Record keeping in two types of relationships. *Journal of Personality and Social Psychology, 47,* 549–577.

Clark, M. S. (1986). Evidence of the effectiveness of manipulations of communal and exchange relationships. *Personality and Social Psychology Bulletin, 12,* 414–425.

Clark, M. S., & Chrisman, K. (1994). Resource allocation in intimate relationships: Trying to make sense of a confusing literature. In M. J. Lerner & G. Mikula (Eds.), *Entitlement and the Affectional Bond: Justice in Close Relationships* (pp. 65–88). New York: Plenum.

Clark, M. S., & Grote, N. K. (1998). Why aren't indices of relationship costs always negatively related to indices of relationship quality? *Personality and Social Psychology Review, 2,* 2–17.

Clark, M. S., & Isen, A. M. (1982). Toward understanding the relationship between feeling states and social behavior. In A. H. Hastorf &

A. M. Isen (Eds.), *Cognitive social psychology* (pp. 73–108). New York: Elsevier.

Clark, M. S., & Mills, J. (1979). Interpersonal attraction in exchange and communal relationships. *Journal of Personality and Social Psychology, 37,* 12–24.

Clark, M. S., & Mills, J. (1993). The difference between communal and exchange relationships: What it is and is not. *Personality and Social Psychology Bulletin, 19,* 684–691.

Clark, M. S., Mills, J., & Corcoran, D. M. (1989). Keeping track of needs and inputs of friends and strangers. *Personality and Social Psychology Bulletin, 15,* 533–542.

Clark, M. S., & Pataki, S. P. (1995). Interpersonal processes influencing attraction and relationships. In A. Tesser (Ed.), *Advanced Social Psychology* (pp. 282–331). New York: McGraw-Hill.

Clark, M. S., & Waddell, B. (1985). Perception of exploitation in communal and exchange relationships. *Journal of Social and Personal Relationships, 2,* 403–413.

Clark, R., Anderson, N. B., Clark, V. R., & Williams, D. R. (1999). Racism as a stressor for African Americans. *American Psychologist, 54,* 805–816.

Clark, R. D., III, & Maass, A. (1988). The role of social categorization and perceived source credibility in minority influence. *European Journal of Social Psychology, 18,* 347–364.

Clark, R. D., III, & Word, L. E. (1972). Why don't bystanders help? Because of ambiguity? *Journal of Personality and Social Psychology, 24,* 392–400.

Clarke, V. A., Lovegrove, H., Williams, A., & Macpherson, M. (2000). Unrealistic optimism and the Health Belief Model. *Journal of Behavioral Medicine, 23,* 367–376.

Clément, R., Noels, K. A., & Deneault, B. (2001). Interethnic contact, identity, and psychological adjustment: The mediating and moderating roles of communication. *Sex Roles, 57,* 559–577.

Cline, V. B., Croft, R. G., & Courrier, S. (1973). Desensitization of children to television violence. *Journal of Personality and Social Psychology, 27,* 360–365.

Coates, L. (1997). Causal attributions in sexual assault trial judgments. *Journal of Language and Social Psychology, 16,* 278–296.

Coats, E. (1998). www.stolaf.edu/cgi-bin/mailarchivesearch. pl?directory=/home/www/people/huff/SPSP&listname=archive98

Cohen, S. (1978). Environmental load and the allocation of attention. In A. Baum, J. S. Singer, & S. Valins (Eds.), *Advances in environmental psychology* (Vol. 1, pp. 1–29). Hillsdale, NJ: Erlbaum.

Cohen, S. (1996). Psychological stress, immunity, and upper respiratory infections. *Current Directions in Psychological Science, 5,* 86–90.

Cohen, S., Evans, G. W., Krantz, D. S., & Stokols, D. (1980). Physiological, motivational, and cognitive effects of aircraft noise on children. *American Psychologist, 35,* 231–243.

Cohen, S., Evans, G. W., Krantz, D. S., Stokols, D., & Kelly, S. (1981). Aircraft noise and children: Longitudinal and cross-sectional evidence on adaptation to noise and the effectiveness of noise abatement. *Journal of Personality and Social Psychology, 40,* 331–345.

Cohen, S., Frank, E., Doyle, W. J., Skoner, D. P., Rabin, B. S., & Gwaltney, J. M., Jr. (1998). Type of stressors that increase susceptibility to the common cold in healthy adults. *Health Psychology, 17* (3), 214–223.

Cohen, S., Glass, D. C., & Singer, J. E. (1973). Apartment noise, auditory discrimination, and reading ability in children. *Journal of Experimental Social Psychology, 9,* 407–422.

Cohen, S., & Herbert, T. B. (1996). Health psychology: Psychological factors and physical disease from the perspective of human psychoneuroimmunology. *Annual Review of Psychology, 47,* 113–142.

Cohen, S., Tyrrell, D. A. J., & Smith, A. P. (1991). Psychological stress in humans and susceptibility to the common cold. *New England Journal of Medicine, 325,* 606–612.

Cohen, S., Tyrrell, D. A. J., & Smith, A. P. (1993). Negative life events, perceived stress, negative affect, and susceptibility to the common cold. *Journal of Personality and Social Psychology, 64,* 131–140.

Cohen, S., & Wills, T. A. (1985). Stress, social support, and buffering. *Psychological Bulletin, 98,* 310–357.

Cohn, L. D. & Adler, N. E. (1992). Female and male perceptions of ideal body shapes. *Psychology of Women Quarterly, 16,* 69–79.

Collins, N. L., & Read, S. J. (1990). Adult attachment, working models, and relationship quality in dating couples. *Journal of Personality and Social Psychology, 58,* 644–663.

Collins, R. L. (1996). For better or worse: The impact of upward social comparison on self-evaluations. *Psychological Bulletin, 119,* 51–69.

Collins, W. A., & Sroufe, L. A. (1999). Capacity for intimate relationships: A developmental construction. In W. Furman, C. Feiring, & B. B. Brown (Eds.), *Contemporary perspectives on adolescent romantic relationships.* New York: Cambridge University Press.

Coltrane, S., Archer, D., & Aronson, E. (1986). The social-psychological foundations of successful energy conservation programs. *Energy Policy, 14,* 133–148.

Condon, J. W., & Crano, W. D. (1988). Inferred evaluation and the relation between attitude similarity and interpersonal attraction. *Journal of Personality and Social Psychology, 54,* 789–797.

Conway, M., & Dubé, L. (2002). Humor in persuasion on threatening topics: Effectiveness is a function of audience sex role orientation. *Personality and Social Psychology Bulletin, 28,* 863–873.

Conway, M., & Ross, M. (1984). Getting what you want by revising what you had. *Journal of Personality and Social Psychology, 47,* 738–748.

Cook, S. W. (1984). Cooperative interaction in multiethnic contexts. In N. Miller & M. Brewer (Eds.), *Groups in contact: The psychology of desegregation.* New York: Academic Press.

Cook, S. W. (1985). Experimenting on social issues: The case of school desegregation. *American Psychologist, 40,* 452–460.

Cooley, C. H. (1902). *Human nature and social order.* New York: Scribner's.

Cooper, J. (1998). Unwanted consequences and the self: In search of the motivation for dissonance reduction. In E. Harmon-Jones & J. S. Mills, *Cognitive dissonance theory: Revival with revisions and controversies.* Washington, DC: American Psychological Association.

Cooper, W. H., Gallupe, R. B., Pollard, S., & Cadsby, J. (1998). Some liberating effects of anonymous electronic brainstorming. *Small Group Research, 29,* 147–178.

Cordova, D. I., & Lepper, M. R. (1996). Intrinsic motivation and the process of learning: Beneficial effects of contextualization, personalization, and choice. *Journal of Educational Psychology, 88,* 715–730.

Corenblum, B., & Annis, R. (1993). Development of racial identity in minority and majority children: An affect discrepancy model. *Canadian Journal of Behavioral Science, 25,* 499–521.

Corenblum, B., Annis, R., & Young, S. (1996). Effects of own group success or failure on judgments of task performance by children of different ethnicities. *European Journal of Social Psychology, 26,* 777–798.

Corenblum, B., & Stephan, W. G. (2001). White fears and Native apprehensions: An integrated threat theory approach to intergroup attitudes. *Canadian Journal of Behavioural Science, 33,* 251–268.

Corneil, W., Beaton, R., Murphy, S., Johnson, C., & Pike, K. (1999). Exposure to traumatic incidents and prevalence of post-traumatic stress symptomatology in urban firefighters in two countries. *Journal of Occupational Health Psychology, 4,* 131–141.

Cosmides, L., & Tooby, J. (1992). Cognitive adaptations for social exchange. In J. H. Barkow, L. Cosmides, & J. Tooby (Eds.), *The adapted mind: Evolutionary psychology and the generation of culture* (pp. 163–228). New York: Oxford University Press.

Cotton, J. L. (1981). *Ambient temperature and violent crime.* Paper presented at the meeting of the Midwestern Psychological Association, Chicago.

Cotton, J. L. (1986). Ambient temperature and violent crime. *Journal of Applied Social Psychology, 16,* 786–801.

Cottrell, N. B. (1968). Performance in the presence of other human beings: Mere presence, audience, and affiliation effects. In E. C. Simmel, R. A. Hoppe, & G. A. Milton (Eds.), *Social facilitation and imitative behavior* (pp. 91–110). Boston: Allyn & Bacon.

Cottrell, N. B., Wack, K. L., Sekerak, G. J., & Rittle, R. (1968). Social facilitation in dominant responses by the presence of an audience and the mere presence of others. *Journal of Personality and Social Psychology, 9,* 245–250.

Courneya, K. S., & Friedenreich, C. M. (1997). Determinants of exercise during colorectal cancer treatment: An application of the theory of planned behavior. *Oncology Nursing Forum, 24,* 1715–1723.

Courneya, K. S., & Friedenreich, C. M. (1999). Utility of the theory of planned behavior for understanding exercise during breast cancer treatment. *Psycho-Oncology, 8,* 112–122.

Craig, W. M., & Pepler, D. J. (1997). Observations of bullying and victimization in the school yard. *Canadian Journal of School Psychology, 13,* 41–60.

Cramer, K. M., Nickels, J. B., & Gural, D. M. (1997). Uncertainty of outcomes, prediction of failure, and lack of control as factors explaining perceived helplessness. *Journal of Social Behavior and Personality, 12,* 611–630.

Crandall, C. S., D'Anello, S., Sakalli, N., Lazarus, E., Wieczorkowska, G., & Feather, N. T. (2001). An attribution-value model of prejudice: Anti-fat attitudes in six nations. *Personality and Social Psychology Bulletin, 27,* 30–37.

Crandall, C. S., Eshelman, A., & O'Brien, L. (2002). Social norms and the expression and suppression of prejudice: The struggle for internalization. *Journal of Personality and Social Psychology, 82,* 359–378.

Crawford, C., & Krebs, D. L. (1998). *Handbook of evolutionary psychology.* Mahwah, NJ: Erlbaum.

Crites, S. L., Jr., Fabrigar, L. R., & Petty, R. E. (1994). Measuring the affective and cognitive properties of attitudes: Conceptual and methodological issues. *Personality and Social Psychology Bulletin, 20,* 619–634.

Crombag, H. F. M., Wagenaar, W. A., & Van Koppen, P. J. (1996). Crashing memories and the problem of "source monitoring." *Applied Cognitive Psychology, 10,* 95–104.

Cross, S. E. (1995). Self-construals, coping, and stress in cross-cultural adaptation. *Journal of Cross-Cultural Psychology, 26,* 673–697.

Cross, S. E., Bacon, P. L., & Morris, M. L. (2000). The relational-interdependent self-construal and relationships. *Journal of Personality and Social Psychology, 78,* 791–808.

Cross, S. E., & Madson, L. (1997). Elaboration of models of the self: Reply to Baumeister and Sommer (1997) and Martin and Rubble (1997). *Psychological Bulletin, 122,* 51–55.

Cross, S. E., & Madson, L. (1997). Models of the self: Self-construals and gender. *Psychological Bulletin, 122,* 5–37.

Crowley, A. E., & Hoyer, W. D. (1994). An integrative framework for understanding two-sided persuasion. *Journal of Consumer Research, 20,* 561–574.

Croyle, R. T., & Jemmott, J. B., III. (1990). Psychological reactions to risk factor testing. In J. A. Skelton & R. T. Croyle (Eds.), *The mental representation of health and illness* (pp. 121–157). New York: Springer-Verlag.

Crutchfield, R. A. (1955). Conformity and character. *American Psychologist, 10,* 191–198.

Csikszentmihalyi, M., & Figurski, T. J. (1982). Self-awareness and aversive experience in everyday life. *Journal of Personality, 50,* 15–28.

Cunningham, M. R. (1986). Measuring the physical in physical attractiveness: Quasi-experiments on the sociobiology of female facial beauty. *Journal of Personality and Social Psychology, 50,* 925–935.

Cunningham, M. R., Barbee, A. R., & Pike, C. L. (1990). What do women want? Facialmetric assessment of multiple motives in the perception of male facial physical attractiveness. *Journal of Personality and Social Psychology, 59,* 61–72.

Cunningham, M. R., Roberts, A. R., Barbee, A. P., Druen, P. B., & Wu, C. (1995). "Their ideas of beauty are, on the whole, the same as ours": Consistency and variability in the cross-cultural perception of female physical attractiveness. *Journal of Personality and Social Psychology, 68,* 261–279.

Curtis, R. C., & Miller, K. (1986). Believing another likes or dislikes you: Behaviors making the beliefs come true. *Journal of Personality and Social Psychology, 51,* 284–290.

Cusumano, D. L., & Thompson, J. K. (1997). Body image and body shape ideals in magazines: Exposure, awareness, and internalization. *Sex Roles, 37,* 701–721

Czaczkes, B., & Ganzach, Y. (1996). The natural selection of prediction heuristics: Anchoring and adjustment versus representativeness. *Journal of Behavioral Decision Making, 9,* 125–139.

Dabbs, J. M., Carr, T. S., Frady, R. L., & Riad, J. K. (1995). Testosterone, crime, and misbehavior among 692 male prison inmates. *Personality and Individual Differences, 18,* 627–633.

Dabbs, J. M., Jr., Ruback, R. B., Frady, R. L., Hopper, C. H., & Sgoutas, D. S. (1988). Saliva testosterone and criminal violence among women. *Personality and Individual Differences, 7,* 269–275.

Dahl, D. W., Gorn, G. J., & Weinberg, C. B. (1998). Condom carrying behavior among college students. *Canadian Journal of Public Health, 89,* 368–370.

D'Angelo, A. M. (2000, February 14). No charges in bridge fall. *North Shore News.* www.nsnews.com/issues00/w021400/ 02110001.html

Darke, P. R., Chaiken, S., Bohner, G., Einwiller, S., Erb, H., & Hazlewood, J. D. (1998). Accuracy motivation, consensus information, and the law of large numbers: Effects on attitude judgment in the absence of argumentation. *Personality and Social Psychology Bulletin, 24,* 1205–1215.

Darley, J. M. (1995). Constructive and destructive obedience: A taxonomy of principal-agent relationships. *Journal of Social Issues, 51,* 125–154.

Darley, J. M., & Akert, R. M. (1993). *Biographical interpretation: The influence of later events in life on the meaning of and memory for earlier events.* Unpublished manuscript, Princeton University.

Darley, J. M., & Batson, C. D. (1973). From Jerusalem to Jericho: A study of situational and dispositional variables in helping behavior. *Journal of Personality and Social Psychology, 27,* 100–108.

Darley, J. M., & Fazio, R. H. (1980). Expectancy confirmation processes arising in the social interaction sequence. *American Psychologist, 35,* 867–881.

Darley, J. M., & Latané, B. (1968). Bystander intervention in emergencies: Diffusion of responsibility. *Journal of Personality and Social Psychology, 8,* 377–383.

Darwin, C. (1872). *The expression of emotions in man and animals*. London: John Murray.

Darwin, C. R. (1859). *The origin of species*. London: John Murray.

Davidson, A. R., & Jaccard, J. J. (1979). Variables that moderate the attitude behavior relation: Results of a longitudinal survey. *Journal of Personality and Social Psychology, 37*, 1364–1376.

Davies, M. F. (1997). Belief persistence after evidential discrediting: The impact of generated versus provided explanations on the likelihood of discredited outcomes. *Journal of Experimental Social Psychology, 33*, 561–578.

Davies, R. (1988). *The lyre of Orpheus*. New York: Penguin Books.

Davies, R. (1991). *Murther and walking spirits*. Toronto: McClelland and Stewart.

Davis, C., Lehman, D., Cohen Silver, R., Wortman, C., & Ellard, J. (1996). Self-blame following a traumatic event: The role of perceived avoidability. *Personality and Social Psychology Bulletin, 22*, 557–567.

Davis, C. G., & Lehman, D. R. (1995). Counterfactual thinking and coping with traumatic life events. In N. J. Roese & J. M. Olson (Eds.), *What might have been: The social psychology of counterfactual thinking* (pp. 353–374). Mahwah, NJ: Erlbaum.

Davis, C. G., Lehman, D. R., Wortman, C. B., Silver, R. C., & Thompson, S. C. (1995). The undoing of traumatic life events. *Personality and Social Psychology Bulletin, 21*, 109–124.

Davis, D. D., & Harless, D. W. (1996). Group versus individual performance in a price-searching experiment. *Organizational Behavior and Human Decision Processes, 66*, 215–227.

Davis, K. E., & Jones, E. E. (1960). Changes in interpersonal perception as a means of reducing cognitive dissonance. *Journal of Abnormal and Social Psychology, 61*, 402–410.

Davis, M. H., & Stephan, W. G. (1980). Attributions for exam performance. *Journal of Applied Social Psychology, 10*, 235–248.

Davison, K. P., Pennebaker, J. W., & Dickerson, S. S. (2000). Who talks? The social psychology of illness support groups. *American Psychologist, 55*, 205–217.

Davitz, J. (1952). The effects of previous training on post-frustration behavior. *Journal of Abnormal and Social Psychology, 47*, 309–315.

Dawes, R. M. (1980). Social dilemmas. *Annual Review of Psychology, 31*, 169–193.

Dawes, R. M. (1998). Behavioral decision making and judgment. In D. Gilbert, S. Fiske, & G. Lindzey (Eds.), *The handbook of social psychology* (4th ed., Vol. 1, pp. 497–548). New York: McGraw Hill.

De Dreu, C. K. W., Harinck, F., & Van Vianen, A. E. M. (1999). Conflict and performance in groups and organizations. In C. L. Cooper & I. T. Robertson (Eds.), *International review of industrial and organizational psychology* (Vol. 14, pp. 369–414). Chichester, England: American Ethnological Press.

De Dreu, C. K. W., Weingart, L. R., & Kwon, S. (2000). Influence of social motives on integrative negotiation: A meta-analytic review and test of two theories. *Journal of Personality and Social Psychology, 78*, 889–905.

De Waal, F. (1996). *Good natured: The origins of right and wrong in humans and other animals*. Cambridge, MA: Harvard University Press.

Dean, K. E., & Malamuth N. M. (1997). Characteristics of men who aggress sexually and of men who imagine aggressing: Risk and moderating variables. *Journal of Personality and Social Psychology, 72*, 499–455.

Deaux, K. (1993). Reconstructing social identity. *Personality and Social Psychology Bulletin, 19*, 4–12.

Deaux, K., & Emswiler, T. (1974). Explanations of successful performance of sex-linked tasks: What is skill for male is luck for the female. *Journal of Personality and Social Psychology, 29*, 80–85.

Deaux, K., & LaFrance, M. (1998). Gender. In D. T. Gilbert, S. T. Fiske, & G. Lindzey (Eds*.), The handbook of social psychology* (4th ed., Vol. 1, pp. 788–828). New York: McGraw-Hill.

DeBono, K. G., & Snyder, M. (1995). Acting on one's attitudes: The role of a history of choosing situations. *Personality and Social Psychology Bulletin, 21*, 629–636.

Deci, E. L., & Flaste, R. (1995). *Why we do what we do: The dynamics of personal autonomy*. New York: G. P. Putnam's Sons.

Deci, E. L., Koestner, R., & Ryan, R. M. (1999a). A meta-analytic review of experiments examining the effects of extrinsic rewards. *Psychological Bulletin, 125*, 627–668.

Deci, E. L., Koestner, R., & Ryan, R. M. (1999b). The undermining effect is a reality after all—extrinsic rewards, task interest, and self-determination: Reply to Eisenberger, Pierce, and Cameron (1999) and Lepper, Henderlong, and Gingras (1999). *Psychological Bulletin, 125*, 692–700.

Deci, E. L., & Ryan, R. M. (1985). *Intrinsic motivation and self-determination in human behavior*. New York: Plenum.

Deci, E. L., & Ryan, R. M. (Eds.). (2002). *Handbook of self-determination research*. Rochester, NY: University of Rochester Press.

DeJong, W., & Winsten, J. A. (1989). *Recommendations for future mass media campaigns to prevent preteen and adolescent substance abuse*. Unpublished manuscript, Center for Health Communication, Harvard School of Public Health.

DeMarco, P. (1994, September 28). "Dear diary," *New York Times*, p. C2.

Dennett, D. C. (1991). *Consciousness explained*. Boston: Little, Brown.

DePaulo, B. M. (1994). Spotting lies: Can humans learn to do better? *Current Directions in Psychological Science, 3*, 83–86

DePaulo, B. M., & Friedman, H. S. (1998). Nonverbal communication. In D. Gilbert, S. Fiske, & G. Lindzey (Eds.), *The handbook of social psychology* (4th ed., Vol. 2, pp. 3–40). New York: McGraw Hill.

DePaulo, B. M., Kenny, D. A., Hoover, C. W., Webb, W., & Oliver, P. (1987). Accuracy of person perception: Do people know what kinds of impressions they convey? *Journal of Personality and Social Psychology, 52*, 303–315.

DePaulo, B. M., Lassiter, G. D., & Stone, J. I. (1983). Attentional determinants of success at detecting deception and truth. *Personality and Social Psychology Bulletin, 8*, 273–279.

DePaulo, B. M., & Pfeiffer, R. L. (1986). On-the-job experience and skill at detecting deception. *Journal of Applied Social Psychology, 16*, 249–267.

DePaulo, B. M., Stone, J. I., & Lassiter, G. D. (1985). Deceiving and detecting deceit. In B. R. Schlenker (Ed.), *The self and social life* (pp. 323–370). New York: McGraw-Hill.

Desmond, E. W. (1987, November 30). Out in the open. *Time*, pp. 80–90.

Desportes, J. P., & Lemaine, J. M. (1988). The sizes of human groups: An analysis of their distributions. In D. Canter, J. C. Jesuino, L. Soczka, & G. M. Stephenson (Eds.), *Environmental social psychology* (pp. 57–65). Dordrecht, Netherlands: Kluwer.

Deutsch, M. (1973). *The resolution of conflict: Constructive and destructive processes*. New Haven, CT: Yale University Press.

Deutsch, M. (1990). Cooperation, conflict, and justice. In S. A. Wheelan, E. A. Pepitone, & V. Abt (Eds.), *Advances in field theory* (pp. 149–164). Newbury Park, CA: Sage.

Deutsch, M. (1997). Comments on cooperation and prejudice reduction. At the symposium on: Reflections on 100 Years of Social Psychology, April 1997, Yosemite National Park, CA.

Deutsch, M., & Gerard, H. G. (1955). A study of normative and informational social influence upon individual judgment. *Journal of Abnormal and Social Psychology, 51*, 629–636.

Deutsch, M., & Krauss, R. M. (1960). The effect of threat upon interpersonal bargaining. *Journal of Abnormal and Social Psychology, 61,* 181–189.

Deutsch, M., & Krauss, R. M. (1962). Studies of interpersonal bargaining. *Journal of Conflict Resolution, 6,* 52–76.

Devine, P. (1998). Moving beyond attitude change in the study of dissonance-related processes. In E. Harmon-Jones & J. S. Mills, *Cognitive dissonance theory: Revival with revisions and controversies.* Washington, DC: American Psychological Association.

Devine, P. G. (1989a). Automatic and controlled processes in prejudice: The roles of stereotypes and personal beliefs. In A. R. Pratkanis, S. J. Breckler, & A. G. Greenwald (Eds.), *Attitude structure and function* (pp. 181–212). Hillsdale, NJ: Erlbaum.

Devine, P. G. (1989b). Stereotypes and prejudice: Their automatic and controlled components. *Journal of Personality and Social Psychology, 56,* 5–18.

Devine, P. G., & Monteith, M. J. (1999). Automaticity and control in stereotyping. In S. Chaiken & Y. Trope (Eds.), *Dual-process theories in social psychology* (pp. 339–360). New York: Guilford Press.

Dickerson, C., Thibodeau, R., Aronson, E., & Miller, D. (1992). Using cognitive dissonance to encourage water conservation. *Journal of Applied Social Psychology, 22,* 841–854.

Diener, E. (1980). Deindividuation: The absence of self-awareness and self-regulation in group members. In P. B. Paulus (Ed.), *Psychology of group influence* (pp. 209–242). Hillsdale, NJ: Erlbaum.

Diener, E., & Wallbom, M. (1976). Effects of self-awareness on antinormative behavior. *Journal of Research in Personality, 10,* 107–111.

Dienesch, R. M., & Liden, R. C. (1986). Leader-member exchange model of leadership: A critique and further development. *Academy of Management Review, 11,* 618–634.

Dijksterhuis, A., & van Knippenberg, A. (1996). The knife that cuts both ways: Facilitated and inhibited access to traits as a result of stereotype activation. *Journal of Experimental Social Psychology, 32,* 271–288.

Dillard, J. P. (1991). The current status of research on sequential-request compliance techniques. *Personality and Social Psychology Bulletin, 17,* 283–288.

Dion, C. (2000). *My story, my dream.* Toronto, ON: HarperCollins.

Dion, K., Berscheid, E., & Walster (Hatfield), E. (1972). What is beautiful is good. *Journal of Personality and Social Psychology, 24,* 285–290.

Dion, K., Pak, A., & Dion, K. (1990). Stereotyping physical attractiveness. *Journal of Cross Cultural Psychology, 21,* 158–179.

Dion, K. K. (2002). Cultural perspectives on facial attractiveness. In G. Rhodes (Ed.). *Facial attractiveness: Evolutionary, cognitive, and social perspectives* (pp. 239-259). Westport, CT: Ablex Publishing.

Dion, K. K., & Dion, K. L. (1996). Cultural perspectives on romantic love. *Personal Relationships, 3,* 5–17.

Dion, K. K., & Dion, K. L. (2001). Gender and relationships. In R. K. Unger (Ed.). *Handbook of the psychology of women and gender* (pp. 256–271). New York: John Wiley & Sons.

Dion, K. K., & Dion, K. L. (2001). Gender and cultural adaptation in immigrant families. *Journal of Social Issues, 57,* 511–521.

Dion, K. L. (1985). Social distance norms in Canada: Effects of stimulus characteristics and dogmatism. *International Journal of Psychology, 20,* 743–749.

Dion, K. L. (1999). Ms. as a title of address. In H. Tierney (Ed.). *Women's studies encyclopedia: Revised and expanded edition* (Vol. 2, G–P, pp. 954–957). Westport, CT: Greenwood Press.

Dion, K. L. (2000). Canada. In A. E. Kazdin (Ed.). *Encyclopedia of psychology* (Vol. 2, pp. 5–12). Washington, D.C.: American Psychological Association & New York: Oxford University Press.

Dion, K. L. (2001). Immigrants' perceptions of discrimination in Toronto: The Housing New Canadians project. *Journal of Social Issues, 57,* 523–539.

Dion, K. L. (2002). The social psychology of perceived prejudice and discrimination. *Canadian Psychology, 43,* 1–10.

Dion, K. L. (in press). Prejudice, racism, and discrimination. In M. J. Lerner (Ed.). *Comprehensive handbook of psychology. Vol. 5. Personality and social psychology.* New York: John Wiley & Sons.

Dion, K. L., & Dion, K. K. (1973). Correlates of romantic love. *Journal of Consulting and Clinical Psychology, 41,* 51–56.

Dion, K. L., & Dion, K. K. (1987). Belief in a just world and physical attractiveness stereotyping. *Journal of Personality and Social Psychology, 52,* 775–780.

Dion, K. L., & Dion, K. K. (1993). Gender and ethnocultural comparisons in styles of love. *Psychology of Women Quarterly, 17,* 463–473.

Dion, K. L., Dion, K. K., & Pak, A. W. (1992). Personality-based hardiness as a buffer for discrimination-related stress in members of Toronto's Chinese community. *Canadian Journal of Behavioural Science, 24,* 517–536.

Dion, K. L., & Kawakami, K. (1996). Ethnicity and perceived discrimination in Toronto: Another look at the personal/group discrimination discrepancy. *Canadian Journal of Behavioural Science, 28,* 203–213.

Dion, K. L., & Schuller, R. A. (1991). The Ms. stereotype: Its generality and its relation to managerial and marital status stereotypes. *Canadian Journal of Behavioural Science, 23,* 25–40.

Dix, T. (1993). Attributing dispositions to children: An interactional analysis of attribution in socialization. *Personality and Social Psychology Bulletin, 19,* 633–643.

Dodge, M. K. (1984). Learning to care: Developing prosocial behavior among one- and two-year-olds in group settings. *Journal of Research and Development in Education, 17,* 26–30.

Dodson, C. S., Johnson, M. K., & Schooler, J. W. (1997). The verbal overshadowing effect: Why descriptions impair face recognition. *Memory and Cognition, 25,* 129–139.

Doi, T. (1988). An experimental investigation of the validity of the characteristic space theory and the measurement of social motivation. *Japanese Journal of Experimental Social Psychology, 27,* 139–148.

Dolin, D. J., & Booth-Butterfield, S. (1995). Foot-in-the-door and cancer prevention. *Health Communication, 7,* 55–66.

Dollard, J. (1938). Hostility and fear in social life. *Social Forces, 17,* 15–26.

Dollard, J., Doob, L., Miller, N., Mowrer, O. H., & Sears, R. R. (1939). *Frustration and aggression.* New Haven, CT: Yale University Press.

Donakowski, D. W., & Esses, V. M. (1996). Native Canadians, First Nations, and Aboriginals: The effect of labels on attitudes toward Native peoples. *Canadian Journal of Behavioural Science, 28,* 86–91.

Donnerstein, E. (1980). Aggressive erotica and violence against women. *Journal of Personality and Social Psychology, 39,* 269–272.

Donnerstein, E., & Berkowitz, L. (1981). Victim reactions in aggressive erotic films as a factor in violence against women. *Journal of Personality and Social Psychology, 41,* 710–724.

Donnerstein, E., & Donnerstein, M. (1976). Research in the control of interracial aggression. In R. G. Green & E. C. O'Neal (Eds.), *Perspectives on aggression* (pp. 133–168). New York: Academic Press.

Donnerstein, E., & Linz, D. (1994). Sexual violence in the mass media. In M. Costanzo, S. Oskamp et al. (Eds.), *Violence and the law: Claremont symposium on applied social psychology, Vol. 7* (pp. 9–36). Thousand Oaks, CA: Sage.

Donnerstein, E., Slaby, R. G., & Eron, L.D. (1994). The mass media and youth aggression. In L. D. Eron, J. H. Gentry, & P. Schlegel (Eds.),

Reason to hope: A psychological perspective on violence and youth (pp. 219-250). Washington, DC: APA Press.

Dotto, L. (2000, February/March). The seven second solution. *Equinox*, pp. 32–43.

Double deception [Letter to the editor]. (2000, April 1). *Winnipeg Free Press*.

Dougherty, M. R. P., Gettys, C. F., & Ogden, E. E. (1999). MINERVA-DM: A memory process model of judgments of likelihood. *Psychological Review, 106,* 180–209.

Dovidio, J. F. (1984). Helping behavior and altruism: An empirical and conceptual overview. In L. Berkowitz (Ed.), *Advances in experimental social psychology* (Vol. 17, pp. 361–427). New York: Academic Press.

Dovidio, J. F., Evans, N., & Tyler, R. B. (1986). Racial stereotypes: The contents of their cognitive representations. *Journal of Experimental Social Psychology, 22,* 22–37.

Dovidio, J. F., & Gaertner, S. L. (1996). Affirmative action, unintentional racial biases, and intergroup relations. *Journal of Social Issues, 52,* 51–75.

Dovidio, J. F., Piliavin, J. A., Gaertner, S. I., Schroeder, D. A., & Clark, R. D. III. (1991). The arousal: cost-reward model and the process of intervention. In M. S. Clark (Ed.), *Review of personality and social psychology* (Vol. 12, pp. 86–118). Newbury Park, CA: Sage.

Dowd, M. (2000, September 13). Grilled over rats. *New York Times,* p. A31.

Drigotas, S. M., Safstrom, C. A., & Gentilia, T. (1999). An investment model of dating infidelity. *Journal of Personality and Social Psychology, 77,* 509–524.

Dryer, D. C., & Horowitz, L. M. (1997). When do opposites attract? Interpersonal complementarity versus similarity. *Journal of Personality and Social Psychology, 72,* 592–603.

Duck, J., Hogg, M., & Terry, D. (1995). Me, us and them: Political identification and the third-person effect in the 1993 Australian federal election. *European Journal of Social Psychology, 25,* 195–215.

Dunn, D. S., & Wilson, T. D. (1990). When the stakes are high: A limit to the illusion of control effect. *Social Cognition, 8,* 305–323.

Dunning, D., Griffin, D. W., Milojkovic, J., & Ross, L. (1990). The overconfidence effect in social prediction. *Journal of Personality and Social Psychology, 58,* 568–581.

Dunning, D., & Hayes, A. F. (1996). Evidence of egocentric comparison in social judgment. *Journal of Personality and Social Psychology, 71,* 213–229.

Dunning, D., & Stern, L. B. (1994). Distinguishing accurate from inaccurate eyewitness identifications via inquiries about decision processes. *Journal of Personality and Social Psychology, 67,* 818–835.

Dutton, D. G. (1995). *The domestic assault of women: Psychological and criminal justice perspectives.* Vancouver, BC: UBC Press.

Dutton, D. G., & Aron, A. P. (1974). Some evidence for heightened sexual attraction under conditions of high anxiety. *Journal of Personality and Social Psychology, 30,* 510–517.

Dutton, D. G., & Hart, S. D. (1992a). Evidence for long-term, specific effects of childhood abuse and neglect on criminal behavior in men. *International Journal of Offender Therapy and Comparative Criminology, 36,* 129–137.

Dutton, D. G., & Hart, S. D. (1992b). Risk markers for family violence in a federally incarcerated population. *International Journal of Law and Psychiatry, 15,* 101–112.

Duval, S., & Wicklund, R. A. (1972). *A theory of objective self-awareness.* New York: Academic Press.

Dweck, C. S. (1999). *Self-theories: Their role in motivation, personality, and development.* Bristol, PA: Taylor & Francis.

Eagly, A. H. (1987). *Sex differences in social behavior: A social-role interpretation.* Hillsdale, NJ: Erlbaum.

Eagly, A. H., Ashmore, R. D., Makhijani, M. G., & Longo, L. C. (1991). What is beautiful is good, but … : A meta-analytic review of research on the physical attractiveness stereotype. *Psychological Bulletin, 110,* 109–128.

Eagly, A. H., & Carli, L. L. (1981). Sex of researchers and sex-typed communications as determinants of sex differences in influenceability: A meta-analysis of social influence studies. *Psychological Bulletin, 90,* 1–20.

Eagly, A. H., & Chaiken, S. (1975). An attribution analysis of communicator characteristics on opinion change: The case of communicator attractiveness. *Journal of Personality and Social Psychology, 32,* 136–244.

Eagly, A. H., & Chaiken, S. (1993). *The psychology of attitudes.* Fort Worth, TX: Harcourt Brace Jovanovich.

Eagly, A. H., & Chaiken, S. (1998). Attitude structure and function. In D. T. Gilbert, S. T. Fiske, & G. Lindzey (Eds.), *The handbook of social psychology* (4th ed., Vol. 1, pp. 269–322). New York: McGraw-Hill.

Eagly, A. H., & Crowley, M. (1986). Gender and helping behavior: A meta-analytic review of the social psychological literature. *Psychological Bulletin, 100,* 283–308.

Eagly, A. H., & Johnson, B. T. (1990). Gender and leadership style: A meta-analysis. *Psychological Bulletin, 108,* 233–256.

Eagly, A. H., & Karau, S. J. (1991). Gender and the emergence of leaders: A meta-analysis. *Journal of Personality and Social Psychology, 60,* 685–710.

Eagly, A. H., Karau, S. J., & Makhijani, M. G. (1995). Gender and the effectiveness of leaders: A meta-analysis. *Psychological Bulletin, 117,* 125–145.

Eagly, A. H., Makhijani, M. G., & Klonsky, B. G. (1992). Gender and the evaluation of leaders: A meta-analysis. *Psychological Bulletin, 111,* 3–22.

Eargle, A., Guerra, N., & Tolan, P. (1994). Preventing aggression in inner-city children: Small group training to change cognitions, social skills, and behavior. *Journal of Child and Adolescent Group Therapy, 4,* 229–242.

Eberman, C., & McKelvie, S. J. (2002). Vividness of visual memory and source memory for audio and text. *Applied Cognitive Psychology, 16,* 87–95.

Eden, D., & Zuk, Y. (1995). Seasickness as a self-fulfilling prophecy: Raising self-efficacy to boost performance at sea. *Journal of Applied Psychology, 80,* 628–635.

Edmonds, S. (2000, May 5). Judge agrees anthrax vaccine unsafe. *The Canadian Press.* www.canoe.ca/Health0005/05_ anthrax.html (July 26, 2000).

Edwards, D. J. A. (1975). Returning a dropped object: Effect of response cost and number of potential helpers. *Journal of Social Psychology, 97,* 169–171.

Edwards, K. (1990). The interplay of affect and cognition in attitude formation and change. *Journal of Personality and Social Psychology, 59,* 202–216.

Edwards, K., & Smith, E. (1996). A disconfirmation bias in the evaluation of arguments. *Journal of Personality and Social Psychology, 71,* 5–24.

Edwards, K., & von Hippel, W. (1995). Hearts and minds: The priority of affective versus cognitive factors in person perception. *Personality and Social Psychology Bulletin, 21,* 996–1011.

Eibl-Eibesfeldt, I. (1963). Aggressive behavior and ritualized fighting in animals. In J. H. Masserman (Ed.), *Science and psychoanalysis: Vol. 6. Violence and war.* New York: Grune & Stratton.

Eisenberg, N., Guthrie, I. K., Murphy, B. C., Shepard, S. A., Cumberland, A., & Carlo, G. (1999). Consistency and development of prosocial dispositions: A longitudinal study. *Child Development, 70,* 1360–1372.

Eiser, J. R., & Ford, N. (1995). Sexual relationships on holidays: A case of situational disinhibition. *Journal of Social and Personal Relationships, 12,* 323–339.

Ekman, P. (1965). Communication through nonverbal behavior: A source of information about an interpersonal relationship. In S. S. Tomkins & C. E. (Eds.), *Affect, cognition, and personality* (pp. 390–442). New York: Springer-Verlag.

Ekman, P. (1992). *Telling lies: Clues to deceit in the marketplace, politics, and marriage* (rev. ed.). New York: Norton.

Ekman, P. (1993). Facial expression and emotion. *American Psychologist, 48,* 384–392.

Ekman, P. (1994). Strong evidence for universals in facial expressions: A reply to Russell's mistaken critique. *Psychological Bulletin, 115,* 268–287.

Ekman, P., & Davidson, R. J. (Eds.) (1994). *The Nature of Emotion: Fundamental Questions.* New York: Oxford University Press.

Ekman, P., & Friesen, W. V. (1969). The repertoire of nonverbal behavior: Categories, origins, usage, and coding. *Semiotica, 1,* 49–98.

Ekman, P., & Friesen, W. V. (1971). Constants across cultures in the face and emotion. *Journal of Personality and Social Psychology, 17,* 124–129.

Ekman, P., & Friesen, W. V. (1975). *Unmasking the face.* Englewood Cliffs, NJ: Prentice Hall.

Ekman, P., & Friesen, W. V. (1986). A new pan-cultural facial expression of emotion. *Motivation and Emotion, 10,* 159–168.

Ekman, P., Friesen, W. V., & Ellsworth, P. (1982a). Does the face provide accurate information? In P. Ekman (Ed.), *Emotion in the human face* (pp. 56–97). Cambridge, England: Cambridge University Press.

Ekman, P., Friesen, W. V., & Ellsworth, P. (1982b). What are the similarities and differences in facial behavior across cultures? In P. Ekman (Ed.), *Emotion in the human face* (pp. 128–143). Cambridge, England: Cambridge University Press.

Ekman, P., Friesen, W. V., O'Sullivan, M., Chan, A., Diacoyanni-Tarlatzis, I., Heider, K., Krause, R., LeCompre, W. A., Pitcairn, T., Ricci-Bitti, P. E., Scherer, K., Tomita, M., & Tzavras, A. (1987). Universals and cultural differences in the judgments of facial expressions of emotions. *Journal of Personality and Social Psychology, 53,* 712–717.

Ekman, P., & O'Sullivan, M. (1988). The role of context in interpreting facial expression: Comment on Russell & Fehr (1987). *Journal of Experimental Psychology: General, 117,* 86–88.

Ekman, P., O' Sullivan, M., & Frank, M. G. (1999). A few can catch a liar. *Psychological Science, 10,* 263–266.

Ekos Research Associates and Canadian Policy Research Networks. (1999, April). *Analysis of Volunteering: Results from the 1997 National Survey of Giving, Volunteering and Participating.* Applied Research Branch: Strategic Policy, Human Resources Canada.

Elig, T. W., & Frieze, I. H. (1979). Measuring causal attributions for success and failure. *Journal of Personality and Social Psychology, 38,* 270–277.

Elliot, G. R., & Eisdorfer, C. (1982). *Stress and human health: Analysis and implications of research.* New York: Springer.

Elliot, J. (1977). The power and pathology of prejudice. In P. Zimbardo & F. Ruch (Eds.), *Psychology and life,* 9th ed., diamond printing. Glenview, IL: Scott Foresman.

Ellsworth, P. C., & Mauro, R. (1998). Psychology and law. In D. Gilbert, S. Fiske, & G. Lindzey (Eds.), *The handbook of social psychology* (4th ed., Vol. 2, pp. 684–732). New York: McGraw Hill.

Elvers, A. (2002). Katy Simons: An exceptional spirit. *University of Winnipeg Journal,* Fall/Winter, 13.

Emery, R. E., & Wyer, M. M. (1987). Divorce mediation. *American Psychologist, 42,* 472–480.

Endo, Y., Heine, S. J., & Lehman, D. R. (2000). Culture and positive illusions in close relationships: How my relationships are better than yours. *Personality and Social Psychology Bulletin, 26,* 1571–1586.

Eraker, S. A., & Politser, P. (1988). How decisions are reached: Physicians and the patient. In J. Dowie & A. S. Elstein (Eds.), *Professional judgment: A reader in clinical decision making* (pp. 379–394). Cambridge, England: Cambridge University Press.

Erdelyi, M. H. (1994). Hypnotic hypermnesia: The empty set of hypermnesia. *International Journal of Clinical and Experimental Hypnosis, 42,* 379–390.

Eron, L. D. (1982). Parent-child interaction, television violence, and aggression of children. *American Psychologist, 37,* 197–211.

Eron, L. D. (1987). The development of aggressive behavior from the perspective of a developing behaviorism. *American Psychologist, 42,* 425–442.

Eron, L. D., Huesmann, L. R., Lefkowitz, M. M., & Walder, L. O. (1996). Does television violence cause aggression? In: D. F. Greenberg (Ed.), *Criminal careers, 2,* 311–321. The international library of criminology, criminal justice, and penology. Aldershot, England: Dartmouth Publishing Company Limited.

Esser, J. K. (1998). Alive and well after 25 years: A review of groupthink research. *Organizational Behavior and Human Decision Processes, 73,* 116–141.

Esses, V., Jackson, L., & Armstrong, T. (1998). Intergroup competition and attitudes toward immigrants and immigration: An instrumental model of group conflict. *Journal of Social Issues, 54,* 699–724.

Esses, V. M., & Dovidio, J. F. (2002). The role of emotions in determining willingness to engage in intergroup contact. *Personality and Social Psychology Bulletin, 28,* 1202–1214.

Esses, V. M., Dovidio, J. F., Jackson, L., & Armstrong, T. L. (2001). The immigration dilemma: The role of perceived group competition, ethnic prejudice, and national identity. *Journal of Social Issues, 57,* 389–412.

Esses, V. M., & Gardner, R. C. (1996). Multiculturalism in Canada: Context and current status. *Canadian Journal of Behavioural Science, 28,* 145–152.

Esses, V. M., Haddock, G., & Zanna, M. P. (1993). Values, stereotypes, and emotions as determinants of intergroup attitudes. In D.M. Mackie & D.L. Hamilton (Eds.), *Affect, cognition, and stereotyping: Interactive processes in group perception.* San Diego, California: Academic Press, Inc.

Esses, V. M., & Zanna, M. P. (1995). Mood and the expression of ethnic stereotypes. *Journal of Personality and Social Psychology, 69,* 1052–1068.

Estabrooks, P., & Carron, A. V. (1999). The influence of the group with elderly exercisers. *Small Group Research, 30,* 438–452.

Ester, C. (1995). Responding to school violence: Understanding today for tomorrow. *Canadian Journal of School Psychology, 11,* 108–116.

Estrada-Hollenbeck, M., & Heatherton, T. F. (1998). Avoiding and alleviating guilt through prosocial behavior. In J. Bybee (Ed.), *Guilt and children* (pp. 215–231). San Diego, CA: Academic Press.

Evans, G. W. (2000). Environmental stress and health. In A. Baum, T. Revenson, & J. E. Singer (Eds.), *Handbook of health psychology.* Mahwah, NJ: Erlbaum.

Evans, G. W., Bullinger, M., & Hygge, S. (1998). Chronic noise exposure and physiological response: A prospective study of children living under environmental stress. *Psychological Science, 9,* 75–77.

Evans, G. W., Lepore, S. J., & Schroeder, A. (1996). The role of interior design elements in human responses to crowding. *Journal of Personality and Social Psychology, 70,* 41–46.

Evans, W. N., Neville, D., & Graham, J. D. (1991). General deterrence of drunk driving: Evaluation of American policies. *Risk Analysis, 11,* 279–289.

Ezekiel, R. S. (1995). *The racist mind: Portraits of American neo-Nazis and Klansmen.* New York: Viking.

Fabrigar, L. R., & Petty, R. E. (1999). The role of affective and cognitive bases of attitudes in susceptibility to affectively and cognitively based persuasion. *Personality and Social Psychology Bulletin, 25,* 363–381.

Fabrigar, L. R., Priester, J. R., Petty, R. E., & Wegener, D. T. (1998). The impact of attitude accessibility on elaboration of persuasive messages. *Personality and Social Psychology Bulletin, 24,* 339–352.

Falck, R., & Craig, R. (1988). Classroom-oriented, primary prevention programming for drug abuse. *Journal of Psychoactive Drugs, 20,* 403–408.

Fazio, R. H. (1989). On the power and functionality of attitudes: The role of attitude accessibility. In A. R. Pratkanis, S. J. Breckler, & A. G. Greenwald (Eds.), *Attitude structure and function* (pp. 153–179). Hillsdale, NJ: Erlbaum.

Fazio, R. H. (1990). Multiple processes by which attitudes guide behavior: The MODE model as an integrative framework. In M. P. Zanna (Ed.), *Advances in experimental social psychology* (Vol. 23, pp. 75–109). San Diego: Academic Press.

Fazio, R. H. (1995). Attitudes as object-evaluation associations: Determinants, consequences, and correlates of attitude accessibility. In R. Petty, & J. Krosnick (Eds.), *Attitude strength: Antecedents and consequences* (pp. 247–282). Hillsdale, NJ: Erlbaum.

Fazio, R. H. (2000). Accessible attitudes as tools for object appraisal: Their costs and benefits. In G. Maio & J. Olson (Eds.), *Why we evaluate: Functions of attitudes* (pp. 1–36). Mahwah, NJ: Erlbaum.

Fazio, R. H., Jackson, J. R., Dunton, B. C., & Williams, C. J. (1995). Variability in automatic activation as an unobstrusive measure of racial attitudes: A bona fide pipeline? *Journal of Personality and Social Psychology, 69,* 1013–1027.

Fazio, R. H., Ledbetter, J. E., & Towles-Schwen, T. (2000). On the costs of accessible attitudes: Detecting that the attitude object has changed. *Journal of Personality and Social Psychology, 78,* 197–210.

Fazio, R. H., Powell, M. C., & Williams, C. J. (1989). The role of attitude accessibility in the attitude-to-behavior process. *Journal of Consumer Research, 16,* 280–288.

Feeney, J. A., & Noller, P. (1990). Attachment style as a predictor of adult romantic relationships. *Journal of Personality and Social Psychology, 58,* 281–291.

Fehr, B. (1988). Prototype analysis of the concepts of love and commitment. *Journal of Personality and Social Psychology, 55,* 557–579.

Fehr, B. (1993). How do I love thee? Let me consult my prototype. In S. Duck (Ed.), *Individuals in relationships* (pp. 87–120). Newbury Park, CA: Sage.

Fehr, B. (1994). Prototype-based assessment of laypeople's views of love. *Personal Relationships, 1,* 309–331.

Fehr, B. (1996). *Friendship processes.* Thousand Oaks, CA: Sage Publications.

Fehr, B. (2001). The status of theory and research on love and commitment. In G. Fletcher and M. Clark (Eds.). *The Blackwell handbook of social psychology: Interpersonal processes.* Oxford, UK: Blackwell Publishers.

Fehr, B., & Baldwin, M. (1996). Prototype and script analyses of laypeople's knowledge of anger. In G. J. O. Fletcher, and J. Fitness (Eds.), *Knowledge structures in close relationships: A social psychological approach.* Mahwah, New Jersey: Lawrence Erlbaum Associates, Publishers.

Fehr, B., Baldwin, M., Collins, L., Patterson, S., & Benditt, R. (1999). Anger in close relationships: An interpersonal script analysis. *Personality and Social Psychology Bulletin, 25,* 299–312.

Fehr, B., & Broughton, R. (2001). Gender and personality differences in conceptions of love: An interpersonal theory analysis.

Fehr, B., & Russell, J. A. (1991). The concept of love viewed from a prototype perspective. *Journal of Personality and Social Psychology, 60,* 425–438.

Fein, S., McCloskey, A. L., & Tomlinson, T. M. (1997). Can the jury disregard that information? The use of suspicion to reduce the prejudicial effects of pretrial publicity and inadmissable testimony. *Personality and Social Psychology Bulletin, 23,* 1215–1226.

Fein, S., & Spencer, S. J. (1997). Prejudice as self-image maintenance: Affirming the self through derogating others. *Journal of Personality and Social Psychology, 73,* 31–44.

Feingold, A. (1990). Gender differences in effects of physical attractiveness on romantic attraction: A comparison across five research paradigms. *Journal of Personality and Social Psychology, 59,* 981–993.

Feingold, A. (1992a). Good-looking people are not what we think. *Psychological Bulletin, 111,* 304–341.

Feldman-Summers, S., & Kiesler, S. B. (1974). Those who are number two try harder: The effect of sex on attributions of causality. *Journal of Personality and Social Psychology, 38,* 846–855.

Felmlee, D. H. (1995). Fatal attractions: Affection and dissatisfaction in intimate relationships. *Journal of Social and Personal Relationships, 12,* 295–311.

Feshbach, N. (1978, March). *Empathy training: A field study in affective education.* Paper presented at the meetings of the American Educational Research Association, Toronto, Ontario, Canada.

Feshbach, N., & Feshbach, S. (1969). The relationship between empathy and aggression in two age groups. *Developmental Psychology, 1,* 102–107.

Feshbach, N. D. (1989). Empathy training and prosocial behavior. In J. Groebel & R. A. Hinde (Eds.), *Aggression and war: Their biological and social bases* (pp. 101–111). New York: Cambridge University Press.

Feshbach, N. D. (1997). Empathy: The formative years—implications for clinical practice. In A. C. Bohart & L. S. Greenberg (Eds.), *Empathy reconsidered: New directions in psychotherapy* (pp. 33–59). Washington, DC: American Psychological Association.

Feshbach, N. D., & Cohen, S. (1988). Training affect comprehension in young children: An experimental evaluation. *Journal of Applied Developmental Psychology, 9,* 201–210.

Feshbach, S. (1971). Dynamics and morality of violence and aggression: Some psychological considerations. *American Psychologist, 26,* 281–292.

Festinger, L. (1954). A theory of social comparison processes. *Human Relations, 7,* 117–140.

Festinger, L. (1957). *A theory of cognitive dissonance.* Stanford, CA: Stanford University Press.

Festinger, L., & Carlsmith, J. M. (1959). Cognitive consequences of forced compliance. *Journal of Abnormal and Social Psychology, 58,* 203–211.

Festinger, L., & Maccoby, N. (1964). On resistance to persuasive communications. *Journal of Abnormal and Social Psychology, 68,* 359–366.

Festinger, L., Riecken, H. W., & Schachter, S. (1956). *When prophecy fails*. Minneapolis: University of Minnesota Press.

Festinger, L., Schachter, S., & Back, K. (1950). *Social pressures in informal groups: A study of human factors in housing*. New York: Harper & Bros.

Festinger, L., & Thibaut, J. (1951). Interpersonal communication in small groups. *Journal of Abnormal and Social Psychology, 46,* 92–99.

Fiedler, F. (1967). *A theory of leadership effectiveness*. New York: McGraw-Hill.

Fiedler, F. (1978). The contingency model and the dynamics of the leadership process. In L. Berkowitz (Ed.), *Advances in experimental social psychology* (Vol. 11, pp. 59–112). Orlando, FL: Academic Press.

Fiedler, K., Walther, E., & Nickel, S. (1999). Covariation-based attribution: On the ability to assess multiple covariations of an effect. *Personality and Social Psychology Bulletin, 25,* 607–622.

Fincham, F. D., & Bradbury, T. N. (1993). Marital satisfaction, depression, and attributions: A longitudinal analysis. *Journal of Personality and Social Psychology, 64,* 442–452.

Finger, K., & Pezdek, K. (1999). The effect of cognitive interview on face identification accuracy: Release from verbal overshadowing. *Journal of Applied Social Psychology, 84,* 340–348.

Finney, P. D. (1987). When consent information refers to risk and deception: Implications for social research. *Journal of Social Behavior and Personality, 2,* 37–48.

Fischer, W. F. (1963). Sharing in preschool children as a function of amount and type of reinforcement. *Genetic Psychology Monographs, 68,* 215–245.

Fischhoff, B. (1975). Hindsight foresight: The effect of outcome knowledge on judgment under uncertainty. *Journal of Experimental Psychology: Human Perception and Performance, 1,* 288–299.

Fishbein, M., & Ajzen, I. (1975). *Belief, attitude, intention, and behavior: An introduction to theory and research*. Reading, MA: Addison-Wesley.

Fishbein, M., Chan, D., O'Reilly, K., Schnell, D., Wood, R., Beeker, C., & Cohn, C. (1993). Factors influencing gay men's attitudes, subjective norms, and intentions with respect to performing sexual behaviors. *Journal of Applied Social Psychology, 23,* 417–438.

Fiske, A. P., Kitayama, S., Markus, H. R., & Nisbett, R. E. (1998). The cultural matrix of social psychology. In D. Gilbert, S. Fiske, & G. Lindzey (Eds.), *The handbook of social psychology* (4th ed., Vol 2, pp. 915–981). New York: McGraw Hill.

Fiske, S., & Depret, E. (1996). Control, interdependence, and power: Understanding social cognition in its social context. In W. Stroebe & M. Hewstone (Eds.), *European Review of Social Psychology, 7,* 31–61. New York: Wiley.

Fiske, S. T. (1989a). Examining the role of intent: Toward understanding its role in stereotyping and prejudice. In J. S. Uleman & J. A. Bargh (Eds.), *Unintended thought* (pp. 253–283). New York: Guilford.

Fiske, S. T. (1989b). *Interdependence and stereotyping: From the laboratory to the Supreme Court (and back)*. Invited address, American Psychological Association, New Orleans.

Fiske, S. T. (1993). Social cognition and social perception. *Annual Review of Psychology, 44,* 155–194.

Fiske, S. T., & Taylor, S. E. (1991). *Social cognition* (2nd ed.). New York: McGraw-Hill.

Flanagan, C. A., Bowes, J. M., Jonsson, B., Csapo, B., & Sheblanova, E. (1998). Ties that bind: Correlates of adolescents' civic commitments in seven countries. *Journal of Social Issues, 54,* 457–475.

Fletcher, G. J. O., & Ward, C. (1988). Attribution theory and processes: A cross-cultural perspective. In M. H. Bond (Ed.), *The Cross-Cultural Challenge to Social Psychology*. Newbury Park, CA: Sage.

Fletcher, J. F., & Chalmers, M. (1991). Attitudes of Canadians toward affirmative action: Opposition, value pluralism, and nonattitudes. *Political Behavior, 13,* 67–95.

Flowers, M. L. (1977). A lab test of some implications of Janis' groupthink hypothesis. *Journal of Personality and Social Psychology, 35,* 888–897.

Fong, G. T., Krantz, D. H., & Nisbett, R. E. (1986). The effects of statistical training on thinking about everyday problems. *Cognitive Psychology, 18,* 253–292.

Forgas, J. P., & Bower, G. H. (1987). Mood effects on person-perception judgments. *Journal of Personality and Social Psychology, 53,* 53–60.

Foster, M., & Matheson, K. (1999). Perceiving and responding to the personal/group discrimination discrepancy. *Personality and Social Psychology Bulletin, 25,* 1319–1329.

Foster, M. D., & Dion, K. L. (2001, June). Hardiness and responses to perceived discrimination: Buffer or denial? In K. L. Dion (Chair). *Social psychology of prejudice: Cognitive perspectives*. Symposium conducted at the American Psychological Association Convention, Toronto, Ontario.

Fox, J. (1980). Making decisions under the influence of memory. *Psychological Review, 87,* 190–211.

Frank, M. G., & Gilovich, T. (1988). The dark side of self and social perceptions: Black uniforms and aggression in professional sports. *Journal of Personality and Social Psychology, 54,* 74–85.

Frank, M. G., & Gilovich, T. (1989). Effect of memory perspective on retrospective causal attributions. *Journal of Personality and Social Psychology, 57,* 399–403.

Fredrickson, B. L., Roberts, T., Noll, S. M., Quinn, D. M., & Twenge, J. M. (1998). That swimsuit becomes you: Sex differences in self-objectification, restrained eating, and math performance. *Journal of Personality and Social Psychology, 75,* 269–284.

Freedman, D., Pisani, R., Purves, R., & Adhikari, A. (1991). *Statistics* (2nd ed.). New York: Norton.

Freedman, J. (1965). Long-term behavioral effects of cognitive dissonance. *Journal of Experimental and Social Psychology, 1,* 145–155.

Freedman, J. L., & Fraser, S. C. (1966). Compliance without pressure: The foot-in-the-door technique. *Journal of Personality and Social Psychology, 4,* 195–202.

Freedman, J. L., Martin, C. K., & Mota, V. L. (1998). Pretrial publicity: Effects of admonition and expressing pretrial opinions. *Legal and Criminological Psychology, 3,* 255–270.

Freud, S. (1930). *Civilization and its discontents* (Joan Riviere, Trans.). London: Hogarth Press.

Freud, S. (1933). *New introductory lectures on psycho-analysis*. New York: Norton.

Fried, C., & Aronson, E. (1995). Hypocrisy, misattribution, and dissonance reduction: A demonstration of dissonance in the absence of aversive consequences. *Personality and Social Psychology Bulletin, 21,* 925–933.

Friedkin, N. E. (1999). Choice shift and group polarization. *American Sociological Review, 64,* 856–875.

Friedman, H. S. (1993). Interpersonal expectations and the maintenance of health. In P. D. Blank (Ed.), *Interpersonal expectations: Theory, research, and applications* (pp. 179–193). New York: Cambridge University Press.

Friesen, W. V. (1972). *Cultural differences in facial expressions in a social situation: An experimental test of the concept of display rules.* Unpublished dissertation, University of California, San Francisco.

Frodi, A. (1975). The effect of exposure to weapons on aggressive behavior from a cross-cultural perspective. *International Journal of Psychology, 10,* 283–292.

Fu, G., Lee, K., Cameron, C. A., & Xu, F. (2001). Chinese and Canadian adults' categorization and evaluation of lie- and truth-telling about prosocial and antisocial behaviors. *Journal of Cross-Cultural Psychology, 32,* 720–727.

Fuller, T. D., Edwards, J. N., Vorakitphokatorn, S., & Sermsri, S. (1996). Chronic stress and psychological well-being: Evidence from Thailand on household crowding. *Social Science and Medicine, 42,* 265–280.

Funder, D. C., & Colvin, C. R. (1988). Friends and strangers: Acquaintanceship, agreement, and the accuracy of personality judgment. *Journal of Personality and Social Psychology, 55,* 149–158.

Furnham, A., & Gunter, B. (1984). Just world beliefs and attitudes toward the poor. *British Journal of Social Psychology, 23,* 265–269.

Fury, G., Carlson, E. A., & Sroufe, L. A. (1997). Children's representations of attachment relationships in family drawings. *Child Development, 68,* 1154–1164.

Gabriel, S., & Gardner, W. L. (1999). Are there "his" and "hers" types of interdependence? The implications of gender differences in collective versus relational interdependence for affect, behavior, and cognition. *Journal of Personality and Social Psychology, 77,* 642–655.

Gaertner, S. L., & Dovidio, J. F. (1986). The aversive form of racism. In J. F. Dovidio & S. L. Gaertner (Eds.), *Prejudice, discrimination, and racism: Theory and research* (pp. 61–89). New York: Academic Press.

Gagné, F. M., & Lydon, J. E. (2001). Mind-set and close relationships: When bias leads to (in)accurate predictions. *Journal of Personality and Social Psychology, 81,* 85–96.

Gagnon, A., & Bourhis, R. Y. (1996). Discrimination in the minimal group paradigm: Social identity or self-interest? *Personality and Social Psychology Bulletin, 22,* 1289–1301.

Gallup, G. G. (1977). Self-recognition in primates: A comparative approach to the bidirectional properties of consciousness. *American Psychologist, 32,* 329–338.

Gallup, G. G. (1993). Mirror, mirror on the wall which is the most heuristic theory of them all? *New Ideas in Psychology, 11,* 327–335.

Gallup, G. G. (1994). Monkeys, mirrors, and minds. *Behavioral and Brain Sciences, 17,* 572–573.

Gallup, G. G. (1997). On the rise and fall of self-conception in primates. In J. G. Snodgrass & R. L. Thompson (Eds.), *The self across psychology: Self-recognition, self-awareness, and the self-concept.* New York: New York Academy of Sciences Press.

Gallup, G. G., & Suarez, S. D. (1986). Self-awareness and the emergence of mind in humans and other primates. In J. Suls & A. G. Greenwald (Eds.), *Psychological perspectives on the self* (Vol. 3, pp. 3–26). Hillsdale, NJ: Erlbaum.

Gangestad, S. W. (1989). Uncompelling theory, uncompelling data. *Behavioral and Brain Sciences, 12,* 525–526.

Gangestad, S. W. (1993). Sexual selection and physical attractiveness: Implications for mating dynamics. *Human Nature, 4,* 205–235.

Gao, G. (1993, May). An investigation of love and intimacy in romantic relationships in China and the United States. Paper presented at the annual conference of the International Communication Association, Washington, DC.

Gao, G. (1996). Self and other: A Chinese perspective on interpersonal relationships. In W. B. Gudykunst, S. Ting-Toomey, & T. Nishida (Eds.), *Communication in Personal Relationships Across Cultures* (pp. 81–101). Thousand Oaks, CA: Sage.

Garb, H. N. (1996). The representativeness and past-behavior heuristics in clinical judgment. *Professional Psychology: Research and Practice, 27,* 272–277.

Gardner, R. C., MacIntyre, P. D., & Lalonde, R. N. (1995). The effects of multiple social categories on stereotyping. *Canadian Journal of Behavioural Science, 27,* 466–483.

Gardner, W. L., Pickett, C. L., & Brewer, M. B. (2000). Social exclusion and selective memory: How the need to belong influences memory for social events. *Personality and Social Psychology Bulletin, 26,* 486–496.

Garfinkle, H. (1967). *Studies in ethnomethodology.* Englewood Cliffs, NJ: Prentice Hall.

Gavanski, I., & Hoffman, C. (1987). Awareness of influences on one's own judgments: The roles of covariation detection and attention. *Journal of Personality and Social Psychology, 52,* 453–463.

Geen, R. (1994). Television and aggression: Recent developments in research and theory. In D. Zillmann, J. Bryant, A. C. Huston (Eds.), *Media, children, and the family: Social scientific, psychodynamic, and clinical perspectives* (pp. 151–162). Hillsdale, NJ: Erlbaum.

Geen, R. (1998). Aggression and anti-social behavior. In D. Gilbert, S. Fiske, & G. Lindzey (Eds.), *The handbook of social psychology* (4th ed., Vol. 2, pp. 317–356). New York: McGraw Hill.

Geen, R. G. (1989). Alternative conceptions of social facilitation. In P. B. Paulus (Ed.), *Psychology of group influence* (2nd ed., pp. 15–51). Hillsdale, NJ: Erlbaum.

Geiselman, R. E., & Fischer, R. P. (1989). The cognitive interview technique for victims and witnesses of crime. In D. C. Raskin (Ed.), *Psychological methods in criminal investigation and evidence* (pp. 191–215). New York: Springer.

Gelinas-Chebat, C., & Chebat, J. (1992). Effects of two voice characteristics on the attitudes toward advertising messages. *Journal of Social Psychology, 132,* 447–459.

George, J. M. (1990). Personality, affect, and behavior in groups. *Journal of Applied Psychology, 75,* 107–116.

George, J. M., & Brief, A. P. (1992). Feeling good–doing good: A conceptual analysis of the mood at workÑorganizational spontaneity relationship. *Psychological Bulletin, 112,* 310–329.

Gerard, H. B. (1953). The effect of different dimensions of disagreement on the communication process in small groups. *Human Relations, 6,* 249–271.

Gerard, H. B., & Mathewson, G. C. (1966). The effects of severity of initiation on liking for a group: A replication. *Journal of Experimental Social Psychology, 2,* 278–287.

Gerard, H. B., Wilhelmy, R. A., & Conolley, E. S. (1968). Conformity and group size. *Journal of Personality and Social Psychology, 8,* 79–82.

Gerdes, E. P. (1979). College students' reactions to social psychological experiments involving deception. *Journal of Social Psychology, 107,* 99–110.

Gibbons, F. X. (1978). Sexual standards and reactions to pornography: Enhancing behavioral consistency through self-focused attention. *Journal of Personality and Social Psychology, 36,* 976–987.

Gibbons, F. X., Eggleston, T. J., Benthin, A. C. (1997). Cognitive reactions to smoking relapse: The reciprocal relation between dissonance and self-esteem. *Journal of Personality and Social Psychology, 72,* 184–195.

Gibbs, J. P. (1985). Deterrence theory and research. *Nebraska Symposium on Motivation, 33,* 87–130.

Giesler, R., Josephs, R., & Swann, W. (1996). Self-verification in clinical depression: The desire for negative evaluation. *Journal of Abnormal Psychology, 105,* 358–368.

Gifford, R. (1991). Mapping nonverbal behavior on the interpersonal circle. *Journal of Personality and Social Psychology, 61,* 279–288.

Gifford, R. (1994). A lens-mapping framework for understanding the endcoding and decoding of interpersonal dispositions in nonverbal behavior. *Journal of Personality and Social Psychology*, 66, 398–412.

Gigerenzer, G. (1993). The bounded rationality of probabilistic mental models. In K. I. Manktelow & D. E. Over (Eds.), *Rationality: Psychological and philosophical perspectives* (pp. 284–313). London: Routledge.

Gigerenzer, G., & Goldstein, D. G. (1996). Reasoning the fast and frugal way: Models of bounded rationality. *Psychological Review, 103,* 650–669.

Gilbert, B. (1990, April). Earth Day plus 20, and counting. *Smithsonian,* pp. 47–55.

Gilbert, D. T. (1991). How mental systems believe. *American Psychologist, 46,* 107–119.

Gilbert, D. T. (1993). The assent of man: Mental representation and the control of belief. In D. M. Wegner & J. W. Pennebaker, (Eds.), *The handbook of mental control* (pp. 57–87). Englewood Cliffs, NJ: Prentice Hall.

Gilbert, D. T. (1998a). Ordinary personology. In D. T. Gilbert, S. T. Fiske, & G. Lindzey (Eds.), *The handbook of social psychology* (4th ed., Vol. 2, pp. 89–150). New York: McGraw-Hill.

Gilbert, D. T. (1998b). Speeding with Ned: A personal view of the correspondence bias. In J. M. Darley & J. Cooper (Eds.), *Attribution and social interaction* (pp. 5–36). Washington, DC: American Psychological Association.

Gilbert, D. T., Giesler, R. B., & Morris, K. A. (1995). When comparisons arise. *Journal of Personality and Social Psychology*, 69, 227–236.

Gilbert, D. T., & Malone, P. S. (1995). The correspondence bias. *Psychological Bulletin, 117,* 21–38.

Gilovich, T. (1991). *How we know what isn't so: The fallibility of human reasoning in everyday life.* New York: Free Press.

Gilovich, T., & Medvec, V. H. (1995). The experience of regret: What, when, and why. *Psychological Review, 102,* 379–395.

Gilovich, T., Medvec, V. H., & Chen, S. (1995). Commission, omission, and dissonance reduction: Coping with regret in the "Monty Hall" problem. *Personality and Social Psychology Bulletin, 21,* 182–190.

Gilovich, T., Medvec, V. H., & Savitsky, K. (2000). The spotlight effect in social judgment: An egocentric bias in estimates of the salience of one's own actions and appearance. *Journal of Personality and Social Psychology, 78,* 211–222.

Gimlin, D. (1994). The anorexic as overconformist: Toward a reinterpretation of eating disorders. In K. A. Callaghan (Ed.), *Ideals of Feminine Beauty: Philosophical, Social, and Cultural Dimensions* (pp. 99–111). Westport, CN: Greenwood.

Gire, J. T. (1997). The varying effect of individualism-collectivism on preference for methods of conflict resolution. *Canadian Journal of Behavioral Science, 29,* 38–43.

Glass, D. C., & Singer, J. E. (1972). *Urban stress: Experiments on noise and social stressors.* New York: Academic Press.

Godin, G., & Kok, G. (1996). The theory of planned behavior: A review of its application to health related behaviors. *American Journal of Health Promotion, 11,* 87–98.

Godin, G., Maticka-Tyndale, E., Adrien, A., Manson-Singer, S., Willams, D., & Cappon, P. (1996). Cross-cultural testing of three social cognitive theories: An application to condom use. *Journal of Applied Social Psychology, 26,* 1556–1586.

Goethals, G. R., & Darley, J. M. (1977). Social comparison theory: An attributional approach. In J. M. Suls & R. L. Miller (Eds.), *Social comparison processes: Theoretical and empirical perspectives* (pp. 259–278). Washington, DC: Hemisphere/Halsted.

Goffman, E. (1955). On face-work: An analysis of ritual elements in social interaction. *Psychiatry, 18,* 213–231.

Goffman, E. (1959). *Presentation of self in everyday life.* Garden City, NY: Doubleday Anchor Books.

Goffman, E. (1967). *Interaction ritual.* Garden City, NY: Doubleday.

Goffman, E. (1971). *Relations in public.* New York: Basic Books.

Gold, J. A., Ryckman, R. M., & Mosley, N. R. (1984). Romantic mood induction and attraction to a dissimilar other: Is love blind? *Personality and Social Psychology Bulletin, 10,* 358–368.

Goldstein, J. H., & Arms, R. L. (1971). Effect of observing athletic contests on hostility. *Sociometry, 34,* 83–90.

Goleman, D. (1982, January). Make-or-break resolutions. *Psychology Today,* p. 19.

Gollwitzer, P. M. (1986). *Public vs. private self-symbolizing.* Unpublished manuscript, Max-Planck Institute for Psychological Research, Munich, Germany.

Gollwitzer, P. M., & Wicklund, R. A. (1985). Self-symbolizing and the neglect of others' perspectives. *Journal of Personality and Social Psychology, 48,* 702–715.

Gonzales, M. H., Aronson, E., & Costanzo, M. (1988). Using social cognition and persuasion to promote energy conservation: A quasi-experiment. *Journal of Applied Social Psychology, 18,* 1049–1066.

Gonzalez, R., Ellsworth, P. C., & Pembroke, M. (1993). Response biases in lineups and showups. *Journal of Personality and Social Psychology*, 64, 525–537.

Gopaul-McNicol, S.-A. A. (1987). A cross-cultural study of the effects of modeling, reinforcement, and color meaning word association on doll color preference of Black preschool children and White preschool children in New York and Trinidad. *Dissertation Abstracts International, 48,* 340–341.

Gorassini, D. R., & Olson, J. M. (1995). Does self-perception change explain the foot-in-the-door effect? *Journal of Personality and Social Psychology, 69,* 91–105.

Gordon, A. K., & Miller, A. G. (2000). Perspective differences in the construal of lies: Is deception in the eye of the beholder? *Personality and Social Psychology Bulletin, 26,* 46–55.

Gould, S. J. (1997, June 26). Evolution: The pleasures of pluralism. *The New York Review,* pp. 47–52.

The Governor General of Canada. (1999, December 22). Governor General announces 19 decorations for bravery. www.gg.ca/ appointments/99dec22_e.html (September 10, 2000).

Graham, K., & Wells, S. (2001a). The two worlds of aggression for men and men. *Sex Roles, 45,* 595–622.

Graham, K., & Wells, S. (2001b). Aggression among young adults in the social context of the bar. *Addiction Research & Theory, 9,* 193–219.

Graham, K., West, P., & Wells, S. (2000). Evaluating theories of alcohol-related aggression using observations of young adults in bars. *Addiction, 95,* 847–863.

Granberg, D., & Brown, T. (1989). On affect and cognition in politics. *Social Psychology Quarterly, 52,* 171–182.

Grant, P. R. (1992). Ethnocentrism between groups of unequal power in response to perceived threat to social identity and valued resources. *Canadian Journal of Behavioural Science, 24,* 348–370.

Grant, P. R. (1993). Reactions to intergroup similarity: Examination of the similarity-differentiation and the similarity-attraction hypothesis. *Canadian Journal of Behavioral Science, 25,* 28–44.

Graybar, S. R., Antonuccio, D. O., Boutilier, L. R., & Varble, D. L. (1989). Psychological reactance as a factor affecting patient compliance to physician advice. *Scandinavian Journal of Behaviour Therapy, 18,* 43–51.

Great Lakes: Chemical hot spot. (2000, August 24). www.ec.gc.ca/water/en/manage/polle_hotspt.htm.

Greenberg, J., & Pyszczynski, T. (1985). The effect of an overheard slur on evaluations of the target: How to spread a social disease. *Journal of Experimental Social Psychology, 21,* 61–72.

Greenberg, J., Pyszczynski, T., & Solomon, S. (1986). The causes and consequences of the need for self-esteem: A terror management theory. In R. F. Baumeister (Ed.), *Public self and private self* (pp. 189–212). New York: Springer-Verlag.

Greenberg, L. (1979). Genetic component of bee odor in kin recognition. *Science, 206,* 1095–1097.

Green-Demers, I., Pelletier, L. G., Stewart, D. G., & Gushue, N. R. (1998). Coping with the less interesting aspects of training. Toward a model of interest and motivation enhancement in individual sports. *Basic and Applied Social Psychology, 20,* 251–261.

Greene, D., Sternberg, B., & Lepper, M. R. (1976). Overjustification in a token economy. *Journal of Personality and Social Psychology, 34,* 1219–1234.

Greenglass, E. R. (1991). Type A behavior, career aspirations, and role conflict in professional women. In M. J. Strube (Ed.), *Type A Behavior.* Newbury Park, CA: Sage.

Greening, L., & Chandler, C. C. (1997). Why it can't happen to me: The base rate matters, but overestimating skill leads to underestimating risk. *Journal of Applied Social Psychology, 27,* 760–780.

Greenwald, A. G., & Banaji, M. R. (1989). The self as a memory system: Powerful, but ordinary. *Journal of Personality and Social Psychology, 57,* 41–54.

Greenwald, A. G., Spangenberg, E. R., Pratkanis, A. R., & Eskenazi, J. (1991). Double-blind tests of subliminal self-help audiotapes. *Psychological Science, 2,* 119–122.

Griffin, D., & Buehler, R. (1993). Role of construal processes in conformity and dissent. *Journal of Personality and Social Psychology, 65,* 657–669.

Griffin, D., & Buehler, R. (1999). Frequency, probability, and prediction: Easy solutions to cognitive illusions. *Cognitive Psychology, 38,* 48–78.

Griffin, D., Gonzalez, R., & Varey, C. (2001). The heuristics and biases approach to judgment under uncertainty. In A. Tesser (Ed.). *Blackwell handbook of social psychology* (Vol. 1, pp. 207–235). Oxford, UK: Blackwell Publishers.

Griffin, D., & Tversky, A. (1992). The weighing of evidence and the determinants of confidence. *Cognitive Psychology, 24,* 411–435.

Griffin, D. W., & Ross, L. (1991). Subjective construal, social inference, and human misunderstanding. In L. Berkowitz (Ed.), *Advances in experimental social psychology* (Vol. 24, pp. 319–359). San Diego, CA: Academic Press.

Griffin, E., & Sparks, G. G. (1990). Friends forever: A longitudinal exploration of intimacy in same-sex pairs and platonic pairs. *Journal of Social and Personal Relationships, 7,* 29–46.

Griffitt, W., & Veitch, R. (1971). Hot and crowded: Influences of population density and temperature on interpersonal affective behavior. *Journal of Personality and Social Psychology, 17,* 92–98.

Grills, B. (1997). *Falling into you: The story of Céline Dion.* Kingston, ON: Quarry Press.

Groenland, E. A. G., & Schoormans, J. P. L. (1994). Comparing mood-induction and affective conditioning as mechanisms influencing product evaluation and choice. *Psychology and Marketing, 11,* 183–197.

Grove, L. (1997, August 21). A man named Sissy. *Washington Post,* pp. C1; C4.

Grusec, J. E. (1991). The socialization of altruism. In M. S. Clark (Ed.), *Review of personality and social psychology* (Vol. 12, pp. 9–33). Newbury Park, CA: Sage.

Grusec, J. E., Kuczynski, L., Rushton, J. P., & Simutis, Z. M. (1979). Modeling, direct instruction, and attributions: Effects on altruism. *Developmental Psychology, 14,* 51–57.

Guay, F., Boivin, M., Hodges, E. V. E. (1999). Social comparison processes and academic achievement: The dependence of the development of self-evaluations on friends' performance. *Journal of Educational Psychology, 91,* 564–568.

Gudykunst, W. B., Ting-Toomey, S., & Nishida, T. (1996). *Communication in Personal Relationships across Cultures.* Thousand Oaks, CA: Sage Publications.

Guerin, B. (1986). Mere presence effects in humans: A review. *Journal of Experimental Social Psychology, 22,* 38–77.

Guerin, B. (1993). *Social facilitation.* Cambridge, England: Cambridge University Press.

Guimond, S. (1999). Attitude change during college: Normative or informational social influence? *Social Psychology of Education, 2,* 237–261.

Guimond, S. (2000). Group socialization and prejudice: the social transmission of intergroup attitudes and beliefs. *European Journal of Social Psychology, 30,* 335–354.

Guimond, S., & Dubé, L. (1989). *La representation des causes de l'inferiorité economique des québequois francophones. Canadian Journal of Behavioural Science, 21,* 28–39.

Guimond, S., & Palmer, D. L. (1996). The political socialization of commerce and social science students: Epistemic authority and attitude change. *Journal of Applied Social Psychology, 26,* 1985–2013.

Guisinger, S., & Blatt, S. J. (1994). Individuality and relatedness: Evolution of a fundamental dialect. *American Psychologist, 49,* 104–111.

Gully, S. M., Devine, D. J., & Whitney, D. J. (1995). A meta-analysis of cohesion and performance: Effects of level of analysis and task interdependence. *Small Groups Research, 26,* 497–520.

Gustafson, R. (1989). Frustration and successful vs. unsuccessful aggression: A test of Berkowitz' completion hypothesis. *Aggressive Behavior, 15,* 5–12.

Haddock, G., Rothman, A. J., & Schwarz, N. (1996). Are (some) reports of attitude strength context dependent? *Canadian Journal of Behavioral Science, 28,* 313–316.

Haddock, G., & Zanna, M. P. (1994). Preferring "housewives" to "feminists": Categorization and the favorability of attitudes toward women. *Psychology of Women Quarterly, 18,* 25–52.

Haddock, G., & Zanna, M. P. (1997). Impact of negative advertising on evaluations of political candidates: The 1993 Canadian federal election. *Basic and Applied Social Psychology, 19,* 205–223.

Haddock, G., & Zanna, M. P. (1998). Assessing the impact of affective and cognitive information in predicting attitudes toward capital punishment. *Law and Human Behavior, 22,* 325–339.

Haddock, G., Zanna, M. P., & Esses, V. M. (1993). Assessing the structure of prejudicial attitudes: The case of attitudes toward homosexuals. *Journal of Personality and Social Psychology, 65,* 1105–1118.

Haddock, G., Zanna, M. P., & Esses, V. M. (1994). The (limited) role of trait-laden stereotypes in predicting attitudes toward Native peoples. *British Journal of Social Psychology, 33,* 83–106.

Hadjistavropoulos, T., & Genest, M. (1994). The understanding of the role of physical attractiveness in dating preferences: Ignorance or taboo? *Canadian Journal of Behavioral Science, 26,* 298–318.

Hafer, C. L. (2000a). Do innocent victims threaten the belief in a just world? Evidence from a modified Stroop task. *Journal of Personality and Social Psychology, 79,* 165–173.

Hafer, C. L. (2000b). Investment in long-term goals and commitment to just means drive the need to believe in a just world. *Personality and Social Psychology Bulletin, 26,* 1059–1073.

Hafer, C. L. (2002). Why we reject innocent victims. In M. Ross & D. T. Miller (Eds.) *The justice motive in everyday life* (pp. 109–126). New York: Cambridge University Press.

Hafer, C. L., Reynolds, K. L., Obertynski, M. A. (1996). Message comprehensibility and persuasion: Effects of complex language in counter attitudinal appeals to laypeople. *Social Cognition, 14,* 317–337.

Haidt, J., & Keltner, D. (1999). Culture and facial expression: Open-ended methods find more faces and a gradient of recognition. *Cognition and Emotion, 13,* 225–266.

Hall, E. T. (1969). *The hidden dimension.* Garden City, NY: Doubleday.

Halperin, I. (1997). *Céline Dion: Behind the fairytale. A very very unauthorized biography.* Boca Raton, FA: Boca Publications Group.

Hamill, R. C., Wilson, T. D., & Nisbett, R. E. (1980). Ignoring sample bias: Inferences about populations from atypical cases. *Journal of Personality and Social Psychology, 39,* 578–589.

Hamilton, V. L., Sanders, J., & McKearney, S. J. (1995). Orientations toward authority in an authoritarian state: Moscow in 1990. *Personality and Social Psychology Bulletin, 21,* 356–365.

Hamilton, W. D. (1964). The genetical evolution of social behavior. *Journal of Theoretical Biology, 7,* 1–52.

Han, S., & Shavitt, S. (1994). Persuasion and culture: Advertising appeals in individualistic and collectivistic societies. *Journal of Experimental Social Psychology, 30,* 326–350.

Haney, C., Banks, C., & Zimbardo, P. (1973). Interpersonal dynamics in a simulated prison. *International Journal of Criminology and Penology, 1,* 69–97.

Hansen, C. H., & Hansen, R. D. (1988). Finding the face in the crowd: An anger superiority effect. *Journal of Personality and Social Psychology, 17,* 917–924.

Hanson, I., & Hampton, M. R. (2000). Being Indian: Strengths sustaining First Nations Peoples in Saskatchewan residential schools. *Canadian Journal of Community Mental Health, 19,* 127–142.

Hansson, R. O., & Slade, K. M. (1977). Altruism toward a deviant in a city and small town. *Journal of Applied Social Psychology, 7,* 272–279.

Harackiewicz, J. M. (1979). The effects of reward contingency and performance feedback on intrinsic motivation. *Journal of Personality and Social Psychology, 37,* 1352–1363.

Harackiewicz, J. M., & Elliot, A. J. (1993). Achievement goals and intrinsic motivation. *Journal of Personality and Social Psychology, 65,* 904–915.

Harackiewicz, J. M., & Elliot, A. J. (1998). The joint effects of target and purpose goals on intrinsic motivation: A mediational analysis. *Personality and Social Psychology Bulletin, 24 (7),* 675–689.

Haritos-Fatouros, M. (1988). The official torturer: A learning model for obedience to the authority of violence. *Journal of Applied Social Psychology, 18,* 1107–1120.

Harkness, A. R., DeBono, K. G., & Borgida, E. (1985). Personal involvement and strategies for making contingency judgments: A stake in the dating game makes a difference. *Journal of Personality and Social Psychology, 49,* 22–32.

Harmon-Jones, E. (1998). Is feeling personally responsible for the production of aversive consequences necessary to cause dissonance effects? In E. Harmon-Jones & J. S. Mills, *Cognitive dissonance theory: Revival with revisions and controversies.* Washington, DC: American Psychological Association.

Harmon-Jones, E., & Mills, J.S. (1998). *Cognitive dissonance theory: Revival with revisions and controversies.* Washington, DC: American Psychological Association.

Harries, K. D., & Stadler, S. J. (1988). Heat and violence: New findings from Dallas field data, 1980–1981. *Journal of Applied Social Psychology, 18,* 129–138.

Harris, B. (1986). Reviewing 50 years of the psychology of social issues. *Journal of Social Issues, 42,* 1–20.

Harris, M. (1974). Mediators between frustration and aggression in a field experiment. *Journal of Experimental and Social Psychology, 10,* 561–571.

Harris, M. B., Benson, S. M., & Hall, C. (1975). The effects of confession on altruism. *Journal of Social Psychology, 96,* 187–192.

Harris, P. (1996). Sufficient grounds for optimism? The relationship between perceived controllability and optimistic bias. *Journal of Social and Clinical Psychology, 15,* 9–52.

Harrison, J. A., & Wells, R. B. (1991). Bystander effects on male helping behavior: Social comparison and diffusion of responsibility. *Representative Research in Social Psychology, 19,* 53–63.

Hart, A. J., & Morry, M. M. (1997). Trait inferences based on racial and behavioral cues. *Basic & Applied Social Psychology, 19,* 33–48.

Hart, D., & Damon, W. (1986). Developmental trends in self-understanding. *Social Cognition, 4,* 388–407.

Harter, S. (1993). Causes and consequences of low self-esteem in children and adolescents. In: Baumeister, R., Ed., *Self-esteem: The puzzle of low self-regard.* New York: Plenum, pp. 87–116.

Hartshorne, H., & May, M. A. (1929). *Studies in the nature of character: Studies in service and self-control* (Vol. 2). New York: Macmillan.

Hartstone, M., & Augoustinos, M. (1995). The minimal group paradigm: Categorization into two versus three groups. *European Journal of Social Psychology, 25,* 179–193.

Hartup, W. W., & Laursen, B. (1999). Relationships as developmental contexts: Retrospective themes and contemporary issues. In W. A. Collins & B. Laursen (Eds.), *Relationships as developmental contexts: Minnesota Symposia on Child Psychology* (Vol. 30, pp. 13–35). Mahwah, NJ: Erlbaum.

Hassebrauck, M., & Buhl, T. (1996). Three-dimensional love. *Journal of Social Psychology, 136,* 121–122.

Hastie, R. (1980). Memory for behavioral information that confirms or contradicts a personality impression. In R. Hastie, T. M. Ostrom, E. B. Ebbesen, R. S. Wyer, D. L. Hamilton, & D. E. Carlston (Eds.), *Person memory: The cognitive basis of social perception* (pp. 141–172). Hillsdale, NJ: Erlbaum.

Hastie, R., & Pennington, N. (1991). Cognitive and social processes in decision making. In L. B. Resnick, J. M. Levine, & S. D. Teasley (Eds.), *Perspectives on socially shared cognition* (pp. 308–327). Washington, DC: American Psychological Association.

Hastie, R., & Pennington, N. (1995). The big story: Is it a story? In R. S. Wyer, Jr. (Ed.), *Knowledge and memory: The real story. Advances in social cognition* (Vol. 8, pp. 133–138). Hillsdale, NJ: Erlbaum.

Hastie, R., & Pennington, N. (2000). Explanation-based decision making. In T. Connolly & H. R. Arkes (Eds.), *Judgment and decision making: An interdisciplinary reader* (2nd ed., pp. 212–228). New York: Cambridge University Press.

Hastie, R., Penrod, S. D., & Pennington, N. (1983). *Inside the jury.* Cambridge MA: Harvard University Press.

Hatfield, E., Greenberger, E., Traupmann, J., & Lambert, P. (1982). Equity and sexual satisfaction in recently married couples. *Journal of Sex Research, 18,* 18–32.

Hatfield, E., & Rapson, R. L. (1993). *Love, sex, and intimacy: Their psychology, biology, and history.* New York: Harper Collins.

Hatfield, E., & Sprecher, S. (1986a). *Mirror, mirror: The importance of looks in everyday life.* Albany: State University of New York Press.

Hatfield, E., & Sprecher, S. (1986b). Measuring passionate love in intimate relationships. *Journal of Adolescence, 9,* 383–410.

Hatfield, E., & Sprecher, S. (1995). Men's and women's preferences in marital partners in the United States, Russia, and Japan. *Journal of Cross-Cultural Psychology, 26,* 728–750.

Hatfield, E., & Walster, G. W. (1978). *A new look at love.* Reading, MA: Addison-Wesley.

Haugtvedt, C. P., & Wegener, D. T. (1994). Message order effects in persuasion: An attitude strength perspective. *Journal of Consumer Research, 21,* 205–218.

Hausenblas, H. A., Carron, A. V., & Mack, D. E. (1997). Application of the theories of reasoned action and planned behavior: A meta-analysis. *Journal of Sport and Exercise, 19,* 36–51.

Hawa, R., Munro, B. E., & Poirier, M. (1998). Information, motivation and behaviour as predictors of AIDS risk reduction among Canadian first-year university students. *Canadian Journal of Human Sexuality, 7,* 9–18.

Hazan, C., & Shaver, P. (1987). Romantic love conceptualized as an attachment process. *Journal of Personality and Social Psychology, 52,* 511–524.

Hazan, C., & Shaver, P. (1994a). Attachment as an organizational framework for research on close relationships. *Psychological Inquiry, 5,* 1–22.

Hazan, C., & Shaver, P. (1994b). Deeper into attachment theory. *Psychological Inquiry, 5,* 68–79.

Hazelwood, J. D., & Olson, J. M. (1986). Covariation information, causal questioning, and interpersonal behavior. *Journal of Experimental Social Psychology, 22,* 276–291.

Health Canada. (2002, June 28). Smoking rates continuing to drop. www.hc-sc.gc.ca/english/media/relases/2002/2002_52.htm.

Hébert, Y., Bernard, J., deMan, A. F., & Farrar, D. (1989). Factors related to the use of condoms among French-Canadian university students. *The Journal of Social Psychology, 129,* 707–709.

Heckhausen, J., & Schulz, R. (1995). A life-span theory of control. *Psychological Review, 102,* 284–304.

Hedge, A., & Yousif, Y. H. (1992). Effects of urban size, urgency, and cost on helpfulness. *Journal of Cross-Cultural Psychology, 23,* 107–115.

Heider, F. (1958). *The psychology of interpersonal relations.* New York: Wiley.

Heine, S. J. (2001). Self as cultural product: An examination of East Asian and North American selves. *Journal of Personality, 69,* 881–906.

Heine, S. J. (under review). In search of East Asian self-enhancement.

Heine, S. J., Kitayama, S., & Lehman, D. R. (2001). Cultural differences in self-evaluation: Japanese readily accept negative self-relevant information. *Journal of Cross-Cultural Psychology, 32,* 434–443.

Heine, S. J., & Lehman, D. R. (1995). Cultural variation in unrealistic optimism: Does the West feel more vulnerable than the East? *Journal of Personality and Social Psychology, 68,* 595–607.

Heine, S. J., & Lehman, D. R. (1997a). Culture, dissonance, and self-affirmation. *Personality and Social Psychology Bulletin, 23,* 389–400.

Heine, S. J., & Lehman, D. R. (1997b). The cultural construction of self-enhancement: An examination of group serving biases. *Journal of Personality and Social Psychology, 72,* 1268–1283.

Heine, S. J., & Lehman, D. R. (1999). Culture, self-discrepancies, and self-satisfaction. *Personality and Social Psychology Bulletin, 25,* 915–925.

Heine, S. J., Lehman, D. R., Markus, H. R., & Kitayama, S. (1999). Is there a universal need for positive self-regard? *Psychological Review, 106,* 766–794.

Heine, S. J., & Renshaw, K. (2002). Interjudge agreement, self-enhancement, and liking: Cross-cultural perspectives. *Personality and Social Psychology Bulletin, 28,* 578–587.

Heine, S. J., Takata, T., & Lehman, D. R. (2000). Beyond self-presentation: Evidence for self-criticism among Japanese. *Personality and Social Psychology Bulletin, 26,* 71–78.

Hejmadi, A., Davidson, R. J., & Rozin, P. (2000). Exploring Hindu Indian emotion expressions: Evidence for accurate recognition by Americans and Indians. *Psychological Science, 11,* 183–187.

Helgeson, V. S. (1994). The effects of self-beliefs and relationship beliefs on adjustment to a relationship stressor. *Personal Relationships, 1,* 241–258.

Helgeson, V. S., & Cohen, S. (1996). Social support and adjustment to cancer: Reconciling descriptive, correlational, and intervention research. *Health Psychology, 15,* 135–148.

Helgeson, V. S., & Fritz, H. L. (1999). Cognitive adaptation as a predictor of new coronary events after percutaneous transluminal coronary angioplasty. *Psychosomatic Medicine, 61,* 488–495.

Henderson-King, E., & Nisbett, R. E. (1996). Anti-black prejudice as a function of exposure to the negative behavior of a single black person. *Journal of Personality and Social Psychology, 71,* 654–664.

Hendrick C., Hendrick, S. S., Foote, F. H., & Slapion-Foote, M. J. (1984). Do men and women love differently? *Journal of Social and Personal Relationships, 1,* 177–195.

Hendrick, S. S., & Hendrick, C. (1986). A theory and method of love. *Journal of Personality and Social Psychology, 50,* 392–402.

Hendrick, S. S., & Hendrick, C. (1992). *Liking, loving and relating* (2nd ed.). Pacific Grove, CA: Brooks/Cole.

Hendrick, S. S., & Hendrick. C. (1995). Gender differences and similarities in sex and love. *Personal Relationships, 4,* 281–297.

Hendrick, S. S, Hendrick, C., & Adler, N. L. (1988). Romantic relationships: Love, satisfaction, and staying together. *Journal of Personality and Social Psychology, 54,* 980–988.

Henley, N. M. (1977). *Body politics: Power, sex, and nonverbal communication.* Englewood Cliffs, NJ: Prentice Hall.

Hennessey, B. A., Amabile, T., & Martinage, M. (1989). Immunizing children against the negative effects of reward. *Contemporary Educational Psychology, 14,* 212–227.

Hennessey, B. A., & Zbikowski, S. M. (1993). Immunizing children against the negative effects of reward: A further examination of intrinsic motivation focus sessions. *Creativity Research Journal, 6,* 297–307.

Henry, R. A. (1995). Using relative confidence judgments to evaluate group effectiveness. *Basic and Applied Social Psychology, 16,* 333–350.

Her Majesty the Queen v. Warren Paul Glowatski. (1999, June 2). *British Columbia Superior Courts Reasons for Judgements Database.* (Docket No. 95773). www.courts.gov.bc.ca/jdb%2Dtxt/sc/99/08/s99%2D0836.txt (June 29, 2000).

Herold, E. S., & Mewhinney, D. (1993). Gender differences in casual sex and AIDS prevention: A survey of dating bars. *The Journal of Sex Research, 30,* 36–42.

Hersh, S. M. (1970). *My Lai 4: A report on the massacre and its aftermath.* New York: Vintage Books.

Hertwig, R., Gigerenzer, G., & Hoffrage, U. (1997). The reiteration effect in hindsight bias. *Psychological Review, 104,* 194–202.

Herzog, T. A. (1994). Automobile driving as seen by the actor, the active observer, and the passive observer. *Journal of Applied Social Psychology, 24,* 2057–2074.

Hess, U., Banse, R., & Kappas, A. (1995). The intensity of facial expression is determined by underlying affective state and social situation. *Journal of Personality and Social Psychology, 69,* 280–288.

Hess, U., Philippot, P., & Blairy, S. (1998). Facial reactions to emotional facial expressions: Affect or cognition? *Cognition and Emotion, 12,* 509–531.

Heunemann, R. L., Shapiro, L. R., Hampton, M. C., & Mitchell, B. W. (1966). A longitudinal study of gross body composition and body conformation and their association with food and activity in the teenage population. *American Journal of Clinical Nutrition, 18,* 325–338.

Hewstone, M., & Jaspars, J. (1987). Covariation and causal attribution: A logical model of the intuitive analysis of variance. *Journal of Personality and Social Psychology, 53,* 663–672.

Higgins, E. T. (1987). Self-discrepancy: A theory relating self and affect. *Psychological Review, 94,* 319–340.

Higgins, E. T. (1989). Knowledge accessibility and activation: Subjectivity and suffering from unconscious sources. In J. S. Uleman & J. A. Bargh (Eds.), *Unintended thought* (pp. 75–123). New York: Guilford Press.

Higgins, E. T. (1989). Self-discrepancy theory: What patterns of self-beliefs cause people to suffer? In L. Berkowitz (Ed.), *Advances in experimental social psychology* (Vol. 22, pp. 93–136). New York: Academic Press.

Higgins, E. T. (1996). Knowledge application: Accessibility, applicability, and salience. In E. T. Higgins and A. R. Kruglanski (Eds.), *Social psychology: Handbook of basic principles.* New York: Guilford, pp. 133–168.

Higgins, E. T. (1999). Self-discrepancy: A theory relating self and affect. In R. F. Baumeister (Ed.), *The self in social psychology* (pp. 150–181). Philadelphia: Psychology Press.

Higgins, E. T., & Bargh, J. A. (1987). Social cognition and social perception. *Annual Review of Psychology, 38,* 369–425.

Higgins, E. T., Bond, R. N., Klein, R., & Strauman, T. (1986). Self-discrepancies and emotional vulnerability: How magnitude, accessibility, and type of discrepancy influence affect. *Journal of Personality and Social Psychology, 51,* 5–15.

Higgins, E. T., & Brendl, C. M. (1995). Accessibility and applicability: Some "activation rules" influencing judgment. *Journal of Experimental Social Psychology, 31,* 218–243.

Higgins, E. T., Klein, R., & Strauman, T. (1987). Self-discrepancies: Distinguishing among self-states, self-state conflicts, and emotional vulnerabilities. In K. M. Yardley & T. M. Honess (Eds.), *Self and identity: Psychosocial perspectives* (pp. 173–186). New York: Wiley.

Higgins, E. T., Rholes, W. S., & Jones, C. R. (1977). Category accessibility and impression formation. *Journal of Experimental Social Psychology, 13,* 141–154.

Hill, A. J., Boudreau, F., Amyot, E., Dery, D., & Godin, G. (1997). Predicting the stages of smoking acquisition according to the theory of planned behavior. *Journal of Adolescent Health, 21,* 107–115.

Hill, A. J., Oliver, S., & Rogers, P. J. (1992). Eating in the adult world: The rise of dieting in childhood and adolescence. *British Journal of Clinical Psychology, 31,* 95–105.

Hilton, A., Potvin, L., & Sachdev, I. (1989). Ethnic relations in rental housing: A social psychological approach. *Canadian Journal of Behavioural Science, 21,* 121–131.

Hilton, J. L., & Darley, J. M. (1991). The effects of interaction goals on person perception. In M. P. Zanna (Ed.), *Advances in experimental social psychology* (Vol. 24, pp. 235–267). San Diego, CA: Academic Press.

Hippler, H. J., Schwarz, N., & Sudman, S. (Eds.). (1987). *Social information processing and survey methodology.* New York: Springer-Verlag.

Hirt, E. R., & Markman, K. D. (1995). Multiple explanation: A consider-an-alternative strategy for debiasing judgments. *Journal of Personality and Social Psychology, 69,* 1069–1086.

Hoaken, P. N. S., & Pihl, R. O. (2000). The effects of alcohol intoxication on aggressive responses in men and women. *Alcohol and Alcoholism, 35,* 471–477.

Hobbes, T. (1986). *Leviathan.* Harmondsworth, England: Penguin Press. (Original work published 1651)

Hobden, K. L., & Olson, J. M. (1994). From jest to antipathy: Disparagement humor as a source of dissonance-motivated attitude change. *Basic and Applied Social Psychology, 15,* 239–249.

Hobfoll, S. E., & Vaux, A. (1993). Social support: Social resources and social context. In L. Goldberger & S. Breznitz (Eds.), *Handbook of stress: Theoretical and clinical aspects* (2nd ed., pp. 685–705). New York: Free Press.

Hodson, G., & Sorrentino, R. M. (1997). Groupthink and uncertainty orientation: Personality differences in reactivity to the group situation. *Group Dynamics, 1,* 144–155.

Hoeksema–van Orden, C. Y. D., Gaillard, A. W. K., & Buunk, B. P. (1998). Social loafing under fatigue. *Journal of Personality and Social Psychology, 75,* 1179–1190.

Hoffman, A. J., Gillespie, J. J., Moore, D. A., Wade-Benzoni, K. A., Thompson, L. L., & Bazerman, M. H. (1999). A mixed-motive perspective on the economics versus environmental debate. *American Behavioral Scientist, 42,* 1254–1276.

Hoffman, C., Lau, I., & Johnson, D. R. (1986). The linguistic relativity of person cognition: An English-Chinese comparison. *Journal of Personality and Social Psychology, 51,* 1097–1105.

Hoffman, M. L. (1981). Is altruism a part of human nature? *Journal of Personality and Social Psychology, 40,* 121–137.

Hofstede, G. (1984). *Culture's consequences: International differences in work-related values.* Newbury Park, CA: Sage.

Hofstede, G. (1986). Cultural differences in teaching and learning. *International Journal of Intercultural Relations, 10,* 301–320.

Hoge, W. (1997, September 5). Responding to Britain's sorrow, Queen will address the nation; Hurt by criticism, Royal family mourns openly. *The New York Times,* pp. A1; A6.

Hogg, M. A. (1992). *The Social Psychology of Group Cohesiveness: From Attraction to Social Identity.* London, England: Harvester-Wheatsheaf.

Hogg, M. A. (1993). Group cohesiveness: A critical review and some new directions. In W. Stroebe & M. Hewstone (Eds.), *European review of social psychology* (Vol. 4, pp. 85–111). Chichester, England: Wiley.

Hogg, M. A., & Abrams, D. (1988). *Social identifications.* London: Routledge. (cf. Chapter 3)

Hogg, M. A., & Hains, S. C. (1998). Friendship and group identification: A new look at the role of cohesiveness in groupthink. *European Journal of Social Psychology, 28,* 323–341.

Hollander, E. P. (1958). Conformity, status, and idiosyncrasy credit. *Psychological Review, 65,* 117–127.

Hollander, E. P. (1960). Competence and conformity in the acceptance of influence. *Journal of Abnormal and Social Psychology, 61,* 361–365.

Hollander, E. P. (1985). Leadership and power. In G. Lindzey & E. Aronson (Eds.), *Handbook of social psychology* (3rd ed., Vol. 2, pp. 485–537). New York: McGraw-Hill.

Holmes, J. G., Miller, D. T., & Lerner, M. J. (2002). Committing altruism under the cloak of self-interest: The exchange fiction. *Journal of Experimental Social Psychology, 38,* 144–151.

Holmes, T. H., & Rahe, R. H. (1967). The social readjustment rating scale. *Journal of Psychosomatic Research, 11,* 213–218.

Holtz, R. (1997). Length of group membership, assumed similarity, and opinion certainty: The dividend for veteran members. *Journal of Applied Social Psychology, 27,* 539–555.

Holtzworth-Munroe, A., Bates, L., Smutzer, N., & Sandin, E. (1997). A brief review of the research on husband violence. *Aggression and Violent Behavior, 2,* 65–99.

Homans, G. C. (1961). *Social behavior: Its elementary forms.* New York: Harcourt Brace & World.

Honts, C. R. (1994). Psychophysiological detection of deception. *Current Directions in Psychological Science, 3,* 77–82.

Hornstein, H. A. (1991). Empathic distress and altruism: Still inseparable. *Psychological Inquiry, 2,* 133–135.

Horvarth, P. (1996). Nuclear weapons concerns, agency beliefs, and social responsibility values in disarmament activism. *Peace and Conflict: Journal of Peace and Psychology, 2,* 17–35.

House, J. S., Robbins, C., & Metzner, H. L. (1982). The association of social relationships and activities with mortality: Prospective evidence from the Tecumseh Community Health Study. *American Journal of Epidemiology, 116,* 123–140.

House, R. J. (1971). A path-goal theory of leadership effectiveness. *Administrative Science Quarterly, 16,* 321–338.

Houston, D. A., & Fazio, R. H. (1989). Biased processing as a function of attitude accessibility: Making objective judgments subjectively. *Social Cognition, 7,* 51–66.

Hovland, C. I., Janis, I. L., & Kelley, H. H. (1953). *Communication and persuasion: Psychological studies of opinion change.* New Haven, CT: Yale University Press.

Hovland, C. I., & Sears, R. R. (1940). Minor studies in aggression: 6. Correlation of lynchings with economic indices. *Journal of Psychology, 9,* 301–310.

Hovland, C. I., & Weiss, W. (1951). The influence of source credibility on communication effectiveness. *Public Opinion Quarterly, 15,* 635–650.

Howard, D. J. (1997). Familiar phrases as peripheral persuasion cues. *Journal of Experimental Social Psychology, 33,* 231–243.

Hsu, S. S. (1995, April 8). Fredericksburg searches its soul after clerk is beaten as 6 watch. *Washington Post,* pp. A1, A13.

Huesmann, L. R. (1982). Television violence and aggressive behavior. In D. Pearly, L. Bouthilet, & J. Lazar (Eds.), *Television and behavior: Vol. 2. Technical reviews* (pp. 220–256). Washington, DC: National Institute of Mental Health.

Huesmann, L. R., & Miller, L. S. (1994). Long-term effects of repeated exposure to media violence in childhood. In L. R. Huesmann (Ed.), *Aggressive behavior: Current perspectives* (pp. 153–186). New York: Plenum.

Huffman, K. T., Grossnickle, W. F., Cope, J. G., & Huffman, K. P. (1995). Litter reduction: A review and integration of the literature. *Environment and Behavior, 27,* 153–183.

Hughes, J. N., & Hasbrouck, J. E. (1996). Television violence: Implications for violence prevention. *School Psychology Review, 25,* 134–151.

Huguet, P., Galvaing, M. P., Monteil, J. M., & Dumas, F. (1999). Social presence effects in the Stroop task: Further evidence for an attentional view of social facilitation. *Journal of Personality and Social Psychology, 77,* 1011–1025.

Hui, C. H., & Triandis, H. C. (1986). Individualism-collectivism: A study of cross-cultural researchers. *Journal of Cross-Cultural Psychology, 17,* 225–248.

Hull, J. G. (1981). A self-awareness model of the causes and effects of alcohol consumption. *Journal of Personality and Social Psychology, 90,* 586–600.

Hull, J. G., & Young, R. D. (1983). Self-consciousness, self-esteem, and success-failure as determinants of alcohol consumption in male social drinkers. *Journal of Personality and Social Psychology, 44,* 1097–1109.

Hull, J. G., Young, R. D., & Jouriles, E. (1986). Applications of the self-awareness model of alcohol consumption: Predicting patterns of use and abuse. *Journal of Personality and Social Psychology, 51,* 790–796.

Hunsberger, B. (1995). Religion and prejudice: The role of religious fundamentalism, quest, and right-wing authoritarianism. *Journal of Social Issues, 51,* 113–129.

Hunsberger, B. (1996). Religious fundamentalism, right-wing authoritarianism and hostility toward homosexuals in non-Christian religious groups. *The International Journal for the Psychology of Religion, 6,* 39–49.

Hunt, G. T. (1940). *The wars of the Iroquois.* Madison: University of Wisconsin Press.

Hurley, D., & Allen, B. P. (1974). The effect of the number of people present in a nonemergency situation. *Journal of Social Psychology, 92,* 27–29.

Huston, A., & Wright, J. (1996). Television and socialization of young children. In T. M. MacBeth (Ed.), *Tuning in to young viewers: Social science perspectives on television* (pp. 37–60). Thousand Oaks, CA: Sage

Hutchinson, R. R. (1983). The pain-aggression relationship and its expression in naturalistic settings. *Aggressive Behavior, 9,* 229–242.

Hutton, R. B., Mauser, G. A., Filiatrault, P., & Ahtola, T. A. (1986). Effects of cost-related feedback on consumer knowledge and consumption behavior: A field experimental approach. *Journal of Consumer Research, 13,* 327–336.

Hynie, M., & Lydon, J. E. (1995). Women's perceptions of female contraceptive behavior: Experimental evidence of the sexual double standard. *Psychology of Women Quarterly, 19,* 563–581.

Hynie, M., & Lydon, J. E. (1996). Sexual attitudes and contraceptive behavior revisited: Can there be too much of a good thing? *Journal of Sex Research, 33,* 127–134.

Hynie, M., Lydon, J. E., Cote, S., & Wiener, S. (1998). Relational sexual scripts and women's condom use: The importance of internalized norms. *Journal of Sex Research, 35,* 370–380.

Iacono, W. G., & Patrick, C. J. (1999). Polygraph ("lie detector") testing: The state of the art. In A. K. Hess & I. B. Weiner (Eds.), *The handbook of forensic psychology* (2nd ed., pp. 440–473). New York: Wiley.

Ickes, W., Patterson, M. L., Rajecki, D. W., & Tanford, S. (1982). Behavioral and cognitive consequences of reciprocal versus compensatory responses to preinteraction expectancies. *Social Cognition, 1,* 160–190.

Imrich, D. J., Mullin, C., & Linz, D. (1995). Measuring the extent of prejudicial pretrial publicity in major American newspapers: A content analysis. *Journal of Communication, 45,* 94–117.

Inglehart, M. R. (1991). *Reactions to critical life events: A social psychological analysis.* New York: Praeger.

Intrieri, R. C., & Morse, J. M. (1997). A sequential analysis of verbal and nonverbal interaction of two long-term care residents. *The Journal of Applied Gerontology, 16,* 477–494.

Isen, A. M. (1987). Positive affect, cognitive processes, and social behavior. In L. Berkowitz (Ed.), *Advances in experimental social psychology* (Vol. 20, pp. 203–253). San Diego, CA: Academic Press.

Isen, A. M. (1999). Positive affect. In T. Dalgleish & M. J. Power (Eds.), *Handbook of cognition and emotion* (pp. 521–539). Chichester, England: Wiley.

Isen, A. M., & Levin, P. A. (1972). Effect of feeling good on helping: Cookies and kindness. *Journal of Personality and Social Psychology, 21,* 384–388.

Isenberg, D. J. (1986). Group polarization: A critical review and meta-analysis. *Journal of Personality and Social Psychology, 50,* 1141–1151.

Iwata, O. (1992). A comparative study of person perception and friendly altruistic behavior intentions between Canadian and Japanese undergraduates. In S. Iwawaki, Y. Kashima, & K. Leving (Eds.), *Innovations in cross cultural psychology.* Amsterdam, Netherlands: Swets & Zeitlinger.

Izard, C. (1969). The emotions and emotion constructs in personality and culture research. In R. B. Cattell (Ed.), *Handbook of modern personality theory* (pp. 496–510). Chicago: Aldine.

Izard, C. E. (1994). Innate and universal facial expressions: Evidence from developmental and cross-cultural research. *Psychological Bulletin, 115,* 288–299.

Jackson, E. L. (1985). Environmental attitudes and preferences for energy resource options. *Journal of Environmental Education, 17,* 23–30.

Jackson, E. L. (1987). Outdoor recreation participation and views on resource development and preservation. *Leisure Sciences, 9,* 235–250.

Jackson, J. (1981, July 19). Syndicated newspaper column.

Jackson, J. M., & Williams, K. D. (1985). Social loafing on difficult tasks: Working collectively can improve performance. *Journal of Personality and Social Psychology, 49,* 937–942.

Jackson, J. S., Brown, T. N., Williams, D. R., Torres, M., Sellers, S. L., & Brown, K. (1996). Racism and the physical and mental health status of African Americans: A thirteen-year national panel study. *Ethnicity and Disease, 6,* 132–147.

Jackson, J. S., & Inglehart, M. R. (1995). Reverberation theory: Stress and racism in hierarchically structured communities. In S. E. Hobfoll & M. W. de Vries (Eds.), *Extreme stress and communities: Impact and intervention* (pp. 353–373). Dordrecht, Netherlands: Kluwer Academic Publishers.

Jackson, J. W. (1993). Realistic group conflict theory: A review and evaluation of the theoretical and empirical literature. *Psychological Record, 43,* 395–413.

Jackson, L. A. (1992). *Physical Appearance and Gender: Sociobiological and Sociocultural Perspectives.* Albany, NY: State University of New York Press.

Jackson, L. A., Hunter, J. E., & Hodge, C. N. (1995). Physical attractiveness and intellectual competence: A meta-analytic review. *Social Psychology Quarterly, 58,* 108–122.

Jackson, L. M., & Esses, V. M. (1997). Of scripture and ascription: The relation between religious fundamentalism and intergroup helping. *Personality and Social Psychology Bulletin, 23,* 893–906.

Jackson, T., Towson, S., & Narduzzi, K. (1997). Predictors of shyness: A test of variables associated with self-presentation models. *Social Behavior and Personality, 25,* 149–154.

Jacobs, D. (1998, October 16). Pesticides: On the farm, in the fields. *Ottawa Citizen.* www.npwrc.usgs.gov/narcam/info/news/Jacobs2.htm.

Jacobs, P., & Landau, S. (1971). *To serve the devil* (Vol. 2, p. 71). New York: Vintage Books.

Jacowitz, K. E., & Kahneman, D. (1995). Measures of anchoring in estimation tasks. *Personality and Social Psychology Bulletin, 21,* 1161–1166.

James, J. M., & Bolstein, R. (1992). Large monetary incentives and their effect on mail survey response rates. *Public Opinion Quarterly, 56,* 442–453.

James, W. (1890). *The principles of psychology.* New York: Holt.

Jamieson, D. W., Lydon, J. E., & Zanna, M. P. (1987). Attitude and activity preference similarity: Differential bases of interpersonal attraction for low and high self-monitors. *Journal of Personality and Social Psychology, 53,* 1052–1060.

Janes, L. M., & Olson, J. M. (2000). Jeer pressure: The behavioral effects of observing ridicule of others. *Personality and Social Psychology Bulletin, 26,* 474–485.

Janis, I. L. (1972). *Victims of groupthink.* Boston: Houghton Mifflin.

Janis, I. L. (1982). *Groupthink* (2nd ed.). Boston: Houghton Mifflin.

Janis, I. L., & Feshbach, S. (1953). Effects of fear-arousing communications. *Journal of Abnormal and Social Psychology, 49,* 78–92.

Jankowiak, W. (1995). Introduction. In W. Jankowiak (Ed.), *Romantic Passion: A Universal Experience?* (pp. 1–19). New York: Columbia University Press.

Janzen, L. (2001, May 13). Police photos, lineups faulted in Sophonow case. *Winnipeg Free Press,* p. A3.

Jecker, J., & Landy, D. (1969). Liking a person as a function of doing him a favor. *Human Relations, 22,* 371–378.

Jepson, C., & Chaiken, S. (1990). Chronic issue-specific fear inhibits systematic processing of persuasive communications. *Journal of Social Behavior and Personality, 5,* 61–84.

Job, R. F. S. (1988). Effective and ineffective use of fear in health promotion campaigns. *American Journal of Public Health, 78,* 163–167.

Johnson, D. W., & Johnson, R. T. (1987). *Learning together and alone: Cooperative, competitive, and individualistic learning* (2nd ed.). Englewood Cliffs, NJ: Prentice Hall.

Johnson, D. W., & Johnson, R. T. (1989). *A meta-analysis of cooperative, competitive, and individualistic goal structures.* Hillsdale, NJ: Erlbaum.

Johnson, H. (2001). Contrasting views of the role of alcohol in cases of wife assault. *Journal of Interpersonal Violence, 16,* 54–72.

Johnson, J. T., & Boyd, K. R. (1995). Dispositional traits versus the content of experience: Actor/observer differences in judgments of the "authentic self." *Personality and Social Psychology Bulletin, 21,* 375–383.

Johnson, M. K., Hashtroudi, S., & Lindsay, D. S. (1993). Source monitoring. *Psychological Bulletin, 114,* 3–28.

Johnson, M. K., Raye, C. L., Wang, A. Y., & Taylor, T. H. (1979). Fact and fantasy: The roles of accuracy and variability in confusing imaginations with perceptual experiences. *Journal of Experimental Psychology: Human Learning and Memory, 5,* 229–240.

Johnson, R. (1981). Perceived physical attractiveness of supporters of Canada's political parties: Stereotype or in-group bias? *Canadian Journal of Behavioural Science, 13,* 320–325.

Johnson, T. E., & Rule, B. G. (1986). Mitigating circumstance information, censure, and aggression. *Journal of Personality and Social Psychology, 50,* 537–542.

Joiner, T. E., Jr., & Wagner, K. D. (1995). Attributional style and depression in children and adolescents: A meta-analytic review. *Clinical Psychology Review, 15,* 777–798.

Jones, C., & Aronson, E. (1973). Attribution of fault to a rape victim as a function of the respectability of the victim. *Journal of Personality and Social Psychology, 26,* 415–419.

Jones, D., & Hill, K. (1993). Criteria of facial attractiveness in five populations. *Human Nature, 4*, 271–296.

Jones, E., & Kohler, R. (1959). The effects of plausibility on the learning of controversial statements. *Journal of Abnormal and Social Psychology, 57,* 315–320.

Jones, E. E. (1990). *Interpersonal perception.* New York: Freeman.

Jones, E. E., & Davis, K. E. (1965). From acts to dispositions: The attribution process in social psychology. In L. Berkowitz (Ed.), *Advances in experimental social psychology* (Vol. 2, pp. 219–266). New York: Academic Press.

Jones, E. E., & Harris, V. A. (1967). The attribution of attitudes. *Journal of Experimental Social Psychology, 3,* 1–24.

Jones, E. E., & McGillis, D. (1976). Correspondent inferences and the attribution cube: A comparative reappraisal. In J. H. Harvey, W. J. Ickes, & R. F. Kidd (Eds.), *New directions in attribution research* (Vol. 1, pp. 389–420). Hillsdale, NJ: Erlbaum.

Jones, E. E., & Nisbett, R. E. (1972). The actor and the observer: Divergent perceptions of the causes of behavior. In E. E. Jones, D. E. Kanouse, H. H. Kelley, R. E. Nisbett, S. Valins, & B. Weiner (Eds.), *Attribution: Perceiving the causes of behavior* (pp. 79–94). Morristown, NJ: General Learning Press.

Jordan, M., & Sullivan, K. (1995, September 8). A matter of saving face: Japanese can rent mourners, relatives, friends, even enemies to buff an image. *Washington Post*, pp. A1, A28.

Josephson, W. (1987). Television violence and children's aggression: Testing the priming, social script, and disinhibition prediction. *Journal of Personality and Social Psychology, 53,* 882–890.

Judd, C., & McClelland, G. (1998). Measurement. In D. Gilbert, S. Fiske, & G. Lindzey (Eds.), *The handbook of social psychology* (4th ed., Vol. 1, pp. 180–232). New York: Random House.

Judd, C. M., & Park, B. (1988). Out-group homogeneity: Judgments of variability at the individual and group levels. *Journal of Personality and Social Psychology, 54,* 778–788.

Jussim, L. (1986). Self-fulfilling prophecies: A theoretical and integrative review. *Psychological Review, 93,* 429–445.

Jussim, L. (1989). Teacher expectations: Self-fulfilling prophecies, perceptual biases, and accuracy. *Journal of Personality and Social Psychology, 57,* 469–480.

Jussim, L. (1991). Social perception and social reality: A reflection-construction model. *Psychological Review, 98,* 54–73.

Juveniles committing fewer violent crimes. (1997, Oct. 3). *Charlottesville Daily Progress*, pp. A1; A9.

Kafer, R., Hodkin, B., Furrow, D., & Landry, T. (1993). What do the Montreal murders mean? Attitudinal and demographic predictors of attribution. *Canadian Journal of Behavioral Science, 25,* 541–558.

Kahn, M. (1966). The physiology of catharsis. *Journal of Personality and Social Psychology, 3,* 278–298.

Kahneman, D., & Miller, D. T. (1986). Norm theory: Comparing reality to its alternatives. *Psychological Review, 93,* 136–153.

Kahneman, D., & Tversky, A. (1973). On the psychology of prediction. *Psychological Review, 80,* 237–251.

Kahneman, D., & Tversky, A. (1982). The simulation heuristic. In D. Kahneman, P. Slovic, & A. Tversky (Eds.), *Judgment under uncertainty: Heuristics and biases* (pp. 201–208). New York: Cambridge University Press.

Kahneman, D., & Tversky, A. (1983). Can irrationality be intelligently discussed? *The Behavioral and Brain Sciences, 6,* 509–510.

Kalin, R., & Berry, J. W. (1996). Interethnic attitudes in Canada: Ethnocentrism, consensual hierarchy and reciprocity. *Canadian Journal of Behavioural Sciences, 28,* 253–261.

Kallgren, C. A., Reno, R. R., & Cialdini, R. B. (2000). A focus theory of normative conduct: When norms do and do not affect behavior. *Personality and Social Psychology Bulletin, 26,* 1002–1012.

Kallgren, C. A., & Wood, W. (1986). Access to attitude-relevant information in memory as a determinant of attitude-behavior consistency. *Journal of Experimental Social Psychology, 22,* 328–338.

Kalven, H., Jr., & Zeisel, H. (1966). *The American jury.* Boston: Little, Brown.

Kappas, A. (1997). The fascination with faces: Are they windows to our soul? *Journal of Nonverbal Behavior, 21,* 157–162.

Karau, S. J., & Williams, K. D. (1993). Social loafing: A meta-analytic review and theoretical integration. *Journal of Personality and Social Psychology, 65,* 681–706.

Karau, S. J., & Williams, K. D. (1995). Social loafing: Research findings, implications, and future directions. *Current Directions in Psychological Science, 5,* 134–140.

Kashy, D. A., & DePaulo, B. M. (1996). Who lies? *Journal of Personality and Social Psychology, 70,* 1037–1051.

Kassarjian, H., & Cohen, J. (1965). Cognitive dissonance and consumer behavior. *California Management Review, 8,* 55–64.

Katz, D. (1960). The functional approach to the study of attitudes. *Public Opinion Quarterly, 24,* 163–204.

Kawakami, K., Dion, K. L., & Dovidio, J. F. (1998). Racial prejudice and stereotype activation. *Personality and Social Psychology Bulletin, 24,* 407–416.

Kebbell, M. R., & Wagstaff, G. F. (1998). Hypnotic interviewing: The best way to interview eyewitnesses? *Behavioral Sciences and the Law, 16,* 115–129.

Keelan, J. P. R., Dion, K. L., & Dion, K. K. (1994). Attachment style and heterosexual relationships among young adults: A short-term panel study. *Journal of Social and Personal Relationships, 11,* 201–214.

Kelley, H. H. (1950). The warm-cold variable in first impressions of persons. *Journal of Personality, 18,* 431–439.

Kelley, H. H. (1955). The two functions of reference groups. In G. E. Swanson, T. M. Newcomb, & E. L. Hartley (Eds.), *Readings in social psychology* (2nd ed., pp. 410–414). New York: Holt.

Kelley, H. H. (1967). Attribution theory in social psychology. In D. Levine (Ed.), *Nebraska Symposium on Motivation* (Vol. 15, pp. 192–238). Lincoln: University of Nebraska Press.

Kelley, H. H. (1973). The process of causal attribution. *American Psychologist, 28,* 107–128.

Kelley, H. H. (1983). Love and commitment. In H. H. Kelley, E. Berscheid, A. Christensen, J. H. Harvey, T. L. Huston, G. Levinger, E. McClintock, L. A. Peplau, & D. R. Peterson (Eds.), *Close relationships* (pp. 265–314). New York: Freeman.

Kelley, H. H., & Thibaut, J. (1978). *Interpersonal relations: A theory of interdependence.* New York: Wiley.

Kelly, A. E., Klusas, J. A., von Weiss, R. T., & Kenny, C. (2001). What is it about revealing secrets that is beneficial? *Personality and Social Psychology Bulletin, 27,* 651–665.

Kelly, J. R., & Karau, S. J. (1999). Group decision making: The effects of initial preferences and time pressure. *Personality and Social Psychology Bulletin, 25,* 1342–1354.

Kelman, H. C. (1997). Group processes in the resolution of international conflicts: Experiences from the Israeli–Palestinian case. *American Psychologist, 52,* 212–220.

Keltner D. (1995). Signs of appeasement: Evidence for the distinct displays of embarrassment, amusement, and shame. *Journal of Personality and Social Psychology, 68,* 441–454.

Keltner, D., & Buswell, B. N. (1996). Evidence for the distinctness of embarrassment, shame, and guilt: A study of recalled antecedents and facial expressions. *Cognition and Emotion, 10*, 155–171.

Kenny, D., Kashy, D., & Bolger, N. (1998). Data analysis in social psychology. In D. Gilbert, S. Fiske, & G. Lindzey (Eds.), *The handbook of social psychology* (4th ed., Vol. 1, pp. 233–268). New York: McGraw-Hill.

Kenny, D. A. (1994). Using the social relations model to understand relationships. In R. Erber & R. Gilmour (Eds.), *Theoretical Frameworks for Personal Relationships* (pp. 111–127). Hillsdale, NJ: Erlbaum.

Kenrick, D. T., & Keefe, R. C. (1992). Age preferences in mates reflect sex differences in human reproductive strategies. *Behavioral and Brain Sciences, 15*, 75–133.

Kenrick, D. T., & MacFarlane, S. W. (1986). Ambient temperature and horn honking: A field study of the heat/aggression relationship. *Environment and Behavior, 18,* 179–191.

Kent, M. V. (1994). The presence of others. In A. P. Hare, H. H. Blumberg, M. F. Davies, & M. V. Kent (Eds.), *Small group research: A handbook* (pp. 81–105). Norwood, NJ: Ablex.

Kerr, N. L. (1995). Social psychology in court: The case of the prejudicial pretrial publicity. In G. G. Brannigan & M. R. Merrens (Eds.), *The social psychologists: Research adventures* (pp. 247–262). New York: McGraw-Hill.

Kerr, N. L., & Kaufman-Gilliland, C. M. (1994). Communication, commitment, and cooperation in social dilemmas. *Journal of Personality and Social Psychology, 66,* 513–529.

Kerr, N. L., & Kaufman-Gilliland, C. M. (1997). ". . . and besides, I probably couldn't have made a difference anyway": Justification of social dilemma defection via perceived self-inefficacy. *Journal of Experimental Social Psychology, 33,* 211–230.

Kerr, N. L., & Stanfel, J. A. (1993). Role schemata and member motivation in task groups. *Personality and Social Psychology Bulletin, 19,* 432–442.

Ketelaar, T., & Ellis, B. J. (2000). Are evolutionary explanations unfalsifiable? Evolutionary psychology and the Lakatosian philosophy of science. *Psychological Inquiry, 11,* 1–21.

Key, W. B. (1973). *Subliminal seduction.* Englewood Cliffs, NJ: Signet.

Key, W. B. (1989). *Age of manipulation: The con in confidence and the sin in sincere.* New York: Holt.

Kiesler, C. A., & Kiesler, S. B. (1969). *Conformity.* Reading, MA: Addison-Wesley.

Kihlstrom, J. F. (1987). The cognitive unconscious. *Science, 237,* 1445–1452.

Kihlstrom, J. F., & Klein, S. B. (1994). The self as a knowledge structure. In R. S. Wyer & T. K. Srull (Eds.), *Handbook of social cognition. Vol. 1: Basic processes* (pp. 153–206). Hillsdale, NJ: Erlbaum.

Killen, J. D. (1985). Prevention of adolescent tobacco smoking: The social pressure resistance training approach. *Journal of Child Psychology and Psychiatry, 26,* 7–15.

Kim, M. P., & Rosenberg, S. (1980). Comparison of two structural models of implicit personality theory. *Journal of Personality and Social Psychology, 38,* 375–389.

Kim, U., & Berry, J. W. (1993). *Indigenous Psychologies: Research and Experience in Cultural Context.* Newbury Park, CA: Sage.

Kim, U., Triandis, H. C., Kagitcibasi, C., Choi, S. C., & Yoon, G. (Eds.) (1994). *Individualism and Collectivism: Theory, Method and Applications.* Thousand Oaks, CA: Sage.

King, A. S. (1971, September). Self-fulfilling prophecies in training the hard-core: Supervisors' expectations and the underprivileged workers' performance. *Social Science Quarterly,* pp. 369–378.

Kirchmeyer, C., & Bullin, C. (1997). Gender roles in a traditionally female occupation: A study of emergency, operating, intensive care, and psychiatric nurses. *Journal of Vocational Behavior, 50,* 78–95.

Kirkpatrick, L. A., & Davis, K. E. (1994). Attachment style, gender, and relationship stability: A longitudinal analysis. *Journal of Personality and Social Psychology, 66,* 502–512.

Kirkpatrick, L. A., & Hazan, C. (1994). Attachment styles and close relationships: A four-year prospective study. *Personal Relationships, 1,* 123–142.

Kirschner, R. H., Eckner, F., & Baron, R. C. (1986). The cardiac pathology of sudden unexplained nocturnal death in Southeast Asian refugees. *Journal of the American Medical Association, 256,* 2819–2918.

Kitayama, S., & Markus, H. R. (1994). Culture and the self: How cultures influence the way we view ourselves. In D. Matsumoto (Ed.), *People: Psychology from a cultural perspective* (pp. 17–37). Pacific Grove, CA: Brooks/Cole.

Klein, W. M. (1996). Maintaining self-serving social comparisons: Attenuating the perceived significance of risk-increasing behaviors. *Journal of Social and Clinical Psychology, 15,* 120–142.

Klenke, K. (1996). *Women and leadership: A Contextual Perspective.* New York: Springer.

Kliewer, W., Lepore, S. J., & Evans, G. W. (1990). The costs of Type B behavior: Females at risk in achievement situations. *Journal of Applied Social Psychology, 20,* 1369–1382.

Knapp, M. L., & Hall, J. A. (1997). *Nonverbal Communication in Human Interaction.* New York: Harcourt Brace College Publishers.

Knox, R. E., & Inkster, J. A. (1968). Postdecision dissonance at post time. *Journal of Personality and Social Psychology, 8,* 319–323.

Koehnken, G., Malpass, R. S., & Wogalter, M. S. (1996). Forensic applications of line-up research. In S. L. Sporer, R. S. Malpass, & G. Koehnken (Eds.), *Psychological issues in eyewitness identification* (pp. 205–231). Mahwah, NJ: Erlbaum.

Koestner, R., & Losier, G. F. (2002). Distinguishing three ways of being internally motivated: A closer look at introjection, identification, and intrinsic motivation. In E. L. Deci & R. M. Ryan (Eds.). *Handbook of self-determination research* (pp. 101–121). Rochester, NY: University of Rochester Press.

Kogan, N., & Wallach, M. A. (1964). *Risk-taking: A study in cognition and personality.* New York: Holt.

Kohn, A. (1993). *Punished by rewards.* Boston: Houghlin Mifflin.

Kojetin, B. A. (1993). Adult attachment styles with romantic partners, friends, and parents. Unpublished doctoral dissertation, University of Minnesota, Minneapolis.

Kollack, P., Blumstein, P. & Schwartz, P., (1994). The judgment of equity in intimate relationships. *Social Psychology Quarterly, 57,* 340–351.

Komorita, S. S., & Parks, C. D. (1995). Interpersonal relations: Mixed-motive interaction. *Annual Review of Psychology, 46,* 183–207.

Komorita, S. S., Parks, C. D., & Hulbert, L. G. (1992). Reciprocity and the induction of cooperation in social dilemmas. *Journal of Personality and Social Psychology, 62,* 607–617.

Koopman, C., Hermanson, K., Diamond, S., Angell, K., & Spiegel, D. (1998). Social support, life stress, pain and emotional adjustment to advanced breast cancer. *Psycho-Oncology, 7,* 101–111.

Koriat, A., Goldsmith, M., & Pansky, A. (2000). Toward a psychology of memory accuracy. *Annual Review of Psychology, 51,* 481–537.

Korte, C. (1980). Urban-nonurban differences in social behavior and social psychological models of urban impact. *Journal of Social Issues, 36,* 29–51.

Krajick, K. (1990, July 30). Sound too good to be true? Behind the boom in subliminal tapes. *Newsweek, 116,* 60–61.

Krakow, A., & Blass, T. (1995). When nurses obey or defy inappropriate physician orders: Attributional differences. *Journal of Social Behavior and Personality, 10,* 585–594.

Kramer, G. P., Kerr, N. L., & Carroll, J. S. (1990). Pretrial publicity, judicial remedies, and jury bias. *Law and Human Behavior, 14,* 409–438.

Krauss, R. M., & Deutsch, M. (1966). Communication in interpersonal bargaining. *Journal of Personality and Social Psychology, 4,* 572–577.

Kremer, J. F., & Stephens, L. (1983). Attributions and arousal as mediators of mitigation's effects on retaliation. *Journal of Personality and Social Psychology, 45,* 335–343.

Kressel, K., & Pruitt, D. G. (1989). A research perspective on the mediation of social conflict. In K. Kressel & D. G. Pruitt (Eds.), *Mediation research: The process and effectiveness of third party intervention* (pp. 394–435). San Francisco: Jossey-Bass.

Kristiansen, C. M., & Giulietti, R. (1990). Perceptions of wife abuse: Effects of gender, attitudes toward women, and just-world beliefs among college students. *Psychology of Women Quarterly, 14,* 177–189.

Krosnick, J. A., & Alwin, D. F. (1989). Aging and susceptibility to attitude change. *Journal of Personality and Social Psychology, 57,* 416–425.

Krosnick. J. A., Li, F., & Lehman, D. R. (1990). Conversational conventions, order of information acquisition, and the effect of base rates and individuating information on social judgments. *Journal of Personality and Social Psychology, 59,* 1140–1152.

Krueger, J., Ham, J. J., & Linford, K. (1996). Perceptions of behavioral consistency: Are people aware of the actor-observer effect? *Psychological Science, 7,* 259–264.

Kruglanski, A. W. (1989). *Lay epistemics and human knowledge.* New York: Plenum.

Kruglanski, A. W., & Mayseless, O. (1990). Classic and current social comparison research: Expanding the perspective. *Psychological Bulletin, 108,* 195–208.

Kruglanski, A. W., & Webster, D. M. (1991). Group members' reactions to opinion deviates and conformists at varying degrees of proximity to decision deadline and of environmental noise. *Journal of Personality and Social Psychology, 61,* 212–225.

Kruglanski, A. W., & Webster, D. M. (1996). Motivated closing of the mind: "Seizing" and "freezing." *Psychological Review, 103,* 263–283.

Krull, D. (1993). Does the grist change the mill? The effect of the perceiver's inferential goal on the process of social inference. *Personality and Social Psychology Bulletin, 19,* 340–348.

Kubitschek, W. N., & Hallinan, M. T. (1998). Tracking and students' friendships. *Social Psychology Quarterly, 61,* 1–15.

Kulik, J., & Brown, R. (1979). Frustration, attribution of blame, and aggression. *Journal of Experimental Social Psychology, 15,* 183–194.

Kunda, Z. (1990). The case for motivated reasoning. *Psychological Bulletin, 108,* 480–498.

Kunda, Z. (1999). *Social cognition: Making sense of people.* Cambridge, MA, US: The MIT Press.

Kunda, Z., Davies, P. G., Adams, B. D., & Spencer, S. J. (2002). The dynamic time course of stereotype activation: Activation, dissipation, and resurrection. *Journal of Personality and Social Psychology, 82,* 283–299.

Kunda, Z., Fong, G. T., Sanitioso, R., & Reber, E. (1993). Directional questions about self-conceptions. *Journal of Experimental Social Psychology, 29,* 63–86.

Kunda, Z., & Oleson, K. C. (1995). Maintaining stereotypes in the face of disconfirmation: Constructing grounds for subtyping deviance. *Journal of Personality and Social Psychology, 68,* 565–579.

Kunda, Z., & Oleson, K. C. (1997). When exceptions prove the rule: How extremity of deviance determines the impact of deviant examples on stereotypes. *Journal of Personality and Social Psychology, 72,* 965–979.

Kunda, Z., Sinclair, L., & Griffin, D. (1997). Equal ratings but separate meanings: Stereotypes and the construal of traits. *Journal of Personality and Social Psychology, 72,* 720–734.

Kunkel, D., Wilson, B., Donnerstein, E., Blumenthal, E., et al. (1995). Measuring television violence: The importance of context. *Journal of Broadcasting and Electronic Media, 39,* 284–291.

Kunz, P. R., & Woolcott, M. (1976). Season's greetings: From my status to yours. *Social Science Research, 5,* 269–278.

Kuo, Z. Y. (1961). Genesis of the cat's response to the rat. In *Instinct* (p. 24). Princeton, NJ: Van Nostrand.

Kurdek, L. A. (1992). Assumptions versus standards: The validity of two relationship cognitions in heterosexual and homosexual couples. *Journal of Family Psychology, 16,* 164–170.

Kuykendall, D., & Keating, J. P. (1990). Altering thoughts and judgments through repeated association. *British Journal of Social Psychology, 29,* 79–86.

Kwok, D. C. (1995). The self-perception of competence by Canadian and Chinese children. *Psychologia: An International Journal of Psychology in the Orient, 38,* 9–16.

Kwong, M. J., Bartholomew, K., & Dutton, D. G. (1999). Gender differences in patterns of relationship violence in Alberta. *Canadian Journal of Behavioural Science, 31,* 150–160.

La France, M. & Hecht, M. (1999). Option or obligation to smile: The effects of power and gender in facial expression. In P. Philippot, R. S. Feldman, & E. J. Coats (Eds.), *The social context of nonverbal behavior* (pp. 45–70). New York: Cambridge University Press.

La Gaipa, J. J. (1982). Rules and rituals in disengaging from relationships. In S. Duck (Ed.), *Personal relationships: Vol. 4. Dissolving personal relationships* (pp. 189–210). London: Academic Press.

Lalancette, M. F., & Standing, L. (1990). Asch fails again. *Social Behavior and Personality, 18,* 7–12.

Lalonde, R. N., Moghaddam, F. M., & Taylor, D. M. (1987). The process of group differentiation in a dynamic intergroup setting. *Journal of Social Psychology, 127,* 273–287.

Lamb, C. S., Jackson, L. A., Cassiday, P. B., & Priest, D. J. (1993). Body figure preferences of men and women: A comparison of two generations. *Sex Roles, 28,* 345–358.

Lambert, A. J., & Raichle, K. (2000). The role of political ideology in mediating judgments of blame in rape victims and their assailants: A test of the just world, personal responsibility, and legitimization hypotheses. *Personality and Social Psychology Bulletin, 26,* 853–863.

Langer, E. J., & Rodin, J. (1976). The effects of choice and enhanced personal responsibility for the aged: A field experiment. *Journal of Personality and Social Psychology, 34,* 191–198.

Langer, P. A. (1986). *Preventing domestic violence against women.* Washington, DC: U.S. Department of Justice, U.S. Government Printing Office.

Langlois, J. H., Kalakanis, L., Rubenstein, A. J., Larson, A., Hallam, M., & Smoot, M. (2000). Maxims or myths of beauty? A meta-analytic and theoretical review. *Psychological Bulletin, 126,* 390–423.

Langlois, J. H., & Roggman, L. A. (1990). Attractive faces are only average. *Psychological Science, 1,* 115–121.

Langlois, J. H., Roggman, L. A., & Musselman, L. (1994). What is average and what is not average about attractive faces? *Psychological Science, 5,* 214–220.

LaPiere, R. T. (1934). Attitudes vs. actions. *Social Forces, 13,* 230–237.

L'Armand, K., & Pepitone, A. (1975). Helping to reward another person: A cross-cultural analysis. *Journal of Personality and Social Psychology, 31,* 189–198.

Larson, J. R., Jr., Christensen, C., Franz, T. M., & Abbott, A. S. (1998). Diagnosing groups: The pooling, management, and impact of shared and unshared case information in team-based medical decision making. *Journal of Personality and Social Psychology, 75,* 93–108.

Larson, J. R., Jr., Foster-Fishman, P. G., & Franz, T. M. (1998). Leadership style and the discussion of shared and unshared information in decision-making groups. *Personality and Social Psychology Bulletin, 24,* 482–495.

Latané, B. (1981). The psychology of social impact. *American Psychologist, 36,* 343–356.

Latané, B. (1987). From student to colleague: Retracing a decade. In N. E. Grunberg, R. E. Nisbett, J. Rodin, & J. E. Singer (Eds.), *A distinctive approach to psychological research: The influence of Stanley Schachter* (pp. 66–86). Hillsdale, NJ: Erlbaum.

Latané, B., & Darley, J. M. (1968). Group inhibition of bystander intervention. *Journal of Personality and Social Psychology, 10,* 215–221.

Latané, B., & Darley, J. M. (1970). *The unresponsive bystander: Why doesn't he help?* Englewood Cliffs, NJ: Prentice Hall.

Latané, B., & Dabbs, J. M. (1975). Sex, group size, and helping in three cities. *Sociometry, 38,* 108–194.

Latané, B., & L'Herrou, T. (1996). Spatial clustering in the conformity game: Dynamic social impact in electronic games. *Journal of Personality and Social Psychology, 70,* 1218–1230.

Latané, B., & Nida, S. (1981). Ten years of research on group size and helping. *Psychological Bulletin, 89,* 308–324.

Latané, B., Nowak, A., & Liu, J. (1994). Measuring emergent social phenomena: Dynamism, polarization, and clustering as order parameters of social systems. *Behavioral Science, 39,* 1–24.

Latané, B., Williams, K., & Harkins, S. (1979). Many hands make light work: The causes and consequences of social loafing. *Journal of Personality and Social Psychology, 37,* 822–832.

Lau, R. R., & Russell, D. (1980). Attributions in the sports pages: A field test of some current hypotheses about attribution research. *Journal of Personality and Social Psychology, 39,* 29–38.

Laughlin, P. R. (1980). Social combination processes of cooperative problem-solving groups as verbal intellective tasks. In M. Fishbein (Ed.), *Progress in social psychology* (Vol. 1, pp. 127–155). Hillsdale, NJ: Erlbaum.

Laver, Ross. (1994, October 17). Apocalypse now. *Maclean's,* p. 14.

Lavine, H., Sweeney, D., & Wagner, S. H. (1999). Depicting women as sex objects in television advertising: Effects on body dissatisfaction. *Personality and Social Psychology Bulletin, 25,* 1049–1058.

Lavoie, F., Robitaille, L., & Hébert, M. (2000). Teen dating relationships and aggression. *Violence Against Women, 6,* 6–36.

Lawler, E. J., & Thye, S. R. (1999). Bringing emotions into social exchange theory. *Annual Review of Sociology, 25,* 217–244.

Lazarus, R. S. (1966). *Psychological stress and the coping process.* New York: McGraw-Hill.

Lazarus, R. S. (1993). Why we should think of stress as a subset of emotion. In L. Goldberger & S. Breznitz (Eds.), *Handbook of stress: Theoretical and clinical aspects* (2nd ed., pp. 21–39). New York: Free Press.

Lazarus, R. S. (2000). Toward better research on stress and coping. *American Psychologist, 55,* 665–673.

Lazarus, R. S., & Folkman, S. (1984). *Stress, appraisal, and coping.* New York: Springer-Verlag.

Leary, M. R. (1995). *Self-presentation: Impression management and interpersonal behavior.* Madison, WI: Brown & Benchmark.

Leathers, D. G. (1997). *Successful Nonverbal Communication: Principles and Applications.* Boston: Allyn & Bacon.

Lee, F., Hallahan, M., & Herzog, T. (1996). Explaining real-life events: How culture and domain shape attributions. *Personality and Social Psychology Bulletin, 22,* 732–741.

Lee, J. A. (1973). *The colors of love: An exploration of the ways of loving.* Don Mills, Ontario: New Press.

Lee, J. A. (1988). Love-styles. In R. J. Sternberg & M. L. Barnes (Eds.), *The psychology of love* (pp. 38–67). New Haven, CT: Yale University Press.

Lee, K., Cameron, C. A., Xu, F., Fu, G., & Board, J. (1997). Chinese and Canadian children's evaluations of lying and truth telling: Similarities and differences in the context of pro- and antisocial behaviors. *Child Development, 68,* 924–934.

Lee, Y., & Seligman, M. E. P. (1997). Are Americans more optimistic than the Chinese? *Personality and Social Psychology Bulletin, 23,* 32–40.

Lefrançois, R., Leclerc, G., Hamel, S., & Gaulin, P. (2000). Stressful life events and psychological distress of the very old: Does social support have a moderating effect? *Archives of Gerontology and Geriatrics, 31,* 243–255.

Lehman, D. R., Davis, C. G., DeLongis, A., & Wortman, C. B. (1993). Positive and negative life changes following bereavement and their relations to adjustment. *Journal of Social and Clinical Psychology, 12,* 90–112.

Leippe, M., & Eisenstadt, D. (1998). A self-accountability model of dissonance reduction: Multiple modes on a continuum of elaboration. In E. Harmon-Jones & J. S. Mills, *Cognitive dissonance theory: Revival with revisions and controversies.* Washington, DC: American Psychological Association.

Leippe, M. R., & Eisenstadt, D. (1994). Generalization of dissonance reduction: Decreasing prejudice through induced compliance. *Journal of Personality and Social Psychology, 67,* 395–413.

Leippe, M. R., Manion, A. P., & Romanczyk, A. (1992). Eyewitness persuasion: How and how well do fact finders judge the accuracy of adults' and children's memory reports? *Journal of Personality and Social Psychology, 63,* 181–197.

Leishman, K. (1988, February). Heterosexuals and AIDS. *Atlantic Monthly.*

Lemieux, R., & Hale, J. L. (1999). Intimacy, passion, and commitment in young romantic relationships: Successfully measuring the triangular theory of love. *Psychological Reports, 85,* 497–503.

Lemyre, L., & Smith, P. M. (1985). Intergroup discrimination and self-esteem in the minimal group paradigm. *Journal of Personality and Social Psychology, 49,* 660–670.

Lepore, L., & Brown, R. (1997). Category and stereotype activation: Is prejudice inevitable? *Journal of Personality and Social Psychology, 72,* 275–287.

Lepper, M. (1995). Theory by numbers? Some concerns about meta-analysis as a theoretical tool. *Applied Cognitive Psychology, 9,* 411–422.

Lepper, M. (1996). Intrinsic motivation and extrinsic rewards: A commentary on Cameron and Pierce's meta-analysis. *Review of Educational Research, 66,* 5–32.

Lepper, M. R., Greene, D., & Nisbett, R. E. (1973). Undermining children's intrinsic interest with extrinsic reward: A test of the overjustification hypothesis. *Journal of Personality and Social Psychology, 28,* 129–137.

Lepper, M. R., Keavney, M., & Drake, M. (1996). Intrinsic motivation and extrinsic rewards: A commentary on Cameron and Pierce's meta analysis. *Review of Educational Research, 66,* 5–32.

Lerner, M. J. (1980). *The belief in a just world: A fundamental decision.* New York: Plenum.

Lerner, M. J. (1991). The belief in a just world and the "heroic motive": Searching for "constants" in the psychology of religious ideology. *International Journal for the Psychology of Religion, 1,* 27–32.

Lerner, M. J., & Grant, P. R. (1990). The influences of commitment to justice and ethnocentrism on children's allocations of pay. *Social Psychology Quarterly, 53,* 229–238.

Lerner, M. J., & Miller, D. T. (1978). Just world research and the attribution process: Looking back and ahead. *Psychological Bulletin, 85,* 1030–1051.

Leung, K. (1996). Beliefs in Chinese culture. In M. H. Bond (Ed.), *The handbook of Chinese psychology* (pp. 247–262). Hong Kong: Oxford University Press.

Leung, K., & Bond, M. H. (1984). The impact of cultural collectivism on reward allocation. *Journal of Personality and Social Psychology, 47,* 793–804.

Leventhal, H., Watts, J. C., & Pagano, F. (1967). Effects of fear and instructions on how to cope with danger. *Journal of Personality and Social Psychology, 6,* 313–321.

Levi, P. (1986). *"Survival in Auschwitz"; and "The Reawakening: Two memoirs."* New York: Summit Books.

Levin, D. T. (2000). Race as a visual feature: Using visual search and perceptual discrimination tasks to understand face categories and the cross-race recognition deficit. *Journal of Experimental Psychology: General, 129,* 559–574.

Levine, J. M. (1989). Reaction to opinion deviance in small groups. In P. B. Paulus (Ed.), *Psychology of group influence,* (2nd ed., pp. 187–231). Hillsdale, NJ: Erlbaum.

Levine, J. M., & Moreland, R. L. (1998). Small groups. In D. Gilbert, S. Fiske, & G. Lindzey (Eds.), *The handbook of social psychology* (4th ed., Vol. 2, pp. 415–469). New York: McGraw Hill.

Levine, J. M., & Thompson, L. (1996). Conflict in groups. In E. T. Higgins & A. W. Kruglanski (Eds.), *Social psychology: Handbook of basic principles* (pp. 745–776). New York: Guilford.

Levine, M. P., & Smolak, L. (1996). Media as a context for the development of disordered eating. In L. Smolak, M. P. Levine, & R. Striegel-Moore (Eds.), *Developmental psychopathology of eating disorders: Implications for research, prevention, and treatment* (pp. 235–257). Mahwah, NJ: Erlbaum.

Levine, R., Sato, S., Hashimoto, T., & Verma, J. (1995). Love and marriage in eleven cultures. *Journal of Cross Cultural Psychology, 26,* 554–571.

Levine, R. A., & Campbell, D. T. (1972). *Ethnocentrism: Theories of conflict, ethnic attitudes, and group behavior.* New York: Wiley.

Levine, R. V., Martinez, T. S., Brase, G., & Sorenson, K. (1994). Helping in 36 U.S. cities. *Journal of Personality and Social Psychology, 67,* 69–82.

Levy, J. S., & Morgan, T. C. (1984). The frequency and seriousness of war: An inverse relationship? *Journal of Conflict Resolution, 28,* 731–749.

Lewin, K. (1943). Defining the "field at a given time." *Psychological Review, 50,* 292–310.

Lewin, K. (1947). Frontiers in group dynamics. *Human Relations, 1,* 5–41.

Lewin, K. (1948). *Resolving social conflicts: Selected papers in group dynamics.* New York: Harper.

Lewin, K. (1951). Problems of research in social psychology. In D. Cartwright (Ed.), *Field theory in social science* (pp. 155–169). New York: Harper & Row.

Lewis, M., & Brooks, J. (1978). Self-knowledge and emotional development. In M. Lewis & L. Rosenblum (Eds.), *The development of affect* (pp. 205–226). New York: Plenum.

Leyens, J. P., Camino, L., Parke, R. D., & Berkowitz, L. (1975). Effects of movie violence on aggression in a field setting as a function of group dominance and cohesion. *Journal of Personality and Social Psychology, 32,* 346–360.

L'Heureux-Dubé, C. (2001). Beyond the myths: Equality, impartiality, and justice. *Journal of Social Distress and the Homeless, 10,* 87–104.

Liang, D. W., Moreland, R., & Argote, L. (1995). Group versus individual training and group performance: The mediating role of transactive memory. *Personality and Social Psychology Bulletin, 21,* 384–393.

Liberman, A., & Chaiken, S. (1992). Defensive processing of personally relevant health messages. *Personality and Social Psychology Bulletin, 18,* 669–679.

Lichtenstein, S., Fischhoff, B., & Phillips, L. D. (1982). Calibration of probabilities: The state of the art to 1980. In D. Kahneman, P. Slovic, & A. Tversky (Eds.), *Judgment under uncertainty: Heuristics and biases* (pp. 306–334). New York: Cambridge University Press.

Liebert, R. M., & Baron, R. A. (1972). Some immediate effects of televised violence on children's behavior. *Developmental Psychology, 6,* 469–475.

Lim, T.-S., & Choi, S.-H. (1996). Interpersonal relationships in Korea. In W. B. Gudykunst, S. Ting-Toomey, & T. Nishida (Eds.), *Communication in Personal Relationships across Cultures* (pp. 122–136). Thousand Oaks, CA: Sage.

Lin, Y. H. W., & Rusbult, C. E. (1995). Commitment to dating relationships and cross-sex friendships in America and China. *Journal of Social and Personal Relationships, 12,* 7–26.

Lindsay, D. S. (1994). Memory source monitoring and eyewitness testimony. In D. F. Ross, J. D. Read, & M. P. Toglia (Eds.), *Adult eyewitness testimony: Current trends and developments* (pp. 27–55). New York: Cambridge University Press.

Lindsay, R. C. L. (1994). Expectations of eyewitness performance: Jurors' verdicts do not follow from their beliefs. In D. F. Ross, J. D. Read, & M. P. Toglia (Eds.), *Adult eyewitness testimony: Current trends and developments* (pp. 362–384). New York: Cambridge University Press.

Lindsay, R. C. L., & Wells, G. L. (1985). Improving eyewitness identifications from lineups: Simultaneous versus sequential lineup presentation. *Journal of Applied Psychology, 70,* 556–564.

Lindsay, R. C. L., Wells, G. L., & Rumpel, C. M. (1981). Can people detect eyewitness-identification accuracy within and across situations? *Journal of Applied Psychology, 66,* 79–89.

Linville, P. W., Fischer, G. W., & Fischhoff, B. (1993). AIDS risk perceptions and decision biases. In J. B. Pryor & G. D. Reeder (Eds.), *The social psychology of HIV infection* (pp. 5–38). Hillsdale, NJ: Erlbaum.

Linville, P. W., Fischer, G. W., & Salovey, P. (1989). Perceived distributions of characteristics of in-group and out-group members: Empirical evidence and a computer simulation. *Journal of Personality and Social Psychology, 57,* 165–188.

Linz, D. G., Donnerstein, E., & Penrod, S. (1984). The effects of multiple exposures to filmed violence against women. *Journal of Communication, 34,* 130-147.

Linz, D. G., Donnerstein, E., & Penrod, S. D. (1988). Effects of long-term exposure to violent and sexually degrading depictions of women. *Journal of Personality and Social Psychology, 55,* 758–768.

Lippmann, W. (1922). *Public opinion.* New York: Free Press.

Litt, M. D. (1988). Self-efficacy and perceived control: Cognitive mediators of pain tolerance. *Journal of Personality and Social Psychology, 54,* 149–160.

Lloyd, S. A., & Cate, R. M. (1985). The developmental course of conflict in dissolution of premarital relationships. *Journal of Social and Personal Relationships, 2,* 179–194.

Lockwood, P. (2002). Could it happen to you? Predicting the impact of downward social comparison on the self. *Journal of Personality and Social Psychology, 82,* 343–358.

Lockwood, P., & Kunda, Z. (1997). Superstars and me: Predicting the impact of role models on the self. *Journal of Personality and Social Psychology, 73,* 91–103.

Lockwood, P., & Kunda, Z. (1999). Increasing salience of one's best selves can undermine inspiration by outstanding role models. *Journal of Personality and Social Psychology, 76,* 214–228.

Lockwood, P. & Kunda, Z. (2000). Outstanding role models: Do they inspire or demoralize us? In A. Tesser, R. B. Felson, & J. M. Suls (Eds.). *Psychological perspectives on self and identity* (pp. 147–170). Washington, D.C.: American Psychological Association.

Loftus. E. (1974). Reconstructing memory. The incredible eyewitness. *Psychology Today, 8,* 116–119.

Loftus, E. (1983). Silence is not golden. *American Psychologist, 38,* 564–572.

Loftus, E. F. (1979). *Eyewitness testimony.* Cambridge, MA: Harvard University Press.

Loftus, E. F. (1993). The reality of repressed memories. *American Psychologist, 48,* 518–537.

Loftus, E. F., & Hoffman, H. G. (1989). Misinformation and memory: The creation of new memories. *Journal of Experimental Psychology: General, 118,* 100–104.

Loftus, E. F., & Ketcham, K. (1994). *The myth of repressed memory: False memories and allegations of sexual abuse.* New York: St. Martin's Press.

Loftus, E. F., Miller, D. G., & Burns, H. J. (1978). Semantic integration of verbal information into a visual memory. *Journal of Experimental Psychology: Human Learning and Memory, 4,* 19–31.

London, P. (1970). The rescuers: Motivational hypotheses about Christians who saved Jews from the Nazis. In J. R. Macaulay & L. Berkowitz (Eds.), *Altruism and helping behavior* (pp. 241–250). New York: Academic Press.

Lonner, W., & Berry, J. (Eds.). (1986). *Field methods in cross-cultural research.* Beverly Hills, CA: Sage.

Lord, C. G., Lepper, M. R., & Preston, E. (1984). Considering the opposite: A corrective strategy for social judgment. *Journal of Personality and Social Psychology, 47,* 1231–1243.

Lord, C. G., Ross, L., & Lepper, M. (1979). Biased assimilation and attitude polarization: The effects of prior theories on subsequently considered evidence. *Journal of Personality and Social Psychology, 37,* 2098–2109.

Lord, C. G., Scott, K. O., Pugh, M. A., & Desforges, D. M. (1997). Leakage beliefs and the correspondence bias. *Personality and Social Psychology Bulletin, 23,* 824–836.

Lore, R. K., & Schultz, L. A. (1993). Control of human aggression. *American Psychologist, 48,* 16–25.

Lorenz, K. (1966). *On aggression* (M. Wilson, Trans.). New York: Harcourt, Brace & World.

Losier, G. F., & Koestner, R. (1999). Intrinsic versus identified regulation in distinct political campaigns: The consequences of following politics for pleasure versus personal meaningfulness. *Personality and Social Psychology Bulletin, 25,* 287–298.

Lott, A. J., & Lott, B. E. (1974). The role of reward in the formation of positive interpersonal attitudes. In T. Huston (Ed.), *Foundations of interpersonal attraction.* New York: Academic Press.

Luby, V., & Aron, A. (1990, July). A prototype structuring of love, like, and being in love. Paper presented at the Fifth International Conference on Personal Relationships, Oxford, UK.

Ludwig, T. D., Gray, T. W., & Rowell, A. (1998). Increasing recycling in academic buildings: A systematic replication. *Journal of Applied Behavior Analysis, 31,* 683–686.

Lumsdaine, A. A., & Janis, I. L. (1953). Resistance to "counterpropaganda"; produced by one-sided and two-sided "propaganda" presentations. *Public Opinion Quarterly, 17,* 311–318.

Lundy, D. E., Tan, J., & Cunningham, M. R. (1998). Heterosexual romantic preferences: The importance of humor and physical attractiveness for different types of relationships. *Personal Relationships, 5,* 311–325.

Lupaschuk, D., & Yewchuk, C. (1998). Student perceptions of gender roles: Implications for counsellors. *International Journal for the Advancement of Counseling, 20,* 301–318.

Lupfer, M. B., & Layman, E. (1996). Invoking naturalistic and religious attributions: A case of applying the availability heuristic? The representativeness heuristic? *Social Cognition, 14,* 55–76.

Lussier, Y., Sabourin, S., & Turgeon, C. (1997). Coping strategies as moderators of the relationship between attachment and marital adjustment. *Journal of Social and Personal Relationships, 14,* 777–791.

Luus, C. A. E., & Wells, G. L. (1994a). Eyewitness identification confidence. In D. F. Ross, J. D. Read, & M. P. Toglia (Eds.), *Adult eyewitness testimony: Current trends and developments* (pp. 348–361). New York: Cambridge University Press.

Lyall, S. (1997, September 5). A ruler who lives firmly by the rules. *The New York Times,* pp. A1; A6.

Lydon, J. (1999). Commitment and adversity: A reciprocal relation. In A. Jeffrey & J. Warren (Eds.). *Handbook of interpersonal commitment and relationship stability.* New York, NY: Plenum Publishers.

Lydon, J. Zanna, M. P., & Ross, M. (1988). Bolstering attitudes by autobiographical recall: Attitude persistence and selective memory. *Personality and Social Psychology Bulletin, 14,* 78–86.

Lydon, J. E., Meana, M., Sepinwall, D., Richards, N., & Mayman, S. (1999). The commitment calibration hypothesis: When do people devalue attractive partners? *Personality and Social Psychology Bulletin, 25,* 152–161.

Lydon, J. E., & Zanna, M. P. (1990). Commitment in the face of adversity: A value-affirmation approach. *Journal of Personality and Social Psychology, 58,* 1040–1047.

Lykken, D. T. (1998). A tremor in the blood: Uses and abuses of the lie detector. New York: Plenum.

Lysak, H., Rule, B. G., & Dobbs, A. R. (1989). Conceptions of aggression: Prototype or defining features? *Personality and Social Psychology Bulletin, 15,* 233–243.

Maccoby, E. E. (1990). Gender and relationships: A developmental account. *American Psychologist, 45,* 513–520.

Maccoby, E. E., & Jacklin, C. N. (1974). *The psychology of sex differences.* Stanford, CA: Stanford University Press.

MacCoun, R. J. (1989). Experimental research on jury decision-making. *Science, 244,* 1046–1050.

MacDonald, G., Zanna, M. P., & Holmes, J. G. (2000). An experimental test of the role of alcohol in relationship conflict. *Journal of Experimental Social Psychology, 36,* 182–193.

MacDonald, T., & Ross, M. (1999). Assessing the accuracy of predictions about dating relationships. How and why do lovers' predictions differ from those made by observers? *Personality and Social Psychology Bulletin, 25,* 1417–1429.

MacDonald, T., Zanna, M., & Fong, G. (1996). Why common sense goes out the window: Effects of alcohol on intentions to use condoms. *Personality and Social Psychology Bulletin, 22,* 763–775.

MacDonald, T. K., Fong, G. T., Zanna, M. P., & Martineau A. M. (2000). Alcohol myopia and condom use: Can alcohol intoxication be associated with more prudent behaviour? *Journal of Personality and Social Psychology, 78,* 605–619.

MacDonald, T. K., & Martineau, A. M. (2002). Self-esteem, mood, and intentions to use condoms: When does low self-esteem lead to risky health behaviors? *Journal of Experimental Social Psychology, 38,* 299–306.

MacDonald, T. K., & Zanna, M. P. (1998). Cross-dimension ambivalence toward social groups: Can ambivalence affect intentions to hire feminists? *Personality and Social Psychology Bulletin, 24,* 427–441.

Mackie, D. M. (1987). Systematic and nonsystematic processing of majority and minority persuasive communications. *Journal of Personality and Social Psychology, 53,* 41–52.

Maclean, N. (1983). *A river runs through it.* Chicago: University of Chicago Press.

Madon, S., Jussim, L., & Eccles, J. (1997). In search of the powerful self-fulfilling prophecy. *Journal of Personality and Social Psychology, 72,* 791–809.

Magaro, P. A., & Ashbrook, R. M. (1985). The personality of societal groups. *Journal of Personality and Social Psychology, 48,* 1479–1489.

Magoo, G., & Khanna, R. (1991). Altruism and willingness to donate blood. *Journal of Personality and Clinical Studies, 7,* 21–24.

Maier, N. R. F., & Solem, A. R. (1952). The contribution of a discussion leader to the quality of group thinking: The effective use of minority opinions. *Human Relations, 5,* 277–288.

Maio, G. R., Bell, D. W., & Esses, V. M. (1996). Ambivalence in persuasion: The processing of messages about immigrant groups. *Journal of Experimental Social Psychology, 32,* 513–536.

Maio, G. R., Esses, V. M., & Bell, D. W. (1994). The formation of attitudes toward new immigrant groups. *Journal of Applied Social Psychology, 24,* 1762–1776.

Maio, G. R., & Olson, J. M. (1995). Relations between values, attitudes, and behavioral intentions: The moderating role of attitude function. *Journal of Experimental Social Psychology, 31,* 266–285.

Maio, G. R., & Olson, J. M. (1998). Attitude dissimulation and persuasion. *Journal of Applied Social Psychology, 27,* 1063–1084.

Maio, G. R., Olson, J. M., & Bush, J. E. (1997). Telling jokes that disparage groups: Effects on the joke teller's stereotypes. *Journal of Applied Social Psychology, 27,* 1986–2000.

Major, B. (1980). Information acquisition and attribution process. *Journal of Personality and Social Psychology, 39,* 1010–1023.

Malamuth, N. (1983). Human sexuality. In D. Perlman & P. C. Cozby (Eds.), *Social psychology.* New York: Holt, Rinehart & Winston.

Malamuth, N. M. (1981). Rape fantasies as a function of exposure to violent sexual stimuli. *Archives of Sexual Behavior, 10,* 33–47.

Malamuth, N. M. (1986). Predictors of naturalistic sexual aggression. *Journal of Personality and Social Psychology, 50,* 953–962.

Malamuth, N. M., & Briere, J. (1986). Sexual violence in the media: Indirect effects on aggression against women. *Journal of Social Issues, 42,* 75–92.

Malamuth, N. M., & Check, J. U. (1981). The effects of mass media exposure on acceptance of violence against women: A field experiment. *Journal of Sex Research, 15,* 436–446.

Malamuth, N. M., Linz, D., Heavey, C. L., Barnes, G., & Acker, M. (1995). Using the confluence model of sexual aggression to predict men's conflict with women: A 10-year follow-up study. *Journal of Personality and Social Psychology, 69,* 353–369.

Malle, B. F., & Horowitz, L. M. (1995). The puzzle of negative self-views: An exploration using the schema concept. *Journal of Personality and Social Psychology, 68,* 470–484.

Malle, B. F., & Knobe, J. (1997). Which behaviors do people explain? A basic actor-observer asymmetry. *Journal of Personality and Social Psychology, 72,* 288–304.

Malpass, R. S., & Devine, P. G. (1981). Eyewitness identification: Lineup instructions and the absence of the offender. *Journal of Applied Psychology, 66,* 482–489.

Mandal, M. K., Bryden, M. P., & Bulman-Fleming, M. B. (1996). Similarities and variations in facial expressions of emotions: Cross-cultural evidence. *International Journal of Psychology, 31,* 49–58.

Mandel, D. R., & Lehman, D. R. (1996). Counterfactual thinking and ascriptions of cause and preventability. *Journal of Personality and Social Psychology, 71,* 450–463.

Mandler, G. (1975). *Mind and emotion.* New York: Wiley.

Manis, M., Shedler, J., Jonides, J., & Nelson, T. E. (1993). Availability heuristic in judgments of set size and frequency of occurrence. *Journal of Personality and Social Psychology, 65,* 448–457.

Manstead, A. S. R. (1997). Situations, belongingness, attitudes, and culture: Four lessons learned from social psychology. In G. McGarty & H. S. Haslam (Eds.), *The message of social psychology: Perspectives on mind and society* (pp. 238–251). Oxford: Blackwell.

Maracek, J., & Mettee, D. R. (1972). Avoidance of continued success as a function of self-esteem, level of esteem certainty, and responsibility for success. *Journal of Personality and Social Psychology, 22,* 90–107.

Marion, R. (1995, August). The girl who mewed. *Discover,* pp. 38–40.

Markey, P. M. (2000). Bystander intervention in computer-mediated communication. *Computers in Human Behavior, 16,* 183–188.

Markman, K. D., Gavanski, I., Sherman, S. J., & McMullen, M. N. (1995). The impact of perceived control on the imagination of better and worse possible worlds. *Personality and Social Psychology Bulletin, 21,* 588–595.

Markus, H. (1977). Self-schemata and processing information about the self. *Journal of Personality and Social Psychology, 35,* 63–78.

Markus, H., & Kitayama, S. (1991). Culture and the self: Implications for cognition, emotion, and motivation. *Psychological Review, 98,* 224–253.

Markus, H. R., Kitayama, S., & Heiman, R. J. (1996). Culture and "basic" psychological principles. In E. T. Higgins & A. W. Kruglanski (Eds.), *Social psychology: Handbook of basic principles* (pp. 857–913). New York: Guilford.

Markus, H. R., & Nurius, P. (1986). Possible selves. *American Psychologist, 41,* 954–969.

Markus, H. R., Smith, J., & Moreland, R. L. (1985). Role of the self-concept in the social perception of others. *Journal of Personality and Social Psychology, 49,* 1494–1512.

Markus, H. R., & Zajonc, R. B. (1985). The cognitive perspective in social psychology. In G. Lindzey & E. Aronson (Eds.), *Handbook of social psychology* (3rd ed., Vol. 1, pp. 137–230). New York: McGraw-Hill.

Marlowe, D., & Gergen, K. J. (1970). Personality and social behavior. In K. J. Gergen & D. Marlowe (Eds.), *Personality and social behavior* (p. 1–75). Reading, MA: Addison-Wesley.

Marshall, V. W., Clarke, P. J., & Ballantyne, P. J. (2001). Instability in the retirement transition. *Research on Aging, 23,* 379–409.

Martin, A. J., Berenson, K. R., Griffing, S., Sage, R. E., Madry, L., Bingham, L. E., & Primm, B. J. (2000). The process of leaving an abusive relationship: The role of risk assessments and decision certainty. *Journal of Family Violence, 15,* 109–122.

Martin, K. A., & Leary, M. R. (1999). Would you drink after a stranger? The influence of self-presentational motives on willingness to take a health risk. *Personality and Social Psychology Bulletin, 25,* 1092–1100.

Martin, L. L., Seta, J. J., & Crelia, R. (1990). Assimilation and contrast as a function of people's willingness and ability to expend effort in forming an impression. *Journal of Personality and Social Psychology, 59,* 27–37.

Martz, J. M. (1991). Giving Batson's strawman a brain . . . and a heart. *American Psychologist, 20,* 162–163.

Maticka-Tyndale, E. (1992). Social construction of HIV transmission and prevention among heterosexual young adults. *Social Problems, 39,* 238–252.

Maticka-Tyndale, E., Herold, E. S., & Mewhinney, D. (1998). Casual sex on spring break: Intentions and behaviors of Canadian students. *Journal of Sex Research, 35,* 254–264.

Maticka-Tyndale, E., Herold, E. S., & Mewhinney, D. (2001). Casual sex on spring break: Intentions and behaviors of Canadian students. In R. F. Baumeister (Ed.). *Social psychology and human sexuality: Key readings in social psychology* (pp. 173–186). Philadelphia, PA: Psychology Press.

Matthews, K. A. (1988). Coronary heart disease and Type A behaviors: Update on and alternative to the Booth-Kewley and Friedman (1987) quantitative review. *Psychological Bulletin, 104,* 373–380.

Maupin, H. E., & Fisher, R. J. (1989). The effects of superior female performance and sex-role orientation on gender conformity. *Canadian Journal of Behavioral Science, 21,* 55–69.

McAlister, A., Perry, C., Killen, J., Slinkard, L. A., & Maccoby, N. (1980). Pilot study of smoking, alcohol, and drug abuse prevention. *American Journal of Public Health, 70,* 719–721.

McAllister, H. A. (1996). Self-serving bias in the classroom: Who shows it? Who knows it? *Journal of Educational Psychology, 88,* 123–131.

McArthur, L. (1972). The how and what of why: Some determinants and consequences of causal attribution. *Journal of Personality and Social Psychology, 22,* 171–193.

McArthur, L. Z. (1990). *Social perception.* Pacific Grove, CA: Brooks/Cole.

McArthur, L. Z., & Baron, R. M. (1983). Toward an ecological theory of social perception. *Psychological Review, 90,* 215–238.

McArthur, L. Z., & Berry, D. S. (1987). Cross cultural agreement in perceptions of babyfaced adults. *Journal of Cross-Cultural Psychology, 18,* 165–192.

McCann, S. J. (1992). Alternative formulas to predict the greatness of U.S. presidents: Personological, situational, and zeitgeist factors. *Journal of Personality and Social Psychology, 62,* 469–479.

McCann, S. J. H. (2001). The precocity-longevity hypothesis: Earlier peaks in career achievement predict shorter lives. *Personality and Social Psychology Bulletin, 27,* 1429–1439.

McCarthy, J. F., & Kelly, B. R. (1978). Aggressive behavior and its effect on performance over time in ice hockey athletes: An archival study. *International Journal of Sport Psychology, 9,* 90–96.

McCauley, C. (1989). The nature of social influence in groupthink: Compliance and internalization. *Journal of Personality and Social Psychology, 57,* 250–260.

McClelland, D. C. (1975). *Power: The inner experience.* New York: Irvington.

McCloskey, M., & Zaragoza, M. (1985). Misleading postevent information and memory for events: Arguments and evidence against memory impairment hypotheses. *Journal of Experimental Psychology: General, 114,* 1–16.

McConahay, J. B. (1981). Reducing racial prejudice in desegregated schools. In W. D. Hawley (Ed.), *Effective school desegregation.* Beverly Hills, CA: Sage.

McConahay, J. B. (1986). Modern racism, ambivalence, and the Modern Racism Scale. In J. F. Dovidio & S. L. Gaertner (Eds.), *Prejudice, discrimination, and racism: Theory and Research* (pp. 91–125). New York: Academic Press.

McCrae, R. R., Yik, M. S. M., Trapnell, P. D., Bond, M. H., & Paulhus, D. L. (1998). Interpreting personality profiles across cultures: Bilingual, acculturation, and peer rating studies of Chinese undergraduates. *Journal of Personality and Social Psychology, 74,* 1041–1055.

McDonald, H. E., & Hirt, E. R. (1997). When expectancy meets desire: Motivational effects in reconstructive memory. *Journal of Personality and Social Psychology, 72,* 5–23.

McDonald, J., & McKelvie, S. J. (1992). Playing safe: Helping rates for a dropped mitten and a box of condoms. *Psychological Reports, 71,* 113–114.

McFarland, C., & Buehler, R. (1997). Negative affective states and the motivated retrieval of positive life events: The role of affect acknowledgment. *Journal of Personality and Social Psychology, 73,* 200–214.

McFarland, C., & Buehler, R. (1998). The impact of negative affect on autobiographical memory: The role of self-focused attention to moods. *Journal of Personality and Social Psychology, 75,* 1424–1440.

McFarland, C., & Miller, D. (1990). Judgments of self-other similarity. *Personality and Social Psychology Bulletin, 16,* 475–484.

McFarland, C., & Miller, D. T. (1994). The framing of relative performance feedback: Seeing the glass as half empty or half full. *Journal of Personality and Social Psychology, 66,* 1061–1073.

McFarlane, J., Martin, C. L., & Williams, T. M. (1988). Mood fluctuations: Women versus men and menstrual versus other cycles. *Psychology of Women Quarterly, 12,* 201–233.

McGregor, C., Darke, S., Ali, R., & Christie, P. (1998). Experience of non-fatal overdose among heroin users in Adelaide, Australia: Circumstances and risk perceptions. *Addiction, 93,* 701–711.

McGuire, A. M. (1994). Helping behaviors in the natural environment: Dimensions and correlates of helping. *Personality and Social Psychology Bulletin, 20,* 45–56.

McGuire, W. J. (1964). Inducing resistance to persuasion. In L. Berkowitz (Ed.), *Advances in experimental social psychology* (Vol. 1, pp. 192–229). New York: Academic Press.

McGuire, W. J. (1968). Personality and susceptibility to social influence. In E. F. Borgatta & W. W. Lambert (Eds.), *Handbook of personality theory and research* (pp. 1130–1187). Chicago: Rand McNally.

McHugo, G. J., & Smith, C. A. (1996). The power of faces: A review of John T. Lanzetta's research on facial expression and emotion. *Motivation and Emotion, 21,* 85–120.

McKelvie, S. J. (1995). Biases in the estimated frequency of names. *Perceptual and Motor Skills, 81,* 1331–1338.

McKelvie, S. J. (1997). The availability heuristic: Effects of fame and gender on the estimated frequency of male and female names. *Journal of Social Psychology, 137,* 63–78.

McKelvie, S. J., & McLellan, B. (1993). "Effects of age and gender on perceived facial attractiveness." Reply. *Canadian Journal of Behavioral Science, 26,* 205–209.

McKelvie, S. J., & McLellan, B. (1994). Effects of age and gender on perceived facial attractiveness: Reply. *Canadian Journal of Behavioural Science, 26,* 205–209.

McKenna, K. Y. A., & Bargh, J. A. (2000). Plan 9 from cyberspace: The implications of the Internet for personality and social psychology. *Personality and Social Psychology Review, 4,* 57–75.

McKenzie-Mohr, D., Nemiroff, L. S., Beers, L., & Desmarais, S. (1995). Determinants of responsible environmental behavior. *Journal of Social Issues, 51,* 139–156.

McNatt, D. B. (2000). Ancient Pygmalion joins contemporary management: A meta-analysis of the result. *Journal of Applied Psychology, 85,* 314–322.

Mead, G. H. (1934). *Mind, self, and society.* Chicago: University of Chicago Press.

Medvec, V. H., Madey, S. F., & Gilovich, T. (1995). When less is more: Counterfactual thinking and satisfaction among Olympic medalists. *Journal of Personality and Social Psychology, 69,* 603–610.

Medvec, V. H., Madey, S. F., & Gilovich, T. (2002). When less is more: Counterfactual thinking and satisfaction among Olympic medalists. In T. Gilovich, D. Griffin, & D. Kahneman (Eds.). *Heuristics and biases: The psychology of intuitive judgment* (pp. 625–635). Cambridge, UK: Cambridge University Press.

Meeus, W. H. J., & Raaijmakers, Q. A. W. (1995). Obedience in modern society: The Utrecht Studies. *Journal of Social Issues, 51,* 155–175.

Meier, D. (1995). *The power of their ideas.* New York: Beacon.

Meindl, J. R., & Lerner, M. J. (1984). Exacerbation of extreme response to an out-group. *Journal of Personality and Social Psychology, 47,* 71–83.

Melara, R. D., DeWitt-Rickards, T. S., & O'Brien, T. P. (1989). Enhancing lineup identification accuracy: Two codes are better than one. *Journal of Applied Psychology, 74,* 706–713.

Memon, A., & Stevenage, S. V. (1996). Interviewing witnesses: What works and what doesn't? *Psycholoquy, 7* witness-memory.1.memon.

Menec, V. H., & Chipperfield, J. G. (1997). The interactive effect of perceived control and functional status on health and mortality among young-old and old-old adults. *Journal of Gerontology: Psychological Sciences, 52B,* 118–126.

Menec, V. H., Chipperfield, J. G., & Perry, R. (1999). Self-perceptions of health: A prospective analysis of mortality, control, and health. *Journal of Gerontology: Psychological Sciences, 54B,* 85–93.

Menec, V. H., Perry, R. P. (1998). Reactions to stigmas among Canadian students: Testing attribution-affect-help judgment model. *Journal of Social Psychology, 138,* 443–453.

Menec, V. H., Perry, R. P., Struthers, C. W., Schonwetter, D. J., Hechter, F. J., & Eichholz, B. L. (1994). Assisting at-risk college students with attributional retraining and effective teaching. *Journal of Applied Social Psychology, 24,* 675–701.

Merikle, P. M. (1988). Subliminal auditory messages: An evaluation. *Psychology and Marketing, 5,* 355–372.

Merton, R. K. (1948). The self-fulfilling prophecy. *Antioch Review, 8,* 193–210.

Messick, D., & Liebrand, W. B. G. (1995). Individual heuristics and the dynamics of cooperation in large groups. *Psychological Review, 102,* 131–145.

Metcalfe, J. (1998). Cognitive optimism: Self-deception or memory-based processing heuristics? *Personality and Social Psychology Review, 2,* 100–110.

Mewhinney, D. M., Herold, E. S., & Maticka-Tyndale, E. (1995). Sexual scripts and risk taking of Canadian university students on spring break in Daytona Beach, Florida. *Canadian Journal of Human Sexuality, 4,* 273–288.

Meyer, P. (1999). The sociobiology of human cooperation: The interplay of ultimate and proximate causes. In J. M. G. van der Dennen & D. Smillie (Eds.), *The Darwinian heritage and sociobiology: Human evolution, behavior, and intelligence* (pp. 49–65). Westport, CT: Praeger.

Meyerowitz, B. E., & Chaiken, S. (1987). The effect of message framing on breast self-examination attitudes, intentions, and behavior. *Journal of Personality and Social Psychology, 52,* 500–510.

Michalos, A. C., & Zumbo, B. D. (2001). Ethnicity, modern prejudice, and the quality of life. *Social Indicators Research, 53,* 189–222.

Michaels, J. W., Blommel, J. M., Brocato, R. M., Linkous, R. A., & Rowe, J. S. (1982). Social facilitation and inhibition in a natural setting. *Replications in Social Psychology, 2,* 21–24.

Middleton, W., Harris, P., & Surman, M. (1996). Give 'em enough rope: Perception of health and safety risks in bungee jumpers. *Journal of Social and Clinical Psychology, 15,* 68–79.

Milgram, S. (1963). Behavioral study of obedience. *Journal of Abnormal and Social Psychology, 67,* 371–378.

Milgram, S. (1969, March). The lost letter technique. *Psychology Today,* pp. 30–33, 67–68.

Milgram, S. (1970). The experience of living in cities. *Science, 167,* 1461–1468.

Milgram, S. (1974). *Obedience to authority: An experimental view.* New York: Harper & Row.

Milgram, S. (1976). Obedience to criminal orders: The compulsion to do evil. In T. Blass (Ed.), *Contemporary social psychology: Representative readings* (pp. 175–184). Itasca, IL: F. E. Peacock.

Mill, D., Gray, T., & Mandel, D. R. (1994). Influence of research methods and statistics courses on everyday reasoning, critical abilities, and belief in unsubstantiated phenomena. *Canadian Journal of Behavioral Science, 26,* 246–258.

Millin, L. (2002, August 7). Just forget recovered memory. *Winnipeg Free Press,* p. A12

Miller, A. F. (1995). Constructions of the obedience experiments: A focus upon domains of relevance. *Journal of Social Issues, 51,* 33–53.

Miller, A. G. (1986). *The Obedience Experiments: A Case Study of Controversy in Social Science.* New York: Praeger.

Miller, A. G., Ashton, W., & Mishal, M. (1990). Beliefs concerning the features of constrained behavior: A basis for the fundamental attribution error. *Journal of Personality and Social Psychology, 59,* 635–650.

Miller, C. E., & Anderson, P. D. (1979). Group decision rules and the rejection of deviates. *Social Psychology Quarterly, 42,* 354–363.

Miller, C. T. (1982). The role of performance-related similarity in social comparison of abilities: A test of the related attributes hypothesis. *Journal of Experimental Social Psychology, 18,* 513–523.

Miller, D. T., & McFarland, C. (1986). Counterfactual thinking and victim compensation: A test of norm theory. *Personality and Social Psychology Bulletin, 12,* 513–519.

Miller, D. T., & McFarland, C. (1987). Pluralistic ignorance: When similarity is interpreted as dissimilarity. *Journal of Personality and Social Psychology, 53,* 298–305.

Miller, D. T., & Ratner, R. K. (1996). The power of the myth of self-interest. In L. Montada & M. Lerner (Eds.), *Current societal concerns about justice* (pp. 25–48). New York: Plenum.

Miller, D. T., & Ross, M. (1975). Self-serving biases in the attribution of causality: Fact or fiction? *Psychological Bulletin, 82,* 213–225.

Miller, D. T., & Taylor, B. R. (2002). Counterfactual thought, regret, and superstition: How to avoid kicking yourself. In T. Gilovich, D. Griffin, & D. Kahneman (Eds.). *Heuristics and biases: The psychology of intuitive judgment* (pp. 367–378). Cambridge, UK: Cambridge University Press.

Miller, D. T., Turnbull, W., & McFarland, C. (1990). Counterfactual thinking and social perception: Thinking about what might have been. In M. P. Zanna (Ed.), *Advances in experimental social psychology* (Vol. 23, pp. 305–331). San Diego, CA: Academic Press.

Miller, J. G. (1984). Culture and the development of everyday social explanation. *Journal of Personality and Social Psychology, 46,* 961–978.

Miller, J. G., Bersoff, D. M., & Harwood, R. L. (1990). Perceptions of social responsibilities in India and the United States: Moral imperatives or personal decisions? *Journal of Personality and Social Psychology, 58,* 33–47.

Miller, N., & Campbell, D. T. (1959). Recency and primacy in persuasion as a function of the timing of speeches and measurements. *Journal of Abnormal and Social Psychology, 59,* 1–9.

Mills, J. (1958). Changes in moral attitudes following temptation. *Journal of Personality, 26,* 517–531.

Mills, J., & Clark, M. S. (1982). Communal and exchange relationships. In L. Wheeler (Ed.), *Review of personality and social psychology* (Vol. 2, pp. 121–144). Beverly Hills, CA: Sage.

Mills, J., & Clark, M. S. (1994). Communal and exchange relationships: Controversies and research. In R. Erber & R. Gilmour (Eds.), *Theoretical Frameworks for Personal Relationships* (pp. 29–42). Hillsdale, NJ: Erlbaum.

Mischel, W., Cantor, N., & Feldman, S. (1996). Principles of self-regulation: The nature of willpower and self-control. In E. T. Higgins & A. W. Kruglanski (Eds.), *Social psychology: Handbook of basic principles* (pp. 329–360). New York: Guilford.

Misconceptions about why people obey laws and accept judicial decisions. (1997, Sept.). *American Psychological Society Observer, 5,* 12–13, 46.

Mitchell, K. J., & Johnson, M. K. (2000). Source monitoring: Attributing mental experiences. In E. Tulving & F. I. Craik (Eds.), *Oxford handbook of memory* (pp. 179–195). New York: Oxford University Press.

Moghaddam, F. M., Taylor, D. M., & Wright, S. C. (1993). *Social psychology in cross-cultural perspective.* New York: Freeman.

Mohamed, A. A., & Wiebe, F. A. (1996). Toward a process theory of groupthink. *Small Group Research, 27,* 416–430.

Montemayor, R., & Eisen, M. (1977). The development of self-conceptions from childhood to adolescence. *Developmental Psychology, 13,* 314–319.

Moore, D. (2000). Mother and brother speak about Michel Trudeau's life and death and promote awareness of the danger that caused his death. Canadian Press. January 14.

Moore, T. E. (1995). Subliminal self-help tapes: An empirical test of perceptual consequences. *Canadian Journal of Behavioural Science, 27,* 9–20.

Moran, G., & Cutler, B. L. (1991). The prejudicial impact of pretrial publicity. *Journal of Applied Social Psychology, 21,* 345–367.

Moreland, R. L. (1987). The formation of small groups. In C. Hendrick (Ed.), *Review of personality and social psychology* (Vol. 8, pp. 80–110). Newbury Park, CA: Sage.

Moreland, R. L. (1999). Transactive memory: Learning who knows what in work groups and organizations. In L. L. Thompson & J. M. Levine (Eds.), *Shared cognition in organizations: The management of knowledge* (pp. 3–31). Mahwah, NJ: Erlbaum.

Moreland, R. L., Argote, L., & Krishnan, R. (1996). Socially shared cognition at work: Transactive memory and group performance. In J. L. Nye & A. M. Brower (Eds.), *What's social about social cognition?* (pp. 57–84). Thousand Oaks, CA: Sage.

Moreland, R. L., & Beach, R. (1992). Exposure effects in the classroom: The development of affinity among students. *Journal of Experimental Social Psychology, 28,* 255–276.

Moreland, R. L., & Zajonc, R. B. (1982). Exposure effects in person perception: Familiarity, similarity, and attraction. *Journal of Experimental Social Psychology, 18,* 395–415.

Morgan, D. G., & Stewart, N. J. (1998). High versus low density special care units: Impact on the behaviour of elderly residents with dementia. *Canadian Journal on Aging, 17,* 143–165.

Morgan, H. J., & Shaver, P. R. (1999). Attachment processes and commitment to romantic relationships. In J. M. Adams & W. H. Jones, *Handbook of interpersonal commitment and relationship stability* (pp. 109–124). New York: Klewer.

Morris, M. W., & Peng, K. (1994). Culture and cause: American and Chinese attributions for social and physical events. *Journal of Personality and Social Psychology, 67,* 949–971.

Morris, W. N., & Miller, R. S. (1975). The effects of consensus-breaking and consensus-preempting partners on reduction of conformity. *Journal of Experimental Social Psychology, 11,* 215–223.

Morry, M. M., & Staska, S. L. (2001). Magazine exposure: Internalization, self-objectification, eating attitudes, and body satisfaction in male and female university students. *Canadian Journal of Behavioural Science, 33,* 269–279.

Morry, M. M., & Winkler, E. (2001). Student acceptance and expectation of sexual assault. *Canadian Journal of Behavioural Science, 33,* 188–192.

Morse, D. R., Martin, J., & Moshonov, J. (1991). Psychosomatically induced death: Relative to stress, hypnosis, mind control, and voodoo: Review and possible mechanisms. *Stress Medicine, 7,* 213–232.

Moscovici, S. (1985). Social influence and conformity. In G. Lindzey & E. Aronson (Eds.), *Handbook of social psychology* (Vol. 2, pp. 347–412). New York: McGraw-Hill.

Moscovici, S. (1994). Three concepts: Minority, conflict, and behavioral style. In S. Moscovici, A. Mucchi-Faina, & A. Maass (Eds.), *Minority Influence* (pp. 233–251). Chicago: Nelson-Hall.

Moscovici, S., & Nemeth, C. (1974). Minority influence. In C. Nemeth (Ed.), *Social psychology: Classic and contemporary integrations* (pp. 217–249). Chicago: Rand McNally.

Moskalenko, S., & Heine, S. (in press). Watching your troubles away: Television viewing as a stimulus for subjective self-awareness. *Personality and Social Psychology Bulletin.*

Moyer, K. E. (1976). *The psychobiology of aggression.* New York: Harper & Row.

Moyer, K. E. (1983). The physiology of motivation: Aggression as a model. In C. J. Scheier & A. M. Rogers (Eds.), *G. Stanley Hall Lecture Series* (Vol. 3). Washington, DC: American Psychological Association.

Mullen, B. (1986). Atrocity as a function of lynch mob composition: A self-attention perspective. *Personality and Social Psychology Bulletin, 12,* 187–197.

Mullen, B., Anthony, T., Salas, E., & Driskell, J. E. (1994). Group cohesiveness and quality of decision making: An integration of tests of the groupthink hypothesis. *Small Group Research, 25,* 189–204.

Mullen, B., Brown, R., & Smith, C. (1992). Ingroup bias as a function of salience, relevance, and status: An integration. *European Journal of Social Psychology, 22,* 103–122.

Mullen, B., & Cooper, C. (1994). The relation between group cohesiveness and performance: An integration. *Psychological Bulletin, 115,* 210–227.

Mummery, W. K., & Wankel, L. M. (1999). Training adherence in adolescent competitive swimmers: An application of the theory of planned behavior. *Journal of Sport and Exercise Psychology, 21,* 313–328.

Münsterberg, H. (1908). *On the witness stand: Essays on psychology and crime*. New York: Doubleday, Page.

Muraven, M., & Baumeister, R. F. (2000). Self-regulation and depletion of limited resources: Does self-control resemble a muscle? *Psychological Bulletin, 126*, 247–259.

Muraven, M., Baumeister, R. F., & Tice, D. M. (1999). Longitudinal improvement of self-regulation through practice: Building self-control through repeated exercise. *Journal of Social Psychology, 139*, 446–457.

Muraven, M., Tice, D. M., & Baumeister, R. F. (1998). Self-control as limited resource: Regulatory depletion patterns. *Journal of Personality and Social Psychology, 74*, 774–789.

Murdoch, D., Pihl, R. O., & Ross, D. (1990). Alcohol and crimes of violence: Present issues. *The International Journal of Addictions, 25*, 1065–1081.

Murray, S. L., Bellavia, G., Feeney, B., Holmes, J. G., & Rose, P. (2001). The contingencies of interpersonal acceptance: When romantic relationships function as a self-affirmational resource. *Motivation and Emotion, 25*, 163–189.

Murray, S. L., Haddock, G., and Zanna, M. P. (1996). On creating value-expressive attitudes: An experimental approach. In Seligman, Olson, & Zanna (Eds.), *The psychology of values: The Ontario symposium* (Vol. 8). Mahwah, NJ: Lawrence, Erlbaum.

Murray, S. L., & Holmes, J. G. (1993). Seeing virtues in faults: Negativity and the transformation of interpersonal narratives in close relationships. *Journal of Personalityand Social Psychology, 65*, 707–722.

Murray, S. L., & Holmes, J. G. (1997). A leap of faith? Positive illusions in romantic relationships. *Personality and Social Psychology Bulletin, 23*, 586–604.

Murray, S. L., & Holmes, J. G. (1999). The (mental) ties that bind: Cognitive structures that predict relationship resilience. *Journal of Personality and Social Psychology, 77*, 1228–1244.

Murray, S. L., Holmes, J. G., Bellavia, G., Griffin, D. W., & Dolderman, D. (2002). Kindred spirits? The benefits of egocentrism in close relationships. *Journal of Personality and Social Psychology, 82*, 563–581.

Murray, S. L., Holmes, J. G., Dolderman, D., & Griffin, D. W. (2000). What the motivated mind sees: Comparing friends' perspectives to married partners' views of each other. *Journal of Experimental Social Psychology, 36*, 600–620.

Murray, S. L., Holmes, J. G., & Griffin, D. W. (1996a). The benefits of positive illusions: Idealization and the construction of satisfaction in close relationships. *Journal of Personality and Social Psychology, 70*, 79–98.

Murray, S. L., Holmes, J. G., & Griffin, D. W. (1996b). The self-fulfilling nature of positive illusions in romantic relationships: Love is not blind, but prescient. *Journal of Personality and Social Psychology, 71*, 1155–1180.

Murray, S. L., Holmes, J. G., MacDonald, G., & Ellsworth, P. C. (1998). Through the looking glass darkly? When self-doubts turn into relationship insecurities. *Journal of Personality and Social Psychology, 75*, 1459–1480.

Mussen, P., & Eisenberg-Berg, N. (1977). *Roots of caring, sharing, and helping: The development of prosocial behavior in children*. San Francisco: Freeman.

Mussweiler, T., Strack, F., & Pfeiffer, T. (in press). Overcoming the inevitable anchoring effect: Considering the opposite compensates for selective accessibility. *Personality and Social Psychology Bulletin*.

Myers, D. G., & Arenson, S. J. (1972). Enhancement of dominant risk tendencies in group discussion. *Psychological Reports, 30*, 615–623.

Nadler, A., & Fisher, J. D. (1986). The role of threat to self-esteem and perceived control in recipient reactions to help: Theory development and empirical validation. In L. Berkowitz (Ed.), *Advances in experimental social psychology* (Vol. 19, pp. 81–123). New York: Academic Press.

Nario, M. R., & Branscombe, N. R. (1995). Comparison processes in hindsight and causal attribution. *Personality and Social Psychology Bulletin, 21*, 1244–1255.

Nasco, S. A., & Marsh, K. L. (1999). Gaining control through counterfactual thinking. *Personality and Social Psychology Bulletin, 25*, 556–568.

Nathanson, S. (1987). *An eye for an eye? The morality of punishing by death*. Totowa, NJ: Roman & Littlefield.

Neal, A. (2000, July 7). The handbag. *The other story* [Radio show]. www.ottawa.cbc.ca/theotherstory/handbag.html (November 14, 2000).

Neisser, U. (1976). *Cognition and reality: Principles and implications of cognitive psychology*. San Francisco: Freeman.

Nemeroff, C. J., Stein, R. I., Diehl, N. S., & Smilack, K. M. (1995). From the Cleavers to the Clintons: Role choices and body orientation as reflected in magazine article content. *International Journal of Eating Disorders, 16*, 167–176.

Nemeth, C. J., & Chiles, C. (1988). Modeling courage: The role of dissent in fostering independence. *European Journal of Social Psychology, 18*, 275–280.

Neuberg, S. L. (1988). Behavioral implications of information presented outside of awareness: The effect of subliminal presentation of trait information on behavior in the Prisoner's Dilemma game. *Social Cognition, 6*, 207–230.

Neuberg, S. L. (1994). Expectancy-confirmation processes in stereotype-tinged social encounters: The moderating role of social goals. In M. P. Zanna & J. M. Olson (Eds.), *Psychology of prejudice: The seventh annual Ontario Symposium on Personality and Social Psychology*. Hillsdale, NJ: Erlbaum.

Newby-Clark, I. R., McGregor, I., & Zanna, M. P. (2002). Thinking and caring about cognitive inconsistency: When and for whom does attitudinal ambivalence feel uncomfortable? *Journal of Personality and Social Psychology, 82*, 157–166.

Newcomb, T. M. (1961). *The acquaintance process*. New York: Holt, Rinehart & Winston.

Newman, L. S. (1991). Why are traits inferred spontaneously? A developmental approach. *Social Cognition, 9*, 221–253.

Newman, L. S. (1996). Trait impressions as heuristics for predicting future behavior. *Personality and Social Psychology Bulletin, 22*, 395–411.

Newman, L. S., & Uleman, J. S. (1993). When are you what you did? Behavior identification and dispositional inference in person memory, attribution, and social judgment. *Personality and Social Psychology Bulletin, 19*, 513–525.

Newtson, D. (1974). Dispositional inferences from effects of actions: Effects chosen and effects forgone. *Journal of Experimental Social Psychology, 10*, 489–496.

Ng, W., & Lindsay, R. C. L. (1994). Cross-racial facial recognition: Failure of the contact hypothesis. *Journal of Cross-Cultural Psychology, 25*, 217–232.

Nguyen, M., Beland, F., Otis, J., & Potvin, L. (1996). Diet and exercise profiles of 30- to 60-year-old male smokers: Implications for community heart health programs. *Journal of Adolescent Health, 21*, 107–115.

Nichols, J. G. (1975). Casual attributions and other achievement-related cognitions: Effects of task outcome, attainment value, and sex. *Journal of Personality and Social Psychology, 31*, 379–389.

Nickel, R. (2002). Chief hurt by results. *Brandon Sun.* October 24. www.brandonsun.com/index.php?id=1664. (October 24, 2002)

Niedenthal, P. M., & Beike, D. R. (1997). Interrelated and isolated self-concepts. *Personality and Social Psychology Review, 1,* 106–128.

Nisbett, R. E. (1993). Violence and U.S. regional culture. *American Psychologist, 48,* 441–449.

Nisbett, R. E., Fong, G. T., Lehman, D. R., & Cheng, P. W. (1987). Teaching reasoning. *Science, 238,* 625–631.

Nisbett, R. E., Krantz, D. H., Jepson, C., & Kunda, Z. (1983). The use of statistical heuristics in everyday inductive reasoning. *Psychological Review, 90,* 339–363.

Nisbett, R. E., & Ross, L. (1980). *Human inference: Strategies and short-comings of human judgment.* Englewood Cliffs, NJ: Prentice Hall.

Nisbett, R. E., & Wilson, T. D. (1977a). Telling more than we can know: Verbal reports on mental processes. *Psychological Review, 84,* 231–259.

Nisbett, R. E., & Wilson, T. D. (1977b). The halo effect: Evidence for unconscious alteration of judgments. *Journal of Personality and Social Psychology, 35,* 250–256.

Noels, K. A., & Clément, R. (1996). Communicating across cultures: Social determinants and acculturative consequences. *Canadian Journal of Behavioural Science, 28,* 214–228.

Noels, K. A., Clément, R., Pelletier, L. G. (1999). Perceptions of teachers' communicative style and students' intrinsic and extrinsic motivation. *The Modern Language Journal, 83,* 23–34.

Norris, F. H., & Kaniasty, K. (1996). Received and perceived social support in times of stress: A test of the social support deterioration model. *Journal of Personality and Social Psychology, 71,* 498–511.

Nowak, A. & Latané, B. (1994). Simulating the emergence of social order from individual behavior. In N. Gilbert & J. Doran (Eds.), *Simulating societies: The computer simulation of social processes* (pp. 63–84). Chicago: University of Chicago Press.

Nowak, A., Szamrej, J., & Latané, B. (1990). From private attitude to public opinion: A dynamic theory of social impact. *Psychological Review, 97,* 362–376.

Oakes, P. J., & Turner, J. C. (1980). Social categorization and intergroup behavior: Does minimal intergroup discrimination make social identity more positive? *European Journal of Social Psychology, 10,* 295–301.

O'Connor, K. M., & Carnevale, P. J. (1997). A nasty but effective negotiation strategy: Misrepresentation of a common-value issue. *Personality and Social Psychology Bulletin, 23,* 504–515.

O'Farrell, T. J., & Murphy, C. M. (1995). Marital violence before and after alcoholism treatment. *Journal of Consulting and Clinical Psychology, 63,* 256–262.

Ogloff, J. R., & Vidmar, N. (1994). The impact of pretrial publicity on jurors: A study to compare the relative effects of television and print media in a child sex abuse case. *Law and Human Behavior, 18,* 507–525.

O'Hara, J. (2000, March 6). The hell of hazing. *Maclean's,* 50-52.

Ohbuchi, K. (1988). Arousal of empathy and aggression. *Psychologia: An International Journal of Psychology into the Orient, 131,* 177–186.

Ohbuchi, K., Kameda, M., & Agarie, N. (1989). Apology as aggression control: Its role in mediating appraisal of and response to harm. *Journal of Personality and Social Psychology, 56,* 219–227.

Ohbuchi, K., & Sato, K. (1994). Children's reactions to mitigating accounts: Apologies, excuses, and intentionality of harm. *Journal of Social Psychology, 134,* 5–17.

O'Leary, A. (1990). Stress, emotion, and human immune function. *Psychological Bulletin, 108,* 363–382.

O'Leary, J., & Covell, K. (2002). The tar ponds kids: Toxic environments and adolescent well-being. *Canadian Journal of Behavioural Science, 34,* 34–43.

Oliner, S. P., & Oliner, P. M. (1988). *The altruistic personality: Rescuers of Jews in Nazi Europe.* New York: The Free Press.

Olson, J. M., Maio, G. R., & Hobden, K. L. (1999). The (null) effects of exposure to disparagement humor on stereotypes and attitudes. *Humor: International Journal of Humor Research, 12,* 195–219.

Olson, J. M., Roese, N. J., & Zanna, M. P. (1996). Expectancies. In E. T. Higgins & A. W. Kruglanski (Eds.), *Social psychology: Handbook of basic principles* (pp. 211–238). New York: Guilford.

Olson, J. M., & Zanna, M. P. (1993). Attitudes and attitude change. *Annual Review of Psychology, 44,* 117–154.

Olsson, N. (2000). A comparison of correlation, calibration, and diagnosticity as measures of the confidence-accuracy relationship. *Journal of Applied Psychology, 85,* 504–511.

Olweus, D. (1994). *Bullying at school: What we know and what we can do.* London: Blackwell Publishers.

Olweus, D. (1995a). Annotation: Bullying at school: Basic facts and effects of a school based intervention program. *Journal of Child Psychology and Psychiatry, 35,* 1171–1190.

Olweus, D. (1995b). Bullying or peer abuse at school: Facts and interventions. *Current Directions in Psychological Science, 4,* 196–200.

Olweus, D. (1995c). Bullying or peer abuse in school: Intervention and prevention. In G. Davies, S. Lloyd-Bostock, M. McMurran, & C. Wilson (Eds.), *Psychology, law, and criminal justice: International developments in research and practice* (pp. 248–263). Berlin, Germany: Walter de Gruyter.

Olweus, D. (1996). Bullying at school: Knowledge base and an effective intervention program. In C. Ferris & T. Grisso (Eds.), *Understanding aggressive behavior in children.* New York Academy of Sciences, Annals of the New York Academy of Sciences, Vol. 794 (pp. 265–276). New York: Academy of Sciences.

Olweus, D. (1997). Tackling peer victimization with a school-based intervention program. In D. Fry & K. Bjorkqvist (Eds.), *Cultural variation in conflict resolution: Alternatives to violence* (pp. 215–231). Mahwah, NJ: Erlbaum.

O'Neill, P. (2000). Cognition in social context. In J. Rappaport & E. Seidman (Eds.). *Handbook of community psychology* (pp. 115–132).

Orbell, J. M., van de Kragt, A. J. C., & Dawes, R. M. (1988). Explaining discussion-induced comparison. *Journal of Personality and Social Psychology, 54,* 811–819.

Osbeck, L. M., Moghaddam, F. M., & Perrault. (1997). Similarity and attraction among majority and minority groups in a multicultural context. *International Journal of Intercultural Relations, 21,* 113–123.

Oskamp, S. (1995). Applying social psychology to avoid ecological disaster. *Journal of Social Issues, 51,* 217–238.

Oskamp, S., Burkhardt, R. I., Schultz, P. W., Hurin, S., & Zelezny, L. (1998). Predicting three dimensions of residential curbside recycling: An observational study. *Journal of Environmental Education, 29,* 37–42.

Ostrom, T., & Sedikides, C. (1992). Out-group homogeneity effects in natural and minimal groups. *Psychological Bulletin, 112,* 536–552.

Otten, C. A., Penner, L. A., & Waugh, G. (1988). That's what friends are for: The determinants of psychological helping. *Journal of Social and Clinical Psychology, 7,* 34–41.

Otto, A. L., Penrod, S. D., & Dexter, H. R. (1994). The biasing impact of pretrial publicity on juror judgments. *Law and Human Behavior, 18,* 453–469.

Ovcharchyn, C. A., Johnson, H. H., & Petzel, T. P. (1981). Type A behavior, academic aspirations, and academic success. *Journal of Personality*, *49*, 248–256.

Page, S. (1998). Accepting the gay person: Rental accommodation in the community. *Journal of Homosexuality, 36,* 31–39.

Page, S. (1999). Accommodating persons with AIDS: Acceptance and rejection in rental situations. *Journal of Applied Social Psychology, 29,* 261–270.

Palmer, D. L. (1996). Determinants of Canadian attitudes toward immigration: More than just racism? *Canadian Journal of Behavioural Science, 28,* 180–192.

Palmer, D. L. (2000). *Canadian attitudes in the wake of the boats from China.* Submitted to Citizenship and Immigration Canada.

Pancer, S. M., Brown, S. D., Gregor, P., Claxton-Oldfield, S. P. (1992). Causal attributions and the perception of political figures. *Canadian Journal of Behavioral Science, 24,* 371–381.

Pancer, S. M., & Pratt, M. W. (1999). Social and family determinants of community service involvement in Canadian youth. In M. Yates & J. Youniss (Eds.), *Roots of civic identity: International perspectives on community service and activism in youth.* Cambridge, United Kingdom: Cambridge University Press.

Pandey, J. (1990). The environment, culture, and behavior. In R. Brislin (Ed.), *Applied cross-cultural psychology* (pp. 254–277). Thousand Oaks, CA: Sage.

Paolucci-Oddone, E., Genius, M., & Violato, C. (2000). A meta-analysis of the published research on the effects of pornography. In C. Violato (Ed.). *The changing family and child development* (pp. 48-59). Burlington, VT: Ashgate Publishing.

Parke, R. D., Berkowitz, L., Leyens, J. P., West, S. G., & Sebastian, R. J. (1977). Some effects of violent and nonviolent movies on the behavior of juvenile delinquents. In L. Berkowitz (Ed.), *Advances in experimental social psychology* (Vol. 10, pp. 135–172). New York: Academic Press.

Patch, M. E., Hoang, V. R., & Stahelski, A. J. (1997). The use of meta-communication in compliance: Door-in-the-face and single-request strategies. *Journal of Social Psychology, 137,* 88–94.

Patrick, C. J., & Iacono, W. G. (1989). Psychopathy, threat, and polygraph test accuracy. *Journal of Applied Psychology, 74,* 347–355.

Patterson, A. (1974, September). *Hostility catharsis: A naturalistic quasi-experiment.* Paper presented at the meeting of the American Psychological Association, New Orleans.

Patterson, L. A., Cameron, J. E., & Lalonde, R. N. (1996). The intersection of race and gender: Examining the politics of identity in women's studies. *Canadian Journal of Behavioural Science, 28,* 229–239.

Paulhus, D. L. (1987). Effect of group selection on correlations and factor patterns in sex role research. *Journal of Personality and Social Pscyhology, 53,* 314–317.

Paulhus, D. L. (1998). Interpersonal and intrapsychic adaptiveness of trait self-enhancement: A mixed blessing? *Journal of Personality and Social Psychology, 74,* 1197–1208.

Paulhus, D. L., & Bruce, M. N. (1992). The effect of acquaintanceship on the validity of personality impressions: A longitudinal study. *Journal of Personality and Social Psychology, 63,* 816–824.

Paulhus, D. L., & Morgan, K. L. (1997). Perceptions of intelligence in leadership groups: The dynamic effects of shyness and acquaintance. *Journal of Personality and Social Psychology, 72,* 581–591.

Paulhus, D. L., & Reynolds, S. (1995). Enhancing target variance in personality impressions: Highlighting the person in person perception. *Journal of Personality and Social Psychology, 69,* 1233–1242.

Paulus, P. B, & Dzindolet, M. T. (1992). The effects of prison confinement. In P. Suedfeld & P. E. Tetlock (Eds.), *Psychology and social policy* (pp. 327–341). New York: Hemisphere.

Paulus, P. B., McCain, G., & Cox, V. (1981). Prison standards: Some pertinent data on crowding. *Federal Probation, 15,* 48–54.

Peirce, R. S., Frone, M. R., Russell, M., & Cooper, M. L. (1996). Financial stress, social support, and alcohol involvement: A longitudinal test of the buffering hypothesis in a general population survey. *Health Psychology, 15,* 38–47.

Pelham, B. W. (1991). On confidence and consequence: The certainty and importance of self-knowledge. *Journal of Personality and Social Psychology, 60,* 518–530.

Pelletier, L. G. (2002). A motivational analysis of self-determination for pro-environmental behaviors. In E. L. Deci & R. M. Ryan (Eds.). *Handbook of self-determination research* (pp. 205–232). Rochester, NY: University of Rochester Press.

Pelletier, L. G., Dion, S., Tuson, K., & Green-Demers, I. (1999). Why do people fail to adopt environmental protective behaviors? Toward a taxonomy of environmental amotivation. *Journal of Applied Social Psychology, 29,* 2481–2504.

Pelletier, L. G., Fortier, M. S., Vallerand, R. J., & Briere, N. M. (1996). *Perceived autonomy support, motivation, and persistence in physical activity: A longitudinal investigation.* Unpublished manuscript, University of Ottawa.

Pennebaker, J. W. (1982). *The psychology of physical symptoms.* New York: Springer-Verlag.

Pennebaker, J. W. (1990). *Opening up: The healing powers of confiding in others.* New York: William Morrow.

Pennebaker, J. W. (1997). Writing about emotional experiences as a therapeutic process. *Psychological Science*, *8,* 162–166.

Pennebaker, J. W., Barger, S. D., & Tiebout, J. (1989). Disclosure of traumas and health among Holocaust survivors. *Psychosomatic Medicine, 51,* 577–589.

Pennebaker, J. W., & Beale, S. K. (1986). Confronting a traumatic event: Toward an understanding of inhibition and disease. *Journal of Abnormal Psychology, 95,* 274–281.

Pennebaker, J. W., Colder, M., & Sharp, L. K. (1990). Accelerating the coping process. *Journal of Personality and Social Psychology, 58,* 528–537.

Pennebaker, J. W., & Harber, K. D. (1993). A social stage model of collective coping: The Loma Prieta earthquake and the Persian Gulf War. *Journal of Social Issues, 49,* 125–145.

Pennebaker, J. W., & Sanders, D. Y. (1976). American graffiti: Effects of authority and reactance arousal. *Personality and Social Psychology Bulletin, 2,* 264–267.

Pennebaker, J. W., & Seagal, J. D. (1999). Forming a story: The health benefits of narrative. *Journal of Consumer Psychology, 55,* 1243–1254.

Penner, L. A., & Finkelstein, M. A. (1998). Dispositional and structural determinants of volunteerism. *Journal of Personality and Social Psychology, 74,* 525–537.

Penner, L. A., Fritzsche, B. A., Craiger, J. P., & Freifeld, T. S. (1995). Measuring the prosocial personality. In J. Butcher & C. Spielberger (Eds.), *Advances in personality assessment* (Vol. 10, pp. 147–163). Hillsdale, NJ: Erlbaum.

Pennington, N., & Hastie, R. (1988). Explanation-based decision making: Effects of memory structure on judgment. *Journal of Experimental Psychology: Learning, Memory, and Cognition, 14,* 521–533.

Pennington, N., & Hastie, R. (1990). Practical implications of psychological research on juror and jury decision making. *Personality and Social Psychology Bulletin, 16,* 90–105.

Ramsey, S. J. (1981). The kinesics of femininity in Japanese women. *Language Sciences, 3,* 104–123.

Rapoport, A., & Chammah, A. M. (1965). *Prisoner's Dilemma: A study in conflict and cooperation.* Ann Arbor: University of Michigan Press.

Raps, C. S., Peterson, C., Jonas, M., & Seligman, M. E. P. (1982). Patient behavior in hospitals: Helplessness, reactance, or both? *Journal of Personality and Social Psychology, 42,* 1036–1041.

Read, J. D., Connolly, D., & Turtle, J. W. (2001). Memory in legal contexts: Remembering events, circumstances, and people. In R. A. Schuller, & J. R. P. Ogloff (Eds.). (2001). *Introduction to psychology and law: Canadian perspectives* (pp. 95–125). Toronto: University of Toronto Press.

Reeves, R. A., Baker, G. A., Boyd, J. G., & Cialdini, R. B. (1991). The door-in-the-face technique: Reciprocal concessions vs. self-presentational explanations. *Journal of Social Behavior and Personality, 6,* 545–558.

Regan, P. C. (1998). Of lust and love: Beliefs about the role of sexual desire in romantic relationships. *Personal Relationships, 5,* 139–157.

Regan, P. C., & Berscheid, E. (1997). Gender differences in characteristics desired in a potential sexual and marriage partner. *Journal of Psychology and Human Sexuality*, *9*, 25–37.

Regan, P. C., & Berscheid, E. (1999). *Lust: What we know about human sexual desire.* Thousand Oaks, CA: Sage.

Regan, P. C., Snyder, M., & Kassin, S. M. (1995). Unrealistic optimism: Self-enhancement or person positivity? *Personality and Social Psychology Bulletin*, *21*, 1073–1082.

Regehr, C., Cadell, S., & Jansen, K. (1999). Perceptions of control and long-term recovery from rape. *American Journal of Orthopsychiatry, 69,* 110–115.

Rehm, J., Steinleitner, M., & Lilli, W. (1987). Wearing uniforms and aggression: A field experiment. *European Journal of Social Psychology, 17,* 357–360.

Reichl, A. J. (1997). Ingroup favouritism and outgroup favouritism in low status minimal groups: Differential responses to status-related and status-unrelated measures. *European Journal of Social Psychology, 27,* 617–633.

Reifman, A. S., Larrick, R., & Fein, S. (1988). *The heat-aggression relationship in major-league baseball.* Paper presented at the meeting of the American Psychological Association, San Francisco.

Reis, H. T., Nezlek, J., & Wheeler, L. (1980). Physical attractiveness in social interaction. *Journal of Personality and Social Psychology, 38,* 604–617.

Reis, H. T., & Patrick, B. C. (1996). Attachment and intimacy: Component processes. In E. T. Higgins & A. W. Kruglanski (Eds.), *Social psychology: Handbook of basic principles* (pp. 523–563). New York: Guilford Press.

Reis, H. T., Wheeler, L., Speigel, N., Kernis, M. H., Nezlek, J., & Perri, M. (1982). Physical attractiveness in social interaction 2: Why does appearance affect social experience? *Journal of Personality and Social Psychology, 43,* 979–996.

Reis, T. J., Gerrard, M., & Gibbons, F. X. (1993). Social comparison and the pill: Reactions to upward and downward comparison of contraceptive behavior. *Personality and Social Psychology Bulletin, 19,* 13–20.

Reiter, S. M., & Samuel, W. (1980). Littering as a function of prior litter and the presence or absence of prohibitive signs. *Journal of Applied Social Psychology, 10,* 45–55.

Rempel, J. K., Ross, M., & Holmes, J. G. (2001). Trust and communicated attributions in close relationships. *Journal of Personality and Social Psychology, 81,* 57–64.

Reno, R., Cialdini, R., & Kallgren, C. A. (1993). The transsituational influence of social norms. *Journal of Personality and Social Psychology, 64,* 104–112.

Reynolds, L. (2000). Some folks call Tillie "a miracle worker." *Winnipeg Free Press.* March 22: D3.

Rheingold, H. L. (1982). Little children's participation in the work of adults: A nascent prosocial behavior. *Child Development, 53,* 114–125.

Rhodes, N., & Wood, W. (1992). Self-esteem and intelligence affect influenceability: The mediating role of message reception. *Psychological Bulletin, 111,* 156–171.

Rholes, W. S., Newman, L. S., & Ruble, D. N. (1990). Understanding self and other: Developmental and motivational aspects of perceiving persons in terms of invariant dispositions. In E. T. Higgins & R. M. Sorrentino (Eds.), *Handbook of Motivation and Cognition: Foundations of Social Behavior*, (Vol. 2). New York: Guilford.

Richards, J. M., & Gross, J. J. (1999). Composure at any cost? The cognitive consequences of emotion suppression. *Personality and Social Psychology Bulletin, 25,* 1033–1044.

Richardson, D., Hammock, G., Smith, S., & Gardner, W. (1994). Empathy as a cognitive inhibitor of interpersonal aggression. *Aggressive Behavior, 20,* 275–289.

Richardson, H. R. L., Beazley, R. P., Delaney, M. E., & Langille, D. E. (1997). Factors influencing condom use among students attending high school in Nova Scotia. *Canadian Journal of Human Sexuality, 6,* 185–196.

Ringelmann, M. (1913). Recherches sur les moteurs animés: Travail de l'homme. *Annales de l'Institut National Argonomique,* 2e srie, tom 12, 1–40.

Riordan, C. A. (1978). Equal-status interracial contact: A review and revision of a concept. *International Journal of Intercultural Relations, 2,* 161–185.

Roberts, K. P. (1996). How research on source monitoring can inform cognitive interview techniques. *Psycholoquy, 7* witness-memory.15.roberts.

Roberts, W., & Strayer, J. (1996). Empathy, emotional expressiveness, and prosocial behavior. *Child Development, 67,* 449–470.

Robins, R. W., Spranca, M. D., & Mendelsohn, G. A. (1996). The actor-observer effect revisited: Effects of individual differences and repeated social interactions on actor and observer attributions. *Journal of Personality and Social Psychology*, *71*, 375–389.

Rodin, J. (1986). Aging and health: Effects of the sense of control. *Science, 233,* 1271–1276.

Rodin, J., & Langer, E. J. (1977). Long-term effects of a control-relevant intervention with the institutional aged. *Journal of Personality and Social Psychology, 35,* 897–902.

Roesch, S. C., & Amirkhan, J. H. (1997). Boundary conditions for self-serving attributions: Another look at the sports pages. *Journal of Applied Social Psychology*, *27*, 245–261.

Roese, N. J. (1994). The functional basis of counterfactual thinking. *Journal of Personality and Social Psychology, 66,* 805–818.

Roese, N. J. (1997). Counterfactual thinking. *Psychological Bulletin, 121,* 133–148.

Roese, N. J., Hur, T., & Pennington, G. L. (1999). Counterfactual thinking and regulatory focus: Implications for action versus inaction and sufficiency versus necessity. *Journal of Personality and Social Psychology, 77,* 1109–1120.

Roese, N. J., & Olson, J. M. (1993). Self-esteem and counterfactual thinking. *Journal of Personality and Social Psychology, 65,* 199–206.

Roese, N. J., & Olson, J. M. (1994). Attitude importance as a function of repeated attitude expression. *Journal of Experimental and Social Psychology, 30,* 39–51.

Roese, N. J., & Olson, J. M. (1995). Outcome controllability and counter-factual thinking. *Personality and Social Psychology Bulletin, 21,* 620–628.

Roese, N. J., & Olson, J. M. (1996). Counterfactuals, causal attributions, and the hindsight bias: A conceptual integration. *Journal of Experimental Social Psychology, 32,* 197–227.

Roese, N. J., & Olson, J. M. (1997). Counterfactual thinking: The inter-section of affect and function. In M. Zanna (Ed.), *Advances in experi-mental social psychology* (Vol. 29). San Diego, CA: Academic Press.

Roese, N. J., & Sande, G. N. (1993). Backlash effects in attack politics. *Journal of Applied Social Psychology, 23,* 632–653.

Rogers, P. (1998). The cognitive psychology of lottery gambling: A theo-retical review. *Journal of Gambling Studies, 14,* 111–134.

Rogers, R. (1983). Cognitive and physiological processes in fear appeals and attitude change: A revised theory of protection motivation. In J. T. Cacioppo & R. E. Petty (Eds.), *Social psychophysiology: A source-book* (pp. 153–176). New York: Guilford Press.

Rohan, M., & Zanna, M. (1996). Value transmission in families. In C. Seligman, J. Olson, & M. Zanna (Eds.), *The psychology of values: The Ontario symposium on personality and social psychology, Vol. 8,* pp. 253–276. Mahwah, NJ: Erlbaum.

Rosch, E., & Lloyd, B. (1978). (Eds.) *Cognition and categorization.* Hillsdale, NJ: Erlbaum.

Rose, V. G., & Ogloff, J. R. P. (2001). Evaluating the comprehensibility of jury instructions: A method and an example. *Law and Human Behavior, 25,* 409–431.

Rosen, S., Bergman, M., Plester, D., El-Mofty, A., & Satti, M. (1962). Prebycusis study of a relatively noise-free population in the Sudan. *Annals of Otology, Rhinology, and Laryngology, 71,* 727–743.

Rosenbaum, M. E. (1986). The repulsion hypothesis: On the nondevel-opment of relationships. *Journal of Personality and Social Psychology, 51,* 1156–1166.

Rosenberg, L. A. (1961). Group size, prior experience, and conformity. *Journal of Abnormal and Social Psychology, 63,* 436–437.

Rosenberg, M. J., Davidson, A. J., Chen, J., Judson, F. N., & Douglas, J. M. (1992). Barrier contraceptives and sexually transmitted diseases in women: A comparison of female-dependent methods and condoms. *American Journal of Public Health, 82,* 669–674.

Rosenberg, S., Nelson, S., & Vivekananthan, P. S. (1968). A multidimen-sional approach to the structure of personality impressions. *Journal of Personality and Social Psychology, 9,* 283–294.

Rosenblatt, P. C. (1974). Cross-cultural perspectives on attraction. In T. L. Huston (Ed.), *Foundations of interpersonal attraction* (pp. 79–99). New York: Academic Press.

Rosenhan, D. L. (1970). The natural socialization of altruistic autonomy. In J. R. Macaulay & L. Berkowitz (Eds.), *Altruism and helping behav-ior* (pp. 251–268). New York: Academic Press.

Rosenhan, D. L. (1973). On being sane in insane places. *Science, 179,* 250–258.

Rosenman, R. H. (1993). Relationship of the Type A behavior pattern with coronary heart disease. In L. Goldberger & S. Breznitz (Eds.), *Handbook of stress: Theoretical and clinical aspects* (2nd ed., pp. 449–476). New York: Free Press.

Rosenthal, A. M. (1964). *Thirty-eight witnesses.* New York: McGraw-Hill.

Rosenthal, R. (1994). Interpersonal expectancy effects: A 30-year per-spective. *Current Directions in Psychological Science, 3,* 176–179.

Rosenthal, R. (1995). Critiquing Pygmalion: A 25-year perspective. *Current Directions in Psychological Science, 4,* 171–172.

Rosenthal, R., & Jacobson, L. (1968). *Pygmalion in the classroom: Teacher expectation and student intellectual development.* New York: Holt, Rinehart & Winston.

Ross, L. (1977). The intuitive psychologist and his shortcomings: Distortions in the attribution process. In L. Berkowitz (Ed.), *Advances in experimental social psychology* (Vol. 10, pp. 173–220). Orlando, FL: Academic Press.

Ross, L. (1998). Comment on Gilbert. In J. M. Darley & J. Cooper (Eds.), *Attribution and social interaction* (pp. 53–66). Washington, DC: American Psychological Association.

Ross, L., Amabile, T. M., & Steinmetz, J. L. (1977). Social roles, social control, and biases in social perception. *Journal of Personality and Social Psychology, 35,* 485–494.

Ross, L., Lepper, M. R., & Hubbard, M. (1975). Perseverance in self per-ception and social perception: Biased attributional processes in the debriefing paradigm. *Journal of Personality and Social Psychology, 32,* 880–892.

Ross, L., & Nisbett, R. E. (1991). *The person and the situation: Perspectives of social psychology.* New York: McGraw-Hill.

Ross, L., & Samuels, S. M. (1993). *The predictive power of personal reputa-tion versus labels and construal in the Prisoner's Dilemma game.* Unpublished manuscript, Stanford University.

Ross, L., & Ward, A. (1995). Psychological barriers to dispute resolution. In M. P. Zanna (Ed.), *Advances in experimental social psychology* (Vol. 27, pp. 255–304). San Diego, CA: Academic Press.

Ross, L., & Ward, A. (1996). Naive realism: Implications for social con-flict and misunderstanding. In T. Brown, E. Reed, & E. Turiel (Eds.), *Values and knowledge.* Hillsdale, NJ: Erlbaum.

Ross, L. R., & Spinner, B. (2001). General and specific attachment repre-sentations in adulthood: Is there a relationship? *Journal of Social and Personal Relationships, 18,* 747–766.

Ross, M. (1989). Relation of implicit theories to the construction of per-sonal histories. *Psychological Review, 96,* 341–357.

Ross, M., & McFarland, C. (1988). Constructing the past: Biases in per-sonal memories. In D. Bar-Tel & A. Kruglanski (Eds.), *The social psychology of knowledge* (pp. 299–314). New York: Cambridge University Press.

Ross, M., McFarland, C., Conway, M., & Zanna, M. P. (1983). Reciprocal relation between attitudes and behavior recall: Committing people to newly formed attitudes. *Journal of Personality and Social Psychology, 45,* 257–267.

Ross, M., & Olson, J. M. (1981). An expectancy-attribution model of the effects of placebos. *Psychological Review, 88,* 408–437.

Ross, M., & Sicoly, F. (1979). Egocentric biases in availability and attribu-tion. *Journal of Personality and Social Psychology, 45,* 257–267.

Ross, M., & Wilson, A. E. (2002). It feels like yesterday: Self-esteem, valence of personal past experiences, and judgments of subjective distance. *Journal of Personality and Social Psychology, 82,* 792–803.

Ross, M., Xun, W. Q. E., & Wilson, A. E. (2002). Language and the bicul-tural self. *Personality and Social Psychology Bulletin, 28,* 1040–1050.

Ross, W., & La Croix, J. (1996). Multiple meanings of trust in negotia-tion theory and research: A literature review and integrative model. *International Journal of Conflict Management, 7,* 314–360.

Roszell, P., Kennedy, D., & Grabb, E. (1989). Physical attractiveness and income attainment among Canadians. *Journal of Psychology, 123,* 547–559.

Rotenberg, K. J. (1998). Stigmatizations of transitions in loneliness. *Journal of Social and Personal Relationships, 15,* 565–576.

Rothbaum, F., & Tsang, B. Y.-P. (1998). Lovesongs in the United States and China: On the nature of romantic love. *Journal of Cross-Cultural Psychology, 29,* 306–319.

Rothman, A. J. (2000). Toward a theory-based analysis of behavioral maintenance. *Health Psychology, 19,* 64–69.

Rothman, A. J., & Hardin, C. D. (1997). Differential use of the availability heuristic in social judgment. *Personality and Social Psychology Bulletin, 23,* 123–138.

Rothman, A. J., Martino, S. C., Bedell, B. T., Detweiler, J. B., & Salovey, P. (1999). The systematic influence of gain- and loss-framed messages on interest in and use of different types of health behavior. *Personality and Social Psychology Bulletin, 25,* 1355–1369.

Rothman, A. J., & Salovey, P. (1997). Shaping perceptions to motivate healthy behavior: The role of message framing. *Psychological Bulletin, 121,* 3–19.

Rothman, A. J., Salovey, P., Antone, C., Keough, K., & Martin, C. D. (1993). The influence of message framing on intentions to perform health behaviors. *Journal of Experimental Social Psychology, 29,* 408–432.

Rotton, J., & Frey, J. (1985). Air pollution, weather, and violent crimes: Concomitant time-series analysis of archival date. *Journal of Personality and Social Psychology, 49,* 1207–1220.

Rousseau, J. J. (1930). *The social contract and discourses.* New York: Dutton.

Rubin, Z. (1970). Measurement of romantic love. *Journal of Personality and Social Psychology, 16,* 265–273.

Rubin, Z. (1973). *Liking and loving: An invitation to social psychology.* New York: Holt, Rinehart & Winston.

Rubin, Z., Peplau, L. A., & Hill, C. T. (1981). Loving and leaving: Sex differences in romantic attachments. *Sex Roles, 7,* 821–835.

Ruble, D. N., & Feldman, N. S. (1976). Order of consistency, distinctiveness, and consistency information and causal attribution. *Journal of Personality and Social Psychology, 31,* 930–937.

Rudman, L. A., & Borgida, E. (1995). The afterglow of construct accessibility: The behavioral consequences of priming men to view women as sexual objects. *Journal of Experimental Social Psychology, 31,* 493–517.

Ruggiero, K., & Taylor, D. (1997). Why minority group members perceive or do not perceive the discrimination that confronts them: The role of self-esteem and perceived control. *Journal of Personality and Social Psychology, 72,* 373–389.

Ruggiero, K. M., & Taylor, D. M. (1995). Coping with discrimination: How disadvantaged group members perceive the discrimination that confronts them. *Journal of Personality and Social Psychology, 68,* 826–838.

Rule, B. G., Taylor, B. R., & Dobbs, A. R. (1987). Priming affects of heat on aggressive thoughts. *Social Cognition, 5,* 131–143.

Rusbult, C. E. (1980). Commitment and satisfaction in romantic associations: A test of the investment model. *Journal of Experimental Social Psychology, 16,* 172–186.

Rusbult, C. E. (1983). A longitudinal test of the investment model: The development (and deterioration) of satisfaction and commitment in heterosexual involvements. *Journal of Personality and Social Psychology, 45,* 101–117.

Rusbult, C. E. (1991). *Commitment processes in close relationships: The investment model.* Paper presented at the meeting of the American Psychological Association, San Francisco.

Rusbult, C. E. (1993). Understanding responses to dissatisfaction in close relationships: The exit-voice-loyalty-neglect model. In S. Worchel & J. A. Simpson (Eds.), *Conflict Between People and Groups: Causes, Processes, and Resolutions* (pp. 30–59). Chicago: Nelson-Hall.

Rusbult, C. E., & Buunk, A. P. (1993). Commitment processes in close relationships: An interdependence analysis. *Journal of Social and Personal Relationships, 10,* 175–204.

Rusbult, C. E., & Martz, J. M. (1995). Remaining in an abusive relationship: An investment model analysis of nonvoluntary dependence. *Personality and Social Psychology Bulletin, 21,* 558–571.

Rusbult, C. E., Martz, J. M., & Agnew, C. R. (1998). The investment model scale: Measuring commitment level, satisfaction level, quality of alternatives, and investment size. *Personal Relationships, 5,* 357–391.

Rusbult, C. E., & Van Lange, P. A. M. (1996). Interdependence processes. In E. T. Higgins & A. W. Kruglanski (Eds.), *Social Psychology: Handbook of Basic Principles* (pp. 564–596). New York: Guilford.

Rusbult, C. E., Yovetich, N. A., & Verette, J. (1996). An interdependence analysis of accommodation processes. In G. J. O. Fletcher & J. Fitness (Eds.), *Knowledge Structures in Close Relationships: A Social Psychological Approach* (pp. 63–90). Mahwah, NJ: Erlbaum.

Rushton, J. P. (1975). Generosity in children: Immediate and long-term effects of modeling, preaching, and moral judgment. *Journal of Personality and Social Psychology, 31,* 459–466.

Rushton, J. P. (1989). Genetic similarity, human altruism, and group selection. *Behavioral and Brain Sciences, 12,* 503–559.

Russell, B., & Branch, T. (1979). *Second wind: The memoirs of an opinionated man.* New York: Ballantine Books.

Russell, G. W. (1983). Psychological issues in sports aggression. In J. H. Goldstein (Ed.), *Sports violence.* New York: Springer-Verlag.

Russell, G. W., & Arms, R. L. (1998). Toward a social psychological profile of would-be rioters. *Aggressive Behavior, 24,* 219–226.

Russell, J. A. (1994). Is there universal recognition of emotion from facial expressions? A review of the cross-cultural studies. *Psychological Bulletin, 115,* 102–141.

Russell, J. A., & Fehr, B. (1987). Relativity in the perception of emotion in facial expressions. *Journal of Experimental Psychology: General, 116,* 223–237.

Russell, J. A., & Fehr, B. (1988). The role of context in interpreting facial expression: Reply to Ekman and O'Sullivan. *Journal of Experimental Psychology: General, 117,* 89–90.

Russell, J. A., & Fehr, B. (1994). Fuzzy concepts in a fuzzy hierarchy: Varieties of anger. *Journal of Personality and Social Psychology, 67,* 186–205.

Russell, J. A., Suzuki, N., & Ishida, N. (1993). Canadian, Greek, and Japanese freely produced emotion labels for facial expressions. *Motivation and Emotion, 17,* 337–351.

Rutter, D. R., Quine, L., & Albery, I. P. (1998). Perceptions of risk in motorcyclists: Unrealistic optimism, relative realism, and predictions of behaviour. *British Journal of Psychology, 89,* 681–696.

Ryan, B., Jr. (1991). *It works! How investment spending in advertising pays off.* New York: American Association of Advertising Agencies.

Ryan, R. M., & Deci, E. L. (1996). When paradigms clash: Comments on Cameron and Pierce's claim that rewards do not undermine intrinsic motivation. *Review of Educational Research, 66,* 33–38.

Sacks, O. (1987). *The man who mistook his wife for a hat and other clinical tales.* New York: Harper & Row.

Salovey, P., Mayer, J. D., & Rosenhan, D. L. (1991). Mood and helping: Mood as a motivator of helping and helping as a regulator of mood. In M. S. Clark (Ed.), *Prosocial behavior: Review of personality and social psychology* (Vol. 12, pp. 215–237). Newbury Park, CA: Sage.

Salovey, P., & Rodin, J. (1985). Cognitions about the self: Connecting feeling states and social behavior. In P. Shaver (Ed.), *Self, situations, and social behavior: Review of personality and social psychology* (Vol. 6, pp. 143–166). Beverly Hills, CA: Sage.

Salovey, P., Rothman, A. J., Detweiler, J. B., & Steward, W. T. (2000). Emotional states and physical health. *American Psychologist, 55,* 110–121.

Salovey, P., Rothman, A. J., & Rodin, J. (1998). Social psychology and health behavior. In D. Gilbert, S. Fiske, & G. Lindzey (Eds.), *The handbook of social psychology* (4th ed., Vol. 2, pp. 633–683). New York: McGraw-Hill.

Samyn, P. (2002, November 8). Love of U.S. at a new low: Number of Canadians who have unfavourable opinion has doubled: poll. *Winnipeg Free Press,* pp. A1–A4.

Sande, G., Goethals, G., Ferrari, L., & Worth, L. (1989). Value guided attributions: Maintaining the moral self-image and the diabolical enemy-image. *Journal of Social Issues, 45,* 91–118.

Sande, G. H., Goethals, G. R., & Radloff, C. E. (1988). Perceiving one's own traits and others': The multifaceted self. *Journal of Personality and Social Psychology, 54,* 13–20.

Sande, G. N., Ellard, J. H. & Ross, M. (1986). Effect of arbitrarily assigned status labels on self-perceptions and social perceptions: The mere position effect. *Journal of Psychology and Social Psychology, 50,* 684–689.

Sanders, G. S. (1983). An attentional process model of social facilitation. In A. Hare, H. Bumberg, V. Kent, & M. Davies (Eds.), *Small groups.* London: Wiley.

Sanders, G. S., & Simmons, W. L. (1983). Use of hypnosis to enhance eyewitness memory: Does it work? *Journal of Applied Psychology, 68,* 70–77.

Sanger, D. E. (1993, May 30). The career and the kimono. *New York Times Magazine,* pp. 18–19.

Sanitioso, R., Kunda, Z., & Fong, G. T. (1990). Motivated recruitment of autobiographical memories. *Journal of Personality and Social Psychology, 59,* 229–241.

Sanna, L. J. (1992). Self-efficacy theory: Implications for social facilitation and social loafing. *Journal of Personality and Social Psychology, 62,* 774–786.

Sansone, C., & Harackiewicz, J. M. (1996). "I don't feel like it": The function of interest in self-regulation. In L. L. Martin & A. Tesser (Eds.), *Striving and feeling: Interactions among goals, affect, and self-regulation* (pp. 203–228). Mahwah, NJ: Erlbaum.

Sansone, C., & Harackiewicz, J. M. (1997). *"Reality" is complicated: Comment on Eisenberger and Cameron.* Unpublished manuscript, University of Utah.

Sarason, I. G., Sarason, B. R., & Pierce, G. R. (1990). (Eds.). *Social support: An interactional view.* New York: Wiley.

Sastry, J., & Ross, C. E. (1998). Asian ethnicity and the sense of personal control. *Social Psychology Quarterly, 61,* 101–120.

Sato, T., & Cameron, J. E. (1999). The relationship between collective self-esteem and self construal in Japan and Canada. *Journal of Social Psychology, 139,* 426–435.

Saunders, J. W. S. (2001). Experts in court: A view from the bench. *Canadian Psychology, 42,* 109–118.

Savitsky, K. (1998). SPSP Email List Archive. www.stolaf.edu/cgi-bin

Savitsky, K., Medvec, V. H., Charlton, A. E., & Gilovich, T. (1998). "What, me worry?" Arousal, misattribution, and the effect of temporal distance on confidence. *Personality and Social Psychology Bulletin, 24,* 529–536.

Saxe, L. (1994). Detection of deception: Polygraph and integrity tests. *Current Directions in Psychological Science, 3,* 69–73.

Saxe, L., Dougherty, D., & Cross, T. (1985). The validity of polygraph testing: Scientific analysis and public controversy. *American Psychologist, 40,* 355–366.

Schachter, S. (1951). Deviation, rejection, and communication. *Journal of Abnormal and Social Psychology, 46,* 190–207.

Schachter, S. (1959). *The psychology of affiliation.* Stanford, CA: Stanford University Press.

Schachter, S. (1964). The interaction of cognitive and physiological determinants of emotional state. In L. Berkowitz (Ed.), *Advances in experimental social psychology* (Vol. 1, pp. 49–80). New York: Academic Press.

Schachter, S. (1977). Nicotine regulation in heavy and light smokers. *Journal of Experimental Psychology: General, 106,* 5–12.

Schachter, S., & Singer, J. E. (1962). Cognitive, social, and physiological determinants of emotional states. *Psychological Review, 69,* 379–399.

Schacter, D. L. (1995, April). Memory wars. *Scientific American,* pp. 135–139.

Schacter, D. L. (1996). *Searching for memory: The brain, the mind, and the past.* New York: Basic Books.

Schafer, M., & Crichlow, S. (1996). Antecedents of groupthink: A quantitative study. *Journal of Conflict Resolution, 40,* 415–435.

Schaller, M., Asp, C. H., Rosell, M. C., & Heim, S. J. (1996). Training in statistical reasoning inhibits formation of erroneous group stereotypes. *Personality and Social Psychology Bulletin, 22,* 829–844.

Schaller, M., & Conway, L. G. III. (1999). Influence of impression-management goals on the emerging contents of group stereotypes: Support for social-evolutionary process. *Personality and Social Psychology Bulletin, 25,* 819–833.

Schaller, M., & Conway, L. G. III. (2001). From cognition to culture: The origins of stereotypes that really matter. In G. B. Moskowitz (Ed.). *Cognitive social psychology: The Princeton symposium on the legacy and future of social cognition* (pp. 163–176). Mahwah, NJ: Lawrence Erlbaum.

Schaller, M., & Conway, L. G. III, & Tanchuk, T. L. (2002). Selective pressures on the once and future contents of ethnic stereotypes: Effects of the communicability of traits. *Journal of Personality and Social Psychology, 82,* 861–877.

Schaller, M., & O'Brien, M. (1992). "Intuitive analysis of covariance" and group stereotype formation. *Personality and Social Psychology Bulletin, 18,* 776–785.

Scheier, M. F., & Carver, C. S. (1987). Dispositional optimism and physical well-being: The influence of generalized outcome expectancies on health. *Journal of Personality, 55,* 169–210.

Scheier, M. F., Carver, C. S., & Bridges, M. W. (1994). Distinguishing optimism from neuroticism (and trait anxiety, self-mastery, and self-esteem): A revision of the Life Orientation Test. *Journal of Personality and Social Psychology, 67,* 1063–1078.

Scheier, M. F., Matthews, K. A., Owens, J., Magovern, G. J., Lefebvre, R. C., Abbott, R. A., & Carver, C. S. (1990). Dispositional optimism and recovery from coronary artery bypass surgery: The beneficial effects of physical and psychological well-being. *Journal of Personality and Social Psychology, 57,* 1024–1040.

Schlenker, B. R. (1980). *Impression management: The self-concept, social identity, and interpersonal relations.* Monterey, CA: Brooks/Cole.

Schlenker, B. R., & Britt, T. W. (1999). Beneficial impression management: Strategically controlling information to help friends. *Journal of Personality and Social Psychology, 76,* 559–573.

Schlenker, B. R., Britt, T. W., & Pennington, J. (1996). Impression regulation and management: Highlights of a theory of self-identification. In R. M. Sorrentino & E. T. Higgins (Eds.), *Handbook of motivation and cognition* (Vol. 2, pp. 118–147). New York: Guilford.

Schlenker, B. R., & Pontari, B. A. (2000). The strategic control of information: Impression management and self-presentation in daily life. In A. Tesser, R. B. Felson, & J. M. Suls (Eds.). *Psychological perspectives on self and identity* (pp. 199–232). Washington, D.C.: American Psychological Association

Schmidt, D. E., & Keating, J. P. (1979). Human crowding and personal control: An integration of the research. *Psychological Bulletin, 86,* 680–700.

Schneider, D. J. (1973). Implicit personality theory: A review. *Psychological Bulletin, 79,* 294–309.

Schneider, M. E., Major, B., Luhtanen, R., & Crocker, J. (1996). Social stigma and the potential costs of assumptive help. *Personality and Social Psychology Bulletin, 22,* 201–209.

Schoeneman, T. J., & Rubanowitz, D. E. (1985). Attributions in the advice columns: Actors and observers, causes and reasons. *Personality and Social Psychology Bulletin, 11,* 315–325.

Schooler, J. W. (1999). Seeking the core: The issues and evidence surrounding recovered accounts of sexual trauma. In L. M. Williams & V. L. Banyard (Eds.), *Trauma and memory* (pp. 203–216). Thousand Oaks, CA: Sage.

Schooler, J. W., & Eich, E. (2000). Memory for emotional events. In E. Tulving & F. I. M. Craik (Eds.), *The Oxford handbook of memory* (pp. 379–392). Oxford: Oxford University Press.

Schooler, J. W., & Engstler-Schooler, T. Y. (1990). Verbal overshadowing of visual memories: Some things are better left unsaid. *Cognitive Psychology, 22,* 36–71.

Schooler, J. W., Fiore, S. M., & Brandimonte, M. A. (1997). At a loss *from* words: Verbal overshadowing of perceptual memories. *Psychology of Learning and Motivation, 37,* 291–340.

Schriesheim, C. A., Tepper, B. J., & Tetrault, L. A. (1994). Least preferred co-worker score, situational control, and leadership effectiveness: A meta-analysis of contingency model performance predictions. *Journal of Applied Psychology, 79,* 561–573.

Schroeder, D. H., & Costa, P. T., Jr. (1984). Influence of life event stress on physical illness: Substantive effects or methodological flaws? *Journal of Personality and Social Psychology, 46,* 853–863.

Schuller, R. A., & Hastings, P. A. (1996). Trials of battered women who kill: The impact of alternative forms of expert evidence. *Law and Human Behavior, 20,* 167–187.

Schuller, R. A., & Paglia, A. (1999). An empirical study: Juror sensitivity to variations in hearsay conveyed via expert evidence. *Law and Psychology Review, 23,* 131–152.

Schuller, R. A., & Yarmey, M. (2001). The jury: Deciding guilt and innocence. In R. A. Schuller, & J. R. P. Ogloff (Eds.). (2001). *Introduction to psychology and law: Canadian perspectives* (pp. 157–187). Toronto: University of Toronto Press.

Schultz, P. W., Oskamp, S., & Mainieri, T. (1995). Who recycles and when? A review of personal and situational factors. *Journal of Environmental Psychology, 15,* 105–121.

Schulz, R. (1976). Effects of control and predictability on the physical and psychological well-being of the institutionalized aged. *Journal of Personality and Social Psychology, 33,* 563–573.

Schulz, R., & Hanusa, B. H. (1978). Long-term effects of control and predictability-enhancing interventions: Findings and ethical issues. *Journal of Personality and Social Psychology, 36,* 1202–1212.

Schuman, H., & Kalton, G. (1985). Survey methods. In G. Lindzey & E. Aronson (Eds.), *Handbook of social psychology* (3rd ed., Vol. 1, pp. 635–697). New York: McGraw-Hill.

Schwartz, S. H. (1992). Universals in the content and structure of values: Theoretical advances and empirical tests in 20 countries. In M.

P. Zanna (Ed.), *Advances in experimental social psychology* (Vol. 25, pp. 1–65). San Diego, CA: Academic Press.

Schwartz, S. H., & Gottlieb, A. (1976). Bystander reactions to a violent theft: Crime in Jerusalem. *Journal of Personality and Social Psychology, 34,* 1188–1199.

Schwarz, N. (1998). Accessible content and accessibility experiences: The interplay of declarative and experiential information in judgment. *Personality and Social Psychology Review, 2,* 87–99.

Schwarz, N., Bless, H., Strack, F., Klumpp, G., Rittenauer-Schatka, H., & Simmons, A. (1991). Ease of retrieval as information: Another look at the availability heuristic. *Journal of Personality and Social Psychology, 61,* 195–202.

Schwarz, N., Groves, R. M., & Schuman, H. (1998). Survey methods. In D. Gilbert, S. Fiske, & G. Lindzey (Eds.), *The handbook of social psychology* (4th ed., Vol. 1, pp. 143–179). New York: Random House.

Scott, D. (1999). Equal opportunity, unequal results: Determinants of household recycling intensity. *Environment and Behavior, 31,* 267–290.

Scott, J. P. (1958). *Aggression.* Chicago: University of Chicago Press.

Scott. S. (2002). The man who reads faces. *Elm Street.* October: 78–91.

Sears, D. O. (1981). Life stage effects on attitude change, especially among the elderly. In S. B. Kiesler, J. N. Morgan, & V. K. Oppenheimer (Eds.), *Aging: Social change* (pp. 183–204). New York: Academic Press.

Secord, P. F., & Backman, C. W. (1964). *Social psychology.* New York: McGraw-Hill.

Sedikides, C., & Anderson, C. A. (1994). Causal perceptions of intertrait relations: The glue that holds person types together. *Personality and Social Psychology Bulletin, 21,* 294–302.

Sedikides, C., Campbell, W. K., Reeder, G. D., & Elliot, A. J. (1998). The self-serving bias in relational context. *Journal of Personality and Social Psychology, 74,* 378–386.

Sedikides, C., & Skowronski, J. J. (1997). The symbolic self in evolutionary context. *Personality and Social Psychology Review, 1,* 80–102.

Segal, M. W (1974). Alphabet and attraction: An unobtrusive measure of the effect of propinquity in a field setting. *Journal of Personality and Social Psychology, 30,* 654–657.

Séguin, C., Pelletier, L. G., & Hunsley, J. (1999). Predicting environmental behaviors: The influence of self-determined motivation and information about perceived environmental health risks. *Journal of Applied Social Psychology, 29,* 1582–1604.

Seijts, G. H., & Latham, G. P. (2000). The effects of goal setting and group size on performance in a social dilemma. *Canadian Journal of Behavioral Science, 32,* 104–116.

Seligman, M. E. P. (1975). *Helplessness: On depression, development, and death.* San Francisco, CA: W. H. Freeman.

Seligman, M. E. P., & Schulman, P. (1986). Explanatory style as a predictor of productivity and quitting among life insurance agents. *Journal of Personality and Social Psychology, 50,* 832–838.

Selye, H. (1956). *The stress of life.* New York: McGraw-Hill.

Selye, H. (1976). *Stress in health and disease.* Woburn, MA: Butterworth.

Seppa, N. (1997). Children's TV remains steeped in violence. *APA Monitor, 28,* p. 36.

Sergios, P. A., & Cody, J. (1985). Physical attractiveness and social assertiveness skills in male homosexual dating behavior and partner selection. *Journal of Social Psychology, 125,* 505–514.

Seta, J. J., Seta, C. E., & Wang, M. A. (1990). Feelings of negativity and stress: An averaging-summation analysis of impressions of negative life experiences. *Personality and Social Psychology Bulletin, 17,* 376–384.

Shackelford, T. K., & Buss, D. M. (1996). Betrayal in mateships, friendships, and coalitions. *Personality and Social Psychology Bulletin, 22,* 1151–1164.

Shapiro, P. N., & Penrod, S. D. (1986). Meta-analysis of facial identification studies. *Psychological Bulletin, 100,* 139–156.

Sharan, S. (1980). Cooperative learning in small groups. *Review of Educational Research, 50,* 241–271.

Sharp, F. C. (1928). *Ethics.* New York: Century.

Sharpe, D., Adair, J. G., & Roese, N. J. (1992). Twenty years of deception research: A decline in subjects' trust? *Personality and Social Psychology Bulletin, 18,* 585–590.

Sharpe, D., & Taylor, J. K. (1999). An examination of variables from a social-developmental model to explain physical and psychological dating violence. *Canadian Journal of Behavioural Science, 31,* 165–175.

Shaver, P. R., Wu, S., & Schwartz, J. C. (1992). Cross-cultural similarities and differences in emotion and its representation. In M. S. Clark (Ed.), *Review of personality and social psychology: Vol. 13. Emotion* (pp. 175–212). Newbury Park, CA: Sage.

Shavitt, S. (1989). Operationalizing functional theories of attitude. In A. R. Pratkanis, S. J. Breckler, & A. G. Greenwald (Eds.), *Attitude structure and function* (pp. 311–337). Hillsdale, NJ: Erlbaum.

Shavitt, S. (1990). The role of attitude objects in attitude function. *Journal of Experimental Social Psychology, 26,* 124–148.

Shaw, J. I., & Skolnick, P. (1995). Effects of prohibitive and informative judicial instructions on jury decision making. *Social Behavior and Personality, 23,* 319–325.

Shaw, J. I., & Skolnick, P. (1999). Weapon focus and gender differences in eyewitness accuracy: Arousal versus salience. *Journal of Applied Social Psychology, 29,* 2328–2341.

Sheehan, P. W., & Tilden, J. (1984). Real and simulated occurrences of memory distortion in hypnosis. *Journal of Abnormal Psychology, 93,* 259–265.

Sheldon, K. M. (1999). Learning the lessons of tit-for-tat: Even competitors can get the massage. *Journal of Personality and Social Psychology, 77,* 1245–1253.

Shepperd, J. A. (1995). Remedying motivation and productivity loss in collective settings. *Current Directions in Psychological Science, 4,* 131–134.

Sherif, M. (1936). *The psychology of social norms.* New York: Harper.

Sherif, M. (1966). *In common predicament:Social psychology of intergroup conflict and cooperation.* Boston: Houghton Mifflin.

Sherif, M., Harvey, O. J., White, J., Hood, W., & Sherif, C. (1961). *Intergroup conflict and cooperation: The robber's cave experiment.* Norman: University of Oklahoma, Institute of Intergroup Relations.

Sherman, I. W., & Berk, R. A. (1984). The specific deterrent effects or arrest for domestic assault. *American Sociological Review, 49,* 261–272.

Sherman, J. W., & Klein, S. B. (1994). Development and representation of personality impressions. *Journal of Personality and Social Psychology, 67,* 972–983.

Sherman, L. W. (1992). The influence of criminology on criminal law: Evaluating arrests for misdemeanor domestic violence. *Journal of Criminal Law and Criminology, 83,* 1–45.

Sherrod, D. R. (1974). Crowding, perceived control, and behavioral aftereffects. *Journal of Applied Social Psychology, 4,* 171–186.

Sherrod, D. R., & Cohen, S. (1979). Density, personal control, and design. In A. Baum & J. R. Aiello (Eds.), *Residential crowding and design* (pp. 217–227). New York: Plenum.

Shestowsky, D., Wegener, D. T., & Fabrigar, L. R. (1998). Need for cognition and interpersonal influence: Individual differences in impact on dyadic decisions. *Journal of Personality and Social Psychology, 74,* 1317–1328.

Shih, M., Ambady, N., Richeson, J. A., Fujita, K., & Gray, H. M. (2002). Stereotype performance boosts: The impact of self-relevance and that manner of stereotype activation. *Journal of Personality and Social Psychology, 83,* 638–647.

Shih, M., Pittinsky, T. L., & Ambady, N. (1999). Stereotype susceptibility: Identity salience and shifts in quantitative performance. *Psychological Science, 10,* 80–83.

Shotland, R. L., & Straw, M. K. (1976). Bystander response to an assault: When a man attacks a woman. *Journal of Personality and Social Psychology, 34,* 990–999.

Shultz, T. R., Léveillé, E., Lepper, M. R. (1999). Free choice and cognitive dissonance revisited: Choosing "lesser evils" versus "greater goods." *Personality and Social Psychology Bulletin, 25,* 40–48.

Sidanius, J., Levin, S., & Pratto, F. (1996). Consensual social dominance orientation and its correlates within the hierarchical structure of American society. *International Journal of Intercultural Relations, 20,* 385–408.

Siero, F. W., Bakker, A. B., Dekker, G. B., & van den Burg, M. T. C. (1996). Changing organizational energy consumption behavior through comparative feedback. *Journal of Environmental Psychology, 16,* 235–246.

Sigal, J. J., & Weinfeld, M. (2001). Do children cope better than adults with potentially traumatic stress? A 40-year follow-up of Holocaust survivors. *Psychiatry, 64,* 69–80.

Signorielli, N., Gerbner, G., & Morgan, M. (1995). Violence on television: The cultural indicators test. *Journal of Broadcasting and Electronic Media, 39,* 278–283.

Silver, L. B., Dublin, C. C., & Lourie, R. S. (1969). Does violence breed violence? Contributions from a study of the child abuse syndrome. *American Journal of Psychiatry, 126,* 404–407.

Silvera, D. H. (2000). The effects of cognitive load on strategic self-handicapping. *British Journal of Social Psychology, 39,* 65–72.

Silverstein, B., Perdue, L., Peterson, B., & Kelly, E. (1986). The role of the mass media in promoting a thin standard of bodily attractiveness for women. *Sex Roles, 14,* 519–532.

Sime, J. D. (1983). Affiliative behavior during escape to building exits. *Journal of Environmental Psychology, 3,* 21–41.

Simmie, S. (1999, November 20). Pumping up the "level of cruelty". *Toronto Star,* p. A3.

Simon, H. A. (1990). A mechanism for social selection and successful altruism. *Science, 250,* 1665–1668

Simonton, D. K. (1984). *Genius, creativity, and leadership: Historiometric inquiries.* Cambridge, MA: Harvard University Press.

Simonton, D. K. (1985). Intelligence and personal influence in groups: Four nonlinear models. *Psychological Review, 92,* 532–547.

Simonton, D. K. (1987). *Why presidents succeed: A political psychology of leadership.* New Haven, CT: Yale University Press.

Simonton, D. K. (1992). Presidential greatness and personality: A response to McCann (1992). *Journal of Personality and Social Psychology, 63,* 676–679.

Simonton, D. K. (1999). Significant samples: The psychological study of eminent individuals. *Psychological Methods, 4,* 425–451.

Simpson, G. E., & Yinger, J. M. (1958). Racial and cultural minorities: An analysis of prejudice and discrimination. New York: Harper.

Simpson, J. A. (1990). Influence of attachment styles on romantic relationships. *Journal of Personality and Social Psychology, 59,* 971–980.

Simpson, J. A., & Kenrick, D. T. (Eds.) (1997). *Evolutionary social psychology.* Mahwah, NJ: Erlbaum.

Simpson, J. A., Rholes, W. S., & Philips, D. (1996). Conflict in close relationships: An attachment perspective. *Journal of Personality and Social Psychology, 71,* 899–914.

Sinclair, G. (2000, June 30). Home-grown heroes. *Winnipeg Free Press,* p. A1, A4.

Sinclair, L., & Kunda, Z. (1999). Reactions to a black professional: Motivated inhibition and activation of conflicting stereotypes. *Journal of Personality and Social Psychology, 77,* 885–904.

Sinclair, L., & Kunda, Z. (2000). Motivated stereotyping of women: She's fine if she praised me but incompetent if she criticized me.

Sinclair, R. C., Mark, M. M., & Clore, G. L. (1994). Mood-related persuasion depends on (mis)attributions. *Social Cognition, 12,* 309–326.

Singh, D. (1993). Adaptive significance of female physical attractiveness: Role of waist to hip ratio. *Journal of Personality and Social Psychology, 65,* 293–307.

Sistrunk, F., & McDavid, J. W. (1971). Sex variable in conforming behavior. *Journal of Personality and Social Psychology, 17,* 200–207.

Skarlicki, D. P., Ellard, J. H., & Kelln, B. R. C. (1998). Third-party perceptions of a layoff: Procedural, derogation, and retributive aspects of justice. *Journal of Applied Psychology, 83,* 119–127.

Skinner, B. F. (1938). *The behavior of organisms.* New York: Appleton-Century-Crofts.

Skinner, E. A. (1995). *Perceived control, motivation, and coping.* Thousand Oaks, CA: Sage.

Skinner, E. A. (1996). A guide to constructs of control. *Journal of Personality and Social Psychology, 71,* 549–570.

Slavin, R. (1996). Cooperative learning in middle and secondary schools. (Special section: Young adolescents at risk) *Clearing House 69,* 200–205.

Slavin, R. E. (1980). Cooperative learning and desegregation. Paper presented at the meeting of the American Psychological Association.

Sloan, J. H., Kellerman, A. L., Reay, D. T., Ferris, J. A., Koepsell, T., Rivara, F. P., Rice, C., Gray, L., & LoGerfo, J. (1988). Handgun regulations, crime, assaults, and homicide: A tale of two cities. *New England Journal of Medicine, 319,* 1256–1261.

Slovic, P., & Lichtenstein, S. (1971). Comparison of Bayesian and regression approaches to the study of information processing in judgment. *Organizational Behavior and Human Performance, 6,* 649–744.

Slugoski, B. R., & Wilson, A. E. (1998). Contribution of conversation skills to the production of judgmental errors. *European Journal of Social Psychology, 28,* 575–601.

Slusher, M. P., & Anderson, C. A. (1989). Belief perseverance and self-defeating behavior. In R. Curtis (Ed.), *Self-defeating behaviors: Experimental research, clinical impressions, and practical implications* (pp. 11–40). New York: Plenum.

Smart, L., & Wegner, D. M. (1999). Covering up what can't be seen: Concealable stigma and mental control. *Journal of Personality and Social Psychology, 77,* 474–486.

Smith, A. E., Jussim, L., & Eccles, J. (1999). Do self-fulfilling prophecies accumulate, dissipate, or remain stable over time? *Journal of Personality and Social Psychology, 77,* 548–565.

Smith, D. D. (1976). The social content of pornography. *Journal of Communication, 26,* 16–24.

Smith, K. D., Keating, J. P., & Stotland, E. (1989). Altruism reconsidered: The effect of denying feedback on a victim's status to empathic witnesses. *Journal of Personality and Social Psychology, 57,* 641–650.

Smith, M. B., Bruner, J., & White, R. W. (1956). *Opinions and personality.* New York: Wiley.

Smith, M. C. (1983). Hypnotic memory enhancement of witnesses: Does it work? *Psychological Bulletin, 94,* 387–407.

Smith, R. E., Wheeler, G., & Diener, E. (1975). Faith without works: Jesus people, resistance to temptation, and altruism. *Journal of Applied Psychology, 5,* 320–330.

Smith, S. S., & Richardson, D. (1983). Amelioration of deception and harm in psychological research: The important role of debriefing. *Journal of Personality and Social Psychology, 44,* 1075–1082.

Smith, V. L., & Ellsworth, P. C. (1987). The social psychology of eyewitness accuracy: Misleading questions and communicator expertise. *Journal of Applied Psychology, 72,* 294–300.

Smith, V. L., Kassin, S. M., & Ellsworth, P. C. (1989). Eyewitness accuracy and confidence: Within- versus between-subjects correlations. *Journal of Applied Psychology, 74,* 356–359.

Snyder, C. R., Irving, L. M., & Anderson, J. R. (1991). Hope and health. In C. R. Snyder & D. R. Forsyth (Eds.), *Handbook of clinical and social psychology* (pp. 285–305). New York: Pergamon.

Snyder, M. (1984). When belief creates reality. In L. Berkowitz (Ed.), *Advances in experimental social psychology* (Vol. 18, pp. 247–305). Orlando, FL: Academic Press.

Snyder, M., & DeBono, K. G. (1989). Understanding the functions of attitudes: Lessons for personality and social behavior. In A. R. Pratkanis, S. J. Breckler, & A. G. Greenwald (Eds.), *Attitude structure and function* (pp. 339–359). Hillsdale, NJ: Erlbaum.

Snyder, M., & Ickes, W. (1985). Personality and social behavior. In G. Lindzey & E. Aronson (Eds.), *Handbook of social psychology* (3rd ed., pp. 883–947). New York: Random House.

Snyder, M., & Swann, W. B., Jr. (1978). Hypothesis-testing procedures in social interaction. *Journal of Personality and Social Psychology, 36,* 1202–1212.

Snyder, M., Tanke, E. D., & Berscheid, E. (1977). Social perception and interpersonal behavior: On the self-fulfilling nature of social stereotypes. *Journal of Personality and Social Psychology, 35,* 656–666.

Soames, R. F. (1988). Effective and ineffective use of fear in health promotion campaigns. *American Journal of Public Health, 78,* 163–167.

Solomon, L. Z., Solomon, H., & Stone, R. (1978). Helping as a function of number of bystanders and ambiguity of emergency. *Personality and Social Psychology Bulletin, 4,* 318–321.

Somerfield, M. R., & McCrae, R. R. (2000). Stress and coping research. *American Psychologist, 55,* 620–625.

Sommers, E. K., & Check, J. V. (1987). An empirical investigation of the role of pornography in the verbal and physical abuse of women. *Violence and Victims, 2,* 189–209.

Son Hing, L. S., Li, W., & Zanna, M. P. (2002). Inducing hypocrisy to reduce prejudicial responses among aversive racists. *Journal of Experimental Social Psychology, 38,* 71–78.

Sontag, S. (1978). *Illness as metaphor.* New York: Farrar, Straus & Giroux.

Sontag, S. (1988). *AIDS and its metaphors.* New York: Farrar, Straus & Giroux.

Sorensen, J., Wrinkle, R. Brewer, V., & Marquart, J. (1999). Capital punishment and deterrence: Examining the effect of executions on murder in Texas. *Crime and Delinquency, 45,* 481–493.

Sorrels, J. P., & Kelley, J. (1984). Conformity by omission. *Personality and Social Psychology Bulletin, 10,* 302–305.

Sorrentino, R. M. (1991). Evidence for altruism: The lady is still in waiting. *Psychological Inquiry, 2,* 147–150.

Sorrentino, R. M., & Field, N. (1986). Emergent leadership over time: The functional value of positive motivation. *Journal of Personality and Social Psychology, 50,* 1091–1099.

South, S. J., & Lloyd, K. M. (1995). Spousal alternatives and marital dissolution. *American Sociological Review, 60,* 21–35.

Span, P. (1994, December 14). The gene team: Innocence project fights injustice with DNA testing. *Washington Post,* pp. C1, C14.

Spencer, S., Steele, C. M., & Quinn, D. (1997). *Under suspicion of inability: Stereotype threat and women's math performance.* Unpublished manuscript, Stanford University.

Spencer, S. J., Josephs, R. A., & Steele, C. M. (1993). Low self-esteem: The uphill battle for self-integrity. In R. F. Baumeister (Ed.), *Self-esteem and the puzzle of low self-regard* (pp. 21–36). New York: Wiley.

Spencer, S. J., Steele, C. M., & Quinn, D. M. (1999). Stereotype threat and women's math performance. *Journal of Experimental Social Psychology, 35,* 4–28.

Spiegel, D., Bloom, J. R., Kraemer, H. C., & Gottheil, E. (1989). Psychological support for cancer patients. *Lancet, 2,* 1447.

Spiegel, H., & Spiegel, D. (1987). *Trance and treatment: Clinical uses of hypnosis.* Washington, DC: American Psychiatric Press. (Original work published in 1978.)

Spitzberg, B. H., & Rhea, J. (1999). Obsessive relational intrusion and sexual coercion victimization. *Journal of Interpersonal Violence, 14,* 3–20.

Spitzer, B. L., Henderson, K. A., & Zivian, M. T. (1999). Gender differences in population versus media body sizes: A comparison over four decades. *Sex Roles, 40,* 545–565.

Sporer, S. L. (1994). Decision times and eyewitness identification accuracy in simultaneous and sequential lineups. In D. F. Ross, J. D. Read, & M. P. Toglia (Eds.), *Adult eyewitness testimony: Current trends and developments* (pp. 300–327). New York: Cambridge University Press.

Sporer, S. L., Koehnken, G., & Malpass, R. S. (1996). Introduction: 200 years of mistaken identification. In S. L. Sporer, R. S. Malpass, & G. Koehnken (Eds.), *Psychological issues in eyewitness identification* (pp. 1–6). Mahwah, NJ: Erlbaum.

Sporer, S. L., Penrod, S., Read, D., & Cutler, B. (1995). Choosing, confidence, and accuracy: A meta-analysis of the confidence-accuracy relation in eyewitness identification studies. *Psychological Bulletin, 118,* 315–327.

Sprecher, S. (1994). Two sides to the breakup of dating relationships. *Personal Relationships, 1,* 199–222.

Sprecher, S. (1998). The effect of exchange orientation on close relationships. *Social Psychology Quarterly, 61,* 230–231.

Sprecher, S., & Fehr, B. (1998). The dissolution of close relationships. In J.H. Harvey (Ed.), *Perspectives of loss: A sourcebook.*

Sprecher, S., Felmlee, D., Metts, S., Fehr, B., & Vanni, D. (1998). Factors associated with distress following the breakup of a close relationship. *Journal of Social and Personal Relationships, 15,* 791–809.

Sprecher, S., & Metts, S. (1989). Development of the "Romantic Beliefs Scale" and examination of the effects of gender and gender-role orientation. *Journal of Social and Personal Relationships, 6,* 387–411.

Sprecher, S., & Schwartz, P. (1994). Equity and balance in the exchange of contributions in close relationships. In M. J. Lerner & G. Mikula (Eds.), *Entitlement and the Affectional Bond: Justice in Close Relationships* (pp. 11–42). New York: Plenum.

Sprink, K. S., & Carron, A. V. (1994). Group cohesion effects in exercise classes. *Small Group Research, 25,* 26–42.

Stangor, C., & McMillan, D. (1992). Memory for expectancy-congruent and expectancy-incongruent information: A review of the social and social developmental literatures. *Psychological Bulletin, 111,* 42–61.

Staples, S. L. (1996). Human response to environmental noise: Psychological research and public policy. *American Psychologist, 51,* 143–150.

Stasser, G. (2000). Information distribution, participation, and group decision: Explorations with the DISCUSS and SPEAK models. In D. R. Ilgen & C. L. Hulin (Eds.), *Computational modeling of behavior in organizations: The third scientific discipline* (pp. 135–161). Washington, DC: American Psychological Association.

Stasser, G., Stewart, D. D., & Wittenbaum, G. M. (1995). Expert roles and information exchange during discussion: The importance of knowing who knows what. *Journal of Experimental and Social Psychology, 31,* 244–265.

Stasser, G., & Titus, W. (1985). Pooling of unshared information in group decision making: Biased information sampling during discussion. *Journal of Personality and Social Psychology, 48,* 1467–1478.

Statistics Canada. (1997). Causes of death—Shelf tables. Ottawa, ON: Ministry of Industry. No. 84F0208XPB.

Statistics Canada. (1999, January 29). *The Daily.*

Statistics Canada. (1999, July 18). Crime statistics. *The Daily.* www.statcan.ca/Daily/English/000718/d000718a.htm (July 25, 2000).

Statistics Canada. (2000). *Family violence in Canada: A statistical profile.* Ottawa, ON: Ministry of Industry. No. 85-224-XIE.

Staub, E. (1974). Helping a distressed person: Social, personality, and stimulus determinants. In L. Berkowitz (Ed.), *Advances in experimental social psychology* (Vol. 7, pp. 293–341). New York: Academic Press.

Staub, E. (1989). *The Roots of Evil: The Origins of Genocide and Other Group Violence.* Cambridge, England: Cambridge University Press.

Steblay, N. M. (1987). Helping behavior in rural and urban environments: A meta-analysis. *Psychological Bulletin, 102,* 346–356.

Steblay, N. M., Besirevic, J., Fulero, S. M., & Jimenez-Lorente, B. (1999). The effects of pretrial publicity on juror verdicts: A meta-analytic review. *Law and Human Behavior, 23,* 219–235.

Steele, C. (1997). A threat in the air: How stereotypes shape intellectual identity and performance. *American Psychologist, 52,* 613–629.

Steele, C., & Aronson, J. (1995). Stereotype vulnerability and intellectual performance. In E. Aronson, (Ed.), *Readings about the social animal (7th ed.).* New York: Freeman.

Steele, C. M. (1988). The psychology of self-affirmation: Sustaining the integrity of the self. In L. Berkowitz (Ed.), *Advances in experimental social psychology* (Vol. 21, pp. 261–302). New York: Academic Press.

Steele, C. M., & Aronson, J. (1995). Stereotype-threat and the intellectual test performance of African-Americans. *Journal of Personality and Social Psychology, 69,* 797–811.

Steele, C. M., Hoppe, H., & Gonzales, J. (1986). *Dissonance and the lab coat: Self-affirmation and the free choice paradigm.* Unpublished manuscript, University of Washington.

Steele, C. M., & Liu, T. J. (1981). Making the dissonance act unreflective of the self: Dissonance avoidance and the expectancy of a value affirming response. *Personality and Social Psychology Bulletin, 7,* 383–387.

Steele, C. M., Spencer, S. J., & Josephs, R. (1992). *Seeking self-relevant information: The effects of self-esteem and stability of the information.* Unpublished manuscript, University of Michigan.

Steele, C. M., Spencer, S. J., & Lynch, M. (1993). Self-image resilience and dissonance: The role of affirmational resources. *Journal of Personality and Social Psychology, 64,* 885–896.

Steiner, I. D. (1972). *Group process and productivity.* New York: Academic Press.

Stern, L. B., & Dunning, D. (1994). Distinguishing accurate from inaccurate eyewitness identifications: A reality monitoring approach. In D. F. Ross, J. D. Read, & M. P. Toglia (Eds.), *Adult eyewitness testimony: Current trends and developments* (pp. 273–299). New York: Cambridge University Press.

Stern, M., & Hildebrandt, K. A. (1986). Prematurity stereotyping: Effects on mother-infant interaction. *Child Development, 57,* 308–315.

Sternberg, R. J. (1986). A triangular theory of love. *Psychological Review, 93,* 119–135.

Sternberg, R. J. (1988). *The triangle of love.* New York: Basic Books.

Sternberg, R. J. (1997). Construct validation of a triangular love scale. *European Journal of Social Psychology, 27,* 313–335.

Sternberg, R. J., & Beall, A. E. (1991). How can we know what love is? An epistemological analysis. In G. J. O. Fletcher & F. D. Fincham (Eds.), *Cognition in close relationships* (pp. 257–278). Hillsdale, NJ: Erlbaum.

Stewart, D. D., & Stasser, G. (1995). Expert role assignment and information sampling during collective recall and decision making. *Journal of Personality and Social Psychology, 69,* 619–628.

Stewart, M., Craig, D., MacPherson, K., & Alexander, S. (2001). Promoting positive affect and diminishing loneliness of widowed seniors through a support intervention. *Public Health Nursing, 18,* 54–63.

Stewart, W., & Barling, J. (1996). Daily work stress, mood, and interpersonal job performance: A mediational model. *Work and Stress, 10,* 336–351.

Stice, E., & Shaw, H. E. (1994). Adverse effects of the media-portrayed thin-ideal on women and linkages to bulimic symptomology. *Journal of Social and Clinical Psychology, 13,* 288–308.

Stipek, D. & Gralinski, J. H. (1991). Gender differences in children's achievement-related beliefs and emotional responses to success and failure in mathematics. *Journal of Educational Psychology, 83,* 361–371.

Stoff, D. M., & Cairns, R. B. (Eds.) (1996). *Aggression and violence: Genetic, neurobiological, and biosocial perspectives.* Mahwah, NJ: Erlbaum.

Stogdill, R. M. (1974). *Handbook of leadership.* New York: Free Press.

Stone, J., Aronson, E., Crain, A. L., Winslow, M. P., & Fried, C. (1994). Inducing hypocrisy as a means of encouraging young adults to use condoms. *Personality and Social Psychology Bulletin, 20,* 116–128.

Stormo, K. J., Lang, A. R., & Stritzke, W. G. K. (1997). Attributions about acquaintance rape: The role of alcohol and individual differences. *Journal of Applied Social Psychology, 27,* 279–305.

Storms, M. (1973). Videotape and the attribution process: Reversing actors' and observers' points of view. *Journal of Personality and Social Psychology, 27,* 165–175.

Storms, M. D., & Nisbett, R. E. (1970). Insomnia and the attribution process. *Journal of Personality and Social Psychology, 16,* 319–328.

Strack, F., & Hannover, B. (1996). Awareness of influence as a precondition for implementing correctional goals. In P. M. Gollwitzer & J. A. Bargh (Eds.), *The psychology of action: Linking cognition and motivation to behavior* (pp. 579–596). New York: Guilford.

Strack, F., & Mussweiler, T. (1997). Explaining the enigmatic anchoring effect. *Journal of Personality and Social Psychology, 73* (3), 437-446.

Strauss, M. A., & Gelles, R. J. (1980). *Behind closed doors: Violence in the American family.* New York: Anchor/ Doubleday.

Stroebe, W., & Stroebe, M. (1996). The social psychology of social support. In E. T. Higgins & A. W. Kruglanski (Eds.), *Social psychology: Handbook of basic principles* (pp. 597–621). New York: Guilford.

Strube, M., & Garcia, J. (1981). A meta-analysis investigation of Fiedler's contingency model of leadership effectiveness. *Psychological Bulletin, 90,* 307–321.

Studer, J. (1996). Understanding and preventing aggressive responses in youth. *Elementary School Guidance and Counseling, 30,* 194–203.

Stuster, J. W., & Blowers, M. A. (1995). *Experimental evaluation of sobriety checkpoint programs.* Report No. DTNH22-91-C-07204. Washington, DC: National Highway Safety Administration.

Suedfeld, P., Conway, L. G. III., & Eichorn, D. (2001). Studying Canadian leaders at a distance. In O. Feldman & L. O. Valenty (Eds.). *Profiling political leaders: Cross- cultural studies of personality and behavior* (pp. 3-19). Westport, CT: Prager Publishers/ Greenwood Publishing Group.

Sullivan, M. J. L., Rouse, D., Bishop, S., & Johnston, S. (1997). Thought suppression, catastrophizing, and pain. *Cognitive Therapy and Research, 21,* 555–568.

Suls, J., & Fletcher, B. (1983). Social comparison in the social and physical sciences: An archival study. *Journal of Personality and Social Psychology, 44,* 575–580.

Suls, J. M., Martin, R., & Wheeler, L. (2000). Three kinds of opinion comparison: The triadic model. *Personality and Social Psychology Review, 4,* 219–237.

Suls, J. M., & Miller, R. L. (Eds.). (1977). *Social comparison processes: Theoretical and empirical perspectives.* Washington, DC: Hemisphere/Halstead.

Summers, G., & Feldman, N. S. (1984). Blaming the victim versus blaming the perpetrator: An attributional analysis of spouse abuse. *Journal of Social and Clinical Psychology, 2,* 339–347.

Sundstrom, E., Bell, P. A., Busby, P. L., & Asmus, C. (1996). Environmental psychology. *Annual Review of Psychology, 47,* 485–512.

Support Concern and Resources for Eating Disorders. (2002). Eating disorder: Statistics and facts. www.eating-disorder.org/ facts.html. (December 17, 2002)

Swann, W. (1996). *Self-traps: The elusive quest for higher self-esteem.* New York: W. H. Freeman & Co.

Swann, W. B., Bosson, J. K., & Pelham, B. W. (2002). Different partners, different selves: Strategic self-verification of circumscribed identities. *Personality and Social Psychology Bulletin, 28,* 1215–1228.

Swann, W. B., Jr. (1990). To be adored or to be known? The interplay of self-enhancement and self-verification. In R. M. Sorrentino & E. T. Higgins (Eds.), *Motivation and cognition* (pp. 404–448). New York: Guilford Press.

Swann, W. B., Jr., & Ely, R. J. (1984). A battle of the wills: Self-verification versus behavioral confirmation. *Journal of Personality and Social Psychology, 46,* 1287–1302.

Swann, W. B., Jr., & Hill, C. A. (1982). When our identities are mistaken: Reaffirming self-conceptions through social interaction. *Journal of Personality and Social Psychology, 43,* 59–66.

Swann, W. B., Jr., Hixon, G., & De La Ronde, C. (1992). Embracing the bitter "truth": Negative self-concepts and marital commitment. *Psychological Science, 3,* 118–121.

Swann, W. B., Jr., & Pelham, B. W. (1988). *The social construction of identity: Self-verification through friend and intimate selection.* Unpublished manuscript, University of Texas-Austin.

Swann, W. B., Jr., & Schroeder, D. B. (1995). The search for beauty and truth: A framework for understanding reactions to evaluations. *Personality and Social Psychology Bulletin, 21,* 1307–1318.

Swann, W. B., Jr., Stein-Seroussi, A., & McNulty, S. E. (1992). Outcasts in a white-lie society: The enigmatic worlds of people with negative self-concepts. *Journal of Personality and Social Psychology, 62,* 618–624.

Swap, W. C. (1977). Interpersonal attraction and repeated exposure to rewarders and punishers. *Personality and Social Psychology Bulletin, 3,* 248–251.

Sweeney, P. D., Anderson, K., & Bailey, S. (1986). Attributional style in depression: A meta-analytic review. *Journal of Personality and Social Psychology, 50,* 974–991.

Swim, J., & Sanna, L. (1996). He's skilled, she's lucky: A meta-analysis of observers' attributions for women's and men's successes and failures. *Personality and Social Psychology Bulletin, 22,* 507–519.

Symons, C. S., & Johnson, B. T. (1997). The self-reference effect in memory: A meta-analysis. *Psychological Bulletin, 121,* 371–394.

Symons, D. (1979). *The evolution of human sexuality.* New York: Oxford University Press.

Tafarodi, R. W., Kang, S., & Milne, A. B. (2002). When different becomes similar: Compensatory conformity in bicultural visible minorities. *Personality and Social Psychology Bulletin, 28,* 1131–1142.

Tafarodi, R. W., & Swann, W. B. (1996). Individualism-collectivism and global self-esteem: Evidence for a cultural trade-off. *Journal of Cross-Cultural Psychology, 27,* 651–672.

Tait, E. (2002, November 18). Bombers' defence "blew it." *Winnipeg Free Press,* p. C4.

Tajfel, H. (1982a). *Social identity and intergroup relations.* Cambridge, England: Cambridge University Press.

Tajfel, H. (1982b). Social psychology of intergroup relations. *Annual Review of Psychology, 33,* 1–39.

Tajfel, H., & Billig, M. (1974). Familiarity and categorization in intergroup behavior. *Journal of Experimental Social Psychology, 10,* 159–170.

Tajfel, H., & Turner, J. C. (1979). An integrative theory of social contact. In W. Austin & S. Worchel (Eds.), *The social psychology of intergroup relations.* Monterey, CA: Brooks/Cole.

Tanford, S., & Penrod, S. (1984). Social influence model: A formal integration of research on majority and minority influence processes. *Psychological Bulletin, 95,* 189–225.

Tang, K. (2000). Cultural stereotypes and the justice system: The Canadian case of R. v. Ewanchuk. *International Journal of Offender Therapy and Comparative Criminology, 44,* 681–691.

Tang, S., & Hall, V. C. (1995). The overjustification effect: A meta-analysis. *Applied Cognitive Psychology, 9,* 365–404.

Taylor, D., Ruggiero, K. M., & Louis, W. R. (1996). Personal/group discrimination discrepancy: Towards a two-factor explanation. *Canadian Journal of Behavioural Science, 28,* 193–202.

Taylor, D. M., & Gardner, R. C. (1969). Ethnic stereotypes: There effects on the perception of communicators of varying credibility. *Canadian Journal of Psychology, 23,* 161–173.

Taylor, D. M., Wright, S. C., Moghaddam, F. M, & Lalonde, R. M. (1990). The personal/group discrimination discrepancy: Perceiving my group, but not myself, to be a target fro discrimination. *Personality and Social Psychology Bulletin,* 16, 254–262.

Taylor, S. E. (1981). A categorization approach to stereotyping. In D. L. Hamilton (Ed.), *Cognitive processes in stereotyping and intergroup relations* (pp. 418–429). Hillsdale, NJ: Erlbaum.

Taylor, S. E. (1981). The interface of cognitive and social psychology. In J. Harvey (Ed.), *Cognition, social behavior, and the environment* (pp. 189–211). Hillsdale, NJ: Erlbaum.

Taylor, S. E. (1989). *Positive illusions: Creative self-deception and the healthy mind.* New York: Basic Books.

Taylor, S. E. (1995). *Health psychology* (3rd ed.). New York: McGraw-Hill.

Taylor, S. E., & Brown, J. (1988). Illusion and well-being: A social psychological perspective on mental health. *Psychological Bulletin, 103,* 193–210.

Taylor, S. E., & Brown, J. D. (1994). Positive illusions and well-being revisited: Separating fact from fiction. *Psychological Bulletin, 116,* 21–27.

Taylor, S. E., & Crocker, J. (1981) Schematic bases of social information processing. In E. T. Higgins, C. P. Herman, & M. P. Zanna (Eds.), *Social cognition: The Ontario Symposium* (Vol. 1, pp. 89–134). Hillsdale, NJ: Erlbaum.

Taylor, S. E., & Falcone, H. (1982). Cognitive bases of stereotyping: The relationship between categorization and prejudice. *Personality and Social Psychology Bulletin, 8,* 426–432.

Taylor, S. E., & Fiske, S. T. (1975). Point of view and perceptions of causality. *Journal of Personality and Social Psychology, 32,* 439–445.

Taylor, S. E., Klein, L. C., Lewis, B. P., Gruenewald, T. L., Gurung, R. A. R., & Updegraff, J. A. (2000). Biobehavioral responses to stress in females: Tend-and-befriend, not fight-or-flight. *Psychological Review, 107,* 411–429.

Taylor, S. E., Lichtman, R. R., & Wood, J. V. (1984). Attributions, beliefs about control, and adjustment to breast cancer. *Journal of Personality and Social Psychology, 46,* 489–502.

Taylor, S. E., Repetti, R. L., & Seeman, T. (1997). Health psychology: What is an unhealthy environment and how does it get under the skin? *Annual Review of Psychology, 48,* 411–447.

Taylor, S. P., & Leonard, K. E. (1983). Alcohol and human physical aggression. In R. Geen & E. Donnerstein (Eds.), *Aggression: Theoretical and empirical reviews.* New York: Academic Press.

Tedeschi, J. T. (Ed.). (1981). *Impression management theory and social psychological research.* New York: Academic Press.

Teger, A. L., & Pruitt, D. G. (1967). Components of group risk taking. *Journal of Experimental Social Psychology, 3,* 189–205.

Tesser, A. (1980). Self-esteem maintenance in family dynamics. *Journal of Personality and Social Psychology, 39,* 77–91.

Tesser, A. (1988). Toward a self-evaluation maintenance model of social behavior. In L. Berkowitz (Ed.), *Advances in experimental social psychology* (Vol. 21, pp. 181–227). Orlando, FL: Academic Press.

Tesser, A., Campbell, J., & Mickler, S. (1983). The role of social pressure, attention to the stimulus, and self-doubt in conformity. *European Journal of Social Psychology, 13,* 217–233.

Tesser, A., Martin, L., & Mendolia, M. (1995). The impact of thought on attitude extremity and attitude-behavior consistency. In R. Petty & J. Krosnick, (Eds.) *Attitude strength: Antecedents and consequences* (pp. 73–92). Ohio State University series on attitudes and persuasion, Vol. 4. Mahwah, NJ: Lawrence Erlbaum Associates, Inc.

Tesser, A., & Paulus, D. (1983). The definition of self: Private and public self-evaluation management strategies. *Journal of Personality and Social Psychology, 44,* 672–682.

Tesser, A., & Smith, J. (1980). Some effects of friendship and task relevance on helping: You don't always help the one you like. *Journal of Experimental Social Psychology, 16,* 582–590.

Tetlock, P. E. (1992). The impact of accountability on judgment and choice: Toward a social contingency model. In M. P. Zanna (Ed.), *Advances in experimental social psychology* (Vol. 25, pp. 331–376). San Diego, CA: Academic Press.

Tetlock, P. E., Peterson, R. S., McGuire, C., Chang, S., & Field, P. (1992). Assessing political group dynamics: A test of the groupthink model. *Journal of Personality and Social Psychology,* 63, 403–425.

Thibaut, J., & Walker, L. (1975). *Procedural justice: A psychological analysis.* Hillsdale, NJ: Erlbaum.

Thibaut, J. W., & Kelley, H. H. (1959). *The social psychology of groups.* New York: Wiley.

Thibodeau, R., & Aronson, E. (1992). Taking a closer look: Reasserting the role of the self-concept in dissonance theory. *Personality and Social Psychology Bulletin, 18,* 591–602.

Thill, E. E., & Curry, F. (2000). Learning to play golf under different goal conditions: Their effects on irrelevant thoughts and on subsequent control strategies. *European Journal of Social Psychology, 30,* 101–122.

Thøgersen, J. (1996). Recycling and morality: A critical review of the literature. *Environment and Behavior, 28,* 536–538.

Thomas, M. (1982). Physiological arousal, exposure to a relatively lengthy aggressive film, and aggressive behavior. *Journal of Research in Personality, 16,* 72–81.

Thomas, M. H., Horton, R., Lippincott, E., & Drabman, R. (1977). Desensitization to portrayals of real-life aggression as a function of exposure to television violence. *Journal of Personality and Social Psychology, 35,* 450–458.

Thomas, W. I. (1928). *The child in America.* New York: Alfred A. Knopf.

Thompson, C. P., Skowronski, J. J., Larsen, S. F., & Betz, A. (1996). *Autobiographical memory: Remembering what and remembering when.* Mahwah, NJ: Erlbaum.

Thompson, J. K., & Heinberg, L. J. (1999). The media's influence on body image disturbance and eating disorders: We've reviled them, now can we rehabilitate them? *Journal of Social Issues, 55,* 339–353.

Thompson, L. (1995). They saw a negotiation: Partisanship and involvement. *Journal of Personality and Social Psychology, 68,* 839–853.

Thompson, L. (1997). *The mind and heart of the negotiator.* Englewood Cliffs, NJ: Prentice-Hall.

Thompson, L., & Hrebec, D. (1996). Lose-lose agreements in interdependent decision making. *Psychological Bulletin, 120,* 396–409.

Thompson, R. (2000, May 5). Love hurts: Virus wreaks global havoc. *National Post.*

Thompson, S. C., Nanni, C., & Levine, A. (1994). Primary versus secondary and central versus consequence-related control in HIV-positive men. *Journal of Personality and Social Psychology, 67,* 540–547.

Thompson, S. C., Sobolew-Shubin, A., Galbraith, M. E., Schwankovsky, L., & Cruzen, D. (1993). Maintaining perceptions of control: Finding perceived control in low-control circumstances. *Journal of Personality and Social Psychology, 64,* 293–304.

Thomsen, C. T., & Borgida, E. (1996). Throwing out the baby with the bathwater? Let's not overstate the overselling of the base rate fallacy. *Behavioral and Brain Sciences, 19,* 39–40.

Tice, D. (1993). The social motivations of people with low self-esteem. In: Baumeister, R. *Self-esteem: The puzzle of low self-regard.* New York: Plenum Press, pp. 37–53.

Ting, J., & Piliavin, J. A. (2000). Altruism in comparative international perspective. In J. Phillips, B. Chapman, & D. Stevens (Eds.), *Between state and market: Essays on charities law and policy in Canada* (pp. 51–105). Montreal and Kingston, Ontario: McGill-Queens University Press.

Ting-Toomey, S., & Chang, L. (1996). Cross cultural interpersonal communication: Theoretical trends and research directions. In W. B. Gudykunst, S. Ting-Toomey, & T. Nishada (Eds.), *Communication in personal relationships across cultures.* Thousand Oaks, CA: Sage.

Toch, H. (1980). *Violent men* (rev. ed.). Cambridge, MA: Schenkman.

Toch, T. (1992, November 9). Homeroom sweepstakes. *U.S. News & World Report,* pp. 86–89.

Toi, M., & Batson, C. D. (1982). More evidence that empathy is a source of altruistic motivation. *Journal of Personality and Social Psychology, 43,* 281–292.

Tollestrup, P., Turtle, J., & Yuille, J. (1994). Actual victims and witnesses to robbery and fraud: An archival analysis. In D.F. Ross, J.D. Read, & M.P. Toglia (Eds.), *Adult eyewitness testimony: Current trends and developments.* New York: Cambridge University Press.

Tomes, J. L., & Katz, A. N. (1997). Habitual susceptibility to misinformation and individual differences in eyewitness memory. *Applied Cognitive Psychology, 11,* 233–251.

Tougas, F., Brown, R., Beaton, A., & St-Pierre, L. (1999). Neosexism among women: The role of personally experienced social mobility attempts. *Personality and Social Psychology Bulletin, 25,* 1487–1497.

Tougas, F., Brown, R., Beaton, A. M., & Joly, S. (1995). Neosexism: Plus ça change, plus c'est pareil. *Personality and Social Psychology Bulletin, 21,* 842–849.

Trafimow, D., & Schneider, D. J. (1994). The effects of behavioral, situational, and person information on different attribution judgments. *Journal of Experimental Social Psychology, 30,* 351–369.

Trafimow, D., & Wyer, R. S. (1993). Cognitive representation of mundane social events. *Journal of Personality and Social Psychology, 64,* 365–376.

Trapnell, P. D., & Campbell, J. D. (1999). Private self-consciousness and the five-factor model of personality: Distinguishing rumination from reflection. *Journal of Personality and Social Psychology, 76,* 284–304.

Trappey, C. (1996). A meta-analysis of consumer choice and subliminal advertising. *Psychology and Marketing, 13,* 517–530.

Traupmann, J., Petersen, R., Utne, M., & Hatfield, E. (1981). Measuring equity in intimate relations. *Applied Psychology Measurement, 5,* 467–480.

Travis, C. B., Phillippi, R. H., & Tonn, B. E. (1989). Judgment heuristics and medical decisions. *Patient Education and Counseling, 13,* 211–220.

Travis, C. B., & Yeager, C. P. (1991). Sexual selection, parental investment, and sexism. *Journal of Social Issues, 47,* 117–129.

Tremblay, R. E., Schaal, B., Boulerice, B., Arseneault, L., Soussignan, R. G., Paquette, D., & Laurent, D. (1998). Testosterone, physical aggression, dominance, and physical development in early adolescence. *International Journal of Behavioral Development, 22,* 753–777.

Triandis, H. C. (1989). The self and social behavior in differing cultural contexts. *Psychological Review, 96,* 506–520.

Triandis, H. C. (1990). Cross-cultural studies of individualism and collectivism. In J. J. Berman (Ed.), *Nebraska Symposium on Motivation, 1989* (pp. 41–133). Lincoln: University of Nebraska Press.

Triandis, H. C. (1994). *Culture and social behavior.* New York: McGraw-Hill.

Triandis, H. C. (1995). *Individualism and Collectivism.* Boulder, CO: Westview Press.

Trimpop, R. M., Kerr, J. H., Kirkcaldy, B. D. (1999). Comparing personality constructs of risk-taking behavior. *Personality and Individual Differences, 26,* 237–254.

Triplett, N. (1898). The dynamogenic factors in pace making and competition. *American Journal of Psychology, 9,* 507–533.

Trivers, R. (1985). *Social evolution.* Menlo Park, CA: Benjamin-Cummings.

Trivers, R. L. (1971). The evolution of reciprocal altruism. *Quarterly Review of Biology, 46,* 35–57.

Tropp, L. R., & Wright, S. C. (2001). Ingroup identification as the inclusion of ingroup in the self. *Personality and Social Psychology Bulletin, 27,* 585–600.

Tseëlon, E. (1995). *The presentation of woman in everyday life.* Thousand Oaks, CA: Sage.

Turner, C., & Leyens, J. (1992). The weapons effect revisited: The effects of firearms on aggressive behavior. In P. Suedfeld & P. Tetlock (Eds.), *Psychology and social policy* (pp. 201–221). New York: Hemispheres.

Turner, C., & Simons, L. (1974). Effects of subject sophistication and evaluation apprehension on aggressive responses to weapons. *Journal of Personality and Social Psychology, 30,* 341–348.

Turner, C., Simons, L., Berkowitz, L., & Frodi, A. (1977). The stimulating and inhibiting effects of weapons on aggressive behavior. *Aggressive Behavior, 3,* 355–378.

Turner, J. C., Hogg, M. A., Oakes, P. J., Reicher, S. D., & Wetherell, M. S. (1987). *Rediscovering the social group: A self-categorization theory.* Oxford, UK: Blackwell Publishers.

Turner, M. E., Pratkanis, A. R., Probasco, P., & Leve, C. (1992). Threat, cohesion, and group effectiveness: Testing a social identity maintenance perspective on groupthink. *Journal of Personality and Social Psychology, 63,* 781–796.

Tversky, A., & Kahneman, D. (1973). Availability: A heuristic for judging frequency and probability. *Cognitive Psychology, 5,* 207–232.

Tversky, A., & Kahneman, D. (1974). Judgment under uncertainty: Heuristics and biases. *Science, 185,* 1124–1131.

Twenge, J. M., Baumeister, R. F., Tice, D. M., & Stucke, T. S. (2001). If you can't join them, beat them: Effects of social exclusion on aggressive behavior. *Journal of Personality and Social Psychology, 81,* 1058–1069.

Tyler, T. R. (1990). *Why people obey the law.* New Haven: Yale University Press.

Tyler, T. R., Boeckmann, R. J., Smith, H. J., & Huo, Y. J. (1997). *Social justice in a diverse society.* Boulder, CO: Westview Press.

Uchino, B. N., Uno, D., & Holt-Lunstad, J. (1999). Social support, physiological processes, and health. *Current Directions in Psychological Science, 8,* 145–148.

Uehara, E. S. (1995). Reciprocity reconsidered: Gouldner's "moral norm of reciprocity" and social support. *Journal of Social and Personal Relationships, 12,* 483–502.

Uleman, J. S., & Moskowitz, G. B. (1994). Unintended effects of goals on unintended inferences. *Journal of Personality and Social Psychology, 66,* 490–501.

Uranowitz, S. W. (1975). Helping and self-attributions: A field experiment. *Journal of Personality and Social Psychology, 32,* 852–854.

Valins, S. (1966). Cognitive effects of false heart-rate feedback. *Journal of Personality and Social Psychology, 4,* 400–408.

Vallerand, R. J. (1997). Toward a hierarchical model of intrinsic and extrinsic motivation. *Advances in Experimental Social Psychology, 29,* 271–360.

Vallerand, R. J., Fortier, M. S., & Guay, F. (1997). Self-determination and persistence in real-life setting: Toward a motivational model of high school dropout. *Journal of Personality and Social Psychology, 72,* 1161–1176.

Vallerand, R. J., & Ratelle, C. F. (2002). Intrinsic and extrinsic motivation: A hierarchical model. In E. L. Deci & R. M. Ryan (Eds.). *Handbook of self-determination research* (pp. 37–63). Rochester, NY: University of Rochester Press.

Vallone, R. P., Griffin, D. W., Lin, S., & Ross, L. (1990). The overconfident prediction of future actions and outcomes by self and others. *Journal of Personality and Social Psychology, 58,* 582–592.

Vallone, R. P., Ross, L., & Lepper, M. R. (1985). The hostile media phenomenon: Biased perception and perceptions of media bias in coverage of the Beirut massacre. *Journal of Personality and Social Psychology, 49,* 577–585.

van de Vijver, F., & Leung, K. (1997). *Methods and data analyses for cross-cultural research.* Thousand Oaks, CA: Sage.

Van Overwalle, F., & De Metsenaere, M. (1990). The effects of attribution-based intervention and study strategy training on academic achievement in college freshmen. *British Journal of Educational Psychology, 60,* 299–311.

Van Vugt, M. (2001). Community identification moderating the impact of financial incentives in a natural social dilemma: Water conservation. *Personality and Social Psychology Bulletin, 27,* 1440–1449.

Van Yperen, N. W., & Buunk, B. P. (1994). Social comparison and social exchange in marital relationships. In M. J. Lerner & G. Mikula (Eds.), *Entitlement and the affectional bond: Justice in close relationships* (pp. 89–116). New York: Plenum.

Vanneman, R. D., & Pettigrew, T. (1972). Race and relative deprivation in the urban United States. *Race, 13,* 461–486.

VanOostrum, N., & Horvath, P. (1997). The effects of hostile attribution on adolescents' aggressive responses to social situations. *Canadian Journal of School Psychology, 13,* 729–738.

Vaske, J. J., Donnelly, M. P., Petruzzi, J. P. (1996). Country of origin, encounter norms, and crowding in a front country setting. *Leisure Sciences, 18,* 161–176.

Vidmar, N. (1974). Retributive and ulitarian motives and other correlates of Canadian attitudes toward the death penalty. *Canadian Psychologist, 15,* 337–356.

Vidyasgar, P., & Mishra, H. (1993). Effect of modelling on aggression. *Indian Journal of Clinical Psychology, 20,* 50–52.

Vissing, Y., Straus, M., Gelles, R., & Harrop, J. (1991).Verbal aggression by parents and psychosocial problems of children. *Child Abuse and Neglect, 15,* 223–238.

Voas, R. B., Holder, H. D., & Gruenewald, P. J. (1999). The effect of drinking and driving interventions on alcohol-related traffic crashes within a comprehensive community trial. *Addiction, 92,* S221–S236.

Voissem, N. H., & Sistrunk, F. (1971). Communication schedules and cooperative game behavior. *Journal of Personality and Social Psychology, 19,* 160–167.

Von Hippel, W., Jonides, J., Hilton, J. L., & Narayan, S. (1993). Inhibitory effect of schematic processing on perceptual encoding. *Journal of Personality and Social Psychology, 64,* 921–935.

Vorauer, J. D. (2001). The other side of the story: Transparency estimation in social interaction. In G. B. Moskowitz (Ed.). *Cognitive social psychology: The Princeton symposium on the legacy and future of social cognition* (pp. 261–276). Mahwah, NJ: Erlbaum.

Vorauer, J. D. (in press). Dominant group members in intergroup interaction: Safety or vulnerability in numbers? *Personality and Social Psychology Bulletin.*

Vorauer, J. D., & Cameron, J. J. (in press). So close, and yet so far: Does collectivism foster transparency overestimation? *Journal of Personality and Social Psychology.*

Vorauer, J. D., & Claude, S. D. (1998). Perceived versus actual transparency of goals in negotiation. *Personality and Social Psychology Bulletin, 24,* 371–385.

Vorauer, J. D., Hunter, A. J., Main, K., & Roy, S. (2000). Meta-stereotype activation: Evidence from indirect measures for specific evaluative concerns experienced by members of dominant groups in intergroup interaction. *Journal of Personality and Social Psychology, 78,* 690–707.

Vorauer, J. D., & Kumhyr, S. M. (2001). Is this about you or me? Self- versus other-directed judgments and feelings in response to intergroup interaction. *Personality and Social Psychology Bulletin, 27,* 706–719.

Vorauer, J. D., Main, K., & O'Connell, G. B. (1998). How do individuals expect to be viewed by members of lower status groups? Content and implications of meta stereotypes. *Journal of Personality and Social Psychology, 75,* 917–937.

Vorauer, J. D., & Miller, D. T. (1997). Failure to recognize the effect of implicit social influence on the presentation of self. *Journal of Personality and Social Psychology, 73,* 281–295.

Voraurer, J. D., & Ross, M. (1999). Self-awareness and feeling transparent: Failing to suppress one's self. *Journal of Experimental Social Psychology, 35,* 415–440.

Wagstaff, G. F. (1989). Forensic aspects of hypnosis. In N. P. Spanos & J. F. Chaves (Eds.), *Hypnosis: The cognitive-behavioral perspective.* Buffalo, New York: Prometheus Books.

Wakefield, S., & Elliott, S. J. (2000). Environmental risk perception and well-being: effects of the landfill siting process in two southern Ontario communities. *Social Science & Medicine, 50,* 1139–1154.

Wall, A., Hinson, R. E., & McKee, S. A. (1998). Alcohol outcome expectancies, attitude toward drinking and the theory of planned behavior. *Journal of Studies on Alcohol, 59,* 409–419.

Wall, G. (1995). Barriers to individual environmental action: The influence of attitudes and social experiences. *Canadian Review of Sociology and Anthropology, 32,* 465–489.

Wallach, M. A., Kogan, N., & Bem, D. J. (1962). Group influences on individual risk taking. *Journal of Abnormal and Social Psychology, 65,* 75–86.

Walsh, M., Hickey, C., & Duffy, J. (1999). Influence of item content and stereotype situation on gender differences in mathematical problem solving. *Sex Roles, 41,* 219–240.

Walster, E. (1966). Assignment of responsibility for an accident. *Journal of Personality and Social Psychology, 3,* 73–79.

Walster, E., Aronson, V., Abrahams, D., & Rottman, L. (1966). Importance of physical attractiveness in dating behavior. *Journal of Personality and Social Psychology, 5,* 508–516.

Walster, E., & Festinger, L. (1962). The effectiveness of "overheard" persuasive communication. *Journal of Abnormal and Social Psychology, 65,* 395–402.

Walster, E., Walster, G. W., & Berscheid, E. (1978). *Equity: Theory and research.* Boston: Allyn & Bacon.

Walters, V., Lenton, R., French, S., Eyles, J., Mayr, J., & Newbold, B. (1996). Paid work, unpaid work and social support: A study of the health of male and female nurses. *Social Science Medical, 43,* 1627–1636.

Wang, T., Brownstein, R., & Katzev, R. (1989). Promoting charitable behavior with compliance techniques. *Applied Psychology: An International Review, 38,* 165–184.

Wänke, M., Schwarz, N., Bless, H. (1995). The availability heuristic revisited: Experienced ease of retrieval in mundane frequency estimates. *Acta Psychologica, 89,* 83–90.

Wasswa, H. (2002, March 16). Uganda cult deaths remain a mystery. Associated Press. www.rickross.com/reference/tencommandments/tencommandments117.html. (October 22, 2002)

Watkins, D., Adair, J., Akande, A., Gerong, A., McInerney, D., Sunar, D., Watson, S., Wen, Q., & Wondimu, H. (1998). Individualism-collectivism, gender and the self-concept: A nine-culture investigation. *Psychologia: An International Journal of Psychology in the Orient, 41,* 259–271.

Watkins, D., Akande, A., Fleming, J., Ismail, M., Lefner, K., Regmi, M., Watson, S., Yu, J., Adair, J., Cheng, C., Gerong, A., McInerney, D., Mpofu, E., Singh–Sengupta, S., & Wondimu, H. (1998). Cultural dimensions, gender, and the nature of self-concept: A fourteen-country study. *International Journal of Psychology, 33,* 17–31.

Watson, D., & Pennebaker, J. W. (1989). Health complaints, stress, and distress: Exploring the central role of negative affectivity. *Psychological Review, 96,* 234–254.

Watson, J. (1924). *Behaviorism.* Chicago: University of Chicago Press.

Watson, R. I. (1973). Investigation into deindividuation using a cross-cultural survey technique. *Journal of Personality and Social Psychology, 25,* 342–345.

Watson, W. E., Johnson, L., Kumar, K., & Critelli, J. (1998). Process gain and process loss: Comparing interpersonal processes and performance of culturally diverse and non-diverse teams across time. *International Journal of Intercultural Relations, 22,* 409–430.

Webber, R., & Crocker, J. (1983). Cognitive processes in the revision of stereotypic beliefs. *Journal of Personality and Social Psychology, 45,* 961–977.

Weber, E. U., Bockenholt, U., Hilton, D. J., & Wallace, B. (1993). Determinants of diagnostic hypothesis generation: Effects of information, base rates, and experience. *Journal of Experimental Psychology: Learning, Memory, and Cognition, 19,* 1151–1164.

Webster, D. M. (1993). Motivated augmentation and reduction of the overattributional bias. *Journal of Personality and Social Psychology, 65,* 261–271.

Wegener, D. T., & Petty, R. E. (1994). Mood management across affective states: The hedonic contingency hypothesis. *Journal of Personality and Social Psychology, 66,* 1034–1048.

Wegener, D. T., & Petty, R. E. (1995). Flexible correction processes in social judgment: The role of naive theories in corrections for perceived bias. *Journal of Personality and Social Psychology, 68,* 36–51.

Wegener, D. T., & Petty, R. E. (1996). Effects of mood on persuasion processes: Enhancing, reducing, and biasing scrutiny of attitude-relevant information. In L. L. Martin & A. Tesser (Eds.), *Striving and feeling: Interactions between goals and affect* (pp. 329–362). Mahwah, NJ: Erlbaum.

Wegener, D. T., Petty, R. E., & Smith, S. M. (1995). Positive mood can increase or decrease message scrutiny: The hedonic contingency view of mood and message processing. *Journal of Personality and Social Psychology, 69,* 5–15.

Wegner, D. M. (1989). *White bears and other unwanted thoughts: Suppression, obsession, and the psychology of mental control.* New York: Viking.

Wegner, D. M. (1992). You can't always think what you want: Problems in the suppression of unwanted thoughts. In M. P. Zanna (Ed.), *Advances in experimental social psychology* (pp. 193–225). San Diego, CA: Academic Press.

Wegner, D. M. (1994). Ironic processes of mental control. *Psychological Review, 101,* 34–52.

Wegner, D. M. (1995). A computer network model of human transactive memory. *Social Cognition, 13,* 319–339.

Wegner, D. M. (in press). *The illusion of conscious will.* Cambridge, MA: MIT Press.

Wegner, D. M., Ansfield, M., & Pilloff, D. (1998). The putt and the pendulum: Ironic effects of the mental control of action. *Psychological Science, 9* (3), 196–199.

Wegner, D. M., & Bargh, J. A. (1998). Control and automaticity in social life. In D. Gilbert, S. Fiske, & G. Lindzey (Eds.), *The handbook of social psychology* (4th ed., Vol. 1, pp. 446–498). New York: McGraw Hill.

Wegner, D. M., Erber, R., & Bowman, R. E. (1995). *Sexism and mental control: When thought and speech betray egalitarian beliefs.* Unpublished manuscript, University of Virginia.

Wegner, D. M., Erber, R., & Raymond, P. (1991). Transactive memory in close relationships. *Journal of Personality and Social Psychology*, *61*, 923–929.

Wegner, D. M., Wenzlaff, R., Kerker, M., & Beattie, A. E. (1981). Incrimination through innuendo: Can media questions become public answers? *Journal of Personality and Social Psychology, 40*, 822–832.

Wegner, D. M., & Wheatley, T. (1999). Apparent mental causation: Sources of the experience of will. *American Psychologist, 54*, 480–492.

Wehrle, T., Kaiser, S., Schmidt, S., & Scherer, K. R. (2000). Studying the dynamics of emotional expression using synthesized facial muscle movements. *Journal of Personality and Social Psychology, 78*, 105–119.

Weiner, B., Amirkhan, J., Folkes, V. S., & Verette, J. A. (1987). An attributional analysis of excuse giving: Studies of a naive theory of emotion. *Journal of Personality and Social Psychology, 52*, 316–324.

Weingardt, K. R., Toland, H. K., & Loftus, E. F. (1994). Reports of suggested memories: Do people truly believe them? In D. F. Ross, J. D. Read, & M. P. Toglia (Eds.), *Adult eyewitness testimony: Current trends and developments* (pp. 3–26). New York: Cambridge University Press.

Weinstein, N. D. (1980). Unrealistic optimism about future life events. *Journal of Personality and Social Psychology, 39*, 806–820.

Weinstein, N. D., & Klein, W. M. (1996). Unrealistic optimism: Present and future. *Journal of Social and Clinical Psychology*, *15*, 1–8.

Weir, W. (1984, October 15). Another look at subliminal "facts." *Advertising Age*, p. 46.

Weiss, R. S. (1973). *Loneliness: The experience of emotional and social isolation*. Cambridge, MA: MIT Press.

Wekerle, C., & Wall, A. (2002). Introduction: The overlap between relationship violence and substance abuse. In C. Wekerle, & A. Wall (Eds.). *The violence and addiction equation* (pp. 1–21). New York: Taylor & Francis.

Wells, G. L. (1984). The psychology of lineup identifications. *Journal of Applied Social Psychology, 14*, 89–103.

Wells, G. L. (1992). Naked statistical evidence of liability: Is subjective probability enough? *Journal of Personality and Social Psychology, 62*, 739–752.

Wells, G. L. (1993). What do we know about eyewitness identification? *American Psychologist, 48*, 553–571.

Wells, G. L., & Bradfield, A. L. (1998). "Good, you identified the suspect": Feedback to eyewitness reports distorts their reports of the witnessing experience. *Journal of Applied Social Psychology, 83*, 360–376.

Wells, G. L., Lindsay, R. C. L., & Ferguson, T. (1978). Accuracy, confidence, and juror perceptions in eyewitness identification. *Journal of Applied Psychology, 64*, 440–448.

Wells, G. L., Lindsay, R. C. L., & Ferguson, T. J. (1979). Accuracy, confidence, and juror perceptions in eyewitness identification. *Journal of Applied Psychology, 64*, 440–448.

Wells, G. L., & Luus, C. A. E. (1990). Police lineups as experiments: Social methodology as a framework for properly conducted lineups. *Personality and Social Psychology Bulletin, 16*, 106–117.

Wells, G. L., Malpass, R. S., Lindsay, R. C. L., Fisher, R. P., Turtle, J. W., & Fulero, S. M. (2000). From the lab to the police station. *American Psychologist, 55*, 581–598.

Wells, G. L., Small, M., Penrod, S. D., Malpass, R. S., Fulero, S. M., & Brimacombe, C. A. E. (1998). Eyewitness identification procedures: Recommendations for lineups and photospreads. *Law and Human Behavior, 22*, 603–645.

Wells, G. L., Wright, E. F., & Bradfield, A. L. (1999) Witnesses to crime: Social and cognitive factors governing the validity of people's reports. In R. Roesch, S. D. Hart, & J. R. P. Ogloff (Eds.), *Psychology and law: The state of the discipline* (pp. 53–88). New York: Kluwer.

Wells, S., Graham, K., & West, P. (1998). "The good, the bad, and the ugly": Responses by security staff to aggressive incidents in public drinking settings. *Journal of Drug Issues, 28*, 817–836.

Wells, S., Graham, K., & West, P. (2000). Alcohol-related aggression in the general population. *Journal of Studies on Alcohol, 61*, 626–632.

Wells, W. D. (Ed.), (1997). *Measuring advertising effectiveness*. Mahwah, NJ: Erlbaum.

Wenzel, M. (2000). Justice and identity: The significance of inclusion for perceptions of entitlement and the justice motive. *Personality and Social Psychology Bulletin, 26*, 157–176.

Werner, C., & Parmelee, P. (1979). Similarity of activity preferences among friends: Those who play together stay together. *Social Psychology Quarterly, 42*, 62–66.

Weyant, J. M. (1996). Application of compliance techniques to direct-mail requests for charitable donations. *Psychology and Marketing, 13*, 157–170.

Whatley, M. A., Webster, J. M., Smith, R. H., & Rhodes, A. (1999). The effect of a favor on public and private compliance: How internalized is the norm of reciprocity? *Basic and Applied Social Psychology, 21*, 251–259.

Wheeler, L., & Kim, Y. (1997). What is beautiful is culturally good: The physical attractiveness stereotype has different content in collectivistic cultures. *Personality and Social Psychology Bulletin, 23*, 795–800.

Wheeler, L., Koestner, R., & Driver, R. (1982). Related attributes in the choice of comparison others: It's there, but it isn't all there is. *Journal of Experimental Social Psychology, 18*, 489–500.

Wheeler, L., & Kunitate, M. (1992). Social comparison in everyday life. *Journal of Personality and Social Psychology*, *62*, 760–773.

Wheeler, L., Martin, R., & Suls, J. (1997). The proxy model of social comparison for self-assessment of ability. *Personality and Social Psychology Review, 1*, 54–61.

White, H. (1997). Longitudinal perspective on alcohol and aggression during adolescence. In M. Galanter (Ed.), *Recent developments in alcoholism, Vol. 13: Alcohol and violence: Epidemiology, neurobiology, psychology, family issues* (pp. 81–103). New York: Plenum.

White, L. K. (1990). Determinants of divorce: A review of research in the eighties. *Journal of Marriage and the Family, 52*, 904–912.

White, R. K. (1977). Misperception in the Arab–Israeli conflict. *Journal of Social Issues, 33*, 190–221.

Whitley, B. E., & Frieze, I. H. (1985). Children's causal attributions for success and failure in achievement settings: A meta-analysis. *Journal of Educational Psychology, 77*, 608–616.

Whitley, B. E., Jr. (1999). Right-wing authoritarianism, social dominance orientation, and prejudice. *Journal of Personality and Social Psychology, 77*, 126–134.

Whitney, K., Sagrestano, L., & Maslach, C. (1994). Establishing the social impact of individuation. *Journal of Personality and Social Psychology, 66*, 1140–1153.

Whorf, B. L. (1956). *Language, thought, and reality*. New York: Wiley.

Wicker, A. W. (1969). Attitudes versus actions: The relationship between verbal and overt behavioral responses to attitude objects. *Journal of Social Issues, 25*, 41–78.

Wicklund, R., & Brehm, J. (1998). Resistance to change: The cornerstone of cognitive dissonance theory. In E. Harmon-Jones & J. S. Mills, *Cognitive dissonance theory: Revival with revisions and controversies.* Washington, DC: American Psychological Association.

Wicklund, R. A. (1975). Objective self-awareness. In L. Berkowitz (Ed.), *Advances in experimental social psychology* (Vol. 8, pp. 233–275). New York: Academic Press.

Wicklund, R. A., & Frey, D. (1980). Self-awareness theory: When the self makes a difference. In D. Wegner & R. Vallacher (Eds.), *The self in social psychology* (pp. 31–54). New York: Oxford University Press.

Wicklund, R. A., & Gollwitzer, P. M. (1982). *Symbolic self-completion.* Hillsdale, NJ: Erlbaum.

Wiedenfeld, S. A., O'Leary, A., Bandura, A., Brown, S., Levine, S., & Raska, K. (1990). Impact of perceived self-efficacy in coping with stressors on components of the immune system. *Journal of Personality and Social Psychology, 59,* 1082–1094.

Wiggins, J. S. (1979). A psychological taxonomy of trait-descriptive terms: The interpersonal domain. *Journal of Personality and Social Psychology, 37,* 395–412.

Wiggins, J. S. (1993). Agency and communion as conceptual co-ordinates for the understanding and measurement of interpersonal behavior. In D. Chicchetti & W. Grove (Eds.), *Thinking clearly in psychology: Essays in honor of Paul E. Meehl.* Minneapolis, MN: University of Minnesota Press.

Wiggins, J. S., & Holzmuller, A. (1981). Further evidence on androgyny and interpersonal flexibility. *Journal of Research in Personality, 15,* 67–80.

Wilder, D. A. (1984). Intergroup contact: The typical member and the exception to the rule. *Journal of Experimental Psychology, 20,* 177–194.

Wilder, D. A. (1986). Social categorization: Implications for creation and reduction of intergroup bias. In L. Berkowitz (Ed.), *Advances in experimental social psychology* (Vol. 19, pp. 291–355). New York: Academic Press.

Wilder, D. A., & Shapiro, P. N. (1989). Role of competition-induced anxiety in limiting the beneficial impact of positive behavior by an out-group member. *Journal of Personality and Social Psychology, 56,* 60–69.

Williams, K., Harkins, S., & Latané, B. (1981). Identifiability as a deterrent to social loafing: Two cheering experiments. *Journal of Personality and Social Psychology, 40,* 303–311.

Williams, K. D., Loftus, E. F., & Deffenbacher, K. A. (1992). Eyewitness evidence and testimony. In D. K. Kagehiro & W. S. Laufer (Eds.), *Handbook of psychology and law* (pp. 141–166). New York: Springer-Verlag.

Williams, K. R., & Hawkins, R. (1986). Perceptual research on general deterrence: A critical review. *Law and Society Review, 20,* 545–572.

Williams, R. B., Jr. (1987). Refining the Type A hypothesis: Emergence of the hostility complex. *American Journal of Cardiology, 60,* 27J–32J.

Williams, R. H., & Ross, M. H. (1980, March–April). Drilling for oil and gas in our houses. *Technology Review,* pp. 24–36.

Williams, S. S., Kimble, D. L., Covell, N. H., Weiss, L. H., Newton, K. J., Fisher, J. D., & Fisher, W. A. (1992). College students use implicit personality theory instead of safer sex. *Journal of Applied Social Psychology, 22,* 921–933.

Williamson, G. M., & Clark, M. S. (1989). Providing help and desired relationship type as determinants of changes in moods and self-evaluations. *Journal of Personality and Social Psychology, 56,* 722–734.

Williamson, G. M., & Clark, M. S. (1992). Impact of desired relationship type on affective reactions to choosing and being required to help. *Personality and Social Psychology Bulletin, 18,* 10–18.

Wilson, A. E., & Ross, M. (2000). The frequency of temporal-self and social comparisons in people's personal appraisals. *Journal of Personality and Social Psychology, 78,* 928–942.

Wilson, A. E., & Ross, M. (2001). From chump to champ: People's appraisals of their earlier and current selves. *Journal of Personality and Social Psychology, 80,* 572–584.

Wilson, D. K., Purdon, S. E., & Wallston, K. A. (1988). Compliance in health recommendations: A theoretical overview of message framing. *Health Education Research, 3,* 161–171.

Wilson, T. D. (1985). Strangers to ourselves: The origins and accuracy of beliefs about one's own mental states. In J. H. Harvey & G. Weary (Eds.), *Attribution in contemporary psychology* (pp. 9–36). New York: Academic Press.

Wilson, T. D. (1994). The proper protocol: Validity and completeness of verbal reports. *Psychological Science, 5,* 249–252.

Wilson, T. D. (in press). *Strangers to ourselves: Self-insight and the adaptive unconscious.* Cambridge, MA: Harvard University Press.

Wilson, T. D., & Brekke, N. C. (1994). Mental contamination and mental correction: Unwanted influences on judgments and evaluations. *Psychological Bulletin, 116,* 117–142.

Wilson, T. D., Centerbar, D. B., & Brekke, N. C. (2001). Mental contamination and the debiasing problem. In T. Gilovich, D. W. Griffin, & D. Kahneman (Eds.), *The psychology of judgment: Heuristics and biases.* New York: Cambridge University Press.

Wilson, T. D., Gilbert, D. T., & Wheatley, T. (1998). Protecting our minds: The role of lay beliefs. In V. Yzerbyt, G. Lories, & B. Dardenne (Eds.), *Metacognition: Cognitive and social dimensions* (pp. 171–201). Thousand Oaks, CA: Sage.

Wilson, T. D., Houston, C. E., Etling, K. M., & Brekke, N. (1996). A new look at anchoring effects: Basic anchoring and its antecedents. *Journal of Experimental Psychology: General, 125,* 387–402.

Wilson, T. D., Houston, C. E., & Meyers, J. M. (1998). Choose your poison: Effects of lay beliefs about mental processes on attitude change. *Social Cognition, 16* (1), 114–132.

Wilson, T. D., Laser, P. S., & Stone, J. I. (1982). Judging the predictors of one's own mood: Accuracy and the use of shared theories. *Journal of Experimental Social Psychology, 18,* 537–556.

Wilson, T. D., & Linville, P. W. (1982). Improving the academic performance of college freshmen: Attribution therapy revisited. *Journal of Personality and Social Psychology, 42,* 367–376.

Wilson, T. D., & Linville, P. W. (1985). Improving the performance of college freshmen using attributional techniques. *Journal of Personality and Social Psychology, 49,* 287–293.

Wilson, T. D., Lisle, D., Schooler, J., Hodges, S. D., Klaaren, K. J., & LaFleur, S. J. (1993). Introspecting about reasons can reduce post-choice satisfaction. *Personality and Social Psychology Bulletin, 19,* 331–339.

Wilson, T. D., & Stone, J. I. (1985). Limitations of self-knowledge: More on telling more than we can know. In P. Shaver (Ed.), *Review of personality and social psychology* (Vol. 6, pp. 167–183). Beverly Hills, CA: Sage.

Winslow, R. W., Franzini, L. R., & Hwang, J. (1992). Perceived peer norms, casual sex, and AIDS risk prevention. *Journal of Applied Social Psychology, 22,* 1809–1827.

Winter, D. G. (1987). Leader appeal, leader performance, and the motive profiles of leaders and followers: A study of American presidents and elections. *Journal of Personality and Social Psychology, 52,* 196–202.

Wittenbrink, B., Judd, C. M., & Park, B. (1997). Evidence for racial prejudice at the implicit level and its relationship with questionnaire measures. *Journal of Personality and Social Psychology, 72,* 262–274.

Wolfgang, A., & Wolofsky, Z. (1991). The ability of new Canadians to decode gestures generated by Canadians of Anglo-Celtic backgrounds. *International Journal of Intercultural Relations, 15,* 47–64.

Wood, J. V. (1989). Theory and research concerning social comparisons of personal attributes. *Psychological Bulletin, 106,* 231–248.

Wood, J. V. (1996). What is social comparison and how should we study it? *Personality and Social Psychology Bulletin, 22,* 520–537.

Wood, J. V., & Dodgson, P. G. (1996). When is self-focused attention an adaptive coping response? Rumination and overgeneralization versus compensation. In I. G. Sarason, G. R. Pierce, and B. R. Sarason (Eds.), *Cognitive interference: Theories, methods, and findings.* Mahwah, NJ: Lawrence Erlbaum Associates, Publishers.

Wood, J. V., Michela, J. L., & Giordano, C. (2000). Downward comparison in everyday life: Reconciling self-enhancement models with the mood-cognition priming model. *Journal of Personality and Social Psychology, 79,* 563–579.

Wood, J. V., Taylor, S. E., & Lichtman, R. R. (1985). Social comparison in adjustment to breast cancer. *Journal of Personality and Social Psychology, 49,* 1169–1183.

Wood, J. V., & VanderZee, K. (1997). Social comparisons among cancer patients: Under what conditions are comparisons upward and downward? In B. P. Buunk and F. X. Gibbons (Eds.), *Health, coping, and well-being: Perspectives from social comparison theory.* Mahwah, NJ: Lawrence Erlbaum Associates, Publishers.

Wood, W. (1987). Meta-analytic review of sex differences in group performance. *Psychological Bulletin*, *102*, 53–71.

Wood, W., Christensen, P. N., Hebl, M. R., & Rothgerber, H. (1997). Conformity to sex-typed norms, affect, and the self-concept. *Journal of Personality and Social Psychology, 73*, 523–535.

Wood, W., & Eagly, A. H. (2000). A call to recognize the breadth of evolutionary perspectives: Sociocultural theories and evolutionary psychology. *Psychological Inquiry, 11,* 52–55.

Wood, W., Lundgren, S., Ouelette, J. A., Busceme, S., & Blackstone, J. (1994). Minority influence: A meta-analytic review of social influence processes. *Psychological Bulletin, 115,* 323–345.

Wood, W., Wong, F. Y., & Chachere, G. (1991). Effects of media violence on viewers' aggression in unconstrained social interaction. *Psychological Bulletin, 109,* 371–383.

Word, C. O., Zanna, M. P., & Cooper, J. (1974). The nonverbal mediation of self-fulfilling prophecies in interracial interaction. *Journal of Experimental Social Psychology, 10,* 109–120.

Worth, L. T., & Mackie, D. M. (1987). Cognitive mediation of positive affect in persuasion. *Social Cognition*, *5*, 76–94.

Wortman, C. B., & Brehm, J. W. (1975). Response to uncontrollable outcomes: An integration of reactance theory and the learned helplessness model. In L. Berkowitz (Ed.), *Advances in experimental social psychology* (Vol. 8, pp. 277–336). New York: Academic Press.

Wright, E., Rule, B., Ferguson, T., McGuire, G., & Wells, G. (1992). Misattribution of dissonance and behaviour-consistent attitude change. *Canadian Journal of Behavioural Science, 24,* 456–464.

Wright, E. F., Luus, C. A. E., & Christie, S. D. (1990). Does group discussion facilitate the use of consensus information in making causal attributions? *Journal of Personality and Social Psychology*, *59*, 261–269.

Wright, E. F., MacEachern, L., Stoffer, E., & MacDonald, N. (1996). Factors affecting the use of naked statistical evidence of liability. *The Journal of Social Psychology, 136,* 677–688.

Wright, L. (1994). *Remembering Satan.* New York: Knopf.

Wright, R. (1994). *The moral animal: Why we are the way we are: The new science of evolutionary psychology.* New York: Random House.

Wright, S. C. (1997). Ambiguity, social influence, and collective action: Generating collective protest in response to tokenism. *Personality and Social Psychology Bulletin, 23,* 1277–1290.

Wright, S. C., Aron, A., McLaughlin, T., & Ropp, S. A. (1997). The extended contact effect: Knowledge of cross-group friendships and prejudice. *Journal of Personality and Social Psychology, 73*, 73–90.

Wright, S. C., Taylor, D., Moghaddam, F. (1990). Responding to membership in a disadvantaged group: From acceptance to collective protest. *Journal of Social and Personality Psychology, 58,* 994–1003.

Wyer, R. S., & Srull, T. K. (1989). *Memory and cognition in its social context.* Hillsdale, NJ: Erlbaum.

Wyer, R. S., Jr. (1988). Social memory and social judgment. In P. R. Solomon, G. R. Goethals, C. M. Kelley, & B. R. Stephens (Eds.), *Perspectives on memory research.* New York: Springer-Verlag.

Yarmey, A. D. (2001a). Expert testimony: Does eyewitness memory research have probative value for the courts? *Canadian Psychology, 42*, 92–100.

Yarmey, A. D. (2001b). Police investigations. In R. A. Schuller, & J. R. P. Ogloff (Eds.). (2001). *Introduction to psychology and law: Canadian perspectives* (pp. 59–94). Toronto: University of Toronto Press.

Yarmey, A. D., Yarmey, A. L., Yarmey, M. J., & Parliament, L. (2001). Commonsense beliefs and the identification of familiar voices. *Applied Cognitive Psychology, 15*, 283–299.

Yarmey, A. D., Yarmey, M. J., & Yarmey, A. L. (1996). Accuracy of eyewitness identifications in showups and lineups. *Law and Human Behavior, 20,* 459–477.

Yik, M. S., Bond, M. H., & Paulhus, D. L. (1998). Do Chinese self-enhance or self-efface? It's a matter of domain. *Personality and Social Psychology Bulletin, 24,* 399–406.

Yik, M. S. M., Meng, Z., & Russell, J. A. (1998). Adults' freely produced emotion labels for babies' spontaneous facial expressions. *Cognition and Emotion, 12*, 723–730.

Yik, M. S. M., & Russell, J. A. (1999). Interpretation of faces: A cross-cultural study of a prediction from Fridlund's theory. *Cognition and Emotion, 13,* 93–104.

Yovetich, N. A., & Rusbult, C. E. (1994). Accommodative behavior in close relationships: Exploring transformation of motivation. *Journal of Experimental Social Psychology*, *30*, 138–164.

Yudko, E., Blanchard, D., Henne, J., & Blanchard, R. (1997). Emerging themes in preclinical research on alcohol and aggression. In M. Galanter (Ed.), *Recent developments in alcoholism, Vol. 13: Alcohol and violence: Epidemiology, neurobiology, psychology, family issues* (pp. 123–138). New York: Plenum.

Zaccaro, S. J., Foti, R. J., & Kenny, D. A. (1991). Self-monitoring and trait-based variance in leadership: An investigation of leader flexibility across multiple group situations. *Journal of Applied Psychology*, *76*, 308–315.

Zahn-Waxler, C., Radke-Yarrow, M., & King, R. A. (1979). Child rearing and children's prosocial initiations toward victims of distress. *Child Development, 50,* 319–330.

Zajonc, R. B. (1965). Social facilitation. *Science, 149,* 269–274.

Zajonc, R. B. (1968). Attitudinal effects of mere exposure. *Journal of Personality and Social Psychology, 9,* Monograph Suppl. No. 2, Pt. 2.

Zajonc, R. B. (1980). Compresence. In P. B. Paulus (Ed.), *Psychology of group influence* (pp. 35–60). Hillsdale, NJ: Erlbaum.

Zajonc, R. B., Heingartner, A., & Herman, E. M. (1969). Social enhancement and impairment of performance in the cockroach. *Journal of Personality and Social Psychology, 13,* 83–92.

Zajonc, R. B., & Sales, S. M. (1966). Social facilitation of dominant and subordinate responses. *Journal of Experimental Social Psychology, 2,* 160–168.

Zanna, M., & Cooper, J. (1974). Dissonance and the pill: An attribution approach to studying the arousal properties of dissonance. *Journal of Personality and Social Psychology, 29,* 703–709.

Zanna, M., Goethals, G. R., & Hill, J. (1975). Evaluating a sex-related ability: Social comparison with similar others and standard setters. *Journal of Experimental Social Psychology, 11,* 86–93.

Zanna, M., & Rempel, J. K. (1988). Attitudes: A new look at an old concept. In D. Bar-Tal & A. W. Kruglanski (Eds.), *The social psychology of attitudes* (pp. 315–334). New York: Cambridge University Press.

Zanna, M. P., & Fazio, R. H. (1982). The attitude-behavior relation: Moving toward a third generation of research. In M.P. Zanna, E. T. Higgins, & C. P. Herman (Eds.), *Consistency in social behavior: The Ontario Symposium* (Vol. 2, pp. 283–301). Hillsdale, NJ: Erlbaum.

Zanna, M. P., & Sande, G. N. (1987). The effects of collective actions on the attitudes of individual group members: A dissonance analysis. In M. P. Zanna, J. M. Olson, C. P. Herman's (Eds.), *The Ontario Symposium* (Vol. 5: Social Influence).

Zanot, E. J., Pincus, J. D., & Lamp, E. J. (1983). Public perceptions of subliminal advertising. *Journal of Advertising, 12,* 39–45.

Zebrowitz, L. A. (1997). *Reading Faces: Window to the Soul?* Boulder, CO: Westview Press.

Zebrowitz, L. A., & Montepare, J. M. (1992). Impressions of babyfaced individuals across the life-span. *Developmental Psychology, 28,* 1143–1152.

Zebrowitz-McArthur, L. (1988). Person perception in cross-cultural perspective. In M. H. Bond (Ed.), *The cross-cultural challenge to social psychology* (pp. 245–265). Newbury Park, CA: Sage.

Zillman, D., & Bryant, J. (1984). Effects of massive exposure to pornography. In N. M. Malamuth & E. Donnerstein (Eds.), *Pornography and sexual aggression* (pp. 115–138). Orlando, FL: Academic Press.

Zillmann, D. (1978). Attribution and misattribution of excitatory reactions. In J. H. Harvey, W. J. Ickes, & R. F. Kidd (Eds.), *New directions in attribution research* (Vol. 2, pp. 335–370). Hillsdale, NJ: Erlbaum.

Zimbardo, P., & Andersen, S. (1993). Understanding mind control: Exotic and mundane mental manipulations. In M. D. Langone (Ed.), *Recovery from cults* (pp. 104–125). New York: Norton.

Zimbardo, P. G. (1970). The human choice: Individuation, reason, and order versus deindividuation, impulse, and chaos. In W. J. Arnold & D. Levine (Eds.), *Nebraska Symposium on Motivation: 1969* (Vol. 17, pp. 237–307). Lincoln: University of Nebraska Press.

Zine, J. (2001). Muslim youth in Canadian schools: Education and the politics of religious identity. *Anthropology & Education Quarterly, 32,* 399–423.

Zuber, J. A., Crott, H. W., & Werner, J. (1992). Choice shift and group polarization: An analysis of the status of arguments and social decision schemes. *Journal of Personality and Social Psychology, 62,* 50–61.

Zuwerink, J., Monteith, M., Devine, P., & Cook, D. (1996). Prejudice toward Blacks: With and without compunction? *Basic and Applied Social Psychology, 18,* 131–150.

CREDITS

Chapter 1

Text and Art: p. 13: Figure 1.1 adapted from L. Ross and S. M. Samuels, *The Predictive Power of Personal Reputation versus Labels and Construal in the Prisoner's Dilemma Game*. Unpublished manuscript, Stanford University, © 1993. Reprinted by permission of Lee Ross.
Photos and Cartoons: p. 1: Jane Wooster Scott, "Springtime in Central Park"/Collection of Howard Berkowitz/SuperStock, Inc.; **p. 2:** © Derek Kennedy; **p. 5:** Jeff McIntosh/CP Photo Archive; **p. 6:** Sayyid Azim/CP Photo Archive; **p. 12:** © B. Seitz/Photo Researchers, Inc; **p. 16L:** © Archives of the History of American Psychology, The University of Akron; **p. 16M:** © Archives of the History of American Psychology, University of Akron; **p. 16R:** © AP/Wide World Photos; **p. 17:** PMO Photo; **p. 19:** Courtesy of the University of Vermont; **p. 21:** © Innervision; **p. 25TL:** © Kopstein/Monkmeyer Press; **p. 25BL:** © Frank Siteman/The Picture Cube.

Chapter 2

Text and Art: p. 34: From Latane and Darley, *Witness of the Genovese Murder*, p. 78. Copyright 1987. **p. 42–43:** From "Some folks call Tillie 'a miracle worker'," *Winnipeg Free Press*, March 22, 2000. Reprinted with permission. **p. 43:** From a letter to the editor, *Winnipeg Free Press*, April 1, 2000. Reprinted with permission. **p. 57:** Figure 2.2 from "Canadian code of ethics for psychologists," Canadian Psychological Association, 1991, and "Ethical principles of psychologists and code of conduct," *American Psychologist*, 47, pp. 1597–1611, Copyright 1992 by the American Psychological Association. Adapted with permission.
Photos and Cartoons: p. 28: © Harvey Dinnerstein, "Underground, Together" 1996. Oil on canvas, 90 × 107¼ in. Photograph courtesy of Gerold Wunderlich & Co., New York, NY; **p. 30:** © AP/Wide World; **p. 35:** © 1985 FarWorks, Inc/Distributed by Universal Press Syndicate. All rights reserved; **p. 38:** Zephyr Picture/MaXx Images Inc.; **p. 39:** © Myrleen Ferguson/PhotoEdit; **p. 44:** © Literary Digest; **p. 43:** Joe Bryska/Winnipeg Free Press; **p. 51:** © Jim West; **p. 53:** Universal Press Syndicate © 1996 G. B. Trudeau; **p. 56:** © 1993 FarWorks, Inc./Distributed by Universal Press Syndicate. All rights reserved.

Chapter 3

Text and Art: p. 64: Figure 3.1 adapted from Carli, L. L. (1999). Cognitive reconstruction, hindsight, and reactions to victims and perpetrators. *Personality and Social Psychology Bulletin, 25*, 966–979; **p. 69:** Figure 3.3 from "Category accessibility and impression formation" by E. T. Higgins, W. S. Rholes, and C. R. Jones, in *Journal of Experimental Social Psychology*, 13, pp. 141–154. © 1977 by Academic Press. Reproduced by permission of the publisher; **p. 70:** Figure 3.4 from Ross, et al., "Perseverance in self-perception and social perception: Biased attributional processes in the debriefing paradigm," *Journal of Personality and Social Psychology, 32*, pp. 880–892. Copyright 1975 by the American Psychological Association. Adapted by permission. **p. 72:** Figure 3.6 from Rosenthal and Jacobson, *Pygmalion in the Classroom: Teacher Expectation and Student Intellectual Development*. Copyright 1968 Holt, Rinehart, & Winston. **p. 79:** Figure 3.7 from Schwarz, et al., "Ease of retrieval as information: Another look at the availability heuristic," *Journal of Personality and Social Psychology, 61*, pp. 195–202. Copyright 1991 by the American Psychological Association. Adapted by permission. **p. 83:** Figure 3.8 from Hamill, et al., "Ignoring sample bias: Inferences about population from atypical cases," *Journal of Personality and Social Psychology, 39*, pp. 578–589. Copyright 1980 by the American Psychology Association. Adapted by permission. **p. 86:** Figure 3.9 from Gilbert, D. T. (1991). How mental systems believe. *American Psychologist, 46*, 107–119. Adapted by permission.

Chapter 4

Text and Art: p. 99: Excerpt from P. DeMarco, "Dear Diary," from *The New York Times*, September 28, 1994. © 1994 by The New York Times Company. Reprinted by permission. **pp. 103–104:** From Carroll & Russell, "Do facial expressions signal specific emotions? Judging emotion from the face in context," *Journal of Personality and Social Psychology, 70*, 205–218. Copyright 1996 by the American Psychological Association. Reprinted by permission. **p. 107:** Excerpt from *Social Psychology* by Daniel Perlman and P. Chris Cozby, copyright 1983 by Holt, Rinehart and Winston, reprinted by permission of the publisher. **p. 110:** Figure 4.1 from Hoffman et al., "The linguistic relativity of person cognition: An English/Chinese comparison," *Journal of Personality and Social Psychology*, 51, pp. 1097–1105. Copyright 1986 by the American Psychological Association. Adapted by permission. **p. 117:** Figure 4.3 adapted from Jones and Harris, "Attribution of attitudes," *Journal of Experimental Psychology*, 3. Copyright 1967. Reprinted by permission of Academic Press. **p. 118:** Figure 4.4 from Taylor, et al., "Point of view and perception of causality," *Journal of Personality and Social Psychology*, 32. Copyright 1975 by the American Psychological Association. Adapted by permission. **p. 119:** Figure 4.5 adapted from Taylor and Fiske, 1975. **p. 121:** Reprinted by permission of Rhona Raskin, Clinical Counsellor/Advice Columnist; **p. 122:** Figure 4.7 from Storms, "Videotape and the attribution process: Reversing actors' and observers' points of view," *Journal of Personality and Social Psychology*, 27. Copyright 1973 by the American Psychological Association. Adapted by permission. **p. 123:** Figure 4.8 adapted from Storms, 1973. **p. 125:** © Winnipeg Free Press, July 3, 2000. Reprinted with permission. **p. 133:** Paulhus, D. L., & Bruce, M. N. (1992). The effect of acquaintanceship on the validity of personality impressions: A longitudinal study. *Journal of Personality and Social Psychology, 63*, 816–824.
Photos and Cartoons: p. 98: Kazimir Severinovic Malevic (1878–1935), Russian, "Three Girls." Russian State Museum, St. Petersburg, Russia/Superstock Inc.; **p. 100L&R:** © CBS Photo Archive; **p. 102:** © Dr. Paul Ekman/Human Interaction Laboratory; **p. 105L&R:** © Dr. Paul Ekman/Human Interaction Laboratory; **p. 107:** © AP/Wide World; **p. 109L:** © Chris Schwarz/Ponopresse; **p. 109R:** © F. de LaFosse/Sygma; **p. 112:** © SuperStock, Inc.; **p. 119:** © Paul Conklin/Photo Edit; **p. 125:** © Rusty Barton.

Chapter 1 (right column continuation)
Photos and Cartoons: p. 61: Alejandro Xul Solar, "Patria B." Photo © Christie's Images; **p. 62:** Photograph by KC Armstrong; **p. 65:** © Archive Photos; **p. 66L:** © A. J. Warner from "The Darker Brother"; **p. 66R:** © A. J. Warner from "The Darker Brother"; **p. 75:** © Irven de Vore/Anthro–Photo File; **p. 78:** © Charles Thatcher/Tony Stone Images; **p. 82L:** © Jamey Stillings/Tony Stone Images; **p. 82R:** © Joe Sohm/The Image Works; **p. 88:** © Doug Martin/Photo Researchers, Inc.; **p. 92L:** Andrew Medichini/CP Photo Archive; **p. 92R:** Adrian Wyld/ CP Photo Archive.

Chapter 5

Text and Art: p. 143: Adapted from Campbell, et al., "Self-concept clarity: Measurement, personality correlates, and cultural boundaries," *Journal of Personality and Social Psychology, 70*, p. 145. Copyright 1996 by the American Psychological Association. Reprinted by permission. **p. 146:** Excerpt from S. E. Cross, P. L. Bacon, and M. L. Morris, "The relational-interdependent self-construal and relationships," *Journal of Personality and Social Psychology, 78*, pp. 791–808. © 2000 by the American Psychological Association. Reprinted with permission. **p. 147:** Figure 5.1 from S. Gabriel and W. L. Gardner, "Are there 'his' and 'hers' types of interdependence? The implications of gender differences in collective versus relational interdependence for affect, behavior, and cognition," *Journal of Personality and*

Social Psychology, 77, pp. 642–655. © 1999 by the American Psychological Association. Reprinted with permission. **p. 150:** Figure 5.2 from Carver and Scheier, *Attention and Self-Regulation: A Control Theory Approach to Human Behavior.* Copyright 1981. Reprinted by permission of Springer-Verlag. **p. 151:** Adapted from Trapnell, P.D., & Campbell, J.D. (1999). Private self-consciousness and the five-factor model of personality: Distinguishing rumination from reflection. *Journal of Personality and Social Psychology, 76*, p.293. Copyright 1999 by the American Psychological Association. Reprinted with permission. **p. 158:** Figure 5.3 from Greene, et al., "Overjustification in a token economy," *Journal of Personality and Social Psychology, 34*. Copyright 1976 by the American Psychological Association. Adapted by permission. **p. 158:** From B. Russell and T. Branch, *Second Wind: The Memoirs of an Opinioned Man.* Copyright 1979. Reprinted by permission of Ballantine Books. **p. 159:** Figure 5.4 from Hennessey, et al., "Immunizing children against the negative effect of reward: A further examination of intrinsic motivation focus sessions," *Creativity Research Journal, 6,* pp. 297–307. Copyright 1993. Reprinted by permission of Albex Publishing Corp. **p. 170:** Figure 5.6 from Lockwood, P. & Kunda, Z. (1999). Increasing salience of one's best selves can undermine inspiration by outstanding role models. *Journal of Personality and Social Psychology*, 76, p. 217. Copyright 1999 by the American Psychological Association. Reprinted with permission. **Photos and Cartoons: p. 138:** Victor Brauner, "Additivite Spatiale," Photo © Christie's Images. © 1998 Artists Rights Society (ARS). New York/ADAGP, Paris; **p. 140:** © Kharen Hill/Image Network; **p. 141:** © Harper Collins Archives; **p. 145:** © Japan Pool/AP/Wide World Photos; **p. 152:** Frascino © 1977 The New Yorker Collection. All rights reserved. **p. 154:** © Jay Thomas/International Stock Photography, Ltd.; **p. 157:** © 1995 PEANUTS, reprinted by permission of United Feature Syndicate, Inc.; **p. 158:** AP/Wide World Photos; **p. 163:** © Capilano Suspension Bridge and Park; **p. 167TL:** © Mark Baldwin; **p. 167TR:** © Mark Baldwin; **p. 167B:** © Eric Berndt/Unicorn Photos; **p. 170:** Hamilton from The New Yorker Collection. All rights reserved. **p. 173L:** Michel PONOMAR-EFF/PONOPRESSE; **p. 173R:** Ryan Remiorz/CP Photo Archive.

Chapter 6

Text and Art: p. 184: Figure 6.2 adapted from Tesser, A., & Smith, J. (1980). Some effects of friendship and task relevance on helping: You don't always help the one you like. *Journal of Experimental Social Psychology, 16,* pp. 582–590. **p. 185:** Figure 6.3 from C. M. Steele, H. Hoppe, and J. Gonzalez, *Dissonance and the Lab Coat: Self-Affirmation and the Free Choice of Paradigm.* Unpublished manuscript, University of Washington, Copyright 1986. Reprinted by permission of the author. **p. 189:** Figure 6.4 based on Heine, S. J., Takata, T., & Lehman, D. R. (2000). Beyond self-presentation: Evidence for self-criticism among Japanese. *Personality and Social Psychology Bulletin, 26,* pp. 71–78. **p. 200:** Figure 6.6 from Aronson and Mills, "The effect of severity of initiation on liking for a group," *Journal of Abnormal and Social Psychology*, 1959. **p. 203:** Figure 6.7 from Stone, Aronson, Crain, Winslow, and Fried, "Inducing hypocrisy as a means of encouraging young adults to use condoms," *Personality and Social Psychology Bulletin.* Copyright 1993 Sage Publications. Reprinted by permission. **p. 206:** Figure 6.8 from "Long-term behavioral effects of cognitive dissonance" by J. Freedman in *Journal of Experimental Social Psychology, 1,* pp. 145–155. © 1965 by Academic Press. Reproduced by permission of the publisher. **p. 207:** Figure 6.9 from Zanna, et al., "Dissonance and the pill: An attribution approach to studying the arousal properties of dissonance," *Journal of Experimental Social Psychology*, 29. Copyright 1974 by the American Psychological Association. Adapted by permission. **p. 209:** Figure 6.10 from Jecker and Landy, "Liking a person as a function of doing him a favor." *Human Relations, 22*, pp. 371–378. Copyright 1969. Reprinted by permission of Plenum Publishing Company. **Photos and Cartoons: p. 176:** Jasper Johns, "Target with Plaster Casts." 51" × 44" × 3⅞", encaustic and collage on canvas with plaster casts, 1955. Collection of David Geffen, Los Angeles. © Jasper Johns/Licensed by VAGA, New York, NY; **p. 177:** © Michael Ponomareff/Ponopresse; **p. 179:** © Eyewire; **p. 181:** © Tony Freeman/PhotoEdit; **p. 193:** © Peanuts reprinted by permission of United Feature Syndicate, Inc.; **p. 194:** © Jonathan Nourok/PhotoEdit; **p. 197:** © D & I MacDonald/The Picture Cube; **p. 199:** © DND Photo/Sgt. Matheson (Neg# IHC88-12-2); **p. 201:** © Vincent Graziani/International Stock Photography, Ltd.; **p. 205:** © D. Wiggett/First Light; **p. 210:** The Canadian Press/DND/HO-93; **p. 211:** © AP/Wide World Photos; **p. 212:** The Canadian Press/Dan Loh.

Chapter 7

Text and Art: p. 230: Figure 7.2 adapted from Ajzen/Fishbein, *Understanding and Predicting Social Behavior*. Copyright 1980 (1985?). Adapted by permission of Prentice Hall, Inc., Upper Saddle River, NJ. **p. 245:** Figure 7.6 from Schwarz, et al., "Mood and Persuasion: A Cognitive Response Analysis," *Personality and Social Psychology Bulletin*, Vol. 16, No. 2, June 1990, pp. 331–345. Reprinted by permission of the author. **p. 248:** Figure 7.7 adapted from Shavitt, "The role of attitude objects in attitude function," *Journal of Social Psychology*, 26, pp. 124–148. Copyright 1990. Reprinted by permission. **Photos and Cartoons: p. 218:** Federico Zandomeneghi, "La Lecture," oil on canvas, 26 × 32⅜" Christie's Image/SuperStock; **p. 219:** Jose Luis Pelaez, Inc./CORBIS/MAGMA; **p. 222:** © Robert Kusel/Tony Stone Images; **p. 227:** © Gregg Adams/Tony Stone Images; **p. 229:** The Canadian Press/Mathew McCarthy; **p. 233:** © Sexuality Education Resource Centre, Winnipeg; **p. 236:** Courtesy McNeil Consumer Healthcare; **p. 244:** Chuck Savage/First Light; **p. 246:** © David Young-Wolff/PhotoEdit; **p. 247:** © Miele. Reprinted by permission of Miele; **p. 249:** © Authentic Old Ads; **p. 251T:** Hamilton © 1984 The New Yorker Collection. All rights reserved; **p. 251B:** © American Association of Advertising Agencies; **p. 255:** © M. Siluk/The Image Works.

Chapter 8

Text and Art: p. 263: Figure 8.1 adapted from Sherif, *The Psychology of Social Norms*. Copyright 1936 by HarperCollins Publishers. Reprinted by permission. **p. 269:** Figure 8.2 from Bueler, R. & Griffin, D. (1994). Change-of-meaning effects in conformity and dissent: Observing construal processes over time. *Journal of Personality and Social Psychology, 67*, p. 989. Copyright 1994 by the American Psychological Association. Reprinted with permission. **p. 272:** Figure 8.3 from Asch, "Studies of independence and conformity: A minority of one against a unanimous majority," *Psychological Monographs*, 70 (9, Whole No. 416). **p. 273:** Figure 8.4 adapted from Asch, "Symposium on preventive and social psychiatry." **p. 276:** Figure 8.5 adapted from S. E. Asch, "Opinions and social pressure," *Scientific American*, 193, pp. 31–35, 1955. **p. 295:** Figure 8.8 from S. Milgram, *From Obedience to Authority.* Copyright 1974. Reprinted by permission of HarperCollins Publishers, Inc. **p. 297:** Figure 8.9 from S. Milgram, *From Obedience to Authority.* Copyright 1974. Reprinted by permission of HarperCollins Publishers, Inc. **Photos and Cartoons: p. 259:** Milton Dacosta, "Menina Ajoelhada," photo © Christie's Images; **p. 260:** © Peter Blashill/The Province; **p. 261:** © 1995, Washington Post Writers Group; **p. 266:** The New York Times, Oct. 31, 1938, Copyright © 1938 The New York Times Company; **p. 272:** © William Vandivert; **p. 278:** Bill Becker/CP Photo Archive; **p. 281:** © Keith Morison/PDI; **p. 283L:** © Marie Hansen/Life Magazine; **p. 283R:** © Michael Newman/PhotoEdit; **p. 284:** © Kobal Collection; **p. 285:** © The New York Times/NYT Graphics; **p. 289:** © Universal Press Syndicate; **p. 291:** © Antman/The Image Works; **p. 292:** © "Ron Haeberle/Life Magazine: © 1969 Time-Warner, Inc."; **p. 293:** Johnny Florea/Life Magazine: © Time-Warner, Inc.; **p. 294L:** © Copyright: © 1965 by Stanely Milgram. From *Obedience* (film), distributed by the Pennsylvania State University PCR, Courtesy of Alexandra Milgram; **p. 294R:** © Copyright © 1965 by Stanely Milgram. From *Obedience* (film), distributed by the Pennsylvania State University PCR, Courtesy; **p. 299:** Bill Aron/PhotoEdit.

Chapter 9

Text and Art: p. 311: Figure 9.1 from Zajonc, et al., "Social enhancement and impairment of performance in the cockroach," *Journal of Personality and Social Psychology*, 13. Copyright 1969 by the American Psychological Association. Adapted by permission. **p. 314:** Figure 9.2 from Cotrell, et al., "Social facilitation in dominant responses by the presence of an audience and the mere presence of others," *Journal of Personality and Social Psychology*, 9. Copyright 1968 by the American Psychological Association. Adapted by permission. **p. 316:** Figure 9.3 from Jackson, et al., "Social Loafing on difficult tasks," *Journal of Personality and Social Psychology*, 49. Copyright 1985 by the American Psychological Association. Adapted by permission. **p. 322:** Figure 9.4 from Stasser, et al., "Pooling of unshared information in group decision making: Biased information and sampling during discussion," *Journal of Personality and Social Psychology, 48*. **p. 323:** Figure 9.5 adapted from Janis, *Victims of Groupthink*. Copyright 1982 by Houghton Mifflin and Company. Reprinted by permission. **p. 326:** Try It! from Wallach, et al., An example of an item from the choice Dilemmas Questionnaire, *Journal of Abnormal and Social Psychology*, 65. **p. 331:** Figure 9.6 from Jackson, "Deindividuation and valence of cues," *Journal of Personality and Social Psychology*, 49. Copyright 1985 by the American Psychological Association. Adapted by permission. **p. 336:** Figure 9.7 from Deutsch and Krauss, "The effect of threat upon interpersonal bargaining," *Journal of Abnormal and Social Psychology*, 1960, pp. 181–189. **p. 337:** Figure 9.8 from Deutsch & Krauss, "Studies of interpersonal bargaining," *Journal of Conflict Resolution, 6*, pp. 52–76. Copyright 1962. Reprinted by permission of Sage Publications.

Photos and Cartoons: p. 303: Fernand Leger (1881–1955), French, "Construction Workers," SuperStock, Inc.; **p. 304L:** © Louise Richard; **p. 304R:** The Canadian Press/Mike Pinder; **p. 305:** © John Boykin/PhotoEdit; **p. 307:** Philip G. Zimbardo, Inc.; **p. 309:** © 1997, The Washington Post. Reprinted with permission; **p. 313:** Scott Montgomery/Stone; **p. 317:** © Tony Freeman/PhotoEdit; **p. 319:** The Canadian Press/Rick Madonik; **p. 324:** © NASA/John F. Kennedy Space Center; **p. 329a:** Supreme Court of Canada/Philippe Landreville; **p. 329b:** Topham/The Image Works; **p. 329c:** Alain Nogues/Sygma; **p. 329d:** © The Bettmann Archive; **p. 329e:** Jean-Marc Carisse; **p. 338:** © Michael Newman/PhotoEdit; **p. 340:** The Canadian Press/Joe Gibbons.

Chapter 10

Text and Art: p. 348: Figure 10.1 from reprinted from *Social Pressures in Informal Groups* by Leon Festinger, Stanley Schachter, and Kurt Back with the permission of the publishers, Stanford University Press. Copyright 1950 by Leon Festinger, Stanley Schachter, and Kurt Back. **p. 349:** Figure 10.2 from R.L. Moreland and R. Beach, "Exposure effects in the classroom: The development of affinity among students," *Journal of Experimental and Social Psychology, 28*, pp. 255–276. Copyright 1992. Reprinted by permission. **p. 352:** Figure 10.3 from Curtis, et al., "Amount of liking," *Journal of Personality and Social Psychology*, 51. Copyright 1986 by the American Psychological Association. Adapted by permission. **p. 362:** Figure 10.4 adapted from Sternberg, *The Triangle of Love*. Copyright 1988. Reprinted by permission of HarperCollins Publishers, Inc. **p. 364:** Table 10.2 from Fehr, B. (1988). Prototype analysis of the concepts of love and commitment. *Journal of Personality and Social Psychology*, 55, pp. 557–579. Copyright 1988 by the American Psychological Association. Reprinted with permission. **p. 370:** Table 10.3 adapted from APA Adapted from Bartholomew, K. & Horowitz, L.M. (1991). Attachment styles among young adults: A test of a four-category model. *Journal of Personality and Social Psychology*, 61, pp. 226–244. Copyright 1991 by the American Psychological Association. Reprinted with permission. **p. 375–376:** Figure 10.5 and 10.6 adapted from Rusbult, "A longitudinal test of the investment model," *Journal of Personality and Social Psychology, 45*. Copyright 1983 by the Amerian Psychological Association. Adapted by permission.

Photos and Cartoons: p. 344: Bharati Chaudhuri (b. 1951), "Invisible Tension," 1992, SuperStock, Inc.; **p. 346:** Inc.Ted Kawalerski Photography/The Image Bank/Getty Images; **p. 347:** © Michael

Newman/PhotoEdit; **p. 350:** © Michael Newman/PhotoEdit; **p. 354TL:** © Evan Agostini/Gamma Liaison; **p. 354TM:** © Popperfoto/Archive Photos; **p. 354TR:** © S. Shapiro/Gamma Liaison; **p. 354BL:** © Jeff Manzetti/AP/Wide World Photos; **p. 354BM:** © Charles William Bush/NBC, Inc./Kobal Collection; **p. 354BR:** © Aaron Rapoport/Fox/Kobal Collection; **p. 356:** Judith H. Langlios/Dept. of Psychology/University of Texas, Austin; **p. 359:** © Buddy Mays/International Stock Photography, Ltd.; **p. 360:** Reprinted with special permission of King Features Syndicate; **p. 366:** © Bob Daemmrich/Stock Boston; **p. 367:** © SuperStock, Inc.; **p. 370:** © Elizabeth Crews/The Image Works; **p. 377L:** © UPI/Bettmann; **p. 377R:** © Wojnarowicz/The Image Works.

Chapter 11

Text and Art: p. 388: Reprinted with permission of The Associated Press. **p. 396:** Figure 11.1 from Batson, *The Altrusim Question: Toward a Social Psychological Answer*. 1991 Lawrence Erlbaum Associates. **p. 397:** Figure 11.2 from M. Toi and C. D. Batson, "More evidence that empathy is a source of altruistic motivation*," Journal of Personality and Social Psychology*, 43, pp. 281–292. Copyright 1982. Reprinted by permission. **p. 407:** Figure 11.3 from Darley, et al., "Bystander intervention in emergencies: Diffusion and responsibility*," Journal of Personality and Social Psychology*, 8. Copyright 1968 by the American Psychological Association. Adapted by permission. **p. 408:** Figure 11.4 adapted from Latané & Darley, *The Unresponsive Bystander: Why Doesn't He Help?* Copyright 1970. Reprinted by permission of Simon & Schuster. **p. 415:** Figure 11.5 from Hendrick, et al., *Romantic Love*, p. 69. Copyright 1992 by Sage Publications, Inc. Reprinted by permission of Sage Publications, Inc.

Photos and Cartoons: p. 388: Romare Bearden, "The Piano Lesson," 1983, collage and watercolor, 29" x 22", © Romare Bearden Foundation/Licensed by VAGA, New York, NY; **p. 389L:** Joe Byrska/Winnipeg Free Press; **p. 389R:** Winnipeg Free Press; **p. 391:** © Rhoda Sidney/The Image Works; **p. 394:** © B. Lambert/Sygma; **p. 397:** © 1995 Watterson/Distributed by Universal Press Syndicate; **p. 398:** © United Press International, Inc.; **p. 403:** © Elena Rooraid/PhotoEdit; **p. 406:** © New York Times Pictures; **p. 406inset:** © New York Times Pictures; **p. 410:** © Steve McCurry/Magnum Photos; **p. 414:** © Charles Gupton/Stock Boston; **p. 417:** Erlanson Productions/The Image Bank/Getty Images; **p. 418:** Aneal Vohra/MaXx Images Inc.

Chapter 12

Text and Art: p. 440: Figure 12.1 from Berkowitz, et al., "Weapons as aggression eliciting stimuli," *Journal of Personality and Social Psychology*, 7. Copyright 1967 by the American Psychological Association. Adapted by permission. **p. 444:** Figure 12.2 from Liebert, et al., "Some immediate effects of televised violence on children's behavior," *Developmental Psychology*, 6. Copyright 1972 by the American Psychological Association. Adapted by permission. **p. 452:** Figure 12.3 from Archer, et al., *Violence and Crime in Cross National Perspective*. Copyright 1984. Reprinted by permission of Yale University Press. **p. 458:** Figure 12.4 from Archer and Gartner, "Violent Acts and Violent Times: A Comparative Approach to Postwar Incident Rates," *American Sociological Review, 41*. Copyright 1976. Reprinted by permission. **p. 462:** Figure 12.5 from Baron, "The Reduction of Human Aggression: A Field Study on the Influence of Incompatible Responses," *Journal of Applied Social Psychology*, 6. Copyright 1976. Reprinted by permission.

Photos and Cartoons: p. 423: Frank Romero, "Freeway Wars," 1990, serigraph, 31½" × 38", © Frank Romero, Nicolas and Cristina Hernandez Trust Collection, Pasadena, California; **p. 424:** Skyrage Foundation; **p. 428:** Dick Hemingway; **p. 431:** Emile Wamsteker/AP/Wide World Photos; **p. 433:** Dana Fradon © 1985 from the New Yorker Collection. All rights reserved.; **p. 435:** © Jonathan Nourok/Photo Edit; **p. 442:** © Albert Bandura/Stanford University; **p. 443:** Adrian Wyld/CP Photo Archive; **p. 447:** © John Coletti/Stock Boston; **p. 448:** © 1973 Universal Press Syndicate; **p. 451:** © Catherine Ursillo/Photo Researchers; **p. 455:** © Photo Researchers; **p. 457L:** U.S. Army Photo; **p. 457R:** From " Faces of the Enemy" by Sam Keen/Harper & Row: © 1986; **p. 461:** The Canadian Press.

Chapter 13
Text and Art: p. 467: © Mary Young. **p. 473:** Figure 13.1 adapted from Bond, et al., "Response to violence in a psychiatric setting," *Personality and Social Psychology Bulletin*, 14, pp. 448–458. Copyright 1988. Reprinted by permission of Sage publications. **p. 482:** Figure 13.2 from Quattrone, et al., "The perception of variability within ingroups and outgroups: Implications for the law of small numbers," *Journal of Personality and Social Psychology, 38*. Copyright 1980 by the American Psychological Association. Adapted by permission. **p. 486:** Figure 13.4 from APA Sinclair, L. & Kunda, Z. (1999). "Reactions to a black professional: Motivated inhibition and activation of conflicting stereotypes," *Journal of Personality and Social Psychology, 77*, pp. 885–904. © 1999 by the American Psychological Association. Reprinted with permission. **p. 495:** Figure 13.5 from Palmer, D.L. (1996). "Determinants of Canadian attitudes toward immigration: More than just racism?" *Canadian Journal of Behavioural Science, 28*, pp. 180–192. Copyright 1996. Canadian Psychological Association. Reprinted with permission. **p. 508:** Figure 13.7 from Ruggiero, K.M. & Taylor, D.M. (1995). "Coping with discrimination: How disadvantaged group members perceive the discrimination that confronts them," *Journal of Personality and Social Psychology, 68*, pp. 826–838. © 1995 by the American Psychological Association. Reprinted with permission. **p. 513:** Figure 13.8 adapted from Sherif, "Intergroup conflict and cooperation: The Robber's Cave Experiment." Copyright 1961. Reprinted by permission of O.J. Harvey.
Photos and Cartoons: p. 467: © Eileen Ogemah c.1954, courtesy of Louis Ogemah; **p. 468:** © Mary Young; **p. 470:** © Garvey/Monkmeyer; **p. 472:** Ziegler © 1994 from the New Yorker Collection. All rights reserved.; **p. 476:** Drawing by Alain, © 1951, The New Yorker: 25th Annual Album, Harper & Bros.; **p. 478:** © Gary Rush (McGill Sports Info); **p. 483:** Photograph courtesy of Ron Baxter Smith; **p. 490:** PhotoEdit/Bill Aron; **p. 494:** The Canadian Press/Jacques Boissinot; **p. 497:** The Canadian Press/Paul Darrow; **p. 505:** © 1992 Gary Hallgren; **p. 511:** The Canadian Press/Adrian Wyld; **p. 515:** © Siteman/Monkmeyer.

Social Psychology in Action 1
Text and Art: p. 525: Table SPA 1.1 reprinted by permission of the publisher from "The Social readjustment rating scale," by Holmes and Rahe, *Journal of Psychosomatic Research*, 11, pp. 213–218. Copyright 1967 by Elsevier Science, Inc. **p. 527:** Figure SPA 1.1 from Cohen, et al., "Psychological Stress and Susceptibility to the Common Cold," *New England Journal of Medicine*, 325. Copyright 1991. Reprinted by permission. **p. 529:** From Langer, et al., "The effects of choice and enhanced personal responsibility for the aged: A field experiment," *Journal of Personality and Social Psychology*, 34. Copyright 1976 by the American Psychological Association. Adapted by permission. **p. 536:** Figure SPA 1.5 from Wilson, et al., "Improving the academic performance of college freshman: Attribution therapy revisited," *Journal of Personality and Social Psychology*, 49. Copyright 1982 by the American Psychological Association. Adapted by permission.
Photos and Cartoons: p. 520: Ernst Kirchner, "Portrait of the Poet Frank," oil on canvas, 27½" × 23⅝", Christie's Images, SuperStock;

p. 526TL: © Robert Brenner/PhotoEdit; **p. 526TR:** © Peter Southwick/Stock Boston; **p. 526BL:** © Thomas Hoepker/Magnum Photos; **p. 526BR:** © Elena Rooraid/PhotoEdit; **p. 528:** The Canadian Press/Chris Mikula; **p. 534:** DILBERT reprinted by permission of United Feature Syndicate, Inc.; **p. 539:** Edward Koren © 1989 from The New Yorker Collection. All rights reserved.; **p. 540:** Phill Snel/CP Photo Archive; **p. 541:** © Bruce Ayres/Tony Stone Images; **p. 531L:** © Donna Day/Tony Stone Images; **p. 531R:** © Billy E. Barnes/PhotoEdit; **p. 546:** Health Canada.

Social Psychology in Action 2
Text and Art: p. 556: Figure SPA 2.1 from Glass and Singer, *Urban Stress: Experiments on Noise and Social Stressors*. Copyright 1972 by Academic Press. Reprinted by permission. **p. 560:** Figure SPA 2.2 from Sherrod, "Crowding, Perceived Control and Behavior Aftereffects," *Journal of Applied Psychology*, 4. Copyright 1974. Reprinted by permission. **p. 565:** Table SPA 2.1 from Orbell, et al., "Explaining discussion-induced comparison," *Journal of Personality and Social Psychology*, 54. Copyright 1988 by the American Psychological Association. **p. 572:** Figure SPA 2.4 from Cialdini, et al., " A focus theory of normative conduct: Recycling the concept of norms to reduce littering in public," *Journal of Personality and Social Psychology*, 58. Copyright 1990 by the American Psychological Association. Adapted by permission.
Photos and Cartoons: p. 552: © Janet Nipi Ikuutaq; **p. 553:** © Cameramann/The Image Works; **p. 554:** © Warren Faidlay/International Stock Photography Ltd.; **p. 557:** © David Young-Wolff/PhotoEdit; **p. 559:** © Robert Brenner/PhotoEdit; **p. 563:** © 1991The New Yorker Collection. All rights reserved.; **p. 567:** © Pedrick/The Image Works; **p. 570:** © Maurice and Sally Landre; **p. 573:** © Eva Omes.

Social Psychology in Action 3
Text and Art: p. 581: Figure SPA 3.1 from Lindsay, et al., "Can people detect eyewitness identification," *Journal of Applied Psychology, 66*. Copyright 1981 by the American Psychological Association. Adapted by permission. **p. 603:** Table SPA 3.1 adapted from Pennington and Hastie, "Explanation based decision making: Effects of memory structure on judgement," *Journal of Experimental Psychology: Learning, Memory, and Cognition*, 14, pp. 521–533. Copyright 1988 by the American Psychological Association.
Photos and Cartoons: p. 577: Trevor Goring; **p. 579L:** The Canadian Press/Ken Gigliotti; **p. 579C:** The Canadian Press/Winnipeg Sun; **p. 579R:** The Canadian Press/Aaron Harris; **p. 583T:** © Paul Buckowski/AP/Wide World Photos; **p. 583B:** © James Schnepf/Gamma-Liaison; **p. 586:** © Courtesy of Elizabeth Loftus; **p. 589:** © 1985 Far Works, Inc. Dist. by Universal Press Syndicate; **p. 594:** © Mark C. Burnett/Photo Researchers; **p. 596:** © Forsyth/Monkmeyer; **p. 599:** The Canadian Press/Jacques Boissinot; **p. 604:** © Film Stills Archives Collection, The Museum of Modern Art, New York; **p. 608:** © A. Ramey/Photo Edit.

NAME INDEX

SUBJECT INDEX